W9-CMR-799

A Companion to the Philosophy of Language

Blackwell Companions to Philosophy

This outstanding student reference series offers a comprehensive survey of philosophy as a whole. Written by today's leading philosophers, each volume provides lucid and engaging coverage of the key figures, terms, topics, and problems of the field. Taken together, they provide the ideal basis for course use, representing an unparalleled work of reference for students and specialists alike.

Already published:

A Companion to Ethics
Edited by Peter Singer

A Companion to Aesthetics
Edited by David Cooper

A Companion to Epistemology
Edited by Jonathan Dancy and Ernest Sosa

A Companion to Contemporary Political Philosophy
Edited by Robert E. Goodin and Philip Pettit

A Companion to the Philosophy of Mind
Edited by Samuel Guttenplan

A Companion to Metaphysics
Edited by Jaegwon Kim and Ernest Sosa

A Companion to Philosophy of Law and Legal Theory
Edited by Dennis Patterson

A Companion to Philosophy of Religion
Edited by Philip Quinn and Charles Taliaferro

A Companion to the Philosophy of Language
Edited by Bob Hale and Crispin Wright

A Companion to the World Philosophies
Edited by Eliot Deutsch and Ron Bontekoe

Forthcoming:

A Companion to the Philosophy of Science
Edited by William Newton-Smith

A Companion to Feminist Philosophy
Edited by Alison Jagger and Iris Young

A Companion to Continental Philosophy
Edited by Simon Critchley and William Schroeder

Blackwell Companions to Philosophy

A Companion to the Philosophy of Language

Edited by
BOB HALE
and
CRISPIN WRIGHT

First published 1997

2 4 6 8 10 9 7 5 3 1

Blackwell Publishers Ltd
108 Cowley Road
Oxford OX4 1JF
UK

Blackwell Publishers Inc.
350 Main Street
Malden, Massachusetts 02148
USA

British Library Cataloguing in Publication Data

A CIP catalogue record for this book is available from the British Library.

Library of Congress Cataloging in Publication Data

A Companion to the philosophy of language / edited by Bob Hale and Crispin Wright.
p. cm. – (Blackwell companions to philosophy)
Includes bibliographical references and index.
ISBN 0-631-16757-9
1. Language and languages – Philosophy. I. Hale, Bob.
II. Wright, Crispin, 1942– III. Series.
P106.C5945 1997
149'.94–dc20 96-41009
CIP

Typeset in $10^1/_2$ on $12^1/_2$pt Photina
by Best-set Typesetter Ltd, Hong Kong
Printed in Great Britain by T. J. International, Cornwall

This book is printed on acid-free paper.

Contents

Preface

The recent proliferation of dictionaries and encyclopaedias of philosophy has resulted in no shortage of companionship for the philosophical tourist whose desire is merely for a short excursion. Our *Companion* is intended as a guide for a more determined and ambitious explorer. Thus this is no alphabetized compendium of brief statements of the principal theoretical positions, concepts and protagonists in recent and contemporary philosophy of language, but comprises, rather, twenty-five extended essays on a nucleus of the most central issues in the field, each of which has seen and continues to see important work.

All of our contributors are active in research on their selected topics. Each was invited to contribute an essay somewhat along the lines of the *State of the Art* series which *Mind* initiated in the mid-1980s: a survey and analysis of recent trends in work on the topic in question, offering a bibliography of the more important literature and incorporating a substantial research component. Accordingly these are essays for a philosophically experienced – advanced undergraduate, graduate or professional – readership. Each essay is, however, written so as to presuppose a minimum of prior knowledge of its specific subject matter, and so offers both a self-contained overview of the relevant issues and of the shape of recent discussion of them and, for readers who want it, an up-to-date preparation for extended study of the topic concerned. There are, naturally, numerous points of connection among the essays, some of which will be obvious enough from their titles or from a quick glance at their opening sections; others have been indicated by explicit cross-referencing. We have attempted, in the Glossary, to provide concise explanations of all of the more important technical or semi-technical terms actually employed in the various essays, and of a good number of other terms of art which, though not actually used by any of our contributors, figure centrally in other published work on the issues. The result, as we hope, is an anthology which will both stimulate research in the philosophy of language and provide an up-to-date textbook for its advanced teaching for many years to come.

Few would now subscribe to the idea which prevailed for a while in some Anglo-American philosophical circles during the 1970s, that the philosophy of language is First Philosophy, and that great issues in, for instance, metaphysics, epistemology and the philosophy of mind, are to be resolved by, in effect, recasting them as matters for treatment within the theory of meaning. But there is no doubt that philosophy of language continues to occupy a position of central importance in contemporary philosophy, nor that some of the best and most influential philosophical writing of the latter half of this century, by some of the foremost philosophical thinkers of our time, has been accomplished in this area. The threefold division into which we have organized the chapters closely reflects the landscaping which these leading authors have given to the subject. Part I, on *Meaning and Theories of Meaning*, comprises essays which are all concerned, in one way or another, with issues connected to the nature of language mastery that have loomed large in the writings of Davidson, Dummett and Grice. Part II, on *Language, Truth and Reality*, pivots around more metaphysical issues to do with meaning: with the ongoing debate about meaning-scepticism that has drawn on the writings of Kripke, Putnam, Quine and Wittgenstein, and with the connections between issues to do with meaning and the various debates about realism, whose excavation has been led by Dummett. Finally, Part III, on *Reference, Identity and Necessity*, focuses on issues which take centre stage in – or at least, loom large in the stage-setting for – Kripke's *Naming and Necessity*. Together the three parts cover almost every topic that anyone familiar with contemporary work in the philosophy of language would expect to receive extensive discussion in a volume of this kind. There are nevertheless some vacancies which we would have liked, ideally, to have filled. There is, for example, no essay focusing on the concept of a *criterion* which the first generation of commentary elicited from Wittgenstein's *Philosophical Investigations*, nor – perhaps more grievous – did we succeed in the end in commissioning a suitable study of semantic externalism or of notions of supervenience.

It remains to express our gratitude to our contributors, both for their patience with our editorial suggestions and for the excellence of their contributions and valuable assistance with glossary entries; to our publishers for bearing with us while we put together a volume which has been inevitably subject to many delays; to the secretarial staff of the Philosophy Departments of the Universities of St Andrews and Glasgow for assistance with the preparation and standardization of typescripts; and to each other.

Bob Hale and Crispin Wright

Notes on Contributors

Anita Avramides is the Southover Manor Trust Fellow in Philosophy at St Hilda's College, Oxford. She is the author of *Meaning and Mind: An Examination of a Gricean Account of Language* (MIT Press, 1989). Her main interests include the philosophy of mind and language, with a special interest in the problem of other minds.

Paul Artin Boghossian is Professor of Philosophy and Chairman of the Philosophy Department at New York University. He has published several papers on the philosophy of mind and the philosophy of language, on such topics as rule-following , mental representation, realism about psychological states, self-knowledge and the nature of colour experience.

Edward Craig is Reader in Modern Philosophy at the University of Cambridge, and has been a Fellow of the British Academy since 1993. He is the author of *The Mind of God and the Works of Man* (OUP, 1987) and *Knowledge and the State of Nature* (OUP, 1990), as well as articles on various topics in the theory of knowledge and philosophy of language. He is Chief Editor of the Routledge *Encyclopedia of Philosophy*.

Graeme Forbes is Celia Scott Weatherhead Distinguished Professor at Tulane University, New Orleans, USA. He is currently working on an electronic edition of his *The Metaphysics of Modality* (OUP, 1985) and on a monograph about referential opacity. He is also the author of *Languages of Possibility* (Blackwell, 1989) and the textbook *Modern Logic* (OUP, 1994).

Bob Hale is Professor of Metaphysical Philosophy in the University of Glasgow. His philosophical interests lie mainly in the philosophy of mathematics and the philosophy of logic and language. His previous publications include *Abstract Objects* (Blackwell, 1987) and several articles in these areas.

Jane Heal is a Reader in Philosophy at the University of Cambridge and a Fellow of St John's College. Her interests are mainly in philosophy of language and philosophy of mind. Her previous publications include her book *Fact and Meaning* (Blackwell, 1989) and several journal articles in these areas.

Barry Loewer is Professor of Philosophy at Rutgers University. His published work lies mainly in the philosophy of mind and psychology, the philosophy of quantum mechanics and metaphysics.

E. J. Lowe is Professor of Philosophy and Head of the Philosophy Department at the University of Durham, specializing in metaphysics, philosophy of mind and philosophical logic. He is author of *Kinds of Being: A Study of Individuation, Identity and the Logic of Sortal Terms* (Blackwell, 1989), *Locke on Human Understanding* (Routledge, 1995), and *Subjects of Experience* (Cambridge University Press, 1996).

Alexander Miller completed his Ph.D. at the University of Michigan (Ann Arbor) in 1995 and has been Lecturer in Philosophy at the University of Birmingham since January 1996, having lectured previously at the University of Nottingham in 1994 and 1995. He works mainly on the philosophy of language and mind, metaphysics, and metaethics.

Richard Moran is Professor of Philosophy at Harvard University, having previously taught at Princeton University. He works primarily in the areas of moral psychology, the philosophy of mind and language, and aesthetics.

Harold Noonan is Reader in Philosophical Logic at the University of Birmingham. He has published two books – *Objects and Identity* (Martinus Nijhoff, 1979) and *Personal Identity* (Routledge, 1989) – and various articles on topics in the philosophy of mind, philosophy of language and philosophy of logic.

Christopher Peacocke is Waynflete Professor of Metaphysical Philosophy at the University of Oxford, and also holds a Leverhulme Personal Research Professorship. Until 1998, he is a regular Visiting Professor at the Department of Philosophy at New York University. He is the author of *A Study of Concepts* (MIT, 1992) and of papers in the philosophy of language, mind, psychology and logic. He is currently working on a book on metaphysics and epistemology. He is a Fellow of the British Academy.

John Perry is the H. S. Stuart Professor of Philosophy at Stanford University, and Director of the Center for the Study of Language and Information. His publications include *A Dialogue on Personal Identity and Immortality* (Hackett, 1978), *Situations and Attitudes* (with Jon Barwise, MIT Press, 1983) and various articles on the philosophy of language.

Mark Richard works in the philosophy of language, logic, and mind. He is the author of *Propositional Attitudes* (Cambridge University Press, 1990), an associate editor of *Linguistics and Philosophy*, and currently associate professor and chair of the Philosophy Department at Tufts University.

R. M. Sainsbury is Stebbing Professor of Philosophy at King's College, London. He is the Editor of *Mind* and the author of *Russell* (Routledge, 1979), *Logical Forms* (Blackwell, 1991) and *Paradoxes* (Cambridge, second edition 1995).

John Skorupski is Professor of Moral Philosophy at the University of St Andrews and was previously Professor of Philosophy at the University of Sheffield. He is the author of *English-Language Philosophy 1750–1945* (Oxford, 1993). Currently he is working on a study of the epistemology and metaphysics of the normative domain, which will include among other topics an examination of the notions of meaning and aprioricity.

Robert Stalnaker is Professor of Philosophy in the Department of Linguistics and Philosophy at MIT. He is the author of *Inquiry* (MIT Press, 1984), and of articles on intentionality and the foundations of semantics and pragmatics.

Jason Stanley is an Assistant Professor at the Sage School of Philosophy, Cornell University. His interests include the philosophy of language, the history and philosophy of logic, the history of analytic philosophy, epistemology, and the philosophy of mind.

Charles Travis is Professor of Philosophy at the University of Stirling. He has published extensively on the philosophy of language and the philosophy of mind. His most recent work includes his book *The Uses of Sense* (Oxford, 1989), together with numerous articles devoted to related issues. He is currently working on a book on thoughts and attitudes.

Ralph Walker teaches philosophy at Magdalen College, Oxford, where he has been a Fellow and Tutor since 1972. His publications include *Kant* (1978) and *The Coherence Theory of Truth* (1989). He is at present writing a book arguing that the moral law, and prescriptive principles of certain other kinds, are in a very strong sense objectively real.

David Wiggins is Wykeham Professor of Logic in the University of Oxford. He was previously Professor of Philosophy at Birkbeck College, London, and before that Fellow and Praelector of University College, Oxford. His principal publications are *Sameness and Substance* (Blackwell, 1980) and *Needs, Values, Truth* (Blackwell, second edition 1993). He is a Fellow of the British Academy.

Timothy Williamson is Professor of Logic and Metaphysics at the University of Edinburgh. He was previously a Fellow in Philosophy at University College, Oxford. He is the author of *Identity and Discrimination* (Blackwell, 1990), *Vagueness* (Blackwell, 1994) and articles in journals of philosophy and logic.

Crispin Wright is Professor of Logic and Metaphysics at the University of St Andrews. He was previously Nelson Professor of Philosophy at the University of

Michigan. His principal publications are *Wittgenstein on the Foundations of Mathematics* (Duckworth, 1980), *Frege's Conception of Numbers as Objects* (Aberdeen University Press, 1983), *Truth and Objectivity* (Harvard, 1992) and *Realism, Meaning and Truth* (Blackwell, second edition 1993). He is a Fellow of the British Academy and of the Royal Society of Edinburgh.

PART I

MEANING AND THEORIES OF MEANING

1

Meaning and truth conditions: from Frege's grand design to Davidson's

DAVID WIGGINS

1. However close it may have lain beneath the surface of some earlier speculations about language, the idea that to understand a sentence is to have grasped its truth-condition was first made explicit by Frege, for whom it was simply an unemphasized consequence of his general approach to questions of meaning. In the transition from logical positivism to modern analytical philosophy, the idea came near to being mislaid entirely. It was brought back into a new prominence in the late 1960s by Donald Davidson. Having rediscovered the idea for himself and in his own way, Davidson pressed its claims as a principle in the philosophy of mind and meaning, and as the only proper basis on which to conduct serious semantic investigations.

In advance of considering more recent claims about meaning, it will be useful to mark certain moments in the formulation and reformulation of the original insight of the truth-conditional theory. In a historical framework, even the bare skeleton of one furnished here, truth-conditional notions may be expected to transcend our more immediate sources of information about them as well as our more ephemeral disputations.

2. What is it for a declarative sentence to mean something, or have a sense? For Frege, to answer such a question was not, as it was later for Carnap or his inheritors, an all-important end in itself. Nor was answering it part of a comprehensive effort to arrive at a philosophical account of the relation of language to mind, as it is for Davidson and his inheritors. For Frege, it was a means, a propaedeutic for the understanding of the specific thing whose status and nature centrally concerned him, namely arithmetical judgements. Nevertheless, despite the special character of this original interest, Frege saw the question of the meaning of a declarative sentence as a general one, requiring not so much the introduction of a *calculus ratiocinator* (he said) as the creation of something more resembling a Leibnizian *lingua characteristica*. ("My intention was not to represent an abstract logic in formulas, but to express a content through written signs in a more precise and clear way").[1] What Frege took the answer to his question to require was a general notion of meaning that could be correlative with the general idea of the understanding of a sentence. The conception he formed was of the *Sinn* or *sense* of a sentence that was to be understood thus or so, the sentence itself being seen as

something built up by iterable modes of combination from component words, each of which had its own contributory sense. The senses of part and whole were to be such that the latter could be determined from the former (plus an account of the modes of grammatical combination involved in the construction of the sentence).

The culmination of Frege's efforts may be found in Volume 1, Section 32 of the *Grundgesetze der Arithmetik*,[2] where he declares that there is both sense and reference for every sentence of his 'concept-writing' or 'ideography', his *Begriffsschrift*. The *Begriffsschrift* is the constructed language whose operations are to shadow the workings of natural language and, in matters of difficulty like the foundations of arithmetic, to regulate or supplant natural language. The reference of a sentence of *Begriffsschrift* is its truth value, and the sense of the sentence is the thought that the sentence expresses.

But how exactly does a thought attach to a sentence? And what is a thought? Well, which thought it is that a sentence expresses and how the thought attaches to the sentence will depend upon nothing other than this: under what conditions is the sentence to count as true? Or, as Frege describes the matter for the artificial language he has just finished constructing,

> It is determined through our stipulations [for the linguistic expressions and devices comprising the language of *Begriffsschrift*] under what conditions [any sentence of *Begriffsschrift*] stands for the True. The sense of this name [of a truth-value, i.e. the sense of this sentence], that is the thought, is the sense or thought that these conditions are fulfilled. The names [expressions], whether simple or composite, of which the [sentence or] name of a truth-value is constituted contribute to the expression of a thought, and this contribution [of each constituent] is its sense. If a name [expression] is part of the name of a truth value [i.e. is part of a sentence], then the sense of the former, the name [expression], is part of the thought expressed by the latter [the sentence].

This statement comes at the end of Frege's detailed explanations of *Begriffsschrift*. But its import is potentially perfectly general, and the stipulations of sense for the expressions of his invented language simulate what it is for the expressions of a natural language to have a given or actual (not merely stipulated) sense. The institution of the *Begriffsschrift* – a project Frege had begun in preparation for his books on the foundations of arithmetic (1884,[3] 1893[4]) and published in part in 1879,[5] but then resumed and substantially corrected in the work of 1893, from which we have just quoted – at once illuminates natural language, albeit only in microcosm, and extends it. It illuminates it by displaying clearly the workings of a distinct language abstracted from natural language, namely the concept-script in which Frege hoped to make newly perspicuous all questions of "inferential sequence". The purposes this serves are akin to the practical and theoretical purposes that the construction of an artificial hand with a specialized function might have for a community of beings whose normal members had natural hands with less specialized functions.

3. Given Frege's concern with "a formula-language for pure [i.e. non-empirical] thought", it is unsurprising that, as he said, he "confined [him]self for the time being to expressing [within it] relations that are independent of the particular characteristics of objects" (*Begriffsschrift*, 1879, preface). Properties and relations that were not so independent registered in the *Begriffsschrift* only in the form of generality-indicating letters such as Φ or Ψ that prescinded from all particular content.[6] Nevertheless, Frege did envisage successive relaxations of this ordinance, and he spoke of possible extensions of his formula language to embrace the sciences of geometry, motion, mechanics and so on.

Given the universality and generality of the insights that originate with Frege, what we now have to envisage is the final extension of *Begriffsschrift*, namely the extension which, for purposes rather different from Frege's, will even furnish it with the counterpart of such ordinary sentences as "the sun is behind cloud" (say). In the long run, the extended *Begriffsschrift* might itself be modified further, to approximate more and more closely to the state of some natural language. In the interim, however, in the transition from Frege's to our own purposes, it stands as an illustrative model of something more complicated.

In such an extension as the one we are to imagine, a sentence like "the sun is behind cloud" will have a sense if and only if it expresses a thought. For the particular thought that the sun is behind cloud to attach to this English sentence (for it to attach to such a social artefact as this, produced and held fast in its temporal, historic and social setting, Frege need not forbid us to say) will be for the sentence to be so placed in its total (historical and customary-cum-linguistic) context that it stands [in some situation] for the True just in case [in that situation] the sun is behind cloud. Putting the matter in a way that is not Frege's but will readily consist with his way, he who understands the sentence is party to a practice that makes this the condition under which the sentence counts as true.

Once so much is said, what mystery remains about what a thought is? The thought expressed by a sentence is expressed by it in virtue of ordinary linguistic practices (the practices that we have imagined will be encapsulated in the definitions or elucidations of the empirical terms to be introduced into the extended *Begriffsschrift*), which expose the sentence to reality, and its author to the hazard of being wrong, in one way rather than another way.

4. The truth-conditional thesis, so seen, can be detached from more questionable features of Frege's semantical doctrine, such as the idea that a sentence is a complex sign standing for objects called the True or the False, or is a name of a truth-value. Wittgenstein does detach it (an act of retrieval for which he is too rarely commended) in *Tractatus Logico-Philosophicus* (1921):[7]

> 4. 022 A sentence in use (Satz) shows how things stand if it is true. And it says that they do so stand.
>
> 4. 024 To understand a sentence in use means to know what is the case if it is true.
>
> 4. 061 A sentence in use is true if we use it to say that things stand in a certain way, and they do.

These are striking formulations, more general than Frege's and not radically dependent upon Wittgenstein's picture-theory of meaning. But now it seems we must attend to a problem that neither Frege nor Wittgenstein addressed explicitly. It is the problem (which still excites controversy in connection with Donald Davidson's version of the truth-conditional view of meaning)[8] that not just any true equivalence in the form [s is true if and only if p] can suffice to show that s actually *means* that p.

Suppose that the sentence "the sun is behind cloud" is now true. Then all sorts of other things have now (as matters stand) to be the case. It is daytime, the sun has risen, it is not dark, more people are awake than asleep, and millions of automobiles are emitting smoke into the atmosphere, and so on – all this in addition to the sun's being behind cloud. For these are the invariable consequences or accompaniments, in the world as it is, of its being daytime and the sun's having actually risen (in order that it be obnubilated or not obnubilated). It is only to be expected, then, that, where *s* makes such a particular historical statement as it does, in a manner dependent upon some historical context, any of these extra things may in that context be added *salva veritate* to the right-hand side of the biconditional "*s* is true if and only if the sun is behind cloud and . . .". (It is certain that any necessary truth or natural law can be added so.) It is only by virtue of knowing already what *s means* that one would pick on the "sun is behind cloud" conjunct, from out of the mass of things that also hold when the "sun is behind cloud" is true, to be the clause to give the proper truth-condition for *s*. It follows that, to put down what a given utterance of a sentence *s* means and impart its meaning to someone, we need to be in a position to signal some 'intended' or 'privileged' or 'designated' condition on which its truth depends. Only where '*s* is true iff p' signals on its right-hand side an intended, privileged or designated condition, can we conclude from this biconditional's obtaining that the utterance of *s* means that p.

5. One way to try to put all this on the proper basis and lend a point to some particular condition's being marked out as the semantically pertinent condition is to recast Frege's and Wittgenstein's thesis as follows:

> Sentence s has as its use to say that p – or s means that p – just if whether s is true or not *depends specifically upon* whether or not p.

But this is not really the end of the difficulty. For one of the things that the truth of "the sun is behind cloud" (as said at a given particular time and place) depends specifically upon, in one ordinary and standard sense of "depend", might perhaps (at that time and place) be low atmospheric pressure plus the obtaining of other meteorological conditions. None of this, however, is what the sentence actually says (or even, in its context, implies). And for the same reason we cannot improve the formulation just given by ruling that the truth of the sentence has to depend *only* upon the designated condition. It cannot depend "only" on that condition, in the ordinary sense of "depend". For it will have to depend (in that ordinary sense) on everything that the satisfaction of the intended condition itself depends upon.

6. Consider now what Frege might have said in reply to this difficulty, pointing to things already done in *Grundgesetze*. To increase the generality of his reply, however, let us suppose (as before), that the language of his *Begriffsschrift* has been formally expanded to enable one to say "the sun is behind cloud" and all sorts of similar empirical things. Each new primitive expression ('sun', 'cloud', etc.) will have had a reference stipulated for it in accordance with an empiricized extension of Frege's canon for definitions (see *Grundgesetze*, 1893, I, section 33). In each case, the sense of the new primitive expression will consist in the fact that its reference is stipulated thus or so.[9] By virtue of this, it will have been contrived that the sense of any complex expression can be determined from its structure and from the referential stipulations governing each constituent expression. But now, in the light of all this, Frege is entitled to insist that, if we stick scrupulously to what actually flows from the full and appointed referential stipulations for all the individual expressions and devices of the extended *Begriffsschrifft* – let us call the set that consists of them Θ(Bg+) – then we shall never be able to arrive at an unwanted biconditional like 'the sentence "the sun is behind cloud on 25 June 1993" is true if and only if on 25 June 1993 the sun is behind cloud and the sun has risen and there is low pressure and more people are awake than asleep and . . .' (or its counterpart in Bg+). For the stipulations for the extended *Begriffsschrift* furnish no way to derive such a biconditional; and the intended condition will be the condition that the appointed stipulations do suffice to deliver.[10] Not only that. In concert, these stipulations, which license nothing about low pressure as part of the truth-condition for *s*, will *spell out* the specific particular dependence that had to be at issue in the restatement of the Frege–Wittgenstein thesis.

No wonder, then, that we can hear ' "the sun is behind cloud" is true if and only if the sun is behind cloud' as more or less equivalent to 'The truth of "the sun is behind cloud" semantically depends upon whether or not the sun is behind cloud'. For we hear ' "The sun is behind cloud" is true if and only if the sun is behind cloud' as something delivered to us by whatever plays the part for English that the Fregean stipulations Θ(Bg+) will play for the extended *Begriffsschrift*. What we are saying is, in effect, this:

[*s* means in Bg+ that p] is equivalent to $\vdash_{\theta(Bg+)}$ [True *s* if and only if p].

There is nothing strange or scandalous in the suggestion that we hear the conditional as nested in this way within an operator "⊢" whose presence has to be understood. Countless conditionals we utter are intended by us to be understood as presupposing some norm or tendency that we could roughly identify but do not attempt to describe in the form of an explicit generalization. In so far as some residue of a philosophical problem still persists, the place to which it escapes is the characterization of "⊢" and the idea of a set of referential specifications Θ(Bg+) that imply this or that equivalence in the form [True *s* if and only if p]. The point that is left over, which we shall have to attend to in due course, is that, although Θ(Bg+) would *exemplify* such a set, Θ(Bg+) could scarcely stand in for a general characterization of what a referential specification *is*. We need $\vdash_{\theta(L)}$ for variable L.

7. It will consolidate the position now arrived at to pause here to show – if not in Frege's symbolism (which continues to daunt typesetters and readers equally) or even in exact accordance with every particular of Frege's own view of predication[11] – how, more exactly and in more detail, the claim might be made good that Frege can pick out the particular sort of dependence that he needs to secure between the obtaining of the condition that p and *s*'s truth. Let us do so by giving the referential specification of the semantics of a tiny sublanguage L(1) of English that might be the counterpart of some small fragment of the extended *Begriffsschrift* (or Bg+).

Suppose the constituent strings of L(1) are simply the following:

(1) The sun is behind cloud
(2) Not (the sun is behind cloud), [which is said aloud as follows: the sun is not behind cloud]
(3) The moon is behind cloud
(4) Not (the moon is behind cloud), [which is said aloud as follows: the moon is not behind cloud],

together with all possible conjunctions of (1), (2), (3) and (4). Then we can determine the sense of an arbitrary string of L(1) by the following provisions:

Terms:	T(1)	"The sun" is a term and stands for the sun.
	T(2)	"The moon" is a term and stands for the moon.
Predicates:	P(1)	"Behind cloud" is a predicate and stands for behind cloud.[12]
Connectives:	C(1)	"Not" is a unary connective; where A is a string of L, "not" + A is true if and only if A is not true.
	C(2)	"And" is a binary corrective; [A + "and" + B] is true if and only if A is true and B is true.

Syncategorematic Expressions: "Is" is a syncategorematic expression, whose role is to signal the fundamental mode of combination exemplified in R(1) below.

Rule of Truth: R(1) A sentence that is of the form [t + "is" + Φ], i.e. a sentence consisting of a term t, such as "the sun" or "the moon", followed by the syncategorematic expression, "is", followed by a predicate expression, Φ, such as "behind cloud", is true if and only if what t stands for is what Φ stands for[13] [i.e. the reference of t has the property that Φ stands for].

Now let us put these rules together and note their effect. Given the sentence ["the moon" + "is" + "behind cloud"] = [The moon is behind cloud], we can agree, by R(1), that the sentence is true if and only if what "the moon" stands for is what "behind cloud" stands for, which last we can show to be true (see T(2) and P(1)) if and only if the moon is behind cloud. That does not make news – no more than news is made when, having multiplied 13 by 25 and got 325, you then divide 325 by 13 and get 25. But it verifies something. Similarly, as Davidson would point out here on Frege's behalf, our semantic derivation helps verify something, namely that, so far as they go, T(1), T(2), P(1), C(1), C(2) and R(1) represent a correct reckoning of the semantic resources of L(1).

What is achieved would have looked more impressive, no doubt, if L(1) had been a fragment of French and our referential specification had been done in English. Such a specification is something we can more easily imagine someone's failing to get right. There is no question, however, of a specification of this sort's looking impressive (or its needing to do so) – unless it solves neatly and correctly a known grammatical difficulty or casts some light, however indirect, on a real obscurity in the workings of a given language. Note too that for purposes of these derivations from T(1), T(2), P(1) and R(1), nothing at all depends on the meaning of "stand for". (See note 27.)

8. This completes the referential specification or semantic theory $\Theta^{L(1)}$ for a language L(1), which is a specimen sublanguage of Bg+. (More strictly speaking, L(1) is the natural language counterpart of a sublanguage of Bg+.) It leaves nothing to chance in the idea that, where *s* is an L(1) sentence, *s* means in L(1) that p if and only if the biconditional [True *s* if and only if p] flows from $\Theta^{L(1)}$. It illustrates what it would take to complete the answer to the problem mentioned in § 5. In the context of Frege's own particular purposes in the *Grundgesetze der Arithmetik*, let this serve as a model for the complete defence of what Frege wanted to say there about sentence sense. For all he needed to be able to do in that work was to illustrate there his complete grasp of and control over the sense of a *Begriffsschrift* sentence. There is no relevant doubt, either theoretical or practical, of that grasp.[14]

9. In *Tractatus* 4. 024 Wittengenstein is heir to Frege's idea of sentence sense, and he tries to prescind from the particularities of *Begriffsschrift* in order to make a general claim. Then in 4. 061 he attempts to bring real, live speakers into the picture. Once we take their presence seriously, however, we shall notice a new kind of difficulty – the first (but not the last) of several.

Consider the Latin sentence *alea jacta est*. Like its standard translation into English, *the die is cast*, the sentence is true if and only if a die has been thrown. This requires, inter alia, that there be a real die and someone who has thrown it. But it is safe to say that what speakers have normally used the Latin or the English sentence to state or to intimate – to say in the full and ordinary sense of 'say' – is nothing of that sort. The normal use of the sentence is to say the sort of thing that Julius Caesar said by *alea jacta est* when he broke the laws of the Roman Republic and, instead of disbanding his troops, led them towards Rome across the boundary marked by the river Rubicon. We who follow Caesar use the English sentence to assert that, in doing some act or other such as crossing that stream, we have committed ourselves irrevocably.

What is the difficulty here? The difficulty this creates for the Frege–Wittgenstein characterization of sense is that it shows that there is no simple route from the ordinary or normal use of a sentence like "alea jacta est" – or from what people usually say by uttering it – back to its strictly or narrowly linguistic meaning.

The proper response to this problem is to concede something. We must adjust the Frege–Wittgenstein thesis to read as follows:

> Sentence *s* has as its use in L(i) to say *literally* (to say in the thinnest possible acceptation of 'say') that p – thus *s* means that p in the narrowest strictest sense of 'means' – if and only if the referential specifications specific to the language L(i) [e.g. the sorts of specification given in § 7] rule that whether *s* is true or not depends upon whether or not p.

This reformulation simply spells out the intention that Frege or Wittengenstein could have voiced. But what it suggests is that, to implement that intention, we have to embed our new formulation in some larger, more comprehensive theory, the sort of theory for which we have to look forward to the work of J. L. Austin.[15] This can persevere in the Fregean explication of the literal meaning of a sentence as consisting in its sense or truth-condition. But the fuller kind of saying that we find in the *the die is cast* example is something that the comprehensive theory will have to explain by building upwards and outwards from literal meaning characterized after the fashion of provisions like T(1), T(2), P(1), C(1), C(2) and R(1). A neo-Austinian theory may suggest that, by doing the *rhetic act* of uttering something which has as its sense (and means literally) in language L(i) that the die has been thrown, and by performing thus the *locutionary act* of saying that the die is thrown, a speaker can perform a further speech act, namely an *illocutionary act*, tantamount in force to the declaration or intimation that he is irrevocably committed. By saying one thing, then (here a false thing), Caesar conveys something else, which proves to have been a true thing.

10. There is much more to say about this, but not here or now. Here I have only to show how one might place in a single focus the Frege–Wittgenstein conception of sense, in the condition in which it was available by 1921, and the different researches of J. L. Austin. (See also Chapter 3, INTENTION AND CONVENTION, § 3.) These were undertaken some thirty years after the *Tractatus*, in a framework of theoretical expectations both at odds with the concerns of *Grundgesetze* and *Tractatus* and uninformed, alas, by attention to anything very much that these works had in common. But the justification for my act of anachronism is that, unless we use Austin's work to *delimit* the area in which Frege, Russell and the early Wittgenstein wanted to operate, their theories will be plagued with irrelevant objections. There is a host of questions about meaning their theories cannot even purport to answer. Nevertheless, that is not a point against them – *provided* that the theories do not positively prevent answers from being given to these other questions. It cannot be

emphasized too strongly, however, that the theory of literal sense as fixed by truth-conditions must be such that it can be fitted into the larger framework that embraces both the non-literal use of declarative sentences and the literal use of ordinary non-declarative sentences.[16]

11. So much, then, for the question of the intended truth-condition, and so much now for what "the die is cast" normally says in English, as two heads of objection to the unrefined truth-conditional view of saying. The answer to the first objection had the effect of drawing attention to the phenomenon of semantic compositionality, to which we shall return. The second, which motivated the isolation of the strict or literal sense of an expression, will force the philosopher of language into a far less restrictive and abstractive interest than heretofore in the social and linguistic phenomena of communication. Evidently this is an interest well-calculated to match the interest to which Wittgenstein gives voice, in a passage too rarely heeded as already expressive of his constant attitude to such questions, at *Tractatus* 4. 002:

> Everyday language is a part of the human organism and is no less complicated than it. . . . The tacit conventions on which the understanding of everyday language depends are enormously complicated.

In due course it will prove that an even more radical reorientation towards the behavioural and the social lies in store for us, when we return to the problem of properly generalizing the Fregean doctrine beyond the case of one specified language. Since such problems did not exercise Wittgenstein, however, who writes 4. 022, 4. 024 and 4. 061 in the manner of one who has already achieved full philosophical generality, let us tell some of the rest of the story, before we return to the generality problem.

The thing that principally troubled Wittgenstein about 4. 024, to judge from what he wrote in the period after the *Tractatus*, was the non-operational character of the neo-Fregean conceptions of sense and truth that he had espoused in the *Tractatus*. By the time of writing *Philosophische Bemerkungen*, what he prefers to say is this:

> To understand the sense of a *Satz* means to know how the issue of its truth or falsity is to be decided (*Philosophische Bemerkungen*, IV. 43).[17]

This new formulation looks backwards one decade at the doctrine of *Tractatus*. It is no less easily recognizable as the antecedent of the infamous claim advanced by the logical positivists of the 1930s, which dominated the thirties and forties and had an even longer period of influence in the philosophy of science, namely that the sense of a sentence is nothing more nor less than the method of its verification. (For further discussion of this, see Chapter 2, MEANING, USE, VERIFICATION.)

Equally, however, the new formulation is the antecedent of a more durable claim that Wittgenstein came to advance, namely, that ("for a large class of cases") to understand a linguistic expression is simply to grasp its use in the language. (See the *Blue* and *Brown Books* and see the two decades' worth of philosophy books by others that were influenced by this formulation.) As verificationism fell out of favour, this doctrine rushed in to fill the vacuum that was left by its disappearance.[18] Then, as the limitations came to be perceived of the doctrine of meaning as use, the next idea that rushed into the vacuum was Grice's idea that the meaning of a declarative utterance was a function of speakers' intentions to use that sentence to induce (by the recognition of that intention) this or that belief. The Fregean idea was destined to be rediscovered for philosophy and accorded an attention it had never previously enjoyed – but scarcely immediately.[19] For English speakers, it remained more or less buried until 1959, when Michael Dummett's article "Truth" disinterred it and put it back into circulation.[20] This limited circulation was yet further limited by the fact that Dummett expressed reservations of his own (not dissimilar to those we have attributed to Wittgenstein) about the acceptability of the thesis in the form in which Frege had had it. (See Chapter 12, REALISM AND ITS OPPOSITIONS, §§ 1 and 2.)

12. So much then for the shift that Wittgenstein himself seems to have initiated away from the doctrine of *Tractatus* 4. 024, and so much for the philosophy of language that worked itself out downstream of Frege, Russell and early Wittgenstein over the period between 1921 and the 1960s, when Davidson's philosophy of language first became visible. But now let us go back to the point in the argument that we had reached at the end of § 8.

In § 8, having expounded *Grundgesetze*, 1. 32, we were saying that Frege or Wittgenstein would have been well-placed to defend the truth conditional thesis against the objections mentioned in § 4 by formulating it as follows: in *Begriffsschrift* extended (or its sublanguage L(1)), *s* can be used to say literally that p if and only if the equivalence [True *s* if and only if p] flows from the referential stipulations for the language Bg+ (or L(1)). The difficulty that this left over was this: that the most that this positive doctrine will ever enable us to *put on the page* is an account of what it is for a sentence to say-in-the-language-of-Begriffsschrift(+) that p, or

> *s* can be used to say-literally-in-Bg(+) that p – or *s* means-literally-in-Bg(+) that p – if and only if it is derivable from the referential-stipulations-for-Bg(+) (specified thus T(1), T(2), P(1), C(1), C(2), R(1). . . .) that *s* is a true-(Bg(+))-sentence if and only if p.

This points at something general about truth and meaning, namely the thing that Wittgenstein gets across in 4. 024. But how can we fully articulately say this general thing? How can we extricate "mean literally", "say literally" or "referential stipulation" from these hyphenations with "Bg(+)"?

13. One manageable objective we might set ourselves is this: to arrive at the generalization we need by satisfying all the necessary conditions to supplant the constant "Bg(+)" by a variable "L(i)". If we proceed in this way, we can transcend Bg(+) and we can make explicit the thing that the (Bg(+))-relative condition only shows.

Looking back at what we then have to generalize and free from relativity to

Bg(+), it will appear that the chief obligation we now incur is to dispense with the reference to particular stipulations such as T(1), T(2), P(1), . . . , etc. Instead, we have to say explicitly what sort of thing a referential stipulation is. And perhaps the most natural first suggestion will be that we should advance on the following basis:

> *s* means that p in L(i) if and only if there is a Θ for L(i), namely $\Theta^{L(i)}$, that associates each expression of L(i) with its proper value, and this $\Theta^{L(i)}$ implies that *s* is true if and only if p.

Such a proposal will resonate in multiple ways with a common theme in a variety of semantical traditions. (Davidson calls it the building-block proposal.) The only trouble is that, in practice, it has never been brought convincingly to life. There is nothing both general and foundational to be said, simply in terms of reference, about how "and", "not", "Caesar" and "behind cloud" all have their meaning. We cannot dispense, in semantics, with something like the idea of reference. Equally, however, we cannot make out of the idea of reference the whole basis for the semantics of the sentence. From a standing start, we cannot even explain in such terms what distinguishes a sentence from a mere list. Frege himself never at any point dispensed with the idea of reference. But he also insisted, in the Preface to *The Foundations of Arithmetic*, that "only in the context of a sentence does a word mean or stand for anything". Somewhere near the beginning of our account we have to render it more intelligible than our first suggestion will, that sentences have sense, and can be used not merely to list items of reference but to *say* things.

14. Noting that truth and meaning are symmetrically relativized in the elucidation of meaning we offered at the end of § 12, we shall see that there is a different suggestion we can explore. Not only did $\Theta^{L(1)}$ in § 7 state the meanings of each sentence of the language L(1). As a by-product of doing that, it fixed systematically and non-accidentally correctly the extension of the predicate "true" as restricted to L(1) sentences. "The sun is behind cloud" is true if and only if the sun is behind cloud, "The moon is behind cloud" is true if and only if the moon is behind cloud, etc. (Such biconditionals are sometimes called *partial definitions* of 'true sentence of L(i)'.) We need not know which sentences are the true ones or constitute the actual extension of "true-in-L(1)". But we do have a systematic way to state the principle on which that extension is assembled and, in that however strange or philosophically unwonted sense, we have a "definition" of 'true-in-L(1)'.

So the new thought is this: why not underwrite the *Tractatus* 4. 024 generalization by saying the following?:

> for any *s*, *s* can be used to say literally in L(i) that p – *s* means literally in L(i) that p – if and only if it is derivable from the definition of *true sentence of* L(i) that s is true if and only if p.

It will be quickly noticed that here we are characterizing literal meaning in terms of "definition", a notion that surely appears equally semantical and equally difficult.

But the hope must be that there is some way to say what a definition of true L(i) sentence is otherwise than by making some general definition of definition.

15. Having had recourse, in this last transposition, to the idea of a definition of truth in L(i), the time has come to turn our attention away from the main trend of semantic speculation in analytical philosophy, away from Jena, Cambridge and Vienna, towards Lwów, Warsaw and the study that Tarski called the "methodology of the deductive sciences", which was one part of Tarski's contribution to the prewar development of mathematical logic.[21]

The change of orientation is at first surprising. We are inclined but not necessitated in this direction by the formal shape of the problem we have been considering, which relates only to the conceptual lacuna that divides *Grundgesetze* 1. 32 from *Tractatus* 4. 024. Other directions are thinkable. Yet, given the actual influences that have formed the semantical speculations of nowadays (Davidson's and others), there is no real alternative, however oblique Tarski's concerns are to Davidson's, and however small the immediate progress we may appear to make by following this new route.

Let us begin by asking the question how it can have come about, if the theory of Fregean sense was in no way Tarski's preoccupation, that Tarski should have been interested in identifying a set of axioms for a language L(i) that delivered theorems given in the form [s is true in L(i) if and only if p]. Why was Tarski interested in axioms delivering the theorems of which philosophers of language like Davidson want to say that they determine the sense or contribution of each of the expressions of L(i)? The answer is that, although Tarski was not interested in meaning as such, he was interested, and interested in a special way, in truth.[22] He was interested in the idea of truth neither after the fashion of the traditional logic – truth simply as the thing that valid inference preserves – nor after the fashion of philosophers who are exercised by the more mysterious and perennial questions about truth. The sort of thing Tarski was interested in doing was to find ways to compare and contrast the class of true formulas of a given formal language with the class of formulas that the rules and axioms make provable there. Embarking on inquiries of this kind, what Tarski needed was a systematic account of what determined the extension of the concept *true*.[23] (Such a systematic account, given in what I have invited the reader to see as a modernization of the method of Frege's *Grundgesetze*, is what he called a 'definition'.) But that was not everything he needed. He also needed to find assurance that his account of truth would not be undermined by the ancient paradoxes that exploited that idea, Epimenides's paradox, for instance[24] (cp. Tarski, 1931, p. 110, and 1936, p. 252).

Let us take the second of these problems first. Tarski's analysis of the liar paradox and its variants suggested to him that the best way to safeguard the construction he had in mind was to begin with some particular object-language that was itself free from all semantic notions. Once the object-language itself was made determinate, semantic concepts[25] such as satisfaction and truth, as restricted to that object-language, and designation, similarly restricted,[26] could be introduced into the metalanguage for that language by defining each concept deliberately, with full formal correctness, in terms drawn from the object-language (or translations of the same into the metalanguage), from elementary set theory and from the formal morphology of the object-language, as given in the metalanguage.[27] On these terms, one could assure oneself that, if the object-language was immune from paradox, then the metalanguage would be immune too.

16. So far so good. But on what principle was a restricted, paradox-free notion of truth, the concept *true sentence of L(i)*, to be positively characterized? What was the philosophical or intuitive substance of the idea? For his thoughts about this, Tarski turned (by his own account[28]) to his teacher Tadeusz Kotarbinski's book *Elementy Teorji Poznania*, where we find the following passage (itself reminiscent of *Tractatus* 4. 061):

> Let us pass to the classical doctrine and ask what is [to be] understood by "[a sentence's or thought's] accordance with reality". The point is not that a true thought should be a good copy or [fac]simile of the thing of which we are thinking, as a printed copy or photograph is. Brief reflection suffices to recognize the metaphorical nature of such a comparison. A different interpretation of 'accordance with reality' is required. We shall confine ourselves to the following explanation: "John judges truly if and only if things are thus and so: and things are in fact thus and so."[29]

Spelling out this explanation for the case of some particular sentence, we have

John judges truly in saying "snow is white" if and only if
(1) John is right in saying "snow is white" if and only if snow is white
(2) snow is indeed white.

But then it seems we can have, more simply[30]

"Snow is white" is true if and only if snow is white.

The chief thing that it seems a definition of "true in L(i)" must do in order to conform to Kotarbinski's requirements is to imply one such equivalence in respect of each sentence of L(i).[31]

But now, having come this far, we shall be moved to ask: how otherwise can the definition of truth in L(i) furnish the thing Kotarbinski required, or ensure the complete eliminability of "true sentence of L(i)" that is required for the explicit definition of "true sentence of L(i)" that Tarski desired, than by doing first the sort of thing we have seen that $\Theta^{L(1)}$ did? This is how Tarski's path comes to cross the path that we have seen Frege's and Wittgenstein's thoughts as marking out. The parties go in different directions, but at the intersection there is one common thing each party needs in order to arrive where it is headed. Each party needs to be involved, for any language that comes into consideration, in something like the exercise conducted in § 7. (Of course, Wittgenstein, attempting a more ambitious thing, needs to depend on the possibility of doing more than this: a matter to which we shall return.)

17. In the light of this, how is the problem to be solved of saying what a referential specification is? Well, if there is this convergence, then Tarski must have the same problem under a different name if he is to say what a definition of truth is. Tarski has to say what such a definition must be like in order to be adequate. The problem is solved as follows:

> A formally correct definition $\Theta^{L(i)}$ of the predicate "true" as applied to L(i) sentences is *materially adequate* if and only if, for every sentence sentence *s* of L(i), Θ implies a biconditional (or so-called T-sentence) in the form [True *s* if and only if p], where 'p' holds a place for a translation of *s* into the metalanguage ML(i).

Tarski calls this provision – which is evidently not itself statable at any level lower that the meta-metalanguage – Convention T.[32] It is simply the generalization of Kotarbinski's desideratum.[33] Similarly, then, a referential specification for L(i) assigns a value to every expression in L(i): and a set of such assignments is materially adequate under the very same condition as Tarski gives. It must yield a T sentence for each sentence of L(i). And each T-sentence must in the same way be translational, which is to say that, in each case, 'p' must hold a place for a translation of *s* into the metalanguage.

18. Does this represent any progress? For Tarski, it is progress, because Tarski's only objective is to arrive at a non-accidentally and recognizably correct definition of true sentence of L(i). The word "translation" is not being used here in a manner that offends against Tarski's professed attitude to semantic notions. It occurs only in the meta-metalanguage, or (as one might fancifully say) in Kotarbinski's and Tarski's philosophy of truth. Occurring there, it presupposes only this: that a logician can recognize when the sentence given on the right-hand side of a T-equivalence is faithful to the meaning of the sentence mentioned on the left. Nevertheless, because Convention T includes within it a semantical term coordinate with *meaning, definition* and the rest, anyone who is concerned with the idea of meaning for its own sake still faces the same old question. How can we eliminate the semantical term from Convention T – or how can we analyse or dismantle it there?

Here at last we can resume the story that we have already carried up to 1959, which was the moment when Michael Dummett put the truth-conditional insight back into circulation. If anybody had been concerned with the question of how to make Wittgenstein's generalization 4. 024 work, then Tarski's construction would have served him perfectly – unless he had had such an obsessive concern with the nature of meaning itself that it was not sufficient to trace the small circle that joins the ideas of truth, meaning and translation. The trouble is that perfectly properly, indeed *ex officio*, philosophy is imprisoned within that obsession.

19. To understand Donald Davidson's revival of the general idea of meaning as given by truth-conditions, and the distinctive advance that this made possible, it helps to appreciate the immediate background of his speculations. This was not any concern on Davidson's part with the theory common to early Wittgenstein (to

whom Davidson rarely, if ever, referred) and Frege (to whose doctrines Davidson evidently regarded Alonzo Church as the complete guide, although this guide completely omitted all mention of Frege's truth-conditional insight). The background was more topical, namely Davidson's doubts about Carnap's methods of extension and intension,[34] his considered rejection of the answer to the question of linguistic meaning provided by H. P. Grice's reduction of semantic notions to psychological ones such as belief and intention,[35] and Davidson's attachment to the speculative framework furnished by W. V. Quine's book *Word and Object* (1960) – most especially the question of what a thinker from outside a community of speakers would need to avail himself of if he were to try to make sense of utterances in their unknown language. What Davidson wanted was to retain Quine's naturalistic approach to such questions, to align himself with Quine's objection to all "museum myths" of meaning, but to do so without commitment to Quine's talk of ocular irradiation, neural impacts upon subjects and the rest. According to Davidson, the thing that impinges on subjects had better be the world itself, the world that is common to both interpreter and subjects.

Seeking for some framework within which to give a systematic account of the information (or putative information) that an interpreter would need to amass and draw upon in order to interpret others, and to frame his hypotheses about the meanings of his subjects' uttered sentences, and seeking at the same time to sweep away the supposed obscurity of '*s* means that p', the construction Davidson found himself reaching for was in effect none other than Tarski's:

> Let us try treating the position occupied by 'p' [in 's means that p'] extensionally: to implement this, sweep away the obscure 'means that', provide the sentence that replaces 'p' with a proper sentential connective, and supply the description that replaces s with its own predicate. The plausible result is
>
> (T) *s* is T if and only if p.
>
> It is worth emphasizing that the concept of truth played no ostensible role in stating our original problem [the problem of a theory of meaning for a given language]. That problem upon refinement led to the view that an adequate theory of meaning [for the language spoken by the interpreter's subjects] must characterize a predicate meeting certain conditions. It was in the nature of a discovery that such a predicate would apply exactly to the true sentences. . . . A Tarski-type truth definition supplies all we have asked so far of a theory of meaning.[36]

The discovery is of course a rediscovery, the rediscovery of the thing that Frege and Wittgenstein had articulated and that Davidson failed to credit to Frege. If Frege's original insight had not been correct, there could have been no such discovery. Working within Quine's framework, however, the attitude Davidson had towards Tarski was as follows. Taking translation for granted (or taking "means in L(i)" for granted), Tarski had defined "true sentence of L(i)". Conversely, then, why should not Davidson take truth in L(i) for granted, in order to define "means in L(i)"? The only residual problem was to dispense with Tarski's use of the word "translation".

20. Davidson's first thought about the problem seems to have been that he could secure everything he needed if he were simply to omit the requirement that the T-sentences generated by $\Theta^{L(i)}$ in the form [*s* is true if and only if p] should provide translations on the right-hand side of the L(i) sentence *s* mentioned on the left. Could he not stipulate instead that absolutely all the T-sentences that $\Theta^{L(i)}$ generated should be true? But it is now pretty clear that the condition is not sufficient.[37]

From the beginning of all Davidson's speculations, however, shaped as they were by Quine's *Word and Object*, the correct solution to this problem was always at hand. Perhaps Davidson's best account of this solution is the one given in his "Radical Interpretation" (1973).[38] But there is a real point here in giving a Davidsonian solution in a variant that is not open to the objections that so many critics have urged against Davidson's own formulation.[39] The distinctive features of the variant presentation are chiefly due to Richard Grandy and John McDowell.[40]

If the interpreter of the utterance of a sentence is to say what it means, then he has to find out under what conditions the sentence, being the sentence it is, counts as true. To say so much is to say little more than Frege said. The next thought one will have, however, is less Fregean. It is that linguistic behaviour is a proper part of behaviour. But, if so, there ought to be some other than purely semantic way of specifying what it is for a radical interpreter to succeed in interpreting alien people. Surely the interpreter's linguistic efforts are part of the larger effort to interact successfully with others, to coordinate one's efforts with theirs (where appropriate), to make sense of them and so on. But, if we can enlarge a little in such terms, namely terms that are not *specifically* semantical, upon what such an interpreter must then be attempting to achieve, and if the interpretation of speech is simply one proper part of the larger thing the interpreter seeks to understand, then here at last we shall find the substantive non-semantic constraint upon $\Theta^{L(i)}$ we have been looking for.

> A definition of truth in L(i) will be materially adequate if it generates a T-sentence for each sentence s of L(i) and collectively the T-sentences that the definition implies, when experimentally applied to individual utterance by the speakers of L(i), advance unimprovably the effort to make total sense of the speakers of L(i).

The notion of total sense is not a semantic notion, but it *subsumes* one. One person's making sense of another is a matter of their participative interaction in a shareable form of life, of their homing upon the same objects, of their being in a position (*ceteris paribus*) to succeed in joint enterprises, and so on. In so far as we make sense of others, we deploy a mode of understanding that can be redescribed, however artificially, as follows. There is a store of everyday predicates of human subjects, of features of the environments that impinge on subjects, and of the events that are counted as the actions or conduct of such subjects. When we deploy this mode of understanding, we seek in response to circumstances, including the speech or conduct of subjects, to distribute predicates of these and other kinds across features of reality, mental states and actions in such a way that: (1) the propositional attitudes we ascribe to subjects, specifying the content of these attitudes, are intelligible singly and jointly in the light of the the reality to which we take subjects (or their informants, or their informants' informants . . .) to have been exposed; and (2) the actions (and actions of speaking) that we ascribe to subjects are intelligible in the light of the propositional attitudes we ascribe to them.[41]

In the form in which we now have it, the new elucidation of meaning finally bridges the gap between Frege's doctrine and Wittgenstein's. Of course it inherits all the well-known difficulties of the ideas of understanding, explaining, making intelligible, imaginative projection or identification. But these difficulties are there anyway. The proposal not only depends upon these ideas. It assists us by helping to trace their interrelations.

21. The conclusion to which we have been drawn is that what it is for a sentence to mean that the sun is behind cloud and to be available to say that the sun is behind cloud, is as complicated as this. It involves a biconditional, '"The sun is behind cloud" is true if and only if the sun is behind cloud', which is imbedded within the scope of an operator whose presence indicates that this biconditional is derivable from the whole system by which we make sense to one another and make sense of one another. What we have here is the idea of a significant language as a system that correlates strings of repeatable expressions with the states of affairs that the strings can draw attention to or get across, this system itself being a subsystem of the larger system by which social beings participate in their shared life. There is nothing abstruse in that. It is because we grasp it so readily (I think), both in philosophy and before philosophy, that we can hear a T-sentence given in the form "s is true if and only if p" as the output of such a system. When we grasp that, it is tantamount to our grasping something intuitively similar to the "⊢" that played the part we described in the Fregean elucidation of the meaning of *Begriffsschrift* sentences.

22. Objection may be made because, in the formulation I have set down here, *s* can only have it as its literal use to say that p if *all* suitably constrained theories imply that *s* is true if and only if p. What reason is there to suppose that this condition is non-vacuously satisfiable? The objection is a good one, because the formulation does seem to foreclose a matter that ought to have been left open. It seems better on reflection to postpone such questions until we have a fuller account of what it is to make sense of the shared life and conduct of L-speakers. This is a question of the indeterminacy of interpretation – or translation, as Quine says. (See Chapter 16, THE INDETERMINACY OF TRANSLATION.) In the interim, perhaps we should rule that it is sufficient for *s* to mean that p that *some* unimprovable theory that meets all the constraints should entail the biconditional [*s* is true if and only if p].

23. It may be objected that the idea of translation that our final proposal purported to remove surreptitiously returns with the idea of an interpreter's 'making sense'

of other people. But to this the theorist of truth-conditions must reply by simply reiterating his claim that the idea of making sense that we find here is a much wider one than the idea of linguistic interpretation. The presence or absence of this more general thing can be demonstrated non-linguistically. The ideas of making sense of and being made sense of embrace and subsume the ideas of saying and the interpretation of saying, and they involve them illuminatingly with coeval, collateral ideas of explanation and understanding – even (as you may say, if you are as convinced as I am of the indispensability of these further things to the full story) with the idea of participation by interpreter and subjects in a shared form of life, and the idea of explanation as *Verstehen.*

24. A third objection might take the following form. After all the changes and emendations consequential upon earlier objections, should not all residues of the idea of compositionality itself have been expelled from the final formulation? "Truth itself is unduly emphasized in your construction," the objector may say. 'One might accept this for argument's sake as the result of your foolish concentration upon declarative utterances. But, even in the cases where truth really does belong, it is surely not necessary to insist that the interpretive biconditional should be generated by the recursively or compositionally generated definition of truth that you envisage for the language L(i). If we are simply helping ourselves now to the idea of what it requires to "make total sense" of speakers, *Verstehen* and the rest, why cling to this residue of Fregean compositionality?'

To this I would reply that the meaning we are interested in understanding is linguistic meaning, the non-natural meaning possessed by sentences that will be further saturated by context of utterance (etc.) – the meaning with which sentences of what we recognize as languages are invested. (See Chapter 3, INTENTION AND CONVENTION, § 5ff.) Generally speaking, what makes interpretation possible is the fact that the language to which the sentences belong can be treated as *pre-existing* any particular speaker or hearer and any particular act of communication. It is something that speakers and hearers need to know about already. The compositionality that theories of L(i)-sense or definitions of 'true sentence of L(i)' have to reflect is a property of the language L(i) itself, L(i) and its properties being something irreducible to any psychological, social or pre-linguistic fact or facts about individual speakers or individual situations of communication.[42]

25. In opposition to such claims as the one just entered, many have tried to see the clauses of the definition of 'true sentence of L(i)' as answerable, in the last analysis, to psychological or neurolinguistic facts about speakers. On further reflection, some among those who are tempted by such an approach have shied away from the manifest embarrassments of getting involved in all that. And, backing off, they have preferred to say (as John Foster and Donald Davidson have more or less agreed in saying[43]) that the "theory" corresponding to the definition of true sentence of L(i) "explicitly states something knowledge of which *would suffice* for interpreting utterances by speakers of the language".[44] There are doubts about this kind of formulation. My own view would be that the question it answers should never have been permitted to arrive at the point where it could exact either this or any

remotely similar answer. The thing the definition of truth for L(i) is answerable to is how things are with the social object that is the language L(i) – not how things are with the speakers past and present in virtue of whose existence that language is extant. The question for anyone who would define truth for L(i) is this: how have we to see L(i) – how must we parse it and segment it – in order to understand why its sentences mean this or that? How do we have to see L(i) in order to get principles by which we work out what its more complicated or obscure L(i) utterances mean? Again, why do L(i) sentences have to be translated into foreign tongues on *this* principle rather than that principle in order to arrive at a passable version of what was originally said? In so far as purposes such as working out what sentences mean and discerning principles of translation do not force us into one sort of grammatical description rather than another, there may be indeterminacy about the properties of L(i). But that is nothing new. Nor does it render it indeterminate which object the language L(i) is. L(i) is a historically given thing, changeable no doubt, and always in process, but a persisting social object nevertheless. It is not in any reprehensible sense a vague or indeterminate (that is mythical) object.

26. One last question. What, then, after all these twists and turns, was the advantage of going by the Tarskian route to our final destination? One alternative might have been to reflect that we never really define or reduce anything in philosophy. So someone might ask: why not gloss the notion of meaning in a free-wheeling fashion by simply using it and involving it with all the collateral notions that are imported by the idea of interpretation?[45] Such, after all, is the method of philosophical elucidation – the method we have learned not to hope to improve upon.

There is much to agree with in this objection – the Davidsonian account is an exercise in elucidation too – except that the principal contention seems wrong. It seems wrong to suggest that we should deny truth its foundational place in the elucidation of meaning. For there is a real advantage in going by the Fregean and Tarskian way. It is true that Tarski's construction, which consolidates Frege's, is conditioned in the first instance by Tarski's deep suspicion of primitive semantic notions, and this is a suspicion one may not share. But suspicion of the semantical as such is not the only possible reason one might have to applaud the fact that Tarski gives his construction in terms of simple truth (*not* truth in a structure/model),[46] that he introduces semantic notions deliberately and in a measured fashion, and defines notions like satisfaction and the valuation function (*) by fixing their extension. One may applaud all this not because one thinks semantic notions really *are* suspect, but because an account of meaning that builds on Tarski's construction *helps to show how meaning is possible*. By seeing the definition of "true sentence of L(i)", for any language L(i) as needing to be built up in this careful and austere fashion, while the output of the definition is constrained in a manner that is irreducibly non-austere (and as messy as the social always will be), we can understand something about how it is possible for there to be such a thing as the semantical, and on what conditions it is possible, namely the existence of both the compositional (in the small) *and* the social (in the large).

Notes

1 'On the object of my concept-writing' (1883) in *Nachgelassene Schriften*, translated in *Posthumous Writings*. For the concept-writing itself, see *Begriffsschrift, eine der arithmetischen nachgelbildeten Formelsprache des reinen Denkens* (Halle 1879).

2 See *Grundgesetze der Arithmetik* (1893). In this work, section 32 and the preceding sections consolidate, codify and complete the doctrines of (direct) sense and reference explored and expounded in 'Ueber Sinn und Bedeutung', pp. 25–50. (Assiduously avoid the paperback, in which the translation has been revised and mismatched with the standard Fregean terminology that is adopted in this Companion.)

3 *Die Grundlagen der Arithmetik.*

4 See *Grundgesetze der Arithmetik* (1893).

5 See *Begriffsschrift* (1879), n. 1.

6 In view of the confusion surrounding this mathematical term, Frege did not call them 'variables'.

7 *Tractatus Logico-Philosophicus* (1921). I translate *Satz* here not as 'proposition' but as 'sentence in use', in order to mark and preserve the continuity (as well as the discontinuity) with Frege, who always used *Satz* to mean what we now mean by 'sentence'. I think Wittgenstein effectively answers the complaint that Frege has nothing to say about what it is to understand a sentence or grasp a thought. For this complaint – justifiable enough, perhaps, when directed against such traditional accounts as the one given in Church (see § 04 of *Introduction to Mathematical Logic*, Princeton, 1994) – see e.g. Dennett, *The Intentional Stance*, p. 123: 'Frege does not tell us anything about what grasping a thought consists in.' In fact, it would be much fairer to complain against him (if one thinks this a matter for complaint) that, by introducing the thought as that which one grasps by virtue of grasping the acceptance/rejection conditions of something linguistic, Frege must acquiesce, not in a vacuous platonism of *noeta*, but in a potentially highly controversial quasi-linguistic view of thinking, namely the view of thinking as the soul's internal dialogue with itself. Interestingly, this view really is Platonic (as well as plausible, when modestly construed): 'The soul when it thinks is simply conversing with itself, asking itself questions and answering, affirming and denying. . . . So I define one's thinking as one's speaking – and one's thought as speech that one has had – not with someone else or aloud but in silence with oneself,' Plato, *Theaetetus* 189^{E}–190^{A}. On this and cognate matters, see now Dummett, 'The philosophy of thought and the philosophy of language'.

8 For Davidson's version, see 'Truth and Meaning'. For various formulations of this and cognate apparent difficulties, see Ayer, 'Truth'; Wiggins, 'On sentence-sense, word-sense, and difference of word sense', pp. 18–19; Strawson, *Meaning and Truth*, Inaugural Lecture, Oxford 1969; and Foster, 'Meaning and Truth Theory'. See also Davidson's 'Reply to Foster', on which see below, n. 37.

9 Here I borrow an expository idea from Michael Dummett. See his *Frege: Philosophy of Language*, pp. 227–8.

10 They might, however, suffice to derive *some* unwanted biconditionals, e.g. those like [True [A *or* A] if and only if A is true *and* A is true], which can be derived by exploiting the simplest resources of ordinary deduction. To exclude such biconditionals we must rule that a biconditional in the form '*s* stands for the True if and only if p' be derived from the stipulations by a certain canonical proof procedure that exploits the sense-giving stipulation for each constituent of *s* and then halts, abstaining from needless detours through logical equivalences that are not needed for the deduction of the first

biconditional. Alternatively, we must adapt Θ and weaken the deductive apparatus that it uses to arrive at the point where we can show that ⊢Θ *s* is true iff (. . .). It may perhaps be possible to adapt Θ to deliver everything that is needed by means of the substitutions that are licensed by equivalences and identities. Richard Grandy has discussed this approach.

11 For some discussion of these issues, see my 'On the sense and reference of predicate expressions', with reference there to V. Dudman and P. Sen.

12 N.b. no quotation marks here: see n. 13 and reference below.

13 For the use of the relative pronoun 'what' in connection with the references of predicates, see Frege, *Posthumous Writings*, p. 122.

14 In so far as doubts persist, they relate to Axiom V of the system of *Grundgesetze* and the paradox generated by Frege's construction of arithmetic, not to the notions of sense and reference as such.

15 For J.L. Austin's theory of locutionary, illocutionary and perlocutionary acts see *How to Do Things with Words*. A rhetic act is an act of using vocables with a contextually determinate sense and reference and in such a way that one can be reported as saying that –. For the connection between the locutionary and the rhetic, for the connection between Austin's researches and post-Austinian developments and for much else besides that belongs in the areas I have so roughly blocked in, see Hornsby, 'Things done with words'.

16 If the inner core of a theory of sense for a given language is stated truth-conditionally, then the immediately adjacent next outer portion of that larger theory comprises the theory of the other linguistic moods of L(i). This will identify linguistic acts as acts of specifically *asserting that* [the sun is behind cloud, say], *asking whether* [the sun is behind cloud] or *enjoining* (again in the thinnest possible sense, and however vaingloriously in this particular case) *that* [the sun be behind cloud]. Cp. McDowell, 'Truth conditions, bivalence and verificationism', p. 44, who assigns this task to a 'theory of force' (note that this is not Dummett's usage of that expression: 'Truth conditions', p. 416). For the reasons why one might hive this task off from a theory of force in Austin's more general sense, see Davidson, 'Moods and performances', pp. 109–21. See also Hornsby, 'Things done with words'.

17 *Philosophical Remarks*, ed. by Rush Rhees, transl. by R. Hargreaves and R. White: Blackwell, 1975.

18 My recollection from being an undergraduate at Oxford during the 1950s at the time when Austin was giving the lectures he then called *Words and Deeds (1954–5)*, but before the appearance of Grice's article 'Meaning' (1957), is that in that period the doctrine then current about the meaning of words and sentences was simply a generalization of the Wittgensteinian thesis that meaning was use. There was no audible trace of the idea that to know the meaning of a sentence was to know what it would take for it to be true. To judge by my experience three years later in the Princeton philosophy department, the situation was very much the same in North America.

19 It is true that in the 1950s, Frege's writings were being translated. But neither *The Foundations of Arithmetic* nor 'On sense and reference' (the one paper which Carnap, Quine, Feigl and Sellars had made familiar to all professional philosophers) explained what the sense of a sentence was to be. Nor did any of Geach's and Black's other *Selections*. It is true, too, that *Tractatus* 4. 024 was legible enough. But by its apparent archaism the picture theoretical framework obscured the doctrine.

20 Dummett, 'Truth'. It is noteworthy that, in the several decades here under consideration, Wittgenstein's is the one clear, philosophically salient formulation of the

connection that Frege discerned between sense and truth-condition. Frege's doctrine on this point is conspicuous by its absence from expositions where we might have expected to find it, such as those of Alonzo Church at § 04 of his introduction to *Introduction to Logic* (Princeton 1956) and Rudolf Carnap at § 33 of *Der Logische Aufbau der Welt.* (For Carnap's own insufficiently remarked final return to a Fregean position, without explicit acknowledgment to Frege, see *Introduction to Semantics*, p. 22.)

I have wondered whether it is something connected with the blind spot I seek to explain in the text that accounts for the strange neglect of Richard L. Cartwright's definitive improvement of Quine's criterion of ontological commitment, namely his reformulation of this in terms of rules of truth. See Cartwright's 'Ontology and the theory of meaning', an article that rehearses and resolves difficulties that were still under active discussion a whole decade later.

21 By 'methodology of the deductive sciences' was meant, *inter alia*, the systematic study of such notions as *sentence, consequence, definition, deductive system, equivalence, axiom system independence, consistency*, and *completeness*.

22 See Tarski, 'The concept of truth in formalized languages'; also 'The semantic conception of truth' and 'Truth and proof'.

23 Having determined the extension of these concepts, of the true and the provable, he could inquire in the metalanguage whether they coincided. Tarski showed that the metalinguistic definition of 'provable in L(i)' – a purely syntactical notion – could be defined within L(i); but that, for any L(i) of sufficient expressive power, the definition of 'true in L(i)' could not be stated in L(i). The true and the provable could not, then, coincide.

24 See especially pp. 110 and 252 of Tarski, 'The concept of truth'; see also 'Truth and proof'.

25 That is, as Tarski puts it, 'concepts which, roughly speaking, express certain connections between the expressions of a language and the objects and states of affairs referred to by those expressions'.

26 Or rather, the extensionally defined counterpart of reference, namely the valuation or asterisk function as it is defined for each L(i). For the importance of not beginning by calling this function that of 'reference', see McDowell, 'Physicalism and primitive denotation'.

27 The metalanguage is the language in which one may speak of whatever the object language speaks of and also of the expressions of the object language in their relation to what the object language speaks of.

28 See the Bibliography to Tarski, 'The concept of truth'.

29 *Elementy Teorji Poznania*, pp. 106–7 in the English translation. Note that neither Kotarbinski nor Tarski takes this schema to be the recipe for a redundancy or deflationist or (as Tarski says) nihilistic theory of truth. Indeed, Tarski sometimes claimed to be coming to the rescue of the correspondence theory – though this claim must be taken with a pinch of salt. (Nothing in Tarski's theory can vindicate the idea that truth is to be defined in terms of a relation between sentences and states of affairs. Nor is there anything essential to the Tarskian construction that will vindicate the classical conception of truth as bivalent. Such questions remain open.)

30 For the claim about Tarski and Kotarbinski, see Wiggins, *Needs, Values, Truth*, pp. 333–4. (In addition to making general reference to Kotarbinski's book, Tarski refers also to lectures in Warsaw by Lesniewski. But the main burden of that acknowledgment seems to relate to the semantic paradoxes.)

31 For the failure of several current proposals to deliver this result by the method (which

is not Tarski's official method) of simply conjoining 'partial definitions', see § 2 of Milne's 'Tarski on truth and its definition'.

32 Cp. 'The concept of truth', p. 187.

33 Material adequacy is adequacy to the subject-matter, which is truth. It therefore entails *non-accidental* fidelity to the extension of the predicate. To think of the material conditional/bi-conditional will excite wrong associations. See Tarski (1931), p. 129.

34 See Davidson, 'Carnap's Methods of Intension and Extension'.

35 See again Grice, 'Meaning'. See also Chapter 3, INTENTION AND CONVENTION.

36 See 'Truth and Meaning', 1967.

37 It can be proved that, if there is one theory that provides a true T-sentence for each sentence of the language L(i), then there will automatically be a second such theory, and the interpretations to be read off the second theory will be different from those to be read off the first. See Evans's and McDowell's editorial introduction to *Truth and Meaning* (Oxford, 1976). Their finding is not superseded by the footnote that Davidson added in 1982 to the *Inquiries* reprint of 'Truth and Meaning' – p. 26, n. 10 – however illuminating the footnote might be in other ways.

38 See also Chapter 8, RADICAL INTERPRETATION.

39 Objections have mostly related to Davidson's free-wheeling use of the idea of an interpreter's needing to find what sentences a subject *holds-true*. It must be noted, however, that Davidson has persisted in this part of his original presentation, and has developed it further in his Dewey lectures, *Journal of Philosophy*, 1990.

40 See Grandy, 'Reference, meaning and belief'; Evans and McDowell, editorial introduction to *Truth and Meaning*; McDowell, 'Bivalence and Verificationism', § 1; and McDowell, 'On the Sense and Reference of a Proper Name'.

41 See McDowell, op. cit.; also for some further suggestions, see Wiggins, *Sameness and Substance*, p. 222, and *Needs, Values, Truth*, ch. 4 (ad init.).

42 That is to say that I see language as a social object with a past, a present and a future, something that is for each generation of speakers an *objet trouvé*, with words and modes of combination possessed contingently of this, that or the other meaning. Languages are not, on this conception, abstract objects defined by their syntax or semantics. (As Nietzsche remarks, nothing with a history can be defined.) What the syntax and semantics (as of t) are answerable to is the state of this language (as of t), not the states of the speakers who aspire to speak that language.

43 See their respective contributions to Evans and McDowell, *Truth and Meaning*.

44 That is to say that they shy away from representing that this is the theory that speakers actually use. Davidson, however (who has so much to lose from misunderstanding here), has not, when he has spoken of speakers and interpreter's 'theories', exercised all the caution I should have counselled on this matter. See, for one instance among several, 'A nice derangement of epitaphs'.

45 See e.g. the approach to meaning of Sainsbury, 'Understanding and theories of meaning', pp. 127–44; and of Davies, *Quantification, Meaning and Necessity*.

46 On this point, see again Milne, 'Tarski on truth and its definition'.

References

Austin, J.L. 1965: *How to Do Things with Words*, ed. J.O. Urmson. Oxford: Oxford University Press.

Ayer, A.J. 1953: 'Truth'. *Revue Internationale de Philosophie*, 25.

Carnap, R. 1928: *Der Logische Aufbau der Welt*. Berlin: Weltkreis-Verlag.

Carnap, R. 1944: *Introduction to Semantics*. Cambridge, Mass.: Harvard University Press.
Cartwright, R.L. 1954: 'Ontology and the theory of meaning', *Philosophy of Science*, 21/4.
Church, A. 1956: *Introduction to Mathematical Logic*. Princeton: Princeton University Press.
Coffa, Alberto L. 1991: *The Semantic Tradition from Kant to Carnap*. Cambridge: Cambridge University Press.
Davidson, D. 1967: 'Truth and meaning'. *Synthese*, *17*. Reprinted in his *Inquiries into Truth and Interpretation*, 1984. Oxford: Oxford University Press.
——1973: 'Radical interpretation', *Dialectica*, 27, 313–28. Reprinted in his *Inquiries into Truth and Interpretation*, 1984. Oxford: Oxford University Press.
——1976: 'Reply to Foster'. In *Truth and Meaning: essays in semantics*, ed. J. McDowell and G. Evans, 1976. Oxford: Oxford University Press.
——1979: 'Moods and performances'. Ibid.
——1963: 'Carnap's methods of intension and extension'. In P.A. Schilpp (ed.), *The Philosophy of Rudolf Carnap*, La Salle, Ill. London: Cambridge University Press.
——1986: 'A nice derangement of epitaphs'. In E. Le Pore (ed.), *Truth and Interpretation*. Oxford: Blackwell.
——1990: 'The Structure and Content of Truth'. *Journal of Philosophy*, 87/6, 279–328.
Davies, M.K. 1981: *Meaning, Quantification and Necessity*. London: Routledge.
Dennett, D. 1987: *The Intentional Stance*. Cambridge, Mass.: Bradford Books.
Dummett, M.A.E. 1958: 'Truth'. *Proceedings of the Aristotelian Society*, 59, 141–62.
——1973: *Frege: Philosophy of Language*. London: Duckworth.
——1986: 'The philosophy of thought and the philosophy of language'. In *Mérites et limites des méthodes logiques en philosophie*. Paris: Vrin et Fondation Singer Polignac.
Foster, J. 1976: 'Meaning and truth theory'. In J. McDowell and G. Evans (eds), *Truth and Meaning: essays in semantics*, 1976. Oxford: Oxford University Press.
Frege, G. 1879: *Begriffsschrift, eine der arithmetischen nachgelbildeten Formelsprache des reinen Denkens*. Halle: Trans. in Terrell Ward Bynum, *Conceptual Notation and Related Articles*, 1972. Oxford: Clarendon Press.
——1883: 'On the object of my concept-writing'. In *Nachgelassene Schriften*. Translated by P. Long and R. White in H. Hermes, F. Kambartel and F. Kaulbach (eds), *Posthumous Writings*, 1979. Oxford: Blackwell.
——1884: *Die Grundlagen der Arithmetik, eine logisch-mathematische Untersuchung über den Begriff der Zahl*. Breslau: Trans. by J.L. Austin, *The Foundation of Arithmetic*, 1950. Oxford: Blackwell.
——1892: 'Ueber Sinn und Bedeutung', *Zeitschrift für Philosophie und philosophische Kritik*, 100 , 25–50. Trans. in H. Feigl and W. Sellars (eds), *Readings in Philosophical Analysis*, 1949, New York; and in P.T. Geach and M. Black (trans. and eds), *Translations from the Philosophical Writings of Gottlob Frege*, 1952. Oxford: Blackwell.
——1893: *Grundgesetze der Arithmetik, begriffsschriftlich abgeleitet*, vol. 1. Jena: Verlag Hermann Pohle.
Grandy, R. 1973: 'Reference, meaning and belief'. *Journal of Philosophy*, 70, 439–52.
Grice, H.P. 1957: 'Meaning'. *Philosophical Review*, 66, 377–88.
Hornsby, J. 1988: 'Things done with words'. In Jonathan Dancy, J.M.E. Moravcsik and C.C.W. Taylor (eds), *Human Agency: Language and Duty: essays for J.O. Urmson*, Stanford, CA: Stanford University Press.
Kotarbinski, T. 1929: *Elementy Teorji Poznania*. Lwów. English translation, *Gnosiology: the scientific approach to the theory of knowledge*, trans. from the 2nd Polish edn by Olgierd Wojasiewicz, ed. by G. Bidwell and C. Pinder. Oxford and New York: Pergamon Press, 1966.

McDowell, J. 1976: 'Truth conditions, bivalence and verificationism'. In *Truth and Meaning*, eds. Evans and McDowell, Oxford 1976.

——1977: 'On the sense and reference of a proper name'. *Mind*, 86, 159–85.

——1978: 'Physicalism and primitive denotation'. *Erkenntnis*, 13, 131–52.

Milne, P. 1994/5: 'Tarski on truth and its definition'. Forthcoming.

Quine, W.V.O. 1960: *Word and Object*. Cambridge, Mass.: MIT Press.

Sainsbury, R.M. 1979/80: 'Understanding and theories of meaning'. *Proceedings of the Aristotelian Society*, 80, 127–44.

Strawson, P.F. 1969: *Meaning and Truth*. Inaugural lecture, Oxford; reprinted in Strawson, *Logico-Linguistic Papers*, 1971. London: Methuen.

Tarski, A. (1931): 'On definable sets of real numbers'. In *Logic, Semantics and Metamathematics*, trans. J.H. Woodger. Oxford: Oxford University Press, 1955.

——1936: 'The concept of truth in formalized languages'. In *Logic Semantics and Metamathematics*, trans. J.H. Woodger. Oxford: Oxford University Press, 1955.

——1944: 'The semantic conception of truth'. *Philosophy and Phenomenological Research*, 4, 341–76.

——1967: 'Truth and proof'. *Scientific American*, 220, 63–77.

Wiggins, D. 1971: 'On sentence-sense, word-sense, and difference of word sense'. In Steinberg and Jacobovits (eds.), *Semantics: An interdisciplinary reader*. Cambridge: Cambridge University Press.

——1980: *Sameness and Substance*. Oxford: Blackwell.

——1984: 'On the sense and reference of predicate expressions'. *Philosophical Quarterly*, 34/136, 311–28.

——1991: *Needs, Values, Truth*. Oxford: Blackwell, 2nd edn.

Wittgenstein, L. 1921: 'Logisch-philosophische Abhandlung'. *Annalen der Naturphilosophie*. Repr. and trans. as *Tractatus Logico-Philosophicus*, 1922.

——1958: *Blue and Brown Books*. Oxford: Blackwell. New York/London: Kegan Paul, Trench, Trubner.

——1975: *Philosophical Remarks*, ed. R. Rhees and trans. R. Hargreaves and R. White. Oxford: Blackwell.

Suggestions for further reading

Davidson has not only proposed an interpretive cum truth-conditional understanding of declarative meaning that inherits the role of Frege's account of these matters – on this consult his (1967), (1976), (1973) and (1989) works – and made important suggestions about how we should bring the meanings of declarative and other utterances into a general framework – see (1979) – but he has also made detailed proposals about the framing of truth-definitions for sub-languages of English that exemplify the difficulties posed by particular modes of combination, most notably the constructions involving reported speech and adverbial qualification. It will be instructive for anyone with an interest in the truth conception to consult some or all of his papers: 'The logical form of action sentences', 'On saying that', 'Theories of meaning and learnable languages' (all in his *Inquiries into Truth and Interpretation*), and 'Adverbs of action', in B. Vermazen and M.B. Hintikka (eds), *Essays on Davidson: Actions and Events* (Oxford: Oxford University Press, 1985).

In connection with these problems as well as with the broadly Davidsonian or neo-Fregean approach to meaning, the reader should study McDowell and Evans's editorial preface to *Truth and Meaning*; McDowell (1977) and (1978) (see above); E. LePore (ed.), *Truth and Interpretation* (Oxford: Oxford University Press, 1986); and Wiggins, '"Most" and

"All": some comments on a familiar programme and on the logical form of quantified sentences', in M. Platts (ed.), *Reference, Truth and Reality* (London: Routledge and Kegan Paul, 1980).

For a better understanding of truth in general, see Tarski's (1967) *Scientific American* article, and his (1936) paper, up to, say, definition 23. For a textbook account of truth, satisfaction and the modern idea of truth in an interpretation, see E. Mendelson's *Introduction to Mathematical Logic* (Princeton: van Nostrand, 1964), pp. 50–3.

2

Meaning, use, verification[1]

JOHN SKORUPSKI

1 Meaning as use

1.1 Introductory

Language has been the focus of the analytic tradition in twentieth-century philosophy. A good deal of that philosophizing about language has drawn its inspiration from a simple-sounding idea: to understand a word is to know how to use it. The formulation is particularly associated with Wittgenstein. But the idea itself has had immensely wide influence. It was important in logical empiricism – the empiricism of Vienna in the thirties – and also in ordinary language philosophy in Oxford after the Second World War. It can be traced to the nineteenth century: for example, one might see it as a central feature of Peirce's pragmatist conception of meaning, or as a generalization on the reflections of philosophically minded mathematicians and scientists, in the latter part of the nineteenth century, about the meaning of scientific and mathematical calculi. (Notable among many were Mach, Poincaré and Hilbert.) From the idea that use exhausts meaning important consequences have seemed to flow: the elimination of metaphysics, the dissolution of sceptical paradoxes – the pseudo-problematic nature of certain classical philosophical questions.

However, this essay will not trace the nineteenth- and twentieth-century sources of the idea.[2] Nor will it examine the question of its grand philosophical implications, though these possible implications are of major importance. Our task here will be simply to assess the idea itself. We shall examine how it leads to a distinctive conception of meaning which I will call the 'epistemic conception' (1.3–5). Verificationism, an influential doctrine about meaning associated with the Vienna Circle, may be presented as a special case of this conception: 2.1–3 will consider what verificationism is, its difficulties, and whether there can be a non-verificationist but still epistemic conception of meaning. In 3.1–2 I will argue that important insights contained in the epistemic conception can be retained even if we treat them as insights about the normative nature of concepts rather than as insights about the form of language-rules. And I will consider the effect of doing this on an influential doctrine whose modern form is closely associated with the epistemic conception of meaning – the doctrine that the a priori is the analytic.

1.2 Meaning and use in Wittgenstein

'Meaning is use' says that use, function in a language, *completely* exhausts meaning. To understand an expression or sentence is to master its use within a grammatically structured means of communicating, that is, a language. No more is required for full understanding than whatever is required for that. But although this formulation is particularly associated with Wittgenstein, what he intended by it is a matter of controversy.[3] The invocation of use evoked a cluster of ideas, and commentators have highlighted different elements in this cluster.

Wittgenstein begins the *Philosophical Investigations* (2nd edn, 1958) with a critique of a conception of language according to which

> Every word has a meaning. This meaning is correlated with the word. It is the object for which the word stands. § 1 (p. 2[e])

If we are mesmerized by the idea of meaning as a 'correlation' between a word and another thing, we misconceive what it is to understand a language.

Wittgenstein has many things to say against this mesmeric conception. He is particularly concerned to draw attention to the diversity of language uses, the variety of speech acts linguistic utterances can be used to perform – the many things you can do with words. Language is not just used to assert and describe. Nor are words just used to designate things. But we shall not be concerned with various important points he makes about the diversity of language-use. (Baker and Hacker, 1980, provide a comprehensive commentary.) Our topic can be pinned down by distinguishing two criticisms of the correlational model. The first, widely made by many philosophers interested in language at least from Bentham onwards, is that certain expressions which seem to designate something may turn out, on analysis of their use in sentences in which they occur, not to do so. This is shown by producing a paraphrase of sentences in which the expressions occur, which preserves the meaning of the sentences but eliminates the expressions. This point does not put in question the correlational model of meaning as such.

The other point is more thoroughgoing and deeper. It is that the model of designator and thing designated is a philosophically misleading prototype of meaning. In making this point, one does not need to deny that that a designation or 'semantic value' is associated with every ineliminable non-empty term, in virtue of its meaning. For example, the word 'yellow' will designate the property *yellow* – or a Fregean concept or the class of yellow things, or whatever the right account of its semantic value is – and we will understand that (inexplicitly) when we understand 'yellow'. But we can ask what it is to have that understanding. The *sentence*, 'The English word "yellow" designates the property *yellow*', cannot be employed to explain the meaning of 'yellow' to someone who does not understand the word. Its meaning can be explained to someone who already understands another language, by using *that* language (' "Yellow" en anglais signifie *jaune*.'). But to someone who does not already understand another language it must be explained in other ways. Attending to the ways in which the meaning of words is actually explained gives us an overview of their use and thus of the rules which govern that use. These rules constitute their meaning in the language.[4]

This line of argument for the conception of meaning as use will be a main topic in what follows. I will call it 'the Constitutive Argument', since it is about what constitutes such metalinguistic knowledge as that 'yellow' in English designates yellow. We return to it in 1.5 and again in 3.1–2. But finally in this section I want to note a point which is often connected with the Constitutive Argument in Wittgenstein's discussions of language – and also with his reflections on rule-following. In *Philosophical Remarks* (1975), for example, Wittgenstein says

> in a certain sense, the use of language is something that cannot be taught, i.e. I cannot use language to teach it in the way in which language could be used to teach someone to play the piano. – And that of course is just another way of saying: I cannot use language to get outside language. (p. 54)

Now if the use of language is what cannot be taught, and meaning is use, one might conclude that meaning cannot be taught. But Wittgenstein only says that in a certain sense it cannot be taught. What does he mean? Any rule or instruction given for the use of a word must be given in language, understood broadly to cover all signs. Signs can only convey meaning if at some point there is a natural uptake of how they are being used. It is that natural uptake which cannot be taught – it is a condition of the possibility of teaching a language to someone that teacher and pupil share it. In this sense "Language must speak for itself" (Wittgenstein, 1974, p. 40). In grasping a language-rule, I grasp its applications – but this cannot require grasping further rules determining what its application to particular cases is. A being which grasps and applies rules must have spontaneous normative responses about the *right* way to apply a rule in a given case: responses not determined by a further rule. That normative dimension of understanding a sign cannot be conveyed by instruction in rules, but is presupposed by the very process of instruction.

We shall come back to this point as well in 3.1–2. For the moment I simply note its compatibility with the previous one, which was that rules which constitute the meaning of a sign should be thought of as rules for its use. Nothing we have said so far precludes the possibility that such rules of use may be stated explicitly and systematically for a whole language, yielding thereby a theory of meaning for that language. Wittgenstein would probably have opposed such a view. But although it is true that rules of use presuppose normative responses which are not themselves codifiable as rules, that in no way shows that the rules do not exist or cannot be systematically exhibited.

So we turn now to the idea that meaning-rules are rules of *use*, rules for doing things with words.

1.3 The priority thesis and the epistemic conception of meaning

Consider the speech act of assertion. It may or may not be the case that an account of it has to be given before we can give an account of other uses of language. It is at least clear that the assertoric use is a main use of language, for which there must be rules of use.

The most straightforward assumption to make about those rules would be that they combine to specify when a sentence in a language is correctly assertible. So where L is a language and S is a sentence in L, the specification has the form

(RA) S is correctly used to make an assertion in L if and only if . . .

Let us call the condition indicated by the dots on the right-hand side of 'if and only if' the *assertion condition*. Rules for the use of a word would contribute to determine assertion conditions for sentences containing that word.

In (RA) the notion of correctness is being used in a particular sense. It is correct, in the relevant sense, to use the sentence to make an assertion just if one is *justified* in making the assertion thereby conveyed – but questions of such matters as etiquette are not at issue. What is meant is that one is justified in thinking that assertion *true*. And the word 'true' is to be taken in its broadest sense, the sense in which any assertion whatsoever formally aims at truth. Truth in this sense may be partially characterized as a property F, such that for any assertion A whatsoever, if it is shown that there is no adequate ground to hold that A has F, reason (as against etiquette, discretion etc.) requires withdrawal of A.

Why does the relevant notion of correctness relate in this way to the broad notion of truth? Because of what may be called the basic principle of the practice of assertion:

(A) One correctly uses a sentence to make an assertion if and only if one is justified in believing, of the proposition expressed by that use of the sentence, that it is true.[5]

Let us call this kind of correctness 'epistemic justification' – one uses a sentence correctly if one is epistemically justified in using it to make an assertion. So now we conclude that, in general, the assertion condition of a sentence will have to spell out its basic form of epistemic justification.[6]

In 2.3 we ask whether, even granted a conception of meaning as use, a sentence's meaning should be thought of as given *exhaustively* by its assertion conditions, or whether account should also be taken of the inferences it licenses. But perhaps our initial assumption – that rules fixing the assertoric use of a language should issue in direct specifications of the RA form – has been too speedy anyway? Look again at principle (A). It says that what one asserts and what one believes to be true is a proposition, not a sentence. If we reflect on that it may well strike us that the (RA) form over-ambitiously combines two tasks which should be kept separate. One task, that of the theory of meaning proper, is to specify for any sentence in L what proposition it expresses. (In the course of doing that in a finite systematic way, the theory will also have to specify for any expression in L what concept it expresses.) Another task is to give an account, for various kinds of propositions, of when one is justified in believing them to be true. This second task does not belong to the theory of meaning, but to epistemology.

Philosophers in the thirties (Wittgenstein and the Vienna Circle) who took it that the way to specify the meaning of a sentence was (RA) also rejected this division between semantics and epistemology.[7] How are these theses connected?

A grounding idea is that *there is no language-independent account to be given of concepts and propositions.* To talk of concepts or propositions is simply to talk indirectly of the use of expressions and sentences in languages – classes of same-use expressions and sentences. Grasping a concept is understanding (the use of) an expression in a language. Grasping a proposition is understanding (the use of) a sentence in a language. Attitudes to propositions and concepts are attitudes to sentences and expressions in a language. We cannot *explain* understanding an expression or sentence as knowing what concept or proposition it expresses – as though that concept or proposition were an entity independent of language, and 'understanding what concept or proposition is expressed' were a matter of knowing the correlation between the bits of language which do the expressing and the pre-existing non-linguistic item which is expressed.

Call this thesis the *priority thesis.*[8] It says that an account of concepts and concept-possession is dependent on an account of language-rules and language-understanding. It does not deny that it can be useful to talk of concepts and propositions. It is not denying the *truth* of principle (A). It is a positive thesis about what such talk amounts to. Talking about concepts and propositions is a way of talking about language-understanding, without specifying the particular language. It has a negative side – concepts and propositions have no explanatory role in the epistemology of understanding. We do not *explain* how a person understands the meaning of a word by saying that he or she possesses the concepts it expresses and knows that it expresses that concept. For possessing the concept just is knowing how to use the word (or some synonym) and that is what constitutes understanding it.

It is the priority thesis which seems to produce the conclusion that semantics and epistemology are one and the same. We may call this the *identity thesis*; for it denies that there are language-independent concepts which generate their own language-independent epistemic norms. There are only rules of language. Epistemic norms, the subject-matter of epistemology, are simply rules of classes of language – the subject-matter of semantics.

As I have noted, the slogan 'meaning is use' can be associated with a cluster of ideas in Wittgenstein's work, and its interpretation is controversial. It is clear that he himself directs it against the correlational model, and that he presents instead a conception of understanding as grasping language-rules which are like rules for making moves in a game. So he is not envisaging a reductive account of language-understanding in non-intensional terms, as some have thought (see e.g. Horwich, 1995). To say that understanding consists in mastery of rules which are like rules of a game is still to give an intensional account – an account which attributes to language-users judgements about whether, for example, it is permissible or correct to utter a sentence. But we also thought it unlikely that Wittgenstein himself intended his emphasis on use to yield a systematic theory of meaning for a language. In order to leave that interpretative question clearly open, it will help to have a name other than 'use theory' for the view which does aspire to develop the idea of meaning as use systematically. Various names have been used – 'criterial semantics' (Baker, 1974, Peacocke, 1981), or 'anti-realist semantics' (Wright, 1987, ch. 7); 'verificationist semantics' (Putnam, 1983), or 'justificationist theory of meaing' (Dummett, 1993b). A first statement of this view is that ground-rules of meaning (for assertoric sentences) take the (RA) form, and that accounts of the meanings of words in a language must be given in such a way as to entail statements of that form for each assertoric sentence in L. Let us call it, non-commitally, the *epistemic conception of meaning* (EM): 'conception', in that it proposes what the *form* of a theory of meaning should be; 'epistemic', because the meaning-rules it envisages state when assertion of a sentence is epistemically justified. This is only a first statment of EM: in 2.3, as I said, we shall consider the possibility of broadening it beyond this initial, verificationist form, letting it take into account what inferences assertion of a sentence justifies. But this form will do for the moment.[9]

The priority thesis seems to lead to the identity thesis and thus to EM. In identifying rules of language-use with rules of epistemic justification it gives EM a particularly sharp and central role in philosophy. Just one story now gives a unified account of the meaning and the epistemology of L. The epistemic conception of meaning might just as well be called the semantic conception of epistemology. In effect it does away with the traditional philosophical discipline of epistemology. That does not make 'epistemic' a misleading word – it abolishes epistemology *because* it is an epistemic conception of meaning.[10]

This kind of view is central to logical empiricism. Logical empiricism held that there are only factual propositions – the province of science – and recommendations about how to speak or, more generally, what to do. There are no non-factual propositions, and there are no factual propositions which lie beyond the province of science. A language is a set of recommendations, or rules. The rules stipulate when a sentence in the language is assertible.

Think of the assertion condition as specifying an information state of the language-user. It can consist in justified beliefs or in states of experience. An important point is that every aspect of this state is accessible to the language-user. Whether or not one is in a state of experience, has a belief, has a justification for that belief – all this must be reflexively transparent if the rule is to be a rule of *use*. It must be possible in principle for me to tell, by reflection on my state of information alone, what it is and whether it warrants assertion of a sentence. If rules of use did not have this form I could not directly apply them: I would have to have a further criterion to tell whether the antecedent of the rule obtains.

Distinguish this from another point: must there be an effective procedure for deciding whether evidence warranting assertion of a sentence can be obtained or not? That is, must it always be possible to enlarge one's information state, by a specifiable method, to a point where one can authoritatively assert either that evidence warranting its assertion is available or that it is not? No. The requirement is that it should be transparent whether a sentence is assertible in an information state. *That* question must be effectively decidable. But the sentence itself need not in any sense be effectively decidable. One must be able to tell whether one's information state warrants the assertion 'There is evidence warranting assertion of S'.[11] If it does not, it's not required that one has a procedure for getting into an information state which decides the issue.

1.4 *The truth-conditional conception of meaning*

So the suggestion is that the priority thesis leads to EM, via the identity thesis. But we must now consider an analysis of meaning which seems to show that the suggestion is wrong. If this analysis is satisfactory, then the priority thesis does not entail the identity thesis, and therefore does not force EM.

The proposer of this analysis agrees that there must be rules which determine the correct assertoric use of sentences in L. But he insists on the point made in the previous section (1.3) – those rules need only determine, for any particular sentence which can be used to make an assertion, *what* that assertion is. His claim is that we can formulate rules which do that, without making explanatory appeal to grasp of concepts and propositions, and without casting them in the RA form. They will be cast in such a way as to yield, instead, a statement for each assertoric sentence of the condition under which it expresses a truth (in the broad sense of truth invoked in 1.3). Such an account, he argues, tells us what each assertoric sentence says – and remains consistent with the priority thesis.

So instead of specifications of meaning of the RA form, this theory of meaning proposes to make do with specifications of the form

(RT) S is true in L if and only if *p*

('is true in L' means 'expresses a truth when used literally and assertorically in L'.)

Let us call this a *truth-conditional* theory of meaning. Like any other theory, it will need to make use of the compositionality of meaning: the fact that the meaning of a sentence is a function of the meaning of its constituent expressions. And it is this feature of the theory – its appeal to compositionality – which is supposed to yield an account of understanding compatible with the priority thesis.

Consider for example the sentence, 'Ammonia smells.' Its meaning depends on the meaning of 'ammonia' and 'smells' and its syntactic structure. How might we spell out this dependence? Suppose the meaning of the words is given by 'dictionary' rules like this:

(1) 'Ammonia' is true (in English) of ammonia
(2) 'smells' is true (in English) of *x* if and only if *x* smells

And the syntactic structure is given by this 'compositional' rule:

(3) 'Fa' is true (in English) if and only if 'F' is true of that which 'a' is true of

Substituting 'ammonia' and 'smells' into (3) and using (1) and (2) we can deduce that

'Ammonia smells' is true (in English) if and only if ammonia smells.

So we know this equivalence solely on the basis of knowledge of those semantic rules of English in virtue of which (1)–(3) hold, plus the very basic logic involved in deriving it. That being so, the suggestion now goes, we know that the English sentence 'Ammonia smells' expresses the proposition that ammonia smells. For suppose that English sentence 'Ammonia smells' expresses a proposition P. Then I ought to be able tell that 'Ammonia smells' is true if and only if P is, just by knowing the semantic rules of English plus the basic metalogic of the theory. But let P = (say) the proposition that water is odourless. Then although it is true that ammonia smells if and only if water is odourless, I need to *know* that in order to recognize that

'Ammonia smells' is true in English if and only if water is odourless.

Although, in this example, the biconditional which I need to know is a posteriori, the point does not turn on that. Consider, for example, the proposition that 2 + 2 = 4 if and only if 3 + 3 = 6. This may be known a priori. But I still need to *know* it, as well as dictionary and compositional rules, to know that

'2 + 2 = 4' is true in English if and only if 3 + 3 = 6.

In general, a sentence S in L expresses the proposition that *p* just if, by virtue of semantic conventions of L alone, S is true if and only if *p*. If I know an instance of this biconditional for every sentence in L which has an assertoric use, and I know it compositionally – through a grasp of the semantic value of the terms from which it is formed – then I have a complete grasp of L's assertoric power. So there seems to be no need to appeal to an account of the *assertion* conditions of sentences in L to account for the assertoric uses to which L may be put. The truth-conditional theory itself, so far as we have sketched it, seems consistent with the priority thesis. It does not mention concepts or propositions in explaining what it is to understand a language.[12] Moreover, it seems to provide a language-relative account of how one comes to know a proposition. Knowing the semantic conventions of L is knowing, for any sentence in L, what proposition it expresses. Which one? The one that is true solely on condition that that sentence expresses a truth. So grasping the proposition that ammonia smells can consist in understanding English and then grasping it as the proposition which is true solely on condition that 'Ammonia smells' expresses a truth in English. (Or it can consist in understanding some other language L and grasping it as the proposition which is true solely on condition that the sentence in L which is in fact synonymous with 'Ammonia smells' expresses a truth.)

Thus the truth-conditional theory seems to be consistent with the priority thesis, in that it does not make explanatory appeal to the notion of language-independent concepts and propositions. On the other hand it does not seem to require endorsement of the identity thesis either. It dovetails with the basic law of assertion, (A): I know that it is correct to assert a sentence S in L if and only if I have reason to think it expresses a truth – and the truth-conditional theory tells me what the truth-condition of S in L is. To know the *assertion* conditions of S in L I must both know its truth-condition, and also know the epistemology which links with that truth-condition. But that latter knowledge, knowledge of the appropriate epistemology, is not given by the truth-conditional theory of meaning itself. So the argument from the priority thesis to EM seems to break down.[13]

1.5 *'Full-bloodedness'*

If it does break down, that must mean that the identity thesis is stronger than the priority thesis. It must mean that the priority thesis can be upheld consistently with a firm distinction between epistemic norms and rules of language. But can it be?

It is certainly true, as argued in the previous section, that if we know that

'Ammonia smells' is true (in English) if and only if ammonia smells

and we know that on the basis of knowledge of semantic conventions of English and very basic logic alone, then we know what proposition the sentence expresses – i.e. that ammonia smells. But, as Michael Dummett (1974) has stressed, we can still ask what it *is* to know that 'Ammonia smells' is true (in English) if and only if ammonia smells. Call the proposition which is known – it is a metalinguistic proposition about English – 'M'. There is a difference between knowing M, and knowing that the metalinguistic *sentence* which expresses it is true. I could know that this sentence in the metalanguage (which in this case is itself English) expresses a truth without knowing what the object-language sentence meant, because I could know it to be true in English without grasping the proposition it expresses. (Compare: knowing that 'Lublin jest polskim miastem' expresses a truth in Polish, because you have been told authoritatively that it does, but not knowing what proposition it expresses.)

Can this point be deployed against the truth-conditional theory and in favour of EM? Is it an application of the Constitutive Argument (1.2)? To deploy it in favour of EM one must take as one of its premises the priority thesis – which the truth-conditional theorist considered in 1.4 claimed to accept. The priority thesis says that to explain what it is to grasp a particular proposition is to give an account of what it is to understand some particular sentence or other. Now suppose we try to combine that with the claim that understanding 'Ammonia smells' is to be *explained* as consisting in a grasp of M. By the priority thesis, grasping M must then in turn be explained as consisting in understanding some sentence. What sentence? Well, we could say that grasp of M is explained by giving an account of what it is to understand 'Ammonia smells' itself – but that would now put us in an explanatory circle. Apparently, then, we have to say that grasp of M is explained by giving an account of what it is to understand a sentence which expresses M. And then, by the same argument, we shall have to say that understanding that metalinguistic sentence will in turn be explained as grasping the higher-level metalinguistic proposition which specifies its truth-condition. Obviously, this won't do. It cannot be the case that every language is understood only by prior understanding of a metalanguage in which biconditionals about truth-conditions of sentences in the language are expressed.

But the choice between a vicious circle and a vicious regress arises from the attempt to combine the priority thesis with the claim that understanding a sentence is to be *explained* as consisting in a grasp of the metalinguistic proposition which specifies its truth-condition. Thus, if we accept the priority thesis we must reject that claim.

This spelling-out of the Constitutive Argument makes the priority thesis one of its premises. Similar reasoning forces rejection of the claim that understanding a word is to be *explained* as consisting in a grasp of a metalinguistic proposition – one which specifies its semantic value, or specifies the concept it expresses. Thus we are led to the conclusion that the theory of meaning must, in Dummett's words, be 'full-blooded' and not merely 'modest'. A modest theory of meaning, he says, is

> not intended to convey the concepts expressible in the object-language, but to convey an understanding of that language to one who already had those concepts.

while a full-blooded theory should,

> in the course of specifying what is required for a speaker to grasp the meaning of a given word, . . . explain what it is for him to possess the concept it expresses. (1993a, p. viii)

The point is that if we accept the priority thesis then we must reject the idea that understanding a word or a sentence can quite generally be explained as grasping a metalinguistic proposition which exhibits its meaning by specifying its semantic value or its truth condition. On the contrary, we shall have to be able to say that grasping a metalinguistic proposition of that kind can consist in understanding the word or sentence which it is about. For example, grasping M can consist – if one's home language is English – in understanding 'Ammonia smells': the very same understanding as is involved, in that case, in grasping the proposition *ammonia smells*.[14] Explaining what it is to possess a concept or grasp a proposition becomes a task for the theory of meaning, and not for some other branch of philosophy. Hence there must be a part of the theory of meaning which does more than simply stating what expressions of the language are true of and deriving from that truth-conditions for sentences of the language. There *may* be a truth-conditional part of this kind, but there must also be a part which goes beyond it. And this part will conform to the epistemic conception of meaning.

But if we take this part to consist in the specification of assertion conditions for sentences in the language, won't the argument we have just considered apply to it as well? Won't it equally show that understanding 'Ammonia smells' cannot consist in knowing the proposition that 'Ammonia smells' is assertible iff . . . ?

To this the EM theorist's response is that knowing the assertion conditions of a sentence can consist in a *practical* ability to tell when it is right to utter it assertorically: to recognize information states as warranting or not warranting that kind of utterance of the sentence.[15] Precisely the same ability could, of course, be invoked to explain what it is to know the truth-conditions of a sentence. But that is the EM theorist's point. To respond in this way would concede that grasping truth-conditions is not something over and above, independent of, mastery of assertion conditions. EM anchors understanding to a practical normative response.

Now all of this has proceeded on the assumption that the priority thesis is correct. But why cannot we reject that thesis, and accept an account of concepts and propositions which is not language-relative?

The most significant approach of this kind is *Platonism*. I use the term to refer to the view that concepts and propositions are non-spatio-temporal entities known by non-perceptual intuition. Platonism, combined with a truth-conditional view of meaning, may seem to offer an explanation of understanding. To know that 'straight' is true in English of straight things is to grasp, by non-perceptual intuition, the concept of straightness and to know that it is expressed by the English word 'straight'.

One can object, in this purported explanation of understanding, to the appeal to non-empirical intuition of concepts and propositions. But there is a different and clinching consideration – I will call it the 'no-intrinsic-meaning argument'. Wittgenstein uses it in various places, such as the following:

> In attacking the formalist conception of arithmetic, Frege says more or less this: these petty explanations of the signs are idle once we *understand* the signs. Understanding would be something like seeing the picture from which all the rules followed, or a picture that makes them all clear. But Frege does not seem to see that such a picture would itself be another sign, or a calculus to explain the written one to us. (1974, p. 40)

Wittgenstein's point is that there is no such thing as an object which has intrinsic meaning, that is, which (a) has meaning irrespective of having that meaning conferred on it and (b) is such that knowing it and knowing its meaning are one and the same. Even if we had access to objects in a Platonic third world, and had a mapping of terms and sentences onto these objects, that would do nothing for us unless those objects were already signs – signs which had intrinsic meaning. (If their meaning were not intrinsic, the questions of what it is for them to have meaning and what it is for us to understand that meaning would again arise.) The same would go for a picture in the world of physical or mental representations. The objection does not have to do with the particular world we are talking about. It is not a positivistic or even a naturalistic objection. (Blackburn, 1984, ch. 2 sets out a version of it and applies it to Fodor's 'language of thought' hypothesis.)

It is certainly a devastating argument against the view that a person's understanding of language is to be explained in terms of his or her possession of concepts and propositions – *if possession of concepts and propositions is taken to be quasi-*

perceptual access to a class of objects. So taken, concept-possession could not *in principle* have a justificatory or explanatory role. But we have not shown that the only alternative to a language-relative account of concept-possession is one which treats concepts as intrinsically meaningful objects, mysteriously accessible to us. That would have to be shown, if we sought to derive the priority thesis from the no-intrinsic-meaning argument alone. Sometimes Wittgenstein seems to appeal to a dichotomy between an account of understanding which invokes access to intrinsically meaningful objects and one which invokes only grasp of language-rules:

> the mere fact that we have the expression 'the meaning' of a word is bound to lead us wrong: we are led to think that the rules are responsible to something not a rule, whereas they are responsible only to rules. (Reported in Moore, 1959, p. 258)

The apparent suggestion here is that if we avoid reifying 'the meaning' of a word into an intrinsically meaningful object then we have to accept that the rules governing its use constitute its meaning and are not 'responsible' to anything else. But may there not be a middle way – an account of concepts which neither reifies them nor makes them language-relative – and, given such an account, will it not be the case that a word which expresses a concept will have its meaning in the language set by rules which are 'responsible' to, or dovetail with, language-independent features of that concept? An account fitting this description would be this: to grasp a concept is to respond to a pattern of epistemic norms. It is to be disposed to accept a particular pattern of thought-transitions as primitively justified. Epistemic norms, however, are not themselves rules of language. A theory of meaning for a language is not in the business of describing them; that is a matter for the theory of concepts (or epistemology). Thus the theory of meaning can describe the rules of the language truth-conditionally, and will dovetail with an account of concepts which is neither language-relative nor Platonistic but characterizes possessing concepts as acknowledging patterns of epistemic norms.

Such an approach certainly has to reject the priority thesis, but it still accepts the no-intrinsic-meaning argument against Platonism. It provides, one might say, a full-blooded theory of concepts and a modest theory of meaning. So the question arises whether there is a case for the priority thesis which is independent of the no-intrinsic-meaning argument. We will return to these matters in 3.1–2. But first we must examine further the conception which, as it now seems, is indeed forced if the priority thesis is accepted: that is, the epistemic conception of meaning.

2 Verificationism

2.1 *Verificationism: meaning and truth*

In the thirties, verificationist conceptions of meaning were advanced by Wittgenstein and by philosophers of the Vienna Circle. But the connection between verificationism and EM is not straighforward. There can be non-epistemic versions of a verificationist view of meaning. And there can be non-verificationist forms of the epistemic conception of meaning. In considering these points we shall have to develop an account of EM which goes beyond the initial statement of it in 1.3.

I will use the term 'verificationism' to refer to a view of *meaning*, not, at least directly, to a view of truth. Verificationism is the view that understanding a sentence consists in grasping what information states would verify it. An information state verifies a sentence just if a person in that state is warranted in asserting it. All significant sentences have assertion conditions – their meaning can be displayed in the RA form.

In contrast, a verificationist view of *truth* holds that truth is verifiability. A sentence is true if and only if it is verifiable, that is, if and only if there is evidence warranting its assertion. To say that there is such evidence is to say, roughly, that a state of information warranting assertion of the sentence can be reached by us through an investigation which improves our current state of information – as it bears on the question of the sentence's truth or falsity – as much as it is actually possible to improve it.[16]

The difficulties with such a view of truth are notorious. Consider, for example, the two sentences 'Charlemagne's favourite colour was magenta', and 'Human beings cannot grow above 12 feet tall'. As far as the verificationist conception of *meaning* is concerned, both sentences have a meaning. We know what kinds of evidence would warrant their assertion – for example, a text from the time of Charlemagne, which in general had the marks of reliability, and which recorded that Charlemagne often commented that his favourite colour was magenta; inductive evidence that human beings never reach 12 feet together with theoretical considerations (e.g. relations between the height of an animal, its volume, mass and muscular power, considerations of evolutionary fitness) which indicate that they could not. But we also know that evidence of that kind may not actually be available. It may not be possible to improve our information to the point where we are warranted either in asserting or in denying these sentences. Do we want to say that in that case those sentences are neither true nor false? Does a sentence's possession of truth-value depend on such contingencies?

To be sure, there are various ways of spelling out the word 'possible' in the phrase 'improving our information as much as it is possible to do'. Verificationists about truth characteristically idealize the notion of verifiability. For example, they may idealize the computing abilities of the agent which does the verifying, or its ability to move in space and time. But such idealized notions of verifiability cannot be identical with the concept of assertibility which is required for a verificationist view of meaning of the *epistemic* type. (This qualification will be explained in a moment.) For there the concept required, as was said in 1.3, is that of an assertion condition. And whether or not the assertion condition of a sentence obtains – whether or not the sentence is assertible in the language-user's information state – is something that must be transparent to the language-user. This transparent notion of assertibility cannot be identical with any non-transparent notion of verifiability – one which requires hypotheses about what would be assertible by an ideal agent.

There is, in fact, no straightforward route from a verificationist conception of meaning of this epistemic kind to a verificationist account of truth. It requires an unobvious philosophical argument to make the connection. (For arguments intended to make the connection see Dummett, 1959a and 1978b, Wright, 1987; 'Introduction', for criticism, see Skorupski, 1988.) On the other hand, there is a route from verificationism about truth to a non-epistemic type of verificationism about meaning.

A historical excursus will provide helpful background here. In conversations which he had in the late twenties with Schlick and others from the Vienna Circle, Wittgenstein took a very strict verificationist line about meaning. The record made by Friedrich Waismann of these conversations contains many formulations of it – for example, 'The sense of a proposition is the method of its verification' (Wittgenstein, 1979, p. 79; cp. e.g. p. 227). Wittgenstein takes the notion of verifying a sentence quite strictly to mean '*indefeasibly* establishing its truth'. He describes (in Waismann's record) two conceptions of verification. According to one, the one he rejects, I cannot verify a proposition, for example 'Up there on the cupboard there is a book', completely.

> A proposition always keeps a back-door open, as it were. Whatever we do, we are never sure that we were not mistaken.
>
> The other conception, the one I want to hold, says, 'No, if I can never verify the sense of a proposition completely, then I cannot have meant anything by the proposition either. Then the proposition signifies nothing whatsoever.'
>
> In order to determine the sense of a proposition, I should have to know a very specific procedure for when to count the proposition as verified. (Wittgenstein, 1979, p. 47)

Applying the procedure must yield a definite and indefeasible result. A consequence of this view is that general 'propositions', which are not verifiable in the strict sense, have to be treated as 'hypotheses' rather than as genuine propositions.

But why must we adopt this very strict notion of verification? Why cannot verification just consist in achieving a state of information which warrants assertion? And why cannot that verifying state be defeasible? We know what kind of evidence would justify assertion of 'Charlemagne's favourite colour was magenta', or 'Human beings cannot grow above 12 feet tall'. We also know that that sort of evidence could be defeated by further evidence. We know that these sentences always 'keep a back door open', that there can be no such thing as verifying them 'completely'. In short, why can't we work with 'defeasibly justify assertion of', not 'conclusively establish the truth of'?

Whatever the reason for Wittgenstein's extremism in these Viennese discussions, his remarks usefully highlight the difference between two quite distinct philosophical perspectives from which verificationism can grow.

In one of these, it emerges from a combination of two things. The first is a conception of meaning which holds that a sentence has meaning by picturing a state of affairs (so, a species of the truth-conditional view). The second is an ontology which conceives of reality as a totality of states of affairs, thought of as immediately encounterable in experience. To understand a sentence is, then, to be able to picture – and for this kind of verificationism this means to be able to imagine experiencing or observing – the state of affairs which makes it true. And to verify a sentence or its negation is, so to speak, to run through the totality to the appropriate point and check by direct observation whether or not the state of affairs pictured by the sentence obtains. Verification, conceived in this way, is conclusive.

Here the central idea is that understanding a sentence is being able to represent to oneself what it would be like to encounter in experience the state of affairs which makes it true. Its affinity with Wittgenstein's *Tractatus* philosophy is suggestive. Though the Tractarian knowing subject is a highly elusive item, it is not implausible to think of it as being able to sweep at will through the states of affairs, or configurations of Tractarian objects, to which elementary sentences correspond, directly checking whether or not any elementary sentence is true.

But this last idea, with its phenomenalistic implication, could be loosened. The loosened version says that if one can describe, at least 'in principle', what it would be like to have this encounter, the sentence is verifiable. It may not be possible to arrange to have the encounter, but the state of affairs is at least ideally verifiable – one can imagine a knower ideally transported to the site of the state of affairs and having the encounter. And now we have a verificationist notion of *truth* which can combine with a truth-conditional view of meaning to yield a kind of verificationism about meaning. Call this the positivistic route to verificationism. It rests on a positivist ontology of the real as the in-principle observable, and the verificationism which results is not a species of the epistemic conception of meaning.

But Wittgenstein does not say in these conversations that the meaning of a sentence is the picturable state of affairs which would verify it, render it true. His emphasis is on *methods* of verification. When he says on p. 227 (Wittgenstein, 1979) 'The sense of a proposition is the method of its verification,' he is quoted as continuing:

> A method of verification is not the means of establishing the truth of a proposition; it is the very sense of a proposition . . . To specify it is to specify the sense of a proposition. You cannot look for a method of verification. A proposition can only say what is established by the method of its verification.[17]

The next paragraph plays on the idea of thought as a movement with a determinate direction, set off in search of an answer to a question. The sense of both the question and the answer is given by the direction of the search (direction-sense).[18] Connectedly, Wittgenstein insists that different methods of verification ('thought-movements' with different directions) produce different senses. Such a view is not suggested by the positivistic route to verificationism. For as far as that conception goes I might be able to travel in various ways to the point of verification, the point at which I check by direct inspection whether or not the relevant state of affairs obtains. Equally, Wittgenstein's remark that you cannot look for a method of verifying a proposition – that is, first understand it and then look around for ways of verifying it – does not sit well with that positivistic conception.

Overall, then, it seems that what Wittgenstein presents in these conversations is a strictly operational kind of verificationism, a species of EM.[19] But without an underlying positivist (and indeed phenomenalist) impetus, there is no case for such strict operationism. The arguments for EM as such do not enforce it. Later Wittgenstein greatly broadened his operationist version of EM, taking into account the consequences for practice of an assertion as well as the operations which license it. To understand an assertion it is not enough to be told when you're licensed to make it: you need to know what it's a license to *do*, what consequences flow from it, ultimately for action.

The result is a fully liberalized, and pragmatized, conception of meaning as use. Understanding a word or sentence is knowing what can be done with it in communication and action, knowing the rules which govern its role in our practices of assertion and inference. The use of a sentence is as much a matter of the practical conclusions you can draw from an assertion of it as of the conditions under which you can assert it. The epistemic conception of meaning has now been framed in its full breadth. It is not derived *from* the idea that truth is verifiability. (The contemporary version of this line of thought, from verificationism about truth to verificationism about meaning, is to read 'is true' in a truth-conditional theory of meaning as equivalent to 'is assertible'. It is presented and discussed in Wright, 1987, chs. 1, 2 and 9; see also Strawson, 1977). Nor does it provide any obvious route *to* a link between verifiability and truth. In both cases the alternative, present in this tradition since the Viennese thirties, is to endorse some deflationary view of truth. EM can realistically recognize that some – or, indeed, all – of the ways in which we acquire warrants for asserting a sentence are defeasible. An inquiry which was good enough to justify the assertion may be superseded by further inquiry which defeats that assertion, that is, leads to an improved information state in which the assertion is no longer justified. The epistemic conception, comprehensively stated, is compatible with such defeasibility in a way that the strict verificationism enunciated in the passage from Wittgenstein quoted above is not.

In fact if we adopt this comprehensive epistemic conception of meaning (for short I will call it 'the comprehensive EM') we have to reject not only strict verificationism but verificationism as such. For to say that evidence defeasibly warrants an assertion that *p* is to accept as intelligible 'There is evidence warranting the assertion that *p* but it is not the case that *p*'. This sentence must have meaning since it appears as a constituent in 'It is logically possible that there is evidence warranting the assertion that *p* but it is not the case that *p*'. The latter sentence is one which we are justified in asserting if we are justified in holding that there can be evidence that *p* which is sufficient but defeasible. It is the way we express, in the language, the proposition that evidence is defeasible. Yet the constituent sentence itself is never verifiable. Thus, if a sentential constituent of a meaningful sentence must itself be meaningful, we have a sentence in the language which is meaningful but not verifiable. So we cannot liberalize verificationism to allow for defeasible verifications: if we liberalize it we have to go beyond it.

We return to this point in 2.3. But first we will consider what account the comprehensive EM can give of the meaning of the logical operators. They are of great importance – witness the fact that sentences like the one above, whose intelligibility refutes verificationism, contain them.

2.2 The meaning of the logical operators

We can give an account of the meaning of logical operators (the operators of sentential logic, and the quantifiers of predicate logic), as of any other expressions, contextually: by giving an account of the way they contribute to the meaning of sentences in which they occur. But on the verificationist view of meaning, an account of the meaning of complex sentences containing the logical operators will have to take the RA form. So our account of the meaning of logical operators, on the verificationist view, must spell out how they contribute to the assertion conditions of sentences in which they occur. And it is natural to think that the way in which they contribute is by mapping the assertion conditions of the constituent clauses of the complex sentence onto an assertion condition for the complex sentence itself; just as in a truth-conditional theory they map the truth-conditions of the constituent clauses onto a truth-condition for the complex sentence itself. Call this the 'assertion-condition-functional' (ACF) view of their meaning, as opposed to the truth-condition-functional (TCF) view of their meaning advanced by the truth-conditional approach. As Dummett famously put it:

> *We no longer explain the sense of a statement by stipulating its truth-value in terms of the truth-values of its constituents, but by stipulating when it may be asserted in terms of the conditions under which its constituents may be asserted.* (Dummett, 1959a; pp. 17–18 in 1978a. Emphasis in the original.)

The ACF view leads to the conclusion that verificationism will require rejection of classical logic. For consider 'P or it is not the case that P', and compare its truth condition – it is true if either 'P' is true or 'It is not the case that P' is true – with the assertion condition it will have on Dummett's proposal: it is assertible if either 'P' is assertible or 'It is not the case that P' is assertible. This latter account of the meaning of 'or' will allow us to assert 'Either magenta was Charlemagne's favourite colour or it was not' *only* if we have evidence warranting the assertion that it was or evidence warranting the assertion that it wasn't. Classical logic, on the other hand, allows us to assert the sentence outright. To save classical logic, one might try supplementing one's account of the meaning of 'or'. For example, we could say that a sentence of the form 'p or q' would be assertible just where 'p' is assertible, or 'q' is assertible, *or where 'q' = 'not-p'*.

There are serious obstacles to this suggestion; but they need not concern us.[20] For, whatever one's view may be about the desirability or otherwise of maintaining classical logic, there is something wrong with the idea that an account of the logical operators must be ACF. The point turns on this: evidence that there is no evidence that *p* does not warrant asserting that it is not the case that *p*. For example, we may have sufficient warrant to assert that there is no evidence that Charlemagne's favourite colour was magenta; but that does not justify us in denying that Charlemagne's favourite colour was magenta. Now consider a pair of sentences of the form '*p*' and 'It is assertible that *p*'. They have the same assertion conditions; any information state which warrants assertion of the one warrants assertion of the other. Consider next the pair 'It is not the case that *p*' and 'It is not assertible that *p*'. These clearly do not have the same assertion conditions, for the reasons just given. It follows that an ACF account of the meaning of 'not' cannot be acceptable.

On any view, it is not part of our practice to regard a demonstration that there is no evidence that *p* as tantamount to a warrant for asserting 'It is not the case that *p*'. The reason is obvious. The world is not totally surveyable by us. There are true propositions about it which we do not have the evidence to assert. Evidence can sometimes be sufficient, though defeasible; but it can also be simply insufficient.

So, also, 'If *p* then *q*' cannot mean, for example, 'If it is verifiable that *p* then it is verifiable that *q*.' For let '*q*' = 'there is no evidence that *p*'. The sentence, 'If *p* then there is no evidence that *p*' is perfectly intelligible and may indeed be assertible. ('If the Prime Minister is a master-criminal there is no evidence that he is. For a master criminal is totally effective in covering his traces.')[21] Both '*p*' and 'there is evidence that *p*' have assertion conditions, but the assertion conditions of the conditional cannot be a function of them.

But does the comprehensive EM have to give an ACF account of 'not' and 'if'? Well, there is no ban on its using the word 'true' in formulating assertion conditions for complex sentences. For it does not deny that a person who understands a sentence S in L can thereby be said to know that S is true in L if and only if *p* (where the sentence which replaces '*p*' has the same semantic content as S). On the contrary, it says that knowing that metalinguistic proposition just is understanding S (see 1.5) – and understanding S in turn, according to a comprehensive EM, consists in mastery of its use in the language – of when it is assertible and what can be inferred from it.

So a comprehensive EM does not require that accounts of the meaning of logical operators must be ACF. It can allow that users of L who understand, and thus grasp the truth-conditions of, elementary sentences in L (those not containing the operators) may also have a truth-functional understanding of the operators. This view, incidentally, does not require that the meaning of those elementary sentences is unaffected by the introduction of operators into L. If introducing an operator into L changes the inferential power of a sentence which does not contain that operator, it also changes its use in L and thus its meaning. But this does not offend the compositional principle, that the meaning of a sentence is determined by the meaning of its constituents. That principle does not preclude the possibility that introducing a new operator into L changes the meaning of sentences in L. It only says that the meaning of a sentence formed with the new operator is a function of the meaning of its constituent sentences.

Let me illustrate by reference to the word 'not'. A truth-functional specification of its meaning will say: 'It is not the case that p' is true if and only if 'p' is not true. If I know that, I can infer that

> 'It is not the case that p' is assertible if and only if it is assertible that 'p' is not true.

So I know the assertion condition of 'It is not the case that *p*' – so long as I can recognize the conditions which warrant denial of 'p' (i.e. assertion that 'p' is not true). But I cannot, from the assertion condition of a given sentence, mechanically derive the assertion condition for its denial, and hence not the condition for assertion of its negation either. So this is an account of the assertion condition of 'It is not the case that *p*' which is not ACF. Nothing in the comprehensive EM requires that a semantics for the word 'not' should equip me with the ability to recognize when denial of any arbitrary English sentence is justified, solely as a function of its assertion condition. A semantic theory for English tells me that the correct way to negate an English sentence '*p*' is by saying 'It is not the case that *p*'. It registers the semantic complexity of negations by delivering truth conditions for negations as a function of truth conditions of the sentences negated. In doing so it enshrines the substantive principle that negation of S is justified just if denial of S is: a fundamental normative feature of our inferential practice. But semantic theory has no mission to tell me any more than that. Of course, on the epistemic conception of meaning there must still in principle be an account of one's understanding of the assertion conditions for denial of various kinds of sentence. But these may be very multifarious and will not be functions of the assertion conditions for ' "P" is true'. The same goes for the other truth-functional operators.[22]

2.3 *Beyond verificationism*

We noted in 2.1 that verificationism cannot be liberalized without being rejected. Liberalization means recognizing that the best available evidence may (a) be insufficient and (b) when sufficient at present, may yet in future be defeated.

For example we are entirely justified in saying that Charlemagne's favourite colour may have been magenta even if there is no evidence warranting the assertion that it was or was not. And we are also justified in saying that, while there are currently sufficiently good scientific grounds for thinking that nothing can travel faster than light, it remains possible that theoretical advances in future may defeat them.

More generally, we are justified in holding that (1) there are sentences which are true even though no-one has sufficient evidence for asserting that they are, and (2) that there are sentences which we have sufficient evidence to assert, but which are not true. Both these general propositions, about our ignorance and fallibility, are justified as internal consequences of our overall commonsense and scientific conception of the physical world (of which classical logic is currently a part), our place in it, the way we get causal signals from it, and so on. The intelligibility and truth of (1) and (2) cannot be denied; but at the same time there can be no warrant for asserting any of their instances.

So those instances, for example ' "Charlemagne's favourite colour was magenta" is true but there is insufficient evidence to assert "Charlemagne's favourite colour was magenta" ', or 'We are justified in asserting "Nothing can travel faster than light" but that sentence is not true', have no free-standing assertoric role in the language. There are no circumstances which justify their assertion. Their only role is as constituents in complex assertions; embedded, for example, in the context "It is possible that . . .", "It could be true that . . .", or in conditionals or negations. But it is still a role: and it is a grasp of that role which, according to the comprehensive EM, constitutes our mastery of their meaning.

The truth in verificationism is that where a sentence can have free-standing assertoric use, grasp of its meaning requires mastery of that use. But some complex sentences formed by sentential operators have a meaning only in virtue of their role in inference and their embedding in more complex sentences still. Where a sentence has a free-standing assertoric use, a person who understands it will know that it has that use and thus will have a grasp of its assertion conditions. But where a sentence does not have such a use, but can still figure in embeddings and inferences, that is what is grasped by someone who understands it.

3 Rules and norms

3.1 Concepts as cognitive roles

In 2.1–3 we attempted to set out EM in its broadest, most plausible, form. But we must now go back to the questions raised at the end of 1.5. That section argued that the priority thesis amounts to the identity thesis and imposes an epistemic conception of meaning or, otherwise put, a semantic conception of epistemology. We saw how Wittgenstein's no-intrinsic-meaning argument destroys any conception of meanings or concepts as intrinsic signs. But we also saw that the no-intrinsic-meaning argument seems to fall short of establishing the priority thesis and thus EM.

Grasping the meaning of a word cannot consist in cognizing an intrinsically meaningful object. But this does not refute the simple point that to understand a word *is* to possess a concept and know that the word expresses the concept. It merely shows that possessing the concept is not a matter of cognizing any such object. The right response to Wittgenstein's no-intrinsic-meaning argument may be a better account of concept-possession than that of the Platonist (or the 'language-of-thought' theorist).

A better account is that to possess a concept is to acknowledge certain cognitive moves as justified. Grasping concepts is acknowledging norms. By analogy to the slogan that meaning is use, one may say that *concepts are cognitive roles*. The no-intrinsic-meaning argument does not decide the choice between the two slogans.

Are the slogans complementary, or does one make the other redundant? It is a question of the difference between norms and language-rules. By a 'norm' I mean a true normative proposition about reasons. An *epistemic* norm is about reasons to believe – about the relation '. . . gives *x* reason to believe that *p*'. So the slogan 'Concepts are cognitive roles' says that to possess a concept is to acknowledge a pattern of epistemic norms. In contrast, a rule is not a *proposition* at all. It cannot be said to be true or false. It is the content of an explicit stipulation or implicit convention. The priority thesis comes down to saying that we cannot treat purported epistemic norms as ultimately distinct from *rules* of a language. Talk of norms constituting a concept must reduce to talk of language-rules constituting the meanings of words.

The no-intrinsic-meaning argument does not establish this thesis. We must look elsewhere – to that extraordinarily influential assumption which (as we noted in 1.3, in discussing the priority and identity theses) was made by Viennese logical empiricism. It was also made by Oxford ordinary-language philosophy, and indeed Quinean naturalism. The assumption is that all propositions are factual. Assertoric and judgable content is factual content.[23] In that case, if there are normative propositions there must be a domain of 'normative facts'. Well, we do talk about 'the fact that' one ought to come to the assistance of distressed people, or 'the fact that' one ought to accept the simplest explanation of the data. But we are not, I think, indulging in ontology. There is a substantial, ontologically committing use of the word 'fact': in this use of the word the idea of 'normative fact' seems to be a kind of category mistake. The stubborn thought that makes it seem a category mistake is a cousin, one might say, of the no-intrinsic-meaning argument. It is the thought that no fact, in any world (natural or non-natural), is intrinsically normative. Acknowledging a norm cannot *consist* in recognizing a fact. Norms are no more facts than meanings are things. But it is in this ontologically committing sense of 'fact' that the claim that all propositions are factual is to be understood.

If all propositions are factual and there are no normative facts, normative utterances, such as 'You ought to come to the assistance of distressed people', or 'You ought to accept the simplest explanation of the data' cannot be assertions but must rather be understood as recommendations, proposals, prescriptions and so forth. In particular, then, it can become plausible to hold that the alleged epistemic norms which constitute concepts should really be seen as prescriptions as to the use of words. But this conclusion is not enforced by the powerful double-barrelled weapon that says no object is intrinsically meaningful and no fact intrinsically normative. It requires the further claim that all assertoric content is factual. Only then do we get the dichotomy of facts and rules which generates the priority thesis and EM.

Although Wittgenstein often seems to assume the dichotomy (as in the passage quoted on p. 40) it is also Wittgenstein, especially in his later thinking, who effectively drives a wedge through it in his reflections on what it is to follow a rule. He highlights the point, noted in 1.2, that to apply a rule is to exercise normative judgement. What view he takes of it, having highlighted it, is a matter of dispute. Here I am assuming, contrary to some readings of his philosophy of language, that he does not intend to *deny* that the question, 'Has the rule been applied correctly?', can have a true answer. His view is not the nihilist one that there is no true answer, or the extreme-conventionalist one that the answer in every case expresses a decision. He accepts that it can be determinately true that if you're following the rules of English you ought to call this patch here 'yellow' (though there can also be vague or indeterminate cases). I also assume – contrary, admittedly, to much current discussion – that Wittgenstein was not a reductionist. It was not his view that 'If you're following the rules of English you ought to call this patch here "yellow" ' has a non-normative truth-condition, consisting, say, in a fact about the speech-dispositions or mental states of certain language-users. But if nihilism, radical conventionalism and reductionism are all false then we have here an example of a normative judgement which corresponds to no fact (in the ontologically committing sense).[24] The upshot is that a thinker who follows rules must grasp norms *as well as* facts and rules. Commitment to the existence of norms is thus entailed by our very description of an entity as a rule-follower – if there are rules, the dichotomy of facts and rules is not exhaustive.

Applying a rule involves a spontaneous normative capacity which is reducible neither to judgements about what is the case nor to familiarity with conventions or stipulations. But why should interpretative normative judgements, judgements about the right way to apply a rule to a case, be the *only* instances of true normative propositions? We naturally and stably converge on many primitive judgements about what there is reason to think, feel or do. Spontaneity and stability of normative judgement is present in all these cases. They are genuine judgements; no more is needed to show they have genuine propositional content.

Now we can formulate a real contrast between an epistemic conception of meaning and an epistemic conception of content (or concepts). Both hold that a truth-conditional theory of meaning must be supplemented if one wants a full account of language-understanding. And both can be said to hold that the supplement must be an account of concepts as cognitive roles. But EM takes it that an account of the cognitive roles of concepts reduces to an account of rules for use of expressions in a language. It holds that the required supplement is still *semantic*. On this view, there is a level of semantic theory which describes conventions for introducing and eliminating terms in a language. Conventions stipulating when a sentence is assertible and what is inferable from it are determined by them. They constitute the language, and the level of semantic theory at which they are stated – call it 'the cognitive-role level' – is more fundamental than the truth-conditional level. In contrast, an epistemic conception of content ('EC' for short) takes the objectivity of norms seriously, and holds that an account of concepts can consist in an account of the epistemic norms regulating their introduction and elimination in one's thinking. Such an account – a theory of epistemic norms – is not a level of semantic theory, for it does not purport to describe rules of a language. It denies the identity of semantics and epistemology. As far as the semantics of a language is concerned, it can hold that a truth-conditional account is fully adequate.[25]

Many questions are raised by this approach; a number of them are analogous to questions which arise for a comprehensive EM. Thus one can ask how a theory of epistemic norms, as well as a theory of linguistic rules of use, copes with the phenomenon of defeasibility; and one can ask how concept-constituting norms, or rules, determine an extension for a concept. These are crucial questions, but they will not be pursued here. The next and final section takes up a very important and attractive corollary of EM: the account it yields of how a priori knowledge derives from grasp of meaning.

3.2 Aprioricity and normativity

An epistemic conception of meaning greatly enlarges the empiricist idea that apriority is analyticity – that an a priori warrant for an assertion is one obtainable from a grasp of its meaning alone. Because it introduces rules of language at the cognitive-role level it is able to give a new account of analyticity which differs from what one might call the Kant/Mill account.

In the latter, a class of sentences is identified as uncontroversially empty of content, or a class of inferences as uncontroversially 'merely apparent'; and then these, together with sentences or inferences reducible to them by explicit definitions, are defined as analytically true. Take, for example, 'Anyone who is a father is a parent' or, 'He's a father. Therefore he's a parent'. The explicit definition is '"x is a father" = Df "x is male and x is a parent"'. The contentless sentence might be 'A father is a father', and the inferences acknowleged as merely apparent would in this case include and-elimination. But as Mill particularily emphasized, this account of analyticity does not guarantee that *all* logic is analytic. It is not uncontroversial that all logically valid inferences are merely apparent, even if it is uncontroversial that and-elimination is. (If even this is rejected, the class of analytic truths is even smaller: e.g. 'Tomorrow is the day after today'.) In this respect, the Kant/Mill account contrasts with the 'Kant/Frege' account, which characterizes analyticity outright as derivability, with explicit definitions, from logic. However, it does not (in Frege's case at least) claim that analyticity is truth by virtue of meaning alone, or that analytic propositions are empty of content; and it is therefore unacceptable to a clear-headed empiricist. In contrast to both of these approaches, then, the new account of the a priori generated by EM *does* simultaneously claim that all logic is analytic and that analyticity is truth by virtue of meaning alone. It promises an empiricist account of the aprioricity of logic and mathematics. This has been perhaps its most influential feature.[26]

In the new account, as in the Kant/Mill account, a sentence is a priori or analytic when a justification for asserting it can be derived exclusively from a grasp of its meaning. But the rules which constitute that meaning will now include introduction and elimination rules statable only at the cognitive-role level. An example will explain what I mean. Consider the following introduction rule for the English word 'yellow':

(1) The occurrence of a visual experience as of a yellow object in one's visual field warrants, in the absence of defeating information, assertion of the sentence in English 'There's something yellow there'.

This is a rule formulated at the cognitive-role level. In contrast, if (as is plausible) 'yellow' is semantically simple, then a truth-conditional semantics for English will contain only the following dictionary rule:

(2) ' "yellow" is true (in English) of *x* if and only if *x* is yellow'.

Notice that as I have formulated (1) the relation *warrants assertion of* holds between a state of visual experience – something which is not a sentence – and a sentence. Many philosophers, both friends and foes of EM, would find this unacceptable. They assume or argue that the relation can only hold between sentences.[27] But the only relevant constraint on an object which satisfies '. . . warrants assertion of S', where 'S' can be any sentence, seems to be that it must have content and be transparent (in the sense of 1.3). A visual experience or a memory has content and is transparent, and so it satisfies that constraint. Some rules at the cognitive-role level will link warrants for asserting sentences to warrants for asserting other sentences (specifically, in the case of logical connectives, metalinguistic sentences – see 2.2). But if a language has empirical content at all it must contain rules linking the assertibility of certain sentences in the language to the language-user's experience and memory. In the spirit of stating EM in the most liberal way possible, we should allow that a fully comprehensive EM account can include them.

Consider now the following normative proposition:

(3) The occurrence of a visual experience as of a yellow object in one's field of vision justifies, in the absence of defeating information, a judgement that there's something yellow there.

This is not a metalinguistic statement of a rule of English as (1) is, but a normative proposition stated in English. What is the relation between them? The EM theorist must maintain that (3) is in some way an expression of (1) alone. It cannot be a genuine normative proposition. Rather, sentence (3) is 'assertible a priori' in English because its warrant derives solely from a rule of the language – for English the rule will be (1), while for other languages which have a sentence synonymous to (3) it will be a rule analogous to (1). Let us allow, for the sake of argument, that the details of this can be filled in coherently. However it is done, the crucial point is that it provides an explanation of how a priori knowledge of (3) is possible, in a way that no appeal to (2) could do. I have a priori knowledge of (3) in virtue of grasping rule (1), or some analogous rule in another language.

In short, EM generates a new account of aprioricity as analyticity, because it postulates introduction and elimination rules at the cognitive-role level. Indisputably, this is important and new – a major twentieth-century contribution to philosophy. But is it right? *Does* the aprioricity of (3) depend in any way on there being a rule of English expressible by (1), or some analogous rule for another language? Well, it's far from obvious that it does depend on that. Do we want to say that (3) is 'a priori'? What makes us want to say it is, if we do, does not seem to stem from the fact that some language, English or another, contains some rule. Rather, the essential point is simply that we converge, on critical reflection, in finding (3) primitively or spontaneously compelling. It is a fundamental epistemic norm: it expresses a primitive normative response. Acknowledging it does not consist in learning any linguistic convention or stipulation. It's the other way round: training in linguistic conventions *assumes* such primitive normative responses. In teaching (2) we assume the existence of belief-forming dispositions responsive to (3). And once a person had learned (2) he or she would see the truth of (1), understood now not as a language rule but as a consequence of (2) and (3).

On the other hand, we have accepted the point that no fact is intrinsically normative. So acknowledging (3) does not consist in knowledge of any fact, natural or non-natural. What, then, is its epistemology? As for any other fundamental norm, be it of belief, action or feeling, it is the epistemology of reflective examination and critical convergence. That is the epistemology characteristic of the normative: it is not the epistemology appropriate to propositions which depict the existence of a state of affairs.

This takes us to the brink of controversial epistemological questions which are not on our agenda here. For present purposes it is enough to pin down how EC, the view that concepts are patterns of epistemic norms, differs from EM, the view that they are patterns of language-rules. EC requires the thesis that the normative and the factual are both domains of judgement, consisting of propositions with truth-value. If this is defensible, then we can say that (3) expresses a norm partially constitutive of the concept *yellow*. We can also say it is a 'conceptual truth' – at any rate it is concept-constituting and it is true. *But its status as a conceptual truth in this sense in no way explains how it might be a priori*. The way it is known to be true is the way that any fundamental norm is known to be true; its epistemology is that appropriate to fundamental norms in general. It is not *because* it is a conceptual truth, constitutive of the concept *yellow*, that it is true. Thus EC does not belong to that class of views which takes certain truths to be 'a priori' and seeks to *explain* that status by saying that they are conceptual (truths, that is, which go beyond the Kant/Mill prototype of analyticity). But this does not matter. If concepts are constituted by norms of reasoning, and if we can get a satisfactory account of normative knowledge, we do not *also* need a substantive theory of the a priori which goes beyond Kant/Mill analyticity. An account of normative knowledge will do what an account of the a priori was meant to do.[28]

I assumed earlier (3.1) that Wittgenstein is neither a nihilist nor a radical conventionalist nor a reductionist about rule-following. If all this is right then the later Wittgenstein needs a distinction between rules and norms of the kind made here. His own reflections on rule-following show that to avoid this trilemma one must go beyond the Viennese dichotomy of facts and rules. It is that dichotomy, together with the points that no object has intrinsic meaning and no fact is intrinsically normative, that produces the package of EM, the linguistic theory of the a priori and radical conventionalism about logic and rule-following. But did Wittgenstein go beyond it? Reading his later writings on 'grammar' and 'rules' it is hard to come up with an answer. Michael Dummett attributes the whole package to Wittgenstein (see e.g. Dummett, 1959a, 1994; cp. Stroud, 1965). Others disagree. They faithfully reflect Wittgenstein's own murkiness. In a valuable discussion of Wittgenstein's notion of a criterion, for example, Hacker (1990) comments thus:

> To say that *q* is a criterion for W is to give a partial explanation of the meaning of 'W', and in that sense to give a rule for its correct use. The fact that the criterial relation between *q* and W may be neither arbitrary (in one sense at least) nor stipulated, that in innumerable cases we could not resolve to abandon the normative relationship without a change in our form of life, and in many cases could not abandon it at all, does not imply that it is empirical, let alone that it is a matter of *Wesensschau*. We may concede that certain concepts are deeply embedded in our lives, occupy a pivotal role in our thought and experience, yet still insist that their use is rule-governed, a matter of *nomos* rather than *phusis*. (p. 552)

Note how the line of thought here goes from acknowledging that the relationship is 'normative' to the conclusion that – however inescapable for us, however felt as a constraint rather than a stipulation – it must yet be a 'rule', a matter of convention rather than nature. But why cannot it be acknowledged that it is normative without being in *any* sense a convention? It is hard to see what could be at work here other than the philosophical thesis that all propositions, judgable contents, are factual.

It may be impossible to tell how far Wittgenstein thought his way past this thesis. On the one hand he was not (in his later thought) burdened by the realist semantic assumptions about truth and reference which lead to it. But on the other hand his constant insistence that 'training' determines the 'logical grammar', or framework, of our language-games at least suggests that he did not repudiate the Viennese dichotomy of facts and rules. For one is 'trained' to observe rules: the process of acknowledging a norm – spontaneously, autonomously – is a process of education, not 'training'.

At any rate, if we reject the thesis that all judgable content is factual, we can acknowledge that the normative is a domain of the understanding, something we judge of – but yet that norms are still like rules in this respect: we do not find them in the world. They are presupposed in cognition of a world – and that view still has certain strong affinities with Wittgenstein's later philosophy, even if it is not his. For example, what he says about logic would also apply to this view of norms. For them, as for 'logic',

> There is not any question at all . . . of some correspondence between what is said and reality; rather is logic antecedent to any such correspondence. (Wittgenstein, 1978, 1. 156: p. 96)

Certainly this a very important and controversial philosophical claim. The question in the end, of course, is not who thought it but whether it is true, and if so, how or why.

Notes

1 I am grateful to Bob Hale and Crispin Wright for many very useful discussions (including some illuminating disagreements) about the issues dealt with in this chapter.

2 I shall refer to its development in Wittgenstein's thought, since his discussions of it remain influential and exemplary. A balanced historical account would also examine the important ideas of a number of his contemporaries; for example, Rudolf Carnap and Moritz Schlick in the development of Viennese verificationism and Friedrich Waismann for his influence on the development of ordinary language philosophy (e.g. Carnap, 1936, 1937, 1949 and 1967; Schlick, 1936 and 1979, Vol. 2; Waismann, 1945, and Wittgenstein, 1979).

3 In the *Tractatus* (Wittgenstein, 1961, 6. 211) he merely notes, 'In philosophy the question, "What do we actually use this word or this proposition for?" repeatedly leads to valuable insights.'

The characterization of a word's meaning as its use in a language becomes prominent in his conversations with Schlick and others between 1929 and 1932 and in lectures and writing of the thirties. For example, in *Philosophical Grammar* (Wittgenstein, 1974): 'We ask "How do you use the word, what do you do with it" – that will tell us how you understand it' (p. 87); 'The use of a word in the language is its meaning . . . Grammar describes the use of words in the language' (p. 60). Further, description of use is description of *rules* of use, like description of 'rules of a game': '"I can use the word 'yellow'" is like "I know how to move the king in chess"' (p. 49). Wittgenstein retains this conception even when he drops his verificationism (on which see 2.1).

4 'the meaning of a word is what the explanation of its meaning explains . . . "What 1 c.c. of water weighs is called '1 gram' – Well, what *does* it weigh?" . . . Meaning, in our sense, is embodied in the explanation of meaning.' (Wittgenstein, 1974, pp. 59–60).

5 You need to know this basic principle to lie (to seek to make someone believe something is true which you know to be false, by asserting it).

6 'It is what is regarded as the justification of an assertion that constitutes the sense of the assertion.' (Wittgenstein, 1974, p. 81.)

7 Here I use 'semantics' broadly, as equivalent to 'theory of meaning' (or if the term 'meaning' is resisted, of 'language-use'). In this broad sense it is not distinguished from syntax but includes it.

8 I borrow the name from Michael Dummett (e.g. Dummett, 1993c, ch. 2), but the account of the idea in what follows is my own.

9 EM should also be distinguished from conceptual role semantics (see Field, 1977, and Peacocke, 1981 and ed. 1993, for a selection of representative articles). They often sound similar, and similar issues, for example about reference and truth, arise for them. The difference is that EM describes understanding in terms of grasp of rules, while conceptual role semantics describes it solely in terms of assertoric and inferential dispositions. The difference disappears if grasp of rules reduces to assertoric and inferential dispositions – whether or not it does is *one* of the issues at stake in the rule-following considerations (see Chapter 15, RULE-FOLLOWING, OBJECTIVITY AND MEANING).

10 What is abolished is the idea of epistemology as the study of norms of belief, understood as distinct from linguistic conventions or proposals. 'Epistemology' can still remain as the name for conceptual analysis of what kind of fact is asserted to hold when one says, for example, that a person *knows* that so-and-so is the case.

11 Warrant, incidentally, comes in degrees. That is important, and a comprehensive theory would need to take it into account. However, it will not be considered here.

12 It may mention them in giving truth-conditions for sentences which themselves mention concepts and propositions. But while this might show that they enter its ontology, it would not show that it makes explanatory appeal to them in exhibiting what language-understanding is.

13 This attempt to show that truth-conditional semantics is consistent with the priority thesis is loosely based on earlier discussions by Davidson and others of the philosophy underlying his programme for semantics. See Davidson (1984); Evans and McDowell (eds., 1976), 'Introduction', and Davidson's reply to Foster therein.

14 This line of thought implies either (a) a 'deflationary', 'redundancy', or 'minimalist' theory of truth (a theory of the kind discussed e.g. in Horwich 1990) or (b) a verificationist theory of truth (see 2.1). So the disjunction of (a) and (b) *follows* from the priority thesis. A separate issue is whether a truth-conditional theory which clear-headedly *rejects* the priority thesis has to adopt some theory of truth robuster than (a) (including (b) among these robuster theories). Some argue that it does have to do so (see Peacocke, 1993b, p. xvi); I do not myself think that is so.

15 Remember that we are talking here of a *normative* response: there is no attempt in this account of understanding to reduce or eliminate normative attitudes to language-use.

16 Contemporary philosophers who have influentially espoused a view of truth like this include Putnam (1990) and Wright; but Wright now accepts it only for some areas of discourse – see his concept of 'superassertibility' in Wright (1992). Interestingly, it is not prominent in either Wittgenstein or the Vienna Circle. Schlick is closest to it. Neurath inclined to coherentism or to questioning the very respectability of the concept of truth; Carnap (1949), relying on Tarski's semantic characterization of truth, defended truth as a respectable concept but explicitly distinguished it from assertibility. Wittgenstein inclined to a deflationary view of it. As remarked in note 15, both the verificationist and the deflationary view are consistent with the priority thesis.

17 This passage comes from a section copied by Stein from notes which Waismann circulated as a transcript of Wittgenstein's views (see editor's introduction, p. 20).

18 "The direction of a thought-movement is defined by the logical place of the answer." Note the continuity with *Tractatus* 6.5 and 6.51; cp. Wittgenstein (1975, pp. 66 and 174: 'The meaning of a question is the method of answering it', and 'Every proposition is the signpost for a verification'.

19 In Waismann's own theses (included in Wittgenstein 1979 as Appendix B) the 'positivistic' kind of verificationism is rather more prominent – "To understand a proposition means to to know how things stand if the proposition is true" – but the operationist conception is simultaneously stressed.

20 The suggestion is canvassed by Crispin Wright in 'Anti-realism and revisionism', *Realism, Meaning and Truth*, pp. 317–41. Cp. Skorupski (1988) section VI, pp. 516–23.

21 Further discussion of related issues, together with further reading, can be found in Wright (1987), pp. 309–16 ('Could Thatcher be a master-criminal'?). Note, however, that Wright's discussion is about the implications for an 'epistemically constrained' notion of truth, whereas here the issue concerns EM and its account of the meaning of logical operators.

22 In this section I have skirted obscure and much-discussed issues about 'holism', 'anti-realism' and classical logic. A recent statement of Dummett's view (which is opposed to

that taken here) is Dummett (1991), chs. 8–12. Compare Wright, 'Anti-realism', section VI in Wright (1987). The line I have taken is discussed a little more extensively in §§ I–VII of Skorupski (1993a).

23 'What else but a fact can a statement express? In what sense could something be called "true" or "false" if it does not designate an existing or nonexisting fact?' (Carnap, 1967, p. 341).

24 It does not correspond to the fact that the patch *is* yellow. Rather, the English sentence 'The patch is yellow' can express a fact because the normative proposition 'If you're following the rules of English you ought to call this patch "yellow"' can be determinately true.

25 Two writers who argue for an epistemic theory of content – though in quite different and, indeed, unrelated ways – are John Pollock and Christopher Peacocke. Peacocke's theory has been developed in a number of writings, most recently at book length in Peacocke (1992). An accessible account of Pollock's view is in Pollock (1987). Also, those writers in the Davidsonian truth-conditional tradition who hold that interpreting the meaning of a speaker's utterances requires that one attribute norms of rationality to the speaker, in effect yoke a truth-conditional semantics to an epistemic theory of content. See Davidson (1984).

26 For further discussion of these matters see Coffa (1991) and Skorupski (1993b). See also Chapter 14, ANALYTICITY.

27 The dispute goes right back to the Vienna Circle. Neurath announced that '*Statements are compared with statements*, not with "experiences", "the world", or anything else' (Neurath, 1959, p. 291). Schlick replied: 'It is my humble opinion that we can compare anything to anything if we choose' (Schlick, 1979, Vol. 2, p. 401). See Jacob (1984). A non-linguistic version of the Neurathian doctrine is that only a belief can provide a reason for a belief: see e.g. Davidson (1986). For recent discussions of how experience provides reasons for belief see McDowell (1994) and Millar (1991).

28 Peacocke argues that a theory of concepts cast in terms of norms of reasoning can yield a substantive account of the a priori which differs from the EM account of analyticity discussed in this section. His account does not seem to me to be successful, but neither does it seem to me to be needed for his project of stating possession conditions for concepts. See Peacocke (1993a), Skorupski (1995) and Peacocke (1996).

References

Baker, G.P. 1974: 'Criteria: A new foundation for semantics', *Ratio*, 16, 156–89.

——and Hacker, P.M.S. 1980: *Wittgenstein, Understanding and Meaning*. Oxford: Basil Blackwell.

Blackburn, S. 1984: *Spreading the Word: Groundings in the Philosophy of Language*. Oxford: Oxford University Press.

Carnap, R. 1936 and 1937: 'Testability and meaning', *Philosophy of Science*, 3, 419–71; 4, 1–40.

——1949: 'Truth and confirmation', in Feigl and Sellars (1949). Translation, with adaptations, of 'Wahrheit und Bewahrung', *Actes du Congrès International de Philosophie Scientifique* (1936).

——1967: 'Pseudo-problems in philosophy: the heteropsychological and the realism controversy', in R. Carnap, *The Logical Structure of the World*, trans. by Eolf A. George. London: Routledge and Kegan Paul.

Coffa, Alberto 1991: *The Semantic Tradition from Kant to Carnap: To the Vienna Station.* Cambridge: Cambridge University Press.
Davidson, Donald 1984: *Inquiries into Truth and Interpretation.* Oxford: Clarendon Press.
——1986: 'A coherence theory of truth and knowledge', in E. Lepore (ed.), *Truth and Interpretation.* Oxford: Blackwell.
Dummett, Michael 1959a: 'Truth', *Proceedings of the Aristotelian Society*, 59. Reprinted in Dummett (1978a).
——1959b: 'Wittgenstein's philosophy of mathematics', *Philosophical Review*, 68. Reprinted in Dummett (1978a).
——1974: 'What is a theory of meaning?' in Samuel Guttenplan (ed.), *Mind and Language* Oxford: Oxford University Press. Reprinted in Dummett (1993a) as 'What is a theory of meaning? (I)', with an appendix.
——1978a: *Truth and Other Enigmas.* London: Duckworth.
——1978b: 'The philosophical basis of intuitionistic logic', in Dummett (1978a).
——1991: *The Logical Basis of Metaphysics.* London: Duckworth.
——1993a: *The Seas of Language.* Oxford: Oxford University Press.
——1993b: 'Realism and anti-realism' in Dummett (1993a).
——1993c: *Origins of Analytical Philosophy.* London: Duckworth.
——1994: 'Wittgenstein on necessity: some reflections', in Bob Hale and Peter Clark (eds), *Reading Putnam.* Oxford: Oxford University Press. Also in Dummett (1993a).
Evans, G. and McDowell, J. (eds) 1976: *Truth and Meaning: Essays in Semantics.* Oxford: Clarendon Press.
Feigl, H. and Sellars, W. (eds) 1949: *Readings in Philosophical Analysis.* New York: Appleton-Century-Crofts.
Field, Hartry 1977: 'Logic, meaning and conceptual role', *Journal of Philosophy*, 74, 347–75.
Hacker, P.M.S. 1990: *Wittgenstein, Meaning and Mind: An Analytical Commentary on the Philosophical Investigations*, vol. 3. Oxford: Basil Blackwell.
Horwich, Paul 1990: *Truth.* Oxford: Basil Blackwell.
——1995: 'Meaning, use and truth', *Mind*, 104, 355–68.
Jacob, Pierre 1984: 'The Neurath–Schlick controversy', *Fundamenta Scientiae*, 5, 351–66.
McDowell, John 1994: *Mind and World.* Cambridge, Mass.: Harvard University Press.
Millar, Alan 1991: *Reasons and Experience.* Oxford: Oxford University Press.
Moore, G.E. 1959: 'Wittgenstein's lectures in 1930–33', *Philosophical Papers.* London: George Allen and Unwin.
Neurath, Otto 1959: 'Sociology and physicalism', in A.J. Ayer (ed.), *Logical Positivism.* Glencoe, Ill.: Free Press, London: Allen and Unwin.
Peacocke, Christopher 1981: 'The theory of meaning in analytic philosophy', in G. Floistad (ed.), *Contemporary Philosophy*, vol. 1. *Philosophy of Language, Philosophical Logic.* The Hague: Martinus Nijhoff.
——1992: *A Study of Concepts.* Cambridge, Mass.: MIT Press.
——1993a: 'How are a priori truths possible?' *European Journal of Philosophy*, 1, 175–99.
——(ed.) 1993b: *Understanding and Sense*, vol. 1. Aldershot: Dartmouth.
——1996: 'Can a theory of concepts explain the a priori? A reply to John Skorupski's critical notice of *A Study of Concepts*', *International Journal of Philosophical Studies*, 4, 154–60.
Pollock, John 1987: *Contemporary Theories of Knowledge.* London: Hutchinson.
Putnam, Hilary 1983: 'Computational psychology and interpretation theory', in Putnam's *Realism and Reason: Philosophical Papers*, vol. 3. Cambridge: Cambridge University Press.

——1990: *Realism with a Human Face*. Cambridge, Mass.: Harvard University Press.

Schlick, M. 1936: 'Meaning and verification', *The Philosophical Review*, 45. Reprinted in Feigl and Sellars (eds) 1949, and Schlick (1979) vol. 2.

——1979: *Philosophical Papers* (2 vols.), edited by Henk L. Mulder and Barbara F.B. van de Velde-Schlick, trans. by Peter Heath. Dordrecht: Reidel.

Skorupski, John 1988: 'Realism, meaning and truth' (critical review of Wright, *Realism, Meaning and Truth*), *Philosophical Quarterly*, 38, 500–25.

——1993a: 'Anti-realism, inference and the logical constants', in J. Haldane and C. Wright (eds), *Realism and Reason*. Oxford: Oxford University Press.

——1993b: *English-Language Philosophy 1750–1945*. Oxford: Oxford University Press.

——1995: 'Possessed by concepts' (critical notice of Christopher Peacocke, *A Study of Concepts*), in *International Journal of Philosophical Studies*, 3, 143–64.

Strawson, P.F. 1977: 'Scruton and Wright on anti-realism, etc.', *Proceedings of the Aristotelian Society*, 77, 15–22.

Stroud, Barry 1965: 'Wittgenstein and logical necessity', *Philosophical Review*, 74, 504–18.

Waismann, Friedrich 1945: 'Verifiability', *Proceedings of the Aristotelian Society*, Supplementary vol. 19.

Wittgenstein, L. 1958: *Philosophical Investigations*, 2nd edition, ed. G.E.M. Anscombe and R. Rhees, trans. by G.E.M. Anscombe. Oxford: Basil Blackwell.

——1961: *Tractatus Logico-Philosophicus*, trans. by D.F. Pears and B.F. McGuinness. London: Routledge and Kegan Paul.

——1974: *Philosophical Grammar*, ed. Rush Rhees, trans. by Anthony Kenny. Oxford: Blackwell.

——1975: *Philosophical Remarks*, ed. Rush Rhees, trans. by Raymond Hargreaves and Roger White. Oxford: Blackwell.

——1978: *Remarks on the Foundations of Mathematics*, 3rd edition, ed. G.H. von Wright, Rush Rhees and G.E.M. Anscombe, trans. by G.E.M. Anscombe. Oxford: Blackwell.

——1979: *Wittgenstein and the Vienna Circle*, conversations recorded by Friedrich Waismann, ed. Brian McGuiness, trans. by Joachim Schulte and Brian McGuiness. Oxford: Basil Blackwell.

Wright, C. 1987: *Realism, Meaning and Truth*. Oxford: Basil Blackwell.

——1992: *Truth and Objectivity*. Cambridge, Mass.: Harvard University Press.

3

Intention and convention

ANITA AVRAMIDES

1 Intention and convention in language

Individuals perform intentional actions, and among these are linguistic acts. Individuals also perform conventional actions, and among these, as well, are linguistic acts. Some philosophers have taken these facts as the starting-point for an understanding of language and meaning.

No one would deny that intentions must have a place in a completed account of linguistic meaning, but only some have insisted that reference to speakers and their intentions is of fundamental importance in the understanding of language (see § 2). One philosopher who gives a clearly defined and central place to speakers and their intentions when accounting for meaning is H. P. Grice. In his 1957 paper, "Meaning", Grice proposes an analysis of meaning in terms of a speaker's intention to produce a response in an audience. Grice's analysis of meaning is an analysis of speaker meaning (see §§ 6 and 7). Grice further proposes that we use this analysis of speaker meaning as the foundation of an account of linguistic meaning. One difference between the two sorts of meaning is this: linguistic meaning is timeless, while speaker meaning is tied to a particular occasion of utterance. One way of effecting the transition from speaker meaning to linguistic meaning is to introduce the notion of convention. David Lewis (1969) and Stephen Schiffer (1972) have constructed an analysis of the notion of convention which dovetails nicely with Grice's work on meaning (see §§ 9 and 10).

According to Lewis, "it is a platitude that language is ruled by convention" (1969, p. 1). The problem with platitudes is that they can be so taken for granted that it is often difficult to say what precisely they mean. The idea that language is conventional can be traced back to the ancient Greeks. In *De Interpretatione* Aristotle wrote, 'A name is a spoken sound significant by convention. . . . I say "by convention" because no name is a name naturally but only when it has become a symbol.' According to John Lyons (1968, p. 4), the ancient Greeks took convention to be the result of custom or habit, itself the result of either tacit agreement or social contract which, in that it was man-made, men could alter without affecting the efficacy of language. This view of language was set in opposition to that of the naturalist. A naturalist view of language is claimed to have been held by Cratylus and is reported by Socrates in the Platonic dialogue concerned with language, *Cratylus*. Characteristically, Socrates makes the point by appeal to analogy: "To what does the carpenter look in making the shuttle? Does he not look to that which is naturally fitted to act as a shuttle?. . . . Then, as to names, ought not our legislator also to know how to put the true natural name of each thing into sounds and syllables?" A natural name is onomatopoeic, or has a part which is imitative or suggestive of what it refers to (see Lyons, p. 5).

For philosophers today the debate is no longer between the conventionalist and the naturalist. In some sense, all philosophers are conventionalists. Reflecting on the positions of Cratylus and Aristotle, it is possible to discern two basic ideas in the thought that language is conventional. First there is the rejection of the Cratylian idea that words have a natural meaning in favour of the idea that there is an *arbitrary* association between a word and its meaning. Further to this is the positive idea that speakers exercise a degree of rational, or intentional, control over their language. It is the first of these ideas – that the association between a word and its meaning is arbitrary – which has the greatest claim to being a platitude. It is this that no philosopher today denies. All too often, however, it is the *further* idea – that speakers exercise rational control over the meaning of their words – which is taken to be necessary for convention. And it is to this idea that many object (see § 10).

Some of those who object to the more full-blooded notion of convention are opposed also to an account of meaning which depends on the concept of intention. This may be because intention-based semantics is also thought to give a speaker some sort of rational control over the meaning of their words (see Grandy and Warner, 1989, for a good discussion of the way in which meaning is, for Grice, a reason-governed activity). Whatever the reason for entwining the fates of these two ideas, it should be remembered that they are essentially distinct.

2 Use theories *vs*. formal theories

Traditionally there have been two approaches to the understanding of language, each of which accords an essentially different place to speakers and their intentions. One approach is associated with formal theories of meaning, the other with what is sometimes referred to as 'use theories' of meaning. It will help to clear the way for a discussion of the Gricean, intention-based approach if we first review this traditional distinction.

Formal theories of meaning are primarily concerned with the formal structure of language and the interrelations between sentences. They aim, *inter alia*, to explain how, from a finite stock of semantic primitives, a user of the language can understand and construct a potentially infinite variety of sentences. Formal theorists study language in abstraction from the imprecisions and ambiguities of daily use. Such theories were prominent in the first part of the twentieth century, encouraged by developments in formal logic. More recently, formal theories of meaning have been proposed by, among others, Donald Davidson (1984) and Michael Dummett (1975). Both Davidson and Dummett agree that a formal approach is the correct approach to linguistic meaning, and they both agree that a theory of meaning should be constructed in such a way as to conform to certain general principles. Both Davidson and Dummett agree that a formal approach to linguistic meaning is correct, and they both agree that a theory of meaning should be constructed in such a way as to conform to certain general principles. Davidson and Dummett part company over the question of which principles should guide the construction of the formal theory. As a result, Davidson ends up employing a Tarski-style theory of truth in his account of meaning, while Dummett rejects a truth-conditions theory in favour of one based on verification conditions. (See Chapter 1, MEANING AND TRUTH CONDITIONS, Chapter 2, MEANING, USE, VERIFICATION, Chapter 8, RADICAL INTERPRETATION, and Chapter 12, REALISM AND ITS OPPOSITIONS.)

Despite the formal nature of these theories of meaning, they do accord some role to speakers and their intentions. Latterly, formal theorists have proposed that a completed account of meaning should be taken to consist in a series of layers (see, for example, Wiggins, 1971): the fundamental level is labelled 'semantics' and accounts for the strict meaning of an utterance; the next level is labelled 'pragmatics' and accounts for an utterance's force; further levels are brought in to account for perlocutionary effect, tone, conversational implicature, etc. The claim, then, is that formal theories are only applicable at the level of semantics; reference to speakers and their intentions are to be brought in at the next level – that of pragmatics.

In contrast to the formal theorists, the use theorists put central emphasis on speakers and what they do in their account of meaning. They are not content to let mention of speakers and their intentions be relegated to the level of pragmatics. The debate is over the core; use theorists see themselves as offering an account of semantics (see Loar, 1976, p. 150). This approach to meaning is associated with the writings of J. L. Austin, the later Wittgenstein and Grice. John Searle (1971, pp. 6–7) has written that the influence of these philosophers

> recasts the discussion of many of the problems in the philosophy of language into the larger context of human action and behaviour generally. . . . Instead of seeing the relations between words and the world as something existing *in vacuo*, one now sees them as involving intentional actions by speakers.

According to these philosophers one cannot abstract away from the imprecision of natural language, but must study language in its natural habitat, so to speak. By placing the emphasis on speakers and their intentions, these use theorists place less emphasis on sentence structure; they concentrate on giving an account of whole sentences. However, just as formal theorists eventually turn their attention to intentions, so use theorists do eventually turn their attention to structure once the basic analysis is in place. It is often said that the weakness in the formal approach is in the way it handles intention, while the weakness of the intention-based approach is in the way it handles structure (see § 8).

The weakness of one approach may be thought to be the strength of another. A union of the two has sometimes been thought to cover all desiderata. This is a good idea in principle; in practice, however, there are difficulties. There can be no reconciliation with an approach which is considered misguided, and many have thought this about the Gricean approach to meaning (see § 4). Furthermore, for many philosophers the battle rages over the core. P. F. Strawson (1971, p. 172) characterizes this battle as a "Homeric struggle". Strawson himself enters the fray on the side of the use theorist. He does allow both the use and the formal theorist a place in an overall account of meaning, but he places the use theorist closer to the philosophical foundations of meaning.

Strawson points out that both theorists may accept some of the ground of the other: both may accept that the meaning of sentences of a language is largely determined by the semantic and syntactic rules of that language; and both may accept that those who share knowledge of a language have at their disposal a useful means of communicating. Strawson characterizes the difference between the theorists in this way: the use theorist insists, and the formal theorist denies, that the nature of the rules can be understood only by reference to the function of communication. Strawson then attempts to show that the use theorist must be correct by considering the formal, truth conditions, theory of Davidson, and arguing that these truth conditions cannot be understood without reference to the act of communication which they facilitate. The line of thought which leads Strawson to this conclusion goes as follows. The truth condition theorist claims that to give "necessary and sufficient conditions for the truth of every sentence . . . is a way of giving the meaning of a sentence" (Davidson, 1984, p. 24). According to Strawson, such an account gives us an understanding of meaning only if we have some understanding of truth – not just truth in this or that language, but truth in general. The first thing we notice when we try to give some account of truth in general is this: "one who makes a statement or assertion makes a true statement if and only if things are as, in making that statement, he states them to be" (Strawson, 1971, p. 180). When we put this together with the idea that meaning can be specified in terms of truth-conditions, we get the following: to specify the meaning of an indicative sentence is to specify how things are stated to be by someone who makes a statement by uttering it. What we run up against here is the speech act of statement-making, and the content of such a speech act. Strawson then writes (1971, p. 181):

> Here the [use] theorist . . . sees his chance. There is no hope of elucidating the notion of the content of such speech acts without paying some attention to the notions of those speech acts themselves. . . . And we cannot, the theorist maintains, elucidate the notion of stating or asserting except in terms of audience-directed intention. For the fundamental case of stating or asserting . . . is that of uttering a sentence with a certain intention.

Strawson's conclusion is that reference to speakers and their intentions is of fundamental importance in the understanding of language.

John McDowell (1980) has a certain sympathy with the use theorist, but thinks Strawson grants such a theorist too much ground. In particular, McDowell objects to the employment of a Gricean *analysis* to account for meaning. Strawson's mistake, according to McDowell, is to take the formal theorist to be giving a kind of analysis of meaning in term of truth conditions. McDowell agrees that, had the formal theorist embarked on the task of analysis, it would indeed be short-sighted to stop before offering some analysis of the notion of truth employed in the original analysis. However, analysis is not the business of the formal theorist. Once we see this, claims McDowell, we can see as well that the *further* analysis of truth which Strawson insists upon is unnecessary. McDowell agrees with Strawson that the theorist of meaning must mention kinds of action which are standardly intentional and directed towards audiences. However, he believes that this can be done without employing the method of analysis anywhere in the account of meaning. (This idea is developed in § 4, below.)

Despite their differences, McDowell and Strawson agree that the study of meaning involves us in the study of speech acts of various sorts. It was Grice who introduced a detailed analysis of these acts in terms of speakers' intentions, but it was J. L. Austin who emphasized the need for philosophers of language to appreciate that speakers of a language *do* things with words.

3 Austin and the use of language

Austin's 1955 William James Lectures were published in 1962 under the title *How to Do Things With Words*. According to Geoffrey Warnock (1989), Austin claimed to have formed his views on this topic as early as 1939. In his early thinking about language Austin distinguishes what he calls "performative" from what he calls "constative" utterances. The "typical or paradigm case" of a constative utterance is a descriptive utterance, or a statement (1962, p. 132). Austin initially identifies a constative as an utterance which states a fact and is true or false. He then proceeds to point out that there are utterances which masquerade as constatives, as statements of fact, but which are "intended as something quite different" (1962, p. 3). In other words, there are utterances which are grammatically constructed along the same lines as a statement of fact, and yet are importantly different from such statements. Austin specifies two of these differences:

(1) The masquerading utterances do not describe – or *constate* – anything; they are not true or false, and
(2) The utterance of one of these masqueraders is, or is part of, the doing of an action, which would not normally count as saying something.

Austin gives the name "performative" to these masquerading utterances. He begins by drawing attention to *explicit* performatives, that is, to utterances which are explicit about the action which they serve to perform. Examples include the following:

(1) I promise to meet you at 5 o'clock.
(2) I bet you £10 *Princess Precious* will win the race.
(3) I name this ship the *Queen Elizabeth*.
(4) I do thee wed.

If I say "I promise to meet you at 5 o'clock", this is not a description of a promise, it is an act of promising. My utterance is not truth-evaluable. Austin writes,

> [This] needs argument no more than that 'damn' is not true or false: it may be that the utterance 'serves to inform you' – but that is quite different. To name the ship *is* to say (in the appropriate circumstances) the words 'I name, etc.'. When I say, before the registrar or altar, etc. 'I do,' I am not reporting on a marriage: I am indulging in it. (1962, p. 6)

One important feature of a performative utterance is this: the utterance itself is not sufficient for the completion of the (speech) act; in addition, a certain 'setting' is required. Austin refers to this as the condition of convention. About this he writes: "There must exist an accepted conventional procedure having a certain conventional effect, that procedure to include the uttering of certain words by certain persons in certain circumstances" (1962, p. 14). It is to these conventions that Austin is referring, above, when he says that the words "I name, etc." must be said in the appropriate circumstances, and the words "I do" must be said before an altar or a registrar. Austin says little in support of this condition, which he takes to be obvious.

Thus we find in Austin an early example of the explicit introduction of the notion of convention into semantics. However, the notion of convention which Austin takes to be necessary for the completion of a performative utterance must be distinguished from that centrally under discussion in this essay. Austin is not here referring to *linguistic* conventions, but to *social* conventions. These social conventions must be in place for the utterance to be successful or "felicitous". This leads us to note yet another feature which, according to Austin, differentiates performative from constative utterances: performatives, which require the existence of (social) conventions, are either felicitous (successful) or infelicitous (unsuccessful); constatives, which do not require the stage setting provided by conventions, are either true or false.

By the time he came to write *How To Do Things With Words* Austin believed this distinction between constatives and performatives itself to be infelicitous. The problem arises when one tries to be more precise about the differences between these two kinds of utterance. Austin considers whether there might not be some criterion (or criteria) of grammar or of vocabulary which could be used to distinguish performative from constative utterances, but concludes that the same sentence used on different occasions may be used either as one or the other.

For example, I may promise simply by saying, "I shall be there at 5 o'clock"; or I may warn you simply by saying, "The bull is dangerous." In other words, Austin came to recognize that performatives need not take an explicit form. At one point Austin considers whether it would be possible to distinguish performatives by arguing that, in the case where a performative cannot, as it stands, be distinguished in point of grammar or vocabulary from a constative utterance, we can bring out or make explicit the performative nature of the utterance. Thus, if someone says, "I shall be there," we could ask if this is a promise. If the answer is "yes", we can take the original utterance to be a performative. It should, then, be possible in principle to make a list of performative verbs. At this point, however, Austin runs up against a problem. Is "I approve" an example of an explicit performative, or does it have descriptive meaning? And what are we to make of utterances beginning with "I state that"? Furthermore, Austin soon came to appreciate that one cannot uphold the distinction between performatives and constatives, as he initially believed, by pointing out that the former are felicitous or infelicitous while the latter are true or false. Several considerations led him to conclude that both kinds of utterance can be thought to be open to both kinds of evaluation (see 1962, p. 55 and pp. 132–46). Finally, and most importantly, Austin came to the conclusion that in the case of *all* (or almost all) utterances there is an element of saying and there is an element of doing.

With his ill-fated distinction between constative and performative utterances Austin was exploring the relationship between saying and doing, and in what sense to say something may be to do something. Having been unable to sustain a constative-performative distinction, he chooses to make a fresh start on the problem. He writes (1971, p. 20), "What we need, perhaps, is a more general theory of . . . speech-acts, and in this theory our constative–performative antithesis will scarcely survive."

Austin begins again, this time guided by the idea that "to say something is in the full and normal sense to do something" (1962, p. 94). He calls the saying of something in this normal sense the performance of a locutionary act, and he breaks this up into the following sub-acts: the phonetic (uttering noises), the phatic (uttering words with a certain construction), and the rhetic (uttering words with a certain meaning). Austin adds that "to perform a locutionary act is also and *eo ipso* to perform an illocutionary act" (1962, p. 98). He defines an illocutionary act as the performance of an act *in* saying something (as opposed to a locutionary act *of* saying something). The illocutionary act determines the way we use our words: to ask a question, give information, issue a warning, and the like. Further to these acts, Austin notes that when we perform a locutionary act we may also perform an act of another kind; we may, by our utterance, have a certain kind of effect on our audience. For example, I might, by my utterance, persuade, annoy, frighten or amuse another. Austin labels acts of this type 'perlocutionary' acts. A perlocutionary act is an act done *through*, or *by*, the locutionary act.

Austin now proposes to uphold a threefold distinction where before he had attempted to uphold a twofold one. In his 1964 paper "Intention and Convention in Speech Acts", P. F. Strawson investigates two aspects of this three-fold distinction. The first has to do with the place of convention, the second concerns the effect of the utterance on an audience.

In his discussion of the distinction between illocutionary and perlocutionary acts Austin writes that "the former may, for rough contrast, be said to be *conventional* . . . but the latter could not". There clearly is a link here between illocutionary acts and performatives. And just as with performatives, it would seem that Austin's reference to conventions is a reference to extra-linguistic conventions. The question Strawson raises is this: Is it the case that all illocutionary acts do involve such extra-linguistic conventions? Strawson accepts that when one utters the words "I do thee wed", or "Checkmate", a certain social convention must be in place. However, he cannot see what convention is involved when one utters with the force of a warning, "The ice over there is thin." Strawson concludes that only *some* illocutionary acts are conventional in this sense. As for the rest, we may call them "conventional", but "only in so far as *the means to perform [them]* are conventional" (1971, p. 165). In such cases illocutionary force is exhausted by meaning; there is no appeal to extra-linguistic conventions. Strawson emphasises that there are, roughly, two kinds of case: there are illocutionary acts which require the existence of certain social conventions, and there are others (perhaps the majority) which do not require this. (For a further discussion of illocutionary acts and convention also see Warnock, 1989, and Recanati, 1987.)

The second aspect of Austin's threefold distinction which Strawson discusses is the way in which illocutionary acts may be thought to have effects. Perlocutionary acts straightforwardly involve an effect on an audience (e.g. my utterance may have the effect of amusing you), but the way effects are involved in an illocutionary act is very different from this. Consider the case where I utter the words, "There is a bull in the field" with the illocutionary force of a warning. In order for this illocutionary act to be successful, a certain effect must be achieved, that is, my audience must hear my utterance and understand it as a warning. If this effect is not achieved, the illocutionary act is unsuccessful. In other words, to speak with a certain illocutionary force is not *eo ipso* to perform a certain illocutionary act. The latter requires an effect – what Austin called "uptake" on the part of the audience. (It should be noted that for the illocutionary act to be considered complete the warning need not be heeded, just understood.)

Strawson seeks further to clarify in what sense the performance of illocutionary acts involves the securing of uptake. In order to understand further the idea of securing uptake, or of *understanding*, Strawson suggests that we deploy a Gricean analysis of meaning. Where Grice is primarily interested in the analysis of speaker meaning, Strawson is interested in the analysis of hearer's understanding. Strawson proposes to adapt Grice's analysis. The suggestion, very roughly, is this:

> For an audience A to understand an utterance x, A must recognize the speaker S's intention that S's utterance of x produce a certain response in A.

Just as the original Gricean analysis is subject to counterexample and in need of emendation (see §§ 6 and 7), so the Strawsonian analysis of understanding will require emendation. Strawson's point is that some such analysis will give substance to the idea of audience uptake which is required for the successful completion of an illocutionary act. Strawson's suggestion also provides an explicit link from Austin's work on speech acts to Grice's analysis of meaning.

4 The analysis of meaning

The idea emphasized by Austin, whether by reference to performatives or to illocutionary acts, is that in speaking we perform *actions* of various kinds. By way of development of this idea we may add that actions are intentional events performed by persons. Austin's work broke much ground, but it shied away from precision. As we have just seen, Strawson attempted to introduce precision into Austin's work by proposing a union of it with the work of Grice (suitably amended). There are those, however, who would argue that the analytic precision introduced by Grice and Griceans is a wrong turning in the idea that meaning is use. The later Wittgenstein has been interpreted as holding that such analytic rigours are very much out of place in philosophy. Perhaps influenced by Wittgenstein, some philosophers have opposed analysis when the subject under consideration is meaning.

Michael Dummett (1975, pp. 97–8) has suggested that our concept of meaning is too unclear to be the subject of analysis. In the case of meaning, a theory specifying the meanings of the expressions in the language is all we can hope for. Thus, Dummett takes the side of the formal theorists, and relegates mention of speakers and their intentions to the level of pragmatics. Dummett contrasts the case of meaning with that of knowledge, and argues that in the latter case analysis is appropriate. It is an interesting question to which concepts the method of analysis is fruitfully applied. In opposition to Dummett, I have suggested that analysis is appropriately and fruitfully applied to the concept of meaning. Grice and others have done much by way of clarification of this concept – for example, by disentangling different senses of "to know", and by suggesting a priority among types of meaning: speaker meaning, sentence meaning, word meaning, meaning over time, etc. (see § 5). With this work in mind, I have argued that our concept of meaning is not as unclear as Dummett suggests (see Avramides, 1989, ch. 1.).

As we saw in § 2, John McDowell also resists the introduction of analyses of meaning. He writes (1980, p. 124), "we lack an argument that meaning constitutes the sort of philosophical problem which requires analysis for its solution". Like Dummett, McDowell favours theory-building over analysis; however, where Dummett favours a theory based on verification conditions, McDowell follows Davidson in favouring one based on truth conditions. Despite his partiality for theory-building, McDowell does not proceed by first constructing a core, truth, theory and building out to include reference to speaker's intentions. Rather, he suggests that we begin with a picture of the whole – a picture which includes both sense and force – and that we work our way back to a core, truth, theory which can help to explain the structural and recursive features of language. Proceeding in this way will guarantee that the truth theory we end up with at the core is in fact a theory of meaning for speakers of that language.

McDowell takes issue with Strawson (cf. § 2 above), and via Strawson with Grice, over the way intentions figure in an account of meaning. He accuses Strawson of commitment to an analysis of meaning which aims to provide a "reductive account of kinds of speech acts in terms of the intentions of their performers" (1980, p. 131). A reductive analysis is one which gives an explanation of the notion of speaker meaning in terms of some *conceptually prior* notion of speaker intention. McDowell suggests that in the place of analysis we aim to provide an account of meaning which gives "a perspicuous mapping of interrelations between concepts". Rather than say that meaning consists in a speaker's intention to produce a response in an audience by means of the audience's recognition of the speaker's intention (Grice), McDowell suggests that we see speech acts as intentional performances on the part of speakers to say such-and-such to an audience, which speech acts are recognized – or understood – by that audience. McDowell's suggestion eschews the idea of conceptual priority.

In the course of developing his proposal, McDowell makes reference to the work of John Searle (1969). Like McDowell, Searle rejects the Gricean idea that a hearer must recognize a speaker's intention and suggests, instead, that what is essential to meaning is the hearer's understanding. It is interesting to note that, in his criticism of Grice, Searle refers to the Austinian idea of an illocutionary act. As we saw in § 3 above, what is requisite to the achievement of an illocutionary act is audience uptake – that is, audience understanding; recognition of the speaker's intention is neither here nor there. McDowell and Searle on the one hand, and Grice and Strawson on the other, propose two different ways of developing the Austinian idea that we do things with words.

It seems to me that McDowell offers an interesting alternative to Grice's work, but does not succeed in providing us with a reason to reject the Gricean method of analysis. It is a mistake to hold that analyses are necessarily reductive, and hence incompatible with an attempt to examine the interrelations between concepts. I have argued (in 1989, ch. 1, § 3) that analyses are susceptible of two different interpretations. The one is reductive, the other I labelled "reciprocal". I associate the first with John Wisdom, who held that the aim of analysis is to reach a new level of concept, one more basic or more fundamental than the other. The second I associate with the work of G. E. Moore (1966, p. 168) who held that "the chief use of analysis in the way of clearness, is only the clearness which it produces when you are doing philosophy itself". In a reciprocal analysis, conceptual priority is replaced by conceptual interdependence. Which interpretation one gives of the analysis is not something that can be represented in the original analysis. It does, however, effect the further understanding of the concepts employed on the right-hand side of the original analytic biconditional. What determines the interpretation we give is our understanding of the concepts involved.

Once these two interpretations have been distinguished it is possible to ask which sort of analysis Grice intended. Grice himself writes in such a way as to make it difficult to answer this question. Griceans such as Stephen Schiffer (1982) and Brian Loar (1981) clearly advocate a reductive interpretation. In 1989 I defended a reciprocal interpretation. An analysis of meaning under a reciprocal interpretation is one way of achieving the "perspicuous mapping of interrelations between concepts" which McDowell seeks. As far as I can see, McDowell does not here have an argument against the Gricean method of analysis.

In the introduction to their collection of essays *Truth and Meaning*, Gareth Evans and John McDowell put forward an argument which, if successful, would count against even the weaker, non-reductive, interpretation of Grice's work. Their claim is that the analysis does not correctly reflect the "phenomenology of language". Language is habitual and unreflective, while the analysis is very complex and suggests a highly reflective form of behaviour. Griceans would accept the observation about language use, but argue that squaring with the phenomenology is not their goal. They do not hold that the analysis reflects a conscious process undergone either by speakers or their audience. Schiffer (1982) has argued that our behaviour reveals that audiences in fact have what he calls "tacit expectations" concerning those they listen to, and speakers exploit these expectations in the noises they choose to use. Furthermore, it could be said that the analysis represents something true of the speaker – not something of which she is consciously aware. David Armstrong (1971) has suggested that the analysis may represent a rational reconstruction rather than any kind of psychological reality. This idea has also been attributed to Grice (see Grandy and Warner, 1989, pp. 8–15).

It may be that the sense in which the analysis of meaning represents a wrong turning in the development of the fundamentally correct idea that meaning is an act performed by speakers lies deeper than any of the above arguments have delved. Indeed, it may involve a commitment to a certain way of doing philosophy, one which eschews the rigours of analysis. The problem with this way of approaching things, however, is that it would apply equally to the rigours of theory building as to those of analysis. The difficulty with the philosophers' views I have considered here is that they want to retain a theory of meaning while rejecting the (Gricean) analysis of *meaning*. For this reason their arguments are directed against an analytic approach to meaning – allowing for the possibility of an analysis of some other concept. However, I am not yet persuaded of these objections to the analysis of our concept of meaning.

5 Grice's account of non-natural meaning

Grice begins his 1957 paper with the observation that the word "means" has (at least) two different senses: a natural sense (as in "Those spots mean measles", or "Black clouds mean rain"); and a non-natural sense (as in "By that gesture Sam meant that he was fed up", or "His remark meant . . ."). One distinguishing feature of these two uses of the word "means" is this: the natural use is factive – that is, it commits the speaker to a certain fact (i.e. that someone has or will have the measles, or that it will rain); the non-natural use is non-factive (for example, Sam's gesture may mean that he is fed up, but Sam may not be fed up).

In "Meaning" Grice simply sets aside natural uses of "means" and develops an analysis of non-natural meaning. In a much later paper, "Meaning Revisited", he suggests that non-natural meaning is a descendent of, or is derived from, natural meaning. Grice explains how this may come about by considering a special case of natural meaning: a groan. A groan is a natural sign of pain when it is produced involuntarily by an individual. An involuntarily produced groan will lead an observer to believe that the groaner is in pain or discomfort (cf. the case of observing black clouds). Now in certain circumstances an individual may groan *voluntarily*.

The most obvious case of a voluntarily produced groan is where there is a desire to deceive. In such cases, however, because of the association between a voluntarily produced groan and deception, any tendency on the part of an observer to come to believe that the groaner is in pain is undermined. The move from natural to non-natural meaning comes about, suggests Grice, when the groan is produced voluntarily and an observer still takes this as reason to believe the groaner is in pain and *not* as evidence of deception. This happens when the groan is voluntarily produced with the intention that it be recognized as a voluntary act, and is recognized as such. Grice suggests that the move from natural meaning to non-natural meaning is complete when the groaner (henceforth the speaker) is taken by the observer (henceforth the hearer) to be trustworthy.

In this way Grice shows that there is a conceptual link from natural to non-natural meaning. It should be noted that Grice's story is not intended as a description of a historical or developmental process. It should also be noted that non-natural meaning is not necessarily limited to such natural devices. Any device that will communicate the speaker's intentions will do.

Grice intends the distinction between natural and non-natural meaning to do roughly the same work as the more traditional distinction between natural and conventional signs (1989, p. 215). One difference which inclines Grice to favour the natural – non-natural distinction is this: there may be cases of meaning which are not signs (for example, words) and which are not conventional (for example, some gestures and cases of meaning on a particular single occasion). Thus, Grice's analysis of non-natural meaning is designed to cover more than conventional linguistic meaning. The basic Gricean analysis is of speaker meaning on a particular occasion. The move to standard, or timeless, meaning is achieved by the introduction of the notion of convention at a later stage in the development of the analysis. The basic analysis is also of whole-utterance meaning. The meaning of the utterance parts, the words, is also addressed by Griceans at a later stage. In the sections which follow I give a brief outline of the various stages in the development of the Gricean analysis.

6 The sufficiency of the analysis

Griceans aim to construct an analysis which provides conditions which are both necessary and sufficient for speaker meaning. The initial idea for the analysis comes from Grice, but the analysis has developed in response to counter-examples provided by, among others, Jonathan Bennett, Brian Loar, Stephen Schiffer, and P. F. Strawson.

The basic idea is to give an analysis of non-natural speaker-meaning of a whole utterance on a particular occasion in terms of, roughly, a speaker's intention to produce a certain response in an audience. This, however, is too rough; as it stands, there is nothing that reflects the fact that what is being analysed is an act of *communication* between a speaker and a hearer. We move closer towards an analysis of an act of communication if we say, not only that a speaker must have an intention to produce a response in an audience, but that the audience must recognize this intention. Yet even this is not adequate to account for communication, since the audience may indeed recognize the speaker's intentions, but not come to have the intended response *because* of this recognition. To capture this it must be added that the audience's recognition of the speaker's intention should function as at least part of the reason for the response. Furthermore, the audience must come to have its response as the result of its recognition that the speaker's utterance has a certain feature (note that: the Gricean literature, "utterance" must be understood to cover not only spoken syllables and the written word, but also gestures). Each of these emendations to the basic analysis is in response to specific counter-examples which can be found in Schiffer (1972) and Grice (1989, essays 5, 6 and 14).

At this point the basic analysis looks like this:

(1) Speaker S meant something in uttering x if and only if S uttered x intending:
  (a) that x have a certain feature, f
  (b) that A recognize that x has f,
  (c) that A infer at least in part from the fact that x has f that S uttered x intending:
  (d) that S's utterance of x produce response r in A,
  (e) that A's recognition of S's intention (d) should function as at least part of A's reason for r.

(Note: This formulation of the analysis largely follows Schiffer (1972). Grice's own formulation of the analysis can be found in Grice (1989), essays 5, 6, and 14.)

At this point the analysis is still not sufficient for meaning. In other words, counter-examples can still be devised which reveal that all the above-mentioned conditions may be satisfied and yet, intuitively, the case is not one of meaning. The kind of problem was first identified by P. F. Strawson (1971, p. 156) and is captured by the following counter-example: Let's say that S intends, by the act of arranging convincing-looking evidence that p, to bring it about that an audience, A, believes that p. Say, also, that S arranges this evidence knowing that A is watching him do this, and knowing as well that A will take the arranged evidence as evidence that p. If we add to the story that S also knows that A does *not* know that S knows that A is watching, then this case cannot be taken to be a case of genuine communication. Strawson identifies the problem as follows: although A will take S to be trying to bring it about that A believes that p, A will not take S as trying to 'let him know' or 'tell' him something. The point is that, in this case, A comes to believe that p because he reasons that S would not be doing what he is doing unless he intended A to come to believe that p as a result of seeing S arrange the evidence. There is a slight deception on S's part which results in a lack of openness between S and A about what is going on. Strawson then suggests, "It seems a minimum further condition of his trying to [communicate with A] that [S] should not only intend A to recognize his intention to get A to think that p, but that he should also *intend A to recognize his intention to get A to recognize his intention* to get A to think that p" (1971, p. 157).

This condition is, then, built into the basic analysis in the following way:

(2) S meant something in uttering x iff S uttered x intending:
(a)–(e) and
(f) that A should recognize S's intention (c).

The addition of condition (f) does get around the kind of problem which Strawson's counter-example brought to light. However, Strawson also suggests that, unless the analysis contains a condition which ensures that a kind of openness is maintained between speaker and audience, we may find this kind of problem recurring. Strawson does not actually introduce the term "openness", but he does suggest the idea (1971, p. 157). Neither does he suggest any way of ensuring openness. The term "openness" can be found in Simon Blackburn's discussion of the Gricean analysis (see Blackburn, 1984, ch. 4).

Strawson was correct. Soon further counter-examples were being devised which showed that conditions (a)–(f) are not sufficient conditions of (speaker) meaning. These further counter-examples are extremely complex and ingenious. It is not necessary here to repeat them (although they may be found in Schiffer, 1972, pp. 18–19). What is important to understand is that these further counter-examples represent more complex examples of the sort of deceit we can see from the original Strawsonian counter-example.

One way of blocking this sort of counter-example would be to add, for each counter-example, a further condition of the sort that Strawson added to block his counter-example, sometimes labelled "backward-looking" intentions. The problem with this solution is it leaves us waiting for the next ingenious counter-example. In other words, adding further intentions is an *ad hoc*, defensive move. We need to grasp the nettle that Strawson observed, and build into the analysis a condition which will ensure sufficiency on this score. Strawson was acute in his observation that we need in the analysis a condition which ensures that "it [is] clear to both" speaker and audience what is going on, as well as that it is "clear to them both that it [is] clear to them both".

Stephen Schiffer has proposed building into the basic analysis a condition which aims to ensure that this sort of counter-example can no longer be brought against the analysis. Schiffer labels this the "mutual-knowledge condition" (see Schiffer, 1972, II. 2). Roughly, a speaker, S, and an audience, A, mutually know that p if and only if S knows that p, and A knows that p, and S knows that A knows that p, and A knows that S knows that p, and S knows that A knows that S knows that p, and A knows that S knows that A knows that p, and so on. This "and so on" is both important and controversial. It is important because without this it could be argued that we would be no better off with this new mutual knowledge condition than we were with the earlier series of "backward-looking" intentions. Writing in a condition with the words "and so on" basically is saying that we could iterate knowledge conditions indefinitely here. This, however, is controversial because it can be argued to involve a regress, no better than the regress involved in the defensive further conditions of intention mentioned earlier. However, Schiffer has defended the regress involved in the mutual knowledge condition, claiming that this regress is "perfectly harmless" (1972, p. 32).

Schiffer offers the following example to illustrate the phenomenon of mutual knowledge and to give assurance of the harmless nature of the regress involved: Two people, A and B, are seated at a table with a candle between them. Assuming that A and B have normal sense faculties, normal intelligence, and normal perceptions, and that they both have their eyes open, we can say that both A and B know that there is a candle before them. Furthermore, given these same assumptions we can say that each of A and B knows that the other knows that there is a candle before him, *and so on*. This regress is claimed to be harmless because it involves knowledge that two (or more) people may uncontroversially be thought to have about one another given certain situations and certain general features of those situations. Schiffer takes his point to have been established, and adds that the phenomenon illustrated by the two people seated before a candle is an entirely general one which does not depend upon any features particular to the viewing of a candle. He then points out that the phenomenon is also to be found in cases of communication. It is precisely the absence of such mutual knowledge which, in Schiffer's opinion, is at the root of the counter-examples from Strawson onwards.

Schiffer proposes to build into the basic analysis this condition of mutual knowledge in the following way:

> (3)(2) S meant something by uttering x iff S uttered x, intending thereby to realize a certain state of affairs E that S intends to be such that if E obtains, S and a certain audience mutually know that E obtains and that E is conclusive (or at least good) evidence that S uttered x intending:
> (a) to produce a certain response, r, in A,
> (b) that A's recognition of S's intention (a) function as at least part of A's reason for A's response r, and
> (c) to realize E.

The analysis, on the surface, now looks substantially altered from that in (1). However, close inspection will satisfy that (3) is indeed (1) with the incorporation of a mutual knowledge condition. In particular, the feature *f* referred to in (1) has been absorbed into the state of affairs *E* in (3). Concerning *E* Schiffer writes, "Typically, E will essentially involve the fact that S, a person having such and such properties, uttered a token of type x having a certain feature(s) f, in the presence of A, a person having such and such properties, in certain circumstances, C" (1972, p. 39).

This condition of mutual knowledge has been the subject of much criticism. Some of it comes from Schiffer himself, who now rejects the Gricean account of meaning which he once did so much to promote (see Schiffer, 1987). It has been objected that the regress is not harmless, and, further, that it is psychologically implausible that speakers have any such knowledge – either explicitly or tacitly. Alan Coady (1976) has suggested that it won't be possible to find a property possession of which will suffice for knowledge. He points out that a "visually normal" person (the property suggested by Schiffer) may be facing a candle on a table, and have well-sighted eyes focused on the candle, but fail to know that there is a candle before him because he may be daydreaming.

There are alternatives to the mutual knowledge condition. Grice himself eschews mutual knowledge in favour of a condition which in effect guarantees that the speaker *not* have, what Grice calls, "sneaky" intentions. A sneaky intention is one which encourages a hearer to come to have a belief as the result of recognizing a certain feature of the speaker's utterance, while the speaker's true intentions are otherwise. The evidence-arranger in Strawson's counter-example has a sneaky intention. Grice suggests that we build into the analysis a condition which states that the speaker *not* have certain sorts of intentions (see Grice, 1989, essay 18).

There is yet another suggestion for dealing with the deception which generates counter-examples to the sufficiency of the proposed analysis. This suggestion leads to the simplest overall formulation of the analysis, and can be found in Harman (1974). Harman's suggestion is this:

(4) S intends that an audience A will respond in a certain way r at least partly by virtue of A's recognition of this very intention.

All that this version of the analysis requires is that we accept self-referential intentions. (A slightly different formulation, also employing self-referential intentions, can be found in Blackburn, 1984, ch. 4.) A self-referential intention is one which has itself within its scope. Harman's appeal to self-referential intentions avoids the need for a *series* of intentions of the sort we find in (1), augmented by a series of "backward-looking" intentions to accommodate the possibility of complex deceptions. A formulation of the Gricean analysis which incorporated self-referential intentions would, then, be one way of handling such cases of deception and incorporation into the analysis of a mutual knowledge condition would be another. Harman suggests that the mutual knowledge condition itself can be argued to involve a kind of self-reference. In the light of this, Harman suggests that we sweep aside complexity and accept self-reference at a much earlier stage along the lines of (3) above.

Despite the simplicity which such intentions introduce into the analysis, self-referential intentions have been rejected by some on the grounds that they involve a "reflexive paradox", and by others on the grounds that they involve a regress. (For a discussion of self-referential intentions see Recanati, 1987, pp. 192–9, and also Blackburn, 1984, ch. 4, § 2.)

This covers, in rather broad brush-strokes, the sufficiency of the analysis of (speaker) meaning. It is interesting to note that it is the possibility of deception which has made the formulation of sufficient conditions for (speaker) meaning so difficult. The possibility of deception lies, we might say, at the very heart of meaning. This is not surprising when we recall the suggested conceptual link between natural and non-natural meaning outlined by Grice (see § 5 above). The move from natural to non-natural meaning comes about, on this suggestion, when an involuntary act comes to be produced voluntarily. And the most obvious case of such voluntary acts would be, suggests Grice, for the purpose of deception. On this view deception may be thought to lie at the heart of meaning – the very thing revealed by the Gricean attempt to analyse meaning.

I shall not pursue the sufficiency of the analysis any further here. Rather, I shall turn, in the following section, to a brief examination of the necessity of the proposed analysis.

7 The necessity of the analysis

Objections to the necessity of the Gricean analysis of meaning are designed to show that there are cases of meaning which, intuitively, do not satisfy the conditions for speaker meaning discussed in § 6. There are, roughly, two kinds of counter-example to the necessity of the analysis. One kind is designed to show that there may be cases of (speaker) meaning where the speaker does not intend to produce a response in a particular audience. Here are a few examples:

(1) Diary entries.
(2) A sign with the words: Private Property, Keep Out.
(3) Rehearsing a speech or conversation.
(4) Soliloquies.
(5) Writing notes to clarify a problem.

Grice (1989, essay 5, § 5) and Schiffer (1972, chs. II.2 and III) have both suggested a way of responding to this sort of counter-example. Grice is characteristically terse and modest in the number of counter-examples he considers, while Schiffer's discussion of this sort of counter-example is highly detailed and thorough. I would say that they are in agreement in their proposed emendations to the analysis. However, since each formulates the analysis in a slightly different way, the proposed amended analysis looks a little different in each case. For simplicity, I shall follow Grice here.

Grice's way with this sort of counter-example is to recommend that the analysis be amended in such a way as to incorporate the idea that the speaker produce his utterance with the intention of producing something which *would* produce a certain response in appropriate circumstances in an audience who has a certain property. (For Grice's version of the analysis, suitably amended, see Grice, 1989, p. 114; to see how the same emendations would fit into Schiffer's version of the analysis, see Avramides, 1989, pp. 64–5.) The sort of property Grice has in mind includes the following: is a passerby who sees this notice; is a snoop who read this diary; is identical with the speaker (1989, p. 114). Grice notes that the analysis, so amended, will cover cases of speaker meaning where (a) the speaker thinks there may, at some future time, be a particular person who may encounter S's utterance, or (b) the speaker pretends to address some imagined audience or type of audience, or (c) the speaker intends to produce a certain response in a "fairly indefinite kind of audience were it the case that such an audience was present" (1989, p. 113). If one accepts the Grice–Schiffer line with this sort of counter-example to the necessity of the analysis of speaker meaning, one would be in a position to say that, strictly speaking, there aren't any cases of meaning where the speaker has no audience-directed intention.

There is a second kind of counter-example which aims to challenge the necessity of the analysis of (speaker) meaning. To understand this kind of counter-example we must return to the basic Gricean analysis (as described in § 6 above). The basic analysis stipulates that the speaker intends to "produce a response in an audience", and that this be by means of the audience's "recognition of the speaker's intention to produce that response". The second kind of counter-example is designed to show that there are cases of (speaker) meaning where the speaker has an intention to produce a certain response, but where it is no part of the speaker's intention that part of the audience's reason for his response is that the speaker intends to produce that response in that audience. (See formulation (2a) and (2b) of the analysis in § 6 above.) Here are some examples:

(1) A student giving the correct answer to a teacher in the course of a *viva voce* examination.
(2) A husband confessing an infidelity to his wife when confronted by her with incontrovertible evidence.
(3) A passerby giving directions to a tourist, indifferent to whether or not the tourist believes anything he says.
(4) Someone reminding a friend of the name of a mutual friend's baby by saying "Rose" (or by holding up a rose).
(5) A lecturer delivering a philosophy lecture. (He does not intend the lecture to produce in his audience the belief that the lecturer believes the content of the lecture.)

Schiffer has suggested that in cases like (1) and (2) the speaker may be said to mean something in an "extended or attenuated sense, one derived from and dependent upon the primary sense captured in the [analysis]" (1972, III, 3). In (1) the student means something in an extended sense because, Schiffer offers, he produces his utterance *as if* he were genuinely "telling" the teacher something. In the case of (2) Schiffer suggests that the husband's confession may said to be producing his utterance *as if* he were "telling" his wife something. In this case the confession may act as a means of "getting things out into the open". Schiffer points out that case (3) simply requires that we point out that, while appearing indifferent, the speaker may arguably have a momentary or fleeting intention to produce a belief in his audience. Finally, Schiffer accommodates cases like (4) and (5) by rewriting the analysis in such a way as to accommodate the fact that what the speaker intends is to produce in an audience the *activated* belief that p. This move clearly accommodates cases like (4), where the audience can be said to know the baby's name, but needs to be prompted or reminded. This move will also cover cases like (5) where the lecturer may be said (ideally, at least) to get the student to understand that certain propositions are consequences of other propositions one already believes. (It should be noted that in his response to alleged counter-examples of types (4) and (5) Schiffer is indebted to Grice, 1989, essay 5, § 4.)

At the end of the day, both kinds of counter-example to the necessity of the analysis of (speaker) meaning can be accommodated either by a more careful understanding of the example or a small emendation to the analysis. It has to be said that both Grice and Schiffer have written up the development of the analysis in a way which obscures the final results. A careful reading, however, reveals that the analysis is robust and can accommodate counter-examples.

For those who are still worried that the task of coming up with conditions which are at the same time strong enough for sufficiency and weak enough for necessity is too much to require, the following will, perhaps, placate (see also § 4 above):

> [Many] concepts . . . do not have absolutely knock down necessary and sufficient condition. . . . But this insight into the looseness of our concepts . . . should not lead us into a rejection of the very enterprise of philosophical analysis; rather the conclusion to be drawn is that certain forms of analysis, especially analysis into necessary and sufficient conditions, are likely to involve (in varying degrees) idealization of the concept analyzed. This approach has the consequence that counterexamples can be produced . . . which do not fit the analysis. . . . Their existence does not 'refute' the analysis, rather they require an explanation of why and how they depart from the paradigm case. (Searle, 1969, p. 55)

Searle's reflections on analysis fit with Grice's own suggestion that what we are doing when we construct an analysis of meaning is describing an "optimal state" (see Grice, 1989, essay 18). Grandy and Warner (1989, pp. 25–6) sum up Grice's idea of an optimal state in such a way as to make it chime in with Searle's comments on analysis. Grandy and Warner suggest that "to spot exceptions and resolve conflicts as well as handle situations not covered by the rules, one needs to know what the . . . optimum is" (1989, p. 26). Grice introduces the notion of an optimal state as a way of introducing the notion of value into semantics; the notion can also help us to defend the analysis against certain alleged counter-examples.

8 Structure

Thus far the Gricean analysis is designed to give an account of the speaker meaning of whole utterances. Sentence structure was set aside until the basic analysis had been developed. Until the issue of structure has been addressed, the analysis is open to the following objection: in any given language there will be an infinite number of unuttered, yet meaningful, sentences (see Platts, 1979). This objection arises as the result of the following fact of language: sentences of a language can be generated by the combination and recombination of a finite number of semantic elements in accordance with certain rules. The meaning of a sentence is a function of the meaning of its parts, the words. (This is a feature of language much emphasized by formal theorists of meaning: see § 2 above.)

One obvious way to address this objection would be to amend the analysis so that it makes mention of speakers and their intentions, not in relation to whole sentences, but in relation to sentence parts. This sort of approach is tentatively proposed by Grice (1989, essay 6). The suggestion is that speakers would have knowledge of what Grice calls "resultant procedures" regarding both the constituent elements of some utterance (for example, that "Tom" denotes Tom) and their rules of combination. There is, however, a problem with this suggestion. It not only attributes to speakers a great deal of knowledge, but it attributes to them as well possession of certain concepts (for example, the concept of denotation) which they are unlikely to have. Grice notes the problem, and proposes that we simply accept that "in some sense" we do know these rules. He acknowledges that the proper understanding of what exactly this sense is remains an "unsolved mystery" (see Chapter 7, TACIT KNOWLEDGE).

Loar (1981, ch. 10) proposes a more sophisticated version of Grice's suggestion. Following David Lewis (1983, essay 11), Loar identifies, for each language, a grammar which generates sentences of the language on the basis of repeatable constituents, combining operators and a representing operation. The notion of a grammar which is at work here is not purely syntactic; it is, rather, semantically interpreted. This grammar may be represented by a Tarski-style truth theory for a language. Now, there are infinitely many grammars which could be the grammar of a given language. Which grammar is the grammar of a given language is a matter of which has been "internalized" by the speakers of the language (see Loar, 1981, p. 259). Loar's idea of a grammar replaces Grice's notion of a resultant procedure. The idea of an *internalized* grammar, however, gains us little insight into Grice's unsolved mystery.

At this point formal theorists may see their opportunity and argue that an appeal to resultant procedures, or grammars, is little more than a return to the apparatus of formal theories of meaning (see Coady, 1976). It could be argued that, when it comes to accounting for structure, what we find is that it is the formal theorist who is closer to the philosophical foundations of meaning. This conclusion would be in direct opposition to that of Strawson (see § 2, above).

At this point it is tempting to conclude that it may be less illuminating to answer the question of whether the formal or the use theorist is closer to the philosophical foundations of meaning, than to set about exploiting the virtues of each theory in an attempt to understand meaning and language. It is manifestly clear that speakers perform intentional acts of meaning, and that the content of these acts have a structure which is well represented by formal theories of meaning. It may no longer be helpful to see the opposition between formal and use theorists on the scale of a "Homeric struggle"

9 Linguistic meaning

Whatever one thinks of the merits of the analysis thus far to account for *speaker* meaning, as it stands – even after the considerations of the previous three sections – it is still insufficient to account for *linguistic* meaning. Linguistic meaning is timeless; that is, it does not depend on the particular occasion of use. In 1989, essay 6, Grice considers the analysis of timeless meaning for an individual, and then extends this to account for timeless meaning within a group or community of speakers. By building up to linguistic meaning in this way we can see better what is involved in the idea of timeless meaning. Grice's first suggestion is that we analyse an individual's timeless meaning by appeal to that individual's "habit" or "policy" of uttering certain sounds when intending a hearer to believe that. . . . The problem is that the speaker may have other means of getting a hearer to believe that . . . , or may use the very same words when intending a hearer to believe something quite different. In other words, appeal to a speaker's habit or policy is neither necessary nor sufficient for timeless meaning.

Grice then considers the idea of an individual "having a certain procedure in his repertoire" to utter certain sounds when intending a hearer to believe that. . . . To approach the idea of timeless meaning for a group of individuals, Grice suggests that the individual's procedure conforms to the general practice in a group. Grice then crudely defines the notion of "having a procedure in one's repertoire" by saying that such an individual has a standing readiness (or willingness) to do (or say) such-and-such. This formulation is not susceptible to the objections encountered with the idea of policies and habits. It does, however, run up against the following problem. Consider the exceedingly prim Aunt Mathilda. While it is true to say that the sentence "She is a whore" means that she is a whore, it is *not* true that Aunt Mathilda has any inclination to utter these words in any circumstance whatsoever.

Having noticed this objection, Grice turns away from any further attempt to develop his account of timeless meaning. By the time Schiffer came to write his account of it, another idea had begun to gain currency, that of convention. Following the work of David Lewis, Schiffer suggests that we can bring together the notion of convention (suitably defined) with the already-developed analysis of speaker meaning to produce an account of timeless (or linguistic) meaning. Very roughly, we can say that,

(5) An utterance x (timeless) means that p in a community if and only if there prevails in that community a convention to use x in order to s-mean that p. (The analysis of speaker meaning outlined in § 6 would slot into the place of "s-mean".)

To many (if not all) Griceans it seemed that Lewis's notion of convention was exactly what the analysis of meaning required for its completion. It only remains for us to understand the notion of convention which Schiffer employs in the move from speaker meaning to linguistic meaning.

10 Convention

The notion of convention which Schiffer employs in the account of timeless meaning is one whose analysis is largely borrowed from Lewis (1969). Lewis's account in turn develops an idea put forward by David Hume in his *Treatise of Human Nature* (III, ii, 2). Concerning convention, Hume writes:

> It is only a general sense of common interest; which sense all the members of the society express to one another, and which induces them to regulate their conduct by certain rules. I observe, that it will be for my interest to leave another in the possession of his goods *provided* he will act in the same manner with regard to me. He is sensible of a like interest in the regulation of his conduct. When this common sense of interest is mutually expressed, and is known to both, it produces a suitable resolution and behaviour. And this may properly enough be called a convention or agreement betwixt us, tho' without the interposition of a promise; since the actions of each have a reference to those of the other, and are performed upon the supposition, that something is to be performed on the other part.

Lewis builds on Hume's idea of common interest by bringing to bear work developed by T. C. Schelling (*The Strategy of Games*) concerning games of strategy (as opposed to games of skill or chance). Games of strategy present us with "coordination problems"; that is, situations where two or more people must choose a course of action, where the best course of action for each is dependent upon what each expects the other to do. The solution to a coordination problem has been labelled a "coordination equilibrium".

I shall briefly outline a very simple coordination problem which gives rise to a convention. Two people, A and B, are cut off in the middle of an important telephone conversation. Each believes that each wants the conversation to continue, and neither has any special interest in being the one to call back. The problem is this: if both dial back, the line will be blocked; if neither dials back, their interests will not be served. A coordination equilibrium is achieved if A and B succeed in adopting a strategy which is such that no other strategy would have made either of them better off. In the telephone case such an equilibrium is achieved if A and B both consider the other's expectations concerning redialling. In this case, as well as considering the other's expectations, A and B are in a position to exploit a certain feature of the situation which is known to both, and known by both to be known to both: the fact that the original caller has the telephone number to hand. A coordination equilibrium is achieved when the original caller dials back and the line is restored. Convention is achieved when, in response to a *recurring* coordination problem, participants not only employ the same strategy, but employ the same strategy *because it has been employed in the past in such situations and is known by all participants to have worked as a solution to the problem*. It is only when this stage is reached that we may speak of *conventional* regularities. A convention is, according to this analysis, a self-perpetuating regularity in behaviour.

Lewis then offers the following definition of convention (this account is taken from Lewis 1983, pp. 164–5):

> A regularity R, in action or in action and belief, is a *convention* in a population P if, and only if, within P, the following conditions hold (or at least they almost hold; a few exceptions to the 'everyone's' can be tolerated).
> (1) Everyone conforms to R.
> (2) Everyone believes that the others conform to R.

(3) This belief that the others conform to R gives everyone a good and decisive reason to conform to R himself.
(4) There is a general preference for general conformity to R rather than slightly-less-than-general conformity – in particular, rather than conformity by all but one.
(5) There is at least one alternative R′ to R such that the belief that the others conformed to R′ would give everyone a good and decisive reason to conform to R′ likewise; such that there is a general preference for general conformity to R′ rather than less-than-general conformity to R; and such that there is normally no way of conforming to R and R′ both.
(6) Conditions (1)–(5) are a matter of common knowledge (that is, they are known to everyone, it is known that they are known to everyone, and so on).

These conditions are reasonably straightforward; however, a few, brief, explanatory notes are in order. Condition (3) mentions reasons which, according to Lewis, may be practical (where conforming to R is a matter of acting in a certain way) or which may be epistemic (where conforming to R is a matter of believing in a certain way). Condition (4) serves to distinguish cases of convention from cases of deadlock conflict, where there is conformity to R along with a wish that others do not conform to R. Condition (5) mentions R′, an alternative to R. An alternative is something such that it could have been the regularity followed in the place of R. R′ is subject to all the condition of R. The existence of R′ is what ensures that a convention is *arbitrary*. Finally, condition (6) mentions the notion of *common knowledge*, which is, essentially, the same idea that we found in § 6 above, and called *mutual knowledge*. (For a further discussion of the notion see Heal, 1978.) The knowledge required in this condition may be "merely potential: knowledge that would be available if one bothered to think hard enough", or it may be "irremediably nonverbal knowledge" (Lewis, 1969, p. 63). Several philosophers have criticised Lewis's condition (6) on the grounds that it requires too much of speakers (see, for example, Grandy, 1977). Lewis's reply is that "like it or not, we have plenty of knowledge we cannot put into words" (1969, p. 64).

It should be noted that Lewis is concerned with the analysis of convention *per se*; convention in language is a special case of this more general notion. Schiffer (1972) has argued that, although it is correct to see conventions generally as arising in response to coordination problems, the case of language should be viewed differently. According to Schiffer, linguistic conventions arise, not in response to a coordination problem, but because of the need of each participant to communicate. This, however, is a minor variation on a theme. The theme involves accepting that speakers of a language exercise a degree of rational control over which sounds they employ to communicate their intentions to an audience.

To say that our linguistic practices are under the rational control of language users has, for some, conjured up pictures of rational assemblies, of language users convening to adopt conventions. Thus we find Quine writing in objection to the idea that language is conventional:

> When I was a child I pictured our language as settled and passed down by a board of syndics, seated in grave convention along a table in the style of Rembrandt. This picture remained for a while undisturbed by the question what language the syndics might have used in their deliberations, or by dread of vicious regress. (Preface to Lewis, 1969)

It was in reply to just such objections that Lewis developed his analysis of convention. The central point of Lewis's analysis is to show that there is no regress because there need be no deliberation. Conventions arise because of a common interest (cf. Hume Treatise III, ii, 2, quoted above).

Lewis has successfully shown that conventions need not be the result of explicit agreement. Nevertheless, there are those who still object to the rational underpinning which Lewis's account gives to the notion of convention. Tyler Burge has argued that his account of convention "takes too little note of the extent of the unconscious element in many conventions" and overlooks the fact that conventions are perpetuated as much by "inertia, superstition and ignorance" as by "enlightened self-interest" (1975, pp. 253–5). Burge rejects *any* idea of rational control by speakers. He concludes that our linguistic practices are conventional, but that this amounts to no more than to say that the linguistic rules which a community uses are arbitrary. Burge suggests that we understand the arbitrary nature of these conventions in the following way: firstly, that the rules a person follows are not determined by any psychological, biological or sociological law, but are "historically accidental"; and secondly, that the rules are not uniquely the best way to fulfil their social functions.

Others have questioned whether Lewis's definition correctly captures our ordinary, quite general, concept of convention. Jamieson (1975) outlines cases of convention which do not conform to Lewis's definition. Gilbert (1989) also examines the conditions in his definition, asking whether these capture our 'everyday' concept of convention, and concludes that they do not. Furthermore, she questions the degree of rational agency implied by Lewis's account, and concludes "that the power of rationality is not as great as some have thought". She then proceeds to offer her own account of social convention, with an application to language (1989, ch. 6).

Davidson (1984, essay 18, and 1986) adopts the most radical position of all on the issue of convention, claiming that "convention does not help explain what is basic to linguistic communication" (1984, p. 280). Davidson's position is more radical still, as he also rejects the idea that linguistic practices are rule-governed regularities, while allowing that, in the interpretation of another, it may be useful to suppose their language to be rule-governed and conventional. We may construct a theory – Davidson calls it a "prior theory" – of the other's language which incorporates such conventional regularities (see Davidson, 1986, p. 442). According to Davidson, although the prior theory may be *useful*, it should not be taken to reflect anything shared by speakers of the language.

> Knowledge of conventions of language is thus a practical crutch to interpretation, a crutch we cannot in practice afford to do without – but a crutch which, under

> optimum conditions for communication, we can in the end throw away, and could in theory have done without from the beginning. (1984, p. 279)

The theory which, according to Davidson, can get along without the crutch of convention is what he calls the "passing theory" (1986, p. 442). What the passing theory draws on is the interpreter's "intuition, luck, skill . . . taste and sympathy" (1984, p. 279), and none of this is codifiable – much less conventional. Davidson concludes (1986, p. 446) that "there is no such thing as a language, not if a language is anything like what many philosophers and linguists have supposed. There is, therefore, no such thing to be mastered, learned or born with."

Davidson's position *appears* to be at odds with both use and formal theories of meaning. That it should be odds with the use theorist is not surprising, as Davidson has explicitly rejected such theories (see 1984, essays 9–11). That it should be at odds with formal theories is harder to fathom, since, as we have seen in § 2 above, Davidson is an explicit advocate of a formal, truth, theory of meaning. It may be, however, that closer examination of his work will reveal no real incompatibility. (For a discussion of this matter see Hacking, 1986 and Dummett, 1986.)

Davidson's rejection of the idea that language is conventional follows from his rejection of the idea that linguistic practice embodies rule-governed regularities. What Davidson does not reject is the idea that "the use of a particular sound to refer to, or mean, what it does is *arbitrary*" (1984, p. 265). With reference to the ancient Greek debate (see § 1), we could say that Davidson is on the side of Aristotle and not Cratylus. Neverthless, Davidson chooses to disassociate himself entirely from the idea of convention. What he is in fact disassociating himself from is the notion of convention as it has come to be understood by some philosophers today – a notion often associated with use theories of meaning, as well as with the idea that language embodies regularities.

Despite the fact that the idea that language is conventional fits so neatly with the idea that semantics is intention-based, these two ideas are basically independent of one another. The Gricean analysis of timeless meaning may appeal to convention, but it need not. Grice himself rejects the idea of convention (1989, p. 298), and, as we have seen above, offers the seeds of an alternative account of timeless meaning in a community of speakers. And many of those who hold that language is conventional would not uphold a Gricean analysis of meaning (for example Burge, or Dummett).

Where analyses are produced there is a temptation to concentrate on looking for counter-examples to them. This is of value, and it helps us to find the correct shape for the analysis. There are, however, other, deeper, questions raised by any analysis, which can be obscured by all the attention to detail. This obscuration has been especially true of the Gricean analysis of meaning, but is to some extent also true of the Lewisian account of convention. These deeper questions include the following. In what sense can speakers of a language be said to know any of the things the analyses commit the speaker to knowing? (See again Chapter 7, TACIT KNOWLEDGE.) Do we need to give a reductive interpretation of the Gricean analysis of meaning; and, if not, what does this tell us about the relationship between our concepts of semantics and of psychology? What ontological commitment, if any, do these analyses entail? In other words, do they commit a creature to the possession of (sophisticated) thoughts in the absence of language? Shifting the focus away from the analyses and from the production of counter-examples and on to these sorts of questions will further our understanding of the way in which attention to how we use language can help us to understand meaning.

References

Armstrong, D. 1971: "Meaning and communication". *Philosophical Review*, 81, 427–47.
Austin, J.L. 1962: *How To Do Things With Words*. Oxford: Oxford University Press.
——1971: "Performative-Constative", in J. Searle (ed.), *The Philosophy of Language*. Oxford: Oxford University Press.
——1979: *Collected Papers*. Oxford: Oxford University Press.
Avramides, A. 1989: *Meaning and Mind: An Examination of a Gricean Account of Meaning*. Cambridge, Mass.: MIT Press.
Bennett, J. 1976: *Linguistic Behaviour*. Cambridge: Cambridge University Press.
Blackburn, S. 1984: *Spreading the Word*. Clarendon Press, Oxford.
Burge, T. 1975: "On knowledge and convention". *Philosophical Review*, 84, 249–55.
Coady, A. 1976: "Review of Schiffer's *Meaning*". *Philosophy*, 102–9.
Davidson, D. 1984: *Inquiries into Truth and Interpretation*. Oxford: Oxford University Press.
——1986: "A nice derangement of epitaphs". In *Truth and Interpretation: Perspectives on the Philosophy of Donald Davidson*, ed. E. Lepore. Oxford: Basil Blackwell.
Dummett, M. 1975: "What is a theory of meaning?", *Mind and Language*, ed. S. Guttenplan. Oxford: Oxford University Press.
——1986: '"A Nice Derangement of Epitaphs": some comments on Davidson and Hacking'. In *Truth and Interpretation: Perspectives on the Philosophy of Donald Davidson*, ed. E. Lepore. Oxford: Basil Blackwell.
Evans, G. and McDowell, J. (eds.) 1976: *Truth and Meaning*. Oxford: Clarendon Press.
Gilbert, M. 1989: *On Social Facts*. Princeton: Princeton University Press.
Grandy, R. 1977: "Review of Lewis' *Convention: A Philosophical Study*", *The Journal of Philosophy*, 74, 129–39.
——and Warner, R. (eds.) 1989: *Philosophical Grounds of Rationality: Intentions, Categories, Ends*. Oxford: Oxford University Press.
Grice, H.P. 1957: 'Meaning', *Philosophical Review*, 66, 377–88.
——1989: *Study in the Way of Words*. Cambridge, Mass.: Harvard University Press.
Hacking, I. 1986: "The parody of conversation". In *Truth and Interpretation: Perspectives on the Philosophy of Donald Davidson*, ed. E. Lepore. Oxford: Basil Blackwell.
Harman, G. 1974: Review of *Meaning* by S. Schiffer, *Journal of Philosophy*, 70, 224–9.
Heal, J. 1978: "Common knowledge", *Philosophical Quarterly*, 28, 116–31.
Jamieson, D. 1975: "David Lewis on Convention", *Canadian Journal of Philosophy*, 5, 73–81.
Lewis, D. 1969: *Convention: A Philosophical Study*. Cambridge, Mass.: Harvard University Press.
——1983: "Languages and Language", *Philosophical Papers*, Vol. 1. Oxford: Oxford University Press.
Loar, B. 1976: "Two theories of meaning". In *Truth and Meaning*, ed. G. Evans and J. McDowell. Oxford: Clarendon Press.
——1981: *Meaning and Mind*. Cambridge: Cambridge University Press.

Lyons, J. 1968: *Introduction to Theoretical Linguistics*. Cambridge: Cambridge University Press.

McDowell, J. 1980: "Meaning, communication, and knowledge". In *Philosophical Subjects: Essays Presented to P.F. Strawson*, ed. Z. Van Straaten. Oxford: Clarendon Press.

Moore, G.E. 1966: "The Justification of Analysis". In *Lectures on Philosophy*, ed. C. Lewy. London: George Allen and Unwin.

Platts, M. 1979: *Ways of Meaning*. London: Routledge and Kegan Paul.

Recanati, R. 1987: *Meaning and Force: The Pragmatics of Performative Utterances*. Cambridge: Cambridge University Press.

Schiffer, S. 1972: *Meaning*. Oxford: Clarendon Press.

——1982: "Intention-based semantics", *Notre Dame Journal of Philosophy*, 43, 119–56.

——1987: *Remnants of Meaning*. Cambridge, Mass.: MIT Press.

Searle, J. 1969: *Speech Acts: An Essay in the Philosophy of Language*. Oxford: Oxford University Press.

——1971: Editorial Introduction to *The Philosophy of Language*. Oxford: Oxford University Press.

Strawson, P.F. 1964: 'Intention and convention in speech acts', *Philosophical Review*, 73, 439–60.

——1971: *Logico-Linguistic Papers*. London: Methuen.

Warnock, G.J. 1989: *J.L. Austin*. London: Routledge.

Wiggins, D. 1971: "On sentence-sense, word-sense, and difference of word-sense". In *Semantics: An Interdisciplinary Reader in Philosophy, Linguistics, and Psychology*, ed. L.A. Jacobovits and D.D. Steinberg. Cambridge: Cambridge University Press.

4

Pragmatics

CHARLES TRAVIS

Here are two non-equivalent characterizations of pragmatics. Pragmatics (first version) concerns the linguistic phenomena left untreated by phonology, syntax and semantics. Pragmatics (second version) is the study of properties of words which depend on their having been spoken, or reacted to, in a certain way, or in certain conditions, or in the way, or conditions, they were.[1]

Here are two equally non-equivalent characterizations of semantics. Semantics (first version) is, by definition, concerned with certain relations between words and the world, and centrally with those on which the truth or falsity of words depends: thus David Lewis's slogan, "Semantics with no treatment of truth conditions is not semantics."[2] Semantics (second version) is defined by this idea: "A theory of meaning for a language should be able to tell us the meanings of the words and sentences which comprise that language."[3] So what a semantic theory of English, say, must do is, for each English expression, provide a specification of what it means. Semantics in general would be an account of the nature of such particular theories, or of their subject matter.

Combine these different ideas, and you get a substantial thesis: such things as English sentences *have* statable conditions for truth, and meanings can be given in or by stating these. That *might* be wrong. Perhaps, as J. L. Austin suggested, questions of truth arise at a different level entirely from that of expressions of a language. Perhaps conditions for truth depend, pervasively, on the circumstances in which, or the way in which, words were produced. If so, then on the second version of pragmatics and the first version of semantics, semantic questions are pragmatic ones; whereas semantics (second version), however it is to be done, would have little or nothing to do with truth conditions. Call this the pragmatic view.

This essay argues that the pragmatic view is the right one; that it is intrinsically part of what expressions of (say) English mean that any English (or whatever) sentence may, on one speaking of it or another, have any of indefinitely many different truth conditions, and that any English (or whatever) expression may, meaning what it does, make any of many different contributions to truth conditions of wholes in which it figures as a part. I will first set out the reasons for thinking so, then discuss a few of the most significant consequences.

The issue also emerges in asking what words are for. On one view, bracketing ambiguity, indexicals and demonstratives (see Chapter 23, INDEXICALS AND DEMONSTRATIVES), for each declarative English sentence there is a thought which is the one it expresses; its role in English is to express that one. On the pragmatic view this is just what is not so. Independent of ambiguity, indexicality, and so on, what meaning does is to make a sentence a means for expressing *thoughts* – not some *one* thought, but any of myriad different ones. Meaning does that in making a sentence a particular description of how things are, so a means for describing things as that way. Any description admits of many different applications. The same description, applied differently, yields different thoughts. A right application, where there is one, is fixed by circumstances of producing the description, not just by the description itself. If a sentence may thus equally well express any of many thoughts, conditions for the truth of one of these cannot be conditions for the truth of the *sentence*.

1 Semantic properties

There are properties words have, and would have, no matter how we understood them. Being spoken loudly or at 3 p.m. are two. Then there are properties words have, or would have, on one understanding of them, but would lack on another – properties words have, if at all, only in virtue of their being rightly understood in the way they are. I want to consider two classes of such properties.

The first sort of property is one of relating in a given way to truth (or falsity). Properties of being true (false) if, given, of, or only if, thus and so, or thus, or the way things are, are all within this class. (They are all properties words might have on one understanding, and lack on another.) For future convenience, I exclude being true or false *simpliciter* from this class, though I include being true (false) given the way things are. I call these properties *truth-involving*, and any set of them a *truth-condition*.

The second sort are properties identified without mention of truth, and on which truth-involving properties depend. Such properties include such things as describing X as Y, calling X Y, saying X to be Y, and speaking of X. The words 'is red', for example, speak of being red and, on a speaking, may have called something red. These properties identify *what* words say. I will call them *content-fixing*, and any set of them a *content*.

One might wonder whether content-fixing properties are not really truth-involving ones in disguise – whether, for example, to call something red is not just to say (of it) what is true of such-and-such things, and true of a thing under such-and-such conditions. In what follows, we will find out whether that is so.

The properties indicated so far might reasonably be called semantic, not worrying overly for the moment about boundaries between syntax and semantics. I will call them that, and any set of them a *semantics*. The latitude allowed here means that not every semantics in the present sense is one words might have. Some semantic properties may exclude others. Calling something a fish, for example, may exclude, *tout court*, saying what is true of my piano. Call a semantics some words *might have* coherent, keeping in mind that a semantics might thus be coherent on some occasions for speaking, while not on others.

We can raise questions about a semantics, or sort of semantics, without saying which items might have it – whether, for example, English sentences or something else might do so. One thing we may ask of a given semantics is whether it *requires* any further semantics – whether there is a semantics which any words with it must have. Or we may ask whether it is supplementable in a variety of – perhaps mutually exclusive – ways; whether words with it may, for all that, have any of various further semantics.

It is interesting to ask, in particular, whether the semantics an English sentence has in meaning what it does is compatible with any of many supplementations, specifically with any of a variety of truth conditions. To answer that we need not first say what semantics meaning does confer. We need only find a number of speakings of the sentence on each of which it had whatever semantics its meaning does confer; on each of which, as much as any of the others, those words *did* mean what they do mean. In specific cases we may convince ourselves of that much without knowing just *which* properties meaning confers.

2 The pragmatic view

Is what a sentence means compatible with semantic variety – specifically variety in truth conditions – across its speakings? Consider this sentence:

(1) The leaves are green.

The words 'are green', meaning what they do, are means for calling things green. Similarly, meaning what they do, 'The leaves', when spoken as in (1), purport to speak of some leaves. What its (present) tense means makes (1), on a speaking, purport (roughly) to speak of things at the time of that speaking. Consider speakings of (1) in which the words did all this, and in all other respects (if any) meant what they *mean*. Does that much semantics require them to have just *one* full semantics on all such speakings? Or is that much compatible with semantic variety, and, specifically, with those words having, on different speakings, any of many truth conditions?

A story. Pia's Japanese maple is full of russet leaves. Believing that green is the colour of leaves, she paints them. Returning, she reports, 'That's better. The leaves are green now.' She speaks truth. A botanist friend then phones, seeking green leaves for a study of green-leaf chemistry. 'The leaves (on my tree) are green,' Pia says. 'You can have those.' But now Pia speaks falsehood.

If the story is right, then there are two distinguishable things to be said in speaking (1) with the stipulated semantics. One is true; one false; so each would be true under different conditions. That semantics is, then, compatible with semantic variety, and with variety in truth involving properties. So what the words of (1) mean is compatible with various distinct conditions for its truth.

But is the story right? There are just two grounds for rejecting it. First, one might reject its data by claiming that both speakings of (1), above, share a truth value, require the same for truth, and are true of the same. Second, one might accept the phenomena as presented, but claim that they *are* accounted for by what (1) means – either by some ambiguity in (1), or by some particular way in which what (1) means makes what it says depend systematically on the circumstances of its speaking.

Consider the first option. Either the stipulated semantics makes (1) true of painted leaves, or it makes (1) false of them, *punkt*. If one of these disjuncts is right, appearances to the contrary may be explained in any of a variety of ways. The first task, though, is to choose. Which disjunct is right? One must choose in a principled way. What the words mean must make one or the other disjunct plainly, or at least demonstrably, true.

What we know about what words mean will not solve this problem of choice. Nothing we know about what '(is) green' means speaks to this question: If an object is painted green, should its colour count as what it would be without the paint, or rather as what it has been coloured by painting it? Nor is it plausible that some further development in natural science might resolve this issue. So, it seems, the first option must be rejected. Nor, as we shall see, are colours an unfair example. There are similar problems for any simple predicate, ones left unsolved by what the words in question mean.

We must, then, begin on the second option. Its simplest version is that (1) is ambiguous, or that the words 'are green' are: in one of their senses, they are true of leaves painted green, in another, false of leaves merely painted green. Does 'is green' have such senses in English? I do not think so. But there is a more important question. Suppose it does. Would that yield a different answer to our question about semantic variation?

It would change the answer if the only occasion for saying both true and false things of given leaves in speaking (1) were in case they were painted. But there are indefinitely many more occasions than that provides for saying either of two distinct things in so speaking. Suppose the leaves were not painted (or were painted red), but had a fluorescent green mould growing on them. Or suppose they are painted, but in pointillist style: from a decent distance they look green, but up close they look mottled. Is that a way of painting leaves green? It might sometimes, but only sometimes, so count. So there would be two distinct things to be said in the presumed 'paint counts' sense of 'is green'. And so on.

The above need not be the *only* ambiguity in the English 'is green'. But if words are ambiguous in English, there must be a way of saying just what these ambiguities are; so a fact as to how many ways ambiguous they are. The pair of speakings we considered differed in that each invoked a different understanding of what it would be for leaves to be green. There is no reason to think that there is any limit to possible understandings of *that*, each of which might be invoked by some words which spoke on that topic. There is not only an understanding on which painting might make it so, but also one on which painting might make it, so as long as it is not in too loose a pointillist style, or too shiny. And so on, *ad infinitum*. If 'green' has, say, thirteen senses, there are, for each of them, various possible (and invokable) understandings of what it would be for leaves to be green in *that* sense. If so, then ambiguity is not a way of avoiding the present conclusion.

It is sometimes said: there is no *uniform* standard for things being green; it is one thing for an apple to be green, another for a tomato to be green, and so on. That idea, though, gets nowhere with the present problem. Throughout the question has been what it is true to say of *leaves*.

Finally, it might be said that the phenomena show 'green' to be a vague term. Perhaps it is in some sense, though we have so far seen no more reason to say so than there is to say the same of any term. But it is hard to see how vagueness is to the point. In one sense, perhaps, words are vague if there is not enough in a correct understanding of them for deciding whether, given the way the things they speak of are, they ought to count as true or false. The *English* sentence (1) is certainly in that condition. But one *speaking* of it may clearly state what is true, while another clearly states what is false. That can only be so if the semantics of (1) on some speakings of it is substantially richer than that fixed for it by the meanings of its constituents, and richer in different ways for different such speakings. So what (1) says on a speaking, of given leaves, etc., is not determined merely by what it, or its parts, mean.

I take the English sentence (1) to illustrate, in the respects noted, what is generally so of a language's sentences – indeed, to illustrate how a sentence of a language *must* function. I have no space for more examples; nor for a satisfying account of why that should be.[4] The reader might anyway test the claim with some further examples of his or her own.

3 Domestications

The above, if correct, answers the initial question: what a sentence means, or what its parts do, is compatible with semantic variety; with variety in what such words say or said, and with variety in their truth-involving properties. One might think that compatible with the traditional view, in which semantics is both the study of what words mean and, centrally, of the conditions for their truth; that all said so far is consistent with the meanings of words determining the conditions for their truth; and even that the general point has long been recognized. One might still think, in other words, that the point may be domesticated within a framework in which what words mean still fixes, in an important sense, what they say wherever spoken. I will discuss two plans for such domestication.

The first plan turns on the idea of ellipsis: some words are to be understood as short for others. A particular 'He'll come', for example, may be rightly construed as a shortened 'He'll come to the party'. Assuming ellipsis were pervasive, how might it help? If (1) may be used to say any of many things, it must, on different speakings, be elliptical for different things: on each it says what that for which it is then elliptical would say. For this explanation to domesticate the phenomena, the things for which (1) is elliptical must not themselves exhibit semantic variation of the sort that (1) did. For example, if a given instance of (1) is elliptical for 'The leaves are green beneath the paint', there must not be more than one thing to be said in *those* words. If the phenomena are as I suggest, this assumption is wrong. I leave this suggestion at that.

The second suggestion revolves around this idea: what words mean *does* determine what they say.[5] But it does not do so *simpliciter*. Rather, it does so as a function of some set of factors, or parameters, in speakings of the words. The parameters allow for different things to be said in different such speakings. Such was always in the plan for linking sentences with truth conditions.

The plan is illustrated by Frege's treatment of the present tense. Frege notes that a speaking of (1) in July might be true, while one in October was false.[6] He observes, correctly, that different things would have been said in each such speaking. One thing this shows is that the tensed verb refers to a specific time or interval, and different ones on different speakings; the words say the leaves to be green at that time.

Frege thought that more was shown. First, that for the present tense the time referred to is always the time of speaking. Second, that where present-tense words are spoken, there is a factor – the time they were spoken – and a function, fixed by what they mean, from values of it to the time they spoke of: in fact, the identity function. So third, that what (1) means determines a function from variables in its speakings to thoughts expressed on those speakings.

Frege's view might be generalized. What *some* words say, or contribute to what is said in using them, varies across speakings of them. Where this is so, the meaning of the words does two things. First, it determines on just what facts about a speaking the semantic contribution of the words so spoken depends. Second, it determines just how their semantics on a speaking depends on these facts. Specifically, it determines a specifiable function from values of those factors to the semantics the words would have, if spoken where those values obtain.

The above is a hypothesis. *If* it is true, then while the words (1) may say different things on different speakings, what those words mean determines how they so vary. It determines that the words say thus and so where such-and-such factors take on such-and-such values, for any values those factors may take on (where the thus and so said is what would be true under such-and-such conditions). If that is so, it is reasonable to say that what words mean determines what they say, and when they, or that, would be true. It does so by determining effectively how other facts about their speaking matter to such questions.

But is the hypothesis true? First note that semantics is not history. Sentence (1) will have been spoken only a finite number of times before the heat death of the universe. Suppose that each such time something in particular was said. Then, of course, there is a function from parameters of *those* occasions to what was said in (1) on them. There are many such functions, from many such parameters. That is not semantics. What we wanted to know was: if you spoke (1) on such-and-such occasion (as may or may not actually be done), what *would* you say? The question was whether what (1) means provides an answer to that. The historical remark about actual occasions does nothing towards showing that it does.

The point was that the words 'is green', while speaking of being green, may make any of many semantic contributions to wholes of which they are a part, different contributions yielding different results as to what would count as things being as they are said to be. Are there parameters in speakings of those words which determine just which semantic contribution they would make when? Is there a function such that for each assignment of values to those parameters, there is one particular contribution the words *would* inevitably make, spoken where those values hold? I will not demonstrate here that there are no such things. But there need not be: perhaps for any set of parameters, further possible factors would yield more than one distinguishable thing to be said for fixed values of those.

There are several respects in which the present phenomena are *unlike* central cases where the parameter approach seems promising. One difference is this. In central cases, such as 'I' and 'now', pointing to given parameters seems to be a part of the terms meaning what they do. It is part of the meaning of 'I', and its use in English, that it is a device for a speaker to speak of himself. That suggests speakers as a relevant parameter. If there is no unique semantic contribution, 'I' makes for a fixed value of that parameter, the meaning of 'I' fixes no function from *that* to contributions made in speaking it. By contrast, it is not part of what 'green' means, so far as we can tell, that speakings of it speak of, or refer to, such-and-such parameters. If its contribution, on a speaking, to what is said *is* a function of some parameters – say, implausibly,[7] the speaker's intentions – saying so is not part of saying what 'green' means. The parameter approach does not *automatically* suggest itself here as it did with 'I'.

This difference between 'I' and 'green' shows up when it comes to saying what was said. Consider a speaking of the words 'I am in Paris'. Ignore any possibilities for various contributions by 'in Paris', or by the present tense at a time. Then, knowing nothing more about the speaking, we know that, in it, it was said *that* the speaker, whoever s/he may be, was, at the time of speaking, whenever that was, in Paris. However in the dark we may be on those points, we *do* thus specify which fact (or non-fact) was stated. Not so for speakings of (1). Suppose that Pia spoke those words, and that *we* say of that, 'Pia said that the leaves she spoke of were, at the time of speaking, green.' We will not have said *what* Pia stated unless *our* 'green' made some definite contribution to what *we* said about Pia. But, as we have seen, 'green' may make any of many contributions of the needed sort. If it made one such in *our* words and a different one in Pia's then what we said about her is *false*. We may, for example, have said her to say what would be false of green-painted leaves, while what she said would be true of that. The information contained in the meanings of the words she used is thus not enough for specifying, however uninformatively, *which* fact (or non-fact) she stated.

In speaking (1) literally, one does what then counts as calling leaves green. That may be one thing that sometimes counts as 'saying that the relevant leaves were green'. But *such* a use of 'say that', if there is one, does not purport to specify which fact (or non-fact) was stated. It says nothing that allows us to associate what was said with a truth condition for it. So it does not point to a function, fixed by meaning, from speakings to thoughts expressed in them.

A second contrast between present phenomena and such things as 'I' and 'now', traditionally conceived, is suggested by this remark of Frege's:

> the content of a sentence often goes beyond the thought expressed by it. But the opposite often happens too; the mere wording, which can be made permanent by

> writing or the gramophone, does not suffice for the expression of the thought. . . . If a time indication is conveyed by the present tense, one must know when the sentence was uttered in order to grasp the thought correctly. Therefore the time of utterance is part of the expression of the thought. . . . The case is the same with words like 'here' and 'there'. In all such cases the mere wording, as it can be preserved in writing, is not the complete expression of the thought; the knowledge of certain conditions accompanying the utterance, which are used as means of expressing the thought, is needed for us to grasp the thought correctly. Pointing the finger, hand gestures, glances may belong here too.[8]

We begin with the idea that sentences are related to thoughts in this way: for each sentence there is a thought which is the thought it expresses.[9] With indexicality, we lose that idea. There is no particular thought which is the one the sentence 'I am here' expresses. Perhaps, though, we may regain that idea if we permit ourselves to generalize the ordinary notion of a sentence. Ordinarily, we think of a sentence as a string of words. Suppose, though, we drop that idea. Let us call something a symbol if it has two features. First, it is individuated by purely non-semantic features, as a word might be individuated by its shape.[10] Second, it has semantic properties, where we will take that to be so if it makes a definite, specifiable semantic contribution to the whole, or wholes, of which it is a part. We might regard a (generalized) sentence as a structured set of symbols in this sense. So, if Frege is right about its semantic contribution, a time of utterance may be a symbol, and hence a constituent of a sentence in this sense. An utterance 'The leaves are green' in July would then count as a different sentence from an utterance, 'The leaves are green' in October – an odd, but coherent way to speak.

If the only deviations from the rule that, for each sentence, there is the thought it expresses are represented by the sort of case Frege has in mind, then we may now regain the initial idea in this form: for each *generalized* sentence, there is a thought which is the thought it expresses. But the phenomena exhibited by (1) cannot be domesticated in this way. There is no identifiable feature of a speaking of (1) which counts as a symbol in the present sense, and whose semantic contribution to the speaking is identifiable with precisely the set of truth-involving properties (1) would have so spoken. If the phenomena (1) exhibits are pervasive, then even a generalized sentence, no matter what extra symbols it contained, might be used to say any of many things.

Wittgenstein held that any symbol is open to different interpretations; and that under different circumstances, different identifications of its content would be correct. That is the moral of his discussion of rules and what they instruct (*Investigations*, §§ 84–7). His arguments apply as well to generalized symbols as to others. If he is right, then the demonstration omitted here, that the parameter approach *cannot* work, is anyway to be found.

4 Implicature

> Suppose that I were the doctor and a patient came to me, showed me his hand and said: 'This thing that looks like a hand isn't just a superb imitation – it really is a hand'

and went on to talk about his injury – should I really take this as a piece of information, even though a superfluous one?[11]

I am sitting with a philosopher in the garden; he says again and again, 'I know that that's a tree,' pointing to a tree that is near us. Someone else arrives and hears this, and I tell him: 'This fellow isn't insane. We are only doing philosophy.'[12]

Wittgenstein cites some bizarre things to say. We do not say such things, barring very special occasion to do so. But what does that mean? Suppose one says them anyway. Despite the oddity, might one have spoken truth?

The philosopher does acrobatics recklessly close to the tree. 'That's a tree over there,' someone warns. 'I know that's a tree,' he replies testily. 'Well, then, shouldn't you be more careful?' Here the philosopher speaks truth. So, one might reason, he *does* know these things. But one cannot cease to know things, or so it seems, *just* by moving from one conversation to another. So however bizarre saying so may be in other cases, for all that, he speaks truth there too. So one might reason.

But this is a bad argument. For it *may* be that words like 'I know I'm wearing shoes' vary their semantics from speaking to speaking. If some speakings of them speak truth, that does not mean that all will. We cannot generally reason: Pia spoke truth when she called the leaves green; so if I call them green, I will speak truth too. That was the moral of § 2. The point would be, not that the philosopher ceases to know something by changing conversations, but rather, that on one occasion he counts as knowing such-and-such, on another not.

There is, though, a form of account on which many bizarre things we 'would not say', would, for all that, be true. The idea is due to H. P. Grice. The starting-point is the observation that saying is only one of numerous ways for words, or speakers of them, to represent things as so. There is also implying, suggesting, insinuating, presupposing, and so on. *That* insight did not originate with Grice. Grice, though, concerned himself with a particular class of such representations, which he called implicatures, using the verb 'implicate' for the sort of representing in question. Implicatures come in two sorts: conventional and conversational. Conventional implicatures are features of the meanings of the terms involved. They are illustrated by 'Pia dissuaded Tod from leaving', and 'Sam struggled to reach the lectern'. The first represents Tod as at least having thought of leaving; the second represents Sam as facing some obstacle to reaching the lectern. But the first does not *say* that Tod had thought of leaving, nor the second that there was an obstacle. That does not yet mean, that, for example, the second might be *true* were there no obstacle. It leaves it obscure what could make it so. But it may facilitate arguing the point. In any event, just as to use 'It's green' to mean what it does *is* to call something green, so to use 'struggle' to mean what it does, in a case like the above, is to suggest or imply that there is an obstacle. Grice suggests that it is difficult to produce words with a conventional implicature without implicating that. Such implicatures are not, or hardly, what Grice calls 'cancellable'. That he takes to be a main identifying feature of them.

Some implicatures, Grice notes, arise only on certain speakings of words, so *are* cancellable. These Grice calls conversational implicatures, and he explains them thus (though in much greater detail than given here). In normal conversation, we represent ourselves as observing certain maxims, and may be supposed to do so. Grice calls these *conversational maxims*. Examples are: be co-operative, be brief, be informative, and be relevant. Sometimes a speaker *seems* to violate some of these maxims. But it may be that he would not have if such-and-such, and it may be unreasonable to take the speaker to be violating them. We may then reason thus. The speaker said that P (in saying 'W'). Saying P (or saying it in 'W') would violate the maxims unless Q. The speaker was not violating the maxims. So (according to him) Q.

A speaker may intend for us to avail ourselves of some inference of this sort, to a given conclusion that (according to him) Q. It may be part of the proper understanding of his words that he so intends. In that case, the speaker has, or his words have, conversationally implicated that Q. For example, Pia may say, 'Jones submitted a sequence of English sentences, divided into paragraphs, and titled "What is truth?"'. If this is merely a way of saying that Jones submitted an essay, then it violates the maxim of brevity. Pia would not do *that*. So, by the suggested sort of inference, we may conclude that there is, according to Pia, something which distinguishes Jones's work from a proper essay – perhaps its incoherence. It may have been given to be understood that we were so to reason. In that case, the conclusion was conversationally implicated.

The notion of conversational implicature points to a particular sort of understanding some words, on some speakings, may bear. Nothing in the pragmatic view suggests that there should not be such understandings. Note, though, that, as Grice insists, for Q to be conversationally implicated in words 'W', Q must follow from what 'W' said, or the fact that 'W' said it, or both. So we might ask what Grice thinks words say. He is quite clear about that:

> In the sense in which I am using the word *say*, I intend what someone has said to be closely related to the conventional meaning of the words (the sentence) he has uttered. Suppose someone to have uttered the sentence *He is in the grip of a vice*. . . . One would know that he had said, about some particular male person or animal x, that at the time of the utterance . . . either (1) x was unable to rid himself of a certain kind of bad character trait or (2) some part of x's person was caught in a certain kind of tool or instrument . . . But for a full identification of what the speaker had said, one would need to know (a) the identity of x, (b) the time of utterance, and (c) the meaning on the particular occasion of utterance, of the phrase *in the grip of a vice* [a decision between (1) and (2)].[13]

This is just the rejected conception of saying. On it, for example, bracketing lexico-syntactic ambiguity, we can always form a guaranteed-true report, in indirect speech, of what was said in any arbitrary speaking of given words: if the words were 'The leaves are green', then that the relevant leaves were, at the relevant time, green. To think that is to miss the possibility of occasion-sensitivity in the content of 'green'. So Grice's conception of saying cannot be assumed in any argument directed against an instance of the pragmatic view.

Grice aimed to resuscitate views fallen into disrepute, largely through what were, in effect, early applications of the pragmatic view. For example, the idea of conversational implicature was first developed specifically in aid of reviving some notion of a sense datum. With that in mind, let us return to the bizarre remarks with which this section began. Consider 'I know that that's a tree'. It would usually be bizarre to say that, for example, where the tree was in plain view and no doubt of any kind had arisen as to whether it was a tree. Grice invites us to entertain the possibility that the reason we would not say such a thing in such circumstances is that if we did, we would conversationally implicate something not so. He means that idea to encourage us to ask whether what would be said if one did so speak is anyway something true, or rather something false; and to expect one choice or the other to be *correct*.

In using 'know' bizarrely we *may* conversationally implicate something (though there is a problem if conversationally implicating that Q absolutely requires saying that P). But the pragmatic view offers another explanation of why, in some situations, we would not say 'I know that . . .'. Suppose that 'know' may make any of many distinct semantic contributions to wholes of which it is a part, and varies its contribution from one speaking to another. Then, describing someone as he is at a time, we would, on some occasions, say something true in saying him to know that X is a tree, and, on other occasions, say something false in saying *that*. For there are various things to be said in so describing him. In that case, circumstances of a speaking of 'N knows . . .' may confer on it a supplement to the content provided by the meanings of the terms alone. For some such supplements, the result will be stating truth; for others it will be stating falsehood. But *some* circumstances may fail to confer a supplement of either of these sorts. Words produced in such circumstances would have a content still supplementable in either way. But a content still so supplementable can require neither truth nor falsity. Speak, in those circumstances of N knowing that it's a tree, and one will fail both at saying what is true and at saying what is false. Nothing either so or not-so will have been said to be so. Recognizing that, where it is so, may make one refrain from so speaking. In that case, the idea, encouraged Grice, that if we said it anyway we would at least say something true or else something false, is simply a mistake. In that case, conversational implicature could not be a consequence of the fact of having said *that* such and such. There is no such fact.

That the content of words is consistently supplementable in more than one way is not in itself a block to those words stating truth. It is so only where different such supplements, or different ones within some range of reasonable ones, yield different results as to truth – where, that is, the content to be supplemented is compatible both with truth and with falsity. So it just *might* be that if you say irrelevantly, pointing at your brogues, 'Those things are shoes', there is no compelling reason to deny that you have spoken truth (though the situation changes if you are wearing four-eyelet low moccasin boots, or even just moccasins). That is typically not how it is for philosophically sensitive terms like 'know'. That is one lesson the long history of scepticism teaches us. (If there must be an *occasion-insensitive* answer, just when *does* someone count as knowing there is a tree before him?)

This last point shows the problem in applying the notion of implicature where it is meant to carry philosophic baggage, notably where it is meant as a way of dismissing claims about what 'we would not say' as philosophically irrelevant. Where those claims point to occasion-sensitivity they are philosophically highly relevant. It is all very well to insist, for example, that either Sam does or doesn't now know that he is wearing shoes, full stop; and that if you said, bizarrely, 'Sam knows he is', you would either state truth or state falsity. Sooner or later, though, one must choose. Which is it? If, applying the pragmatic view, we carefully assemble a perspicuous view of the *different* things we at least take ourselves to say to be so, on different occasions for speaking of Sam, in saying him to know precisely that, then *either* there is a principled way of choosing between them (or choosing a further candidate) by appealing to what is recognizably so about what 'know' means, *or* they show that no one answer to the question is the right one occasion-independently. Prospects for the first alternative are dim.

5 Metaphysics

The English 'is green' speaks of a certain way for things to be: green. One might say that it speaks of a certain property: (being) green. If we do say that, we must also say this about that property: what sometimes counts as a thing's having it sometimes does not, so that there are, or may be, things which, on some occasions for judging, count as having the property, and on others do not. If for a property to have an extension (at a time) is for there to be a definite set of things (at that time) which are just those things (then) with that property, then this property does not have an extension, even at a time. Better put, it makes no sense to speak of 'its extension'.

Is all this just vagaries of the English 'is green'? Two related questions arise. First, might there be predicates which did not vary their contributions to what was said with them in the way that 'is green' does? If we said such a predicate to speak of a property, that property *would* have an extension, at least at a time. Such a predicate could not vary its contributions to wholes so that, in ascribing that property to an object (at a time) it would be possible to speak truth and also possible to speak falsehood. So there would be no call for saying of anything that it sometimes counted, and sometimes didn't, as having (at a given time) that property. Second, can we preserve the idea that (genuine) properties have extensions by supposing that predicates like 'is green' simply refer to different properties on different occasions (and that it is by their thus varying their referent that they make different contributions to different wholes)?

Why might one want properties to have extensions? First, one might think that we can gain this for properties by definition – by 'property' we just mean what has an extension – and that extensions are convenient means for counting properties (as one or two). Second, one might take such a view of properties as mere sane realism. We cannot change, say, the way a cow is by thinking about it. As a rule, the cow stays just as it is no matter how we think of it. And we may read, or misread, that sane thought thus: those ways for things to be which are, or count as, ways the cow is count as ways the cow is no matter how we think about the cow, or them. So for any genuine way for things to be, either the cow is that way (at a time), or it is not, *punkt*. The same goes for any other object. In which case genuine ways for things to be have extensions (at times). But whatever there is in favour of this line of thought, I suggest that both our questions merit negative answers.

I begin with the first. I will state the main point, though there is here no space for detailed argument. Once we fix what 'is green' speaks of – green – we then note that there are different possible understandings of what it would be for an object (or some objects) to be *that* way (green). These are possible understandings in that they represent what one *might* regard as a thing's being green. So, for each, some item may be said, in calling it green, to be green on *that* understanding of its being so. And for each, that may be the *right* understanding (on some occasion) of what being green would come to. 'Is green' provides a particular description for things, expresses a certain concept. What is said in using it depends not only on what that description is, but on how that description, or that concept, is, or would be, applied in fitting it to particular circumstances of its use.

Suppose, now, that we identify an understanding of being green – say, the understanding on which an item was said to be green in some particular speaking of 'is green'. We now introduce a predicate – say, 'is green*' – which, by stipulation, is to mean *is green on that understanding of being green*. This predicate speaks, as it were, of a finer-grained property than 'is green' (as such) does. May *this* predicate make different contributions to what is said in wholes of which it is part? It may if there are different possible understandings of what it would be to be green on that understanding; two different things to be said as to whether such-and-such *is* being green on that understanding of what it would be to be so. As far as we can tell, this always will be so. We understand, for example, that paint is to count as changing colour, and not as hiding it. We now encounter a rather poor paint job: you *could* say that it covered the original colour, but you could view the original colour as still showing through enough that the object had not yet been made the colour of the paint, even on the indicated understanding of its being that colour. An understanding of being green, in so far as we can identify one, seems unable to foreclose in principle on the possibility of differing, but, apart from particular surroundings, equally sane and sensible views of what *that* understanding entails.

A predicate about which the pragmatic view was wrong would be one which did not admit of different possible understandings of what it would be for some item to fit the description which that predicate provides (or for the description to fit some item). The right understanding of it would foresee every eventuality in or to which the description might be applied. There is reason to think that no such predicate is available to human beings, at least given the way we in fact cognitively conduct our affairs. Again, what is said in applying a given description depends on *how* it is applied, and how, in given circumstances, it ought to be.

Now for the second question. First, if the first point is correct, then no understanding *we* could have of being green, so none that might attach to a particular use of 'is green', would be one on which 'is green' spoke of a property, if a property must have an extension. To paraphrase Wittgenstein, we refine our concepts, or understandings, for particular purposes – so that *in fact*, in the situations we face or expect, unclarity as to what to do or say does not arise. In doing that we neither reach, nor aim at, that absolute clarity on which we would speak of what had definite extensions. Where 'is green' has made different contributions to different wholes, we may identify different things for it to have spoken of each time – being green on this understanding, and being green on that one. So we may see the predicate as varying its reference across speakings of it. But we must not mistake these different things for properties with extensions. Second, if we cannot have a predicate for which the pragmatic view does not hold, then, equally, we have no means for specifying properties to which extensions may sensibly be ascribed. In any event, the phenomenon we have to deal with is not merely that predicates vary their contributions to wholes, but also that, whatever a predicate may be said to speak of – being such-and-such – what would sometimes count as an item's being *that* other times would not.

6 Perspective

Given words may have any of many semantics, compatibly with what they mean. Words in fact vary their semantics from one speaking of them to another. In that case, their semantics on a given speaking cannot be fixed simply by what they mean. The circumstances of that speaking, the way it was done, must contribute substantially to that fixing. As pointed out earlier, this does not mean that there is a function from certain parameters of speakings to semantics, taking as value for each argument the semantics words would have where those values held. It thus also does not mean that there might be a precise theory, generating, for each semantics words might have, necessary and sufficient conditions for their having that. Still, we may describe how circumstances do their work.

Here is one thought. The words 'is green' are a means which English provides for calling things green (describing them as green, etc.). If, in speaking English, you want to call an item green, those words will do. Speak them literally, seriously, and so forth, and you will then count as having done just that. The truth of what you say in calling an item green should turn precisely on whether the way that item is then counts as its being green. These two remarks jointly identify which truth-involving properties any such words must have: they are true of, and only of, those ways for things to be which counted, at their speaking, as the item they spoke of being green. Similarly for other English predicates.

Where you called an item green, the truth of your remark turns on whether it *then* counted as being green. On different occasions, different ways for an item to be would count as its being green. That variation means that, on different occasions, calling an item green will confer different truth-involving properties on your words. Consider two occasions which differ in this respect. On each, words which call an item green will have some set of truth-involving properties, which is, therefore, a possible set of such properties for words with that content to have. Those truth-involving properties, and the property of calling that item green, cohere on at least some occasions for so describing things. But those truth-involving properties *cannot* be those of words with that content produced on the other. That would not correspond to what, on the other, counts as something's being green. So each of the above semantics, available as it is on some occasions, is unavailable on others. I can sometimes speak truth in calling painted leaves green; but I cannot do so in circumstances where their being so painted does not count as their being green.

Let us pursue this thought. Consider:

(2) Today is a sunny day.

Spoken on day D, (2) would, typically, speak of day D. It would also identify the day it speaks of in a particular way: it speaks of that day as the day of its speaking, and represents it as identified by that fact. Since some speaking of (2) has both the semantic properties just mentioned, the two jointly form a semantics which is at least sometimes coherent. Let D* be the day after D. Words produced on D* could not have the semantics just mentioned. They could not speak of D and say it to be sunny while, on their proper understanding, identifying the day they speak of as the day of their speaking. On day D, we may express, or think, a thought with both those features. On other days (in normal circumstances) we cannot. Let us say that words with a semantics which is only sometimes available, in the above sense, express a perspectival thought, and have a perspectival content.

Now the point of the discussion of 'is green' may be put this way. Perspectival thought is the normal and pervasive case. On one occasion, we call an item green (at a time), and thereby produce words with such-and-such truth-involving properties. On another occasion, we may, if we like, say the same item to be green (at that same time). But our doing that may require that our words have quite different truth-involving properties. Those of our first remark may not correspond to what would count, on the occasion of this further speaking, as that item's being green. If that is right, it is fair to suppose that perspectival thoughts are the typical sort of thoughts we think. One might say: we relate cognitively to the world in essentially perspectival ways.

Now consider two minor puzzles. First, I have said there is something true, and also something false, to be said of given leaves, and their condition at a given time, in saying them to be green. How can this be? Consider the true thing to be said. What could make it true, other than the fact that the leaves are green? But, if that is a fact, how could one speak falsehood in saying no more nor less than that about them? Second, if there *are* those two things to be said, then *say* them, or rather, state the true one and deny the false one. To do so, you would have to call the leaves green, and then deny that they are that, as in 'The leaves are green, and the leaves are not green'. But that is a contradiction, so cannot be true. So what the pragmatic view requires that it be true to say is something it could not be true to say. So the view is wrong.

The first puzzle's rhetorical question has a non-rhetorical answer. What could make given words 'The leaves are green' true, other than the presumed 'fact that the leaves are green', is the fact that the leaves *counted* as green on the occasion of that speaking. Since what sometimes counts as green may sometimes not, there may still be something to make other words 'The leaves are green' false, namely, that on the occasion of *their* speaking, those leaves (at that time) did not count as green.

As for the second puzzle, we are challenged to say something literally unsayable – *not*: sayable-but-false, but rather not sayable at all. We ought to decline the challenge. On some occasion, words which call given leaves (at a time) green may (thereby) have truth-involving properties in virtue of which they are true. On some other occasion, words which deny those same leaves to be green may similarly be true. But given the way (described above) in which occasions work to forge a link between content-fixing properties and truth-involving ones, there is no occasion on which both these feats could be accomplished at once; so none on which 'The leaves are green and the leaves are not green' could have the semantics which a conjunction of those two truths would have to have. If the occasion is one on which the way those leaves are counts as their being green, then no words could have the semantics of the true denial; and *mutatis mutandis* if on the occasion the way the leaves are does not count as their being green. Each of the thoughts provided for above is a *perspectival* thought; and, in virtue of its perspectival character, unavailable to be expressed at all on any occasion on which the other is expressible.[14] The nature of semantic variation thus allows us to decline the challenge.

These are banal examples. In philosophy, neglect of perspectival thought often leads to more excitement. A philosopher may sense, for example, that our concepts apply as they do against a background of our natural reactions; if we naturally viewed things *quite* differently, we might apply the concepts we now have so as to speak truth in saying what it would not now be true to say. Asked to express some such truths, the philosopher is reduced to nonsense. Naturally enough. He was describing other perspectives. Some things said truly from them are not so much as expressible at all from his own.

7 Thoughts

Frege writes,

> Without offering this as a definition, I mean by 'a thought' something for which the question of truth can arise at all.[15]

Thoughts, for Frege, are not words. For him words are true only in a derivative sense: just in case they express a thought which is. For words are always open to, and in need of, interpretation. They are true, if at all, only on a given understanding of them (even if it is their proper understanding). Words 'Mary had a little lamb' may be a remark on husbandry, or one on gastronomy and, perhaps, true if understood the first way, false if understood in the second. Truth and falsity seem to correspond to understandings words may have, rather than to the words themselves (which Frege conceives as a quite different matter). It is the understandings, as opposed to the words, which settle questions of truth and falsity. So, on his view, it is for understandings, and not for words, that questions of truth and falsity arise. Words, apart from an understanding, could not be true or false at all.

If words admit of interpretations, then conceivably they may bear different understandings on different occasions for understanding them. Such shifts in interpretation could bring with them shifts in truth value. So if words were the primary objects for which questions of truth arose, it would be conceivable, for any sort of semantic object, that one and the same item should count as true on one occasion for assessing it, false on another.

Thoughts, for which questions of truth are, strictly speaking, to arise, are meant to be free in principle of both of the above features. They are to be absolutely immune to interpretation; and they are to be true or false absolutely, independent of the ways, if any, in which they enter into our thinking. On Frege's view, only such semantic objects could be material for logic.

We may extend the notion of semantic property so that thoughts have a semantics too. The semantic features of a thought will be just those features by which one thought may be distinguished from another. Among these will be such things as being about eating ovine, and such things as being true if Mary ate a bit of ovine, hence, on the above plan, both truth-involving and content-fixing properties. Its truth-involving properties are meant to be just those its content requires. Moreover, it is meant to have all this semantics intrinsically: any thought, no matter how encountered, is that thought iff it has that semantics. This means that the content of a thought – unlike the content of words – must determine its truth-involving properties *inexorably* (to coin a term): there are no two sets of truth-involving properties such that an item with that content might have the one but not the other, and also vice versa; there is *one* set of truth-involving properties which is *the* set any item with that content *must* have. For if not, then a thought's having that content might, on some occasions, make it count as having one set of truth-involving properties, and on others make it count as having another, counter to the tenet that every thought has its truth-involving properties intrinsically.

Why must thoughts have inexorable content? Suppose C is a non-inexorable content. Then there might be an item with C and truth-involving properties T, and an item with C and distinct truth-involving properties T*. But truth-involving properties are meant to be those which content requires. So these must be two items differing in further content-fixing features. This means that an item with C is, so far, open to interpretation: it might, for all that, bear any of several distinct understandings. That is to say: it might, for all that, be, or (if words) express, or represent, any of several distinct thoughts. So C is not the (whole) content of a thought.

Thoughts are identified precisely by their semantics, whereas words are identified by shape, syntax or spelling, or by the event of their production. The identity of words leaves their content open. So the content of given words must depend on further factors: on the character of their surroundings. This leaves it open that their surroundings might, on some occasions of considering them, count as conferring one semantics on the words, while on other such occasions those surroundings might count as conferring another. In that way, the semantics of words – how they are rightly understood – may be an occasion-sensitive affair. By contrast, the semantics of a given thought is meant to depend on *nothing*. So there are no such possibilities for variation across occasions in the semantics a given thought *counts* as having.

Thoughts, as thus conceived, are not open to interpretation. They are what Wittgenstein called 'shadows': semantic items interpolated between words and the states of affairs that make words true or false, and somehow more closely tied to those states of affairs than mere words could be. About shadows, Wittgenstein said:

> Even if there were such a shadow it would not bring us any nearer the fact, since it would be susceptible of different interpretations just as the expression is.[16]

How could this be true of thoughts? Could thoughts admit of interpretation? If so, how?

There are too many strands in our inherited notion of a thought to unravel them here. But here is a sketch of a framework for relevant issues. To begin, one *might* think to buy the semantic absoluteness of a thought – its immunity to interpretation – by stipulation. Wherever I would say something to be so in saying 'S', and it is determinate what, I may, it seems, refer to a thought in saying 'the thought that S'. I may also say, correctly, it seems: 'The thought that S is true iff S'. In saying that, I ascribe a set of truth-involving properties to the thought I refer to; in fact, whatever such properties my words 'S' then had. For I say the thought to be true exactly where what is so according to my words 'S' is so. So, it seems, we might stipulate that the thought I thus refer to is precisely the one with those truth-involving properties.

This is not quite enough. A thought cannot *just* have truth-involving properties. It must have a content. What content should that be? Here we come up against another strand in the conception of a thought. A thought is meant to be something that can be expressed in various words, or speakings, on various occasions. If you now express a thought, I can later express that very thought virtually whenever I like. On any plausible version of that view, words W and W* may express the same thought while differing in content. Frege gives this example:

> If someone wants to say today what he expressed yesterday using the word 'today', he will replace this word with 'yesterday'. Although the thought is the same, its verbal expression must be different in order that the change of sense which would otherwise be effected by the differing times of utterance may be cancelled out.[17]

The word 'today' brings with it a different contribution to content than the word 'yesterday'. Frege's two sentences are not alike in content-fixing properties. Yet, for good reason, Frege takes it that the one sentence, produced under certain circumstances, would express the same thought as the other sentence produced under certain others. If so, then the content-fixing properties of that thought are liable to vary across occasions.

The question is: just *how* may content vary while words express the same thought? One idea would be that W and W* express the same thought only if they apply the same concepts to the same objects. But this will not do. It does not even allow for Frege's example. It collapses completely if we return to the notion of perspective. On some occasions, in calling given leaves green one would state truth; on others, in calling those leaves green one would state falsehood (and not because the leaves changed). Apply a given concept to the leaves in different surroundings, and you will produce words with very different truth-involving properties. The semantics of some such words, produced in given surroundings, is unavailable in other surroundings for any words. Words with the *content* of those words, in the other surroundings, may have truth-involving properties so different that, at least for some purposes, we cannot take them to have expressed the same thought. The false remark about the leaves, for example, was not the same thought as the true remark. So if, in the changed surroundings, one wants to express the same thought again, one must *not* speak of the same concepts and objects. What it would take to express the same thought again is nothing more nor less than an adequate paraphrase. If the original words were 'The leaves are green', then, depending on surroundings, an adequate paraphrase might be 'The leaves are painted green'.

There is no space here for an account of what makes paraphrases adequate. But here are two remarks. First, adequate paraphrases may need to share crucial or relevant truth-involving properties; but they are unlikely to share *all* truth-involving properties. In remote enough circumstances, leaves may be green in the sense in which they were said to be in a given 'The leaves are green', but not painted green (perhaps dyed); though, for current purposes, 'The leaves are painted green' was an adequate paraphrase. Second, suppose on an occasion I express a thought in saying 'The leaves are green'. Then whether, on another occasion, words W are an adequate paraphrase of what I said may well depend on the occasion for the paraphrase, and perhaps, too, on the occasion for considering that occasion.

Thoughts viewed from this position lose their claims to have some *one* semantics intrinsically, and to be immune to interpretation. If, with perspective in mind, we ask what would count as producing some given thought again, and if we consider all the occasions for posing that question, we see how *that* thought may count on some occasions as having semantics which it would not count as having on others. For it may on some occasions admit of paraphrases it does not admit of on others. Nor need it ever have an inexorable content. To see how thoughts admit of interpretation, one need only know how to look for occasions for interpreting them.

8 Concluding remarks

There is much left to discuss, but no space left to discuss it. It is thus time to commend the subject to the reader. The pragmatic view gives a substantially different form to virtually every philosophic problem, not just in philosophy of language, but wherever puzzles arise. The new form may make some of these problems more tractable. For a start we will need new conceptions of logical form, and of such related notions as intensionality. These may yield new things to say on such questions as whether 'if–then' is transitive. We may then take a fresh look at what we say of people in ascribing propositional attitudes to them, and at understanding itself. Such a look, I predict, would make philosophy of psychology take a fresh course. It is also worth a look, from the pragmatic view, at problems of knowledge, of explanation, of freedom and responsibility, and so on. Some of this work is begun. There is much left to explore.

Notes

1 See e.g. Donald Kalish, "Semantics", in *The Encyclopedia of Philosophy*, Macmillan, New York, 1967.
2 Lewis, "General semantics", in *Semantics of Natural Language*, D. Davidson and G. Harman, eds. (Reidel, Dordrecht, 1972), p. 169.
3 Mark Platts, introduction to *Reference, Truth and Reality*, Routledge and Kegan Paul, London, 1980, p. 2.
4 For some more discussion see my *The Uses of Sense* (Oxford, Oxford University Press, 1989), especially ch. 1.
5 Throughout I leave lexico-syntactic ambiguity aside.
6 I modify Frege's example slightly. His discussion is in "The thought", *Logical Investigations* (Basil Blackwell, Oxford, 1977), p. 27.
7 See my "Annals of analysis", *Mind*, 100 (April 1991), pp. 237–64, for further discussion.
8 Frege, 'The thought', pp. 10–11.
9 Once again, ignore lexico-syntactic ambiguity.
10 Strictly speaking, this is false of words (consider e.g. homonyms). But ignore that for now.
11 Ludwig Wittgenstein, *On Certainty* (Blackwell, Oxford, 1969), § 461.
12 Ibid., § 467.
13 Grice, "Logic and Conversation", in *Studies In The Way of Words* (Harvard University Press, Cambridge, Mass., 1989), p. 25.
14 More precisely, any occasion on which a thought with the semantics of the first is expressible is *ipso facto* one on which a thought with the semantics of the second is not. I do not mean to prejudge questions of thought-identity.
15 Frege, 'The thought', p. 4.
16 Reported by G.E. Moore in "Wittgenstein's Lectures in 1930–33", *Mind*, 63 (1954), pp. 1–15, repr. in *Philosophical Occasions 1912–1951*, ed. by James C. Klagge and Alfred Nordmann, Hackett, Ind. and Cambridge, 1993, p. 59.
17 Frege, 'The thought', p. 10.

Bibliography

Austin, J.L., "Truth", in J.L. Austin, *Philosophical Papers* (Oxford University Press, Oxford, 1961).
——"How To Talk", in *Philosophical Papers*.
——"Other Minds", in *Philosophical Papers*.
——*How To Do Things With Words* (Harvard University Press, Cambridge, Mass., 1962).

——*Sense and Sensibilia* (Oxford University Press, Oxford, 1962).
Barwise, J. and Perry, J., *Situations and Attitudes* (MIT Press, Cambridge, Mass., 1983).
Cartwright, Richard, "Propositions" and "Propositions again", in his *Philosophical Essays* (MIT Press, Cambridge, Mass., 1987).
Dummett, Michael, "Mood, force and convention", in his *The Seas of Language* (Oxford University Press, Oxford, 1993).
Fauconnier, Gilles, *Mental Spaces* (MIT Press, Cambridge, Mass., 1985).
Frege, Gottlob, "The thought", in *Logical Investigations* (Blackwell, Oxford, 1977).
Grice, H.P., "Logic and conversation", in P. Cole and J. Morgan (eds), *Syntax and Semantics*, Vol. 3 (Academic Press, London, 1975), reprinted in H.P. Grice, *Studies in the Way of Words* (Harvard University Press, Cambridge, Mass., 1989).
——"Further notes on logic and conversation", in Cole and Morgan; reprinted in *Studies in the Way of Words*.
——"Retrospective epilogue", in *Studies in the Way of Words*.
Lewis, David, "General Semantics", in Davidson, D. and Harman, G. (eds), *Semantics of Natural Language* (Reidel, Dordrecht, 1972).
Kaplan, D., "Demonstratives", in J. Almog et al. (eds), *Themes From Kaplan* (Oxford University Press, Oxford, 1989).
Sperber, Dan, and Wilson, Deirdre, *Relevance* (Blackwell, Oxford, 1986).
Stalnaker, Robert, "Pragmatics", in Davidson, D. and Harman, G. (eds), *Semantics of Natural Language* (Reidel, Dordrecht, 1972).
Strawson, P.F., *Introduction to Logical Theory* (Methuen, London, 1952).
Travis, Charles, "Annals of analysis", *Mind*, 100 (April 1991), 237–64.
——*The Uses of Sense* (Oxford University Press, Oxford, 1989).
——"Meaning's role in truth", *Mind*, 105 (July 1996), 451–66.
Wittgenstein, Ludwig, *On Certainty* (Blackwell, Oxford, 1969).
——*Philosophical Investigations* (Macmillan, New York, 1953).
Ziff, Paul, "Understanding", in *Understanding Understanding* (Cornell University Press, Ithaca, NY, 1972).
——"What is said", in *Understanding Understanding*.

5

A guide to naturalizing semantics

BARRY LOEWER

Semantic predicates – *is true, refers, is about, has the truth-conditional content that p* – are applicable both to natural-language expressions and to mental states. For example, both the sentence "The cat is crying" and the belief that the cat is crying are about the cat and possess the truth-conditional content that the cat is crying. It is widely thought that the semantic properties of natural-language expressions are derived from the semantic properties of mental states.[1] According to one version of this view, the sentence "The cat is crying" obtains its truth conditions from conventions governing its use, especially its being used to express the thought that the cat is crying. These conventions are themselves explained in terms of the beliefs, intentions, and so forth of English speakers.[2] In the following I will assume that some such view is correct and concentrate on the semantic properties of mental states.[3]

In virtue of what do mental states possess *their* semantic properties? What makes it the case that a particular mental state is about the cat and has the truth conditions that the cat is crying? The answer cannot be the same as for natural-language expressions, since the conventions that ground the latter's semantic properties are explained in terms of the semantic properties of mental states. If there is an answer, that is, if semantic properties are real and are not fundamental, then it must be that they are instantiated in virtue of the instantiation of certain non-semantic properties. Recently a number of philosophers, whom I will call "Semantic Naturalizers," have attempted to answer this question in a way that they take to be compatible with *Naturalism*. Naturalism's central contention is that everything there is, every individual, property, law, causal relation, and so on is ontologically dependent on natural individuals, properties, and so forth. It is not easy or straightforward to spell out the notion of ontological dependence; but for the purposes of this discussion I will understand it as including the claim that for each instantiation of property M there are instantiations of natural properties and relations, P, P*, . . . , that together with natural laws and causal relations among the P instantiations *metaphysically* entail M's instantiation. This characterization is intended to capture the idea that M is instantiated *in virtue of* the P instantiations. Or, to put it metaphorically, Naturalism is the thesis that for God to create our world He needed only to have created the naturalistic entities and laws. Everything else follows from these.[4]

Naturalists are seldom explicit concerning exactly which properties are the natural ones. Their working account is that the natural properties are those expressed by predicates appropriately definable in terms of predicates that occur in true theories of the natural sciences.[5] Most contemporary naturalists think that all natural-science properties are identical to, or are exemplified in virtue of the exemplification of, fundamental physical properties. These are the properties that occur in laws of fundamental physics. This version of naturalism is physicalism; all God needed to do to create our world is to create the physical properties and laws and set the physical initial conditions. Whether or not they accept physicalism, Semantic Naturalizers assume that certain modal notions, specifically law, causation, and probability, are naturalistically respectable. Whether these notions can be grounded in contemporary physics (or physics and the other natural sciences), or even whether they may presuppose semantic concepts, is not without controversy. Of course, if these notions presuppose semantic notions then they cannot form the basis for a physicalistic or naturalistic reduction of semantics. At best one would have a metaphysical reduction of semantics.[6] Since this issue is seldom addressed by Semantic Naturalizers, and discussing it would involve us in controversial issues in metaphysics, I will, for the most part, ignore it in the following.

Semantic Naturalism is a *metaphysical* doctrine about the status of semantic properties.[7] Semantic Naturalizers also endorse an *epistemic* thesis that I will call "perspicuous semantic naturalism." It is the view that, at least in some cases, the metaphysical connections between naturalistic and semantic properties are sufficiently systematic and transparent to allow us to see that certain naturalistic conditions are sufficient for certain semantic properties. If Semantic Naturalizers can find naturalistic conditions that are metaphysically sufficient for semantic properties, and know that they have found such conditions, they would show how semantic naturalism can be true and thus place the semantic within the natural order. This Guide reviews recent naturalization proposals and the prospects of the naturalization project.

Although Naturalism in something like the above sense is widely endorsed in contemporary philosophy, there is also an active tradition that is inhospitable to semantic naturalism. Adherents to this tradition think that semantic and natural properties are so radically different from each other as to preclude the former from holding in virtue of the latter. Two lines of thought have been especially influential in this regard. One is that semantic properties are essentially normative. A putative example is that it is constitutive of the concept *cat* that it ought to be applied only to cats. Further, it is claimed, such essential normativity cannot be accounted for in purely naturalistic terms.[8] The second line of thought is that the principles that govern the attribution of semantic predicates lead to the indeterminacy of the semantic attributions even given all possible relevant evidence. For example, given all of a person's verbal dispositions (the supposed totality of relevant evidence), principles of attribution license alternative assignments of truth conditions and references to that person's sentences and terms. It is a verificationist step, but perhaps one that is not inappropriate in this case, to the conclusion that there is no fact of the matter (within the range of indeterminacy) concerning reference and truth conditions.[9]

There is not a philosophical consensus concerning how far, if any distance at all, these considerations go in undermining semantic naturalism. However, any adequate account of semantic properties will need to account both for the normativity that content properties possess and for the determinacy of reference and truth conditions. We will see these issues coming up in various ways in our survey of naturalistic theories.

But first we should note the consequences if semantic naturalism is false. Those who believe that it is false respond in two ways. One is to claim that there are no semantic properties (or that they are never instantiated). This view, Semantic Eliminativism (Churchland, 1981), thus preserves naturalism at the expense of semantics. The other response is to claim that there are semantic properties but they are metaphysically independent of natural properties. This view, Semantic Dualism (Davidson, 1982, esp. pp. 207–24, 245–60, McDowell, 1994), thus preserves semantics at the expense of naturalism. Neither option is very pretty. Eliminativism strikes some philosophers as self-refuting (Boghossian, 1990) and others (Fodor, 1987) merely as obviously false in light of the success of folk-psychological and cognitive-science explanations that employ semantic concepts.[10] Semantic dualism seems incompatible with semantic properties playing a genuine causal role in producing behavior. If, as is widely believed, the natural sciences are causally complete, then there seems to be no room for causation (of physical effects) in virtue of properties metaphysically independent of natural properties (Papineau, 1993, Loewer, 1995). So the situation seems to be that while there are reasons to worry that semantic naturalism might be false, there are also reasons to doubt the alternatives. The semantic naturalist will resolve this paradox if he can produce a naturalization of semantic properties. That would be enough to quell doubts concerning semantic naturalism, since we would then know that the gap between the semantic and the natural can be bridged.

The mental states that have been the focus of naturalization proposals are the propositional attitudes: desire, belief, and perception (perceptual belief) (see Chapter 9, PROPOSITIONAL ATTITUDES). There are two parts to naturalizing a particular kind of propositional attitude. First is the specifying of natural facts in virtue of which it is an attitude of that particular type, such as a belief or a desire. Second is the specifying of the natural facts in virtue of which it has its semantic properties, such as its particular truth conditional content. With regard to the first part, the view held by most semantic naturalizers is that the property of being a particular kind of attitude, such as being a belief, is a *functional* property (Fodor, 1987). Functional properties are higher-level properties instantiated by an individual x in virtue of x (or x's parts) and other entities instantiating lower-level properties that are lawfully or causally related to each other in certain specified ways.

Most semantic naturalizers also think that the property of being a belief (or other propositional attitude) involves an internal mental representation, and that this representation bears the state's semantic properties.[11] On this view, for example, the belief that the cat is crying involves a relation to an internal representation that has the truth-conditional content that the cat is crying. Some semantic naturalizers further propose that mental representations are elements in a *language* of thought, "Mentalese."[12] On this view, complex mental representations are composed of names, predicates, logical particles, and so on, arranged in syntactic structures. Naturalizing the semantics of Mentalese consists in specifying the natural facts in virtue of which simple Mentalese expressions possess their semantic properties, and then showing how the semantic properties of complex expressions are determined by their structure and the semantic properties of their constituents (Field, 1972 and 1978). While not every Semantic Naturalizer buys the language of thought hypothesis, it will often be convenient to presuppose it in what follows.

There are two conceptions of semantic content that have figured in recent discussions of naturalizing content, called "broad content" and "narrow content." "Broad content" refers to the usual truth-conditional content of intentional mental states. Hilary Putnam (1975) posed thought experiments that have been taken to show that the usual truth-conditional content of certain thoughts fails to supervene on the thinker's intrinsic physical properties. Putnam imagined two people, Oscar and twin-Oscar, who are identical with respect to their intrinsic neurophysiological properties, but who differ in the following ways. Oscar lives on Earth and speaks English. Twin-Oscar lives on a twin-Earth and speaks twin-English. The primary difference between earth and twin-earth is that on the latter planet the liquid that fills the oceans, that quenches thirst, and so on is not H_2O but XYZ, a chemical compound indistinguishable from H_2O without chemical analysis. Putnam claims that Oscar's and twin-Oscar's utterances of "water is . . ." and the thoughts that each expresses with the sentence differ in their truth conditions. Oscar's thought is true iff H_2O is . . . and twin-Oscar's thought is true iff XYZ is. . . . If this is correct, then intentional properties, at least in some cases, do not supervene on intrinsic neurophysiological properties or any properties that supervene on them (such as computational or syntactic properties). This view, *semantic externalism*, is now widely held for thoughts that involve natural-kind concepts like *water*.

"Narrow content" is a term introduced to designate content properties that do supervene on intrinsic neurophysiological properties (Fodor, 1981 and 1987). While Oscar and twin-Oscar's thoughts differ in broad content, they agree in narrow content. Some philosophers (Fodor, 1987) have argued that only narrow-content properties are implicated in intentional causation, and for this reason are required by an intentional science; but there is little agreement concerning exactly how to characterize it, or even whether there are such properties (Stalnaker, 1991). In any case, most of the naturalization proposals concern broad properties, specifically reference and truth-conditional content, so that will be our focus here.

What naturalistic facts are plausible candidates to serve as metaphysically sufficient for the semantic properties of mental representations? Putnam's twin-Earth thought experiments and Kripke's well-known theory of proper names (Kripke, 1972) both suggest that causal relations are involved in determining the references of predicates and names (see Chapter 21, REFERENCE AND NECESSITY, section 4). Their considerations seem to carry over to mental representations corresponding to predicates and names. It is plausible that Oscar's mental representation "water" refers to H_2O partly in virtue of the fact that H_2O has caused or is apt to cause Oscar to think water thoughts. And it is also plausible that part of the account of what makes a person's mental representation "Aristotle" refer to Aristotle is that it possesses a causal history that originates with a baptism of Aristotle. Neither Putnam nor Kripke are sympathetic to the naturalization project, but their work is often taken as the starting-point for naturalistic proposals. Causation and kindred notions like law, counterfactuals, and probability seem to be the "right stuff," if there is right stuff, out of which to try to build naturalistic accounts of intentionality.[13]

The crude causal theory

I will begin our survey of specific naturalization proposals with the crude causal theory (CCT) for the reference of Mentalese predicates f. No one has ever held the CCT, but it will be useful to describe it and note its most obvious defects, since these are the problems that more sophisticated accounts are designed to solve.

(CCT) It is metaphysically necessary that (if tokens of f are caused by and only by instances of the property F then f refers to F).

The obvious problem with the CCT is that it doesn't allow for the possibility of tokening f or a sentence containing f that is not caused by F. This is called "the problem of error," since if f occurs as part of the perceptual belief that x is a f, then since f is caused by F it follows that the belief is true. But of course, a perceptual belief, such as the belief that x is a cat, may be caused by a small dog, not by a cat. The problem of error is a special case of the disjunction problem. The CCT implies that whether or not f is a component of a belief the disjunction of all the causes of f's tokens are the reference of f; so if f is caused by cats, small dogs, utterances of "cat," and so on, then CCT says that f refers to the property of being a cat or a small dog or an utterance of "cat" and so on. Clearly many of the causes of f need not be included within what it refers to. A naturalist successor to the CCT will need to find some way of naturalistically distinguishing the reference constituting causes from the others.

A second problem is that semantic relations are apparently more fine-grained than causal relations. This is the "fine-grainedness problem:" f may refer to F and not G even though F and G are metaphysically or nomologically co-instantiated. For example, the properties of being triangular and of being trilateral are apparently distinct, but necessarily co-instantiated. Triangular things cause tokens of f just in case trilateral things do, but a predicate can refer to one property but not the other. Quine (1960) pointed out a pervasive type of property co-instantiation. When and only when the property of being a rabbit is instantiated, so is the property of being an undetached rabbit part. When one of these properties is causally linked to f, so is the other. This makes it quite difficult to see how a causal theory can account for the difference between thinking that 'there goes a rabbit' and thinking 'there goes an undetached rabbit part'.

Dretske's information-theoretic account

Fred Dretske (1981) proposed a close relative of the CCT that identifies the truth conditions of a belief state with part of the information that the state carries under certain circumstances. The notion of information can be defined this way: state type T carries information of type p iff there is a nomological or counterfactual regularity (perhaps a *ceteris paribus* law) to the effect that if a T occurs p obtains.[14] So, for example, the height of mercury in a thermometer carries information about the ambient temperature. Dretske's idea is to construct the content of beliefs out of the information that they carry under certain circumstances. An initial and crude formulation of the theory is:

(DRET) It is metaphysically necessary that (if B carries the information that p then B has the truth condition that p).[15]

Versions of both the fine-grainedness and the error problem cause trouble for DRET. If B carries the information p and p implies q then it also carries the information that q. But, of course, one can believe that p without believing that q, even though p implies q. Dretske responds to this problem by identifying the content of a belief with the *maximal* information that it carries under certain circumstances. This is a little progress, but it leaves untouched the problem that if p and q are nomologically or metaphysically co-occurring then any state that carries information that p carries the information that q. So according to DRET, no belief can have the exact content that there is a rabbit, since any state that carries the information that there is a rabbit also carries the information that there is an undetached rabbit part. Notice that it is of no avail to protest that a given believer might not even have the concept *undetached*, since that doesn't affect the fact that his belief-state still carries the information that there is an undetached rabbit part. Dretske's attempts to handle this problem are not successful.[16]

The error problem arises for DRET in this way. According to DRET, the belief that p always carries the information that p, which means that whenever the belief is tokened it is true. Dretske's proposal for solving the error problem is to identify a subclass of the actual tokenings of B as the bearers of the information that constitutes B's truth-conditions. Tokens of B outside of this class have the same truth-conditional content as those within the class, although they may not carry the same information. This permits (but doesn't obligate) the latter tokens to be false. Dretske's initial specification of the class of tokens of the belief state that fix its truth-conditional content is the class of tokens that occur and are reinforced during what he calls "the learning period." His idea is that during this period a type of mental state becomes a reliable indicator of p, and so comes to have the content that p. So Dretske's official account is

(DRET*) It is metaphysically necessary that (if the maximal information carried by B during the learning period is p then any instance of B has the truth condition p).

DRET* allows for errors, but its naturalistic credentials are questionable. The trouble is that *learning* seems to be a semantic notion. Dretske may think that it is possible to characterize the learning period non-semantically, but he can't just take this for granted. In any case, even if the learning period could be characterized naturalistically, the account is implausible, at least for some beliefs. There are some beliefs that are learned in circumstances in which the information they carry is not the belief's content. For example, when a child learns to token a belief with a content about tigers by seeing pictures of tigers, her belief-states carry information about pictures, although their content is about tigers. Dretske's account will end up assigning the wrong truth-conditional contents to these beliefs.[17]

Optimal conditions accounts

A different way of specifying a belief's content is in terms of the information it would carry under epistemically optimal conditions (Stampe, 1977, Stalnaker, 1984, and Fodor, 1990). The core idea of this approach is that there is a class of beliefs for which there are conditions – the epistemically optimal conditions – under which a person has the belief just in case it is true.

(OPT) It is metaphysically necessary that (if B is a belief of kind K then there are epistemically optimal conditions C_B such that B's truth condition is p if, were C_B the case, then B would nomologically covary with p).

So, for example, if for subject A there is a belief state B, that under optimal conditions covaries with the presence of a red ball located in front of her, then B's content is that there is a red ball in front of A. In this case appropriate optimal conditions are that A's eyes are open, she is attending to what she sees, the lighting is good, and so on.

OPT allows for errors, since tokens of B that don't occur in epistemically optimal conditions need not be true. It also seems to supply truth-conditions with normative force, at least if epistemically optimality is a normative notion. But, like Dretske's theory, its specification of the meaning constituting conditions is not naturalistic. "Epistemically optimal" is clearly an intentional predicate. It is not at all clear that epistemically optimal conditions can be specified without reference to semantic notions. Different conditions are "optimal" for different beliefs. For example, epistemically optimal conditions for the perceptual belief that there is a red ball in the room include good lighting; but optimal conditions for the belief that there is a firefly in the room is that the lights are off. This example makes it obvious that the optimal conditions for acquiring true beliefs depends on the belief's content. Of course the naturalizer cannot appeal to the content of a belief in characterizing optimal conditions.

Not only are epistemically optimal conditions for a belief sensitive to the belief's content, but for most beliefs, if they possess optimal conditions at all, these conditions involve other beliefs. Whether or not a person's belief-state reliably covaries with a state of affairs depends on what other beliefs that person has. For example, a person who fails to believe that fossils are derived from once-living organisms, or who believes that the earth is 6,000 years old, will not reliably form beliefs about the age of a fossil. If there are optimal conditions for forming beliefs concerning the age of fossils, those conditions will involve having certain beliefs and not having certain other beliefs. To assume that optimal conditions can be characterized naturalistically looks as though it begs the naturalization problem rather than solving it.[18]

Teleological theories

Teleological theories propose to explain the truth-conditional content of mental states, especially certain desires and beliefs, in terms of their biological functions. A crude teleological theory (CTT) for belief is:

(CTT) It is metaphysically necessary that (if O is an organism and B is one of its belief states and it is B's biological function to carry the information that p then B has the truth conditions that p).[19]

The concept of a biological function is defined in terms of natural selection (Wright, 1973, Neander, 1991) along the following lines: it is the function of biological system S in members of species s to F iff S was selected by natural selection because it Fs.[20] S was selected by natural selection because it Fs just in case S would not have been present (to the extent it is) among members of s had it not increased fitness (that is, the capacity to produce progeny) in the ancestors of members of s.[21] So CTT says that if B was selected because it carried the information that p, then B has the truth condition that p.

CTT is naturalistic and allows for error. In fact, it is compatible with almost all tokens of B being false, since all that is required is that B was selected because it carried the information that constitutes its content; and that could be so even if most past and no present tokens of B are true. It also seems to supply truth-conditional content with normativity. Just as a heart ought to pump blood, B ought to be tokened only if it carries the information that p. There are, however, a number of problems with CTT. One is that it directly applies only to beliefs composed out of innate concepts, since only beliefs involving innate concepts could possess a biological function. Perhaps the notion of biological function can be extended beyond features selected by natural selection; but that remains to be seen. A second, and more worrying problem, is that it either fails to assign determinate contents or assigns contents that are much too thick-grained to be the truth-conditions of beliefs. This problem has been discussed mostly with respect to the belief, or proto-belief, of animals, especially a frog's (the hope being that extension to a human's will come when the bugs are worked out).

Suppose that B is an internal state of a frog that is responsive to stimuli and that controls the frog's snapping behavior. Tokens of the state B in the frog's ancestors generally carried a great deal of information including: that flies are present, that small moving black things are present, that food is present, and so on. Furthermore, since these various conditions were reliably co-instantiated in the environment in which the frog evolved, they are all equally good candidates to be the information that it is the function of B to carry. So CTT implies either that B's content is indeterminate among components of the package or that its content is the whole package of information.

It is not clear whether this is an objection to teleological accounts, since it is not clear what beliefs or desires, if any, frogs have. But it is an objection if teleological accounts are incapable of delivering more fine-grained contents than the one they apparently attribute to the frog. More elaborate theories of content that promise to solve this problem are due to Millikan (1984, 1986, and 1989) and Papineau (1993). Both accounts, especially Millikan's, are rather elaborate. Here I will just briefly sketch Papineau's approach.

(PAPB) If D is a desire and B a belief and p is the (minimal?) state of affairs whose obtaining guarantees that actions based on B and D satisfy D then B has the truth-condition p.

If we suppose that the frog desires to catch a fly, and that this desire together with B lead to his snapping, then B's truth-conditional content is the minimal state of affairs that will guarantee that snapping will result in catching a fly. In this case it is a belief with something like the content *if I snap then I will catch a fly.* Of course, PAPB is not naturalistic, since it appeals to the concept of satisfying a desire and that is a semantic concept. Papineau attempts to remedy this by providing a naturalistic account of the contents of desires.

(PAPD) If q is the minimal state of affairs such that it is the biological function of D is to operate in concert with beliefs to bring about q then D is the desire that q.

Papineau's idea is that if the desire of type D was selected because it contributed by acting in concert with beliefs to bringing about q, then q is D's content. Let's suppose that the content of A's desire D is that she eats an apple. On a particular occasion D (together with beliefs) may cause the moving of A's hand, A's eating an apple, A's eating a fruit, and A's being nourished. Papineau suggests that the moving of the hand (to grasp the apple) isn't among D's functions, since there are occasions when D was selected (A's ancestors who possessed D had increased fitness, or D was reinforced in A) even though D didn't cause their hands to move. On the other hand, Papineau supposes that whenever D was selected D ate an apple, ate a fruit, was nourished, and so on. He suggests that the most specific of these features of the behavior which led to D's being selected is D's content; that is, eating an apple.

There are a number of worries that one might have concerning Papineau's account. One is that it applies, at best, only to certain beliefs and desires. PAPB provides contents only to means–ends beliefs (although Papineau suggests how the account can be extended to other beliefs). Many desires could not have been selected for by natural selection, since they are desires that possess impossible satisfaction-conditions, or desires for situations that have never obtained, or have obtained too recently to be selected. It is hard to see how the desire to not have any children (or the desire that no-one has any children) could have been selected for on the basis of bringing about its content. Perhaps these objections are not all that damaging if PAPD is intended just as a sufficient condition that applies to a certain class of desires. But then we will need a naturalistic specification of that class of desires. More damaging to PAPD is that possessing the function of bringing about x is not a sufficient condition for D's being the desire to bring about x. Suppose that D is the desire to eat an apple. It is compatible with this that there have been occasions when D led not to apple-eating but to pear-eating (some ancestors of A mistook pears for apples). It is plausible that eating pears (pears being as nutritious as apples) led to increased fitness, in which case D's function is to cause (together with beliefs) eating apples or pears. PAPD yield the result, contrary to our assumption, that D is the desire to eat apples or pears. There seems to be no reason why a desire could not have as its function causing, together with beliefs, some situation that differs from its content. If PAPD is incorrect then PAPB, even if it is correct, is no longer adequate as a naturalization of belief.

It is plausible that the human cognitive system contains subsystems that have the functions of producing states that bring about certain effects, and producing other states that carry certain information (and work in concert with the first kind of state to produce effects). But there is no reason to suppose that these states are individuated exactly in the same way that beliefs and desires are. Truth-conditional content seems much more determinate and fine-grained than anything that teleology is capable of delivering. This is made obvious by considering that there cannot be any selectional advantage for creatures whose beliefs are about rabbits over those whose beliefs are about undetached rabbit parts; yet our contents are so fine-grained as to distinguish these belief-states.

Fodor's asymmetric dependence theory

Fodor (1990b) proposed a variant of the causal (or informational) account that is intended to be a naturalization of the reference of a simple Mentalese predicate. It appeals to the idea that the meaning-constituting causes are those which, in a sense to be soon explained, are resilient. It will simplify exposition of his theory to define two technical notions. The law $Q \rightarrow C$ (Qs cause Cs) *asymmetrically depends* on the law $P \rightarrow C$ just in case if Ps didn't cause Cs then Qs would not cause Cs but if Qs didn't cause Cs then Ps would still cause Cs. *C locks onto P* just in case (1) it is a law that Ps cause Cs, (2) there are Qs (= Ps) that cause Cs, and (3) for any $Q \neq P$, if Qs cause Cs then Qs causing Cs asymmetrically depends on Ps causing Cs.[22] If C locks onto P then $P \rightarrow C$ is resilient in that it survives the breaking of $Q \rightarrow C$ for Qs other than P. Fodor's proposal, then, is:

(ADT) It is metaphysically necessary that (if C locks onto P then C refers to P).

Suppose that it is a law that cows cause "Cow"s (or rather the word's Mentalese counterpart), that other things also cause "Cow"s, and that such causal relations asymmetrically depend on the 'cow → "Cow" ' law. Then, according to ADT, "Cow" refers to cow. ADT handles the error and disjunction problems this way. Horses on a dark night can cause "Cow"s even though the horses on dark nights are not among the reference-constituting causes of "Cow;" that is, the law that horses on a dark night → "Cow"s depends on the law that cows → "Cow"s. If a horse caused "Cow" is a constituent of the belief "There is a cow," then the belief is false. Of course, this account of error is correct only if ADT is correct. If ADT is not correct then it may count some erroneous beliefs as true, or some true beliefs as erroneous.

Fodor provides some commentary along with the theory that helps to understand it. One point is that the law connecting a property to a predicate that refers to it is a *ceteris paribus* law. That is, it holds only as long as certain unspecified conditions obtain. Presumably this means that only under certain kinds of circumstances do cows actually cause A's mental representation "Cow." Presumably these conditions are that cows are perceptually salient to A, A's perceptual system is in good working order, and so on. A second point involves the dependence relation between causal laws. Sometimes Fodor says that it is a basic relation among laws that cannot be explained in other terms. But sometimes he explains it in terms of counterfactuals; Q → C depends on P → C just in case if P → C had not obtained then neither would Q → C have obtained. Fodor insists that the counterfactual be understood *synchronically*, not *diachronically*. If A learned to recognize cows on the basis of pictures of cows, then it may be that cow → "Cow" depends diachronically on cow-picture → "Cow." That is, it is true that if there hadn't been causal connection between pictures of cows and A's "Cow"s, there wouldn't be a connection between cows and A's "Cow"s. But Fodor thinks that synchronic dependence goes in the opposite direction. Once A has acquired "Cow" then cow → "Cow" is more resilient than cow-picture → "Cow." A third point is that the account of reference is *atomic*. By this is meant that it is metaphysically possible for A's Mentalese predicate C to lock onto P, even if C bears no inferential or causal relations to any of A's other symbols, or even if A's Mentalese vocabulary contains only the predicate C. Fodor welcomes this surprising feature of his account, since he thinks that there are reasons to hold that inferential or causal relations among thoughts are not constitutive of the thought's semantic properties (Fodor and Lepore, 1992).

There are two questions that need answers to evaluate Fodor's theory. First, is it genuinely naturalistic? And, secondly, is C locking onto P really a sufficient condition for C's referring to P? Answering these questions is made difficult by the fact that the central notions in Fodor's account – *ceteris paribus* laws and asymmetric dependence between laws – are technical notions that are not clearly defined.

There are two places to worry whether ADT is genuinely naturalistic. First, supposing that it is a law that P → C then it is reasonable to believe that its *ceteris paribus* conditions include having and not having certain other intentional states.

We noticed a similar point in our discussion of optimal-conditions theories. Does this make P →C non-naturalistic? Not necessarily. If the fact that P →C is a law is naturalistically reducible, then it too is a naturalistic fact. But do we have any reason other than the belief that semantic naturalism is true to think that P →C is naturalistically reducible?

Second, and more worrying, is whether the dependency relations that Fodor requires are naturalistic. These dependency relations are not themselves the subject of any natural science; so Fodor cannot claim, as the teleosemanticist does, that he is explaining a semantic notion in terms of a scientifically respectable notion, that is, a biological function. Further, it is not obvious that the synchronic counterfactuals that Fodor appeals to when explaining asymmetric dependence have truth-conditions that can be specified non-intentionally. Why is Fodor so certain that the counterfactual (synchronically construed) *if cow → "Cow" were broken then cow-picture → "Cow" would also be broken* is true? Perhaps if the first law were to fail "Cow" would change its reference to cow-picture and so the second law would still obtain. If so, then while "Cow" refers to 'cow,' ADT would say that it refers to 'cow-picture.'[23] Fodor cannot respond by saying that in understanding asymmetric dependence the counterfactual should be understood as holding the actual reference of "Cow" fixed, since that would be introducing a semantic concept into the explanation of asymmetric dependence. I do not think that these points show that ADT is not naturalistic; but they do show that the burden is on Fodor to argue for the naturalistic credentials of the dependency relation. Fodor sometimes seems tempted to just take the dependency relation to be metaphysically primitive and declare that it is part of the natural order (Fodor, 1991). One could see some irony in calling on such elaborate metaphysical notions to defend scientific naturalism.

Is the fact that C locks onto P sufficient for C to refer to P? It is difficult to answer this question without having a clear characterization of asymmetric dependence. The intrepid philosopher who thinks that she has devised a counter-example to ADT runs the risk of being told by its inventor that she has gotten the dependency relations wrong. There are a number of such putative counter-examples in the literature (Baker, 1991, Boghossian, 1991, Adams and Aizawa, 1994, Gates, 1995) and answers to the counter-examples by Fodor (1991, 1994).[24] Instead of going into the details of these objections I will sketch two general worries about the account.

We attribute propositional attitudes to one another on the basis of folk-psychological generalizations and general information about what people tend to believe, desire, and so forth under certain circumstances. So, for example, if A is a normal human being looking at a cow 100 feet away, then we expect A to believe that there is a cow in front of her. If, in fact, there is not a cow but a cleverly made cardboard cow-façade, then we expect A to at first believe that there is a cow, but that when she moves closer to the cardboard cow and examines it she will cease to believe that there is a cow. Our ability to attribute beliefs, desires, and so on to each other depends, at least in part, on generalizations like these. When testing a theory of intentionality we appeal to such generalizations. We ask whether it is possible for the putative naturalistic sufficient condition for A's believing that p to be satisfied while our folk-psychological generalizations give the result that A doesn't believe that p. The problem I see with ADT is not that there are clear cases in which C locks onto P, but C fails to refer to P; it is rather that, as far as I can see, ADT doesn't engage folk psychology. For all we know, an assignment of beliefs to A employing ADT and an assignment employing the usual folk-psychological principles may diverge radically. I am not arguing that they must or do diverge, but that Fodor has provided no reason to think they don't. The worry isn't an idle one, since it is not at all clear what asymmetric dependence has to do with our folk-psychological principles of belief-attribution. If ADT is to carry conviction we need some account of why it is that the contents it assigns will match those assigned by folk psychology.[25]

The second problem is the familiar one of the inscrutability of reference that seems to bedevil all naturalistic theories. If cow → "Cow"s is a law, then so is undetached-cow-part → "Cow" (and laws involving various other properties metaphysically co-instantiated with cow: Quine, 1960). Neither one of these putative laws asymmetrically depends on the other since they hold in exactly the same possible worlds. So it looks like if a predicate locks onto any property it either locks onto all those properties that are metaphysically co-instantiated, or onto the disjunction of all these properties (Gates, 1995).

One response to the problem is to declare that properties like undetached-cow-part, temporal state of a cow, and so on are not eligible to enter into laws and causal relations. Without a naturalistic justification of this claim the response is another instance of borrowing from metaphysics to buy naturalism. Fodor, to his credit, has not taken this route, but has suggested an addition to ADT to cope with the problem (Fodor, 1994). He argues that the inferential relations among sentences containing the predicate "Cow" will differ (for a thinker whose Mentalese contains the truth-functional connectives) depending on whether "Cow" refers to cow or to undetached cow part. By adding further conditions on the inferential relations borne by sentences to each other, he proposes to specify sufficient conditions for "Cow" to refer to cow (and no other property). The account is too complex to deal with in detail here. I will just say that, at best, Fodor's proposal excludes some properties from being the references of "Cow," but fails to single out cow as the unique reference.

Causal-role semantics

Causal-role (aka "conceptual role" and "inferential role") semantics (CRS) is another approach to naturalizing semantics that deserves mention, albeit only a brief one here. The mention is brief because although causal-role semantics has been in the air for some time (Sellars, 1974, Harman, 1982, Field, 1978, Loar, 1981, and Block, 1986) no-one has actually proposed a CRS that is naturalistic and assigns specific truth-conditions to mental states or representations. The basic idea of CRS is that the semantic properties of a mental representation are partially constituted by certain causal or inferential relations between that and other mental representations. If only causal relations among mental representations are taken into account, then at best CRS is an account of narrow content. To turn it into an account of broad content, causal relations between mental representations and external items need to be added.

CRS should be distinguished from theories of interpretation like Davidson's (1984) that also ground truth-conditions in causal relations among mental representations (or natural-language representations) and external events. Davidson's theory of radical interpretation places constraints on the contents of a person's propositional attitudes. The most important one is that a correct theory of interpretation should assign mostly true beliefs. But the account is not a naturalization, since the semantic concept *truth* is used in formulating the constraint. (On Davidson's theory, see further Chapter 8, RADICAL INTERPRETATION.)

The immediate difficulty with CRS is that most of the actual causal roles of a person's sentence A do not seem necessary for it to possess its truth conditions. For example, A's Mentalese sentences "There is a cat" and "There is an animal" might have their usual truth-conditions even though A has no disposition to infer the latter from the former. Given externalism, CRS cannot adequately specify sufficient conditions for a sentence to possess particular truth-conditions solely in terms of its causal connections to other sentences. It will also need to invoke causal connections with external items. But this brings it back to the problem of specifying exactly which causal connections are content-constituting. CRS has made no distinctive contribution to answering this question naturalistically. The prospects for a naturalized CRS do not look good (Fodor and Lepore, 1992).

CRS seems to fare better as an account of what makes it the case that logical expressions possess their meanings. For example, it is plausible that dispositions to infer S from S#R, and to infer S#R from the pair of premisses S and R, are relevant to making it the case that "#" is conjunction. But elaborating this into a naturalistic sufficient condition of "#" to be conjunction is not completely straightforward. The most obvious difficulty is characterizing those causal relations that count as *inferences* without appealing to *truth*.

Conclusion

None of the naturalization proposals currently on offer are successful. We have seen a pattern to their failure. Theories that are clearly naturalistic (such as CCT) fail to account for essential features of semantic properties, especially the possibility of error and the fine-grainedness of content. Where these theories are sufficiently explicit we have seen that they are subject to counter-examples. In attempting to avoid counter-examples, semantic naturalists place restrictions on the reference (or truth-condition) constituting causes or information. But in avoiding counter-examples these accounts bring in, either obviously or surreptitiously, semantic and intentional notions, and so fail to be naturalistic.

Of course, the failure of naturalization proposals to date does not mean that a successful naturalization will not be produced tomorrow. But another possibility, and one that philosophers have recently begun to take seriously (such as McGinn,

1993), is that while semantic naturalism is true, we may not be able to discover naturalistic conditions that we can *know* are sufficient for semantic properties; that is, perspicuous semantic naturalism may be false. It may be that the naturalistic conditions that are sufficient for semantic properties are too complicated or too unsystematic for us to be able to see that they are sufficient. Or, it may be that there is something about the nature of semantic concepts that blocks a clear view of how the properties they express can be instantiated in virtue of the instantiation of natural properties. This position, though it may be correct, is not by itself intellectually satisfying. The least we would like to know is exactly why we cannot know which natural properties are sufficient for semantic properties.[26] As of now, we don't know whether semantic naturalism is true and, if it is true, we don't know whether we can know, of any particular proposed naturalization, that it is correct; though, as we have seen, we can know of some that they are incorrect.[27]

Notes

1 Proponents of this view include Grice (1957), Lewis (1969), and Fodor (1975). For a contrary view see Davidson (1984), who holds that mental and public language semantic properties are interdependent, and that neither is metaphysically prior to the other.

2 The program of accounting for the semantic properties of natural language in terms of those of mental states is identified with Paul Grice (1957) and Stephen Schiffer (1972). A detailed account in terms of conventions can be found in Lewis (1969). See also Chapter 3, INTENTION AND CONVENTION.

3 So in the following, "semantic property" means semantic property of an intentional mental state or event.

4 The proposition that Fx is metaphysically entailed by conditions K just in case K together with a characterization of the nature of F logically imply Fx. The best-understood example of this is the realization of a functional property F by lower-level property instantiations. In this case it logically follows from the functional nature of F, the nature of the Ps and causal relations among the Ps that whenever the Ps are instantiated M is also instantiated.

5 This characterization is vague with respect to what counts as an appropriate definition, as a property, and the natural sciences. Removing the vagueness raises a number of problems that would take us too far afield to discuss.

6 Hilary Putnam (see e.g. 1992) has long maintained that causal and nomological concepts are inextricably bound up with intentionality, and for this reason attempting to naturalize semantics is a misconceived project.

7 Although it is a metaphysical doctrine, it is also contingent, since its truth doesn't rule out possible worlds in which some properties are instantiated but not in virtue of the instantiations of natural properties.

8 There are two issues that are often mentioned by those who think that normativity considerations derail semantic naturalism. One is that grasping a concept involves being in a mental state that obligates one to applying the concept only to items in its extension. It is difficult to see how any purely natural state can entail such an obligation (Kripke, 1982 and Boghossian, 1989; see also Chapter 15, RULE-FOLLOWING, OBJECTIV-

ITY AND MEANING). The other consideration is the claim that the attribution of intentional concepts is constrained by normative principles of rationality and charity (see Chapter 8, RADICAL INTERPRETATION). Davidson (1980, 1984) starts with this claim and tries to fashion it into an argument against the existence of nomic connections between intentional and non-intentional properties. There is little agreement about exactly what Davidson's argument is or even whether its conclusion conflicts with naturalism. Even so it has been influential, and is often cited or repeated by those skeptical of naturalization (McDowell, 1994).

9 Quine's (1960) arguments for the indeterminacy of translation and for the inscrutability of reference, and Putnam's (1978) so-called "model theoretic argument" are instances of this line of thought (see Chapter 16, THE INDETERMINACY OF TRANSLATION, and Chapter 17, PUTNAM'S MODEL-THEORETIC ARGUMENT AGAINST METAPHYSICAL REALISM).

10 A sophisticated version of eliminativism maintains that robust semantic properties don't exist (or are uninstantiated) but that deflationary semantic predicates can be used to specify reference and truth conditions. A robust semantic property is a property that may enter into causal explanations and exists independently of our concepts and definitions. In contrast, a deflationary truth predicate, "DT", for a language L is defined by providing a list of the conditions under which the predicate applies; e.g. "Snow is white" is DT iff snow is white; "Snow is green" is DT iff snow is green; etc. More generally (p)("p" is DT iff p) where the quantifier is substitutional. An important feature of DT is that, unlike robust truth, it applies only to the language for which it is defined. There is no reason to suppose that items in the extension of a deflationary predicate have anything, in particular causal and explanatory powers, in common. It seems to follow that deflationary semantic notions cannot be employed in causal explanations or play an explanatory role in an intentional cognitive science. The attraction of deflationism (the view that the only instantiated semantic predicates are deflationary ones) is that it both allows us to use semantic predicates for certain purposes (e.g. for infinite conjunction and disjunction) and is compatible with Naturalism. Skepticism concerning deflationism arises from the worry that deflationary truth and reference are too thin to do the work that we want done by semantic concepts. For recent discussion see Horwich (1990) and Field (1986 and 1994).

11 Proponents of this view usually distinguish between explicit and implicit propositional attitudes. Only the former involve relations to mental representations. The latter are dispositions to produce explicit attitudes (Fodor, 1987, ch. 1).

12 Field (1978) and Fodor (1975 and 1987) are important sources of this view. Fodor proposes it as an empirical hypothesis that provides the best explanation of certain features of human thought, specifically systematicity and the capacity to engage in logical reasoning.

13 Causation, laws, counterfactuals, etc. are not themselves items mentioned in physics, and it is controversial whether they supervene on physical facts. Even so, Fodor and other naturalizers would consider it a successful naturalization if they could show that intentional properties supervene on these properties. However, Putnam (1992) has complained that notions of law and causation presuppose intentional notions. While this may be true on some accounts of these notions, it is not true on others. For example, on some accounts probabilities are rational degrees of belief. Obviously, explaining semantic properties of beliefs in terms of degrees of belief would not contribute to naturalization. On other accounts probabilities are objective, mind-independent features of the world. In this case there seems to be no danger of circularity, though one

may wonder at employing so metaphysical a notion in the cause of naturalism. However, these issues are too complicated to develop here.

14 Dretske (1981) characterizes information in terms of probabilistic relations. There are numerous problems with his account that are avoided by the characterization used here. Also see Loewer (1987).

15 Dretske's formulation characterizes belief functionally as states that guide behavior in certain ways. He doesn't commit himself to a language of thought account of beliefs.

16 This is forcefully argued in Gates (1995).

17 Dretske (1988) suggests a teleological characterization of the state tokens whose information fixes the beliefs content. His basic idea is that those instances of the belief state that produces behavior that is reinforced are the ones whose informational content fixes the belief's semantic content. While this is a naturalistic characterization of the class, it is questionable whether it assigns appropriate contents. It is easy to imagine situations in which a false token of a belief produces behavior that is reinforced. For further discussion of Dretske's theory see Loewer (1987) and McLaughlin (1993).

18 This point is developed in Loewer (1987) and more thoroughly in Boghossian (1991).

19 Some teleological accounts employ a more general characterization of informational account. S carries the information that p iff $P(p/S \text{ occurs}) > P(p/S \text{ doesn't occur})$.

20 Selection by conditioning (i.e. by reinforcement) also figures in accounts of function devised by some teleosemanticists (Dretske, 1988).

21 For example, the biological function of the heart is to pump blood (not to make a thumping sound) since it is that property of pumping blood (not making a thumping sound) that accounts via natural selection for the presence of hearts. Notice that something may have the function to F even if it doesn't F or seldom Fs. It should be noted that it doesn't follow that every biological sytem that does something useful has that as its function (or that it has any function). Only those things that a system does that lead to an increase in fitness are its functions. So, for example, it is not obvious that e.g. certain cognitive abilities are the product of any function.

22 Fodor sometimes also adds the requirement that the law $P \rightarrow C$ is instantiated. This is supposed to give the result that Oscar's Mentalese "water" refers to H_2O and twin-Oscar's Mentalese "water" refers to XYZ. However, this addition may not be needed if the dependency relations concerning laws involving Oscar's and twin-Oscar's mental expressions are different.

23 Boghossian (1991) argues that locking on is either not sufficient for reference or is not naturalistic. His argument shows that to get the counterfactuals that underlie the locking-on relation to come out right, the similarity relation relative to which they are evaluated must take into account *semantic similarities.*

24 One of Boghossian's counter-examples to Fodor's theory is particularly persuasive. He imagines a natural kind concept K and laws $X \rightarrow K$ and $Y \rightarrow K$ where X and Y are different substances that are nomologically indistinguishable by us (they behave differently only in black holes). It may then be that neither of these laws asymmetrically depend on the other. Fodor's theory would have the consequence that K refers to the disjunction X v Y. But surely in the imagined situation K might refer only to X in virtue of the role it plays in physical theory.

25 This point is developed at length in different ways by Carl Gillett and Andrew Milne in dissertations at Rutgers.

26 Boghossian (1990) argues that belief holism (the fact that which situations are apt to

cause one to acquire a particular belief depends on one's other beliefs) prevents us from certifying that any naturalistic condition on content-constituting causes or information is correct.

27 I am grateful to Paul Boghossian, Jerry Fodor, Gary Gates, Carl Gillett and Fritz Warfield for helpful discussion and (not always heeded) advice.

References and further reading

Adams, F. and Aizawa, K. (1994), "Fodorian semantics", in *Mental Representation*, ed. Stich and Warfield. Oxford: Blackwell, pp. 223–42.

Baker, L. (1991), "Has content been naturalized?", in Loewer and Rey (1991), pp. 17–32.

Block, N. (1986), "Advertisement for a semantics for psychology", in *Studies in the Philosophy of Mind*, eds. P. French, T. Uehling and H. Wettstein. *Midwest Studies in Philosophy*, 10. Minneapolis: University of Minnesota Press.

Boghossian, P. (1989), "The rule following considerations", *Mind* 83, pp. 507–49.

——(1990), "The status of content", *Philosophical Review* 99, pp. 157–84.

——(1991), "Naturalizing content", in Loewer and Rey (1991), pp. 65–86.

Churchland, P. (1981), "Eliminative materialism and the propositional attitudes", *Journal of Philosophy* 78, pp. 67–90.

Davidson, D. (1980), *Essays on Actions and Events*. Oxford: Clarendon Press.

——(1984), *Inquiries into Truth and Interpretation*. Oxford: Clarendon Press.

Dretske, F. (1981), *Knowledge and the Flow of Information*. Cambridge, Mass.: MIT Press.

——(1988), *Explaining Behavior*. Cambridge, Mass.: MIT Press.

Field, H. (1972), "Tarski's theory of truth", *Journal of Philosophy* 69, pp. 347–75.

——(1977), "Logic, meaning, and conceptual role", *Journal of Philosophy* 74, pp. 379–409.

——(1978), "Mental representation", *Erkenntnis* 13, pp. 9–61.

——(1986), "The deflationary conception of truth", in *Fact, Science, and Value*, eds G. McDonald and C. Wright. Oxford: Blackwell, pp. 55–117.

——(1994), "Deflationist views of meaning and content", *Mind* 103, pp. 249–85.

Fodor, J. (1975), *The Language of Thought*. New York: Thomas Y. Cromwell.

——(1981), "Methodological solipsism", in *Representations: philosophical essays on the foundations of cognitive science*. Brighton: Harvester.

——(1987), *Psychosemantics: the problem of meaning in the philosophy of mind*. Cambridge, Mass.: MIT Press.

——(1990a), "Psychosemantics, or where do truth conditions come from", in *Mind and Cognition*, ed. W. Lycan. Oxford: Blackwell, pp. 312–38.

——(1990b), *A Theory of Content and Other Essays*. Cambridge, Mass.: MIT Press.

——(1991), "Replies", in Loewer and Rey (1991), pp. 255–319.

——(1994), *The Elm and the Expert*. Cambridge, Mass.: MIT Press.

——and Lepore, E. (1992), *Holism: a shopper's guide*. Oxford: Blackwell.

Gates, Gary (1995), "The price of information", forthcoming in *Synthese*.

Grice, P. (1957), "Meaning", *Philosophical Review* 66, pp. 377–88.

Harman, G. (1982), "Conceptual role semantics", *Notre Dame Journal of Formal Logic* 23, pp. 242–56.

Horwich, P. (1990), *Truth*. Oxford: Blackwell.

Kim, J. (1993), *Supervenience and Mind*. Cambridge: Cambridge University Press.

Kripke, S. (1972), *Naming and Necessity*. Cambridge, Mass.: Harvard University Press.

——(1982), *Wittgenstein on Rules and Private Language*. Cambridge, Mass.: Harvard University Press.

Lewis, D. (1969), *Convention*. Cambridge, Mass.: Harvard University Press.

Loar, B. (1981), *Mind and Meaning*. Cambridge: Cambridge University Press.

Loewer, B. (1987), "From information to intentionality", *Synthese* 70, pp. 287–317. Reprinted in Stich and Warfield (1994).

——(1995), "An argument for strong supervenience", in *New Essays on Supervenience*, ed. E. Savellos. Cambridge: Cambridge University Press, pp. 218–25.

——and Rey, G. (1991), *Meaning in Mind: Fodor and his Critics*. Oxford: Blackwell.

McDowell, J. (1994), *The Mind and the World*. Cambridge, Mass.: Harvard University Press.

McGinn, C. (1982), "The structure of content", in *Thought and Object*, ed. A. Woodfield. Oxford: Oxford University Press.

——(1993), *Problems in Philosophy: The Limits of Inquiry*. Oxford: Blackwell.

McLaughlin, B., ed. (1993), *Dretske and his Critics*. Oxford: Blackwell.

Millikan, R. (1984), *Language, Thought, and Other Biological Categories*. Cambridge, Mass.: MIT Press.

——(1986), "Thoughts without laws; cognitive science with content", *Philosophical Review* 95, pp. 47–80.

——(1989), "Biosemantics", *Journal of Philosophy* 86, pp. 281–97. Reprinted in Stich and Warfield (1994).

——(1991), *White Queen Psychology and Other Essays for Alice*. Cambridge, Mass.: MIT Press.

Neander, K. (1991), "Functions as selected effects: the conceptual analyst's defense", *Philosophy of Science* 58, pp. 169–84.

——(1995), "Misrepresentation and malfunction", *Philosophical Studies*, 79, pp. 109–41.

Papineau, D. (1993), *Philosophical Naturalism*. Oxford: Blackwell.

Pietroski, P. (1993), "Intentionality and teleological error", *Pacific Philosophical Quarterly*, 73, pp. 267–82.

Putnam, H. (1975), *Mind Language and Reality (Philosophical Papers Vol. 2)*. Cambridge: Cambridge University Press.

——(1978), *Meaning and the Moral Sciences*. London: Routledge and Kegan Paul.

——(1992), *Renewing Philosophy*. Cambridge, Mass.: Harvard University Press.

Quine, W.V. (1960), *Word and Object*. Cambridge, Mass.: MIT Press.

Schiffer, S. (1972), *Meaning*. Oxford: Oxford University Press.

Sellars, W. (1974), "Meaning as functional classification", *Synthese* 61, pp. 64–79.

Stampe, D. (1977), "Towards a theory of linguistic representation", *Midwest Studies in Philosophy* 2, pp. 42–63.

Stalnaker, R. (1984), *Inquiry*. Cambridge, Mass.: MIT Press.

——(1991), "Semantics for the language of thought", in Loewer and Rey (1991), pp. 229–37.

Stich, S. and Warfield, T. (1994), *Mental Representation*. Oxford: Blackwell.

Wright, L. (1973), "Functions", *Philosophical Review*, 84, pp. 139–68.

6

Meaning and privacy

EDWARD CRAIG

1 Introduction: the two questions and their consequences

It has been widely held that certain states of sentient creatures are private, in the technical sense that their nature cannot be known by anyone other than the subject who experiences them. For instance, the phenomenal quality of perceptual states has often been seen in this light. "I know you call that colour by the same name, but I can't know whether you see it in the same way as I do" is a position familiar to most students of philosophy, both amateur and professional. Involved, clearly, are issues in both the philosophy of mind and epistemology, but it is not the purpose of this chapter to go into these in depth; for the moment the reader should assume – or at least be prepared to entertain the hypothesis – that there are indeed states which are private in the sense defined. We may call them epistemically private items (EPI).

A general question arises about the role, if any, of such EPI in the meaning of language. A highly influential tradition makes the meaning of a word depend on the nature of the "idea" associated with it, whilst treating ideas as items before the consciousness of speakers and their hearers, hence as strong candidates for epistemic privacy. Much recent argument, on the other hand, denies that the epistemically private can have any such part to play, and that it is precisely the fact of its privacy that rules it out of semantics.

The debate thus broadly characterized focuses not on one question, however, but two, close enough to be conflated by the unwary, yet quite different enough for all hope of clarity to be gone if they are not carefully distinguished. One concerns the semantics of the "public" language, the one in which we communicate, or apparently succeed in communicating, with each other; the other is the notorious question about the possibility of a "private" language, that is to say a language used by a person for the sole purpose of communicating with their own (later) self, and in principle unusable for communication with anybody else. We shall have to ask

(1) whether the nature of our EPI affects, or can affect, the semantics of a natural language used for inter-personal communication,
(2) whether there can be a private language, in which a person records facts about their EPI for their own later information.

The content of the first of these questions is easy enough to grasp, even if the arguments that are brought to bear on it may be less so. But a "private" language sounds like a highly artificial construction, and a little time must therefore be spent inquiring just what such a language is supposed to be.

The *locus classicus* is Ludwig Wittgenstein's *Philosophical Investigations* § 243:

> The words of this language are to refer to what can only be known to the person speaking; to his immediate private sensations. So another person cannot understand the language.

As an introduction to the concept of a private language this passage is not without its difficulties. The first sentence appears to commit itself to at least a limited scepticism about the contents of other minds, though it is probably better read as a definition of the concept of privacy, with the plausible assumption added that if there is anything private in this sense, the phenomenal quality of states of consciousness will be so. The second sentence implicitly brings in another assumption: that A can understand B only if he *knows* the nature of the objects B is referring to. We shall later see that this is open to question, with the result that it may make a difference whether we take "private language" to be defined by the first sentence of the quotation or the second. By no means all the literature on the topic pays due attention to this possibility.

Since the assimilation of Wittgenstein's *Philosophical Investigations* (1953) it has been common, indeed almost standard, to answer both questions in the negative: EPI have no role to play in the semantics of any public language; and there can be no such thing as a private language. Moritz Schlick, in a series of lectures delivered in London in 1932, in effect had made both these claims. More recently Michael Dummett (Dummett, 1973) has offered reasons in favour of the negative thesis about EPI and public language; the extent to which these arguments are new, and the extent to which they reformulate or adapt points from earlier literature, will be considered in what follows.

The two questions have not, in the main, been pursued for their own sakes, but rather because negative answers to them have been thought to entail important consequences in the philosophy of mind, the theory of knowledge and metaphysics.

One major question affected, bridging the first two of these areas, is that of scepticism about knowledge of other minds – which dissolves as unstatable if the answer to (2) is negative. Another, obviously central to the philosophy of mind, is that of the true meanings of prima facie EPI-words, which is obviously much affected by a "No" to (1).

(It might be thought that (1) was capable of resolving or dissolving scepticism about other minds without the assistance of (2). For if those ("private") aspects of our mental states on which the sceptic may with good prospects focus attention have no effect on what any word of our common language means, it would seem to follow that we cannot say anything to each other about those aspects, hence cannot pose the question of whether they are the same in others as they are in ourselves. But this overlooks the fact that, without a negative answer to (2), it still remains a possibility that each of us can formulate for ourselves the question "Are their EPI like mine?", and then doubt whether we can know the answer.)

In epistemology, a "No" to (2) poses problems for those "foundationalist" theories which purport to ground knowledge on beliefs about items that might be taken to be EPI; also for doctrines which "analyse" propositions about the prima facie public into propositions about the prima facie private, such as phenomenalism. It could be said that so long as (2) only speaks of what can/cannot be *said*, it doesn't affect these doctrines (which only require assumptions about what can be *thought*); but – apart from the fact that the implied distinction between being sayable and being thinkable may prove troublesome – one must consider that we shall find arguments being deployed against a private language which attack the notion of thought about one's EPI in the first instance, and language only derivatively.

Further (and more recently), the answer to (1) has been suggested (by Dummett) to be of critical importance in a central question of ontology: that of the debate between Realists and Anti-Realists. (See Chapter 12, REALISM AND ITS OPPOSITIONS.) A negative answer, in Dummett's view, leaves the Anti-Realist in the ascendant. Later on we shall briefly consider whether (1) really is central for the Realism *vs.* Anti-Realism debate.

2 Private states and public language: the possibility

Michael Dummett has denied that EPI can play any role in the semantics of the public language. For this view he advances a group of three closely related arguments, which we may call respectively the arguments from Communicability, from Acquisition and from Manifestation.

Suppose that what I mean by some expression of the public language is affected by the nature of certain states epistemically private to me. Then, argues Dummett, that expression has a meaning which I will not be able to communicate to anyone else. Because the states are private, nobody else can know their nature, hence neither can they know what I mean by that expression. Others do not understand it, therefore it is not, after all, an instrument of the public language, which is by definition a vehicle of interpersonal understanding.

The Argument from Acquisition asks us to consider the position of learners acquiring the use of a language, some of whose expressions depend for their meaning on the nature of their teachers' EPI. Since *ex hypothesi* this is something they cannot know, they cannot make the associations needed to know what the expressions mean; in other words, they cannot acquire a grasp of the language.

The Argument from Manifestation looks at the same situation from the point of view of those who, like the teacher, have to judge whether or not the learners now use the expressions of the language with the accepted meanings. But if these meanings are affected by speakers' EPI, there is nothing the learners can do to "manifest" their understanding, no way in which they can let the competent speaker know that they have learnt their lesson properly.[1]

In short, if EPI affect meaning, then what anyone means is unknowable to anyone else, and language cannot serve mutual understanding or communication.

Hence it is not a public language. Anyone who thinks that interpersonal communication is of the essence of language will be prepared to drop the word "public" from that sentence, and say that such a "language" is not a language, *tout court*; but so long as the possibility of a private language is undefeated we should stop at the narrower conclusion.[2]

It will be noted that all these arguments turn on the same point: if the meaning of other speakers' expressions depends on the nature of their EPI it cannot be known. They are thus very close relations of an argument that has frequently been directed at the classical empiricist theory of meaning. That theory equated meanings (and thoughts) with image-like items entertained before the mind's eye, that is to say with some of the strongest candidates for epistemic privacy; so it had the intolerable consequence that nobody could know what anyone else meant or thought.

The most direct approach to the arguments from Communicability, Acquisition and Manifestation will therefore be to ask two questions. First, is it true that if EPI have a role in semantics there can be no interpersonal knowledge of the meanings of the expressions in whose semantics they figure? Second, if that be so, how much does it matter? – is it the catastrophe that the arguments imply it to be, or can a supporter of EPI-semantics just take it in his stride?

The answer to the first question must be yes, since it follows straight from the definition of an EPI, given the principle that if A is an essential constituent of B, the nature of B can be known only if that of A is knowable too. But there is a complication which should be considered, if only to avoid being confused by it. This is the thought that until we have inspected the cases for and against scepticism about Other Minds, the traditional "Argument from Analogy" and the like, it must remain an open question whether we can know what someone else means, even if their meaning is determined, or partially determined, by their inner states.

In one respect the introduction of this thought at this point is just an irrelevance, for it is aimed not so much at the thesis that EPI can play no role in public-language semantics as at the question of whether there are any EPI at all, any facts about persons which are epistemically private in the defined sense. But in another respect, the matter of the *application* of the thesis rather than its internal logic, it is very much to the point, since it asks whether there is in fact anything at all about us which the thesis would, if true, exclude from semantics and pronounce incommunicable. We shall return to this later, though only briefly. Responses to scepticism about other minds are very varied, as are the conceptions of the mental which they trade upon or promote, so that a serious discussion of these possibilities would lead us too far away from our topic of the relation between private states and meaning.

So let us for the moment accept the obvious affirmative answer to our first question, and move to the second. One reason for announcing a catastrophe sufficient to discredit the position it follows from runs: Understanding someone is knowing what they mean. So if I don't know what you mean then I don't understand you. Hence any theory which makes the meaning of expressions of the public language dependent on EPI in effect denies that we understand each other when using these expressions; and that means that, by definition, they are not elements of the public language at all.

It may be doubted, however, whether understanding someone is necessarily to be equated with knowing what they mean. Accounts of the concept of knowledge vary, and some allow that knowledge exists where others deny it, so that any casual equation of understanding with knowledge of meaning needs more rigorous investigation. We may approach this, whilst keeping in touch with our main question, by considering the possible effects of what I shall call "Burke's Assumption":[3] we naturally assume that others have, in broadly similar external circumstances, broadly similar internal states. In so far as the latter are epistemically private there is no question of our knowing whether, or when, the assumption is true, but nevertheless it is one we all naturally make. Under exceptional circumstances (Fred can't see which traffic light is on, Mabel can't tell whether that is a trombone or a flute – whatever the incentive we offer them to get it right), we start to adjust our beliefs, but this is a departure from our first, firm inclinations. And let us assume further, that these assumptions are in fact mostly right.

Given Burke's Assumption, it will often be the case that speaker and hearer, teacher and pupil have the same, true beliefs about the qualities of each others' EPI; and hence there will no barrier in principle, and usually none in fact, to each arriving at the same, true beliefs about what the other means, even though their EPI affect their meaning. Is this enough for the operation of a public language in the semantics of which EPI have a role? And if it is enough, what of the assumptions that were necessary to allow us to reach this position?

To begin with the first question. We still have to admit that none of our speakers *knows* that the others mean what he takes them to mean. But this would not seem to prevent anyone from understanding anyone else. There is no particular reason to think that to understand correctly one must know that one understands correctly. And there seems to be no reason to deny that such true beliefs about the meanings that others attach to their expressions are enough to constitute understanding. After all, speakers will be expressing the thoughts that their hearers confidently take them to be expressing, and why should that be held to fall short of understanding them? They do not have any guarantee of mutual understanding, but why should there not be understanding without a guarantee?

Perhaps the objection is a rather different one, however. Whatever may or may not be required for understanding, it remains the case that we *do* know that we understand each other. And that rules out all theories which cast publicly unknowable items in any essential semantic role.

With this we are back at the point we touched on earlier, and the proponent of EPI-driven semantics has two lines of reply. One would be to adopt, at least as a defensive measure, some "externalist" account of knowledge such as reliabilism, and then point out that if we do make such assumptions as Burke suggested, and these assumptions are, in the main, correct, then our methods of coming to beliefs about other people's EPI are reliable, and the beliefs accordingly are knowledge; the supposed EPI aren't private after all. It still applies, admittedly, that if there are any states of persons about which others have no reliable ways of coming to true beliefs, then they really are EPI and can have no effect on the public language; but whether there are any, and if so which, becomes a very obscure and perhaps from the very nature of the case uninvestigatable question.

The trouble with this blocking response is that it relies on a particular, by no means uncontroversial, account of the concept of knowledge. And even if this account be accepted, the objector to EPI-semantics might well not agree that his worries had been adequately addressed. What the objector is really saying that there must surely be (quite independently of the correct analysis of "S knows that p", even if such a thing exists), is some good reason – something which we can see to be a good reason without needing to know already that the beliefs are true. And it is precisely this which there cannot be, with respect to our belief in mutual understanding, if EPI have any effect on meaning.

This argument will be as strong as the claim made by our objector, that there must be some reason (of an "internalist" kind) for this belief. How strong is that? Perhaps not very strong, for there is a plausible line of thought that sheds a good deal of doubt on it. Reaching a belief by reasoning to it from premises antecedently believed is a slow and uncertain process, easily thrown off course. Seeing that for practical purposes many beliefs are needed quickly, and with the degree of conviction necessary to give rise to immediate and decisive action, evolutionary development is not likely greatly to have favoured it over "blind", as it were mechanical methods of acquiring beliefs. Once a certain level of sophistication has been reached, the power of reasoning, used at the right time and place, may become a most valuable way of extending our stock of beliefs; but there are no grounds for thinking that it took much part in the beginnings of human mental activity when our basic types of belief and methods of forming them were being developed. What happened then was that we grew some successful psychological hardware. But that means that when we now consider some class of beliefs (such as those involved in Burke's Assumption), we are not entitled to *assume* that they must be retrospectively certifiable by any process of rational inference; they may turn out to be so, and then again they may not. And one thing we should certainly not do is think that they must be rationally certifiable just because we find them so convincing.

If allowed, this argument seriously weakens the claim that, since it would mean that in many cases we could give no good reason for thinking that we understand each other, EPI can have no part in semantics. For perhaps we can give no such reason. But some may think that the argument ought not to be allowed, after all. They can point to the unquestionable fact that there are many beliefs that we almost certainly would not have unless we could give reasons for them, and then they *may* be able to argue that the belief in mutual understanding is likely to be one of them. How to turn this possibility into a concrete proposal, however, is not obvious; and the present writer knows of no published attempt to do so.

Those who think that the nature of speakers' EPI may, without disaster, be assigned a role in the meaning of expressions of the public language thus seem to have the better of this phase of the argument, if only perhaps for the time being: at least until further arguments are brought, they can stave off the objection that their proposal puts our confidence in mutual understanding beyond the scope of rational support. But there is another, quite different line of attack against which they will also have to defend themselves.

The idea was to achieve mutual understanding, without banishing EPI from semantics, by relying on Burke's Assumption. More explicitly, we were to suppose that we all have a strong tendency to attribute to others EPI like our own under like circumstances, and that this tendency mostly leads us to true beliefs. The first type of objection focused on the *consequences* of this supposition, and turned on the question of whether they were unacceptably sceptical or not. The second type of objection is directed at Burke's Assumption itself: does it really make sense? Whether true or false, Burke's Assumption makes essential use of the notion of interpersonal comparison of inner states: we generally assume, it says, that those of others are similar to our own. It has been argued, however, and in more than one way, that this notion is in fact incoherent.

One such line of argument comes, unsurprisingly, from verificationism. Any doctrine which links meaningfulness at all closely to verifiability, whatever may be the exact nature of the link, is bound to find difficulty in alleged comparisons between the EPI of different persons. For since no subject can, in principle, have knowledge of both terms, any such comparison is as good an example of unverifiability-in-principle as can be found in a sentence that neither introduces "nonsense" vocabulary nor flouts any basic rule of grammar. If verificationism doesn't exclude this as meaningless, how could it exclude anything that we wouldn't all exclude anyway?

Nothing can safely be concluded from this, however. Notoriously, it proved extremely difficult even to formulate the verification principle in any way fully satisfactory to its proponents; so it is hardly surprising that the few published attempts to argue for its acceptance have turned out inconclusive. In any case, those likely to accept directly verificationist lines of thought are nowadays far fewer than was the case a generation ago. (See Chapter 2, MEANING, USE, VERIFICATION.) A much more fashionable assault on Burke's Assumption issues from Wittgenstein's discussion of rules and what it is to follow them.

Saul Kripke (1982) has offered an argument inspired by Wittgenstein's writings on rule-following, if not actually to be found in them. Suppose that a speaker uses a word on some occasion in the same way, that is to say with the same meaning, as he has used it on an earlier occasion. There must be something in virtue of which his present use of the word is consistent with previous uses (rather than having another, new meaning on this occasion). What could this something be? It cannot be either a publicly observable fact about him or his behaviour, or a fact about his inner mental state.[4] So it cannot be a fact solely about *him* at all, but must include something about the behaviour of other speakers of his community, to the effect that they would speak as he does in these circumstances, or regard his way of speaking as correct. The notion of sameness or consistency of meaning therefore demands the existence of some communal practice and is illusory without it.

If this be true (a very difficult buck which I here thankfully pass), then there is certainly a prima facie threat to the participation of EPI in semantics. I think we may take it that meaning is not a property of totally isolated utterances, but arises because expressions, and ways of combining them, are used consistently in accordance with specific rules. It follows that something can be a factor in the meaning of an expression only if it relates in a consistent way to the use of that expression, which means that, whatever it is, there must be a coherent notion of its being "the same thing again" or "another of the same sort". Is there any such notion where EPI are concerned? On the assumptions we are making about the outcome of the rule-following debate, that reduces to the question of whether, as regards the description of EPI, there is such a thing as communal agreed practice. And the temptation is to say no, precisely because they are private.

Before succumbing to it, however, there is a somewhat convoluted line of thought which we need to follow through. To start with, note that the principle about communal practice will surely have to be hypothetical in form, a matter of how others *would* describe something if they were well-placed to do so. Otherwise we invite the result that if some potholer is the only person ever to see a certain underground rock-formation, he cannot possibly describe it, either correctly or incorrectly. So perhaps our question should be not: how do others describe my EPI? but rather: how would others describe my EPI if they were well-placed to do so?

Now this might seem the right moment to say that others never are or could be well-placed to describe my EPI, precisely because they are private to me. So our conditional ("If others were well-placed . . .") isn't assessable, even in principle, and the original temptation beckons again. Easiest would be just to give in to it; but we shouldn't, because if Burke's Assumption is true, then we frequently are well-placed to describe other people's EPI. Perhaps we aren't *as well-placed as they are*, but why should that be necessary? For after all, the requirement we allowed ourselves to start from, provisionally accepting it as a consequence of the rule-following debate, was the need for "communal practice". It would be a further thing to demand that this communal practice be based on *knowledge* of the items being described. Whether it could be justified or not could only be settled by a detailed scrutiny of the arguments about rules; but since it has not been established uncontroversially that even our provisional assumption really does follow from them, the prospects for a yet stronger version specifying knowledge as an essential basis of the communal practice must be quite doubtful.

It appears likely, then, that this type of attack on Burke's Assumption merely begs the question; its pivotal claim, that no relevant communal practice exists, can be made only when it has *already* been shown that Burke's Assumption is false, or incoherent. The possibility that EPI may have a part to play in the semantics of a public language remains open.

Another line of attack begins with the arguments against the possibility of a private language. If these arguments show that we cannot communicate with ourselves (or perhaps it should be "our later selves") about our EPI, then surely *a fortiori* we cannot communicate with others? But even this question is cloudy. It was pointed out earlier that the *locus classicus*, Wittgenstein's *Philosophical Investigations* § 243, actually offers two definitions of a private language. Wittgenstein appears to have assumed that a language in which someone speaks of "what can only be known to the person speaking; . . . his immediate private sensations" would necessarily be one which others could not understand. But our argument so far suggests that this may well be mistaken, in which event the two definitions fall apart and clarity demands that we look at them and their consequences separately.

Fortunately we can quickly clear the air, at least to some extent. If a private language be defined as "a language which only one speaker can, in principle, understand", then its alleged impossibility can have no effect at all on the question of whether EPI can figure in the semantics of a language which many people can understand, *unless* we take it that such a language would refer to the speaker's EPI, and that that is the ultimate reason for its impossibility. Otherwise the notion of an epistemically private item will simply not get a foothold in the logic of the argument, and our investigation reaches a dead end. In effect, we find ourselves forced back to the definition of a private language in terms of EPI.

So: if a private language, understood as one in which speakers refer to their own EPI, had been shown to be impossible, wouldn't it follow that EPI had no role in the public language either? But still the mists won't disperse, because we have to answer that we can't yet say: it will depend on just why a private language is impossible. If the agreed reason is that for EPI there is no legitimate notion of "being the same" or "being of the same kind", then will this not affect the private and public questions equally?[5] Perhaps, but only if the reasons for declaring there to be no such notion apply to the public case as strongly as to the private case. If they are verificationist reasons, then surely they do; it is hard to imagine how interpersonal verification could be thought possible when intrapersonal verification was not. But what if they are reasons drawn from the rule-following debate, to the effect that meaningfulness calls for a social practice, in other words a multiplicity of speakers? Wouldn't they have force only against the private language, leaving the public language, where by definition there is more than one speaker, untouched?

If we find that last line of thought convincing, however, then that can only be because we are still conflating the two definitions of a private language. The definition we are now supposed to be concentrating on doesn't say anything about a private language having only one speaker; it defines a private language as one in which you refer to your own EPI. And the crucial point is that until our earlier arguments about understanding and Burke's Assumption have been decisively refuted, it remains possible that the public language may be a private language as well; for if the public language permits us to talk to each other about our EPI, then why not also to ourselves? The idea may sound paradoxical, but only if we are still caught up in the second half of Wittgenstein's unfortunate double definition, and so feel that a private language *must* be a language with only one speaker.

Contrary to much recent thought, then, it begins to seem quite possible that there are no conclusive reasons for banning EPI from the factors that can give expressions of the public language their meaning. But that only brings us to the next two questions: provisionally accepting that it is *permissible* to do so, should we ever *actually* involve EPI in our account of meaning? And what difference will it make if we do?

3 Private states and public language: the effects

The immediately obvious candidates for EPI-affected semantics are expressions which purport to describe sensations (like "itch" or "headache"), and those standing for properties at least plausibly thought of as powers to produce sensations of certain kinds (such as "red" or "shrill"). Here it is tempting to think that what a speaker means depends on the phenomenal quality of his experiences; and most people would take the view that, whereas there may be other examples, if there are to be any at all then these must be amongst them.

But even here there can seem to be two options. One is to give in happily to the temptation. The other is to stick to the idea that the function of the public language is the adjustment and coordination of behaviour, and that anything surplus to that, whatever its standing, is no part of linguistic meaning; so that provided we agree about what is to be called "red", stop at red lights, anticipate sweetness in red apples, we agree on the meaning of "red", and would do even if our respective visual experiences were quite different. Plenty that is epistemically private is going on, on this view, when we see red lights or have headaches; but whatever its significance for human life it doesn't affect the meanings of any of the expressions we use to talk to each other.

Coming at the present stage of the argument, however, this seems unmotivated. If we have already agreed that nothing bars EPI from playing a semantic role in principle, isn't it merely doctrinaire to insist that they never do so in fact? The restrictive view of the function of language described in the last paragraph has usually stemmed from a decision that only what is public can be of any import in semantics, and there is no obvious reason to stick to it if that decision is itself in doubt. Admittedly it is sometimes useful to distinguish between understanding a speaker's words and understanding the speaker, in the sense of knowing what it is like for them to be in the situation that their words describe: you may know exactly what is meant by my utterance "There's a snake coming towards me", whilst having no idea how I feel about it. But what principally makes the distinction useful in this case is that what I have said may be true *however* I feel about it; so it has no application to a case in which what I am doing is describing my feelings.

Anyone prepared to go this far, and to allow that private states may affect, indeed be objects of, public discourse, is already quite a long way away from what has become, since the *Philosophical Investigations*, more or less the standard position. But most recent interest in the question about the semantic role of private states arises from the belief, advocated by Michael Dummett, that a very deep and general metaphysical issue depends on it: whether it is permissible to take a realist view of the world.

That issue is naturally, if vaguely, understood in terms of the world's dependence on, or independence of, human styles of thought and methods of investigation. But Dummett would have it understood, at least in the first instance, as a question about the right form for a theory of meaning: should the meaning of a sentence ultimately be characterized in terms of its truth-conditions, or in terms of the conditions under which we regard it as assertible? We need not here concern ourselves with Dummett's reasons for recommending this question as a fruitful entrance to the debate about realism, but can concentrate on his view that a decision against any possible role for EPI promotes the "assertibility-conditions" approach to semantics. (See Chapter 12, REALISM AND ITS OPPOSITIONS.)

Grasp of meaning, once any part is denied to EPI, must consist in the capacity for some kind of publicly accessible behaviour. So argues Dummett, and he goes on to say what that behaviour must be: recognition of the circumstances under which the sentence can properly be asserted. We may think we understand sentences whose truth-conditions, if they obtain, we cannot recognize as obtaining. If so, we delude ourselves, since under those circumstances our understanding could not be manifested, but would have to consist in some epistemically private feature of our minds, in breach of the principle that EPI have no legitimate business in semantics. Assertibility-conditions, not truth-conditions, must therefore be primary in a theory of meaning.

This argument certainly has some force, once we accept the ban on the private from which it starts. But two corners have to be negotiated before it can be fully convincing, and they should at least be signposted here. First, we have to consider whether the explicit recognition of the fact that certain conditions obtain really is the *only* sufficient way of manifesting grasp of the meaning of a sentence. Secondly, it may be asked whether such "explicit" recognition really is as publicly accessible a phenomenon as the proposed use of it demands.

Neither question is easily resolved. The first is obscured by the point that manifestation must mean manifestation to someone, in this case other speakers of the relevant part of the language, which is to say other human beings familiar with the subject matter. But do we not then need to know in advance that we cannot entertain unverifiable thoughts? For if we can, may there not be numerous ways in which someone can manifest to others that he is thinking some such thought, and using a certain sentence to express it? If this is a thought we can entertain, perhaps we also have a shared pattern of reactions to it, a pattern that can signal to others that a speaker is indeed expressing it.

The second question raises the problem of the nature of intensional states. Recognizing something, in this case the obtaining of certain truth-conditions, is not just a matter of assenting *when* they obtain, but of doing so *because* they obtain, and because *they* obtain rather than because of some other conditions which accompany them. Thus the notion of recognition brings with it something which might be called the "perspective" of the subject who does the recognizing; and it is not obvious that this can be accounted for in terms restricted solely to publicly available features of the subject and the situation. Perhaps it can, but complex issues are involved.

So it should not be thought that anti-realism in the theory of meaning follows directly from the thesis that EPI can play no part in semantics. On the other hand, it would be just as bad a mistake to think that if that thesis is shown to be groundless we can at once help ourselves to meaning–theoretic realism. True, it would then have been shown that if we can entertain thoughts about states of affairs whose existence we could not in principle detect, those states of affairs could be the truth-conditions of sentences of a mutually understandable public language, regardless of whether entertaining such a thought called for the occurrence of certain private states. But we would still not have addressed the question of what it would be to think such a thought; nor would that question necessarily be any easier just because we were allowed to appeal to EPI in answering it.

4 The possibility of a private language

We now return to the second question broached at the beginning of this chapter: the possibility of a language in which a subject can, comprehensibly at any rate to himself, express thoughts about his own private states. This question is for historical reasons now inseparably connected with certain passages from Wittgenstein's *Philosophical Investigations*, and any treatment of it must take account of them; but they will be used here simply as the obvious door to the debate, and no attempt will be made to decide any of the trickier questions of Wittgensteinian exegesis.

It was remarked in Section 1 that Wittgenstein introduces the notion of a private language with a double definition; its words are to "refer to what can only be known to the speaker" (his "immediate private sensations") – and it is a language which no one else can understand. It will be obvious from Section 2 that I would wish to drop the second clause from consideration as causing far more trouble than it is worth. We shall concentrate on the idea of a language with terms that refer to a speaker's own EPI, and the crucial question is whether even the speaker himself could understand it, whether it really could be a language even for him.

But that way of putting it, though it has become standard, still does not reliably capture quite what most philosophers have had in mind when thinking about private language. What is essential is not so much the idea of terms that have the speaker's EPI for their *reference*, but rather of terms whose sense or meaning depends in some degree on the nature of the EPI of the person using them. It is, of course, true that some such terms, by virtue of their meaning, may well be usable to refer to the speaker's EPI; and is also true that Wittgenstein's most famous example is about the (purported) use of just such a term to record recurrences of a particular type of sensation.[6] Nevertheless, the wider formulation just suggested will serve us better. It covers more possibilities; it gives a closer parallel with the question about EPI and public-language semantics discussed in earlier sections; and the arguments of the private-language debate as actually conducted apply to it at least as well as they do to the version which, by following the standard translation of *Philosophical Investigations* § 243, makes the notion of reference sound primary.

All who argue the impossibility of a private language, and all those who defend private language against them, seem agreed on one central point: that meaningfulness requires the rule-governed, or at the very least consistent, use of a symbol; so that whatever it is about the use of a word which determines its meaning must be capable of *recurrence*, of being the *same again*. That principle has an obvious consequence for the words of a private language: epistemically private items, or those aspects of them which affect the meanings of the private vocabulary, must be the sort of thing which can repeat: it must be possible for there to be *another thing of that kind*. And this simple commitment is, according to various arguments, the Achilles' heel of the idea of a private language.

One such line of argument makes appeal to verificationism. Whether it is to be found in Wittgenstein is a matter of controversy, but there is little room for doubt that verificationism was at least one of the planks on which Schlick rested certain negative claims about private language (though he did not use that expression) in lectures given in London in 1932.[7] The critical question for him was, anticipatably, whether a colour seen today was of *the same* shade as one seen yesterday. What did it mean? That was to be determined, he said, by looking at the way in which an answer could be tested. So long as we were allowed to resort to such things as the opinions of other people, the persistence of the coloured object and the empirically determinable probability of its having changed colour, no special problem arose. But it was quite otherwise, Schlick held, in a case in which there was nothing to appeal to beyond the memory of the person making the judgement. In that case we should

> have to declare it impossible to distinguish between a trustworthy and a deceptive memory; we therefore could not even raise the question whether it was deceptive or not; there would be no sense in speaking of an "error" of our memory. . . . I recall it so, and that is final; in our supposed case I cannot go on asking: do I remember correctly? for I could not possibly explain what I meant by such a question.[8]

Not even in communication with oneself, Schlick concluded, can words convey the nature of a private experience.[9]

Now in so far as this argument rests on the principle that the meaning of a statement is its method of verification, few philosophers nowadays will rush to endorse it; even fewer in so far as it is felt to rest on an application of the "Picture Theory of Meaning".[10] And, as all readers of Wittgenstein will have recognized, the above passage bears a striking resemblance to parts of the *Philosophical Investigations*, striking enough to raise the question whether Wittgenstein really added anything new. But it is widely held that he did: that the *Investigations* contain an argument to the impossibility of a private language that makes no use of either the picture theory or of the verification principle.

This argument is usually located in § 258, where Wittgenstein asks how the user of the private language is to give meaning to its signs. An inward ostensive definition, with the attention concentrated on the relevant private item, will be just an idle ceremony of no semantic consequence unless it brings about consistent usage:

the "speaker" really does thereafter apply the sign correctly, that is to say in connection with EPI of *that* type. The trouble is that

> in the present case I have no criterion of correctness. One would like to say: whatever is going to seem right to me is right. And that only means that here we can't talk about "right".

In that event, Wittgenstein leaves us to conclude, there is no difference between a language and what merely seems to its "speaker" to be a language. And that only means that here we can't talk about a language. What vitiates private language is the collapse, in the case of EPI, of the distinction between "seems" and "is".

A distraction at this stage is the notion, introduced in § 258, of an ostensive definition. Earlier in the *Philosophical Investigations*[11] Wittgenstein discusses the business of giving meaning by ostension, arguing that its effectiveness depends on a great deal of cooperation from the recipient of the definition, who needs the right antecedent mental "set" if he is to discern what kind of thing is being pointed out as a example of the term. It is often suggested, not implausibly in view of §§ 257–8, that these thoughts about ostensive definition are part of Wittgenstein's weaponry against private language.

If they are, it is because, in Wittgenstein's opinion, ostensive definition can work only under conditions which the private linguist doesn't satisfy. Such at least seems to be the message of § 257: "a great deal of stage-setting in the language is presupposed". And the implication of the last sentence of the paragraph is that the stage-setting in this case has to come from the public language, in particular from its use of the word "pain".

This raises a little swarm of questions. In the first place, is what is at issue here the possibility of a private language as, following *Philosophical Investigations* § 243, we defined it earlier? Or is it rather the possibility of having a private language whilst not speaking any public language? For it looks as if the most that § 257 will show is the impossibility of the latter, and not of the former. (If the would-be private linguist does have the use of the word "pain" in public English, why should he not build on it a term designed to express the particular character of certain pains of his?)

Second, we should note that though ostensive definition calls for prior "stage-setting", it cannot always call for prior stage-setting *in a language*, since otherwise we could never get started. So the claim that our private linguist requires part of the public language as his stage, rather than just a particular mental set, needs special argument and shouldn't be accepted without it.

Thirdly, we should notice the way in which § 257 begins: we are to imagine a special situation, in which human beings have pains but show no outward signs of having them. Now it is quite reasonable to suppose that, under those circumstances, that part of the public vocabulary could not be taught, and so would not exist. So if there were good grounds to think that "stage-setting" of that kind would be necessary for the inner ostensive definition to work, then a private language might well turn out to be impossible. But that would have been shown to hold, we have to remember, only for the imaginary circumstances posited at the beginning of the paragraph. We could then react in two ways: we could either say that this shows nothing at all about the impossibility of a private language under the actual conditions of human life, or we could modify our understanding of what a private language is supposed to be.

The necessary modification would be to think of an EPI not just as something the nature of which could be known only to its experiencing subject, but to require also that there should be no outward sign of its occurrence. Such an extra load on the concept of an EPI would render the thesis that private language is impossible, weaker and very much less important. This can be seen by reflecting that it could be accepted by the most unreconstructed Cartesians, provided that they were prepared to say that some outwardly observable feature of the material body went along with every inward feature of the mental substance of the mind, and that they would not then have to alter their views about the nature of the mental in any way at all. It would therefore be much more to the point if we could show the impossibility of private language on the old, unrevised concept of the epistemically private.[12]

Back then to the argument from the collapse of the seems/is distinction. Why is it held to have collapsed? Why shouldn't whether this EPI of mine really is of the same kind as that of yesterday be one question, whether it seems to me to be the same another? One line, we have seen, is to say that the only way to verify an answer to the first question is to ask the second – and then conclude that the two questions can't, after all, be distinguished. No more about the verificationism of that argument; but it is worth asking whether its other premise ('the only way to verify an answer to the first question is to ask the second') is true.

It could be said that the only way to verify an answer to any question at all is to find out whether it seems to us to be the right answer. But for most questions that will be true only if "seeming to us to be the right answer" is allowed to describe the result of a complex procedure in which several avenues of inquiry lead us to the same point. (What we seem to see coincides with what we seem to hear, with what Fred and Mabel seem to be telling us, and with our memory of what is normal under the circumstances seeming to obtain, for instance.) It is this that gives the seems/is distinction content: it becomes possible that something might seem, by one investigative route, what it turned out (on the witness of the other routes) not to be. And what causes the trouble for the private linguist is that in the case of an EPI there is none of this complexity, only a once-and-for-all judgement, unanswerable to any further investigation, that it seems to be of the right kind. But is that true? Must all judgements about EPI have this "one-track", structureless character?

Some writers have thought not, but suggest that there is no reason of principle why EPI should not fall into patterns and exhibit regularities.[13] One might add that there is a powerful *de facto* reason why they should: since they are our perceptual states, they must exhibit all manner of regularities if we are to perceive a stable and regular world, as of course we do. And if so, there will be more than one question which the private linguist can ask when trying to decide whether a particular item was of a certain type or not. Besides just "Did it strike me as being of that type?", there is also "Did it seem to be accompanied by the items that usually – as it seems to me – accompany items of that type?" A response to this would have to take one of two courses: either to retreat, saying that the argument only applied to such EPI as don't fall into any such patterns, whilst allowing a private language to encompass all that do; or to argue that the existence of such patterns would have no tendency to reinstate the seems/is distinction.

If we are hoping for a robust version of the anti-private-language thesis, only the second option will be of much interest. Its proponents must tread carefully, lest their reasons for denying the seems/is distinction in the private case get out of hand and threaten the distinction for public objects, thus undermining public language as well. The threat is serious enough, since it might well be thought that the only thing that enables us to make a distinction at all between seeming to be and actually being is the existence of *various ways* in which a given proposition may seem to be true, so that we can think of being true as the concurrence of the different ways of seeming true.

Suppose, then, that this debate turns out in favour of the seems/is distinction for EPI and their properties. Would that reinstate private language? Not by itself. Perhaps two EPI of mine do each possess the feature F, but in order that my word W should apply to them both something else is needed: that W really is my word for F-ness. It is not enough that I do in fact utter W whenever this type of EPI occurs. (I may say "Ouch" whenever a certain type of EPI afflicts me; that does not make "Ouch" *mean* that sort of inner state.) Somehow, most likely to do with my intentions regarding it, I must have given the word W meaning. So: under what conditions can there be meaning, and stable intentions, and does the private linguist fulfil them?[14]

It can certainly be doubted. Saul Kripke (1982) ties the rejection of private language to Wittgenstein's views on following rules, drawing attention in particular to *Philosophical Investigations* § 201–2 and seeing it as an outcome of the material beginning around § 139. Here we are harking back, of course, to the position sketched in Section 2: meaning requires consistency of use, and consistency can be understood only against the background of communal practice. Therefore no facts about an isolated individual are sufficient to confer meaning; and isn't the speaker of a private language isolated in the relevant sense?

If we take a private language to be one which only its speaker can understand, presumably the answer is yes. But we have seen reason to ignore that part of Wittgenstein's double definition, and think of private language as defined by the epistemic privacy of the objects to which its terms refer. Then the question is less straightforward, since it seems possible (at least until Burke's Assumption can be refuted) that there may be communal linguistic practice relating to EPI; this because Burke's Assumption would allow us to have, and express, beliefs about the private states of others, even though we cannot *know* what these states are like. It will allow us to confirm, from our own impressions, others' statements about their EPI, even to reject their claims on occasion, at least where insincerity or inattention is suspected. So a private language still seems possible; indeed, it looks possible that the public language may also be a private one, in that each of us can use it for referring to their EPI.

Can it be countered at this stage that what we have just described does not count as a communal practice in the required sense, because the required sense demands a practice amongst (so to speak) epistemically equal partners? Without going further into the concept of epistemic equality, it does seem reasonable to agree that Burke's Assumption will not provide it; but will the argument from rule-following really justify the demand? After all, the practice described above is not a mere sham, in which one person makes a statement about their EPI and everyone else respectfully parrots it; the participants are making independent judgements, even if one of them has a favoured vantage point. The rule-following arguments are fascinating; they are also complex and controversial, and there must be some room for doubt as to whether they prove the necessity for a communal practice at all. To demand a proof of the need for a community of *epistemically equal* individuals is to impose a substantial further burden on them. Perhaps they can bear it; but that needs to be shown carefully and explicitly.

Two relatively minor points should be mentioned. Christopher Peacocke has proposed what he calls the "Discrimination Principle", claiming that it rules out private language.[15] He states it as follows:

> for each content a speaker may judge, there is an adequately individuating account of what makes it the case that he is judging that content rather than any other.[16]

If, then, p and q are different judgements, there must be something about the act of judging that p which distinguishes it from the act of judging that q. And there are propositions which the supporter of private language will have to claim it possible to judge, which, however, do not satisfy the Discrimination Principle with respect to some other proposition which he is committed to distinguishing from them.

We need not enter into the details of the argument. For whilst this approach may offer a *framework* for discussion of the possibility of a private language, or of many other issues, it cannot by itself settle anything. The Discrimination Principle is nothing but a special case of the trivial truth that if two things are different in respect of a certain property (in this case two judgements in respect of their content), then there is some difference between them relevant to the property in question. And from this nothing can follow as to which particular judgements are legitimate, which spurious, until we add some more substantial premises telling us which factors can be relevant to the content of a judgement. But that falls little short of saying: until we add a theory of meaning. The Discrimination Principle leaves everything still to be contested.

Finally, there is one early approach that can with some confidence be written off: the private-language argument is not, and never really has been, based on scepticism about the memory when exercised about previous EPI. A. J. Ayer (Ayer, 1954) appears to have taken it in this way, and consequently had little difficulty in disposing of it with the counter that reliance on memory was equally necessary for the verification of utterances in the public language. Certain it is that this line has no prospects whatever unless backed up by reasons for thinking memory especially fallible in the private case. And this is not what has been argued – not by Schlick, and not, on any plausible account of his intentions, by Wittgenstein. Their view was not that our memory is especially likely to fail us where the properties of past EPI are in question; it was, rather, that there are no genuine statements or thoughts, and hence nothing for the memory to report, whether truly or falsely, reliably or not.

Notes

1 For further discussion of these arguments, see Chapter 12, REALISM AND ITS OPPOSITIONS, § 2.

2 We can see already the need to treat the private-language question separately; for all the above arguments turn on the unknowability of an EPI by *others*, and so clearly do not apply to the case of a private language, where there are no others to be considered.

3 In Craig (1982) I called this "the assumption of uniformity". Readers should take it that only the ugly name has been changed. Edmund Burke wrote (1757, p. 13):

> We do and must suppose, that as the conformation of their organs are nearly, or altogether the same in all men, so the manner of perceiving external objects is in all men the same, or with little difference.

4 Here I just baldly state the next major lemma of the argument. Fuller discussion will be found elsewhere in this volume: see Chapter 15, RULE-FOLLOWING, OBJECTIVITY AND MEANING, section 2.

5 Given, that is, the assumption that meaningfulness always involves rules, so that whatever is relevant to meaning must be capable of playing the same role consistently.

6 See *Philosophical Investigations*, § 258.

7 See Schlick (1938), pp. 177–9.

8 Ibid., p. 179.

9 Schlick favours putting all this in terms of a distinction between "Form" and "Content", thus introducing complexities which I have here attempted to skirt round. His main thesis throughout this sequence of lectures is that language can convey only Form, never Content, and this he bases on a view of meaning not wholly unrelated to the notorious "Picture Theory" of Wittgenstein's *Tractatus Logico-Philosophicus*, to the effect that an utterance can only express a fact if it shares its Form. Some may like to read the lectures with this connection in mind.

10 See n. 9 above.

11 See *Philosophical Investigations*, § 28 and following.

12 It might be thought that the revision cannot be avoided, since only events which had no corresponding outward sign could be epistemically private in the original sense. But this seems wrong; the fact that an inner state has an externally observable correlate means that others have a clue as to when it is occurring, but that is far from saying that the outward sign is so revealing that they can know from it what the inner event is like.

13 See e.g. Harrison (1974), ch. 6, esp. § 37.

14 In this connection see Wright (1991).

15 Peacocke (1988), esp. pp. 491–3.
16 Ibid., p. 468.

Bibliography

Ayer, A.J. (1954), 'Could language be invented by a Robinson Crusoe?' *Proceedings of the Aristotelian Society*, Supplementary vol. 28, pp. 63–94. Also reprinted in Jones (1971), pp. 50–61.

Blackburn, S.W. (1984), 'The individual strikes back', in *Synthese* 58, pp. 281–301.

Burke, E. (1757; 1990 edn), *A Philosophical Enquiry into the Origin of our Ideas of the Sublime and Beautiful*. Oxford: Oxford University Press.

Craig, E.J. (1982), 'Meaning, use and privacy', *Mind* 91, pp. 541–64.

——(1986), 'Privacy and rule-following', in *Language, Mind and Logic*, ed. J. Butterfield. Cambridge: Cambridge University Press.

——(1991), 'Advice to philosophers: three new leaves to turn over', *Proceedings of the British Academy* 76, pp. 265–81.

Dummett, M.A.E. (1973), 'The philosophical basis of intuitionistic logic', reprinted in his *Truth and Other Enigmas*, London: Duckworth (1978), pp. 215–47.

Harrison, R. (1974), *On What There Must Be*. Oxford: Clarendon Press.

Jones, O.R. (ed.) (1971), *The Private Language Argument*. London: Macmillan.

Kripke, S. (1982), *Wittgenstein on Rules and Private Language*. Oxford: Basil Blackwell.

Peacocke, C. (1988), 'The limits of intelligibility: a post-verificationist proposal', *The Philosophical Review* 97, pp. 463–96.

Schlick, M. (1938), '*Form and content, an introduction, to philosophical thinking*', in *Gesammelte Aufsätze*. Vienna.

Wittgenstein, L. (1953), *Philosophical Investigations*, trans. G.E.M. Anscombe. Oxford: Basil Blackwell.

Wright, C.J.G. (1987), 'Introduction', in *Realism, Meaning and Truth*. Oxford: Blackwell, esp. pp. 13–23.

——(1991), 'Wittgenstein's Later Philosophy of Mind: Sensation, Privacy and Intention', in *Meaning Scepticism*, ed. Klaus Puhl. Berlin: Walter de Gruyter.

7

Tacit knowledge

ALEXANDER MILLER

1 Introduction

Competent speakers of a natural language know what the sentences of that language mean. A theory of meaning for a natural language, if correct, specifies what each well-formed declarative sentence of that language means.[1] Thus, the following question naturally suggests itself: what sort of relationship, if any, obtains between speakers of, and a correct theory of meaning for, a given natural language? In this paper I shall examine a number of answers that have been given in response to this question. In particular, I shall be considering whether any account of the relationship can provide an adequate justification for what has been an article of faith of those engaged in the construction of systematic theories of meaning for natural languages: the requirement that such theories be compositional. A theory of meaning is compositional if and only if (a) it has only finitely many proper (non-logical) axioms, and (b) each of the meaning-delivering theorems ("meaning-specifications") served up is generated from the axiomatic base in such a way that the semantic structure of the sentence concerned is thereby exhibited.[2]

What motivation is there for seeking compositional semantic theories in preference to their more readily available, non-compositional counterparts? Why should the construction of a semantic theory be constrained by the requirement that it reflect the semantic structure of the language concerned? As Crispin Wright notes, in a wide-ranging survey of these issues (1986; see also his 1980, Chapter 15, 1981, and 1988), the answer generally given to this question is that the construction of such theories is supposed to take us some way towards providing answers to each of the following three questions:

(1) How is it possible, given the finitude of their capacities, for speakers of a natural language to understand a potential infinity of sentences?
(2) How is it possible to *learn* a natural language?
(3) How is it possible to understand utterances of previously unencountered sentences?

In what follows I shall ignore (1), and look only at (2) and (3). It is not clear to me what the claim that speakers understand a potentially infinite number of sentences amounts to and, in any case, as we shall see, Gareth Evans makes it clear that the demand for compositionality in semantic theories has nothing essentially to do with this alleged "potential infinity": it can be levelled with equal force at theories dealing with languages containing only a finite number of possible sentences. I shall proceed as follows. I begin, in Section 2, with Michael Dummett's idea that answers to (2) and (3) might be facilitated if competent speakers of a natural language can be credited with *tacit knowledge* of the axiomatic base of a compositional theory of meaning for their language. I shall then explain that viewing tacit knowledge of semantic axioms as a bona fide propositional attitude-state is implausible, because a plausible constraint (outlined by Evans and Wright) on a state's being a propositional attitude is thereby violated. In Section 3 I examine Gareth Evans's suggestion that ascription of tacit knowledge of a semantic theory can be empirically well-founded, so long as we are clear that in ascribing it we are not ascribing a set of genuine propositional attitudes but only a set of *mere dispositions*, one for each primitive expression of the language, to the speaker. Crispin Wright has raised a number of objections against Evans's account, and in Section 4 I shall show that Evans's suggestion, as developed and modified by Martin Davies, has the resources to respond to those objections. Section 5 briefly looks at how the modified account can provide answers to questions (2) and (3) above. In Section 6 I argue that Wright's alternative to Davies's mirror constraint actually *presupposes* it. I finish, in Section 7, by considering whether the project of constructing semantic theories in accordance with the mirror constraint is in tension with Wittgenstein's reflections on rule-following.

2 Tacit knowledge and propositional attitudes

Dummett writes:

> A theory of meaning will, then, represent the practical ability possessed by a speaker as consisting in his grasp of a set of propositions; since the speaker derives his understanding of a sentence from the meanings of its component words, these propositions will most naturally form a deductively connected system. The knowledge of these propositions that is attributed to a speaker can only be an implicit knowledge. In general, it cannot be demanded of someone who has any given practical ability that he have more than an implicit knowledge of those propositions by means of which we give a theoretical representation of that ability. (Dummett, 1976, p. 70)

It is clear from this passage that tacit knowledge of a semantic theory's axiomatic base is taken by Dummett to be a species of knowledge: that the state of tacitly knowing an axiom of such a theory is taken to be a propositional attitude state, a state which represents the information codified in that axiom. As Wright comments,

> The explanatory ambitions of a theory of meaning would seem to be entirely dependent upon the permissibility of thinking of speakers of its object language as knowing the propositions which its axioms codify and of their deriving their understanding of (novel) sentences in a manner mirrored by the derivation, in the theory, of the appropriate theorems. (Wright, 1986, p. 207)

It is *tacit* knowledge because competent speakers will generally be unable to formulate the theory of meaning whose axiomatic base they tacitly know, and will generally be unable to recognize a correct formulation of the theory of meaning if it is presented to them. But for all that, it is still knowledge, and knowledge of propositions. It is easy to see how this contributes to answering (2) and (3) above. Say that a language L is learnable when it is possible for its speakers "to come to know the meanings of all the sentences of L by way of exposure and projection" (Davies, 1981, p. 60). Thus, we can say that a language is learnable when one needs explicit training with only a relatively small number of sentences in order to secure competence with a possibly very large set of sentences outwith that set. So we can see that to say that a language is learnable is just to say that speakers can understand novel utterances, without explicit training in their use. Question (2) collapses, therefore, for natural languages at any rate, into (3). And there is no problem for Dummett in answering (3): speakers can understand novel utterances because they have at their disposal the information, codified in their tacit knowledge of the theory of meaning for the relevant language, of the semantic properties of the sentence's parts. This tacit knowledge provides them with the resources for understanding the sentence, in the same way that the axioms of the theory of meaning provide the resources for the derivation of a meaning-specification for the relevant sentence.

There is, no doubt, much to be said about Dummett's idea. But for the rest of this section I want to focus on a set of arguments whose upshot is that, whatever tacit knowledge of the axiomatic base of a semantic theory is, it cannot be construed as a genuine propositional attitude or intentional state.

Evans and Wright have argued that there is a necessary condition which all genuine intentional states must satisfy to qualify as such, and that putative states of tacit knowledge of meaning-theoretic axioms do not satisfy this condition. In order to motivate this condition they ask us to contrast, on the one hand, the belief that a man might have to the effect that a certain substance is poisonous, with the disposition that a rat might have to avoid a similarly contaminated substance. Can we describe the rat as having a genuine belief that the substance is poisonous? Evans and Wright suggest not: for whereas in the case of the man the belief is, to use Evans's phrase, "at the service of many distinct projects", and can interact with others of his beliefs and desires to produce new beliefs and desires, none of this obtains in the case of the rat's disposition. In the case of the man, for instance, the belief could be at the service of projects such as killing an adversary, retaining good health or getting out of an obligation by taking a small dose, to name but a few. None of this is possible in the case of the rat: the putative "belief" is harnessed to the single "project" of avoidance of the substance. This is supposed to be a reflection of the fact that propositional attitudes and intentional states, such as beliefs and desires, come in *articulated systems* or *holistic networks*. And it is because genuine beliefs come in such networks and can thus interact with other beliefs, that they can indeed be at the service of many distinct projects. For example, the man's belief that the substance is poisonous can be at the service of the project of getting out of a particular obligation because that belief can, together with the beliefs that a small amount of the substance causes only a mild illness and that a mild illness will release him from the obligation, lead to the belief that taking a small amount of the substance will enable him to avoid fulfilling the obligation.

A crude version of the constraint suggested by the Evans–Wright discussion might therefore run as follows:

> *Constraint 1:* A state P of an agent W is a genuine propositional attitude or intentional state only if P can interact with others of W's propositional attitudes and intentional states to produce new propositional attitudes – thus putting P at the service of many distinct projects of the agent.[3]

Where does this leave the tacit knowledge a speaker might have of a meaning-theoretic axiom? Evans and Wright both claim that such a state of a speaker violates the constraint above. Far from being at the service of many distinct projects, the tacit knowledge is, says Evans,

> exclusively manifested in speaking and understanding a language; the information is not even potentially at the service of any other project of the agent, nor can it interact with any other beliefs of the agent (whether genuine beliefs or other "tacit" beliefs) to yield further beliefs. (Evans, 1981, p. 133)

While Wright puts it like this:

> The (implicit) knowledge of a meaning-theoretic *axiom* would seem to be harnessed to the single project of forming beliefs about the content of sentences which contain the expression, or exemplify the mode of construction, which it concerns.

He asks the following (rhetorical) question:

> What is supposed to be the role of *desire*? What is the (implicit?) desire which explains why the subject puts his axiomatic beliefs to just this use, and what are the different uses to which they might be put if his desires were different? (Wright, 1986, pp. 227–8)

No plausible answers to these questions suggest themselves, so the conclusion is that states of tacit knowledge of semantic axioms cannot plausibly be viewed as propositional attitudes. Evans appears to view the objection as applying to tacit knowledge *tout court*, that is, not only to states of tacit knowledge of axioms but also to states of tacit knowledge of meaning-theoretic *theorems*, which codify the rules governing the use of whole sentences. But Wright quite clearly sees the objection as applying only to tacit knowledge of the axioms; as he says, "someone who is credited with implicit knowledge of a meaning-delivering theorem may express his knowledge in an indefinite variety of ways, including, in appropriate contexts, lying, assent, and silence". So no reason emerges "to doubt the propriety of crediting [speakers] with implicit knowledge of the content of meaning-delivering theorems" (Wright, 1986, p. 227 and pp. 237–8). Thus, Wright's defence of genuinely intentional tacit knowledge of meaning-specifying theorems is in effect a claim that tacit knowledge of such theorems can be inferentially integrated with the rest of the agent's propositional attitudes in the manner required by Constraint 1.[4] But how can my semantic belief concerning the meaning of a given sentence interact with my propositional attitudes to give rise to new propositional attitudes? An example should suffice to convince us that this is indeed possible. I have a certain intentional state, the possession of which is constitutive of my understanding of the sentence "Catriona is getting married to Seamus on Saturday": this intentional state can interact with my belief that Catriona is getting married to Sean on Saturday to lead to the belief that the sentence "Catriona is getting married to Seamus on Saturday" is false; or it can interact with my desire to annoy Patrick (an unsuccessful suitor of Catriona's) to lead to the belief that I ought to utter "Catriona is getting married to Seamus" in Patrick's presence; and so on. Examples can quite easily be multiplied: this shows how the tacit knowledge of semantic theorems, unlike the tacit knowledge of semantic axioms, can indeed be at the service of many distinct projects of the agent concerned.

Let's suppose, as seems plausible, that Wright is correct in claiming that the objection just considered does not apply to states of tacit knowledge of the meaning-specifying theorems, for the reason stated. Then the following question suggests itself: why cannot we view the tacit knowledge of an axiom as a genuine intentional state after all, in virtue of the fact that although it is *directly* harnessed to the single project of forming beliefs about the content of sentences in which it figures, it can make an *indirect* contribution to the other projects of the agent *via* the states of tacit knowledge of the theorems corresponding to those sentences? The state of tacit knowledge of an axiom *is* at the service of many of the agent's projects because the project to which it is *directly* harnessed is itself at their service. Or equivalently, a state of "tacit knowledge" of an axiom can lead inferentially to a vast number of other propositional attitudes because it *can* lead inferentially to genuine intentional states (i.e. those that consist in implicit knowledge of the appropriate theorems), which *in turn* can lead to almost any other intentional state, modulo the other intentional states which we suppose the agent to possess.

So what is important in determining whether a state is a genuine propositional attitude is not the *number* of intentional states to which it can give rise, or the number of the agent's projects which it is at the service of; rather, what is crucial is the nature of the potential *routes* from the given state to the rest of the propositional attitudes, and the nature of the potential routes via which the information in question is placed at the service of a multiplicity of the agent's projects. I suggest, then, that in order to draw the required distinction in such a way that tacit knowledge of semantic axioms is excluded, we need something along the lines of the following amended version of Constraint 1:

> *Constraint 2:* A state P of an agent W is a genuine propositional attitude or intentional state *only if* P can interact *directly* with others of W's propositional attitudes and intentional states to produce new propositional attitudes – thus putting P *immediately* at the service of many distinct projects of the agent.

Of course, the questions facing us now are: (a) what exactly do we mean by "directly" as it appears in Constraint 2?, and (b) does Constraint 2 provide us with a plausible means of drawing the distinction between intentional and non-intentional states?

Let's attempt to answer (a) first. We can say that a cognitive state P interacts directly with a given propositional attitude only if the interaction takes place without the mediation of some other propositional attitude R in the causal generation of which P plays a part. Getting clear on why states of tacit knowledge of axioms fail to satisfy the constraint will help secure our grip on this notion of directness. Such a state can interact with other states only via the states of tacit knowledge concerning the sentences in which the expression corresponding to the axiom figures, because of Frege's insight that a speaker's understanding of a subsentential expression can be manifested only through the use that he makes of whole sentences in which that expression figures: it is always by means of complete sentences that we perform linguistic acts or, more figuratively, make moves in a given language game. Thus, suppose that there is a cognitive state of mine which represents the information that a given predicate, e.g. "horse", has such-and-such satisfaction conditions. Suppose also that I hear someone utter the sentence "I have a horse with five legs". Then I might form the belief either that the person in question simply has an understanding of the predicate which differs from mine, or that he has a very rare and unusual sort of horse. But these beliefs can be formed *only* via my implicit knowledge of the meaning of the whole sentence "I have a horse with five legs", because it is only in the context of a whole sentence that a linguistic act involving the predicate can be effected.

So, tacit knowledge of an axiom can never (with one exception) interact directly with other putative intentional states, because it always has to interact with them via states of tacit knowledge of the appropriate meaning-theoretic theorems, in whose causal generation it plays a part. The one exception is, of course, its interaction with the states of tacit knowledge of the theorems themselves: but this is not sufficient on its own for the satisfaction of Constraint 2.

But now for question (b): is the fact that a given state fails to satisfy Constraint 2 good grounds for refusing to describe that state as genuinely intentional? Two further questions we might ask in attempting to decide on the plausibility of Constraint 2 are: (1) is there any good a priori motivation for the constraint?, and (2) does the constraint rule out the states which intuitively ought to be ruled out?

I won't spend a great deal of time on (2). I will limit myself to noting, firstly, that no genuine belief state can be ruled out by Constraint 2 since I can move from the belief that P to almost any other belief that Q quite simply, by coming to possess the belief that $P \rightarrow Q$ and drawing out the appropriate inference: where the interaction between the belief that P and the belief that $P \rightarrow Q$ needn't take place via any further intentional state causally generated by the belief that P.[5] And, secondly, that the constraint does appear to rule out at least some of Stich's intuitive examples of subdoxastic states; in the case of Hess's experiment with the retouched photographs, for example, it seems that it is only via the conscious belief that the pupil sizes have been enlarged in one picture that the states representing information about pupil size can interact with other of the agents' propositional attitudes.[6]

So I would tentatively suggest that we can give an affirmative answer to (2). But what about (1)? Why should a state which fails to satisfy Constraint 2 be discounted from being a genuine intentional state? I think this latter question can only be answered after some reflection on the role played by the postulation of intentional states in the rationalistic explanation of human behaviour. Some sorts of behaviour exhibited by a human agent call for explanation in terms of the beliefs, desires, and other propositional attitudes possessed by that agent, and the use of language is clearly one such kind of behaviour. So we attempt rationalistically to explain a person's use of his language by crediting him with a range of intentional states. The crucial point is that once we have credited him with intentional states corresponding to the theorems of a correct theory of meaning for his language, we have everything we need in order to run the appropriate explanation: crediting the speaker with intentional states corresponding to the *axioms* adds nothing whatsoever to the rationalistic explanation of the speaker's behaviour provided by ascribing to him intentional states concerning the rules for the use of whole sentences. The explanatory redundancy of the ascription of states of tacit knowledge of the axioms is guaranteed by the fact that they only ever play a part in explaining behaviour via states of tacit knowledge of theorems: if it were possible for states of tacit knowledge of axioms to interact directly with other intentional states, then this crucial point about explanatory redundancy could not be made.

So it seems that room can be found for the states corresponding to semantic axioms only within a causal explanation of speakers' behaviour, and accordingly we can view such states only as causal states which play a part in the proximate causal history of the (intentional) states corresponding to the theorems in the semantic theory. Ascribing to speakers intentional states corresponding to various parts of the axiomatic base would simply be to load our explanatory theory with more baggage than is warranted by its explanatory brief: if P only ever interacts with other propositional attitudes via a state P* of which it is a causal antecedent, and if describing P as intentional exceeds the explanatory demands on the theory – in the sense that describing P as an intentional state makes *no* contribution whatsoever to that explanation – then it seems that the most that we can claim concerning P is that it is a causal state which plays a part in the proximal causal history of P*.

This seems to rule out Dummett's idea that states of tacit knowledge of the axioms of a semantic theory can be viewed as genuine propositional attitudes. Is there an alternative way of construing the relationship between speakers and the axiomatic base of the semantic theory, and can we still justify the demand for compositionality? Evans's alternative to Dummett attempts to answer these questions, so it is to Evans's discussion that we now turn.

3 Tacit knowledge and dispositional states

Evans's discussion proceeds with reference to the relatively simple, and finite, language L consisting of ten names "a", "b", "c", . . . , which stand for Harry, John, Bill, . . . , and ten predicate expressions "F", "G", "H", . . . , which stand for happiness, baldness, heaviness, ... L thus has 100 syntactically admissible sentences, each consisting of the concatenation of a name with a predicate.

Suppose that a semantic theorist sets out to find the correct theory of meaning for this language. One constraint is that the theory settled for should have the right *output*: the meaning-specifying theorems which it issues in should be *correct*. Suppose that what the semantic theorist is after is a correct, Davidson-style truth-conditions theory for L. Then we will regard the theory as acceptable if it delivers the following set of truth-conditions specifications:

> "Fa" is true-in-L iff Harry is bald
> "Fb" is true-in-L iff John is bald
> . . . .
> "Ga" is true-in-L iff Harry is happy
> . . . .
> "Oj" is true-in-L iff Michael is anxious.

But then the following problem arises. Call two theories which issue in the same set of truth-conditions specifications *extensionally equivalent*. Then the following two theories for L will be extensionally equivalent:

> T1: the *listiform* theory, which has 100 axioms, one for each individual sentence of L (i.e. simply the full list of truth-conditions specifications given immediately above).
>
> T2: the articulated theory consisting of 21 axioms, one for each of the proper names (e.g. "a" denotes Harry), one for each of the predicates (e.g. an object satisfies 'F' iff it is bald), and an axiom for the subject-predicate mode of combination (e.g. "a sentence coupling a name with a predicate is true iff the object denoted by the name satisfies the predicate").

T2 is clearly closer in spirit than T1 to the theories which semanticists have in fact been attempting to construct for natural languages; but Wright's demand for a motivation for compositionality can now be stated as follows: given that the constraint that a theory issue in the correct truth-condition specifications is not by itself sufficiently strong to discriminate in favour of T2, can any further constraints be imposed which will provide a motive for the preference of T2 to T1? In other words, can there ever be empirically respectable evidence which will discriminate between two extensionally equivalent theories?[7]

Evans suggests the following constraint: the theory should aspire to provide not just the correct truth-conditions specifications, but also a description of the *dispositions* corresponding to each of the expressions for which that theory has a proper axiom. So if we find that speakers have 100 dispositions of the relevant type we will be justified in opting for T1, whereas if we find that they have twenty such dispositions, the acceptance of T2 will be warranted. But what are the dispositions "of the relevant type" alluded to above? In the case of T1, the dispositions corresponding to its primitive expressions (the expressions to which it devotes an individual axiom) are easy to specify: each disposition is simply "a disposition to judge utterances of the relevant sentence-type as having such-and-such truth-conditions" (Evans, 1981, p. 124). T2 is more problematic because its primitive expressions are not whole sentences, but rather proper names and predicate expressions, and it is only sentences which can be said to have truth-conditions. As a consequence, the dispositions corresponding to the primitive expressions of T2 have to be interdefined. Evans suggests characterizing the dispositions as follows:

> We might say that a speaker U tacitly knows that the denotation of "a" is Harry iff he has a disposition such that:
> (Πϕ)(Πψ) if:
>
> (i) U tacitly knows that an object satisfies ϕ iff it is ψ
> (ii) U hears an utterance having the form ϕ^a,
>
> then U will judge that the utterance is true iff Harry is ψ.
>
> Connectedly, we say that a speaker tacitly knows that an object satisfies "F" iff it is bald iff he has a disposition such that:
> (Πx)(Πα) if
>
> (i) U tacitly knows that the denotation of α is x,
> (ii) U hears an utterance having the form F^α, then U will judge that the utterance is true iff x is bald.
>
> In these formulations, "Π" is a universal substitutional quantifier, with variables having the following substitution classes: ϕ, names of predicate expressions of the (object) language, α, names of names of the (object) language; ψ, predicate expressions of our language (the metalanguage), and "x", proper names of our language. (Evans, 1981, pp. 124–5)

How can we tell whether or not a speaker has the dispositions possession of which constitutes tacit knowledge of T1 or of T2? Evans suggests three sources of empirical evidence.

The first source is connected with Evans's insistence that the notion of a disposition involved in his account has to be taken in a full-blooded way: the ascription of a disposition is not to be regarded merely as a statement that some regularity obtains:

> These statements of tacit knowledge must not be regarded as simple statements of regularity, for if they were, anyone who correctly judged the meanings of complete sentences would have a tacit knowledge of T2. When we ascribe to something the disposition to V in circumstances C, we are claiming that there is a state S which, when taken together with C, provides a causal explanation of all the subjects V-ing (in

> C). So we make the claim that there is a common explanation to all these episodes of V-ing. Understood in this way, the ascription of tacit knowledge of T2 . . . involves the claim that there is a single state of the subject which figures in a causal explanation of why he reacts in a regular way to all the sentences containing the expression.
>
> . . .
>
> The decisive way to decide which [ascription of tacit knowledge] is correct is by providing a causal, presumably neurophysiologically based, explanation of comprehension. With such an explanation in hand, we can simply see whether or not there is an appeal to a common state or structure in the explanation of the subject's comprehension of each of the sentences containing the proper name "a". (Evans, 1981, pp. 125–7)

In addition, we can also examine the patterns of acquisition of knowledge of the meanings of sentences manifested in the linguistic behaviour of L-speakers. For example, evidence suggestive of tacit knowledge of T1 would be that even when a speaker has acquired dispositions to judge correctly of the truth conditions of Ga and Fc, he is not thereby (in the absence of further training and exposure) disposed to judge correctly of the truth-conditions of Gc. Evidence suggestive of tacit knowledge of T2 would be that he *is*, under the same conditions, so disposed.

Further evidence is provided by the patterns of loss of knowledge of meanings exhibited in speakers of L. If such a speaker is initially competent with each of the 100 sentences of L and if, by knocking out his competence with, say, Hd, we thereby disturb his competencies with all other sentences containing the expressions "H" and "d", then tacit knowledge of T2 will be ascribable. But if the other competencies remain undisturbed by the speaker's loss of competence with Hd, then the ascription of tacit knowledge of T1 will be in order.

It seems, then, that we have found an empirically respectable way of deciding which of T1 and T2 should be accepted for the language L. It is perhaps worth noting that at this stage the central idea underlying Evans's account seems to be the following: the derivational structure of a theory of meaning (the canonical routes from its axioms to its theorems) should in some sense reflect the causal structure found among the competencies of the speakers of the language under scrutiny (the causal routes leading from the dispositions associated with the language's names and predicates to the intentional states associated with the whole sentences of the language). In the remainder of this paper I shall elaborate upon and question the constraint motivated by this central idea.

4 Wright's attack on Evans

In this section I outline three criticisms that Wright has raised against Evans's dispositionalist account of tacit knowledge of semantic axioms, and the responses that have been offered by Martin Davies on Evans's behalf. I shall argue that the responses offered by Davies to two of Wright's criticisms are unsuccessful as they stand, and sketch my own alternative defence of Evans against them. I will then show how Davies's response to the third objection is plausible as it stands.

Wright's first objection to Evans concerns characterization of the dispositions which constitute tacit knowledge of T2. We can see from the quotations above that the dispositions corresponding to the names and predicate expressions of L have to be interdefined, i.e. the dispositions which constitute tacit knowledge of the denotation conditions of the proper names of the language are defined in terms of tacit knowledge of the satisfaction conditions of L's predicate expressions; and the dispositions which constitute tacit knowledge of the satisfaction conditions of the predicates are defined in terms of tacit knowledge of the denotation conditions of L's proper names. Why is this a problem? As Wright puts it, "to characterize a disposition ought to be to characterize both what it is a disposition to do and the circumstances under which it will be manifest" (Wright, 1986, p. 233). Suppose, e.g., that we are trying to give a dispositional account of ductility, and that we come up with: X is ductile iff the observable phenomena $c_1, \ldots, c_n$ occur under background circumstances C. Suppose further that the conditions C include the possession by X of the additional dispositions $d_1, \ldots, d_k$. Wright's point is that if, in characterizing the manifestations distinctive of some one of the further dispositions d_i, say, we *have* to refer to background circumstances *which include the assumption that X is ductile*, we will have said thereby *nothing whatsoever* as to what ductility consists in: we will simply have failed to say what ductility is.

This point seems to me to be fundamentally correct, and its easy to see how it applies to Evans's account of tacit knowledge of T2. Take the disposition which constitutes tacit knowledge of the denotation of the name "a". What we are after in characterizing this disposition is something of the form: X tacitly knows that the denotation of "a" is Harry iff observable phenomena $c_1, \ldots, c_n$ occur under background conditions C. In this case the background conditions include the possession by X of the further dispositions $d_i, \ldots$ = tacit knowledge of the satisfaction conditions of certain of the predicate expressions of L. But a characterization of the distinctive manifestations of the d_i's is possible only if we make reference to background conditions in which X is assumed to have tacit knowledge of the denotation conditions of the names of L, and it is precisely *this* species of tacit knowledge which we are trying to explicate. So our account turns out to be viciously circular, and we fail altogether in our attempt to say what tacit knowledge that the denotation of "a" is Harry consists in.

Wright himself is not pessimistic about the possibility of a solution to this problem:

> I offer the point more as something which someone who wished to advance Evans's account should say something about than as an objection. Perhaps a more sophisticated account of the notion of a disposition would remove the worry; my own suggestion would be that Evans's proposal should have proceeded by reference to states of a different sort – his real interest, after all, is in the underlying 'categorical' bases. (Wright, 1986, p. 233).

And Davies subsequently offers what seems to be a respectable way around the trouble threatened by Evans's characterization. Davies suggests that we cast our account of tacit knowledge in terms of "underlying explanatory states", rather than in terms of dispositions; instead of defining tacit knowledge in terms of the dispositions a speaker has concerning truth, satisfaction and denotation conditions, we define it in terms of the states which make up the "categorical bases" underlying those dispositions.[8] The speaker with tacit knowledge of T2 will not now be characterized as having twenty dispositions defined *à la* Evans, but as being the bearer of twenty *causal explanatory states*, each of which is the basis of one of those dispositions. This allows us to state the constraint that was breaking through the clouds at the end of Section 3:

> If, and only if, a speaker who has dispositions to judge correctly of the truth conditions of $S_1, \ldots, S_n$ is thereby (and without any further training or exposure) disposed to judge correctly of the truth-conditions of S, should the semantic resources sufficient for the canonical derivation of truth-conditions specifications for $S_1, \ldots, S_n$ be sufficient for the canonical derivation of a truth-condition specification for S.

Under our first revision of Evans's account in terms of underlying states, this becomes what Davies terms the *mirror constraint*:

> If, and only if, the operative states implicated in the causal explanation of a speaker's beliefs about the meanings of $S_1, \ldots, S_n$ are jointly sufficient for a causal explanation of his belief about the meaning of S, should the semantic resources sufficient for a canonical derivation of truth-conditions specifications for $S_1, \ldots, S_n$ be sufficient for the canonical derivation of a truth-condition specification for S.

However, I have the following worry about whether this does satisfactorily avoid Wright's problem concerning interdefinability and vicious circularity: if our only means of *individuating* the categorical bases underlying the dispositions is via the dispositions which they underlie, then doesn't the problem simply carry over into the revised account in terms of causally operative states? Is it possible to characterize the causally operative state which underlies my disposition concerned with the denotation condition of the name "a" *without* referring to the causal states underlying the disposition I have connected with the satisfaction conditions of L's predicates? If not, and if this holds vice versa, then I suggest that we have again failed to say what tacit knowledge that the denotation of "a" is Harry consists in, because we will have failed to individuate the causal state, possession of which allegedly constitutes that tacit knowledge. So we are faced with the following dilemma: either we must provide an account of how the operative states can be individuated without reference to the dispositions which it is claimed they underlie – which account is at present lacking – or, on the other hand, the problem that arose for Evans's account arises again for Davies's proposed revision.

Is Wright's objection, then, fatal to Evans's account? We would be over-hasty in concluding that it is: Davies's switch to talk of underlying causal states and categorical bases, indeed, does nothing to remove the circularity which Wright focuses on, but how *vicious* is that circularity? I will suggest that the circularity here will infect any constitutive account of the mastery of individual subsentential expressions, no matter whether that account is couched in terms of dispositions, underlying causal states, or in terms of anything else we care to choose. This should raise our suspicions about whether circularity can be regarded as a *defect* in such an account.

Any account of what competence with a name consists in will have to contain resources sufficient for an account of what competence with the sentences containing that name consists in, since it is only in the use of whole sentences that competence with the name can be manifested. This means that we will also require an account of what competence with predicate expressions consists in; and when we try to give this latter account – an account of what understanding the sentences containing the predicates consists in – we find ourselves back at the point we started out from, requiring an account of what competence with names consists in. Thus, *any* account of what competence with a name consists in requires an account of what competence with predicate expressions consists in, and vice versa.

This points to the proper line of response to Wright's objection. Isn't it the case that something analogous to this interdefinability property is possessed by beliefs and desires? Intentional action requires both beliefs and desires to be present, and, more generally, beliefs, desires and propositional attitudes are ascribable to an agent only in systems, and not individually. When we attempt to give, say, a constitutive account of the belief which partially rationalizes a certain action, we stand in need of a similar account of the appropriate desire, and vice versa. But we would not take this to signal the impossibility of providing a constitutive account of either belief or desire: rather, the conclusion drawn is that the relationship between the beliefs, desires and the behavioural facts which ground their ascription is irreducibly *holistic* (see Chapter 10, HOLISM). How, then, do we say what beliefs and desires are? I think, roughly speaking, that there are two components to this. Firstly, by showing how the propositional attitude ascriptions relate *to each other* – by giving the a priori principles which constrain the relations *between* the various sorts of propositional attitude; and secondly, by giving the interpretative principles which link the propositional attitudes holistically to the behavioural facts which ground their ascription (see Fricker 1981). In summary, we individuate a propositional attitude not by picking it out individually, but by giving its place in the network of propositional attitudes which form part of any agent's mental armoury. So the fact that we *can't* pick out such states in isolation from the entire network in which they occur needn't give us too much cause for concern.

I suggest that an analogous point is available in the case of states of tacit knowledge. All the interdefinability focused on by Wright shows is that tacit knowledge, too, has to be ascribed in a holistic fashion. We do not give an account of what tacit knowledge of, say, a name "a" consists in, apart from an account of what constitutes tacit knowledge of the complete axiomatic base: and we give such an account by delineating the constraints which govern the ascription of tacit knowledge of the axiomatic base *as a whole*. This is where the mirror constraint has a crucial part to play: faced with a semantic theory T, we decide whether or not a speaker should be ascribed tacit knowledge of T by seeing whether the theory meets the mirror constraint with respect to that speaker; in other words, by seeing whether the derivational structure *of the whole theory* is isomorphic in the relevant sense to the causal structure found in that speaker's overall competence. Just as we give an account of what beliefs are by giving their location within a wider network of propositional attitudes, we give an account of what tacit knowledge is by showing how the causal states in question are located in a wider causal structure: having given the structure, we need say nothing more about the composition of the individual states. The mental, unlike the metallurgical, is essentially holistic.[9]

I now move on to look at Wright's second objection to Evans's account of tacit knowledge. I will argue that although the solution which Davies proposes *is* a good solution to a problem which Evans perhaps ought to have taken account of, it simply fails altogether to engage with Wright's objection in the deeper form in which he originally raised it. I will then show how Davies ought to have responded to Wright's deeper objection.

Davies summarizes the objection thus:

> The second objection relates to the account of tacit knowledge as a certain kind of causal structure. Suppose that a subject knows (tacitly or in the ordinary sense) what the various sentences of L mean; and suppose that underlying those pieces of knowledge there is indeed a causal structure of the kind which, on Evans's account, is required for tacit knowledge of T2 – the articulated theory. Wright asks why such a subject would not be at least as well described by a two-part theory. The first part would be the *semantic* theory T1 – the listiform theory; the second part would be 'some appropriate hypotheses of a *non-semantic* sort, about the presumed causal substructure of the dispositions which T1 describes'. Why, in short, does mere *causal* structure justify articulation in a *semantic* theory? (Davies, 1987, p. 443–4).

The suggested problem seems to be that not all attributions of causal explanatory structure will be pertinent to the ascription of tacit knowledge to the speaker concerned; and in order to bring this point home Davies provides an example of a case in which "a pattern of breakdown is intuitively misleading as to the attributability of tacit knowledge . . . [but where] . . . the evidence is not obviously misleading as to the presence of some kind of causal structure" (Davies, 1987, p. 451).

Consider the speaker C who has a language system which performs derivations in an explicit representation of the semantic theory T1 – the matrix in Figure 1 is supposed to show how the representations of the 100 axioms of T2 are arranged, and each of its elements represents an information storage unit. Now we elaborate the example somewhat and suppose that in order to function properly the individual units of the matrix have to be supplied with certain nutrients, which flow through the matrix in channels. Suppose also that there are two types of nutrient X and Y, that the X nutrient flows through the matrix in ten channels $X_a, \ldots, X_j$ "each of which serves the ten storage units for the ten sentences containing a single

			G	H	I	J	K	L	M	N	O
Xa	a	Fa	Ga	Ha	Ia	Ja	Ka	La	Ma	Na	Oa
Xb	b	Fb	Gb	Hb	Ib	Jb	Kb	Lb	Mb	Nb	Ob
Xc	c	Fc	Gc	Hc	Ic	Jc	Kc	Lc	Mc	Nc	Oc
Xd	d	Fd	Gd	Hd	Id	Jd	Kd	Ld	Md	Nd	Od
Xe	e	Fe	Ge	He	Ie	Je	Ke	Le	Me	Ne	Oe
Xf	f	Ff	Gf	Hf	If	Jf	Kf	Lf	Mf	Nf	Of
Xg	g	Fg	Gg	Hg	Ig	Jg	Kg	Lg	Mg	Ng	Og
Xh	h	Fh	Gh	Hh	Ih	Jh	Kh	Lh	Mh	Nh	Oh
Xi	i	Fi	Gi	Hi	Ii	Ji	Ki	Li	Mi	Ni	Oi
Xj	j	Fj	Gj	Hj	Ij	Jj	Kj	Lj	Mj	Nj	Oj

Figure 1.

name", and that in a similar fashion the Y nutrient flows in ten channels $Y_F, \ldots, Y_O$ "each of which serves the ten storage units for the ten sentences containing a single predicate". The supposition crucial for the example is that each of the storage units will *fail* to function if it doesn't get its supply of *each* of the nutrient types, so that "failure of a unit prevents nutrient flow through at least one of the channels serving that unit".

The difficulty should now be clear: we want to say that if the speaker has tacit knowledge of any theory then he must have tacit knowledge of T1, but the patterns of breakdown likely to occur in his linguistic behaviour will suggest the ascription of tacit knowledge of T2, for example if his competence with Gg is knocked out; and because of the implications this has for the channels of nutrient flow his competencies either with all other sentences containing G or with all other sentences containing g, or both, will be knocked out also.

Davies's first point seems basically correct: not all causal structure will be germane to the attribution of tacit knowledge, so we need some account which will enable us to discriminate between causal structure that is thus relevant, and causal structure that is not. Nutritional structure is causal structure, but is intuitively irrelevant to the ascription of tacit knowledge. Why is this so? Davies suggests that this is because "the causal explanatory structure in the example is in no way *sensitive* to the *information* stored in the units", and that this lack of sensitivity is manifested in the fact that the patterns of *revision* of semantic beliefs is unlikely to follow the patterns of semantic decay: 'we do not expect that *revision* of C's belief about the meaning of "Fa" would go hand in hand with corresponding revisions of his beliefs about other sentences' (Davies, 1987, p. 453). So we need to revise our account of causal structure, and with it the mirror constraint, in such a way that the required sensitivity to informational content is introduced. In accordance with the remarks above, this is introduced via the notion of revision, so that the mirror constraint is modified thus:

> If, and only if, the operative states implicated in the causal explanation of a speaker's beliefs about the meanings of $S_1, \ldots, S_n$ are jointly sufficient for a causal explanation of his belief about the meaning of S; *and* those first states together with the revision of the speaker's belief about the meaning of S provide an explanation of the speaker's corresponding revisions in his beliefs about the meanings of $S_1, \ldots, S_n$ – should the semantic resources sufficient for the canonical derivation of truth-conditions specifications for $S_1, \ldots, S_n$ be sufficient for the canonical derivation of a truth-condition specification for S.

But does the introduction of the notion of sensitivity to information really solve the difficulty which Wright raised? I want to suggest that it does not, and that in fact Davies has misunderstood the character of Wright's objections here.

Wright's problem was *not* that some patterns of causal structure were irrelevant to tacit knowledge ascriptions, but that *even if* we could find a good constitutive account of tacit knowledge in which some form of causal structure *was* relevant to its ascription, this still would not justify articulation in the derivational structure of a semantic theory. Even if we *grant* the assumption that certain of the causal interrelations amongst speakers' competencies *are* worth describing, the objection raised is that we needn't run the risk of having the structure of these interrelations reflected indirectly via the derivational structure of a theory of meaning. Such structure could equally well be described (in the case of language L) by a listiform theory like T1, supplemented with a rider along the following lines: speakers are generally able to understand novel utterances provided they only involve familiar semantic primitives, and changes in their semantic beliefs about a sentence tend to be associated with changes in their semantic beliefs about all sentences containing one or more of the semantic primitives figuring in that sentence. More *detail* can then be obtained via the recursive syntax which was initially wedded to the listiform semantic theory. It might be worthwhile to pause briefly and investigate precisely how the relevant detail can be brought to light.

Wright suggests that the recursive syntax will provide this detail on the condition that it itself satisfies the mirror constraint. Now what does it mean to say that a *syntax* satisfies the mirror constraint? I suggest the following reconstrual of the mirror constraint for syntactical theories:

> If, and only if, the causal states implicated in the causal explanation of a speaker's beliefs about the meanings of $S_1, \ldots, S_n$ are jointly sufficient for a causal explanation of his belief about the meaning of S; *and* those first states together with the revision of the speaker's belief about the meaning of S provide an explanation of the speaker's corresponding revisions in his beliefs about the meanings of $S_1, \ldots, S_n$ – should the syntactic resources sufficient for the canonical derivation of well-formedness specifications for $S_1, \ldots, S_n$ be sufficient for the canonical derivation of a well-formedness specification for S.

If a syntactical theory satisfies this then *its* derivational structure (the canonical routes from its axioms to its specifications of well-formedness) will mirror with at least as much clarity the causal structure of speakers' competencies which was initially mirrored in the derivational structure of the semantic theory. It is important to note that this objection holds good even where the causal structure *is* sensitive to the informational content stored in the units of the representation of a semantic theory. Davies betrays his misunderstanding of this point in the following passage:

> It may be that by Wright's lights, no refinement of the notion of causal structure could ever justify the idea that a *semantic* theory should mirror that structure. But, to the extent that any refinement ensures that the salient causal structure can be described as an information-processing structure, this extreme view will be hard to sustain. (Davies, 1987, p. 454)

I disagree with this: even if we find that the salient causal structure can in fact be described as an information processing structure, the objection still stands. The problem is not one of answering the question of how *causal* structure justifies articulation in a semantic theory, but rather of answering the question of how causal structure justifies articulation in a *semantic* theory.

Thus, notwithstanding the fact that Davies's revised account provides a useful sharpening-up of the notion of causal structure considered as relevant to the attribution of tacit knowledge, I would suggest that that revision leaves Wright's objection, properly read, completely untouched.

How, then, can we deal with Wright's objection? Wright's thought was that causal structure can be reflected by a purely syntactical – i.e. non-semantic – theory, and that therefore some additional reasons have to be provided to ground the preference for reflection in theories of meaning. I think we can undercut Wright here by *denying* that he has shown how to reflect the salient causal structure in a non-semantic theory. Let's look more closely at the conjunction: listiform semantic theory plus syntactical theory which meets the mirror constraint. The latter part of the conjunction will reflect the same causal structure as any semantic theory which satisfies the mirror constraint. But is it really *non-semantic* in nature? I would say that it is not – that if we stipulate that the syntactical theory must meet the mirror constraint (as modified to apply to such theories) then it is no longer *purely* syntactical. Agreed, the theorems which form the output of this theory are concerned solely with the well-formedness or otherwise of the sentences of the language. But what a theory is *about*, what *sort* of theory a given theory *is*, is determined not only by the content of the sentences which make up its output, but also by the constraints in accordance with which that output is generated. Suppose, for example, we have a theory A whose output consists of sentences detailing the amount of money possessed by a sample of 100 Scottish women, and a theory B whose output consists of sentences detailing the amount of money possessed by a sample of 100 people, but which has been constructed in accordance with the constraint that the people included in the sample space should all be Scottish women. Then, even though theory B's output is couched in pronouncements of the form "Person X has £x" which feature no mention of Scotland or women, there is a clear sense in which that theory is still *about* Scottish women. To get back to the linguistic case, we should note that the mirror constraint is a *semantic* constraint – it makes reference to beliefs about the *meanings* of sentences and to relations that obtain between these beliefs. So, any theory which is required to satisfy the mirror constraint will be a semantic theory to the extent that it will encode semantic information, including, despite appearances, any theory whose output mentions only the grammaticality of the language's sentences.

I thus deny that Wright has shown how the relevant causal structure can be reflected by a non-semantic theory: what he has given us is, in fact, an account of how that structure can be reflected in another *semantic* theory. Indeed, it is perhaps misleading even to speak of *another* semantic theory: just as the theory B above seems to be little more than a *reformulation* of the theory A, given the extensional equivalence of T1 and T2, the conjunction of T1 with a recursive "syntax" which is really partially semantic seems to me to be little more than a reformulation of the explicitly semantic T2.

I now look at the third objection which Wright raises against Evans. According to Evans's original account, the job of the theory of meaning is to describe the dispositions which speakers have, corresponding to each of the expressions for which that theory provides a separate axiom. But if this is *all* that the theory is meant to do, then the twenty-first axiom of T2 – the compositional axiom – ought to be redundant, because someone who only has the dispositions described by the other twenty axioms will thereby be disposed to judge correctly of the truth-conditions of the sentences of L. This is again a consequence of the fact that the dispositions connected with the names and predicates are interdefined. However, without the compositional axiom the theory T2 will be paralyzed: it will be impossible to derive any truth-conditions specifications for the sentences of L. So "Evans has not shown how we are to construe an articulated semantic theory as a description of speakers' dispositions" (Davies, 1987, p. 444).

The way out of this difficulty is again to switch from talk of dispositions to talk of the states underlying those dispositions, and of the reflection of causal explanatory structure via the satisfaction of the mirror constraint. The job of the theory of meaning is now viewed not as the description of dispositions, but as the reflection of a certain sort of causal structure. There is, then, no obstacle preventing the theory T2 from satisfying the mirror constraint, and hence no obstacle to its reflecting the structure in question and thus doing its proper job.

Let me try to clarify this point with the aid of one of Davies's examples. Consider another semantic theory T3, which has the same axioms as T2 for the proper names of L, but differently styled axioms for its predicates. These axioms will instead be of the form:

> A sentence coupling a name with the predicate "F" is true iff the object denoted by that name is bald.

As Davies puts it, "What T3 does is to parcel out the content of T2's compositional axiom among the ten predicates of the language" (1987, p. 445), so that T3 is not open to Wright's objection even when we take the Evans line about the description of dispositions. More importantly, when we take the line in terms of causally operative states and reflection of causal structure, it seems that there is nothing to choose between the ascription of tacit knowledge of T2 and the ascription of tacit knowledge of T3. To see this, define a relation of *DS-equivalence* (equivalence in point of derivational structure) on theories of meaning as follows:

> Two (extensionally equivalent) theories Tk and Tm are DS-equivalent iff, for any sentences $S_1, \ldots, S_n$, S: the semantic resources in Tk which suffice for the canonical derivation of truth-conditions specifications for $S_1, \ldots S_n$ suffice also for the canonical derivation of a truth-condition specification for S if and only if the semantic resources in Tm which suffice for the canonical derivation of truth-conditions specifications for $S_1, \ldots, S_n$ suffice also for the canonical derivation of a truth-condition specification for S.

Then it turns out that T2 and T3 are DS-equivalent, for "although T2 has an extra axiom relative to T3, the use of this resource in T2 is constant across all derivations of meaning-specifications for whole sentences" (Davies, 1987, pp. 446–7). I'll clarify this by means of an example. In T2 the semantic resources sufficient for the derivation of a truth-condition specification for Ga and Fb are sufficient also for the derivation of a truth-condition specification for Fa:

Ga	(1)	"a" denotes Harry	(axiom for "a")
	(2)	an object satisfies G iff it is happy	(axiom for "G")
	(3)	a sentence coupling a name with a predicate is true iff the object denoted by the name satisfies the predicate	(compositional axiom)
	(4)	"Ga" is true iff Harry is happy	(from (1), (2) and (3))
Fb	(1)	"b" denotes John	(axiom for "b")
	(2)	an object satisfies "F" iff it is bald	(axiom for "F")
	(3)	compositional axiom	(as above)
	(4)	"Fb" is true iff John is bald	(from (1), (2) and (3))
Fa	(1)	"a" denotes Harry	(axiom for "a")
	(2)	an object satisfies F iff it is bald	(axiom for "F")
	(3)	compositional axiom	(as above)
	(4)	"Fa" is true iff Harry is bald	(from (1), (2) and (3))

We can see that the resources used in T2 in the derivations of the specifications for Ga and Fb were the axioms for "a", "b", "F", "G" and the compositional axiom. These give all we need in order to derive a specification for Fa. Now, because of the way the compositional axiom is built into the axioms for the predicates in T3, the same thing holds in T3. Witness,

Ga	(1)	"a" denotes Harry	(axiom for "a")
	(2)	a sentence coupling a name with the predicate "G" is true iff the object denoted by the name is happy	(axiom for "G")
	(3)	"Ga" is true iff Harry is happy	(from (1) and (2))
Fb	(1)	"b" denotes John	(axiom for "b")
	(2)	a sentence coupling a name with the predicate "F" is true iff the object denoted by the name is bald	(axiom for "G")
	(3)	"Fb" is true iff John is bald	(from (1) and (2))
Fa	(1)	"a" denotes Harry	(axiom for "a")
	(2)	axiom for "F"	(as above)
	(3)	"Fa" is true iff Harry is bald	(from (1) and (2))

Here the resources used in the derivations of specifications for Ga and Fb were the axioms for "a", "b", "F" and "G". And again, these give us all we need in order to derive a specification for "Fa". We could do this again for all the appropriate sentences of L, and this would amount to a conclusive proof of Davies's assertion that T2 and T3 are DS-equivalent.

We thus find ourselves in the following position: because of the DS-equivalence of T2 and T3, either both theories satisfy the mirror constraint for a given speaker, or neither do; so that the 5 percent difference – the difference between the twenty axioms of T3 and the twenty-one axioms of T2 – *doesn't* in fact matter. Given that we are not concerned with the description of dispositional states apart from their position in a causal web whose structure we are concerned to reflect, the fact that we can describe that causal structure in causal theories which do not devote an individual axiom to name–predicate concatenation is innocuous: it does not vitiate its reflection in theories which *do* contain such an axiom.

However, as Davies realizes, there is now another objection in the offing. Suppose we are trying to decide whether a given articulated semantic theory satisfies the mirror constraint with respect to a particular speaker of L. Suppose also that that speaker revises his belief concerning "Fb" from "John is bald" to "John is baldish". In accordance with the mirror constraint, we will check whether he revises his beliefs about " Fa", "Ga" and "Gb" *correspondingly*. But what counts as the *corresponding* revision of, say, "Gb"? Is it the null revision, which leaves the speaker with the belief that "Gb" means that John is happy, or is it the revision which leaves him with the belief that John is happyish? No one of these answers seems to be uniquely correct, and according to Davies this latent indeterminacy is a time-bomb which threatens the stability of his proposed account of tacit knowledge. But this threat seems to dissipate somewhat when we note that the indeterminacy can in fact be resolved "according as we look at the semantic properties of a language through the grid of one theory rather than the other" (Davies, 1987, p. 459). Precisely how this resolution is achieved can be seen from the following quotation from an earlier paper of Davies's – to say that the revision of the semantic belief concerned with S_i corresponds (considered from the viewpoint of a particular semantic theory) to the revision in the semantic belief concerned with S is to say that:

> If A were to revise his belief about the meaning of S in that respect of the meaning which the semantic theorist discerns as a deductive consequence [in the semantic theory in question] of the presence in S of the syntactic item Γ assigned the semantic property Δ, and if what A believed about the meaning of S as the result of this revision were to be the deductive consequence of a revision of Δ to Δ*, then A would revise his belief about the meaning of S_i (and the meanings of any other sentences containing Γ) in such a way as would be the deductive consequence (in the theory in question) of the assignment to Γ of Δ* rather than Δ. (Davies, 1981a, p. 149)

Given this, we can now say which revisions merit the ascription of tacit knowledge of T2, and which merit the ascription of T3. And it seems that these will not coincide:

> If we consider T2, then there are two possible changes in the proper axioms, each of which would result in "Fb" being assigned the meaning that John is baldish. A change in T2's axiom for "F" has one pattern of consequences: a change in the 21st axiom – the compositional axiom – has a different, and more extensive pattern of consequences. If we consider T3, on the other hand, then there is only one possible change to the proper axioms which would result in "Fb" being assigned the meaning that John is baldish. (Davies, 1987, p. 459)

So, our original account, in which the ascription of tacit knowledge of T2 simply was ascription of tacit knowledge of T3, and vice versa, will have to be revised in such a way as to take this into account. For consider the following two speakers A and B

> For whom, a form of the language of thought hypothesis is true. For these speakers, language comprehension – in particular, the assignment of meaning to sentences – is a matter of derivations in a semantic theory explicitly represented in a special purpose language processing system. Suppose that speaker A conducts on his inner blackboard derivations in theory T2, while speaker B conducts derivations in theory T3 . . . For the purposes of tacit knowledge ascriptions speakers A and B are grouped together. (Davies, 1987, pp. 447–8)

But now:

> Just as theory T2 with its 21 axioms provides an extra locus of content sensitivity over theory T3 with its 20 axioms, so the causal explanatory structure in speaker A provides an extra locus of systematic revision over the causal explanatory structure in speaker B. So, not altogether surprisingly, it is speaker A – conducting inner derivations in theory T2 – who meets the condition for tacit knowledge if the indeterminacy is resolved by looking at the language through the grid of T2. And it is speaker B who meets the condition if the indeterminacy is resolved by looking at the language through the grid of theory T3. (Davies, 1987, p. 459)

What is going on here? The suggestion is that *only if* we have a one-to-one correspondence between the axioms of a theory of meaning and the explanatory loci of systematic revision which go towards making up the causal explanatory structure in a speaker can we spell out satisfactorily the notion of systematic revision amongst the implicit semantic beliefs that constitute that speaker's linguistic competence. For if the axioms for the language's expressions and the speaker's competencies with those expressions correspond with each other one by one, then since "for each axiom of rule, the required notion of *systematic revision* can be spelled out in a quite determinate way", similarly, determinate sense can be made of the notion of systematic changes in the nature of the speaker's competencies, that is, in his revisions of his semantic beliefs. If this is correct then the 5 percent difference *will* matter – A will be viewed as having tacit knowledge of T2 (and not of T3) while B will be viewed as having tacit knowledge of T3 (and not of T2).

Although I am suspicious of the details of Davies's example of the speakers A and B – it is unclear, for instance, whether A really has the twenty-one causal explanatory states required for tacit knowledge of T2 (what state now corresponds to the compositional axiom?), and witness the hardly uncontroversial assumption about the language-of-thought hypothesis – I think we can accept that he has provided a good argument to the effect that a speaker with causal states underlying Evans's dispositions can only be ascribed tacit knowledge of T3 and not T2, because in the latter case we would have no means of resolving the indeterminacy which surrounds the possible revisions which such a speaker could make in his semantic beliefs. However, as Davies himself points out, this amounts only to a minor revision, and certainly not to a wholesale rejection, of the account of tacit knowledge which has its roots in Evans's suggestions. As Davies puts it, "the form of Evans's original proposal shines through" (1987, p. 461).

5 The mirror constraint and understanding novel utterances

Can the imposition of the mirror constraint help us understand speakers' capacities to understand novel utterances, provided they include only familiar semantic primitives and modes of construction? Suppose that a speaker can come to understand S after exposure to the sentences $S_1, \ldots, S_n$, that loss of competence with S occasions loss of competence with at least some of $S_1, \ldots, S_n$, and that a revision of a speaker's belief concerning the meaning of S occasions corresponding revisions in his beliefs about the meanings of each of $S_1, \ldots, S_n$. Then, on the basis of this evidence we shall claim that: the operative states implicated in the causal explanation of the speaker's beliefs about $S_1, \ldots, S_n$ are jointly sufficient for a causal explanation of his belief about the meaning of S, and those first states, together with his revision of his belief about the meaning of S, are sufficient for an explanation of the corresponding revisions in his beliefs about the meanings of $S_1, \ldots, S_n$. Of course, to make such a claim is not yet to *provide* the causal explanation alluded to, so that we are still left with the question: how is it possible that the operative states implicated could be thus sufficient? It is precisely this question that is answered by showing how the semantic resources sufficient for the canonical derivation of meaning-specifications for $S_1, \ldots, S_n$ are sufficient for the canonical derivation of a meaning-specification for S, by the provision of a semantic theory in which they are so sufficient. That is, the move from the operative states to the belief about the content of the novel utterance is viewed as being explained by the provision of a theory which generates, on the basis of the information represented by the relevant operative states – represented by the axioms of the theory – a meaning-specifying theorem which gives the content of the novel utterance in question. So, the provision of a compositional theory of meaning is supposed to make explicable the notion that a speaker could come to form an implicit belief about the content of a novel utterance on the basis of a pre-existing set of causally operative states, because the route from the operative states to the belief about content is reflected by the derivational route from the axiomatic base of the semantic theory to the appropriate meaning-specification. Thus, the construction of a compositional semantic theory, and the notions that speakers might have, in the requisite sense, tacit knowledge of such a theory, is supposed to help answer the question as to how it is possible for speakers to understand utterances of previously unencountered sentences.[10] Davies thus goes beyond Evans, who claims that "the notion of tacit knowledge of a structure reflecting theory of meaning, explained as I have explained it, cannot be used to explain the capacity to understand new sentences" (1981, p. 134). I shall return to this difference between Evans and Davies in the final section.

6 Wright's proposal

In addition to the objections responded to in Section 4, Wright complains that whereas the account of tacit knowledge given by Evans – and by implication, the development of that account via the imposition of Davies's mirror constraint – requires the semantic theorist to pay attention to empirical facts about language acquisition, loss and revision, *actual* semantic theorizing seems to have proceeded in happy ignorance of such facts. Loath to conclude that the right conception of the semantic theorist's task "has not greatly impinged upon the consciousness of workers in the field", Wright proposes an alternative account of what theorists of meaning ought to be doing, which is claimed to harmonize better with their actual *modus operandi*. In this section I briefly outline Wright's alternative proposal, and argue that it presupposes, rather than undercuts, the Evans–Davies account which proceeds via the imposition of the mirror constraint.

Speakers are able to understand novel utterances provided they include only familiar semantic primitives; and the semantic theorist's task is to give an answer to the question, "how do they do it?". Wright sees this question as dividing into two sub-questions: (a) how is it possible for there to be a device which could, when fed with information concerning the visible or audible structure of a sentence, process that information in such a way that a theorem about the meaning of the sentence is generated? and (b) how is it possible for such a device actually to be embodied in normal, competent speakers of a natural language? Question (a) is conceived of as being answerable a priori, independently of the empirical evidence upon which

Evans and Davies lay so much stress: it will have been answered when a suitable "computer program" has been written, the writing of which will not demand elevation from the armchair. Wright thus thinks that if we view semantic theorists as attempting to answer Question (a) in the manner he describes, the discrepancy between the account of what their project is, and what they actually do, will vanish. And he views the provision of an answer to (a) as an essential prerequisite for any attempted answer to (b):

> The sort of understanding of the actual capacities of speakers which is called for would be achieved exactly when enough was known about them to enable us to understand how in detail they embody such a device. And, of course, there can be no such understanding before we have formed the appropriate theoretical conception of the powers which the device must have. Doing that requires writing the computer program. (Wright, 1986, p. 236)

However, it seems to me that Wright has overlooked something crucial here. Given that we are interested in answering the question "How do *they* do it", even after (a) and (b) have been answered there remains the further question: (c) do they, in reality, embody the device whose theoretical powers the computer program describes? An affirmative answer to this question is crucial if the answers given to (a) and (b) are to have any explanatory value: an account of the theoretical powers of the device and an account of how it might be *possible* for speakers to embody it will have no explanatory value as an answer to the question "how do they do it?" if they do not actually embody the device in question. Questions (a) and (b) together tell us how it *could* be done, but what we are really after is an account of how it *is* done, and for this we need an answer to (c). And, of course, the provision of an answer to (c) is an empirical matter, dependent on the sort of empirical evidence concerning language acquisition and loss Evans and Davies focus on: whether or not a speaker actually does embody a particular information-processing mechanism is a matter which is amenable to empirical investigation. We will not view a particular speaker as embodying a particular information-processing mechanism unless the derivational structure of that mechanism is isomorphic to the causal-explanatory structure, the existence of which is suggested by the appropriate sorts of empirical data.

So if semantic theorists are out to answer the question "how do they do it?" of our capacity to understand novel utterances, they are at some point going to have to pay attention to empirical detail. The question is, of course, where? Two broad answers to the question suggest themselves. The semantic theorist could begin to pay attention to such detail at the final stage of his enterprise: having written the appropriate computer program, and having shown – somehow or other – that it is possible for it to be embodied in speakers, he could then *go on* to ask whether or not they actually do embody it. And it is at this final stage that the usual sources of empirical evidence will be crucial. The semantic theorist would thus be attempting to answer the questions (a), (b) and (c) in a straightforwardly linear fashion. But it is clear that this could be an extremely inefficient way of going about things: once answers to (a) and (b) have been provided, there is no guarantee that the required affirmative answer to (c) will be forthcoming. The semantic theorist could write out his program, argue that it is possible for the information-processing device to be embodied in actual speakers, and then discover – to his horror – that it is in fact *not* actually embodied. And this could happen time and time and time again. Of course, he might get an affirmative answer to (c) on one of his early attempts after all; but it is clear that if he is proceeding in the linear fashion described, this could only have the status of a happy accident.

An alternative, and much more efficient, way of proceeding would be to write the computer program out as before, but this time in accordance with empirical constraints which ensure that, once (a) and (b) have been answered, no obstacle remains to the production of an affirmative answer to (c). In effect, this involves writing the computer program – constructing the theory of meaning – in accordance with some constraint along the lines of the mirror constraint. The semantic theorist is thus still viewed as attempting to answer the questions (a), (b) and (c), but no longer in the simple linear fashion described above. We answer (a) and (b) subject to the constraint that there is an affirmative answer to (c) via the imposition of something like the mirror constraint, and we are justified in so doing because without an affirmative answer to (c) the answers to (a) and (b) will have no explanatory value as answers to the question, "How do they do it?". There is no point in writing a program describing the theoretical powers of an information-processing device which we do not embody if the whole aim of the enterprise is to achieve an understanding of how *we* can understand novel utterances.

My conclusion is thus that, far from providing an account of the semantic theorist's task which does not involve the imposition of the mirror constraint, Wright's suggestions, in the end, only serve to highlight the need for the imposition of that very constraint.[11]

7 Tacit knowledge and rule-following

In the above, I have been attempting to defend the suggestion that the construction of theories of meaning should be subject to Davies's mirror constraint. But there is at least one major problem outstanding which anyone wishing to embrace the account I have defended would have to face up to. I cannot do more than briefly mention this problem here. It stems from the fact that our account attempts to give an explanation of language mastery – in particular of the capacity to understand novel utterances – in *cognitive-psychological* terms. In Wright's words, it is an ability we are conceived to have

> because we are appropriately related to a finite body of *information* which may be inferentially manipulated in such a way as to entail, for each novel string on which we can exercise our "linguistic-creative" power, appropriate theorems concerning its grammaticalness and content,

which commits us to

> the picture of language as a kind of syntactico-semantic mechanism, our largely unconscious knowledge of which enables us to compute the content which, independently and in advance of any response of ours, it bestows on each ingredient sentence . . . [and in which] the mechanism does the generating and the competent adult keeps track of what (and how) it generates. (Wright, 1989, pp. 233 and 238)

Prima facie, this seems like an accurate description of our account: the information codified in the causal states corresponding to semantic axioms is conceived of as settling in advance, and independently of anything we go on to say or do, the content of the totality of admissible sentences in the language.

But why should this be a problem? What is wrong with the picture of language as a syntactico-semantic mechanism whose output competent speakers are able to track? Wright's suggestion is that it is precisely this sort of picture of the ability constitutive of language mastery which is the ultimate target of Wittgenstein's remarks in the *Investigations* and elsewhere on the nature of rule-following: that if we try to construe language mastery as an ability to track states of affairs constituted independently and in advance of what we say or do, we shall find ourselves unable to give any coherent account of the epistemology of the tracking accomplishment. (For further discussion, see Chapter 15, RULE-FOLLOWING, OBJECTIVITY AND MEANING, Section 4.) Thus, the question which we will have to leave unanswered here is: *does the account of tacit knowledge which uses the mirror constraint actually commit us, as Wright suggests, to conceptions of meaning and linguistic understanding which the rule-following considerations would counsel us against?* Perhaps one way to try to avoid an affirmative answer to this question would be to retain Davies's version of the mirror constraint as it stands, but drop the claim that the causal-explanatory states corresponding to semantic axioms have informational content – that they represent information – which somehow settles in advance the content of the intentional states constitutive of sentential understanding. It is difficult to assess this suggestion in the absence of an account of what the relationship between the causal states and the axioms is, and of when causal states which are not genuinely intentional can be claimed to have informational content.[12] John Campbell takes Evans to be suggesting that the causal states underlying language mastery have no such content:

> [Evans suggests that] the discernment of structure by a description of understanding is in effect a discernment of non-psychic, purely neural structure . . . [and that] there is no *psychological* machinery which typically explains a speaker's perception of the meaning of the heard sentence. (1982, p. 24)

Davies, on the other hand, is explicit in his desire to take the opposing view:

> We ought to explore the differences between propositional attitudes *and other information-containing cognitive states.* (1986, p. 140; see also his 1989)

Deciding who is right will require a full account of the sort of content possessed by "subdoxastic states", together with an account of the conditions under which such content should be described. This question should, perhaps, be the starting-point for any future discussion of the notion of tacit knowledge. But if Campbell's interpretation is the correct one, there might still be a way of holding on to the mirror constraint, while avoiding the conceptions of meaning and understanding which Wittgenstein would have us question.[13]

Notes

1 We should distinguish between two senses of the phrase "theory of meaning". This could signify, on the one hand, a theory relating to a single language which attempts to state the meaning of every sentence in that language; or, on the other, a theory relating to language in general, which "attempts to analyse, elucidate, or determine the empirical content of the concept of meaning in general" (Sainsbury, 1979, p. 127). In this essay we will be concerned exclusively with theories of meaning in the former sense. I shall assume that a natural language is one which is learned by training and projection from that training.

2 In what follows I assume that the meaning-specifications have the form of truth-condition specifications, in the manner of essays 1–5 of Davidson (1984). (See also Chapter 1, MEANING AND TRUTH CONDITIONS. This assumption has been widely disputed: see Dummett (1975) and (1976). But I do not enter into these issues in this chapter: for our present purposes, nothing of importance hinges on the outcome of that particular debate.

3 Stephen Stich (1978) suggests a necessary condition on a cognitive state's counting as a genuine belief which is very similar in spirit to the constraint which we just extracted from the Evans–Wright discussion. Stich uses the notions of *inferential integration* and *insulation*. Whereas genuine beliefs form inferentially integrated subsystems of an agent's cognitive states (in the sense that there are *many* inferential routes, both deductive and inductive, from a given belief to any other belief), *subdoxastic* states, in contrast, are inferentially insulated from the vast majority of the subjects' genuine beliefs, in the sense that a subdoxastic state will be linked inferentially to only a very limited range of the agent's beliefs.

4 Might there be other reasons for finding the notion of tacit knowledge of meaning delivering theorems problematic? How could the theorems encapsulate a rule governing the use of sentences, followed even by competent speakers who do not register the theorem in consciousness? As Wright puts it (1986, p. 218), 'How can a principle function as a rule if those who engage in the practice which it is supposed to regulate have no consciousness of it?' Wright convincingly rejects this line of objection to tacit knowledge of theorems. In addition, we might add that if Wittgenstein's rule-following considerations have taught us anything, it is that the following question is no easier to answer: how can a principle function as a rule if those who engage in the practice which it is supposed to regulate *are* in fact conscious of it?

5 Note that it would be a mistake to think that a similar argument could reinstate tacit knowledge of a meaning-theoretic axiom as a genuine propositional attitude, since tacit knowledge of an axiom A can equally interact with a multiplicity of other states, namely, those corresponding to the sentences in which the expression governed by A appears. There is no real analogy with the example concerning genuine beliefs, since the states corresponding to the axioms will be implicated only in the causal explanation of the agent's possession of the states corresponding to the theorems. No such implica-

tion need hold in the belief example: e.g. the belief that P might not play any part in the causal generation of the belief that P → Q. ("Interact", as it appears in constraint 2, really concerns *rationalistic* explanation: to say that state A interacts with state B to lead to state C is to say that state A and state B together rationalistically explain the presence of the state C. The crucial point about the axiom-theorem case will then be that the citation of the state corresponding to the axiom will be redundant, so far as rationalistic explanation is concerned: see below.)

6 Hess took two photographs of the same girl, enlarged the pupils of her eyes in only one of them, and then showed the two pictures to a range of male subjects who were unaware of the change. Hess found that the males consistently described the girl as looking more attractive in the altered picture, although they were unable to say in what the difference consisted. The idea is that there must have been causal states of the males containing information about relative pupil size which played a part in the causal production of the explicit beliefs about relative attractiveness, although those causal states are not to be counted as genuine beliefs in themselves. For a fuller discussion of the Hess experiment, see Stich (1978, pp. 503, 505–6, and 511).

7 Note that the analogue of the listiform theory for a language with an infinite number of sentences is provided by an infinitary axiom schema: A is T iff P, 'where "P" may be replaced by any declarative sentence of the object language and "A" by the quotational name of that sentence' (Wright, 1986, p. 211).

8 We ought to note, in fairness to Evans, that this seems to be precisely what he was after in the first place – witness his claim that dispositions have to be given a full-blooded characterization.

9 Note that this holism does not imply that we shall not be able to pair explanatory states with individual axioms.

10 Given my remarks at the start of Section 2, this shows that the construction of semantic theories in accordance with the mirror constraint can also help to answer the question about learnability.

11 So although I do not want to go so far as to claim that "the right account has not greatly impinged upon the consciousness of workers in the field", I would suggest that the most efficient way of implementing that account seems to have eluded many of its practitioners.

12 Note, though, that if we take this line we appear to lose the possibility of explaining, in cognitive-psychological terms, our capacity to understand novel utterances.

13 A fuller discussion of tacit knowledge would also have to include a discussion of "the doctrine of essential linguistic structure", as discussed in Fricker (1981) and Sainsbury (1979). I hope to take up this issue in a future paper. I would like to thank Michael Clark, Martin Davies, John Divers, Jim Edwards, Bob Hale, Bob Kirk, Greg McCulloch, Joe Mendola, Mark Sainsbury, Laura Schroeter, Roger Squires, Jim Stuart, Stephen Read and Crispin Wright for very helpful comments and discussion.

References and further reading

Campbell, J. (1982), "Knowledge and understanding", *Philosophical Quarterly* 32, pp. 17–34.

Davidson, D. (1984), *Inquiries into Truth and Interpretation*. Oxford: Oxford University Press.

Davies, M. (1981), *Meaning, Quantification, and Necessity: Themes in Philosophical Logic*. London: Routledge.

Davies, M. (1981a), "Meaning, structure, and understanding", *Synthese* 48, pp. 135–61.
——(1986), "Tacit knowledge and the structure of thought and language", in C. Travis (ed.), *Meaning and Interpretation*. Oxford: Blackwell, pp. 127–58.
——(1987), "Tacit knowledge and semantic theory: can a 5% difference matter?", *Mind* 96, pp. 441–62.
——(1989), "Tacit knowledge and subdoxastic states", in A. George (ed.), *Reflections on Chomsky*. Oxford: Basil Blackwell, pp. 131–52.
Dummett, M. (1975), "What is a theory of meaning?", in S. Guttenplan (ed.), *Mind and Language*. Oxford: Oxford University Press, pp. 97–138.
——(1976), "What is a theory of meaning? (2)", in G. Evans and J. McDowell (eds), *Truth and Meaning*. Oxford: Oxford University Press, pp. 67–137.
Evans, G. (1981), "Semantic theory and tacit knowledge", in S. Holtzmann and C. Leich (eds), *Wittgenstein: To Follow a Rule*. London: Routledge, pp. 118–37.
Fricker, E. (1981), "Semantic structure and speakers' understanding", in *Proceedings of the Aristotelian Society*, 8, pp. 49–66.
Sainsbury, R.M. (1979), "Understanding and theories of meaning", in *Proceedings of the Aristotelian Society*, 80, pp. 127–44.
Stich, S. (1978), "Beliefs and subdoxastic states", in *Philosophy of Science* 45, pp. 499–518.
Wright, C. (1980), *Wittgenstein on the Foundations of Mathematics*. London: Duckworth.
——(1981), "Rule-following, objectivity, and the theory of meaning", in *Holtzmann and Leich, Wittgenstein*: *To Follow a Rule*, pp. 99–117.
——(1986), "Theories of meaning and speakers' knowledge", in his *Realism, Meaning, and Truth*, Oxford: Blackwell, pp. 204–38.
——(1988), "How can the theory of meaning be a philosophical project?", in *Mind and Language* 1/1, pp. 31–44.
——(1989), "Wittgenstein's rule-following considerations and the central project of theoretical linguistics", in George, *Reflections on Chomsky*, pp. 233–64.

8

Radical interpretation

JANE HEAL

1 A bird's-eye view of some options

To engage in radical interpretation is to set about investigating the meanings of utterances in some completely unknown language. It has been suggested that reflection on how such interpretation should proceed will throw light on the nature of meaning. The most influential proponent of this idea is Donald Davidson (1984, especially essays 9–12). This chapter will therefore be much concerned with his proposals. But it aims also to locate his views in a broader context and to consider alternative approaches.

The structure of this essay is as follows. The remainder of this section discusses the location of radical interpretation within the broader field of philosophy, and identifies some of the options and their presuppositions. Section 2 outlines the ideas of Davidson; and sections 3, 4 and 5 consider their contrasts with alternative views, seeking to identify the crucial issues.

Two things need clarification at the start. The first is that the epistemological appearance of the enterprise, if taken too seriously, could be misleading. To think that we should get illumination on the ontology or metaphysics of some concept by asking how judgements using it are established is characteristically an empiricist view. But talk of 'what one would need to know in order to establish such-and-such' may also be a mere rhetorical device for the vivid presentation of independently motivated metaphysical proposals. We should regard our reflections on the imagined procedures of radical interpretation in the second way and not the first. This is clearly the approach of Davidson and others; the investigations they speak of are highly idealized, and neither they nor we wish to commit ourselves at the outset to controversial aspects of empiricism (see Davidson, 1990, and Lewis, 1983, pp. 110–11).

A second point needing early clarification is that our quarry is not just the notion of linguistic meaning but also a broader notion of meaning or representational content, in which such content may be attributed to psychological states as well as to linguistic items. We are to think about what fixes the content of a person's thoughts as well as about how we could identify the meaning of what he or she says. Davidson takes it that thought cannot occur without language, and that language is the primary vehicle of thought (1984, Essay 11). So for him it follows immediately that investigation of the nature of thought and investigation of the nature of language are one and the same. But even those philosophers who do not accept this are likely to agree that thought and language are closely linked. It seems impossible that, for a language-using creature, there could be two entirely independent sets of facts, one about what he or she thinks and one about the meaning of what he or she says.

What exactly is 'radical interpretation'? And what is presupposed by the idea that it is possible? Its proponents seem to mean by the phrase an inferential process which starts from information, *all* of which is non-semantic, and ends with attribution of rich and varied meanings. Thus Davidson says that radical interpretation must start from 'evidence that can be stated without essential use of such linguistic concepts as meaning, interpretation, synonymy and the like' (1984, p. 128). Lewis characterizes the matter thus: 'At the outset we know nothing about [our subject's] beliefs, desires and meanings . . . Our knowledge . . . is limited to our knowledge of him as a physical system . . . Now, how can we get from that knowledge to the knowledge we want [sc. the knowledge of meanings]?' (Lewis, 1983, p. 108).

To give this description is not to say that radical interpretation cannot have among its starting-points some general principles about meaning, in the form of explicit or implicit instructions on how to process the non-semantic information presented. Clearly without such general principles we should be completely hamstrung. But the starting information is not to contain any attributions of actual particular meanings, even to expressions of one's own language, since on Davidson's fully developed theory our knowledge of the meanings in our own first language is based on radical interpretation.

We can see why this restriction on the nature of the evidence might be imposed by someone who wishes to use reflection on radical interpretation to cast light on the metaphysics of meaning, that is, on the nature of meaning as a phenomenon and on its relation to other kinds of fact. If we imagine ourselves interpreting non-radically – inferring to meanings from a mixed body knowledge containing facts about meaning as well as non-semantic facts – it may be that we can, on reflection, discover some distinctive patterns of relation between our non-semantic premises and our conclusions. It will, however, be difficult to build much upon this for metaphysical purposes (to use it, for example, to build theories of the relation of the semantic to the physical) until we are clear what has been the distinctive contribution of the additional semantic premises. But it is precisely the nature of the semantic which we are trying to clarify. And thus we risk going round in a circle. The claim here is not that any philosophical enterprise of this shape is bound to be hopeless; the claim is only that it is apparent that metaphysical conclusions could much more easily be drawn if the inferences were 'radical' in the sense outlined.

We can now see clearly at least one presupposition of the idea that radical interpretation is possible; it is that rich meaning notions are not an essential part of the basic observational vocabulary with which we approach the world. We may speak colloquially of hearing a person say that something is the case, or seeing that a person is thinking such-and-such. But, says the believer in radical interpretation, this is a mere useful idiom, not to be taken seriously. What is really observationally apparent must be something less committal, for example that certain sounds or movements were produced in certain patterns, having such-and-such causes, and the like. Facts about meaning are somehow based on or inferred from such facts.

Let us for the moment accept that there could be such a radically non-semantic starting-point as the one imagined. There are now broadly two possibilities for how the attempted working-out of meanings might go. First we could maintain a form of dualism. On this view, possession of meaning by a physical vehicle is a matter of that vehicle being suitably related to some unobservable entity, or itself having some unobservable property. Perhaps, for example, it is the effect of some intrinsically representational state of a Cartesian mind. (This is the theory of substance dualism.) Or perhaps it has in itself another hidden or mental aspect. (This would be the theory of a 'double-aspect' property dualism.) The investigation of meanings on this hypothesis is very similar to the investigation of micro-organisms or invisible dwarf companions to visible stars. Only it is not quite like this, because dualistically conceived meanings are also thought of as *in principle* unobservable, even with microscopes or spaceships. They are thought of as causing public manifestations, but being essentially linked, in a distinctive and epistemologically privileged way, to their subject. There are many familiar lines of argument against dualist positions, for example the fact that they produce 'other minds' problems and that they make it difficult to give an intelligible account of mind–body interactions.

Those philosophers who write on radical interpretation and whose work we shall consider take it for granted, however, that dualism is not a serious option. This means that, for them, the other possibility is the one which must be accepted. This possibility is that all the facts that are relevant to meaning are there in the non-semantic (that is, the physical or material) assemblage. Meaning is not, as in dualism, something independent of this assemblage but is, on the contrary, something fixed and constituted (in so far as it is fixed and constituted) by the non-semantic. So any materialist theory of mind which is non-eliminativist and which addresses itself seriously to the question of intentional content is a theory of radical interpretation.

It is not the case that the believer in the possibility of radical interpretation who also rejects dualism is committed to any simple-minded form of reductionism. He or she is not committed, for example, to the idea that semantic statements can be translated or unpacked one by one into packages of non-semantic ones. As we shall see, Davidson's proposal is very different from anything of this kind. But it is the case that the believer in radical interpretation is committed to the idea that the semantic arises from, or is constituted by, some kind of appropriate complexity in the non-semantic. For want of a better word, I shall say that he or she is committed to the reducibility of the semantic to the non-semantic. But it is to be remembered that what is involved is reducibility in some extremely broad sense.

The difficulties of dualism have given a bad name to the whole idea of non-reductive accounts of meaning (in the very broad sense of 'reduction' just gestured at). The bulk of philosophical writing on meaning (in the analytic tradition) has thus been concerned to pursue the radical interpretation strategy. But are dualism (in which a hidden and separate meaning is inferred *behind* the non-semantic surface) or a reductive materialist view (in which it is discerned *in* the patterns of the non-semantic) the only options? What if we abandon the assumption common to the materialist accounts and dualism, namely that meaning is not observable, while retaining dualism's commitment to non-reductionism? This gives us a view on which meaning is a public and observable property of certain sounds, marks or movements, but a non-physical one. So the concept of meaning is a descriptive and factual one, and also, very importantly, a basic observational one. But it is not part of that predominantly quantitative and value-free conceptual scheme we have built up for describing, predicting and explaining the behaviour of inanimate objects; rather, it belongs to a different but equally fundamental area of thinking, namely the one we use in our relations with other persons. This line of thought is favoured by those with Wittgensteinian sympathies. If we accept this view it is likely that the idea of the imagined starting-point for radical interpretation, a starting-point in which a person knows plenty of non-semantic facts but no semantic facts at all, will come to seem incoherent. The starting-point for any thinking is one in which we are observationally aware of the world as containing both semantic and non-semantic facts.

This option will seem to many extremely wild, because it clashes with certain widespread but often unarticulated assumptions about fundamental matters like fact, truth and perception; so to make it seem even coherent, let alone plausible, we would need to reappraise our views on these topics. But before considering whether we need to embark on that unsettling enterprise, we should surely see whether we cannot find something more immediately congenial in the radical-interpretation camp.

We have then at least the following questions to ask. Is radical interpretation possible? If it is, what are the strengths and weaknesses of the particular variants proposed? If it is not, why does it fail and what should we put in its place?

On this last question, let us remember that in addition to dualism and the Wittgensteinian option sketched we have at our disposal also such views as eliminativism and instrumentalism. The first of these says that psychological concepts, including those of content and meaning, are so confused and/or scientifically ill-grounded that nothing answers to them, and hence no theory of their (true) applicability is required (Churchland, 1988; Stich, 1983). The second says that talk of meaning and content is a useful tool but not to be factually interpreted (Dennett, 1979 and 1987).

For various reasons, our entry-point into these issues will be consideration of the views of Davidson. The topic we are considering got its name from him, and some important themes emerged in his writings. Focusing on them allows us to identify interesting points of contrast between different theories of radical interpretation. But it is also arguably the case that his view, if correct, contains the seeds of its own destruction, in that it leads to unacceptable claims about the indeterminacy of meaning, and might thus lead us to question the validity of the whole radical-interpretation project.

It is, however, difficult to see at first reading what is of central importance in Davidson's work, because the form of his proposal is substantially but unhelpfully influenced by its history. We turn therefore in section 2 to a brief sketch of its development and summary of its mature form.

2 From 'truth and meaning' to 'radical interpretation'

A distinction it is useful to have clear is that between providing an analysis of a concept, an account which clarifies its links with other concepts and hence its metaphysics, and providing what I shall call a 'calculus' for that concept, a set of rules for working out if it is applicable to an item on the basis of information about the composition of that item. (See Heal, 1978, for more on this distinction.) For example, consider the claim that sodium nitrite is poisonous to octopuses. A person can show that she knows very well what this means – by unpacking the claim in terms of what will happen to octopuses who ingest sodium nitrite. But this person may be in no position to say whether the claim is true or not, because she has no sodium nitrite or no octopuses, or cannot get the latter to eat the former. Another person might, by contrast, be in a position to rule on the truth of the claim, because he is in possession of a set of instructions for calculating to what creatures, if any, a chemical compound is poisonous, from a canonical specification of the elements in the compound and their mode of bonding. This person might, however, not fully understand the claim, because for him 'poisonous' is little more than a dummy predicate and he has no grip on its relations to eating, illness and so forth.

For many concepts, as for 'poisonous', analysis is independent of calculus. It is a contingent matter whether or not there is a calculus of poisonousness. And even if there is a calculus one can understand 'poisonous' very well without suspecting this, let alone knowing what it is. But for meaning things are different. And this is the starting point for Davidson's discussion in 'Truth and Meaning' (Davidson 1984, Essay 2; see also Chapter 1, MEANING AND TRUTH CONDITIONS: FROM FREGE'S GRAND DESIGN TO DAVIDSON'S). He is concerned to emphasize that an item cannot have sentential-type meaning, that is, be the vehicle for a complete linguistic move, unless it is complex. Any such sentence must be built up from words which, together with their arrangement, determine the meaning of the whole.

His arguments rest heavily upon the fact that natural languages allow for the construction of indefinitely many new sentences. In them a finite number of words are built together in increasingly complicated arrangements by application (repeated if need be) of a finite stock of constructions. Unless we see sentences as built in this way it is entirely mysterious how finite creatures like ourselves could have the language-speaking and -understanding capacities which we do.

These considerations are weighty; and we can cite others which point in the same direction. Even if a language had only a finite number of sentences there would, I suggest, be reasons for thinking that sentence-style meaning requires the existence of words or word-like complexity in the sentences. It is central to the notion of meaning (for contingent a posteriori sentences at least) that meaning is one thing and truth value another. Imagine now some item which has a meaning of this kind and is also false – for example, an item which means 'snow is green'. Try to suppose also that this item entirely lacks semantic complexity in its properties or relations; its having the meaning it does is a one-off matter, and not bound up with any systematic connection with any other meaning-bearing items. We seem here to have something completely unintelligible. The difficulty is not merely epistemological – how could we tell that the item had this meaning? – but also constitutive: what could there be about it which fixes that it is about snow or about greenness? One-word indexical sentences, like 'Fire!', do not provide a counter-example to this claim. What is required for a linguistic move is a token, and each token of this sentence does exhibit two separable features, namely its type and its spatio-temporal location, which contribute independently to fixing the claim made by the whole.

So Davidson's starting-point in 'Truth and Meaning' is the fact that 'S means that p', when unpacked, turns out to commit us to the idea that S is a complex item which will have a number of different features, each with its own semantic role, which jointly determine the meaning of S. Let us go along with him in assuming that the features are the presence of identifiable words. This is not obligatory. The features could be things such as colour, size or shape, or they could be relational properties. But the word-hypothesis simplifies exposition without distorting the issues we are concerned with here.

But if S contains words then it must be (potentially at least) part of a language. There must be (the possibility of) other words which could replace some of the words in S, and so the possibility of other sentences which could be built from different combinations of those words. So 'S means that p' turns out to have the following implication: S belongs to a language, that is, a system of meaningful items, for which a meaning calculus can be given which supplies 'S means that p' as an output theorem. Davidson, in 'Truth and Meaning' conceives his task to be that of unpacking further what any such meaning calculus would have to be like.

Suppose that S is 'a is F', that we know that it means that a is F and that we are convinced that 'a' and 'is F' are the semantically relevant subparts. An adequate meaning calculus will assign properties to 'a', to 'is F' and to concatenation; these property assignments will be (some of) the axioms of the meaning calculus, and they must entail as a theorem

'a is F' means that a is F.

What might they be like? Well, says Davidson, we already know of one sort of axiom set which will do exactly this job, namely that employed in a Tarski-style theory of truth. (See Tarski, 1956. For useful expositions see Haack, 1978, and Evnine, 1991.) All this might merely lead to the thought that a Tarskian calculus of truth conditions and a Davidsonian calculus of meaning will employ the same shape of machinery. It does not yet entitle us to suppose that the notion of meaning can be unpacked into or analysed in terms of the notion of truth. But this is the bold step which Davidson proposes. He suggests that we abandon Tarski's requirement that the theorems must have on their right-hand sides something with the same meaning as the sentence mentioned on the left, and that we instead demand only that theorems be true biconditionals about truth conditions. His conjecture is that this, together with the remaining constraint of using finite semantic structure to generate a theorem about every sentence, must narrow down the number of acceptable calculi to such an extent that anything which satisfies the constraints will, in fact, serve as a calculus of meaning.

The proposal, in summary, is this:

'S means that p' unpacks into
'S is part of a language and a correct truth conditions calculus for this language can be set up which delivers "S is true iff p" as a theorem.'

(Let us enter a caveat here. Davidson denies, 1976, p. 35, that this was his proposal, and he implies that he all along intended further constraints. But however this may be, the line of interpretation I have sketched is the most natural reading of 'Truth and Meaning', and is what most of its readers took Davidson to be saying.)

The proposal is one about the conceptual connection between the notion of meaning on the one hand and the notions of word, language, structure, calculus and truth on the other. It claims to offer insight into meaning, but not by invoking anything to do with radical interpretation. Why, then, have we spent so much time on it? Because Davidson's later view is, in part, an attempt to rescue the earlier theory; and the later view retains, unnecessarily to my mind, certain features of the earlier one. These are features which many have found particularly implausible, and they have hindered appreciation of other, more important new elements introduced in the later theory. So unless we know a little of the history we shall not understand properly what is going on.

One damning objection to the early proposal which soon became apparent is this (Foster, 1976; see also Chapter 1, MEANING AND TRUTH CONDITIONS: FROM FREGE'S GRAND DESIGN TO DAVIDSON'S). An acceptable truth-conditions calculus for a language can generate the true theorem that S is true iff p, when it is quite clear that S does *not* mean that p. For example, if the properties P and Q by chance characterize all and only the same things, then a calculus of truth conditions which assigns Q to a predicate 'F' will do just a well as one which assigns P. Yet looking at the speakers of the language, it may be far more plausible that they are speaking about Q than about P; P might be something these speakers could not be aware of, such as a microstructural property, or it might be some gerrymandered compound property like 'having Q while 2 + 2 = 4', which is, of course, coextensive with 'having Q'.

Davidson's moves in 'Radical Interpretation' provide a response to this. He there offers a proposal about meaning which retains a central element of the earlier work, but locates it in an importantly different setting. The retained element is the idea that to say 'S means that p' is to say that S belongs to a language for which an empirically acceptable calculus of truth conditions delivers 'S is true iff p' as a theorem. But the empirical conditions which make a calculus acceptable are spelt out differently. The demand now is not that the calculus supply true biconditionals about truth conditions; it is that it deliver theorems which lead to the speaker of the language satisfying the *Principle of Charity*. We shall return to this in a later section. But what it says is roughly the following: *if* we use our candidate calculus to interpret our subject – that is, whenever the calculus says something of the form 'S is true iff p' and the subject says S, then we take him to be expressing the belief that p – *then* he comes out as by and large a sensible fellow, with a mainly correct view of the world.

This condition may now enable us to distinguish between the two calculi (the one which linked 'F' with property P and the one which linked it with property Q) that were mentioned earlier. It may be that the overall psychology attributed to the subject using Q reveals him as much more coherent and intelligible than the one using P.

We could, then, just add the Principle of Charity to the earlier empirical condition (that the calculus deliver a correct account of truth conditions) and leave the overall proposal otherwise untouched. It may seem as if this is what Davidson does. And indeed, his later proposal could be summarized in the form of words we used earlier, with the addition of the extra clause.

But it is important to realize that, at the same time as the Principle of Charity comes on the scene, another change takes place in Davidson's thought, namely a shift of attention from the case of thinking about one's own language to that of thinking about a strange language. The home-language case drops away out of explicit consideration. When mentioned, it is presented as just another case of radical interpretation, but one where familiarity disguises this fact from us. The effect of this is that the way of understanding what it is for something to be a correct calculus of truth conditions which was earlier called upon is no longer available. When we are thinking about the home language we can presuppose an implicit understanding of sentences. This makes it straightforward to test theorems delivered by a candidate theory. Suppose I am already a speaker of English, and I am asked whether '"Snow is white" is true iff rubies contain carbon' is a true biconditional. I may not know the answer instantly, but at least I know what I have to do to find out. But when we change the case to an unknown language, matters are very different. Suppose the candidate theory delivers '"Skuppit gromper" is true iff rubies contain carbon'. How am I to tell whether this is a true biconditional about truth conditions?

It is easy not to notice how big the shift is between the position of 'Truth and Meaning' and that of 'Radical Interpretation'. The fact that a very similar formulation can be offered may suggest that all that has happened is that Charity has been added in as an extra constraint. But a crucial point is that with the change of focus from the home case to the alien, the earlier account of empirical correctness needs replacement. And with its replacement, the whole shape of the enterprise changes. The earlier project aims for an account of linguistic meaning in terms of truth. It tries to illuminate the intensional semantic notion of meaning by unpacking its links with the extensional notion of truth, together with the notions of structure and calculus. This project works within a circle of semantic concepts and it applies only to linguistic items; views about the nature of persons and psychological states are not brought in at all. The second project is, by contrast, in many ways more ambitious. It offers to give an account of *both* meaning *and* truth, which are now put back together as an inextricable pair, neither of which is more fundamental than the other. And the account it offers is extended to apply to psychological states as well as to linguistic items. The story it offers, to put matters extremely briefly, sees meaning, language, truth and thought all as needing to be explained in terms of patterns discernible in uninterpreted behaviour.

Let me now spell out in more detail the fully fledged, later proposal. First some preliminaries. It is supposed that we can identify prior to interpretation the class of sentences which the subject holds true, that is, those he or she is willing to assert sincerely. Patterns of recurrent elements can be discerned in those sentences. The patterns are of such a kind that a finite calculus of truth conditions can be set up which covers all sentences of the language. This is to say that we can hit on a finite number of axioms which assign semantic properties to the recurrent elements in such a way that we can derive for every sentence some theorem assigning it truth conditions. The pattern of actions and utterances is also such that use of this calculus as a tool for attributing attitudes makes the subject come out as satisfying the Principle of Charity. Let us call such a calculus 'an empirically correct theory of truth' for the language in question. Now we can state the proposal thus:

> 'S means that p' unpacks as
> 'S is true iff p' is a theorem of an empirically correct theory of truth for the language containing S.

And

> 'A thinks that p' unpacks as
> There is some S which A holds true and S means that p.

Davidson draws the following conclusions from this account: that meaning is a normative notion, implicated with what he elsewhere calls 'the constitutive ideal of rationality' (1980, p. 223) and that meaning is to some extent indeterminate, in that alternative calculi of truth conditions could well be set up which satisfied all the constraints equally well. We shall consider the first of these claims in section 4 and the second in section 5. But we turn first to another matter.

3 The basis for radical interpretation

How does this approach compare with other theories which share the basic assumption of the radical interpretation programme, namely that meaning must somehow be based in or derived from the non-meaningful?

Most other approaches of such character have in common a broadly functionalist and naturalistic orientation. They suppose that the nature of psychological notions is to be elucidated by pointing to their causal role *vis-à-vis* behaviour. They thus tend to share a sympathy with the idea of unpacking semantic relations in terms of causal relations. For a person to be thinking that a is F is for him or her to be in a state with suitable causal relations to a and to F-ness. Where they differ is in the spelling-out of what 'suitable' means. Some call on the idea of a language of thought, in which individual words have semantics fixed by their individual causal histories (Field, 1978; Fodor, 1975 and 1987). Some give an important role to the aetiology of internal structures in natural selection (Millikan, 1984; Papineau, 1987). Others call upon the notion of information (Dretske, 1981). Here I cannot hope to do justice to the variety and ingenuity of theories proposed (see Chapter 5, A GUIDE TO NATURALIZING SEMANTICS). Instead I shall ask where they, or large subgroups of them, seem likely to come into conflict with the Davidsonian view sketched at the end of section 2, in the hope that this will bring into focus at least some of the interesting issues in the area.

One immediate point of contrast stands out, namely that most theories other than Davidson's would take as their base not a set of facts about 'holding true', but the totality of physical facts. In defence of his starting-point Davidson writes, '[Holding true] is an attitude an interpreter may plausibly be taken to be able to identify before he can interpret, since he may know that a person intends to express a truth in uttering a sentence without having any idea *what* truth' (1984, p. 135). The general claim here is, however, implausible, and the reason given for it (that it is *sometimes* possible to know that a person intends to express a truth without knowing which) does little to support it. A theory of radical interpretation should be applicable to giant octopuses or superbeings emerging from their spaceships as well as to newly encountered human beings. But consideration of such non-human cases makes clear that identification of something as a holding true requires ability to distinguish voluntary from involuntary and linguistic from non-linguistic behaviour. There is every reason to suppose that making these distinctions will involve simultaneously making rich hypotheses about the contents of beliefs and purposes. A similar point can be made in connection with speech acts other than sincere assertion, such as commands, stories and irony (1984, p. 135). Davidson does mention these, but he underplays the fact that distinguishing them from sincere assertions (which we shall have to do if we are to identify the holdings true before interpretation) also requires attributions of rich and complex intentions.

So, in brief, Davidson's proposed radical interpretation starts in a place which is either not available or is not radical. Moreover, even if that place were available, his methodology would have us ignore evidence about the placement of speech in the context of non-linguistic action. But such placement might surely give us useful clues to meaning. And indeed Davidson himself, at another point (1984, p. 162) remarks that a theory of interpretation cannot stand alone, but will need to be integrated within a more comprehensive theory of thought and action.

Why, then, should Davidson have chosen as basic this unsatisfactory 'holding true' notion? One explanation is the powerful influence on him of the Quinean radical translation model. (See Chapter 16, THE INDETERMINACY OF TRANSLATION.) But another is the desire to carry forward as much as possible of the shape of the 'Truth and Meaning' theory. There we assumed that we started with an identified body of sentences for which we know truth conditions, namely the sentences of our own language. The test of a proposed calculus was then simply whether it delivered correct statements about truth conditions for these sentences. The nearest we can get to this position, if we shift to a radical situation, is to imagine, first, that linguistic behaviour at the start neatly differentiates itself from the rest, and second, that we can establish by observation the conditions under which each sentence is held true. On those assumptions (and – *very* importantly, given *also* that holding-true conditions for the most part coincide with actual truth conditions: see the next section) then we can proceed very much as we did on the 'Truth and Meaning' story. But the moral of the discussion of non-human cases is that this is not a persuasive line. A desire to duplicate the earlier structure as far as possible has led to the implausible idea that sentences held true can be isolated from the rest of behaviour prior to interpretation. The totality of physical facts would be a much less tendentious place to start.

Davidson's proposal, then, needs modification in at least two ways. The first is the change in the imagined starting-point, and the second is the need to take account of the relation of linguistic behaviour to its context in action. The upshot of such changes would be a theory rather like that proposed by Lewis (1983). The idea is, briefly, this: to say 'A thinks that p' or 'A's utterance S means that p' is correct provided that these claims would be delivered by an acceptable overall theory of A's behaviour; a theory is acceptable if it attributes beliefs, desires, intentions and meanings to A (and thus licenses redescription of some mere movements, noise-makings and so on as actions and utterances) in such a way that (1) A has a language with a finitely specifiable and reasonably simple semantic structure; (2) A has, by and large a true, rational and epistemologically defensible view of the world (that is, he satisfies the Principle of Charity); and (3) A comes out as doing and refraining in action (including linguistic action) in the way expected of a rational person with the intentional states attributed.

What is there in this which might still provoke objections? The Davidsonian idea that there is a link between meaning on the one hand and system or structure on the other is still very much in play. The proposal assumes that nothing can be seen as a meaning-bearer (whether an action expressive of intention or an utterance expressive of belief) unless it is part of a repertoire of other possible items with which it is contrasted. Methodologically, we are exhorted to use these contrasts and the circumstances of their occurrence as key diagnostic elements for interpretation. And this, the insight stressed at the start of section 2, is not, it seems to me, something with which any theory of meaning need quarrel. (However, the most unlikely quarrels are pursued. See Fodor and Lepore, 1992, esp. ch. 3.)

A potentially more controversial feature of the proposal is that it has a behaviourist flavour. What licenses and makes true attributions of meaning is a certain sort of patternedness in observable behaviour. It is not a trivial matter that behaviour should be amenable to redescription in terms of a rational psychology, any more than it is a trivial matter that a certain set of intricately shaped and coloured flat wooden shapes should fit together in a jigsaw to present a recognizable picture. In both cases it is a matter of individual items locking together, literally or metaphorically, in the right kind of way. And we can imagine sets of items which do not fit. But some might wonder whether such a merely surface feature of behaviour was a sufficient condition of thought and meaning, and whether we should not demand also that there be inner causal mechanisms answering in structure to the beliefs and desires attributed.

We shall return to this issue. But first we shall consider another possible source of disquiet, namely the role given in the proposal to the Principle of Charity. Is the Principle, as some have thought, hopelessly parochial? Is it over-optimistic about the likely success of thought? And what does it have to do with some supposed normative aspect to meaning?

4 Interpretation, charity, holism and norms

To start with, let us look at the early history of the Principle of Charity, when it was, rightly, found unattractive. We should, said Davidson, insist a priori that an interpreter find a calculus 'which yields, so far as possible, a mapping of sentences held true (or false) by the aliens on to sentences held true or false by the linguist' (1984, p. 27). What this amounts to is that we must make the assumption that pretty well everything we say, and also pretty well everything the aliens say, is true. (Davidson explicitly draws out these anti-sceptical implications of his position in 1984, Essay 14. See also Evnine, 1991, ch. 8.)

Why does Davidson make this recommendation? Following our earlier line, a conjecture is that it is because this is the simplest way of converting the 'Truth and Meaning' proposal for use on an unknown language. For my home language I am able to test whether a truth-conditions calculus is empirically acceptable by seeing whether the theorems it delivers are true. I can do this on a one-by-one basis, using my taken-for-granted knowledge of my own language together with ability to find out about the world. But when we deal with an unknown language, this method is inapplicable. Since I do not understand the sentences I do not know what to enquire into to test a claim about their truth conditions. (We have already touched on this point earlier, in section 2.) But if I could just *equate* the aliens' being willing or unwilling to assert a sentence with that sentence's being true or false then this lack of understanding need not handicap me. I do not need to investigate the truth of their sentence directly in order to test a candidate calculus; I need only to find out whether the aliens *hold* the sentence true and then, simply assuming that it *is* true, I find out whether the conditions which the calculus assigns to it do obtain. If they obtain, then the theory is confirmed. Doubtless I must make some allowance for the possibility of the aliens making occasional errors. But if I can insist a priori that such mistakes must be extremely rare, then the above simple testing strategy is available.

The early formulation of the Principle of Charity, however, produced objections. It seems to involve the claims, firstly that we already have pretty well all the thoughts there are to have (because any set of thoughts can be mapped on to ours), and secondly that our beliefs are pretty well one hundred per cent correct. These claims appear to underrate the possibilities both for ignorance and for error.

The first claim is in fact not essential to the proposed method. Davidson need not deny our possible ignorance of many aspects of the universe, and he ought to allow that the process of interpretation could be one of substantial learning about the world, that is, it need not merely be one of pairing things we already know with things the alien subject knows. What is more crucial is the claim of substantial correctness in all systems of thought, including our own current one, since it is this claim which underpins the rough equation of 'the subject holds S true' with 'S is true' in our investigative methodology. This second claim is objectionable, however, in that it is either highly implausible or hopelessly unclear. If it is taken to mean that the *actual* sincere utterances of any group of persons must be largely true, it is implausible. It rules out the idea that an extensive part of the lives of a group of persons should be concerned with the pursuit of some chimerical and theoretically ill-based enterprise. How can we rule out a priori the idea that our societies might have evolved in such a way as to doom most of us to think and speak, a large proportion of the time, about alchemy, astrology or historical materialism? But if we shift instead to consider merely *possible* utterances and our willingness to assent to them, the content of the claim becomes extremely unclear, as Davidson himself later hints (1984, p. 136). Possible utterances form an indefinitely large set, and so quantitative claims about proportions of truth and falsity in the set have no obvious meaning.

So it looks as if 'Truth and Meaning' is again exerting an unfortunate influence, and has led Davidson to an indefensible position. Before considering whether anything can be rescued, we need to distinguish two different roles for a principle like the Principle of Charity. (Useful moves in this direction are made in Malpas, 1988.) One role is played at the start of the attempt to interpret. Davidson claims that interpretation of words and attribution of beliefs combine to explain utterance. But, he says, we cannot access the beliefs expressed in an utterance prior to and independent of grasp on the meaning of the utterance. Nor can we do the reverse. We need, therefore, to make some initial assumption, in order to begin to test and elaborate any theory. Davidson's way out of the impasse is that we should start by taking it that the beliefs of the other are the same as ours.

There is much that is attractive here. Even those who think that non-linguistic behaviour can provide very strong or conclusive evidence for certain beliefs (and hence would reject the detailed Davidsonian proposal, with its stress on language) may recognize an analogous problem in the way in which belief and desire co-operate to produce action. Thus it is a plausible thought that any interpretive enterprise will have to start off by trying out some assumptions in order to break into a circle. And it is also plausible that a good place to start is with the idea that the others are like us.

One alternative to the Principle of Charity, following this line of thought, is sometimes called the Principle of Humanity. It does not recommend us to attribute to our subject as a starting hypothesis the very thoughts we ourselves actually have. But it suggests a close variant, namely the thoughts we would have had, if we had been through someone else's life experiences (Grandy, 1973; Lewis, 1983). This, indeed, looks a useful suggestion and better than straight Charity. If all that was at issue was methodological advice on how to start out interpreting, perhaps we should stop here.

But it is not all that is at issue. However useful as a tip on how to *start*, neither Humanity nor Charity tells us where we shall *end up*. What if our initial assignment of thoughts based on the principle does not work out? What if further investigation makes it seem likely that our subject has different sensory apparatus and/or different emotions and interests from us, and so has significantly different views from any we do or would have had? In these circumstances we must modify our starting hypothesis. And we need at this point to know what constraints there are upon the shape of theory we may move on to, and how to evaluate rival emendations.

Let us now look at one of Davidson's own later remarks. He stresses (as do proponents of the Principle of Humanity) that any interpretation must allow for intelligible error. He writes:

> It is impossible to simplify the considerations that are relevant [i.e. to assessing a proposed theory] for everything we know or believe about the way evidence supports belief can be put to work in deciding where the theory can best allow error and what errors are least disruptive of understanding. The methodology of interpretation is, in this respect, nothing but epistemology seen in the mirror of meaning. (1984, p. 169)

The important theme here is that any set of thoughts we attribute to a subject must come with (or with the possibility of) some intelligible epistemology. This principle, if correct, applies not only to what we guess when we start out interpreting, but to hypotheses at all stages. Something else stressed by Davidson, and which is part of the same line of thought, is the prominent role given to indexical utterances in providing some anchorage for interpretive theories. We must be able to see some utterances as expressing perceptual judgements about the world around the subject.

What does this insistence on the need for plausible epistemology stand opposed to? Rejection of dualism about meaning is one of the deep-lying assumptions of the enterprise. Classical dualism moves from belief in the *non-reducibility* of facts about psychology (including facts about content and meaning) to claims of their *independence* from the physical. Such independence would allow us to evade the proposed epistemological constraints. We do not, on a dualist view, have to tell a story about how the subject could, so to speak, have got in touch with what we say he is thinking about. We are allowed to suppose that it just is a fact that he is thinking about it. So on a dualist view, content may float free of public facts about a creature's constitution and placement in the world. This is what leads to its constant implicit threat of scepticism, both about other minds and about the external world.

Let us, however, not identify rejection of dualism with acceptance of empiricism. It is one thing to be very unhappy to attribute to a person a thought about some state of affairs which we believe he or she has had no opportunity to perceive, hear of or theoretically conjecture. It is another to suppose that some sensory reduction can be given for all thoughts. (See Davidson, 1990 for a discussion of the difference.)

Can we say anything else general about sets of thoughts? Yes, says Davidson. We should recognize the so-called 'holism of meaning'. This is the claim that an intentional state with content cannot exist in isolation, but requires the presence in the subject of many other intentional states with suitable contents. For example, anyone who wonders whether the bank is open must believe a fair number of general things, such as that other people exist, that goods are produced and exchanged and that money exists; and he or she must also have some suitable beliefs about such things as the nature and location of the bank in question.

This view, the holism of meaning, has some resemblance to the claim, argued earlier in section 2, of the necessity for any meaning-bearer to be itself complex and to be placed in a system. But they are not the same view. The mere claims of complexity and systematicity carry no immediate implications about the kind of content which is to be carried by the other elements in the system, while the view currently under consideration emphasizes the need for particular kinds of conceptual content to be present. The relation between the two theses deserves more discussion than it can be given here (The word 'holism' is sometimes used also in connection with the view about the joint operation of belief and meaning in giving rise to utterance. But this is a third, and different view. See also Chapter 10, HOLISM.)

The holism of meaning thesis is offered in support of the Principle of Charity, that is, the idea that there must be 'massive agreement' between our thoughts and any other possible set of thoughts and that we must in consequence be substantially right. It is argued that it implies that disagreement cannot exist except against a background of agreement. To redeploy the earlier example, there cannot be disagreement over whether the bank is open unless there is agreement on at least some things, like the existence of other people, the exchange of goods, the existence of money, and so on. So the idea of detecting pervasive error in another thinker (whether we interpret others or they interpret us) is incoherent.

This is the argument. But it does not, in fact, help us with the trouble we had earlier in applying quantitative notions like 'massive agreement' to indefinitely large sets of beliefs; and hence it does not help in seeing exactly what the content of the claim is. Without detailed supplementary information (about how much agreement is required to underpin one disagreement, about whether one agreed set of beliefs can underpin more than one disagreement, and so forth) nothing follows about quantities. Such supplementation is unlikely to be forthcoming. We would do well, then, simply to jettison the quantitative style of claim.

What if anything then remains of the Principle of Charity? Let us first re-express the original insight of meaning holism. It is that for an item to bear a certain meaning it is required that it exist in a setting of other items bearing related meanings. Thus it is only when a rationally coherent and related group of items exists, a group which can be taken to represent some extended portion of a world, that we can attribute content to any member of it.

Let us pause to emphasize something important at this point. Nothing that has been said requires us to insist that a particular thought requires some given, fixed set of other thoughts. We may do so, if we are sympathetic to the idea of analytic truth. But we could instead demand something weaker, namely only that there be *some* suitable setting to anchor a given content. As an analogy, consider what is required for a dot in a cartoon-style picture to represent a living human eye. One might think (adopting the analytic model) that there had to be a dot for the other eye, a line for the mouth, a circle for the face, or at least a reasonable subset of these. But this is not correct. We can imagine a dot which represents the eye of someone peering through a hole in a screen, where none of the rest of the body is depicted. What is required is that there is enough detail in the rest of the picture to make clear that this is what is happening. Similarly for content, one could speculate. We can attribute a given belief in the absence of its usual accompaniments in us, provided there is some other suitable setting to anchor its meaning. And perhaps there are no ways of cataloguing and systematically studying what 'suitable settings' there could be.

So to return to our current question of whether anything useful can be salvaged from the Principle of Charity. We have so far expressed the holism of meaning in terms which suggest that it is relevant only to small subsets within a set of thoughts. But the implications of the holism are wider. The thoughts which are, so to speak, at the edge of one set will need to be in the middle of another. And thus the idea of the 'suitable setting' will spread to encompass the totality of thoughts. The upshot is that the set must, as a whole, be more or less coherent and so represent what could be one world. We cannot have a fragment here and another contradictory fragment there without losing grip on the idea that it is one mind, one subject's point of view, that we are capturing.

If we now combine this thought with the earlier anti-dualist one we arrive at the following view. Any set of thoughts we attribute to a subject must be a recognizable representation (however incomplete or distorted) of this one world which we share with him or her. It must be something with which we can to some degree sympathize, in that we can see it as the outcome of rationality, i.e. cognitive competence in a broad sense, trying to get to grips with this world. This muted version of Charity may be a far cry from a claim of massive agreement and general correctness, but it is not negligible.

Having thus thrown out the early version of the Principle of Charity and summarized what seems important in the later version, let us now turn back to the other question we have been pursuing and ask whether there is anything in the Principle, as now understood, to raise objections from those who hold other, for example functionalist, views about radical interpretation.

The anti-dualist strand, with its emphasis on the 'externalist' idea that the content of a meaningful item is to be in part at least fixed by its context (for example, external causal links) is thoroughly congenial. (For more on the many varieties of externalism see McGinn, 1989.) Some theorists explicitly reject the idea of meaning holism (see, for example, Fodor, 1987, ch. 3; and Fodor and Lepore, 1992). But most functionalists would have no difficulty in endorsing this view also. The central functionalist idea is that psychological terms are elements in some folk proto-theory for explaining behaviour; their meaning is explained by reference to their explanatory roles in this theory *vis-à-vis* observable behaviour and, importantly, *vis-à-vis* each other. The holist idea of linking content to place in some suitable pattern seems a natural development of this. For such a functionalist just as for Davidson, rationality, the existence of appropriate inferential and content links, is built into the very nature of the psychological. (See Evnine, 1991, pp. 111–12.)

Where, then, could any clash arise? The crucial question is this. Can the key notion of rationality be given at some level a naturalistic, such as a physical, unpacking; or is it centrally a normative notion of a kind which resists such capture? It would be generally agreed that it is normative; it has to do with thinking as one ought, that is, in such a way as to promote the goals of thought. But this does not preclude the existence of a non-normative equivalent. To use a familiar old example, a knife's being good may, given the acknowledged purpose of knives and the causal facts about the world, amount to its having certain physical properties (of weight, shape, sharpness and so on). Is there something describable in the language of the natural sciences which in a similar sense is what rationality 'amounts to'?

Some may think that we already have such a thing, and that it is given by an amalgam of the (syntactic) rules of inference provided by (a favoured) deductive logic, inductive logic and decision theory. This, however, seems over-optimistic, given the disputes, paradoxes and unclarities in these subjects. We also need to remember that acquisition of knowledge about the universe does not always take the form of adding empirical information within a fixed conceptual and logical structure, but may involve modification of concepts and hence of patterns of inter-judgemental linkages (consider non-Euclidean geometry, Einsteinian revelations on space and time and so on). We are not in a position to say that there are no more conceptual upsets ahead; so we cannot now plausibly claim that we know, definitively and completely, what rationality amounts to.

But all the same, is there such a thing as what it amounts to? This is a very close relative of the question that arose above as to whether any notion of analyticity is defensible (see Chapter 14, ANALYTICITY) and, connectedly, of whether there is some limit to the 'suitable settings' which meaning holism requires. Obtaining a reasoned answer to these questions could well require us to have a view on such things as whether there is one complete and final truth about the universe and one set of concepts which that truth demands for its expression, whether there is any hope of human beings attaining that truth, whether (or in what sense) we could be rational if we were constitutionally debarred by the structure of our minds from attaining it, and what the connection is between rationality in theoretical matters (arriving at the truth) and rationality in practical matters (arriving at good decisions). Those who favour an ultimately physicalist account of rationality will incline to assume something optimistic about the possibilities of disentangling theoretical from practical reason and arriving at the complete truth about the universe, while others will be sceptical on these matters. Some sceptics, like Davidson, seem to think that it is in principle impossible that there should be a physicalistic unpacking. Other sceptics, like the instrumentalist, Dennett, seem to think that there is such an unpacking, but that our finitude constitutionally debars us from realizing it and consequently our 'rationality' and 'thought' are merely useful fictions.

We can return here briefly to tie up one loose end, namely why Davidson's proposal has, as remarked towards the end of section 3, a behaviourist flavour. We can see now that it is not an attractive option for one who is sceptical about a naturalistic unpacking of 'rational' to appeal to internal structures. If there was a fixed structure to rationality then there would be some fixed set of thoughts associated by meaning holism with any given thought, namely that set which the one and only true rationality requires it to be linked with. And it would be natural to insist that a subject who has the thought must contain some physical realization of (at least some part of) the relevant set and its supporting causal linkages. So on this view internal mechanisms would be important. But, on the other hand, if there is no fixed structure of rationality, then it is unclear what importance internal mechanisms could have. The only thing that can matter is whether the totality of utterances and behaviour can be redescribed in terms of some one of the (perhaps indefinitely many and exceedingly various) rational psychologies. Any investigation into the inner mechanisms which subserve the intelligible behaviour must follow after the attempt to make sense of that behaviour. The presence of inner mechanisms cannot be used as a separate and prior constraint on whether a subject possesses a certain thought. (Compare here Davidson's rejection of psycho-physical laws in 1980, Essay 11.)

5 Indeterminacy of meaning, holism and molecularity

We have so far been presenting most of our theories, Davidson's included, as though they were straightforward accounts of what non-semantic facts constituted some semantic fact. But we must now grapple with a final complication, namely that the Davidsonion approach seems to imply indeterminacy (1984, pp. 100–1, 153–4). On his view, to say that a noise has a certain meaning is to say that a subject's behaviour can be systematized by a certain kind of theory. But the crucial problem is that there is no guarantee that there is only one way of systematizing a given body of behaviour. The assignment of meanings to individual moves or noises is merely a record of the fact that the behaviour as a whole can be arranged in a certain sort of pattern. But the fact that the pieces of behaviour can be arranged in one pattern cannot rule out the possibility of arranging them also in another one. Consider as an analogy the pieces of a jigsaw. We are used to unique-arrangement jigsaws. But there is no conceptual necessity to this, and an ingenious toy-maker could manufacture (perhaps already has manufactured) multiple-arrangement ones. To label an utterance 'a saying that it is raining' is, on the Davidsonian story, like labelling a jigsaw piece 'a mountain summit piece'. In other words, such a labelling tells us that there is at least one overall satisfactory arrangement in which the utterance or piece could play the designated role. But, to re-emphasize, that is no conceptual bar to the existence of another arrangement in which it plays another role. Indeed Davidson goes further and endorses an argument designed to prove that if there is one adequate linguistic interpretation then there must be alternative satisfactory interpretations. His argument (1984, Essay 16) is a close relative of some given by Quine (1960, ch. 2 and 1969, Essay 2). (See also Chapter 16, THE INDETERMINACY OF TRANSLATION, and Chapter 17, PUTNAM'S MODEL-THEORETIC ARGUMENT AGAINST METAPHYSICAL REALISM, Dummett, 1975, and Heal, 1989.)

We could embrace this conclusion and the anti-realist implications which it has for the notion of meaning. But many philosophers find this conclusion intuitively incredible (such as Lewis, 1983, p. 118). We may note two reasons at least for being unhappy with it. The first is that it seems to threaten the possibility of a realist metaphysical stance in general. (For more detailed arguments to this effect see Heal 1989, ch. 6.) The second reason is that it undermines our central notions of deliberation and reason-giving. Let me expand on this a little.

We take it for granted, pre-philosophically, that we are capable of arriving at new thoughts by rational inference from our current thoughts, for example by working out what further things are certainly or probably true of the world, given what we already know. To use the jigsaw model, we think of ourselves as, in part, self-building jigsaws, where gaps get filled in or new pieces are added round the edge in the light of the parts of the scene already pictured. But on Davidson's story existing pieces do not have determinate content of the kind which would enable them to be the rational bases for such extensions. On his view, the contents they are to be assigned await determination in the light of the later pieces. The patterns to which we must look in assigning meaning are patterns spread out across time, including the future, and not merely across space. Thus features of later utterances, features which fix what overall patterns they and the earlier ones can form, are partly constitutive of the earlier utterances having the meanings they do. To put matters very picturesquely, the meaning of an individual utterance is not fully present in it at the time when it occurs, but exists, in part, in the future. What goes on now is such that it could have one meaning in the light of one line of future development, and would have another given some alternative.

Now suppose that we want an explanation of the appearance of some later pieces and we want an explanation which is causal or quasi-causal, in the sense that it has to do with the development of some process through time and explains later stages by citing conditions wholly present at earlier times. It is a consequence of the Davidsonian view (as sketched immediately above) that such an explanation cannot invoke the notion of meaning, because the meaning is not, on that story, present at the time of the utterance to do any causing. Commonsense, however, is strongly committed to the possibility of such meaning-invoking and quasi-causal explanation. It is thus committed to what Dummett calls 'molecularity' in a theory of meaning – that is, the idea that grasp of individual concepts (and relatedly the having of determinate individual thoughts into which those concepts are assembled) has some real ontological and explanatory priority *vis-à-vis* the total assemblage of thoughts at which a person arrives (Dummett, 1975). Davidson's holism precisely denies this. So, somewhat paradoxically, Davidson's strong insistence on the rationality of thought as it is spread out through time threatens to deprive us of any dynamic rationality in determination of our futures.

It is the commonsense conviction of molecularity which gives such power and attractiveness to those functionalist theories which emphasize the causal role and determinate nature of inner structures. So one strategy for avoiding the unwelcome indeterminacy would pursue those questions about the nature of rationality which were mentioned at the end of the last section. Such a strategy would also emphasize the importance of determinate causal connections between aspects of the world and states of persons in fixing semantic relations. The hope would be that some acceptable naturalistic theory, using these kinds of materials, can be built. (For more on semantic naturalism, see Chapter 5, A GUIDE TO NATURALIZING SEMANTICS.)

But there is a different move which has been proposed by philosophers influenced by Wittgenstein and sceptical of the success of the naturalistic programme (see McDowell, 1981, 1982, 1984; Heal, 1989; Mulhall, 1990). They propose rejection of the initial assumption made in section 1, which grounded the whole search for a theory of radical interpretation, that possession of meaning had to be an inferred or constructed state of affairs and is such that it cannot be simply observed. Let us turn to look at this more closely.

It is surely true that we could be in a situation of needing to engage in something like 'radical interpretation'. That is to say, we could be (a) confronted with some complex moving physical object, which might plausibly be taken to be a thinking, talking creature but (b) not yet certain that the creature is indeed a thinker or talker. In such a case there is nothing for it but to assemble what information we can about the creature's behaviour and circumstances – information which can be stated without commitment on what it thinks and means, because *ex hypothesi* we do not as yet have firm views about this – and to see what we can conjecture.

But it does not follow immediately from this that meaning is always and essentially a theoretical or inferred matter. Consider a parallel case. I may be confronted by an array of colours and shapes, but unclear as to whether I am seeing a material object. I may then try to assemble facts about the nature of the array and how it changes under various circumstances, in order to help me decide. These facts will be statable without commitment to a view about whether I am seeing an object and/or its nature. We need not conclude, however, that sense-datum theories in their classic form should be resurrected, and that material-object statements should be seen as inferred from or constructed out of sense-datum ones. One crucial idea in seeing that it need not follow is that the investigation of sensory experience will often itself presuppose facts about material objects and our uncontroversial perception of them. For example, it may take the form of seeing what happens *when I put on my spectacles* or *when I move my head*. It is extremely doubtful that we can, in turn, take these conditions to be inferred from or constructed from sense data; and if they cannot, what we arguably have is a conceptual scheme in which both material-object and perceptual-experience judgements are, in different and interlocking ways, 'observational', and in which neither can be regarded as more fundamental than the other.

Could it be the case that some analogous possibility holds for meaning? On such a view, claims about physical items, with their causes, circumstances, patterns and so on would have conceptual links with claims about meanings (just as claims about perceptual experience have conceptual links with claims about material objects), but the latter would not be reducible to the former. And both would be fundamental and observational elements of our conceptual repertoire. On such an approach, it might be possible to combine respect for the normative and holistic elements Davidson stresses with the molecularity and determinacy to which common sense is committed (see McDowell, 1981, 1982, 1884 and 1986; and Heal, 1989).

It is, however, becoming clearer than ever that our questions about the nature of meaning and the possibility of radical interpretation are linked with other fundamental philosophical questions. Of the views sketched in this paper, different ones will seem attractive, depending upon one's sympathies on certain basic matters; and adjudication between the options discussed is possible only in the light of the persuasiveness of large-scale philosophical positions.

References

Churchland, P.M. 1988: *Matter and Consciousness*. Cambridge, Mass.: MIT Press.
Davidson, D. 1976: 'Reply to Foster', in G.A. Evans and J. McDowell (eds), *Truth and Meaning*, pp. 33–41.
——1980: *Essays on Actions and Events*. Oxford: Clarendon Press.
——1984: *Inquiries into Truth and Interpretation*. Oxford: Clarendon Press.
——1990: 'Meaning, truth and evidence', in *Perspectives on Quine*, eds R. Barrett and R. Gibson. Oxford: Basil Blackwell, pp. 68–79.
Dennett, D. 1979: *Brainstorms*. Hassocks, Sussex: Harvester Press.
——1987: *The Intentional Stance*. Cambridge, Mass.: MIT Press.
Dretske, F. 1981: *Knowledge and the Flow of Information*. Cambridge, Mass.: MIT Press.
Dummett, M. 1975: 'What is a theory of meaning?', in *Mind and Language*, ed. S. Guttenplan. Oxford: Clarendon Press, pp. 97–122.
Evans, G.A. and McDowell, J. (eds) 1976: *Truth and Meaning*. Oxford: Clarendon Press.
Evnine, S. 1991: *Donald Davidson*. Cambridge: Polity Press.
Field, H. 1978: 'Mental representation', *Erkenntnis* 13, pp. 9–61.
Fodor, J. 1975: *The Language of Thought*. New York: Thomas Y. Crowell.
——1987: *Psychosemantics*. Cambridge, Mass.: MIT Press.
——and Lepore, E. 1992: *Holism: A Shopper's Guide*. Oxford: Blackwell.
Foster, J.A. 1976: 'Meaning and truth theory', in G.A. Evans and J. McDowell (eds), *Truth and Meaning*, pp. 1–32.
Grandy, R.E. 1973: 'Reference, meaning and belief', *Journal of Philosophy* 70, pp. 439–52.
Haack, S. 1978: *Philosophy of Logics*. Cambridge: Cambridge University Press.
Heal, J. 1978: 'On the phrase "theory of meaning"', *Mind* 87, pp. 359–75.
——1989: *Fact and Meaning*. Oxford: Basil Blackwell.
Lewis, D.K. 1983: *Philosophical Papers*, 2 vols, Oxford: Oxford University Press, Vol. 1.
Malpas, J.E. 1988: 'The nature of interpretive charity', *Dialectica* 42, pp. 17–36.
McDowell, J. 1981: 'Anti-realism and the epistemology of understanding', in *Meaning and Understanding*, eds H. Parrett and J. Bouveresse. New York: Walter de Gruyter, pp. 225–48.
——1982: 'Criteria, defeasibility and knowledge', *Proceedings of the British Academy*, 68, pp. 455–79.
——1984: 'Wittgenstein on following a rule', *Synthese* 58, pp. 325–63.
——1986: 'Functionalism and anomalous monism', in *The Philosophy of Donald Davidson: Perspectives on Actions and Events*, ed. E. Lepore and B. McLaughlin. Oxford: Basil Blackwell, pp. 385–98.
McGinn, C. 1989: *Mental Content*. Oxford: Basil Blackwell.
Millikan, R. 1984: *Language, Thought and Other Biological Categories*. Cambridge, Mass.: MIT Press.
Mulhall, S. 1990: *On Being in the World*. London: Routledge.
Papineau, D. 1987: *Reality and Representation*. Oxford: Basil Blackwell.
Quine, W.V.O. 1960: *Word and Object*. Cambridge, Mass.: MIT Press.

Quine, W.V.O. 1969: *Ontological Relativity and Other Essays*. New York: Columbia University Press.

Stich, S. 1993: *From Folk Psychology to Cognitive Science*. Cambridge, Mass.: MIT Press.

Tarski, A. 1956: 'The concept of truth in formalised languages', in *Logic, Semantics and Metamathematics*. Oxford: Clarendon Press, pp. 152–278.

9

Propositional attitudes

MARK RICHARD

Propositional attitudes and philosophy of language

What are propositional attitudes? An informal answer is that they are relations – like belief, fear, hope, knowledge, understanding, assuming, and so on – between minds and propositions. A somewhat sharper answer identifies propositional attitudes with those sorts of mental states which (normally) have truth conditions (or the like) in virtue of their involving a representation of such.[1] We can distinguish among propositional attitudes in terms of their differing connections to behavior, to perception, and to one another.

A variety of objections (which for want of space we don't discuss) might be raised to this characterization. Some philosophers have wanted to reserve the term 'propositional attitude' for states which are "in principle accessible" to consciousness, or that are "inferentially integrated" with other propositional attitudes (see Chapter 10, HOLISM, and Chapter 7, TACIT KNOWLEDGE, section 2). At issue is the status of the states ascribed to us by theories in linguistics and cognitive science.[2] Some say that some perceptual states (seeing a lion dance, for example) satisfy our definition, but are importantly different from propositional attitudes (because they are relations to events or other concrete entities).[3]

Some of the contention and research surrounding attitudes, and sentences ascribing propositional attitudes (APAs, for short), results from their importance to epistemology, philosophy of mind, and action theory. Why has philosophy of language been so concerned with attitudes and their ascription?

Perhaps the primary reason has been the view that propositional attitudes are relations to *propositions*, which are closely related to meanings, and are therefore critical to an account of what it is to understand a language. On the simplest plausible version of this view,

(1) Propositional attitudes are binary relations between individuals and propositions, relations picked out by attitude verbs such as 'believes', 'says', 'wishes'.[4]

(2) A use of a (declarative) sentence *expresses* a single proposition, save in cases in which the sentence is semantically defective, as perhaps sentences with empty names are.[5]

(3) Propositions have truth values, modal properties such as necessity, and truth conditions. Sentence-uses inherit these from the proposition they express.

(4) In a use of an APA *a Vs that S*, V an attitude verb, *that S* names the proposition expressed by S (on that use); the ascription is true provided that what *a* names is related, by the relation *V* picks out, to the proposition.[6]

(5) There is an (axiomatizable) account assigning, to a sentence type S and a context of use c, the proposition which is what the sentence literally says, as used in c, and which is what's named in c by *that S*.

(6) A sentence's meaning is given by a rule which enables one to tell, given appropriate non-linguisitic information about a context or a use (for example, who is speaking, what time it is) what proposition the sentence expresses. To be a competent speaker is to know such a rule.

The spirit of (1) through (4) informs a good deal of what Frege and Russell had to say about language, truth, and thought. Something like (5) informs the work of those of us who count Tarski and Montague, as well as Russell and Frege, as founders of modern philosophy of language.

Call (1) through (5) the *relational account* of attitudes and their ascription. It is a short step from the relational account to the idea that when a sentence is used (literally) to convey information, the information conveyed is the proposition the sentence expresses. After all, the information conveyed by Sam's literal use of S is naturally identified with both what's said by S and (given the relational account) with the referent of the 'that' clause in a true use of 'In uttering S, Sam (literally) said that T'. Given that the role of a semantic theory is in large part to give an account of how sentences are used to convey information, it follows that a good deal of semantics will be concerned with explaining the association of objects of propositional attitudes with sentences and their uses.[7]

David Kaplan has recently popularized (6); he calls the sort of rule in question the *character* of a sentence.[8] It is controversial in ways that (1) through (5) are not: perhaps a person can be a competent speaker of English in virtue of having syntactic knowledge and a variety of abilities which needn't add up to propositional knowledge of the rules assigning propositions to sentence uses.[9]

Some reject the relational account's implication that semantics is about what's said. For example, Davidson identifies theories of meaning with theories giving a Tarskian account of truth.[10] But even the dissenters recognize, in one way or another, the importance of another problem posed by attitude ascriptions. This is what Max Cresswell has called the *hyperintensionality* of APAs: Expressions which have the same possible-worlds intension – and so, in general, can be substituted for one another outside of APAs and quotational contexts – can generally not be so exchanged in APAs. This anomaly constitutes a second reason why APAs are important to the philosophy of language.[11]

This problem might well be divided into two sub-problems. First of all, what otherwise appear to be logical laws apparently fail when applied to APAs.[12] If the argument from A to B is logically valid, then *If A, then A* and *If A, then B* are logically equivalent, no matter how hairy the proof of the latter might be. So

Donald knows that if A, then B

comes from

Donald knows that if A, then A

by substitution of logical equivalents. But few think pairs so related must be equivalent in truth value. The first problem of hyperintensionality, then, is to explain what transformations within the scope of attitude-verbs are logically valid.

Notoriously, proper names of the same thing are intersubstitutable within modal contexts *salva veritate*, but are not in the scope of attitude verbs. For example,

Odile thinks that Twain is dead
Odile thinks that Clemens is dead

apparently needn't agree in truth value. In fact, even expressions, like 'yell' and 'shout', which appear to be *synonyms* are not intersubstitutable within the scope of attitude verbs. Tyler may take 'yell' and 'shout' to be synonyms, but think that there are people who understand these expressions – and so have beliefs about yelling and shouting – but who have doubts that every shout is a yell. It is quite plausible that in this case

Tyler thinks that some doubt that all who shout yell

may be true, while

Tyler thinks that some doubt that all who shout shout

is not. But the latter comes from the former by substitution of (apparent) synonyms for synonyms.[13]

That even substitution of apparent synonyms fails within attitude ascriptions presents a *prima facie* counter-example to the claim that natural languages have semantics which satisfy a non-trivial principle of compositionality, on which the semantic properties of a complex expression are determined, in a way which can be spelled out in a finite theory, by the semantic properties of its parts and by its syntax. For synonyms, one would have thought, have identical semantic properties. The second problem which the hyperintensionality of attitude ascriptions poses is that of finding an account of the semantic properties of expressions which provides a satisfactory account of the truth-conditions of attitude ascriptions (and other constructions, of course), while also allowing for a compositional account of the semantics of natural languages.

This last problem has proven remarkably difficult. Indeed, the arguable failure of all attempts to arrive at a satisfactory account of APAs has moved Stephen Schiffer (1987) to argue that natural languages simply have no compositional semantics, in the sense of an axiomatizable theory which characterizes the conditions under which a use of an arbitrary sentence of the language is true or false.

Propositions and structure

Much of the work on APAs centers upon the construction and deconstruction of accounts of propositions. The next sections review some standard accounts of propositions, and standard objections thereto.

A belief, assertion, or other attitude partitions possibilities into two classes: those in which it is true, and the rest. One picture of propositions identifies them with such partitions. The view that propositions are sets of possible worlds is a version of this picture; so is the picture of propositions as sets of situations. The proposition expressed by S is the set of worlds (or situations) in which S is true. Unlike most views which read the structure of a sentence onto the proposition it expresses, such views allow that difference of vocabulary or structure is not a bar to sentences saying the same thing. And since a non-linguistic mental state may (in virtue of its relations to evidence and behavior) partition possibilities, this view makes ascription of belief to non-human animals relatively unproblematic.

However, logically equivalent sentences are true in the same worlds; so the identification of propositions with sets of worlds does not solve the problem of hyperintensionality. For example, on this account, when A is a logical consequence of B, then it is impossible to know that B without knowing that A and B. Although there have been some ingenious attempts to defend the possible-worlds account against such consequences, few seem to have been convinced. The identification of propositions with sets of situations runs into analogous difficulties.[14]

Headway can be made if we assume that propositions have a structure which reflects the structure of the sentences which express them. If what's said by a sentence is also individuated in terms of contributions made by the parts of the sentence, then logically equivalent sentences may, when they have different structures or their parts make different contributions, say different things. Thus we reach the view that propositions are structured like the sentences that express them, with a proposition's constituents corresponding to (certain) constituents of the sentences expressing it.[15]

Given that propositional structure is derived from, or at least reflected by, sentence stucture, it seems that the main problem an account of propositions has to answer is, What sorts of things are the constituents of propositions? A natural first answer is that they are the workaday semantic values of expressions: individuals, properties, and relations, and various things corresponding to connectives and logical operatives, if we select values as Russell would have us; possible-worlds intensions, if we select such values as does the possible-worlds semanticist.

This answer, however, runs into problems, if we assume that what a sentence says is (roughly speaking) determined by "putting" semantic values contributed by expressions into the appropriate positions in the structure contributed by the sentence. For example, there is no difference in the propositional structure contributed by 'Twain is dead' and 'Clemens is dead'; neither is there is any difference in the semantic values of the sentence's parts, on either of the above accounts of semantic values.[16] But, as we observed above, it seems that one can believe what one of the sentences says while not believing what the other does.

Direct reference

To the consternation of many, the idea that co-referential names and demonstratives make identical propositional contributions – so that the proposition that Twain is dead in fact *is* the proposition that Clemens is – has enjoyed a good deal of popularity in the last 15 years.[17] "Direct reference" (sometimes called Russellian, Millian, or naïve) accounts of propositions gained currency in good part as a result of arguments by Donnellan, Kripke, Putnam, and Kaplan against Fregean and descriptional accounts of the semantics of proper names and natural kind terms.

At the core of many of these arguments was the simple, but compelling observation that, for example, what's said by 'Twain is dead' is, of necessity, true if and only if *Twain* is dead; what's said by 'Clemens is dead' is, of necessity, true if and only if *Clemens* is dead; and thus the truth-conditions of the claims, that Twain is dead and that Clemens is dead, are the same.[18] They thus made it implausible, given the identity of what a sentence says and the object of the belief it expresses, that there is any (contingent) truth-conditional content which distinguishes the object of the belief that Twain's dead from that of the belief that Clemens is. But if there isn't this sort of difference between the objects of the beliefs, one might argue, it is not clear that there's any difference at all between them.[19]

Furthermore, given that names are not synonymous with descriptions and do not have Fregean senses – conclusions that many have drawn on the basis of the above-mentioned arguments – it seems that the only contribution a name might make to what a sentence says is its referent. Given this and plausible principles of compositionality, the direct-reference view seems to follow.[20]

Against direct-reference accounts, one might argue that if a speaker sincerely and understandingly dissents from a belief ascription, saying *I do not believe that S*, she must be correct about this; but this would not be so if the direct-reference view were correct. However, dissent does not imply disbelief. Suppose that A is watching B, who is across the street on the phone. A is also speaking to B on the phone, though A is not aware that the person seen is the person spoken to. Suppose that A can truly say, pointing across the way, *I believe that she is happy*. Then B can say, to herself or through the phone, *The man watching me believes that I am happy*. If B can thus speak truly to A, A can speak truly, though the phone, to B, saying *The man watching you believes that you are happy*. Since A can also say truly *I am the man watching you*, a use of *I believe that you are happy* by A would also be true, even though A, we may suppose, would dissent.[21]

Direct-reference views, of course, conflict with strongly held intuitions of speakers. Speakers do not see the facts that Hesperus is Phosphorus, and that the ancients knew that Hesperus was Hesperus, as giving us any reason at all for thinking that the ancients knew that Hesperus was Phosphorus. Advocates of direct reference counter that these intuitions can be explained by distinguishing between what a sentence-use literally says and what it might convey by non-semantic means. They suggest that (a) to have a propositional attitude is to be related to a Russellian proposition "under" a way of apprehending such; (b) while information about how a proposition is believed is typically conveyed by an APA, it is conveyed as a conversational implicature or via some other pragmatic, non-semantic, mechanism; (c) speakers' intuitions, while sensitive to the information a sentence-use conveys, are often unable to distinguish between what is conveyed as a matter of truth-conditional content and what is conveyed pragmatically. Suggestion (a) is made plausible by appeal to the above-mentioned attacks on Fregeanism. Suggestion (c) is independently plausible. And the distinction drawn in (b), between semantically and pragmatically conveyed information, is one which any comprehensive theory of language will have to draw. So unless we have an account that handles the data better than the direct-reference account, we should adopt it.[22]

I don't find this line of defense satisfactory, for it forces us to say that attempts to explain or predict behavior by ascribing propositional attitudes, if taken literally, *cannot* be successful. For it is the "way" a belief or desire is held that is relevant to its role in governing behavior, not (merely) its Russellian content. That Smith wants Twain dead, and that he believes that if he shoots, Twain will die, gives us not the slightest reason to think that Smith will shoot, given that the APAs are to be understood as the direct-reference theorist would have us understand them. For Smith might hold the desire under "Twain is dead", hold the belief under "if I shoot, then Clemens will die", and not accept "Twain is Clemens". Given the central role behavior explanation has in the practice of ascribing attitudes, it seems asking too much to ask us to relegate such explanations to the realm of pragmatic by-effects.[23]

Fregeanism

Probably the most popular view of attitude ascriptions is one or another version of Fregeanism. Relevant to our present concerns are the following of Frege's views: Sentences and their significant parts have both *reference* and *sense*. The former are (roughly) what would nowadays be called extensions; the latter are "ways of thinking" or "modes of presentation" of references. Frege's own examples of senses of proper names are often given by associating definite descriptions with names, encouraging the widespread view that sense corresponds to some sort of descriptive conceptualization. In any case, it is the sense of an expression that is responsible for its having whatever reference it has. Senses are also the objects of propositional attitudes and the references of 'that' clauses. Thus, *a believes that S* is true just in case *a* bears the belief relation to the sense named by *that S*.[24]

Such an account can deny that whoever thinks that Twain is dead thinks that Clemens is dead. If Odile associates different ways of thinking with the names 'Twain' and 'Clemens', she will associate different senses (different *thoughts*, in Fregean lingo) with 'Twain is dead' and 'Clemens is dead'. Unless she accepts that Twain is Clemens, there is nothing that would force her, in such a case, to believe one thought, given only that she believes the other.

The idea that sense, as a way of conceptualizing or thinking of something, determines reference has come in for persistent criticism in the last 20 years. The arguments that names are rigid designators alluded to in the last section were explicitly directed against such a view of sense. Now, the Fregean might simply concede to Kripke, Kaplan, Donnellan, and others that sense does not determine reference, or the modally relevant properties of an expression.[25] He could still say that expressions have sense. He might simply say that sense is semantically irrelevant *except* in linguistic contexts sensitive to it: propositional-attitude constructions, those created by 'seek', 'imagine', and other such verbs, and perhaps a few others ('means that'). Perhaps as an ecumenical gesture, the Fregean could allow that in such contexts expressions stand for something cobbled out of sense *and* reference. For example, perhaps 'Twain' in my use of 'Flo thinks that Twain is Clemens' would have as a reference the pair <Mark Twain, the sense I associate with 'Mark Twain'>. Thus, it might be said, we have the advantages of a Fregean account of attitude ascriptions without the drawbacks of an implausible account of reference.

Sense, however, is idiosyncratic, in so far as speakers may use a single name to refer to an individual, but associate quite different senses with the name. Suppose you have a belief you express with 'Frege was German'. I should be able to ascribe it to you by echoing you, saying 'You think that Frege was German'. But if the 'that'-clause names the thought *I* express with 'Frege was German' it seems that the ascription won't be true, since you, having a different sense for 'Frege', don't believe *my* thought that Frege was German.[26]

One might suggest that in *a believes that S*, the 'that'-clause names a sense which *a* associates with S. One problem with this is logical: It renders the argument *You think that Frege was German; Jo thinks whatever you do; so Jo thinks that Frege was German* invalid, since the 'that' clause now designates flaccidly. One might hold that a use of *that S* names the speaker's sense for S, and say that *a believes that S* is true iff a has a belief object that is *similar* to the one the 'that'-clause names. But this again runs afoul of the fact that I can report the beliefs of others by echoing their words, as when the other expresses belief saying 'Frege was German', and I say 'the other believes that Frege was German'. For I can do this even when the other thinks of Frege in ways quite unlike the way in which I think of him.[27]

Even if the Fregean account of attitude *ascription* is in error, a Fregean might say, still, attitudes *themselves* are relations to the sort of thing which Frege had in mind when he spoke of sense. But what are senses? A goodly number of Fregeans have suggested that, at least in the case of proper names, the notion of sense can be cashed out in terms of the notion of a *mental file or dossier*.[28] Roughly, the idea is that a way of thinking of something is a way of keeping track of or a locus of information about it. On this conception of sense, co-referential names will have the same sense when their user directs information "tagged" with either to the same locus of information; thus, names a speaker knows to co-refer will typically have the same sense.

Whether this be Frege's notion or not, it is unclear that propositional attitudes can be individuated in terms of it. For one thing, assertions seem much more finely individuated: to say that Twain sleeps is not to say that Clemens does, even if speaker and audience have a single Twain/Clemens dossier. (For what one says does not shift simply because one's audience does; but one who understands what I say with 'Twain sleeps' and 'Clemens sleeps' may find only one claim informative.) Since there is pressure to identify the objects of beliefs and assertions (we can say what others think and think what others say), such considerations also count against individuating beliefs in terms of such a notion of sense.

Some contemporary Fregeans have argued that Frege's view of sense and reference is quite different from the view criticized by Kripke, Kaplan, and others. They say that the sense of a proper name is tied to what it presents in such a way that it is impossible for the sense to present anything other than that referent. As Gareth Evans explained the idea, my way of thinking of an object is characterized by describing how that mode of thought relates me to it; for you to think about something in the same way, the same description has to apply to you (save that references to me are replaced by references to you). Since the description refers to the object of thought, the way of thinking is one whose use (and thus existence) depends on its object.

A fanciful example: My sense for 'Frege' relates me to Frege because it is associated with (or is) information my teacher, Terry Parsons, conveyed to me, and which he gained by talking to Frege. It is impossible for such a description to be true of anyone unless Frege exists (and unless Terry Parsons exists, for that matter). So it's not possible for someone to think of something with my sense for 'Frege' unless these objects exist. Furthermore, if the description applies to you, it applies because you think of *Frege*, so my sense for 'Frege' can't pick out anything but him.[29]

It is commonly thought that a *virtue* of Frege's view, over that discussed in the last section, is that it can assign a thought to a sentence with an empty name, without committing itself to the existence of a reference for the name. On Evans's account a name without reference is without sense, since there is no x such that the name represents a way of thinking of *x*. So sentences in which a referenceless name occurs have no sense, either. Whether this is ultimately objectionable depends in part on whether we should suppose (for example) that the same sort of explanation of Smith's behavior is to be given, when (1) Smith *sees* a cat, thinks "that's nice", and is moved to pet, and (2) Smith *hallucinates* a cat, thinks "that's nice", and is moved to pet.[30]

Evans's view seems at odds with the relatively unexceptional claims that (A) necessarily, the proposition that Frege is a mathematician is true iff Frege is a mathematician, and (B) Frege might have been a mathematician though Terry Parsons never existed (and so nothing was related to him). Call my sense for 'Frege' f; call the proposition I express with 'Frege is a mathematician' p. Evans's view seems to be (C) necessarily, f presents something only if it is related to Terry Parsons. But (D) since p is the thought which results from applying the sense of 'is a mathematician' to f, necessarily, p is true only if f presents something that is a mathematician. Combined with (A), these claims imply that p can be true only if something is related to Parsons, which conflicts with (B).

Perhaps Evans would reject (D). But (D) seems part of the Fregean doctrine that sense determines reference; to this extent, Evans's view is not Fregean.

Attitudes, utterances, and sentences

If ascribing an attitude is not relating someone to a Russellian proposition or Fregean thought, what is it? Perhaps in ascribing attitudes we are talking about linguistic entities – sentences or utterances, for example. If so, we can (in principle) account for hyperintensionality. Even if 'I shout' and 'I yell' are synonymous, they are different sentences; to say that Mary is related to one needn't commit us to her being related to the other. So if (for example)

Mary hopes that I yell

says that Mary is related to the sentence 'I yell', it need not imply that Mary hopes that I shout. Another attraction of such views, at least for some, is an ontological one: Those suspicious of properties, possible worlds, or other "intensional entities" have hoped to make extensional sense of the attitudes by seeing them as relations to sentence tokens, utterances, or some other linguistic ersatz for propositions.

One well-known linguistic account of APAs is Davidson's paratactic one.[31] Davidson took the 'that' in 'says that' as a demonstrative, picking out the ensuing sentence-utterance. An indirect-speech report says that some utterance of its subject *samesays* the demonstrated utterance, with samesaying one or another relation of synonymity. Thus

[D] Derrida said that man is irrational

has the form and truth conditions of

[D1] Some utterance of Derrida's samesays that. Man is irrational.

where the demonstrative names the utterance of the sentence following. It is, on Davidson's view, no more the task of semantics to explicate the samesaying relation than to explicate relations picked out by other transitive verbs.

Lepore and Loewer observe that we can generalize this account to other propositional attitudes, by quantifying over states which stand to those attitudes as utterances stand to sayings.[32] For example

[S] Searle thinks that glass is transparent

has a logical form suggested by

[S1] There's a belief b of Searle's which has-the-same-content-as that. Glass is transparent.

They suggest identifying the belief states with neural ones.

The paratactic account is often thought to be committed to a manifestly false account of truth conditions. If [D]'s truth conditions are those of [D1]'s, then [D] cannot be true unless an English utterance exists, for [D1] involves reference, via 'that', to such. But Derrida could have said, man is irrational though no English utterances exist. Lepore and Loewer reply that u may samesay u′ even if u′ does not exist. This requires that utterances have their semantic properties essentially. If they are physical events, this may not be plausible. (For another response, see the end of this section.)

The paratactic account is fairly non-conservative as far as logical intuitions go. Burge points out that even arguments of the form *a believes that A. So, a believes that A* are not formally valid on Davidson's account, since the demonstratives they supposedly contain *must* vary in reference.[33] The account has also been criticized on syntactic grounds, as it makes binding like that occurring in 'Every boy said that he is a fine fellow' mysterious.[34]

Perhaps the best-known account of ascriptions like [D] and [S] on which they are ascriptions of relations to sentence types is Carnap's.[35] The account makes use of the notion of intensional isomorphism: Roughly, and slightly inaccurately, sentences are intensionally isomorphic provided they have the same syntactic structure and their simplest interpreted constituents have, pointwise, the same possible-worlds intension. Carnap's suggestion was (roughly) that [D] is true provided

> [D2] Derrida assertively uttered a sentence intensionally isomorphic to 'man is irrational'

Ascription [S] is true if, roughly, Searle is disposed to assent to some sentence intensionally isomorphic to 'glass is transparent'. These proposals are members of two large families of sententialist accounts of such ascriptions, other members being obtained either by replacing intensional isomorphism with some other relation between sentences (translation, for example), or by replacing the relation the subject of the attitude has towards the sentence most directly realizing her belief – replacing *is disposed to assent to* with *has a neural copy of*, for example.[36]

Church's objections to Carnap's proposal are taken by many to be decisive.[37] Church had, in essence, two objections to Carnap. First of all, he complained that [D2] did not "convey the same information" as [D], since one gives the content of Derrida's assertion without revealing his words, while the other gives his words but not the content. Church reinforced the point by observing that literal translations of [D] and [D2] into German would clearly convey different things to a German speaker.

If we take Carnap's account as an attempt to spell out truth conditions (thought of as sets of possible worlds or truth-supporting situations), this objection simply misses the point.[38] There is no reason to suppose that an illuminating account of the truth conditions of (a use of) a sentence S and (the use of) S itself will convey the same information. For example, a correct account of the truth conditions of 'some dogs bark' is given thus:

> Some of the things to which 'dog' applies are things to which 'bark' applies.

But this does not convey the same information as 'some dogs bark.' Indeed, an illuminating account (say, in terms of structure) of what proposition S expresses will typically fail to convey the same information as S.

Church's other objection to Carnap's account was, in essence, this. Example [D] and its German translation are not intensionally isomorphic, since they involve reference to different expressions (of English and German respectively). So 'Leo thinks that Derrida said that man is irrational' and its German translation can be expected to vary in truth-conditions or even truth-value – Leo might be disposed to assent to an isomorph of [D] without being disposed to assent to an isomorph of its German translation. The objection assumes that a sentence and its translation can't diverge in truth value, but surely this is false. 'He thinks Phil's a groundhog' and 'He thinks Phil's a woodchuck' may diverge in truth-value; but they are both translated by the same sentence in French, which has but a single word for the woodchuck.[39]

Church did point out a serious problem for *Carnap's* version of sententialism; but it is not clear that he uncovered a problem with *every* version of sententialism. For example, it is not clear why a sententialist who held

> *a believes that S* is true iff what *that S* names (the sentence S) translates a sentence "in a's belief-box"

should be perturbed by Church's objection.

Some generic objections to sententialism should be mentioned in passing.[40] It's commonly alleged that sententialism is defeated by the fact that a sentence can mean different things in different languages. For all we know, there is a language L in which 'pigs fly' says that dogs bark. Thus 'pigs fly' translates (into L) a sentence ('dogs bark') which is in my belief-box. Thus, on the account of the truth-conditions just displayed, it is true that I think that pigs fly, since the sentence 'pigs fly' translates a sentence realizing one of my beliefs. But I don't think that pigs fly.

There are natural ways of individuating sentences on which such objections have no force. We might identify words with sets of utterance-tokens by speakers. English's 'pig' then turns out to be the set of all English 'pig' tokens. If sentences are structured collections of words, the objection fails, since L's words and English's words are surely different.

The second objection is this: If propositions are sentences, then that Smith thinks that fleas are disgusting entails that the sentence 'fleas are disgusting' exists. But Smith might have the belief without the sentence existing. A sententialist needn't accept the claim about entailment. Presumably there is a cross-world relation, *sentence S as used in w translates sentence T as used in w′*. S (in w) stands in this relation to T (in w′) in virtue of uses of S in w being similar in appropriate ways to those of T in w′. Such similarity does not require that S in fact exist in w′. (The contents of my bathtub don't have to exist in w′ in order for the underlying kind of my bathtub's actual contents to be the same as the underlying kind of some sample of liquid in w′.) A sententialist who endorsed a translational account of attitude ascription might simply say that *a believes that S* when used at a world w is true at world w′ just in case (1) there is at w′ a sentence T which realizes at w′ one of a's beliefs and, (2) S as used at w translates T as used at w′.

The view, that what *that S* provides in *a believes that S* is (individuated in terms of) a sentence, is a view about the semantics of belief ascription. It must be distinguished from the view that beliefs and other attitudes are realized, in the mind or brain, by states which are sentence-like in important ways: *psychological sententialism*, as it might be called.

On this view, the psychological states which realize propositional attitudes (a) have syntactic structure and parts with semantic properties like those of natural-language sentences; (b) have truth-conditions which can be assigned by something like a compositional induction on their structures. Views that we have a "language of thought", and must have such to be thinkers, are usually committed to this (and much more besides).

Psychological and semantic sententialism are independent doctrines. We could classify unstructured states with structured labels like sentences (semantic but not psychological sententialism). It is a priori possible that representing a state of affairs requires representing its constituents in a sentence-like way, though the point of attitude ascription is merely to report of how a person partitions possibilities (psychological but not semantic sententialism).

One line of argument for psychological sententialism claims that our best cognitive models of attitudes are ones on which they are computational states operating on sentence-like objects with properties (a) and (b).[41] Some have suggested that the "productivity" of the attitudes requires psychological sententialism: She who can entertain the thought that something bothered John, and can have the desire that Mary touch nothing, must also have the ability to entertain the thought that John touched something, and the ability to have the desire that Mary bother nothing. This is explained if the states are realized by a system of states with something like natural-language syntax and semantics; it is not so easy to see what other explanation there might be.

That the best models of attitudes are sentential is quite controversial.[42] Even without appeal to contentious psychological models, we should be leary of the above arguments. Attitudes involved in higher cognitive processes in humans are plausibly thought to be sentential for reasons given by these arguments. But one may wonder whether all belief (like) states of monkeys (which are motivational, involve considerable discriminatory ability, but need not contribute much to something like an ability to reason) are well-modeled by sententialist models.[43] Neither do such states have the sort of "compositional complexity" alluded to above.

Opponents of psychological sententialism claim it is false to our conception of the attitudes, a conception of them as states with a certain functional role (usually a role captured by colloquial, or folk, psychology) which have representational content. For it is perfectly possible to have representational content without being sententially structured; representational properties, for example, might be assimilated to one or another causal relational property. In my opinion, this argument ignores important aspects of our concepts of the attitudes. Attitudes *are* states with certain kinds of motivational roles and representational content; but an attitude is required to have a certain *kind* of representational content. An attitude represents a state of affairs – a congeries of individuals, properties, and relations – *by* representing its constituent individuals, properties, and relations.

Evidence that we think of attitudes as being realized by *structured* representations is given (a) by the naturalness with which we accede to the idea that, for example, having the belief that Bush lost to Clinton requires having a representation of Bush and one of Clinton; and (b) by the unsatisfactoriness of accounts of attitude-ascription which identify the semantic object of belief with an unstructured object, like a set of possible worlds. We reject such accounts because we take it as obvious that states of affairs can be necessarily or logically equivalent without beliefs with those states as objects being identical. This means that the states which realize those beliefs must themselves be different. While it doesn't *follow* from this that belief states realize beliefs by being sentence-like representations of a state of affairs, such considerations, along with (a), make psychological sententialism plausible.[44]

Attitudes and context

We have yet to find a satisfactory account of APAs. This section reviews some recent proposals. While they differ in particulars, they are united by the idea that attitude ascription involves some sort of *context sensitivity*, and that it is by appeal to this that we should explain hyperintensionality.

Kripke (1979) recounts the sad story of Pierre, who was raised in Paris but taken under dark circumstances to London. As a child, Pierre read (in French) of the city Londres, and accepted as true the French *Londres est jolie*, presumably expressing a belief therewith. He still accepts this sentence. Pierre learned English directly in London; it never occurred to him that he was in the city he called *Londres*. Finding his circumstances mean, he assents to 'London isn't pretty', and presumably expresses a belief with it.

Kripke poses a puzzle about belief with the case. He observes that we seem committed to a disquotational principle about belief, something like *If a normal English speaker, on reflection, sincerly assents to 'p', then he believes that p.* If this is true, its analogues in other natural languages are truths, too. We seem committed to the view that translations of truths express truths. The first principle, and the facts, commit us to saying that Pierre believes that London is not pretty. An analogue of the first principle, and the facts, commits us to the truth in French of *Pierre croit que Londres est jolie.* The translation principle, then, commits us to saying that Pierre believes that London is pretty. But, as Kripke observes, Pierre may be supposed to be fully rational, a man committed to consistency at all costs, and so on. So he presumably does not have contradictory beliefs.

Kripke seems to think that there must be a univocal, "context-free" answer to the question, Does Pierre or does he not believe that London is pretty? If we suppose that this is so, Kripke's case is indeed puzzling. For when we concentrate on Pierre's "French thoughts", it seems obvious that we should say that Pierre thinks that the town is pretty, and that he does not think that it is not pretty; when we consider his English thoughts, it is evident that he thinks that it is not pretty.

Perhaps Kripke's case is not so much a puzzle as a dramatic demonstration that ascriptions of propositional attitudes are contextually sensitive; perhaps the truth of 'Pierre thinks that London is pretty' depends in part on how things are with Pierre *and* in part on how things are in the context in which the sentence is used.

A number of recent accounts of attitude ascriptions see claims about the attitudes as contextually sensitive. *Sentential-role* accounts take a use of

(P) Pierre believes that London is pretty

to be true just in case Pierre has a belief similar, in some contextually salient role, to that the user would normally voice with 'London is pretty'. *Translational* accounts see (P) as true, provided the 'that'-clause, or what it names, provides an adequate translation of something which realizes one of Pierre's thoughts (or of one of his thoughts *simpliciter*); since what counts as an acceptable translation may vary from context to context, (P) may vary in truth across contexts. *Implicit reference* accounts see uses of sentences like (P) as involving a tacit reference by the speaker to a way of thinking, a mental particular (a particular representation or word in the language of thought), or a property of such. Since different speakers may make references to different ways of thinking or representations, uses of (P) may differ in truth.[45]

In Stephen Stich's version of the sentential-role story, belief states can resemble each other in terms of reference, functional role, and ideology, with ideological resemblance determined by the referential and functional similarities of the "networks" in which the states are embedded. Various similarity measures match such states along these dimensions; contextual differences in interest and emphasis select among these measures. Thus (P)'s truth-conditions shift, as do its users' attention and interest. Functional role and ideological setting might be seen as aspects of Fregean sense; Russellian propositions are a little like reifications of referential roles. So this view is a *bit* like the view that attitude ascriptions may relate one to either a Fregean sense or a Russellian proposition.

This approach makes our general success in explaining behavior by ascribing attitudes hard to explain. Presumably it is a belief's functional role that is most relevant in behavior explanation, and so similarity of such roles looms large in behavior explanation. But our behavior explanations are failures if they don't respect the referential properties of others' beliefs. Suppose we disagree about what's best for colds: You think pseudoepherine, I think oxymetazoline. Neither of us has much of a theory about his medication beyond thinking the stuff is the best for colds. 'I shall get some oxymetazoline' has for me the functional role that 'I shall get some pseudoepherine' has for you. Suppose that you are going to the store for pseudoepherine, Mary asks why you're leaving, and I say 'he wants to get some oxymetazoline'. If only similarity in functional role is relevant, this is true on Stich's account. But it's not true.

One response would say that referential similarity is always required in belief ascription, and, additionally, functional similarity is required in behavior explanation. But then I just *can't* explain your behavior to Mary, because nothing in my repertoire matches your motivation in reference and functional roles. But if I say 'he wants to get some pseudoepherine', I explain your behavior quite well. If we say that *only* referential similarity is required in behavior explanation, the Russellian's problems with this topic recur.

Translational accounts of (P) take it as true when its 'that' clause provides a contextually adequate translation of one of Pierre's thoughts, or something realizing them. The author's version of such an account begins by assuming that some (weak) version of psychological sententialism is correct.[46] Thus, each of Pierre's beliefs is realized by a sentence-like mental state whose parts, in context, determine a Russellian content. Call what results from pairing the parts of a "sentence" realizing a belief with their contextually determined referents a *thought*. Pretend for now that beliefs are realized by natural-language sentence tokens (which we think of as ordered sets). Then among Pierre's thoughts are

⟨⟨'est jolie', the property of being pretty⟩, ⟨'Londres', London⟩⟩

and

⟨⟨'not', the negation function⟩, ⟨⟨'is pretty', being pretty⟩, ⟨'London', London⟩⟩.[47]

Call the pairings in thoughts, of representations with what they represent, *annotations*.

Thoughts are pairings of (the parts of) representations with what they represent. The 'that' clauses of attitude ascriptions also determine such pairings. For example, the 'that' clause of (P) provides us with

⟨⟨'is pretty', being pretty⟩, ⟨'London', London⟩⟩.

Call the pairings named by 'that' clauses *RAMs*.[48] In ascribing an attitude, we offer the RAM our 'that' clause determines as a representation or translation of one of the believer's thoughts; the ascription is true provided that the proffered RAM is an acceptable translation of such a thought, according to currently prevailing standards.

What is translation, and how might the standards governing it shift across contexts? Translation preserves Russellian content.[49] So a RAM p translates a thought q only if p and q, when stripped of the words or representations within them, determine the same Russellian proposition.[50] What else is required in translation? This varies with interests, mutual knowledge, and conversational background. For instance, it may be common knowledge that some of Pierre's beliefs are realized *en français*, and are the focus of discussion. If so, one may expect a restriction along the lines of

> In discussing Pierre, 'London' can be used only to represent representations which Pierre voices with 'Londres'.

With such a restriction in place, (P) will be true, while

(P′) Pierre believes that London is not pretty

will not. Other contexts provide restrictions which make (P′) true and (P) false.[51]

Call the sort of restriction just discussed – that in an ascription of attitude to x, an expression can only represent a representation of x's with a particular property P – a *restriction on translation*. Context contributes a collection of restrictions on translation. An ascription *A believes that S* is true in context c, provided A has a thought q which can be translated (consistent with all c's restrictions) using the RAM that S.

This account attempts to preserve the virtues of direct-reference accounts – their compatibility with "the new theory of reference", their eschewal of "ways of thinking" as meanings or semantic values of expressions – with the idea that in ascribing an attitude we are *somehow* speaking of ways of thinking. It does this by holding that the words in a 'that' clause have two functions. One is to secure a Russellian referent: In (P), 'London' secures London. The other role is to stand as proxy for the representations of others: 'London' in (P) is a proxy for a way of thinking of London.

It is possible to get some of the effect of the account, without requiring such yeoman service of the words in a belief ascription, if we suppose that in using (P) we refer to Pierre's representations, but not via some expression in (P). (Tacit reference is not unheard of; John Perry's example is the apparent reference to a location in uses of 'it's snowing'.)[52] If (P) involves tacit reference to Pierre's representations, then the semantic value of the predicate

(P1) believes that London is pretty

on a true use of (P) might be something like the property

S_1: believing the Russellian proposition that London is pretty under the representation FR

where FR names Pierre's "French representation" of London's pulchritude. Since different uses of (P) may involve different references, simultaneous use of (P) may differ in truth value.

So say Perry and Mark Crimmins. They hold that sometimes we refer to particular representations, sometimes to their properties. On some uses of (P), the semantic value of (P1) might turn out to be not S_1 but

S_2: believing the Russellian proposition that London is pretty under a representation that includes a representation with property P*: being typically expressed by Pierre in French.

If there is reference to representations or their properties in belief ascription, then there will be reference to aspects of propositional structure and to how representations "fill" these. This is necessary to differentiate between believing that Hesperus rose before Phosphorus and believing that Phosphorus rose before Hesperus; it's only by saying which representation is responsible for filling which position (*role*, in Crimmins and Perry's parlance) that the difference between the two beliefs can be explained. A full-blown account of a use of (P) involving reference to P* has it making a claim something like this:

> There are representations r and k such that Pierre believes the proposition that London is pretty under r, k is a part of r, and k, which has P*, is responsible for London filling role u

where role u is the "subject role" of the proposition that London is pretty.

Both the translational and the referential account, in effect, see attitudes as complex relations between an individual, a representation, and a representational content, with the latter being something like a Russellian proposition. Each sees attitude ascriptions as involving some hidden logical structure – quantification over ways of translating, in the case of the translational account; reference to representations or properties thereof, in the case of the referential account.

In my opinion, the implicit-reference account does not give an acceptable account of the logical properties of attitude ascriptions. Since the representations implictly referred to may shift from premiss to conclusion, the account must say that the argument 'Smith thinks snow is white, so Smith thinks snow is white' is not valid. Worse yet, my use of 'Smith thinks snow is white' may be false not because Smith fails to believe the proposition that snow is white, but because he does not believe it under the representation I refer to. Thus there are contexts in which 'Jones believes that snow is white' and 'Smith believes whatever Jones does' are true (taking the latter to be regimented 'For all p: if Jones believes p under some r, then Smith believes p under some r'), but 'Smith believes that snow is white' is false.

On the translational account, x satisfies *believes that London is large* just if 'London is large' adequately translates one of x's thoughts. Though the standards of adequacy in translation may vary from context to context, these standards are "built in" to the semantic value of the attitude-verb in a context. The verb's context-independent meaning is a rule which takes a collection of restrictions on translation, and returns a rule which pairs off individuals with the RAMs which translate one of their thoughts. Because of the predicate's univocality in context, the arguments just discussed are, on a translational account, valid.

Such objections may not be decisive; one might hold that our intuitions about validity are no more infallible than those about truth conditions.[53] I do believe that the translational or referential account gives the essentials of a correct account of attitude ascription.

Appendix: *de dicto, de re,* and *de se*

It is common to distinguish between *de dicto* and *de re* attitudes or attitude ascriptions. Those who do so may have any of a number of distinctions in mind. The most straightforward distinction is a syntactic one exhibited by

(1a) John believes that Ned is tall.
(1b) John believes of Ned that he is tall.

and

(2a) John believes that Ned is tall.
(2b) There's some x such that x is Ned and John believes that x is tall.

In the b-sentences, the clause governed by 'believes' contains (elements like) variables which are bound from without. These are *de re* ascriptions. *De dicto* ascriptions, like the a-sentences, are ones in which the content sentence (the sentence which 'that' introduces) contains no variables bound from the outside.[54]

The terminology arises thus: *De dicto* ascriptions report that the believer has what a sentence says – a *dictum*, or proposition – as the object of an attitude. *De re* ascriptions relate the believer to a thing (or *res*) – Ned, in our examples – specified independently of how the believer conceptualizes it. Note that from (1b) and 'Ned is Ed' we can infer 'John believes of Ed that he is tall', while (1a) and the identity do not seem to imply 'John believes that Ed is tall'.

Say that when ascriptions are related as are

(3a) x believes that t is F
(3b) x believes of t that it is F

with 'it' in (3b) referring back to t, b is the *de re* ascription corresponding to a. Since arbitrary (positive) noun phrases can occur in the position of *t*, a *de dicto* ascription and the corresponding *de re* ascription are independent. That you believe that some dogs have fleas neither implies nor is implied by the claim that you believe of some dogs that they have fleas. (You may have the first belief without the ability or willingness to identify or describe any particular thing as having fleas; you may identify Rex the dog as something beflead, but think him a skunk and that only skunks have fleas, thereby having the second belief but not the first.) Likewise, that you wish that the winner of the lottery be heavily taxed apparently neither implies nor is implied by the claim that you wish, with respect to the winner of the lottery, that he be heavily taxed.[55]

Limiting attention to cases in which *t* is replaced with something other than a quantifier – say, a demonstrative, indexical, or proper name – it is plausible that a *de dicto* ascription implies the corresponding *de re* ascription, for it is plausible that (for example) (1b) follows from (1a). Only the Millian holds that implication holds in the other direction.

Some accounts of attitudes make some attitudes dependent on objects external to the believer. A Russellian account of propositions, on which Odile is a part of the proposition that Odile said hello, will usually hold that it's impossible to believe that Odile said hello, if she does not exist.[56] The *de re* senses which some Fregeans introduce (see page 203) cannot exist unless what they (in fact) present exists. To have such a sense as a belief object is to have a belief which depends upon a particular object. A second use of the term *de re attitude* applies it to states which are object-dependent in this way – an attitude towards something (a Russellian proposition, *de re* sense, whatever) which is itself ontologically dependent upon an object which the belief is about.

This use of the terminology is different from the first. Sentence (1a) reports a *de re* attitude on a Millian or Evansean view, since on these views the proposition that Ned is tall cannot exist unless Ned does. But sentence (1a) is not a *de re* ascription.

A third use of the terminology arises as a result of the view that some belief involves an epistemically significant relation to an object. Russell held that if a proposition contained an object as a constituent, one couldn't believe the proposition unless one were *acquainted* with that object; acquaintance, in turn, could only be had with objects about which one, in some important sense, could not be deluded.[57] Even though no-one now accepts quite so stringent a requirement, it is commonly thought that object-dependent propositions can be believed only by those with some fairly significant epistemic contact with their constituents.[58] Many writers use '*de re* belief' in such a way that *de re* belief is a kind of belief whose possession requires having one or another epistemically interesting rapport with the object or objects the belief is about.

Does having an object-dependent belief (*de re* in the second sense) require having intimate epistemic contact with the relevant objects (*de re* in the third)? I would say not, as anyone who understands a sentence with a proper name of me may have object-dependent beliefs about me, but such a person need have no particularly interesting epistemic relation to me. An objection runs thus: On your view, someone without such contact with an object x – say, someone one who can (only) describe x – can come to have object-dependent beliefs about it just by "christening" x with a name stipulated to always "introduce" x into the belief it expresses. This implies that someone with only descriptive knowledge of x can be in exactly the same epistemic relation to x as someone who has object-dependent knowledge of x. But this is absurd, since someone who has object-dependent knowledge knows something that someone with only descriptive knowledge doesn't.

This argument succeeds only if it is allowed that introducing a name for an object does not change epistemic relations to the object. But introducing a name (when one previously had none) does create a new epistemic link with the nominata: After the christening, one has a means to *refer* to the object, and express propositions in which the object occurs, while before one did not. Of course, the sort of link a christening opens to the object can't be exploited to gain "interesting extensions" of one's knowledge in the way that other epistemic links (perception, introspection, relations established via third-party testimony) can be. But that doesn't mean that the link doesn't exist, as the argument must assume in order to go through.

There is apparently a difference between what is typically reported by

(4a) John believes that he himself is tall

and

(4b) John believes that John [or: that man] is tall,

even if 'John' (or 'that man') refers to John himself. If John doesn't realize that he is John (or that man) – because of amnesia or some other circumstance – the a- and b-sentences might diverge in truth value. For if John is suffering from amnesia, he can think (to himself) *I am tall*, while thinking *But John (that man) is not tall.* Assuming that inferences like that from (1a) to (1b) are valid, this argument also shows that what's reported by (4a) isn't (merely) a *de re* belief, either. The term *belief de se* is often used to refer to the sort of belief about oneself typically reported in English using the 'she herself' locution.[59]

What, exactly, is (4a) telling us about John? According to Frege "everyone is presented to himself in a particular and primitive way, in which he is presented to no-one else."[60] In saying this, Frege had in mind a "distinctively first-person" way of thinking of oneself, which typically accompanies one's 'I'-thoughts.[61] One view is that a *de se* ascription to x ascribes to x a thought which involves x's private mode of self-thought.[62]

One way to avoid private thought-objects in an account of thought *de se* treats 'he himself' (and analogous uses of simpler pronouns like 'he') as functioning somewhat as predicate abstractors, so that the logical form of (4a) is suggested by

(4c) John believes λx(x is tall)

One then says that *de se* belief involves a distinctive way of ascribing a property (*self-ascribing* it). All believers can self-ascribe properties, and all properties are (in principle) open to self-ascription. But of course only you can *self*-ascribe being tall to yourself.

David Lewis takes this line, and holds that *all* attitudes are relations to properties; what appears to be "purely propositional belief" (such as the belief that $2 + 5 = 4$) is self-ascription of "propositional properties" (being such that $2 + 5 = 4$). He argues that this provides a superior account of belief. For suppose there were propositionally omniscient gods, Ed and Fred, who knew every true proposition. For example, Ed knows that Ed lives in Shutesbury and eats corn, while Fred lives in Leveritt and eats peas; Fred knows this, too. Lewis argues that since they may know all the propositions without knowing who they are (Ed may know that Ed eats corn while wondering *But am I Ed?*), some knowledge is a relation to something besides a proposition.

One can concede that the gods would be ignorant in such a case, without thereby conceding that the objects of the attitudes fail to be truth-bearers. 'There is something which Ed does not know' is true if a sentence of the form 'Ed does not know that S' is true. A translational account of attitude ascriptions (see p. 211ff.) can allow that for any sentence S which is free of the 'he himself' locution (or cognates), if S is true, then 'Ed knows that S' is true in the two-gods story. This seems to get at what Lewis has in mind in describing the case as one in which Ed is propositionally omniscient.[63] And it is consistent with the falsity of 'Ed knows that he himself is Ed', if 'he himself' is so restricted that in ascriptions to Ed it can only represent 'I' or other "first-person" modes of reference.[64]

Notes

1 The caveat 'normally' allows us to hold that one might believe, say, that Zeus was a god, though the belief would be without truth conditions due to a reference failure of 'Zeus' or a corresponding part of the representation realizing the belief. It is unclear that we can avoid such a rider, since there need not be only finitely many ways in which a representation might fail to have truth conditions. The parenthetical 'or the like' allows, for instance, that attitudes like desire and wishing have objects with satisfaction, not truth, conditions.

2 Chomsky (1965, 1986) holds that we know the grammar of our language, though the knowledge is not conscious or inferentially integrated with conscious knowledge. Stich (1978) criticizes him on these points. Fodor (1975) exuberantly postulates propositional attitudes without regard to conscious access or cognitive integration; Searle (1990) holds that representation without the possibility of conscious access is impossible.

3 See, for instance, Higginbotham (1983), which presents an alternative to accounts in Barwise (1981) and Barwise and Perry (1983). Barwise and Perry take seeing a lion dance to be a relation between a "scene" and a perceiver, but (in 1983) assimilate the objects of the attitudes to the objects of perception. Neale (1988) discusses Higginbotham's account.

Martin (1992) argues that visual perception may involve representation without (so to speak) the kind of conceptualization required for a propositional attitude, as when I see an object without immeadiately registering its presence or properties.

4 Attitude verbs presumably pick out relations between individuals, propositions, and times; strictly, attitudes themselves are such relations. For simplicity, tense and time are ignored throughout.

5 There are important differences between assigning semantic properties to expression types in a context and assigning them to expression tokens or their utterance. Most of the sequel slurs this distinction. And I generally suppress reference to the fact that expressions are sensibly assigned semantic values only relative to a context of use.

6 Italicization is used as a device for talking about expressions. (Precisely: It functions as a method of quasi-quotation, in Quine's sense.) Single quotes are used to mention expressions.

7 This line of thought can be found in Salmon (1986a) and Soames (1987a).

8 Kaplan (1977); see also Chapter 23, INDEXICALS AND DEMONSTRATIVES.

9 See Higginbotham (1992), Soames (1992) for discussion.

10 Davidson (1967). Some identify the task of a theory of meaning with giving an account of truth conditions, which they in turn identify with assigning sets of worlds or situations to the sentences, which are in turn identified with what sentences say. See, for example, Montague (1974).

11 Hyperintensionality is distinct from what Quine calls *opacity*. As Quine defines the notion, a linguistic context $e(\ldots)$ is opaque provided there are singular terms t and t' such that $t = t'$ is true, but $e(t)$ and $e(t')$ have different extensions. The opacity of 'believes that . . . won' follows from the assumptions that definite descriptions are terms, and that 'the lottery winner = the man in the corner', 'Jo thinks that the lottery winner won', and 'Jo doesn't think that the man in the corner won' are all true. That 'believes that . . . won' is hyperintensional does not follow from this. Conversely, the hyperintensionality of 'believes that this is . . .' can be demonstrated by means of a suitable pair of necessarily equivalent predicates, but its opacity can't.

12 Precisely: Transformations which are valid within the scope of modal operators fail within the scope of attitude verbs.

13 See Mates (1950) and Burge (1978); compare Yagisawa (1984).

14 On propositions as sets of worlds, see Stalnaker (1984, 1987), Powers (1978), Richard (1990), and Cresswell (1985). Soames (1984a, 1987a) objects to situation semantics' account of propositions; some of his points are anticipated in Richard (1983). An alternative account identifies propositions with collections of possible and impossible worlds (or situations). See Soames (1987a) for criticism and Edelberg (1994) for a defense.

15 Lewis (1972) and Cresswell (1985) are possible worlds semanticists using structured propositions. Salmon (1986a) and Soames (1987a, 1989) adopt a Russellian view on which the structure of the proposition that *S* generally recapitulates that of *S* itself. Of course, many linguistic views of propositions identify propositions with structured (linguistic or quasi-linguistic) items; among the many examples are Segal (1989), Richard (1990), and Larson and Ludlow (1993).

16 Given the almost universally accepted claim that names rigidly desiginate their bearers; for discussion see Chapter 22, RIGID DESIGNATION, and Chapter 21, REFERENCE AND NECESSITY.

17 Salmon (1986a), Soames (1984b, 1987a, 1989), Richard (1983, 1987a, and McKay (1979) are examples. David Kaplan (1977) is the fountainhead of contemporary enthusiasm for this sort of view.

18 A little more precisely, the arguments made it plausible that such terms are rigid designators of their bearers, and thus the modal properties of the propsitions expressed by *A(t)* and *A(t′)* are identical, if t and t′ name the same thing and the dotted position in *A(. . .)* does not occur in the scope of a device of quotation or attitude verb. See Kripke (1972), Kaplan (1977), Donnellan (1972, 1974), and Putnam (1975).

19 In this argument, 'object of belief' should be understood as shorthand for 'what's named by the "that" clause in a belief ascription'.

20 But see Crimmins (1992) for discussion of this line of argument.

21 This argument is in Richard (1983). Soames (1987a) suggests that it generalizes to show that co-referential proper names are intersubstitutable in APAs. Forbes (1987), Richard (1990), and Crimmins (1992) offer various suggestions as to why the argument does not establish a direct reference view.

22 Such views owe a great deal to Grice (1990) and Kripke (1977). Versions are in Richard (1983, 1987a); Soames (1984a, 1987;) Salmon (1986a); and Berg (1988).

23 Richard (1987a) tries to square folk psychology with the direct reference view. Richard (1990) and Crimmins (1992) argue that the view's inability to account for the literal truth of folk psychology is a serious flaw.

24 See Frege (1952), especially 'On sense and reference'.

25 Graeme Forbes (1989) has suggested that sense determines actual reference, and that contexts like *necessarily*, . . . are extensional, the extension of a sentence being a state of affairs. He then adopts an account of sense like that of Evans discussed below. Richard (1993a) and Crimmins (1993) discuss Forbes' account.

26 See Kripke (1979) and Richard (1987b).

27 See Richard (1988, 1990). One hears the response that (a) I cannot understand the other unless I know that she uses 'Frege' to refer to Frege, but (b) I cannot know this unless there is some similarity in the way the other and I think of Frege. Response (b) is wrong. For example, I might know on the basis of third-party testimony that you use

'Frege' for Frege; or I might know that you are an American and in situation F, and that Americans in situation F use 'Frege' for Frege. It is also unclear why I *must* understand the other in order to correctly ascribe a belief to her.

28 See Evans (1982) and Forbes (1989). The idea arguably originates in Kaplan (1969).

29 See Evans (1982) and McDowell (1984).

30 For discussion, see Evans (1982), Segal (1989), and Recannati (1993).

31 Davidson (1969).

32 Lepore and Loewer (1989).

33 Burge (1986).

34 See Higginbotham (1986) and Hand (1991). Hand also observes that for many cases involving negative polarity and infinitives, positing (the utterance of) a discrete sentence with the content of the ascribed attitude is implausible.

35 Carnap (1946).

36 Intensional isomorphism (and relations like translation) are not dyadic but actually quadratic relations between two sentences and two languages.

37 Church (1950).

38 Admittedly, Carnap himself did not seem to take it in this way.

39 See Richard (1990). A different response is given in Leeds (1979).

40 See Schiffer (1987) for an inventory. Richard (1995) attempts to meet serious objections to sententialism in a way that would be acceptable to those with broadly nominalistic inclinations.

41 Perhaps the most influential arguments are in Fodor (1975, 1987); those mentioned in the text are suggested by him. A sampling of the literature is in Block (1981) and Rosenthal (1991).

42 McLaughlin (1993) gives an introduction to current debate.

43 A summary of some relevant observation and experiment is Cheney and Sefarth (1990).

44 For discussion see Stalnaker (1984), Dennett (1987), Richard (1990), and Crimmins (1992).

45 Stich (1983) and Boer and Lycan (1986) present sentential role accounts. The latter is discussed in Richard (1990). Richard (1989, 1990, 1993a and b) develops a translation account. Grandy (1986) offers an earlier translational account. Schiffer (1979) suggests an implicit reference account, in which tacit reference is (apparently) made to intersubjectively accessible ways of thinking of objects and properties. Perry and Crimmins (1989) and Crimmins (1992) develop the version discussed below.

46 See Richard (1989, 1990, and 1993b).

47 Here the quotation names should be thought of as names of particular token representations of Pierre's which are instance of the quoted types.

48 Short for *Russellian Annotated Matrix*. Soames suggests 'annotated proposition' as a better name. Note that in describing RAMs, quote names name expression types.

49 It would be possible to deny this and still preserve something of the spirit of the account suggested here. One might say that the *normal* or *default* mode of translation is one which preserves Russellian content. One would go on to suggest that, just as the intentions of speakers might require a use of 'London is pretty' in 'Pierre thinks London is pretty' to represent one of Pierre's 'French thoughts', so might these require a use of 'this is a very pleasant place' to represent a thought expressed by '*hier ist est sehr gemutlich*', though the Russellian content of '*gemutlich*' and 'pleasant' in their respective languages are not identical.

Two developments suggest themselves. The less radical simply allows that in context, correlations (the functions which map parts of RAMs to parts of thoughts) may occasionally map ⟨e,x⟩ to ⟨f,y⟩ when x is not y. More radically, the atomistic account of translation used in the text would be replaced by a more holistic one, in which correlations are replaced by functions which map whole RAMs to whole thoughts.

50 Slightly more precisely: Translation requires that there be a *correlation* function f which maps the annotations in RAMs to annotations in thoughts such that q can be obtained from p by replacing p's parts with their image under f. The text supresses complications arising with iteration of attitude verbs. See Richard (1990).

51 The restriction in the text is really on the use of the annotation ⟨'London', London⟩.

A more detailed account of the nature of contextual restrictions is in Richard (1993c). There it is proposed that context associates a (possibly null) "theory" about how a representation functions in thought with each pair of an individual u and expression e; the contextual restriction on a use of e in an ascription of attitude to u is that e can be used to represent only a representations r of u's such that the theory associated with u and e is substantially correct when taken as a theory about r.

52 See Perry (1986). Perry and Crimmins (1989), and Crimmins (1992) give the account sketched below.

53 For critical discussion of translational and implicit reference accounts, see Crimmins (1992), Richard (1993b, 1995b), Saul (1993), Schiffer (1992), and Soames (1995).

54 Slightly more precisely, *de re* ascriptions contain elements (pronouns or variables) which are within the scope of the complementizer for the attitude verb, and which are either bound to a noun phrase outside the complementizer's scope, or have an antecedent outside the complementizer from which they acquire their reference. (This definition may not not capture quite the class of ascriptions each author who uses the terminology calls *de re*.)

55 This has been denied by various latitudinarian accounts of *de re* attitudes; see Chisholm (1976) for an example. See Kaplan (1969) and Sleigh (1967) for discussion.

56 This assumes that it's impossible to have the belief unless the proposition exists, and that it's impossible for a proposition to exist unless its parts do.

57 See Russell (1911, 1912).

58 Much of the discussion of Kripke's examples of contingent a priori knowledge seems to be driven by the assumption that object dependent knowledge requires epistemic rapport. See, for example, Donnellan (1979) and Forbes (1989). See also Kaplan (1969, 1977, 1978, and 1989), and Richard (1993a).

59 Castenada (1966, 1967) first brought out the importance of the divergence between the a and b sentences. It has been extensively discussed in the literature; important examples are Perry (1979), Lewis (1979), and Chisholm (1981). Boer and Lycan (1980) deny that there is a difference in the truth conditions of 4a and b; Boer and Lycan (1986) retract this.

60 Frege (1979).

61 Why, one might ask, must this way of thinking be private? According to Frege, a way of thinking presents no more than one thing. Presumably Frege assumes that the way of thinking in question would 'seem first-person' to whomever used it – so that if I were to use the mode of thought you use with 'I' to think of x, I would have to do the sort of thing I do when I think to myself ***I*** *am tall*. This all seems to imply that if I could use your private mode of self thought, I could think that you are tall by thinking ***I*** *am tall*, which seems absurd.

62 Evans (1981), Peacocke (1981), McGinn (1983), and Forbes (1987) present Fregean accounts of *de se* thought.

63 This ignores presumable (but irrelevant) limitations of expressive capacity in English.

64 Alternatives to Fregean and the Lewis/Chisholm account of *de se* belief can be found in Perry (1979), Stalnaker (1981), and Richard (1983).

References and further reading

Almog, Joseph *et al.* 1989: *Themes from Kaplan*. Oxford: Oxford University Press.

Anderson, C. Anthony 1983: The paradox of the knower. *Journal of Philosophy*, 80, 338–55.

—— 1987: Review of Bealer's *Quality and Concept*. *Journal of Philosphical Logic*, 16. 115–64.

—— 1989: Russellian intensional logic. In Almog *et al.* 1989.

Asher, Nicholas 1986: Belief in discourse representation theory. *Journal of Philosophical Logic*, 15, 137–89.

Barwise, Jon 1981: Scenes and other situations. *Journal of Philosophy*, 78, 369–97.

—— 1989: Situations, facts, and true propositions. In *The Situation in Logic*. Stanford, Calif: CSLI.

—— and Etchemendy, John 1987: *The Liar*. Oxford: Oxford University Press.

Barwise, Jon and Perry, John 1983: *Situations and Attitudes*. Cambridge, Mass.: MIT Press.

Bealer, George 1982: *Quality and Concept*. Oxford: Oxford University Press.

Berg, Jonathan 1988: The pragmatics of substitutivity. *Linguistics and Philosophy*, 11, 355–70.

Block, Ned 1981: *Readings in the Philosophy of Psychology*, Vols 1 and 2. Cambridge, Mass.: Harvard University Press.

Boer, Steven and Lycan, William 1980: Who, me? *Philosophical Review*, 89, 427–66.

—— 1986: *Knowing Who*. Cambridge, Mass.: MIT Press.

Burge, Tyler 1977: Belief *De Re*. *Journal of Philosophy*, 74, 338–62.

—— 1978: Belief and synonymity. *Journal of Philosophy*, 75, 119–38.

—— 1979: Individualism and the mental. In P. French *et al.* (eds), *Midwest Studies in Philosophy*, 4. Minneapolis: Univ. of Minnesota Press, 73–121.

—— 1982: Other bodies. In Woodfield (1982).

—— 1986: On Davidson's 'Saying That'. In E. LePore (ed.) *Truth and Interpretation*. Oxford: Oxford University Press.

Carnap, Rudolf 1946: *Meaning and Necessity*. Chicago: University of Chicago Press.

Castenada, Hector-Neri 1966: 'He': A study in the logic of self-consciousness. *Ratio*, 8, 130–57.

—— 1967: Indicators and quasi-indicators. *American Philosophical Quarterly*, 4, 85–100.

Cheney, Dorothy and Seyfarth, Robert 1990: *How Monkeys See the World*. Chicago: University of Chicago Press.

Chisholm, Roderick 1976: *Person and Object*. La Salle, Ill.: Open Court.

—— 1981: *The First Person*. Minneapolis: University of Minnesota Press.

Chomsky, Noam 1965: *Aspects of the Theory of Syntax*. Cambridge, Mass.: MIT Press.

—— 1986: *Knowledge of Language: Its Nature, Origin, and Use*. New York: Prager.

Church, Alonzo 1950: On Carnap's analysis of statements of assertion and belief. Reprinted in Linsky (1971).

Cresswell, Max 1985: *Structured Meanings: The Semantics of Propositional Attitudes*. Cambridge, Mass.: MIT Press.

Crimmins, Mark 1992a: *Talk about Beliefs*. Cambridge, Mass: MIT Press.

Crimmins, Mark 1992b: Context in the attitudes. *Linguistics and Philosophy*, 15, 185–98.
——1993: Forbes' so-labelled neo-Fregeanism. *Philosophical Studies*, 69, 115–29.
Cummins, Robert 1989: *Meaning and Mental Representation*. Cambridge, Mass.: MIT Press.
Davidson, Donald 1967: Truth and Meaning. In Davidson (1984).
——1969: On saying that. In Davidson (1984).
——1984: *Essays on Truth and Interpretation*. Oxford: Oxford University Press.
Dennett, Daniel 1981: *Brainstorms*. Cambridge, Mass.: MIT Press.
——1987: *The Intentional Stance*. Cambridge, Mass.: MIT Press.
Dretske, Fred 1981: *Knowledge and the Flow of Information*. Cambridge, Mass.: MIT Press.
Donnellan, Keith 1972: Proper names and identifying descriptions. In D. Davidson and G. Harman (eds), *Semantics for Natural Language*. Dordrecht: Reidel.
——1974: Speaking of Nothing. *Philosophical Review*, 83, 3–31.
——1979: The contingent *a priori* and rigid designators. In P. French *et al.* (eds), *Contemporary Perspectives in the Philosophy of Language*. Minneapolis: University of Minnesota Press.
Edelberg, Walter 1994: Propositions, circumstances, and objects. *Journal of Philosophical Logic*, 23, 1–34.
Evans, Gareth 1981: Understanding demonstratives. In H. Parret and J. Bouveresse (eds), *Meaning and Understanding*. Berlin: de Gruyter.
——1982: *The Varieties of Reference*. Oxford: Oxford University Press.
Field, Hartry 1977: Logic, meaning, and conceptual role. *Journal of Philosophy*, 74, 379–409.
——1978: Mental representation. *Erkenntnis*, 13, 9–61.
Fodor, Jerry 1975: *The Language of Thought*. New York: Thomas Y. Crowell.
——1981: *Representations*. Cambridge, Mass.: MIT Press.
——1987: *Psychosemantics*. Cambridge, Mass.: MIT Press.
Forbes, Graeme 1987: Indexicals and intensionality: a Fregean perspective. *Philosophical Review*, 96, 3–31.
——1989: *Languages of Possibility*. Cambridge, Mass.: Basil Blackwell.
——1990: The indispensibility of sinn. *Philosophical Review*, 99, 535–63.
——1993: Solving the iteration problem. *Linguistics and Philosophy*, 16, 311–30.
Frege, Gottlob 1952: *Translations from the Philosophical Writings*. Translated by Max Black and Peter Geach, Oxford: Oxford University Press.
——1984: Thoughts. In B. McGuinness (ed.), *Collected Papers on Mathematics, Logic, and Philosophy*. Oxford: Blackwell. Reprinted in Salmon and Soames (1988).
Grandy, Richard 1986: Some misconceptions about belief. In Grandy and Warner (eds), *Philosophical Grounds of Rationality: Intentions, Categories, Ends*. Oxford: Oxford University Press.
Grice, Paul 1990: *Studies in the Ways of Words*. Cambridge, Mass.: Harvard University Press.
Hand, Michael 1991: On saying that again. *Linguistics and Philosophy*, 14, 349–65.
Higginbotham, James 1983: The logic of perceptual reports: an extensional alternative to situation semantics. *Journal of Philosophy*, 80, 100–27.
——1986: Linguistic theory and Davidson's program in semantics. In E. LePore (ed.), *Truth and Interpretation: Perspectives on the Philosophy of Donald Davidson*. Oxford: Basil Blackwell.
——1991: Belief and logical form. *Mind and Language*, 6, 344–69.
——1992: Truth and understanding. *Philosophical Studies*, 65, 3–21.
——1993: *Language and Cognition*. Oxford: Blackwell.
Hintikka, Jakko 1962: *Knowledge and Belief*. Ithaca, NY: Cornell University Press.

Kaplan, David 1969: Quantifying in. In D. Davidson and G. Harman (eds), *Words and Objections*. Dordrecht: Reidel. Reprinted in Linsky (1971).

——1977: *Demonstratives. Draft #2*. Dittograph. Reprinted in Almog *et al.* (1989).

——1978: Dthat. In P. Cole (ed.), *Syntax and Semantics 9*. New York: Academic Press.

——1986: Opacity. In L. Hahn and P. Schlipp (eds), *The Philosophy of W.V. Quine*. La Salle, Ill.: Open Court.

——1989: Afterthoughts. In Almog *et al.* (1989).

Kripke, Saul 1972: *Naming and Necessity*. In D. Davidson and G. Harman (eds), *Semantics for Natural Language*. Dordrecht: Reidel. Reprinted in 1980 as a mongraph by Harvard University Press.

——1977: Speaker's referene and semantic reference. In P. French *et al.* (eds), *Midwest Studies in Philosophy*, 2. Minneapolis: University of Minnesota Press.

——1979: A puzzle about belief. In A. Margalit (ed.), *Meaning and Use*. Dordrecht: Reidel. Reprinted in Salmon and Soames (1988).

Larson, Richard and Ludlow, Peter 1993: Interpreted logical forms. *Synthese*, 95, 305–55.

Leeds, Stephen 1979: Church's translation argument. *Canadian Journal of Philosophy*, 9, 43–51.

Lepore, E. and Loewer, B. 1989: You can say *that* again. In P. French *et al.* (eds), *Midwest Studies in Philosophy*, 14, 338–56.

Lewis, David 1970: How to define theortetical terms. *Journal of Philosophy*, 67, 427–46. Reprinted in Lewis (1983).

——1972: General semantics. In D. Davison and G. Harman (eds) (1972). Reprinted in Lewis (1983).

——1974: Radical interpretation. *Synthese* 23, 331–44. Reprinted in Lewis (1983).

——1979: Attitudes de dicto and de se. *Philosophical Review*, 88, 513–43. Reprinted in Lewis (1983).

——1983: *Collected Papers*, Vol. 1. Oxford: Oxford University Press.

Linsky, Leonard (ed.) 1971: *Reference and Modality*. Oxford: Oxford University Press.

——1985: *Oblique Contexts*. Chicago: University of Chicago Press.

Loar, Brian 1981: *Mind and Meaning*. Cambridge: Cambridge University Press.

——1987: Subjective intentionality. *Philosophical Topics*, 15, 89–124.

McDowell, John 1977: On the sense and reference of a proper name. *Mind*, 86, 159–85. Reprinted in M. Platts (ed.), *Reference, Truth, and Reality*. London: Routledge and Kegan Paul.

——1984: *De Re* senses. *Philosophical Quarterly*, 34, 283–94.

McGinn, Colin 1982: The structure of content. In Woodfield (1982).

——1983. *The Subjective View: Secondary Qualities and Indexical Thoughts*. Cambridge: Cambridge University Press.

MacKay, Tom 1979: On proper names in belief ascriptions. *Philosophical Studies*, 39, 287–303.

——1991: Representing *De Re* beliefs. *Linguistics and Philosophy*, 14, 711–39.

McLaughlin, Brian 1993: The connectionism/classicism battle to win souls. *Philosophical Studies*, 71, 163–90.

Marcus, Ruth Barcan 1981: A proposed solution to a puzzle about belief. In P. French *et al.* (eds), *Midwest Studies in Philosophy*, 6. Minneapolis: University of Minnesota Press.

——1983: Rationality and believing the impossible. *Journal of Philosophy*, 80, 321–37.

Martin, M.G.F. 1992: Perception, concepts, and meaning. *Philosophical Review*, 101, 745–63.

Mates, Benson 1950: Synonymity. *University of California Publications in Philosophy*, 25. Reprinted in L. Linsky (ed.), *Semantics and the Philosophy of Language*. Urbana: University of Illinois Press.

Milikan, Ruth 1984: *Language, Thought, and Other Biological Categories*. Cambridge, Mass.: MIT Press.

Montague, Richard 1974: *Formal Philosophy*, ed. R. Thomason. New Haven: Yale University Press.

Moravcsik, Julius 1990: *Thought and Language*. London: Routledge.

Morton, Adam 1980: *Frames of Mind*. Oxford: Oxford University Press.

Neale, Stephen 1988: Events and 'logical form'. *Linguistics and Philosophy*, 11, 303–22.

Parsons, Terence 1981: Frege's hierarchies of indirect senses and the paradox of analysis. In P. French *et al.* (eds), *Midwest Studies in Philosophy*, 6. Minneapolis: University of Minnesota Press.

Peacocke, Christopher 1981: Demonstrative thoughts and psychological explanation. *Synthese*, 49, 187–217.

Perry, John 1977: Frege on demonstratives. *Philosophical Review*, 86, 474–97.

——1979: The case of the essential indexical. *Noûs*, 13, 3–21. Reprinted in Salmon and Soames (1988).

——1980: Belief and acceptence. In P. French *et al.* (eds), *Midwest Studies in Philosophy*, 5.

——1986: Thought without representation. *Proceedings of the Aristotelian Society*, Suppl. Vol., 60, 263–83.

Perry, John, and Crimmins, Mark 1989: The prince and the phone booth: reporting puzzling beliefs. *Journal of Philosophy*, 86, 685–711.

Powers, Larry 1978: Knowledge by deduction. *Philosophical Review*, 87, 337–71.

Prior, A.N. 1971: *Objects of Thought*. Oxford: Oxford University Press.

Putnam, H. 1963: Brains and behavior. In Putnam (1975b).

——1966: The mental life of some machines. In Putnam (1975b).

——1967: The nature of mental states. In Putnam (1975b).

——1970: Is semantics possible? In Putnam (1975b).

——1975a: The meaning of 'meaning'. In Putnam (1975b).

——1975b: *Mind, Language, and Reality. Collected Papers*. Vol. 2 Cambridge: Cambridge University Press.

——1988: *Representation and Reality*. Cambridge, Mass.: MIT Press.

Quine, W.V. 1956: Quantifiers and propositional attitudes. *Journal of Philosophy*, 53, 177–187. Reprinted in Linsky (1971).

——1960: *Word and Object*. Cambridge, Mass.: MIT Press.

Recannati, François 1993: *Direct Reference*. Cambridge: Basil Blackwell.

Richard, Mark 1983: Direct reference and ascriptions of belief. *Journal of Philosophical Logic*, 12, 425–52. Reprinted in Salmon and Soames (1988).

——1987a: Attitude ascriptions, semantic theory, and pragmatic evidence. *Proceedings of the Aristotelian Society*, 87, 243–62.

——1987b: Quantification and Leibniz's law. *Philosophical Review*, 96, 555–78.

——1988: Taking the Fregean seriously. In D. Austin (ed.), *Philosophical Analysis: A Defense by Example*. Dordrecht: Reidel.

——1989: How I say what you think. In P. French *et al.* (eds), *Midwest Studies in Philosophy*, 14, 317–37. Notre Dame, Ind.: University of Notre Dame Press. Reprinted in Higginbotham (1993).

——1990: *Propositional Attitudes*. Cambridge: Cambridge University Press.

——1993a: Sense, necessity, and belief. *Philosophical Studies*, 69, 243–63.
——1993b: Attitudes and context. *Linguistics and Philosophy*, 16, 123–48.
——1993c: Attitudes, indexicality, and propositions. Series of lectures given at the National University of Mexico, Mexico City.
——1995a: Propositional quantification. In J. Copeland (ed.), *Logic and Reality*. Oxford: Oxford University Press.
——1995b: Defective contexts, accommodation, and normalization. *Canadian Journal of Philosophy*, 25, n. 4, 551–70.
Rosenthal, David (ed.) 1991: *The Nature of Mind*. Oxford: Oxford University Press.
Russell, Bertrand 1903: *Principles of Mathematics*. London: Allen and Unwin.
——1911: Knowledge by acquaintance and knowledge by description. *Proceedings of the Aristotelian Society*, 11. Reprinted in Salmon and Soames (1988).
——1912: *The Problems of Philosophy*. Oxford: Oxford University Press.
——1918: *The Philosophy of Logical Atomism*. In R. Marsh (ed.), *Logic and Knowledge*. London: George Allen and Unwin.
Salmon, Nathan 1986a: *Frege's Puzzle*. Cambridge, Mass.: MIT Press.
——1986b: Reflexivity. *Notre Dame Journal of Formal Logic*, 27, 401–29. Reprinted in Salmon and Soames (1988).
——1989: Illogical belief. In J. Tomberlin (ed.), *Philosophical Perspectives 3*. Atascadero, Cal.: Ridgeview Publishing Company.
——1992: Reflections on reflexivity. *Linguistics and Philosophy*, 15, 53–63.
Salmon, Nathan, and Soames, Scott 1988: *Propositions and Attitudes*. Oxford: Oxford University Press.
Saul, Jennifer 1993: Still an attitude problem. *Linguistics and Philosophy*, 16, 423–35.
Schiffer, Stephen 1979: Naming and knowing. In French *et al.* (eds), *Midwest Perspectives in the Philosophy of Language*, 2, 28–44.
——1987: *Remnants of Meaning*. Cambridge, Mass.: MIT Press.
——1990a: The mode-of-presentation problem. In C. Anderson and J. Owens (eds), *Propositional Attitudes*. Stanford, Ca.: CSLI.
——1990b: The relational theory of belief. *Pacific Philosophical Quarterly*, 71, 240–5.
——1992: Belief ascription. *Journal of Philosophy*, 89, 499–521.
Searle, John 1990: Consciousness, explanatory inversion, and cognitive science. *Behavioral and Brain Sciences*, 13, 585–98.
Segal, Gabriel 1989: A preference for sense and reference. *Journal of Philosophy*, 86, 73–89.
——1990: The return of the individual. *Mind*, 98, 39–57.
Sleigh, Robert 1967: On quantifying into epistemic contexts. *Noûs*, 1, 1–31.
Soames, Scott 1984a: Lost innocence. *Linguistics and Philosophy*, 8, 59–71.
——1984b: What is a theory of truth? *Journal of Philosophy*, 81, 411–29.
——1987a: Direct reference, propositional attitudes, and semantic content. *Philosophical Topics*, 15 (n. 1), 47–88. Reprinted in Salmon and Soames (1988).
——1987b: Substitutivity. In J.J. Thomson (ed.), *On Being and Saying: Essays for Richard Cartwright*. Cambridge, Mass.: MIT Press.
——1989: Semantics and semantic competence. In J. Tomberlin (ed.), *Philosophical Perspectives*, 3. Atascadero, Cal: Ridgeview Publishing Company.
——1990: Pronouns and propositional attitudes. *Proceedings of the Aristotelian Society*, 90, 191–212.
——1992: Truth, Meaning, and Understanding. *Philosophical Studies*, 65, 17–35.
——1995: Beyond singular propositions? *Canadian Journal of Philosophy*, 5, n. 4, 515–49.

Stalnaker, Robert 1976: Propositions. In A. MacKay and D. Merrill (eds), *Issues in the Philosophy of Language*. New Haven, Conn.: Yale University Press.
——1978: Assertion. *Syntax and Semantics*, 9, 315–32.
——1981: Indexical belief. *Synthese*, 49, 129–51.
——1984: *Inquiry*. Cambridge, Mass.: MIT Press.
——1987: Semantics for belief. *Philosophical Topics*, 15 (no. 1), 177–90.
Stich, Stephen 1978: Beliefs and subdoxastic states. *Philosophy of Science*, 45, 499–518.
——1979: Do animals have beliefs? *Australasian Journal of Philosophy*, 57, 79–91.
——1983: *From Folk Psychology to Cognitive Science*. Cambridge, Mass: MIT Press.
Wettstein, Howard 1991: *Has Semantics Rested Upon a Mistake?* Stanford, Calif.: Stanford University Press.
Woodfield, Andrew 1982: *Thought and Object: Essays on Intentionality*. Oxford: Oxford University Press.
Yagisawa, Takashi 1984: The pseudo-Mates argument. *Philosophical Review*, 93, 407–19.

10

Holism

CHRISTOPHER PEACOCKE

The question must arise whether a doctrine which is attributed to all of Quine, Putnam, Davidson, Rorty, Gadamer and Heidegger is possibly a doctrine which comes in more than one version. Even the most ardent taxonomist is likely to draw back from classifying the various actual and possible positions which emerge from the very tangled history of recent discussions of holism. I will be approaching the matter by addressing a series of questions, starting with those which are most likely to arise in the mind of those philosophers who regard holism with a mixture of fascination and suspicion.[1]

1 What is meaning holism?

Here is a highly general formulation of global holism about meaning, a formulation acceptable to holists of many different stripes:

> (GH) The meaning of an expression depends constitutively on its relations to all other expressions in the language, where these relations may need to take account of such facts about the use of these other expressions as their relations to the non-linguistic world, to action and to perception.

This is a constitutive thesis about what it is for an expression to have a certain meaning. It is neither an epistemological thesis, nor a psychological thesis; though of course if it is correct, it will have consequences for both psychology and epistemology. It goes far beyond the less controversial claim that in assessing the evidence that a given expression has a certain meaning, we must take account of the properties of any sentence in which the expression occurs, regardless of what else is in that sentence.

(GH) is non-committal in at least two respects. First, different theorists who are both committed to accepting (GH) may emphasize different relations to the non-linguistic world as partially constitutive of meaning. Some theorists accepting (GH) may give a special status to observable states of affairs; others may not. Empiricism is not written into, nor entailed by, (GH). Second, one who holds (GH) is not committed to saying that one can make explicit, in a non-circular way, the relations to all other expressions in which a given expression must stand if it is to have a given meaning. Interpretationism is the doctrine that in saying what it is for a particular expression to have a given meaning, a fundamental place must be given to the fact that under optimal interpretation of the language in which the expression occurs, the expression is assigned that meaning. According to the interpretationist there may be more to be said about optimal interpretation in general, and more to be said about various particular meanings. But neither of these, according to the interpretationist, will amount to a full account of what it is to grasp a given meaning unless they actually mention optimal interpretation itself. This is not the place for a discussion of the important question of the correctness of interpretationism, and one of its possible motivations, a certain subjectivism about propositional attitudes and contents (as in McDowell, 1986, and possibly Davidson himself). All that matters for present purposes is that it is prima facie consistent for a global holist about meaning to be an interpretationist. (For discussion of Davidson's position, see Chapter 8, RADICAL INTERPRETATION.)

Global holists who, unlike interpretationists, believe that grasp of a particular meaning can be made explicit without presupposing the understander's grasp of that meaning can make use of the notion of an *understanding-condition* in specifying meanings. An understanding-condition is an explicit statement of the condition a person must meet to understand a given expression, a statement which does not at any point take for granted understanding of the expression in question, nor possession of the concept it expresses. We can formulate the global holism of these theorists in:

(GHE) For a thinker to meet the understanding-condition for any expression E, there must exist certain other expressions $E_1, \ldots, E_n$, such that

(a) the understander meets a certain specifiable, non-circular condition $R(E, E_1, \ldots, E_n)$; this condition may concern the use of the expressions $E_1, \ldots, E_n$, and it may concern their relations to the non-linguistic world; and
(b) the expressions $E, E_1, \ldots, E_n$ exhaust the expressions in the understander's language.

Global holism of the sort captured in (GHE) itself comes in several kinds. One kind is that variety which recognizes certain methods of establishing sentences containing a given expression, or certain methods of deriving consequences from them, as canonical. It writes these methods into the relevant understanding-conditions. One example of a global holism with canonical methods, (GHEC), restricted to the language of mathematics, would be the "pure mathematical holism" mentioned by Dummett, which identifies truth with provability by any of the canonical methods acknowledged in classical mathematics (Dummett, 1991, p. 226). Since some sentences can be proved outright by classical methods, we have in this example one of the extreme forms of holism attacked by Dummett, according to which understanding another person's expression sometimes involves knowing which sentences containing it he holds true (Dummett, 1975, Appendix). This framework of classification also formally leaves space for a further kind of case, that of a kind of holism which does not accept the designation of any methods as canonical (GHENC). Such, for instance, would be the position of a global holist who thinks that we can usefully speak only of similarity of meaning, not of identity of meaning, and who holds that two sentences are more similar in meaning the greater the overlap in accepted methods of establishing them.

Those already well-acquainted with this territory will recognize that (GHE) is the natural formulation of that kind of global holism when the apparatus of possession conditions, as a means of individuating concepts, is adapted to the case of linguistic meaning (Peacocke, 1992). I have chosen this formulation for its bearing on the issue of the circularity of global holism. Those who reject all forms of global holism, but still accept the possibility of explicit formulations of understanding-conditions, commonly propose that there is a certain non-trivial, partial ordering of all the expressions of a language. This ordering has the property that to elucidate the meaning of an expression at any given place in the ordering, it is not necessary to mention its relations to expressions later in the ordering. Since the global holist will say that there is no such ordering, it is natural to wonder whether a global holist can avoid circularity in his account of meaning. Dummett, for one, characterizes holism as "the doctrine that any meaning-theory is inevitably circular" (1991, p. 241). In fact the availability of the above form (GHE) should indicate that there is no structural obstacle of principle to the global holist's giving non-circular accounts of the understanding of particular expressions. For instance, one form of global holism might state that to understand a certain expression, one must appreciate that sentences containing it can be established by a certain finite family of methods, where a statement of the methods involves all the other concepts expressed in the language. This may not be plausible – it will be discussed below – but provided that the methods can be specified without presuming on any prior understanding of the expression in question, it is not circular. A global holist who possesses such non-circular specifications may rightly insist that he admits and employs the notion of the content of a given individual sentence. For him, that content will be fixed by the meaning specifications for the components of the sentence, together with the way in which they compose the sentence.

Quine is not a holist of any of the sorts so far distinguished, for he has always acknowledged a level of observational vocabulary for which he would say that all of the above theses are false. Quine's holism is captured by the preceding formulations only if we understand the talk of expressions, and variables ranging over them, as restricted to the non-observational part of the language. We are clearly entering here the realm in which holism comes in degrees. A position may be classified as more holistic the fewer restrictions we have to place on the talk of expressions in order for the position to be classified as holistic according to the characterizations above. This matter of degree arises also for conceptual-role theories of meaning, as advocated in Block (1986), Harman (1982) and Sellars (1974), which state that for an expression to have a particular meaning is for it to have a certain role in its user's psychology. A conceptual-role theory of meaning will similarly be more holistic the fewer restrictions it places on those features of an expression's total role which it regards as individuative of the expression's meaning. The limiting case at the end of the spectrum of increasingly holistic alternatives is that in which no restrictions are placed on those features of the conceptual role of an expression which contribute to individuating its meaning. Acceptance of this limiting case is naturally accompanied by scepticism that the strict relation of intersubjective synonymy of expressions – at least for that aspect of meaning captured by holistic conceptual role – is ever, in fact, satisfied (cp. Field, 1977).

I turn now to consider grounds which have been offered in support of meaning holism.

2 Does the Duhem-Quine Thesis provide a ground for meaning holism?

This question must be split into two parts:

(a) Is the Duhem-Quine Thesis true? (If it is not, it will not be a ground for anything.)
(b) If the Duhem-Quine Thesis is true, does it support meaning holism?

Actually we should distinguish the Duhem thesis from the Quine thesis. Duhem wrote:

> the physicist can never subject an isolated hypothesis to experimental test, but only a whole group of hypotheses; when the experiment is in disagreement with his predictions, what he learns is that at least one of the hypotheses constituting this group is unacceptable and ought to be modified; but the experiment does not designate which one should be changed. (Duhem, 1962, p. 187)

Two points emerge from Duhem's discussion. First, Duhem's thesis is specific to hypotheses of physics. He explicitly contrasted the physicist's situation with that of a physiologist who wishes to confirm that a nerve is a motor nerve, rather than a sensory nerve (ibid., p. 182). Second, in Duhem's account it is the experiments which are said to confirm, or to be in conflict with, a group of hypotheses. Quine's thesis, which he says "was well argued by Duhem" (Quine, 1961, p. 41, n. 17), is by contrast not confined to physics; and for Quine what confirms or conflicts with groups of hypotheses are not the results of experiments but rather (in the 1951 version) sense experiences.[2] Quine wrote:

> our statements about the external world face the tribunal of sense experience not individually but only as a corporate body. (Ibid., p. 41)

And, further on in the same paper:

> Even a statement very close to the periphery [of our field of beliefs] can be held true in the face of recalcitrant experience by pleading hallucination. (Ibid., p. 43)

Duhem could not have offered that ground on behalf of *his* thesis. The possibility of pleading hallucination arises no less for the physiologist than for the physicist. A thesis defensible on such grounds could not discriminate between those two disciplines.

In Quine's later formulations, the talk of sense experiences gives way to talk of stimuli. With this comes his notion of the stimulus-meaning of a sentence for a speaker, which is the ordered pair of its affirmative and negative stimulus-meanings. Its affirmative stimulus-meaning is "the class of all stimulations (hence evolving ocular irradiation patterns between properly timed blindfoldings) that would prompt his assent" (Quine, 1960, p. 32). Negative stimulus-meaning is defined similarly, with "dissent" in place of "assent". In this later framework, the Quine thesis becomes the claim that sentences about the external world cannot be assigned stimulus-meanings one-by-one, but only collectively, in sets.

This version of the Quine thesis is plausible, but it supports holism about meaning only if meaning is to be elucidated in terms of stimulus-meaning. Identity of stimulus-meaning is far from necessary for identity of meaning. Creatures with very different sensory systems could mean the same thing, on an occasion, by an utterance of the sentence "This edge is straight", even though their different patterns of sensory receptors preclude identity of stimulus-meaning. Nor do the sensory systems have to be radically different for the point to hold. For someone who knowingly has a serious case of astigmatism, the stimulus-meaning of "That line is straight" will differ from its stimulus-meaning for his better-sighted friend. Yet the sentences have the same meaning for both. The lesson of such simple examples is twofold. Meaning must be keyed more strongly to the environment; and we cannot hope to capture the nature of a person's grasp of meaning by looking solely at incoming information, to the neglect of the person's later use of that information, including ultimately its effects on his actions. Invited on many occasions to endorse a firmer separation of meaning from stimulus-meaning, Quine has persistently held fast to his later formulations: "I did intend the stimulus meaning to capture the notion of meaning – for the linguistic community in the case of an observation sentence, and for the individual speaker in the case of many other occasion sentences" (Quine, 1986, pp. 427–8).

Does Duhem's thesis imply a form of meaning holism? We can formulate the crucial question more generally, and also more explicitly. Let us say that a given branch of discourse *has the Duhemian property* just in case it is only whole groups of statements in that branch of discourse which are confirmed by experiments or observable states of affairs, rather than individual statements. So a branch of discourse is Duhemian if and only if it is as Duhem thought physics to be. We can now formulate our question thus: are the distinctive terms of a Duhemian branch of discourse such that their understanding-conditions involve all the other terms of the whole language?

There are two reasons we should not give an unrestricted affirmative answer. The first is that there are some examples of areas of discourse which have the Duhemian property, but where the most plausible explanation of the phenomenon does not involve any global holism about the meaning of its distinctive terms. One example is discourse about persons' intentional states, and the actions they explain. Any particular action may potentially be explained by indefinitely many combinations of beliefs and desires. Even if one is given in advance both that a particular event is an intentional action, and is given the description under which it is intentional, nothing follows about which mental states of the person whose action it is were operative in producing the action. In general, actions are produced only by combinations of beliefs and desires. Correlatively, their occurrence can confirm or disconfirm only whole sets of hypotheses about the agent's mental states. There is disagreement about what grasp of the scheme of explanation of intentional states involves – whether it involves approximate laws, or whether it involves some irreducible notion of making something intelligible, to mention two of the options. But it cannot be plausibly suggested that the concepts of all the other sciences have to be brought in to explain what is involved in mastery of the scheme of intentional states. Any evidence may, indeed, be relevant to such questions as that of whether certain normal conditions, which may be required for perception, or reasoning, or intentional action are met; but this is holism of the evidence, not meaning holism.

What holds for intentional psychology may also hold for other areas of discourse. The language a person employs may be divisible into many different parts, and the discourse of each part may have the Duhemian property, without any form of global meaning-holism being true of the language as a whole.

The second reason against saying that any Duhemian branch of discourse supports a form of global holism is more fundamental, and indeed, if correct, suggests that the first reason may already be implicitly conceding too much. Why should the meaning of a theoretical hypothesis, or of a set of them, be elucidated in terms of its or their consequences for observable states of affairs at all? A scientist may formulate this hypothesis: "There are particles of matter less than 0.000001 mm in diameter, which exert tiny forces on each other." It is initially quite implausible that in order to understand this hypothesis, the scientist must know observational tests for sets of hypotheses containing it. On the contrary, attaining knowledge of observational tests for this or any other hypothesis takes reasoning and creative thought. Such knowledge usually comes after understanding of the hypothesis, and so cannot be identified with the understanding. The capacity for understanding the hypothesis is present as soon as the thinker has a general notion of size, its measurement, of matter and of forces. This understanding must indeed ultimately connect the measurement of size at various points with the observable, and a detailed account of the nature of that connection should be given. But it is one thing to state that such connections must exist for anyone who understands measurement: it is quite another to say that the meaning of a set of hypotheses is given in terms of their observational consequences. Grasp of systems of measurement for the various physical magnitudes mentioned in the special theory of relativity no doubt involves some indirect connection of values of these magnitudes with observables. But it took further thought to devise an observational test of the theory.

From the standpoint of this second reason, the first reason implicitly conceded too much in not contesting the claim, even for the non-global holism of the scheme of intentional explanation, that the meaning of its hypotheses are given by connections with the actions they explain. It can equally take creative thought to reason out what actions would be evidence, in the context of others a subject possesses, of a given propositional attitude. In this case, too, knowledge of what would be evidence is subsequent to understanding of the sentence which attributes the given attitude. Knowledge of what would be evidence cannot be identified with understanding that sentence.

3 Does revisability support meaning holism?

The rational revisability of statements has loomed large in discussions of holism. In "Two Dogmas of Empiricism", Quine argued that on the conception of empirical content he presents there, "no statement is immune to revision" (Quine, 1961, p. 43). In Putnam's discussion of "the considerations that lead *me* to embrace meaning holism", he highlights the rational, non-stipulative revisability of a vast range of statements (Putnam, 1986, pp. 406ff.). I turn now to consider the relations between revisability and holism; and also to distinguish two rather different sources of revisability.

Meaning holism does not by itself imply unlimited revisability. Those forms of meaning holism which admit certain canonical methods – the forms which accept (GHEC) of § 1 above – actually preclude unlimited revisability, since according to them suitable uses of the canonical methods will not be revisable. The same holds for more limited forms of holism which admit canonical methods. Canonical methods are in effect acknowledged in Quine's later thought, in which those principles to which assent is ensured by his 'verdict tables' are taken as having an innocent kind of analyticity (Quine, 1974, pp. 77–80). Only those forms of meaning holism which do not distinguish any methods at all as canonical entail unlimited revisability. It is a real question whether these forms can make any sense of the immediate acceptance of certain statements as being required by reason, and of certain transitions as being required by reason. Some of these forms are certainly excluded by the fact that we could never rationally revise statements of the form "If *p*, then *p*".

Does Duhem's thesis imply some kind of revisability which in its turn supports meaning holism? It cannot, if the considerations of the previous section were correct. I argued that Duhem's thesis does not imply meaning holism. If that is right, Duhem's thesis can hardly imply something which in turn implies meaning holism. But it is well worth considering what kinds of revisability are present in Duhemian areas of discourse (in the sense of the preceding section), in order to distinguish them from examples of revisability which have a different source.

A paradigm case of revisability of the sort which impressed Duhem is the attribution of a particular numerical value to a theoretical magnitude, ascribed to a particular object (or region) at a particular time. When this sort of attribution is made on the basis of experimental data, it seems indisputable that the attribution would have to be revised if, as could well be the case, we came rationally to change our mind about the principles linking the theoretical magnitude with the observable properties of the experimental setup. But besides being no challenge to central laws of logic, revisability of such particular ascriptions of theoretical magnitudes to particular objects is also consistent with the unrevisability of statements of certain very general characteristics of theoretical magnitudes or properties. A magnitude that has theoretical links neither with mass nor repulsion and attraction could hardly be the magnitude of force. Something which has nothing to do with heritable characteristics could hardly be a gene. Duhem's thesis does not exclude such simple examples of unrevisability.

Revisability with a rather different source can be illustrated if we take, first, perceptual demonstratives. Consider the perceptual-demonstrative "that plant", which is in a suitable context a way of thinking of a particular plant made available by the plant's being presented to the thinker in perception in a particular way. The thinker may radically revise his view of various statements of the form "that plant is thus-and-so", without "that plant" losing its reference nor, more importantly for our concerns, its sense. These radical revisions may involve change of belief about the plant's origins, its sources of energy, its mode of reproduction, its lack (or otherwise) of magical properties; and much else. Revision on any of these matters does not affect the sense of the demonstrative expression, because no such revision undermines the foundation of the availability of the perceptual-demonstrative way of thinking of the object, viz. its being, in virtue of its causal relations to his perceptual state, the one which is presented to him in a certain way in perception. More generally, we can describe a kind of sense (or mode of presentation) as *causally-linked* if a correct statement of what is required for something to be the reference of a sense of that kind mentions the causal relations of that thing to the thinker. Perceptual-demonstratives constitute just one of many causally linked kinds of sense. Another type is that of recognitionally based senses; a further kind is that whose instances have their references fixed in part by their being the dominant sources of certain dossiers of information.[3] In these, as in other causally linked cases, recognition of radical error, and hence radical revision of beliefs, is consistent with constancy of sense. Many of Putnam's most striking examples of revisability are ones which turn on a causally linked way of thinking of some property or magnitude (Putnam, 1986).

Rational revisability made possible by causally linked senses does not seem to me to give any grounds for meaning holism in the sense distinguished in § 1 above. Examples of such rational revisability are consistent with the predicates whose ascription is revised having understanding-conditions which do not make reference to the whole language. Nor is it plausible that the understanding-conditions of the expressions with causally linked senses presupposes understanding of all the rest of the language. The crucial element in the understanding-conditions for those expressions is that the thinker's use of them be suitably answerable to information coming via the causal channel or channels which make available to the thinker the example of the causally linked kind in question. A thinker with only a fairly primitive vocabulary and conceptual repertoire can be making use of the same instance of a causally linked kind as a powerful theoretician.

Quine's arguments for holism and his insistence on extensive revisability have been linked in his writings with a rejection of analyticity, understood as truth "purely in virtue of meaning". If we reject the holism, and assert that revisability is more limited than Quine allows, are we thereby committed to the existence of sentences true purely in virtue of meaning? We are not. It is entirely open to one who rejects holisms of a Quinean sort to agree none the less that no sense can be made of truth purely in virtue of meaning. Any sentence, if true, can be said to be true in virtue of its disquoted truth-condition, as Quine himself has long insisted. From the standpoint of more recent approaches to meaning, the possibility of any sentence's being "true purely by virtue of meaning" remains highly questionable. Suppose we have a truth-conditional approach to meaning. Then for each of the expressions in a sentence, its meaning is given by its axiom in that theory of truth which can serve as a meaning-theory for the language. What could being "true purely in virtue of meaning" amount to in this framework? The best candidate would be that the truth of a sentence so classified is derivable solely from the axioms of the truth theory dealing with the individual components of the sentence. But in that case, it is certain that no sentences are true purely in virtue of meaning, because the meaning-theoretic axioms have to be supplemented with logic if theorems are to be derived from them. Under this elaboration of "truth in virtue of meaning", a logical truth can be shown to be true in virtue of the meaning of its component, *plus* logic. This does not look like an alternative to the principle that every sentence is true in virtue of its disquoted truth condition; rather, it looks like a special case of it. Indeed, the most obvious way to derive the outright truth of a logical truth in the truth theory is first to derive a T-sentence for it; then to prove outright, using logic alone, that the right-hand side of the T-sentence holds; and then to apply modus ponens right-to-left on the biconditional which constitutes the T-sentence. All this amounts to is showing that the sentence has a (canonical) truth-condition, and that its truth-condition holds.

What does, arguably, come with limited revisability and canonical methods is not analyticity, but rather a form of the a priori. It is plausible that semantic values are assigned to expressions in such a way that canonical methods involving those expressions are always truth-preserving. If this is correct, application of a canonical method will be truth-preserving, however the actual world may turn out to be. This sounds very close to a traditional form of the a priori (cp. Peacocke, 1993a). But it does not resuscitate truth-purely-in-virtue-of-meaning. A conditional sentence whose antecedent captures the input, and whose consequent expresses the output, of a canonical method can be said to be a priori; but it is still true in virtue of the holding of its disquoted truth-condition. Similarly, a canonical form of inference is truth-preserving because every instance is such that, if the truth-conditions of its premisses are met, so are those of its conclusion. Recognition of canonical methods and a rejection of holism about meaning does not require one to side with Carnap on the possibility, or even the intelligibility, of truth purely by convention.[4] (For further relevant discussion, see Chapter 14, ANALYTICITY.)

4 Do interpretational and compositional considerations support meaning holism?

In a famous paper, 'Truth and Meaning', Davidson wrote:

> If sentences depend for their meaning on their structure, and we understand the meaning of each item in the structure only as an abstraction from the totality of

> sentences in which it features, then we can give the meaning of any sentence (or word) only by giving the meaning of every sentence (and word) in the language. (Davidson, 1984, p. 22)

This is naturally read as a statement of global holism about meaning. But when considering the doctrine that the meaning of an expression is understood as an abstraction from the totality of sentences in which it occurs, we need to distinguish a constitutive from an epistemological version. The constitutive version states that *what it is* for an expression to have a certain meaning is to be explained by mentioning what can be abstracted from properties of whole sentences in which it occurs. It may help to draw a parallel with another constitutive thesis of abstraction. It is very tempting to hold that what it is for a given number to measure a particular object's mass (or other physical magnitude) is to be explained by mentioning the way in which that number simply codes a certain place that the object has in a system of physical relations which do not involve numbers. The numerical value of the physical magnitude does no more than abstract from a certain place in a system of relations. Representation theorems of the sort proved in the theory of measurement then allow us to say this: for an object to have a certain number as its mass is simply for it to be mapped to that number by the unique mass function which (a) takes a certain object as the unit mass, and (b) conforms to the two principles that the mass of x = the mass of y iff x has-the-same-mass as y, and that for non-overlapping objects, the mass of their sum is the sum of their masses. The constitutive thesis of abstraction for numerical values of physical magnitudes is very attractive. We seem completely unable to offer any constitutive account of what it is for an object to have, say, a mass of 5 grams which does not mention such abstraction. This is to agree with Field in denying what he calls 'heavy-duty Platonism' (Field, 1989, pp. 186–93).

The weaker, epistemological version of the thesis of abstraction for the case of meaning agrees that in coming to know the meaning of an expression we do not understand, evidence from the use of any sentence containing the expression may be relevant. But this point about evidence does not support global holism about meaning. Rather, evidence about any sentence containing an expression may be relevant to learning which one of several non-globally individuated meanings it possesses. Considerations in favour of the stronger, constitutive thesis must go beyond those which could equally be accommodated by the epistemological thesis.

There are two closely related problems for the holistic, constitutive thesis of abstraction in the case of meaning. The first problem is whether there exists any meaning-free level of properties and relations of sentences from which their meanings can be abstracted without dependence on meaning-involving notions. It is true that in Davidson's earlier accounts of radical interpretation, the fundamental level of evidence available to a radical interpreter was said to be that of holding a sentence true, an attitude which, it was emphasized, can be known to be present without knowing what the sentence means. In the earlier work, the constraint on a theory of truth as providing an interpretation of the language was said to be that of maximizing true belief, under the theory of truth in question (the "Principle of Charity"). This constraint, too, is stated without attributing, or making hypotheses about, particular meanings. Davidson's later writings formulate the constraint on acceptable interpretations as that of maximizing intelligibility. As Grandy (1973) and McGinn (1977) emphasized, this diverges from the Principle of Charity. It is acceptable to attribute intelligible error; it is unacceptable to attribute inexplicably correct belief. Fulfilment of the constraint of maximizing intelligibility must involve the fulfilment of constraints for each particular content *p* which may be judged. If the belief that *p* is ascribed under an interpretation of the language-user's linguistic and non-linguistic behaviour, then the language-user's behaviour and attributed attitudes must be intelligible in the light of his believing the particular content that *p*. This is disanalogous to the relation between numerical values of physical properties and the underlying non-numerical physical relations from which they are abstracted. (It is as if there were particular constraints relating to an object's having a mass of 5 grams which any assignments of mass had to satisfy! See further Chapter 8, RADICAL INTERPRETATION.) In particular, this constraint on ascriptions of beliefs that *p*, and the general constraint of maximizing intelligibility, simply use intentional notions. They are not meaning-free accounts of how constitutive abstractionism might be true.

This difference between a constitutive abstractive thesis about meaning and other constitutive abstractive theses need not be fatal if the constraints relating to particular contents could be elucidated without taking for granted the notion of meaning or content. One could conceive, for example, of an alliance between the constitutive abstractionist about meaning and a conceptual-role theorist of meaning, one who insists that meaning is captured only by global conceptual role. This leads us, though, to the second problem.

Accounts have gradually been emerging of what is involved in mastering various particular concepts – in particular demonstratives (Evans, 1982), logical concepts and observational concepts (Peacocke, 1992). These accounts have not adverted to the global conceptual role of the concept treated. They have, rather, concerned certain canonical circumstances for applying the concept, and certain canonical commitments involved in applying it. If these accounts are, even in principle, along the right lines, then it is not true that the meanings of words expressing these concepts are constitutively dependent upon properties of all the sentences in which they occur. For one who accepts such accounts, it is their existence which makes the case of meaning unlike that of the assignment of numbers as values of physical magnitudes (at least in the respect we have been discussing).

Interpretationists and others would, of course, doubt that these accounts can be completely correct if they purport to exhaust what individuates a meaning or concept. But this doubt need not push an interpretationist in the direction of global holism. It is open to the interpretationist to say that what makes it the case that a word expresses a particular observational concept is dependent upon the intelligibility of a person's use of the expression in certain perceptual circumstances, together with what he is intelligibly prepared to infer from the applicability of the expression in other circumstances. Similarly, the doubts of non-interpretationist objectors about the exhaustiveness of the offered accounts are more likely to concern their (somewhat) reductive features than their failure to embrace global holism.

It is important to note two points about the position which accepts the merely epistemological version of the abstractionist claim, while rejecting the stronger constitutive, holistic version. First, the merely epistemological version can still endorse the view that interpretation is answerable to global constraints of rational intelligibility. The core of the intelligibility requirements for each meaning attributed can be given by the thinker's satisfaction of the non-holistic possession condition for the concept expressed by an expression with that meaning. The totality of such requirements for each meaning attributed gives a global set of requirements for an interpretation, a set answerable to the interpretee's use of any sentence in his language. The non-holistic interpretationist is then equally entitled to make the point that interpretation is answerable to global constraints of rational intelligibility. The global background constraint of maximizing intelligibility as applied to non-linguistic as well as linguistic actions is also applicable throughout the enterprise of interpretation. It, too, is independent of holism about meaning.

The second point to note is that the merely epistemological version of the abstraction claim can insist that an expression has linguistic meaning only if it is capable of combining with others to form complete sentences (when it is not already a complete sentence), and that this is so as a constitutive matter. Such an uncontroversial doctrine does not entail global holism about meaning. It also neither entails nor precludes less extensive holisms.

Reference and satisfaction are thought of very differently under the constitutive and the merely epistemological versions of the abstraction claim. Under the constitutive, holistic version, the correctness of attributions of referential relations to terms and of satisfaction conditions to predicates is exhausted by their role in contributing to the truth conditions ascribed to individual sentences by a theory of truth. Consistently with his constitutive version of the abstractionist claim, this is precisely Davidson's position:

> these notions [satisfaction, reference – CP] we must treat as theoretical constructs whose function is exhausted in stating the truth conditions for sentences. . . . A theory of this kind . . . assigns no empirical content directly to relations between names or predicates and objects. These relations are given a content *indirectly* when the T-sentences are. . . . [Reference] plays no essential role in explaining the relation between language and reality. (Davidson, 1984, pp. 223, 225)

On Davidson's view, a particular truth theory "can be supported by relating T-sentences, and nothing else, to the evidence" (ibid., p. 223).

There are at least three possible views about the role of reference in the explanation of facts about the truth-conditions of whole sentences. It seems to me that the correct view is intermediate between two extremes. At one extreme, we have the view which treats the role of reference as entirely analogous to the role of microproperties and microentities in the physical explanation of macrophenomena. If we have a realistic attitude to these physical theories, we will insist that the content of a statement about microphenomena is not exhausted by its role in the theory. We will also insist that it is neither constitutive nor necessary of microphenomena that they play that role in the explanation of macrophenomena. The macrophenomena might not even exist, consistently with the existence of the microphenomena and entities appealed to. The properties of carbon atoms explain the macroproperties of diamonds, but carbon atoms with their microproperties could still exist even were there not to be any diamonds. Davidson does in fact compare his own view of the status of the relation of reference, as expressed in the passages quoted in the preceding paragraph, with the status of the postulation of a fine structure in physical phenomena which explains macrophenomena (ibid., p. 222). But the points just made about a realistic attitude to physical theories seem to me to show that a parallel with physical theory could be accepted by someone with a Davidsonian attitude to reference only if he took some form of instrumentalistic attitude to statements about microphenomena.

It does not seem correct simply to assimilate the role of axioms of reference in a semantic theory to axioms postulating microproperties and microentities in a physical theory. It should be agreed, even by the merely epistemological abstractionist, that, as an a priori and constitutive matter, the correctness of an axiom stating the reference of an atomic expression in a language is answerable to facts about complete sentences containing the expression. Truths about the relation of reference for atomic expressions cannot have the same metaphysical, constitutive independence of facts about the truth-conditions of complete sentences which microphenomena have from (at least certain) macrophenomena. It certainly seems that we cannot make sense of an atomic expression having a certain reference except in so far as its doing so contributes to the semantic properties of complete sentences in which it occurs. For this reason, there is at least one respect in which the view of reference which accompanies the merely epistemological version of the abstractionist doctrine need not be treating the concept of reference "as a concept to be given an independent analysis or interpretation in terms of non-linguistic concepts" – which is what Davidson was concerned to avoid (Davidson, 1984, p. 219).

At the other extreme we have the view that if the T-sentences of two semantic theories are the same, and are both well-confirmed, then the two theories are equally good. This is an extreme form of instrumentalism about the semantic properties of subsentential expressions. This view has been vigorously contested – refuted, it seems to me – in the literature on tacit knowledge (see for instance Davies, 1987; Evans, 1981). The arguments are discussed elsewhere in this volume (see Chapter 7, TACIT KNOWLEDGE). What is important here is that there is a middle position between extreme instrumentalism, and the view that treats semantic theory as analogous to physical theory. Claims about the reference of an atomic expression are constitutively and a priori answerable to facts about whole sentences containing it. But when a particular referential axiom for an expression *a* is correct, the explanation of a person's use and understanding of sentences containing *a* has a certain structure. Suppose a proposed axiom states that *a* denotes Paris. If speakers of the language happily assert all sorts of sentences of the form "*a* is thus-and-so" without checking on anything about Paris, and without taking themselves as answerable to anything about Paris, that is strong evidence against the proposed axiom. Generally, in the enterprise of maximizing intelligibility, a proposed axiom which states that an expression refers to a certain object is answerable to the role of the properties of that object in the explanation of speakers' sincere assertions containing the expression. More specifically, when the axiom "*a* denotes Paris" is correct for a language as understood by a given person, there is a common component in the explanation of all the various cases of his understanding of a sentence containing *a* as meaning something about Paris. The common component of each explanation is just his possession of the information stated in the axiom "*a* denotes Paris".

There is a great deal more to be said on many aspects of this middle position, but I hope enough has been said for us to be able to identify the two properties which distinguish it from the two extremes. On the middle position, it will be agreed that there is a sense in which it is a priori that: if *a* denotes Paris, and *f* is true of anything just in case it is elegant, then *fa* is true iff Paris is elegant. A full statement of the a priori, constitutive features of the relation of reference preclude assimilation of its status to something analogous to that of theoretically postulated relations in physics. But these a priori links in no way rule out the possibility that a person's possession of the information that *a* denotes Paris contributes causally to the explanation of his knowledge that *fa* means that Paris is elegant. There is such explanation when understanding is suitably structured; and so the middle position is also distinguished from the other, instrumentalist, extreme.

5 Global holism, justification and semantic value

Dummett describes the holist thus:

> For the holist, we ought not to strive to command a clear view of the working of our language, because there is no clear view to be had. We have a haphazard assembly of conventions and rules, and there are no principles which govern our selection of them or render them any more appropriate than any others we might adopt. (Dummett, 1991, p. 241)

But we should, Dummett holds, subject any language to a critical scutiny which

> aims at a systematic means of ascribing *content* to the expressions and sentences of the language, in terms of which accepted modes of operating with it (including the rules of inference observed) can be justified, or, better, are evidently justified. (p. 241)

It was not written into our original formulations of holism – (GH), (GHE) and their variants – that such justification is unavailable. We also noted, towards the end of § 1, that certain types of holist could endorse the notion of the content of an individual sentence. So we should consider separately types of holism which do, and types of holism which do not, make the claim that content-based justification is impossible. Let a *warranting* form of holism about meaning be a form which meets these two conditions. (1) The form of holism is committed to holding that there is a notion of justification on which certain assertions, made in appropriate circumstances, are warranted, in part by virtue of their meaning (and similarly for certain transitions between sentences). (2) This relation of justification is sufficiently powerful to rule out certain otherwise apparently satisfactory, fundamental specifications of alleged meanings (or understanding-conditions) as legitimate. We can say that a form of holism is *warrant-free* if it is committed to holding that there is no notion of justification meeting the conditions (1) and (2). It is a warrant-free holism which "sanctions the claim that we have a right to adopt whatever logical laws we choose" (Dummett, 1991, p. 227).

A warranting holism may be either conservative or revisionary of our actual judgemental and inferential practices, according as actual practices do or do not meet the standard of justification favoured by the warranting holism. The scope for a revisionary warrant-free holism is much narrower. Some such scope no doubt exists. For example, a warrant-free holist may also believe in a form which classifies some methods of forming judgements as canonical; so the actual inferential practice of an individual may be criticized as not properly related to the canonical methods for the communal language. But this is a very limited kind of case. What warrant-free holists cannot coherently do is to criticize a practice as not meeting the requirements for justification, where justification is of the sort mentioned in conditions (1) and (2).

Our question must now be: is either warranting holism or warrant-free holism about meaning tenable?

Warrant-free holism faces the problem of the existence of rules for certain expressions which lack meaning. These rules are in no way circular or infinitely regressive; but they fail to determine a meaning for the expressions they treat. Intuitively, they fail precisely because what is said in the proposed rules makes it impossible to see what the contribution of these expressions to the content of complete sentences containing them could possibly be. The most well-known and spectacular case of this is the example of Prior's connective *tonk*, whose alleged sense is introduced by the two rules that from A one can infer $AtonkB$, and from $AtonkB$ one can infer B (Prior, 1960). The rules for *tonk*, if accepted, clearly lead to the provability of all formulae. There are, though, other examples in which a proposed set of "rules" is not inconsistent (nor leads to radically non-conservative extensions of systems to which it is added), but fails to determine a meaning.

In earlier work, I mentioned the example of a spurious quantifier Q (Peacocke, 1993b). Q is said to have the same introduction rule as the existential quantifier: from $A(t)$, one can infer $QxA(x)$, subject to the usual restriction on the variables. Q is also said not to have any other introduction rules, and it is further said that the analogue of the existential elimination rule is invalid for it. There is a powerful intuition that no meaning is fixed by these rules. What could $QxA(x)$ possibly mean? It must mean something that can be inferred from any instance. Yet it cannot mean the existential quantification of $A(x)$, otherwise the elimination rule would be valid. It cannot mean something equivalent to the holding of an alternation consisting of that existential quantification with some further condition *p*. For then there should be a further introduction rule, that $QxA(x)$ can be inferred from *p* – yet there were said to be no further underived introduction rules. This argument that *Q* has no meaning is quite general, and applies under both constructivist and more realistic conceptions of content. The example is one of many. Similar points could be elaborated for the equally problematic connective "*Ü*", which was introduced and exposed by Dummett (1991, pp. 288–90). *Ü* is supposed to have the same introduction rule as ordinary alternation, but a more restricted elimination rule. The reader can develop an argument entirely parallel to that given for *Q* that there can be no contribution to the meaning of complete sentences containing it made by *Ü*.

It is highly plausible that what is wrong with all of these spurious connectives and operators is that the specifications placed upon them prevent them from having semantic values, appropriately related to their specifications, which contribute to the determination of the truth value of complete sentences in which they occur. The rules for *tonk*, for example, place inconsistent requirements upon the truth value of *AtonkB*, for the line of the truth table in which *A* is true and *B* is false. If *AtonkB* is counted as true under those conditions, then the second rule for *tonk* will lead from true premisses to a false conclusion when *A* is true and *B* is false. But if *AtonkB* is counted as false under those same conditions, the first rule will then lead from truth to falsity.

It is at this point that the warranting holist is likely to intervene in the discussion, and advertise the virtues of his position. After all, he may say, if the defect of these spurious connectives is the impossibility of giving a coherent account of their contribution to semantic value, then what is wrong with them is not obviously anything to do with holism. So why should there not be a warranting holism which, unlike warrant-free holism, insists that any specification of a genuine meaning (perhaps by means of an understanding-condition) must admit a corresponding account of its contribution to semantic value, but which remains a form of holism none the less?

Warranting holism faces two closely related problems, which I call the *overdetermination* problem and the *overdiscrimination* problem. We can illustrate the overdetermination problem for the simple case of "and". It is plausible that the understanding-condition for this expression of English involves some kind of mastery of the introduction and elimination rules for conjunction, and that (for a realist, at least) the semantic value of "and" is that classical truth-function which makes those rules always truth-preserving. But for a thinker who possesses the concept of probability, "and" will feature in other principles too. Such a thinker will have some form of mastery of the principle that if *A* and *B* are independent propositions, then prob(*A*&*B*) = prob(*A*) · prob(*B*). If we ask what semantic value for "&" would make this principle always correct, again the classical truth-function for conjunction is the answer. So the total set of principles essentially involving "&", acceptance of which is required if the thinker is to understand the expressions they contain, overdetermines the required semantic value.

Why is this a problem? It is a problem for the warranting holist, because it is a datum which can easily be exploited by an opponent of global holism about meaning. The opponent will say that this state of affairs is symptomatic of the fact that only a subset of principles essentially containing "&" are constitutive of its meaning (the introduction and elimination rules). It is they which fix its semantic value, which is then drawn upon and presupposed by someone who starts using the concept of probability in combination with logical connectives like conjunction. This is why the principles of probability can be justified without appealing to those principles themselves as partially fixing the semantic values of the logical constants, the anti-holist will say. Our warranting holist may reply that all principles essentially containing "&" are equally on a par. But that reply is quite implausible about "&".

The overdetermination problem is on one side of a coin which has the overdiscrimination problem on its other side. The more principles we include as individuative of the meaning of an expression in a person's language, and thereby as contributing to the determination of its semantic value, the wider is the range of cases in which we are precluded from identifying its meaning with that of an expression in the language of a person with either a much richer or a much narrower vocabulary. In one of his earlier writings on the topic, Dummett ascribes to the holist the view that "deduction is useful, because by means of it we can arrive at conclusions, even conclusions of the simplest logical form, which we could not arrive at otherwise" (Dummett, 1978, p. 303). But in fact that is precisely what we cannot do on the holist's view of meaning. According to the holist, when we enrich our vocabulary the meaning of all our expressions changes, and a conclusion we reach with the methods involving a new concept, though it may be grammatically the same as one formulable in the old vocabulary, does not actually have the same meaning as its orthographically identical predecessor. As a result of this overdiscrimination of meanings, the territory in which a global holist can also justifiably, by his own lights, apply a notion of warrant that is unavailable on the warrant-free conception is really quite limited.

6 Local holisms and their source

Sometimes, perhaps always, a thing (property, relation) is individuated in part by its relations to other things, properties or relations. What it is to be that thing, property or relation cannot be properly explained without mentioning those other things, properties or relations. I mention three kinds of case, each familiar from discussions in different areas. First, what it is to be a particular place cannot be explained without mentioning the network of spatial relations in which the place stands. A second plausible example involves mass and force. What it is for something to be the physical magnitude of mass cannot be elucidated without alluding to the fact that things with mass require the action of a force for a change in their motion, and are capable of exerting forces when their state of motion changes. Conversely, the physical magnitude of force is individuated in part by its connections with the physical magnitude of mass. Third, the property of having a certain linguistic meaning is individuated in part by its connections with the property of believing something with the same content. It is partially constitutive of meaning that it can be used to express beliefs (and even, I would argue, knowledge).[5]

All these claims about what is constitutive or individuative of an object, property or relation are, in the first instance, claims about things at the level of reference, rather than at the level of sense. They are claims about the things or properties themselves, rather than about those things or properties as thought of in a certain way. It is true that one often formulates such points by saying, for example, "The concept of mass is the concept of a property which, when instantiated requires the action of a force for . . .". But when one uses such a formulation, one is employing that concept or way of thinking of mass which makes explicit the way in which the property to which it refers is individuated. I say that the claims are "in the first instance" about things at the level of reference, because the point I wish to emphasize does not preclude the possibility that further philosophical analysis may reveal that these constitutive facts about the level of reference may ultimately themselves have an explanation which involves other facts about the level of sense. A parallel may help to make the point. Kripke's arguments have made a strong case that it is necessary, of Peter Serkin, that his father is Rudolf Serkin (Kripke, 1980). This is a *de re* claim about Peter Serkin himself, and not about some mode of presentation of him, and it is arguably constitutive. In any case, let us suppose that it is so, for the sake of the illustration. It does not follow that the ultimate source of *de re* necessities of origin is not some a priori principle stating that continuant objects necessarily have their actual origins, a principle whose a priori status traces back in part to the sense of "continuant object". That is a separate question, and neither a positive nor a negative answer to it undermines the fact that the original essentialist claim about Peter Serkin involves the man himself, and not some concept of him.

In our three examples, there will be a local holism for the meanings of expressions for (and equally for concepts of) places and spatial relations; for expressions for mass and force; and for expressions for meaning and belief. In each case, what it is to understand an expression for one of these things will have to be given simultaneously with an account of what is involved in understanding (or at least possessing a concept of) the other. These local holisms are entailed by the conjunction of two plausible claims. The first claim is that when one thing (property, relation) rather than another is the reference of a word, there must be some fact about the use of that word which, possibly together with the way the world is, fixes it and nothing else as the word's reference. We can call such a fact about the use of the word or concept "the reference-fixing fact". The second claim is that the reference-fixing facts for words referring to the things and properties in our three examples involve the language-user's rudimentary grasp of the constitutive relations of the thing or property in question to other things or properties. If these claims are sound, then local holisms of meaning are derivative from holisms at the level of the individuation of properties and things.

Grasp of these interrelations is not, of course, and could not be, the only element in an account of mastery of these expressions. There are practical components, involved in the explanation of spatial actions, in the understanding of expressions for places and spatial relations. The same holds for mass and force. Some would argue that there are first-person elements in the grasp of the concepts of meaning and belief. But in all three cases, it is plausible that understanding expressions for the things or properties comprising the local holism involves some form of knowledge of their role in theories capable of explaining respectively, in the three examples, spatial facts, mechanical facts and facts about intentional action.

* * *

Even if the general arguments for meaning holism are not convincing, there remain a great many intriguing questions about more local holisms. Some of these questions are questions about particular examples. What, for instance, is the relation between practical spatial abilities and mastery of concepts of places and spatial relations? Can a family of practical abilities also display a form of holism? Beyond the questions about particular examples, there are also general questions about kinds of local holism, to which the answers about particular examples are pertinent. Is it always possible in principle to specify the nature of the connections a thinker has to grasp between the properties and objects involved in a local holism without presupposing some mastery of the very concepts involved in the holism? If not, that would seem to count in favour of a version of anti-reductionism about mastery of those concepts. And whatever the answer to that general question, what could or should be the shape of a computational psychology which explains, at the sub-personal level, mastery of a local holism? As far as I know, all these questions are open. Even if global holism is false, the topic of holism deserves to be with us for some time to come.

Notes

1 The arguments for meaning holism have recently been subjected to a lively critique in Fodor and LePore (1992). Though Fodor, LePore and I agree in our major conclusions, the arguments for them are rather different, and also venture into different territories. For those wanting a critical overview of discussions about meaning holism, I believe that Fodor and LePore's book and the present paper will be found complementary, rather than intersubstitutable..

2 Moulines (1986) and Vuillemin (1986) each provide an interesting discussion of the first of these differences between Duhem and Quine, but both pass over the second difference.

3 For an important discussion of the sense of natural kind terms pertinent to these points, see Wiggins (1980, pp. 78–84).

4 It should be noted that my rather strict use of 'analytic' diverges from that of Fodor and LePore (1992). As far as I can see, many of the claims Fodor and LePore make about the analytic/synthetic distinction are ones I would formulate as claims about the a priori/a posteriori distinction (and would also then accept). This point applies in particular to

their discussion of the view that there is no principled distinction between the propositions a person has to believe in order to believe a given content and those he does not (ibid., p. 24ff.). It is plausible that rejection of that view does involve some commitment to the existence and applicability of an a priori/a posteriori distinction. It is not at all so clear that it involves commitment to the applicability of the notion of truth-purely-in-virtue-of-meaning.

5 If meaning and belief do indeed form a local holism, those who have argued from interpretational considerations to meaning holism have mistakenly taken an admittedly important local holism for a global holism.

References

Block, N. 1986: Advertisement for a semantics for psychology. In *Midwest Studies in Philosophy X: Studies in the Philosophy of Mind*, ed. P. French, T. Uehling, and H. Wettstein. Minneapolis: University of Minnesota Press.

Davidson, Donald 1984: *Inquiries into Truth and Interpretation*. Oxford: Clarendon Press.

Davies, M. 1987: Tacit knowledge and semantic theory: can a five per cent difference matter? *Mind*, 96, 441–62.

Duhem, P. 1962: *The Aim and Structure of Physical Theory*. Translated by Prince Louis de Broglie. New York: Athenaeum.

Dummett, M. 1975: What is a theory of meaning? (I). In *Mind and Language*, ed. S. Guttenplan. Oxford: Clarendon Press.

——1978: *Truth and Other Enigmas*. London: Duckworth.

——1991: *The Logical Basis of Metaphysics*. Cambridge, Mass.: Harvard University Press.

Evans, G. 1981: Semantic theory and tacit knowledge. In *Wittgenstein: To Follow a Rule*, ed. S. Holtzman and C. Leich. London: Routledge.

——1982: *The Varieties of Reference*. Oxford: Oxford University Press.

Field, H. 1977: Logic, meaning and conceptual role. *Journal of Philosophy*, 74, 347–75.

——1989: *Realism, Mathematics and Modality*. Oxford: Blackwell.

Fodor, Jerry and LePore, E. 1992: *Holism: A Shopper's Guide*. Oxford: Blackwell.

Grandy, R. 1973: Reference, meaning and belief. *Journal of Philosophy*, 70, 439–52.

Harman, G. 1982: Conceptual role semantics. *Notre Dame Journal of Formal Logic*, 23, 242–56.

Kripke, S. 1980: *Naming and Necessity*. Oxford: Blackwell.

McDowell, J. 1986: Functionalism and anomalous monism. In *Actions and Events: Perspectives on the Philosophy of Donald Davidson*, ed. E. LePore and B. McLaughlin. Oxford: Blackwell.

McGinn, C. 1977: Charity, interpretation and belief. *Journal of Philosophy*, 74, 521–35.

Moulines, C. 1986: The ways of holism. *Noûs*, 20, 313–32.

Peacocke, C. 1992: *A Study of Concepts*. Cambridge, Mass.: MIT Press.

——1993a: How are a priori truths possible? *European Journal of Philosophy*, 1, 175–99.

——1993b: Proof and truth. In *Reality: Representation and Projection*, ed. J. Haldane and C. Wright. New York: Oxford University Press.

Prior, A. 1960: The runabout inference-ticket. *Analysis*, 21, 38–9.

Putnam, H. 1986: Meaning holism. In *The Philosophy of W.V. Quine*, ed. L. Hahn and P. Schilpp. La Salle, Illinois: Open Court.

Quine, W. 1960: *Word and Object*. Cambridge, Mass.: MIT Press.

——1961: Two dogmas of empiricism. In *From a Logical Point of View*, Cambridge, Mass.: Harvard University Press.

——1974: *The Roots of Reference*. La Salle, Illinois: Open Court.
——1986: Reply to Hilary Putnam. In *The Philosophy of W. V. Quine*, ed. P. Schilpp. La Salle, Illinois: Open Court.
Sellars, W. 1974: Meaning as functional classification. *Synthese*, 27, 417–37.
Vuillemin, J. 1986: On Duhem's and Quine's theses. In *The Philosophy of W.V. Quine*, ed. P. Schilpp. La Salle, Illinois: Open Court.
Wiggins, D. 1980: *Sameness and Substance*. Oxford: Blackwell.

11

Metaphor

RICHARD MORAN

Metaphor enters contemporary philosophical discussion from a variety of directions. Aside from its obvious importance in poetics, rhetoric, and aesthetics, it also figures in such fields as philosophy of mind (as in the question of the metaphorical status of ordinary mental concepts), philosophy of science (as in the comparison of metaphors and explanatory models), in epistemology (as in analogical reasoning), and in cognitive studies (as in the theory of concept-formation). This article will concentrate on issues metaphor raises for the philosophy of language, with the understanding that the issues in these various fields cannot be wholly isolated from each other. Metaphor is an issue for the philosophy of language not only for its own sake, as a linguistic phenomenon deserving of analysis and interpretation, but also for the light it sheds on non-figurative language, the domain of the literal which is the normal preoccupation of the philosopher of language. A poor reason for this preoccupation would be the assumption that purely literal language is what most language-use consists in, with metaphor and the like sharing the relative infrequency and marginal status of songs or riddles. This would not be a good reason not only because mere frequency is not a good guide to theoretical importance, but also because it is doubtful that the assumption is even true. In recent years, writers with very different concerns have pointed out that figurative language of one sort or another is a staple of the most common as well as the most specialized speech, as the brief list of directions of interest leading to metaphor would suggest. A better reason for the philosopher's concentration on the case of literal language would be the idea that the literal does occupy some privileged theoretical place in the understanding of language generally, because the comprehension of figurative language is itself dependent in specific ways on the literal understanding of the words used. This is at least a defensible claim and, if true, we might then hope for an understanding of figurative language from a theory of literal meaning, combined with an account of the ways in which the figurative both depends on and deviates from it.

The light such an investigation may shed on non-figurative language will derive from the issues which even this mere sketch of their relation raises for the philosophy of language. We will want to know, for instance, about the specific nature of the dependence of the figurative on the literal; and how the comprehension of figurative language is related to, and different from, the understanding of the literal meanings of the words involved. If the theory of meaning in language is, at the least, closely allied with the theory of what understanding such things as sentences consists in, then a question raised by metaphor is how understanding as applied to metaphorical speech is related to understanding in this semantic sense, and whether the same kind of knowledge, such as whatever it is that 'knowing a language' consists in (see Chapter 7, TACIT KNOWLEDGE), applies in similar ways in the two cases. We will want to consider reasons for and against speaking of a difference in *meaning* in connection with metaphor, and whether such distinctive meaning is to be sought for on the level of the word, sentence, or utterance; on the level of semantics, pragmatics (see Chapter 4, PRAGMATICS), or somewhere else.

1 Figurative and non-figurative: metaphor, idiom and ambiguity

The familiar subject–predicate form ('X is a wolf, the sun, a vulture . . . ') comprises but one class of metaphors, and neglects various other grammatical forms (such as 'rosy-fingered dawn' or 'plowing through the discussion'), not to mention metaphoric contexts which don't involve assertion at all. And, in general, short, handy examples will not help much in the understanding of, say, literary metaphors whose networks of implications are not discernible outside the verbal environment of a particular text or genre. None the less, even such simple cases can help us to make some provisional distinctions between metaphor and other figurative and non-figurative language. For instance, idioms, such as 'to kick the bucket' or 'to butter someone up', resemble metaphors in calling for a special reading. If one understands such expressions correctly, one will not expect reference to have been made to any actual bucket or real butter. In a word, they are to be taken figuratively and not literally. (This is so even though, for instance, there is hardly anything wildly paradoxical in the idea of someone kicking a genuine bucket). But although they both involve giving figurative readings to an utterance, there are important differences in how one comprehends the meaning of an idiomatic expression and the meaning of a metaphor. If you don't know what 'vulture' means or what plowing is, you won't be able to interpret their metaphorical expressions at all. And what one does when one interprets the metaphor is employ what one knows about vultures and what is believed about them to determine what the utterance means on this occasion. This is part of what is meant by the previous suggestion that the comprehension of figurative language is dependent on the literal understanding of the words used.

If idiom is to count as a case of figurative language (which it seems it should, since we can distinguish what it is literally to kick the bucket and the very different thing usually meant by the expression), then this claim of dependence on the literal will have to be amended. For an understanding of the literal meanings of the words that make up an idiom is of very limited usefulness in understanding what is meant, and is sometimes even positively detrimental to such understanding. Someone unfamiliar with the expression will not get very far by employing his understanding of what is known or believed about such things as buckets to figure out what the expression means. And further, if she does know a great deal about the literal meaning of a word like 'moot', for instance, then, other things being equal, this may well render her less rather than more likely to understand what is meant by the (American) idiomatic labeling of something as a 'moot point' – that is, that the point is of no current practical import and not worth discussing. What this means is that the meaning of an idiomatic expression is not a function of the meanings of the individual words that compose it; unlike metaphors, they are simply taught to us as wholes, rather than being a matter of individual interpretation on an occasion. (For such reasons, it has been said that "an idiom has no semantic structure; rather it is a semantic primitive." Davies, 1982, p. 68. See also Dammann, 1977.) And again, unlike metaphors, their meaning is simply given: there is no 'open-ended' quality to the idiom's meaning, no special suggestiveness, no call for its creative elaboration. There is a simple, stable answer to the question of what 'kick the bucket' means idiomatically, and that is why dictionaries can have special sections in them for idioms, but not for metaphors (see Cavell, 1969).

Finally, the contrast with idiom enables us to distinguish some issues here concerning paraphrase. It is often said that metaphors, or at least poetic, 'live' metaphors, are not subject to paraphrase, and this is often taken to mean that they are not translatable into another language. However, there is one sense in which it is idioms and not metaphors which resist translation into another language. The overall effectiveness of certain literary metaphors will, to be sure, be influenced by certain language-specific phonetic features; but none the less, referring metaphorically to someone as, say, 'shoveling food into his mouth' will be possible wherever they have shovels and food, and words for these things. By contrast, translating the words of the idiom 'to kick the bucket' into Spanish or Korean will not be likely to get across your meaning, or any other meaning. The reason for this, again, is the 'semantic primitiveness' of idiomatic phrases. Since an idiom's meaning is not built up from the meaning of its individual words, this meaning will not be conveyed in another language by means of word-by-word translation (see Dammann, 1977). Naturally, this doesn't mean that some perfectly good sense of 'translation' is not appropriate here. If 'kick the bucket' is one way in English of saying that someone died, then there will be perfectly good ways of translating that idea into Spanish or Korean. So resistance to word-by-word translation is not the same as the inability to express the meaning of the idiom in words of another language.

One way in which the issue of the translatability of poetic metaphor is vexed is through confusion about what might be meant by the idea of a word's acquiring a specifically 'metaphorical meaning'; and this idea will be discussed at some length later. But, in addition, there is some lack of clarity about the relation between paraphrase and translation. If all we mean by paraphrase is the ability to say what one means in other words, then it does seem true that there is a difference between idiom and metaphor here. For, as described above, the idiomatic meaning of some expression can be given in other words in a quite straightforward and definite manner. (Many idioms are euphemisms, after all, whose literal equivalents are all too straightforward.) By contrast, the paraphrase of a live metaphor is much less definite, more open-ended, more dependent on context (including the individual speaker), and more open to the creative interpretation and elaboration of the hearer. What should be noted, however, is that these are all features of the paraphrase of metaphor within a language, and do not carry over any immediate implications for the translation of metaphors across languages. Familiar ideas about the 'essential incompleteness' of any prose paraphrase of metaphor should not cloud the issue, for there is no reason in principle why the very same indefiniteness and open-ended character of a metaphor in English should not show up in its version in another language. Translation need have nothing to do with reducing the live metaphor to a prose paraphrase. And if it is argued that even good translation will not capture all and only the connotations and associations of the original metaphor, it may be replied that to the extent that this is true at all, it will apply to cases of perfectly literal language as well, from '*Gemütlichkeit*' to 'priggish'. To sum up: within a language the idiomatic meaning of an expression may be completely given by its literal equivalent, whereas the live metaphor is not reducible to its prose paraphrase; and across languages, an idiom cannot be translated word by word, but only as a fused whole; whereas word-by-word translation of a metaphorical expression may, in fortunate circumstances, preserve the same suggestiveness and 'open texture' as the original. In so far as metaphor involves comparison of things and ideas with other things and ideas, it is something less specifically language-bound than is idiom.

In this respect metaphors also differ from puns, homonyms, and ordinary ambiguity in language. A pun in English, like 'heart' and 'hart', may be metaphorically exploited by a poet, but is only a homophonic accident until it is so exploited. A translation of the play into another language may well display the same metaphoric comparison, but naturally the phonetic motivation for making just this comparison will be lost with the homophony. Sometimes homophonic words are not only pronounced the same but are also spelled the same, and then we have true homonyms, like 'cape' for a body of land and an article of clothing. An inscription such as 'cape' is ambiguous between the two meanings, which need not be etymologically related at all, and once again this ambiguity may be metaphorically exploited. But neither puns nor homonyms are in themselves examples of figurative language. 'Cape' has (at least) two meanings, but they are both perfectly literal ones, and understanding one of the meanings provides no interpretive clue to the other one.

2 Metaphorical meaning

Even this brief characterization raises deep theoretical issues, in so far as it has appealed to some notion of 'figurative meaning' at various different stages. In metaphor we interpret an utterance as meaning something different from what the words would mean, taken literally. Often we will want to say that a statement which is wildly false when taken literally is quite true when taken figuratively. And from here it is natural to reason in the following way. Truth-values cannot vary unless *truth-conditions* vary, and if the truth-conditions of an utterance are what determine its meaning, then the literal and the metaphorical interpretations of an utterance amount to differences in meaning (see Chapter 1, MEANING AND TRUTH CONDITIONS). The words, or the utterance, have one meaning when intended or taken literally, and another when spoken metaphorically. In addition it was argued, in connection with idiom, that a metaphor can be translated into another language while preserving its metaphorical meaning, and in his original (1962) paper Max Black takes this to imply that "to call a sentence an instance of metaphor is to say something about its meaning, not about its orthography, its phonetic pattern, or its grammatical form" (p. 28).

Thus, some of the motivation for talking about 'meaning shift' in connection with metaphor is clear enough; and it seems equally undeniable that, quite often, everyday metaphorical speech is successful at communicating something different from what the words, on their literal interpretation, would mean. But our brief characterization of metaphor, especially in its contrast with idiom and common ambiguity, already raises some serious questions for this way of talking about metaphor. For it was pointed out that, unlike the cases of 'kick the bucket' or 'cape', the different reading we give to 'vulture' (when used, say, to refer to a certain kind of human predator) is directly dependent on our understanding of the literal meanings of the individual words. Unlike an ambiguous word like 'cape', then, in metaphor the two meanings must be related somehow. When a *token* of 'cape' is reinterpreted as having one meaning rather than another, the meaning assigned to it on the first reading is excluded, and nothing in the first reading (other than one's dawning sense of its inappropriateness) plays a role in bringing one to the second interpretation. In principle, and often enough in practice, the reader could have hit on the correct interpretation the first time, without considering any possible ambiguity, and nothing would have been thereby lost in her comprehension of what was said.

Such cases of ambiguity explain some of the motivation for individuating words according to sameness of meanings, rather than according to sameness of spelling or pronunciation. (Hence, on this view, the two 'capes' count as different words.) For a speaker does not clarify her intentions by saying she employed the same word, 'bank' (encompassing both meanings), on one occasion to refer to part of the river and on another occasion to refer to where she keeps her money. There is no point expressed in using the 'same word' in these different ways; for the two words are hardly more related in meaning than are 'kinder' in English and *Kinder* in German. In neither this case nor the case with 'bank' need the orthographic identity ever have occurred to the speaker in order to use the words correctly and to communicate her meaning fully.

Contrast this with the case of metaphor. If we think of the words of a metaphorical expression as undergoing a 'meaning-shift' of some kind, it will have to involve a difference of meaning very different from that involved in ordinary ambiguity. For when an expression is interpreted metaphorically, the first interpretation (the literal one) is not canceled or removed from consideration. The literal meaning of 'vulture' is not dispensable when we interpret it metaphorically in its application to some friend or relation. The literal meaning must be known to both the speaker and the audience for the metaphorical point of the epithet to be made. It has everything to do with clarifying the speaker's intentions that she chose this word, with its literal meaning applying to a kind of bird, to refer to this other thing which is not a bird; and when we start to figure out the reason why the speaker is using this word with its literal meaning in this context, we have begun to interpret what she is intending to get across metaphorically. Simply characterizing metaphor in terms of a change of meaning fails to capture the role of the original, literal meaning.

But the dependence of the metaphorical on the literal runs deeper than this, and raises further doubts about the appropriateness of the idea of 'meaning-shift' in metaphor; for the description of interpretation given so far might apply just as well to a situation in which a person is speaking in a kind of code, in which someone has to interpret her utterance in such a way that certain words are to be replaced by specific other ones. He might conjecture that 'vulture' is one of these words, and hit upon the right substitution for it. In such a case we might well speak of the word 'vulture' being given a different meaning or application in this context.

The case of metaphor differs from this in several ways. First, and perhaps most obviously, there is nothing corresponding to a code for a live metaphor, and no rules to appeal to for going from the literal to the metaphorical meaning. Further, in the case of genuine codes the original meaning of the words will normally be incidental, at best, to the new meaning; and in fact, a coined expression with no previous meaning in the language may do just as well, if not better. In metaphor, on the other hand, if we are to speak of a new meaning, this meaning will be something reachable only through comprehension of the previously established, literal meanings of the particular words that make it up. And this dependence of the metaphorical on the literal is rather special, in ways that exacerbate difficulties with the view of metaphor as involving a change of meaning. For the first (literal) reading of the expression does not just provide clues to help you get to the second one, like a ladder that is later kicked away, but instead it remains somehow 'active' in the new metaphorical interpretation. It is not similar to a case in which we first got the meaning wrong and have now successfully disambiguated it. Rather, the literal meaning of 'vulture' remains an essential part of the meaning of the metaphorical expression, otherwise one will have no sense of what metaphorical comparison is intended. If something like 'meaning-shift' is involved in this, then we must explain how the literal meaning of 'vulture' could play any role at all in the generation and comprehension of the metaphorical meaning, if it is this very same original meaning that is supposed to have changed (or, to speak a bit less confusingly, if the word has now taken on a different meaning).

It might be thought that we could avoid this problem by referring to an expansion rather than a change of meaning. That way we could retain and rely on the original meaning of the words, and still describe what is going on in terms of some change of meaning. So, for instance, 'vulture' still refers to the same birds it always did, but now, in addition, it also refers to a certain kind of person. The problem with this idea is that while it describes a certain process of linguistic change, it simply isn't what is meant by live metaphor. Words commonly expand and contract in application over time, and this process can take many forms, some of which may indeed involve metaphor at some stage. But the process itself is not inherently metaphorical, and it can proceed for any number of reasons. In earlier times, the word 'engine' applied more narrowly to instruments of war and torture, and not generally to any mechanism that converts energy into force or motion. This expansion in application does not make the latter, contemporary use metaphorical, even if we think that, for instance, certain relations of perceived similarity played a role in the expansion. And in any case, what any such analysis of 'meaning change' in terms of merely extended application leaves out of consideration is the point insisted on above, the special dependence of the metaphorical on the literal which makes the literal meaning of a word such as 'vulture' still 'active' in the comprehension of its metaphorical use. We are still in need of an account of this 'activity', to be sure, but there is certainly an essential functional role for the awareness of the literal meaning of 'vulture' in the comprehension of its metaphorical use which has no parallel in the understanding of various other predicates with extended applications. So we still lack an explanation of what could be meant in speaking of 'change of meaning' in connection with metaphor.

These questions will require answers just as much on an account that appeals to speaker-meaning rather than semantic meaning (Searle, 1979, and Black, 1979), as it will also on 'extensionalist' accounts, which eschew talk of 'meanings' altogether in favor of reference to different applications of labels (see Goodman, 1968, Elgin, 1983, and Scheffler, 1979).

3 Davidson and the case against metaphorical meaning

How might we characterize the dependence of the metaphorical on the literal, specifically the way in which the literal meaning is still 'alive' in the metaphorical application, and avoid making reference to a new metaphorical meaning? And, on the other hand, if we do avoid all such reference, how can we account for the difference in truth value between the utterance taken literally and taken metaphorically? Further, if we drop all reference to meaning, then it will be quite unclear how we can make sense of the idea that we correctly understand the speaker as saying (or meaning) something different from what her words literally mean, or that we see metaphor as a vehicle of communication at all.

In a paper that has attracted a great deal of commentary, Donald Davidson (1979) has taken this step, and has argued that we should indeed cease talking about figurative meaning in connection with metaphor altogether; and he seems prepared to accept the consequences that follow from this rejection. Early on, he states the thesis of the paper as the claim that "metaphors mean what the words, in their most literal interpretation, mean, and nothing more" (p. 246). He does not mean to deny that metaphor accomplishes many of the same things that philosophers and literary critics have claimed for metaphor (such as the special suggestive power of poetic metaphor, or its capacity to produce insight of a sort that may not be capturable in plain prose), but he denies that these accomplishments have anything to do with content or meaning of a non-literal sort. It will be useful to look more closely at Davidson's paper, for it is an especially forthright and radical response to many of the same problems in accounting for 'metaphorical meaning' that have emerged elsewhere in recent literature on the subject. At the same time we can gain a better appreciation of the costs as well as the benefits of rejecting 'metaphorical meaning'. (Davidson's paper is discussed in Cooper, 1986, Davies, 1982, Fogelin, 1988, Moran, 1989, and Stern, 1991, and there are responses by Black and Goodman in Sacks, 1979.)

The argumentative structure of the paper is not always easy to interpret, but Davidson gives a number of reasons for the denial of metaphorical meaning, some of which are related to the argument given above and which contrast metaphor with common ambiguity. He further argues that positing metaphorical meanings does nothing to explain how metaphors function in speech. If, as he says, a metaphor makes us attend to certain covert features of resemblance (p. 247), it tells us nothing about how this is accomplished to claim that the words involved have some figurative meaning in addition to the literal one. It is not only more accurate simply to say that a fresh metaphor typically produces such effects (in whatever causal manner anything else might do so), but it also more economical, for we are thereby spared the need to account for what these special meanings are and where they come from. In an ordinary, literal context, appeal to meaning can be genuinely explanatory because there we can have a firm grip on the distinction between what the words mean in the language and what they may be used to do on a particular occasion (to lie, for example, or to encourage, or to complain). However, if we think of what metaphorical language is used for (such as to make us appreciate some incongruous similarity) as itself being a kind of 'meaning', we lose any sense of this distinction. And yet one of the theoretical virtues of appeal to semantic meaning in the first place is that it enables us to explain something of how these words, with this established meaning and in this context, can be used to perform this particular function on this occasion. That is, a particular established meaning provides both constraints on and possibilities for what a word or phrase may be used to do, and for this reason appeal to such meaning (once it is determined by a given context) can be genuinely explanatory of what the phrase is on this occasion used for. But the only meaning which is distinct and independent of the use on this occasion, and which could play any such explanatory role, is the literal meaning of the phrase. (Various writers have criticized Davidson's argument for assuming a concept of literal meaning that is utterly independent of context, but it seems clear that this is not his view: see p. 260.)

In addition, Davidson argues, when we think of metaphor in terms of the communication of a specific propositional content, we can only have in mind the most dead of dead metaphors, such as referring to the 'leg' of a table. And these, he suggests, are not properly metaphors at all. If the expression 'figurative meaning' points to anything at all, it indicates some special power of metaphor, some striking quality that may be productive of insight or creative elaboration on the part of the audience. The failure to capture anything about the distinctively figurative functioning of live metaphor Davidson sees as a further defect of the idea discussed earlier, that the meaning or application of a term is 'extended' in a metaphorical context. For if we say that the literal application of an expression such as 'vulture' is extended, we have first of all said something false, or at best misleading: as if, now, both some birds and some people were straightforwardly vultures, the way both vultures and sparrows are straightforwardly birds. And in addition, for our trouble, we have failed thereby to capture anything figurative about the whole process. And then, on the other hand, if we say that the metaphorical application of the term has been extended, then we seem to have got no further in our analysis. For we now owe an explanation of what a metaphorical application is, and specifically, how it differs from any other type of application of a term.

(For a different perspective on what are normally thought of as dead metaphors, see Lakoff and Johnson, 1980.)

4 Paraphrase and propositional status

The concentration on live metaphor is bound up with another strand of Davidson's case against metaphorical meaning, but one for which it is difficult to determine the weight he wants to give to the various considerations he brings forward. Whatever makes a poetic metaphor 'live', it is certainly in large part a function of its power of suggestiveness, the fact that the interpretation of live metaphor is open-ended, indeterminate, and not fixed by rules. As Davidson says at the beginning of his essay, 'there are no instructions for devising metaphors; there is no manual for determining what a metaphor "means" or "says"; there is no test for metaphor that does not call for taste' (p. 245). The creative indeterminacy of live metaphor is one reason why live and dead metaphors differ with respect to the possibilities for paraphrase, or for specifying the meaning in other words. We can fully state what is meant by the 'shoulder' of a road, precisely to the extent that there isn't anything figurative left to the expression. With genuine, or poetic, metaphor the case is quite different, and at various points Davidson seems to be asking, 'How could the sort of open-ended, non-rule-governed character of live metaphor possibly apply to anything legitimately called a meaning?' When we encounter difficulties in applying paraphrase to live metaphor, the reason for this is simply that "there is nothing there to paraphrase" (p. 246). If there were anything said or asserted in the metaphorical expression beyond what it literally states, then it would be just the sort of thing that does submit to paraphrase. As it is, however, what it provides us with beyond the literal is not anything propositional at all.

> It should make us suspect the theory that it is so hard to decide, even in the case of the simplest metaphors, exactly what the content is supposed to be. The reason it is often so hard to decide is, I think, that we imagine there is a content to be captured when all the while we are in fact focusing on what the metaphor makes us notice. If what the metaphor makes us notice were finite in scope and propositional in nature, this would not in itself make trouble; we would simply project the content the metaphor brought to mind on to the metaphor. But in fact there is no limit to what a metaphor calls to our attention, and much of what we are caused to notice is not propositional in character. (1979, pp. 262–3)

In this passage, however, Davidson seems to allow that reference to a kind of meaning distinct from the literal would be legitimate if what the utterance got across were "finite in scope and propositional in nature". Then, presumably, we could get a handle on paraphrase, and we could start talking about what was said and what was meant. It was said earlier that it is difficult to settle how much

Davidson wants to rest on these considerations; and the reason for this is that, although they run through the entire paper, he also freely admits that it may just as well be said of literal language that its interpretation is not determined by rules (p. 245), and that what it gets across to the audience is often not "finite in scope" (p. 263, n. 17). And, certainly, no theorist wants to deny meaning or cognitive content there. (As far as putting into other words goes, we might also ask how one would paraphrase many perfectly literal statements, such as 'The sky is blue' or 'I can hear you now'.) Nor should simple vagueness or indeterminacy in interpretation be thought of as crucial to the issue of meaning, for vagueness itself can be something fixed by the dictionary-meaning of a term. For instance, 'house' is a word with a perfectly straightforward meaning, but which allows for a zone of indeterminacy as to just which structures shall count as houses (for discussion of different conceptions of vagueness, see Chapter 18, SORITES.)

If there is to be a genuine case against metaphorical meaning along these lines, then, it seems that we should see the crux of the issue not as concerning indefiniteness as such, but as concerning the question of whether we may speak of propositional content in connection with metaphor. It is certainly true, as Davidson says, that "much of what we are caused to notice is not propositional in character"; but it does not follow from this that the figurative process does not communicate anything that is propositional as well. It seems clear that part of what traditionally raises philosophers' suspicions about the propositional content of poetic metaphor is not the assumption of an incompatibility of content with indeterminacy, but rather the connection of this aspect of the figurative dimension of metaphor with ideas of ineffability, or the essential inability to capture this dimension in words other than those of the specific metaphor itself. When a content or a thought is held to be ineffable, and not simply indeterminate, it is felt that, although one may have a perfectly definite content in mind, it cannot be fully expressed in words. (In fact, in various contexts the sense of indescribability is a response to the highly determinate character, the utter specificity, of what one has in mind.) Or, as in the case of certain poetic metaphors, it may be felt that the idea may be verbally expressed, but only in these very words; or only indirectly expressed, or incompletely hinted at. This sense is certainly something different from simple vagueness, and does raise different questions for the idea that what live metaphor does is communicate some special propositional content. If we agree with Davidson that this problem removes any justification for looking for propositions expressed by metaphorical utterances, then we may still say all we like about the various non-cognitive effects of such utterances, but we will no longer be able to describe metaphor in terms of communication, meaning, or content.

However, ineffability of the sort under consideration here concerns a claim about the specifically linguistic representation of a thought, and does not immediately place something outside the bounds of the propositional unless we have already agreed that a proposition is something essentially linguistic or sentential. Only then will it seem obvious that accepting an equivalent prose paraphrase is necessary for any part of the metaphor to count as a propositional content. Davidson could be correct when he says, "A picture is not worth a thousand words, or any other number. Words are the wrong currency to exchange for a picture" (p. 263), but it wouldn't follow from this that a picture cannot itself be a representation of a propositional content. For on one standard view of what propositions are, they are "functions from possible worlds into truth values" (Stalnaker, 1972); and on such an account – whether or not it takes reference to 'possible worlds' at face value (see Chapter 19, MODALITY, section 3) – pictures, maps, memories, or anything else that represents the world as being a particular way can qualify as propositional representations. (We may thus, in Stalnaker's words, "abstract the study of propositions from the study of language".) If one takes this wider view of what a proposition is, there may be less resistance to considering the possibility of someone with a particular cognitive content in mind, but who is either unwilling or unable to accept an equivalent of it in prosaic language. We could accept Davidson's point about translation into another representational medium, without accepting the identification of the propositional with the sentential.

In fact, for purposes of this discussion, there would be little to complain of in the restriction of propositional content to the meaning of sentences, so long as we kept in mind the various different ways in which the content of a sentence may be indicated and determined in a context, including making essential reference to something extra-linguistic. We may note that many belief-reports are only partially verbal reports, with the essential content of the belief being indicated in some other way:

> Many of our beliefs have the form: 'The color of her hair is –', or 'The song he was singing went –', where the blanks are filled with images, sensory impressions, or what have you, but certainly not words. If we cannot even say it with words but have to paint it or sing it, we certainly cannot believe it with words. (Kaplan, 1971, p. 142)

Thus, to bring us a little closer to the case of metaphor, a sentence like 'He said it in this voice just like Akim Tamiroff' is in perfectly good order, and expresses a genuine thought. But, of course, it will not communicate much to someone who has never heard of Akim Tamiroff. This particular person and the experience of his voice are essential to the content of the proposition. To someone who has never heard this voice, the speaker may quite straightforwardly be unable to communicate what she means. And it is all too easy to imagine being unable to provide any descriptive equivalent, and that no substitute expression will capture what you want to say. Yet it would certainly be wrong to conclude from this that the speaker has not said or meant anything. (For a defense of the idea of metaphorical meaning, which makes extensive use of the comparison with demonstratives, see Stern, 1985 and 1991. See also Chapter 23, INDEXICALS AND DEMONSTRATIVES.)

Similarly, with a metaphorical expression like the well-worn example of Juliet and the sun, reference to the sun is essential to the determination of the content of what Romeo has in mind, and his reluctance to accept any prose paraphrase as capturing all that he means is not itself any reason to deny that he does have something in mind which he is seeking to express in words. Nor would it be right to say that although he does have some content in mind (since we reject the simple sentential view of cognitive content), there must be some confusion involved in trying to express it verbally. Hence, to qualify a concession made earlier for the sake of argument, words may sometimes be the wrong medium of exchange for a picture, but it depends on what we are expecting the words to do. We may not be entirely satisfied with any descriptive translation of what was said in either the Akim Tamiroff or the Juliet cases, but even so it won't follow that "the attempt to give literal expression to the content of the metaphor is simply misguided" (Davidson, 1979, p. 263). As with any attempt to put one's thoughts and feelings into words, it may matter a great deal to try to go as far as one can in this direction. If we can't make sense of this kind of effort at descriptive and expressive fidelity, then we can't make sense of the kind of struggle that goes into the composition of poetic metaphor in the first place, let alone more everyday efforts to put the non-verbal world of experience into words.

(These considerations relate to the debate since Aristotle over whether metaphor and simile are essentially different figures. Fogelin, 1988, and Dammann, 1977, both defend a 'comparativist' view of metaphor, and insist on the distinction between figurative and non-figurative comparisons.)

5 Metaphor and communication

The discussion thus far has suggested that neither vagueness nor the indeterminacy of the interpretation of metaphor provide good reasons for denying that metaphor has a cognitive content beyond the literal. And, further, even if the difficulties or inadequacies of paraphrase are attributed to a degree of 'ineffability' (and not just indeterminacy) in what is seeking expression, this need not mean that we are not dealing with a genuine propositional content. Naturally, these considerations do not by themselves constitute an account of figurative meaning. Many difficulties remain in making sense of meaning and content as applied to metaphor, and these include various problems that were left hanging in the earlier discussion. For instance, we still need to describe a sense of 'meaning' as applied to metaphor which doesn't reduce to ordinary ambiguity or the expansion of application of a term. We have not yet explained the special dependence of the figurative meaning on the literal meaning, a dependence that has so far only been described metaphorically as the literal meaning's still remaining 'alive' in the figurative context (that is, unlike a code). And very little has been said so far to relate the sense of 'meaning' at stake here to more familiar uses of the term in ordinary speech and in more formal uses in the philosophy of language.

But lest we lose heart at the prospect of these and other problems for explicating the sense of figurative 'meaning', it would be worthwhile to remind ourselves of how serious the consequences would be of endorsing a fully non-cognitive account of metaphor of the sort Davidson and others have recommended. (The most comprehensive defense of the rejection of metaphorical meaning is David Cooper's 1986 book, *Metaphor*, especially Chapter 2.) It is important to Davidson's view that it not be seen as 'no more than an insistence on restraint in using the word "meaning"', but rather as a rejection of the idea that "associated with a metaphor is a definite cognitive content that its author wishes to convey and that the interpreter must grasp if he is to get the message" (p. 262). So, to begin with, any such theory is burdened with the same problems as is non-cognitivism elsewhere in philosophy (see Chapter 19, MODALITY, section 4, and Chapter 12, REALISM AND ITS OPPOSITIONS, section 4). There will be nothing for understanding or misunderstanding a metaphorical utterance to consist in, nothing to the idea of getting it right or getting it wrong when we construe what the 'figurative meaning' might be. Related to this are non-cognitivism's familiar problems with making sense of the apparent facts of agreement and disagreement in the domain in question; for the rejection of any distinctive content to a metaphorical utterance obscures understanding of what, for instance, the negation or denial of such an utterance can mean, and such a denial will, in the ordinary case, be a denial of the utterance taken figuratively. If there is nothing to the idea of a distinctive figurative content, then there's nothing for the speaker's audience to be agreeing with or dissenting from, except for the statement taken literally, and agreement or disagreement with that statement is not to the point. Further, if the figurative dimension involves no difference in meaning, but instead simply 'nudges us into noticing some resemblance', then it's hard to say what differences of meaning we can point to between 'Juliet is the sun', 'Imagine Juliet as the sun', or even 'Juliet is not (or is no longer) the sun'. All three sentences succeed in linking the two ideas, but they hardly say the same thing. We might compare such problems with the difficulty for moral non-cognitivism in providing an account of the functioning of moral terms in conditional contexts, when some moral predicate is not being asserted, but is used in the context of reasoning and argument. (For more on these and other criticisms of non-cognitivism as applied to metaphor, see Bergmann (1982), Elgin (1983), Kittay (1987), and Tirrell (1989), as well as the papers mentioned previously in connection with Davidson.)

The cost of the denial of any specifically metaphorical content, then, seems rather steep, and the case for the banishment of metaphor from the realm of meaning to that of 'use' or the brute effects of utterance seems flawed. It is true that there are many things done in speech that do not involve communication and meaning, but are more purely causal effects of utterance (although, of course, communication is causal in its own way too). We are told, for instance, that metaphor gets us to notice things (similarities or incongruities, or whatever). And it is in terms of such particularities of use that Davidson compares metaphor with the use of language to lie, persuade, or complain. However, a few things must be noted about this comparison. First, it is not at all clear that metaphor is a 'use' of language in this sense at all. It would not, for instance, serve as any explanation why someone said what she did simply to say she was speaking metaphorically. Further, lying or complaining can count as "belong[ing] exclusively to the domain of use" (p. 247) rather than meaning, precisely because whether one says 'It's raining out' to lie or to complain does not affect the truth-conditions of the utterance. But, of course, whether the truth-conditions of an utterance may indeed differ on a metaphorical interpretation is just the point at issue, and cannot be begged at this point.

And when we do speak of metaphor as producing various effects, it is important to note in the context of this discussion that it accomplishes these effects in a quite particular manner, one which involves a relationship between a speaker and an audience, and an interconnected network of beliefs about intentions, expectations, and desires; in short, just the sort of situation that Paul Grice and others have argued is what differentiates a situation of meaning and communication from the other various ways in which beliefs may be acquired (see Chapter 3, INTENTION AND CONVENTION, especially section 5). As Davidson notes, plenty of things, like a bump on the head, can get one to notice or appreciate something, even something profound, and we don't think of all such cases as involving anything like meaning or communication. However, metaphorical speech counts as genuinely communicative (of a content beyond the literal) because, among other things, the figurative interpretation of the utterance is guided by assumptions about the beliefs and intentions of the speaker, intentions which, among other things, satisfy the Gricean formula (intending that the intention be recognized by means of this very utterance). And because we are in this way dependent on beliefs about the speaker's beliefs there is a purchase on the ideas of understanding and misunderstanding what was meant, none of which applies when some non-Intentional causal phenomenon succeeds in making one appreciate some fact.

The dependence of the hearer on beliefs about the speaker has several layers. To take the utterance as metaphorical in the first place requires assumptions about the beliefs and intentions of the speaker. Then, even the non-assertoric dimensions of the reception of metaphor (framing one thing in terms of another, the clash of images, and so on) are dependent on what we take the relevant dimensions of the comparison or contrast to be. Lacking any idea of the intended salient features of, say, music, food, and love, we would fail to have so much as a non-assertoric comparison or contrast of these elements, let alone a metaphorical assertion. And finally, the interpretation of the utterance involves assumptions about the speaker's beliefs about the various elements, including her beliefs about their salience to the audience, and about what, if any, particular attitude toward these things is expressed by the metaphor. None of these dependencies obtain with respect to all the other various ways in which the phenomena of the world can cause one to be struck by something or other, and that is the primary reason why we speak of communication, understanding, and misunderstanding in the one set of cases and not the other.

6 Pragmatics and speaker's meaning

These and other considerations have led many writers on the subject to identify the meaning of a metaphorical utterance with what is called the speaker's meaning, in contrast with the semantic meaning, of the sentence. The latter notion concerns the meaning of a sentence in a given language, and is standardly understood to be a function of either its truth-conditions or *assertability conditions*, assuming a certain context. Speaker's meaning, by contrast, concerns what a speaker on an occasion may employ a sentence to imply or communicate, a content that may diverge more or less widely from the content assigned to the sentence by the language. Hence, in ironic speech, for example, a speaker may utter the words 'That was a brilliant thing to say', in order to communicate something quite different from what the sentence-type means in English. (The example of irony shows the usefulness of separating the issue of 'meaning-change' – which patently does not apply to the words of an ironic utterance – from the issues of communication and cognitivity.)

Speaker-meaning will typically be an instance of what Grice has called 'conversational *implicature*'. Very briefly, Grice sees linguistic behavior as guided by a general Cooperative Principle, which divides into various more particular maxims, such as 'Do not say what you believe to be false', or 'Be relevant', and which speakers expect to be obeyed in conversational exchange. Naturally, any such maxim may fail to be observed on a given occasion (people do tell lies, for instance). But what is important to Grice's story is the different ways in which a maxim may not be observed. For it may be that it is not followed either through sheer carelessness, or because the speaker is 'opting out' of the conversational exchange altogether, or, most importantly here, the speaker may 'flout' a maxim. In such a case the speaker makes it manifestly clear that, on one level at least, she is intentionally violating some maxim. In the above example of speaking ironically, the speaker takes it to be clear to the audience that she does not think what was just said was brilliant, and yet here she is, uttering a sentence with that very meaning. Hence she is flouting one of Grice's 'Maxims of Quality' ('Do not say what you believe to be false'). At this point it is up to the hearer to construe what the point of the utterance could be, and what other proposition(s) may be intended. The general assumption of the Cooperative Principle is retained, but the hearer now looks for what proposition may be implicated by this utterance. Thus conversational implicature is a means of communicating something different from the literal, semantic meaning of the sentence uttered.

Taking this general approach, John Searle takes the general formula for metaphor to be: A speaker utters a sentence with (semantic) meaning 'S is P', but does so in order to convey (or 'implicate') a different proposition, namely 'S is R'. In Searle's example (1979), someone says 'X is a block of ice' in order to convey the very different proposition that X is emotionally unresponsive and so forth. In most cases it will be the manifest or categorical falsity of the sentence taken literally that cues the audience to interpret the utterance as implicating something metaphorically. The main questions for which Searle takes a theory of metaphor to be responsible are, then, how an utterance is recognized as metaphorical (rather than ironic, say), and what principles the hearer employs to compute the speaker's meaning from the meaning of the sentence uttered, combined with the context of utterance.

An account of this general form may, then, offer us a sense of 'meaning' as applied to metaphor, which does not entail that a linguistic entity as such somehow contains within itself a metaphorical as well as a literal (semantic) meaning, but one which is none the less a sense of 'meaning' which bears some important relation to meaning in the strictly semantic sense. It also offers some understanding of the special dependence of the figurative on the literal, in that it is only through comprehension of the literal meaning of the statement that the hearer may reach the secondary meaning 'implicated' by the utterance. And the principles that guide this interpretation will involve appeal to features of resemblance, contrast, context, and emotional attitudes toward the subject that make the relation between literal and figurative meaning very much unlike the relation between a word and its substitution in some code.

In addition, such a view need not subsume 'figurative meaning' under the categories of simple ambiguity and ordinary expansion of meaning. Gricean implicature involves there being some point to the speaker's application of this phrase, with this literal meaning, in this context, in order to convey something quite different. Common ambiguity (such as, say, homonymy) does not involve any such point or communicative intent. Nor need there be any such point in the case of the ordinary expansion of the application of a term. In some cases there may be some such point to the expanding, but often there will not be. When there is some point to the extension (as in, for example, the extending of 'mouth' to parts of bottles and rivers) the motivation may simply concern some perceived similarity between the various things now referred to by the same term (Davidson's example). In those cases the theorist of 'speaker-meaning' will indeed need to distinguish the point of metaphorical speech from that of ordinary expansion of the application of a term without any communicative point; otherwise he fails to distinguish figurative meaning from some forms of ordinary ambiguity. On the other hand, one may not want to distinguish the two cases too sharply, because metaphor is, after all, one of the vehicles of the normal extending of the application of words. Sometimes when metaphors die, their death involves the alteration of the ordinary dictionary-meaning of a term, as in the case of 'mouth'. This phenomenon is, in fact, a further problem for any view that denies any distinct cognitive content to live metaphor. For it is clear that part of the meaning of the word 'mouth' is different now from what it was prior to the development of the metaphor, and yet we would not be able to say where the difference in meaning came from if the metaphor had no content aside from the (old) literal one when the metaphor was alive. By the same token, this would also, of course, oblige the theorist of speaker-meaning, for whom the distinction between it and semantic-meaning is crucial, to say something about the diachronic story of how speaker-meaning becomes 'regularized' over time and merges into an altered semantic-meaning of the term.

There are thus some promising features of this general approach, but its application and explanatory power also seem to have some significant limitations. First of all, it's not clear, on Searle's version of the theory anyway, that much has been said to elucidate the specifically figurative dimension of metaphor. If what one is doing in speaking metaphorically is saying (or making-as-if-to-say) 'S is P' in order to convey the different proposition 'S is R', then it is hard to see how anything in the way of special insight or enhanced apprehension of the subject is achieved in this way. And it doesn't seem enough to make up for the flat quality of the analysis to add, as Searle does, that the speaker may intend "an indefinite range of meanings, S is R1, S is R2, etc." (1979, p. 115). No degree of indefiniteness alone will add up to power or insightfulness. (And if one is skeptical of the claims made for insight and metaphor, the criticism would remain that even the appearance of power or insight – which surely does require explaining – seems to find no place in this account.) Related to this is the problem, common to many accounts that want to emphasize the cognitive aspect of metaphors and their role in assertion, that the account seems derived from the consideration of only the dead and dying among metaphors. And even this class is normally restricted to examples of the familiar subject–predicate form; whereas, clearly, a major part of the theoretical interest in metaphor concerns the desire to understand what is deeply right or expressive or illuminating in such occurrences of live metaphor as in the dense figurative networks of literature, which need not involve any phrases in subject–predicate form, or be part of any statement of fact (either real or pretended). (By comparison, we might ask here how a caricature or a gesture can be 'right', expressive, or illuminating.)

A further way in which the 'live' quality of live metaphor seems to escape this analysis is in the account of how interpretation proceeds and what the derived meaning consists in. For if the meaning of a metaphorical utterance is the speaker's meaning, and the latter is a function of the intentions of the speaker in making the utterance, then the meaning of metaphor in general will be confined to the intentions of the speaker. Interpretation of the metaphor, then, will be a matter of the recovery of the intentions of the speaker. This may do well enough for instances of well-worn metaphor with little suggestive power left, but it gives the wrong picture of the interpretation of live metaphor. As Cooper says, in criticism of the 'speaker's meaning' view, "even a quite definite speaker-intention does not finally determine the meaning of a metaphor" (1986, p. 73). It is consistent with this criticism to insist, as claimed earlier here, that the interpreter of a metaphor is dependent on various assumptions about the beliefs and intentions of the speaker, and that this is required even to achieve a sense of what sort of figurative comparison is relevant. For it does not follow from this claim that the interpretation of metaphor is restricted to the recovery of the speaker's intentions. The interpreter may need to presume various things about the beliefs of the speaker for the metaphor to succeed in picturing one thing in terms of another; but once that perspective has been adopted, the interpretation of the light it sheds on its subject may outrun anything the speaker is thought explicitly to have had in mind. And on the other hand, from the point of view of the speaker, the restriction to speaker-meaning seems inadequate, in that it construes metaphor as a kind of shorthand or mnemonic device for a given set of beliefs that she wishes to convey. What such a picture leaves out of consideration is the role of metaphor in thought, the fact that the composition of live metaphor is undertaken in the expectation that it will lead one's thoughts about the subject in a certain direction: that it will be productive of new thought about it, and is not just a convenient summing up of beliefs one already has.

(The comparison of metaphor with models in science has inspired work on metaphor as a vehicle, and not just a repository, of thought. On this, see various papers in Ortony (1979). This general point, however, is not restricted to the case where a metaphor functions as a kind of explanatory model, but applies as well to the composition of metaphor in everyday and poetic cases, where it is not functioning as a model for explanation. This aspect of 'metaphorical thought' has received considerably less attention in recent philosophy.)

7 Metaphor, rhetoric and relevance

We have arrived, then, at a familiar point of tension for theories of metaphor. On the one hand, there is the desire (widespread, but not universal) to see metaphor as a cognitive phenomenon and hence as having a describable role in such activities as assertion, communication, and reasoning. But on the other hand, theories of metaphor that seek to defend and define this cognitive role often end up obscuring the very features of metaphor that make it an object of theoretical interest in the first place: its figurative power; the role of metaphor in expressing or producing insight of some kind; or the special open-ended role of the interpretation of live metaphor. It is no surprise, then, that 'non-cognitive' theorists like Davidson emphasize the difference between live and dead metaphors, whereas 'cognitive' theorists often either downplay the distinction or deal with examples of metaphor that might as well be dead.

To make progress from here, it may be useful to re-orient our approach to the whole phenomenon, to consider cognition and communication outside the context of strictly linguistic activity, and to begin investigating them from this broader perspective prior to explicit theorizing about the case of metaphor. That is, instead of taking the determinate proposition expressible in a simple sentence as our paradigm, and then asking how closely metaphor may or may not approach this model, we might begin with communicative situations that are non-verbal, indefinite, and unstructured, and ask where we might locate metaphorical speech on a continuum of cases from there to explicit, literal speech. This is more or less the approach taken by Dan Sperber and Deirdre Wilson in their 1986 book, *Relevance*, and in subsequent publications on rhetoric and communication. They see linguistic communication as but one variety of the larger class of what they call 'ostensive–inferential communication', which encompasses "behavior which makes manifest an intention to make something manifest" (p. 49). (Their account has obvious points of contact with Grice's work, as well as important differences with it, and these are discussed in the book.) The breadth of the category of communication they employ, and the distance from the sentential paradigm, can be seen from one of their first examples of ostension, many of whose features have come up for discussion in the case of metaphor. Two people are newly arrived at the seaside, and one of them opens the window of their room and inhales appreciatively and 'ostensively', that is, in a manner addressed to the other person. This person thus has his attention drawn to an indefinite host of impressions of such things as the air, the sea, and memories of previous holidays.

> [Although] he is reasonably safe in assuming that she must have intended him to notice at least some of them, he is unlikely to be able to pin her intentions down any further. Is there any reason to assume that her intentions were more specific? Is there a plausible answer, in the form of an explicit linguistic paraphrase, to the question,

> what does she mean? Could she have achieved the same communicative effect by speaking? Clearly not. (1986, pp. 55–6)

If this sort of situation is accepted as an example of communication, we can see how many of the features of metaphor which are thought to stand in the way of any cognitive account find a natural place here; and the case of explicit, literal, verbal communication looks more like the special case. That is, the way may be open to see some types of verbal communication (such as, for example, figurative language) as sharing many of the features of this non-verbal example. Thus we could see metaphorical speech as involving dependence on beliefs about the speaker's intentions, but not restricted in its interpretation to the recovery of those intentions. We could speak of a content that is communicated, but which is to a significant degree indeterminate, resistant to paraphrase, and open to the elaborative interpretation of the hearer. And, since the account does not assume literalness as a norm, we could avoid the implication of a generally Gricean approach that speaking figuratively, for all its utter pervasiveness in everyday speech, must involve transgression of some sort, or the violation of linguistic rules. Or, to quote Sperber and Wilson (1986, p. 200), "[T]here is no connection between conveying an implicature and violating a pragmatic principle or maxim." (See also Cooper, 1986, on the 'perversity' objection to speaker-meaning theories. It should be noted that the rejection of the normative presumption of literalness does not entail the rejection of the previously described dependence of the figurative on the literal, that is, the idea that knowledge of the literal semantic meanings of the words involved is necessary for the composition or comprehension of metaphor.)

Here we can do no more than indicate a few of the main themes of their approach which relate to the case of figurative language. Sperber and Wilson see implicatures as being conveyed in speech not through a presumption of either literality or obedience to conversational maxims, but through the guarantee of relevance which, they claim, any act of ostensive communication carries with it. Such acts will lie on a continuum of cases from communication of an impression to coded information, from showing to saying. In fact, it is internal to this approach that various dimensions of assessment, normally construed categorically, will be such as to admit of differences of degree: literality and figurativeness, evocativeness, susceptibility to paraphrase, and degree-of-intendedness.

Relevance, as defined by them, concerns the value of information gained, in light of the cognitive 'cost' to the hearer of assimilating that information. (As the quoted example indicates, however, 'information' is a suitably broad notion here too.) The guarantee of relevance may go unfulfilled, of course, but it is different from a maxim that one either seeks to conform to or not. Relevance is guaranteed in the sense that any act of ostensive communication involves a claim on the attention of another person, and any such claim itself communicates the presumption that this attention is somehow worth the effort. Implicatures themselves may be weak or strong, far to seek or immediately obvious, and are related to each other in various ways. In this way, we may begin to have at least a useful description of the functioning of live or poetic metaphor, where the effort at interpretation generates a penumbra of stronger and weaker implications which in turn lead to others, more or less remote from the immediate inferential consequences of the utterance, but which are pursued in so far as the presumption of relevance is rewarded. Dead metaphors will be those with a relatively small network of implications, immediately comprehended at small cost. Along these lines, then, we may begin to be able to say a few things about what the figurative power of poetic metaphor consists in, and what claims can be made for it as both productive and as expressive of insight of various kinds (including, for instance, marking the difference between the 'live' or fully-felt appreciation of some fact, and its merely 'intellectual' apprehension).

* * *

A final note. The alternatives to non-cognitivism discussed here have been drawn from theories of conversation, or the pragmatics of language, rather than from semantic theories for natural languages. However, the semantic/pragmatic distinction in philosophy of language is itself a complex matter and a subject of controversy (see Chapter 4, PRAGMATICS). Thus, mention should be made of recent 'cognitive' accounts which explicitly challenge the assignment of figurative meaning exclusively to either one level of analysis or the other. So, for instance, Kittay (1987) describes her 'semantic field' theory of metaphor as one that moves between semantic and pragmatic accounts. And the work of Stern's mentioned earlier belongs to a broadly semantic account, but finds the analysis of both metaphor and demonstratives to require "a notion of meaning one level more abstract than truth conditions" (1991, p. 40). In these as well as other ways, discussed previously, we can see the theory of figurative language prompting the rethinking of some of the basic concepts in the philosophy of language generally.

References

Bergmann, Merrie 1982: Metaphorical assertions. *Philosophical Review*, 41, 229–45.

Black, Max 1962: Metaphor. *Models and Metaphors: Studies in Language and Philosophy*. Ithaca, NY: Cornell, 25–47.

——1979: 'How metaphors work'. In Sacks (1979), 181–92.

Cavell, Stanley 1976: Aesthetic problems of modern philosophy. *Must We Mean What We Say?* New York: Scribners, 1969; Cambridge: Cambridge University Press, 1976, 73–96.

Cohen, L.J. and Margalit, A. 1972: The role of inductive reasoning in the interpretation of metaphor. In *Semantics of Natural Language*, eds D. Davidson and G. Harman. Dordrecht: D. Reidel.

Cohen, Ted 1975: Figurative speech and figurative acts. *Journal of Philosophy*, 71, 669–84.

Cooper, David 1986: *Metaphor*. Oxford: Blackwell.

Dammann, R.M.J. 1977–8: Metaphors and other things. *Proceedings of the Aristotelian Society*, 78, 125–40.

Davidson, Donald 1979: What metaphors mean. In *On Metaphor*, ed. Sheldon Sacks. Chicago: University of Chicago Press; also reprinted in his *Inquiries into Truth and Interpretation*. Oxford: Oxford University Press, 1984.

Davies, Martin 1982–3: Idiom and metaphor. *Proceedings of the Aristotelian Society*, 83, 67–85.

Elgin, Catherine 1983: *With Reference to Reference*. Indianapolis: Hackett.

Fogelin, Robert 1988: *Figuratively Speaking*. New Haven: Yale.

Goodman, Nelson 1968: *Languages of Art: An Approach to a Theory of Symbols*. Indianapolis: Hackett.

Grice, H.P. 1975: Logic and conversation. *Speech Acts*, Vol. 3 of *Syntax and Semantics*, ed. Peter Cole and Jerry L. Morgan. New York: Academic Press, 41–58.

Isenberg, Arnold 1973: On defining metaphor. In *Aesthetics and Theory of Criticism: Selected Essays of Arnold Isenberg*, eds. Callagan, Cauman and Hempel. Chicago: University of Chicago Press.

Kaplan, David 1971: Quantifying in. In *Reference and Modality*, ed., Leonard Linsky. Oxford: Oxford University Press.

Kittay, Eva Feder 1987: *Metaphor: Its Cognitive Force and Linguistic Structure*. Oxford: Oxford University Press.

Lakoff, George, and Johnson, Mark 1980: *Metaphors We Live By*. Chicago: University of Chicago Press.

Moran, Richard 1989: Seeing and believing: metaphor, image, and force. *Critical Inquiry*, 16, 87–112.

Ortony, Andrew, ed. 1979: *Metaphor and Thought*. Cambridge: Cambridge University Press.

Sacks, Sheldon, ed. 1979: *On Metaphor*. Chicago: University of Chicago Press.

Scheffler, Israel 1979: *Beyond the Letter*. London: Routledge and Kegan Paul.

Searle, John R. 1979: Metaphor. In *Expression and Meaning: Studies in the Theory of Speech Acts*. Cambridge: Cambridge University Press, 76–116.

Sperber, Dan and Wilson, Deirdre 1985–6: Loose talk. *Proceedings of the Aristotelian Society*, 86, 153–71.

——1986: *Relevance: Communication and Cognition*. Cambridge, Mass.: Harvard University Press.

Stalnaker, Robert 1972: Pragmatics. In *Semantics of Natural Language*, 2nd edn, eds D. Davidson and G. Harman. Dordrecht: D. Reidel.

Stern, Josef 1985: Metaphor as demonstrative. *Journal of Philosophy*, 80, 677–710.

——1991: What metaphors do not mean. *Midwest Studies in Philosophy*, 16, eds. P.A. French, T.E. Uehling, Jr., and H.K. Wettstein. Indiana: University of Notre Dame Press, 13–52.

Tirrell, Lynne 1989: Extending: the structure of metaphor. *Noûs*, 23, 17–34.

PART II

LANGUAGE, TRUTH AND REALITY

12

Realism and its oppositions

BOB HALE

In many branches of philosophy, dealing with very different areas of our thought and talk, there occur disputes centred on the tenability of positions described as 'realist'. In the philosophy of science, realism stands opposed to various forms of instrumentalism; mathematical realists, often known as Platonists, are opposed in one way by nominalists, in another by constructivists; moral realists contend with subjectivist tendencies, such as expressivism and projectivism, as well as with error theories; in the theory of meaning itself, realism is under attack from positions which hold that meaning must be explained in terms which preserve an essential link between what we mean and evidence, as well as from meaning-sceptical arguments advanced by Quine, Kripke and others (see Chapter 16, THE INDETERMINACY OF TRANSLATION; Chapter 14, ANALYTICITY; Chapter 19, MODALITY, section 2; Chapter 15, RULE-FOLLOWING, OBJECTIVITY AND MEANING; and Chapter 17, PUTNAM'S MODEL-THEORETIC ARGUMENT AGAINST METAPHYSICAL REALISM). It is scarcely obvious that there is some single type of issue at stake in these disputes (henceforth R/AR disputes), or that there is at least some significant continuity between them. The very diversity of the positions set against realism in these different areas might of itself be thought to point towards the opposite conclusion: that realism amounts to different things in the different cases, so that any attempt at general discussion is doomed to failure. It is not obvious, either, that the various disputes have anything much to do with the philosophy of language, or that there is any reason to expect arguments in the philosophy of language to play a significant part in their resolution.

Against these dampening thoughts may be set – besides the feeling that it is unlikely to be sheer coincidence that the same label is applied to completely disparate positions with no significant similarities whatever – at least two reasons why philosophers of language may properly take an interest in general questions about realism and the forms which opposition to it may assume. First, and most obviously, there is a R/AR dispute (or disputes) within the philosophy of language itself, centred on the tenability of realist theories of meaning. At the very least, it might be expected that scrutiny of R/AR disputes in other areas may illuminate the issues here, if only through contrasts rather than parallels. But second, and more importantly, the notion that debates about other realisms – in science, mathematics, or other areas – may proceed unaffected by arguments in the philosophy of language overlooks the possibility that a successful anti-realist argument in the theory of meaning may ramify into other disputed areas (see Chapter 15, RULE-FOLLOWING, OBJECTIVITY AND MEANING, section 3.)

We begin (§ 1) with an examination of Michael Dummett's influential treatment of these issues, which couples an attempt to identify a common form exemplified by a large, if not exhaustive, range of R/AR disputes with important arguments against a realist position about meaning which – if they are sound, and Dummett's diagnosis of what is at stake in those disputes is correct – promise to resolve the issue in the anti-realist's favour, not only in the theory of meaning itself, but across the board.[1] We then (§ 2) survey the principal negative arguments, advanced by Dummett and others, for semantic anti-realism. In § 3, we turn to the wider question of the bearing of these arguments on R/AR disputes more generally, and review doubts about the adequacy of Dummett's general conception of their common form. Other ways in which the anti-realist case may be prosecuted are reviewed in § 4: classical reductionist positions; error theories; expressivist/projectivist options and quasi-realism; and we conclude (§ 5) with a brief examination of the new perspective on R/AR disputes advocated in recent work by Wright.

§ 1 Dummett's general account of R/AR disputes

Many traditional, and at least some currently active, R/AR disputes appear primarily to concern the existence of entities of some sort – objects of some general type, or perhaps entities which, if there are such, should be taken as belonging to some other category. Medieval realists and their nominalist adversaries, for example, were disagreed over the existence of universals – abstract entities conceived as objective worldly correlates of general terms like 'red' and 'honest' and denoted by corresponding abstract nouns like 'redness' and 'honesty'. The cardinal negative thesis of many modern nominalists has likewise been the denial that there exist any abstract entities – by which they chiefly understood properties or attributes, as opposed to the particular concrete entities they characterize, together with sets or classes. One kind of realism or platonism about mathematics is distinguished by its acceptance of numbers and sets as genuine objects, lying outside space and time but none the less existing independently of our thought. At least part of what is in dispute between scientific realists and their opponents is whether a satisfactory account of theoretical science requires us to see it as describing the properties of unobservable or theoretical entities such as particles, forces and fields. Modal realists of one sort insist that there are possible worlds, distinct from but no less real than the actual world. (See Chapter 19, MODALITY, section 3.)

Dummett's conception of R/AR disputes stands in sharp contrast with the model suggested by such examples. Issues between realists and their opponents are, he contends, usually best characterized *not* as disputes about the *existence of entities* of some problematic sort, but in terms of a certain *class of statements* – those distinctive of the area of thought and talk in question – which he usually labels the 'disputed' class. Further, the disagreement is not – or not primarily – over whether statements of the disputed class are true, since the anti-realist will agree that in many cases they are so; it concerns, rather, the nature or character of the notion of truth which may be applied to them. This last point merits both emphasis and comment. A preference for formulating R/AR disputes in terms of problematic statements rather than problematic entities need, by itself, involve no significant break with the idea that those disputes centrally concern the existence of entities of certain kinds. It need not do so, because the preference might be grounded in the plausible view that general ontological questions (Do there exist so-and-so's?) reduce to, or are at least best approached as, questions partly about the logical form of some appropriate range of statements and partly about their truth-values. Thus one question at issue between mathematical Platonists on the one side and, on the other, nominalists and others is whether numbers, sets, and so on exist. Precisely because we are obviously not concerned with entities which might conceivably be objects of ostension or of any sort of perceptual encounter, or which might announce their presence indirectly through their effects, it is difficult to see how the question of their existence can be non-prejudicially approached, save by equating it with a question about truth and logical form: are there true statements whose proper analysis discloses expressions purporting reference to numbers? General endorsement of this approach to questions of ontology is tantamount to acceptance of Frege's celebrated 'Context Principle' which, construed as a principle about reference, warns against asking after the reference of subsentential expressions outside the context of complete sentences.[2] Dummett is sympathetic to it. But his insistence upon treating R/AR disputes as centred on a class of statements is prelude to a quite different claim about their character. He writes:

> Realism I characterize as the belief that statements of the disputed class possess an objective truth-value, independently of our means of knowing it: they are true or false in virtue of a reality existing independently of us. The anti-realist opposes to this the view that statements of the disputed class are to be understood only by reference to the sort of thing which we count as evidence for a statement of that class . . . The dispute thus concerns the notion of truth appropriate for statements of the disputed class; and this means that it is a dispute concerning the kind of *meaning* which these statements have.[3]

As Dummett goes on to make clear, he thinks that the notion of a statement's having an 'objective truth-value, independently of our means of knowing it . . . in virtue of a reality existing independently of us' is to be understood in a very strong sense. The realist is to be understood as holding not merely that a statement may be true or false without our actually knowing its truth-value, nor even that a statement may be true or false even though we are in fact or in practice unable to tell which, but that there can be a much more radical dislocation of truth-value and our capacity for its recognition – a statement may possess a determinate truth-value without its being possible, even in principle, for us to come to know it.[4] It is for this reason that realism, as Dummett conceives it, amounts to – or at least crucially involves – a thesis about meaning: to adopt a realist view of any area of thought and talk is to conceive of its distinctive statements as endowed with meaning through being associated with evidentially unconstrained truth-conditions, that is, conditions whose satisfaction bears no essential connection, however attenuated, with the possibility of its being recognized by us.

Although the foregoing characterization may be taken as definitive, Dummett very frequently depicts the issue between realists and their opponents in other, ostensibly quite different terms, as concerning the Principle of Bivalence, according to which every statement is either true or false.[5] It is clear that in taking endorsement of unrestricted Bivalence as 'a touchstone for a realistic interpretation of the statements of some given class', Dummett intends no departure from his official characterization. The relations between the two are, however, by no means straightforward. It is, certainly, very plausible to regard unqualified endorsement of bivalence as *sufficient* for realism. For it is a plain fact that our language affords the means of framing various kinds of statement which are not effectively decidable – that is, statements for which there exists no procedure guaranteed to issue, after finitely many steps, in a correct verdict on their truth-values. To insist that such statements are, nevertheless, determinately either true or false would, it seems, require thinking of them as capable of being true, or false, in the absence of evidence either way, and thus as possessed of potentially evidence-transcendent truth-conditions. But realism does not obviously entail a commitment to unrestricted bivalence. It seems that one might decline to endorse bivalence for reasons which appear quite consistent with holding that certain statements may have their truth-values undetectably, say because one took failure of reference on the part of ingredient singular terms to deprive statements of truth-value.[6] A further complication concerns vagueness, which is commonly – though not invariably – taken to cause certain statements to lack determinate truth-value (see Chapter 18, SORITES). These considerations indicate that refusal to endorse bivalence may or may not signal adoption of an anti-realist view, depending upon the specific reasons for that refusal. If realism does involve a commitment to bivalence, it would seem that it can be at most a conditional one, to the effect that any statement is true or false whose ingredient terms are not subject to vagueness or reference-failure. Whether and how this qualified claim can be established, and, in particular, how it might be shown that vagueness and reference-failure are the only grounds on which a realist may properly refuse to endorse bivalence, are hard questions to which, so far as I know, we still want answers. Here they must be left open.

There are, as we have observed, many different areas in which what seems aptly described as a realist position may be defended or opposed. There is no clear presumption that one must be committed to realism across the board, if one seeks to uphold a realist position in any quarter of it. On the contrary, it appears that realism in one area might consist perfectly well with opposition to it in another – that one might, for instance, defend a realist view about theoretical science whilst rejecting realism about ethics, or values generally, or, even more selectively, combine a realist attitude towards some parts of scientific theory (such as classical physics) with anti-realism about other parts (such as quantum mechanics). Certainly there appears little prospect of a quite general argument enforcing adoption of a globally realist stance. A considerable part of the interest and importance of Dummett's configuration of R/AR disputes undoubtedly lies in the fact that it opens up the possibility – which might otherwise appear no less remote – of a quite general argument of the opposing tendency, enforcing global anti-realism across all the disputed areas. For if Dummett is right, realism everywhere depends upon the viability of a realist conception of meaning in terms of potentially evidence-transcendent truth-conditions (hereafter, 'realist truth-conditions' for brevity). Thus any argument against semantic realism as such is potentially quite generally destructive of realist options. There are, accordingly, two main questions requiring attention: (1) Are there compelling arguments – perhaps ones advanced by Dummett himself – against a realist conception of meaning? (2) Has Dummett provided an adequate general characterization of R/AR disputes? In the thirty or so years since Dummett's earliest publications that bear on them, both questions have generated a very considerable amount of critical discussion, of which only the briefest overview can be given here.

§ 2 Arguments against semantic realism

Dummett himself advances two main arguments against the idea that our understanding of disputed statements could consist in our associating them with realist truth-conditions, one focused on the difficulty of seeing how we could *acquire* such an understanding, and the other on the difficulty of seeing how we could *manifest* it. As will quickly become apparent, neither argument purports to be conclusive; each is, rather, to be seen as presenting the realist with a challenge which she appears unable to meet.

According to the *Acquisition Challenge*, our training in the use of language consists in our being taught to accept statements as true in circumstances of such-and-such a sort, and to reject them as false in circumstances of other sorts. This training *necessarily* proceeds in terms of states of affairs which we can *recognize* as obtaining. But how, in that case, are we supposed to come by the conception of evidence-transcendent truth-conditions which the realist postulates? How are we to come to know what it is for a statement of that kind to be true, or false, in virtue of the obtaining of some state of affairs which obtains *undetectably*? The challenge is to explain how we come to assign to statements truth-conditions involving states of affairs which, by their very nature, *can have played no part* in the process by which the meanings of those statements are learned or communicated. If it is conceded that there can indeed be no *ostensive* training that enables us to form such a conception, but suggested that we can nevertheless acquire it through *verbal explanation*, the counter may be given that this merely postpones the problem, since presumably no verbal explanation can be adequate that does not itself employ sentences already understood as having evidence-transcendent truth-conditions – but in that case, how is the proposed explanation to get off the ground?[7]

The *Manifestation Challenge* runs thus: If the meaning of a statement consists in its having certain (possibly evidence-transcendent) truth-conditions, then understanding it (knowing its meaning) is possessing knowledge of such. But knowledge of a statement's meaning cannot, in general, consist in the ability to provide an informative statement, in other words, of what it means (and obviously it can't consist in the ability to state *un*informatively what it means, just by disquoting it).

We may concentrate on the case where knowledge of meaning does not consist in the capacity to give a verbal explanation of meaning, since no such explanation can introduce the possibility of evidence-transcendence. When knowledge of meaning is not verbalizable but implicit knowledge, it must be knowledge of how to use the sentence, and must therefore consist in the speaker's possession of certain practical abilities. But now, by just what practical abilties is an alleged grasp of evidence-transcendent truth-conditions supposed to be manifested? In the case of effectively decidable statements, or of statements which, whenever they are true, are recognizably so, a speaker's implicit knowledge can be identified with his capacity to discriminate between circumstances in which the statement is true and those in which it is not. But it clearly cannot do so in the case of any statement possessed of evidence-transcendent truth-conditions – in this case, there is nothing a speaker can do which fully manifests his supposed grasp of those conditions. Realism thus clashes head-on with the Wittgensteinian equation of meaning with use and of understanding with capacity for correct use.[8]

Attempts to answer the Acquisition Challenge

Truth–value links

Among the types of statement that are problematic, in view of the anti-realist challenge, are statements about the past and about other minds. The realist conception has it that such statements can be determinately true or false in virtue of past states of affairs, or states of mind of others, to which we have no direct access, and for which adequate evidence may be quite simply unavailable. And the challenge is then to explain how we come by this conception. One suggestion is that the truth-values of statements of these problematic kinds are systematically connected with those of statements lying outside the anti-realistically problematic class – in these cases, present-tensed statements and first-person psychological statements. Thus there is a systematic link between the truth-value of a past-tensed statement made at one time, say now, and various corresponding present-tensed statements which were, or could have been, made at earlier times; for example:

> The statement: 'One million years ago, this place *was* covered with ice' is true now if and only if the statement 'This spot *is* covered with ice', made a million years ago, was (or at least would have been) true.

The thought, then, is that understanding this truth-value link is an uncontroversial component in our mastery of tensed discourse. But present-tensed statements are not, as such, anti-realistically problematic, since they relate to conditions which obtain (or don't, as may be) detectably or recognizably. By our grasp of these two things, it is claimed, we can come to understand what it is for past-tensed statements to be true in virtue of states of affairs which are no longer accessible to us.[9]

This response fairly obviously fails to provide a *general* answer to the acquisition challenge, since no such manoeuvre appears feasible in the case of other types of problematic statement, such as unrestricted quantifications over an infinite, or otherwise unsurveyable, totality of objects, such as the natural numbers. Of course, '∀nPn' is true iff all its instances are true. But this is clearly no advance, since whilst the truth-value of each 'Pn' may be unproblematically recognizable, if 'P' is a decidable arithmetic predicate, we enjoy no unproblematic access to the fact, if it is one, that *all* of them are true.[10] But even in cases where the truth-value link gambit appears available, it does not really work. The trouble is that present-tensed statements have unproblematic (detectable) truth-conditions *only in the context of present use*. But the link only helps if we understand what it means to say, for example, 'This spot is covered with ice' *was* true; that is, what is *ceteris paribus* unproblematic is what it is for a present-tensed statement to be *true now*, but what we need, to move from right to left across the truth-value link to knowledge of what it is for a past-tensed statement to be now, but undetectably, true, is understanding of what it is for a present-tensed statement *to have been true* – and this is no less problematic than what we are seeking to explain.[11]

Partial accessibility

We can distinguish between *chronically e-transcendent* statements – such as 'Everything in the universe has doubled in size' and 'The entire universe sprang into existence just five minutes ago, replete with traces of a long and complex past, etc.' – which by their very nature could in no possible circumstances be recognized as true, and statements which, though not *guaranteed* to be so, are, *in favourable cases, detectably* true. Realists may concede that there is no hope of defending their distinctive conception of truth for the former, though claiming that this is no loss, since they are beyond the pale anyway; but they may insist that matters stand otherwise with the latter. Here, they may claim, if a statement of this sort is undetectably true, it is at most *contingent* that it is so. Statements of the same kind are, on occasion, recognizably true: that is, we sometimes have access to states of affairs of the kind which confer truth on them. And this, they may claim, is enough – enough to equip us with a conception of what it is for such statements to be true but undetectably so – this is just for there to obtain a state of affairs of the same kind as we have recognized to obtain in other cases. So it is, McDowell claims, with statements about the past and about the psychological states of others. Although we don't always, or even usually, have direct non-inferential access to past states of affairs, we do sometimes, through memory; and we can on occasion simply and literally observe that another is in pain or violent grief – we may see pain or grief in their face and actions, which express or manifest their state.[12]

Like the preceding response, this is of limited application at best. It is doubtfully available in case of statements about the remote past, beyond the reach of living memory. Further, no response of this sort seems available for spatially or temporally unrestricted contingent generalizations (whether lawlike or accidental), or for quantifications through an infinite domain – in neither case does there appear to be any purchase for the idea of our being sometimes graced with direct access to appropriate truth-conferring state of affairs. Clearly, too, the idea of occasional direct access to others' psychological states may be challenged. But there is a quite general difficulty with the partial access gambit, even in what might seem favourable cases.

First, and obviously, we should distinguish between the (problematic) case of a statement's being *undetectably* true and the (unproblematic) case of a statement's being true, though not as it happens known to be so, simply because we haven't taken steps we could have taken to ascertain its truth-value. We can, plausibly, understand what it is for a statement in the latter case to be true, in terms of there obtaining a state of affairs of the same kind as we have verified to obtain in the case of other statements of that type. But this is not to the point – for it is another, and much stronger, claim that we can come by the notion of undetectable truth by this route.

Second, with this out of the way, we can see that the crucial, but contentious, claim is that statements in respect of which we do *not* enjoy direct access to any truth-conferring state of affairs are *of the same kind* as other statements, such as those about the past, for which we do. Once it is allowed that they *are* of the same kind, it may seem an easy step to the realist's desired conclusion, that we can conceive of the former as true in the same way as the latter, for all that the former are, as it happens, undetectably true. Now they *are* of the same kind in one sense, for they are all statements *about the past*. But this, the anti-realist may protest, is not the point. In another sense, they are *not*: for the former are (allegedly) undetectably true, if true, whereas the latter are, *ex hypothesi*, detectably so. The realist simply *assumes*, but does nothing to show, that this difference *makes no difference*. But that it does make a difference is precisely the content of the acquisition challenge. So the question is begged, not answered.[13]

Enhanced recognitional capacities

The idea that underpins the preceding response, that undetectability of truth-value commonly derives from contingencies of our circumstances or contingent limitations upon our recognitional capacities, is sound enough. There may be some temptation to think it can be exploited to the realist's advantage in a somewhat different way. It may be suggested that we can attain a conception of what it is for statements to be true – though *undetectably* so as far as *we* are concerned – by conceiving of creatures with suitably extended powers of recognition, for whom the obtaining of the relevant truth-conferring states of affairs would *not* be undetectable. Thus far, the moderate anti-realist need have no objection – indeed, unless he is able to appeal to conceivable finite extensions of our powers of recognition, computation, and so on, it is hard to see how he might resist the slide into an implausibly extreme version of anti-realism (strict finitism, in the case of mathematics), according to which the only meaningful statements are those which we can actually verify.[14] But if the suggestion is to serve the realist's ends, it must go beyond envisaging relatively uncontroversial, finite extensions of our detective abilities, to encompass conceiving, for example, of creatures capable of surveying infinite totalities, or 'directly seeing' into the past and future, or into the minds of others. It is not, however, at all clear that we can conceive any such thing in relevant detail – it is one thing to appeal to the idea of creatures whose recognitional capacities *finitely* extend powers we *actually* possess, and quite another to claim that we can conceive of creatures endowed with capacities for which we have *no* actual model, or which constitute *infinite* extensions of our capacities. It may further be objected that even if we could imagine a use for certain sentences, by beings with powers greatly exceeding our own, this does not automatically put us in a position to use those sentences in that way ourselves. To suppose that we could is to suppose that we could employ those sentences with the intention of conforming to standards of correct use, even though we are ourselves entirely unable to tell whether our use accords with them or not. This seems to run afoul of considerations concerning the *normativity* of meaning. To attach a certain meaning to a statement is, in effect, to divide states of affairs into two classes: those in which it is correct to assert the statement, and those in which it is incorrect. To employ the statement with that meaning is, prescinding from complications about insincerity, to use it with the intention of asserting it only in states of affairs of the first kind. But it appears quite generally to make no sense to suppose that an agent intends to ϕ if there is in principle no means available, however indirect, of telling whether or not he has succeeded in ϕ-ing. So in particular, nothing can be made of the suggestion that we intend, in using certain statements, to conform to standards of correctness in use, conformity with which essentially eludes detection *by us*.[15]

Compositionality

A better response might begin by pointing out that the opening claim of the acquisition argument – that our training in the use of language consists in our being taught to accept statements as true in circumstances of such-and-such a sort, and to reject them as false in circumstances of other sorts – is liable to deflect attention from the crucial point that our understanding of most sentences comes, not through any directly forged link between them and recognizable states of affairs in which their assertion is justified, but is the product of prior understanding of their ingredient expressions together with their mode of construction. It may then seem that a very simple response is available: we come by a grasp of realist truth-conditions by coming to understand sentences having those truth-conditions, and we come to understand such sentences in just the way in which we come to understand the vast majority of sentences in our language, by understanding their ingredient words and semantically significant syntax.

The anti-realist must indeed accept that our understanding of sentences of the various kinds central to the dispute – statements about remote regions of space or time, quantifications through infinite or unsurveyably large totalities, counterfactual conditionals, and so on – is, in general, acquired along compositional lines. But he will likely object that the further claim – that that understanding involves the association with those sentences of realist truth-conditions, rather than, say, conditions of justified assertion – is entirely gratuitous. The realist may, and should, concede that the proposed response does not *prove* that we understand the problematic sentences as having realist truth-conditions. But she can point out that it was not intended to do so; the aim was rather to explain, on the *assumption* that our understanding has that character, how we may have acquired it. In the absence of an argument showing that a grasp of realist truth-conditions cannot emerge, via composition, from agreed unproblematic starting points, or an independent argument – perhaps one based on manifestation – for the bankruptcy of the distinctive realist conception of truth-conditions (of which it would be a corollary that we cannot have acquired it), it seems that this is enough to neutralize the acquisition challenge.

Attempts to answer the Manifestation Challenge

Explanatory ascription

Several critics claim that the manifestation challenge may be met, or deflected, by observing that the ascription of knowledge of realist truth-conditions may form part of a successful theoretical explanation of speakers' behaviour. A closely related suggestion is that knowledge of meaning is manifestable in a capacity to interpret the speech-behaviour of others, where this involves, centrally, the correct ascription of beliefs – which may be realist beliefs – which figure, in combination with suitable desires, in explanations of speakers' behaviour.[16] But there is an obvious difficulty with this kind of response. Evidently there is no reason why an anti-realist should not go in for interpretations of linguistic behaviour, or explanations of behaviour in general, in terms of beliefs. It is therefore essential to show, if the proposed reply is to make headway, that such interpretations and explanations must sometimes proceed in terms of specifically realist beliefs.[17] That is, it needs to be indicated what specific aspects of behaviour, or the capacities to which they bear witness, call for explanation in terms of the hypothesis that the subjects of ascription hold beliefs, the content of which demands characterization in terms of realist truth-conditions rather than conditions of warranted assertibility, say; otherwise, the ascription of realist beliefs will merely incorporate so much theoretical slack.[18]

Inferential practice

It may be suggested that a realist understanding of certain statements may be manifested by our employment of distinctively classical principles of reasoning in our willingness to reason by (unrestricted) use of the Law of Excluded Middle, or by Double Negation Elimination, or other patterns of inference rejected by the intuitionists and unjustifiable save on the assumption that the statements are apt for evidence-transcendent truth.

A difficulty with this is that it involves treating our actual inferential practice as sacrosanct. As against this, it may be said that the justification for employing certain principles of inference should be given in terms of the kind of meaning we have conferred upon the statements involved, so that the appeal to inferential practice gets things the wrong way round. Why should we take our unrestricted use of classical logic as showing that we have conferred realist meanings for the sentences involved, rather than as revealing that we have – by a kind of uncritical inertia – illegitimately projected patterns of reasoning that are correct within a restricted domain (say, of decidable statements) to cases which lie outside it? Even if it is granted that a propensity to reason classically betokens a *commitment* to assigning realist truth-conditions to problematic statements, it does not seem that this could suffice to make clear what specific truth-conditions have, putatively, been assigned to them.[19]

Other modes of manifestation?

In case of decidable statements, a speaker may manifest a grasp of truth-conditions in a quite straightforward way, by implementing the appropriate procedure, leading to her recognition of the statement as true, or false, as may be. Where a statement is not effectively decidable, and is in fact true but not recognizably so, a speaker cannot, obviously, manifest a grasp of its truth-condition by determining its truth-value. But the thought is tempting that she may nevertheless demonstrate an appropriate understanding in other ways. Thus Strawson[20] proposes that whilst it is, of course, true – and a truism – that 'grasp of the sense of a sentence cannot be displayed in *response* to unrecognizable conditions', it will be

> enough for the truth-theorist that the grasp of the sense of a sentence can be displayed in response to *recognizable* conditions – of various sorts: there are those which conclusively establish the truth or falsity of the sentence; . . . those which (given our general theory of the world) constitute evidence, more or less good, for or against the truth of the sentence; . . . even those which point to the unavoidable absence of evidence either way.

His thought is that there are various responses to recognizable states of affairs which can be regarded as manifesting a grasp of the sense of a sentence, in addition to recognizing that the condition for its truth definitely does, or definitely does not, obtain.

So there surely are, but this does not seem enough. Here it is crucial to remember that the truth-theorist to whose defence Strawson is (or ought to be) contributing is a realist, who holds that grasp of the sense of a sentence consists, in the case where the sentence is not effectively decidable, in knowledge of its possibly e-transcendent truth-condition. The responses Strawson mentions, however, are entirely consistent with the anti-realist view that, in such cases, understanding the sentence consists in knowing the conditions for its warranted assertion. That is, such responses do not distinctively display grasp of *realist* truth-conditions for the sentence.[21]

Manifestation and manifestees

Manifestation is a relational matter. A chess master may be able to manifest her skills to others with a reasonable knowledge of the game; but she cannot be expected to display all or even any aspects of her virtuosity to those unfamiliar with it. Simon Blackburn claims that the manifestation argument only appears compelling because it tacitly restricts the manifestees to cognitively impoverished creatures, capable only of *observation*. Thus, picking up on Dummett's remark that 'an individual can communicate only what he can be observed to communicate'[22], Blackburn takes this to suggest that the manifestee is to be

> one who is capable of making observations, but no more. But let us suppose that some things lie outside observation: the past, or other peoples' sensations, or sub-atomic particles. Then it is clearly not a sensible requirement that a man should manifest his understanding of these things to someone who is capable of only making observations. . . . Such limited observers make poor audiences. . . . the very word 'manifest' reveals the doubtful nature of this requirement. Like 'display' and 'reveal', it has largely visual overtones: I cannot display or make visible the past events I talk about, the future ones, my own pains and thoughts, let alone electrons or numbers.[23]

But this complaint, it seems to me, misrepresents Dummett's argument. That an anti-realist imposes no restriction to states of affairs which can be observed to obtain, when they do, should be clear from the mathematical case which forms the departure-point for his work. Dummett raises no problem about finitary mathematical statements, although their truth, if they are true, plainly does *not* consist in the obtaining of some *observable* state of affairs. The important distinction is not between the observable and the unobservable, but between effectively decidable statements and others. In the case of any statement whose truth or falsity is an effectively decidable matter, we can equate implicit knowledge of the statement's truth-condition with a capacity to decide it. The case where the statement concerns some literally observable state of affairs is just a special case of this – here there is a particularly simple decision procedure: just look and see (sniff and smell, and so on). It is with non-effectively decidable (non-ED) statements that the problem arises: their being non-ED does not, of course, mean that there cannot be circumstances in which we are able to tell that the condition for their truth is fulfilled or not. Thus to take a famous example, if Goldbach's Conjecture that every even number is the sum of two primes is false, we might one day be confronted with a counter-example; and there is no reason to suppose that, if it is true, it is nevertheless insusceptible of proof – so we could conceivably be in position to recognize it as true. The point is that we have no effective way of bringing about a situation of either kind. It is for this reason that we cannot equate a knowledge of the statement's truth-condition (as the realist conceives it) with a capacity to recognize a proof of it, or a counter-example to it, should we be lucky enough to find ourselves confronted with such. For then the statement would be true if and only there is a proof of it, and false if and only if there is a disproof. But there is no guarantee that a situation of either kind will ever obtain, so the realist could not be justified in taking it that the statement is true or false all the same.[24]

In particular, the suggestion that talk of what can't be made visible – such as numbers – is threatened by the manifestation requirement quite misconstrues its intended force. What has to be capable of manifestation is our supposed knowledge or understanding, not the objects we talk about. If Blackburn's reading of Dummett were right, he ought to find *all* statements about numbers problematic. But of course, he does not: there is no special difficulty in saying what (implicit) knowledge of the truth-condition for example '937 is prime' consists in – it consists in mastery of a procedure for deciding the statement.

Blackburn's key claim – that the argument relies on some unduly restrictive assumption about the capacities of suitable manifestees – is thus indefensible as a reading of Dummett's texts. It might none the less be claimed that the argument has plausibility only under some such restriction. But is that so? Let's suppose the audience is as competent in the use of the statements in question as the speaker. That is, grant what Blackburn would reckon as a suitable audience – someone competent in number theory, say. We can still ask: what recognizable capacities of the speaker constitute his supposed knowledge of what it is for statements involving unbounded quantification over the natural numbers to be true, but undetectably so? Bringing in a suitable audience appears in itself to make no advance on the problem – we still need an answer to the question.[25]

This discussion of the principal anti-realist arguments has been quite selective,[26] and is, it will be only too clear, inconclusive. My aim has been limited to providing little more than an introductory survey of some of the main moves made in this complex, difficult and, in my view, still unresolved debate.

§ 3 The adequacy of Dummett's characterization of R/AR disputes

If Dummett's account of R/AR disputes in general is acceptable, the potential bearing of anti-realist arguments in the theory of meaning upon their resolution is immediate: if successful, such arguments would enforce a globally anti-realist stance. But is it acceptable? Dummett has never maintained that his characterization fits *every* dispute which might be taken to concern the tenability of position describable as realism.[27] His claim has rather been – and continues to be – that it captures what is centrally at issue in an extensive range of such disputes. Few would deny that there are cases to which Dummett's characterization seems entirely apt. The dispute between Platonists and constructivists in the philosophy of mathematics is probably the clearest example. Platonists in this sense uphold – and various species of constructivist challenge – the legitimacy of employing in mathematical reasoning forms of inference enshrined in classical logic, such as Double Negation Elimination and a strong form of Reductio ad Absurdum, which depend for their justification upon the assumption of unrestricted bivalence, and hence upon taking mathematical statements to have realist truth-conditions. But it may be doubted whether the same is true of other R/AR disputes which have commanded interest and attention in recent and ongoing philosophical discussion.

We can distinguish three component claims in Dummett's configuration of R/AR disputes:

(1) such disputes are best understood as concerned with a class of problematic *statements*, rather than with a class of problematic *entities*;
(2) more specifically, what is in dispute is the *character* of the notion of *truth* which may properly be taken to have application to the statements in question;
(3) more specifically still, what is primarily at issue is whether statements of the kind in question may defensibly be held to be capable of being true in a *potentially evidence-transcendent* manner.

Clearly each of these claims presupposes the correctness of – and is, in that sense at least, stronger and more contentious than – its predecessors. Our review of grounds on which the adequacy of Dummett's approach may be doubted can conveniently be organized in terms of them. We begin with some considerations relating to the first claim.

In one of his most recent papers on the present topic,[28] Dummett reiterates his conviction that R/AR disputes are best seen as concerning a class of problematic statements, rather than a class of problematic objects, and offers two reasons for it. The first is that in some cases – the examples given are disputes over the reality of the past or over the future – there is no germane class of objects for the dispute to be about. The second is that even in cases where there is some problematic type of object, as with the Platonist/constructivist dispute about mathematics, it is not the existence of the objects as such that the dispute really concerns, but the objectivity of the statements we make about them. A philosopher who accepts a problematic class of objects – numbers or sets, for example – may yet take an anti-realist view of facts about them; while one who takes objects of that kind to be mind-dependent, perhaps because he views them as products of our intellectual activity, much as Dedekind viewed numbers as our 'free creations', may yet be a realist, in Dummett's sense, about truths concerning them (as Dedekind appears to have been). The significant difference, Dummett claims, is between those who hold that mathematical statements, say, have determinate truth-values independently of our capacity to ascertain them, and those who deny this.[29]

It is natural to protest that, unless it is intended merely as a forceful expression of Dummett's own greater interest in one kind of disagreement than another, the claim that *the* significant difference concerns one's attitude towards recognition-transcendent truth-value is tendentious. It is, of course, *a* difference, and an important one. But granting that much is perfectly consistent with acknowledgement that the disagreement between Platonists and nominalists over the existence of numbers, sets and other kinds of abstract objects centres upon another, equally significant difference, reflecting a different aspect of R/AR disputes. More generally, it is an indisputable historical fact that some R/AR disputes are, at least in part, disputes about the existence of one or another kind of problematic entity. Obvious examples, besides the Platonist/nominalist dispute just mentioned, are the disagreements between realists and their opponents in the philosophy of science over the existence of unobservable entities postulated in advanced scientific theories, and in the philosophy of modality over the existence of possible worlds. The present point is that, even if such disputes are in part about evidence-transcendence, they involve ontological disagreements as well. If neglect of the latter aspect is indeed a consequence of Dummett's reconstruction, that is surely a serious limitation.

In fact, matters are less straightforward than these remarks suggest. Striking a more concessive note, Dummett suggests[30] that a dispute over the existence of certain entities might be represented in his way – that is, as concerned with a problematic class of statements – simply by taking the disputed class to consist of statements purporting reference to those entities. This suggestion accords well with the view briefly adumbrated above[31] that ontological questions are best treated as questions about the logical form and truth-values of some appropriate range of statements. The possibility of thus reconfiguring questions about the existence of entities of some kind as questions about a certain suitably chosen range of statements is certainly enough to show that, if Dummett's approach does indeed involve an unwanted neglect of ontological issues, that is not a defect for which claim (1) is to be held responsible. But that is not, on the face of it, enough to dispose of the charge altogether. For the questions relevant to resolving the ontological issue – questions about the logical form and truth-values of certain statements – are, it seems, quite distinct from those upon which, in line with claims (2) and (3), R/AR disputes should, in Dummett's view, be concerned – questions about the character of the notion of truth applicable to statements in the disputed class. As against this, it might be claimed that what is typically at issue in a philosophical dispute about the existence of entities of some kind is not simply whether or not there are such things as numbers, say, or colours, but whether the entities in question enjoy an objective existence, independent of our thought and talk of them. But the question whether objects of some sort are objective or mind-independent – or so it may plausibly be held – is best regarded as being whether statements purporting reference to those objects are capable of objective, mind-independent truth. Thus questions about the character of the notion of truth having application within the appropriate range of statements are, after all, central to ontological disputes, and the charge that Dummett's approach entirely neglects such disputes is therefore ill-founded.[32]

This last line of defence is, I think, only partially successful. It is certainly plausible that some appropriate notion of objective, mind-independent existence is involved in (most) ontological disputes. And it is hardly less plausible, in my view, that this notion is best elucidated in terms of the idea that statements purporting reference to entities of the problematic kind are apt to be objectively true. But the claim that the notion of objective truth thus involved in ontological questions is invariably the notion of potentially evidence-transcendent truth is surely mistaken. The truth of effectively decidable statements of elementary number theory, taken at face-value, suffices for the existence of indefinitely many natural numbers; but such statements, by their very nature, cannot be candidates for evidence-transcendent truth. This suggests that there has to be some other notion of objective truth, falling short of realist truth in Dummett's sense. We shall return to this point.

Turning now to claim (2), it may be felt that even if reshaping R/AR disputes as concerned with statements (rather than entities) imports no serious loss of generality, its exclusive focus upon the character of the notion of truth having application to them is a good deal less harmless: that the result is to lose contact with what is at issue in earlier disputes about realism. Dummett replies to this charge in a recent paper (1993a). Traditional opposition to realism, he observes, commonly takes the form of *reductionism*. The anti-realist about a given area – schematically, the ostensible subject matter of A-statements – maintains that there are no distinctive A-facts: rather, A-truths can be translated or paraphrased without loss or residue into

B-truths, truths of some other kind which enjoy an (at least relatively) unproblematic ontology and epistemology. Thus the behaviourist denies that there are distinctively mental facts; there are just facts about overt behaviour and circumstances in which it occurs, and truths about minds translate into (complex, subjunctively conditional) truths of the latter sort. According to instrumentalists and operationists – traditional scientific anti-realists – there is no special class of truths about the unobservables of scientific theory, such talk being merely convenient shorthand for talk about observables. The fatal objection to anti-realisms of this reductionist stripe, Dummett reminds us, has been that the translation programmes they enjoin simply cannot be carried through; reductive behaviourism, for example, runs aground over the holistic character of discourse about beliefs, desires and other mental states (see Chapter 10, HOLISM, and Chapter 7, TACIT KNOWLEDGE, section 2), while traditional instrumentalism fails because a suitable division cannot be sustained between observation statements and theoretical ones. But the opposing realisms, he argues, have enjoyed too easy a victory. Intuitionists in mathematics accept the irreducibility of mathematical statements, but oppose realism (as embodied in standard classical mathematics, with its reliance upon unrestricted bivalence) by insisting that their content is exhausted by an account of their justification conditions. By taking this as our model, we can see that there is space for non-reductionist anti-realist positions about the mind, or about science, or in other areas, which involve no commitment to such doom-laden translation programmes. The charge of irrelevance to traditional disputes over realism is thus quite misplaced: what has been done, rather, is to disclose anti-realist options in those disputes which had not been sufficiently noticed.[33]

As against that specific charge, this is a passably effective reply. But misgivings relating to claim (2) may still be felt on a somewhat different score. Let it be granted that focus on the character of the notion of truth applicable to certain statements is well-adapted to plot one kind of non-reductionist opposition to realism (and set aside, pro tem, the question how widely available this kind of anti-realism is): it appears, nevertheless, quite ill-adapted to accommodate other, equally non-reductive forms which opposition to realism may, and in significant cases does, assume. Two such directions of anti-realist thinking, both well-represented in recent discussion, spring readily to mind, neither of which is happily construed as occupied with the character of the notion of truth having application within the discourses they concern.

There is, first, the view – paradigmatically exemplified in the emotive theory of ethical discourse embraced by some logical positivists, and foreshadowed in the writings of Hume[34] – that the seemingly fact-stating, descriptive utterances characteristic of a given region of discourse are not genuine assertions at all, but are rather to be understood as expressive of feelings (whether of approval or disapproval, admiration or distaste) which we project onto the natural goings-on by presenting them in assertoric or propositional style. This projectivist species of anti-realism is to be sharply distinguished from a crude subjectivism according to which ethical utterances are sincere or insincere, true or false *reports* of morally relevant feelings. In its original and purer form, at least, it maintains not that ethical utterances fail to comply with standards of objective truth-telling, but that they are not apt for evaluation as true or false at all. While it finds its most natural, and perhaps its most plausible, application in connection with morals, and evaluative discourse in general, it admits – or is often taken to admit – of extension to other areas. Hume himself may be seen as commending a projectivist treatment of causal necessity; others, following his lead, have advocated similar treatments of other areas – for example, of modality in general (see Chapter 19, MODALITY, sections 3.1 and 4), and even of mathematics.[35]

There is, secondly, a quite different – indeed, opposed – direction of theorizing which accepts the sentences of a problematic discourse as vehicles of genuine statements, aimed at truth, but denies that they can ever attain to it on the ground that reality fails to furnish objects, properties or states of affairs of the kinds their truth demands. Versions of this species of anti-realism – error theories, as they are often called – have been advocated in recent decades in relation to moral discourse by John Mackie and to mathematics by Hartry Field; eliminativist doctrines about ordinary or 'folk-' psychological discourse are perhaps also best viewed as error-theoretical.[36] In sharp contrast with more traditional, reductionist forms of anti-realism, it is held that the statements of the discourse do indeed carry the ontological commitments their surface syntax suggests – to distinctively non-natural moral properties and states of affairs, for example, or to numbers and sets – but that, precisely because there are in reality no such things, those statements are quite generally false.

Whether either of these approaches should ultimately be reckoned the best, or even a sustainable, direction anti-realist intuitions might assume is a question to which we shall return. The present point is, quite simply, that they constitute prima facie playable options for opponents of realism who want no truck with orthodox reductionist strategies – naturalism in ethics or a programme of reinterpreting mathematics as concerned solely with nominalistically acceptable concrete entities – but they are options which can, it seems, find no place in Dummett's configuration of R/AR disputes.[37] Their availability tells, in the first instance, against claim (2). However, since neither the error-theorist's not the expressivist's quarrel with the realist concerns the possibility of holding statements in the disputed class to be capable of evidence-transcendent truth – or subject to bivalence – these examples tell also, albeit indirectly, against claim (3).

A more direct objection to claim (3) – or to taking endorsement of bivalence as the hallmark of realism – focuses upon the phenomenon of vagueness. On one widely accepted view, vague statements are precisely ones which lack determinate truth-values. If that is so, then Dummett's characterization would seem to leave no space for any form of realism about vague discourse.[38] Given the very considerable extent to which vagueness pervades our language, this would constitute a serious limitation. But it is not clear that the objection is decisive. One quite radical response to the objection would be to reject the assumption on which it proceeds, that vagueness involves lack of truth-value. Such is the burden of the epistemic conception of vagueness, which has received some ingenious and determined support in recent work.[39] In this view we hesitate or are reluctant to assert, in problematic cases, that a certain coloured patch is red or that a certain man is thin, not because these statements lack determinate truth-values, but because we do not know what those truth-values are. As Dummett observes, this requires us to hold that our use of vague expressions "confers on them meanings which determine precise applications for them that we ourselves do not know".[40] Finding this supposition implausible, Dummett offers a quite different answer to the objection, contending that the realist should hold that, for every vague statement, there is a range of more precise statements exactly one of which is true and the rest false, while an anti-realist is free to deny this. His thought, it seems, is that while a realist need not endorse an unrestricted principle of bivalence, he can only allow failures where they can be put down to an eliminable lack of precision on our part: if a statement lacks truth-value, that is due not to any indeterminacy in reality but to some looseness in our description.[41] Whether this conception involves no significant departure from the idea that realism is to be characterized in terms of commitment to the possibility of evidence-transcendent truth, or whether, alternatively, unrestricted bivalence may – at least as far as the difficulty over vagueness is concerned – be retained as the mark of realism by upholding an epistemic conception, are delicate questions we shall not try to resolve here.

§ 4 Error theories, projectivism and quasi-realism

Even if an affirmative answer to either of these questions can be sustained, there are, as remarked, lines of attack apparently open to anti-realists which seem not to fit comfortably into Dummett's general characterization of R/AR disputes, since the relevant anti-realist thesis is not that the problematic statements cannot have evidence-transcendent truth-values, but that they are either not really up for assessment as true or false at all (the expressivist/projectivist option) or invariably false (error theories). It may begin to seem that it is not just Dummett's particular focus that distorts or oversimplifies, but that any attempt to identify some one kind of thing that is at issue in all R/AR disputes is unlikely to do justice to the variety of forms opposition to realism – and, correlatively, realism itself – may take. We shall consider in the next section whether the prospects for an illuminating overview are as bleak as our discussion so far suggests. First, it will be convenient and instructive to review, if only and inevitably somewhat briefly and provisionally, the error-theoretic and expressivist options, along with some more sophisticated variants of them.

In its starkest and most uncompromising form, error-theoretic anti-realism would seem to enjoin rejecting the problematic discourse outright, as resting upon presuppositions which, if its negative ontological claims are correct, are recognizably unfulfilled. The continued practice of making moral distinctions, coupled with recognition that the world fails to provide states of affairs of the kind which that practice, properly understood, demands would amount at best to bad faith. If that is a consequence we should find it hard to swallow in the moral sphere, its analogue in the mathematical case seems, if anything, even more clearly intolerable, given the apparent indispensability of mathematics to successful theorizing about the world. For this reason, much interest and importance attaches to the possibility of mitigating the apparently disastrous consequences of pure error-theoretic anti-realism by combining it with a supplementary theory which would explain how, error notwithstanding, we may be rationally justified in continuing to practise the discourse in question. Field[42] may fairly be viewed as arguing for just such a modified error theory about mathematical discourse. Mathematical statements, taken literally and at face-value, are indeed, by his nominalist lights, systematically false, simply because the world fails to contain the numbers, functions, sets, and so on required for their truth.[43] But it is, in his view, a further error to suppose that this deprives them of any respectable employment. Mathematics does not need to be true to be good. What is required – and all that is required – to justify the use of mathematical theories in everyday or scientific theoretical contexts is that such theories should be *conservative*, in the sense that relying upon them in reasoning about non-mathematical matters does not enable us to reach any non-mathematical conclusions from non-mathematical premisses which are not logical consequences of those non-mathematical premisses alone.[44] If this idea can be made to work, it promises at least one significant advantage over more traditional forms of nominalism, by doing away with the need for the kind of reductive translation programme in which – with less-than-encouraging prospects of success – they standardly engage. Whether it *can* be made to work is too large a question for adequate treatment here, but one serious-looking problem merits brief mention. This concerns the belief in conservativeness which supplants a belief in truth as the core of this anti-realist position. The question is whether Field can give a satisfactory account of its content without destabilizing his nominalism. To be conservative, a mathematical theory must be consistent. Since a theory's consistency cannot be explicated in the usual model- or proof-theoretic terms without breaking faith with nominalism, Field must take it to consist in the possibility that its axioms are collectively true. But they are in fact false in his version of nominalism. The implausible upshot would seem to be that the existence/non-existence of numbers and such like must be, in Field's view, not merely a pure contingency, but a metaphysically brute one. Any purported explanation, in nominalistically acceptable terms, of its resolution – either way – would locate non-mathematical states of affairs which would have been otherwise, had the alleged contingency been otherwise resolved, and would thus be in tension with the conservativeness of mathematical theories. The objection, it should be stressed, is not to the notion of brute contingency as such, but to the idea that the (non-) existence of numbers and sets may be properly regarded as exemplifying it.[45]

Expressivism about a discourse avoids this particular difficulty, since it denies that its utterances are genuine statements, properly assessable as true or false. But in its pure form, it runs into others. Typically, the problematic utterances will exhibit many, if not all, of the main features – with, of course, the exception, if expressivism is right, of a capacity for truth-value – of genuine assertion. Moral and modal utterances, for example, happily tolerate embedding under negation, within disjunctions and conditionals, and in reports of propositional attitude. They are at least – however misleadingly – *said* to be true, or false. And, most importantly, they may figure – both atomically and under such embedding – as premisses or conclusions of what are, to all intents and purposes, deductively valid inferences. Since Geach[46] first drew attention to the fact, it has been a commonplace that expressive theories encounter grave difficulty in doing justice to these indisputable aspects of use, as they must if they are to be credible. Whatever attitude or sentiment is expressed by a free-standing utterance of 'Lying is wrong', say, those same words can no longer be held to express it when they figure as antecedent to a conditional, such as 'If lying is wrong, so is getting others to lie.' On the face of it, the antecedent position needs filling with words articulating a condition which may or may not be met, and so by words apt to express not a feeling but a truth. In addition, if 'Lying is wrong' does no more than express a feeling when uttered on its own, it is difficult to see how the ostensibly valid inference from it, together with the above conditional, can be anything other than a crude equivocation.

A sophisticated development of the expressivist/projectivist approach has been forcefully advocated by Simon Blackburn. It is a central objective of his *quasi-realism* to show that acknowledging the expressive/projective basis or origin of moral discourse – to take the case for which his view is most fully worked out – need force no admission that our tendency to talk and think *as if* moral judgements are genuine assertions, having truth-conditions, is misplaced or defective. In his words, quasi-realism seeks to show 'that even on anti-realist grounds, there is nothing improper, nothing "diseased" in projected predicates . . . it tries to earn, on the slender basis [i.e. of projectivist assumptions], the features of moral language (or of the other commitments to which a projective theory might apply) which tempt people to realism'.[47] Earning the right to present our moral or other evaluative commitments in propositional style – as Blackburn would put it – evidently requires, *inter alia*, solving Geach's problem. Blackburn's proposal is that when we assert conditionals with evaluative components, like 'If lying is wrong, so is getting others to lie', we are expressing complex, higher-order evaluative attitudes – in this case, of approval towards combining disapproval of lying with disapproval of getting others to lie. This, he hopes, enables us to explain what is going on when we make evaluative inferences, such as the moral *modus ponens* we have taken as example. Someone who sincerely endorses the premisses approves of combining disapproval of lying with disapproval of getting others to lie, and disapproves of lying. She ought, therefore, to disapprove of getting others to lie (thereby sincerely endorsing the conclusion), since if she does not she will be involved in a kind of attitudinal inconsistency – her attitudes will clash with one another, as Blackburn puts it.[48]

This fails to do justice to the problem. Someone who declines to accept the conclusion that getting others to lie is wrong from the given premisses is to be convicted of *logical* incompetence, and not a merely *moral* fault (failing to have a combination of attitudes of which one approves), as on Blackburn's account of matter.[49] There is, in any case, room for doubt whether the approach can be extended to cover the full range of utterances which are, in Blackburn's view, ripe for projectivist-cum-quasi-realist treatment. It is unclear, for example, that it can deal satisfactorily with 'mixed' conditionals and other compounds involving genuinely factual components alongside evaluative ones, such as 'If Henry said that, he ought to apologize'.[50] Again, a projectivist/quasi-realist treatment of modality has it that 'It is necessary that p' functions to express our own imaginative limitations – something like 'inability to make anything of a possible way of thinking which denies [that p]'[51] – but there seems little prospect of dealing with iterated modalities in this style.

§ 5 Realism and objective truth

Let us take stock a little. We have largely been concerned to assess the adequacy of Dummett's characterization of R/AR disputes. Our discussion suggests that whilst some such disputes are indeed to be seen, as Dummett recommends, as turning upon the tenability of a conception of truth and falsity as potentially evidence-transcendent, there are others where this is not the issue. It seems, for example, that there should be space for a position appropriately describable as realist about (even) effectively decidable mathematical statements. Realists about morals, or about modality, need not, it seems, embrace evidentially unconstrained conceptions of moral or modal fact simply by virtue of their opposition to error-theoretic and expressivist/projectivist accounts of the subject-matter. It merits emphasis that what these and other examples call in question is not, as such, the aptness of Dummett's depiction of realism as 'the belief that statements of the disputed class possess an objective truth-value, independently of our means of knowing it: they are true or false in virtue of a reality existing independently of us': this remains – at least for anyone who accepts that the issues are best seen as primarily concerning a class of problematic statements, rather than a class of problematic entities – as good a schematic characterization of the position as we might hope to give. Rather, what they tell against is the particular, and particularly exacting, interpretation Dummett imposes upon its key ingredient terms – 'objective truth-value', 'independent of our means of knowing' and 'independent reality'. Encashing these notions in terms of potential for evidence-transcendent truth undoubtedly hits off one very strong sense in which the states of affairs a given kind of statement purportedly represents may be held to be objective and independent of our talk and thought. But might there not be other, less demanding but still substantial, conditions whose satisfaction by (true) statements about a given subject matter would suffice for the correctness of (a form of) realism about them? An affirmative answer would invite acceptance of one broadly negative moral: that there need be no one, unique mark of realism uniform across all R/AR disputes – no one thing that is at issue in all of them. But that need not be seen as enforcing the disappointing conclusion that we are confronted with no more than a rag-bag of disparate oppositions, with nothing but a label in common. It need not do so, at least, provided we may view the relevant conditions as reflecting features of – or constraints upon the application of – the notion of truth properly deployed in the various regions of discourse over which realists and anti-realists of one or another kind may disagree. This, in broad outline, is the overall picture recommended in recent work by Crispin Wright, of which we now provide a brief review.

In contrast with expressivists, Wright argues that anti-realists about a given discourse should acknowledge, along with their realist opponents, that its distinctive utterances are genuinely assertoric and so apt for evaluation as true or false; and that, in contrast with error theorists, there is no systematic reason why its assertions should fail to be true. As Wright recognizes, this makes urgent two questions: How can the concession that the relevant utterances are truth-apt, and that many of them are indeed true, 'avoid giving the game to the realist straight away' (unless coupled with some form of reductionist reconstruction of those statements)? And, assuming a satisfactory answer to that question, what *is* in dispute between realists and anti-realists, if both parties agree that the problematic statements are not only truth-apt, but in many cases actually true (as they stand, without benefit of some reductive analysis in terms of statements of some other discourse)? What is left for them to disagree *about?* To answer the first question, Wright circumscribes a notion of truth – *minimal* truth, as he calls it – which is neutral between realists and their opponents. To answer the second, he identifies a number of truth-related issues over which parties who agree on the minimal-truth aptness, or minimal truth, of certain statements may yet diverge – issues where what is in question can be seen as a feature whose possession by those statements would constitute their being *substantially* true in one or another of the ways suggested by the familiar realist idioms of objective or mind-independent truth, or truth in virtue of some sort of correspondence or fit with external reality.

Minimalism

If minimal truth is to serve Wright's purposes, it must be, as he puts it, a 'metaphysically lightweight' notion, unencumbered by any of the features which import realist commitments. But it cannot, he argues, be the metaphysically *weightless* notion which a distinguished tradition initiated by Ramsey and including Wittgenstein, Ayer and most recently Horwich[52] has taken truth to be. According to this conception – *deflationism* – the truth predicate stands for no real property, but is no more than a mere device of disquotation. That is, the effect of applying the truth predicate to a name of a sentence – say, one formed by enclosing the sentence in quotation marks – is to produce a sentence which says no more and no less than can be said by asserting that very sentence on its own without surrounding quotation marks. Thus on this view, the whole meaning of the truth predicate is exhausted by the Disquotation Schema:

(DS) "P" is true if and only if P

Wright argues that deflationism is unstable, because, when coupled with the seemingly undeniable assumption:

(Neg) Every statement, P, has a negation, not-P

it entails inconsistent claims concerning the relations between truth and warranted assertibility. Both are clearly norms of assertoric discourse, in the sense that in making assertions, we aim at truth, and likewise aim to make assertions we are warranted in making. Deflationism is committed via its endorsement of (DS) to accepting the normativity of the truth predicate, in the sense that reason to think a sentence true is reason to assert or accept it. Indeed, (DS) entails that 'true' and 'warrantedly assertible' *coincide* in *normative force*, in the sense that reason to think a statement true is reason to think it warrantedly assertible, and conversely. But deflationism is also committed, by taking the content of the truth predicate to be exhausted by (DS), to holding that the truth predicate is simply a device of assertoric endorsement and hence to denying that truth is a norm of assertion distinct from being warrantedly assertible. However, it follows from (DS), together with (Neg), that truth and warranted assertibility must be distinct norms of assertion, since the predicates expressing them can diverge in extension. For it follows from (DS) together with (Neg) that:

(1) "It is not the case that P" is true if and only if it is not the case that P

And contraposing on (DS) itself, we have:

(2) It is not the case that P if and only if it is not the case that "P" is true

whence, by the transitivity of the biconditional:

(3) "It is not the case that P" is true if and only if it is not the case that "P" is true

But the result of replacing 'is true' by 'is warrantedly assertible' in (3) is clearly incorrect. Provided that a state of information is possible which is neutral with respect to P – that is, which fails to warrant P or its negation – the resulting biconditional fails right-to-left: it may be that neither "P" nor "It is not the case that P" is warrantedly assertible.[53]

Wright contends that the combination of coincidence in normative force with, but potential divergence in extension from warranted assertibility is not only a necessary condition for something to be a genuine truth predicate, but that it is also sufficient. This is (one way to formulate) what he understands by minimalism about truth. It is worth emphasizing that minimalism about truth is, by itself, perfectly consistent with expressivist or error-theoretic anti-realism about a discourse, since it remains, so far, open to the expressivist to deny that the discourse's utterances are genuinely assertoric, and open to the error theorist to grant their assertoric status but still deny that any of them qualify for even minimal truth. Wright does in fact reject both positions. His rejection of expressivism rests upon the further claim that we should adopt a similarly minimal conception of assertion, according to which it suffices for the sentences of a discourse to be assertoric that they exhibit the appropriate syntactical features (embedding under negation, as antecedents of conditionals, in contexts of propositional attitude reports, and so on) and are subjected to 'communally acknowledged standards of proper use' or what he often calls 'discipline'. His rejection of error theories is more qualified, and the reasons for it too subtle and complex for discussion here.[54]

There is one final point that needs to be made about Wright's minimalism if his positive suggestions about what is or should be at issue in R/AR disputes, to which we shall shortly turn, are not to be misunderstood. This is that the minimalist conception is not put forward as an *analysis* of truth, in direct competition with traditional 'theories of truth' like the Correspondence and Coherence Theories (see Chapter 13, THEORIES OF TRUTH). The claim is, rather, that *any* predicate which both satisfies the Disquotation Schema and exhibits certain features – ultimately those enshrined in or derivable from the 'platitudes', as Wright describes them, that to assert a statement is to present it as true, and that any truth-apt content has a significant negation which is likewise truth-apt – should thereby qualify as *a* truth predicate. It is therefore consistent with acknowledging that there is, or even must be, more to say about the content of any predicate endowed with those features. It is, further, consistent with a certain kind of pluralism about truth – with the idea that the more which there is to say may vary from one discourse to another. If that is so, then the possibility lies open that, while we are entitled to claim truth for both moral judgements, say, and statements about the physical properties of things, the kind of truth we (are entitled to) claim for the former is different from the kind we (are entitled to) claim for the latter, and that they differ in ways germane to R/AR disputes.

Cruces

It is a consequence of this last point that there is nothing in Wright's minimalist conceptions of truth and assertion which excludes – and it is clear that there is nothing which requires – that the notion of truth applicable within a given discourse is an evidentially unconstrained one, of the kind to which a Dummettian realist aspires. Here, then, is one crux at which realists and anti-realists may part company, whilst agreeing that the statements in dispute are minimally truth-apt, and that many of them are true. But a great part of the interest and importance of Wright's reconfiguration of the debate lies in its purported identification of a number of other R/AR cruces where neither protagonist is, or need be, committed to the possibility of evidence-transcendent truth. We can get them into a useful perspective by beginning with a few further remarks on the character of the disagreement between the Dummettian realist and her opponent.

This can be redescribed in terms of Wright's notion of *superassertibility*. Roughly, a statement is superassertible if it is warrantedly assertible and is, as a matter of fact, destined to remain so no matter how our state of information is improved. Less roughly, "A statement is superassertible . . . if and only if it is, or can be, warranted and some warrant for it would survive arbitrarily close scrutiny of its pedigree and arbitrarily extensive increments to or other forms of improvement of our information."[55] This notion, and the claims Wright makes for it, demand a much fuller discussion that can be given here; for present purposes, two points are crucial. The first is that – or so, anyway, Wright argues[56] – the predicate "is superassertible" meets the conditions which the minimalist conception holds to be necessary and sufficient for a truth predicate. Reason to think a statement superassertible is reason to think it is warrantedly assertible and conversely, so that 'superassertible' and 'warrantedly assertible' coincide in normative force; but a statement may be warrantedly assertible and yet not superassertible (increments to our information may destroy our warrant), so that the two predicates may diverge in extension. The second is that superassertibility is essentially an evidentially constrained notion: a statement cannot be superassertible unless we can be warranted in taking it to be so. In virtue of the first point superassertibility can, under certain assumptions, provide an interpretation or model of the truth predicate applicable within a given discourse. But, by the second point, if the truth predicate for a discourse admits of potentially evidence-transcendent applications, then it possesses a feature which superassertibility necessarily lacks and so cannot be so interpreted. A Dummettian R/AR dispute is, then, a dispute concerning the capacity of superassertibility to serve as an adequate interpretation of the truth predicate for the problematic region of discourse. The Dummettian realist contends that the truth predicate has a characteristic – that of potential evidence-transcendence – going beyond anything involved in satisfaction of the minimalist platitudes, which enforces a distinction between truth and superassertibility.

In this case, the additional feature of truth for which the realist contends is one which would require us to accept not only that truth and superassertibility are distinct *notions*, but that they diverge, at least potentially, in *extension*. But could there not, Wright now asks, be supplementary characteristics of the truth predicate for a given discourse which demand a *conceptual* distinction between truth and superassertibility without, however, entailing (potential) divergence in their *extensions?* There should be, if Wright's approach is to assuage the misgivings which – as previously suggested – should lead us to doubt the capacity of Dummett's general characterization to do justice to the variety and richness of R/AR disputes. He contends that there are (at least) three such features, each representing ways in which the notion of objectivity for statements of a given discourse might be interpreted, and so apt to form the focus of R/AR disagreement without raising questions about evidence-transcendence.

One issue is whether the discourse satisfies the *Cognitive Command* constraint, which it will do just in case it is a priori that differences of opinion arising within it can be satisfactorily explained only in terms of something worth describing as a cognitive shortcoming in one or other of the disagreed parties.[57] It might, to illustrate with one of Wright's own examples, seem quite obvious that talk of what's funny, or beautiful, fails this test – comic and aesthetic tastes may simply differ; there will doubtless be a causal explanation why I find Buster Keaton hilarious, or Rubens's women beautiful, while you do not – but it need not be one that finds cognitive fault in either of us. Perhaps the same goes for moral judgement, but this is evidently more arguable, and so could be what's at stake between moral realists and their opponents. Rightly or wrongly, virtually all of us will think that stock-market reports, summaries of football results and rainfall records pass the test.[58]

Another – the *Euthyphro contrast*[59] – concerns whether our (cognitively) best judgements in a given area are to be regarded as tracking an independently constituted realm of facts (the realist view); or whether, rather, we should view truth for the discourse's statements as somehow determined by, or constituted out of, our best judgements (the anti-realist option). The label is intended to recall Plato's dialogue, which has Plato maintaining that pious acts are thought to be so by the gods because those acts are pious, while Euthyphro contends for the opposed view, that pious acts are so because the gods take them to be so. Realist and anti-realist may be presumed to agree that there will be a coincidence between the facts of the matter and our judgements made under optimal conditions. The issue then concerns the direction of dependence: are such judgements true because they match up with independently constituted facts, or are those facts themselves no more than a reflection of our best judgements?

How might it be resolved? Wright's plausible suggestion – developing an idea of Mark Johnston's[60] – is, roughly, that the latter view should prevail if it is knowable a priori that the coincidence should hold. Thus it might with some plausibility be held that the truth of judgements about the colours of things simply consists in their being the judgements suitably endowed perceivers would make under optimal conditions, on the ground that it is guaranteed a priori that best-colour judgements co-vary with the colour facts. By contrast, it might be argued that even if our best judgements about the shapes of two- or three-dimensional things match up with the corresponding shape facts, this is a contingent and a posteriori matter. As Wright emphasizes, the suggested test demands much refinement if it is to be acceptable. For example, it would award the verdict too easily to the anti-realist, say about colour facts, if the conditions for optimal judgement were specified merely as 'whatever conditions are needed and sufficient to ensure that our colour judgements are true'. Rather, it must be possible to provide a substantial and independent characterization, reflecting the detailed epistemology of such judgements. It must also be required that the a priori coincidence of best judgement with the facts is not independently guaranteed, simply by our conception of the relevant facts themselves; for example, we may conceive of pain and other sensations as being such that a sincere and unconfused subject is immune to ignorance and error in her present-tense judgements, but would not wish to say, for this reason, that the facts are constituted out of best judgements.

The third issue focuses on *Wide Cosmological Role*:[61] do the facts which true statements of a given kind record have a role to play in explanations of further facts of other kinds, beyond facts about our beliefs and other attitudes, and can they figure in such explanations other than as objects of those attitudes? It might be contended that while moral or modal beliefs, for example, are apt to figure in explanations of our actions, desires and beliefs, moral or modal facts themselves exert no influence on other goings-on; in contrast, facts about the primary qualities of bodies, for example, exert causal influence in the world at large. To the extent that this is so, we might think that this justifies a kind of realism about facts of the latter kind which is unwarranted in regard to the former.

These quite programmatic suggestions prompt a whole host of questions. How are the various realism-relevant conditions – satisfaction of Cognitive Command, passing the Euthyphro test, possession of Wide Cosmological Role, capacity for Evidence-Transcendent truth – related to one another? Is the first the least that can be required for a species of realism, and a precondition for kinds of realism marked off by the others, as Wright suggests? More generally, do these various conditions admit of a linear ordering, corresponding to more or less robust forms of realism? Is the list complete, or are there other realism-relevant conditions to be discerned? How does the classification relate to R/AR disputes about the existence of entitities of problematic kinds? Is the merely minimal truth of statements of arithmetic, for instance, sufficient for the existence of numbers,[62] or should a more substantial kind of truth be demanded? These and other questions must be left for discussion elsewhere, and have indeed already attracted a good deal of critical attention. To conclude, I shall comment briefly on just three doubts Wright's work has provoked.

While Wright's proposal clearly provides a more inclusive framework for the location and pursuit of R/AR disagreements than Dummett's appears to do, it may be held that there remain forms of opposition to realism which elude it. In particular, it has been claimed that the species of irrealism enjoined by the meaning-sceptical argument advanced by Kripke's Wittgenstein does not fit Wright's agenda, on the ground that it involves rejecting even the application of the supposedly neutral notion of minimal truth to statements about the meanings of words.[63] Minimal truth is a prescriptive or normative notion – this is what sets it apart from a merely disquotational one – and this, so it is claimed, requires that a distinction can be drawn between future applications of words which would be correctly judged to accord our present understanding, and those which would not. But that distinction, in this view, is precisely what Kripke's Wittgenstein argues to be vacuous; so he denies that there are even minimal facts about meaning. Even if this is the right way to understand Kripke's sceptic – so that his position falls below the lower bound, as it were, which Wright thinks realists and anti-realists alike should surpass – I doubt that it amounts to a very serious criticism of his approach. Wright is not committed to claiming that *every* self-styled anti-realist will in fact acknowledge the applicability of minimal truth to problematic discourses; he will agree that expressivists about morals, for example, have denied it. It is another question whether rejection of even minimal truth leaves a defensible position. In the present case, he argues that it does not – that semantic irrealism is inherently unstable, because it inflates into a self-defeating global irrealism.[64]

Wright says that any predicate satisfying the platitudes that define minimal truth ought to be recognized as a truth predicate, adding that we should thus be "at least in principle open to the possibility of a pluralist view of truth: there may be a variety of notions . . . which pass the test".[65] This – together with several further remarks in the same vein – might be taken to evince sympathy with a view according to which 'true' is *ambiguous*, bearing one sense in application to a discourse satisfying Cognitive Command, another when the facts recorded by the discourse enjoy Wide Cosmological Role, and so on. Such an ambiguity thesis, like the somewhat parallel doctrine that 'exists' is ambiguous, bearing different senses as applied to feelings, to tables and chairs, or to numbers and sets, may be held to have little to be said for it and much against, and it may, accordingly, be thought a serious objection to Wright's position if it involves its endorsement. Sainsbury[66] makes this point, but suggests that there is no need for Wright to be committed to it; just as what (mis)leads philosophers into postulating an ambiguity in 'exists' can be accommodated by acknowledging instead that feelings, tables and numbers are different kinds of entity, so, he proposes, Wright is best understood as proposing, not that 'true' is ambiguous, but that different kinds of thing are involved in the truth (uniformly understood as minimal) of statements of different types. This seems to involve saying that moral states of affairs (supposing them to be recorded by statements satisfying at most CC) are of a different kind from, say, those recorded by statements about the primary qualities of bodies (assuming these to satisfy WCR). In support of this suggestion, Sainsbury observes that 'true' does not in fact figure in Wright's formulations of CC, WCR, and others. The attractions of this view are obvious, but it is not clear that it speaks adequately to the threatened objection. Minimalism involves the Correspondence Platitude[67] that a statement is true if and only if it corresponds to the facts: it is thus not clear that Wright could avoid regarding 'true' as ambiguous in Sainsbury's way, since a distinction between different kinds of fact will induce, via this platitude, a distinction between kinds of truth. There is also a certain cost: Wright sees himself as preserving what he takes to be sound in Dummett's characterization of R/AR disputes – that is, the idea that they concern the character of the truth predicate applicable within a problematic discourse – whilst freeing it from the exclusive focus on matters of evidence-transcendence and bivalence. But it does not seem possible to do this without retaining the idea that what the truth of statements consists in varies across different discourses. The question is whether that idea enforces an ambiguity thesis. The analogy sometimes drawn between the assertoric use of language and games may be helpful here. Perhaps, as Wright at one point claims, we may view the minimalist platitudes as encapsulating the essential core of a single notion of truth,[68] which may be filled out in different ways in relation to different discourses, somewhat as what constitutes winning may vary across different games, without inducing any ambiguity in the word 'win'.[69]

A third cause for concern, discussed by Wright himself and pressed by some critics,[70] is that CC may fail to amount to a significant constraint over and above the requirements – syntax and discipline – for merely minimal truth. When Wright first formulates CC, he expresses it as a constraint upon *explanation* of disagreements within the discourse:

> A discourse exhibits Cognitive Command if and only if it is a priori that differences of opinion arising within it can be satisfactorily explained only in terms of "divergent input" . . . or "unsuitable conditions" . . . or "malfunction".[71]

But he quickly falls into another formulation, in terms of the idea that any disagreement must "involve something worth describing as a *cognitive shortcoming*".[72]

There is, of course, no harm done by employing the emphasized words as shorthand for the longer list of specific types of failing appearing in the original formulation. But the shift from the requirement that differences of opinion "can be satisfactorily explained only in terms of" cognitive shortcoming to the requirement that such differences must "involve" such shortcoming is not harmless. It invites a charge of trivialization which Wright himself confronts in this form:

> But it *is* a priori that any difference of opinion concerning the comic, when not attributable to vagueness and so on, must involve cognitive shortcoming, since, if all else fails, ignorance or error will at least be involved *concerning the truth value of the disputed statement.*[73]

The charge troubles Wright, who expends much energy and ingenuity in an effort to meet it by arguing that the trivializing move requires defence of an 'intuitional epistemology" invoking a "special faculty . . . apt for the production of non-inferentially justified beliefs essentially involving its [the discourse's] distinctive vocabulary", but that postulation of such a faculty ought to be constrained by considerations of best explanation which are not easily, and certainly not trivially, satisfied. But Wright has – or so it seems to me – conceded more than he need have done. He could have seen off the trivializer much more swiftly, by reverting to the opening formulation of CC. Suppose you and I are disagreed on some comic matter. Let it be granted that there is error – cognitive shortcoming, even – on one side or the other. Still, we are nowhere near to a satisfactory explanation, *in terms of cognitive shortcoming,*[74] of our disagreement, if all we have is that either I have come short, cognitively speaking, in thinking that p – my shortcoming consisting in the bare fact that I think that p when not-p – or you have come short in denying that p, yours consisting in the bare fact that you think that not-p when p. Appeal to this cannot *explain* our disagreement that I think that p when, as you think, it is the case that not-p is precisely *what* we want *explained.* Doubtless there is an explanation to be had why, say, I think that p when, as you think, not-p. If and when such an explanation is located, it may or may not comply with the requirements of CC – but there is so far no ground for thinking that it will, as the would-be trivializer requires.[75]

Notes

1 In a fuller discussion of the major influences on realist and anti-realist thought over the last twenty years or so, our discussion of Dummett's work would be balanced by an equally extensive examination of that of Hilary Putnam. The hard editorial decision to exclude direct discussion of Putnam's work from the present essay was rendered somewhat easier by the inclusion of a separate chapter devoted to one of his central lines of argument (see Chapter 17, PUTNAM'S MODEL-THEORETIC ARGUMENT AGAINST METAPHYSICAL REALISM). Useful remarks about the relations between the positions of these two major figures in the debate are to be found in Putnam's introduction to the third volume of his philosophical papers (Putnam, 1983) and in Dummett (1994).

2 Frege (1884, p. x and § 62); Dummett (1973a, pp. 192–6, 494–500); Dummett

(1982, p. 239); Dummett (1991, chs. 16, 17); Wright (1983, §§ 2, 3, 5, 8); Hale (1987, pp. 10–14, 152–62, 228–30).

3 Dummett (1963, p. 146).

4 Dummett (1963, p. 146; 1969, p. 358; 1973b, p. 224; 1982, p. 230).

5 As Dummett himself emphasizes, it is important to distinguish between Bivalence and the (putative) logical law of Excluded Middle, which asserts validity of the schema 'A or not-A'. It is, in his considered view, the *semantic* principle of Bivalence on which R/AR disputes turn, rather than the logical law of Excluded Middle, which may be validated in other ways – by the adoption of a supervaluational semantics, for example – which involve, as such, no distinctively realist commitment. In earlier writings, it is the latter which is taken to be at issue; but Dummett subsequently declares this to have been a mistake, shifting attention onto Bivalence (cf. Dummett, 1978, p. xxx).

6 Dummett (1963, pp. 155–6) suggests that rejection of the Law of Excluded Middle need involve no departure from realism. But his views on the matter have shifted in respects going beyond those indicated in the preceding footnote (cf. 1982, p. 265, 1993b, pp. 467–8).

7 For formulations of this argument, see especially Dummett (1969, pp. 362–3) and Wright (1993a, p. 13). See also McGinn (1980, p. 26); Tennant (1981); McGinn (1981); Tennant (1984).

8 For formulations of the argument, see Dummett (1976, pp. 79–83, 1973b, pp. 217, 224; Wright (1993a, pp. 16ff., 53–4). In (1973b, pp. 216–18), Dummett gives three arguments – from communication, from knowledge of meaning, and from learning. The last two of these correspond fairly closely to the acquisition and manifestion arguments as described here. An excellent discussion of these arguments is given in Prawitz (1977).

9 For the original suggestion, see Dummett (1969, p. 363); see also Wright (1993a, pp. 89–90) and McGinn (1980, p. 26).

10 For useful remarks about the difficulty of extending the t-v link gambit to quantification over an infinite domain, see Wright (1993a, pp. 89–90).

11 Cf. McDowell (1978, pp. 132–3); see also Wright (1993a, pp. 90–1).

12 Cf. McDowell (1978, pp. 135–6), McGinn (1980, p. 27) and Wright (1993a, Essay 3, esp. pp. 95ff.).

13 A further difficulty concerns the appeal to the distinction between chronically and merely contingently evidence-transcendent truth. Wright (1993a, p. 14) gives a snappy argument to dispel the comfortable appearance that the former category is populated only by a handful of old chestnuts like those cited as examples. Let P be any statement that is contingently undetectably true. Then the statement that it is so will itself be not only true, but *chronically* undetectably true.

14 For discussion of this issue, see Dummett (1975) and Wright (1982).

15 Cf. Dummett (1976, pp. 98–101). Dummett objects that the suggestion 'fails to answer the question how we come to be able to assign to our sentences a meaning which is dependent upon a use to which we are unable to put them'. McGinn (1980, pp. 27–8), apparently taking himself to be rehearsing Dummett's objection, claims that the difficulty lies not in envisaging the required extension of our capacities, but in seeing how they might be manifested. This would make the acquisition challenge dependent on that based on manifestation. If I am right, the former challenge can be upheld without falling back on the manifestation argument, by appealing instead to the essentially normative character of meaning. Wright (1993a, pp. 23–6) develops an independent

argument from normativity against semantic realism. Although McGinn agrees that none of the responses discussed thus far is effective against the acquisition challenge, he rejects it on the ground that it relies on an unacceptable reductionist assumption that 'no conception can enter into understanding a language that is not induced directly by sensorily presented conditions; any going beyond the observational must be impossible or arbitrary' (1980, pp. 28–9). I cannot discuss this objection fully here, but I do not think it can be right – McGinn gratuitously equates what can be recognized with what can be observationally verified, thereby rendering it utterly mysterious how it is that the anti-realist could possibly regard decidable arithmetic statements as unproblematic.

16 Cf. Currie and Eggenburger (1983, p. 271); Scruton (1976); see also Devitt (1983 and 1984, ch. 12), for suggestions of the first line of response, and McGinn (1980, p. 30) for the second.

17 That is, beliefs having realist truth-conditions, as opposed to beliefs in the correctness of realism. The anti-realist will hardly deny that people may manifest realist beliefs in the latter sense.

18 Cf. Wright (1993a, p. 56) for a fuller statement of the difficulty. Among other attempts to meet the Manifestation Challenge by locating a distinctive explanatory advantage in the hypothesis of realist truth-conditions, perhaps the most impressive and rigorously developed is to be found in recent work by Christopher Peacocke. Regrettably, space does not permit discussion of it here. See especially Peacocke (1986, chs. 2 and 3; 1987; 1988 and 1992b). Wright (1993b) criticizes some of Peacocke's specific proposals.

19 It is not entirely uncontroversial that an anti-realist account of meaning must be revisionary of our inferential practice. Dummett has always argued that it would be (cf. also Tennant 1987) but Wright (1981) defends the opposed view. See also his (1986a), which responds to Rasmussen and Ravnkilde (1982). Wright's considered view is that an anti-realist meaning theory will enforce revision (cf. 1992, ch. 2). In effect, there is a dilemma here for the realist who would appeal to actual inferential practice to meet the manifestation challenge: *either* semantic anti-realism must be revisionary of such practice, *or* it need not be; if so, then appeal to the practice begs the question by assuming that it is beyond criticism, as out of line with the kind of meaning we have assigned to our statements; if not, then the appeal falls flat, since the practice is not distinctively realist after all.

20 Strawson (1977, p. 16).

21 This criticism assumes that Strawson is seeking to make out an operational difference between realist and anti-realist practice. But it is possible that he has in mind a somewhat different, and potentially stronger, line of argument according to which, whilst nothing in our linguistic practice as such marks it out as realist, there are theoretical considerations which constrain us to view it as informed by realist conceptions. This line of thought is pursued in Edgington (1985) and J. Campbell (1994).

22 Dummett (1973b, p. 217).

23 Blackburn (1984, pp. 65–6; 1989).

24 Cf. Dummett (1976, pp. 81–2).

25 Cf. Wright (1993a, pp. 20–1).

26 Among important recent work which it has not been possible to discuss here, I should mention Blackburn (1989) and Wright's reply (1989b). A sophisticated attempt to show that acceptance of the manifestation requirement is to be found in Peacocke (1986).

27 Cf. Dummett (1963, pp. 146–7).

28 Dummett (1993b, p. 465). This particularly useful paper summarizes, defends and in places qualifies the general approach first adopted in Dummett (1963) and developed in several papers over the intervening three decades.

29 Dummett (1963, pp. 145–7; 1992, pp. 464–5).

30 Dummett (1963, p. 147).

31 P. 273; cf. also Wright (1993a, pp. 8–9).

32 The charge that Dummett mislocates 'the realism issue' is pressed by Devitt (1983 and 1984, ch. 12). An excellent discussion of the charge is given in Taylor (1987).

33 For this line of reply, see Dummett (1993b, pp. 468–71). For extensive discussion of the contrast between reductionist and non-reductionist forms of anti-realism, and detailed argument for the claim that the latter affords the basis of a sustainable anti-realist challenge in areas besides mathematics, see Dummett (1963, pp. 156–65, and 1982, esp. pp. 239–63).

34 Cf. Hume (1739 Bk. III, Pt. I, Sec. II); Ayer (1946, Introduction, pp. 20–2 and ch. VI).

35 Cf. Blackburn (1984, pp. 210–17; 1986 *passim*).

36 Mackie (1977, ch. 1), Field (1980, pp. 1–16, and 1989, Essays 1 and 2); Churchland (1979); Stich (1983); the special issue of *Mind and Language* 8 (2), 1993 devoted to Eliminativism contains several papers relevant to error-theoretical treatments of psychological discourse.

37 Dummett (1993b) draws a distinction between what he terms 'objectivist' and 'subjectivist' attitudes towards a class of 'apparent assertibles'. A subjectivist about moral utterances takes an expressivist view of them, contending that they serve to voice attitudes or feelings, rather than to make genuine statements. In contrast with this, Dummett says, he was all along concerned with R/AR disputes between parties both of which took an objectivist view of statements in the problematic class, adding that 'the dispute between the subjectivist and the "moral realist" is not one of those to which my comparative method was meant to apply: the issues in that dispute are different and prior to it' (p. 467). Doubtless Dummett is quite right that a significant disagreement about what notion of truth – one that is evidentially constrained or one that is not – has application within the problematic class will take place against the shared assumption that those statements are indeed truth-apt. The fact remains that subjectivism, in Dummett's sense, is one form which opposition to realism may assume, but one which his preferred characterization of R/AR disputes simply passes by. Indeed, it is hard not to read Dummett's remark as implicitly conceding as much.

38 Cf. Wright (1993a, p. 4).

39 Cf. Sorensen (1988, pp. 199–253; 1995); Williamson (1992; 1994a and b); Cargile (1969; 1979, § 36); R. Campbell (1974); and see Chapter 18, SORITES. The epistemicist conception is criticized in Hyde (1995) and also in Wright (1995), to which Sorensen (1995) replies.

40 Cf. Dummett (1993b, p. 468). Indeed, on what may be the most defensible version of the epistemicist view – see Williamson (1992) – it is not merely that we *do not* know the truth-values of vague statements – we *cannot* know them.

41 He writes: "An anti-realist may . . . [hold] that reality itself may be vague, whereas, for the realist, vagueness inheres only in our forms of description". Dummett (1993b, p. 468). For a searching assessment of attempts to make the contrast in this way, see Sainsbury (1995).

42 Cf. Field (1980 and 1989).

43 More accurately, mathematical statements are never non-vacuously true – for whilst those which carry categorical existential commitments, like "There exist prime numbers greater than 10^{17}", will be false, general laws like "a + b = b + a" will, if construed as universally quantified material conditionals (e.g. "For all a, b: if a and b are numbers, then a + b = b + a"), be true, but merely vacuously, precisely because no objects satisfy their main antecedents.

44 A closely related anti-realist position in philosophy of science is van Fraassen's constructive empiricism, according to which good theoretical science aims, not at correct description of unobservable realities, but at empirical adequacy – that is, roughly, at maximizing derivability of correct observationally checkable conclusions from observationally verifiable premisses. See van Fraassen (1980, ch. 1).

45 This necessarily simplified formulation of the objection corresponds closely to that given in Hale (1987, pp. 106–15). For more careful presentations, see Hale and Wright (1992 and 1994). Field (1989, pp. 43–5) attempts to defuse the objection, and (1993) more fully, to which the last-cited paper by Hale and Wright replies.

46 Geach (1965).

47 Blackburn (1984, p. 171). Blackburn (1984, ch. 6) develops his programme, and in several of the essays in his (1993).

48 For a more detailed explanation, together with a sketch of what Blackburn takes to be the underlying logical form of expressive/evaluative compounds, see his (1984, pp. 189–96).

49 Cf. Wright (1988a, p. 33) and Hale (1992). Blackburn (1988) makes a significantly different attempt to preserve a projectivist construal of moral utterances. This later theory cannot be discussed here. It is criticised in detail in Hale (1992). See also Gibbard (1990) and Zangwill (1992).

50 Should this be construed as expressing disapproval of Henry's saying whatever it was without apologizing? Or as expressing approval for combining the belief that Henry said whatever it was with approval for his apologizing? The former seems to lose the distinction between the case where the speaker believes that Henry spoke offensively and that where she wants to leave that question open. The latter looks to run into trouble explaining why we don't assert conditionals with evaluative antecedents and factual consequents, like 'If Henry ought to apologize, he said that.' Both approaches appear committed to locating a hitherto unnoticed ambiguity in the conditional construction.

51 Cf. Blackburn (1984, p. 217).

52 Ramsey (1927); Wittgenstein (1922, 1953); Ayer (1946, pp. 78–90), Horwich (1990).

53 As Wright himself points out, Hilary Putnam's suggested equation of truth with warranted assertibility under ideal epistemic circumstances (cf. his 1981, p. 55) encounters a similar difficulty. But the issue is delicate – see Wright (1992, pp. 37–42).

54 See Wright (1992, pp. 86–7).

55 Wright (1992, p. 48). The notion made its first appearance in his paper "Can a Davidsonian Meaning-Theory be construed in terms of Assertibility?", Essay 14 in Wright (1993a, cf. esp. pp. 411–18).

56 Wright (1992, pp. 44–70).

57 Cf. Wright (1992, chs 2, 3). A fuller specification of the constraint is given on pp. 92–3, where the notion of cognitive shortcoming is fleshed out – the disputants are not to be 'working on the basis of different information (and hence guilty of ignorance or

error . . .), or "unsuitable conditions" (resulting in inattention or distraction and so in inferential error, or oversight of data and so on), or "malfunction" (for example, prejudicial assessment of data, upwards or downwards, or dogma, or failings in other categories . . .)'. Clearly this does not purport to be a finished list. Earlier, related formulations appear in Wright (1980; see pp. 448–9, 1986b and 1989a).

58 It merits emphasis – since statements from a discourse apt for merely minimal truth have to be 'disciplined' (i.e. subject to standards of correct assertion) – that Cognitive Command is a global constraint. *Any* disagreement over one of its statements must be traceable to cognitive shortcoming, if a discourse is to satisfy CC; whereas while particular disagreements within a merely minimally truth-apt discourse may be rationally resolvable, cognitively blameless diagreement is not ruled out a priori. CC – or so Wright intends – is to take up the slack left by minimal truth-aptness.

59 Cf. Wright (1992, pp. 108–39), also Wright (1988b).

60 The source was unpublished material. Johnston (1992, esp. Appendix 3) gives an impression of his later views on the matter.

61 Cf. Wright (1992, pp. 174–201), Divers and Miller (1995) and Oppy (forthcoming).

62 Wright (1992, pp. 28–9).

63 Cf. Edwards (1994, pp. 63–5).

64 See Chapter 15, RULE-FOLLOWING, OBJECTIVITY AND MEANING, sect. 3, and further references given there.

65 Wright (1992, p. 25).

66 Sainsbury (1996); see also Pettit (1996) and Jackson (1994).

67 Wright (1992, pp. 25–7).

68 Wright (1992, p. 38).

69 Cf. Wright (1996).

70 Sainsbury (1996).

71 Wright (1992, pp. 92–3).

72 Wright (1992, p. 93); cf. his reformulation of CC at p. 144.

73 Wright (1992, p. 149).

74 There will, doubtless, be a causal explanation of some sort to be found, but that is beside the point.

75 Two caveats: (a) this suggestion assumes that Wright's later formulations of CC bring no advantage that is lost by reverting to the earlier ones; (b) there may be other ways to press the trivialization threat (cf. Sainsbury 1996 and Williamson 1994a) which cannot be defused by the simple move proposed here, and which call for a fuller discussion than space permits.

Thanks to Jim Edwards and Crispin Wright for very helpful comments.

References and further reading

Ayer, A.J. 1946: *Language, Truth and Logic.* 2nd edn, London: Victor Gollancz.

Blackburn, Simon 1980: Truth, realism and the regulation of theory. *Midwest Studies in Philosophy*, 5, reprinted Blackburn (1993).

——1984: *Spreading the Word: Groundings in the Philosophy of Language.* Oxford: Clarendon Press.

——1986: Morals and modals. In G. Macdonald and C. Wright (eds), *Fact, Science and Morality*. Oxford: Blackwell, reprinted in Blackburn (1993), 119–42.

——1988: Attitudes and contents. *Ethics*, 98, 501–17.

——1989: Manifesting realism. *Midwest Studies in Philosophy*, 14, 29–47.
——1990: Wittgenstein's irrealism. In J. Brandl and R. Haller (eds), *Wittgenstein: ein Neubewehrung*. Vienna: Hölder-Pinchler-Tempky, 13–26.
——1993: *Essays in Quasi-Realism*. New York, Oxford: Oxford University Press.
Campbell, John 1994: *Past, Space, and Self*. Cambridge, Mass., London: MIT Press.
Campbell, Richmond 1974: The sorites paradox. *Philosophical Studies*, 26, 175–91.
Cargile, James 1969: The sorites paradox. *British Journal for the Philosophy of Science*, 20, 193–202.
—— 1979: *Paradoxes*. Cambridge: Cambridge University Press.
Churchland, Paul 1979: *Scientific Realism and the Plasticity of Mind*. Cambridge, New York : Cambridge University Press.
Currie, Gregory, and Eggenburger, Peter 1983: Knowledge and meaning. *Noûs*, 17, 267–79.
Davidson, Donald 1977: Reality without reference. *Dialectica*, 31, reprinted in Davidson (1984).
——1984: *Inquiries into Truth and Interpretation*. Oxford: Clarendon Press.
Devitt, Michael 1983: Dummett's anti-Realism. *Journal of Philosophy*, 80, 73–99.
——1984: *Realism and Truth*. Oxford: Blackwell.
Divers, John, and Miller, Alexander 1994: Rethinking realism: John Haldane and Crispin Wright, eds, *Reality, Representation and Projection*. *Mind*, 103 (412), 519–33.
——1995: Minimalism and the unbearable lightness of being. *Philosophical Papers*, 24 (2), 127–39.
Dummett, Michael 1959: Truth. *Aristotelian Society Proceedings*, 59, reprinted, with additions, in Dummett (1978), 1–24.
——1963: Realism. Reprinted in Dummett (1978), 145–65.
——1969: The reality of the past. *Aristotelian Society Proceedings*, 69, reprinted in Dummett (1978), 358–74.
——1973a: *Frege: Philosophy of Language*. London: Duckworth.
——1973b: The philosophical basis of intuitionistic logic. In H.E. Rose and J.C. Shepherdson (eds) *Logic Colloquium 1973*, reprinted in Dummett (1978), 215–47.
——1975: Wang's paradox. *Synthese*, 30, reprinted in Dummett (1978), 248–68.
——1976: What is a theory of meaning? (2) In Evans and McDowell (eds), *Truth and Meaning*. Oxford: Oxford University Press, 67–137.
——1977: *Elements of Intuitionism*. Oxford Logic Guides, Oxford: Oxford University Press.
——1978: *Truth and Other Enigmas*. London: Duckworth.
——1982: Realism. *Synthese* 52 (1), 55–112, reprinted in Dummett (1993).
—— 1991: *Frege: Philosophy of Mathematics*. London: Duckworth.
——1993a: Realism and antirealism. In Dummett (1993b), 464–78.
——1993b: *The Seas of Language*. Oxford: Oxford University Press.
——1994: Wittgenstein on necessity. In Peter Clark and Bob Hale (eds), *Reading Putnam*. Oxford: Blackwell.
Edgington, Dorothy 1985: Verification and the manifestation of meaning. *Aristotelian Society Suppl*, 59, 33–52.
Edwards, Jim 1994: Debates about realism transposed into a new key: Crispin Wright, *Truth and Objectivity*. *Mind*, 103 (409), 59–72.
Field, Hartry 1980: *Science without Numbers*. Oxford: Basil Blackwell.
——1989: *Realism, Mathematics and Modality*. Oxford: Basil Blackwell.
——1993: The conceptual contingency of mathematical objects. *Mind*, 102 (406), 285–99.

Frege, Gottlob 1884: *Die Grundlagen der Arithmetik.* Breslau: Wilhelm Koebner. Translated into English by J.L. Austin as *The Foundations of Arithmetic,* revised edn. Oxford: Blackwell 1959.

Geach, Peter 1965: Assertion. *Philosophical Review,* 74, 449–65.

Gibbard, Allan 1990: *Wise Choices, Apt Feelings.* Cambridge, Mass.: Harvard University Press.

Haldane, John and Wright, Crispin (eds) 1992: *Reality, Representation and Projection.* Oxford: Oxford University Press .

Hale, Bob 1986: The compleat projectivist. (Critical notice of Blackburn 1984). *Philosophical Quarterly,* 36, 65–84.

——1987: *Abstract Objects.* Oxford: Basil Blackwell.

——1992: Can there be a logic of attitudes? In Haldane and Wright (1992).

Hale, Bob and Wright, Crispin 1992: Nominalism and the contingency of abstract objects. *Journal of Philosophy,* 89, 111–35.

——1994: A reductio ad surdum? Field on the contingency of mathematical objects. *Mind,* 103 (410), 169–84.

Horwich, Paul 1982: Three forms of realism. *Synthese,* 51 (2), 181–202.

——1990: *Truth.* Oxford: Basil Blackwell.

Hume, David 1739: *A Treatise of Human Nature.* Selby-Bigge (ed.) Oxford: Oxford University Press, 1888.

Hyde, Dominic 1995: Review of Williamson (1994b) in *Mind,* 104, 919–25.

Jackson, Frank 1994: Review of Wright (1992). *Philosophical Books,* 35, 162–9.

Johnston, Mark 1992: Objectivity refigured. In Haldane and Wright (1992).

Mackie, John 1977: *Ethics – Inventing Right and Wrong.* Harmondsworth: Penguin.

McDowell, John 1978: On 'The reality of the past'. In C. Hookway and P. Pettit (eds), *Action and Interpretation.* Cambridge: Cambridge University Press.

——1981a: Non-cognitivism and rule-following. In S.H. Holtzman and C.M. Leich (eds), *Wittgenstein: To Follow a Rule.* London: Routledge and Kegan Paul.

——1981b: Anti-realism and the epistemology of understanding. In H. Parret and J. Bouveresse (eds), *Meaning and Understanding.* Berlin, New York: Walter de Gruyter.

McGinn, Colin 1979: An a priori argument for realism. *Journal of Philosophy,* 76, 113–33.

——1980: Truth and use. In Platts (1980), 19–40.

——1981: Reply to Tennant. *Analysis,* 41, 120–22.

——1982: Realist semantics and content ascription. *Synthese,* 52 (1), 113–34.

Oppy, Graham forthcoming: Minimalism, fiction and ethical truth.

Peacocke, Christopher 1986: *Thoughts: An Essay on Content.* Oxford: Basil Blackwell.

——1987: Understanding logical constants: a realist's account'. *Proceedings of the British Academy,* 73, 153–200.

——1988: The limits of intelligibility: a post-verificationist proposal. *Philosophical Review,* 97, 463–96.

——1992a: Truth and Proof. In Haldane and Wright (1992).

——1992b: *A Study of Concepts.* Cambridge, Mass., and London: MIT Press.

Pettit, Philip 1996: contribution to book symposium on Wright 1992 in *Philosophy and Phenomenological Research.*

Platts, Mark (ed.) 1980: *Reference, Truth and Reality.* London: Routledge and Kegan Paul.

Prawitz, Dag 1977: Meaning and proofs: on the conflict between classical and intuitionist logic. *Theoria,* 43, 2–40.

Putnam, Hilary 1981: *Reason, Truth and History.* Cambridge: Cambridge University Press.

——1982: 'Why there isn't a ready-made world'. *Synthese*, 51 (2), 141–68, reprinted in Putnam (1983).
——1983: *Realism and Reason: Philosophical Papers*, Vol. 3. Cambridge: Cambridge University Press.
Ramsey, F.P. 1927: Facts and propositions. *Aristotelian Society Proceedings*, suppl. Vol. 7, 153–70.
Rasmussen, Stig and Ravnkilde, Jens 1982: Realism and logic. *Synthese*, 52, 379–437.
Sainsbury, R.M. 1995: Why the world cannot be vague. Spindel Conference 1994: Vagueness (*The Southern Journal of Philosophy*, 33, Supplement), 1–19.
——1996: contribution to book symposium on Wright (1992) in *Philosophy and Phenomenological Research.*
Scruton, Roger 1976: Truth-conditions and criteria. *Aristotelian Society Supp.*, Vol. 50, 193–216.
Sorensen, Roy 1988: *Blindspots*. Oxford: Oxford University Press.
——1995: Reply to Wright (1995) in supplement to *The Southern Journal of Philosophy*, 33, 161–70.
Stich, Stephen 1983: *From Folk Psychology to Cognitive Science: The Case Against Belief.* Cambridge, Mass.: MIT Press.
Strawson, Peter 1977: Scruton and Wright on anti-realism, etc. *Aristotelian Society Proceedings*, 77, 15–22.
Taylor, Barry 1987: The truth in realism. *Revue Internationale de Philosophie*, 41 45–63.
Tennant, Neil 1981: Is this a proof I see before me? *Analysis*, 41, 115–19.
——1984: Were those disproofs I saw before me? *Analysis*, 44 97–105.
——1987: *Anti-Realism and Logic*. Oxford: Oxford University Press.
van Fraassen, Bas 1980: *The Scientific Image*. Oxford: Oxford University Press.
Wiggins, David 1976: Truth, invention and the meaning of life. *Proceedings of the British Academy*, 62, 331–78.
Williamson, Timothy 1992: Vagueness and ignorance. In *Aristotelian Society Supp.*, 66, 145–62.
——1994a: Critical study of Wright 1992. *International Journal of Philosophical Studies*, 2, 130–44 .
——1994b: *Vagueness*. London and New York: Routledge.
Wittgenstein, Ludwig 1922: *Tractatus Logico-Philosophicus*. London: Routledge and Kegan Paul.
——1953: *Philosophical Investigations*. Oxford: Basil Blackwell.
Wright, Crispin 1980: *Wittgenstein on the Foundations of Mathematics*. London: Duckworth.
——1981: Dummett and revisionism. *Philosophical Quarterly*, 31, 47–67.
——1982: Strict finitism. *Synthese*, 51, reprinted in Wright (1993a).
——1983: *Frege's Conception of Numbers as Objects*. Aberdeen: Aberdeen University Press.
——1984: Can a Davidsonian meaning-theory be construed in terms of assertibility? In Wright (1993).
——1986a: Realism, bivalence and classical logic. In Wright (1993a).
——1986b: Inventing logical necessity. In J. Butterfield (ed), *Language, Mind and Logic*. Cambridge: Cambridge University Press, 187–209.
——1988a: Realism, anti-realism, irrealism, quasi-realism. *Midwest Studies*. 12, 25–49.
——1988b: Moral values, projection and secondary qualities. *Aristotelian Society Suppl.* Vol. 62, 1–26.
——1989a: Necessity, caution and scepticism. *Aristotelian Society Suppl.*, Vol. 63, 203–38.

——1989b: Misconstruals made manifest. *Midwest Studies in Philosophy*, 14, 48–67.
——1992: *Truth and Objectivity*. Cambridge, Mass., and London: Harvard University Press.
——1993a: *Realism, Meaning and Truth*. 2nd edn., Oxford: Basil Blackwell.
——1993b: A note on two realist lines of argument. In Wright (1993a).
——1994a: Reply to Jackson 1994. *Philosophical Books*, 35, 169–75.
——1994b: Reply to Williamson. *International Journal of Philosophical Studies*, 2, 327–41.
—— 1995: The epistemic conception of vagueness. In supplement to *The Southern Journal of Philosophy*, 33, 133–59.
——1996: Contribution to book symposium on Wright (1992) in *Philosophy and Phenomenological Research*.
Zangwill, Nick 1992: Moral modus ponens. *Ratio*, 5 (2), 177–93.

13

Theories of truth

RALPH C. S. WALKER

1 Introduction: problems with correspondence

There are often said to be five main "theories of truth": the correspondence theory, the coherence theory, and the pragmatic, redundancy and semantic theories. It is not really clear how far these theories are in competition with one another, for it is not clear how far they address the same question. However, they are all concerned with truth and falsity as properties of what people say or think. There are other uses of "truth" and "true", as when we speak of a true friend; but these are set aside, perhaps as derivative, at any rate as different.

Various views are held about how the content of what we say or think should be specified, and thus about what the bearers of truth are. Some people would specify it in terms of sentences, pieces of language, as uttered by a particular speaker at a particular time; for them, these would be the bearers of truth. Others would say that truth-bearers are statements or propositions, where these are thought of as what meaningful utterances of sentences express. Others again would say that they are judgements, mental contents which may or may not be expressible in language but which nevertheless embody thoughts. For many purposes this issue is a red herring; where it is not, I shall call attention to the fact. But in general, theories of truth have been concerned with a relation between the world and what we say or think about it; and much of the time it matters little whether the content of our thought is taken to be a judgement, a proposition or just a sentence.

The correspondence theory of truth holds that for a judgement (or, say, a proposition) to be true is for it to correspond with the facts. In a sense this is obvious, but taken in that way the theory is unilluminating. Colloquially, "corresponds with the facts" can function as a long-winded way of saying "is true": so understood, the alleged theory becomes an empty tautology. To have content, it must at least claim that for a judgement to be true is for it to stand in a certain relationship ("correspondence") with something independent of that judgement, a fact or state of affairs in the world. Since this still seems hard to disagree with, it is natural to think that a correspondence theory fully worthy of the name must go on to say something substantial about the relationship of correspondence, and also about the facts or states of affairs with which true judgements correspond. The paradigm of such a theory is Wittgenstein's in the *Tractatus*, and we shall return to it. It is not, however, clear that anything can be said about the correspondence relation, except that it is the relation in which a proposition stands to the world when it is true; nor is it clear that the relevant facts, or states of affairs, can be specified except as those which make a particular proposition true. These are standard objections to the correspondence theory. That they are plausible objections can be borne out by the odd position one can get into if one takes the correspondence theory, in this strong form, really seriously. Russell held such a view, in his Logical Atomist phase, and became much exercised over whether the world contains negative facts or not (Russell, 1956, pp. 211ff.). Is "The Queen is not bald" true in virtue of its correspondence with a special negative fact, or just in virtue of its lack of correspondence with any positive facts? For someone who held the correspondence theory in its strong form this would seem a real issue; others might think the theory had taken us off the rails.

2 The coherence theory and the pragmatic theory

The coherence theory of truth equates the truth of a judgement with its coherence with other beliefs. Different versions of the theory give different accounts of coherence, but in all its forms the point is to exhibit truth as an internal relation between beliefs. The theory holds that the truth, or falsity, of a belief can be determined by discovering whether or not it meets the appropriate test of coherence. In all its forms, again, the coherence in question is coherence with other things that are believed or subscribed to, or at least with other things that would be believed or subscribed to under specifiably ideal circumstances. The coherence theory is therefore not committed to the absurdity of accepting as true an arbitrary set of propositions which happens to be internally coherent. Whatever the standards of coherence may be, it seems likely that alternative sets of propositions will meet them: as Russell (1906–7) pointed out, although the highly respectable Bishop Stubbs died in his bed, the proposition "Bishop Stubbs was hanged for murder" can readily be conjoined with a whole group of others to form a set which passes any plausible coherence test; and indeed, the same can be said of the propositions that make up any good work of realistic fiction. Russell thought this an objection to the coherence theory, but it is not, for the coherence theory is concerned with coherence not amongst arbitrary propositions, but amongst beliefs.

As to whose beliefs, different versions of the theory again hold different things. Some would equate them with the beliefs held by our society; or, perhaps, the beliefs held by humankind in general. Since the beliefs even of a single person will include some that are inconsistent, what is required cannot be coherence with all the beliefs in question but with a majority, or with a majority weighted in some way, perhaps in terms of how deeply they are held. Even so, we normally think that many of our most deeply held beliefs may turn out false, as beliefs in demons have done; and we also think that many of the truths to be discovered in years to come could not be shown to be true simply by their coherence with our present beliefs. Hence some coherence theorists regard truth not as coherence with what we actually do believe, but with what we would believe under idealized circumstances – perhaps, as Peirce (1878) suggested, at the end of all human enquiry. Anyone taking this line must have in mind some non-trivial specification of what these circumstances would be; if they were just "the circumstances under which we would believe the truth" the theory would collapse into vacuity. Other coherence theorists, perhaps more prominent in the past than at present, have met the same difficulties by a different move, regarding truth as coherence not with human beliefs, actual or potential, but with the beliefs of God or of an Absolute Mind.

Coherence theorists differ, again, over how widely they extend their equation of truth with coherence. Some make it cover truth of all kinds; theirs could be called pure coherence theories of truth. Others extend it more narrowly, to cover only truth of a particular kind – moral truth, perhaps, or the truth of theoretical statements in science. Perhaps the commonest position is intermediate between these, and equates truth quite generally with coherence amongst beliefs, except for recognizing a special place for sense-experience. A plausible reading of Kant ascribes such a coherence theory to him, so far as the world of appearances is concerned. The coherence that is equated with truth is, then, a coherence not just amongst beliefs, but also with the deliverances of sense-experience, or, as Kant (1781/7, A218/B266) puts it, "with the material conditions of experience, that is, with sensation". On such a view, certain beliefs will be directly supported by sense-experience, and the truth or falsity of these will be a matter of how well they fit with the experience. There will be others whose relation to sense-experience is less direct, and whose truth is a matter of coherence within the system of beliefs, including, of course, those beliefs directly related to experience. A pure coherence theory, in contrast, would say that even for those beliefs that seem most immediately experiential – "I seem to see something blue" – truth is a matter of coherence, coherence presumably with other beliefs that the subject has or others have at the same or later times (such as the belief that there was an ink-bottle there, that people's impressions of their own experience are usually reliable, and so on).

The pragmatic theory of truth is akin to a coherence theory of this Kantian kind. It holds that the truth of a belief is a matter of whether it "works", that is, whether acting upon it pays off. Acting on it pays off just in case the experiences we have are those the belief led us to expect. Thus the pragmatic theory also makes truth a matter of coherence, but coherence with future experience (Peirce, 1878; James, 1907; Dewey, 1938; and cf. Misak, 1991). The Kantian theory takes this view of one class of beliefs, except that it does not give special weight to future experience over experience past or present. Pragmatists have often moved towards mixed theories of the Kantian type, both by giving equal weight to experience at any time, and by allowing that not all beliefs have their truth-values determined by experience directly: for some, truth is a matter of coherence amongst beliefs. Quine's position is a variant of this (Quine, 1969). For him there is a difference between the two types of belief, but one of degree only. Whether the resulting theory should be called a coherence theory or a pragmatic theory seems arbitrary.

3 Coherence and correspondence

The correspondence theory, the coherence theory and the pragmatic theory are often presented as alternatives only one of which can be true. We have seen something of how the coherence theory and the pragmatic theory relate; but there is no reason why a coherence theorist, or a pragmatist, should not accept the correspondence theory in any of the forms so far described. No sensible coherence theorist will deny that truths correspond with the facts, in that sense of "correspond with the facts" in which it is a synonym for "are true". No coherence theorist need deny the uncontentious claim that for a judgement to be true is for it to stand in a certain relationship, which can be called correspondence, with some state of affairs in the world. As to the more disputable form of correspondence theory, which attempts to elucidate the relationship by saying something substantive and illuminating about the relation of correspondence and about facts or states of affairs, there is no reason why a coherence theorist should not subscribe to that as well – unless, of course, there are considerations against such a theory which render it untenable for anyone.

Why, then, are the coherence and correspondence theories taken to be incompatible? For that we need more precision about what the coherence theory claims. So far I have been describing coherence theorists as "equating" truth with coherence; but that is vague. The coherence theory of truth is the theory that truth is *constituted by* coherence amongst beliefs; likewise, the pragmatic theory of truth is the theory that truth is *constituted by* conformity to (usually future) experience. These theories seek to tell us what the truth of a judgement consists in, or, in other words, to exhibit the essential nature of truth. Neither theory is merely asserting a biconditional, nor even a necessary biconditional. It is uncontroversial that we use coherence amongst beliefs as a test of truth, and that we use conformity to experience in the same way. Without subscribing to either theory of truth, someone might well hold that a belief is true if and only if it passes one or other of these tests. We normally suppose that on the whole our beliefs reflect reality, and that those are true which cohere with experience and with the web of our other beliefs. Even if one believed that the biconditional held necessarily, one might still not be either a pragmatist or a coherence theorist of truth. One might, perhaps, hold that reality was itself coherent as a matter of metaphysical necessity, and that as a matter of the same necessity our beliefs about it are, on the whole, largely true. Something like this was the view of Bradley. Bradley is often said to have held a coherence theory of truth; but that is a mistake, and the mistake lies in the failure to see the difference between a theory that says truth consists in coherence, and one which only says that, of necessity, propositions are true if and only if they meet the coherence test. For Bradley the truth of a judgement consists in its matching reality, though because of the nature of reality a judgement can be true necessarily-iff it satisfies the requirements of coherence (Bradley, 1893, chs. 13–15 and 24). For the coherence theory of truth, on the other hand, it is in the satisfaction of those requirements that the truth of a judgement consists.

A claim about what truth consists in is not usually intended to be analytic. It is not supposed to be a claim about concepts, but rather to be about what that property, truth, really is. In this it resembles the claim that the heat of a body is the mean kinetic energy of its molecules. Neither claim is supposed to be established by considering what we ordinarily mean by our words, or by examining what is "contained in our concepts"; quite how they are to be established is a difficult question, of course, but establishing such things is part of the traditional task of metaphysics. Coherence theorists think philosophical reflection can show that there is nothing else than coherence for truth to amount to. Their claim is therefore that truth is the same property as coherence, but that to characterize it as coherence is more adequate, more illuminating of its nature.

The coherence theory of truth is thus a radical, and at first sight highly counterintuitive, thesis. True propositions can be said to correspond to facts, but since the theory holds that truth consists in coherence, the facts themselves are not independent of this coherence that determines truth. Coherence determines what propositions are true, and therefore what the facts are. Hence the facts are determined by what is believed, or would be under specifiable circumstances; not, of course, that whatever is believed is true, but the truth is what coheres with the main body of beliefs, and can be equated with what would be believed by someone who believed all and only those propositions that so cohere. This is not the view of common sense. The commonsense view is that facts are what they are independently of what anyone believes about them, and independently of what anyone would believe about them under idealized circumstances – unless the idealization were of the trivial kind (such as "under those circumstances in which people would believe what is true"). Truth is, then, a matter of beliefs or propositions matching this independent reality. That gives us another sense, importantly different from the ones noticed before, in which we can speak of a correspondence theory of truth: as a name for this commonsense view. In this sense, unlike the others, the correspondence theory is incompatible with the coherence theory. It asserts just what the coherence theory denies, namely that truth consists in a relation between the proposition in question and something in the world which makes it true, where this something is taken to obtain independently of what anyone believes (or would believe) about it. Like the coherence theory, then, it is a theory about what truth consists in.

The classical proponents of the pragmatic theory are Peirce and James, and it is sometimes difficult to be sure exactly what their theory is; but as I have implied, it (usually) appears also to be a theory about what truth consists in. If it is not, it collapses into the claim that it is by its consonance with (future) experience that we discover what is true; but it would be distinctly misleading to call that epistemological thesis a theory of truth – just as it would be misleading to give that title to the claim that truth is discovered by testing for coherence amongst our beliefs. To the extent to which they reject the coherence theory, pragmatists can accept that truth is a relation between a proposition and something that is independent of what anyone believes; but only because they think of it as constituted, not by beliefs, but by experiences, which they take to be independent of and prior to our beliefs about them. Actually, though, it would be difficult to maintain quite *generally* that the truth of a belief consists in its consonance with experience, because alternative theories – inconsistent with one another – can each predict exactly the same empirical consequences. (Thus the Ptolemaic hypothesis, or the flat-earth theory, can be made to yield all the same predictions as more usual views, with sufficient adjustments to assumptions elsewhere.) Hence the pragmatist must accept coherence as a determinant of truth as well as consonance with experience; coherence, for example, with our ideas about simplicity of theory becomes of central importance for Quine (1969; cf. Peirce, 1878). So the pragmatist's position will be very much the same as that of those coherence theorists who allow a special place for experience; and it will be similarly counter-intuitive. The commonsense view of the matter regards the facts as obtaining independently of anyone's experiences of them, just as it regards them as independent of anyone's beliefs about them. So when "the correspondence theory of truth" is used as a name for this commonsense view, we can take it as holding that truth consists in a relation between a proposition and something in the world that makes it true, where this something obtains independently of anyone's experiences of it and of anyone's beliefs about it.[1]

4 Why pragmatic and coherence theories are attractive

It is no objection to a philosophical position that it is counter-intuitive. Pragmatists and coherence theorists would say that much of the attraction of what I have called the commonsense view derives from failing to distinguish it from "the correspondence theory of truth" in one of the other senses of that term. In any case they adopt their position, not because it seems to be what we normally think, or part of the ordinary meaning of "true", but because they feel there are strong pressures requiring us to accept what they hold about the nature of truth. These pressures are from considerations about knowledge and from considerations about meaning. To a large extent they gain their force from the fact that the commonsense view seems to leave open an awkward possibility: that our thoughts and our beliefs should wholly fail to describe the world around us. This is the possibility raised by Descartes' idea of the *malin génie*. If the world – the facts or the states of affairs that determine the truth-values of our propositions – is wholly independent of our beliefs about it and our experiences of it, what assurance could we ever have that our beliefs are really true?

The obvious answer is that, although the world is independent of our experiences and beliefs, they are not independent of the world. They are caused by it, and this fact somehow enables us to get all the assurance we need. That is what empiricists standardly say; and the reply to them is that the assurance is not provided. For all they can say, the possibility of an alternative causal origin remains, in the *malin génie*. Nothing in the content of our belief or the character of our experience can ever rule this out, for any candidate could have been placed there by the *génie*. Yet to take this suggestion seriously seems absurd. Kant's response was to distinguish between the everyday world of appearances and the world of things in themselves. About the latter we can know nothing. About the former we can know all that we ordinarily think we know, and we know that no *malin génie* deceives us; for the way things are in the world of appearances is determined conjointly by the content of our experience and the a priori principles that govern all our awareness. Truth in the world of appearances is a matter of coherence with these principles and with given experience. The *malin génie* hypothesis can therefore be ruled out, so far as that world is concerned: it does not cohere. Many of Kant's successors, and particularly Hegel, followed a similar line of thought, but rejected the hypothesis of things in themselves as redundant, even vacuous. This left no room for the *malin génie* even in the realm of the unknowable, for there is no such realm. Truth consists in the internal coherence of a system of beliefs. More recently others, some with very different conceptions of the world from Hegel's, have felt drawn to the same conclusion.

Often this has been because people have thought the hypothesis of an unknowable reality to be unintelligible. The verificationists of the Vienna Circle considered that an assertoric sentence could be meaningful only if it were possible to verify it, or perhaps to falsify it. Since it is not possible conclusively to verify, or to falsify, a great many of the things that we commonly say, the present-day proponents of such views require something less: properly to understand an assertoric sentence is to know under what conditions it would be warranted to assert or deny it. They support this with the argument that it is only through the association with its assertibility conditions that the meaning of an assertoric sentence could be taught, and only through the same association that it is possible to discover whether somebody knows how to use it correctly. Language is an instrument of public communication, but if one sought to convey to someone an idea that transcended all possibility of verification, it would be impossible ever to have reason to think one had been rightly understood. This at least is the position of Dummett (1978) and Wright (1987), and perhaps Wittgenstein (see Chapter 2, MEANING, USE, VERIFICATION, and Chapter 12, REALISM AND ITS OPPOSITIONS, section 2).

Neither Dummett nor Wright sees it as leading to the coherence theory of truth, but others have done. Neurath (1931 and 1932–3) and Putnam (1978 and 1983) are perhaps the clearest examples of those who have explicitly adopted coherence theories as the consequence of a verificationist line of thought. It is natural to think them right in seeing the connection. Even if some of our assertoric sentences just describe what is given in experience (something Neurath disputes), clearly most of them make claims which go beyond what is presented; and on a verificationist view of things understanding such a sentence involves grasping a set of rules to the effect that this or that circumstance establishes its truth or renders it warrantedly assertible. Now if one thought of these rules as yielding results which might be correct or incorrect, through their relation to an independent reality, one could resist any kind of coherence theory. But the verificationist does not think of them in that way. It is the rules themselves which determine what is correct or incorrect, for it is the rules which determine what verification is. There is no verification-transcendent reality with which their results can be compared. It is true that for contemporary anti-realists a particular assertion, like "Betty is in pain at *t*", may first be warrantedly assertible (in the light of her pain behaviour) and then cease to be so (when we discover she is being filmed for a TV commercial); but by their own showing there can be no truth of the matter independent of whatever results the procedures of verification yield. If there were, it would have to be something that transcended verification; the possibility would again be opened up that our methods of verification are wrong.

A similar line of argument is sometimes put by saying that our conceptual scheme is, after all, our own. Our concepts, and hence the rules for their application, are provided by ourselves. Not that they are the result of our voluntary choice, of course, but besides the conceptual scheme embodied in our language and our thought there might have been equally viable alternatives. Our scheme is satisfactory, and yields truth about the world, just because it is our scheme itself (or, to be exact, coherence within it) that determines what constitutes truth. On that showing, alternative conceptual schemes might determine an alternative kind of truth; but these we reject, for they are not ours. Putnam often argues in this way, and Quine also, though Quine stresses that it is not just the coherence internal to our conceptual scheme that constitutes truth, but coherence also with experience. Davidson's position develops out of Quine's, but it differs in two essential ways. He attacks Quine for assigning the role he does to experience – beliefs can cohere, or fail to cohere, with other beliefs, but not with experience; and though we have beliefs we call empirical, their truth is determined by coherence amongst beliefs and nothing else. He also rejects the idea of alternative conceptual schemes. Nothing other than our own could constitute a conceptual scheme, for a being who lacked what is essentially our own system of beliefs could not be accounted rational, and neither concepts, beliefs nor the language to express them could properly be ascribed to it (Davidson, 1986; for discussion of Davidson's overall approach, see Chapter 1, MEANING AND TRUTH CONDITIONS, and Chapter 8, RADICAL INTERPRETATION). Davidson's seems to be a neat, clear-cut example of the purest form of coherence theory, though he is no longer willing to call it this himself (Davidson, 1990a and 1990b).

5 Why the coherence theory fails

Despite its initial strangeness, then, there are strong reasons to adopt some version of the coherence theory of truth: reasons which may, indeed, seem compelling. Nevertheless, I think the theory is untenable: it offers an account of what truth consists in, but it is an account which depends on taking for granted the conception of truth.

It claims that the truth of p consists in its coherence with a set of beliefs that are actually held (or would be held, in non-trivially specifiable circumstances). If that were not so – if it claimed that truth amounted simply to coherence within an arbitrary set of propositions – the theory would be open to Russell's objection about Bishop Stubbs. But what about the claim that a certain belief, b_1, is actually held? If we suppose it true, in what does *its* truth consist? It must consist in coherence, for such is the theory; coherence with the other beliefs that are also held. Evidently, though, the same applies to them as well. This means that the Bishop Stubbs objection recurs after all. We can easily denominate an arbitrary set of internally coherent propositions including "Bishop Stubbs was hanged for murder", such that for each proposition p_n in the set, "It is believed that p_n" coheres with the original set. But that does not make it true that p_n is really believed; nor does the coherence of "Bishop Stubbs was hanged for murder" with the set make it true that Bishop Stubbs was hanged for murder.

What the theory requires is that it should be a fact that certain things are believed, a fact that obtains in its own right and not in virtue of some further coherence. A pure coherence theory of truth, which holds that truth *always* consists in coherence, cannot accommodate this. Nor can the impure coherence theory of Kant and the pragmatists, for it makes an exception only for truths about the content of experience. These philosophers treat claims about what people believe as being determined true or false by coherence, for they regard ascriptions of belief as part of our publicly shared theory about people's psychological states, and as having the same sort of status that theoretical claims of any other kind do.

There is in any case something rather unsatisfactory about a coherence theory of truth that is not pure. It is bound to give us a dual conception of truth: in some cases truth consists in coherence, but not in others. It is natural enough to think that we find out about the truth in different ways in different areas – we find out about mathematical truth in one way, truth about the latest news in quite another. We might express that by saying there are different criteria for truth in different areas. But that does not make it natural to think of a dual, or a multiple, conception of what truth is. We can detect warmth by touch or by thermometer, but our conception of it remains univocal. It would seem a lot less misleading to say that what coherence determines is not truth, but something else, which we might call quasi-truth. But then they would have to say that it is only in a very limited sphere that we can claim truth at all. Most of the things that we say are not true or false at all, because truth is correspondence with an independent reality and there is nothing for what we say to correspond to. They are at best quasi-true, or perhaps "useful". Pragmatists have sometimes been prepared to say this; those who take an instrumentalist view of scientific theories have often been willing to say it about the theoretical statements of the sciences. Blackburn, who regards moral and modal "truth" in this way, calls himself a quasi-realist in those areas, and contends that the language (and the logic) of "truth" and "falsity" can be used in these spheres to indicate coherence or the lack of it. Arguably it can. The trouble is that it is misleading, if not positively perverse, to use the word "true" to mark two entirely different relationships. (Wright as well as Blackburn would dissent from what I have just said; they emphasize the similarities rather than the differences in the roles assigned to "true". Blackburn, 1984, ch. 6; Wright, 1992, ch. 4)

6 Frege on defining truth

It may be felt, however, that the objection which was offered against pure coherence theories is too quick. It sounds a bit like the objection which Frege made, against the possibility of defining truth in any way at all, and opinions have differed as to whether Frege's case is convincing.

> If one were to say "A representation is true if it agrees with reality", that would achieve nothing, for in order to apply it one would have to decide, in a given case, whether a representation agreed with reality, or in other words whether it were true that the representation agreed with reality. Thus what is defined must itself be presupposed. The same would apply to every explication of the form "A is true if it has these

> or those properties, or stands to this or that in such-and-such a relation". The question would always arise in the particular case whether it is true that A has these or those properties, or stands to this or that in such-and-such a relation. (Frege, 1969, pp. 139–40)

What Frege calls an attempt to define truth can, I think, fairly be equated with what I have called a theory of what truth consists in. His objection to the correspondence theory, when offered as an account of what truth consists in, is that though it claims the truth of *p* consists in *p*'s correspondence with the facts, it must also admit that whether or not *p* corresponds with the facts is a matter of whether it is *true* that *p* corresponds with the facts. Similarly the coherence theory must admit that the question whether *p* coheres with the beliefs that are held is the same as the question whether "*p* coheres with the beliefs that are held" is itself true. As Frege says, this seems to presuppose the concept that was being defined; and anyone who objects to the coherence theory along these lines will say that the problem with it arises not only over determining what it is for a belief to be actually held (or belong to the appropriate set), but more immediately over determining when one thing coheres with another. For the question whether *p* coheres with *q* is the question whether it is true that *p* coheres with *q*, but the truth of "*p* coheres with *q*" must consist in its coherence with something, say *r*. Its coherence with *r* must itself consist in the coherence (say with *s*) of ' "*p* coheres with *q*" coheres with *r*', and so we are into a vicious regress, even if we set aside the problem of determining values for *q*, *r*, *s* and so on.

But Frege is wrong. An important difference between the correspondence theory and the coherence theory is crucial here. The correspondence theory is a theory of what truth consists in, but not a theory of what facts consist in. It can take the obtaining of a fact as ultimate. It does not have to consist in anything else. The coherence theory, however, has to hold that whether or not a fact obtains is determined by whether or not a certain proposition (the proposition that says this fact obtains) coheres in the appropriate way. The coherence theory is a theory of facts as well as of truth. The correspondence theory is a theory only of truth.

Let us take the correspondence theory first. As an account of what truth consists in, it holds that the truth of *p* consists in a relationship of correspondence between *p* and the facts. It also holds that whether or not this relationship obtains is itself a fact. It does not consist in anything else. In particular, then, it does not consist in the correspondence of "*p* corresponds with the facts" to the facts. Certainly, if *p* does correspond with the facts, then the proposition "*p* corresponds to the facts" will itself correspond to the facts; indeed, its truth – the truth of that *proposition* – consists in that correspondence. But the *fact* that *p* corresponds to the facts is a fact in its own right. Hence although there is certainly a regress of a kind, there is nothing vicious about it, any more than there is anything vicious about the observation that if *p* is true, it is true that *p* is true, and true that it is true that *p* is true. The obtaining of the correspondence relation between *p* and the facts is all that is required for "*p* corresponds with the facts" to correspond with the facts, for what the fact that "*p* corresponds with the facts" has to match is just the fact that the original correspondence relation obtains.

The coherence theorist can try a similar reply. The truth of *p* consists in its coherence with the set of beliefs S; but whether or not *p* coheres with S is something that holds in its own right and does not consist in anything further. Certainly if "*p* coheres with S" is true, its truth consists in its own coherence with S, and the truth of '"*p* coheres with S" coheres with S' consists in coherence again. But from this we no more get a regress that is vicious than we did with the correspondence theory.

This will not do. A coherence theorist might indeed hold that it is a matter of fact, in its own right, whether or not propositions cohere with one another; but to do so would already be to make it impossible for one's coherence theory to be of the pure kind – the kind that offers an account of what truth consists in quite generally. That is because a coherence theory is inevitably a theory of facts as well as of truth. What makes something a fact, for the coherence theorist, is that the corresponding proposition is true, that is, that it coheres in the appropriate way. If it were otherwise, facts and truth would come apart. The truth of "the cat is on the mat" would consist in its coherence; but the fact that the cat is on the mat would obtain, or not obtain, quite independently of this. To hold, then, that whether or not propositions cohere with one another is simply a matter of fact, and not of any further coherence, must be to hold that the truth of "*p* coheres with *q*" does not consist in coherence, and thus to hold to the coherence theory in at best an impure form.

Coherence theorists have not usually been prepared to qualify their position in this way. Their accounts of coherence have differed radically in detail, but the pressures which led them to the coherence theory in the first place have led them also to the view that whatever it is that constitutes coherence must itself be determined by the beliefs that are held. Under "beliefs" here one must include not only the beliefs that the appropriate subjects would adumbrate, but also the rules of inference on which they rely and which decide for them what arguments are good and what arguments are bad. These are as much part of our conceptual scheme as anything else; they are as subject to the manipulation of the *malin génie* as any other beliefs, if the *malin génie* has room to manipulate at all. Hence, in their view, the coherence of our system of beliefs, or of our conceptual scheme, is a property entirely internal to it, the standards of coherence being set by the system itself. That was the theory's apparent advantage: it made truth an entirely internal matter, not a matter of matching an independent reality which seemed beyond our reach, as we could not ensure that our beliefs (and our principles of inference) reflected it correctly. Such a theory we have seen to be untenable. That certain particular beliefs are held, or would be held, under non-trivially specifiable circumstances must simply be a fact, a fact which consists in nothing further and which cannot consist in coherence. If it did, the theory would require the truth of a proposition to consist in its coherence with the set of beliefs which are held; but the truth of the claim that those beliefs are held would have to consist simply in its coherence with that set; and that will not do, for too many alternative sets of beliefs would count as "held" by that criterion, including Russell's remark about the Bishop. To put it in Frege's fashion, the theory requires that "what is defined" (the notion of truth) "must itself be presupposed".

7 The correspondence theory

We have seen that Frege's objection does not touch the correspondence theory of truth. It may be felt, all the same, that the correspondence theory will hardly do, for three connected reasons. In the first place, unless it is spelt out a good deal further it hardly seems to be a *theory* at all: it just says that a true judgement or proposition is one which matches the way things are in a world that is independent of our beliefs about it and our experience of it. Secondly, to show that the pure coherence theory is untenable is not to deprive of their persuasiveness the arguments that led to it. The correspondence theory seems to make the world so independent of our thoughts about it that it renders *utterly mysterious* how we can succeed in knowing about it or even thinking about it, a mystery which is not dispelled by invoking the word "correspondence". Thirdly, this correspondence would have to be something that we constantly aim at, for the aim of our assertions is truth, but we can hardly aim at it without knowing something more substantial about it. As Putnam (1978 and 1983) points out, if we grant that there is a world that is independent of our thoughts about it in the way required, then whatever it is like there is bound to be a large number of relations which hold between it, or the elements of it, and the things that we think and say. If it contains infinitely many elements, Putnam shows that there must be alternative ways of mapping the world on to what we say or think, alternatives which are just as systematic as the relation of correspondence can be supposed to be. By what possible feat could we pick out one of these relationships and decide that *this* is the one that we intend when we talk about correspondence? For detailed discussion of this matter, see Chapter 17, PUTNAM'S MODEL-THEORETIC ARGUMENT AGAINST METAPHYSICAL REALISM.

There have been attempts to give the correspondence theory more content, to meet the first concern at least. Two have been particularly important: that of Wittgenstein's *Tractatus* and that of Austin. For Wittgenstein (1922) the correspondence is a structural isomorphism. Propositions are pictures of facts: to the elements of the proposition correspond the elements of the relevant fact, and the way the elements of a proposition – ultimately, names – are fitted together to form the proposition again corresponds to the way the elements of reality – objects – are fitted together to constitute the fact. This can seem promising: if there is an account to be given of correspondence, what else can it amount to but some such structural isomorphism? Unfortunately, however, it does not succeed. It explains one correspondence (of the proposition with the fact) in terms of others (names with objects, structure of proposition with structure of fact) but since these are unexplained – according to Wittgenstein, inexplicable in principle – no real gain has been made. We may even feel something has been lost, if we feel that Wittgenstein's account of the way propositions are structured is altogether too Procrustean (a conclusion he later reached himself). And the theory has no answer to Putnam's objection. If there is one systematic mapping between propositions and facts that meets Wittgenstein's constraints, there are bound to be other different mappings that meet the same constraints, so that it remains obscure how we manage to intend the right one, and mysterious how we can succeed in knowing about reality.

Austin's correspondence theory is rather different. Statements, he says, are related to the world by conventions of two kinds, demonstrative and descriptive. Descriptive conventions correlate words, as they are standardly used, with "the *types* of situation, thing, event, &c., to be found in the world". Demonstrative conventions correlate words, as they are used on the particular occasion of utterance, with "the *historic* situations, &c., to be found in the world"; they are the conventions that determine reference. Then

> A statement is said to be true when the historic state of affairs to which it is correlated by the demonstrative conventions (the one to which it "refers") is of a type with which the sentence used in making it is correlated by the descriptive conventions. (Austin, 1950, p. 116)

Austin construes "historic" broadly; still, it is arguable that his account is limited, as an account of truth, by its restriction to statements about historic states of affairs. Setting this aside, there is something unsatisfactory about his reliance on "convention", as Strawson (1965) pointed out. Conventions govern language; what they do is to determine what is being said. Certainly, one can distinguish those conventions which one learns when learning a sentence's linguistic meaning – roughly, its Fregean sense – from those which determine its reference on a particular occasion. Taken together, these determine what is being said on the particular occasion; they determine the proposition expressed. But we were concerned with the relation between the proposition and the fact (or "historic state of affairs"). All that Austin tells us about this is that it is true when the relevant state of affairs is as it is said to be. This is disappointing. And if we try to generalize it – to take account of the fact that not every statement picks out a "historic state of affairs" and says that it is of a certain type – we are left only with what Mackie (1973) calls the notion of simple truth: that the statement or proposition is true if, and only if, things are as it says they are.

It is indeed hard to see how the correspondence theory can contrive to say more than this. The idea that the structure of the proposition somehow reflects the structure of the fact is really the only suggestion that seems at all promising, and no doubt Austin, as well as Wittgenstein, was trying to capture it in his account, despite the fact that the two went about it very differently. But complex structures can be said to "reflect" one another in alternative ways, because there are different ways of mapping one on to the other; and another of Strawson's objections to Austin is pertinent against any such theory. Sentences clearly have structure; arguably propositions do as well, since a proposition involves several concepts of different types; but do facts? "Facts," Strawson says, "are what statements (when true) state" (Strawson, 1950, p. 136). He is not denying that there is something in the world that makes a statement true. But the articulation of the world into facts, with a structure that reflects the propositions or the sentences we use to describe it, is simply the result of our way of thinking about it. The structure of the proposition reflects the structure of the fact, because we ascribe to the fact the structure of the proposition. Of course the world does have a structure; as I look around I can see a variety of objects strewn around on the floor, and their spatial arrangement (for example) is perfectly objective. But when I say, "This shirt is white," the corresponding fact can be said to be structured only because we think of the proposition as structured, consisting of a referring subject term and a predicative expression. Otherwise there is nothing specially structured about my shirt's being white; it just is.

The necessary and sufficient condition for *p*'s being true is that things should be as *p* says they are. If we are left with so little, do we still have a "correspondence theory"? There is reason to say so, whether or not we take it in the way that renders it inconsistent with the coherence and pragmatic theories. If we do take it in that way, then a substantial part of the point of calling it a correspondence theory can just be that it does exclude those alternatives: it maintains that truth consists in matching a wholly independent reality, and not in coherence with beliefs or experiences. Three objections were earlier raised to it, as considered in that way, and the first – that it hardly deserves the name of a theory – can thus be dismissed: the feeling that more must be said about correspondence dissolves once it is apparent there is nothing more that can be said. The second and third can, I think, be dismissed as well, though perhaps more tentatively. The third objection was that there will be various different relationships, even systematic ones, between our words or thoughts and the world, and nothing to enable us to pick out one of them as the intended correspondence. But the intended relationship is just that which gives our words the meanings they have, and our concepts their application: then the sentence or proposition is true if things are as it says. Thus the third objection turns into the second, that it is mysterious how we can succeed in thinking or knowing anything about an independent world. On these issues there is much to be said, and this is not the place to say it, except to observe that we do seem perfectly able to say things about an independent world and show them to be true; not, perhaps, by establishing them so securely as altogether to rule out any possibility of deception by a *malin génie*, but then perhaps such a "thin and so to speak metaphysical" doubt (Descartes, 1964–76, vii, 36) need not worry us excessively.

If we take it in the form in which it is *not* inconsistent with the coherence and pragmatic theories, then certainly the "correspondence theory" tells us nothing startling, now that we have seen that the correspondence relation cannot be informatively elucidated. In this mild form it seems uncontroversial: it just tells us that truth is a relationship between what is said or thought and some fact or state of affairs in the world, namely, the relationship that obtains when things are as they are said or thought to be. It is not committed to any ontology of facts, or any account of their structure. It is thus free from the difficulty we noticed right at the outset, of being forced to postulate vast numbers of negative and hypothetical facts for negative and hypothetical propositions to correspond to, or else to give an alternative account of their truth. They also are true when things are as they say. The theory is still however worth stating – worth, even, calling a "theory" – because it appears inconsistent with the redundancy theory, and because on further investigation it turns out not to be quite as uncontroversial as it looks.

8 The redundancy theory

The conflict with the redundancy theory may be more apparent than real. For the redundancy theory (Ramsey, 1927) is not a theory of what truth consists in, but a theory about the meaning of the words "is true". It holds that ". . . is true" can be deleted without loss. One could combine this with the thesis that truth *consists in* a relation of correspondence, because to say that is not necessarily to say anything about what we mean when we use the expression ". . . is true". Correspondence theorists have usually been concerned with what truth consists in, not with the analysis of meanings. There have, however, been exceptions. Austin was one. His account, cleared of the confusion over conventions, reduced to the thesis that a statement or proposition is true if, and only if, things are as it says they are. But Austin would take this, very plausibly, as giving an analysis of what we mean when we say '"Socrates is wise" is true': things are as "Socrates is wise" says they are. This is different from an analysis which allows us just to delete ". . . is true" and forget about it.

The redundancy theorist's alternative analysis also has some initial plausibility so long as we consider only examples of the form "*p* is true", where a value for *p* is specified; or of the form "*p* is false", which the redundancy theorist will analyse as "Not-*p*". Even there, it arouses two sorts of reservation. One is that "*p* is true" does seem to differ, at least in force, from "*p*", adding confirmation or endorsement or something of the sort. The second is that – as Austin claimed – it seems to say something *about p* instead of just asserting it. Wright finds in the idea lying behind these reservations material for a deeper objection: the norms that govern "*p* is true" are, he argues, inevitably different from those that govern the assertion of *p* (Wright, 1992, ch. 1). In any case, though, the theory seems to require amendment (or at least development) as soon as we move on to examples of other kinds, as Ramsey was himself aware. Theories which try to preserve the spirit of the redundancy theory while making such amendments are often called deflationary theories.

What about the self-referential "This statement is true" and "This statement is false"? Here "is true" can hardly just be dropped out, nor can "is false" simply be replaced by a negation. Redundancy theorists have often viewed this as an *advantage* of their analysis, since it makes out such paradox-involving sentences to be incoherent. The point is moot. It is one thing to design an artificial language in which paradox-involving sentences are not well formed, and another to claim that this is true of an ordinary language like ours. The paradoxical character of "This statement is false" is not to be denied, for it can readily be understood by anyone, and a theory which argues it away cannot claim accuracy as an analysis of what we mean. This matter, however, deserves a fuller discussion than it can receive here.

At any rate, the redundancy theory cannot dismiss as ill-formed "The first statement on page 36 is true" or "Whatever the Pope says is true"; nor, indeed, have redundancy theorists ever wished to. They analyse the first as something like "There is some value of *p* such that *p* is the first statement on page 36, and *p*"; the second, as "For all values of *p*, if the Pope says that *p*, then *p*". If we put this more colloquially we get "Things are as the first statement on p. 36 says they are"; "Things are as the Pope says they are". Here, then, the redundancy theory gives the same analysis as the amended Austinian theory.

People have sometimes expressed unease about such formulations. Often they suggest that there is something fishy about the quantification. In such examples the quantified variable occurs twice, but it is not clear that it functions in the same way both times. In its first occurrence – "If the Pope says that *p*" – it is arguable that it stands in for a name: or more exactly, that "that *p*" stands in for a name, the name of a proposition. "That Socrates is wise", or "the proposition that Socrates is wise", designates the proposition that Socrates is wise, and so in general. Indeed, if we express the point in terms of sentences instead of propositions the matter seems clear-cut: the if-clause becomes 'if the Pope says "*p*"', and the readiest device for forming a name of a sentence is to put it between quotation marks. Philosophers are very familiar with quantifiers whose bound variables stand in for names, so this first occurrence of the variable looks unproblematic. But the second cannot be handled in the same way. If it were, we should have to replace *p* again by a name – a sentence in quotes, or a noun phrase referring to a proposition. In that case the then-clause would not be grammatically complete: to make it so we should have to add "is true". This would remove any residual space for the thought that "is true" is in some sense redundant. It would also amount to abandoning any attempt to characterize the truth relation. The thesis, that truth is the relation between a proposition (or a sentence) and the world when things are as it says they are, would turn into the thesis that truth is the relation which stands between a proposition (or sentence) and the world when the proposition (or sentence) is true.

We could try to resolve the problem by using a different kind of quantification. We might construe the quantifiers substitutionally, or we might reflect that just as second-order quantification seems possible in which the variables are replaced by predicative expressions, so there is room for a kind of quantification in which variables are replaced by propositional or sentential expressions (cf. Grover, Camp and Belnap, 1975 = Grover, 1992, ch. 3; see also Grover, 1992, ch. 1). What is really at issue, however, is whether the variable is functioning the same way in both cases. This raises complex problems, but here it will perhaps do to make two observations. One is that if we express the matter in terms of sentences rather than propositions, the variable does appear to function in two ways, so that we need an account of how the two occurrences relate. The other is that if we express it in terms of propositions, it is at least arguable that the variable functions in one way only.

In fact, this seems a highly plausible claim. In the antecedent it is not "*p*" but "that *p*" which looks as if it might name a proposition. The "*p*" itself does not name a proposition but expresses it, just as the "*p*" in the consequent does. In neither case is the proposition asserted, but it is characteristic of propositions that they can occur in just such contexts as these. Propositions are not objects, any more than properties are, and to assimilate the occurrence of propositional expressions to that of names would be no more sensible than to assimilate predicates to names (cf. Prior, 1971, ch. 3; for a different account – perhaps less different than it looks – see Horwich, 1990, esp. pp. 18–21). Confusion is encouraged here by persistence in asking the question, "What then *are* propositions?" with the implied demand that they should turn out to be items like sentences, or sets of sentences, or the ghostly inhabitants of Frege's Third Realm. Propositions are not sentences, but what sentences express; conditions can be specified under which two sentences express the same proposition; but beyond that there is nothing more to be said. (In the same way one can provide conditions for property-identity, but one cannot go further than that in giving a non-circular answer to the question "But what *are* properties?".) There is no gap between understanding the proposition that Socrates is wise and knowing what it would be for Socrates to be wise, so it would be impossible to know that the Pope had expressed that proposition without also knowing what it would be for things to be as it says they are. With sentences it is (perhaps) a different matter: one might know that the Pope had uttered a certain sentence ("Socrates is wise") without knowing anything about what it would be for things to be that way, because one might know he had uttered that sentence but not know what it meant.

Philosophers have often been reluctant to talk about propositions, because of puzzlement over what they are, and over their identity-conditions (see Chapter 24, OBJECTS AND CRITERIA OF IDENTITY; also Chapter 9, PROPOSITIONAL ATTITUDES). They have felt that clarity can only be attained by analysing claims that might appear to be about propositions in such a way that they turn out to be about sentences. If one takes this view, one will feel constrained to adopt the first alternative above, and construe the quantification as really being over sentences. It then seems clear that the two occurrences of the variable do function differently. It is natural, if not unavoidable, to construe 'If the Pope says "Socrates is wise" then Socrates is wise', as containing a reference to a sentence in the antecedent, and then as using that same sentence (and not referring to it) in the consequent. A "sentence" here is of course more than just a string of words; it is a grammatical sentence as uttered on a particular occasion. But to explain the connection between the quoted sentence and the sentence itself, as it occurs in the consequent, we shall have to add an extra clause. The most natural way to do this would be by adding that the sentence "Socrates is wise" means that Socrates is wise: 'If the Pope says "Socrates is wise", and if "Socrates is wise" means that Socrates is wise, then Socrates is wise'. But anyone who rejected the alternative analysis, in which the quantification was taken to be over propositions, would refuse to accept this as adequate on similar grounds. We need an account of the relation between the noun phrase "that Socrates is wise", which in the newly added clause refers to a proposition, and the "Socrates is wise" of the consequent. Such a person would make a parallel objection to any alternative to "means" which still made use of a that-clause. The only possibility, therefore, if the connection is to be expressible at all, is to use the relationship "is true if and only if". If the Pope says "Socrates is wise", and if "Socrates is wise" is true iff Socrates is wise, then Socrates is wise.

This is unfortunate. The redundancy theory held that the meaning of "Whatever the Pope says is true" is captured by "Things are as the Pope says they are"; the apparently undemanding and inoffensive correspondence theory held the same, at least when construed as an account of the meaning of "is true". But whether proposed as an account of the meaning, or as a theory of what truth consists in, it will collapse into circularity if it must, itself, make use of the notion of truth. We cannot explicate truth or "is true" by rendering "Whatever the Pope says is true" as "For every value of *s*, and every value of *p*, if the Pope says *s*, and *s* is true iff *p*, then *p*".

9 The semantic theory

Tarski's (1935 and 1944) "semantic conception of truth" offers a possible way out of this. What Tarski shows is that for a certain rather restricted class of languages, a non-circular explication can be given of "*s* is true iff *p*", for every sentence *s* of the language concerned. It is done by providing a finite set of axioms for the language, and a set of derivation rules which permit one to deduce from the axioms a theorem of the required form – "*s* is true iff *p*" – for each sentence *s* of the language. Here *s* designates a sentence of the language under examination; it does this in terms of its structure, exhibiting it as a concatenation of simpler object-language expressions. The proof itself (and the axioms and theorems) belong to a different language, a metalanguage in which the other language is described. Tarski attached great importance to this distinction between metalanguage and object language, because he was anxious to avoid the problems raised by paradoxes like "This sentence is false". The languages he is concerned with do not permit semantic predicates like "is true" and "is false" to be meaningfully applied, within a given language, to the sentences of that language itself: only (if at all) to the sentences of some other language, for which that language is a metalanguage.

This restriction is enough to prevent Tarski's ideas from applying to ordinary languages in an unqualified form, for clearly these do allow the sort of predication he ruled out. However, it might be possible to carry over his central idea, in some way, into an explication of "is true iff" which would work for an ordinary language. The central idea is that the relationship "is true iff" is fully characterized, for the language concerned, by the axiomatic theory which permits the derivation of theorems of the form "*s* is true iff *p*" for every sentence *s* of the language. The theory does not require a prior understanding of the notion of truth. For that reason, as Tarski sets it out, it does not use the word "true" at all, but rather generates sentences of the form "*s* is T iff *p*", which are often called T-sentences. This relationship – "is T iff" – is then claimed to match our ordinary conception of truth.

The derivation rules that the theory needs are the ordinary rules of deductive logic. The axioms match each of the primitive terms of the object language with a thing or set of things in the world, thus matching the term "Socrates" with Socrates and the term "is wise" with all those things which are wise; they also include clauses which make use of the structure of the object language to enable the derivation of T-sentences. Thus where "*n*" is a name in the object language and "is F" is a one-place predicate, "*n* is F" is T iff the item that is matched with "*n*" is amongst those which are matched with "is F": from which we can infer that "Socrates is wise" is T iff Socrates is wise. Again, "*n* is F and G" is T iff the item which matches *n* is amongst those matched with "is F" and also amongst those matched with "is G", so that "Socrates is wise and sober" is T iff Socrates is wise and Socrates is sober. The relation of matching which the axioms implicitly define is called by Tarski "satisfaction". The satisfaction conditions become much more complex, of course, when one deals with many-place predicates and sentences of more elaborate structure, and the ingenuity of Tarski's account lies in how he deals with the complexity; but the main idea is the same.

Although Tarski says his account "will explain the meaning" of "truth" (Tarski, 1944, p. 351), he is not, of course, offering a conceptual analysis, but an account of what truth consists in. I suggested that it might be helpful to a correspondence theorist who thought it would not do, as it stood, to say the correspondence relation is the relation which holds between a proposition and the world when things are as the proposition says they are, because this involves an improper quantification over propositions. It is now clear that if the correspondence theorist seeks to give an *analysis* of "is true", Tarski's work will not in fact help, because it does not contribute to an analysis. It will not help the redundancy theorist either, since the redundancy theorist also seeks to give an analysis. But to someone who holds a correspondence theory of what truth consists in, it may seem to provide just what is needed. For that reason Tarski's account has sometimes itself been called a correspondence theory.

But does it really provide what is needed? It is more like a counsel of despair. We might hope an account of what truth consists in would tell us something about the nature of truth in general, but on Tarski's view truth does not consist in anything general. His account allows us only to say that truth is a property which characterizes "The cat is on the mat" iff the cat is on the mat, "Socrates is wise" iff Socrates is wise, and so on for all the sentences of the language under discussion. Indeed, for Tarski truth could perfectly well be characterized by a long list of this kind, if the object language were so limited as only to contain a limited number of sentences. The detour through structure and satisfaction is needed only because we want to deal with languages which include indefinitely many sentences, and therefore need an account which has a limited number of axioms but yields an indefinite number of T-sentences. But it tells us nothing *general* about truth at all. A Tarskian truth-theory is a theory for a particular language, enabling us to derive T-sentences for all the sentences of that language. It is the satisfaction axioms for the language L_0 which determine what constitutes truth in L_0; the satisfaction axioms for L_1 which determine what constitutes truth in L_1; and so on. This gives us no general account of what truth consists in, and so it does not give us what we were looking for. A theory of what truth consists in was meant to be an account of what that property, truth, really is: not just truth-in-L_0, or truth-in-L_6. In fact, not only does he not give us what we wanted, Tarski goes further and assures us that we *cannot have* what we wanted. No general account of truth is possible, because it would have to be an account of truth-in-all-languages, including the language in which it is itself expressed. But a language capable of giving an account of "is true" for itself would have to be a language in which Tarski's rigorous distinction between object language and metalanguage was obliterated: a language in which sentences like "This sentence is true" are well-formed, and hence also "This sentence is false".

As already remarked, natural languages just do seem to violate the object-language/metalanguage distinction, and to give meaning to such sentences. Some people have therefore sought to retain Tarski's insights about the relation between truth and satisfaction, while abandoning that distinction and proposing alternative ways of handling the paradoxes. Kripke (1975) offers a particularly interesting attempt at this. However, any such account can still only offer us theories of truth for particular languages, and remains powerless to say anything general about what truth consists in. This is because, like Tarski, they still explicate truth by providing a method of specifying for particular sentences of the language the circumstances in which they are to be called true: truth is the property which belongs to "The cat is on the mat" iff the cat is on the mat, to "Snow is white" iff snow is white, and so on. We could achieve the generality we are looking for only by a more radical move. Instead of introducing satisfaction as implicitly defined by a set of axioms relating the expressions of a particular language with sets of things in the world, we might just say that the satisfaction conditions relate a predicate to the things it applies to, a name to the thing it designates, and so on, and that they therefore yield an account of truth for any language by allowing the derivation of T-sentences for the sentence of that language. But *that* would bring us back to something very familiar. For simple unquantified sentences, what it tells us is that truth is the property a sentence has iff the items it designates have the properties it says they do. More generally, it tells us that truth is the property a sentence has iff things are as the sentence says they are. To say that, of course, is to say something which certain philosophers find objectionable, because of the implicit quantification over propositions: for every sentence *s* and for every proposition *p*, if *s* says that *p*, then *p*.

So we are faced with an alternative. Either we must accept that the correspondence relation can be legitimately, if not very excitingly, expressed by some such formulation as "Things are as *s* says they are", or else we must conclude, with Tarski, that nothing general can be said about truth at all: to the question "What is truth?" there is nothing to be said. At least this would have the merit of explaining why Pilate did not get an answer.

Note

1 Arguably there is room for an intermediate position here – one occupied, according to Wright (1992, ch. 3, and 1995), by the semantic anti-realism explored by Dummett, Putnam and himself. It too holds that truth consists in a relation between a proposition and something in the world that makes it true. It denies the coherence theorist's claim that the world is constituted only by coherence amongst beliefs, and holds instead that the world exists independently of what anyone believes, or would believe, about it. However it maintains also that a statement can represent or describe the world only to the extent that there can, at least in principle, be grounds that would warrant its assertion. And it is only in so far as it can represent or describe the world that a statement is a candidate for truth. Hence, if we use the term "facts" for those aspects of reality in virtue of which true statements are true, the intermediate position would be that although the world is independent of what anyone believes, the facts are not, since what facts there are depends upon our capacities to verify (and hence on what we would believe under specifiable circumstances). This is an interesting idea. Ultimately I think the intermediate position is unstable, but to show that would be too substantial a task for the present context.

References

Books

Blackburn, S.W. 1984: *Spreading the Word* (Oxford: Clarendon Press).

Bradley, F.H. 1893: *Appearance and Reality* (London: Swan Sonnenschein).
Descartes, R. 1964–76: Meditation III. In *Oeuvres de Descartes*, ed. C. Adam and P. Tannery (Paris: Vrin/CNRS, rev. edn).
Dewey, J. 1938: *Logic: the Theory of Enquiry* (New York: Holt).
Dummett, M.A.E. 1978: *Truth and Other Enigmas* (London: Duckworth).
Frege, G. 1969: *Nachgelassene Schriften*, ed. H. Hermes, F. Kambartel and F. Kaulbach (Hamburg: Felix Meiner); trans. P. Long and R. White, *Frege: Posthumous Writings* (Oxford: Blackwell, 1979).
Grover, D. 1992: *A Prosentential Theory of Truth* (Princeton: Princeton University Press).
Horwich, P. 1990: *Truth* (Oxford: Blackwell).
James, W. 1907: *Pragmatism* (New York: Longmans, Green).
Kant, I. 1781, 2nd edn 1787: *Kritik der reinen Vernunft* (Riga: Hartknoch); trans. N. Kemp Smith, *Critique of Pure Reason* (London: Macmillan, 1929).
Mackie, J.L. 1973: *Truth Probability and Paradox* (Oxford: Clarendon Press).
Misak, C. 1991: *Truth and the End of Enquiry* (Oxford: Clarendon Press).
Prior, A.N. 1971: *Objects of Thought* (Oxford: Clarendon Press).
Putnam, H. 1983: *Realism and Reason* (Cambridge: Cambridge University Press).
Quine, W.V.O. 1969: *Ontological Relativity and Other Essays* (New York: Columbia University Press).
Wittgenstein, L. 1922: *Tractatus Logico-Philosophicus* (London: Kegan Paul, Trench, Trubner).
Wright, C. 1987: *Realism, Meaning and Truth* (Oxford: Blackwell).
Wright, C. 1992: *Truth and Objectivity* (Cambridge, Mass.: Harvard University Press).

Articles

Austin, J.L. 1950: Truth. *Proceedings of the Aristotelian Society*, Suppl., 24, 111–28; reprinted in Pitcher (1964), pp. 18–31.
Davidson, D. 1986: A coherence theory of truth and knowledge. In *Truth and Interpretation*, ed. E. LePore (Oxford: Blackwell), pp. 307–19; reprinted in *Reading Rorty*, ed. A. Malachowski (Oxford: Blackwell, 1990), pp. 120–34.
——1990a: Afterthoughts, 1987. In *Reading Rorty*, ed. A. Malachowski (Oxford: Blackwell), pp. 134–8.
——1990b: The structure and content of truth. *Journal of Philosophy*, 87, 279–328.
Grover, D., Camp, J., and Belnap, N. 1975: A prosentential theory of truth. *Philosophical Studies*, 27, 73–125; reprinted in Grover, 1992.
Kripke, S. 1975: Outline of a theory of truth. *Journal of Philosophy*, 72, 690–716; reprinted in *Recent Essays on Truth and the Liar Paradox*, ed. R.M. Martin (Oxford: Clarendon Press 1984), pp. 53–81.
Neurath, O. 1931: Soziologie im Physikalismus. *Erkenntnis*, 2, 393–431; trans. as 'Sociology and physicalism' in *Logical Positivism*, ed. A.J. Ayer (Illinois: Free Press, 1959), pp. 282–317, and as 'Sociology in the framework of physicalism' in Neurath, *Philosophical Papers 1913–1946*, ed. R.S. Cohen and M. Neurath (Dordrecht: Reidel, 1983), pp. 58–90.
——1932–3: Protokollsätze, *Erkenntnis*, 3, 204–14; trans. as 'Protocol sentences' in *Logical Positivism*, ed. A.J. Ayer, pp. 199–208; trans. as "Protocol statements" in Neurath, *Philosophical Papers 1913–1946*, ed. R.S. Cohen and M. Neurath, pp. 91–9.
Peirce, C.S. 1878: How to make our ideas clear. *Popular Science Monthly*, 12, 286–302; reprinted in his *Collected Papers* (Cambridge, Mass.: Belknap Press, 1931–5), Vol. 5, pp. 248–71.

Putnam, H. 1978: Realism and reason. In his *Meaning and the Moral Sciences* (London: Routledge and Kegan Paul), pp. 123–40.
Ramsey, F.P. 1927: Facts and propositions. *Proceedings of the Aristotelian Society*, Suppl. 7, 153–70; reprinted in his *The Foundations of Mathematics* (London, Kegan Paul, Trench, Trubner, 1931), pp. 138–55.
Russell, B. 1906–7: On the nature of truth. *Proceedings of the Aristotelian Society*, 7, 28–49.
——1956: The philosophy of logical atomism. In his *Logic and Knowledge*, ed. R.C. Marsh (London: Allen and Unwin), pp. 177–281.
Strawson, P.F. 1950: Truth. *Proceedings of the Aristotelian Society*, Suppl. 24, 129–56; reprinted in his *Logico-Linguistic Papers* (London: Methuen, 1971), pp. 190–213; also in Pitcher (1964), pp. 32–43.
——1965: Truth: a reconsideration of Austin's views. *Philosophical Quarterly*, 15, 289–301; reprinted in his *Logico-Linguistic Papers* (London: Methuen, 1971), pp. 234–49.
Tarski, A. 1935: Der Wahrheitsbegriff in den formalisierten Sprachen. *Studia Philosophica*, 1, 261–405; reprinted as 'The concept of truth in formalized languages', in his *Logic, Semantics, Metamathematics*, trans. J.H. Woodger (Oxford: Oxford University Press, 1956), pp. 152–278.
——1944: The semantic conception of truth. *Philosophy and Phenomenological Research*, 4, 341–75; reprinted in *Readings in Philosophical Analysis*, ed. H. Feigl and W. Sellars (New York: Appleton-Century-Crofts, 1947), pp. 52–84; also in *Semantics and the Philosophy of Language*, ed. L. Linsky (Urbana: University of Illinois Press, 1952), pp. 13–47.
Wright, C. 1995: Ralph C.S. Walker, the coherence theory of truth. *Synthese*, 103, 279–302.

Further reading

Books

Alston, W.P. 1996: *A Realist Conception of Truth* (Ithaca: Cornell University Press).
Blackburn, S.W. 1993: *Essays in Quasi-Realism* (New York: Oxford University Press).
Bradley, F.H. 1914: *Essays on Truth and Reality* (Oxford: Clarendon Press).
David, M. 1994: *Correspondence and Disquotation* (New York: Oxford University Press).
Devitt, M. 1984: *Realism and Truth* (Oxford: Blackwell); 2nd edn. (Oxford: Blackwell, 1991).
Ellis, B. 1990: *Truth and Objectivity* (Oxford: Blackwell).
Pitcher, G., ed. 1964: *Truth* (Englewood Cliffs, NJ: Prentice-Hall).
Walker, R. 1989: *The Coherence Theory of Truth* (London: Routledge).

Articles

Baldwin, T. 1991: The identity theory of truth. *Mind*, 100, 35–52.
Field, H. 1972: Tarski's theory of truth. *Journal of Philosophy*, 69, 347–75.
——1988: The deflationary conception of truth. In *Fact and Morality*, ed. G. MacDonald and C. Wright (Oxford: Blackwell), pp. 55–117.
Loar, B. 1980: Ramsey's theory of belief and truth. In *Prospects for Pragmatism*, ed. D.H. Mellor (Cambridge: Cambridge University Press), pp. 49–70.
Walker, R. 1995: Verificationism, anti-Realism and idealism. *European Journal of Philosophy*, 3, 257–72.
Wright, C. 1988: Realism, antirealism, irrealism, quasi-realism. *Midwest Studies in Philosophy*, 12, 25–49.

14

Analyticity

PAUL ARTIN BOGHOSSIAN

I

This is what many philosophers believe today about the analytic/synthetic distinction: In his classic early writings on analyticity – in particular, in "Truth by Convention," "Two Dogmas of Empiricism," and "Carnap and Logical Truth" – Quine showed that there can be no distinction between sentences that are true purely by virtue of their meaning, and those that aren't. In so doing, Quine devastated the philosophical programs that depend upon a notion of analyticity – specifically, the linguistic theory of necessary truth, and the analytic theory of a priori knowledge.

Quine himself, so the story continues, went on to espouse far more radical views about meaning, including such theses as meaning-indeterminacy and meaning-skepticism. However, it is not necessary, and certainly not appealing, to follow him on this trajectory. As realists about meaning, we may treat Quine's self-contained discussion in the early papers as the basis for a profound *insight* into the nature of meaning-facts, rather than for any sort of rejection of them. We may discard the notions of the analytic and the a priori without thereby buying in on any sort of unpalatable skepticism about meaning.

Now, I don't know precisely how many philosophers believe all of the above, but I think it would be fair to say that it is the prevailing view. Philosophers with radically differing commitments – including radically differing commitments about the nature of meaning itself – subscribe to it: whatever precisely the correct construal of meaning, so they seem to think, Quine has shown that it will not sustain a distinction between the analytic and the synthetic. Here, merely for purposes of illustration, are two representative endorsements of the view, both of them also containing helpful references to its popularity. The first is by Bill Lycan.

> It has been nearly forty years since the publication of "Two Dogmas of Empiricism." Despite some vigorous rebuttals during that period, Quine's rejection of analyticity still prevails – in that philosophers *en masse* have either joined Quine in repudiating the "analytic/synthetic" distinction or remained (however mutinously) silent and made no claims of analyticity.
>
> This comprehensive capitulation is somewhat surprising, in light of the radical nature of Quine's views on linguistic meaning generally. In particular, I doubt that many philosophers accept his doctrine of the indeterminacy of translation.

Lycan goes on to promise that, in his paper, he is going to

> make a Quinean case against analyticity, without relying on the indeterminacy doctrine. For I join the majority in denying both analyticity and indeterminacy.[1]

Next, here are two other committed realists about meaning, Jerry Fodor and Ernie Lepore, talking about a thesis that, they say,

> almost everybody thinks that there are good reasons to endorse; . . . [namely] . . . that there aren't any expressions that are true or false solely in virtue of what they mean.[2]

Fodor and Lepore go on to claim that this result clearly undermines the idea of a belief or inference that is warranted a priori.

Now, my disagreement with the prevailing view is not total. There is *a* notion of 'truth by virtue of meaning' – what I shall call the metaphysical notion – that *is* undermined by a set of indeterminacy-independent considerations. Since this notion is presupposed by the linguistic theory of necessity, that project fails and must be abandoned.

However, I disagree with the prevailing view's assumption that those very same considerations also undermine the analytic explanation of the a priori. For I believe that an entirely distinct notion of analyticity underlies that explanation, a notion that is epistemic in character. And in contrast with the metaphysical notion, the epistemic notion can be defended, I believe, provided that even a minimal realism about meaning is true. I'm inclined to hold, therefore, that there can be no effective Quinean critique of the a priori that does not ultimately depend on Quine's radical thesis of the indeterminacy of meaning, a thesis that, as I've stressed, many philosophers continue to reject.

All of this is what I propose to argue in this paper. I should emphasize right at the outset, however, that I am not a historian, and my interest here is not historical. Think of me, rather, as asking, on behalf of all those who continue to reject Quine's later skepticism about meaning: Can something like the analytic explanation of the a priori be salvaged from the wreckage of the linguistic theory of necessity?

Belief, apriority and indeterminacy

We need to begin with some understanding, however brief and informal, of what it is to believe something, and of what it is for a belief to count as a priori knowledge.

In my view, the most plausible account of the matter is that believing is a relation to a proposition in the technical sense: a mind-independent, language-independent abstract object that has its truth conditions essentially. Against this background, a belief is true just in case its proposition is true.

However, I don't want to presuppose such a picture of belief in the present context. Not that there would be anything particularly wrong or question-begging about doing so; as Quine himself has made clear, his rejection of propositions is supposed to rest on his critique of analyticity, not the other way around.[3] Nevertheless, in the interests of keeping potential distractions to a minimum, I will work with a picture of belief that is far more hospitable to Quine's basic outlook.

According to this more 'linguistic' picture, the objects of belief are not propositions, but rather interpreted sentences: for a person T to believe that p is for T to hold true a sentence S which means that p in T's idiolect.[4]

Against this rough and ready background, we may say that for T to know that p is for T to justifiably hold S true, with a strength sufficient for knowledge, and for S to be true. And to say that T knows p a priori is to say that T's warrant for holding S true is independent of outer, sensory experience.[5] The interesting question in the analysis of the concept of apriority concerns this notion of warrant: what is it for a belief to be justified, independently of outer sensory experience?

On a minimalist reading, to say that the warrant for a given belief is a priori is just to say that it is justified, with a strength sufficient for knowledge, without appeal to empirical evidence.[6] On a stronger reading, it is to say that, and to say in addition that the justification in question is not defeasible by any future empirical evidence.[7] Which of these two notions is at issue in the present debate?

My own view is that the minimal notion forms the core of the idea of apriority. However, in this paper I will aim to provide the materials with which to substantiate the claim that, under the appropriate circumstances, the notion of analyticity can help explain how we might have a priori knowledge even in the strong sense. A defense of the strong notion is particularly relevant in the present context, for Quine seems to have been particularly skeptical of the idea of empirical indefeasibility.

Before proceeding, we should also touch briefly on the notion of meaning-indeterminacy. In chapter 2 of *Word and Object* Quine argued that, for any language, it is possible to find two incompatible translation manuals that nevertheless perfectly conform to the totality of the evidence that constrains translation. This is the famous doctrine of the indeterminacy of translation. Since Quine was, furthermore, prepared to assume that there could not be facts about meaning that are not captured in the constraints on best translation, he concluded that meaning-facts themselves are indeterminate – that there is, strictly speaking, no determinate fact of the matter as to what a given expression in a language means. This is the doctrine that I have called the thesis of the indeterminacy of meaning.

An *acceptance* of meaning-indeterminacy can lead to a variety of *other* views about meaning. For instance, it might lead to an outright eliminativism about meaning. Or it might be taken as a reason to base the theory of meaning on the notion of likeness of meaning, rather than on that of sameness of meaning.[8] In this paper I am not concerned with the question of what moral should be drawn from the indeterminacy thesis, on the assumption that it is true; nor am I concerned with whether the indeterminacy thesis is true. I am only concerned to show that a skepticism about epistemic analyticity cannot stop short of the indeterminacy thesis, a thesis that, as I have stressed, most philosophers agree in rejecting (see Chapter 16, THE INDETERMINACY OF TRANSLATION).

Analyticity: metaphysical or epistemological?

Traditionally, three classes of statements have been thought to be the objects of a priori knowledge: logical statements, exemplified by such truths as:

Either Brutus killed Caesar or he did not;

mathematical statements, such as:

$7 + 5 = 12$;

and conceptual truths, for instance:

All bachelors are unmarried.

The problem has always been to explain how any statement could be known a priori. After all, if a statement is known a priori, then it must be true. And if it is true, then it must be factual, capable of being true or false. What could possibly entitle us to hold a factual sentence true on a priori grounds?

The history of philosophy has known a number of answers to this question, among which the following has had considerable influence: We are equipped with a special evidence-gathering faculty of *intuition*, distinct from the standard five senses, which allows us to arrive at justified beliefs about the necessary properties of the world. By exercising this faculty, we are able to know a priori such truths as those of mathematics and logic.

The central impetus behind the *analytic* explanation of the a priori is the desire to explain the possibility of a priori knowledge without having to postulate such a special faculty, one that has never been described in satisfactory terms. The question is: How could a factual statement S be known a priori by T, without the help of a special evidence-gathering faculty?

Here, it would seem, is one way: *If mere grasp of* S*'s meaning by* T *sufficed for* T*'s being justified in holding* S *true.* If S were analytic in this sense, then, clearly, its apriority would be explainable without appeal to a special faculty of intuition: mere grasp of its meaning by T would suffice for explaining T's justification for holding S true. On this understanding, then, 'analyticity' is an overtly *epistemological* notion: a statement is 'true by virtue of its meaning' provided that grasp of its meaning alone suffices for justified belief in its truth.

Another, far more metaphysical, reading of the phrase 'true by virtue of meaning' is also available, however, according to which a statement is analytic provided that, in some appropriate sense, it *owes its truth-value completely to its meaning*, and not at all to 'the facts.'

Which of these two possible notions has been at stake in the dispute over analyticity? There has been a serious unclarity on the matter. Quine himself tends to label the doctrine of analyticity an epistemological one, as, for example, in the following passage from "Carnap and Logical Truth":

> the linguistic doctrine of logical truth, which is an epistemological doctrine, goes on to say that logical truths are true purely by virtue of the intended meanings, or intended usage, of the logical words.[9]

However, his most biting criticisms seem often to be directed at what I have called the metaphysical notion. Consider, for example, the object of disapproval in the following famous passage, a passage that concludes the discussion of analyticity in "Two Dogmas":

> It is obvious that truth in general depends on both language and extralinguistic fact. The statement 'Brutus killed Caesar' would be false if the world had been different in certain ways, but it would also be false if the word 'killed' happened rather to have the sense of 'begat'. Thus one is tempted to suppose in general that the truth of a statement is somehow analyzable into a linguistic component and a factual component. Given this supposition it next seems reasonable that in some statements the factual component should be null; and these are the analytic statements. But for all its a priori reasonableness, a boundary between analytic and synthetic statements simply has not been drawn. That there is such a distinction to be drawn at all is an unempirical dogma of empiricists, a metaphysical article of faith.[10]

Now, I think that there is no doubt that many of the proponents of the analytic theory of the a priori, among them especially its positivist proponents, intended the notion of analyticity to be understood in this metaphysical sense; very shortly I shall look at why.

Before doing that, however, I want to register my wholehearted agreement with Quine, that the metaphysical notion is of dubious explanatory value, and possibly also of dubious coherence. I believe that Quine's discrediting of this idea constitutes one of his most enduring contributions to philosophy. Fortunately for the analytic theory of the a priori, it can be shown that it need have nothing to do with the discredited idea.

The metaphysical concept

What could it possibly mean to say that the truth of a statement is fixed exclusively by its meaning and not by the facts? Isn't it in general true – indeed, isn't it in general a truism – that for any statement S,

> S is true iff for some p, S means that p and p?

How could the *mere* fact that S means that p make it the case that S is true? Doesn't it also have to be the case that p? As Harman has usefully put it (he is discussing the sentence 'Copper is copper'):

> what is to prevent us from saying that the truth expressed by "Copper is copper" depends in part on a general feature of the way the world is, namely that everything is self-identical.[11]

The proponent of the metaphysical notion does have a comeback, one that has perhaps not been sufficiently addressed. If he is wise, he won't want to deny the meaning-truth truism. What he will want to say instead is that, in some appropriate sense, our meaning p by S *makes it the case that p.*

But this line is itself fraught with difficulty. For how can we make sense of the idea that something is made true by our meaning something by a sentence?

Consider the sentence 'Either p or not p'. It is easy, of course, to understand how the fact that we mean what we do by the ingredient terms fixes what is expressed by the sentence as a whole; and it is easy to understand, in consequence, how the fact that we mean what we do by the sentence determines whether the sentence expresses something true or false. But as Quine points out, that is just the normal dependence of truth on meaning. What is far more mysterious is the claim that the *truth of what the sentence expresses* depends on the fact that it is expressed by that sentence, so that we can say that what is expressed wouldn't have been true at all, had it not been for the fact that it is expressed by that sentence. There are at least two insurmountable problems in making sense of this idea.

First, any such account would make the truth of what is expressed *contingent*, whereas most of the statements at stake in the present discussion are clearly necessary. Second, such an account would make the truth of the claim expressed contingent *on* an act of meaning, and that is very peculiar. Putting aside the question whether it is so much as intelligible, what plausibility could it conceivably have? Are we to suppose that, prior to our stipulating a meaning for the sentence

Either snow is white or it isn't

it wasn't the case that either snow was white or it wasn't? Isn't it overwhelmingly obvious that this claim was true *before* such an act of meaning, and that it would have been true even if no-one had thought about it, or chosen it to be expressed by one of our sentences?

Why, if this idea is as problematic as I, following Quine, have claimed it to be, did it figure so prominently in positivist thinking about analyticity?

Part of the answer derives from the fact that the positivists didn't merely want a theory of a priori knowledge; they also wanted a reductive theory of necessity. The motivation was not purely epistemological, but metaphysical as well. Guided by the fear that objective, language-independent, necessary connections would be metaphysically odd, they attempted to show that all necessities could be understood to consist in linguistic necessities, in the shadows cast by conventional decisions concerning the meanings of words. Linguistic meaning, by itself, was supposed to generate necessary truth; *a fortiori*, linguistic meaning, by itself, was supposed to generate truth. Hence the play with the metaphysical concept of analyticity.

But this is, I believe, a futile project. In general, I have no idea what would constitute a better answer to the question: What is responsible for generating the truth of a given class of statements? than something bland like 'the world' or 'the facts'; and, for reasons that I have just been outlining, I cannot see how a good answer might be framed in terms of meaning in particular.

So I have no sympathy with the linguistic theory of necessity or with its attendant Conventionalism. Unfortunately, the impression appears to be widespread that there is no way to disentangle that view from the analytic theory of the a priori; or, at a minimum, that there is no way to embrace the epistemic concept of analyticity without also embracing its metaphysical counterpart. I don't know whether Harman believes something of the sort; he certainly gives the impression of doing so in his frequent suggestions that anyone deploying the notion of analyticity would have to be deploying both of its available readings simultaneously:

> It turned out that someone could be taught to make the analytic-synthetic distinction only by being taught a rather substantial theory, a theory including such principles as that meaning can make something true and that knowledge of meaning can give knowledge of truth.[12]

One of the main points of the present paper is that these two notions of analyticity are distinct, and that the analytic theory of the a priori needs only the epistemological notion and has no use whatsoever for the metaphysical one. We can have an analytic theory of the a priori without in any way subscribing to a Conventionalism about anything. It is with the extended defense of this claim that much of the present essay is concerned.

The epistemological concept

Turning, then, to the epistemological notion of analyticity, we immediately confront a serious puzzle: How could any sentence be analytic in this sense? How could mere grasp of a sentence's meaning justify someone in holding it true?

Clearly, the answer to this question has to be *semantical:* something about the sentence's meaning, or about the way that meaning is fixed, must explain how its truth is knowable in this special way. What could this explanation be?

In the history of the subject, two different sorts of explanation have been especially important. Although these, too, have often been conflated, it is crucial to distinguish between them.

One idea was first formulated in full generality by Gottlob Frege. According to Frege, a statement's analyticity (in my epistemological sense) is to be explained by the fact that it is *transformable into a logical truth by the substitution of synonyms for synonyms*. When a statement satisfies this semantical condition, I shall say that it is 'Frege-analytic'.[13]

Now, it should be obvious that Frege-analyticity is at best an *incomplete* explanation of a statement's epistemic analyticity and, hence, of its apriority. For suppose that a given sentence S is Frege-analytic. How might this fact explain its analyticity? Clearly, two further assumptions are needed. First, that facts about synonymy are knowable a priori; and second, that so are the truths of logic. Under the terms of these further assumptions, a satisfying explanation goes through. Given its Frege-analyticity, S is transformable into a logical truth by the substitution of synonyms for synonyms. Facts about synonymy are a priori, so it's a priori that S is so transformable. Furthermore, the sentence into which it is transformable is one whose truth is itself knowable a priori. Hence, S's truth is knowable a priori.

Frege tended not to worry about these further assumptions for two reasons. First, he thought it obviously constitutive of the idea of meaning, that meaning is transparent – that any competent user of two words would have to be able to know a priori whether or not they meant the same. Second, he also thought it obvious that there could be no substantive epistemology for logic – a fortiori, not one that could explain its apriority. As a consequence, he was happy to take logic's apriority for granted. For both of these reasons, he didn't worry about the fact that the concept of Frege-analyticity simply leaned on these further assumptions without explaining them.

I think the jury is still out on whether Frege was right to take these further assumptions for granted. There is certainly a very strong case to be made for the transparency of meaning.[14] And there are well-known difficulties providing a substantive epistemology for something as basic as logic, difficulties we shall have occasion to further review below. Nevertheless, because we cannot simply assume that Frege was right, we have to ask how a complete theory of the a priori would go about filling in the gaps left by the concept of Frege-analyticity.

I shall have very little to say about the first gap. The question whether facts about the sameness and difference of meaning are a priori cannot be discussed independently of the question of what meaning is, and that is not an issue that I want to prejudge in the present context. On some views of meaning – for example, on certain conceptual-role views – the apriority of synonymy is simply a by-product of the very nature of meaning facts, so that no substantive epistemology for synonymy is necessary or, indeed, possible. On other views – for example, on most externalist views of meaning – synonymy is not a priori, so there is no question of a sentence's Frege-analyticity fully explaining its epistemic analyticity.

Since this issue about the apriority of synonymy turns on questions that are currently unresolved, I propose to leave it for now. As we shall see, none of the analyticity-skeptical considerations we shall consider exploit it in any way. (Quine never argues that the trouble with Frege-analyticity is that synonymies are a posteriori.)

Putting aside, then, skepticism about the apriority of synonymy, and, for the moment anyway, skepticism about the very existence of Frege-analytic sentences, let us ask quite generally: What class of a priori statement would an account based on the notion of Frege-analyticity *fail* to explain?

Two classes come to mind. On the one hand, a priori statements that are not transformable into logical truths by the substitution of synonyms for synonyms; and, on the other, a priori statements that are trivially so transformable.

Taking the first class first, there does appear to be a significant number of a priori statements that are not Frege-analytic. For example:

Whatever is red all over is not blue.
Whatever is colored is extended.
If x is warmer than y, then y is not warmer than x.

These statements appear not to be transformable into logical truths by the appropriate substitutions: the ingredient descriptive terms seem not to be decomposable in the appropriate way.

The second class of recalcitrant statements consists precisely of the truths of logic. The truths of logic satisfy, of course, the conditions on Frege-analyticity; but they satisfy them trivially. And it seems obvious that we can't hope to explain our entitlement to belief in the truths of logic by appealing to their analyticity in this sense: knowledge of Frege-analyticity presupposes knowledge of logical truth, and so can't explain it.

How, then, is the epistemic analyticity of these recalcitrant truths to be explained? As we shall see below, the Carnap/Wittgenstein solution turned on the suggestion that they are to be viewed as *implicit definitions* of their ingredient terms. When a statement satisfies this semantical condition, I shall sometimes say that it is 'Carnap-analytic'. However, before proceeding to a discussion of Carnap-analyticity I want to re-examine Quine's famous rejection of the much weaker concept of Frege-analyticity.

II

'Two Dogmas' and the rejection of Frege-analyticity

For all its apparent limitations, the concept of Frege-analyticity is not without interest. Even though Quine made it fashionable to claim otherwise, "All bachelors are male" *does* seem to be transformable into a logical truth by the substitution of synonyms for synonyms, and that fact *does* seem to have something important to do with that statement's apriority. If, then, appearances are not misleading here, and a significant range of a priori statements are Frege-analytic, then the problem of their apriority is *reduced* to that of the apriority of logic and synonymy and, in this way, a significant economy in explanatory burden is achieved.

It was, therefore, an important threat to the analytic theory of the a priori to find Quine arguing, in one of the most celebrated articles of this century, that the apriority of no sentence could be explained by appeal to its Frege-analyticity, because no sentence of a natural language could *be* Frege-analytic.

It has not been sufficiently appreciated, it seems to me, that "Two Dogmas" is *exclusively* concerned with this weaker notion of Frege-analyticity, and not at all with the more demanding project of explaining the apriority of logic. But this is made very clear by Quine:

> Statements which are analytic by general philosophical acclaim are not, indeed, far to seek. They fall into two classes. Those of the first class, which may be called *logically true*, are typified by:
>
> (1) No unmarried man is married.
>
> The relevant feature of this example is that it is not merely true as it stands, but remains true under any and all reinterpretations of 'man' and 'married'. If we suppose a prior inventory of *logical* particles . . . then in general a logical truth is a statement

> that remains true under all reinterpretations of its components other than the logical particles.
>
> But there is also a second class of analytic statements, typified by:
>
> (2) No bachelor is married.
>
> The characteristic of such a statement is that it can be turned into a logical truth by putting synonyms for synonyms. (pp. 22–3)

Quine goes on to say very clearly:

> Our problem . . . is analyticity; and here the major difficulty lies not in the first class of analytic statements, the logical truths, but rather in the second class, which depends on the notion of synonymy. (p. 24)

Most of the rest of 'Two Dogmas' is devoted to arguing that no good sense can be made of such analyticities of the 'second class'.

None of this would make any sense unless Quine were intending in "Two Dogmas" to be restricting himself solely to the notion of Frege-analyticity. Of course, it is the point of two other important papers of his – "Truth by Convention" and "Carnap and Logical Truth" – to argue that there is no non-trivial sense in which *logic* is analytic. We will turn to that issue in due course. Relative to the Fregean notion, however, the logical truths are trivially analytic; and so, given his apparent desire to restrict his attention to that notion in 'Two Dogmas', he simply concedes their 'analyticity' in the only sense he takes to be under discussion. What he wishes to resist in 'Two Dogmas', he insists, is merely the claim that there are any *non-trivial instances of Frege-analyticity.*[15]

Skeptical theses about analyticity

What form does Quine's resistance take? Let's agree, right away, that the result being advertised isn't anything modest, of the form: There are fewer analyticities than we had previously thought. Or, there are some analytic truths, but they are not important for the purposes of science. Or anything else of a similar ilk. Rather, as a very large number of Quine's remarks make clear, the sought-after result is something ambitious, to the effect that the notion of Frege-analyticity is, somehow or other, not cogent. The many admirers of 'Two Dogmas' have been divided on whether to read this as the claim that the notion of Frege-analyticity does not have a well-defined, determinate content, or whether to read it merely as claiming that, although it has an intelligible content, it is necessarily uninstantiated.

I'll call the first claim a *Non-factualism* about analyticity:

> (NF) No coherent, determinate property is expressed by the predicate 'is analytic' (or, since these are correlative terms, the predicate 'is synthetic'); consequently, no coherent proposition is expressed by sentences of the form 'S is analytic' and 'S is synthetic.'

And I'll call the second an *Error Thesis* about analyticity:

(ET) There is a coherent, determinate property expressed by 'is analytic', but it is necessarily uninstantiated; consequently, all sentences of the form 'S is analytic' are necessarily false.[16]

Unfortunately, 'Two Dogmas' doesn't seem to have a clear view about exactly which of these claims it should be read as arguing for.

In favor of the suggestion that Quine's goal is something with the form of a non-factualism about Frege-analyticity there is, first, the fact that the idiom favored by Quine – that there is no distinction between the analytic and the synthetic – sits much better with a non-factualist thesis than it does with an error thesis. The latter claim would be far more happily expressed by saying, "All sentences are necessarily synthetic."

Further, and more importantly, there is the actual character of Quine's *arguments*. As any reader of 'Two Dogmas' knows, much of that article is given over to arguing that we don't really understand what 'is analytic' means, that previous explications either fail to specify its meaning in sufficiently non-circular – hence sufficiently illuminating – terms, or fail to specify it at all.

For example, against the suggestion that 'analyticity' might be understood via a specification of the 'semantical rules' for a language, Quine remarks:

> Let us suppose . . . an artificial language L_0 whose semantical rules have the form explicitly of a specification, by recursion or otherwise, of all the analytic statements of L_0. The rules tell us that such-and-such statements, and only those, are the analytic statements of L_0. Now here the difficulty is simply that the rules contain the word 'analytic' which we do not understand! We understand what expressions the rules attribute analyticity to, but we do not understand what the rules attribute to these expressions.[17]

There are, then, weighty textual reasons for taking Quine to be arguing for something with the form of a NF. Other considerations, however, pull in the opposite direction. The most striking of these occurs in the following passage concerning stipulative definitions, that is, the explicitly conventional introduction of novel notation for the purposes of abbreviation. The passage is framed by a concession on Quine's part that Frege-analyticity would be intelligible, provided the notion of synonymy were. In the case of stipulative definitions, writes Quine,

> the definiendum becomes synonymous with the definiens simply because it has been created expressly for the purpose of being synonymous with the definiens. Here we have a really transparent case of synonymy created by definition; would that all species of synonymy were as intelligible. (p. 26)

This admission, however, in the context of Quine's concession, would appear to be utterly inconsistent with NF. For a NF about Frege-analyticity is committed to the claim that there is no coherent, determinate property of synonymy: no conceivable mechanism could generate an instance of synonymy, for there is no coherent property to generate. *A fortiori*, no stipulational mechanism could.

In fact, even the ET, as stated, is inconsistent with the concession. For according to the ET, although there is such a property as analyticity, of necessity no sentence has it. Yet according to the concession, there could be sentences – namely, those built up in appropriate ways out of the expressions implicated in stipulative definitions – that are analytic. So even the ET needs to be modified, if it is to be made consistent with Quine's admission, thus:

> (ET*) There is a coherent property expressed by 'is analytic', but, with the exception of those instances that are generated by stipulational mechanisms, it is necessarily uninstantiated.

Let me bring the exegetical aspect of this discussion to a premature and artificial close. It is clear that a thesis of either form would result in a philosophically important skepticism about Frege-analyticity. What we need to do is distinguish between the two theses and assess the case that can be made on their behalf.

In actual fact, however, I don't propose to look at Quine's well-known arguments in detail. Instead, my strategy will be to argue that neither a non-factualism about Frege-analyticity, nor an error thesis about it, can plausibly fall short of an outright rejection of meaning itself. Since – along with practically everybody else – I consider such a rejection to be highly implausible, I take this to constitute a *reductio* of Quine's skepticism about Frege-analyticity.

Non-factualism about Frege-analyticity

Let's begin with the non-factualist rejection of Frege-analyticity. Now, to say that there is no such property as the property of Frege-analyticity is essentially to say that, for *any* sentence, there is no fact of the matter as to whether it is transformable into a logical truth by the substitution of synonyms for synonyms. Presumably, this itself is possible only if either there is no fact of the matter about what counts as a logical truth, or no fact of the matter about when two expressions are synonymous. Since the factuality of logic is not in dispute, the only option is a non-factualism about synonymy.

But, now, how can there fail to be facts about whether any two expressions – even where these are drawn from within a *single* speaker's idiolect – mean the same? Wouldn't this have to entail that there are no facts about what each expression means individually? Putting the question the other way: Could there be a fact of the matter about what each expression means, but no fact of the matter about whether they mean the same?[18]

Let's consider this question first against the background of an unQuinean relational construal of meaning, according to which an expression's meaning something is a relation M between it and its meaning, the meaning C. Someone who held that a non-factualism about synonymy could coexist with a determinacy about meaning would have to hold that, although it might be true that some specific word – say, "cow" – bears some specific relation M to some specific meaning C, there is no fact of the matter about whether some *other* word – some other orthographically identified particular – bears precisely the same relation to precisely the same meaning.

But how could this be? How could it conceivably turn out that it is intelligible and true to say that "cow" bears M to C, and that it is not merely false but *nonfactual* to say that some other word – "vache", as it may be – also does? What could be so special about the letters "c", "o", "w"?

The answer, of course, is that there is nothing special about them. If it is factual that one word bears M to C, it is surely factual that some other word does. Especially on a relational construal of meaning, it makes no sense to suppose that a determinacy about meaning could coexist with a non-factualism about synonymy.

The question naturally arises whether this result is forthcoming *only* against the background of a relational construal of meaning. I think it's quite clear that the answer is 'no'. To see why, suppose that instead of construing meaning-facts as involving relations to meanings we construe them thus: "cow" means *cow* just in case "cow" has the monadic property R, a history of use, a disposition, or whatever your favorite candidate may be. Precisely the same arguments go through: it remains equally difficult to see how, given that "cow" has property R, it could fail to be factual whether or not some other word does.

The error thesis about Frege-analyticity

I think, then, that if a plausible skepticism about Frege-analyticity is to be sustained, it cannot take the form of a non-factualism. Does an Error thesis fare any better? According to this view, although there are determinate facts about which sentences are transformable into logical truths by the appropriate manipulations of synonymy, this property is necessarily uninstantiated: it is nomically impossible for there to be any Frege-analytic sentences. Our question is: Does at least this form of skepticism about Frege-analyticity avoid collapse into the indeterminacy doctrine?

Well, I suppose that if we are being very strict about it, we may have to admit that it is barely *logically possible* to combine a denial of indeterminacy with an error-thesis about synonymy; so that we can say that although there are determinate facts about what means what, it is impossible for any two things to mean the same thing. But is such a view plausible? Do we have any reason for believing it? I think not.

Let's begin with the fact that even Quine has to believe that it is possible for two *tokens of the same orthographic type* to be synonymous, for that much is presupposed by his own account of logical truth. As we saw in the passage I quoted above, Quine describes a truth of logic as:

> a statement which is true and which remains true under all reinterpretations of its components other than the logical particles.

Clearly, the idea isn't that such a statement will remain true no matter how the non-logical particles are substituted for, but rather that it will remain true provided that the non-logical particles are substituted for in a uniform way, with multiple occurrences of the same word receiving the same substitution in every case. But what should we count as the same here? As Strawson pointed out, it won't do merely to insist that multiple occurrences of a word be replaced by orthographically uniform replacements; for it certainly seems possible to imagine an orthographically uniform way of substituting for the non-logical particles of 'No unmarried man is married' that results in a falsehood: 'No unilluminated book is illuminated'. And it's hard to see how this is to be fixed without making some use of the idea that the orthographically uniform replacements should express the same meaning.[19]

So even Quine has to admit – what in any event seems independently compelling – that two tokens of the same type can express the same meaning.

What about two tokens of different types? Here again, our own argument can proceed from Quine's own admissions. As we saw, even Quine has to concede that two expressions can mean the same thing, provided that they are explicitly stipulated to mean the same thing. So the skepticism about synonymy has to boil down to the following, somewhat peculiar claim: Although there is such a thing as the property of synonymy; and although it can be instantiated by pairs of tokens of the same orthographic type; and although it can be instantiated by pairs of tokens of distinct orthographic types, provided that they are related to each other by way of an explicit stipulation; it is, nevertheless, in principle impossible to generate instances of this property in some other way, via some other mechanism. For example, it is impossible that two expressions that were introduced independently of each other into the language should have been introduced with exactly the same meanings.

But what conceivable rationale could there be for such a claim? As far as I am able to tell, there is precisely one argument in the literature that is supposed to provide support for this claim. It may be represented as follows:

> Premise: Meaning is radically holistic in the sense that: "What our words mean depends on *everything* we believe, on *all* the assumptions we are making."[20]

Therefore,

> Conclusion: It is very unlikely that, in any given language, there will be two words of distinct types that mean exactly the same thing.

I am inclined to agree that this argument (properly spelled out) is valid, and so, that if a radical holism about meaning were true, then synonymies between expressions of different types would be rare.

However, I note that "rare" does not mean the same as "impossible," which is the result we were promised. And, much more importantly, I am completely inclined to disagree that 'Two Dogmas' provides any sort of cogent argument for meaning holism in the first place.

It's easy to see why, if such a radical meaning holism were true, synonymies might be hard to come by. For although it is not unimaginable, it is unlikely that two words of distinct types will participate in *all* of the same beliefs and inferences. Presumably there will always be some beliefs that will discriminate between them – beliefs about their respective shapes, for example.

But what reason do we have for believing that *all* of a word's uses are constitutive of its meaning?

Many Quineans seem to hold that the crucial argument for this intuitively implausible view is to be found in the concluding sections of 'Two Dogmas'. In those concluding sections, Quine argues powerfully for the epistemological claim that has come to be known as the Quine–Duhem thesis: confirmation is holistic in that the warrant for any given sentence depends on the warrant for every other sentence. In those concluding sections, Quine also assumes a Verificationist theory of meaning, according to which the meaning of a sentence is fixed by its method of confirmation. Putting these two theses together, one can speedily arrive at the view that a word's meaning depends on *all* of its inferential links to other words, and hence at the thesis of meaning-holism.[21]

This, however, is not a very convincing train of thought. First, and not all that importantly, this couldn't have been the argument that *Quine* intended against Frege-analyticity, for this argument for meaning-holism is to be found in the very last pages of 'Two Dogmas', well after the rejection of Frege-analyticity is taken to have been established.

Second, and more importantly, the argument is not very compelling because it depends crucially on a verificationism about meaning, a view that we have every good reason to reject, and which has in fact been rejected by most contemporary philosophers.

Finally, and perhaps most importantly, any such holism-based argument against the possibility of synonymy would need to be supported by something that no-one has ever provided – a reason for believing that yielding such an intuitively implausible result about synonymy isn't itself simply a *reductio* of meaning-holism[22] (see Chapter 10, HOLISM).

III

The analyticity of logic

If the preceding considerations are correct, then there is no principled objection to the existence of Frege-analyticities, and, hence, no principled objection to the existence of statements that are knowable a priori if logical truth is.[23]

But what about logical truth? Is it knowable a priori? And, if so, how?[24]

In the case of some logical truths, the explanation for how we have come to know them will be clear: we will have deduced them from others. So our question concerns only the most elementary laws of sentential or first-order logic. How do we know a priori, for example, that all the instances of the law of non-contradiction are true, or that all the instances of *modus ponens* are valid?

As I noted above, Frege thought it obvious that there could be no substantive answer to such questions; he was inclined, therefore, to take appearances at face value and to simply *assume* the apriority of logic.

What Frege probably had in mind is the following worry. 'Explaining our knowledge of logic' presumably involves finding some *other* thing that we know, on the basis of which our knowledge of logic is to be explained. However, regardless of what that other thing is taken to be, it's hard to see how the use of logic is to be avoided in moving from knowledge of that thing to knowledge of the relevant logical truth. And so it can come to seem as if any account of how we know logic will have to end up being vacuous, presupposing that we have the very capacity to be explained.

Michael Dummett has disputed the existence of a real problem here. As he has pointed out, the sort of circularity that's at issue isn't the gross circularity of an argument that consists of including the conclusion that's to be reached among the premisses. Rather, we have an argument that purports to prove the validity of a given logical law, at least one of whose inferential steps must be taken in accordance with that law. Dummett calls this a "pragmatic" circularity. He goes on to claim that a pragmatic circularity of this sort will be damaging only to a justificatory argument that

> is addressed to someone who genuinely doubts whether the law is valid, and is intended to persuade him that it is. . . . If, on the other hand, it is intended to satisfy the philosopher's perplexity about our entitlement to reason in accordance with such a law, it may well do so.[25]

The question whether Dummett's distinction fully allays Frege's worry is a large one, and I can't possibly hope to settle it here. If something along these general lines can't be made to work, then *any* explanation of logic's apriority – or aposteriority, for that matter – is bound to be futile, and the Fregean attitude will have been vindicated.

However, the question that particularly interests me in the present essay is this: Assuming that the very enterprise of explaining our knowledge of logic isn't shown to be hopeless by Frege's straightforward argument, is there any *special* reason for doubting an explanation based on the notion of analyticity? Quine's enormously influential claim was that there is. I shall try to argue that there isn't – that, in an important sense to be specified later on, our grasp of the meaning of logical claims can explain our a priori entitlement to holding them true (provided that the Fregean worry doesn't defeat all such explanations in the first place).

The classical view and implicit definition

It's important to understand, it seems to me, that the analytic theory of the apriority of logic arose indirectly, as a by-product of the attempt to explain in what a grasp of the meaning of the logical constants consists. Alberto Coffa lays this story out very nicely in his recent book.[26]

What account are we to give of our grasp of the logical constants, given that they are not explicitly definable in terms of *other* concepts? Had they been explicitly definable, of course, we would have been able to say, however plausibly, that we grasp them by grasping their definitions. But as practically anybody who has thought about the matter has recognized, the logical constants are not explicitly definable in terms of other concepts, and so we are barred from giving that account. The question is, what account are we to give?

Historically, many philosophers were content to suggest that the state of grasping these constants was somehow primitive, not subject to further explanation. In particular, such a grasp of the meaning of, say, 'not' was to be thought of as prior to, and independent of, a decision on our part as to which of the various sentences involving 'not' are to count as true. We may call this view, following Wittgenstein's lead, the doctrine of

> *Flash-Grasping:* We grasp the meaning of, say, 'not' "in a flash" – prior to, and independently of, deciding which of the sentences involving 'not' are true.

On this historically influential picture, Flash-Grasping was combined with the doctrine of Intuition to generate an epistemology for logic:

> *Intuition:* Grasp of the concept of, say, negation, along with our intuition of its logical properties, explains and justifies our logical beliefs involving negation – e.g. that 'If not not p, then p' is true.

As Coffa shows, this picture began to come under severe strain with the development of alternative geometries. Naturally enough, an analogous set of views had been used to explain the apriority of geometry. In particular, a flash-grasp of the indefinables of geometry, along with intuitions concerning their necessary properties, was said to explain and justify belief in the axioms of Euclidean geometry.

However, with the development of alternative geometries, such a view faced an unpleasant dilemma. Occupying one horn was the option of saying that Euclidean and non-Euclidean geometries are talking about the *same* geometrical properties, but disagreeing about what is true of them. But this option threatens the thesis of Intuition: If in fact we learn geometrical truths by intuition, how could this faculty have misled us for so long?

Occupying the other horn was the option of saying that Euclidean and non-Euclidean geometries are talking about *different* geometrical properties – attaching different meanings to, say, 'distance' – and so not disagreeing after all. But this option threatens the doctrine of Flash-Grasping. Suppose we grant that a Euclidean and a non-Euclidean geometer attach different meanings to 'distance'. In what does this difference consist? Officially, of course, the view is that one primitive state constitutes grasp of Euclidean distance, and another that of non-Euclidean distance. But in the absence of some further detail about how to tell such states apart, and about the criteria that govern their attribution, this would appear to be a hopelessly *ad hoc* and non-explanatory maneuver.

The important upshot of these considerations was to make plausible the idea that grasp of the indefinables of geometry consists precisely in the adoption of one set of truths involving them, as opposed to another. Applied to the case of logic, it generates the semantical thesis that I'll call

> *Implicit definition:* It is by arbitrarily stipulating that certain sentences of logic are to be true, or that certain inferences are to be valid, that we attach a meaning to the logical constants. More specifically, a particular constant means that logical object, if any, which would make valid a specified set of sentences and/or inferences involving it.

Wittgenstein expressed this reversal of outlook well:

> It looks as if one could *infer* from the meaning of negation that "¬¬p" means p. As if the rules for the negation sign *follow from* the nature of negation. So that in a certain sense there is first of all negation, and then the rules of grammar.
>
> We would like to say: "Negation has the property that when it is doubled it yields an affirmation." But the rule doesn't give a further description of negation, it constitutes negation.[27]

Now, the transition from this sort of implicit definition account of grasp to the analytic theory of the apriority of logic can seem pretty immediate. For it would seem that the following sort of argument is now in place:

(1) If logical constant C is to mean what it does, then argument-form A has to be valid, for C means whatever logical object in fact makes A valid.
(2) C means what it does.

Therefore,

(3) A is valid.

I will return to various questions regarding this form of justification below.[28] For now I want to worry about the fact that neither Carnap nor Wittgenstein was content merely to replace Flash Grasping with Implicit Definition. Typically, both writers went on to embrace some form of irrealism about logic. Intuitively, the statements of logic appear to be fully factual statements, expressing objective truths about the world, even if necessary and (on occasion) obvious ones. Both Carnap and Wittgenstein, however, seemed inclined to deny such an intuitive realism about logic, affirming in its place either the thesis of logical Non-Factualism or the thesis of logical Conventionalism, or, on occasion, both theses at once.

By logical Non-Factualism,[29] I mean the view that the sentences of logic that implicitly define the logical primitives do not express factual claims and, hence, are not capable of genuine truth or falsity. How, on such a view, are we to think of their semantic function? On the most popular version, we are to think of it as prescriptive, as a way of expressing a rule concerning the correct use of logical expressions. By contrast, logical Conventionalism is the view that, although the sentences of logic are factual – although they can express truths – their truth values are not objective, but are, rather, determined by our conventions.

Despite this important difference between them, there is an interesting sense in which the upshot of both views is the same, a fact which probably explains why they were often used interchangeably and why they often turn up simultaneously in the analytic theory of logic. For what both views imply is that, as between two different sets of decisions regarding which sentences of logic to hold true, there can be no epistemic fact of the matter. In short, both views imply an epistemic relativism about logic. Conventionalism implies this because it says that the truth in logic is up to us, so no substantive disagreement is possible; and Non-Factualism implies this because it says that there are no truths in logic, hence nothing to disagree about.

Nevertheless, for all this affinity of upshot, it should be quite plain that the two views are very different from – indeed, incompatible with – each other. Conventionalism is a factualist view: it presupposes that the sentences of logic have truth values. It differs from a realist view of logic in its conception of the *source* of those truth values, not on their existence. Therefore, although it is possible, as I have noted, to find texts in which a rule-prescriptivism about logic is combined with Conventionalism, that can only be a confusion.

The important question is: Why did the proponents of Implicit Definition feel the need to go beyond it all the way to the far more radical doctrines of logical Non-Factualism and/or Conventionalism? Whatever problems it may eventually be discovered to harbor, Implicit Definition seems like a plausible candidate for explaining our grasp of the logical constants, especially in view of the difficulties encountered by its classical rival. But there would appear to be little that *prima facie* recommends either logical Non-Factualism or logical Conventionalism. So why combine these dubious doctrines with what looks to be a plausible theory of meaning?

Apparently, both Carnap and Wittgenstein seem to have thought that the issue was forced, that Implicit Definition logically entailed one or the other anti-realist thesis. It seems quite clear that Carnap, for example, believed that Implicit Definition brought Conventionalism immediately in its wake; and Quine seems to have agreed. What separated them was their attitude towards Conventionalism. Carnap embraced it; Quine, by contrast, seems to have been prepared to reject any premise that led to it, hence his assault on the doctrine of Implicit Definition.

But if this is in fact the correct account of Quine's motivations, then they are based, I believe, on a false assumption, for neither form of irrealism about logic follows from the thesis of Implicit Definition.

I will proceed as follows. First, I will argue that Implicit Definition, properly understood, is completely independent of any form of irrealism about logic. Second, I will defend the thesis of Implicit Definition against Quine's criticisms. Finally, I will examine the sort of account of the apriority of logic that this doctrine is able to provide.

Implicit definition and non-factualism

Does Implicit Definition entail Non-Factualism? It is certainly very common to come across the claim that it does. Coffa, for instance, writes that from the new perspective afforded by the doctrine of Implicit Definition, the basic claims of logic are

> our access to certain meanings, definitions in disguise, devices that allow us to implement an explicit or tacit decision to constitute certain concepts. . . . From this standpoint, necessary claims do not tell us anything that is the case both in the world and in many others, as Leibniz thought, or anything that is the case for *formal* reasons, whatever that might mean, or anything that one is forced to believe due to features of our mind. They do not tell us anything that is the case; so they had better not be called claims or propositions. Since their role is to constitute meanings and since (apparently) we are free to endorse them or not, it is better to abandon the old terminology (a priori "principles", "laws", etc.) that misleadingly suggests a propositional status and to refer to them as "rules". (pp. 265–6)

I have no desire to engage the exegetical issues here; as far as I can tell, the middle Wittgenstein seems very much to have been a non-factualist about the implicit definers of logic, just as Coffa says. What I dispute is that it *follows* from the fact that a given sentence Q is being used to implicitly define one of its ingredient terms, that Q is not a factual sentence, not a sentence that "tells us anything that is the case." These two claims seem to me to be entirely independent of each other.

To help us think about this, consider Kripke's example of the introduction of the term 'meter'. As Kripke imagines it, someone introduces the term into his vocabulary by stipulating that the following sentence is to be true:

(1) Stick S is a meter long at t.

Suppose that stick S exists and is a certain length at t. Then it follows that 'meter' names that length and hence that (1) says that stick S is that length at t, and since it is that length at t, (1) is true.

Knowing all this may not be much of an epistemic achievement, but that isn't the point. The point is that there appears to be no inconsistency whatsoever between claiming that a given sentence serves to implicitly define an ingredient term and claiming that that very sentence expresses something factual.

Similarly, I don't see that there is any inconsistency between supposing that a given logical principle – for instance, the law of excluded middle – serves to implicitly define an ingredient logical constant, and supposing that that very sentence expresses a factual statement capable of genuine truth and falsity.[30]

Implicit definition and conventionalism

So far I have argued that it is consistent with a sentence's serving as an implicit definer that that very sentence come to express a fully factual claim, capable of genuine truth and falsity. Perhaps, however, when implicit definition is at issue, the truth of the claim that is thereby fixed has to be thought of as conventionally determined? Does at least Conventionalism follow from Implicit Definition?[31]

It is easy to see, I suppose, why these two ideas might have been run together. For according to Implicit Definition, 'if, then', for example, comes to mean the conditional precisely by my assigning the truth-value True to certain basic sentences involving it; for example, to

If, if p then q, and p, then q.

And in an important sense, my assigning this sentence the value True is arbitrary. Prior to my assigning it that truth value, it didn't have a complete meaning, for one of its ingredient terms didn't have a meaning at all. The process of assigning it the value True is simply part of what fixes its meaning. Had I assigned it the value False, the sentence would then have had a *different* meaning. So, prior to the assignment there couldn't have been a substantive question regarding its truth value. And after the assignment there couldn't be a substantive question as to whether that assignment was correct. In this sense, then, the sentence's truth value is arbitrary and conventional. Doesn't it follow that Implicit Definition entails Conventionalism?

Not at all. All that is involved in the thesis of Implicit Definition is the claim that the conventional assignment of truth to a sentence determines what proposition that sentence expresses (if any); such a view is entirely silent about what (if anything) determines the truth of the claim that is thereby expressed – *a fortiori*, it is silent about whether our conventions determine it.

Think here again of Kripke's meter stick. If the stick exists and has such-and-so length at t, then it is conventional that 'meter' names that length and, therefore, conventional that (1) expresses the proposition *Stick S has such-and-so length at t.* However, that stick S has that length at t is hardly a fact generated by convention; it presumably had that length prior to the convention, and may continue to have it well after the convention has lapsed.[32]

I anticipate the complaint that the entailment between Implicit Definition and Conventionalism is blocked only through the tacit use of a distinction between a sentence and the proposition it expresses, a distinction that neither Carnap nor Quine would have approved.

Such a complaint would be mistaken, however. The argument I gave relies not so much on a distinction between a sentence and a proposition in the technical sense disapproved of by Quine, as on a distinction between a sentence and *what it expresses.* And it is hard to see how any adequate philosophy of language is to get by without some such distinction.[33] Even on a deflationary view of truth, there is presumably a distinction between the *sentence* 'Snow is white' and that which makes the sentence true, namely, snow's being white. And the essential point for my purposes is that it is one thing to say that 'Snow is white' comes to express the claim that snow is white as a result of being conventionally assigned the truth-value True; and quite another to say that snow comes to be white as a result of our conventions. The first claim is Implicit Definition (however implausibly applied in this case); and the other is Conventionalism. Neither one seems to me to entail the other.

Quine against implicit definition: regress

As I noted above, I am inclined to believe that erroneous opinion on this score has played an enormous role in the history of this subject. I conjecture that had Quine felt more confident that Implicit Definition could be sharply distinguished from Conventionalism, he might not have felt so strongly against it.

In any event, though, whatever the correct explanation of Quine's animus, we are indebted to him for a series of powerful critiques of the thesis of Implicit Definition, critiques that have persuaded many that that thesis, and with it any explanation of the apriority of logic that it might be able to ground, are fundamentally flawed. We must now confront Quine's arguments.

According to Implicit Definition, the logical constants come to have a particular meaning in our vocabulary by our conventionally stipulating that certain sentences (or inferences) involving them are to be true. For instance, let us assume that the meaning for 'and' is fixed by our stipulating that the following inferences involving it are to be valid:

$$(2)\qquad \frac{\text{A and B}}{\text{A}} \qquad \frac{\text{A and B}}{\text{B}} \qquad \frac{\text{A, B}}{\text{A and B}}$$

Now, Quine's first important criticism of this idea occurs in his early paper 'Truth by Convention'.[34] As Quine there pointed out, there are an infinite number of instances of schema (2). Consequently, the inferences of this infinitary collection could not have been conventionally stipulated to be valid singly, one by one. Rather, Quine argued, if there is anything at all to this idea, it must be something along the following lines: We adopt certain general conventions, from which it follows that all the sentences of the infinitary collection are assigned the value Valid. Such a general convention would presumably look like this:

> Let all results of putting a statement for 'p' and a statement for 'q' in 'p and q implies p' be valid.

However, the trouble is that in order to state such a general convention we have had, unavoidably, to use all sorts of logical terms – 'every', 'and', and so on. So the claim, essential to the proposal under consideration, that all our logical constants acquire their meaning via the adoption of such explicitly formulated conventional assignments of validity must fail. Logical constants whose meaning is not fixed in this way are presupposed by the model itself.[35]

This argument of Quine's has been very influential; and I think that there is no doubt that it works against its target as specified. However, it is arguable that its target as specified isn't the view that needs defeating.

For, surely, it isn't compulsory to think of someone's following a rule R with respect to an expression e as consisting in his *explicitly stating* that rule in so many words in the way that Quine's argument presupposes. On the contrary, it seems far more plausible to construe x's following rule R with respect to e as consisting in some sort of fact about x's *behavior* with e.

In what would such a fact consist? Here there are at least a couple of options. According to a currently popular idea, following rule R with respect to e may consist in our being disposed to conform to rule R in our employment of e, under certain circumstances. On this version, the notion of rule-following would have been *reduced* to a certain sort of dispositional fact. Alternatively, one might wish to appeal to the notion of following a given rule, while resisting the claim that it can be reduced to a set of naturalistically acceptable dispositional facts. On such a non-reductionist version there would be facts about what rule one is following, even if these are not cashable into facts about one's behavioral dispositions, however optimal (see Chapter 15, RULE-FOLLOWING, OBJECTIVITY AND MEANING, section 2).

For myself, I am inclined to think that the reductionist version won't work, that we will have to employ the notion of following a rule unreduced.[36] But because it is more familiar, and because nothing substantive hangs on it in the present context, I will work with the reductionist version of rule-following. Applied to the case we are considering, it issues in what is widely known in the literature as a "conceptual role semantics."

According to this view, then, the logical constants mean what they do by virtue of figuring in certain inferences and/or sentences involving them, and not in others. If some expressions mean what they do by virtue of figuring in certain inferences and sentences, then some inferences and sentences are *constitutive* of an expression's meaning what it does, and others aren't. And any CRS must find a systematic way of saying which are which, of answering the question: What properties must an inference or sentence involving a constant C have, if that inference or sentence is to be constitutive of C's meaning?

Quine against implicit definition: constitutive truth

Now, Quine's second objection to Implicit Definition can be put by saying that there will be no way of doing what I said any CRS must do – namely, systematically specify the meaning-constituting inferences. Quine formulated this point in a number of places. Here is a version that appears in 'Carnap and Logical Truth':

> if we try to warp the linguistic doctrine of logical truth into something like an experimental thesis, perhaps a first approximation will run thus: *Deductively irresoluble disagreement as to a logical truth is evidence of deviation in usage (or meanings) of words.* . . . [However] the obviousness or potential obviousness of elementary logic can be seen to present an insuperable obstacle to our assigning any experimental

> meaning to the linguistic doctrine of elementary logical truth. . . . For, that theory now seems to imply nothing that is not already implied by the fact that elementary logic is obvious or can be resolved into obvious steps.[37]

Elsewhere, Quine explained his use of the word "obvious" in this connection thus:

> In "Carnap and Logical Truth" I claimed that Carnap's arguments for the linguistic doctrine of logical truth boiled down to saying no more than that they were obvious, or potentially obvious – that is, generable from obvieties by obvious steps. I had been at pains to select the word 'obvious' from the vernacular, intending it as I did in the vernacular sense. A sentence is obvious if (a) it is true and (b) any speaker of the language is prepared, for any reason or none, to assent to it without hesitation, unless put off by being asked so obvious a question.[38]

Quine's important point here is that there will be no substantive way of distinguishing between a highly obvious, non-defining sentence and a sentence that is an implicit definer. Both types of sentence – if, in fact, both types exist – will have the feature that any speaker of the language will be prepared to assent to instances of them, "for any reason or none." So in what does the alleged difference between them consist? How is distinctive content to be given to the doctrine of Implicit Definition?[39]

Now, there is no doubt that this is a very good question; and the belief that it has no good answer has contributed greatly to the rejection of the doctrine of Implicit Definition. Fodor and Lepore, for example, base the entirety of their recent argument against a conceptual role semantics on their assumption that Quine showed this question to be unanswerable.[40]

If Quine's challenge is allowed to remain unanswered, then the threat to the analytic theory of the a priori is fairly straightforward. For if there is no fact of the matter as to whether S is a sentence that I must hold true if S is to mean what it does, then there is no basis on which to argue that I am entitled to hold S true without evidence.

But that would seem to be the least of our troubles, if Quine's argument is allowed to stand; for what's threatened is not only the apriority of logical truths but, far more extremely, the *determinacy* of what they claim. For as I've already pointed out, and as many philosophers are anyway inclined to believe, a conceptual role semantics seems to be the *only* plausible view about how the meaning of the logical constants is fixed. It follows, therefore, that if there is no fact of the matter as to which of the various inferences involving a constant are meaning-constituting, then there is also no fact of the matter as to what the logical constants themselves mean. And that is just the dreaded indeterminacy of meaning on which the critique of analyticity was supposed not to depend.

The simple point here is that if the only view available about how the logical constants acquire their meaning is in terms of the inferences and/or sentences that they participate in, then any indeterminacy in what those meaning-constituting sentences and inferences are will translate into an indeterminacy about the meanings of the expressions themselves. This realization should give pause to any philosopher who thinks he can buy in on Quine's critique of implicit definition without following him all the way to the far headier doctrine of meaning-indeterminacy.

There has been a curious tendency to miss this relatively simple point. Fodor seems a particularly puzzling case; for he holds all three of the following views. (1) He rejects indeterminacy, arguing forcefully against it. (2) He follows Quine in rejecting the notion of a meaning-constituting inference. (3) He holds a conceptual role view of the meanings of the logical constants. As far as I am able to judge, however, this combination of views is not consistent.[41]

Part of the explanation for this curious blindness derives from a tendency to view Quine's argument as issuing not in an indeterminacy about meaning, but, rather, in a *holism* about it. In fact, according to Fodor and Lepore, the master argument for meaning holism in the literature runs as follows:

(1) Some of an expression's inferential liaisons are relevant to fixing its meaning.

(2) There is no principled distinction between those inferential liaisons that are constitutive and those that aren't. (the Quinean result)

Therefore,

(3) All of an expression's inferential liaisons are relevant to fixing its meaning. (Meaning Holism)

Fearing this argument's validity, and seeing no way to answer Quine's challenge, Fodor and Lepore spend their whole book trying to undermine the argument's first premise, namely, the very plausible claim that at least *some* of an expression's inferential liaisons are relevant to fixing its meaning.[42]

But they needn't have bothered, for I don't see how the master argument could be valid in the first place. The claim that *all* of an expression's inferential liaisons are constitutive of it cannot cogently follow from the claim that it is *indeterminate* what the constitutive inferences are. If it's *indeterminate* what the constitutive inferences are, then it's genuinely *unsettled* what they are. And that is inconsistent with saying that they are *all* constitutive, and inconsistent with saying that *none* are constitutive, and inconsistent with saying that some specified subset are constitutive.

Fodor and Lepore are not alone in not seeing the problem here. Let me cite just one more example. In his comments on an earlier version of the present paper, Harman says:

> Can one accept Quine's argument against analyticity without being committed to the indeterminacy of meaning? Yes and no. By the "indeterminacy of meaning" might be meant an indeterminacy as to which of the principles one accepts determine the meanings of one's terms and which simply reflect one's opinions about the facts. Clearly, Quine's argument against analyticity is committed to that sort of indeterminacy. [However] that by itself does not imply full indeterminacy in the sense of Chapter 2 of *Word and Object*.[43]

As Harman correctly says, Quine has to deny that there is a fact of the matter as to which of T's principles determine the meanings of his terms and which simply reflect T's opinions about the facts – that, after all, is just what it is to deny that there are facts about constitutivity. However, Harman insists, this denial in no way leads to the indeterminacy thesis of chapter 2 of *Word and Object*.

But this is very puzzling. Against the background of a conceptual role semantics, according to which the meaning of T's term C is determined precisely by a certain subset of the principles involving C that T accepts, an indeterminacy in what the meaning-determining principles are will automatically lead to an indeterminacy in what the meaning is, in the full sense of chapter 2 of *Word and Object*. If a subset (not necessarily proper) of accepted principles is supposed to determine meaning; and if there is no fact of the matter as to which subset that is; then there is, to that extent, no fact of the matter as to what meaning has been determined. Since correct translation is supposed to preserve meaning, it follows that there can be no fact of the matter as to what counts as correct translation.

I think there is really no avoiding the severe conclusion that meaning is indeterminate, if the Quinean challenge to constitutivity is allowed to remain unanswered. I'm inclined to think, therefore, that anyone who rejects radical indeterminacy of meaning must believe that a distinction between the meaning-constituting and the non-meaning-constituting can be drawn. The only question is how.

Well, that is not the task of the present paper. Although there are some good ideas about this, I don't have a fully thought-through proposal to present just now.[44] My main aim here is not to *solve* the fundamental problem for a conceptual role semantics for the logical constants; rather, as I have stressed, it is to show that, against the background of a rejection of indeterminacy, its insolubility cannot be conceded.

Pending the discovery of other problems, then, it seems open to us to suppose that a plausible theory of meaning for the logical constants is given by something like the following:

> A logical constant C expresses that logical object, if any, that makes valid its meaning-constituting inferences or sentences.

Implicit definition, justification and entitlement

Now, how does any of this help vindicate the analytic theory of the apriority of logic, the idea that logic is epistemically analytic? Let us consider a particular inference form, A, in a particular thinker's (T) repertoire; and let's suppose that that inference form is constitutive of the meaning of one of its ingredient constants C. How, exactly, might these facts help explain the epistemic analyticity of A for T?

To say that A is epistemically analytic for T is to say that T's knowledge of A's meaning alone suffices for T's justification for A, so that empirical support is not required. And it does seem that a conceptual role semantics can provide us with a model of how that might be so. For given the relevant facts, we would appear to be able to argue as follows:

(1) If C is to mean what it does, then A has to be valid, for C means whatever logical object in fact makes A valid.

(2) C means what it does.

Therefore,

(3) A is valid.

Now, it is true that this is tantamount to a fairly broad use of the phrase "knowledge of the meaning of A," for this knowledge includes not merely knowledge of what A means, strictly so called, but also knowledge of how that meaning is fixed. But this is, of course, both predictable and unavoidable: there was never any real prospect of explaining apriority merely on the basis of a knowledge of propositional content. Even Carnap realized that one needed to know that a given inference or sentence had the status of a 'meaning postulate'.

But isn't it required, if this account is to genuinely explain T's a priori justification for the basic truths of logic, that T know the premisses a priori as well? Yet, it hasn't been shown that T can know the premisses a priori.

It is quite correct that I have not attempted to show that the relevant facts about meaning cited in the premisses are knowable a priori, although I believe that it is intuitively quite clear that they are. I have purposely avoided discussing all issues relating to knowledge of meaning facts. My brief here has been to defend epistemic analyticity; and this requires showing only that certain sentences are such that, *if* someone knows the relevant facts about their meaning, *then* that person will be in a position to form a justified belief about their truth. It does not require showing that the knowledge of those meaning facts is itself a priori (although, I repeat, it seems quite clear to me that it will be).[45]

Isn't it a problem for the aspirations of the present account that a thinker would have to use *modus ponens* to get from the premisses to the desired conclusion?

Not if Dummett's distinction between pragmatic and vicious circularity is credited with opening a space for an epistemology for logic, as discussed above.

Finally, how could such an account possibly hope to explain the man in the street's justification for believing in the truths of logic? For such a person, not only would the relevant meaning facts be quite opaque, he probably wouldn't even be capable of framing them. Yet such a person is obviously quite justified in believing the elementary truths of logic. Thus, so our objector might continue, this sort of account cannot explain our ordinary warrant for believing in logic; at best, it can explain the warrant that sophisticates have.

I think that, strictly speaking, this objection is correct, but only in a sense that strips it of real bite. Philosophers are often in the position of articulating a warrant for an ordinary belief that the man in the street would not understand. If we insist that a person counts as justified only if they are aware of the reason that warrants their belief, then we will simply have to find another term for the kind of warrant that ordinary folk often have and that philosophers seek to articulate. Tyler Burge has called it an "entitlement":

> The distinction between justification and entitlement is this. Although both have positive force in rationally supporting a propositional attitude or cognitive practice, and in constituting an epistemic right to it, entitlements are epistemic rights or warrants that need not be understood by or even be accessible to the subject. . . . The unsophisticated are entitled to rely on their perceptual beliefs. Philosophers may articulate these entitlements. But being entitled does not require being able to justify reliance on these resources, or even to conceive such a justification. Justifications, in the narrow sense, involve reasons that people have and have access to.[46]

When someone is entitled, all the facts relevant to the person's justification are already in place, so to say; what's missing is the reflection that would reveal them.

Just so in the case at hand. If a conceptual role semantics is true, and if A is indeed constitutive of C's meaning what it does, then those facts by themselves constitute a warrant for A; empirical support is not necessary. A can only be false by meaning something other than what it means. But these facts need not be known by the ordinary person. They suffice for his entitlement, even if not for his full-blown justification. This full-blown justification can be had only by knowing the relevant facts about meaning.

Conclusion

Quine helped us see the vacuity of the metaphysical concept of analyticity and, with it, the futility of the project it was supposed to underwrite – the linguistic theory of necessity. But I don't see that those arguments affect the epistemic notion of analyticity that is needed for the purposes of the theory of a priori knowledge. Indeed, it seems to me that epistemic analyticity can be defended quite vigorously, especially against the background of a realism about meaning.

On the assumption that our warrant for believing in elementary logical truths cannot be explained, the outstanding problem is to explain our a priori knowledge of conceptual truths. For this purpose, the crucial semantical notion is that of Frege-analyticity. I have argued that this notion is bound to be in good standing for a meaning realist.

If the project of explaining logic is not ruled hopeless, then I have tried to show how the doctrine that appears to offer the most promising account of how we grasp the meanings of the logical constants – namely, Implicit Definition – can explain the epistemic analyticity of our logical beliefs and, hence, our a priori warrant for believing them. As long as we are not prepared to countenance radical indeterminacy, we should have every confidence that this form of explanation can be made to work.

Appendix: a priori knowledge of the second premise

I have argued that a conceptual role semantics supplies the following sort of warrant for our belief in the elementary truths of logic.

(1) If C is to mean what it does, then A has to be valid, for C means whatever logical object in fact makes A valid.

(2) C means what it does.

Therefore,

(3) A is valid.

In this Appendix I want to propose a reason for holding that the second premise in this argument form is knowable a priori.

The challenge might appear, at first, to be utterly trivial. Surely, we know, for any given C, that it means whatever it means. Suppose C is the word "and"; then, surely, we know a priori that "and" means whatever it means. Indeed, isn't it clear that we know a priori precisely what it does mean, namely, *and*? For any given mentioned constant, isn't disquotation guaranteed to state its meaning accurately?

What all such purely disquotational views of our knowledge of meaning ignore is the possibility that the words we are disquoting fail to have a meaning in the first place. What the disquotational maneuver guarantees is only that, *if* a word has a meaning, then disquotation will state its meaning correctly. However, the disquotational view does not, and cannot, address the question of how we know that the word has a meaning to begin with.

This point is interestingly related to a point made by Harman in the following passage:

> Even if conventional assignments of truth or falsity determine meaning, it does not follow that a sentence is true by virtue of convention. It does not even follow that the sentence is true.[47]

Harman's claim is that, even if we put aside objections to the thesis of Implicit Definition, it wouldn't follow that a meaning-constituting sentence is true. Hence, we couldn't claim to be entitled to S without evidence, just because S is meaning-constituting. Perhaps S is meaning-constituting and not true.

How might this happen? Harman doesn't explain; but it's important to ask. How might it turn out that a sentence that is stipulated to be true, as a way of fixing the meaning of some ingredient term t, nevertheless fail to be true?

One thing is, I think, certain: not by being false. For to be false, S would have to be meaningful. And it is stipulated that, if S expresses any meaning at all, it expresses a true one. Under these assumptions, therefore, S can fail to be true only by expressing no meaning whatever. And this in turn will happen only if one of its ingredient terms fails to express a meaning.

So let us ask: How might it turn out that a set of constitutive rules for a term t fail to determine a meaning for it? I can think of two ways. First, the meaning-constituting role specified for t may impose inconsistent demands on it, thus making it impossible for there to be a meaning that makes true all of its meaning-constituting sentences. A second worry might arise simply against the background of a robust propositionalism, without exploiting worries about inconsistency. For according to a robust propositionalism, meanings are radically mind-independent entities whose existence no amount of defining could ensure. Hence, there may well not be a meaning answering to all the demands placed upon a term by a set of stipulations.[48]

For both of these reasons, then, we cannot immediately conclude from the fact that t is governed by a set of meaning-constituting rules, that t is meaningful.

To put this point in terms of the second premise of the argument-form outlined above, the fact that a given constant C is governed by certain constitutive rules of use doesn't by itself entitle us to conclude that C means what it does, because it doesn't by itself entitle us to conclude that C has a meaning in the first place. Hence, we cannot lean on a disquotational view to vindicate our claim that the second premise is knowable a priori.

A solution

So how are we to proceed? Is there an a priori way of laying to rest a doubt about the meaningfulness of our logical constants? I think we can make a case for the following claim: we are a priori entitled to believe that our basic logical constants are meaningful because we cannot coherently doubt that they are. For the assumption that our constants are meaningful is presupposed in any attempt to claim that they aren't.

I shall assume that, prior to having seen the desirability of introducing an alternative set of logical constants, we start off with a particular, single set of these. For the sake of specificity, let us assume that these constants are classical, that is, that they are governed by classical constitutive rules. As will become clear, this assumption is absolutely inessential to the argument that follows.

Now, consider what a first attempt to formulate a skepticism about the meaningfulness of our constants would look like. The Skeptic wishes to assert that our basic logical constants do not express a meaning. Given the assumption that our constants are classical, the Skeptic's assertion comes down to a claim about the meaningfulness of the basic pair of constants in terms of which all the others can be defined – let's suppose that that pair consists of negation and the conditional. In the case of negation, the Skeptic would appear to want to claim:

(4) $\forall$x (If x is a token of 'not', then x does not have a meaning);

and in the case of 'if, then' this:

(5) $\forall$x (If x is a token of 'if, then', then x does not have a meaning).

The problems with both (4) and (5), however, are not easy to miss. In attempting to state that our basic logical constants fail to be meaningful, both claims have to assume that those very constants *are* meaningful. No one could rationally wish to assert (4) or (5) who did not believe that negation and the conditional are meaningful; yet what (4) and (5) claim is that negation and the conditional are not meaningful (respectively). It would appear, therefore, that any attempt to assert (4) and (5) would be self-defeating: the very act of putting those propositions forward undermines the truth of the propositions that are being put forward.

A number of possible lines of objection need to be considered. First, does the argument especially depend on the particular selection of basic logical constants? Would it work equally well if, say, negation and disjunction had been chosen as the reduction base, rather than negation and the conditional?

It is hard to see how the particular selection can make any difference. It is relatively trivial to show that, regardless of the particular choice of reduction base, the same style of argument goes through, with similar effect.

A second, somewhat more challenging line of objection runs as follows. Let's concede that an assertion of (4) would be self-defeating: we cannot use the constants we have to assert of *them* that they are meaningless.[49] But why couldn't we introduce some *new* constants and use them to formulate a skepticism about the old ones? (Notice that I don't need to make any assumptions about what these prior constants are, whether classical or otherwise.) Such a claim would look like this:

(6) ∀x (If x is a token of 'not', then x does not_N refer),

where the subscript 'N' indicates that the constant is one of the *new* ones. There appears to be nothing self-stultifying about this thesis.

I don't think that this objection works either, though its problems are slightly better hidden. The problem is that the integrity of the old constants is presupposed *in the very act of introducing the new alternatives.*

Recall, we are operating on the assumption that we start off with a determinate set of logical constants. By further, and ultimately optional assumption, these constants are classical. Now we wish to introduce an alternative set of constants, so that we may use them to state, of the old constants, that they are meaningless. Consider how such an introduction would have to go. We would need to say what the constitutive rules governing the new constants are, and that they are *all* of them. That is, we would need to say something along the following lines (where the subscript 'N' indicates that the constant is *new*):

(7) ∀x (If x is a token of 'not_N', then x is subject to rules R1, R2, R3, and no others).

Clearly, however, in this definition the meaningfulness of many of the old constants – in particular, negation, the conditional, and the universal quantifier – is presupposed. And there appears to be no way to cancel that presupposition without jeopardizing the meaningfulness of the new constants with the use of which the skeptical hypothesis is to be formulated. Unless the old constants *are* meaningful, the stipulations will fail to give the new constants a particular meaning. Hence, we cannot coherently suppose both that the new constants have a meaning and that the old ones don't.

As far as I am able to judge, every attempt to formulate a worry about the meaningfulness of our basic logical constants runs into a similar sort of difficulty: every such attempt ends up presupposing the integrity of the constants whose integrity it seeks to question.

An enormous number of questions are left outstanding, none of which can be adequately dealt with here. For one: Is this merely a pragmatic result, or something stronger? Tentative answer: Something stronger. To sustain the claim that the result is merely pragmatic, one would have to make sense of the claim that, although we cannot rationally doubt that our constants are meaningful, it is nevertheless possible that they aren't. However, considerations similar to the ones adduced above would tend to show that we cannot make sense of this thought either.

Another question: Doesn't this argument prove too much? Some of the best recent philosophy has taken the form of claiming that various of the rules of classical logic make unsatisfiable demands on our ability to mean what we do by our words and, hence, that they are incoherent. Isn't any criticism of this form disabled by the above argument?

Not at all. My argument does nothing to preclude the following sort of view: Our constants are essentially intuitionistic – that is, they are governed by a core set of intuitionistic rules. However, some philosophers and mathematicians have mistakenly supposed that they are also subject to certain further rules – they have mistakenly supposed, in other words, that our constants are classical. However, they are mistaken in this: not only are our constants not classical, but they couldn't have been, because creatures like us are incapable of meaning classical constants.

Nothing in my argument prevents someone from adopting the sort of view outlined in the preceding paragraph. What my argument does preclude is the simultaneous assertion that our ordinary constants are classical *and* that they are incoherent. As far as I can see, though, no one with an interest in criticizing classical logic need put his position in that manifestly problematic way.[50,51]

Notes

1 'Definition in a Quinean World', in J. Fetzer, D. Shatz, and G. Schlesinger (eds), *Definitions and Definability: Philosophical Perspectives* (Dordrecht: Kluwer, 1991), pp. 111–31.

2 'Why Meaning (Probably) Isn't Conceptual Role', *Mind and Language*, 6 (1991), 328–43.

3 Consider, for example, the following passage from *The Philosophy of Logic* (Englewood Cliffs, NJ: Prentice Hall, 1970), p. 3:

> My objection to recognizing propositions does not arise primarily from philosophical parsimony – from a desire to dream of no more things in heaven and earth than need be. Nor does it arise, more specifically, from particularism – from a disapproval of intangible or abstract entities. My objection is more urgent. If there were propositions, they would induce a certain relation of synonymy or equivalence between sentences themselves: those sentences would be equivalent that expressed the same proposition. Now my objection is going to be that the appropriate equivalence relation makes no objective sense at the level of

sentences. This, if I succeed in making it plain, should spike the hypothesis of propositions.

4 As I say, I am going to work with this linguistic picture out of deference to my opponents. I would prefer to work with a propositionalist picture of belief. Most of the crucial notions developed in this paper, and much of the argument involving them, can be translated, with suitable modifications, into this propositionalist framework. Thus, even those who believe, as I do, that knowledge is not a matter of knowing that certain sentences are true can find use for the account developed here.

5 The inclusion of the word "outer" here is partly stipulative. I have always found it natural to regard a priori knowledge as encompassing knowledge that is based on no experience as well as knowledge that is based purely on *inner* experience.

6 In the interests of brevity, I shall henceforth take it as understood that "justification" means "justification with a strength sufficient for knowledge".

7 Even this strong notion is not as demanding as many have supposed. For instance, it is consistent with a belief's being a priori in the strong sense that we should have *pragmatic* reasons for dropping it from our best overall theory. For illuminating discussion of the modesty of the notion of the a priori, see Crispin Wright: 'Inventing Logical Necessity', in Butterfield (ed.), *Language, Mind and Logic* (Cambridge: Cambridge University Press, 1984), and Bob Hale, *Abstract Objects* (Oxford: Blackwell, 1986), ch. 6.

8 See Gilbert Harman, *Thought* (Princeton: Princeton University Press, 1973).

9 *The Ways of Paradox* (Cambridge, Mass.: Harvard University Press, 1976), p. 103.

10 'Two Dogmas of Empiricism', in *From a Logical Point of View* (Cambridge, Mass.: Harvard University Press, 1953), pp. 36–7.

11 "Quine on Meaning and Existence I", *Review of Metaphysics*, 21 (1968), 124–51, p. 128. I am indebted to Paul Horwich for emphasizing the importance of this point.

12 "Doubts About Conceptual Analysis", MS, p. 5. See also his "Quine on Meaning and Existence I".

13 See G. Frege (trans. Austin): *The Foundations of Arithmetic*, sec. 3 (Oxford: Blackwell, 1950). (Some may regard the attribution of precisely this notion to Frege controversial. What matters to me is not who came up with the idea, but rather the philosophical role it has played.)

My use of the term 'analytic' in connection with Frege's *semantical* notion as well as with the preceding epistemic and metaphysical concepts may be thought ill-advised. But I do so deliberately, to highlight the fact that the term has been used in the literature in general, and in Quine in particular, to stand for all three different sorts of notion, often without any acknowledgement of that fact. This terminological promiscuity has undoubtedly contributed to the confusion surrounding discussions of this issue.

14 For some discussion, see my "The Transparency of Mental Content", in *Philosophical Perspectives*, 8 (1994), 33–50.

15 Exegetically, this does leave us with a couple of puzzles. First, 'Two Dogmas' does contain a brief discussion of the implicit definition idea, under the guise of the notion of a "semantical rule". Given that, why does Quine insist that he intends only to discuss the notion of Frege-analyticity? Second, the notion of a semantical rule is discussed only in connection with non-logical truths; since, however, the deployment of this idea would be exactly the same in the logical case, why is the analyticity of logic expressly excluded? Third, given that the analyticity of logic is expressly excluded, on what basis does Quine allow himself to draw morals about logic's revisability towards the end of

'Two Dogmas'? I think there is no avoiding the conclusion that, on this and other related issues (see below), 'Two Dogmas' is confused. It would, in fact, have been surprising if these rather tricky problems had all been in clear focus in Quine's pioneering papers.

16 In this context, nothing fancy is meant by the use of such expressions as 'property' and 'proposition'. For present purposes they may be understood in a thoroughly deflationary manner.

I have sometimes been asked why I consider just this particular weakening of a non-factualist thesis, one that involves, problematically from Quine's official point of view, a modal notion? Why not rather attribute to him the following *Very Weak Thesis*:

> (VWT) There is a coherent, determinate property expressed by 'is analytic', but *as a matter of fact*, it has never been instantiated; consequently, all tokens of the sentence 'S is analytic' have been false up to now.

There are two reasons. First, the VWT is not a philosophically interesting thesis; and, second, it could not have been argued for on the basis of a *philosophy* paper – i.e., on the sorts of a priori grounds that Quine offers. So although Quine may not be entitled to precisely the ET, I am going to ignore that and not hold it against him.

17 'Two Dogmas', p. 33.

18 This question was first asked by Grice and Strawson in their "In Defense of a Dogma", reprinted in Grice: *Studies in the Way of Words* (Cambridge, Mass.: Harvard University Press, 1989). Grice and Strawson didn't sufficiently stress, however, that Quine was committed to a skepticism even about *intra*linguistic synonymy, and not just about *inter*linguistic synonymy, for the theory of apriority doesn't much care about the interlinguistic case.

19 Peter Strawson, *Logico-Linguistic Papers* (London: Methuen, 1971), p. 117.

20 Harman, *Thought*, p. 14, emphasis in the original.

21 Recent formulations of this argument may be found in Fodor, *Psychosemantics* (Cambridge, Mass.: MIT Press, 1987), pp. 62ff.; Fodor and Lepore, *Holism: A Shopper's Guide* (Oxford: Blackwell, 1991), pp. 37ff.; Devitt: *Coming to Our Senses*, (New York: Cambridge University Press, 1995), p. 17. None of the authors mentioned approve of the argument.

22 A further 'Two Dogmas'-based argument for meaning holism, this time invalid, will be considered further below, in connection with the discussion of the thesis of Implicit Definition.

23 As before, subject to the proviso about the apriority of synonymy.

24 I am ignoring for now the class of a priori truths that are neither logical nor Frege-analytic. As we shall see, the very same strategy – implicit definition – that can be applied to explain our knowledge of logic can be applied to them as well.

25 *The Logical Basis of Metaphysics* (Cambridge, Mass.: Harvard University Press, 1991), p. 202. Dummett's distinction is deployed in a somewhat different context.

26 A. Coffa, *The Semantic Tradition* (Cambridge: Cambridge University Press, 1991), ch. 14. In the next three paragraphs I follow the general contours of the account that Coffa develops. However, the formulations are mine and they differ in important respects from Coffa's, as we shall see further on.

27 *Philosophical Grammar* (Los Angeles: University of California Press, 1976), pp. 52–3; cited in Coffa, *The Semantic Tradition*.

28 Readers who are acquainted with a paper of mine entitled "Inferential Role Semantics and the Analytic/Synthetic Distinction", *Philosophical Studies* (Spring 1994), pp. 109–

22, will be aware that I used to worry that Implicit Definition could not generate a priori knowledge because of the falsity of something I called "The Principle". The Principle is the thesis that it follows from a sentence's being an implicit definer that that sentence is true. The proper place of this issue in the overall dialectic, and a proposed solution, are discussed in the Appendix to the present chapter.

29 Not to be confused with the non-factualism about Frege-analyticity discussed earlier in the chapter.

30 Someone may object that the two cases are not relevantly analogous. For the meter case is supposed to be a case of the *fixation of reference*, but the logical case an instance of the fixation of meaning. Doesn't this difference between them block the argument I gave?

I don't see that it does. First, the two cases really are disanalogous only if there is an important difference between meaning and reference; yet, as is well-known, there are many philosophers of language who are inclined to think that there isn't any such important difference. Second, it seems to me that even if we allowed for a robust distinction between meaning and reference, the point would remain entirely unaffected. Whether we think of an implicit definer as fixing a term's reference directly, or as first fixing its meaning, which then in turn fixes its reference, seems to me entirely irrelevant to the claim that Implicit Definition does not entail Non-Factualism. As long as both processes are consistent with the fixation of a factual claim for the sentence at issue – as they very much seem to be – the point stands.

31 Certainly many philosophers seem to have thought so. Richard Creath, for example, sympathetically expounds Carnap's view that the basic axioms of logic implicitly define the ingredient logical terms by saying that on this view "the postulates (together with the other conventions) create the truths that they, the postulates express". See his "Carnap's Conventionalism", *Synthese*, 93 (1992), 141–65, p. 147.

32 This point is also forcefully made by Nathan Salmon in "Analyticity and Apriority", *Philosophical Perspectives*, 7 (1993), 125–33, and by Stephen Yablo in his review of Sidelle, *Philosophical Review*, 101 (1992), 878–81.

33 Notice that conventionalists themselves need to make crucial use of such a distinction when they describe their own position, as in the passage cited above from Creath: 'The postulates (together with the other conventions) create the truths that they, the postulates, express.' As Hilary Putnam pointed out some time ago, it's hard to see how distinctive content is to be given to Conventionalism without the use of some such distinction. For a conventionalism merely about linguistic expressions is trivial. A real issue is joined only when the view is formulated as a claim about the truths expressed. See Putnam, "The Refutation of Conventionalism," in his *Mind, Language and Reality: Philosophical Papers* v.2 (New York: Cambridge University Press, 1975).

34 Quine's argument here is officially directed against a Conventionalism about logical truth, that is, against the idea that logical truth is determined by our conventions. This idea we have already rejected in our discussion of the metaphysical concept of analyticity. However, Quine attacks Conventionalism *by* attacking the semantical thesis of Implicit Definition. Hence the need for the present discussion.

35 Quine claims that this argument may also be put as follows: The claim that the sentences of logic lack assignment of truth value until they are conventionally assigned such values must fail. For logic is needed in order to infer from a formulated general convention that the infinitely many instances of a given schema are true. Hence, sentences of logic whose truth value is not fixed as the model requires, are presupposed by the model itself.

It's unclear to me that this is a formulation of precisely the same argument. However, to the extent that it is distinct, it is also addressed by the proposal I put forth below.

36 For discussion, see my "The Rule-Following Considerations", *Mind* (1989), pp. 507–49.

37 'Carnap and Logical Truth', in *The Ways of Paradox*, p. 105.

38 "Reply to Hellman", in Schilpp (ed.), *The Philosophy of W.V.O. Quine* (La Salle: Open Court, 1975), p. 206.

39 For all its influence, it is still possible to find the force of the Quinean point being underestimated by the friends of Implicit Definition. Christopher Peacocke, for example, in a recent, subtle defense of an inferential role semantics claims that what makes the inferences involving the logical constants constitutive is that a thinker finds those inferences "primitively compelling", and does so because they are of those forms. He goes on to explain:

> To say that a thinker finds such instances primitively compelling is to say this: (1) he finds them compelling; (2) he does not find them compelling because he has inferred them from other premises and/or principles; and (3) for possession of the concept in question . . . he does not need to take the correctness of the transitions as answerable to anything else. *A Study of Concepts* (Cambridge, Mass.: MIT Press, 1992), p. 6.

I think it is plain, however, that these conditions are insufficient for answering the Quinean challenge: a non-constitutive, though highly obvious, form of inference may also be found compelling because of its form, and not on the basis of inference from anything else. So these conditions cannot be what distinguish between a constitutive and a non-constitutive inference.

40 "Why Meaning (Probably) Isn't Conceptual Role".

41 For Fodor's views on the mentioned issues, see his *Psychosemantics* (Cambridge, Mass.: MIT Press, 1989) and *The Elm and the Expert* (Cambridge, Mass.: MIT Press, 1994).

42 See Fodor and Lepore: *Holism: A Shopper's Guide* (Oxford: Blackwell, 1993).

43 Harman, "Comments on Boghossian", *APA Symposium on Analytic Truth* (Boston, Mass., December 1994).

44 For a good start, see Peacocke: *A Study of Concepts.*

45 For a discussion of why the second premiss is a priori see the Appendix to the present chapter.

46 Burge, "Content Preservation", *Philosophical Review*, 102 (October 1993).

47 "Quine on Meaning and Existence", pp. 130–1; see also "Truth by Convention", pp. 93–5, and "Carnap and Logical Truth", p. 114.

48 This, I believe, was the basis of Arthur Prior's worry about an inferential role semantics; it was unfortunate that he tried to illustrate his point in a way that misleadingly suggested that his was a worry of the first sort, about consistency. See A. Prior: "The Runabout Inference Ticket", reprinted in Strawson (ed.), *Philosophical Logic* (Oxford: Oxford University Press, 1967).

49 This was suggested to me in conversation by Hartry Field.

50 For much more on all this, see my "Knowledge of Logic" (in preparation).

51 I am grateful to a number of audiences – at MIT, CUNY Graduate Center, Michigan State, the University of Chicago, the SOFIA Conference on Tenerife, the Chapel Hill Colloquium, Dartmouth College, London University and Oxford University. An earlier version of this paper was presented at the NEH Institute on the "Nature of Meaning,"

held at Rutgers University in the summer of 1993. It was there that I first became aware that Christopher Peacocke has been thinking along somewhat similar lines about the a priori – see his "How are A Priori Truths Possible?" presented at the Rutgers conference. Although there are a number of differences between our approaches, and although Peacocke's focus is not on the notion of analyticity, I have benefited from discussing these matters with him. Another philosopher to whom I am grateful for numerous illuminating conversations is Jerry Katz. Although Katz carves up the issues in this area very differently than I do, he deserves an enormous amount of credit for keeping the topic of analyticity alive during a period when it was extremely unfashionable to do so. I also benefited from presenting a version of this chapter as part of a symposium on Analytic Truth, involving Gil Harman, Burton Dreben and W.V.O. Quine, at the 1994 Eastern Division meetings of the APA. I am especially grateful to Gil Harman, Elizabeth Fricker, Hartry Field, Gary Gates, Bill Lycan, Stephen Schiffer and Barry Loewer for their detailed comments on previous versions of this chapter. Special thanks are due to Bob Hale and Crispin Wright for their patience and for their very helpful reactions to several different drafts. For other helpful discussion and commentary, I want to thank Jennifer Church, Jerry Fodor, Albert Casullo, Norma Yunez, Neil Tennant, Peter Unger, Tom Nagel, Paul Horwich, Ned Block, Richard Creath, Allan Gibbard, Stephen Yablo and David Velleman.

Select bibliography

Carnap, R., *Meaning and Necessity* (Chicago: University of Chicago Press, 1947).
Coffa, A., *The Semantic Tradition* (Cambridge: Cambridge University Press, 1991).
Dummett, M., *Truth and Other Enigmas* (London: Duckworth, 1978).
——*Frege: The Philosophy of Language* (London: Duckworth, 1973).
——*Frege: The Philosophy of Mathematics* (Cambridge, Mass.: Harvard University Press, 1991).
Field, H., 'Logic, Meaning and Conceptual Role', *Journal of Philosophy*, 74, 379–409.
Frege, G., *The Foundations of Arithmetic*, trans. Austin (Oxford: Blackwell, 1950).
Grice, H.P., and Strawson, P., 'In Defense of a Dogma', reprinted in Grice, *Studies in the Way of Words* (Cambridge, Mass.: Harvard University Press, 1989).
Harman, G., 'Quine on Meaning and Existence I', *Review of Metaphysics* (1968), 21, 124–51.
Pap, A., *Semantics and Necessary Truth* (New Haven: Yale University Press, 1958).
Peacocke, C., *A Study of Concepts* (Cambridge, Mass.: MIT Press, 1992).
——'How are A Priori Truths Possible?' *European Journal of Philosophy*, 1 (1993), 175–99.
Putnam, H., *Mind, Language and Reality: Philosophical Papers*, Vol. 2 (Cambridge: Cambridge University Press, 1975).
——'Philosophy of Logic', reprinted in *Mathematics, Matter and Method: Philosophical Papers*, Vol. 2 (Cambridge: Cambridge University Press, 1979).
Quine, W.V.O. 'Truth by Convention', reprinted in *The Ways of Paradox* (Cambridge, Mass.: Harvard University Press, 1976).
——'Carnap and Logical Truth', reprinted in *The Ways of Paradox* (Cambridge, Mass.: Harvard University Press, 1976).
——'Two Dogmas of Empiricism', in *From a Logical Point of View* (Cambridge, Mass.: Harvard University Press, 1953).
——*The Philosophy of Logic* (Englewood Cliffs, NJ: Prentice Hall, 1970).

Quine, W.V.O. *Word and Object* (Boston: MIT Press, 1960).

Wright, C., *Wittgenstein on the Foundations of Mathematics* (Cambridge, Mass.: Harvard University Press, 1980).

—— 'Inventing Logical Necessity', in Butterfield (ed.), *Mind, Language and Logic* (Cambridge: Cambridge University Press, 1984).

15

Rule-following, objectivity and meaning

BOB HALE

1 Wittgenstein on meaning, understanding and rules

There is widespread agreement that Wittgenstein advances, in the rule-following sections of *Philosophical Investigations* and *Remarks on the Foundations of Mathematics*,[1] considerations that are quite destructive of certain conceptions of meaning, understanding and rule-following into which we may easily slide when we attempt a general philosophical account of them: that meaning something by a certain expression is a special act or state of mind, accompanying or lying behind writing or speaking; that understanding an expression consists in supplying or adopting an interpretation for it; that following a rule – a rule for the use of a word, say – is a matter of travelling along rails which are already laid down and determine its application in new cases, and so on. And it is equally generally agreed that Wittgenstein's aims, in his discussions of these matters, are not wholly negative and destructive – that he seeks to replace these misconceptions by a better account, armed with which we shall be able to resist the pressures which push us into them: using an expression according to a rule is not founded upon reasons, but that does not mean that there can be no going right (or wrong) in our use of expressions – and the key to understanding how this can be so lies in the idea that to employ an expression with a certain meaning, or according to a rule, is to participate in a custom or practice. It is, in other words, no part of his overall purpose to uphold blanket sceptical conclusions, to the effect that there are no such things as meaning something by a particular expression, as understanding another's words or as employing an expression according to a rule (or as following a rule of any kind). His aim, rather, seems clearly enough to have been to rid us of badly mistaken pictures of what these things are, and to point us towards a proper, less inflated, conception of them.

This much is, I believe, quite uncontroversial. What *is* controversial is the *extent* of the destruction wrought by the negative considerations Wittgenstein advances and, consequentially, the exact character of the conception of meaning, understanding and rule-following – centred on the somewhat elusive ideas of custom and practice – that we may retain in the light of a proper appreciation of their destructive effect. There is, in particular, a sharp opposition between what may be termed 'conservative' readings, which see Wittgenstein as solely concerned to undermine certain seductive misconceptions[2] and count it an error to interpret him as providing support for any sceptical or revisionary theses about meaning and related matters, and more radical ones[3] which claim to find in his writings grounds for calling into question, in one way or another, what may roughly and provisionally be called the objectivity of meaning.

This exegetical issue will not be pursued here.[4] Even if the conservatives are right, the more sceptical lines of thought which Wittgenstein's discussions have suggested to some thinkers quite certainly merit careful attention in their own right, whether or not they can defensibly be attributed to Wittgenstein, or regarded as drawing out consequences of claims to which he uncontroversially commits himself. It is with two of these more sceptical directions of theorizing that we shall be concerned.

2 Kripke on rules

Kripke (1982) interprets central sections of *Philosophical Investigations* (§§ 138–242) as developing a 'sceptical paradox' about meaning. The paradoxical conclusion of the sceptical argument is that there is *no fact about what anyone means by any expression* she uses. Faced with this seemingly outrageous conclusion, we naturally incline to the view that there *must* be something wrong with the argument leading to it: that it relies on some assumption which we can reject, or that it makes some fallacious step. To attempt to sustain this claim is to go for a 'straight solution', which enables us to maintain that there is, after all, some species of fact in which our meaning what we do by our words consists. But Kripke argues – and takes Wittgenstein to have argued – that there can be no such meaning-constitutive facts: the argument, to be reviewed shortly, proceeds by elimination, that is, it considers the various types of fact that might be supposed to play this constitutive role, and tries to show that they cannot do the job required of them. So Kripke advocates instead a 'sceptical solution', that is, a response to the paradox which *accepts* the sceptical conclusion but seeks to explain how we can live with it; in particular, how we can rehabilitate talk of meaning without supposing that there are facts in virtue of which meaning ascriptions (such as statements of the form 'S means such-and-such by E') are true or false.

Kripke develops the sceptical argument in terms of one central example. Suppose '$68 + 57 = ?$' is a question I have never explicitly considered. What answer should I give? I shall almost certainly answer '125'. And I shall naturally suppose that this is not only the arithmetically correct answer, but the one I must give, if my answer is to be in accord with what I have all along meant by '+' or 'plus'. It is, I suppose, a fact that when I used '+' before, I meant a certain definite function – one which has, *inter alia*, the value 125 for the arguments 68, 57, and not some other function, which has a different value for those arguments. In particular it is a fact, surely, that I didn't mean the function Kripke calls 'quus' (for which we shall use the symbol '⊕'), where $m \oplus n = m + n$, provided that $m,n < 57$, but in case m or $n \geq 57$, $m \oplus n = 5$.

Kripke's sceptic maintains that there is no such fact. His argument focuses initially on the claim that '125' is the answer I must give, if I am to be in accord with what I formerly meant by '+'. Granting, pro tem, that there is no problem about my *present* understanding of '+' – that I use it to mean addition – the sceptic presses two questions, one constitutive and one epistemological:

> What makes it the case that up to now I have meant addition rather than, say, quaddition by '+', so that '125' is the answer I should give to '68 + 57 = ?', if I am to be in agreement with what I meant by my previous uses of '+'?
>
> What justifies me in thinking that this is the answer I ought to return, if I am to be in agreement with my past meaning for '+'?

It is crucially important to note that these questions are posed against the background of an idealizing assumption about my cognitive powers. I am assumed to have perfect recall of all potentially relevant aspects of my past linguistic and non-linguistic behaviour, and of all my preceding mental life, any previous thoughts, imaginings, or the like, which may have accompanied my previous uses of '+'. It should be noted also that there is to be no prior restriction upon the type of fact that may be admissibly cited as constitutive of meaning; in particular, there is no Quinean restriction to purely physical or behavioural facts. This idealization sets Kripke's sceptic apart from the traditional variety of epistemological sceptic: if, even under the idealizing assumption, it proves impossible to justify the claim that I meant addition, the conclusion to be drawn is not – with the traditional sceptic – that whilst there may be a determinate fact about what I meant, it lies beyond our epistemic reach, but that there simply is no such fact at all.[5]

The sceptic's answer to both questions is, of course: 'Nothing'. By hypothesis, I have never confronted this particular addition problem before, so that the answer I should now give is not settled by my having previously had the explicit thought, or forming the explicit intention, to answer this question by '125'. Furthermore, my past applications of '+' are finite in number, and it is clearly consistent with my past answers to questions of the form 'm + n = ?' that I meant some other function by '+' (such as ⊕), which coincides with addition over the cases actually encountered, but diverges from it over '68 + 57 = ?'. No finite selection of answers determines to within uniqueness what rule (if any) I was following. The sceptic then argues that no state or event in consciousness – no previous thoughts or imaginings, nor even a special experience of meaning – can constitute the needed fact. First, it is obviously questionable whether there is in fact any single conscious state or event which invariably accompanied my previous uses. Second – and more important – even if there had been, this would be powerless to settle the question unless that state or event in consciousness were itself insusceptible of alternative, quus-like interpretations. In particular, if any past state of consciousness is to prescribe answers in particular as-yet-unencountered cases, it would have to possess a *general* content – a distinctive feeling or mental picture won't do, because it will never be transparent what that requires of me in new cases; rather, it would have to be something like a general thought, such as that the answer I should give to any question of the type 'm + n = ?' is the one which I obtain by counting a collection of m marbles, say, and then a disjoint collection of n marbles, and finally counting the union of these two collections. But this gets us nowhere, unless we assume that there is no parallel problem about what I meant by the terms in which the general rule was formulated. We are just assuming that by 'count' I formerly meant what I now mean by that word, and did not mean *quount*, where quounting the union of two sets gives the same answer as counting them, provided that neither of the sub-collections has more than 56 elements; otherwise, the result of the quount is to be '5'. Keeping this perverse interpretation in play may need further perverse hypotheses about what I meant by such terms as 'union', 'subset', or 'co-extensive'. But there is no evident reason to think they can't be conjured up, with a little ingenuity.[6]

In effect, Kripke's point here is that sooner or later we are going to have to deal with the situation where I am supposed to have attached a certain definite meaning to certain words without giving myself an explanation of them, or rules for applying them, in general terms – so we may as well just suppose that '+' is such.

The thought is tempting that our failure to locate a meaning constituting fact in the details of my past applications of '+', or in the conscious states or events which may be supposed to have accompanied them, results from our looking in the wrong place, for a fact of the wrong sort. My meaning one thing rather than another by my words consists, it may be supposed, in my being *disposed* to apply them in certain ways and not in others. The attraction of this suggestion is that it can be a perfectly good fact that I was disposed to do certain things, not others, even though I did not actually do them – for the circumstances appropriate to exercise of the disposition need not have presented themselves. In particular, it could be that I was all along disposed to answer '125' to the question '57 + 68 = ?', but never actually did so, simply because no events occurred to trigger my additive disposition in this particular way. But the dispositional proposal must be rejected, Kripke argues, for two reasons. First, although it may at first appear that linguistic dispositions have the requisite generality, this is an illusion. There are potentially infinitely many questions of the form 'm + n = ?', but it just isn't true – or so Kripke claims – that for each and every one of them I was disposed to give a certain definite answer. We can only speak correctly of my being disposed to answer this way rather than that, when the numbers to be added are not too big for me to add. In this sense, our dispositions are *finite*. But this means that the dispositional 'solution' doesn't overcome the problem about the finiteness of actual past uses, for the class of answers I did give *or would have given* is still finite; and the sceptic can then undercut the proposed solution by choosing his example so that it lies beyond the reach of my additive (quadditive?) dispositions.[7] Second, the dispositional proposal fails to capture the essentially *normative* aspect of meaning. I may well be disposed to make certain sorts of mistake when doing addition. If what I meant by '+' is identified with what I was disposed to say, in answer to '+' questions, then there is no room for a needed contrast between the answers I *would* have given and those which I *should* have given, the latter being those which accord with my past meaning for '+'. Generally, the claim that some expression means such-and-such has a normative component – it is a claim about the circumstances in which it is, or would be, correct to apply it – which evades capture by an attempted reduction of (putative) meaning-constitutive facts to dispositional facts.[8]

Taking it that the alternatives considered and rejected exhaust the possibilities, Kripke's sceptic concludes that there is no fact constitutive of my *having meant* + rather than ⊕ by '+' in the past, and nothing that could justify my conviction that '125' is the answer I should now give to '68 + 57 = ?', if I am to be faithful to my past meaning for '+'. Furthermore, the conclusion appears to admit of straightforward generalization: if there were a fact in virtue of which I *now* mean + by '+', then – under the idealizing assumption of perfect recall, and so on – I would be able to cite this fact to rebut *tomorrow's* sceptical questions. But I shall clearly be no better placed tomorrow than I am *today*, so there is no such fact. And clearly enough, the sceptical argument doesn't essentially concern me, or the sign '+', so it applies to all other language users and all other expressions. We have the sceptical paradox in full generality: 'There can be no such thing as meaning anything by any word. Each new application we make is a leap in the dark; any present intention could be interpreted so as to accord with anything we may choose to do.'[9]

Kripke's Wittgenstein commends a sceptical solution. The first part of the sceptical solution agrees with the sceptic that there are no facts described or misdescribed by meaning-ascriptions, but says: that doesn't matter, because such statements are *not aimed at stating facts*, but have a quite different, non-fact-stating role. Kripke seeks to make plausible his attribution of this idea to Wittgenstein by linking it to Wittgenstein's abandonment of the truth-conditional theory of meaning found in his *Tractatus* in favour of the conception of meaning as use advocated in his later writings, according to which an account of the use of a declarative sentence will comprise, in Kripke's view, a description of the conditions in which it may be appropriately asserted, together with an explanation of its role in surrounding linguistic and non-linguistic practices. The second part of the sceptical solution brings in the community. The conditions in which it is appropriate to say things like 'Jones means addition by "+"' are essentially communal – the remark is appropriately made when we have found that Jones makes statements using '+' which are in good agreement with the things we are ourselves inclined to say. The point and role of such remarks is to acknowledge him as a fully paid-up member of the community of adders, to convey that he can be relied upon not to come up with bizarre answers (like '5') to addition problems (like '68 + 57 = ?'), and so on.

Kripke's Wittgenstein thinks community involvement is essential to provide for the normativity of meaning. If we just consider Jones on his own, all there is is his inclination to apply the word in a certain way (to respond, unhesitatingly but blindly, to addition questions with certain answers); there is nothing for his usage to be in or out of accord with. There is no room, at the level of the isolated individual's use, for the crucial distinction between what *seems* to him right and what *is* right; so that we cannot speak of right at all.[10] It is only when we bring in the community, and with it the possibility of agreement and disagreement between his use and that of the rest of us, that there can be a question of his applying the word rightly in a particular case. It is essential to realize that Kripke's Wittgenstein is not proposing that there is, after all, a fact constituting my meaning + by '+', but an essentially communal fact: if that were his position, it would clearly be vulnerable to a community-wide version of the sceptical argument, for there would then be no less a problem about what rule the community is following than there is about the individual – there is but a finite stock of previous uses of '+' by the community, and that no more determines what function was meant than does the individual's past usage, and so on.

3 Is semantic irrealism incoherent?

Kripke's argument has, quite justly, received a great deal of critical attention, mostly aimed at making out that the sceptical paradox admits of a straight solution – either one that Kripke overlooks altogether, or one that he considers but fails to rule out. These attempts may be divided into two broad groups. In the first come those which accept the assumption to which, notwithstanding his early insistence that there are to be "no limitations . . . on the facts that may be cited to answer the sceptic",[11] Kripke himself appears to subscribe, that putatively meaning-constitutive facts must be specifiable in non-semantic, non-intentional terms. The main contenders here – aimed at a naturalistic solution – have been attempts to uphold some more or less sophisticated version of dispositional theory, or to show that a broadly causal account of meaning and/or reference escapes the sceptical argument. It has also been claimed that even if Kripke's objections are effective against a dispositional account, they do not dispose of the view that an expression's having a certain meaning consists in its being associated with an appropriate capacity.[12] Others – the second group – take issue with what they see as a substantial reductionist assumption underpinning the sceptical argument, and have accordingly sought to defend the view that semantic facts, or closely related facts about intentions, need not be reducible to facts of some other, naturalistic kind.[13]

Kripke himself describes the sceptical conclusion as 'insane and intolerable'.[14] But he believes that it is none the less a conclusion we have to accept. The sceptical solution, he hopes, enables us to do so. Others have taken a less optimistic view of the sceptical solution, arguing that the sceptical conclusion not only appears to be but really is intolerable. If they are right then there must be something wrong with the argument to it: a straight solution of some sort must be possible. Space does not permit detailed evaluation of the various alternatives which have been canvassed here. In this section I shall, instead, examine some arguments designed to establish the incoherence of the position to which Kripke is led by the sceptical argument. First, however, it will be useful to make some remarks about what that position – semantic irrealism, as I shall call it – involves.

Meaning-statements are made by means of declarative sentences. As such, they may be asserted on their own, and they may equally figure as components in conditionals, disjunctions and other compounds. This is, arguably, by itself enough to ensure that they may with equal propriety be embedded in such contexts as 'It is true that . . .' and 'That . . . is a fact'. It might perhaps be insisted that such embeddings are acceptable only if the embedded sentences express claims which are subject to standards of correctness. I am not myself convinced that that is so, but even if it is, a proponent of the sceptical solution could hardly object on that score to our saying, for example, 'That Jones means addition by "plus" is a fact'. The aim of the sceptical solution is to rehabilitate (talk of) meaning in the face of the sceptical conclusion, by explaining how we can properly and correctly assert things like 'Jones means addition by "plus" '. There is no unavoidable error in ordinary talk of this kind – Kripke is not advocating an 'error theory' of meaning discourse, analogous to John Mackie's error theory of ethical discourse (see Chapter 12, REALISM AND ITS OPPOSITIONS, section 4): the error lies, rather, in prevalent philosophical (mis)interpretations, which construe meaning-statements as genuinely fact-stating or descriptive, having genuine truth-conditions.

It is, then, an obvious thought that for this very reason, it cannot be right simply to deny without qualification that meaning-statements are ever true, or that they state facts. Kripke anticipates such an objection to the sceptical solution's endorsement of the sceptical conclusion, and suggests that it may be defused by appeal to the 'redundancy' theory of truth.[15] His thought seems to be that, since 'it is true that S means that p' has the same content as 'S means that p', we are doing no more in asserting the former than we are in asserting the latter, and so are saying nothing from which a proponent of the sceptical solution need dissent. But this is puzzling.[16] In fact, the point seems to tell in precisely the opposite direction: just because, given a redundancy or deflationary conception of truth (and facts), 'It is true (is a fact) that S means that p' says no more than 'S means that p', there can be nothing wrong with the former – and accordingly, if the sceptical denial that meaning-statements are true or state facts is understood as involving this minimal notion of truth or fact, it must be wrong. The moral – apparently not clearly appreciated by Kripke – is that the sceptical conclusion, if it is to have even a chance of being acceptable, must be understood as invoking some more substantial conception of truth and facts. And if the sceptical solution is to have point, clarification of the more substantial notion(s) of truth and fact whose application to meaning-statements is to be denied becomes a matter of some urgency.[17] Whether a telling objection to Kripke can be erected around this point will be considered later. Meanwhile, I shall reserve the term 'true' for whatever more substantial notion might be taken to be in play, and employ 'correct' for the minimal sense. The sceptical conclusion can then be understood as claiming that meaning-statements are *never true*, but are (at best) *correct*.

More than one thinker has remarked upon the close similarity between the sceptical solution's combination of meaning irrealism with an attempt to rehabilitate meaning discourse by construing it non-descriptively, and more familiar projectivist attempts to save our thought and talk in other areas, such as morality, aesthetics and modality, where the apparent absence of a suitable range of truth-conferring facts seems to preclude a fully realist construal of the discourse.[18] And in one way, given the essentially normative character of the notion of meaning – on which all parties are agreed – together with the plausible claim that there can be no successful reduction of the normative to the purely factual, it may seem that meaning discourse is ripe for projectivist reconstruction (see Chapter 12, REALISM AND ITS OPPOSITIONS, section 4). On the other hand, just because a projectivist treatment of some given region of discourse is a thesis about the kind of meaning attaching to statements belonging to it, it may be doubted whether a non-factualist or projectivist approach can coherently be applied to meaning itself. It may well seem that the philosophical point and advantage of, say, a projective treatment of ethical discourse (perhaps based upon the kind of expressivist reconstrual proposed by the emotive theory) would be substantially compromised, if coupled with the thesis that meaning discourse quite generally, and so any claim about the sort of meaning possessed by ethical statements in particular, is itself not genuinely factual but projective of, say, some attitude we have. These are, of course, no more than vague misgivings. Can they be transformed into a sharp and telling objection to the sceptical solution?

John McDowell wrote:

> It is natural to suppose that if one says 'There is no fact that could consititute its being the case that P', one precludes oneself from affirming that P; . . . Given this supposition, the concession that Kripke says Wittgenstein makes to the sceptic becomes a *denial* that I understand the 'plus' sign to mean one thing rather than another. And now – generalizing the denial – we do seem to have fallen into an abyss: 'the incredible and self-defeating conclusion, that all language is meaningless' (Kripke, 1982, p. 71). It is quite obscure how we could hope to claw ourselves back by manipulating the notion of accredited membership in a linguistic community.[19]

The pessimistic conclusion is, however, too swiftly drawn. As we have seen, it is a condition of the coherence of Kripke's sceptic's argument that he is working with a substantial notion of fact, one for which the correctness of 'It is a fact that P' is precisely *not* guaranteed merely by the assertibility of 'P': that is, a more than merely deflationary or minimal notion of fact. But for this notion we can hardly expect there to be a generally unproblematic transition from 'It is not a fact that P' to denying that P. Kripke will want to hold, on the contrary, that there will be cases in which we can correctly assert that P, when it is not a fact that P. McDowell's 'natural supposition' just begs the question against him. It may be that irrealism about meaning, in contrast with irrealist theses in other areas, such as morals or mathematics, will turn out to suffer from some distinctive species of instability. But if so, further argument is needed to disclose it. Important arguments to the purpose have been advanced by Wright and Boghossian.[20]

Wright argues in two stages: (1) irrealism about meaning leads to global irrealism and (2) global irrealism is incoherent or otherwise directly objectionable. Wright's globalizing argument pivots on what he calls the meaning-truth platitude, that 'the truth value of a statement depends only upon its meaning and the state of the world in relevant respects.' In its original version, from which this formulation of the platitude is taken, it runs thus:

If the truth value of S is determined by its meaning and the state of the world in relevant respects, then non-factuality in one of the determinants can be expected to induce non-factuality in the outcome. (A rough parallel: If among the determinants of whether it is worth while going to see a certain exhibition is how well presented the leading exhibits are, then, if questions of good presentation are not considered to be entirely factual, neither is the matter of whether it is worth while going to see the exhibition.) A projectivist view of meaning is thus, it appears, going to enjoin a projectivist view of what it is for a statement to be true. Whence, unless it is, mysteriously, possible for a projective statement to sustain a biconditional with a genuinely factual statement, the disquotational schema '|P| is true if and only if P' will churn out the result that *all* statements are projective.[21]

Against global projectivism Wright advances several related but distinguishable considerations. An obvious worry, hinted at previously, is that a projectivist treatment of any particular class of statements has point only in so far as it draws a significant contrast between members of that class and other statements which are to be viewed as genuinely fact-stating, or apt for substantial truth. Relatedly, whilst a perfectly good distinction may *turn out* to be empty on one side, it may be doubted whether that could be an a priori matter, as would be the case with the needed distinction between fact-stating and non-fact-stating discourse if the globalizing argument is sound. Thirdly, supposing the distinction satisfactorily drawn, the projectivist will surely want to regard it as a *discovery* that statements in the target class are non-factual – in particular, shouldn't the statement of the conclusion of the sceptical argument be *itself* genuinely factual? Fourth: there will be no *truths* about the (Kripkean) assertion conditions of any sentences, with the result that the premisses of Kripke's version of the argument against private language (relating to the communally-oriented character of the assertion conditions of meaning-statements), and hence also its conclusion, will enjoy a merely projective character.[22]

Boghossian agrees with Wright that irrealism about meaning inflates into global irrealism (though he gives a somewhat different argument for this claim), but he is not persuaded that this is intrinsically objectionable; instead, he argues that meaning irrealism leads directly to self-contradiction, independently of its implicitly global character. The argument[23] starts from a generalization of the point made above: that since any significant, declarative sentence is apt for truth in a merely deflationary sense, a non-factualist thesis about any class of statements cannot be understood as denying that any of those statements are true in that sense, but must be taken to involve a richer, more substantial notion of truth. The non-factualist is, as he puts it, 'committed to holding that the predicate "true" stands for some sort of language-independent property, eligibility for which will not be certified purely by the fact that a sentence is declarative and significant'.[24] He then claims that a judgement that some sentence is or is not (substantially) true cannot but be a genuinely factual judgement. That is: the judgement that S is true (and likewise the judgement that S is not true) must itself be true or false, as opposed to being merely correct or incorrect. But the meaning non-factualist's distinctive thesis is that judgements about what a sentence means are not factual. Since what truth-condition a sentence possesses is a function of its meaning, it follows that judgements about what truth-condition a sentence has are likewise not factual. And since a sentence's having a particular truth-value cannot be a factual matter if its having a certain truth-condition is not, it further follows that a judgement about a sentence's truth-value can never be factual. Thus the meaning non-factualist is committed to denying that it is ever true that S is true. His position is thus self-contradictory.

Does either of these arguments succeed? Obviously enough, the crucial claim in Boghossian's argument is that the judgement that a sentence is (substantially) true must itself be a genuinely factual. But it is anything but obvious that the meaning non-factualist must agree. He is, as we have seen, committed to the intelligibility of a thick (that is, more than merely deflationary) notion of truth; though whether he is further committed to its having a non-empty extension must, at this stage, be regarded as an open question. But acceptance of that much seems perfectly consistent with retention of the thin, merely deflationary notion which we are calling correctness. And so long as both notions are available, why can't the non-factualist hold, apparently with perfect consistency, that metalinguistic attributions of truth, falsity, correctness and incorrectness are all alike, at most correct and never true? Boghossian believes that the non-factualist has not merely to make room for a thick (or as he says 'robust') notion of truth, but that he must *choose* between that and a purely deflationary one:

> It is an assumption of the present paper that the concept of truth is *univocal* . . . We should not confuse the fact that it is now an open question whether truth is robust or deflationary for the claim that it can be both. There is no discernible plausibility in the suggestion that the concept of a correspondence between language and world and the concept of a language-bound operator of semantic ascent might both be versions of the same idea.[25]

Clearly so crucial an assumption stands very much in need of supporting argument; surprisingly, Boghossian provides none, unless you think that the last sentence quoted does more than merely reassert what needs to be established.

This objection coincides pretty well, I think, with one of several developed in more detail by Wright,[26] who insists, as I have done, that the non-factualist is free to wield notions both of truth and correctness. Somewhat ironically, this distinction appears at first to provide the non-factualist with a ready way to interrupt Wright's own attempted reductio at the first, globalizing stage. As Wright's formulation makes plain, the final step involves an application of the Disquotation Scheme for 'true'. More specifically, he appears to have envisaged substituting the right- for the left-hand side of the scheme, to get from:

'"P" is true' is not true

to

'P' is not true

But it now appears that the non-factualist may block this step: when 'P' is true, '"P" is true' will be merely correct, so that the Disquotation Scheme – 'P' is true if and only if P – fails right-to-left.

In fact, this claim relies upon a questionable assumption about the evaluation of conditionals, that is, that a conditional will hold (be true, or at least correct) only if there is no descent in value (from true to correct, say) between its antecedent and consequent. As against this, it may plausibly be claimed that we should require only preservation of designated value (where true and correct are designated, the remaining values not). However, whilst this makes it at least doubtful that the non-factualist can block the globalizing argument by rejecting the Disquotation Scheme outright, it leaves him with the resources for an equally effective rejoinder – indeed, a more satisfactory one, because it allows him to retain the Disquotation Scheme. For if the scheme is secured by adoption of the proposal that what is required for a conditional to hold is not that the consequent is true if the antecedent is, but only that designated values shall be preserved, then instances of the biconditional scheme will not support substitution of their components in complex contexts such as that involved in the globalizing argument.[27]

There is another, more obvious, ground for dissatisfaction with the globalizing argument, at least in Wright's version. For it seems clear that, at least as formulated, the argument given works at best for a sense of 'statement' in which statements can be taken as *both* bearers of meaning *and* bearers of truth value. A proponent of semantic irrealism need not deny that there is, or could be, such a sense of 'statement', provided that he is granted a different sense in which statements have truth values, but cannot sensibly be said to have meanings. Concerning any statement in this sense, he can claim that whether or not it is true *is* a factual matter; or more precisely, that its being so is not threatened by the non-factuality of meaning. It is true enough that whether or not a particular *sentence* is suitable for making a particular statement in this sense depends upon the sentence's having a certain meaning – and that, he holds, is not a factual matter. But the truth value of a statement, in his preferred sense, does not depend upon the meaning of anything. It does not depend upon the meaning of the *statement*, because statements are not the sort of thing to have meanings; and it does not depend upon the meaning of a certain *sentence* – what depends upon a sentence's meaning being, rather, what statement(s) that sentence can be used to make. Thus non-factuality at the level of meaning does not induce non-factuality at the level of truth-value of statements.[28]

This discussion has inevitably been somewhat inconclusive. If what I have argued is right, it has not been shown that irrealism about meaning leads directly to contradiction, independently of its putative tendency to inflate into global irrealism; and it is at least open to question that it does globalize. And even if it does globalize in the way Wright and Boghossian both believe, it remains to be seen whether that leads to its collapse. Wright's arguments are suggestive of instability here, but appear less than decisive.

4 Wright on the rule-following considerations

4.1 The contractual model of meaning and investigation-independence

While Wright is sharply opposed to the semantic-irrealist conclusion which Kripke extracts from the Rule-following Considerations, he advances[29] an argument (for which he claims Wittgensteinian origins) whose conclusion has – rightly or wrongly – been seen as carrying implications for the notion of objectivity which are scarcely less radical, and no more palatable, than Kripke's. The argument is directed not at calling in question the very existence of facts about meaning, but at undermining what Wright takes to be an important misconception of their character. According to the conception under attack – the contractual model of meaning[30] – an expression's having a certain settled meaning consists in its being associated with a definite pattern of application which, once established, extends 'of itself' to new cases quite without any further assistance from us. Learning what the expression means is a matter of 'cottoning on' to such a pattern; our subsequent employment of the expression then either conforms, or fails to conform, with requirements already laid down, as it were, in the contract to which we have become party. Wright's contention is that, for reasons implicit in Wittgenstein's discussions of rule-following, the contractual model is fundamentally flawed and must be replaced by a conception of meaning as shaped by our ongoing use.

That is the immediate conclusion of Wright's argument. If for no other reason, the argument which purports to establish it deserves the closest scrutiny simply because the contractual picture is one which we may find both appealing and entirely natural, and which may, indeed, seem inevitable when we seek to understand what is involved in the normativity of meaning, so that Wright's conclusion is at the very least unsettling. But Wright draws a further conclusion which may appear not merely unsettling, but plainly intolerable. This concerns the way or sense in which ordinary factual statements may be held to be objectively true or false. What, in very general terms, we intend when we take a statement to be objectively true or false, is that its truth-value is in some way independent of our, or anyone else's, opinion. But this somewhat vague idea can be cashed out in various more specific ways. We ought not to be surprised if it should prove that what more precise characterization of it is found acceptable depends upon where one's sympathies lie in the dispute between realists and anti-realists in the theory of meaning (see Chapter 12, REALISM AND ITS OPPOSITIONS, sections 1 and 2). Wright focuses upon one particular conception of objectivity – *investigation-independence* – which we might expect anyone of a realist persuasion to endorse. A realist, in Dummett's sense, about a certain class of statements – that is, one who holds that statements in that class are such that their truth-conditions may be fulfilled, or not, without our being even in principle capable of recognizing as much – evidently regards those statements as objectively true or false. But if a capacity for evidence-transcendent truth is taken as the criterion, the resultant sense of objectivity is very strong indeed. By their very nature, no effectively decidable statements will qualify as having objective truth-values in this sense. And the same, it is natural to suppose, goes for very many other perfectly ordinary statements which, though not effectively decidable in any strict sense, would normally be viewed as capable of objective truth. Assuming that the realist wishes to regard statements of these latter kinds as capable of objective truth, what alternative criterion should he adopt? Wright's plausible suggestion[31] is that he will embrace a notion according to which 'confronted with any decidable, objective issue, there is *already* an answer which, if we investigate the matter fully and correctly, we will arrive at'. For such statements, that is, objectivity of truth-value consists in the possession of a determinate, *investigation-independent* truth-value. But investigation-independence, Wright argues, requires the contractual model of meaning:

> Investigation-independence requires a certain stability in our understanding of our concepts. To think, for example, of the shape of some particular unobserved object as determinate, irrespective of whether or not we ever inspect it, is to accept that there are facts about how we will, or would, assess its shape if we do, or did, so correctly, in accordance with the meaning of the expressions in our vocabulary of shapes; the putative investigation-independent fact about the object's shape is a fact about how we would describe it if on the relevant occasion we continued to use germane expressions in what we regard as the correct way . . . The idea of investigation-independence thus leads us to look upon grasp of the meaning of an expression as grasp of a general pattern of use, conformity to which requires certain determinate uses in so far unconsidered cases. The pattern is thus to be thought of as extending of itself to cases which we have yet to confront.[32]

If this is correct, a successful argument against the contractual model will be equally destructive of the idea that statements are capable of objective truth-value in the sense captured by investigation-independence.

It is obvious that any statement which is evidence-transcendently true or false will be objectively true or false in the sense captured by investigation-independence, but that the converse does not hold. In that sense, the latter is a weaker notion of objectivity than the former. And this, coupled with the fact that the notion of evidence-transcendent truth plays no part in the characterization of the weaker notion, might suggest that someone who rejects realism in Dummett's sense could endorse the claim that there are investigation-independent truths. But if Wright's argument is sound, this is an illusion. For the argument, as we shall see, makes essential use of an anti-realist premiss, so that if he is unable to find fault with it elsewhere, the anti-realist must reject the notion of investigation-independent truth.

4.2 The 1980/1 argument

Can an individual speaker S, in her use of an expression E, defensibly be regarded as attempting to conform to a pattern of application, the requirements of which are already in place? Wright's argument, in its earlier version, divides the question into two.

First, can we defensibly regard S as aiming at conformity to such a pattern *independently* of the possibility of assessment of her performance by others?[33] The difficulty here is to see how it can be justified to describe the situation in terms of S's *recognizing* what her supposed pattern requires her to say, in any particular case, as opposed to her merely being *disposed* to apply E (or not, as may be). The former description is justified only if there is a distinction to be drawn between S's going on as the pattern demands on the one hand, and on the other her merely *seeming* to do so. But S cannot make this distinction for herself, since it is bound to seem to her that her sincere and considered application of E conforms to the requirements of the pattern; and by hypothesis, the distinction is not to be made out on the basis of others' assessment of her performance.

Since the contractual picture cannot be sustained for this case, we move to the question of whether it can make a difference to the situation if we add in, as it were, facts about the agreement, or lack of it, between S and the rest of us over the application of E. Wright argues that it makes no essential difference. Here it is crucial to remember that the question at issue is not whether agreement with the community somehow provides the standard of correctness, but whether bringing in agreement, or lack of agreement, with the community affords a way of keeping the contractual picture in play. As Wright puts it, it is the question: "How does others' agreement with me turn my descriptive disposition into a matter of recognition of conformity with a pattern, recognition of an antecedent fact about how the communal pattern extends to the new case?" The answer, unstated but clearly implied, is that it cannot do so.

Wright restates this last part of the argument in a somewhat different way, which is worth noticing because it corresponds rather more closely to his later, and much terser, formulation.[34] If S's agreement with the rest of us somehow made the crucial difference, so that she could be thought of as recognizing what the shared pattern dictates in a given case, then it should at least make sense for her to claim, should she find herself at loggerheads with the rest of us over the application of E, to recognize that we have gone off track. But the only proper conclusion for S to draw, given that she can find no way to persuade us that we have broken faith with our antecedent pattern, is – or so Wright contends – that she does not (and perhaps never did) know what E means (as we employ it). But if no one can recognize that the community has *gone off* the rails, no one can recognize that the community has *stayed on* them; mere lack of disgreement with the community cannot substantiate the claim to recognize what its supposed pattern requires.

It is tempting, as Wright notes, to think that "a solicitable community of assent just does make the relevant difference". But he gives a supplementary argument[35] which, if good, shows that the temptation must be resisted. On the contractual model, the bearing of communal agreement over the application of E on the correctness or otherwise of S's use has to be understood in a quite particular way. It is not that communal agreement is *constitutive* of correct use. Correctness must consist in conformity with the requirements of the community's pattern, and communal agreement can be at best[36] good inductive evidence for that. In other words, on the contractual model, a community of assent on what should be said in a given case provides the standard against which individual applications of E are to be assessed *only because and in so far as* communal agreement can be taken to be based upon *recognition* of what the community's shared pattern requires. But once this is seen, it should be clear that we have no progress: so far from answering the objection previously urged against the picture of individual, community-independent conformity to an antecedent pattern, bringing in the community merely shifts the target. For what now requires justification is description of the situation in terms of the community's *recognizing* what its supposed pattern requires, in any particular case, rather than in terms of its merely being *disposed*, collectively and non-collusively, to apply E (or not, as may be). The former description is justified only if there is a distinction to be drawn between the community's going on as its pattern demands on the one hand, and on the other, its merely *seeming* to it that it is doing so. As Wright puts it:

> If 'correctness' means ratification-independent conformity with an antecedent pattern, there is apparent absolutely nothing which we can do to make the contrast active between the *consensus description* and the *correct description*.[37]

Of course – and as Wright agrees – we may as a community retrospectively judge that our erstwhile, communally agreed verdict on a particular case was mistaken; but this can give no comfort to the contractualist, since it is obviously wholly tendentious to view this as a matter of our belatedly recognizing that we previously broke faith with the requirements of an antecedently determinate pattern.[38] The necessary contrast between recognizing what our pattern required, and our earlier, collective disposition concerning what to say merely changing, is evidently no less problematic than that between recognizing what our pattern requires us to say now and our present disposition.

Although it will scarcely have escaped the notice of readers already familiar with this debate, it is worth underlining the argument's reliance, in its closing step at least, if not earlier, upon an anti-realist premiss to the effect that there is no sense to the claim that we operate with a distinction – in this case between the supposedly ratification-independent requirements of our pattern of use and how we think we should apply the expression in question – if there is nothing we can do to manifest a grasp of it. Wright himself is under no illusions, of course, about the need for such a premiss, and indeed, stresses the point:

> If those arguments [i.e. the general anti-realist arguments against the intelligibility of attributing grasp of concepts of which there is no distinctive manifestation] are rejected, then there is . . . no obstacle to embracing the investigation-independence of decidable statements. If, and only if, one admits the need to describe how an understanding could be *revealed* of what it is for our consensus verdict . . . to fit the alleged investigation-independent fact of the matter . . . will one feel pressured to reject the 'double-element' conception.[39]

That concludes my summary of Wright's argument in its earlier formulation. It leaves us facing three main questions: (1) is the argument sound? (2) is the rejection of investigation-independence it enjoins tolerable? and (3) if the contractual model is to be scrapped, what should replace it?

4.3 *Horrified reactions*

In view of the apparent innocence of the notion of investigation-independence, it is no surprise that others have seen its rejection not as a salutory corollary of the argument against the contractual model, but as revealing that something must have gone badly wrong, either in the argument Wright builds upon Wittgenstein's discussions of rule-following or in the RFC themselves. Thus John McDowell writes:

> If Wittgenstein's conclusion, as Wright interprets it, is allowed to stand, the most striking casualty is a familiar notion of objectivity. The idea at risk is the idea of things being thus and so anyway, whether or not we choose to investigate the matter in question, and whatever the outcome of any such investigation. That idea requires the conception of how things could correctly be said to be anyway – whatever, if anything, we go on to say about the matter; and this notion of correctness can only be the notion of how the pattern of application that we grasp, when we come to understand the concept in question, extends, independently of the actual outcome of any investigation, to the relevant case. So if the notion of independent-investigation is to be discarded, then so is the idea that things are, at least sometimes, thus and so anyway, independently of our ratifying the judgement that that is how they are. It seems fair to describe this extremely radical consequence as a kind of idealism.[40]

Although McDowell thinks that we cannot accept Wright's conclusion, and is thus committed to denying the *soundness* of the argument leading to it, he does not dispute its *validity*. In fact, he is committed to its validity, because he takes it to form the core of an effective 'transcendental argument against anti-realism' which reduces to absurdity the anti-realist premiss upon which, as we have noted, the argument relies. It would, of course, be wholly tendentious, in the present context, to rest such a *reductio* on the alleged absurdity of the denial of investigation-independence itself. The absurdity lies, rather – or so McDowell contends – in the picture of language to which Wright's argument commits him, on which there is no room for normativity, and so no room for meaning, at all. Of course, Wright does not himself think that his argument leads to this absurd conclusion. But there is no escaping it, McDowell claims, once we accept with Wright that at the individual level there is no going right or wrong in our use of words save in the context provided by communal assessment of individual use, and that as far as the community as a whole is concerned there is no authority to which its collectively agreed use is answerable, and no distinction to be drawn between the 'consensus description' and the 'correct description', so that we cannot say that it 'goes right or wrong', only that it 'just goes'. For this entails a picture of language use on which, 'at the basic level', human beings are merely 'vocalizing in certain ways in response to objects', no doubt to the accompaniment of certain 'feelings of constraint, or convictions of the rightness of what they are saying', but at which 'there is no question of shared commitments – of the behaviour . . . being subject to the authority of anything outside themselves . . . How, then, can we be entitled to view the behaviour as involving, say, calling things "yellow", rather than a mere brute meaningless sounding off?' And once we are committed to this picture of the 'basic' level, stripped of normativity altogether, there is no hope of reinstating it via the notion that individuals are subject to communal correction. As McDowell puts it,

> The problem for Wright is to distinguish the position he attributes to Wittgenstein from one according to which the possibility of going out of step with our fellows gives us the *illusion* of being subject to norms, and consequently the *illusion* of entertaining and expressing meanings.[41]

This attempt to turn Wright's argument on its head is, it seems to me, a complete failure. McDowell plainly takes it that when Wright observes that there is no standard against which the whole community's practice may be assessed, he is advancing this as his own view. But Wright is doing no such thing; he is himself offering a *reductio* of the idea that correct use is a matter of conformity with a ratification-independent pattern. McDowell appears entirely to have overlooked the crucial point that the conclusion that there is no distinction between the consensus verdict and the correct verdict is drawn on that hypothesis – hence Wright's conditional: 'If "correctness" here means ratification-independent conformity with an antecedent pattern, there is apparent absolutely nothing we can do to make active the contrast between the consensus description and the correct description'. Wright's argument as I understand it is that if communal correctness were a matter of conformity with such a pattern then, unless whether or not the community goes right is to be a verification-transcendent matter, there would have to be a distinction between the community's recognizing what its pattern requires and its merely thinking that it does. Since no content can be assigned to *this* contrast, there can be no content either to the distinction between the consensus verdict and the correct verdict, *on this supposition about what correctness consists in.* Given the obvious unacceptability of the conclusion to which it leads, we should reject that supposition.

Somewhat differently, Michael Dummett, in effect,[42] agrees with Wright that "an unflinching application of Wittgenstein's ideas about rules" leads us to deny that there can be pre-determinate, investigation-independent facts; since he finds this conclusion incredible, he concludes that 'the "rule-following considerations" embody a huge mistake'. Wittgenstein was

> right to observe that, for the most fundamental of the rules that we follow, there is nothing *by which* we judge something to be a correct application of them. It certainly does not follow from this that, if we never do make such a judgement in some particular instance, there is no specific thing that would have been a correct application: to draw that inference, you need a general internalist premiss, that there is nothing to truth beyond our acknowledgement of truth.[43]

But this premiss, Dummett complains, is totally implausible; to appeal to it in this context is simply to beg the question.

Since Dummett is discussing Wittgenstein, and not Wright, it would be unjust to complain of a failure to engage the latter's argument. But it is pertinent to observe that Wright's argument is, on the face of it, an argument of precisely the kind whose possibility Dummett denies, since it manifestly does not appeal to any premiss to the effect that there is no more to truth than its being acknowledged.

The immediate reason why Dummett finds the rejection of investigation-independence incredible is that it appears to involve denying, in the case of an elementary calculation, that there is in advance of its being carried out any determinately correct result. Another reason that might be given (to which Dummett attaches great importance, both in the paper from which I have quoted and in earlier writings) is that it appears impossible to account satisfactorily for the value or usefulness of deductive inference without appealing to a distinction between a statement's being true and its being actually verified or recognized as true, and hence, it may seem, without invoking the possibility of investigation-independent truth. Indeed, this may be seen as a special case of a quite general difficulty. For it may seem that if Wright's conclusion stands, nothing approaching justice can be done to the conception we all have of human enquiry in general as a process of *discovery*. These are matters for genuine concern, to which – so far as I have been able to see – nothing in Wright's earlier presentations of the argument speaks. Pending explanation of how it might be alleviated, we have a strong motive for hoping, if not for suspecting, that there is after all a flaw in his argument.

4.4 Wright's strengthened argument

In fact, there is a flaw in it. The first part of the argument, aimed at showing that there can be no substance to the idea that an individual speaker is aiming at conformity to a pattern of use *independently* of the possibility of assessment of her performance by others, seems to me compelling. We should also agree that the contractual conception requires the possibility of community-wide (and so of near-community-wide) departure from its pattern for a given expression. But Wright's next claim – that the only conclusion a lone dissenter could properly draw, on finding herself unable to bring the rest of us round, is that she no longer understands the crucial expression, and so cannot be a competent critic of the rest of the community's use – is far from clearly correct. On the contrary, it appears that there is plenty of room for a proponent of the contractual view to resist it. No doubt I should be disconcerted to find the rest of the community lined up against me. But it is far from self-evident that, were this to happen, it must be that *I* have gone astray, and cannot be that *they* have done so. We can surely envisage circumstances in which the opposite would be the case. It is, for instance, at least conceivable that everyone else has, perhaps as a result of exposure to some insidious form of radiation which I have escaped, suffered eye or brain damage which makes red things look yellow to them, or which has somehow scrambled whatever neural assemblies are associated with their capacity to use colour terms. Of course, this supposition is far-fetched; but it appears at least to make sense, and that is all that is required.

Reformulating the argument once again, Wright claims:

> none of us, if he finds himself on his own about a new candidate for ϕ-ness, *and with no apparent way of bringing the rest of us around*, can sensibly claim to recognize that the community has here broken faith with its antecedent pattern of application for ϕ; the proper conclusion for him is rather that he has just discovered that he does not know what ϕ means.[44]

The italicized words are evidently crucial, since Wright's claim would clearly be preposterous without them. Even with them, the claim that a charge of community-wide error simply makes no sense would be unwarranted if the key words meant merely that there does not appear to be any way in which the isolated individual can persuade the rest that they have gone wrong. Earlier, Wright speaks of the individual being *incorrigibly* out of line, suggesting that there is, without qualification, no way in which he can bring the community around. But now, it seems to me, we need to be a lot clearer about just what supposition it is that we are being invited to entertain, before we can say what follows. Why is it that he can't do that? Are we also to suppose that the situation is, as it were, symmetrical – so that there is, equally, no way in which the community can bring the individual round to its way of thinking? If so, then unless it is further being assumed that one or other party is the victim of some cognitive malfunction which, however, mysteriously resists exposure, we are in effect being asked to suppose that the individual goes one way and the community the other, without either being cognitively at fault: but then it seems that the supposition effectively begs the key question, of whether or not there is a fact of the matter to be recognized.

Wright agrees that his earlier argument needs reinforcement at this point, and seeks to provide it in the later, refurbished version. This proceeds in two stages, corresponding to a distinction Wright draws between basic statements and others. Very roughly,[45] the former are statements involving only demonstratives together with concepts whose mastery consists in the possession of some appropriate recognitional capacity – concepts for which "competent use standardly presupposes no more than normal sensory capacities and ostensive teaching", such as concepts of colour, taste or pitch. In the first stage, Wright deploys a strengthened version of the argument we have been considering, restricted in scope to basic statements; the second stage then generalizes the conclusion – if basic statements lack objectivity of meaning, so must the remainder. The first-stage argument proceeds, in essentials, as before. But now Wright adds a supplementary argument to close off the gap opened up by the apparent possibility that the lone dissenter is right, the rest of his community having indeed gone astray in their application of basic concepts, perhaps as a result of the deleterious effects of some environmental contaminant upon their capacity to apply them reliably, or for some similar reason. What, in more detail, would it be like, he asks, for there to be available reason to think that everyone (else) had gone astray in their application of basic concepts?

Wright's argument starts from the idea that, if this is a genuine possibility, we should be able to see how a sustainable case could be made for thinking it to have been realized. We may suppose that the lone dissenter can put up a case of this sort: he points to (a) evidence that the rest have been exposed to a certain environmental contaminant and (b) evidence that when others have been exposed to this contaminant in the past, their basic judgements of the relevant sort have been distorted. Against such a case, a doubt of the following kind may be raised: the evidence (b) involves the claim that the affected subjects' basic judgements were distorted, and the basis for this claim is that those judgements were found to be at odds with basic judgements made by others who were not affected. The case assumes that we are warranted in taking it that the judgements made by those who were not affected were indeed correct. But might not those very judgements themselves have been the product of widespread error? Unless and until adequate reason can be provided to discount this possibility, the case the lone dissenter has sought to make is worth nothing. Wright's counter-claim is, in effect, that the possibility could only rationally be discounted by appeal to something like this principle, as being analytic of the notion of basic statement:

> If there is widespread non-collusive agreement on the truth of a basic statement S and there is adequate reason to suppose that the parties to this widespread agreement understand the concepts involved in S, and are functioning normally in normal conditions for exercise of the appropriate recognitional capacities, and there is no further evidence germane to the case, then anyone apprised of all these facts has adequate grounds for regarding S as true.[46]

The snag is that the objectivist about meaning can hardly regard this principle as analytic; on her view, it can be at best a contingent truth, and that will not be enough to see off the challenge. In short, the attempt to sustain the contractual model by appealing to the possibility of widespread communal error opens the doors to scepticism.

I shall not here try to evaluate this argument; Wright has, in my view, made a powerful case which – so far as I know – has yet to receive an effective reply. And if he is right, the case against objectivity of meaning relies, in its final form, on no specifically anti-realist premiss. I leave the reader to ponder it, and turn instead to my second main – and by now, pressing – question.

4.5 Investigation-independence and objectivity of judgement

The *term* 'investigation-independent fact' is indeed strongly suggestive of a familiar enough and, for all that it calls for philosophical articulation, seemingly indispensable notion of objectivity; so much so that the suggestion that we should deny that there are any such facts may strike us as the philosophical equivalent of red-rag-waving. I shall try to explain why the bulls should stand their ground.

Preparatory to introducing the notion of *objectivity of judgement* – as distinct from that of objectivity of meaning – Wright says:

> Cognition is *relational*: it is a matter of arriving at true opinions in a manner *sensitive* to states of affairs whose obtaining is somehow independent of one's so arriving. Moreover, such a sensitivity must be conceived as essentially fallible.[47]

Obviously the crucial words here are 'somehow independent'. In what does the independence of cognized states of affairs consist? Part of what is involved, at least, is that in any particular case where a subject S comes to know (and so forms a true opinion) that p, it should be the case that the state of affairs in virtue of which it is true that p does not depend in any way at all on S's coming to believe that p; or, indeed, on S's or anyone else's coming to hold any opinion on the matters in question. That is, we conceive of the relevant state of affairs as such that its obtaining is consistent with universal ignorance of its doing so. That is one component in the notion of objectivity of judgement, as Wright characterizes it. This is naturally expressed in counterfactual terms: whenever a subject S is properly described as coming to know that p, it would (still) have been the case that p, even if neither S nor anyone else had investigated the matter, or formed any opinion on it. It seems to follow that endorsement of objectivity of judgement for a type of statement entails accepting that there are relevant states of affairs which obtain or not, independently of investigation, in this sense at least: it is the case that p (or not) independently of whether anyone ever did or will carry out an investigation to determine whether or not p (and a fortiori, independently of the result of any such investigation, were one (to be) carried out).

Taking in the other component which Wright includes in the idea of objectivity being charted – that is, the essential fallibility of judgement – the objectivist about judgement is committed to there being true claims of this sort:

(1) It is the case that p & it would (still) have been the case that p, even if no one had carried out an investigation to determine whether or not p, and even if someone had carried out an investigation, but one that issued in the verdict that not-p.

How about the case where we are concerned with some decidable, but as yet uninvestigated matter? What kind of claim should the objectivist about judgement make then? Well, suppose the question is whether some large integer *k* is or is not prime. Then the objectivist can say this:

> *k* is either prime or not. If *k* is prime, then even if no one ever investigates, it is prime, and were anyone to investigate but come up with a different answer, she would be mistaken; and if *k* is not prime, then again, even if no one ever investigates, it is not prime, and were anyone to investigate but come up etc.

Generally, where decidable but as yet uninvestigated matters are in question, the objectivist about judgement may register the sense in which they concern objective states of affairs by asserting an appropriate statement of the form:

(2) Either p or not-p. If p, then even if no one ever investigates, p, and were anyone to investigate but come up with any other answer, she would be wrong; and if not-p, then again, even if no one ever investigates, not-p, and etc.

The crucial point for present purposes is that counterfactuals of the kind embedded in these claims are precisely *not* counterfactuals about *what expressions it would be (have been) correct to apply in certain circumstances*. As such, they contrast sharply with the kind of counterfactual in terms of which investigation-independence is characterized by Wright – "the [investigation-independent] fact about the object's shape is a fact about how we would describe it if . . . we continued to use germane expressions in what we regard as the correct way."[48]

An objectivist about judgement can assert claims of both kinds of the forms (1) and (2). This marks one clear sense in which he can regard certain statements as being true or false in virtue of states of affairs obtaining, or not, independently of investigation. If that is right, then we should question McDowell's right to the following transition, integral to the argument by which he persuades himself that a "familiar and intuitive notion of objectivity" requires the contractual conception of meaning:

> The idea at risk is the idea of things being thus and so anyway, whether or not we choose to investigate the matter, and whatever the outcome of any such investigation. That idea requires the conception of how things could correctly be said to be anyway – whatever, if anything, we in fact go on to say about the matter.[49]

For endorsement of conditionals of types (1) and (2) seems quite enough to hit off the idea of objectivity (of things being thus and so anyway . . .). But those conditionals – at least on the face of it – say nothing about how things could correctly be said to be.

It may be replied that this is a mere artefact of formulation: surely the objectivist ought not to make any bones about accepting these reformulations:

(3) It is true to say that p & it would (still) have been true to say that p, even if no one had carried out an investigation to determine whether or not p, and even if someone had carried out an investigation, but one that issued in the verdict that not-p.

(4) Either it is true to say that p or it is true to say that not-p. If it is true to say that p, then even if no one ever investigates, it is true to say that p; and if it is true to say that not-p, then again, even if no one ever investigates, it is true to say that not-p.

Well, of course he should accept them, since their acceptability is guaranteed by the equivalence of 'p' with 'it is true to say that p'. But the effect of securing McDowell's first transition by appeal to the equivalence thesis is simply to put in question the next transition in his argument; that is, from the second sentence, just quoted, to:

> and this notion of correctness can only be the notion of how a pattern of application that we grasp . . . extends, independently of any investigation, to the relevant case.

This transition would be good if, but only if, we could pass from (3) to:

(5) It is true to say that p & it would (still) have been correct to assert 'p', even if no one had carried out an investigation to determine whether or not p, and even if someone had carried out an investigation, but one that issued in the verdict that not-p.

or something to that effect. For it is only if some such transition to a (counterfactual) claim about what words it would have been correct to use is allowable that endorsement of objectivity in the sense of the premiss can be made out to involve commitment to the idea of a pattern of application (of some words) extending independently of investigation. But it should be quite clear that the object-linguistic counterfactual simply does not entail its metalinguistic counterpart. In short, McDowell's argument is vitiated by a simple equivocation on 'how things could correctly be said to be'. The second step in his argument is good only if this says something about what words it would be correct to use; the first is good only if it does not.

If what I have said is right, there is after all a gap, discernible by one who rejects objectivity of meaning, between the truth of a statement and its actual verification. Contrary to first appearances, denying that there are investigation-independent facts (in the sense in which Wright does deny this) does not involve denying that, when we correctly perform an elementary calculation, the correctness of our result is independent of our performance. In that sense we can agree with Dummett that there is, in advance of our carrying it out, a determinately correct result. And more generally, when we make a valid inference from true premisses to the conclusion that p, the truth of our conclusion does not wait upon our coming to it; it can, *without presupposing the contractual model*, be acknowledged that it would still have been the case that p, even if we had not drawn the inference. In that sense, by making the inference we acquire knowledge of a fact of which we had previously been ignorant but which was already there to be known. There is, to be sure, more to be said before we can lay claim to a satisfying explanation of the usefulness of deductive inference.[50] But this much is, it seems to me, enough to dispel the appearance that no such account can be forthcoming if the contractual model of meaning is abandoned.

5 Concluding remarks

I have concentrated here on two discussions, both of which enlist Wittgenstein's rule-following considerations in support of radical and highly revisionary conclusions about the objectivity of meaning – conclusions which may appear to entail, and have been taken to entail, consequences for the objectivity of truth and judgement which are no less radical and revisionary. My principal concern has been to argue that, however unpalatable these conclusions – Kripke's semantic irrealism and Wright's rejection of the contractual model and investigation-independence – may seem, we have as yet no compelling demonstration of their unacceptability, and thus have no advance right to think that the arguments leading to them must be unsound. I should like to conclude with some remarks about how we should view the situation.

First, whilst we have as yet no decisive ground for thinking semantic irrealism unstable, it is quite another question whether any argument Kripke gives, or might have given, compels its acceptance. The greater part of Kripke's argumentation – and certainly the most convincing part of it – is directed against attempts to explain, in naturalistically reductive terms, what it is to mean something by an expression. To the extent that it is effective, it secures its effect by taking undisputed features of the concept of meaning – generality of application and normativity – and showing that they elude explanation on the proposed naturalistic basis. Clearly no argument of this kind could undermine a view according to which semantic, or more generally intentional phenomena are irreducible. To establish semantic irrealism requires no less than a demonstration that indispensable features of the concept of meaning cannot be jointly instantiated. The closest Kripke comes to providing one is in his dismissive discussion of the idea that meaning something is a *sui generis* 'unique introspectible state'; but this comes nowhere near to a demonstration that severally essential ingredients in the concept of meaning cannot coexist. Furthermore, the required features are, as Wright reminds us, apparently coherently co-exemplified in our standard intuitive notion of intention. We have no a priori guarantee that that notion could not turn out to be incoherent; but no reason to think it so is yet in sight.

Matters stand otherwise, it seems to me, with Wright's conclusion. Here we are faced with a prima facie compelling argument for the bankruptcy of the contractual model to which, so far as I have been able to see, no effective counter has been provided. And if I am right, horrified reactions to the ensuing rejection of investigation-independence can be seen to be misplaced, once that notion is properly separated from a more modest notion of objectivity which can perfectly well survive without contractual underpinning. What does then become pressing is the need for a satisfying, detailed account of how we may view meaning as – in Wright's own, somewhat opaque phrase – 'shaped by features of our ongoing linguistic behaviour'. This is one direction in which we have a good way yet to travel, before we can reckon ourselves to have appreciated the full significance of Wittgenstein's remarks on rule-following.

Notes

1 Wittgenstein (1967, §§ 138–242; 1978 Part VI).
2 McDowell (1984), Baker and Hacker (1984a and b; 1985).
3 Kripke (1982), Wright (1980; 1981; 1984b), Carruthers (1984).
4 See, in addition to the works cited in the two preceding notes, Peacocke (1981), McGinn (1984), Budd (1984), Pears (1988, chs 16–18), Williams (1991), Luntley (1991) and Wright (1989b, pp. 239–45).

Another important focus of controversy which must be left unexplored here is the exact relationship between Wittgenstein's discussion of rule-following and his arguments against the possibility of a private language. See Chapter 6, MEANING AND PRIVACY.

5 See Kripke (1982, pp. 14–15), Wright (1984a, pp. 762–3) and Boghossian (1989, p. 515).
6 This calls for some qualification: whilst there is, so far as I know, no published attempt to show that perverse Kripkean hypotheses break down when we try to work them through in detail, at least one critic – Neil Tennant – attempts to make such a case in an as yet unpublished sequel to his *Anti-Realism and Logic*.
7 Kripke (1982, pp. 26–28).
8 Ibid., pp. 28–32.
9 Ibid., p. 55.
10 Cf. Wittgenstein (1967, § 258).
11 Kripke (1982, p. 14).
12 For dispositional theories see, for example, Papineau (1987), Fodor (1987; 1991). For doubts about the efficacy of Kripke's objections, see Blackburn (1984a) and Forbes (1983). Attempts to uphold a causal account of meaning or reference in the face of the sceptical argument may be found in Goldfarb (1985) and McGinn (1984, pp. 164–6), who also defends the capacity proposal (pp. 168–75). Chomsky (1986) argues that Kripke improperly restricts the search for meaning-consititutive facts – the claim that you formerly followed a certain rule is a *theoretical* claim, and as such answerable to future evidence, as well as evidence concerning, for example, your past linguistic behaviour or conscious mental life. Boghossian (1989) provides a useful survey and assessment of attempts at a straight solution which accept Kripke's reductionist assumption. See Chapter 5, A GUIDE TO NATURALIZING SEMANTICS.
13 For criticism of Kripke's reductionist leanings and proposals for non-reductive solutions, see Boghossian (1989, pp. 540–9), McGinn (1984, pp. 150–64) and Wright (1984a, pp. 772–7).
14 Kripke (1982, p. 60).
15 Ibid., p. 86. See Chapter 13, THEORIES OF TRUTH, sect. 8.
16 As some commentators, e.g. Blackburn (1984a, p. 285), have remarked.
17 I cannot, for reasons of space, pursue the matter here – for illuminating discussion, see Wright (1992) *passim*. See also Chapter 12, REALISM AND ITS OPPOSITIONS, final section.
18 Cf. Wright (1984b) and Boghossian (1989; 1990).
19 McDowell (1984, p. 330).
20 Cf. Wright (1984a) and Boghossian (1989; 1990).
21 Wright (1984a, p. 769).
22 Ibid., pp. 769–70.
23 Short version, Boghossian (1989); full dress, Boghossian (1990).
24 Boghossian (1989, p. 526).
25 Boghossian (1990, p. 165, n. 17).
26 Cf. Wright (1992a, p. 234; 1993, pp. 318–24).
27 The difficulty has been stated with respect to Wright's version of the globalizing argument – but, as Wright himself points out, somewhat similar troubles afflict Boghossian's version: cf. Wright (1992a, pp. 218–20).
28 Blackburn (1989) makes a similar objection to Boghossian's version of the argument. Doubts about the sufficiency of this kind of response to the globalizing argument are developed in Wright (1992a, pp. 222–6).
29 In his 1980, 1981 and 1984b.
30 In the later paper Wright refers to this doctrine, according to which meanings are conceived of as "fully settled by over-and-done-with behavioural and intellectual episodes", as that of *objectivity of meaning*.

31 Cf. Wright (1981, p. 99).
32 Wright (1981, p. 100).
33 Wright conducts this stage of the argument in terms of the question whether sense can be given to the claim that an individual is being faithful to an idiolectic pattern of application. But as I understand it, what really matters, for this part of the argument, is not whether she is viewed as seeking to suit her performance to a pattern peculiar to herself rather than a shared pattern, but whether others are supposed to be able to evaluate her performance.
34 In Wright (1984b).
35 Cf. Wright (1980, pp. 219–20).
36 At best, as Wright observes (1980, p. 219), it is far from clear how the probability of communal agreement being in or out of line with the requirements of the ratification-independent pattern could be assessed.
37 (1980, p. 219), my emphasis.
38 Cf. Wright:

> Of course, it may happen that the community changes its mind; and when it does so, it does not revise the judgement that the former view enjoyed consensus. But that is a fact about our procedure; to call attention to it is to call attention to the circumstance that we make use of the notion that we can all be wrong, but it is not call attention to anything which gives sense to the idea that the wrongness consists in departure from a ratification-independent pattern. (1980, pp. 219–20)

39 Wright (1980, p. 221).
40 McDowell (1984, p. 325). Whether this is a fair assessment of the import of Wright's argument, and whether, in particular, McDowell is right to identify the familiar intuitive notion of objectivity to which he gives expression with that of investigation-independence, are questions to which we must shortly return.
41 The scattered quotations from McDowell are all taken from his 1984, p. 336.
42 In effect, because Dummett is not explicitly discussing Wright's argument, though it may be that he does in fact have that argument in mind.
43 The quotations are from Dummett (1994, pp. 63–4).
44 Wright (1980, p. 218).
45 This is a very rough description. For a much more careful account, see Wright (1984b, pp. 276–83). A needed further refinement of the notion of basic statement is provided in Wright (1992b, pp. 40–2).
46 Cf. Wright (1984b, p. 288).
47 Ibid., p. 281.
48 Wright (1980, p. 216).
49 McDowell (1984, p. 325).
50 For further discussion, see Dummett (1973; 1991a, pp. 36–42 and 305–6 and 1991b, ch. 7).
51 Thanks to Jim Edwards and Crispin Wright for very helpful comments.

References and suggested reading

Baker, G. and Hacker, P.M.S. 1984a: On misunderstanding Wittgenstein: Kripke's private language argument. *Synthese*, 58 (3), 407–50.

—— 1984b: *Scepticism, Rules and Language*. Oxford: Blackwell.

——1985: *Wittgenstein: Rules, Grammar and Necessity*. Oxford: Blackwell.
Blackburn, S. 1984a: The individual strikes back. *Synthese*, 58 (3), 281–301.
——1984b: *Spreading the Word*. Oxford: Clarendon Press.
——1989: Wittgenstein's irrealism. In Rudolf Haller and Johannes Brandl (eds), *Wittgenstein – Towards a Re-Evaluation*. Vienna: Hölder-Pichler-Tempsky, pp. 13–26.
Boghossian, P.A. 1989: The rule-following considerations. *Mind*, 93 (392), 507–49.
——1990: The status of content. *Philosophical Review*, 99 (2), 157–83.
Budd, M. 1984: Wittgenstein on meaning, interpretation and rules. *Synthese*, 58 (3), 303–23.
Carruthers, P. 1984: Baker and Hacker's Wittgenstein. *Synthese*, 58 (3), 451–79.
Chomsky, N. 1986: *Knowledge of Language*. New York: Prager.
Dummett, M. 1973: The justification of deduction. In Dummett's *Truth and other enigmas*. London: Duckworth 1978.
——1991a: *Frege: Philosophy of Mathematics*. London: Duckworth.
——1991b: *The Logical Basis of Metaphysics*. London: Duckworth.
——1994: Wittgenstein on necessity: some reflections. In Peter Clark and Bob Hale (eds), *Reading Putnam*. Cambridge, Mass. and Oxford: Blackwell.
Fodor, J. 1987: *Psychosemantics: the problem of meaning in the philosophy of mind*. Cambridge, Mass. and London: MIT Press.
——1991: A theory of content. In *A Theory of Content and Other Essays*. Cambridge, Mass.: MIT Press.
Forbes, G. 1983: Scepticism and semantic knowledge. *Proceedings of the Aristotelian Society*, 84, 223–37
Fogelin, R. 1976: *Wittgenstein*. London: Routledge and Kegan Paul.
Goldfarb, W. 1985: Kripke on Wittgenstein on rules. *Journal of Philosophy*, 82, 471–88.
Holtzman, S.H. and Leich, C.M. (eds) 1981: *Wittgenstein: To Follow a Rule*. London: Routledge and Kegan Paul.
Kripke, S.A. 1982: *Wittgenstein on Rules and Private Language*. Oxford and New York: Blackwell.
Luntley, Michael 1991: The transcendental grounds of meaning and the place of silence. In Puhl (1991), 170–88.
McDowell, John 1984: Wittgenstein on following a rule. *Synthese*, 58 (3), 325–63.
McGinn, Colin 1984: *Wittgenstein on Meaning*. Oxford: Blackwell.
Papineau, David 1987: *Reality and Representation*. Oxford: Blackwell.
Peacocke, Christopher 1981: Rule-following: the nature of Wittgenstein's arguments. In Holtzman and Leich (1981).
Pears, David 1988: *The False Prison*. Vol. 2, Oxford: Oxford Unversity Press.
Puhl, Klaus (ed.) 1991: *Meaning scepticism*. Berlin: de Gruyter.
Putnam, Hilary 1981: Convention: a theme in philosophy. *New Literary History*, 13 (1), reprinted in his *Realism and Reason: Philosophical Papers*. Vol. 3, Cambridge: Cambridge University Press (1983).
Williams, Meredith 1991: Blind obedience: rules, community and the individual. In Puhl (1991), 93–125.
Wittgenstein, Ludwig 1967: *Philosophical Investigations*. 3rd edn, Oxford: Blackwell.
——1978: *Remarks on the Foundations of Mathematics*. 3rd edn, Oxford: Blackwell.
Wright, Crispin 1980: *Wittgenstein on the Foundations of Mathematics*. London: Duckworth.
——1981: Rule-following: objectivity and the theory of meaning. In Holtzman and Leich (1981).

Wright, Crispin 1984a: Kripke's account of the argument against private language. *Journal of Philosophy*, 81 (12), 759–78.
——1984b: Rule-following, meaning and constructivism. In Charles Travis (ed.), *Meaning and Interpretation*. Oxford: Blackwell 1986, pp. 271–97.
——1989a: Review of McGinn 1984. *Mind*, 97 (390), 289–306.
——1989b: Wittgenstein's rule-following considerations and the central project of theoretical linguistics. In Alexander George (ed.), *Reflections on Chomsky*. Oxford Blackwell, pp. 233–64.
——1992a: *Truth and Objectivity*. Cambridge, Mass. and London: Harvard University Press.
——1992b: Scientific realism and observation statements. In David Bell (ed.), *Science and Subjectivity*. Berlin: Academie Verlag, pp. 21–46.
——1993: Eliminative materialism: going concern or passing fancy? *Mind and Language*, 8 (2), pp. 316–26.

16

The indeterminacy of translation

CRISPIN WRIGHT

W. V. O. Quine's contention that translation is indeterminate has been among the most widely discussed and controversial theses in modern analytical philosophy. It is a standard-bearer for one of the late twentieth century's most characteristic philosophical preoccupations: the scepticism about semantic notions which is also developed in Kripke's interpretation of Wittgenstein on rules (see Chapter 15, RULE-FOLLOWING, OBJECTIVITY AND MEANING) and which many have read into Putnam's 'model-theoretic' assault on realism (see Chapter 17, PUTNAM'S MODEL-THEORETIC ARGUMENT AGAINST METAPHYSICAL REALISM). The more general concern reflected by these arguments is how space can be found for the reality of meanings – and indeed for other norms, like the ethical – in a world whose fundamentals, as the orthodox wisdom has it, are apt for complete characterization by the methods and vocabulary of physical science.[1]

If Quine's arguments succeed, this is not a concern which we should seek to allay, since there can be no satisfactory answer to it. At least, that will be the position if, with Quine, we take it that if translation is indeterminate, so is meaning itself, so that there are accordingly no genuine facts about meanings for a satisfactory world-view to accommodate. Quine envisages, moreover, that a consequential indeterminacy must spread outwards to infect ordinary "folk" or intentional psychology which comprises states, like beliefs and desires, which are in part identified by their content, as well as modal properties of statements, such as necessity and possibility, which functionally depend upon those statements' meanings (see Chapter 19, MODALITY). Much is at stake, then, in Quine's thesis.

The discussion to follow is organized as follows. Sections 1 and 2 will offer some initial reflections on the content and implications of the indeterminacy thesis, and of the presuppositions that Quine makes in treating it as a stepping-stone to semantic irrealism. Section 3 then distinguishes Quine's two principal arguments[2] for the thesis: the famous 'gavagai' argument ('from Below') of *Word and Object* (1960), and the argument ('from Above') from the underdetermination of empirical theory by data emphasized in "On the reasons for the indeterminacy of translation" (1970), and lays out the essentials of the former. Section 4 appraises this argument in the light of Gareth Evans's discussion in his "Identity and Predication" (1975). Section 5 assesses the cogency of Evans's objections. Section 6 turns to the second and more radical argument, laying out certain basic distinctions and implications; and section 7 is concerned with its appraisal.

Quine's contribution to these issues is, in effect, no less than to have invented them and to have set the agenda for all subsequent discussion. He has continued a vigorous engagement in that discussion, and students of some of his more recent contributions, for instance in *Pursuit of Truth* (1990) or the "Three indeterminacies" paper (1989), will have noted significant developments and changes of emphasis. But these are beyond the purview of this chapter, whose concern is not with scholarship of the perhaps revisionist tendencies of Quine's more recent thought, but simply with the structure, power and philosophical background of the classic Quinean arguments.

1 What does the indeterminacy of translation involve?

It's a commonplace that expressions in one language may resist a fully satisfactory translation into another: that there is, for instance, no exact English equivalent, capturing all its existentialist overtones, of the French *ennui* (a kind of jaded detachment), or the special piquancy of the German *Schadenfreude* (a form of pleasurable excitement at another's misfortune). This commonplace has little to do with Quine's thesis. Quine's claim is not that exact translation is sometimes impossible, but that *there is no such thing as* exact translation: that for any expression, in any language, there will inevitably be a range of alternative translations of it into any particular language each of which, in conjunction with co-ordinating adjustments in the translation of other expressions, will equally well – and *unimprovably* – accommodate all the behavioural data concerning speakers' use of the translated language.[3]

Quine argues his case for this thesis in the context of *radical* translation. Radical translation is the translation of a hitherto wholly untranslated language, about whose syntax, semantics and etymology we are in a position to make no prior assumptions whatever. All we are assumed to have to go on is our observation of the use of the language. More specifically: we are assumed to be able to identify behaviour on the part of its native speakers which constitutes assent to and dissent from particular utterances in the language, and we are assumed to be able to observe the circumstances in which such assent or dissent takes place. We are also allowed to suppose that we are able to interact with native speakers in particular contexts, to put utterances to them in their own language for assent or dissent, and in general to encourage the production of evidential data for our translation, rather than merely passively observe. Quine's claim is that if a project of translation is undertaken under these circumstances, then there are bound to be intuitively incompatible claims about the meanings of (what we identify as) expressions in the natives' language such that, no matter how extensive the data which we proceed to gather, it will in principle never give us a reason to prefer one such claim to another.

Why, it may be wondered, the focus on radical translation? Why is the situation of someone engaged in so unusual a project, on so impoverished a basis of collateral information, of particular interest? Well, consider how it might be that radical translation was indeterminate, yet *non-radical* translation in certain cases – say the translation of some parts of French into English – was a fully determinate matter.

There's no doubt that in translating a French utterance into English, we will make all kinds of assumptions – about the accuracy of dictionaries, the context, the purposes of the speaker and so on – which effectively may uniquely determine the translation of a particular word in it. But what *justifies* these assumptions? Quine's thought is that their justification would ultimately have to come back to what could be appreciated from the vantage-point of the radical interpreter: that anything we – kindred post-Roman Europeans – can properly be said to *know* about French would have to be accessible, at least in principle, to a Martian radical translator of French – always provided the Martian was a good enough linguist and had enough time to gather the relevant observations. For Quine, any presuppositions we make when translating familiar languages into other familiar languages count as items of known fact – in contrast to, say, convention – only if they could in principle be justified by the methods of radical translation. So if radical translation is indeterminate, then all translation is indeterminate in the sense that the choice between alternative schemes of translation may be beyond justification by appeal to anything factual – anything which may be, properly speaking, known.

As remarked, Quine's view is that it follows from the indeterminacy of translation that meaning itself is indeterminate: if there are no facts of the matter about how an expression may be correctly translated into another language, then there are no facts of the matter about what it means. That may seem a natural enough transition. But it depends, of course, upon an additional assumption: that there can be no facts about meaning which are not accessible to a radical interpreter. And that would seem to involve presupposition of two further, potentially contentious theses:

(1) That there is no first/third person asymmetry in the epistemology of understanding: that I can know nothing about what I mean by some particular expression unless you can know it too, by sufficient observation of my linguistic behaviour – although it seems clear that, in the typical case where I do know what I mean by an expression, I do not know it by observing my own behaviour.[4]

(2) That whatever 'methodology' reconstructs a child's actual learning of a first language, the harvest of that methodology – the understanding of meanings in which pursuit of it results – cannot be *richer* than that of the methodology of radical interpretation. For if it were, there would be a way of knowing facts about meanings which radical interpretation couldn't emulate.

Point (1) may seem attractive, as being merely a version of the thesis that one's meanings must be, in principle, publicly available to others – the thesis of the essential manifestability of meaning which is widely accepted in contemporary philosophy of language (for further discussion, see Chapter 12, REALISM AND ITS OPPOSITIONS; Chapter 6, MEANING AND PRIVACY, and Chapter 7, TACIT KNOWLEDGE). But point (2) may seem less obviously agreeable: doesn't it simply overlook the consideration that the actual learning of a first language may deploy any number of unlearned dispositions – including 'grammatical' dispositions, if Chomsky is right, and also what we might call 'similarity dispositions', that is, dispositions to find certain aspects of similarity in presented material salient and others not so – of which the methodology of radical translation, if it is characterized along the above austere lines, will take no account?

Each of these reservations would require extended discussion before a considered verdict could be reached on Quine's passage from indeterminacy of translation to irrealism about meaning. But for the purposes of what follows, we will assume that points (1) and (2) are each sound, and will not pursue such reservations further.

2 Could one live with the indeterminacy of translation?

Let us (provisionally – there are a number of distinctions to be drawn here, which we shall come to below) formulate the thesis as follows:

> For any expression used in a given language, there are at least two incompatible hypotheses about its meaning which equally well – and *unimprovably* – explain all observable aspects of its use in that language.

Suppose this is accepted, and that we are content to conclude from it that, for any two such unimprovable hypotheses about an expression's meaning, there is no fact of the matter as to which of them is correct. Still, it wouldn't seem to follow that there are no facts about meaning at all. The undecidability of the choice between two unimprovable hypotheses is quite consistent with its being definitely *wrong* to choose any of a large number of incompatible alternative hypotheses; the unimprovable hypotheses may be definitely superior to the rest of the bunch, even if the choice between them is underdetermined. So we need to distinguish between weak and strong versions of the indeterminacy thesis:

> *Weak* versions will contend that *some* questions about the meaning of an expression are indeterminate;
> *Strong* versions of the thesis will contend that *all* questions about the meaning of an expression are indeterminate.

Even if we allow that indeterminacy of translation does indeed entail indeterminacy of meaning, it is clearly a strong thesis that is needed if we are to conclude that there are no facts whatever about meaning.

Now, the strong thesis certainly does seem disconcerting; but we should distinguish between better and worse reasons for finding it so. A bad reason would be the thought that all language becomes simply meaningless if we have to take it that meaning is everywhere indeterminate. That's just a confusion: *meaninglessness* is itself a specific–determinate–semantic condition. If there are no determinate facts about meaning, there are no determinate facts about meaninglessness either. But better reasons for disquiet are not far to seek. First, there is the fact that ordinary psychological states, like belief, desire, fear and so on, which feature so pervasively in our thought about ourselves and each other, are identified by their content: any belief is the belief that p, for some p; any desire is the desire that q, for some q. If there are no facts about the meanings of linguistic expressions, the question immediately arises, how could there still be determinate facts about the content of such states? How could *psychological content* survive an argument which was generally destructive of *linguistic content*? But if it cannot, then it seems that the whole fabric of ordinary psychological explanation must collapse.

Second, if there are no facts about meaning, how can there be facts about *truth*? Our ordinary thinking ascribes truth and falsity to various things: to declarative sentences, to propositions and to beliefs. But the latter now come under the general shadow which, as just noted, Quine's thesis casts over the intentional-psychological; and one who regards meaning as strongly indeterminate is hardly likely to be well-disposed towards propositions – that is, *reified linguistic contents*. So it is declarative sentences, it seems, which will have to be the canonical bearers of truth-values in the Quinean scheme of things. But then there is the obvious difficulty that the truth-value of a sentence functionally depends both on the way the world is and on its *meaning*. If there are no determinate facts about meanings, it would appear to follow that truth-values are indeterminate as well.

As remarked, Quine himself has not shrunk from the scorn of intentional psychology to which his position appears to commit him.[5] But the concern about the availability to him of ordinary notions of truth and falsity is quite another matter. If strong indeterminacy is sustained, the truth-value of a sentence – if the notion remains legitimate at all – will have to be determined by factors independent of meaning as traditionally understood. A programme of naturalized semantics might conceivably prove to be at Quine's service here (see Chapter 5, A GUIDE TO NATURALIZING SEMANTICS), though the prospects for such programmes seem anything but encouraging. This difficulty for Quine seems never to have been properly addressed.[6]

3 Quine's arguments for the indeterminacy thesis

Quine has presented two main and quite different styles of argument for the indeterminacy thesis. What has come to be known as the Argument from Below tries to illustrate the predicament of the radical translator by presenting actual concrete alternative translations of certain expressions between which, no matter what behavioural data might be accumulated, it will never be possible to choose rationally. The Argument from Above[7] proceeds, by contrast, on a purely theoretical basis, from the thesis (henceforward the Underdetermination Thesis) that all empirical theory construction is in principle underdetermined by all available data. This second form of argument, in which Quine himself invests the greater confidence,[8] will show, if successful, that translation, and thereby – so we are now allowing – meaning, must be indeterminate even if we lack the wit to construct in detail the sort of illustrations of indeterminacy of which the Argument from Below seeks to provide some examples. In this section we will review some of the twists and turns pursued by the development of the Argument from Below.

As emphasized, Quine is content to grant to the radical interpreter the ability to recognize native speakers' assent to and dissent from sentences formulated in their language, and the ability to interact with them at least to the extent of eliciting assent to or dissent from particular such sentences. In consequence, the translator will be able – except in the most recalcitrant case – to arrive at empirically confirmed generalizations about which types of situation provoke assent to or dissent from instances of a particular sentence-type. Now Quine is content, in *Word and Object*, to resurrect a surrogate for the notion of synonymy which, in "Two dogmas of empiricism", he so roundly rejected: two sentences are said to be *stimulus synonymous* just in case assent to and dissent from them is provoked by the same sensory circumstances. The central contention of the Argument from Below is accordingly that, no matter how ingenious, the translator will never be able to decide rationally between stimulus-synonyms just on the basis of observation of the native speakers' linguistic behaviour. Yet intuitively, stimulus-synonyms may be very different in meaning; indeed, they may not even coincide in extension.

Suppose, to follow in the tracks of Quine's famous example, that a rabbit hops past and the translator hears the natives say, "gavagai". Subsequent investigation discloses that the natives are generally disposed to assent to "gavagai" when rabbits are visibly present, and to dissent from "gavagai" when there is no sign of rabbits. So the translator tentatively notes down the translation of "gavagai" as "Lo! a rabbit" or "There goes a rabbit", or something of the sort. That may seem to be a well-grounded translation, but there are in fact a variety of alternatives which the translator would seem thereby to have overlooked. There are, that is, a number of concepts besides *rabbit* which, in exhibiting the observed patterns of assent and dissent, the natives could just possibly be exercising. Some of these are, respectively, the concepts of:

undetached rabbit part,
instantaneous temporal stage of a rabbit,
rabbithood (the universal),
rabbit-fusion (the scattered physical aggregate of all rabbits), and
rabbiting (taken as analogous to the feature-placing concepts, *thunder* and *rain*).

And the one-word utterance "gavagai", could correspondingly mean any of:

There is an undetached rabbit part.
There is a temporal stage of a rabbit.
Rabbithood is instantiated over there.
There is a part of the rabbit-fusion.
It's rabbiting.

The point Quine is making is not merely that the finiteness of the translator's observations must leave open alternative interpretations. The contention is not merely that, however much data the interpreter gathers, there will be rival translational hypotheses which are consistent with it. It is stronger; namely, that there are *certain specific* translational hypotheses such that, however much data the interpreter gathers, each will remain in play if any does.

Now it's clear – however peculiarly the various mooted translations of "gavagai" may strike us – that Quine's point is correct so long as the data to be considered concern nothing but the conditions which prompt assent to and dissent from the one-word sentence "gavagai". However, the thought immediately occurs that the situation is bound to change for the better as soon as we consider more complex sentential constructions in which "gavagai" features as a constituent. For example, suppose we are in a position to put the question, "How many gavagai are there over there?", or "Is that the same gavagai that we saw five minutes ago?" Then the correct answers are bound to vary according to whether or not "gavagai" means: *rabbit*, or: *undetached rabbit part*, or: *stage of a rabbit* respectively. For one rabbit is many undetached rabbit parts; and stages of a rabbit, unlike rabbits themselves, have no temporal duration.

Quine's reply to this[9] is that our ability to run these tests will, of course, depend on our having independently translated certain constructions of the native language as meaning "how many" and "is the same . . . as". And, he contends, it is quite unclear how one might go about settling the translation of such expressions without *first* settling the interpretation of words like "gavagai" – that is, of sortal predicates – and without identifying the natives' numerals.

That gives pause. Isn't he right? Suppose, for instance, the natives use a word, "qua", which we have come to suspect may be used in concatenation with sortal predicates to ask "how many?" questions. How could we test this hypothesis unless we *already* knew the meanings of a range of such predicates with which it might be concatenated to ask such questions, and could tell whether the answers were as would be appropriate if "how many?" questions were indeed what "qua" was enabling us to put? Indeed there is a further, more specific difficulty. Suppose we have indeed somehow correctly identified the numerals in the natives' language, so that we can tell when the natives are telling us that there is one of a certain kind of object, or three, and so on. And suppose we have settled on the translation of the word, "qua", as it occurs in constructions like "qua gavagai", as meaning something like "how many?" And imagine that we put the question, "qua gavagai?", when a solitary rabbit is visible, and get an answer which we rightly take to mean "one". Even so, it is too quick to suppose that the translation of "gavagai" as *undetached rabbit part*, is thereby defeated. It *is* defeated, of course, if "qua" does indeed precisely mean: how many? But "qua gavagai" could, consistently with its eliciting the same answers as "how many rabbits?", mean not that but rather: *of how many rabbits are there undetached parts over there?* More generally, its role could be this: that if F means *undetached G-part*, then "qua F" means: *of how many Gs are there undetached parts there?* Under that hypothesis, what looked like a crucial experiment ceases to be so.

Quine's contention, in general, is this: if a pair of expressions have the same stimulus-meaning, then even if they intuitively differ in meaning in ways that would impinge differentially on the use of more complex contexts in which they occur, there will always be a *compensating adjustment* to the interpretation of the surrounding context of such a kind that, under the adjustment, the uses once again coincide. More formally: if F and G have the same stimulus-meaning, but differ in intuitive meaning – like "rabbit" and "undetached rabbit part", for instance – in such a way that, with respect to a particular embedding context, "Φ . . .", the patterns of assent to and dissent from "ΦF" and "ΦG" could be expected to differ, there will always be an adjusted interpretation of "Φ . . ." such that the assent/dissent conditions of "ΦG" under the adjustment will coincide with those of "ΦF" when unadjusted.[10]

4 Evans's appraisal of the argument from below

This line of thought, as it stands, is arresting, but hardly sufficiently developed to count as cogent. It deserves thinking through in detail, yet there are few attempts to do so in the secondary literature. However, a distinguished exception is provided by Gareth Evans's paper, "Identity and Predication" (1975). Evans contends that Quine looks in the wrong place for considerations that might prove the superiority of the translation of "gavagai" as *rabbit*. Quine's consideration of contexts in which "gavagai" might occur embedded is restricted to what he calls the "apparatus of individuation" – constructions involving identity, plurals and the numerals. He allows that if we somehow fix on a translation of certain of the natives' expressions within this apparatus, then it will be possible to construct contexts which will discriminate, in principle, among the stimulus-synonyms of "rabbit". His point, then, is that the translation of native expressions into elements of the apparatus of individuation presents a problem which is *co-ordinate with* that of the translation of "gavagai", and that it is in principle impossible to motivate the identification of certain native devices as expressing plurality, identity, and so on, without first fixing the translation of terms like "gavagai". Evans's counter is that we do not actually need to consider the apparatus of individuation at all; rather it can suffice to consider how predicates may be used *in combination*, and how they behave under negation.

Here is an illustration of the sort of thing Evans has in mind. Suppose we have identified two other words in the native language, "odolby", and "thewi", which we observe to be associated with the following patterns of assent in the native speech community:

> There is assent to the one-word sentence, "odolby", just when something blood-stained is visible.
>
> There is assent to the one-word sentence, "thewi", just when something white is visible.

In addition, suppose we have observed the use of a particle, "neg", which seems to act as an operator of negation; that is, we observe:

> There is assent to "neg gavagai" just when no rabbit is salient;
> There is assent to "neg thewi" just when nothing white is salient;

and so on. And now suppose we also observe the following more complex patterns of linguistic behaviour:

> Situations which prompt assent to "gavagai" and "thewi" do not always prompt assent to the conjoined construction, "thewi gavagai". The latter is assented to only when a white rabbit is salient. "Thewi" and "gavagai" will, however, be assented to individually when a brown rabbit sits on the snow.
>
> It is similar with the conjoined constructions, "odolby gavagai" and "odolby thewi" – they are assented to only when a bloodstained rabbit is salient, or when something is salient which is both white and bloodstained.[11]
>
> Likewise, the natives are disposed to assent to "thewi gavagai" and "odolby gavagai" when two rabbits are in view, one white, the other bloodstained; but they will assent to "odolby thewi gavagai" only when one and the same rabbit is both white and bloodstained.

Evans's thought is that observations of this character would suffice to eliminate some of the stimulus-synonyms of "rabbit" as adequate translations of "gavagai". For instance, if "gavagai" really were just a device for reporting an environmental feature – like "it is raining" – and "thewi" were the same, then it would seem to be impossible to interpret the conjoined construction, "thewi gavagai", as anything other than the conjunction of the ingredient claims: it is whiting and it is rabbiting (compare: it's windy and it's raining). And that translation cannot account for the fact that "thewi gavagai" is not assented to unless the "whiting" is restricted to the surface of a *rabbit*.

The translation of "gavagai" as *undetached rabbit part* also seems to be in difficulties under the hypothesized data. What are we to say that "thewi" means in that case? If it just means *white*, then "thewi gavagai" ought to be assented to whenever a rabbit is salient with an undetached white part – say, a white foot. But that isn't what happens. If the one-word sentence "thewi" means *undetached part of a white thing*, on the other hand, then again "thewi gavagai" ought still to be assented to when the white-footed rabbit presents himself, since his toes are undetached parts of a white thing, namely his foot. So that translation fares no better. We might surmount that difficulty by allowing "thewi" to mean *undetached part of a white rabbit*; but then we'd be at a loss to understand the natives' assent to it as they gaze at a snowy but rabbit-free landscape.

"Undetached rabbit part" and "temporal stage of a rabbit" are, like "rabbit", and unlike the feature-placer, "rabbiting", sortal predicates. By contrast, the other items on Quine's list of stimulus-synonyms for "rabbit", that is, "rabbithood" and "rabbit-fusion", are singular terms, standing respectively for an abstract and for a scattered concrete object. It is these interpretations of "gavagai" which, Evans contends, are put in difficulty by the kind of data which he envisages for the natives' particle of negation. Suppose our observations disclose that the assent conditions of compound sentences vary depending on the position within them of "neg"; for instance

> "neg thewi gavagai" is assented to whenever no white rabbit is in view, including the case when no rabbit of any kind is in view, whereas "thewi neg gavagai" is assented to only in the presence of rabbits of other colours.

These facts are nicely explained if we suppose that "thewi" means white, "gavagai" means rabbit and "neg" functions as a device of sentential negation when it takes initial position, and as a device of predicate negation when it immediately succeeds a predicate.[12] But how are the data to be accommodated on the assumption that "gavagai" is, for example, a singular term standing for the universal, rabbithood? On that assumption, the assent conditions of "thewi gavagai" suggest that "thewi" is a predicate of universals roughly equivalent in meaning to "has a white instance here". But in that case we seem to have no way of generating a sentence with the assent conditions hypothesized for "thewi neg gavagai". For the negation particle has nothing smaller to operate on, so to speak, than an atomic predicate of the natives' language; and when it is so restricted, to suppose that it occurs as a predicate negation in that sentence is to predict, falsely, that the sentence should have the assent conditions of "rabbithood does not have a white instance here" – something which should be assented to when there is no rabbit to be seen.

An analogous problem would presumably confront the translation of "gavagai" as *rabbit-fusion*, could we first but find a workable construal in this case of "thewi" as it occurs in sentences like "thewi gavagai". But in fact, as Evans points out, this translation of "gavagai" also inherits the problems associated with the translation *undetached rabbit part*. If "thewi" is a predicate of concrete but spatio-temporally scattered entities, what hypothesis about its meaning will get the assent conditions of "thewi gavagai" right? Not ". . . has a white part here" – because brown rabbits with white tails don't provoke assent to it – nor even ". . . has a white, rabbit-shaped part", because that would leave us bereft of any explanation of the natives' assent to "thewi todagai" in the presence of an Arctic fox.

So far so good, it may seem. Different considerations come into play when Evans comes to the proposed translation *temporal stage of a rabbit*. The sort of difficulty he finds for this proposal[13] is not posed by envisaged data of the foregoing kinds, but has to do with the interpretation of what, in our preferred translation scheme involving rabbits, whiteness and the rest – henceforward the *favoured scheme* – we will naturally take to be simple *tensed* assertions. Suppose, for instance, that the suffix "-p" is naturally taken, in that scheme, as an indicator that a predication is past-tensed.[14] The question Evans raises is how such data is to be accommodated by a translation scheme for the natives' language which treats the predicates in question as predicates of temporal stages.

Evans's (rather terse) discussion here is semi-technical. He envisages an interpreter who is working within something like the framework of a Tarski–Davidsonian recursive theory of meaning (see Chapter 1, MEANING AND TRUTH CONDITIONS: FROM FREGE'S GRAND DESIGN TO DAVIDSON'S) and who first lays down basic clauses which stipulate satisfaction-conditions for *tenseless counterparts* of the natives' predicates; for instance

$$\langle x,t\rangle \text{ satisfy "odolby" (tenseless)}^{15} \leftrightarrow (\exists y)\ (y \text{ is bloodstained at } t\ \&\ x \text{ is a stage of } y)$$

– a pair consisting of a temporal stage, x, and a time, t, satisfy "odolby" if and only if that stage is a stage of something which is bloodstained at that time, and then stipulates satisfaction-conditions for stages and tensed versions of those predicates in terms of these basic clauses; for instance, for the simple present tense (where t_u is the envisaged time of utterance)

x satisfies "odolby" (present tensed) $\leftrightarrow$ $\langle x, t_u \rangle$ satisfy "odolby" (tenseless)

– a stage satisfies (present tensed) "odolby" only if the pair consisting of that stage and the time of utterance satisfies (tenseless) "odolby"; and for the simple past tense

x satisfies "odolbyp" $\leftrightarrow$ $(\exists t')$ (Before t_u, t' & $\langle x, t' \rangle$ satisfy "odolby" (tenseless))

– a stage satisfies "odolbyp" if and only if there is a time earlier than the envisaged time of utterance such that the pair consisting of that stage and that time satisfies (tenseless) "odolby".

Now, an evident effect of the proposed base clause is that *every* stage, x, in the life of a rabbit which is bloodstained at t will be such that $\langle x, t \rangle$ will satisfy (tenseless) "odolby". So any treatment of the tenses along these lines will have the consequence, as Evans observes, that if any temporal stage of a given rabbit satisfies "odolbyp", or (present-tensed) "odolby", then *every* temporal stage of the same rabbit, *no matter when occurring*, will satisfy "odolbyp", or "odolby" – and indeed will satisfy any other tense of the same predicate, if introduced via a clause along the same lines. Evans evidently regards this kind of promiscuity as a decisive difficulty, for he immediately moves to consider a proposal fashioned to avoid it. But he does not say why. We will return to the matter.

The second proposal Evans considers avoids the promiscuity by an obvious modification in the form of the base clauses; thus

x satisfies "odolby" (tenseless) $\leftrightarrow$ $(\exists y)(\exists t)$(y is bloodstained at t & x is a stage of y & x occurs at t)

– a stage satisfies (tenseless) "odolby" if and only if it is a stage of something *which is bloodstained at the time at which that stage occurs*. Clauses for the simple present and past tenses may then proceed:

x satisfies "odolby" (present tensed) $\leftrightarrow$ x satisfies "odolby" (tenseless) & x occurs at t_u

– a stage satisfies (present-tensed) "odolby" if it occurs at the time of utterance and is a stage of something that is bloodstained at the time that stage occurs; and

x satisfies "odolbyp" $\leftrightarrow$ $(\exists z)(\exists t')$((Before t_u, t') & (z occurs at t') & (x occurs later than t') & (x and z are stages of the same thing) & (z satisfies "odolby" (tenseless)))

– a stage satisfies "odolbyp" if it is a later stage of something one of whose earlier stages, occurring before the time of utterance, is a stage of something bloodstained at the time it occurs.

However, Evans foresees a new difficulty for this scheme. According to the proposed clauses, "odolbyp gavagai" should be true just of stages of a rabbit occurring later than a stage in its life when it was bloodstained. What if there no longer *are* any such stages? What if, rather than clean up the bloodstained rabbit, we had destroyed it? In that case, the proposed clause will predict that the natives will no longer assent to "odolbyp gavagai", for there are now no stages to meet the specified condition. But it is easy to imagine how, consistently with the other data envisaged, they might nevertheless give their assent. We have only to imagine that their assent conditions for "odolbyp gavagai" coincide with those of the English sentence, "a rabbit was bloodstained". Evidence of that coincidence, it might seem, would then be powerful evidence for the favoured scheme as against the temporal stage-scheme.

5 Are Evans's objections compelling?

Seemingly the least cogent part of Evans's discussion is his treatment, just reviewed, of the temporal stage-scheme. Even if the detail of his objections were wholly convincing, there would have to be a vague worry whether the problems thereby disclosed for the stage-theorist were not artefacts of avoidable features of the mooted Tarski–Davidson style of semantic-theoretical treatment of tense. But the detail does not seem convincing in any case. The last consideration, that the proposed clauses cannot recover the assertibility of "odolbyp gavagai" in circumstances when no stage of the rabbit in question post-dates its (last) bloodstained stage,[16] seems crucially to overlook an ambiguity in the hypothesized English (stimulus-)equivalent, "a rabbit was bloodstained". The English sentence can, indeed, be read as embedding a past-tensed predication – when it is taken as the existential generalization, for example, of "that rabbit over there was bloodstained", so that the tensing is done, as it were, within the scope of the quantifier. But the reading germane to Evans's possibility, when "a rabbit was bloodstained" is asserted of a now defunct rabbit, reverses the scope-priority: the past tense is now the principal operator in the sentence, and the quantifier occurs within its scope, so that the effect of the claim is rather that *it was the case that*: [a rabbit is bloodstained]. Any semantic treatment of tense which treats the tenses as operators – on tenseless sentences, in the kind of treatment Evans has in mind, but there are other possibilities – has to be open to all the usual possibilities for ambiguity in the scope of such operators. In particular, we have to expect wide and narrow scope possibilities broadly analogous to those presented by negation. The mooted clause for "odolbyp" is a proposal for a *past-tensed predicate*, where the tense operator is given narrow scope. Evans's objection to it, by contrast, is – irrelevantly – that it does not enable us to recover the (apparent) truth-conditions of predications of "odolbyp" in which it is not merely the predicate but the *whole sentence* that falls within the scope of the past tense. The objection is irrelevant because – their overt form notwithstanding – such sentences should no more be construed as containing the kind of use of "odolbyp" which the proposed clause concerns than "it is not the case that a rabbit is white" should be construed as containing an occurrence of "is not white".

The favoured scheme, too will have to cope with this kind of ambiguity; however it does so, there is no reason to think that the stage-theorist will not have exactly analogous resources.

In any case, what exactly was the problem that moved Evans to dismiss the first form of proposal? Why should the kind of promiscuity imposed by the originally mooted clauses be held to be objectionable? The point might seem obvious. Consider the blood-soaked rabbit of note 14 who gets a thorough cleaning. Suppose the natives assent to "odolby gavagai" before the washing, *but not afterwards*. How, if they are talking about temporal stages of the animal, and if "odolby" has the satisfaction-conditions outlined, is this to be explained? If any temporal stage of the rabbit satisfies the utterance of "odolby" before the washing, then all do, no matter when they occur or when the question is raised. So why – if they are talking about properties of temporal stages – do the natives, having earlier assented to "odolby gavagai", not do so later? To be sure, the reference of "gavagai", will then be presumably to stages of the rabbit which post-date its bloodstained period. But, on the treatment proposed, that should make no difference. Since the natives cannot plausibly be taken to have forgotten that the rabbit was bloodstained, or not to have noticed, their temporally selective assent patterns – the very things that motivate viewing them as deploying tenses in the first place – are seemingly at odds with the ascription to them of an ontology of stages and the proposed semantic clauses for "odolby".

This train of thought, however, confuses the form of promiscuity actually entailed by the original type of clauses – promiscuity over stages, as it were – with a form of promiscuity over times. The key point is that those clauses have to be read as dealing with the satisfaction-conditions of actual or envisaged *token utterances* of the tensed predicates they concern; that is the effect of their reference to a time of utterance, t_u.[17] The generalization they actually entail is that if a particular (actual or envisaged) historic token of (present-tensed) "odolby", or "odolbyp", is satisfied by a particular stage in the life of a rabbit, then it is satisfied by all earlier and later stages in the life of that rabbit. That is not to be confused with anything which generalizes from a particular historic token predicate's satisfaction to the satisfaction of other tokens of the same type uttered at *other times*. Nothing of that kind follows from the clauses in question when properly construed. In particular, they entail nothing about whether if a particular token of "odolby" is satisfied by a present stage of a rabbit, then that or later stages of the same rabbit should be regarded as satisfying *a later tokening* of "odolby". So there is nothing in the clauses to jar with the natives' hypothesized unwillingness to apply "odolby" to what they know to be a formerly, but no longer, bloodstained rabbit.[18]

I am not suggesting that Evans himself was guilty of this confusion, only that one who did fall into it might find a spurious plausibility in Evans's brisk dismissal of that particular approach on behalf of the stage-scheme – and that I am not sure what else he may have had in mind.

In any case, it must be reckoned as doubtful how forceful are Evans's objections to the temporal stage-scheme. The matter would assume some importance as far as the Argument from Below is concerned if Evans had indeed disposed of

Quine's other mooted translation schemes, since the temporal stage-scheme would then represent the argument's last chance, at least as far as Quine himself develops it. But at least one recent commentator has questioned quite generally whether Evans's considerations really are successful.[19] A closer review of the matter will turn out to render further discussion of the temporal stage-scheme unnecessary.

Consider again the data envisaged in order to make trouble for the other schemes. For instance, a brown rabbit with a white foot provokes assent to "thewi" and "gavagai" separately but not to the compound, "thewi gavagai". Evans challenges Quine to find an interpretation of "thewi", within the framework of an ontology of undetached parts of things, which explains this. Neither ". . . is white" nor ". . . is part of a white thing" will do; ". . . is part of a white rabbit" – or, more generally, ". . . is part of a white animal" – would explain why the compound sentence doesn't get assented to in the circumstances described; but it would leave us bereft of any explanation why "thewi" gets assented to on its own in the context in question.

There is an obvious counter. Evans is assuming that we have to find *some one general account* of the meaning of "thewi" to account for both simple and compound occurrences of it. But why shouldn't its syntactic/semantic role be *context-sensitive?* It could, for instance, mean *white*, when occurring in one-word sentences, but *undetached part of a white F*, when occurring in immediate concatenation with the word whose correct translation when not so concatenated is *undetached F-part* (and whose role, when conjoined with "thewi", accordingly reduces to that of fixing the parameter, F). Context-sensitive variation in meaning, contrasting with simple ambiguity in so far as the meanings in question are variously cognate to each other, is a familiar phenomenon in natural languages: think, for instance, of the expression "fix" as it occurs in "I'll fix lunch", "he fixed the puncture" and "they fixed the race." Why should not phenomena of that general sort be found in the natives' language too? In effect what would be postulated would be a theory according to which "thewi" had a kind of ambiguity, albeit one in which there was a close relation between its diverse meanings, and where precisely which meaning it took would be determined by its syntactic mode of occurrence. But that doesn't seem outlandish really.

It is similar with the data concerning the use of "neg", represented by Evans as scotching the interpretations of "gavagai" as a singular term standing respectively for rabbithood and the rabbit-fusion. The problem was to find an interpretation of "thewi" which, when "neg" can occur both as external and as internal negation, would rationalize a native's assent to "thewi" when a white rabbit is salient, but to "thewi neg gavagai", when, say, brown rabbits are salient, and to neither when no rabbit is salient. The interpretation ". . . has a white instance here" captures the first datum; but if "neg" is a device of internal negation, it mis-predicts the assent conditions of "thewi neg gavagai". But again, the obvious rejoinder is that we are not constrained to take "neg", occurring as illustrated, as a device of internal negation in the first place. There could be an operator which, in prenex position, functions as sentential negation, but when it occurs as a predicate-suffix, serves not to negate the predicate – to generate its complement – but operates rather *within* that predicate's content. In particular, under the translation scheme which treats "gavagai" as a singular term standing for a universal, the role of "neg" occurring as suffix may be taken as one of generating the complement of the *adverb* – the mode of instantiation – which we interpret predicates like "thewi" and "odolby" as ascribing. So "thewi neg gavagai" is interpreted as saying not that rabbithood doesn't have a white instance here, but that it has a non-white instance here (as it were, *is instantiated non-whitely here*) – precisely what is wanted to save the data described.

How are we to assess the resulting dialectical situation? It is difficult to see one's way clear to the conclusion that *any* pool of data which a sympathizer with Evans might construct, and which would be prima facie recalcitrant for Quine's alternatives to the favoured scheme, could be handled in the quite simple kinds of way illustrated. But what is surely convincing in advance is that the most that the sympathizer with Evans is going to be able to do is to call attention to possible observational data which wouldn't square with *particular* proposed interpretations of some of the expressions concerned; and that it must always be possible in principle to handle such data if one is willing to assign a *variety* of syntactic roles, and/or semantic ambiguities, to the expressions in question. Does this reflection suffice to show that Evans embarked on a lost cause?

It does not. Consider this case. Suppose that alternative schemes along Quinean lines can indeed be constructed which can survive any envisageable addition to our pool of linguistic data, but that whereas the Quinean schemes survive by the postulation of ambiguities of various kinds, the favoured scheme has, by and large, no need for such recourse. Then the latter would be, in a clear sense, *simpler* than the Quinean alternatives. Now, the point is well taken that simplicity cannot be assumed, without further ado, to be an *alethic* – truth-conducive – virtue in empirical theory generally. There is prima facie sense in the idea that of two empirically adequate theories, it might be the more complex that is actually faithful to the reality which each seeks to circumscribe. But the thought that, when it comes to radical interpretation, there is an ulterior psychologico-semantical reality which an empirically adequate translation scheme might somehow misrepresent is, of course, exactly what Quine rejects – exactly what he famously stigmatizes as the myth of the semantic museum.[20] And with that rejection in place, methodological virtues which are not, in realistically conceived theorizing, straightforwardly alethic can now become so. In such cases, the methodologically best theory ought to be reckoned true just on that account. It is therefore not enough for a defender of Quine to seek to save the alternative schemes by postulations which, though still principled and general, are comparatively expensive in terms of ambiguity and other forms of complication. If a simpler scheme is available, that fact is enough to determine that these alternatives are *untrue*, by the lights of the only notion of truth that, in Quine's own view, can engage the translational enterprise.

It's another question whether the particular moves I envisaged fall foul of this point. The alternative interpretation of "neg" just canvassed, for instance, postulates a syntactic ambiguity only where the favoured, internal/external negation-distinguishing interpretation *already* does so, albeit a different ambiguity. And the interpretation of "thewi" – *undetached part of a white F* – to which we had the undetached-parts theorist resort in the attempt to accommodate Evans's assent-data for "thewi gavagai" might actually serve well enough to accommodate the natives' assent patterns to the one-word sentence "thewi" as well ("undetached part of a white something").

That, however, brings us up against a second and this time, I think, decisive consideration, at least if we may take it that the basic clauses of our semantic theory are to assign reference and satisfaction-conditions in ways which are *presumed to correspond to the conceptual repertoire of speakers of the language in question*. For even if the schemes considered turn out not to enjoin any avoidable degree of complication in comparison with the favoured scheme, the fact is that the range of concepts necessary in order to formulate their various clauses in each case includes, but is not included in, the simple range of concepts of observable spatio-temporal continuants and their observable properties which the favoured scheme deploys. So much is obvious in the case of the schemes deploying the concept of the universal rabbithood, and the rabbit-fusion: these are ideas which you do not grasp until you know respectively what qualifies something to be an instance of the universal, and what qualifies it to be a basic part of the fusion. The same point emerges in the clause to which we had the undetached-parts theorist resort for "thewi", and indeed in the various clauses we considered that the temporal-stage theorist might propose.[21]

It is simplicity not in *semantic* theory but in the associated *psychological* theory that is at stake here. Let it be unresolved whether Quine's alternative schemes must issue in semantically more complex theories; it is certain none the less that their implied accompaniment must be additional psychological complexity. The effect is that their situation is therefore doubly unhappy. Not merely do they involve the ascription of superfluous conceptual resources to speakers – resources strictly unnecessary to explain their linguistic performance – but, worse, we have to regard the resources in question as lurking behind, but *inexpressible* in, the actual vocabulary of the natives' language. To have the concept of an undetached rabbit part, you need a concept of the integrated individual of which such parts are parts; to have the concept of a temporal stage of a rabbit, you need to grasp the idea of the spatio-temporal continuant of which such a stage is a stage. Yet the Quinean translation schemes will represent you as talking only of undetached parts, or temporal stages; reference to the *integrated, spatio-temporally persisting rabbit* will elude you so long as your expressive resources are fully captured by these translation schemes.

Such schemes, then, even if they can indeed cope with all the data which a sympathizer with Evans might imagine, and even if they can do so without losing out by canons of simplicity governing the construction of *semantic* theory, must, it seems, fall foul of a basic methodological consideration: that the conceptual repertoire which radical interpretation may permissibly ascribe to speakers should exceed what is actually expressible in their language, as so interpreted, only if its ascription to them is necessary in other ways in order to account for their linguistic competence. Perhaps an Argument from Below could be developed in such a way as to respect this constraint. But Quine's own examples do nothing to suggest how.[22]

6 The Argument from Above: preliminary clarifications

The Argument from Below operates at the level of sub-sentential expressions. Quine sometimes represents this point by the claim that the conclusion of the argument is not the indeterminacy of translation, properly understood, but rather the *inscrutability of terms.* What a proponent of the argument tries to do in the case of "gavagai", for example, is, as we have seen, to propose hypotheses about its syntactic category and reference in such a way that the truth-conditions – and hence assent-conditions – of contexts containing it are left invariant under compensating readjustments in the interpretation of the other expressions which they contain. Even if this is done successfully, the conclusion will still be consistent, therefore, with determinacy in the matter of what truth-conditions a radical interpreter is to assign to natives' utterances. True, it will be left indeterminate exactly what *thoughts* – individuated more finely than merely by their truth-conditions – should be regarded as expressed by particular native utterances. But the slack will extend no further than the existence of some room for manoeuvre within assignments whose truth-conditions are the same. It is doubtless for this reason, rather than to acknowledge any infirmity in the Argument from Below, that Quine writes:

> My *gavagai* example has figured too centrally in discussions with the indeterminacy of translation. Readers see the example as the ground of a doctrine, and hope by resolving the example to cast doubt on the doctrine. The real ground of the doctrine is very different, broader and deeper.[23]

Quine thus seems content to have most – perhaps all – of his eggs in the other basket.[24] And the contention of the Argument from Above is indeed stronger. It is precisely that unimprovable translation manuals may differ not merely in their interpretations of sub-sentential expressions, but in the truth-conditions they assign to sentences, and hence in which of the natives' utterances they will enjoin us – in conjunction with our own collateral beliefs about the world – to regard as true.

Here, though, there are a variety of possible theses of differing strength, which we shall do well to distinguish. Let 'M' range over unimprovable translation manuals – by whatever criteria – for the natives' language, and let 'S' denote a particular sentence of that language; let 'C' range over claims which identify the truth-conditions of sentences, and 'c' range over claims which, while falling short of identification, somehow constrain the identification of sentences' truth-conditions, for example, by saying what their truth-conditions are not. Let's say that S's meaning is:

(1) *strongly determinate* if and only if there is some C such every M makes C about S

(2) *weakly determinate* if and only if there is some c such that every M makes c about S
(3) *weakly indeterminate* if and only if there is no C such that every M makes C about S
(4) *strongly indeterminate* if and only if there is no c such that every M makes c about S

Then any particular sentence S must be in one of three cases:

(A) strongly determinate
(B) weakly determinate and weakly indeterminate
(C) strongly indeterminate

and there are accordingly *seven* possibilities for the sentences, S, of any particular language:

(1) Every S is in case A.
(2) Some S are in case A, some S are in case B, and every S is in one of those two cases.
(3) Some S are in case A, some S are in case B, and some S are in case C.
(4) Some S are in case A, and some S are in case C, and every S is in one of those two cases.
(5) Every S is in case B.
(6) Some S are in case B and some S are in case C, and every S are in one of those cases.
(7) Every S is in case C.

Each of (2) through to (7) represents a possible indeterminacy thesis, of an increasingly radical order.

Now, if a "fact about meaning" is to be anything agreed on by all unimprovable manuals, then it is only (7) which entails that there are no facts about meaning whatever. This is important. I mentioned at the start the underlying physicalist spirit which drives Quine's argument, the perceived difficulty in finding anything for semantical properties to be in what is conceived of an essentially physical world. The thesis of indeterminacy of translation is meant to assuage this concern precisely by showing that semantic facts are *superstition*, and are therefore owed no refuge in the austere ontology of developed physical science. This radical solution will be frustrated should it turn out that Quine's arguments at best support something less thoroughgoing than a thesis of form (7). For in any other situation, there will *be* residual "facts about meaning"; maybe nothing like the rich variety of such facts that an opponent of Quine would intuitively wish to recognize, but facts about meaning all the same. So we should have the worst of both worlds: insufficient semantic facts to do justice to our intuitions of distinctions of meaning, but enough to set up the perceived difficulty for Quine's physicalism.[25]

The taxonomy invites review of a number of issues. First, on determinacy of truth-value. It might be supposed that, whatever form of indeterminacy thesis is maintained, the effect will be to introduce a species of relativity: the truth-value of a sentence whose meaning is absolutely indeterminate will have to be thought of as likewise non-absolute, as relative to whatever the (unimprovable) manual we happen to favour assigns to it as its truth-condition. But actually there is cause for doubt about the stability of this line of thought. For the truth-value of S can be conceived as determinate relative to some particular manual only if it is thought to be determinate *what that manual has to say* about the meaning of S. And the contents of claims in translation manuals ought, by the Quinean, to be regarded as no more determinate than any others.

If relativism is accordingly eschewed, then it seems it must be conceded that any sentence in category C – any strongly indeterminate sentence – must simply be indeterminate in truth-value, at least so long as we continue to conceive of truth-value as a function of truth-conditions. But how about sentences in category B – weakly determinate but weakly indeterminate sentences? Unimprovable manuals will not converge on the assignment of any particular truth-condition to such a sentence. But they will converge in making certain claims which constrain its meaning, in particular claims which rule out certain such assignments. So the possibility is open, at least while the discussion moves at this level of generality, that such a sentence might yet be determinate in truth-value, since it might be that the space of permissible assignments of truth-conditions is sufficiently narrow to ensure that, as matters happen to stand, the sentence will be true no matter which of those assignments is made. It would all depend how far the weak determinacy extended; how many and what strength of meaning-constraining claims about S the unimprovable manuals would converge upon.

A second issue concerns the respective implications of the various possible strengths of indeterminacy thesis for the viability of ordinary intentional psychology. Assume that it is by the interpretation of what they are prepared to assent to that we are to identify by far the greater proportion of the natives' beliefs. Sentences in category C are obviously useless for this purpose. But might at least some measure of propositional-attitude psychology be feasible if our data concerns acceptances and rejections of sentences in category B? In that event we should know insufficient to determine the truth-conditions of the beliefs thereby evinced. But it is not inconceivable that the range of permissible assignments and truth-conditions on which the best manuals converged might be sufficiently restricted to ensure that, at least in certain special circumstances, the only beliefs which we could regard a particular utterance as expressing would all equally well serve the purpose of rationalizing an associated item of behaviour when conjoined with certain plausibly ascribed desires. (For instance, the belief that a certain fruit was nutritious and the belief that it was merely tasty might rationalize many of the same behavioural episodes.) Again, it will all depend on how weak is the weak determinacy involved.

However, I shall not pursue these matters further. The crucial question is: which of the various possibilities, from (2) to (7), are in the range of Quine's Argument from Above? Here is his own classic statement of the argument:

> Now my point about physical theory is that physical theory is underdetermined even by all . . . possible observations. . . . Physical theories can be at odds with each other

> and yet compatible with all possible data even in the broadest sense. In a word they can be logically incompatible and empirically equivalent. This is a point on which I expect wide agreement, if only because the observational criteria of theoretical terms are commonly so flexible and fragmentary. People who agree on this general point need not agree as to how much physical theory is empirically unfixed in this strong sense; some will acknowledge such slack only in the highest and most speculative reaches of physical theory, while others see it as extending even to commonsense traits of macroscopic bodies.
>
> Now let's turn to the radical translation of a radically foreign physicist's theory. As always in radical translation, the starting point is the equating of observation sentences of the two languages by an inductive equating of stimulus meanings. In order afterward to construe the foreigner's theoretical sentences we have to project analytical hypotheses, whose ultimate justification is substantially just that the implied observation sentences match up. But now the same old empirical slack, the old indeterminacy between physical theories, recurs in second intension. Insofar as the truth of physical theory is underdetermined by observables, the translation of the foreigner's physical theory is underdetermined by translation of his observation sentences. If our physical theory can vary though all possible observations be fixed, then our translation of his physical theory can vary though our translations of all possible observation reports on his part be fixed. Our translation of his observation sentences no more fixes our translation of his physical theory than our own possible observations fix our own physical theory.
>
> The indeterminacy of translation is not just an instance of the empirically underdetermined character of physics. The point is not just that linguistics, being a part of behavioural science and hence ultimately of physics, shares the empirically underdetermined character of physics. On the contrary, the indeterminacy of translation is additional. Where physical theories A and B are both compatible with all possible data, we might adopt A for ourselves and still remain free to translate the foreigner either as believing A or as believing B.[26]

What exactly is the structure of this reasoning? Its premise is clearly indicated. It is the Underdetermination Thesis: the thesis, roughly, that all possible observations – all the observations that scientific observers, however idealized, wherever and whenever situated, might gather between them – do not constrain the selection of an explanatory empirical theory to within uniqueness. Alternative, incompatible theoretical accounts are always possible of any data pool, even if of infinite extent. This is the point on which Quine expects "wide agreement", although he earlier envisages possible disagreement about the level at which Underdetermination operates, some accepting that it holds only for the highest reaches of empirical theory, while others possibly allowing that it go for all empirical theorizing, *tout court.* But how exactly is the transition supposed to be effected to the conclusion: the indeterminacy of translation, and of meaning?

Quine, as the reader will have noted, explicitly disavows that it is simply a matter of applying the Underdetermination Thesis to the special case of empirical linguistics: the indeterminacy is to be "additional". But it is a good question why or whether it would matter much if the argument were indeed that direct. No doubt the direct argument would have to confront a very obvious question: why is its legitimate conclusion not merely that theories of meaning are, like all empirical theories, *underdetermined* by the behavioural data? Why the additionally strong conclusion concerning *indeterminacy*? Quine shows no inclination to draw the conclusion that empirical theory as a whole is indeterminate. So what, for a proponent of the direct route, would distinguish empirical theories of *meaning*, making the indeterministic conclusion appropriate in their case? It may be doubted that such a philosopher could have any better answer than to charge that to hold to the opposed view – that meanings may, in cases of indeterminacy of translation, simply lie beyond the reach of empirical detection – is to succumb to the myth of the museum.[27] It is to succumb, that is, to the illusion that, in a world apt for complete description by physical theory, there can possibly be states of affairs apt to confer truth and falsity on claims about meaning other than those constituted in behavioural propensities of language use which, by hypothesis, underdetermine the selection of semantic theory. But the salient point is, then, that this – the repudiation of the myth of the museum – is a point on which Quine is going to have to rely *in any case*, even if the argument follows a subtler path than the one disavowed. The immediate conclusion, whatever exactly the configuration of the subtler route to it, is still only going to be that respect for all possible data will leave the translation of the natives' utterances underdetermined. One wonders, then, what exactly the additional subtlety, whatever exactly it may prove to consist in, really has to contribute. Does it somehow make for a stronger conclusion, a more pervasive or deeper kind of indeterminacy? Or does Quine see some difficulty for the simple, direct argument which the subtler route can finesse? What does "additional" mean?

Whatever the answers to those questions, it's notable that the scope of the argument can in any case extend no further than that of the Underdetermination Thesis which fuels it. Someone who allows, for example, that only very high-level physical theory is subject to underdetermination will be under no pressure to concede indeterminacy of translation except for vocabulary which occurs exclusively in such theory.[28] And even for sentences containing such vocabulary, it will be *weak* indeterminacy, not strong, that will be suggested. For however exactly the argument is supposed to run, just as not any old interpretation of that vocabulary would result in a theory which was adequate to the relevant data, so not any old interpretation results in a translation which may justifiably be regarded as reflecting the putatively perfectly rational native scientists' beliefs. The translation of theoretical terms in the native scientists' language can be no more indeterminate than is the selection of an empirically adequate theory of those data.

Strikingly, therefore, Quine's argument promises at best the *mildest* kind of indeterminacy thesis, one of type (2) in the above taxonomy, according to which a thesis of *weak* determinacy/indeterminacy is made out merely for *some* statements. And indeed, even if the Underdetermination Thesis is extended to all empirical theorizing, the most that is in prospect is a thesis of the indeterminacy of theoretical vocabulary relative to some fixed translation of the 'observation sentences'. The argument will have nothing to say about the determinacy of the meanings of the latter; and about the interpretation of theoretical terms, it will suggest only some degree, and by no means an unrestricted one, of latitude.

7 The Argument from Above: appraisal

Enough of preliminaries. Let us now try to map the course of the purportedly subtler route which Quine officially conceives the argument to follow. It would seem to involve reliance on the following transitional principle:

> If all possible empirical observation underdetermines the choice between theories T1 and T2 (that is, if T1 and T2 are *empirically equivalent*), then a native scientist's responses to his observations will underdetermine the choice between the ascription to him of acceptance of T1 and the ascription to him of acceptance T2.

And that may seem plausible enough. But notice that it does not, by itself, enjoin any conclusions about indeterminacy of translation. It is one thing to suppose that a rational native scientist could quite consistently hold either of two conflicting theories while respecting all possible relevant data. It is another, quite different thing to hold that the sentences by which he expresses whatever theory he does hold may, by an interpreter who respects all relevant data, be translated in different, incompatible ways. The second will follow directly from the first only if the *only* data that the interpreter has to respect concern which data – which observations – the native scientist will have set himself to respect. And that isn't plausible at all, and goes quite unsupported in Quine's presentation. For the project of translation is constrained not just by the need to identify a set of beliefs which, if rational, the native will have arrived at, but to an even greater degree by the need to find plausible *vehicles* of those beliefs in his overt linguistic behaviour. Quine's picture of the situation would seem to be that all we – the interpreters – can have to go on in the end is the native scientist's acceptance of certain observation sentences. Quine generously concedes our translation of these, and allows us the assumption that the native is a fully rational theorist of the range of data which they express, so that, to over-simplify rather absurdly, if just two incommensurable but unimprovable theories are possible of these data, then the native is likely to have alighted upon one of these theories in particular. But Quine seems to be depending on the idea that there can be nothing to provide us with *further* guidance in translating the relevant parts of the native's language, nothing additional to motivate viewing it as expressive of that theory rather than of its competitor. And that seems quite unjustified. As theorists of meaning, we will have to locate a *syntax* in those parts of the native's language, and then do a plausible job of mapping the ingredient concepts of one of the theories or the other on to components of his language identified by that syntax, the mapping to culminate in a satisfactory recursive theory of meaning. Quine gives absolutely no reason to discount the thought that the case for one of the interpretations in particular may simply evaporate as soon as this serious work of interpretation gets under way. Bluntly, it may just prove impossible to find the right kind of phonological or morphological structures in the native's theoretical sentences to subserve the necessary lexicography and semantic mapping.

That is one misgiving. We encounter another when we turn to consider just what status the premise – the Underdetermination Thesis – enjoys. Quine wrote that he expected "wide agreement" on this. And, surely, is it not just obvious that theories incorporate more content than the sum of their observational consequences?[29] So isn't it perfectly intuitive that this body of consequences must be theoretically axiomatizable in a variety of inequivalent ways?

When Quine anticipated little resistance to underdetermination, no doubt that was one kind of thought he was having. For instance, let T be some empirical theory and consider two consistent but mutually incompatible supplementations of it, T1 and T2, neither of which entails any empirically testable consequences over and above those of T. Then the choice between T1 and T2 is clearly underdetermined by all possible observations. It merits emphasis, therefore, that this kind of case is *not at all to the purpose*. If Quine's argument is to work then the relevant kind of case has to be one in which, precisely because all possible observations underdetermine the choice between two theories, there is nothing to motivate the ascription to the, by hypothesis, *fully rational* native scientist of one set of theoretical beliefs rather than the other. But equally, of course, if the argument is to work it is essential that the interpreter can have no good reason to suppose that the native scientist accepts *neither* theory – essential that there is not a better theory dominating both. And in the envisaged kind of case there will be: for if the native scientist is perfectly rational, he won't be inclined to accept any empirical theory the observational support for which extends no further than for a straightforwardly extricated, otherwise decent enough sub-theory: in the example as envisaged, precisely the theory T.

In brief, gerrymandered examples of Underdetermination, where the incompatibility between empirically equivalent theories is sustained only by their containing empirically idle hypotheses, won't drive Quine's argument. What the argument needs, rather, are cases where empirically equivalent but incompatible theories would either cease to be empirically equivalent, or would lose empirical content, if either was somehow truncated just far enough to eliminate the incompatibility. The clash, in other words, at the theoretical level must be owing to components which are *integral* to the theories' respective capacities to predict and explain the relevant range of observational phenomena. It is not an objection to this point that even when it is required that the axioms be finite in number, any given theory is likely to admit of a variety of axiomatizations, and that difficulties are consequently to be expected for any attempt to characterize precisely which of a theory's components should be reckoned integral to it. Since, as we have just noted, the Argument from Above won't run if the Underdetermination Thesis is made incontestable only by its trivialization, the obligation is actually on the *Quinean* to make out what is involved in the non-trivial case. Whatever it may or may not be possible to say by way of further explanation, what the Quinean requires are examples of pairs of unimprovable theories, the acceptance of each of which in its entirety would be justified on the part of one who knew of sufficiently many of its empirical successes but had no inkling of the other.

With this admittedly vague proviso, what exactly is the Underdetermination Thesis? Again, there are a number of claims of differing strengths to consider. Say that an empirical theory is *tight* just in case it is free of empirical slack of the kind just gestured at, so that it is the underdetermination of tight theories by all possible empirical data that is the material contention for Quine's argument. Let 'S' range over statements whose content potentially befits them to participate in tight theory construction, and let 'T', 'T*' range over empirically acceptable, global such theories. Then the following are among the possibilities worth singling out:

(1)	$(\forall T)(\forall S)(S \in T \rightarrow (\exists T^*) \sim (S \in T^*))$	*Total theoretical underdetermination*: every component of any acceptable, tight, global theory is omitted by another acceptable, tight, global theory.
(2)	$(\forall T)(\exists S)(S \in T \ \& \ (\exists T^*) \sim (S \in T^*))$	*Partial underdetermination of any theory*: any acceptable, tight global theory will have some theoretical components which are omitted by another such theory.
(3)	$(\exists S)(\forall T)(S \in T)$	*Partial determination of all theories*: some theoretical statements feature in any acceptable, tight global theory.
(4)	$(\forall T)(\forall S)(S \in T \rightarrow (\forall T^*)(S \in T^*))$	*Total determination of empirical theory*: the theoretical components of any acceptable, tight global theory feature in all such theories.

Now, allowing that the last may be merely utopian, about which (if either) of the first two of these can "wide agreement" be expected? Well, perhaps the history of science throws up some support for an Underdetermination Thesis of type (2). It is possible, for instance, though this is a matter for experts, that Special Relativity Theory and the Lorentzian Theory of Corresponding States share all their testable consequences, and that either might thus in principle be incorporated within an acceptable, tight, global theory.[30] If so, then – since no acceptable, tight, global theory will contain each of these as sub-theories, but must contain some theory of the phenomena which they explain – thesis (2) may be true. But such local examples seem special at best. It is hard to foresee what argument there might be for something stronger than an Underdetermination Thesis of type (2). Thesis (1), let us be clear, asserts that it is in the nature of empirical theory construction that any tight, empirically adequate, global theory will contain *only* dispensable theoretical claims. What reason is there to think that this is so?

For our present purposes, the crucial reflection is that thesis (3) – that such theories will agree on a common core of theoretical claims – is consistent with thesis (2). So unless the Quinean can make thesis (1) stick, the premise of the Argument from Above, whatever its exact detail, is going to be consistent with the idea that an ideally rational native theorist will be bound, if he is able to take account of sufficiently much of the available data, to arrive at certain *specific* theoretical beliefs, just in virtue of the nature of the project in which he is engaged. And if that were so then unless there is some special reason to worry about the identifiability of such beliefs, we may equip ourselves, as hypothetically ideal interpreters, with a knowledge of what they are. So equipped, our attempt to interpret the native scientist will be subject to an additional constraint: that of locating expressions for these privileged beliefs among the theoretical sentences which the native scientist is prepared to accept. This constraint may then motivate assumptions about the syntax and meanings of sub-sentential expressions in the native's theoretical language which may rub off on the translation of sentences expressing beliefs of other kinds. In short, it may be an additional source of determinacy of translation.

Those suppositions may, to be sure, be utterly fanciful. The point is only that the Underdetermination Thesis, if it is anything less than the radical thesis (1), is going to be *consistent* with them, and hence cannot validly enjoin any conclusion about indeterminacy of translation in the kind of way Quine seems to have had in mind. Quine's thought, in essentials, was that an assumed knowledge of the meanings of the natives' observation sentences could no more narrowly constrain the interpretation of their theoretical language than the totality of true observations which they could express in that vocabulary would constrain their selection of an empirical theory. We have already had cause for misgivings about the refusal, implicit in this comparison, to acknowledge the routine syntactic constraints to which radical interpretation is subject. But now it appears that Quine has in any case to rely upon what is, so far as I am aware, a quite unsupported and implausible version of the Underdetermination Thesis. To wit, only thesis (1) will do. For once theory construction is allowed to be partially determinate – thesis (3) – ideal interpreters will be constrained to find, among the sentences which a putatively rational native scientist is prepared to accept, some which serve to express the privileged core of empirically determined theoretical beliefs. It cannot be excluded – at least, not without further argument, yet to be provided – that this constraint would greatly reduce their freedom of interpretation, or even that it would have the effect that the interpretational project is uniquely determined. (Maybe each item of the native's theoretical vocabulary occurs in the privileged core.)

Again, I'm not suggesting optimism about such possibilities. It is merely that the premise for the Argument from Above, to the extent that it is something for which support might be forthcoming from the history of science, is consistent with them, and hence insufficient for Quine's notorious conclusion.

* * *

We have found each of Quine's classic arguments, from Above and Below, to provide less than compelling grounds for either the thesis of the indeterminacy of translation or even, more modestly, for that of the inscrutability of terms.[31] Moreover, as stressed at the beginning, Quine's own views have been modified and, in certain respects, softened since he first formulated the arguments on which we have concentrated. Nevertheless, a conviction of the resistability of those original lines of thought is no cause for complacency on the part of friends of the intensional. Although the thesis has been usually received as a paradox, it should be remembered that, within a broader physicalist framework, the indeterminacy of translation would come, at least at first blush, as a relief – the obviation of any need to locate meanings, and intentional states, within a purely physical world. As it is, an abiding tension between the thoughts on the one hand that *in some sense* the world is exhaustively physical and, on the other, that ordinary talk of meanings and the propositional attitudes ought to be unproblematical, remains, and its reconciliation continues to be one of the great issues facing contemporary philosophy.[32]

Notes

1 The reader should be reminded, however, that while this general concern has undoubtedly conditioned and intensified the reaction to the 'sceptical argument' which forms the core of Kripke's interpretation of Wittgenstein, that argument itself – in contrast to Quine's – makes no explicit behaviourist or physicalist assumption.

2 In fact they are directed at different versions of it, as we shall see.

3 For Quine's own original formulations, see pp. 27ff. of *Word and Object* (Cambridge, Mass.: MIT Press).

4 Large and subtle issues are raised here. At first blush, it may seem obvious that there are first-/third-person asymmetries of this kind; for instance that, even if my linguistic behaviour does underdetermine the translation of my uses of the word "rabbit" – to anticipate Quine's famous example – leaving the radical interpreter with no clearly superior choice among a range of rival interpretations of them, *I* at least can be in no doubt about which, if any, of these rival interpretations is correct. For by "rabbit", I mean of course: *rabbits* – so that's the right interpretation, and anything else is incorrect! But of course the interpreter will expect me to say that. The question, for him, is exactly what knowledge I thereby express. And the question for me – since I would indeed affirm that sentence whatever I meant by "rabbit" – is whether I thereby express any *substantial* piece of knowledge denied to the radical interpreter.

5 Here is a well-known formulation of that scorn:

> One may accept the Brentano thesis [of the irreducibility of intentional idiom] either as showing . . . the importance of an autonomous science of intention, or as showing the baselessness of intentional idioms and the emptiness of a science of intention. My attitude . . . is the second. . . . If we are limning the true and ultimate structure of reality, the canonical scheme for us is the austere scheme that knows . . . no propositional attitudes but only the physical constitution and behavior of organisms. (*Word and Object*, p. 221)

6 Perhaps because it has not been properly appreciated how deep it goes. Someone might think that, so far from posing a problem for Quine, the upshot here – the indeterminacy of truth-value of individual sentences – is merely part and parcel of Quinean holism: the idea, elaborated in §§ 5 and 6 of "Two Dogmas of Empiricism", in *From a Logical Point of View* (Cambridge, Mass.: Harvard University Press) that individual sentences indeed have no meaning except in the context of a larger system – that "the unit of meaning

is the whole of empirical science". Indeterminacy of truth-value at the level of sentences may not seem too shocking a matter if it is theories as a whole, rather than their ingredient statements, that are properly conceived as the bearers of truth and falsity.

This suggestion just invites the question, however, of why the whole dialectic does not then replay itself at the level of theories. After all, isn't a theory just a big sentence? – so isn't the effect of the holism just to caution against thinking of *small* sentences as the bearers of determinate truth-values? Whereas the problem is to recover, once meaning is indeterminate, *any* space for determinacy of truth-value, even for sentences as big as a global physical theory. If, in company with the indeterminacy of meaning, there is nevertheless to be such a thing as determinate truth-value at any level, then Quine officially needs, for items at that level, an account of truth, and of what determines truth, that liberates the notion from dependence upon any semantic parameter.

7 The Above/Below terminology is Quine's own – "On the Reasons for the Indeterminacy of Translation", *Journal of Philosophy*, 67 (1970), p. 183.

8 At least in "On the Reasons for the Indeterminacy of Translation".

9 *Word and Object*, pp. 71–2.

10 The reader may care to think through how the point might apply for Φ = ". . . is the same as . . ." and F = "rabbit" and G = "temporal stage of a rabbit".

11 Evans seems not to have had a problem with the idea that something might be simultaneously both white and bloodstained! A reader who does will be able to construct another example to make the points about to be illustrated.

12 There will be questions, of course, about its scope where it occurs in the latter mode in sentences involving compound predication; the reader may care to think through what patterns of assent and dissent might motivate particular interpretative proposals about the scope conventions in play in the natives' language.

13 See pp. 360–1 of "Identity and Predication", *Journal of Philosophy*, 72 (1975), pp. 343–63.

14 It's straightforward to envisage the sort of data that might prompt the suggestion. Suppose, in full view of a group of native speakers, we take a deeply and thoroughly bloodstained rabbit and wash it completely clean in a stream. Then we put to them each of the following sentences for assent or dissent:

odolby neg gavagai	odolby gavagai
odolbyp gavagai	odolbyp neg gavagai

Finding that the natives assent to both sentences on the left, and dissent from each on the right, would confirm the interpretation of the "-p" suffix as a past-tense indicator. We may suppose this pattern exemplified across a wide range of cases.

15 In order most easily to illustrate Evans's treatment within the framework of the discussion so far, I shall use "odolby" sometimes as present tensed and sometimes as a tenseless counterpart.

16 I am prescinding from the awkwardness, for Evans's purposes, that his objection only engages if the stage-theorist has somehow been stuck with the assumption that the reference of the particular use of "gavagai" is to the last stage in the life of the rabbit in question (i.e. not to an earlier bloodstained stage of that rabbit, or to a stage of a different rabbit). An analogue of that assumption might be more secure if we were concerned with a different example: one whose featured predicate was true only of the last stage in the life of a particular, recently salient rabbit, and of no stage of any other rabbit in the recent experience of our interlocutors. (Evans actually has "running", but that presents the same awkwardness.)

17 This reading is mandated by the reflection that to treat the clauses as concerning *type-predicates* instead would rapidly lead to contradictions. Let y be bloodstained at t_1 but not at t_2, and let x be a stage of y. Then $\langle x,t_1 \rangle$ satisfy "odolby" (tenseless), since there is a y such that y is bloodstained at t_1 and x is a stage of y. Let t_u first be t_1. *Then x satisfies "odolby" (present tensed).* Note that this upshot involves no relativization to the time of utterance. So now let t_u be t_2. There is no y such that y is bloodstained at t_2 and x is a stage of y. *So x does not satisfy "odolby" (present-tensed).* The italicized claims are overtly contradictory; however, the contradiction is merely apparent if we take it that the two occurrences of "odolby" refer to different tokens of the same type.

Could this contradiction have constituted Evans's objection? No, since it is elicited with respect to a single stage, x, and makes nothing of the generalization across stages on which he remarks. In any case it is easily resolved, as we have just seen, without recourse to anything like his second proposal.

An alternative way to avoid the contradiction for an interpreter who for whatever reason wanted his semantic clauses to concern type-predicates rather than tokens, would be to relativize the notion of satisfaction to times. Such a proposal might proceed with clauses along the following lines (which also avoid recourse to tenseless object-language predicates):

(1) x satisfies "odolby" at time t if and only if something is bloodstained at t of which x is a temporal stage.

(2) x satisfies "odolbyp" at time t if and only if there is some time t′, earlier than t, such that x satisfies "odolby" at t′.

And so on. Note that stage-promiscuity would still be a consequence: such a treatment will entail that if any stage satisfies a predicate at a time, then all stages of the same continuant will satisfy that predicate at that time.

18 Another misgeneralization would confuse stage-promiscuity with a kind of *predicate-promiscuity* – the idea that any stage which satisfies a tensed predicate simultaneously satisfies all other tenses of the same predicate. Predicate-promiscuity would likewise be at odds with the natives' selective use of tensed predicates and, as the reader may care to verify, is indeed entailed, via stage-promiscuity, by Evans's first kind of clauses if they are taken to concern type-predicates. But there is no such implication once those clauses are taken to concern tokens – or are replaced by clauses in which satisfaction is relativized to time (cf. note 17).

19 See Christopher Hookway, *Quine* (Oxford, Polity Press, 1988), ch. 9.

20 *Ontological Relativity and Other Essays* (New York, Columbia University Press, 1969), p. 27ff.

21 The development of this point for the case of the feature-placing interpretation is left as an exercise for the reader.

22 This point is also important for the significance of Putnam's permutation argument in his *Reason, Truth and History* (Cambridge, Cambridge University Press, 1981), pp. 32ff.; for discussion, see Chapter 17, PUTNAM'S MODEL-THEORETIC ARGUMENT AGAINST METAPHYSICAL REALISM.

23 "On the Reasons for Indeterminacy of Translation", opening paragraph. The limitation of the Argument from Below to the inscrutability of terms is expressly recognized at p. 182 of the same paper.

24 Though the reader should note the gist of the concluding remarks to "On the Reasons for Indeterminacy of Translation".

25 It is true, of course, that distinctions of meaning which survive Quine's argument will

be ones which can be behaviourally grounded and are thus properly public. But that is not enough to make them hygienic from the physicalist point of view. As I stressed at the beginning, the basic worry for physicalism concerning the semantic is its *normativity*, and public meanings are no less normative for being public. A Quinean argument which, while not actually exploiting the presumed normativity of meanings, somehow or other did away with all semantic facts would save the physicalist the task of accommodating this particular province of normativity; but if a residue of semantic facts remains, then so does the problem.

26 "On the Reasons for the Indeterminacy of Translation", pp. 179–80.

27 See n. 20.

28 Robert Kirk attempts to construct a counter-example to the Argument from Above, exploiting this point: cf. Kirk, "Underdetermination of Theory and Indeterminacy of Translation", *Analysis*, 33, 6 (1973), pp. 198ff.

29 Strictly, of course, empirical theories issue in categorical claims about observational phenomena only when supplemented with observational premises – statements of "initial conditions". The (intentionally) rhetorical question can be preserved by thinking of the observational consequences of a theory as the corresponding conditional statements, whose antecedents specify the initial conditions, and whose consequents encode the theory's prediction for those circumstances.

30 For detailed discussion of this example, see E. Zahar, "Why did Einstein's Programme Supersede Lorentz's?", *British Journal for the Philosophy of Science*, 24 (1973), pp. 95–123 and 233–62.

31 Always provided, that is, that the issue concerning the latter is not taken to be settled just by the possibility that the assignments of sub-sentential reference effected by an empirically adequate semantic theory for a given language may be varied without loss of empirical adequacy – that is, without loss of consistency with observed patterns of assent. If that possibility is all that is at issue, then the matter is, arguably, settled in Quine's favour by a generalization of the sort of permutation argument offered by Putnam: see Chapter 17, PUTNAM'S MODEL-THEORETIC ARGUMENT AGAINST METAPHYSICAL REALISM. But we have observed that semantic theory has to answer to much more than empirical adequacy in that limited sense.

32 Thanks to Bob Hale, Christopher Hookway, Gabriel Segal and Jason Stanley for very helpful comments.

References and further reading

Works by Quine

1953: Two dogmas of empiricism. In *From a Logical Point of View*. Cambridge, Mass.: Harvard University Press.

1960: *Word and Object*. Cambridge, Mass.: MIT Press.

1969: *Ontological Relativity and Other Essays*. New York: Columbia University Press.

1970: On the reasons for the indeterminacy of translation. *Journal of Philosophy*, 67, 178–83.

1974: *The Roots of Reference*. La Salle: Open Court.

1975: On empirically equivalent systems of the world. *Erkenntnis*, 9, 313–28.

1979: Facts of the Matter. In Shahan and Swoyer (eds).

1981: *Theories and Things*. Cambridge, Mass.: Harvard University Press.

1987: Indeterminacy of translation again. *Journal of Philosophy*, 84, 5–10.

1989: Three indeterminacies. In Barrett and Gibson (eds).

1990: *Pursuit of Truth*. Cambridge, Mass.: Harvard University Press.

Works by other authors

The secondary literature is very extensive. The most useful contributions include the following:

Robert Barrett and Roger Gibson (eds) 1989: *Perspectives on Quine*. Oxford: Blackwell.
Simon Blackburn 1975: The identity of propositions. In Simon Blackburn (ed.), *Meaning, Reference and Necessity*. Cambridge: Cambridge University Press.
C. Boorse 1975: The origins of the indeterminacy thesis. *Journal of Philosophy*, 72, 369–87.
M.C. Bradley 1976: Quine's arguments for the indeterminacy of translation thesis. *Australasian Journal of Philosophy*, 54, 24–49.
Noam Chomsky 1969: Quine's empirical assumptions. In Davidson and Hintikka (eds).
Donald Davidson 1973: Radical interpretation. *Dialectica*, 27, 313–27.
—— and Jaakko Hintikka (eds) 1969: *Words and Objections: Essays on the Work of W.V. Quine*. Dordrecht: Reidel.
Gareth Evans 1975: Identity and predication. *Journal of Philosophy*, 72, 343–63.
Dagfinn Føllesdal 1973: Indeterminacy of translation and underdetermination of the theory of Nature. *Dialectica*, 27, 289–301.
Michael Friedman 1975: Physicalism and the indeterminacy of translation. *Noûs*, 9, 353–74.
Roger Gibson 1982: *The Philosophy of W.V. Quine: An Expository Essay*. Tampa: University Presses of Florida.
Gilbert Harman 1969: An introduction to "Translation and Meaning", ch. 2 of *Word and Object*. In Davidson and Hintikka (eds).
—— 1979: Meaning and theory. In Shahan and Swoyer (eds).
Christopher Hookway 1988: *Quine*. Oxford: Polity Press.
Robert Kirk 1973: Underdetermination of theory and indeterminacy of translation. *Analysis*, 33 (6), 195–201.
—— 1986: *Translation Determined*. Oxford: Oxford University Press.
Hilary Putnam 1981: *Reason, Truth and History*. Cambridge: Cambridge University Press; see especially ch. 2, "A Problem About Reference".
Richard Rorty 1972: Indeterminacy of translation and of truth. *Synthese*, 23, 443–62.
Robert Shahan and Chris Swoyer (eds) 1979: *Essays on the Philosophy of W.V. Quine*. Hassocks: Harvester Press.
Barry Stroud 1969: Conventionalism and indeterminacy of translation. In Davidson and Hintikka (eds).
E. Zahar 1973: Why did Einstein's programme supersede Lorentz's? *British Journal for the Philosophy of Science*, 24 , 95–123 and 233–62.

Finally *Synthese*, 27 (1974) includes a symposium on indeterminacy and radical interpretation, with contributions from Davidson, Michael Dummett, Harman, David Lewis and Quine himself.

17

Putnam's model-theoretic argument against metaphysical realism

BOB HALE AND CRISPIN WRIGHT

Metaphysical realism, as Hilary Putnam conceives it, is not a single, monolithic doctrine, but an amalgam of several closely associated philosophical ideas about the relations between language and reality, and between truth and knowledge or justifiable belief. One component on which Putnam places considerable emphasis is that even an ideal theory (a theory that is '*epistemically* ideal *for humans*' – ideal by the lights of the operational criteria by which we assess the merit of theories) may nevertheless be, in reality, false.[1] But commonly, Putnam presents metaphysical realism as involving adherence to three other claims, of which he takes this feature to be a consequence: that 'the world consists of a fixed totality of mind-independent objects', that 'there is exactly one true description of the way the world is' and that 'truth involves some sort of correspondence between words or thought-signs and external things and sets of things'.[2]

The so-called model-theoretic argument has played a leading role in the campaign Putnam has waged, in writings since 1976, against this outlook. Our leading questions will be: What is the argument? How is it best conceived as working? *Does* it work? Section I takes up the first, and gives our reasons for concentrating, thereafter, on the version of Putnam's argument set forth in his *Reason, Truth and History*. In Section II we explain how, in general terms, that argument is best conceived as working. Cursory inspection of Putnam's overall dialectic reveals it to incorporate three sub-arguments, collectively designed to show that the metaphysical realist confronts an insuperable problem over explaining how our words may possess determinate reference. In our next three sections we expound these three sub-arguments in more detail, and offer some critical reflections on them. Section III considers Putnam's version of the Permutation Argument, aimed at showing that reference cannot be determined by fixing the truth-conditions of whole sentences. In Section IV we then review his argument that reference cannot be fixed by our intentions or anything else 'in the head'; and in Section V we review his 'just more theory' argument, designed to show that the metaphysical realist cannot rescue the situation by appeal to causal or other natural connections between our words and the world. Having argued that the last of these arguments fails, we consider in Section VI whether Putnam's dialectical purposes might be better served by other, more specific arguments he has advanced elsewhere, aimed at showing that the project of giving a naturalistic account of reference is hopeless. In

Section VII we consider how the considerations adduced by Putnam might be seen as an argument telling selectively against metaphysical realism; and we conclude, in Section VIII, with a brief assessment of how far Putnam's argument, so viewed, may be taken to succeed.

I

There are significant differences between the versions of Putnam's argument in 'Models and Reality' (1977) and in *Reason, Truth and History* (1981a). Both confront the metaphysical realist with the same challenge – to show how words can stand in the determinate referential relations which his world-view demands. But the latter furnishes the more complete case for thinking the metaphysical realist incapable of meeting it. 'Models and Reality' deploys the Löwenheim–Skolem theorems, and closely related completeness results, to show – if all goes to plan – that no assignment of truth-values (however tightly constrained) to any (however comprehensive) class of whole sentences can suffice to fix the reference of terms and predicates. But there remain, so far as the argument of 'Models and Reality' goes, various ways a metaphysical realist may respond: for example, that speakers' intentions or other intentional states play an essential role; or that, if the reference of words is to be thought of as determined via their role in complete sentences, it is not those sentences' truth-*values*, but their truth-*conditions*, that matter. Further argument, of precisely the kind attempted in *Reason, Truth and History*, is needed to close off such moves.

In broadest outline, Putnam's thought in *Reason, Truth and History* has the following structure: If the world is to be conceived as consisting of 'some fixed totality of mind-independent objects', with truth consisting in 'some sort of correspondence relation between words or thought-signs and external things and sets of things',[3] then there must be determinate referential relations between the words and the things. But if so, the metaphysical realist owes an account of how that can be so. Putnam argues, by reviewing three, putatively exhaustive directions in which it might be sought, that there can be no such satisfactory account:

First, '*what goes on in the head*' *cannot determine what we are referring to.* We can imagine, Putnam suggests, a planet – Twin Earth – very much like Earth, populated by creatures very like ourselves, in surroundings very much like our own. There is, however, an interesting difference – the substance that fills Twin Earth streams and rivers, lakes and puddles, and comes out of Twin Earth taps, and so forth, is not H_2O but has a different chemical composition, XYZ. However, XYZ has just the same phenomenological properties as our water – it looks and tastes the same, and so on, and is, indeed, called 'water' on Twin Earth. If a Twin Earth dweller were somehow transported to Earth, she would not be able to tell our water apart from the liquid she encounters in similar circumstances back on Twin Earth. Her watery thoughts and experiences are, subjectively or 'from the inside', just like ours. In point of *pure* mental states relevant to the use of 'water' – that is, mental states identified neutrally with respect to the existence and character of such external things as might ordinarily get mentioned in their description – Twin Earth dwellers are indistinguishable from us. Yet when they speak of 'water', they are referring to XYZ, whereas we are referring to H_2O. So 'what's in the head' – pure mental states – does not determine reference. Reference varies in a way that cannot be explained by appeal to pure mental states. But to appeal to *impure* – world-involving – states would be just circular.[4]

Second, sub-sentential reference cannot be determined by fixing, via 'operational and theoretical constraints,'[5] either the truth-values *or even the truth-conditions* of whole sentences. This stronger conclusion is now obtained using more modest model-theoretic resources than in 'Models and Reality'. Given one scheme of reference which induces, at each possible world, such-and-such truth-values on complete sentences, we can obtain, by permutation, as many rival schemes as you like, which agree with the 'intended' scheme on the truth-values of whole sentences in *each* world, but diverge over assignments to terms and predicates.

Third, it is no use appealing to any further non-intentional – e.g. causal – condition as the needed source of referential determinacy. Any such appeal must assume, for example, that it is at least determinate what worldly relation our word 'causes' stands for. Saying that we use 'cats' to speak of just those things that stand in such-and-such causal relations to our use of the word is 'just more theory' – and, as such, just as liable to unwanted interpretations as anything else we may say.

II

There has been a tendency for commentators to interpret this train of thought as leading to a sceptical paradox comparable to that developed by Kripke in Wittgenstein's name (see Chapter 15, RULE-FOLLOWING, OBJECTIVITY AND MEANING, section 2): as Kripke's sceptic argues that there are no facts about meaning, so 'Putnam's Paradox' would have it that there are no facts about reference, all candidates for the constitution of such facts – the truth-conditions of sentences, speakers' intentional states, and causal and other forms of natural relationships between words and the world – failing to deliver the appropriately determinate goods. It is consistent with such an interpretation of Putnam's argument that he should think, as he certainly does, that the paradox admits of resolution, much as Kripke holds that there can be a solution to *his* Wittgensteinian paradox. But then the suggested parallel begins to limp. For one thing, it enjoins, taken strictly, that any solution will leave in place its sceptical conclusion – that there are no facts about reference – just as Kripke's sceptical solution leaves in place his sceptical conclusion, that there are no facts about meaning. If this were the intended form of Putnam's message, we should expect to find him explaining why/how it is that his preferred *internal realism*[6] can accept such indeterminacy with equanimity. But that is not what he does. What we find is, rather, the claim that the internal realist has no trouble *discounting* unintended interpretations of the sort that plague metaphysical realism.[7] Moreover, while it is true that metaphysical realism requires determinacy of reference – since without it, there appears to be no making sense of the claim that an ideal theory may yet be false – it appears that an outright demonstration of indeterminacy could not tell *selectively* against metaphysical realism. For while internal realism stops short of claiming that even an ideal theory may be false, it will surely grant that a *less than ideal*, but still consistent, theory may be so. And this seems to require setting aside unintended interpretations just as much as does the metaphysical realist's more ambitious claim.

So what is the intended structure of the argument? It might be supposed that Putnam's purpose is not to explode the notion of reference altogether, but by engineering a *conditional* explosion – by showing that some distinctively metaphysical-realist assumption subserves a proof of indeterminacy – selectively to dispossess the metaphysical realist of the notion. The fact that, as will emerge, no specifically metaphysical-realist assumption oils the wheels of any of the three sub-arguments tells against this line: how, if so, could their combination spell trouble for metaphysical realism but leave internal realism unscathed?[8]

No: the right way to receive Putnam's argument, or so we suggest, is as turning on the crucial claim that *the metaphysical realist distinctively owes an explanatory/constitutive account of reference, but cannot deliver.* Much of what Putnam writes in *Reason, Truth and History* seems to confirm that this is indeed the primarily intended line of attack. The problem about reference, to which chapter 2 in the book is devoted, is repeatedly described as the problem of accounting for *how* the reference of our terms is fixed.[9] The emphasis throughout is on the need for explanation and the metaphysical realist's inability to supply one. Putnam writes:

> Of course the externalist agrees that the extension of 'rabbit' is the set of rabbits . . . But he does not regard such statements as telling us what reference *is*. For him finding out what reference *is*, i.e. what the *nature* of the 'correspondence' between words and things is, is a pressing problem . . . For me there is little to say about what reference is within a conceptual scheme other than these tautologies.[10]

The prevailing thought, then, would seem to be that the metaphysical realist incurs certain explanatory obligations which, for the internal realist, *simply do not arise* – that the internal realist may reasonably stay silent when questions are put about the *constitution* of the reference relation, about what makes it the case that a particular expression has the reference it does.

Why this should be so is a matter to which we shall return. But this, we shall assume, is how the overall gist of the argument should be interpreted.

III

Deferring issues about overall strategy, we now, in this section, review some of the detail of, and air some qualms concerning, perhaps the most arresting of the three ingredient claims in the *Reason, Truth and History* argument: the claim that even the *truth-conditions* of whole sentences containing them are insufficient to determine the references of sub-sentential expressions.

The well-known reasoning in support of this claim affirms that given any domain of objects, and a language used to speak about them, the references/extensions of the sub-sentential expressions of that language may be permuted consistently with invariance in the truth-value assigned at each possible world to – hence in the truth-condition of – each sentence in the language. This is, Putnam suggests – though the claim needs discussion[11] – a generalization of Quine's contention in *Word and Object* that reference is inscrutable, based on the so-called 'Argument from Below' (see section 3 of Chapter 16, THE INDETERMINACY OF TRANSLATION). However, whereas Quine merely made a suggestive case that, for all our use of whole sentences containing it dictates to the contrary, 'rabbit' might refer to undetached rabbit parts, or temporal stages of rabbits, or the universal rabbithood – thus posing, at most, an unanswered challenge – Putnam's argument is wholly general ('rabbit' could, without change in the truth-conditions of any sentence containing it, refer to anything whatever) and, if correct, conclusive.

Let us review the illustration Putnam himself gives of the kind of thing that could be involved in such a systematic reinterpretation. Divide all possible worlds into just three kinds:

(a) worlds in which some cat is on some mat and some cherry is on some tree ('is on' is here tenseless)
(b) worlds in which some cat is on some mat, but no cherry is on any tree
(c) all other worlds.

Now fix the reference of 'cat' in a way which depends on which of these three groups the actual world belongs to. If the actual world is a type (a) world, then 'cat' is to refer to cherries and 'mat' is to refer to trees. If on the other hand the actual world is a type (b) world, then 'cat' is to refer to cats, and 'mat' is to refer to mats. Finally, if the actual world is a type (c) world, then 'cat' is to refer to cherries, and 'mat' is to refer to quarks.[12]

Now reflect that, if the actual world is as a matter of fact an (a)-world, in which some cherry is on some tree, the sentence, 'A cat is on a mat' will be true when the references of 'cat' and 'mat' are so stipulated. It will likewise be true in any (b)-world, since those are worlds in which some cat is on some mat, and, in those worlds, 'cat' and 'mat' have their customary reference. Finally, in (c)-worlds, the sentence will be false, since no cherry is on a quark. But these valuations, note, coincide exactly with those of 'A cat is on a mat' as ordinarily understood, with 'cat' and 'mat' assigned their customary reference. In short: the sentence 'A cat is on a mat' could have exactly the truth-conditions it does even if, for some possible worlds, including the actual world, 'cat' were to refer not to cats, but to cherries – or whatever you like.

Putnam shows[13] that this type of manoeuvre can be complicated so as to embrace simultaneously all the sentences of an entire language. And if sub-sentential reference may be varied in a systematic way without shift in truth-conditions, then whatever – if anything – determines reference, it cannot be the truth-conditions of whole sentences.

This conclusion is apt to seem deeply counter-intuitive. After all, are not the semantics of sub-sentential expressions exhausted by their contribution to the meanings of sentences containing them? So does not the reference of a term, or common noun, say, *have* somehow to be distinctively reflected in the meanings of sentences in which it occurs? The argument gives pause, to say the least. We shall review four broad lines of reservation about it.

One quite common reaction is that Putnam's argument is somehow self-defeating. For in order to receive it as showing the existence of alternative interpretations of a language under which all its sentences retain their truth-conditions, we need already to be able to *grasp* the distinctions, generated by permutation, between the various interpretations. But if we can do that – if we can grasp and distinguish from one another the divergent interpretations on offer – then why can't we just *stipulate* that one among them in particular is the correct one? And why won't that stipulation be sufficient to render reference fully determinate? If, on the other hand, we can't make the requisite distinctions, then we are in no position to follow the reasoning by which Putnam seeks to persuade us that there is a difficulty.

It would be no answer to this to suggest that assumptions of determinacy of reference feature in Putnam's argument only for the purposes of *reductio as absurdum*. They don't. The claim that sentences' truth-conditions underdetermine sub-sentential reference, if supported by showing how particular permutation-based reinterpretations leave truth-conditions invariant, must depend, for its cogency, on a *continuing* grasp of the differences between the assignments of reference respectively involved in the various interpretations – a grasp which is to survive the drawing of Putnam's conclusion, and on which the grounds for that conclusion depend. So the thought may continue to seem impressive: if we understand the differences, then we can stipulate which interpretation is intended.

The main thing wrong with this objection is, rather, that it misconceives the point of Putnam's argument. It assumes that the argument, like Quine's, is properly seen as a *sceptical* one, directed against the determinacy of reference. Now of course, if that were its project, then the argument had better not proceed in a way which effectively presupposes determinacy, or employs materials which can be straightforwardly exploited so as to ensure it. But that is not Putnam's aim. Putnam's aim is to show, rather, that accounting for the determinacy of reference is a problem specifically for a particular kind of philosophical view. Accordingly – just so long as his own position is not vulnerable to the same difficulty – there is no reason why he should not argue in a way that presupposes determinacy. The intended gist of the permutation argument is merely that whatever secures a determinate reference for a particular sub-sentential expression, it is not the truth-conditions of the sentences in which it features. Putnam's position has to be that if any assumption of determinacy of reference is needed by the argument, it is an assumption which will eventually prove quite innocent from an internal-realist point of view. Of course, it's a good question why or whether that is so, and one to which we shall return.[14]

The second reservation is one some critics misguidedly advanced about the argument of 'Models and Reality'; that is, that the model-theoretic results to which that essay appeals are applicable only to first-order languages.[15] Strictly, this is so. It suffices to remark, however, that no such concern about generality affects the permutation argument of *Reason, Truth and History*. Given a permutation of the referents of the terms and compensating reinterpretation of the predicates of a language which preserves the truth-conditions – that is, the truth-values assigned at each possible world – of each of its *atomic* statements, it is obvious enough that the truth-conditions not merely of first-order quantifications of those statements but also of their second-order generalizations, and indeed modalizations, will be likewise preserved.[16]

Perhaps more surprising is that the result will also extend to languages containing *intentional* operators, in particular expressions of propositional attitude. One might think that there would be a difficulty here, and that the scope of Putnam's argument would consequently have to be restricted. But this is not so. Take the hardest case: suppose that belief, for instance, is treated as a relation between a thinker and a *proposition*, and that any interpretation is required to assign as referent to a that-clause precisely that proposition which, in view of the assignments that interpretation makes to its subsentential parts, the clause in question comes to express. Thus, in Putnam's' illustration, 'that a cat is on a mat' comes to refer, in (a)-worlds, to the proposition that a cherry is on a tree and, in (c)-worlds, to the proposition that a cherry is on a quark, whilst keeping its usual reference otherwise (that is, in (b)-worlds). How might we set about gerrymandering an extension for 'X believes that' in order to ensure that 'X believes that a cat is on a mat' retains its actual truth-conditions – is true at just the worlds at which it is actually true – while the referents of 'cat', 'mat' and 'that a cat is on a mat' vary in accordance with the permutation in (this extension of) Putnam's illustration?

What is required, naturally, is that 'X believes that a cat is on a mat' should express a truth in all and only worlds in which X believes that a cat is on a mat. Now, since both cases are logically possible, there will be some (a)-worlds in which X does believe that a cat is on a mat and some in which he does not. We require accordingly that X stands, in just the former, in whatever relation the perverse interpretation assigns to 'believes that' to the proposition that a cherry is on a tree, and fails so to stand in just the latter. Clearly, therefore, we cannot leave the interpretation of 'believes that' invariant. For there have to be (a)-worlds in which X does believe that a cat is on a mat but does not believe that a cherry is on a tree, and in such worlds the truth-value of 'X believes that a cat is on a mat' would accordingly change under the permutation. Hence our reinterpretation will have to assign a new relation to 'believes that'. But what relation? Whatever the relation is, it will have to have the feature that *of necessity* a subject stands in it to the proposition that a cherry is on a tree just when he believes that a cat is on a mat. For if this is not a matter of necessity, then again, there will have to be (a)-worlds in which X does believe that a cat is on a mat, but does not stand in the relation in question to the proposition that a cherry is on a tree; and once again the perverse interpretation will get the truth-value of 'X believes that a cat is on a mat' wrong.

One's first thought is that there may simply be no such relation. But *that is not right*. There is, after all, at least the 'Cambridge' relation, in which a subject stands to the proposition that a cherry is on a tree just in case he believes that a cat is on a mat! One might compare this to the relation in which you stand to Mount Rushmore just in case you have seen a photograph of Snowdon. The crucial point is that permutation-based interpretation works *purely extensionally*. From the extensional viewpoint, the latter relation has been fully specified just when what its extension is has been determined; and we have done that. For all and only our readers who have seen a photograph of Snowdon, the extension is the set of pairs, ⟨You, dear such reader; Mount Rushmore⟩. Similarly, the new relation which our perverse interpretation assigns to 'believes' will be one which has, at each (a)-world, an extension including the pair ⟨X; the proposition that a cherry is on a tree⟩ if and only if that (a)-world is one at which X believes that a cat is on a mat. For (b)-worlds – where 'that a cat is on a mat' is assigned as its referent the proposition that a cat is on a mat – no adjustment in the extension of the usual belief-relation is needed (at least, not in respect of X and the proposition that a cat is on a mat). Finally, at each (c)-world – where 'that a cat is on a mat' is assigned as its referent the proposition that a cherry is on a quark – 'believes' will be assigned an extension which includes ⟨X; the proposition that a cherry is on a quark⟩ if and only if that (c)-world is one at which X believes that a cat is on a mat.

This generality in the scope of the permutation argument is very striking. Arguably, however, the main thing one should conclude from it is how little the kind of 'interpretation' here in play has to do with *real* interpretation, as it were – interpretation in any sense which involves the specification of propositional contents which a thinker might conceivably have in mind. This is, in effect, the area of concern of a different line of objection – what we shall call the 'dilute truth-conditions' objection – to which we now turn. The objection concerns the ability of the permutation argument, even if this is sound as far as it goes, to deliver a conclusion of the intended significance. Since the goal of the argument, or so it may seem, ought to be to show that the reference of a sub-sentential expression is underdetermined by any features of the *meaning* of whole sentences containing it, Putnam must implicitly take it that he can encapsulate any germane notion of the meaning of a sentence in that of its 'truth-conditions'. To be sure, talk of 'truth-conditions' is, indeed, a standard philosophical idiom for gesturing at sentences' content. But Putnam's argument, the objection claims, works with so dilute a notion of 'truth-conditions' that this connection is subverted. Putnam's notion requires no more of truth-conditional equivalents than coincidence in their truth-values in all possible worlds – *strict equivalence*, in the sense of C. I. Lewis – and strict equivalence is intuitively quite consistent with manifest differences in semantic structure and content. In particular, their strict equivalence is insufficient to ensure that a pair of sentences make the same contribution to the content of sentences which embed them. Merely to take a pair of strict equivalents which draw on different conceptual resources – say, 'A and B are parallel' and 'Anything perpendicular to A is parallel to something perpendicular to B' – suffices to open up the possibility of someone who knows one but not the other. It follows that the truth-conditions, hence the content, of – to stay with the particular example – 'X knows that A and B are parallel' and 'X knows that anything perpendicular to A is parallel to something perpendicular to B' also differ. If we assume that the content of those two sentences is determined compositionally, there is then no alternative but to view the semantic contributions, and hence the meanings, of 'A and B are parallel' and 'Anything perpendicular to A is parallel to something perpendicular to B' as likewise different. And if there can be more to the meaning – specifically, the semantic contribution to larger, embedding contexts – of a sentence than whatever it shares with its strict equivalents, then the general thought that the references of sub-sentential expressions may be determined by the *meanings* – in that richer sense, whatever it is – of the sentences which feature them is quite passed over by an argument which shows merely that *truth-conditions*, in Putnam's Lewisian sense, don't determine sub-sentential reference.

How may Putnam reply to this? He had better not challenge the inadequacy of strict equivalence to capture certain finer-grained but still intuitive notions of sameness and difference of sentence-meaning. Rather, what he ought to query is the stated characterization of the goal of the permutation argument: we should take the goal of the argument, that is, as that of showing, not that the reference of sub-sentential expressions is underdetermined by *any* features of the semantics of whole sentences containing them, but that sub-sentential reference is underdetermined by any whole-sentence semantical features *which can be explained without prior reliance on specific relations of sub-sentential reference*. That the reference of sub-sentential expressions might yet be recoverable from certain finer-grained semantical properties of sentences containing them – finer-grained than can be captured by relations of strict equivalence and non-equivalence – is accordingly, Putnam may charge, in no way inconsistent with his goal. For what goes into the constitution of such finer-grained semantic properties of a sentence will be, broadly, its mode of composition and the semantics – including reference – of its sub-sentential ingredients. Indeed, it is unintelligible how sentences could have such finer-grained semantic features in the first place unless we simply take for granted a gamut of relations of reference between sub-sentential expressions and items in the world. In short: the reply should be that while there may indeed be finer-grained conceptions of sentence-meaning than Lewisian strict equivalence, and while the reference of a particular sub-sentential expression may be recoverable from the finer-grained semantics of sentences containing it, this is all back to front from the point of view of answering Putnam's challenge. That challenge is to explain wherein the determinacy of sub-sentential reference is *constituted*. It is therefore irrelevant to appeal to semantical features of whole sentences which themselves depend upon the reference of those sentences' constituents.

Now, there is a possible misgiving about this reply connected with the question, mentioned earlier, of the extent of the analogy between Putnam's argument and Quine's 'Argument from Below'. The points of analogy are that the conclusion of both Putnam's and Quine's arguments may be expressed in the same way, that we can hold fixed the truth-conditions of a sentence while varying the reference of semantic constituents within it; and in both cases such constancy of truth-conditions may be glossed as consisting in the fact that, no matter how the world actually happens to be, the sentence will retain – after reference-permutation or Quinean reinterpretation respectively – the same truth-value as that secured for it by the (presumed) actual reference of its semantic constituents. However, Putnam's illustration would also seem to point to a potentially important difference. The kind of reinterpretation illustrated by the cats-and-cherries example sustains continuity in truth-value only because it is required to be sensitive to *what is actually the case*:

for instance, 'a cat is on a mat' is true, under the illustrated reinterpretation, in both type (a)- and type (b)-worlds only because what it says is *constrained to vary* as a function of which, if either, of those types the actual world belongs to. By contrast, any of Quine's alternative translation schemes for 'gavagai' (see section 3 of Chapter 16, THE INDETERMINACY OF TRANSLATION) will construe what the sentence says *in a uniform manner*, no matter what the actual world is like. In short, you cannot tell, under Putnam's assignment of reference, what 'a cat is on a mat' says unless you know how relevant matters stand in the world. But no such knowledge is needed to know the impact on 'gavagai' of any particular one of Quine's schemes. What follows is that for Putnam, but not for Quine, an *additional* distance would seem to be opened between preservation of truth-conditions and preservation of content: precisely, 'a cat is on a mat' retains its actual truth-conditions under the illustrated permutation – that is, has the truth-value it would actually have no matter which of the three types of world the actual world belongs to – only because what it says is *made to change* depending on which type of world that is. And while it may be acceptable for the argument to ignore differences in truth-conditions which can only be specified by presupposing differences in – and hence determinacy of – sub-sentential reference, it is still vital that the notion of 'truth-conditions' which it employs be as strong as possible consistently with that limitation. Yet the notion of sameness of truth-conditions at work in the permutation argument would seem to have *even less connection* with sameness of meaning than strict equivalence.

This development of the dilute truth-conditions objection probably ought to be open to just the same counter as the original objection. Suppose the objection is right that there is a perfectly good sense in which the effect of a Putnamian – in contrast to a Quinean – reinterpretation will be to have the *content* of a sentence vary as a function of what is actually true. The crucial question, however, is whether this variation in content could be appreciated from a standpoint which takes nothing for granted about sub-sentential reference, but is apprised only of *independently appreciable* semantic properties of whole sentences. What can be known about the semantics of a sentence by someone who knows nothing about the reference of its constituents? Could such a subject know more than its Putnamian truth-conditions, in which possible worlds it would be true and in which false? If not, then the claimed disanalogy between Quine and Putnam would not matter; the permutation argument would still be working with the strongest relevant notion of truth-conditions. Now there are, of course, things other than its Putnamian truth-conditions which someone can know about the semantics of a sentence who does not yet know anything about the reference of its constituents. In particular, there are all the things that are allowed to be available as data for a radical interpreter. Thus it is open to someone who does not yet know the reference of the constituents of 'a cat is on a mat' to observe its *use*, and to note in particular what appear to be its conditions of warranted assent. What he will observe if 'cat' refers to cats and 'mat' to mats is that the circumstances which prompt assent will tend to be those in which some cat is on some mat in a fashion salient to the assentor. But then, as may seem obvious – indeed, the whole point of Putnam's trick – the same pattern will still be expectable if 'cat' and 'mat' are assigned reference as in his illustration. For suppose that is so and you are asked to assent to or dissent from 'a cat is on a mat'. Isn't it still true that you have only to consider whether you have reason to believe that a cat is on a mat? For if you do, then in both cases – when a cherry is on a tree (in which case that is what the sentence will say) and when none is (in which case it will say that a cat is on a mat) – you will have reason to think that 'a cat is on a mat' is true. So, of course, your observable pattern of assent will be the same.

Prima facie, then, the additional dilution would not matter in any case. However the decisive point is that, as the proofs in the Appendix to this chapter make clear, its apparently additional dilution of the notion of truth-conditions is actually an artefact of a dispensable – and it has to be said, misleading – feature of Putnam's illustration. There is no need for a permutation-based reinterpretation to 'kink' the assignments of reference after the fashion of the cats-and-cherries example. To be clear about this, consider a specific domain of objects, D, and, for simplicity's sake, restrict attention to all possible worlds involving just those objects and no others. Suppose we have a language, L, fitted to talk about the elements of D and to ascribe a given range of simple properties of them. A permutation of such a domain is simply a one-to-one mapping of D onto itself in such a way that no object need be correlated with itself; and the reinterpretation of the terms and (1-place) predicates of L associated with such a permutation does no more than have each term of L refer to the object onto which the permutation takes its actual referent, and have each predicate of L take as its new extension the set whose members are exactly the objects onto which the permutation takes the objects in its actual extension. Clearly, no matter what the actual extension of a predicate may be, the actual referent of a term will be a member of it only if its correlate under the permutation is a member of the set assigned to that predicate under the permutation-based reinterpretation. Although certain complications have to be finessed to take account of variation on the domains associated with different possible worlds, and of more complex predicates, this simple train of thought captures the essence of the permutation argument. And it points directly to a *uniform* reinterpretation of each sentence 'Fa' of L which is guaranteed to preserve its truth-value in any possible world. Where *p* is the permutation in question, that reinterpretation will read along the lines of 'the *p*-correlate of a is a member of the set of *p*-correlates of Fs'.

We conclude that Putnam has the resources to handle the dilute truth-conditions objection. But there is a related and fundamental worry still outstanding. The immediate effect of the permutation argument is that truth-conditions in, as we have seen, a somewhat technical sense underdetermine sub-sentential reference. And this result, we have stressed, is not to Putnam's purpose unless it bears interpretation as showing that all aspects of the use of a sentence that might be observed without presupposition about the reference of its constituents underdetermine what that reference may be. Now Putnam himself repeatedly expresses his finding as being that reference is underdetermined by both observational *and theoretical* considerations.[17] That is a very strong claim. It is tantamount to claiming not merely that alternative assignments of sub-sentential reference are *consistent with* all possible uses of a sentence, but that there will be *nothing to choose between them* even when one takes account of all constraints, beyond empirical adequacy, which condition the construction of semantic theory. This has manifestly not been shown. It hardly seems likely, for instance, that, when all theoretical constraints on interpretation have been reckoned with, there still will be nothing to choose between interpreting speakers as expressing thoughts of the form: object a is F, and interpreting them as expressing thoughts of the form: the *p*-correlate – for some permutation, *p*, of the domain – of a is a member of the set of *p*-correlates of Fs! (For more on relevant such wider interpretational constraints, see Chapter 16, THE INDETERMINACY OF TRANSLATION, section 5.) In order for the permutation argument to succeed in showing that *best* interpretation of the use of whole sentences always has a variety of schemes of sub-sentential reference to select from, we have to be shown how to find *alternative extensionally coincident thoughts* to correspond to such monstrosities about *p*-correlates and sets of *p*-correlates – alternatives which it is as plausible, in the light of all relevant theoretical constraints, to interpret a subject as expressing by 'Fa' as the simple thought that a is F; and we have to be shown how to do this in a systematic way, right across the language. In short, to make good the suggestion that whole-sentence use underdetermines sub-sentential reference, permutation-based reinterpretations have to be shown to be, by *all* relevant constraints, as good – or anyway to facilitate reinterpretations which are as good – as standard interpretations. The results about permutation, by themselves, are powerless to show that is so.[18]

IV

We turn now to Putnam's argument that the intentional states of speakers are insufficient to determine the reference of their words. The argument, as we saw, proceeds by dilemma: if intentional states are conceived as 'pure' – so that, for instance, speakers both on Earth and Twin Earth can express the very same belief by 'Water is wet' – then reference may vary even though intentional states remain the same. If, on the other hand, intentional states are taken to be impure, so that the content of the belief that 'Water is wet' will be a function of the actual environment of its holders, then beliefs are now individuated by the actual references of the terms that occur in their expression, and thus presuppose, rather than constitute, such facts.

One cause for concern is whether the considerations offered in support of the first horn of Putnam's pure/impure dilemma can be made to cohere with what, later in the argument, he will want to say about the insufficiency of the sort of naturalistic conception of reference to which some – Hartry Field is an actual case[19] – may be tempted in response to Putnam's overall argument. To appreciate, after all, how reference may vary across environments in which the pure mental states of subjects remain the same, one has to have some conception of how reference *functionally depends* on environmental factors. But if such a conception is in place, then won't it constitute at least the beginnings of an account, independently of any play with speakers' mental states or the truth-conditions of sentences, of what it is that does determine reference? – precisely the kind of account which, according to the third stage of Putnam's argument, cannot be given. Unquestionably there is a fair interpretative question here. The externalism about content which the first horn of the dilemma employs is a long-term theme in Putnam's writing; yet the metaphysical realist is apparently to be denied access to this element in Putnam's own philosophy in his attempt to respond to Putnam's challenge. However, we are entitled to proceed without pursuing that question by the consideration that this part of Putnam's argument in any case has no need to proceed in terms of the pure/impure dilemma.[20] A much simpler reflection will suffice. In order for speakers' intentional states, of whatever sort, to serve to establish the references of linguistic expressions, it has to be the case that the objects assigned to those expressions as their referents are already given as *objects of thought*. It is only as thought about – as referred to in thought – that we can fix, or understand, what it is for a particular object to be the referent of a particular symbol. But the constitutive question being put to the metaphysical realist arises no less for thought than for language. The challenge is to give an explanation of what it is for our thoughts to be of certain objects, rather than others, in the first place. The fact is, accordingly, that there never was any real option of the kind which the pure/impure dilemma is supposed to address. Intentional states cannot constitute reference. That our intentional states already have reference is (an aspect of) the problem, not its solution.

V

If the first two stages of Putnam's argument were to succeed, then the situation would be that no satisfactory constitutive account of reference can proceed in terms of facts concerning our intentional states, or facts about the truth-values, or even truth-conditions, of complete sentences or thoughts. To a metaphysical realist who is also a materialist, however, such conclusions would likely be entirely congenial, merely serving to underline the need for a quite different account of reference in broadly naturalistic terms. That it would be quite mistaken to think that any such account could meet metaphysical realism's needs is the burden of the third component of Putnam's argument.

This comprises, in fact, several distinguishable lines of attack: some of them are directed specifically at the idea that reference can be fixed by causal connections, but others aspire to greater generality, purporting to establish that there can be no 'reductive' explanation of reference in naturalistic terms or, more generally still, that once it is allowed that neither intentional states nor truth-conditions can form the basis of an explanation of how reference can be determinate, it can be seen that nothing else can do so either. The concern of this section will be with the most general – and most notorious – such line of all.

Putnam writes:

> Suppose there is a possible naturalistic or physicalistic *definition* of reference, as Field contends. Suppose
>
> (1) *x refers to y* if and only if *x bears R to y*

> is true, where *R* is a relation definable in natural science vocabulary without using any semantical notions . . . If (1) is true and empirically verifiable, then (1) is a sentence which is itself true even on the theory that reference is fixed as far as (and *only* as far as) it is determined by operational *plus* theoretical constraints. . . .
>
> If reference is only determined by operational and theoretical constraints, however, then the reference of '*x bears R to y*' is itself indeterminate, and so knowing that (1) is true will not help.[21]

Knowing that all instances of (1) are true won't help, Putnam thinks, because, by the permutation argument, they will remain true – and, indeed, will have the same truth-values in all possible worlds – when 'R' is taken instead to stand for a quite different relation R*. In fact, there are as many such alternatives R* as there are permutations of the universe of discourse. So supposing reference to be R has no more explanatory merit than supposing it to be R*. Hence it is merely an illusion that a unique reference relation has been singled out.

This move – of holding any attempted naturalistic characterization of reference to be 'just more theory', hostage to permutative reinterpretation – is one that Putnam repeatedly makes in the closing stage of his various attacks on metaphysical realism.[22] If allowable, it is of course decisive – for it will be available against *any* specific constraint the metaphysical realist may propose, regardless of its precise content, just so long as the constraint is formulated in a language to which the permutation argument applies.[23] The obvious and crucial issue is: is the move fair, or foul?

Well: it is foul, for a reason first stressed by David Lewis.[24] There is a distinction to be made between, on the one hand, an interpretation's *modelling* a proposed constraint – *making a statement of the constraint come out true* – and on the other, the interpretation's *actually conforming to that constraint*. The 'just more theory' gambit seems simply to miss this crucial distinction, taking the former for the latter.

To elaborate a little: Let C be some proposed (naturalistic) constraint on reference generally, L a language, S a sentence of L expressing C and I an interpretation of L. Suppose that I does indeed induce the value *true* on S. It might seem that I must conform to C; for S expresses C, after all, so that if I makes S come out true, isn't that just the same thing as I's conforming to C? Well obviously, not at all: we have no right to assume that, *whatever interpretation* of L is in play, S will (still) express C. Suppose, schematically, that S has the form:

$$\forall x \forall y \forall z\, (\text{speaker}(x)\ \&\ \text{expression}(y)\ \&\ \text{object}(z)) \rightarrow (x \text{ refers to } z \text{ by } y \rightarrow R(x,y,z))$$

One thing that may vary under different interpretations of L is, naturally, the relation assigned to 'R'. We may not take S as expressing C *tout court* – some interpretations will have S expressing C, others won't. An interpretation J under which S fails to express C may still make S come out true. And if we are able to express C in some other language L*, with resources sufficient to discuss the semantics of L, we may be in position to state – and it can be true – that while S is a sentence of L true under J, J does not conform to C.

A supporter of Putnam might reply that this will be a situation we can recognize as obtaining, and to which we can give expression, if, *but only if*, we can fall back on some other language L*, the reference of whose expressions can be assumed to be (sufficiently) determinate – in particular, there will have to be a sentence of L* by means of which we can give determinate expression to the intended constraint C. And it is precisely at this point, it may be alleged, that the metaphysical realist runs into 'just more theory' trouble. For his predicament is that any language, L* no less than L, will raise just the same problem about determinacy of reference. He can't just assume a more inclusive but referentially determinate L* in which it may be asserted that whilst the sentence S does indeed come out true on a whole host of interpretations (of L), all but a few of these are ones under which S fails to express the proposed constraint, to which they, furthermore, fail to conform. And if he can't simply assume that he can convey this thought in words, he cannot assume that he can think it either.[25] The upshot is, the supporter may claim, that while there is indeed a distinction of the sort Lewis proposes, the metaphysical realist cannot avail himself of it in the situation which matters, when any metalanguage, no less than the language with which we are originally concerned, gives rise to just the same difficulty.

But if this is the best reply that can be made, Lewis is right to cry 'Foul!' Just consider the dialectical situation. The metaphysical realist – Field or Devitt, for example – takes up the challenge to say what constitutes determinate relations of reference, only to find that no sooner has he opened his mouth than Putnam gags him with the complaint that he has no right to assume any of his words to be determinate in reference. The resulting situation is therefore really no different from that generated by the boring and jejune variety of meaning-scepticism which challenges an opponent to explain how meaningful discourse is possible, but won't countenance attempted answers because to presume them meaningful is to beg the question against it. Obviously the metaphysical realist has to be presumed capable of contentful – so, determinately referential – speech if he is to respond to Putnam's challenge, or indeed to any challenge at all. The onus legitimately placed upon him is not to *demonstrate that* determinate reference is possible, but to provide a constitutive account which *explains how* determinate reference works. Accordingly, he is perfectly within his rights to assume, at least pro tem, a metalanguage in which a determinate account of the putative mechanics can in principle be given.

VI

If the 'just more theory' move is illicit, that need still be no very serious matter for the overall argument provided there are good independent reasons for doubting that any naturalistic reduction of reference can be provided. Putnam has assembled in different places a variety of more specific arguments to this conclusion, of – so it seems to us – somewhat differing levels of cogency. We shall briefly review two lines in particular.

The first occurs in 'Model-theory and the "Factuality" of Semantics' (1989). The form of naturalistic proposal Putnam there envisages is familiar from such natural scientific identifications as those of water with H_2O or of heat with mean kinetic energy of molecules. By identifying heat with mean molecular energy of motion, we accomplish what seems to be the best available explanation of empirically attested correlations involving variations in the temperature and pressure of a mass of gas whose volume is kept constant and so forth, and take this to sanction the identification. Might it not be, likewise, that by identifying the relation of reference with a certain physical relation, R, holding between tokenings of expressions and the worldly items to which they refer, we may achieve the best explanation of certain aspects of our use of those expressions? That is, why should ordinary scientific methodology not turn out to provide the same kind of case for identification of reference with R as for the identification of water with H_2O, or heat with mean molecular motion?[26]

Putnam's objection[27] is that any such proposal, grounded upon explanatory virtue, is viciously circular. Here is a key passage:

> One difficulty . . . is that this [proposal] uses the notion of *truth*. Our problem . . . was to explain how a particular reference relation – and that means, also, a particular extension for the notion of truth – gets attached to our words. To say that what does the attaching is the fact that certain sentences . . . are *true*, . . . is flagrantly circular. The problem, of course, is that what the semantic physicalist is trying to do is reduce intentional notions to physicalist ones, and this program requires that he not employ any intentional notions in the reduction. But *explanation* is a flagrantly intentional notion.[28]

We can discount what may seem to be the principal complaint in this passage. The general shape of the type of proposal mooted is that it is because a certain physicalistically specifiable relation R holds between our words and their referents that those words do in fact have those referents. It is, therefore, simply a misrepresentation to treat the proposal as asserting that the fact that certain *sentences* are *true* is what explains why our words refer as they do. That is, it seems quite gratuitous to impute to the physicalist the contention that what 'does the attaching' is the fact that a certain sentence (saying that our words bear R to some object) is true, rather than (simply) the fact which that sentence purports to state. This indifference to the distinction between object- and metalinguistic claims merely invites repetition of the main complaint already levelled at the 'just more theory' move.

The point about explanation made in the second half of the passage may seem more telling: if the semantic physicalist is in the business of giving a reductive account of reference in particular, and intentional notions in general, how can it be permissible to deploy intentional notions in so doing? But this too seems to us of doubtful force. Maybe the question would be appropriate if what was at issue was the standard type of *analytic* or *conceptual* reduction, a purported analysis of necessary and sufficient conditions of application. But the mooted form of proposal actually seeks an a posteriori reduction. It is anything but clear that all use of the notion of explanation must be eschewed, if the aim is that of saying what naturalistic relation between words and things in fact underpins reference – if what's on offer is a *theoretical* identification of reference with R, of the same general character as the identification of heat with mean molecular motion.[29] All it seems to be legitimate to impose, by way of a general constraint, is rather that if use is made of an intentional notion in a statement which is part of a programme of physicalistic reductions of intentional notions generally, that use must be of a kind ultimately amenable to that form of reduction. It would be necessary to look at the details to see whether a particular physicalistic construal of reference, or explanation, violated this rather vague constraint. In any case, the constraints on legitimate a posteriori identification of properties and relations still remain to be clearly worked out.

Putnam is on much stronger ground, however, if it may be assumed that the naturalist proposal must ultimately identify reference with some *specific form of causal relationship* between the item or items that stand as the reference of a term and token uses of that term. Putnam himself, of course, has been prominent among those who have emphasized, as against the once orthodox Fregean conception of the matter, the role of causality in the determination of reference in a wide class of cases. But he warns us that neither his own proposal, nor Kripke's similar idea, were intended to explain from a standing start, as it were, how determinate reference is constituted; clearly they could not do so, since both pictures simply assume from the outset that individuals can be 'singled out for the purpose of a "naming ceremony"', and say nothing about how that might be done *ab initio*.[30]

Putnam has expressed various doubts about the viability of a reductive causal theory of reference. As he stresses, it will normally be the case that very many of the objects and events that figure in the causal ancestry of a particular utterance of an expression will not be what it refers to. Further, a term's or predicate's reference may be to, or may include, things with which it is not causally linked – items existing only in the future, for instance, are presumably available to be referred to but as yet sustain no causal relations.[31] Part of the problem for the causal theorist, then, is to single out the right causal relationship. Putnam is sceptical that this can be done in purely naturalistic terms without falling back on intentional notions. As against Evans's version of a causal theory, for example, according to which, roughly, a term refers to the dominant source of our beliefs involving it, he justly observes that the dominant source of our beliefs about electrons, say, may well be physics textbooks, rather than electrons themselves.[32]

Obviously these considerations are not conclusive. To the difficulty about future things, for example, it may be replied that in cases where the term introduced is general (perhaps a natural-kind term) it is to be understood that its extension comprises the causally connected samples and all other things of the same kind.[33] In general, causal theorists will surely agree that work is needed to characterize the appropriate kind of causal link – but why suppose the project to be hopeless?

Well, we suspect the project *is* hopeless. The core difficulty is to restrict, without ineliminable play with antecedent assumptions about its reference, the utterly disorderly mess of items that are apt to elicit tokenings of any given expression. In his Gifford Lectures[34] Putnam discusses probably the most sophisticated attempt to date to accomplish this: the proposal of Jerry Fodor[35] that the extension of a term comprises the smallest class of items which as a matter of natural law cause tokenings of the term, and whose doing so asymmetrically explains all other tokenings of the term. For example, both horses and pictures of horses are apt to cause tokenings of 'horse'; but Fodor's intuition is that horses are the basic cause and therefore qualify as the reference, since it is only because horses cause tokenings of 'horse' that pictures of horses do.

Against this, it may be objected that there really is no clear priority as between 'If horses did not cause tokenings of "horse", neither would pictures of horses' and 'If pictures of horses did not cause tokenings of "horse", neither would horses'. Rather, what seems to be true is that it is because 'horse' refers to horses that *both* horses *and* pictures of horses – and thoughts of horses, and cows in a darkened field, etc., etc. – elicit, *ceteris paribus*, tokenings of 'horse'! In the jargon of possible worlds, the closest worlds in which pictures of horses do not cause tokenings of 'horse' are worlds in which horses don't either.[36] (For a fuller discussion of difficulties with semantic naturalism, see Chapter 5, 'A GUIDE TO NATURALIZING SEMANTICS'.)

VII

Let us try to take stock. First, to summarize the situation of the three sub-arguments of *Reason, Truth and History*. That the metaphysical realist has no option of explicating reference in terms of intentional states we take to be clear. However, the claim of the permutation argument to have shown that reference is underdetermined by features of the use of whole sentences is, as we saw, open to question. Moreover, the 'just more theory' move *is* a foul, and some of Putnam's own specific criticisms of causalist/naturalist proposals about reference are less than conclusive. However, to observe that the permutation argument as it stands is inconclusive for Putnam's purpose is one thing; but to make the kind of positive, constructive case for the determination of reference by whole-sentence semantics which, if such was her strategy, the metaphysical realist would need, is quite another. It is no clearer how such a case might in detail be made. Moreover, if that is not to be the strategy, then a causal account of reference – broadly construed – is the only remaining avenue to explore, yet the literature justifies nothing but pessimism about reconstructibility of semantic notions in non-intentional, causal terms. Putnam, then, may not have strictly proved all of his three lemmas. But he has done enough to issue a very pointed challenge, and one to which it is by no means clear that the metaphysical realist can satisfactorily respond.

Second, it merits emphasis that Putnam's considerations, even if conclusive, would provide no argument for the indeterminacy of reference as such: rather, what they would establish is that *if* referential relations had to be constituted in a certain kind of way – in the truth-conditions of sentences, for instance, or in causal connections – *then* reference would be indeterminate. The proper conclusion would be merely that a constitutive account of reference, of what makes it the case that a particular term, thought or spoken, stands for a particular object or kind, cannot proceed along any of the three lines reviewed. If those lines indeed exhaust the possibilities, then a case would have been made that there can be no fully explicit, reductive account at all of what constitutes the reference of a symbol to any particular item or range of items – at least, none which does not take for granted the determinacy of reference of our thoughts as a background. 'Aboutness' would have to be conceived as primitive.[37]

Such a finding would no doubt be of great interest. But it will have been achieved, if it can be achieved, in a way that has no evident selective bearing on the status of metaphysical realism. The argument, if it can be made good, will be an argument for everybody. Moreover, notions which promise to admit of no reductive account are anyway ten a penny. So the questions remain: why see in the situation a (potential) *problem* to do with reference? And why, if so, a problem *distinctively* for *metaphysical realism*? The crucial task for a would-be sympathetic interpreter of Putnam is to provide convincing answers to these questions. How might such answers run?

To lack a constitutive account – and all prospect of a constitutive account – of a certain kind of subject matter is not, except in special circumstances, to have a reason to distrust its reality. That Putnam himself intends no scepticism about reference is abundantly clear from his willingness to allow that we can perfectly legitimately and fully adequately specify what 'cat', for instance, refers to: its reference is to *cats* (and therefore not to cherries, or to the *p*-correlates of cats under some permutation, *p*)! More generally, if it is granted that the language in which we are to state the reference of a term is an extension of the language to which that term belongs, then a homophonic formulation is a perfectly adequate response to someone who challenges us to individuate the reference of that term. If, however, that assumption is not granted – that is, if object- and metalanguage are distinct and the challenge is to justify the assignment of one scheme of reference to the terms of the object language, rather than to a permutation of it – then there are perfectly ordinary canons of interpretation to justify a preference, for example, for the assignment of cats to be the extension of 'chat' in French, rather than cats* – that is, cherries in a world in which cats are on mats and cherries are on trees. These will be canons which have to do, for instance, with the salience of cats in many of the situations which provoke 'chat'-talk among the French and a corresponding salient absence, for the most part, of cherries. That there are correct and incorrect things to say about what expressions refer to is enough for there to be *truths* – at least on the conception of truth favoured by the internal realist – about reference.

This is the key to the question of the selective bearing of the argument. What, precisely, might be put in doubt by the kinds of consideration reviewed is the existence of truths about reference *in a more substantial sense of* 'truth', a concept of truth whose applicability to claims of a certain kind requires, beyond the unimpeachability of those claims in the light of the ordinary discipline that informs their use, some form of robust *fit* between them and the world. For it is not enough for metaphysical realism merely that there be facts about what the expressions of our language refer to: these facts must be facts as metaphysical realism is wont to conceive *all* facts, facts no less sublime than – since constituted by relations to – the sublimated objects and properties which make up the metaphysical realist's world. There is accordingly no question of resting content with the sort of deflated account of them which is all that is provided by the homophonic platitudes and routine methodology of interpretation for which the internalist about truth may settle.

The metaphysical realist, then, owes a perspective on the nature of relations of reference which allows them to stand behind the routine interpretative methodology and which, indeed, explains its adequacy – explains how it is indeed a way of 'getting onto' or 'tracking' these independently constituted relations; a perspective which allows us to construe the truth of ascriptions of reference along robust correspondence lines, and which generally finds a place for such relations in the world as metaphysical realism conceives it. And there is, if Putnam's argument can succeed, no such perspective possible, because there is then nothing to be said about what reference *is*.[38]

In brief, then, we have a rich and complex argument to the conclusion that reference admits of no reductive account, coupled with the claim that metaphysical realism – but not internal realism – is saddled with a world-view that cannot be properly understood unless such an account can, *per impossibile*, be given. The crucial difference is entirely one of explanatory obligation. For metaphysical realism, reference is a matter of relations between robustly distinct existences, items of language and thought on the one side, and items in a stubbornly alien world on the other; and this conception, Putnam's driving idea has it, entrains a commitment to the possibility of some sort of external perspective on the nature and constitution of this relationship – exactly what, if his argument succeeds in detail, cannot be delivered. So the metaphysical realist must, in the end, be driven to obscurantism: a conviction in the reality of relations constituted, he knows not how, between his thought and a world wholly alien to it.[39]

VIII

Why does internal realism incur no parallel obligation? Can the mere currency of standards of correctness for claims about reference really ensure that no issue arises? It is one thing to get a sense of Putnam's thought on this point; another to determine whether it is really convincing. The key idea seems to be that, as Putnam repeatedly expresses it, 'there is no ready-made world': that the division of the world into particular objects and kinds of thing is somehow coeval with, rather than merely *reflected by*, the divisions among our concepts and the expressions for them. If the kind picked out by a term of ours is thought of as originally constituted quite independently of the use of that term and the conceptual resources associated with it, then the question has to arise: what attaches the term on to just that kind, as opposed to another? That is the question which metaphysical realism is charged to answer. If, by contrast, the kind is regarded as in some way having no being independently of our deployment of those very conceptual resources, then there is no real linkage to explain, any more than it wants an explanation, how the patterns on a slide manage to be congruent with the images it casts upon a blank screen.

This kind of simile is convincing enough in its way. The difficulty is to give it substance in the case that matters – to see what the idea that human conceptual activity 'slices up' the world really comes to.[40] But perhaps on reflection there is room to repudiate the metaphysically realist conception of a 'hooking' of language onto a sortally predeterminate world without recourse, natural though it may be, to opposing constructivist metaphors.[41] The crucial point is that, unless the unity of a range of items is in some way fixed in advance of the institution of using a term of which they are the reference, there is no non-trivial question what makes for the connection between that term and that range: the range of items in question just constitutionally is that for which the term in question stands.

That leaves the metaphysical realist the options of faulting the detail of the stages of the argument, or living with its conclusion: that to conceive of the world in a certain kind of robustly autonomous fashion is to consign the relation between the vehicles of our thought and the taxonomy of the world to unaccountability. Putnam effectively ridicules such an upshot. But ridicule, it may be countered, is no substitute for argument. Any broad philosophical system will have its primitive notions and theses. Further argument may be demanded as to why metaphysical realism may not legitimately go primitive at the interface between language and the world. That is what it must do if intentionality – 'aboutness' – is indeed irreducible, as in effect the three ingredients of Putnam's argument combine (if they are sound) to show. To be sure, no aspirant to a purely physicalist version of metaphysical realism could rest content with primitively intentional relations of aboutness. And Putnam may be right to say that 'materialism is the only *metaphysical* picture that has contemporary "clout". Metaphysics, or the enterprise of describing the "furniture of the world" . . . has been rejected by many analytic philosophers . . . Today, apart from relics, it is only materialists (or "physicalists", as they like to call themselves) who continue the traditional enterprise'.[42] But it remains to be convincingly explained why 'the only sort of metaphysical realism that our time can take seriously'[43] should be a thorough-going physicalism, or why irreducible intentionality should be especially uncomfortable for one of metaphysically realist predilection.

We end with one final reservation about the scope of the argument. If the interpretation offered is sound, then it can engage only a realist who accepts the autonomy of the division of the world into objects and kinds. So far as we can see, it must therefore fail to touch an intermediate, apparently coherent combination of views: the combination which yokes rejection of the idea that there is a 'pre-sliced', 'ready-made world' – that the world divides into kinds of thing, stuff and so on quite independently of our efforts to devise a conceptual scheme in terms of which it may be best described and understood – with acceptance of an evidentially unconstrained conception of truth, that is, with realism in the sense Dummett has made familiar (see Chapter 12, REALISM AND ITS OPPOSITIONS). Putnam has sometimes written as if the latter form of realism must fall to his argument. If we are right, that can be so only if a Dumettian, realist conception of truth must in the end consist in the kind of robust correspondence conception which is the essence of metaphysical realism as Putnam conceives it. However, it is one thing to accept that questions about what words refer to make sense, and have determinate answers, only within a conceptual scheme (so that the words cannot be thought of as having reference to an antecedently determinate world of objects and kinds), and another to claim that we cannot combine those words into statements which may, in principle, possess determinate but undetectable truth-values. If the latter *is* a consequence of the former, further argument is needed to show it.[44,45]

Appendix: permutation results

In his Appendix to *Reason, Truth and History*, Putnam shows how to prove a relatively strong permutation result to the effect that, given an interpretation I of a (first-order) language L, we can construct another ('unintended') interpretation J which preserves the truth-conditions of all the sentences of L (in his sense, under which sentences have the same truth-condition if they have the same truth-value at all possible worlds), whilst varying the extensions of terms and predicates. Here, we first prove a more basic, weaker result (to the effect that, given an interpretation of a first-order language, we can always construct an alternative 'unintended' interpretation which coincides with the given interpretation over the truth-values of all the sentences, while varying the extensions of terms and predicates). We then indicate how the method of proof (which differs somewhat from that employed by Putnam) may be extended to obtain, first, a result essentially the same as Putnam's and then some stronger results, for second-order languages and for languages with modal operators.

Weak permutation

For this, we work with a first-order language L, with logical constants: $\neg$, $\wedge$, $\exists$; terms, comprising individual constants a, b, c, . . . and variables x, y, z, . . . ; and predicate constants F, G, H, ... The atomic sentences are just the strings $Ft_1, \ldots, t_n$, consisting of an n-place F followed by n occurrences of individual terms. If A,B are sentences, so are $\neg A$, $A \wedge B$ and $\exists xA(x)$, where x is any variable and A(x) comes from some sentence A by replacing one or more occurrences of some one individual constant by occurrences of x.

An interpretation I of L consists of a non-empty domain D with assignments of elements of D as denotations of the individual terms and of sets of ordered n-tuples of elements of D, for appropriate choices of n, as extensions of the n-place predicates. Thus to each 1-place predicate, I assigns as extension a subset of D – intuitively, the set of elements of D having the property for which, under I, that predicate is take to stand; to each 2-place predicate, I assigns a set of ordered pairs of elements of D – intuitively, the pairs of elements of D the first of which bears to the second the relation for which, under I, that predicate stands, and so on. '$I(A) = 1$' denotes that A is true under I, and is defined as follows:

$I(Ft_1 \ldots t_n) = 1$	iff	$\langle I(t_1) \ldots I(t_n)\rangle \in I(F)$
$I(\neg B) = 1$	iff	$I(B) \neq 1$
$I(B \wedge C) = 1$	iff	$I(B) = I(C) = 1$
$I(\exists xB(x)) = 1$	iff	there is an interpretation I° which differs from I at most in its assignment to x, such that $I^\circ(B(x)) = 1$

Theorem 1 (weak permutation)

Let I be any interpretation with domain D, and ϕ be any permutation of D. Let I* be any interpretation with the same domain D such that, for every term t, $I^*(t) = \phi(I(t))$, and for every n-place F, $I^*(F) = \{\langle d_1, \ldots, dn\rangle \mid \langle \phi^{-1}(d_1), \ldots, \phi^{-1}(d_n)\rangle \in I(F)\}$. Then for any A, $I(A) = 1 \leftrightarrow I^*(A) = 1$

Strictly, for the purposes of Putnam-type arguments, we need only establish that for given I, D and ϕ, there is at least one interpretation meeting the specified conditions on I*, for which the theorem's consequent holds. However, the proof can proceed more smoothly for the theorem as stated. It is obvious that there *are* (non-trivial) interpretations meeting the antecedent conditions.

Proof is by induction on the degree of A, as measured by the number of logical operators occurring in it. So the induction hypothesis (IH) is that the theorem holds for all wffs of degree <A, and on this hypothesis it is to be proved that the theorem holds for A. More fully stated, IH is:

If I^1 and I^2 are *any* interpretations with the same domain, such that for each term t, $I^2(t) = \phi(I^1(t))$ and for any n-place F, $I^2(F) = \{\langle d_1, \ldots, d_n\rangle \mid \langle \phi^{-1}(d_1), \ldots, \phi^{-1}(d_n)\rangle \in I^1(F)\}$, then for any B of degree <A, $I^2(B) = 1 \leftrightarrow I^1(B) = 1$

A is atomic i.e. $Ft_1 \ldots t_n$ for some n.

$$
\begin{aligned}
I^*(Ft_1 \ldots t_n) = 1 \quad & \text{iff} \quad \langle I^*(t_1) \ldots I^*(t_n)\rangle \in I^*(F) \\
& \text{iff} \quad \langle \phi(I(t_1)) \ldots \phi(I(t_n))\rangle \in I^*(F) \\
& \text{iff} \quad \langle \phi^{-1}(\phi(I(t_1))) \ldots \phi^{-1}(\phi(I(t_n)))\rangle \in I(F) \\
& \text{iff} \quad \langle I(t_1) \ldots I(t_n)\rangle \in I(F) \\
& \text{iff} \quad I(Ft_1 \ldots t_n) = 1
\end{aligned}
$$

Induction step for $\exists$

Suppose $I(\exists xB(x)) = 1$. Then for some I° differing from I in at most its assignment to x, $I°(B(x)) = 1$. Let $I^\#$ be the same as I* except possibly over its assignment to x, where $I^\#(x) = \phi(I°(x))$. It is easily verified that I° and $I^\#$ meet the conditions on I^1 and I^2 in the induction hypothesis, which then yields that $I^\#(B(x)) = 1$. Hence $I^*(\exists xB(x)) = 1$. The steps are obviously reversible.

Other cases for induction are straightforward. ⊡

Theorem 1 ensures that given any assignment of truth-values to the sentences of L, induced by an interpretation I, there will be a quite different interpretation I* of L based on a permutation of I's domain, which induces all the same truth-*values* on L's sentences, but makes quite different assignments to the names and predicates of the language.

Strong permutation

A stronger permutation result will be that given an interpretation I of L, we can get a different interpretation I* that departs from I over its assignments to names and predicates, whilst giving L's sentences the same truth-*conditions* (in the Putnam sense – the sentences of L coincide in truth-value not just at the actual world, but at every possible world, under the two interpretations). To state and prove this stronger result, we need some preliminary stage-setting:

By a world structure we mean a triple $\langle D, W, \sigma \rangle$, where D and W are non-empty sets (intuitively, think of W as the set of all possible worlds, of D as a very inclusive set of objects, containing each object which exists at any of the worlds in W), and σ is a function from W into the non-empty subsets of D (i.e. σ assigns a non-empty subset of objects to each world[46])

Interpretations I are now assignments as follows: for each i and j, I assigns to the term t_i an element of the domain of w_j as its denotation relative to that world, i.e. $I(t_i,w_j) \in \sigma(w_j)$. And to each n-place F, I assigns, relative to each world w_j, a set of ordered n-tuples from the domain of w_j, i.e. $I(F,w_j) \subseteq (\sigma(w_j))^n$.

Truth under I is now of course a relation between sentences of L and worlds, defined thus:

Atoms $\quad I(Ft_1 \ldots t_n, wj) = 1 \text{ iff } \langle I(t_1,w_j) \ldots I(t_n,w_j)\rangle \in I(F,w_j)$

Molecules $\quad I(\neg B,w_j) = 1 \text{ iff } I(B,w_j) \neq 1$

$I(B \wedge C,w_j) = 1 \text{ iff } I(B,w_j) = 1 \text{ and } I(C,w_j) = 1$

$I(\exists x B(x),w_j) = 1$ iff there is an interpretation I° which differs from I at most in its assignment to x, such that $I^\circ(B(x),w_j) = 1$

Theorem 2 (strong permutation)

Let I be an interpretation of L. Let the ϕ_j be permutations[47] respectively of each of $\sigma(w_j)$ for all the $w_j \in W$. Let I* be any interpretation of L such that for all i and j, $I^*(t_i,w_j) = \phi_j[I(t_i,w_j)]$ and for every n-place F, $I^*(F,w_j) = \{\langle d_1 \ldots d_n\rangle \mid \langle \phi_j^{-1}(d_1) \ldots \phi_j^{-1}(d_n)\rangle \in I(F, w_j)\}$. Then $I^*(A,w_j) = 1 \leftrightarrow I(A,w_j) = 1$

Proof is again by induction on the degree of A – the foregoing proof of *weak permutation* is readily adapted to show what's required for arbitrary w_j, simply by writing in w_j as an extra parameter as appropriate.

A is atomic i.e. $Ft_1 \ldots t_n$ for some n:

$$
\begin{aligned}
I^*(Ft_1 \ldots t_n,w_j) = 1 \quad & \text{iff } \langle I^*(t_1,w_j) \ldots I^*(t_n,w_j)\rangle \in I^*(F,w_j) \\
& \text{iff } \langle \phi_j(I(t_1,w_j)) \ldots \phi_j(I(t_n,w_j))\rangle \in I^*(F,w_j) \\
& \text{iff } \langle \phi_j^{-1}(\phi_j(I(t_1,w_j))) \ldots \phi_j^{-1}(\phi_j(I(t_n,w_j)))\rangle \in I(F,w_j) \\
& \text{iff } \langle I(t_1,w_j) \ldots I(t_n,w_j)\rangle \in I(F,w_j) \\
& \text{iff } I(Ft_1 \ldots t_n,w_j) = 1
\end{aligned}
$$

As before, the induction step is quite straightforward. Here, for illustration, is the case for $\wedge$:

Suppose $I(B \wedge C,w_j) = 1$. Then $I(B,w_j) = I(C,w_j) = 1$. By IH, $I^*(B,w_j) = I^*(C,w_j) = 1$. Hence $I^*(B \wedge C,w_j) = 1$. Steps obviously reversible.

Strengthening for second-order languages

We extend our first-order language L by permitting binding of (first-level) predicate variables by the second-order existential quantifier $\exists f$ – we use f,g, . . . as predicate variables. An interpretation of our second-order language L^2 will make assignments to them of entities of the same types as are assigned to predicate constants in the first-order case. 'true under I' is defined as for previous cases, except that we add a clause for the second-order quantifier:

$I(\exists fB(f)) = 1$ iff there is an interpretation I° which differs from I at most in its assignment to f, such that $I^\circ(B(f)) = 1$

With this addition, we can straightforwardly extend the weak and strong permutation results to the second-order case – all that is needed is an extra case in the induction, dealing with sentences in which the principal operator is second-order $\exists$. For the second-order extension of Theorem 1, this runs:

Induction step for second-order $\exists$

Suppose $I(\exists fB(f)) = 1$. Then for some I° differing from I in at most its assignment to f, $I^\circ(B(f)) = 1$. Let $I^\#$ be the same as I^* except possibly over its assignment to f, where $I^\#(f) = \{\langle d_1, \ldots, d_n\rangle \in D^n \mid \langle \phi^{-1}(d_1), \ldots, \phi^{-1}(d_n)\rangle \in I^\circ(f)\}$. Then by the induction hypothesis, $I^\#(B(f)) = 1$. Hence $I^*(\exists fB(f)) = 1$. The steps are obviously reversible.

Languages with modal operators

The addition of a modal operator, say $\Box$, to L (or L^2) permits the formation of complex sentences which are not truth-functions of their atomic constituents. That is, we can form sentences B with atomic consituents $A_1 \ldots A_k$ so that B's truth-value at a world w_j is not a function simply of the values of $A_1 \ldots A_k$ at w_j. B's truth-value at w_j is, rather, a function of the values of $A_1 \ldots A_k$ at the other worlds in W.

Does this prevent us from running the permutation argument? Well, it seems that it should *not* do so – just because, while a modal sentence's truth-value at a given world is not a function of the values of its atomic ingredients at *that* world, it *is* a function of their values at other worlds. But we know from *strong permutation* that we can jiggle the assignments to individual constants and predicates in such a way as to obtain an 'unintended' interpretation which agrees with the original interpretation on the truth-values of all the sentences of L (or L^2) at all possible worlds (so that they have the same truth-conditions, in Putnam's sense). It follows from this that adding $\Box$ to L (or L^2), with the usual clause to the effect that $I(\Box B,w_j) = 1$ iff $I(B,w_k) = 1$ for all w_k accessible from w_j, can make no essential difference to the situation. The essential point is this. Given an interpretation I which induces a *pattern* of truth-values on a sentence B across the possible worlds, we can construct a variant interpretation I*, differing from I in its assignments to terms and predicates (and in case of L^2, predicate variables) at those worlds, but agreeing with I on the induced value of B at each world. And that is enough to ensure that I and I* will not diverge over the truth-values of modal functions of B.

Notes

1 'Models and Reality', in Putnam (1983, p. 13).

2 Putnam (1981a, p. 49); cf. also 'A defense of internal realism', in Putnam (1990a, p. 30).

3 Putnam (1981a, p. 49).

4 The Twin Earth argument was first presented in Putnam's 'The Meaning of "Meaning"', see especially Putnam (1975, p. 223) and following. An abbreviated statement of it is given in Putnam (1981a, pp. 22–9). See also pp. 41–3 for the distinction between pure and impure mental states; and Chapter 5, A GUIDE TO NATURALIZING SEMANTICS.

5 By saying that an assignment of truth-values to sentences meets operational constraints, Putnam means, roughly speaking, that it accords with all the observational data that is available in principle. By theoretical constraints he means whatever further methodological constraints – including pragmatic considerations such as simplicity and economy – guide the optimum choice between theories which meet all operational constraints. Cf. 'Models and Reality', in Putnam (1983, pp. 3–6).

6 See Putnam's classic characterization of the 'internalist perspective' (1981a, pp. 49 and following).

7 Thus he writes:

> For an internalist like myself, the situation is quite different. . . . signs do not intrinsically correspond to objects, independently of how those signs are employed . . . 'Objects' do not exist independently of conceptual schemes. *We* cut up the world into objects when we introduce one or another scheme of description. Since the objects *and* the signs are alike *internal* to the scheme of description, it is possible to say what matches what. . . . Indeed, it is trivial to say what any word refers to within the language the word belongs to, by using the word itself. What does 'rabbit' refer to? Why, to rabbits of course. (1981a, p. 52)

See also 'Models and reality', in Putnam (1983, p. 24).

8 This question has exercised some of Putnam's critics, e.g. Blackburn (1994, p. 27), but needlessly, if we are right.

9 See e.g. remarks at pp. 25, 27 and 29.

10 Putnam (1981a, p. 52). Cf. also:

> if the received view is correct, then we would have an elegant *account of how* intensions and extensions are fixed [p. 32, our emphasis] One might say that . . . my 'mental representations' . . . *refer* to cathood . . . this may be true, but it just repeats that reference is fixed in one way rather than another. This is what we want to explain and not the explanation sought. [p. 37] To explain reference in terms of (impure) intention would be circular. And the problem of how *pure* mental states of intending, believing, etc., can . . . constitute reference is just what we have found so puzzling. [p. 43]

11 More about this matter below.

12 Cf. Putnam (1981a, p. 34). Putnam's stipulation for (c)-worlds is a little odd – it would have sufficed to have 'cat' refer to cats and 'mat' refer to mats in this case, since all that's required is that 'A cat is on a mat' be false in (c)-worlds.

13 For formal details, see the Appendix.

14 That said, it's worth observing that, even if Putnam's project were to argue for the indeterminacy of reference *tout court*, it's not clear that the permutation argument would be vulnerable to the stated objection. For the proof of the permutability of reference – illustrations apart – is *entirely general*, and following it need involve consideration of no specific suppositions about the reference of particular expressions in the language: suppositions whose status might then be settled by stipulation. Someone – not Putnam – who wanted to harness the permutation argument to a general scepticism about reference *could* quite coherently carry its conclusion forward in the form of the counterfactual: if there were such a thing as determinate reference, it would not be recoverable from the truth conditions of sentences. And indeed, the overall strategy of arguing for indeterminacy by establishing enough such counterfactuals, with a sufficient variety of consequents ('. . . , it would not be recoverable from speakers' intentions', '. . . , it would not be recoverable from facts about causality', etc.), is a perfectly coherent one. By the same token, though, the concern – for a supporter of Putnam – that the model-theoretic argument may fail stably to focus against metaphysical realism, dissolving instead into 'Putnam's Paradox', is not so easily set aside.

15 See, for instance, Ian Hacking (1983, p. 105); though this may not be quite fair to Hacking, who in the relevant passage is mainly raising a doubt about the first-order formalizability e.g. of physical theory, and is not really emphasizing the failure of the Lowenheim-Skolem Theorem at second order. Cf. Putnam's remarks in note 11 of Putnam (1989, p. 230).

16 Permutation results for second-order languages and languages with the usual modal operators are outlined in the Appendix.

17 See e.g. Putnam (1989, p. 215).

18 There are, however, reasons to qualify the force of this reservation, whose significance will emerge only when more has been done to explain how Putnam's argument can bear selectively on metaphysical realism. See Section VII, and especially n. 38 below.

19 Hartry Field (1972). Field's view is discussed by Putnam (1981a, pp. 45–6; 1978, pp. 14–17, 30–32 and 57–58).

20 A reason for thinking the tension merely apparent will anyway emerge in Section VI below – see also note 30.

21 Putnam (1981a, pp. 45–6).

22 Besides directing it at Field's in the passage quoted, Putnam (1983, p. 18) makes essentially the same move against Evans's version of the causal theory, and (1989, pp. 219–20) against Devitt's appeal to a causal theory.

23 This claim appears to run counter to Putnam's own view, as expressed in 'Model Theory and the "Factuality" of Semantics' (1989). He stresses there that his model-theoretic argument is directed against a limited target – *physicalistic* metaphysical realism. Certainly some of the argumentation rehearsed in that paper relies upon the assumption that the metaphysical realist aspires to a physicalist account of reality – including the circularity argument discussed above. Our point is that the 'just more theory' move is *not* subject to this limitation. A similar point is made by David Lewis (1984, pp. 232–3).

24 Ibid., pp. 224–5.

25 Something like this may well be the intended thrust of Putnam's complaint (1983, p. xi) that the causal realist 'ignores his own epistemological position'.

26 Cf. Putnam (1989, pp. 216–17).

27 Putnam advances two quite distinct objections against the proposal. This is his first objection; we shall discuss the second in due course. Meanwhile, note that the first objection is to any identification of reference with a physicalistic relation, regardless of whether it is made in the interests of defending metaphysical realism.

28 (1989, p. 217). Putnam has 'requirement' where we have 'proposal'. The requirement to which he refers is presumably that if a relation R is to be the 'intended' reference relation, the supposition that R is the reference relation should yield an explanation of facts about our use of words.

29 A more detailed formulation of this argument is given in 'Beyond Historicism' (1983, pp. 290–98 and 292–5). We lack space to discuss it here, but it seems to us that it is vitiated by the same gratuitous assumption that anyone who proposes a 'theoretical identification' of an intentional notion – such as *explanation* or *reference* – is thereby debarred from using the notion in question in arguing for the identification. That this might be a reasonable restriction to impose on attempts at *analytic* reductions of intentional notions seems quite irrelevant.

30 Cf. 'Models and Reality' in Putnam (1983, p. 17). This bears on the interpretative question left dangling in Section IV – it is clearly quite consistent with holding that a causal constraint needs to be met in many (or even all) cases of genuine reference to deny that a full constitutive account of reference may be given in purely causal terms.

31 Here is a relevant passage from 'Model Theory and the "Factuality" of Semantics' at p. 219:

> if *E(T)* is the event of someone's using a token of a term *T*, then there is a good sense of 'causal connection' in which *every* event in the backward light-cone of *E(T)* is 'causally connected' to the event *E(T)*; but it will almost never be the case that the term *T* . . . *refers* to every event in the backward light-cone of *E(T)* (and it will typically be the case that the term does refer to things with which the token is *not* causally connected, e.g., future things).

32 'Models and Reality' in Putnam (1983, p. 18). See Evans (1973, pp. 187–208) for his version of the theory. For some further discussion of this approach, see Chapter 21, REFERENCE AND NECESSITY, esp. sect. 4.

33 Putnam would probably concede that the first difficulty may not be insuperable – cf. his acknowledgement that Evans has a proposal, to which he offers no objection – to deal with this problem: see the footnote on p. 18 of 'Models and Reality', in Putnam (1983). He does press the difficulty a little further, claiming that the distinction between causes and background conditions is inescapably interest-relative; but this shows at best that the relevant causal relations can't be singled out by appeal to that distinction, not that they can't be singled out at all.

34 Putnam (1992, ch. 3).

35 Fodor (1990).

36 Further objections, complementing those brought by Putnam (and those discussed in Chapter 5, A GUIDE TO NATURALIZING SEMANTICS), and including a forceful play with the holism of the mental, are developed by Paul Boghossian (1991).

37 Putnam, of course, is well aware of the possibility of this response to his argument, envisaging it explicitly (1989, p. 220); however, he does not regard acknowledging the primitiveness of reference as a commitment to regarding it as 'simple and

irreducible'. *Representation and Reality* is, in effect, an extended argument to the contrary.

38 The astute reader will note that if these considerations are indeed the key to the question of how Putnam's argument can tell selectively against metaphysical realism, then there actually is little force – in the resultant dialectical setting – in the reservation with which our discussion of the significance of the permutation argument concluded in Section III. That reservation was, in effect, that while permutation-based reinterpretations of a language might be *consistent* with all data concerning the use of its sentences, they would be likely to be dominated by the preferred interpretation once appropriate constraints on the construction of interpretational theories, beyond adequacy to the linguistic data, are allowed their proper influence. But that, if correct, is a point about the methodology of interpretation – something which can be freely acknowledged from the internal realist point of view as conditioning the concept of truth that applies to ascriptions of reference and other semantic claims, but which takes us no closer to the *constitutive* account which the metaphysical realist needs of the nature of reference, conceived as a network of external relations of which methodologically superior interpretation is, at best, a means of discovery.

39 Recall the complaint which Putnam airs against Lewis's positive view, that it amounts to 'saying that we-know-not-what fixes the reference relation we-know-not-how' (1989, p. 220).

40 So far as we are aware, Putnam does not himself explicitly employ the metaphor of 'slicing'. But it is common in discussion of his ideas and implicit in several of his own characterizations of internal realism. For example, '"Objects" do not exist independently of conceptual schemes. *We* cut up the world into objects when we introduce one or another scheme of description.' (Putnam 1981a, p. 52.) Of a piece with this are his frequent characterizations of external or metaphysical realism as involving – via its commitment to the idea that there is, whether we can discover it or not, just one true theory of the world – a belief that there is a 'ready-made world', having an intrinsic or 'built-in' structure, comprising a 'fixed totality of mind-independent objects'. Cf., for example, Putnam (1983, p. 211, and 1981a, p. 49).

41 But an outright repudiation of the idea of sortal predetermination, even if not accompanied by a lurch into constructivist metaphor, would be in at least prima facie conflict with retention of the idea, of which Putnam himself has been a principal advocate, that the world encompasses various *natural kinds*. The apparent tension here runs parallel to that noted earlier, between Putnam's advocacy of an externalist account, in broadly causal terms, of how reference is 'fixed', on the one hand; and on the other, his insistence that no progress can be made on the problem of explaining how reference can be determinate by appeal to causal relations between our words and appropriate bits of the world. So, unless the tension can be argued to be merely apparent, some qualification is needed. We cannot pursue this somewhat delicate issue here, and must content ourselves with one brief cautionary remark. Even supposing that the repudiation of sortal predetermination needs qualification to make space for belief in natural kinds, it would be a mistake, for at least two reasons, to think that this could be exploited to recover a metaphysically realist conception of determinate reference. First, the hypothesis that certain things instantiate a natural kind would, at best, serve to explain the *unity* of a class of things forming the reference or extension of a predicate – as distinct from explaining what *constitutes* reference to that class. (This point may, we suspect, contain the germ of a resolution of the apparent tension – but that is a further issue.) Second, however precisely the envisaged qualification might run, it would be

restricted in scope in a way which would, even prescinding from the previous point, preclude its yielding a fully general solution to the problem with which Putnam confronts the metaphysical realist. Crucially, we could expect no help with explaining how *non*-natural-kind terms can enjoy determinate reference. Essentially the same limitation vitiates David Lewis's proposal (1984, pp. 226–9) that some things, such as rabbits, are more eligible to be the referents of our words than others, such as undetached rabbit parts, and that rival schemes of reference may be ranked as better or worse to the extent that their assignments of referents respect 'nature's joints'. Indeed, the difficulty is not just that appeal to natural divisions could afford an at best partial solution to the general problem; it can be seen, on reflection, that it fails to accomplish even that much – the permutation argument can just as well work to deliver perverse jigglings of perfectly *eligible* referents, and has no need for play with unnatural divisions at all.

42 From 'Why There isn't a Ready-Made World' in Putnam (1983, p. 208).

43 Putnam (1989, p. 220).

44 Indeed, Putnam himself has recently shown signs of a cooling in his opposition to realism as Dummett conceives it (e.g. 1994b, pp. 503 and 510–11).

45 We are indebted to Philip Percival, and to colleagues who attended the Putnam conference in Utrecht in September 1994, especially Putnam himself.

46 The point of this complication is simply to avoid making the needlessly restrictive – and unrealistic – assumption that possible worlds do not differ in point of which objects they contain. In the special case where that assumption holds, we could dispense with the function σ, and need only consider a single permutation ϕ of the domain common to all possible worlds. This special case is, of course, covered by Theorem 2 as stated.

47 Each of the permutations ϕ_j could, of course, be defined to be the restriction to $\sigma(w_j)$ of a single permutation ϕ of the inclusive set D.

References and further reading

Works by Hilary Putnam

1975: The meaning of 'Meaning'. In Putnam's *Mind, Language and Reality: Philosophical Papers.* Vol. 2, Cambridge: Cambridge University Press.

1977: Models and reality. In Putnam (1983).

1978: *Meaning and the Moral Sciences.* Boston and London: Routledge and Kegan Paul.

1981a: *Reason, Truth and History.* Cambridge: Cambridge University Press.

1981b: Beyond historicism. In Putnam (1983).

1981c: Why there isn't a ready-made world. In Putnam (1983).

1983: *Realism and Reason: Philosophical Papers.* Vol. 3, Cambridge: Cambridge University Press.

1988: *Representation and Reality.* Cambridge, Mass.: Bradford/MIT Press.

1989: Model theory and the 'Factuality' of semantics. In Alexander George (ed.), *Reflections on Chomsky.* Oxford: Blackwell.

1990a: A defense of internal realism. In (1990b).

1990b: *Realism with a Human Face.* Cambridge, Mass.: Harvard University Press.

1992: *Renewing Philosophy.* Cambridge, Mass.: Harvard University Press (based on the Gifford Lectures given at St Andrews in 1990).

1994a: Simon Blackburn on internal realism. In Peter Clark and Bob Hale (eds), *Reading Putnam.* Oxford: Blackwell.

1994b: Sense, nonsense and the senses: an enquiry into the powers of the human mind. *Journal of Philosophy*, 91, 445–517 (based on the John Dewey Lectures given at Columbia University in 1994).

Works by other authors

Simon Blackburn 1994: Enchanting views. In Peter Clark and Bob Hale (eds), *Reading Putnam*. Oxford: Blackwell.

Paul Boghossian 1991: Naturalizing content. In B. Loewer and G. Rey (eds), *Meaning in Mind: Fodor and his Critics*. Oxford: Blackwell.

Anthony Brueckner 1984: Putnam's model-theoretic argument against metaphysical realism. *Analysis*, 44(3), 134–40.

Michael Devitt 1983: Realism and the renegade Putnam. *Noûs*, 17, 291–301.

Gareth Evans 1973: The causal theory of names. *Aristotelian Society Suppl. Vol.*, 47, 187–208.

Hartry Field 1972: Tarski's theory of truth. *Journal of Philosophy*, 69, 347–75.

Jerry Fodor 1990: *A Theory of Content*. Cambridge, Mass.: MIT Press.

Ian Hacking 1983: *Representing and Intervening*. Cambridge: Cambridge University Press.

David Lewis 1984: Putnam's paradox. *Australasian Journal of Philosophy*, 62(3), 221–36.

18

Sorites

R. M. SAINSBURY AND TIMOTHY WILLIAMSON

1 The early history

The logician Eubulides of Miletus, a contemporary of Aristotle, was famous for seven puzzles. One was the Liar: if a man says that he is lying, is he telling the truth? Another was the Hooded Man: how can you know your brother when you do not know that hooded man, who is in fact your brother? There were also the Bald Man and the Heap. In antiquity they were usually formulated as series of questions. Does one grain of wheat make a heap? Do two grains of wheat make a heap? Do ten thousand grains of wheat make a heap? If you admit that one grain does not make a heap, and are unwilling to make a fuss about the addition of any single grain, you are eventually forced to admit that ten thousand grains do not make a heap. Is a man with one hair on his head bald? Is a man with two hairs on his head bald? Is a man with ten thousand hairs on his head bald? If you admit that a man with one hair is bald, and are unwilling to make a fuss about the addition of any single hair, you are eventually forced to admit that a man with ten thousand hairs is bald. The standard ancient terms for the Heap and the Bald Man were "sorites" (from "soros", a heap) and "phalakros" respectively. Later, "sorites" was used for all such puzzles. They were also known as little-by-little arguments.[1]

Many philosophical doctrines have been suggested as the target Eubulides intended his Heap and Bald Man to destroy: the coherence of empirical concepts, the law of non-contradiction, the law of excluded middle, pluralism, Aristotle's theory of infinity or of the mean. The evidence gives little support to any of these suggestions. Eubulides is indeed said to have attacked Aristotle, but in slanderous terms; the sources do not connect the dispute with any of the puzzles. Aristotle betrays no clear awareness of sorites reasoning in any of his extant works. Some later commentators did consider its use against Aristotle's theory of the mean, but without suggesting that either Eubulides or Aristotle had done so. Eubulides' interests were described as purely logical; if he had a specific target in mind, it is likely to have been a logical one.

Sorites puzzles became a standard weapon of Sceptics in their attacks on Stoic philosophy. A Sceptic does not feel obliged to answer any of the sorites questions; he can simply plead ignorance. If a Stoic is obliged to answer each question "Yes" or "No", he will find himself in an embarrassing position. An obvious focus for Sceptical attack was the Stoic theory of knowledge. It was based on cognitive impressions, which represent real objects with complete accuracy and reliability (compare Descartes' clear and distinct ideas). The Sceptics constructed sorites series from cognitive to non-cognitive impressions, replacing each impression by a virtually indistinguishable one, and took themselves to have undermined Stoic claims to knowledge. Stoic defences against these attacks were mustered by Chrysippus (*c*.280–*c*.207 BCE), the man with the best claim to have initiated propositional logic.

The Stoics firmly accepted the principle of bivalence: every proposition is either true or false. Chrysippus "strained every nerve" to persuade people of it. For any proposition *P* there is one right answer to the question "*P*?", "Yes" or "No"; for any sequence of propositions $P_1, \ldots, P_n$ there is one sequence of right answers to the questions "P_1?", . . . ,"P_n?". The Stoics used "Are *i* few?" as the schematic form of the *i*th sorites question; thus the right answers to the first and last questions are "Yes" and "No" respectively, and there is a last question, "Are *i* few?" rightly answerable "Yes", immediately followed by a first question, "Are $i + 1$ few?" rightly answerable "No": *i* are few and $i + 1$ are not few; *i* is a cut-off point for fewness.

The Stoics distinguished between sentences and the propositions they are used to assert. The argument from bivalence to the existence of a cut-off point assumes that the sentences "One is few", . . . ,"Ten thousand are few" express propositions. However, someone who utters "*i* are few" with the sense "A man with *i* hairs on his head is bald" does assert something, which on the Stoic view requires the sentence to express a proposition. The assumption gave no escape from the argument for a cut-off point. Indeed, there is independent evidence that the Stoics accepted the conclusion of the argument. In other cases which look susceptible to sorites reasoning they insisted on cut-off points; for example, they denied that there are degrees of virtue, holding that one is either vicious or perfectly virtuous. An analogy was drawn with a drowning man as he rises to the surface; he is coming closer to not drowning, but he is not drowning to a lesser degree until he breaks the surface, when he is suddenly not drowning at all. Moreover, in rebutting the sorites argument against cognitive impressions, Chrysippus dealt explicitly with the case "when the last cognitive impression lies next to the first non-cognitive one": cognitiveness has a cut-off point. The Stoics were prepared to apply bivalence to sorites reasoning and swallow the consequences: any difficulty in answering the sorites questions must come from our ignorance of the right answers, not their non-existence. The puzzle is an epistemological one.

One might answer the questions "Is one few?", . . . "Are *i* few?", "Yes", and the questions "Are $i + 1$ few?", . . . "Are ten thousand few?", "No": but one would be guessing. No one has such knowledge of cut-off points; no one knows both that *i* are few and that $i + 1$ are not few. Such a pattern of answers is forbidden by the principle that one should give an answer only if one knows it to be correct. The wise man, the Stoic ideal, conformed to that principle. Since he was infallible rather than omniscient, he would sometimes suspend judgement. The Stoics did not claim to be wise men, still less to be omniscient; they readily admitted that they did not know whether the number of stars was odd or even and that they could not distinguish between very similar hairs or grains (the examples are ancient). Nevertheless, the aim was to avoid error by withholding assent from what one did not know.[2] The Stoic who did not know enough to be wise should suspend judgement more often than the wise man. That fits Chrysippus's recommended response to the sorites. At some point in the interrogation one should fall silent.

If sorites questions puzzled the Stoic simply because he did not always know whether to answer "Yes" or "No", like the question about the number of stars, he could confidently face the interrogation armed only with the three possible answers "Yes", "No" and "I don't know". If he knew *i* to be few he would answer "Yes"; if he knew *i* not to be few he would answer "No"; in every other case he would answer "I don't know". Why should an honest admission of ignorance not completely dissolve the puzzle?

However, Chrysippus did not say that one should admit ignorance; he said that one should fall silent. Under interrogation, saying "I don't know" is quite a different policy from saying nothing. The former but not the latter denies knowledge. This undermines the argument that the Stoic could answer each question "Yes", "No" or "I don't know".

The Stoic is supposed to say only what he knows to be correct. "I don't know" in answer to "Are *i* few?" is tantamount to the assertion "I don't know that *i* are few and I don't know that *i* are not few", just as "Yes" is tantamount to "*i* are few" and "No" to "*i* are not few". Thus the Stoic is supposed to answer "I don't know" only if he *knows* that he doesn't know whether *i* are few. The "Yes"/"No"/"Don't know" strategy requires the Stoic to answer "I don't know" whenever he doesn't know. It is therefore available, on Stoic terms, only if whenever one doesn't know whether *i* are few, one knows that one doesn't know whether *i* are few. For simplicity, one may be assumed to know a proposition just in case it is clear, where the logical consequences of what is clear are themselves clear. The prerequisite for the "Yes"/"No"/"Don't know" strategy is then that if *i* are neither clearly few nor clearly not few, *i* are clearly neither clearly few nor clearly not few. This is equivalent on Stoic terms to a pair of simpler principles:

(1a) If *i* are not clearly few, *i* are clearly not clearly few.
(1b) If *i* are not clearly not few, *i* are clearly not clearly not few.

Principles (1a) and (1b) are simply the relevant instances of the "S5" principle for clarity: if something is not clearly so, it is clearly not clearly so. Thus the "Yes"/"No"/"Don't know" strategy is available only if the S5 principle applies. However, the S5 principle is incorrect for clarity in such cases, for clear fewness is as sorites-susceptible as fewness. One is clearly few; ten thousand are not clearly few. By Stoic logic, there is a cut-off point for clear fewness: for some *i*, $i - 1$ are clearly few and *i* are not clearly few. Where that point comes is no clearer for clear fewness than for fewness. It is very slightly clearer that $i - 1$ are few than that *i* are few. But *i* are too close to being clearly few to be *clearly* not clearly few. One cannot reliably judge whether *i* are clearly few. In particular, one cannot answer the question "Are *i* clearly few?" just by following the policy: if you hesitate to say "Yes", say "No". If that policy worked, one would unhesitatingly judge that *i* were clearly few if and only if *i* were clearly few; whatever one thought was right would be right. But unless one is reasonably cautious, one will sometimes unhesitatingly judge that *i* are clearly few when they are not in fact clearly few (or even few). Most of us say silly things from time to time. On the other hand, if one is reasonably cautious, one will sometimes hesitate over what turns out to be genuinely clear, for fear of a hidden catch. Principle (1a) is false for some *i*. Principle (1b) fails similarly. Silence is the best policy.

When should the Stoic fall silent? Chrysippus seems to have advised that one should fall silent *before* the end of the clear cases. Stoic constraints may imply that one should sometimes give no answer to the sorites question "Are *i* few?" even though *i* are clearly few. If one answers "Yes" whenever that answer is clearly correct, on Stoic assumptions one stops answering "Yes" either when it ceases to be clearly correct or later. In the former case one has located the cut-off point for clarity with perfect accuracy; in the latter one has violated the constraint that all one's answers should be clearly correct. Given the failure of the S5 principle for clarity, one cannot reliably locate the cut-off point for clarity with perfect accuracy; thus one will reliably satisfy the constraint that one's answers should be clearly correct only if one stops answering "Yes" before it has ceased to be the clearly correct answer. One must undershoot in order to avoid the risk of overshooting.

The point generalizes. One would like to satisfy two conditions:

(2a) If "Yes" is a good answer, say "Yes".
(2b) If "Yes" isn't a good answer, don't say "Yes".

The goodness of an answer is some truth-related property of it, and does not simply consist in its being given. There is play between the antecedents and consequents of (2a) and (2b); in an imperfect world they will sometimes come apart. In such a case, one either fails to say "Yes" when "Yes" is a good answer, violating (2a), or says "Yes" when "Yes" is not a good answer, violating (2b). If one regards violations of (2a) and (2b) as equally serious, one may simply aim to say "Yes" when and only when it is a good answer. Other things being equal, one's misses are as likely to fall on one side of the target as on the other, and no matter. But one might regard a violation of (2b) as worse than a violation of (2a); one would rather commit an error of omission by not saying "Yes" when it is a good answer than one of commission by saying "Yes" when it is not a good answer. For example, one might prefer failing to make true or warranted statements to making false or unwarranted ones, and follow a policy of saying nothing when in doubt. One decreases the risk of more serious violations by increasing the risk of less serious ones. At the limit, the price of never violating (2b) is sometimes violating (2a). That is the choice the Stoic makes in falling silent before the end of the clear cases, where clarity is goodness. It was worse to say "Yes" in an unclear case than not to say it in a clear one. Those who take the opposite view should fall silent after the end of the clear cases. The Chrysippan strategy can be seen as resulting from two levels of precaution. At the first level, goodness in (2a) and (2b) is simply truth. The Stoics were not alone in holding it to be worse to give a false answer than to fail to give a true one. For truth, (2a) rather than (2b) is to be violated. This preference motivates the constraint that one should give an answer only if it is clear. But then clarity takes on a life of its own as a cognitive end, and again the Stoic takes the cautious option. Condition (2a) rather than (2b) is to be violated for clarity too.

The Sceptics were not satisfied with Chrysippus's silence; it was most notably attacked half a century after his death by Carneades. "For all I care you can snore, not just become quiescent. But what's the point? In time there'll be someone to wake you up and question you in the same fashion." Chrysippus was dialectically no better off than he would have been had he fallen asleep, and Carneades's attitude was that of a chess-player with what he takes to be a winning strategy, whose opponent simply refuses to make a move (in a game without time-limits).

Suspension of judgement was the Sceptical attitude, and Carneades fastened on the extent to which Chrysippus's strategy allowed it to spread. If Chrysippus suspended judgement in clear cases, on what basis did he object to the Sceptic's suspension of judgement? The question does not reduce the strategy to immediate incoherence, for some sort of reply is open to Chrysippus: do not suspend judgement when the case is clearly clear. Nevertheless, the Stoics were in a very delicate position. Their epistemological caution enlarged the concessions to Scepticism that their bivalent semantics forced them to make under sorites questioning. The concessions did not amount to surrender, for cases remained in which they could still claim knowledge; but these cases were marked off by a disputed no-man's-land rather than a compelling principle.

So far, the Heap and the Bald Man have been presented, as they usually were in antiquity, as series of questions, not as arguments with premises and conclusions. Yet one speaks of them as paradoxes, and a paradox may be defined as an apparently valid argument with apparently true premises and an apparently false conclusion. In argument form, the sorites goes like this:

Premise 1	1 is few
Premise 2	If 1 is few then 2 are few
Premise 3	If 2 are few then 3 are few
. . .	
Premise 10,000	If 9,999 are few then 10,000 are few
Conclusion	10,000 are few

The argument appears to be valid; if its premises are true, its conclusion will be true too. The relevant rule of inference is modus ponens (MP), which allows one to infer *Q* from *P* and "If *P* then *Q*"; its validity is hard to challenge. By MP, "1 is few" and "If 1 is few then 2 are few" entail "2 are few". In the same way, "2 are few" and "If 2 are few then 3 are few" entail "3 are few". After 9,999 applications of MP, one reaches the conclusion "10,000 are few". The premise "1 is few" is apparently true and the conclusion "10,000 are few" apparently false. The gradualness of the sorites series makes each of the conditional premises appear true. Thus the apparently valid argument has apparently true premises and an apparently false conclusion. At least one of these appearances is misleading, for the conclusion cannot be both true and false.

The argument is valid by the standards of orthodox modern logic. It is also valid by the standards of Stoic logic. Two logical principles are at stake. One is MP; it was the first indemonstrable (primitive) form of argument in Stoic logic: "If the first, then the second; but the first; therefore the second". The other is the "Cut" principle that valid arguments can be chained together: thus the valid argument from "1 is few" and "If 1 is few then 2 are few" to "2 are few" can be chained together with the valid argument from "2 are few" and "If 2 are few then 3 are few" to "3 are few", giving a valid argument from "1 is few", "If 1 is few then 2 are few" and "If 2 are few then 3 are few" to "3 are few". The relevant form of Cut was the third Stoic rule for the analysis of complex arguments: "If from two propositions a third is deduced and there are propositions from which one of the premises may be deduced, then the other premise together with these propositions will yield the conclusion".

On Stoic terms, the argument is valid, its first premise true and its conclusion false. Thus not all the conditional premises are true. By the Stoic principle of bivalence, at least one of them is false, despite appearances. At this point there is a complication. The truth and falsity conditions of conditionals were the subject of a fierce controversy that went back to Diodorus and his contemporary, Philo, and was taken up by the Stoics. Philo treated the conditional "If *P* then *Q*" as a truth-function of its components equivalent to "Not: *P* and not *Q*". In contrast, Diodorus held "If *P* then *Q*" to be at least as strong as "Not ever: *P* and not *Q*". Chrysippus went still further; for him, a conditional is true if and only if its antecedent is incompatible with the negation of its consequent. Thus "If *P* then *Q*" is equivalent to "Not possible: *P* and not *Q*". In modern terms, Philo's conditional is material implication, Chrysippus's is strict implication. Later Stoics tended to follow Chrysippus.

In the sorites argument, some conditional premise "If i are few then $i + 1$ are few" is supposed to be false. If the conditional is Chrysippan, it is false if and only if "i are few" is compatible with "$i + 1$ are not few". However, this conclusion looks banal; who thought them incompatible? Chrysippus might cheerfully allow that all the conditional premises, so taken, are false. To know the falsity of such a conditional is not to identify a cut-off point; it is merely to know that a certain point is not debarred from being the cut-off. For some modern philosophers, sorites puzzles arise because vague concepts are subject to tolerance principles which do rule out the possibility of cut-off points and "i are few" does threaten to be incompatible with "$i + 1$ are not few", making the Chrysippan conditional "If i are few then $i + 1$ are few" true.[3] But the Stoics did not take that view, and may not have regarded the argument with Chrysippan conditional premises as genuinely challenging.

The most challenging form of the sorites argument uses the Philonian conditional, for it is the weakest connective to obey MP, which is to say that it is the weakest conditional. If the conditional premises are true on any reading, they are true on this one. Since it was not the standard reading of the conditional, the Stoics had to formulate the premises explicitly as negated conjunctions to confront the argument in its most telling form. Just that was done in standard Stoic accounts.

Once the explicit conditional has been eliminated, MP can no longer be used, but Stoic logic still obliges. The sorites argument with negated conjunctions is valid, its first premise is true and its conclusion false. Thus some premise of the form "Not: i are few and $i + 1$ are not few" is false. By the falsity condition for the Philonian conditional, i are few and $i + 1$ are not few. Thus i is a sharp cut-off point for fewness. Since one cannot identify such a point, one is in no position to deny any of the premises; one can only suspend judgement. The challenge "Which premise is false?" is unfair, for one may be unable to find out even though one knows that at least one premise is false.

What is gained by presenting the sorites as an argument with premises and conclusion? Its logical structure was never the point at issue, for the argument is formally valid according to those whom it threatens, the Stoics, who used arguments with that structure themselves. As for the Sceptics, they could suspend judgement on its logical status; it was enough for their purposes that their opponents took such arguments to be valid. The logical structure provides a convenient way of laying out the problem, but so far nothing more.

It is tempting to argue for a dialectical structure behind the logical façade. One point is that the use of conditionals in the sorites argument is a distraction, since the sorites interrogation shows that one can set the puzzle going in a language whose only resources are "Yes", "No" and simple sentences (without logical connectives such as "if", "and" and "not") in the interrogative mood. Moreover, the argument has been persuasive so far not because its premises commanded assent, but because they forbade dissent. The problem was not that one could say "Not: i are few and $i + 1$ are not few", but that one could not say "i are few and $i + 1$ are not few". One is not presumed to believe the premises of the sorites argument. The point of the questions is to force one to take up attitudes for or against the individual propositions, for any pattern of such attitudes leads one into trouble. Since the premises of the sorites argument seem compelling only when one is interrogated on their components, the question form takes primacy.

The situation is transformed if the premises of the sorites argument can be given positive support. If they can, the argument form takes primacy: the question form leaves too much unsaid. What is more, Chrysippan silence is no longer an adequate response, for it does not undermine the positive support for the premises. Awareness of the need to provide that support is shown by Galen (AD *c*.129–*c*.199): "I know of nothing worse and more absurd than that the being and non-being of a heap is determined by a grain of corn." Chrysippus could not have suspended judgement on the general claim that one grain does not make the difference between a heap and a non-heap. He must deny it, for it contradicts the existence even of an unknown cut-off point. For him, the addition of one grain can turn a non-heap into a heap.

Galen's interest in sorites puzzles was connected with a long-running dispute between Empiricist and Dogmatic (one might say "Rationalist") Doctors. The Empiricist Doctors based their medical knowledge on inductive inferences, holding it to be reliable only if derived from sufficiently many observations; their opponents applied sorites reasoning against the notion "sufficiently many". The Empiricist

Doctors replied that the argument proved too much; if it destroyed the notion of sufficiently many observations, it would by parity of reasoning destroy much of the common sense on which all must rely. They gave the examples of a mountain, strong love, a row, a strong wind, a city, a wave, the open sea, a flock of sheep and a herd of cattle, the nation and the crowd, boyhood and adolescence, the seasons: none would exist if sorites reasoning were to be trusted. The Empiricist Doctors could reasonably claim to know that sorites arguments were unsound, without claiming to know exactly where the flaw lay. Even Chrysippus could not say which premise in negated conjunction form was false.

It was known that for every sorites series which proceeded by adding (as Eubulides' original series seem to have done), a reverse sorites series proceeded by subtracting. Thus examples tend to come in pairs of opposites: rich and poor, famous and obscure, many and few, great and small, long and short, broad and narrow. The awareness of reversibility no doubt helped to check the tendency to think of a sorites puzzle as showing its conclusion to be strange but true, for the conclusion of one sorites argument contradicts the first premise of the reverse argument.

There are also signs of a rather different Empiricist point. The sorites questioner is compared to someone who asks a shoemaker what last will shoe everyone: the question has no answer, for different feet require different lasts. The idea may be that the required number of observations depends on the circumstances of the particular case. There is no general answer to the question, "Are fifty observations enough?" The point has been repeated by modern philosophers, and is correct as far as it goes, but that is not very far; for the questions can be asked about a particular case, and the Empiricist still cannot plausibly claim to know all the answers. The same goes for heaps. Fifty grains may make a heap in one arrangement and not in another; but in any particular process of piling up grains one by one there will be a point at which the right answer to the question "Is this a heap?" is unknown.

As logic declined in later antiquity, so did interest in sorites puzzles. They formed no part of the medieval logic curriculum, perhaps because of their absence from the works of Aristotle. Their revival had to wait for what is usually seen as the corruption of logic in the Renaissance. Lorenzo Valla (1407–57) was one of the chief instigators of a shift from the formal rigour of scholastic logic to the more literary pursuit of humanist dialectic, and his preference for Cicero over Aristotle led him to Cicero's account of sorites arguments. Valla rejected them, on the grounds that even one grain makes some difference, in his original treatment of multiple syllogisms. Unfortunately, later writers did not develop his suggestions. Sorites puzzles were known as curiosities. Logic textbooks used the term "sorites" for all syllogisms with more than two premises. Stoic arguments do not count as multiple syllogisms, for they turn on the logic of propositional connectives such as "if" rather than quantifiers such as "all" and "some". The analogy with the original sense of "sorites" lies in the repetition of steps, but the textbooks did not associate sorites syllogisms with paradoxes in any way.

Leibniz knew of the Heap and the Bald Man. For him, unlike the Stoics, the ideas of heap and baldness exemplify indeterminacy: their limits, like those of colour ideas, have not been fixed. A borderline case is a matter of opinion, different opinions being equally good.[4] In one respect, Leibniz shared the view which has dominated twentieth-century discussions: that the ignorance associated with vagueness is not a matter merely of not knowing where the cut-off lies, but of there being nothing to know.

2 Recent approaches

In the first half of the twentieth century sorites paradoxes aroused little interest. An exception is Russell's 1923 article. He takes the paradoxes seriously, and responds as follows:

> [if a hairy man goes bald] it is argued [that] there must have been one hair the loss of which converted him into a bald man. This, of course, is absurd. . . . there are men of whom it is not true to say they must either be bald or not bald. The law of excluded middle is true when precise symbols are employed, but it is not true when symbols are vague. (pp. 85–6)[5]

More recently, sorites puzzles have been discussed in the form of apparently sound arguments with apparently false conclusions, and philosophers such as Dummett and Wright have advanced grounds for the premises. As noted earlier, this renders Chrysippan silence by itself an insufficient response: the grounds for the premises must be rebutted.

The recent tradition has largely ignored the epistemic view of vagueness, assuming, by contrast, that borderline cases, initially characterized as those where we do not know what to say in answer to a sorites question, are cases in which there is no fact of the matter to be known. Such a view cannot avoid commitment to indeterminacy at the semantic level: for some sentences there is no fact of the matter whether they are true, and for some predicates and some objects, no fact of the matter whether the former apply, or fail to apply, to the latter. So we will refer to the "no fact of the matter" conception of vagueness as the "semantic" conception. (The conception may be coupled with different views about the ontological status of the absence of determinate fact. On one view, once the semantics have been properly formulated, there is nothing more to be said; on another view, the semantic indeterminacy reflects some real indeterminacy in the non-linguistic world itself.)

Developing the semantic conception of vagueness requires abandoning classical semantics or logic. In the context of the rise in the current century of formal methods, it is not surprising that a number of non-classical systems have been designed to accommodate vagueness, semantically conceived; and we will shortly survey some of these theories.

First, however, we present three schemata of sorites-paradoxical arguments (§ 2.1). Secondly, we examine arguments which have been given for the truth of their premises or the falsehood of their conclusions (§ 2.2). Thirdly, we review some formal treatments of vagueness (§ 2.3); and fourthly, we remind the reader of the attractions of the epistemic view of vagueness, but also indicate a potential source of difficulty for the view (§ 2.4).

2.1 *Three forms of paradoxical arguments*

With no sand you cannot make a heap of sand; and if you have just one more grain, you cannot make a heap from what is not a heap. Hence there are no heaps of sand. The argument could be schematized so as to fit the standard pattern of argument by mathematical induction, with quantifiers ranging over the natural numbers and "x'" abbreviating "$x + 1$":

(A) $\varphi(0)$
$\forall x(\varphi x \rightarrow \varphi x')$ (QP)
$\overline{\forall x \varphi x}$

We refer to the quantified premise as QP. This schema yields the heap paradox itself if we replace "φx" by "a collection of x grains cannot make a heap no matter how it is arranged".

Imagine a painted wall hundreds of yards or hundreds of miles long. The left-hand region is clearly painted red, but there is a subtle gradation of shades, and the right-hand region is clearly yellow. The strip is covered by a small double window which exposes only a small section of the wall at any one time. It is moved progressively rightwards, in such a way that at each move after the initial position the left-hand segment of the window exposes just the area that was in the previous position exposed by the right-hand segment. The window is so small relative to the strip that in no position can you tell any difference in colour between what the two segments expose. After each move, you are asked to say whether what you see in the right-hand segment of the window is red. You must certainly answer "Yes" at first. At each subsequent move you can tell no difference between a region you have already called red and the one for which the new question arises. It seems that you must after every move call the next region red, and thus, absurdly, find yourself calling a clearly yellow region red.

This form of sorites can also be moulded to schema (A). One could stipulate that the successive positions of the right-hand segment of the window are numbered upwards from 0, and replace "φ" by ". . . numbers a red region". Equally, and with no difference of substance, we can regard the numerals as simply naming the successive regions, and replace "φ" simply by "red".

One does not need to argue by mathematical induction to have sorites paradoxes. We could, as we saw in § 1 (p. 462) write out, say, 10,000 singular conditionals instead of QP, and use modus ponens to derive the absurd result that a collection of 10,000 grains, however arranged, cannot make a heap. The schema is:

(B) $\varphi(0)$
$\varphi(0) \rightarrow \varphi(1)$

$$\begin{array}{l} \ldots \\ \underline{\varphi(9{,}999) \rightarrow \varphi(10{,}000)} \\ \varphi(10{,}000) \end{array}$$

We do not need to use either conditionals or quantifiers in the premises, for example:[6]

$$\text{(C)}\quad \begin{array}{l} \varphi(0) \\ \underline{\neg\, \varphi(10{,}000)\qquad\qquad} \\ \exists x(\varphi x \,\&\, \neg\, \varphi x') \quad \text{(QC)} \end{array}$$

An instance might be: A man with 0 hairs on his head is bald, and a man with 10,000 hairs on his head is not; therefore there is some number of hairs such that a man with that number of hairs is bald and a man with one more hair is not. The supposed absurdity is the derivation of the existence of a sharp boundary, represented by the quantified conclusion (QC).

In all cases, the arguments appear to be sound, yet they have what appear to be false conclusions.

The availability of these different formulations, and others we have not mentioned, puts constraints on what sort of solution is acceptable. A reasonable initial hope is that there is a single correct approach to all forms of sorites. If this hope can be fulfilled, it would be no good merely to argue, with schema (A) in mind, that the principle of mathematical induction does not hold for vague predicates, for this would not touch sorites arguments exemplifying schemata (B) and (C).[7] Equally, it would not do to suppose that one need only point out that by adopting an intuitionistic logic, one can deny the QP of (A) without thereby being committed to the seemingly unacceptable classical equivalent of its negation, $\exists x(\varphi x \,\&\, \neg\, \varphi x')$;[8] for paradoxical arguments modelled on the other schemata are not touched by this point.

2.2 *Arguments for the premises or against the conclusions*

We will consider two kinds of argument: (a) from the nature of observation; and (b) from the nature of vagueness.

2.2.1 Observational predicates

Perhaps one can always apply "red" or at least "looks red" correctly, under suitable circumstances, just by looking. If so, then if under such circumstances two things look the same, and the predicate is true of one, it is true of the other. With "red" or "looks red" inserted as before into the replacement for "φ", this line of thought justifies the conditional premises in schema (B), the QP in (A), and the negation of the conclusion of (C) (that is, not-QC). The conditionals would be justified by the fact that, given that adjacent regions on the wall look the same, the truth of an antecedent of the form "x is (or looks) red" would be enough for the truth of a consequent corresponding to "x' is (or looks) red". The QP of (A) would be justified by the fact that, given the same feature of the wall, "red" (or "looks red") must apply to both or neither of adjacent regions; and this would also establish the falsehood of the QC of (C).

Since the truth values of the atomic premises and conclusions are uncontroversial, this would take care of all that is controversial in showing that the arguments have true premises and false conclusions. If one takes this result at face value one must regard classical logic, and any other logic upon which arguments moulded on any of the schemata (A)–(C) are valid, as incorrect.

"Red" (or "looks red") is meant to be an example of a more general phenomenon: the "observationality" of certain predicates. Dummett suggests that an observational predicate is one "whose application is determined by mere observation" (1975, p. 261), and "can be decided merely by the application of our sense-organs" (p. 265). Dummett takes it to be a consequence of the observationality of a predicate like "red" that it is "governed by the principle that, if I cannot discern any difference between the colour of *a* and the colour of *b*, and I have characterized *a* as red, then I am bound to accept a characterization of *b* as red" (p. 264). The justification is that a predicate could not be applied simply on the basis of how things look, and so could not be observational, if an indistinguishable difference could determine the predicate's differential applicability.

To use this thought to ensure paradoxical truth-values for the elements of sorites arguments, we could define the observationality of φ as follows:

> if α satisfies φ and, under normal circumstances for observation for φ, β is indistinguishable from α, then β satisfies φ.

If adjacent members of a sorites series count as indistinguishable, this ensures that observational predicates are paradoxical. But it is questionable whether there are any non-trivial observational predicates, thus defined. Consider "looks red" as a strong candidate. Suppose that α and β are indistinguishable under, say, standard lighting conditions etc. Then one might argue: their indistinguishability entails that they look the same; so if α looks red, so does β; so the condition for "looks red" being observational is met. So there is at least one observational predicate.

The notion of indistinguishability is crucial to this argument, but it has not been adequately explained. To show the complexity, consider a case in which regions on the wall are exposed to a subject in a random order (the "random sorites"), and he is asked to say of each region whether it looks red. We then score the result by writing a "Y" beneath a region if the subject said "Yes" with respect to that region, an "N" if he said "No", and a "0" otherwise. What would the score of a perfectly rational subject look like, assuming conditions of observation to be normal for "looks red", and assuming that his eyesight and mastery of the predicate are both perfect? There will certainly be a "Y" beneath at least one of the left-hand regions, and an "N" beneath at least one of the right-hand regions; there will be no "0" to the left of a Y, and no "N" to the left of a "0". But there will certainly be a Y-region, call it α, which has a "0" or "N" adjacent to it and to its right, that is, at α'.

Given the assumptions about the rationality of the subject and the perfect conditions for observation, one might conclude that he has not made a mistake about how things looked to him, even though distinct rational subjects, and the same subject on different occasions, will draw the line in different places. This means that there is no mistake in supposing that α satisfies "looks red" and α' does not. We could infer that adjacent regions of the wall are not, after all, indistinguishable, for a rational subject, without error, made a distinction between them. In that case, we will be hard put to find sorites series with indistinguishable members, and so will be hard put to use the notion of observationality to justify the premises of arguments of types (A) and (B).

Alternatively, we might insist that the adjacent regions of the wall are indistinguishable (for example, because they look the same when co-presented), but then we must say that "looks red" does not satisfy the envisaged condition for being an observational predicate.

Either way, observationality has no impact on the sorites paradoxes.[9] This is what one would have predicted on the supposition that all sorites paradoxes should be accounted for in the same way, for there are many sorites-paradoxical predicates which have little claim to observationality, such as "child", "dog", "know" and "few". Even for those for which observationality is at issue, like "red" or even "heap", we can generate a sorites series in which the adjacent members are discriminable. Intuitively, a patch which differs only just discriminably from a red patch should count as red; and, as we saw, the paradox of the heap is quite impervious to the assumption that the various collections differ in size, in a potentially knowable way.

2.2.2 The nature of vagueness

The semantic conception of vagueness holds that it is of the nature of a vague predicate to draw no sharp boundary between the things to which it applies and those to which it does not. Arguably, this could be expressed precisely as the QP of schema (A), as the conditionals of schema (B), and as a denial of the QC of schema (C). So we have an argument for the paradoxical distributions based on a claim about the nature of vagueness.

Resisting this argument requires, from the perspective of the semantic conception, adjustments to classical logic or classical semantics or both. Perhaps one can persuade oneself that an adequate account of the nature of vagueness should not entail QP. We don't believe a tadpole can turn into a frog in a millisecond, but perhaps we can refrain from holding that it is in general true that anything which is a tadpole at a time is also a tadpole a millisecond later: we see too clearly where that belief would lead. So perhaps there is no immediate argument from the nature of vagueness to the truth-value distributions required to make arguments of type (A) paradoxical.[10] But there is a less immediate argument. Suppose we are happy to resist QP, that is, to hold that it is not true. Then the natural thing to say is that it is false; but this commits us to the truth of its negation, which is classically equivalent to QC: $\exists x(\varphi x \,\&\, \neg\, \varphi x')$. So we sever a direct connection between the nature of vagueness and the paradoxical truth-value distributions, only to force into view a less direct connection. Perhaps we could hold that QP is not true, yet not that it is false; perhaps this would be enough to avoid the unwelcome QC and also avoid the paradox-inducing QP. However, we would need an account of an appropriate non-classical semantics, and a justification for the specific treatment of QP.[11] The general moral, then, is that a semantic view of vagueness requires non-classical semantics and/or non-classical logic.

2.3 Alternative logics and semantics

On the semantic view, it would be desirable to be able to say that QP is not true without being forced to say that QC is true; and desirable to be able to say that at least one conditional from schema (B) fails, without having to say that one of them is false. (The envisaged conditionals are material, so a false one has a true antecedent and a false consequent.)

To do this one would have to abandon bivalence. There are two ways to proceed. We can use a bivalent metalanguage to describe a non-bivalent object language. Well-known examples are given in § 2.3.1 and § 2.3.2. Or we can use a non-bivalent metalanguage to describe our non-bivalent object-language. An example is sketched in § 2.3.3. On the first alternative, we can keep to classical conceptions of sets and models: vagueness is then tamed, described in essentially non-vague terms. On the second alternative, vagueness is never eliminated, never sharply described.

2.3.1 Supervaluations

If an expression is vague, we believe it could, in theory, be replaced by a more precise one. Thus we could replace the vague "child" by the more precise "minor" (meaning person who has not yet reached the day of his or her eighteenth birthday). Not every replacement would be acceptable: if "minor*" is defined as a person who has not yet reached the day of his or her fifth birthday, the word is nowhere near "child", since it would be clear that some children are not minors*. Equally, the expression "minor′ ", defined as a person who had not yet reached his or her thirtieth birthday, would be unacceptable, since it would be clear that some minors′ are not children.

An important line of thought about vagueness is that this notion of an acceptable way of making an expression more precise can be used to specify the meaning of a vague expression: its meaning will be given in terms of all the ways in which it could acceptably be made precise, where an acceptable way is one not precluded by the meaning it has. An acceptable way does not make the extension of the term too narrow, like that of "minor*", or too wide, like that of "minor′ ". A sentence containing a vague expression is to count as true, if it is true however that expression is made precise, and to count as false if it is false however that expression is made precise. This makes room for cases in which the sentence is true on some ways of making it precise, false on others; and, hence, in which it is neither true nor false.

In a classical model, a (unary) predicate is associated with a set of entities from the domain. Using the idea of the previous paragraph, we could associate a vague unary predicate with a range of sets, the sets corresponding to the acceptable ways in which it could be made precise.

This approach has been developed with formal elegance in a kind of model theory called supervaluation theory.[12] In addition to starting from an appealing conception of vagueness, it offers two further charms: it promises a precise description of a vague language; and it promises to preserve classical logic.

Let us think of a model, M, for a language, L, as an ordered pair $\langle D,F\rangle$ of a domain, D, and a family F of valuation functions, each mapping each unary predicate of L on to a subset of D and each name of L on to a member of D. (For simplicity, we will assume that all the non-logical symbols of L are either unary predicates or names.) Suppose that for some predicate, φ, of L, every member f of F meets these conditions:

> if x is in D and is definitely a satisfier of φ then x is in $f(\varphi)$.
> if x is in D and is definitely not a satisfier of φ then x is not in $f(\varphi)$.

Then we shall say that M is *appropriate* for φ. A model is appropriate for a language iff it is appropriate for all its expressions.[13] An appropriate model is *maximal* iff any addition to its family of valuations would render it inappropriate. Maximal models are supposed to represent the semantics of languages with vague predicates.

Within any model, truth-relative-to-a-member-f-of-F (abbreviation: truth$_f$) is defined in the usual classical way:

> $\ulcorner\varphi\alpha\urcorner$ is true$_f$ iff $f(\alpha)$ is in $f(\varphi)$;
> $\ulcorner A \,\&\, B\urcorner$ is true$_f$ iff $\ulcorner A\urcorner$ is true$_f$ and $\ulcorner B\urcorner$ is true$_f$;
> . . . and so on.
> $\ulcorner A\urcorner$ is false$_f$ iff $\ulcorner A\urcorner$ is not true$_f$.

Truth and falsity (relative to a model) are defined by generalizing over valuation-relativized truth: $\ulcorner A\urcorner$ is true in M iff $\ulcorner A\urcorner$ is true$_f$ for every f in F; $\ulcorner A\urcorner$ is false in M iff $\ulcorner A\urcorner$ is false$_f$ for every f in F. Truth and falsity are thus "supervaluations" relative to the basic bivalent valuations in F. This allows for borderline cases to induce a failure of bivalence in maximal models. Suppose that a member α of D is not definitely a satisfier of φ and also not definitely not a satisfier of φ. And suppose that M = $\langle D,F\rangle$ is maximal. This means that there is a member of F, say f_1, such that $f_1(\varphi)$ contains α, and a member of F, say f_2, such that $f_2(\varphi)$ does not contain α. So "$\varphi\alpha$" is true$_{f_1}$ and false$_{f_2}$. So "$\varphi\alpha$" is neither true nor false in this model.

Although supervaluation theory treats the object language as non-bivalent, the law of excluded middle is preserved, that is, the schema $\ulcorner A \vee \neg A\urcorner$ is valid. Consider the instance of it with φ and α as in the previous paragraph. It will be true$_f$ for every f, since for every valuation either $f(\alpha)$ is in $f(\varphi)$ or it is not, and in the first case the disjunction will be true$_f$ in virtue of the truth$_f$ of its first disjunct, and in the second case in virtue of the truth$_f$ of its second. In supervaluation theory, a disjunction can be true without either disjunct being true.

Validity can be defined as usual: an argument is valid iff every model in which all the premises are true is one in which the conclusion is true. The class of valid arguments thus defined is identical with the class of classically valid arguments.[14] Hence arguments following schemas (A), (B) and (C) are all supervaluationally valid; but sorites instances of schemas (A) and (B) are unsound. We will first show how this is so, and then consider what the supervaluational theory has to say about instances of (C).

By the definition of appropriateness, the valuations in an appropriate maximal model will place intuitively definite cases in the extension of any vague predicate, and exclude intuitively definite non-cases from its extension. For "heap", each f will associate the predicate with a set of collections (of grains of sand, say), where one collection is the smallest, and the set also contains all larger ones.[15] In other words, every f will associate the predicate with a sharp threshold, though, because of the predicate's vagueness, the different valuations will associate it with different thresholds. For any f in F, one conditional is false$_f$: the conditional which, for the line drawn by f, has an antecedent referring to an object on one side of the line and a consequent referring to an object on the other. Hence at least one conditional (typically, several conditionals) in the premises of schema (B) will fail to be true.

Similar facts ensure that QP in schema (A) is not merely not true, but false. The singular instances of QP are the conditionals which are the premises of (B). Since every f in F falsifies one of these conditionals, every f falsifies QP.

Many objections have been levelled at supervaluational theories. We list two.

The truth of QC

The supervaluational theory has it that instances of (C) are sound, and thus have a true conclusion, QC: $\exists x(\varphi x \;\&\; \neg\, \varphi x')$. If we find this hard to swallow, we are asked to remember that, in the presence of vagueness, quantifiers do not work in the normal classical way. In particular, using "satisfies" on the lines of "true", there is no sound inference from the truth of QC in the model to the conclusion that there is something in the domain of the model which satisfies "$\varphi x \;\&\; \neg\, \varphi x'$". The supervaluation theorist could claim that only the existence of such an object would amount to the existence of a sharp cut-off; so the truth of QC does not entail a sharp cut-off; so one is confused if one thinks that one wants to deny QC.

By itself, this is unlikely to be very persuasive. It seems plain that one can use our ordinary language to express absence of a cut-off, without having to ascend into the metalanguage, as this response supposes.

However, it is plausible that an object-language account of what it is for a predicate to be vague involves, at least in the first instance, the use of some expression representing definiteness, or, equivalently, vagueness. One wants to say, for example, that "red" is vague because there are things which are neither definitely red nor definitely not red; or that it is vague because there are things concerning which there is no fact of the matter whether they are red or not. More formally, we might say that any vague language could be expected to be capable of expressing its vagueness, perhaps by a sentence operator, "Def", expressing definiteness.[16]

The supervaluation theorist would do well to claim that something like this operator must be used in saying what we want to say about vague predicates and cut-offs: what we really want to say is that there is no *definite* cut-off point. This is properly expressed not by denying QC, but rather by denying "$\exists x$Def(φx & $\neg$ $\varphi x'$)". This means extending supervaluation theory to deal with "Def".

From a supervaluationist's point of view, "Def" should resemble an object-language expression of the notion of truth (by supervaluational lights).[17] Thus "Def A" should be true-on-a-valuation iff A is true (that is, true-on-every-valuation). This makes "Def" in some ways like "□" ("□A" is true-at-a-world iff "A" is true-at-every-world). In particular, taking the analogy in the most straightforward way, "Def" would eliminate vagueness: applied to any sentence, the result is one which is true on all or on no valuations.

However, there are two important points of disanalogy between "Def" and "□". First, if the supervaluationist retains the definition of validity as, in effect, necessary preservation of truth, he must agree that once "Def" is added to the object language, certain classical forms of reasoning (conditional proof, *reductio ad absurdum*, and *or*-elimination) cannot be allowed to be valid.[18] Secondly, if there is higher-order vagueness, then vagueness should not be eliminated by "Def".

Problems with higher-order vagueness

A supervaluational model is intended to divide the sentences of the language into three sets: the truths, the falsehoods and the remainder. There will be adjacent members, α and α', of a sorites series such that α is the last truth in the series and α' the first non-truth. But many find this unacceptable: they claim that there is no more a sharp boundary between the truths and the borderline cases than there is between the truths and the falsehoods.

The notion of a supervaluation is itself vague: it is defined in terms of an acceptable model, which is in turn defined in terms of what definitely falls under a predicate and what definitely does not. These notions admit of borderline cases: the reasons for saying that, for example, there is no fact of the matter whether certain colour patches are red support with no less strength the conclusion that there is no fact of the matter whether certain patches are *definitely* red. Equally, the reasons for thinking that there is no last region of the wall which counts as red support with no less strength the conclusion that there is no last region on the wall which is definitely red. If the conclusion is correct, there will be a valuation such that there is no fact of the matter whether or not it is appropriate.

One ensuing problem is that in an object-language in which there is higher-order vagueness, "Def A" is neither true nor false for some A; so the truth-conditions for "Def" cannot be given in the simple way envisaged earlier ("Def A" is true-on-a-valuation iff A is true). One response draws inspiration from possible-worlds semantics for modality: one would need to introduce an analogue of the accessibility relation, holding between valuations, and this would need to be reflexive (to validate "Def A$\rightarrow$ A") but not transitive (in order not to validate "Def A $\rightarrow$ DefDef A").

A deeper problem is that the supervaluationist's notion of truth as truth-on-all-appropriate-valuations must itself be vague. This means that a potential charm of supervaluation theory is lost: it cannot, after all, give a precise description of a vague language. It also raises the question whether the supervaluational concept of truth is correct. Many believe that truth must satisfy Tarski's disquotation schema:

(T) True (A) iff A.

But then, by reasoning which the supervaluationist endorses, it follows that if A is not true it is false.[19] The supervaluationist category of neither-true-nor-false sentences would vanish, and with it the basic idea of supervaluation theory.[20] So the supervaluationist must deny that his concept of truth is disquotational, and this raises the question whether it is, properly speaking, a concept of *truth* at all.

2.3.2 Degrees of truth

Not all borderline cases for a vague predicate are equal (or so it may reasonably seem). Two patches α and β might both be borderline cases of red, yet one redder than the other: one has a greater degree of redness. So one might be tempted by the following progression: it is closer to the truth to say that α is red than to say that β is red; so truer to say that α is red than to say that β is red; so "α is red" has a greater degree of truth than "β is red".

It is certainly an important feature of many vague predicates, and perhaps of all those which are sorites-susceptible, that the relevant cases are subject to an underlying comparative relation. However, this cannot be taken as any kind of knock-down argument for the existence of degrees of truth, for we have yet to distinguish between the relatively innocuous suggestion that some sentences are nearer to stating the (absolute) truth than others, and the controversial suggestion that some sentences are truer than others. We might make some progress towards the more exotic suggestion by reflecting on the following lines: truth is what one should aim at in belief, but for borderline cases the best you can aim at is degrees of belief; so we must be able to make sense of a notion of degrees of truth.

Whatever the philosophical motivation, semantics based upon degrees of truth have been claimed to dispel sorites paradoxes.[21] In the models $\mu = \langle\delta,\Phi\rangle$ which we now consider, δ is a domain of individuals, and Φ assigns to every name in the language a member of δ, and to each predicate, φ, a J-set, $\Phi(\varphi)$. A J-set is a mapping of members of δ into the real numbers in the closed interval [0,1]. Intuitively, the idea is that the number which is the value of the mapping for the member of δ which is the argument – the "J-value of $\Phi(\varphi)$ for δ" – represents the degree of truth, relative to assignment Φ, associated with affirming φ of that member. The value 1 represents an object to which the predicate definitely applies, the value 0 represents an object to which the predicate definitely does not apply, and the intermediate values represent intermediate cases. Writing $[P]_\Phi = n$ to express the fact that the sentence P is assigned the degree of truth n by function Φ, atomic sentences are assigned degrees of truth by rules like: $[\varphi\alpha]_\Phi$ is the J-value of $\Phi(\varphi)$ for argument $\Phi(\alpha)$. Appropriate models assign J-sets which reflect actual usage, that is, lead to assignments of degrees of truth to atomic sentences which both preserve our intuitive orderings (such as our ordering of how red the patches on the wall are) and conform to our intuitions about definite truths (assigned 1) and definite falsehoods (assigned 0).

The theories we discuss treat the logical constants as degree-functional: that is, the degree of truth of a complex is a function of the degrees of truth of the constituents. There are various possible functions. One standard approach is to stipulate as follows:

$$[\neg P] = 1 - [P]$$
$$[P \,\&\, Q] = \min \{[P],[Q]\}$$
$$[P \vee Q] = \max \{[P],[Q]\}$$
$$[P \rightarrow Q] = 1, \text{ if } [Q] \geq [P], = 1 - ([P] - [Q]) \text{ otherwise.}$$
$$[\forall v A v] = \text{glb}\{[A^a/v]\text{: for all a}\}$$
$$[\exists v A v] = \text{lub}\{[A^a/v]\text{: for all a}\}$$ [22]

The functions give the classical results if the arguments are restricted to 1 and 0. The specific idea behind the equation for $\neg$ is that there is no difference between departing from definite truth (that is, value 1) and approaching definite falsehood, and that predicates have paradigm borderline cases (such as α for φ) for which we want $[\varphi\alpha] = [\neg\,\varphi\alpha]$. The specific idea behind the equation for $\rightarrow$ is that a conditional should fall short of perfect truth to the extent that truth leaks away as between antecedent and consequent.

One standard account of validity within degree theory is based on a generalization of the notion of truth-preservation: a valid argument is one such that every model assigns a degree of truth to the conclusion no lower than that assigned to the lowest-valued premise. However, Edgington (1992) has argued that it would be better to give a different account, based on the idea that validity does not permit additional falsehood: a valid argument is one such that every model assigns a degree of falsehood to the conclusion which does not exceed the sum of the degrees of falsehood it assigns to the premises.

One impact of this view upon the sorites is that arguments of type (A) and type (B) will be seen as having at least one premise which is not entirely true. Thus the truth-values of the components of the conditionals of (B) progressively fall, and a conditional with a consequent less true than its antecedent will not be entirely true. For similar reasons, the QP of (A) is also not entirely true. Hence, on this approach, the impression that the sorites arguments are sound is, for these cases, supposedly dispelled by dispelling the appearance of (fully) true premises.

On the more common definition of degree-theoretic validity, generalizing from truth-preservation, none of the argument patterns we have discussed is valid. For example, type (B) is not, because *modus ponens* is, by this standard, not valid in degree theory. For suppose that $[P] = 0.9$, and $[Q] = 0.8$. Then $[P \rightarrow Q] = 0.9$. So an argument of the form:

$$P, P \rightarrow Q \therefore Q$$

has a lowest-valued premise of 0.9, and a conclusion valued 0.8.

Whichever definition of degree-theoretic validity one uses, arguments of type (C) are invalid, for the premises will have degree 1 and the conclusion a degree of around 0.5. So the apparent soundness of some versions of the sorites arguments is supposedly dispelled, through dispelling the appearance of validity.

However, the degree-theoretic account is open to various objections. We mention three.

It does not do justice to QC

In connection with (C), natural assumptions about the existential quantifier in degree theory have the result that QC does not come out as false (= 0) but only as midway true. A defence of degree theory would have to claim that what should really have degree 0 is not QC itself, but rather "$\exists x$Def(φx & $\neg$ $\varphi x'$)". The required extension of the theory to an object language containing "Def" is not straightforward. If the sentence just quoted is to receive degree 1, it would seem that [DefA] = 0 iff [A] < 1. This means that "Def" would eliminate vagueness, and thus would not allow for higher order vagueness.

Its logic is unintuitive and unmotivated

People have found the assignments of degrees to complexes unintuitive and unmotivated. For example, "$P \vee \neg P$" will be as true as "$P \& \neg P$" when $[P] = 0.5$. Similar unintuitive results are obtained when the sentences stand in non-formal logical relations. Thus suppose Eve is definitely female but a borderline case for being an adult, so that [Eve is an adult] and [Eve is a woman] are both 0.5. Degree theory cannot distinguish between "Eve is a woman if and only if Eve is an adult" and "Eve is a woman if and only if Eve is not an adult", assigning both 1.[23]

Even certain sentences which may be critically involved in some versions of sorites arguments are treated by this degree theory in an unintuitive way. Thus a classical equivalent of QP, "$(\forall x)\neg(\varphi x \& \neg \varphi x')$", will be assigned a value of about 0.5, whereas intuitively it ought to come out as nearly true.

It does not do justice to higher-order vagueness

The degree-theoretic property of having degree of truth 1 is supposed to correspond to some intuitive property (or else the formal semantics cannot connect with the informal judgements of truth and validity which underlie sorites paradoxes). Perhaps it is that of being true, or of being definitely true, or of being completely, definitely and unimpugnably true. Whatever property we choose, we have something unsatisfactory: since having degree 1 is a sharp property, the corresponding truth-related intuitive property must be sharp too. In any sorites series there is a last sentence having truth to degree 1; hence there is also a last sentence with the relevant truth-related intuitive property. But it is natural to suppose that there is no such sharp cut-off: whatever property we consider, true to a certain degree, absolutely true, definitely true or completely, definitely and unimpugnably true, there are no adjacent members of the sorites series one of which lacks, while the other possesses, this property.[24]

2.3.3 A non-bivalent metalanguage

It is hard to see how there could be a more accurate account of what you should aim to do, in using a vague word like "red", than that, if you want to keep to the truth, you should apply it just to red things. This suggests that we should look for a semantic theory which unashamedly uses vague vocabulary in the metalanguage. In particular, we wish to mention a theory recently proposed by Michael Tye (1994).[25]

His proposal is based on three semantic values: true, false and indefinite. The connectives are assigned values as follows: a negation is true iff its component is false, false iff its component is true, otherwise indefinite; a conjunction is true iff both components are, false iff one component is, otherwise indefinite. Universal quantifications are true iff all their instances are, false iff an instance is, otherwise indefinite. So the premises of sorites arguments of schemata (A) and (B) are indefinite, and not true. These argument-patterns are not sound.

Merely having three values is of no help in itself, once higher-order vagueness is admitted, as we saw in the case of supervaluation theory. For example, suppose that in a sorites series of sentences there is a last which is assigned truth. It makes no difference whether the next sentence is assigned falsehood or some other value: either way, we have a boundary where, according to many intuitions, no boundary should be. Tye deals with this by saying that there is no fact of the matter whether all sentences have one of the three truth values. Hence the claim that, for example, there is a last true sentence in a sorites series is vague, and not true. Once again, we would not have the making of soundness in sorites arguments. If this strategy works at all, it should work as well with just two truth-values, distributed in a similarly vague way.

To obtain truth conditions for atomic sentences, Tye associates a predicate with a vague set, a set concerning which there are things for which it is vague whether they are members of it. Thus the approach involves recognizing vague extralinguistic entities, which is controversial.

A problematic feature of his account is that indefiniteness in a component of a complex sentence can render the whole sentence indefinite regardless of its form. Thus "if *P* then *P*" is indefinite if *P* is, yet many find it compelling to regard it as true however things are with *P*. To take an example closer to the sorites, consider the reverse of QP:

RQP $\forall x(\varphi x' \rightarrow \varphi x)$

Applied to the wall, this says that if a region further to the right (towards the yellow end) is red, so is the adjacent region to the left; so it is intuitively true. But on Tye's semantics, it is not true, since the truth of a quantification requires the truth of its instances, and some of these conditionals will have indefinite components, and thus be themselves indefinite. Intuitively, however, RQP is true, and corresponds to what some would see as a constitutive principle: anything redder than a red thing is red.

It is not clear which features of Tye's account are essential. As we have mentioned, the third value could not be essential to dealing with the sorites (even if it is required for the best description of the use of language). It may be that the apparently implausible features can be removed, or shown not to be implausible after all. However, if higher-order vagueness is a genuine semantic phenomenon, there cannot be a precise semantic theory for a vague language. It is plausible to infer, as Tye in effect does, that in this case we must abandon a conception of semantics as making, for every sentence of a language, some definite pronouncement (such as that it is true, false or indefinite): there will have to be sentences for which there is no definite fact of the matter concerning what the semantic theory says about them, and this must be distinguished from the semantic theory saying that there is no definite fact of the matter concerning their semantic value. Thus Tye's approach requires semantic theories to be, in a sense, incomplete.

2.4 The epistemic view[26]

All these problems would be solved on the epistemic view, according to which there really are sharp cut-offs, though we cannot identify them. We cannot identify them because we do not have the required fineness of discrimination: we must allow for a margin of error in our cognitive mechanisms. If we know of a region of the wall that it is red, we could not know of its neighbour to the right that it is not red (even if in fact it is not red); for we could not reliably distinguish shades which differ so little.

Arguments of type (C) are seen as sound demonstrations of the epistemic view. Arguments of types (A) and (B) are valid on the view, and establish the falsehood of a premise by *reductio ad absurdum*. There is no problem about denying QP and accepting QC, and no problem about regarding one of the conditionals in type (B) arguments (though one does not know which) as having a true antecedent and false consequent. One can retain all the simplicity of classical logic and semantics.

The epistemic view thus has plenty to be said for it, yet it often evokes incredulity. Those who see any merit in the rule-following considerations advanced by Wittgenstein, and his denigration of the notion of imperceptible rails upon which the correct usage of language is supposed to run, are likely to be particularly hostile to the epistemic position. However, it is easier to identify generalized hostility than precisely formulated opposing arguments. In this section, we try to give voice to two connected objections.

There is no evidence that vague concepts induce sharp cut-offs

The point of this objection is to claim that the main reasons in favour of the epistemic view are quite general, like arguments of type (C), whereas what would be needed would be a detailed examination of how specific vague concepts actually work. The suggestion is that nothing in the details of how they work would ground the view that they are associated with sharp cut-offs.

However, at least for some vague concepts, close examination reveals some surprisingly rich cut-off determining principles. Consider that paradigm of vagueness, "heap".[27] A heap of φs must be heaped up, and this involves at least one φ stably above another, but not in virtue of glue-like attachment. Thus grains of sand spread out in such a way that no grain is on top of another cannot be a heap, however many grains there are. Moreover, gluing grains together in such a way that some grains are on top of others is not a way of making a heap. It seems to be of the essence of heaps that they are held together by gravity alone. The arrangement must also not be that of a stack: a dry stone wall is not a heap of stones. If we think of roundish things like grains of sand, it would appear that the smallest stable arrangement meeting these conditions requires four of them: three grains close together supporting a fourth on top. Here we arguably have a sharp cut-off. (The governing principles may well not determine the same cut-off for every shape of object.) An argument of this kind is at best suggestive, and it is always open to the conventional theorist to say that we were wrong in counting as vague some predicates for which such cut-off determining principles can be discovered. The conventional theorist may be on safest ground with colour predicates.

The epistemic view does not do justice to the fact that meaning supervenes upon use

"Meaning is use": that is, semantic facts concerning a language supervene on facts about the linguistic behaviour of masters of that language. Can the epistemic view do justice to this?

By "meaning supervenes on use" one might mean just that if two communities used a language in just the same way, then every sentence of the language would have the same meaning in both communities. By this standard, the epistemic theory of vagueness can certainly claim that meaning supervenes on use.

A much more stringent demand is that a theorist should provide explicit details of how meaning supervenes on use. Since no theorist of any kind (whether or not vagueness is at issue) has given any such detailed account, the fact that the epistemic theorist has not should not count against the theory.

However, the supervenience doctrine can be used to generate demands of a strength intermediate between the extremely weak and extremely strong demands of the previous two paragraphs. For there may be a priori principles relating to conditions under which supervenience is possible.

One proposed principle of this kind is verificationism. On the verificationist view, meaning can supervene upon use only through knowledge: a sentence cannot have a meaning such that it would be impossible for those who understand it to determine whether it is true or false. Since the epistemic view holds that it is impossible for us to know where the cut-offs come, the view is inconsistent with the verificationist constraint upon the supervenience relation. However, since verificationism, at least in the strong form envisaged, now has few supporters, it does not pose a serious threat to the epistemic view.

One does not have to be a verificationist to feel qualms about whether the epistemic view can do justice to the supervenience of meaning on use. For example, one might hold that if a predicate stands for a manifest property (one which under some conditions detectably obtains), then under optimal conditions for manifestation, if there is a fact of the matter whether or not it obtains, that fact is detectable. This is not full-blown verificationism, for it is consistent with there being properties which are not manifest, and consistent with it being impossible for us to detect even manifest properties, to the extent that it is impossible for us to bring about optimal conditions. Yet, it might be claimed, we can view a region of the coloured wall under optimal conditions without being able to detect the presence or absence of redness; and the view then delivers that there is no fact concerning whether the region is or is not red.

Clearly the epistemic theorist will take issue with this line of thought, challenging, among other things, what is taken for granted in the notion of optimal condition for manifestation.[28] Until these issues are clarified and resolved, some caution about the epistemic view is called for. However, we are not aware of any decisive refutation of it, and it would provide a breathtakingly simple solution to sorites paradoxes.[29]

Notes

1 The account of the sorites in antiquity draws heavily on Barnes (1982) and Burnyeat (1982). The most important ancient texts are translated in Long and Sedley (1987), vol. 1, 221–5. For more on the history of the sorites see Williamson (1994).

2 The Stoics were not sure that any wise men had lived; they may also have held that only a wise man would know anything at all. Nevertheless, knowledge was what the Stoics aimed at. The argument in the text could still be made with "justified true belief" in place of "knowledge".

3 See below, § 2.2.

4 *Nouveaux Essais*, III v 9 and III vi 27; see Wiggins (1980, p. 124).

5 It is now customary to distinguish between the Law of Excluded Middle, which requires the validity of the schema "Either *A* or not *A*", and the Principle of Bivalence, of which one formulation is that every sentence is true or false. (In § 2.3.1 below we describe a theory which preserves the Law while rejecting the Principle.) Russell is best understood as rejecting the latter.

6 For this formulation, see Rolf (1984, p. 220).

7 Cf. Dummett (1975, pp. 251–2). Kamp (1981, pp. 226–7) provides an independent reason for the same conclusion.

8 Cf. Putnam (1983); Read and Wright (1985); and Putnam (1985).

9 The reason offered here for this conclusion can be found in Wright (1987, p. 283, esp. n. 13), and Williamson (1990, pp. 88–103).

10 In particular, it is reasonable to suggest that our intuitions about vagueness are properly expressed only using some expression for definiteness. Cf. Wright (1987 and 1992).

11 We would, in particular, need an account which allowed that something not true can yield a falsehood, without itself being false.

12 This form of theory was systematically applied to vagueness by Dummett (1975), Fine (1975), Kamp (1975) and Lewis (1970). Fine traces the origins of the idea, as applied to vagueness, to Mehlberg (1958). The use of the expression "supervaluation" goes back to van Fraassen (1966), though he was concerned not with vagueness but with the semantic paradoxes. A glimmering of the idea is found in Russell's suggestion that

vagueness is a matter of a one-many relation between words and world (1923, p. 89). Supervaluation theory can be cast in a bivalent metalanguage, and this may have been part of the theory's appeal. However, it can also be cast in a non-bivalent language, as we in effect point out elsewhere (p. 474 and n. 18).

13 Complex predicates must be included, since an appropriate valuation must respect what Fine (1975) has called "penumbral connections" between predicates. Thus a valuation which ensures that "Eve is a female child" is true must also ensure that "Eve is a girl" is true, to respect the intuition that, definitely, nothing satisfies "x is a female child and not a girl". Vague names, if there are such things, could be treated just like vague predicates: different valuation functions within a model's family may assign them to different things. But for the moment it will be best to imagine that all assignment functions, or at least all appropriate ones, agree on what they assign to names.

14 If the envisaged definition of validity is retained, this depends upon the assumption that "Def" is not in the object language; see p. 474 and n. 18; and see Williamson (1994).

15 This makes the assumption that arrangement is held constant. It follows that if an n-membered collection is a heap, so is any collection with more than n members.

16 Thus Wright (1987 and 1992) suggests that the notion of there being no sharp boundary can be non-paradoxically expressed using such an operator, whereas removing it leads to immediate paradox.

17 This means that it can do something like the work done by the metalinguistic denial that there is something in the domain of the model which satisfies "φx & $\neg$ $\varphi x'$ ".

18 Cf Williamson (1994, pp. 147–53). For example, although one can validly infer "Def A" from "A", if validity is defined in terms of truth-preservation, this does not guarantee the validity of "If A then Def A": if for some model M, some valuation, f, "A" is true$_f$, and for some valuation, g, "A" is false$_g$, then the conditional is false$_f$ and so not true in M, so not valid. The supervaluationist might, therefore, prefer to exploit, in his account of validity, a different similarity with the classical definition. His idea is that questions of truth arise only relative to ways of making precise, and he extends this from atomic sentences to complex ones in terms of making the whole complex sentence precise. In this spirit, he might treat validity similarly, defining it in terms of making precise the whole argument. Then, the right thing to say would be that a valid argument is one for which every valuation verifying the premisses verifies the conclusion. (As sentence connectives are, in supervaluation theory, valuation-functional but not truth-functional, so with arguments.) It would seem that this would restore the classical character of supervaluational validity. (We are grateful to Dominic Hyde for discussion of this point.)

19

(1)	not True (A)	assumed
(2)	True (A) iff A	(T)
(3)	not A	from (1) and (2) by classical prop. logic
(4)	True (not A) iff not A	(T)
(5)	True (not A)	from (3) and (4) by classical prop. logic
(6)	False (A)	from (5), given that a negation is true iff what it negates is false

This argument will not be persuasive for those theorists who adopt some non-classical logics, e.g. those involving distinct notions of negation.

20 For discussions of the relation between supervaluation theory and higher-order vagueness, see Fine (1975, esp. § 5), and Williamson (1994, pp. 156–64). On higher-order vagueness more generally, see Heck (1993) and Wright (1992).

21 A classic formulation is Goguen's (1969).

22 "glb" and "lub" abbreviate "greatest lower bound" and "least upper bound" respectively. These are the infinitary analogues of min and max. "[A^a/v]" abbreviates "the result of replacing every occurrence of "*v*" in "A*v*" by some name not in "A*v*". Cf. Forbes (1985, p. 174).

23 Supervaluation theory, by contrast, treats the first as neither true nor false and the second as false. This is the problem Fine (1975) calls that of "penumbral connection", and he regards the way in which supervaluation theory handles it as an important merit of the theory.

24 Degrees of truth can be defined within the supervaluational approach: roughly, [σ] is the probability of σ being true on a randomly chosen sharpening. Cf. Lewis (1970), Kamp (1975), Edgington (1992), Williamson (1994, pp. 154–6). However, the two accounts differ on the proper treatment of the logical constants, and they have very different philosophical motivations.

25 See also Horgan (1993), who offers a different non-bivalent account in an article which came to our attention too late to be discussed here. We saw above that supervaluation theory could be modifed so as to allow that its concept of a sharpening is vague (and we mentioned that certain objections would still remain); so it could have featured in both the bivalent and non-bivalent categories of our taxonomy.

26 Early postwar versions of the theory can be found in Cargile (1969) and Campbell (1974). For more recent versions, see Williamson (1992), Sorensen (1988, pp. 217–52), Sperber and Wilson (1986) and Williamson (1994, pp. 185–247).

27 Cf . Hart (1991/2), though he does not embrace the epistemic view.

28 Cf. Williamson (1994, pp. 180–4).

29 We thank the Editors, Bob Hale and Crispin Wright, for helpful comments on an earlier draft.

References

Barnes, J. 1982: Medicine, experience and logic. In Barnes et al. (1982).

——Brunschwig, J., Burnyeat, M.F. and Schofield, M. (eds) 1982: *Science and Speculation*. Cambridge: Cambridge University Press.

Burnyeat, M.F. 1982: Gods and heaps. In Schofield and Nussbaum (1982).

——(ed.) 1983: *The Skeptical Tradition*. Berkeley, CA: University of California Press.

Campbell, R. 1974: The sorites paradox. *Philosophical Studies*, 26, 175–91.

Cargile, J. 1969: The sorites paradox. *British Journal for the Philosophy of Science*, 20, 193–202.

Dummett, M. 1975: Wang's paradox. Reprinted in his *Truth and Other Enigmas*. London: Duckworth, 1978, 248–68.

Edgington, D. 1992: Validity, uncertainty and vagueness. *Analysis*, 52, 193–204.

Fine, K. 1975: Vagueness, truth and logic. *Synthese*, 30, 265–300.

Forbes, G. 1985: *The Metaphysics of Modality*. Oxford: Oxford University Press.

van Fraassen, B. 1966: Singular terms, truth value gaps, and free logic. *Journal of Philosophy*, 53, 481–5.

Frede, M. 1983: Stoics and skeptics on clear and distinct impressions. In Burnyeat (1983).

Goguen, J.A. 1969: The logic of inexact concepts. *Synthese*, 19, 325–73.
Hart, W.D. 1991/2: Hat-tricks and heaps. *Philosophical Studies* (Dublin), 33, 1–24.
Heck, R.G. 1993: A note on the logic of (higher-order) vagueness. *Analysis*, 53, 201–8.
Horgan, T. 1993: Robust vagueness and the forced-march sorites paradox. In J. Tomberlin (ed.), *Philosophical Perspectives: Logic and Language*. Atascadero, CA: Ridgeview Publishing Company.
Kamp, J.A.W. 1975: Two theories about adjectives. In E. Keenan (ed.), *Formal Semantics of Natural Language*. Cambridge: Cambridge University Press, 123–55.
——1981: The paradox of the heap. In U. Mönnich (ed.), *Aspects of Philosophical Logic*. Dordrecht: Reidel, 225–77.
Lewis, D. 1970: General semantics. *Synthese*, 22, 18–67; reprinted in Lewis's *Philosophical Papers*, Vol. 1. Oxford: Oxford University Press, 1983.
Long, A.A. and Sedley, D.N. 1987: *The Hellenistic Philosophers*, 2 vols. Cambridge: Cambridge University Press.
Mehlberg, H. 1958: *The Reach of Science*. Toronto: Toronto University Press.
Putnam, H. 1983: Vagueness and alternative logic. *Erkenntnis*, 19, 297–314.
——1985: A quick Read is a wrong Wright. *Analysis*, 45, 203.
Read, S. and Wright, C. 1985: Hairier than Putnam thought. *Analysis*, 45, 56–8.
Rolf, B. 1984: Sorites, *Synthese*, 58, 219–50.
Russell, B. 1923: Vagueness. *Australasian Journal of Philosophy and Psychology*, 1, 84–92; reprinted in his *Collected Papers*, Vol. 9: ed. J. Slater. London: Unwin Hyman, 1988.
Sainsbury, R.M. 1990: Concepts without boundaries. Inaugual lecture published by King's College, London.
Schofield, M. and Nussbaum, M.C. (eds) 1982: *Language and Logos*. Cambridge: Cambridge University Press.
Sorensen, R.A. 1988: *Blindspots*. Oxford: Clarendon Press.
Sperber, D. and Wilson, D. 1986: *Relevance*. Oxford: Basil Blackwell.
Tye, M. 1994: Sorites paradoxes and the semantics of vagueness. In J. Tomberlin (ed.), *Philosophical Perspectives 8: Logic and Language*. Atascadero, CA: Ridgeview Publishing Company, 189–206.
Wiggins, D.R.P. 1980: *Sameness and Substance*. Oxford: Basil Blackwell.
Williamson, T. 1990: *Identity and Discrimination*. Oxford: Basil Blackwell.
——1992: Vagueness and ignorance. *Proceedings of the Aristotelian Society*, Suppl. Vol. 66, 145–62.
——1994: *Vagueness*. London: Routledge.
Wittgenstein, L. 1953: *Philosophical Investigations*. Oxford: Basil Blackwell.
Wright, C. 1987: Further reflections on the sorites paradox. *Philosophical Topics*, 15, 227–90.
——1992: Is higher order vagueness coherent? *Analysis*, 52, 129–39.

PART III

REFERENCE, IDENTITY AND NECESSITY

19

Modality

BOB HALE

1 Preliminary considerations: philosophical issues

1.1 *The importance of modal notions*

The notions of necessity and possibility, of what must be so and what may be so, and the derivative notion of contingency – of what is so but might be otherwise – are ones which very few philosophers find themselves able to do without. It is, to take one arguably fundamental case, hard to see how an adequate explanation of the notion of valid argument, as distinct from that of proof in a specified formal system, might run, save in terms of the idea that the conclusion *must* be true if the premisses are. Even those vigorously sceptical of modal notions seem unable to voice their scepticism without recourse to them. When Quine denies that there are any statements immune from empirical revision – any necessarily true statements, as he construes the notion – he is not claiming that any statement accepted at any time is one which we *will* at some time *in fact* reject; what he is denying is the existence of statements which we *could not* be led to reject. It is difficult to see how his scepticism about necessity could be so much as expressed without employing the notion of possibility. And once a notion of possibility has been granted house-room, the intelligibility of a correlative notion of necessity can hardly be denied. It thus appears that philosophical scepticism about necessity must, if it is not to fall into incoherence, take the form of denying the existence of truths having that character, rather than rejecting the notion altogether. That is not, of course, to deny that the notions of necessity and possibility stand in much need of elucidation; on the contrary, it is surely a central task of a philosophy of modality to provide an account of them.

1.2 *Relative and absolute modalities*

As a first step, we may usefully begin by drawing some distinctions among different notions of necessity and possibility. Probably the single most important distinction to be drawn is between *absolute* and *relative* kinds or senses. Roughly speaking, the distinction here is between a truth's being necessary outright or without qualification, and its being a necessary consequence of some pre-assigned collection of statements which are taken to be true, but not (necessarily or even typically) true by necessity. When philosophers speak of broadly logical necessity or (what is not to be assumed the same thing) metaphysical necessity, they intend an absolute sense of necessity; but when they speak of natural necessity, physical necessity, biological necessity and the like, it appears to be relative necessity that they have in mind. What is usually meant by saying that it is, say, physically necessary that P is that it follows from the laws of physics that P; saying that it is physically possible that P is saying that it is consistent with the laws of physics that P. Since the laws of physics – which need not, of course, be as we suppose them to be – are certain *true* propositions belonging to physics, a proposition cannot be physically necessary without being true; but unless the laws of physics are themselves held to be absolutely necessary, what is physically necessary will not normally be necessarily true in any absolute sense. Similar remarks apply to other relative notions, of course. Clearly, whenever we have a more or less definite body of propositions constituting a discipline D, there can be introduced a relative notion of necessity – expressible by 'It is D-ly necessary that' – according to which a proposition will be D-ly necessary just in case it is true and a consequence of D.

The modal verbs 'must' and 'may' are also commonly employed in *epistemic* senses, as when we say things like 'He must have got off the train at Oxenholme' (when we know that he was aboard when the train left Penrith and was not on it when it arrived at Lancaster) or 'The train may have been delayed.' Such uses may sometimes be correctly explained as involving relative notions – it being epistemically possible that P if it is consistent with what we know that P, and epistemically necessary that P if it follows from things we know that P.[1] But it seems clear that this is not right for all cases: when we assert that, for all we know, Goldbach's Conjecture may be true, but may equally be false, we are not claiming that neither the Conjecture nor its negation is deducible from number-theoretic propositions which we take ourselves to know, but making the far more modest claim that thus far no one has succeeded either in proving that every even number is the sum of two primes or in finding a counter-example.

The notion of consequence employed in characterizing any relative notion of necessity is that of broadly logical consequence. Since, if there are any statements at all that deserve to be regarded as logically necessary, statements recording the connection between the premisses and conclusion of a valid inference are surely among them,[2] our characterization of relative necessity assumes that some truths are broadly logically necessary. It is, however, hard to see how logical necessity itself can be other than an absolute notion. For logical truths to be merely relatively necessary, there would have to be some further truths of which they are (logical) consequences. But first: what could these truths be? Aren't logical truths precisely those which are consequences of the null set of premisses? And second: supposing there is a set K of truths of some other sort, of which logical truths are consequences, what are we to say of the conditionals 'If K then L' where L is any logical truth? How can these conditionals be other than logical truths which are absolutely necessary? It thus appears that, from a philosophical standpoint, it is the absolute notions that are fundamental. The various relative notions presuppose and are to be explained in terms of them, and it is on them that we shall concentrate here. Accordingly, all subsequent references to necessity and possibility are to absolute notions unless otherwise indicated. In addition, discussion will be largely concentrated upon necessity, though much of what is said will apply, with more or less obvious adjustments, to possibility.

1.3 *Comparability and strength of absolute modalities*

The foregoing remarks leave it open that there may be *more than one* absolute notion of necessity. If there *is* more than one – as would be the case, for example, if logical and metaphysical necessity are distinct notions and both are absolute – this gives rise to questions of comparability and relative strength. In saying that two notions of necessity – necessity_1 and necessity_2 – are comparable, I mean simply that either 'it is necessary_1 that A' entails 'it is necessary_2 that A' whatever statement A may be, or conversely. It is clearly a substantial claim that two notions of necessity are comparable. It is more often simply assumed rather than argued that logical necessity is the strongest kind. If attention is restricted to absolute notions and their comparability is assumed, it is hard to see how the common view could seriously be questioned. For if there is an absolute notion of necessity, necessity*, which is distinct from but comparable with logical necessity, either 'It is necessary* that P' entails 'It is logically necessary that P' or conversely. And likewise for the corresponding notions of possibility: either 'It is possible* that P' entails 'It is logically possible that P' or conversely. If necessity* is stronger than logical necessity, then possibility* is weaker than logical possiblity and so does not entail it. But since it is logically possible that P provided that P entails no contradiction, this can only be so if it is possible* for a contradiction to be true. The current vogue for 'true contradictions' notwithstanding, it seems to me that there is no good sense of 'possible' for which this holds. If comparability is not assumed, however, the claim that logical necessity is the strongest kind of necessity calls for further argument.

An argument to the purpose was put forward by Ian McFetridge in a posthumously published essay on logical necessity.[3] As his original argument involves some avoidable complications, I shall give my own version. If there is an absolute notion of necessity than which logical necessity is not stronger, there will likewise be a corresponding notion of possibility than which logical possibility is not weaker; and for this notion of possibility, it will hold that it is possible for the premiss of a valid argument to be true but its conclusion false.[4] Let us use '**Poss** A' to express that it is, in this sense, possible that A. We make the following five assumptions about entailment and '**Poss**' (I write $A \rightarrow B$ for 'A entails B', understood as meaning that there is a valid argument from A to B):

(A1) If $A \rightarrow B$ then $A \;\&\; C \rightarrow B$ and $C \;\&\; A \rightarrow B$
(A2) $A \rightarrow A$
(A3) If $A \rightarrow B$ and $A \rightarrow C$ then $A \rightarrow B \;\&\; C$
(A4) If **Poss** A and $A \rightarrow B$ then **Poss** B
(A5) $\neg$**Poss** $(A \;\&\; \neg A)$

On these assumptions, we can show that if A → B then ¬**Poss** (A & ¬B):

1	(1)	A → B	Assumption
2	(2)	**Poss** (A & ¬B)	Assumption
1	(3)	A & ¬B → B	(1) by A1
	(4)	¬B → ¬B	by A2
	(5)	A & ¬B → ¬B	(4) by A1
1	(6)	A & ¬B → B & ¬B	(3), (5) by A3
1,2	(7)	**Poss** (B & ¬B)	(2), (6) by A4
	(8)	¬**Poss** (B & ¬B)	by A5
1	(9)	¬**Poss** (A & ¬B)	(2), (7), (8) by *reductio ad absurdum*

Remember that **Poss** is any sense of 'possibly' conforming to A4 and A5, so that if our ancillary assumptions about entailment are correct, it follows that there is no such (absolute) sense of 'possibly' in which it is possible that the premiss of a valid argument should be true but its conclusion false. I do in fact hold all five assumptions to be met by entailment and any reasonable notion of possibility. Obviously anyone wishing to impose a quite strong relevance-constraint upon entailment will find A1 unacceptable; and para-consistent logicians will feel free to reject A5. It seems, nevertheless, to be a result of some interest and importance that, without assuming comparability, it can be shown from assumptions which, whilst not quite indisputable, are not grossly immodest, that logical necessity is the strongest absolute notion of necessity.[5]

1.4 The philosophical problem of necessity

What should a philosophical account of the (absolute) notion(s) of necessity accomplish? Michael Dummett provided what many ought to find an apt formulation of the task confronting us:

> The philosophical problem of necessity is twofold: what is its source, and how do we recognize it?[6]

As pinpointing what has been the preoccupation of much philosophical discussion of necessity, Dummett's formulation can scarcely be faulted. Plainly, however, Dummett's questions carry presuppositions which both can be, and actually have been, called into question. One is that there is indeed such a thing as necessity – that the notion of necessity has application. Another, which may still be questioned by one who grants the first presupposition, is that the notion has application in such a way as to give rise to a genuine epistemological problem: in effect, that there is a distinctive class of truths about what is necessary – truths of the form 'It is necessarily true that P' – concerning which it is to be enquired how we (can) know them.

The first presupposition will be the topic of the next section, and the second will be explored in the last two.

2 Quine's scepticism and reactions to it

2.1 *Quine's solution to the problem of necessity*

The burden of Quine's celebrated attack upon the 'first dogma' of empiricism is that there are no statements immune to revision in the face of recalcitrant experience, and so no statements which are analytic in the sense of holding true, come what may. Since Quine makes no distinction between the claim that a statement is analytic and the claim that it is necessary – holding, as he does, that the problem of making sense of the adverb 'necessarily' is one and the same with that of achieving a satisfactory explanation of 'analytic' – his attack is simultaneously one upon the notion of necessity, and his eventual denial that there are any statements which are true come what may is thus a denial that there are any necessary truths. He may thus be seen as rejecting both presuppositions of Dummett's formulation of the problem of necessity. Equally well, he may be seen as offering a negative solution to it. Earlier and contemporary empiricists, including the logical positivists,[7] had accepted that there are necessary truths, knowable a priori, and thus confronted Dummett's problem in spades: how to explain, compatibly with their central thesis that all genuine knowledge derives from sense-experience, first, how there could be such truths and second, how they could be known. Quine's solution was as dramatic as it was radical: there are no necessary truths, hence no satisfiable demand for an account of their source, nor for an explanation how they are known.

2.2 *Quine's scepticism finessed?*

It may well seem that if Quine is right then necessity is, to borrow some words from Hilary Putnam, yet another example of a subject without an object. And that it surely would be, if Quine were right in thinking that there are no statements that are true come what may; for what are necessary truths, if not that? Interestingly, Putnam himself argues, in the paper from which the words are borrowed,[8] that this conclusion is too swiftly drawn. We can grant that Quine's attack is entirely destructive of a certain 'epistemic' notion of necessity – the conception of a true statement as necessary iff not liable to rational revision – and yet still find application for another philosophically important, but non-epistemic, notion. What he has in mind is what many philosophers, following Kripke (and Putnam himself) have called *metaphysical* necessity.[9] The presently relevant point of this shift in thinking about necessity, as Putnam seems here to conceive it, is that it detaches the notion of necessity from that of being knowable a priori (which Putnam, like Quine, understands as requiring unrevisability). According to this way of thinking, it is metaphysically necessary, for example, that water is H_2O (that is, there is no possible world in which water exists but is not this compound of hydrogen and oxygen);[10] but this necessity is something we know – and can only know – a posteriori. And because the claim of necessity does not entrain apriority, it escapes Quine's attack.

Whatever may be said in favour of the notion of metaphysical necessity (or in favour of making space for the conception of necessities knowable only a posteriori), there is an obvious difficulty with this way of rescuing the topic of necessity from Quine's clutches. This emerges as soon as we reflect on how, in more detail, a posteriori necessities are supposed to be known. At least if we follow Kripke's own suggestion – and no-one, to my knowledge, has proposed anything better, or significantly different – our a posteriori knowledge that water is necessarily H_2O is the output of a *modus ponens*, applied to two other pieces of knowledge as premisses: that water is H_2O, and that if water has a certain chemical composition, it has that chemical composition of necessity (that is, its chemical nature is essential to it). On anyone's view, our knowledge of the minor premiss cannot but be a posteriori, and this is why our knowledge of the conclusion is so too. But in Kripke's view, the conditional major premiss is known by 'philosophical analysis'[11] – and is thus, presumably, a necessary truth, known a priori. If that is right, the possibility of a posteriori necessities rests squarely on the shoulders of a priori necessities; it therefore appears to be a complete illusion that Quine's attack on the latter has been finessed.[12]

2.3 More direct defences against Quine's challenge

It thus appears that if we are to take necessity seriously, we have no option but to confront Quine's challenge directly. Full discussion of this issue is beyond the scope of this chapter; but two possible lines of counter-attack may be briefly reviewed.[13]

First, it may be argued that Quine's own position – an uncompromisingly global empiricism in which all statements we accept have the status of empirical hypotheses, up for revision or retention in the light of experience, with the choice being guided by broadly pragmatic considerations[14] – is itself untenable as a direct consequence of his refusal to accord a priori status to any statements whatever. An argument to this general effect – which, so far as I know, has yet to receive an effective counter – has been advanced by Crispin Wright (1986). Wright's central claim is that Quine's position is ultimately unstable because viciously regressive. Among the statements which, in Quine's view, must be up for revision in any (dis)confirmation situation will be certain germane conditionals purporting to record the logical consequences of our currently accepted combination of empirical theory plus underlying logic. In other words, one option when we are confronted with some recalcitrant sequence of experiences will be to retain our threatened empirical theory along with its underlying logic, eliminating recalcitrance by way of rejecting the claim that their combination does, after all, have the troublesome consequences.[15] When, if ever, should we exercise this particular option? Well, presumably, when doing so results in the optimal balance between minimizing clashes with experience and maximizing simplicity and economy of overall theory. To arrive at a rational assessment on that matter, we must see how that option fares in comparison with the various others available. This will involve, *inter alia*, judgements about what the observational consequences are of the various options.

But these in turn will require deploying some hypotheses about the logical consequences attending implementation of the different options. With which hypotheses about their logical consequences should we work? Well, clearly we should work with the *best* such hypotheses. And we should decide what those are by applying Quine's pragmatic criteria; but it was precisely in the course of trying to apply those criteria that we were led to our present question. If we have not come full circle, then we have set off on a vicious infinite regress. If we are ever to be able to apply Quine's pragmatic guidelines some statements must be kept out of the pragmatic melting pot and treated as not being up for empirical revision. If not, then, as Wright in one place puts it, "the pragmatic methodology is drained of all directive content".[16]

Second, and independently of the preceding counter, a defender of necessity might preserve the linkage between it and apriority[17] by severing that (implicit in Quine and explicit in Putnam) between apriority and (absolute) unrevisability. There is no evident reason why we should take ourselves to be immune from error in the a priori detection of necessary truths; on the face of it, having a priori grounds for believing that P is one thing, and being infallible about the matter is another. (See Chapter 14, ANALYTICITY, section I for some further discussion of apriority.)

3 Modal realism 1: realism about possible worlds

As already remarked, it is a further presupposition of Dummett's formulation of the problem of necessity that necessary truths constitute a distinctive class of truths: that there are, in some sense, genuinely modal facts, not reducible to facts of any other kind. In this sense, Dummett's formulation presupposes a realistic attitude towards modality. And as also remarked, realism in this sense has not gone unchallenged. Opposition to it goes at least as far back as Hume, who denied that necessity is anything to be detected among the objects of knowledge, maintaining instead that it is nothing but the projection of our own sentiments or attitudes, themselves induced by patterns in our experience. Hume, of course, had causal or natural necessity in view. But some, following Hume's lead quite closely, have sought to extend his approach to modality in general.[18] Others have evinced less sympathy with Hume's projectivist explanation, but have endorsed the non-cognitivism about necessity on which it builds.[19]

We shall return to this line of anti-realist theorizing. I want first to discuss a different form the realism it opposes may assume which entails, but goes appreciably beyond, the comparatively modest variety just sketched, and which has been the focus of much recent discussion: realism about possible worlds.

3.1 Possible-world semantics

It comes very easily to us to express modal thoughts in the idiom of possible worlds. What is necessarily true is what holds true not only in the actual world, but in all other possible worlds as well; what is possibly true is what holds true in some possible world – perhaps the actual world, but perhaps some merely possible world.

These easy paraphrases form the starting-point of possible-world semantics for modal logics, first developed in the late fifties by Saul Kripke and others. Broadly speaking, an interpretation of an otherwise standard first-order language to which modal operators are added consists of a set, or domain, W, of possible worlds (with one of them, w_α, designated as the actual world) and a set, or domain, I, of individuals, together with functions which assign subsets I_w of I to the elements of W, elements of I to the individual constants (if any) of the language, and, relative to each element of W, subsets of I_w^n to the n-place predicates of the language. Under more or less obvious stipulations for dealing with connectives, quantifiers, and modal operators, we can then define what is required for a formula of the language to be true at a world w in W. A formula is true in the interpretation if true at w_α, and valid if true in all interpretations. In this setting, the condition for $\Box A$ to be true at w_α is that A be true at each w in W, while that for $\Diamond A$ to be true is that A be true at some w in W. A semantical account along these lines *may* be viewed as no more than an algebraic or model-theoretic device, in relation to which metalogical results about the soundness, completeness and so forth of a specified system of modal logic may be established (see Chapter 21, REFERENCE AND NECESSITY, section 2). From such a standpoint we are under no stronger pressure to take the informal accompanying patter about possible worlds as aspiring to literal truth than we are so to regard talk of truth-values intermediate between truth and falsehood as it occurs in the many-valued interpretations by means of which, say, independence results are established. If, however, we are disposed to view possible-world semantics as real semantics – that is, as furnishing genuinely illuminating statements of truth-conditions for modal sentences, and perhaps as forming the basis of explanatory accounts of other concepts, then, or so it seems, we must take the possible-world semantics as attempting, in Alvin Plantinga's memorable phrase, 'to spell out the sober metaphysical truth about modality':[20] we must take seriously the idea that modal statements are, in effect, to be construed as quantifications over a domain of real entities comprising possible worlds. No-one has defended such a realistic attitude towards possible worlds with greater ingenuity and resourcefulness than David Lewis. A full-scale discussion of his position lies well beyond the scope of the present chapter, which must settle for a brief and selective review of the main arguments advanced on either side, and of some of the alternatives to Lewis's uncompromising realism which have been canvassed.

3.2 Arguments for *realism about worlds*

The Paraphrase Argument

In an early defence of realism, Lewis gives some prominence to an argument which represents the central thesis of his realism – that there are possible worlds other than the one we happen to inhabit – as no more than an innocent paraphrase of a very general modal belief from which he expects no-one to dissent:

> It is uncontroversially true that things might have been otherwise than they are. . . . Ordinary language permits the paraphrase: there are many ways things could

> have been besides the way they actually are. On the face of it, this sentence is an existential quantification. It says that there are many entities of a certain description, to wit 'ways things could have been'. I believe that things could have been different in countless ways; I believe permissible paraphrases of what I believe; taking the paraphrase at its face value, I therefore believe in the existence of entities that might be called 'ways things could have been'. I prefer to call them 'possible worlds'.[21]

Given Lewis's insistence, equally prominent in this early discussion, and repeated in subsequent defences, that other possible worlds are (just) more things of the same kind as the actual world, it would seem to follow that the actual world is one of the ways things could have been – the way they are. This strongly suggests what might be called a Tractarian conception[22] of possible worlds, as collections, probably maximal, of possible states of affairs, the actual world being thought of as that collection of possible states of affairs, each of which is realized.

Whatever merit this argument might be thought to possess, it is clear that it can provide absolutely no support for the version of realism which predominates even in *Counterfactuals* (1973), and on which Lewis stabilizes in subsequent writings,[23] according to which worlds are spatio-temporally and (therefore) causally closed systems, typically largely populated by concrete entities of various kinds, the actual world being identified not as a certain collection of states of affairs, but with one particular such system of concrete (and probably also abstract) entities, comprising Lewis and all his surroundings.[24] It is to this rival conception that Lewis appeals (only paragraphs later than the one in which the quoted argument appears), in objecting to the view that (merely) possible worlds are maximally consistent sets of sentences:

> given that the actual world does not differ in kind from the rest, [this view] would lead to the conclusion that our actual world is a set of sentences. Since I cannot believe that I and all my surroundings are a set of sentences . . . I cannot believe that other worlds are sets of sentences either.[25]

Lewis is chary of saying outright whether worlds themselves are concrete entities, pending clarification of the abstract-concrete distinction; but he is confident that, if the distinction can be satisfactorily elucidated at all, it will not be found that the actual world falls on one side of the divide and other possible worlds on the other.

Arguments from explanatory virtue

It is hardly surprising that the Paraphrase Argument disappears from view in Lewis's later defences of his realism, as does the suggestion that realism involves no serious departure from 'common opinion'.[26] Argument of a quite different stripe comes to centre stage – argument broadly to the effect that realism about worlds should command our acceptance by dint of its distinctive explanatory advantages. These, in Lewis's view, are many, various and substantial. Fundamental, of course, must be the claim that by understanding ordinary modal claims as, in effect, quantifications over a domain of possible worlds, we gain an illuminating account of their truth-conditions. Building on this, it may be claimed that a satisfying explanation can be given of uncontroversial facts about validity and invalidity of modal inferences. A simple illustration is afforded by the patently invalid inference from $\Diamond P$ and $\Diamond Q$ to $\Diamond(P\&Q)$. When modal operators are construed as, in effect, quantifiers over a domain of possible worlds, this inference assumes the form: $\exists wP(w), \exists wQ(w) \vdash \exists w(P(w) \& Q(w))$, the invalidity of which is then readily recognizable as a special case of the generally invalid quantificational pattern: $\exists vA, \exists vB \vdash \exists v(A\&B)$. Likewise, the validity of $\Box P, \Box Q \vdash \Box(P\&Q)$ reappears as a special case of the quantificational validity $\forall vA, \forall vB \vdash \forall v(A \& B)$. Lewis is at pains to stress what he sees as the advantages of his realism as a source of good explanations of other philosophically important and perhaps otherwise problematic concepts, besides those involved in modal logic, narrowly conceived. A prominent example is the subjunctive or counterfactual conditional 'If it were the case that P, it would be the case that Q', whose truth-condition is, on Lewis's own account, that Q holds true at all those possible worlds most similar to the actual world at which P holds. Another is the analysis of propositions as sets of possible worlds, under which the proposition that P is identified with the set of possible worlds at which it is true that P. In general terms, the thought is that these and other explanatory advantages cannot be enjoyed without embracing realism about possible worlds themselves.[27]

3.3 Alternatives to and arguments against realism about worlds

There are two fairly obvious ways in which this kind of case for realism may be countered. First, it may be granted that possible-worlds apparatus does indeed bring distinctive explanatory advantages, but argued that these advantages can be enjoyed without engaging in the full-blooded realism about possible worlds which Lewis advocates. Second, it may be argued that the apparent explanatory advantages of possible-world semantics are illusory, because alternative explanations can be provided which make no essential play with possible worlds at all. We shall briefly review some of the main lines of thought which have been advanced under these two broad headings.

Under the first, one early reaction to Lewis's uncompromising or 'extreme' brand of realism was Robert Stalnaker's *moderate realism*. Stalnaker takes Lewis's 'extreme' realism to consist of four theses: in his own words, they are:

(1) Possible worlds exist
(2) Other possible worlds are things of the same sort as the actual world – "I and my surroundings"
(3) The indexical analysis of the adjective 'actual' is the correct analysis[28]
(4) Possible worlds cannot be reduced to something more basic

It is, Stalnaker claims, thesis (2) which 'gives realism about possible worlds its metaphysical bite, since it implies that possible worlds are not shadowy ways things could be, but concrete particulars, or at least entities which are made up of concrete particulars and events' – so that 'even a philosopher who had no qualms about abstract objects like numbers, properties, states and kinds might balk at this proliferation of full-blooded universes which seem less real to us only because we have never been there'.[29] His moderate realism results from rejecting thesis (2), whilst retaining the other three. Rejecting thesis (2) allows us to preserve the identification of the actual world with David Lewis and his surroundings, whilst viewing other possible worlds as no more than ways things might have been, and thus as things of a quite different kind from the actual world. Stalnaker is less than fully explicit on what precisely 'ways things might have been' are, but his view appears to be that they are properties (and so not collections of systems of concrete objects, such as the actual world is).[30] Since properties can be held to exist uninstantiated, this leaves us free to maintain that (merely) possible worlds exist; 'that there really are many ways that things could have been – while denying that there exists anything else that is like the actual world'.[31]

Whatever ontological advantage may be thought to attach to maintaining that merely possible worlds are entities of a radically different kind from the actual world, it has some awkward consequences, at least for anyone who wishes to regard possible-world semantics as providing an illuminating account of the truth-conditions of modal statements. An immediate difficulty arises over the interpretation of modal operators as quantifiers over possible worlds. Since merely possible worlds are to be thought of as properties, it follows that they cannot, as is usually supposed, be first-order quantifiers over objects, but must be (at least) second-order quantifiers over properties.[32] This might, by itself, be thought to render moderate realism a significantly less attractive option (and would, of course, be seen as fatal flaw by those who view higher-order quantification with no less suspicion than Lewisian worlds). But there is a more straightforward difficulty which is quite independent of any hostility towards higher-order quantification. If world quantifiers range over a homogeneous domain of properties, that domain cannot include the actual world; with the result that the semantics will fail to validate such obviously valid inferences as those from a proposition's necessary truth to its truth *simpliciter* (that is, truth in the actual world), and from its truth to its possible truth. This problem was first noticed, so far as I know, by Colin McGinn,[33] who suggests that Stalnaker's only way out is to distinguish between the actual world (now understood as the way things are) and the world (understood as Lewis and his surroundings). But this, McGinn suggests, is an unwelcome move, precisely because the appeal of moderate realism derives, in large part, from its contrast between merely possible worlds as ways things might have been and the actual world as a comprehensive collection of bits and pieces. This is perhaps a fair point against Stalnaker's actual position, but it is worth noticing that there is space for a somewhat different version of moderate realism which escapes the objection.

The difficulty is an immediate consequence of Stalnaker's rejection of thesis (2). But thesis (2), as he understands it, is really two quite independent theses:

(2a) Other possible worlds are things of the same sort as the actual world
(2b) The actual world is David Lewis and his surroundings

Both theses are essential to Lewis's full-blooded realism, and in consequence the rejection of either separately defines a more moderate position. Retention of (2b) coupled with rejection of (2a) – the option Stalnaker actually plumps for – is what leads to the problem just discussed. If, instead, we retain (2a) but reject (2b), the problem does not arise. On this position, every possible world is a way things might have been, the actual world being just that one among them which is the way things happen to be. Moderate realism of this kind can, in contrast with Lewis's, claim the support (for what that is worth) of his paraphrase argument for possible worlds. If ways things might have been are thought of as determined by maximally consistent sets of propositions, realism of this kind enjoins a broadly Tractarian conception of possible worlds and perhaps coincides with a position defended by some contributors to the debate.[34] It is arguably at a considerable advantage over Lewisian realism, since it is clear enough how, on this view, atomic propositions are guaranteed determinate truth-values at each possible world, whereas that is anything but clear, if the actual world consists merely of Lewis and his surroundings, and other worlds are likewise conceived as comprehensive collections of similar bits and pieces, at least unless proposition-like entities are smuggled in under the somewhat opaque heading of 'surroundings'. The view will, of course, have little appeal for those, such as Lewis and Stalnaker, who think propositions are best analysed as sets of possible worlds; but it is more than a little questionable whether that can withstand scrutiny.[35] It should, on the other hand, be congenial to those philosophers who, in broadly Fregean tradition, hold ontological questions to be best conceived as questions about truth and logical form. (See Chapter 12, REALISM AND ITS OPPOSITIONS, section 1.)

A more recent and, in some respects, more radical suggestion, aimed at securing the presumed advantages of construing modal operators as quantifiers over possible worlds at bargain price, is what Gideon Rosen calls *modal fictionalism*. On this proposal[36] we should prefix possible-world paraphrases of modal statements with a non-factive operator which suspends commitment to the possible worlds over which the statement to which it is prefixed quantifies. Much as prefixing 'According to Genesis 19: 26' to 'Lot's wife was turned into a pillar of salt' produces a compound statement which we may assert and believe without committing ourselves to the actual occurrence of the saline transformation of which the component purports to speak, so – the fictionalist proposes – we may seal off the unwanted ontological commitment carried by '$\exists wP^*(w)$' (the possible-worlds version of '$\Diamond P$') by prefixing it with 'According to PW, . . .', where 'PW' denotes some suitable version of possible-worlds theory (such as Lewis's).

It is far from beyond question that embedding possible-world paraphrases of modal statements really does leave us with a theory which enjoys all the supposed advantages of Lewisian realism.[37] Even prescinding from worries on that score, however, the proposal appears to fall foul of a simple dilemma. Observe first that regardless of whether he accepts the conditional 'If PW were true, it would be true that *A*' as a fully adequate explanation of what is meant by 'According to PW, *A*', the fictionalist can hardly deny that each entails the other; or, if he does, then pending an explanation of what he does mean by the latter there is no theory to discuss. The whole point of fictionalism is, of course, to keep open the option of accepting fictionalized versions of quantifications over possible worlds, whilst rejecting the modal realist's ontology, or at least going agnostic. For simplicity, let's suppose the fictionalist wants to go atheist. So he thinks that PW is false. So, does he think it's *contingently* false, or that it's *necessarily* false? If the latter, then he runs into trouble immediately – whatever modal statement P is, his replacement for its possible-world translation is going to be *vacuously* true, simply by virtue of the necessary falsehood of its antecedent. If, instead, he opts for the view that PW, though false, is no worse than contingently so, he must hold that PW might be (or might have been) true. The problem now is to see how this claim, that possibly PW is true, is to be understood. Obviously it cannot be understood in the fictionalist's *preferred* manner; replacing it by a fictionalist ersatz of the usual kind gives us: 'If PW were true, then there would be a world at which PW is true'. Since this is a direct consequence of 'If PW were true at the actual world, it would be true at the actual world', it would be true, as would the latter, even if PW was necessarily false. But then the paraphrase can scarcely be held to capture the content of the claim that PW is possibly true. However, if there is some *other* way to understand this particular modal claim, equally free of commitment to suspect ontology, then it is unclear why modal claims quite generally should not be understood in that way, with the upshot that fictionalization loses its point.[38]

Both of the proposed alternatives to Lewis's realism just discussed make one very important concession to it, namely that ordinary modal idioms are best understood in terms of quantification over possible worlds (though as noted, the fictionalist, at least, appears obliged to recognize a use of some modal idiom which cannot be reduced to such quantification). It is far from clear, however, that so much should be conceded. Several writers have advocated semantical accounts of modality on which modal adverbs are treated as what surface syntactical form suggests they are, that is, a species of sentential operator. These accounts typically take the form of showing how a truth-theory for an object-language including modal operators may be constructed in a metalanguage which itself contains either those same operators (in which case the relevant clauses can be homophonic) or counterparts which are direct translations of the object-language operators.[39]

Lewis has not, as far as I know, explicitly criticized this approach, but it is not hard to guess at his most likely response. In *Counterfactuals* he asks: 'If our modal idioms are not quantifiers over possible worlds, what else are they?', and takes it, apparently, that there are just three significantly different alternatives: (1) to take them as unanalysed primitives, (2) to interpret them as metalinguistic predicates, analysable in terms of consistency (for example, 'Possibly P' means that P is a consistent sentence), and finally (3) to take them as quantifiers, but ones ranging over a domain of some kind of *Ersatze*, such as maximally consistent sets of sentences. Options (2) and (3) fall, he thinks, to the objection that they simply give incorrect results unless 'consistent' is understood as 'possibly true', in which case the theory is circular; (1) he dismisses as 'not an alternative theory at all, but an abstinence from theorizing'.[40] The force of the circularity objection may be doubted, since we have no right to expect philosophically interesting notions always to admit of fully reductive analyses; and there is, in any case, some question whether Lewis is well-placed to press it, since he appears himself to have to rely upon an unanalysed notion of possible world. He might rejoin that whilst 'possible world' is indeed a primitive for him, the notion receives elucidation via its deployment in his theory in a manner akin to that in which it is commonly held that theoretical terms in natural scientific theories do. But this is unconvincing. Whatever its technical utility, possible-worlds theory holds out little promise of illuminating answers to the philosophical questions about necessity and possibility which exercise us: what is the source or ground of possibility, and how in general do we get to know about it?

3.4 Objections to Lewisian realism

A viable alternative to Lewis's realism, perhaps along one of the lines we have considered, which can match whatever explanatory virtues may legitimately be claimed for it would undermine Lewis's main argument for his position; but that would not, of course, constitute a direct argument against it (although some, keen to wield Occam's Razor, might see it as a strong indirect argument). There can be no doubt, however, that the principal spur to attempts to develop such an alternative has been the conviction that full-blooded realism should be avoided if at all possible. The sources of this conviction are many and various. We cannot review them all here, but will conclude this part of our discussion with an examination of one particular line of objection which several thinkers regard as the most important direct argument against Lewis's view, and which, together with Lewis's response to it, broaches questions bearing on wider issues in the philosophy of modality. This is the argument from epistemology. If, as in Lewis's view, we stand in no sort of causal, or other natural, relations with possible worlds other than our own, or with their inhabitants, how can we possibly have knowledge, or even well-grounded beliefs, about them? And if the truth-conditions of ordinary modal propositions are as the modal realist maintains – that is, if they are most perspicuously set forth by paraphrasing them as quantifications over possible worlds – is not the disastrous effect of modal realism that modal knowledge and well-grounded modal belief are rendered impossible?

If it were, in every case, a necessary condition for X to know that P that X's belief that P should be caused by (or stand in some other suitably causal relation with) the fact that P, then the objection would be decisive. It thus appears that the modal realist must deny that knowledge is invariably subject to such a causal constraint.[41] And his position will be the more plausible if he can furnish independent ground for doing so. Lewis contends that mathematical knowledge affords the desired precedent for rejecting a fully general causal requirement. The causal epistemologist's objection to modal realism runs parallel, he claims, to Benacerraf's celebrated dilemma for mathematical knowledge which rests upon the idea that there is a head-on collision between the demands of a broadly causal conception of knowledge on the one hand, and on the other, any account of the truth-conditions of mathematical propositions which has them speaking of causally inert mathematical objects (numbers, sets and so on). It is clear, Lewis thinks, how we should respond to Benacerraf's problem: 'our knowledge of mathematics is ever so much more secure than our knowledge of the epistemology that seeks to cast doubt on mathematics', so it is the latter which must go – 'Causal accounts of knowledge are all very well in their place, but if they are put forward as *general* theories, then mathematics refutes them.'[42]

It would be a perfectly fair objection to Lewis's response as it stands that it simply conflates mathematics with a certain philosophical account of it, according to which the surface syntax of ordinary mathematical statements is to be accepted at face value, with the consequence that numerals and many other mathematical expressions are to be regarded as genuine singular terms, having reference among abstract objects of various kinds. It is the latter, not the former, which is (supposedly) put in doubt by the causal epistemologist's objection. But waive that: even if the case were soundly made that mathematical knowledge should not be seen as demanding causal connections between knowers and what they know, it might still be objected that there is a crucial difference between this case and modality as the modal realist conceives it. Lewis recognizes this: the mathematical objects of which we have knowledge, for all our lack of causal acquaintance with them, are *abstract*, whereas other possible worlds and their occupants are, as Lewis conceives them, no less *concrete* than this world and its occupants. There is, then, space for the counter that it is precisely and only because mathematical entities are abstract that we should not expect mathematical knowledge to satisfy a causal condition, so that the suggested precedent is not enough to get the modal realist off the epistemological hook.[43] Lewis's response is, in effect, that this mis-identifies what it is about the mathematical case that warrants suspension of causal requirements on knowledge.

> causal acquaintance is required for some sorts of knowledge but not for others. However, the department of knowledge that requires causal acquaintance is not demarcated by its concrete subject matter. It is demarcated instead by its contingency. . . . [Perception and] other channels of causal acquaintance set up patterns of causal dependence whereby we can know what is going on around us. But nothing can depend counterfactually on non-contingent matters.

Among the non-contingent matters are what mathematical objects there are, and likewise, what possibilities there are. And this is why the imposition of a causal constraint is inappropriate in both cases alike.[44]

Even if Lewis's claim about how the area within which imposition of a causal constraint upon knowledge should be demarcated is correct, and even if, further, his main argument for realism from its alleged explanatory advantages is successful in its own terms, there would still be room to question whether he has done enough to see off the epistemological challenge. He would have done so only if the latter argument justifies us in taking claims about what possible worlds there are, and what they are like, to report non-contingent matters, and it is far from evident that it does so. It might, to be sure, be held that statements about what is necessary or what is possible (at least, when broadly logical modality is in question) are themselves, if true at all, necessarily so (as in the modal logic S5). But again, that is not enough for Lewis; the issue concerns the modal status not of ordinary modal claims themselves, but of their construals as quantifications over possible worlds as Lewis understands them. Even if it is allowed that an argument to best explanation may warrant taking such claims to be true, it is hard to see how it could justify us in taking them to be *necessarily* true.

Lewis's claim that what marks off the area within which knowledge should satisfy a causal constraint is not concreteness but contingency is plausible, and coheres with a plausible explanation why the line should be drawn where Lewis proposes to draw it. Satisfaction of a causal constraint is to be looked for just when there can, but need not, be a significant co-variation between our beliefs and the facts which confer truth or falsehood upon them. Since non-contingent matters are precisely ones which could not have been otherwise, any counterfactual conditional hypothesizing the falsehood of a non-contingent (that is, a necessary) truth must be vacuously true, whatever its consequent says, for example about what we would then have believed. But then there can be no significant co-variation between the non-contingent facts and our beliefs about them, so there is no sense in requiring that they stand in an appropriate causal relation.

Though plausible, the claim is not beyond question. Indeed, if Kripke and those who follow him are right in their claim that there are necessities – such as that water is H_2O and that heat is mean kinetic energy – which can be known only a posteriori, then it appears to be mistaken. Such apparent counter-examples might be explained away by maintaining that a different notion of necessity is involved in them, but it is not easy to see independent grounds for supposing that to be so. A more plausible reaction would be to modify the principle of demarcation to something along these lines: causal constraints upon knowledge are inappropriate when we are concerned with necessities known, or knowable, a priori. But that suggests that the initial emphasis on non-contingency as such was misplaced, and that the important contrast here is not between necessity and contingency, but between a priori and a posteriori knowledge. That is, it is a truth's being known independently of experience (however that notoriously problematic notion is precisely to be characterized) that renders inappropriate the demand that our knowledge of it should satisfy a causal constraint.[45] It might be suggested that from this improved perspective, Lewis's arguments from explanatory virtue would, other things being equal,[46] be better suited to their purpose than our preceding remarks suggest. There is, it might be claimed, no evident reason in principle why the explanatory virtues of a realistic attitude towards possible worlds should not lie in its underpinning independently plausible analyses of counterfactuals, propositions and other a priori matters. But this sanguine response overlooks a crucial distinction: it may be that there could be a successful argument from explanatory virtue for something which is in fact knowable a priori; but it obviously fails to follow from this, and is anything but clearly true, that such an argument could itself provide us with a priori knowledge.

We have thus far followed Lewis's own discussion of the charge that his position is epistemologically bankrupt largely in presupposing that it will be based upon a causal constraint on knowledge. But it may well seem that his position is in epistemological trouble even if a causalist – or more generally, naturalistic – view of knowledge is *not* assumed. Other worlds, in Lewis's view, are composed of concrete entities possessed of properties and standing in relations to one another of the same general kind as the concrete entities in our world (the actual world). If another world contains knowing subjects anything like us, these subjects know of the doings and undergoings of things in their world much as we know of such things in ours. But because of their utter causal isolation from us, we cannot possibly know of those other worldly goings-on in anything like the ways they are supposed to do, and we must be supposed to know of them in some radically different way. But then whatever account may be proposed, it seems that a yawning chasm is bound to open up between the truth-conditions of ordinary modal statements (as Lewis conceives them) and our knowledge; nothing in the character of our knowledge could in any discernible way reflect the nature of the states of affairs which confer truth upon the propositions known.[47]

It might be replied that the objection misdescribes the propositional objects of our modal knowledge as they are best conceived on Lewis's view. There would indeed be a serious, and perhaps insurmountable, difficulty if our modal knowledge had to consist, or be grounded at a fundamental level, in knowledge of the doings and undergoings *of particular identifiable objects existing in other worlds* – at least on the plausible assumptions that such knowledge would require identifying reference to, or thought of, those objects, and that, in case of concrete objects, no such identifying thought is possible that does not depend, ultimately, on the obtaining of causal or other natural relations between thinker and object. But Lewis's view need not take this shape: what we know, when we know that Possibly P or that Necessarily Q, is, in his view, a *general* proposition: that there is a world having such-and-such a character, or that all worlds satisfy a certain general description. This would be no help, of course, if our knowledge of such general truths had to be grounded in anterior knowledge of truths concerning particular worlds, as would be so if our knowledge that there is a world in which things are thus and so had to derive by existential generalization from the knowledge that things are that way in w_{17}, and our knowledge that in all worlds such-and-such had to be obtained by (ordinary) inductive inference from knowledge of how things are in some finite selection of worlds. It follows immediately that our modal knowledge, as Lewis conceives it, cannot be like our knowledge that there are cities in the UK with more than two million inhabitants, or other-worlders' knowledge of similar truths concerning their own world. But this is a point he might readily accept: there are other instances – which for present purposes may be regarded as uncontentious – in which our knowledge of general truths is not of that kind. The obvious examples are afforded by mathematics where, on a classical view at least, we may come to know general truths of both kinds by non-constructive methods, such as proof by *reductio ad absurdum*. The parallel with mathematical knowledge is, once again, one to which Lewis himself appeals in this context:

> In the mathematical case, . . . we come by our opinions largely by reasoning from general principles that we already accept; sometimes in a precise and rigorous way, sometimes in a more informal fashion, as when we reject arbitrary-seeming limits on the plenitude of the mathematical universe. I suppose the answer in the modal case is similar. I think our everyday modal opinions are, in large measure, consequences of the principle of recombination[48] . . . One could imagine reasoning rigorously from a precise formulation of it, but in fact our reasoning is more likely to take the form of imaginative experiments. We try to think how duplicates of things already accepted as possible . . . might be arranged to fit the description of an alleged possibility. Having imagined various arrangements – not in complete detail, of course – we consider how they might aptly be described.[49]

As a rough account of the phenomenology of ordinary modal thinking, this is scarcely open to dispute. But anyone who was troubled by the appearance of an uncomfortable gulf between, on the one side, any credible story about how we might get to know, or justifiably believe, propositions about what is possible or necessary, and on the other, their Lewisian truth-conditions, is liable to feel short-changed. The idea that the possibility of unicorns, for example, consists in there being some other possible world in which concrete horse-like entities have concrete horn-like appendages plays no essential part in the plausible part of Lewis's story about the exercise of imagination in tandem with his combinatorial principle. That is an account which anyone could offer, without commitment to realism about worlds, to which that realism is at best a gratuitous addition – at best: the case is arguably worse, since it is hard to see how the imaginative exercises which Lewis plausibly identifies as the source of our modal beliefs could possibly equip us with adequate reasons for those beliefs, if they really carried the ontological commitments he ascribes to them.

4 Modal realism 2: the non-cognitivist challenge

We have not tried finally to resolve the issue of realism about possible worlds. For all the heat – and comparatively little light – it has generated, it is, in a fairly clear sense, something of a distraction from the leading questions identified in 1.4. The sense in which those questions presuppose a realist conception of modality appears not to be Lewis's, but a more modest one; what is at issue is, rather, the existence of a genuine class of truths essentially involving modal notions. Or, to put the question another way, does a correct claim of the form 'Necessarily P' state a fact over and above the fact that P? Several recent writers, some of them more or less explicitly following a line of thought suggested by Wittgenstein's remarks on necessity in his *Remarks on the Foundations of Mathematics*, are united in advocating a negative answer to this question, whilst differing both in the considerations they adduce in its support and in their positive accounts of the role or function of necessitated judgements.[50] The principal consequence of the negative thesis is that, when we assert it to be necessary that P, we are not making any claim (over and above the plain claim that P) concerning which there arises any question about how we know it to be true. I shall, accordingly, use the term 'non-cognitivism' to denote the shared negative thesis.

Philosophical doctrines to the effect that the sentences belonging to a given region of discourse do not – syntactical and other appearances to the contrary notwithstanding – genuinely subserve the recording or misrecording of an appropriately corresponding range of facts have, of course, enjoyed a good deal of popularity, especially among philosophers of broadly empiricist sympathies. The obvious examples are sentences used to voice moral and aesthetic judgements. Faced with the more or less manifest inadequacy of attempts to construe such sentences as having naturalistically statable truth-conditions, and the apparently intractable problem of seeing how we might acquire moral or aesthetic knowledge by anything remotely resembling the methods with which – prescinding from radically sceptical doubts – we feel comfortable in other territory, and unwilling to postulate a special realm of 'queer' facts and a suitably attuned, special mode of cognitive access to match, the option can readily appear attractive of supposing that moral and aesthetic talk is not, after all, descriptive and aimed at tracking moral or aesthetic fact, but is best understood in some other way – as expressive of our own moral and aesthetic responses, say, or aimed at influencing the responses and actions of others. While it is clear that they could not be decisive, there is no doubt that similar considerations may play[51] their part in motivating non-cognitivist thinking about modality. We find the same distrust of irreducibly modal fact, and the position derives a good part of its attraction from the perceived inadequacy of attempts to provide a credible epistemology.

One line of thinking here focuses on the role of imagination in the genesis of modal opinion. Very often, we are moved to judge that things *must* be thus and so by the seeming unimaginability or inconceivability of the opposite. Confronted – to take what is arguably a fundamental kind of case – with what qualifies, by ordinary criteria, as a valid deductive inference, and finding ourselves unable to conceive how the premiss could be true without the conclusion being so as well, we move, without much ado, to the belief that we are faced with a necessity. It is hardly surprising that non-cognitivists tend to look askance at this move, the relations between conceivability and possibility and their opposites having long been a matter of philosophical controversy. The non-cognitivist will grant the facts about what we can and can't imagine, and will assure us that he has not the slightest tendency to doubt that if the premiss is true, the conclusion is true as well; but he will protest that he cannot see how that justifies a belief that the conclusion *must* be true, if the premiss is. The limit of our imagination may well have a part to play in explaining our confidence in certain judgements, but it is just another fact about us: what reason is there to see in it a reliable indication not merely of their truth, but of their *necessary* truth?[52]

It seems clear that the cognitivist should concede right away that the step to necessity from our inability to conceive the opposite is problematic, if only because, in general, our being unable to do something may, so far, be properly explained either in terms of some limitation from which we perhaps contingently suffer, or in terms of impossibility inherent in the task, which our inability merely reflects. But that is not to concede that it is merely a confused and broken-backed attempt to inflate facts about our imaginative limitations into objective necessities. If the move is thought of as supplying our basis for thinking that there are such things as necessities at all, and is supposed to yield infallible access to them, then it surely is hopeless. But the cognitivist need not be committed to the implausible claim that we are equipped with an infallible method of detecting necessary truths. And he can insist that we should separate the question of our grounds for holding that there are necessary truths to be appreciated concerning some matter, from the question of how we may be justified in taking some particular proposition to be necessary. It is, for example, one thing to hold that if a number is prime, it is necessarily so, and another to hold, of some particular number, that it is necessarily prime; calculation may provide us with grounds for the latter opinion, but support of quite different kind is needed for the former. If the cognitivist can sustain the distinction in general, and can make the case that there are necessities to be discerned, then he may argue that our inability to imagine things being otherwise can be taken as a fallible, defeasible ground for belief in the necessity in particular cases. These are, of course, very big 'ifs'. The present point is simply that, pending some demonstration that they cannot be discharged, considerations of the kind just rehearsed are bound to be inconclusive, and need not dislodge a determined cognitivist.[53]

Progress on the present issue seems unlikely in the absence of some general, agreed criteria for discriminating between cases in which statements concern some genuinely factual matter – in which correctness is properly seen as consisting in conformity with some range of independently constituted facts, which our opinions, as thereby expressed, may be regarded as in some sense tracking – and cases in which this is not so. A proposal very much to the purpose has been elaborated and defended by Crispin Wright, originally in his book on Wittgenstein's philosophy of mathematics (1980), subsequently in his paper 'Inventing Logical Necessity' (1986), and most recently in his Waynflete Lectures, *Truth and Objectivity* (1992). The general idea underlying Wright's proposal is that statements of a given class are properly viewed as (mis)recording genuine matters of fact – or better, as potentially representing objects of knowledge or at least rationally justifiable opinion – only if there are, a priori, certain kinds of limitation on the possibility of intelligible but unresolved disagreement over their truth-values. (See Chapter 12, REALISM AND ITS OPPOSITIONS, section 5.) Roughly, the thought is that where A is a statement of the kind in question, such disagreement is intelligible only if traceable to the operation of what can be regarded as a cognitive shortcoming in at least one of the parties to it. Besides omitting important refinements, this way of putting it is, of course, objectionably circular. Here is a more careful formulation, taken from the 1986 paper mentioned above:

> Statements of a certain class are apt for the expression of genuine matters of fact only if there are contexts – in which vagueness, or permissible differences in evidence thresholds, are not to the point – in which it is *a priori* that differences in opinion concerning one of the relevant statements can be fully explained only by disclosing . . . some material ignorance, error, or prejudice on the part of some or all of the protagonists.[54]

How, assuming its approximate correctness, does this criterion bear on our present question? It may at first appear that, in contrast, for example, with claims about what is funny or boring, where we are happy enough, on occasion, to write off differences of opinion as due simply to diverging tastes or interests, its application would favour the *cognitivist* about modal matters rather than his opponent. But, as Wright argues, matters are not so straightforward. Can we not conceive of a supremely cautious thinker who agrees with the rest of us on all relevant non-modal matters, but consistently balks at the point where we are disposed to judge something to be not just true in fact, but necessarily so? Suppose, then, that we find ourselves locked in apparently intractable disagreement with such a character over, say, the *necessity* of the conditional corresponding to some simple deductive inference, the *correctness* of which is agreed on both sides. Neither party, it seems, is under any misapprehension of the exact character of the formal transition in question, and both, it seems, are competent in the use of the logical vocabulary involved. Is it a priori that the persistence of our disagreement must, sooner or later, succumb to explanation which convicts him, or us, of some germane ignorance, error or prejudicial assessment of the data? If not, then the non-cognitivist may claim victory. And since the intelligibility of such a disagreement appears not to depend on anything special to our chosen case, it appears that our cautious individual will be at the service of the non-cognitivist in all cases in which we are disposed to think ourselves confronted with a necessary truth.[55]

Actually, that final move, to a globally cautious stance on necessity, is very much open to question. If the argument which Wright himself develops against Quine's global empiricism (sketched in § 2.3) is good, it establishes that there is no coherent epistemology which does not acknowledge some judgements – centrally, judgements about what a given empirical theory *plus* logic entails – as a priori. And if that is so, the question arises of how the possibility of acquiring reason to believe such judgements a priori is to be explained. But then, as Wright himself puts it, "What better basis on which to found a satisfactory account of the possibility of arriving at certain truths by pure thought than on the notion that they hold true in all thinkable circumstances?" (that is, that the truths in question are necessary). It thus appears that there are, after all, reasons to doubt that a globally cautious stance is fully intelligible without supposing its adherent guilty of some cognitive shortcoming: either a failure to acknowledge an indispensable distinction between a priori and empirical methods of appraisal, or a failure to appreciate that this distinction issues from the necessity of some judgements and the contingency of others.[56]

Even if the case just sketched can be made secure, however, cognitivist celebrations would be premature. For on reflection, it seems that an effective case for non-cognitivism might be made *without* relying upon the dubious possibility of *global* caution. The anti-Quinean argument against the intelligibility of a globally cautious attitude does nothing to establish the unintelligibilty of caution in any particular case. Why wouldn't the intelligibility of *local* caution, provided it can strike anywhere, suffice for the non-cognitivist's dialectical purposes? To put the thought another way, why shouldn't the destructive work that was to be done by a single, globally cautious thinker be distributed across a suitably large team of selectively cautious thinkers, each willing to affirm necessity in some cases, while remaining resolutely cautious in others?[57]

There are at least two reasons to doubt that this ingenious twist can accomplish what the non-cognitivist seeks. First, any puzzlement we may have felt about the intelligibility of the globally cautious attitude in relation to particular cases is liable to be compounded by the supposition that caution in selected cases is now coupled with normality (that is, absence of this peculiarly philosophical distaste for modalizing) in others. Are we to suppose, for example, that confronted with *some* valid inferences, our selectively cautious man has no compunction in agreeing that their premisses necessitate their conclusions, and yet in *other* cases, simply refuses point-blank to do so, yet without having anything to say in explanation of his peculiar pattern of necessitated judgements? This begins to seem really unintelligible. If, on the other hand, there is some method in his apparent madness, there ought to be something to be said about the principles that inform his selective judgements; and we may suspect that when it is said, we shall be able to locate some material disagreement on other, non-modal, matters. This difficulty is, clearly, special to the hypothesis of selective caution; the second, which could as well have been raised in relation to global caution, concerns whether cognitively blameless caution really is a fully intelligible attitude in every case. Suppose, for instance, that the cautious man is invited to pronounce upon an explicit formulation of the Law of Non-Contradiction, and responds thus:

> Hm. I am not sure that this is something that I can form a competent opinion about just by reflection. I cannot, I grant, recall any actual example of a statement which was true simultaneously with its negation. And I must confess to some difficulty when I try to be clear about how such a thing might occur. I suspect that it never does occur. Nevertheless, I do not see that this can be a matter for adjudication by a priori methods alone.[58]

As Wright observes, this stance is not intelligible. The reason why not is that its intelligibility would require the cautious man to believe that some further process is needed to establish the falsehood of the negation of a proposition, even after the truth of the original proposition had been established – much as, having calculated the value of $10{,}987 + 3{,}733$, a further process is needed to determine whether it is the same as or distinct from that of 174×80. And that, Wright points out, is absurd: "negation is given as a function on truth-value . . . To suppose that the truth-value of not-P may present an a priori open question when that of P has been settled is merely to display a failure to grasp that negation is, constitutively, a *truth-function*."

If this is right, then there are at least some cases in which caution is simply not an option at all, and is therefore unavailable as means of enforcing a non-cognitivist view of necessity. Clearly crucial questions remain, which we cannot pursue here. So far, it may seem that the non-cognitivist has merely to give up one strategy, but that his position might yet be secured by other arguments. But the damage would be greater, if Wright's criterion could be taken as embodying an acceptable sufficient condition for a statement's enjoying genuinely factual status. For it would then be hard to see how non-cognitivism about a given range of necessitated judgements could be sustained without upholding the intelligibility of the cautious attitude (or something not materially different from it) in those cases. So two pressing questions are: Does Wright's criterion (or some near relative) embody an acceptable *necessary* condition of factuality? and: If so, does it also give an acceptable *sufficient* condition? A third question, which sets the agenda for anyone who hopes to defend affirmative answers to the last two, and is encouraged by the argument of the preceding paragraph, is: How far can considerations of the kind adduced in support of the claim that caution about the a priori/necessary status of the Law of Non-Contradiction is incoherent be duplicated in other putative cases of necessary truth?[59,60]

Notes

1 Since state of information varies from thinker to thinker and time to time, the precise import of such epistemic uses of modal idioms would involve also some relativity to context.

2 See, for example, McFetridge (1990, p. 136).

3 McFetridge (1990, pp. 138–9).

4 Note that this does *not* amount to assuming comparability with logical necessity and possibility.

5 This argument, and its further significance, are discussed in Hale (1996).

6 Dummett (1959, p. 169).

7 Cf. Ayer (1946, ch. 4).

8 Putnam (1983, p. 51).

9 Cf. Putnam (1983, p. 53):

> There is, however, a very different way in which one can try to save the subject of 'necessity' from Quine's attack. Quine, following the logical positivists, assumed that if there was any such thing as 'necessity' then it was either semantical (e.g. 'analyticity') or epistemic ('*apriority*'). To Saul Kripke is due the honor of introducing into the discussion a very different kind of necessity, an objective non-epistemic kind of necessity: *metaphysical necessity*. Or so he called it.

10 Putnam goes on to express some reservations about the strong claim that water is H_2O in all possible worlds, suggesting that 'the "essence" that physics discovers is better thought of as a sort of *paradigm* that other applications of the concept . . . must *resemble* than as a necessary and sufficient condition good in all possible worlds' (1983, p. 64); but he does not see this as undermining the response to Quine's attack.

11 Cf. Kripke (1971, p. 153).

12 It should perhaps be stressed that the point here is purely *epistemological* – that a posteriori knowledge of (metaphysical) necessities depends upon a priori knowledge of what are, presumably, conceptual necessities. It does not appear to require the claim that metaphysical necessity can be *analysed* in terms of conceptual necessity – though of course, if such an analysis could be provided it would supply an independent reason against Putnam's proposal. Alan Sidelle (1989) tries to explain how, compatibly with the view that all necessity derives from conventions, there can be a posteriori necessities such as that water is H_2O. His general idea is that such metaphysical necessities are grounded in 'general principles of individuation' which record analytic, conventionally grounded necessities. An example of the latter would be 'If water has a certain chemical composition, it has that chemical composition necessarily'. Sidelle explicitly distances himself from the logical empiricists' thesis that all necessity is analytic, and appears not to view his general principles as providing the basis for an analysis of metaphysical in terms of analytic necessity. Just as well, since the necessity operator governing the consequent in such principles can hardly be regarded as expressing analytic necessity. We cannot here pursue the question of whether he succeeds in developing a viable alternative which does not simply boil down to the Kripkean explanation of how a posteriori necessities may be known. If he does, that would provide a third reason why Quine's attack on a priori necessity cannot be finessed by Putnam's proposal.

13 For a fuller discussion of the issue, see Chapter 14, ANALYTICITY. A third, and very interesting, attempt to prove that we cannot dispense with the idea that some statements are logically necessary may be found in McFetridge (1990, pp. 153ff.).

14 Roughly, strike the best balance between minimizing 'recalcitrance' (clashes between our total set of accepted statements and experience) and maximizing overall simplicity and economy to theory.

15 Note that this is *not* the option of tinkering with the underlying logic.

16 Wright (1989, p. 222).

17 Perhaps with the exception of the special case of a posteriori *necessities* concerning natural kinds, etc.

18 Cf. Blackburn (1984, pp. 210–17 and 1987), Craig (1985).

19 Cf. Wright (1980, ch. 23 and 1986).

20 Plantinga (1974, p. 125).

21 Lewis (1973, p. 84).

22 Cf. Wittgenstein (1921) 1.1: 'The world is the totality of facts, not of things.'

23 Cf. especially 1986, ch. 1.

24 The lack of fit between the paraphrase argument and Lewis's prevailing conception of worlds is noted by Haack (1977) and Richards (1975).

25 Lewis (1973, p. 86). The objection has no force against the Tractarian conception of possible worlds which best fits the paraphrase argument.

26 Cf. Lewis (1986, p. 133, also p. 100).

27 For a detailed account of what Lewis takes to be the distinctive explanatory pay-offs of his modal realism, see his 1986, ch. 1.

28 According to this analysis, each world is, from the standpoint of its inhabitants, the actual world, and other worlds are merely possible, much as 'here', as employed by a given speaker, denotes where she is, and any other place is, for her there, elsewhere. Just as none of us is tempted to think that here – where we currently are – is the only

place, so no one should be tempted to suppose that this world – the actual world, from our point of view – is the only world. Being real is not to be identified with being actual.

29 Stalnaker (1976, p. 68).

30 It is fairly clear that Stalnaker takes properties to be abstract entities. Actually he says, rather unfortunately in my view, that they are abstract *objects*. This might suggest that he thinks that the actual world is, by contrast, a concrete object. Perhaps this way of making the contrast between the actual world and merely possible worlds could be sustained, if we thought of David Lewis and his surroundings as some kind of physical aggregate, as opposed to a set or collection. But it seems best to understand Stalnaker's view as being that possible worlds are properties, each of which might have been instantiated by the actual world, but only one of which – the way things are – is.

31 Stalnaker (1976, p. 68).

32 Stalnaker's noted tendency to regard properties as (abstract) objects may partly account for his failure to remark on this point. It is not quite clear that possible world quantifiers would have to be higher than second-order. Certainly if W is a predicate specifying a way things might have been, there is no evident reason why W should not involve quantification over first-level properties (i.e. properties of individuals), over properties of such properties, and so on, up to quantifications of arbitrary finite order. But this does nothing to prevent W from expressing a first-level property (which the actual world either has or lacks), any more than the higher-order quantification embedded in 'had all the qualities of a great general' prevents it from standing for a first-level property.

33 See McGinn (1981, p. 159). McGinn raises other objections which will not be discussed here.

34 Cf. Adams (1974), Hintikka (1969) and Plantinga (1974, ch. 4).

35 For defence of analyses of propositions as sets of worlds, see Lewis (1986, ch. 1) and Stalnaker (1984). The preceding sentence in the text indicates one potentially lethal objection. The isssue cannot be pursued here.

36 Cf. Rosen (1990). Rosen's enthusiasm for the position has since been somewhat dampened – see Rosen (1993) and Brock (1993) for a similar problem. Others have been unpersuaded by the objection – see Menzies and Pettit (1994) and Noonan (1994).

37 Cf. Divers (1995).

38 This difficulty is elaborated in Hale (1995a). Rosen seeks to meet it in his (1995), to which Hale (1995b) replies.

39 Cf. Peacocke (1978), Davies (1981, Part III) and Forbes (1985, 1989).

40 Lewis (1973, p. 85).

41 This is a very strong assumption. There is, plausibly, reason enough to reject it, independently of the case in hand – it is, for example, difficult to see how it could fail to preclude the possibility of knowledge of, or justified belief in, perfectly ordinary empirical general truths (see e.g. Hale, 1987, ch. 4, esp. pp. 92–101). But the difficulty can be put, as Hartry Field has observed in connection with mathematical knowledge (see Field, 1989, pp. 230–39) without relying on any such contentious claim about the analysis of the notion of knowledge. The modal realist should agree that we enjoy a significant degree of reliability in our modal beliefs – that we are fairly good at forming beliefs which accord well with the modal facts. On his view, this consists in our being good at forming beliefs which accord well with the facts about what (other) possible worlds there are, and the character of those worlds. If we are thus reliable, this is something which surely calls for explanation. The objection may then be put without

appeal to a specifically causal analysis of knowledge, or reasonable belief; given our lack of causal or other natural relations to other possible worlds, it is hard to see how any satisfactory explanation of the sort required could possibly be constructed.

42 Lewis (1986, p. 109).

43 Ibid., p. 110.

44 Ibid., p. 111.

45 McGinn (1976) actually proposes an explication of the a priori/a posteriori distinction in just such terms. It is important here not to forget that the kind of causal constraint in question is a strong one, to the effect that there must be a suitable causal relation between the putative knower's belief that P and the fact that P. Thus rejecting it for a given range of cases is not setting one's face against the possibility of any kind of causal or naturalistic account of knowledge whatever.

46 Whether other things are equal – and, crucially, whether Lewisian realism really does enjoy a distinctive advantage in such matters – is, of course, a further question.

47 McGinn (1981, pp. 153–8) develops an objection along these lines.

48 "Roughly, the principle is that anything can coexist with anything else, at least provided they occupy distinct spatiotemporal positions. Likewise, anything can fail to coexist with anything else" (Lewis, 1986, p. 88). Lewis is not committed to this initial formulation – it requires, in his view, a proviso to the effect that recombinations must be consistent with "some possible size and shape of spacetime".

49 Lewis (1986, pp. 113–14).

50 Thus Blackburn (1984, ch. 6.5) depicts modal judgements as expressive of attitude, or something like an attitude; Wright (1980, ch. 23) explores the idea that they record decisions; while Craig (1985) speaks in terms of endorsement of a policy. Wright's position has shifted in more recent writings (cf. 1989), in which he grants that necessited judgements are (at least minimally) truth-apt.

51 As they have in fact played. Blackburn's dilemma at his 1987, p. 120, appears to be underpinned by unwillingness to accept irreducible modal facts; the epistemological motive is to the fore in Craig (1985).

52 Cf. Craig (1985, p. 93): "The limit of his imagination . . . is still just another fact about him, and he sees no reason to take it as a guide to what must of *necessity* be the case"; and Wright (1980, p. 453): "you are asking me to affirm that whenever exactly the specified sequence of transformations is correctly followed through on exactly the specified basis, we are bound to achieve this (sort of) result – that no other outcome is possible provided the blueprint is correctly implemented. And that very strong claim, I feel, I am not entitled to make." It is true that Craig and Wright are here describing the position of the Cautious Man – an invention of Wright's, designed to unsettle cognitivists – not that of the non-cognitivist as such. But on the material point – that the uncontroversial facts cannot rationally warrant a judgement of necessity – their views coincide; they differ, principally, in that while the Cautious Man thinks this obliges him to refrain from making necessitated judgements altogether, the non-cognitivist takes it to show that such judgements are not recognitional, but are to be understood as expressing or endorsing a policy or decision of some sort.

53 See Yablo (1993) for an excellent discussion of the standard objections to treating conceivability as a ground for possibility.

54 Wright (1986, pp. 199–200). For an earlier version of Wright's criterion, see his 1980, pp. 448–9. The reference to ignorance and error in the explanans should be understood, of course, as relating to ignorance or error about matters recorded in statements

lying outside the disputed class – else the criterion would be hopelessly circular. Note that these may include facts about the meanings of relevant expressions.

55 Wright (1986, pp. 202ff.).

56 Cf. Wright (1989, pp. 222–3).

57 Wright suggests, not a series of selectively cautious thinkers as here, but a single Eccentric Modalizer (cf. his 1989, pp. 225–8). But so far as I can see, the net effect is the same, as are the problems with the suggestion.

58 This formulation is taken from Wright 1989 (see p. 229), as is the argument that follows.

59 For some – dare I say it? – cautious steps towards an answer to this third question; see the closing nine pages of Wright (1989).

60 Thanks to Crispin Wright and Nick Zangwill for very helpful comments.

References and further reading

Adams, Robert M. 1974: Theories of actuality. *Noûs*, 8, 211–31, reprinted in Loux (1979).

Ayer, A.J. 1946: *Language, Truth and Logic*. 2nd edn, London: Gollancz.

Blackburn, Simon 1984: *Spreading the World*. Oxford: Clarendon Press.

——1987: Morals and modals. In G. Macdonald and C. Wright (eds), *Fact, Science and Morality*. Oxford and New York: Blackwell, pp. 119–41.

Brock, Stuart 1993: Modal fictionalism: A reply to Rosen. *Mind*, 102, 147–50.

Craig, Edward 1985: Arithmetic and fact. In Ian Hacking (ed.), *Essays in Analysis*. Cambridge: Cambridge University Press, 89–112.

Davies, Martin 1981: *Meaning, Quantification and Necessity*. London: Routledge and Kegan Paul.

Divers, John 1995: Modal fictionalism cannot deliver possible world semantics. *Analysis*, 55 (2), 81–9.

Dummett, Michael 1959: Wittgenstein's philosophy of mathematics. *Philosophical Review*, 68, 324–48, and reprinted in Dummett (1978), to which page references are given.

——1978: *Truth and Other Enigmas*. London: Duckworth.

——1994: Wittgenstein on necessity: some reflections. In Peter Clark and Bob Hale (eds), *Reading Putnam*. Oxford and Cambridge, Mass: Blackwell.

Field, Hartry 1989: *Realism, Mathematics and Modality*. Oxford: Blackwell.

Forbes, Graeme 1985: *The Metaphysics of Modality*. Oxford: Clarendon Press.

——1989: *Languages of Possibility: An Essay in Philosophical Logic*. Oxford: Blackwell.

Haack, Susan 1977: Lewis's ontological slum. *Review of Metaphysics*, 33, 415–29.

——1978: *Philosophy of Logics*. Cambridge: Cambridge University Press.

Hale, Bob 1987: *Abstract Objects*. Oxford: Blackwell.

——1989: Necessity, caution and scepticism. *Aristotelian Society Supplementary Vol.* 63, 175–202.

——1995a: Modal fictionalism – a simple dilemma. *Analysis*, 55 (2), 63–7.

——1995b: A desperate fix. *Analysis*, 55 (2), 74–81.

——1996: Absolute necessities. In James Tomberlin (ed.), *Philosophical Perspectives*, 10, forthcoming.

Hintikka, Jaacko 1969: *Models for Modalities*. Dordrecht: Reidel.

Kripke, Saul 1971: Identity and necessity. In Milton Munitz (ed.), *Identity and Individuation*. New York: New York University Press, pp. 135–64.

——1980: *Naming and Necessity*. Oxford: Blackwell.

Lewis, David 1973: *Counterfactuals*. Oxford: Blackwell.
——1986: *On the Plurality of Worlds*. Oxford: Blackwell.
Loux, Michael (ed.) 1979: *The Possible and the Actual*. Ithaca, NY: Cornell University Press.
McFetridge, Ian 1990: *Logical Necessity and Other Essays*. Aristotelian Society Series, Vol. 11, eds John Haldane and Roger Scruton.
McGinn, Colin 1976: A priori and a posteriori knowledge. *Aristotelian Society Proceedings*, 76, pp. 195–208.
——1981: Modal reality. In R. Healey (ed.) *Reduction, Time and Reality*. Cambridge: Cambridge University Press, pp. 143–87.
Menzies, Peter and Pettit, Philip 1994: In defence of fictionalism about possible worlds. *Analysis*, 54, 27–36.
Noonan, Harold 1994: In defence of the letter of fictionalism. *Analysis*, 54, 133–9.
Peacocke, Christopher 1978: Necessity and truth-theories. *Journal of Philosophical Logic*, 7, 473–500.
Plantinga, Alvin 1974: *The Nature of Necessity*. Oxford: Oxford University Press.
Putnam, Hilary 1983: Possibility and necessity. In *Realism and Reason: Philosophical Papers*. Vol. 3, Cambridge: Cambridge University Press, pp. 46–68.
Richards, Tom 1975: The worlds of David Lewis. *Australasian Journal of Philosophy*, 53, 105–18.
Rosen, Gideon 1990: Modal fictionalism. *Mind*, 99, 327–54.
——1993: A problem for fictionalism about possible worlds. *Analysis*, 53, 71–81.
——1995: Modal fictionalism fixed. *Analysis*, 55 (2), 67–73.
Sidelle, Alan 1989: *Necessity, Essence and Individuation*. Ithaca, NY, and London: Cornell University Press.
Stalnaker, Robert 1976: Possible worlds. *Nous*, 10, 65–75, reprinted in Loux (1979).
——1984: *Inquiry*. Cambridge, Mass.: MIT Press.
Wittgenstein, Ludwig 1921: *Tractatus Logico-Philosophicus*. English translation by D.F. Pears and B.F. McGuinness, London and New York: Routledge and Kegan Paul, 1961.
——1978: *Remarks on the Foundations of Mathematics*. Third edn, ed. by G.H. von Wright, R. Rhees and G.E.M. Anscombe; trans. by G.E.M. Anscombe. Oxford: Basil Blackwell.
Wright, Crispin 1980: *Wittgenstein on the Foundations of Mathematics*. London: Duckworth.
——1986: Inventing logical necessity. In J. Butterfield (ed.), *Language, Mind and Logic*. Cambridge: Cambridge University Press.
——1989: Necessity, caution and scepticism. *Aristotelian Society Supplementary Volume*, 63, 203–38.
——1992: *Truth and Objectivity*. Cambridge, Mass., and London: Harvard University Press.
Yablo, Stephen 1993: Is conceivability a guide to possibility? *Philosophy and Phenomenological Research*, 53 (1), 2–42.

20

Essentialism

GRAEME FORBES

1 Concepts

The term "essentialism" in its popular usage is usually qualified in some way, as in "biological essentialism", "gender essentialism", "social essentialism", and so on. The three views just mentioned are typical: they are all views about human nature, and their general thrust is that in certain respects people *have* to be the way that they in fact are, in virtue of, respectively, their genes, their sex, or the social class to which they belong. Usually the respects in question are politically controversial, though there are also interesting examples with no real political overtones, for instance, Chomsky's view that it is part of the "human essence" to be capable of learning only languages whose syntactic rules satisfy the constraints of certain "linguistic universals" (Chomsky, 1988, *passim*). The general idea here is that for each thing of a particular kind there are various apparent possibilities for it which are in fact closed off in virtue of its possessing such-and-such a property, where the property mentioned is characteristic of the kind of essentialism being propounded. For instance, a human being may be said to be unable to partake in interpersonal relationships of a particular emotional timbre because that human being is male.

Contemporary *metaphysical essentialism*, which is our main concern here, consists in a variety of more abstract doctrines of this broad sort. Certain apparent possibilities for things are argued to be not genuine possibilities for them. However, the possibilities are closed off not in virtue of features of the things concerned as specific to them as, say, social class is to human beings in contemporary Western societies, but rather, in virtue of the very nature or identity of the thing. To be more specific, we may explain the idea of a *metaphysically essential property* in terms of Aristotle's "essential/accidental" contrast. According to Aristotle, an accidental property is "something which may possibly either belong or not belong to any one and the self-same thing" (Aristotle, 1928, $102^{b}5$ff.). This can be firmed up in two slightly different ways. Assuming that an accidental property of *x* is a property that *x* in fact possesses, we may say either

(1) *P* is an accidental property of *x* iff (i) *x* in fact possesses *P* but (ii) there is a way things could have gone according to which *x* lacks *P*;

or

(2) *P* is an accidental property of *x* iff (i) *x* in fact possesses *P* but (ii) there is a way things could have gone according to which *x* exists and lacks *P*.

We may then define *P* to be an *essential* property of *x* if *x* in fact possesses *P* but *P* is not an accidental property of *x*. Metaphysical essentialism is more fundamental than the specific kinds of essentialism mentioned above, since these latter typically depend upon (alleged) features of human nature which are themselves accidental, so in ways things could have gone in which human beings do not have those features, they would not have to have the "essential" properties that depend on them.

What hangs on the difference between (1) and (2)? The problem with (1) is that it threatens to make all properties accidental, for an uninteresting reason, at least in the case of things which might not have existed. As we will see, the examples of essential properties that have captured most attention in contemporary philosophy are properties which are *existence-presupposing*: necessarily, if *x* has one of these properties, then *x* exists. But if *x* is a contingent being, one which might not have existed, there are ways things could have gone according to which *x* does not exist, and consequently, in any of these ways things could have gone, *x* lacks all the candidate essential properties, thereby demonstrating that they are not essential to *x* after all. But this seems merely to miss the point, and so one turns to (2) as a superior definition. Unfortunately, (2) also has its flaws, chief among which is that it makes *existence* an essential property, since there is no way things could have gone according to which *x* exists and lacks existence. So neither (1) nor (2) exactly captures the notion we are after. Why this should be so is itself an interesting question to which we shall return. For the moment, we simply observe that if we are to stay with (2), we will want to distinguish between *trivially* and *non-trivially* essential properties, with existence as the paradigm of the trivially essential. How this distinction is to be drawn is itself non-trivial.

The other main concept with which we will be concerned is that of an *individual essence*. Intuitively, the essence of a thing is the collection of its features which determine its identity, which make it the specific thing it is rather than something else. One way of articulating this idea is embodied in the following definition:

(3) *e* is the *(individual) essence* of *x* iff *e* is a set of properties such that each member of *e* is an essential property of *x* and it is not possible for any other object *y* to possess all the properties in *e*.

However, (3) is subject to an irritating technical defect of the same flavor as those afflicting (1) and (2), for there is nothing in any of our definitions which warrants the phrase "*the* essence" in (3). That is, there is no apparent reason why there should not be two different sets of properties *e* and *e′*, each satisfying the condition for being an essence of *x*. So (3) really ought to begin "*e* is *an* essence of *x* iff . . .". We shall return later to recent work of Kit Fine which motivates a different approach to the ideas of essence and essential property by emphasizing these difficulties with (1), (2), and (3). But for the moment we shall stay with the modal approach, the definitions in terms of possibility and necessity, since it is still the orthodoxy.

2 Essentialist theses and arguments for them

The contemporary debate about essentialism was provoked by writings of Kripke (1972, 1980) and Putnam (1975), with subsequent contributions by Fine (Prior and Fine, 1977) and Wiggins (1980). According to Kripke, the origin of an organism *o* is essential to it, and the matter from which an artifact *a* is fashioned is essential to it; or at least, neither the origin of *o* nor the matter of *a* could be entirely different from what it actually is. According to Putnam, the fundamental physical properties of substances are essential to them: a particular substance could not have had a totally different fundamental nature. For instance, there is no way things could go in which an actual chemical compound comes into existence with a molecular structure quite different from the structure it actually has. According to Fine, it is essential to a set to be a set and to have the members it actually has: a set is not to be conceived of as a box, which actually has one range of members, the odd numbers, say, but, if things had gone differently, would have had a different range of members, the even numbers, say (Fine, 1981). Finally, Wiggins has argued for the view that the "natural kind" (if any) to which *x* belongs is essential to *x* (1980, ch. 4). Thus he, Wiggins, as a human being, could not have been a polar bear, or a forest, or a performance of Beethoven's Ninth Symphony.

These claims have struck an intuitive chord in many philosophers. If we grant the essential/accidental distinction in the first place, then it is plausible that it is essential to Wiggins that he is not a performance of Beethoven's Ninth, but not essential to him that he is a professional philosopher (he might have pursued a different career). However, the interesting question concerns not so much whether a particular essentialist thesis is true, but rather what principles are employed in drawing the essential/accidental distinction in particular cases. Indeed, an independently plausible account of the principles should feed back to help decide some of the more controversial theses.

For purposes of uncovering principles we can sort the various doctrines into two groups: those which posit essential connections between specific individuals, such as the connection between a set such as {0} and its member 0 and between a tree and the seed from which it originated, and those which make a thing's kind essential to it, such as the claims that sets are essentially sets and humans essentially human. We begin with the first group, involving essential connections between specific individuals, and we take as a stalking-horse Kripke's proposal about the essentiality of origin, as formulated in the following famous passage (1980, p. 112–13):

> The question really should be . . . could the Queen – could this woman herself – have been born of different parents from the parents from whom she actually came? Could she, let's say, have been the daughter of Mr and Mrs Truman? . . . We can imagine

> discovering [that the Queen was the daughter of Mr and Mrs Truman] . . . But let us suppose that such a discovery is not in fact the case. Let's suppose the Queen really did come from these [her actual] parents . . . can we imagine a situation in which it would have happened that this very woman came out of Mr and Mrs Truman? They might have had a child resembling her in many properties . . . [perhaps] . . . even a child who actually became the Queen of England and was even passed off as the child of other parents. This would not be a situation in which *this very woman* whom we call "Elizabeth II" was the child of Mr and Mrs Truman, or so it seems to me. It would be a situation in which there was some other woman who had many of the properties that are in fact true of Elizabeth . . . How could a person originating from a totally different sperm and egg, be *this very woman*?

The question is somewhat rhetorical, but as Kripke develops his example it has considerable force, and I have never seen a convincing counter-example to the underlying thesis. This thesis is that if an organism o originates from a cell c – a fertilized egg or *zygote*, in the case of human beings – then it is essential to o that it originate from c: o could not exist except by originating from c. We will call this thesis the *essentiality of origin*. However, to find the essentiality of origin plausible and alleged counter-examples to it unconvincing is one thing; but to have a theoretical explanation of why it is true is another.

To find such an explanation we can consider some of the consequences of rejecting the essentiality of origin. If the thesis is false, then even if in the actual world o develops from c, there is a way things could have gone, an *alternative possible world*, in the popular jargon, in which o exists, but as a result of developing from a different cell c'. Let w be such a world, and for the sake of the argument let us suppose that o is as similar as possible in w to the way it is in the actual world. Let us also grant that there are no special connections between how things can go for c and how things can go for c', other than that c and c' cannot both give rise to the same organism in the same possible world. Then there is a world u where c and c' both give rise to organisms; we use r for the organism to which c gives rise in u, and g for the organism to which c' gives rise in u. Let us pick such a u with the special feature that g as it is in u is as similar as possible to o as it is in w. The total set-up is given in Figure 1.

We have refrained from making any suppositions about which, if either, of the organisms in u is identical to o. But in the logic of the situation, there are only three possibilities: (a) o is identical to g; (b) o is identical to r; and (c) o is identical to neither g nor r. The consideration which favors the essentiality of origin is that all three of these options seem to have undesirable consequences, and so the hypothesis which generates them, that there are worlds where o develops from different cells (such as the actual world and w in the figure), is to that extent disconfirmed.

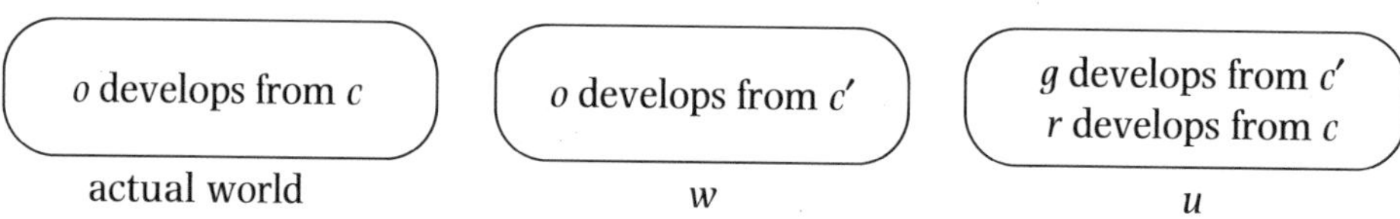

Figure 1

Postponing discussion of (a) for the moment, the problem with (b) and (c) is that the hypothetical non-identity of *o* and *g* is hard to accept, since *o* and *g* are *intrinsic* and *spatio-temporal* duplicates: by this I mean that they have the same nature and occupy the same places at the same times. Indeed, they need differ only in the extrinsic respect that *g* in *u* is existing in a world where *c* gives rise to an organism, while *o* in *w* is not, and in other extrinsic respects which are a consequence of that one. If we were asked to imagine a course of events which differs from *w* in that *c′* gives rise to an organism different from *o*, but that is the totality of the difference – no difference in any features of the two worlds is to be admitted, only a difference in the pure identity of the thing to which *c′* gives rise – we may wonder what content could be given to the idea that *c′* becomes *different* things in the two worlds. But if the idea that the organisms into which *c′* grows in the two worlds are different is of dubious intelligibility in this example, it is hard to see how throwing in *c* and an organism it develops into can make any difference to the intelligibility issue. The objection to world *w*, then, on either (b) or (c), is that it implies the existence of a numerical difference between entities in distinct worlds where there are no intrinsic features of these entities to support the posited difference.

This still leaves the sceptic about the essentiality of origin with (a), that *o* is identical to *g*. However, under plausible assumptions, (a) has the same problematic aspect as (b) and (c). For there seems to be no reason why we cannot choose a world *v* in which *o* develops from *c* in the same way, and at the same places and times, as *r* does in *u*. That is, there is a world *v* in which *o* develops from *c* in such a way as to make it an intrinsic and spatio-temporal duplicate of *r* in *v*, since this only requires that the intrinsic and spatio-temporal features of *r* in *u* are ones all of which could have been possessed by *o*, excluding only those which involve the phenomenon at issue, such as being in a world in which something other than *o* develops from *c*.

This style of argument can be repeated for some of the other examples of essential properties we mentioned earlier. If we allow that a set could have different members, or that an artifact could have been made from entirely different parts, or that a substance could have had different fundamental physical properties, we can, under natural assumptions, generate analogous sorts of duplication without identity, as the reader may confirm. But this leaves us short of a *proof* that these properties are essential. Returning to the essentiality of origin, if intrinsic and spatio-temporal duplication of the sort manifested in our example implies identity, then any view which generates intrinsic and spatio-temporal duplication without identity is to be rejected. But this is insufficient to establish the essentiality of origin, since there are other properties which, if essential to *o*, would rule out intrinsic and spatio-temporal duplication without identity. For example, it might be proposed that the route through space which *o* traces while it exists is essential to *o*. If so, there is no world *v* such as is appealed to in the previous paragraph, and we can settle on (a). For in the actual world, in *w*, and in *u*, *o* must trace the same route; hence in *u*, *r* is spatio-temporally distinguishable from *o* in the actual world, and hence *r*'s route is not a possibility for *o*.

There is, of course, no plausibility in the hypothesis that an ordinary material object's spatio-temporal nature (its location at each time of its existence) is essential to it. The interesting question is why this is so. The kind of relationship in which an organism stands to its originating cell seems bound up with that organism's identity in a special way. It would go too far to say that the relationship is itself identity. A human being, for example, is not *identical* to the zygote from which he or she develops, since the zygote ceases to exist when it divides, while the human being does not cease to exist then. We may, if we wish, speak of a human's *zygotehood* on analogy with childhood (McGinn, 1976), but this simply raises the question of why the identity of the cell that constitutes the body during zygotehood should be any less accidental than the identities of the cells that constitute it during childhood. Nevertheless, the relationships between a set and its members, an organism and its zygote, and an artifact and the matter of which it is constituted (for example, a bronze statue and the bronze from which it is molded) do appear to have a certain affinity: they have an internal aspect which spatio-temporal relations lack. We will return to this later in our discussion of the source of necessity.

The kind of defense given here of the essentiality of origin is less obviously applicable in defense of Putnam's essentialism about the fundamental physical properties of substances. Could water exist in a universe where matter is continuous? Assuming that the fundamental property of water is not just to have a chemical composition of two parts hydrogen to one part oxygen, but rather to have molecules consisting in two hydrogen atoms and one oxygen atom, and hydrogen and oxygen themselves are fundamentally constituted of particles which are not further divisible, there could be nothing in a universe of continuous matter satisfying the description abbreviated by "H_2O". But perhaps water could exist there as the substance fulfilling certain functions actually instantiated by H_2O. Suppose that we can make sense of the idea of functions that are performed by some substance in the actual world and again by some substance in a world where matter is continuous. Then we might argue, on Putnam's side, that this is still not sufficient for identifying the substances. But it will be hard to generate a convincing case of objectionable duplication that comes about as a result of making the identification, for this would require a world in which a substance with the physical structure H_2O exists alongside the substance from the world with continuous matter identified as water on functional grounds. At this point, one is less entitled to confidence in the coherence of the possible situations being stipulated than one is in those of the more straightforward case of organisms and the cells from which they develop. Still, this is only to say that a particular way of defending Putnam's thesis is less effective, not that the thesis itself is incorrect.

We turn briefly to the second group of essentialist theses we distinguished at the beginning of this section, those which say that a thing's kind is essential to it, such as the claims that sets are essentially sets and humans essentially human. These essentialist theses are easier to justify, particularly if we consider extreme cases. What could be meant by the suggestion that, say, {0} could have been a tree instead, or that Wiggins could have been Loch Ness? The problem of making sense of such bizarre hypotheses is not just one of lack of imagination. Indeed, there are fantasies in which persons in some sense "turn into" geographical features. But one does not treat these stories as representing genuine possibilities for the objects concerned; merely the same name is used, on the basis of some far-fetched or peripheral similarity. In the same vein, in explaining the layout of a town to someone over the breakfast table, one might say, "Let this pot of marmalade be the railway station." That does not mean that this pot of marmalade could have been a railway station, much less that particular railway station. The problem is that for it to be a possibility for a pot of marmalade to have been a railway station, or for {0} to have been a tree, we have to be able to conceive of two different states of affairs in which one and the same thing figures, in the first as a pot of marmalade or singleton zero, and in the second as a railway station or an item of flora respectively. However, this in turn means that we would be conceiving of objects and their properties on the model of bare particular and inherence, according to which a thing is a propertyless substratum and can take on any nature you please via the inhering of appropriate properties. But this, if it makes sense at all, is at any rate not the conception which we employ. Articulating our actual conception is another problem, but whatever the right story is in this area (see Wiggins, 1980, ch. 3), one constraint is that it must imply the fundamental unintelligibility of hypotheses which make the broad kind to which a thing belongs an accidental feature of it.

We have considered some examples of interesting essential properties and what might be said in support of them. An individual essence of an object x was defined in (3) to be a collection of essential properties of x such that if at any world an object y possesses all of them, then y is x. The essential properties we have discussed give rise to individual essences in a completely straightforward way only for sets: if x is a set, then *being a set* is part of x's 'natural' essence, and for each y which belongs to x, *having y as a member* is part of x's natural essence, and no other property is part of x's natural essence. By including *being a set* in the essence, we distinguish x from other entities which also have members and which might, as things actually are, have the same members as x, such as a club. The term 'natural' requires some justification, however. It is also an essence of x to be the sole member of $\{x\}$, at least by the lights of (3); but as Fine has urged (Fine, 1994) this essence is not revealing of x's nature: the kind of thing it is and *which* thing of that kind it is. So it is in that sense not the natural essence.

The analogous proposal for organisms is that each organism has its biological kind and the cell or cells from which it developed as its natural essence. But there are two difficulties. First, in view of the mechanisms by which speciation actually occurs, 'kind', at least interpreted as 'species', may be too strong. One would like something more vague here, but how can vagueness enter the specification of a thing's natural essence? Secondly, some cells arise by division of a parent cell. But if y and z arise in this way from x, all three being cells of some kind K, it is not sufficient to specify the essence of y as being of kind K and arising from x, for z is also of kind K and arises from x. However, y is constituted of part of the matter of x (just before division) and z is constituted of the other part, and it certainly seems wrong to say that y could have been constituted of the matter of which z is actually constituted, all else being the same so far as possible. Hence a plausible move in filling out the account of the natural essences of y and z is to add some constraint about what part of the matter of x each can be constituted of. But it also seems that it is too strong to make *exactly* the actual matter from which y is constituted part of y's natural essence. Surely y could have been constituted of slightly more, or slightly less, or slightly different, matter? Again there is the thought that we need to build some kind of vagueness into the specification of essences. We will see in the next section how this might be done.

3 Slippery slopes and primitive thisnesses

The argument of the previous section claimed to ground certain essentialist theses, such as the essentiality of origin, in principles about "identity across possible worlds". The essentialist theses were defended on the grounds that denying them leads, under plausible assumptions, to pairs of worlds containing objects which are intrinsic and spatio-temporal duplicates and yet which are numerically distinct. But this is a poor defense if careful thought reveals that there is actually nothing objectionable about intrinsic and spatio-temporal duplication without numerical identity. We turn now to two arguments which seek to show that indeed there is nothing to object to in such duplication.

The first argument, due in essentials to Chisholm (1968) and sometimes known as Chisholm's Paradox, exploits an intuition of *modal tolerance* in certain features of particular objects (the version I give of Chisholm's Paradox is not quite Chisholm's, since he uses iterated modality; but the moral is the same). A watch, for example, which is actually made from a particular collection of parts, might have been made from a *slightly* different collection; it might have had a different winder, say. More abstractly, imagine that we have an artifact x made of parts $p_1 \ldots p_{20}$, each of which is equally important to its function, and a different artifact y, though of the same design, made of parts $p_{21} \ldots p_{40}$. Suppose we now formulate modal tolerance more precisely as

(4) If a particular make-up is possible for a thing, then a slightly different make-up is also possible for it.

Since x is actually made of $p_1, \ldots, p_{20}$, then trivially, that make-up is possible for it (it could hardly be *impossible*!), and so by one application of (4), x could have been made of $p_1, \ldots, p_{19}, p_{40}$. But then by another application of (4) to this result, x could have been made of $p_1, \ldots, p_{18}, p_{39}, p_{40}$. By a further eight applications of (4), we arrive at the following conclusion:

(5) x could have been made of $p_1, \ldots, p_{10}, p_{31}, \ldots, p_{40}$.

However, exactly the same reasoning leads us to the conclusion that

(6) y could have been made of $p_1, \ldots, p_{10}, p_{31}, \ldots, p_{40}$

since y, being actually made of $p_{21}, \ldots, p_{40}$, could have been made of $p_1, p_{22}, \ldots, p_{40}$ and so on, using (4). Since there seems to be no reason why a situation in which

(5) is true would have to differ in some other way from a situation in which (6) is true, other than in differences logically consequent upon the difference in identity of the things made of $p_1, \ldots, p_{10}, p_{31}, \ldots, p_{40}$ in the respective situations, we have a striking case of duplication without numerical identity. But the logic that leads us to this point is impeccable, hence duplication without identity is unobjectionable.

One response to this is that in fact there is no duplication without identity, since any situation in which x is made of $p_1, \ldots, p_{10}, p_{31}, \ldots, p_{40}$ is *ipso facto* one in which y is made of $p_1, \ldots, p_{10}, p_{31}, \ldots, p_{40}$, and vice versa; it is just that in such a situation, x and y are the *same thing*. But this response is problematic in a number of ways. First, and most to the point in the present context, it is of little use to the essentialist, who will want to say that it is essential to x and to y to be made of a substantial majority of the parts of which they are actually made: a make-up of $p_1, \ldots, p_{10}, p_{31}, \ldots, p_{40}$ should be impossible for both x and y. Secondly, it has the strange implication that as things actually are, x is the same thing as any of the merely possible artifacts which could have been constructed using half of x's parts, for there are possible worlds with artifacts other than x with compositions that stand to $p_1, \ldots, p_{20}$ as x stands to the possible composition $p_1, \ldots, p_{10}, p_{31}, \ldots, p_{40}$. Thirdly, on the usual way of understanding possible situations, it is hard to make sense of two things being identical in a possible situation. On the orthodox approach, we begin with a stock of objects whose possibilities we wish to model, and we represent possible situations involving them by selecting some of the objects and configuring them with atomic properties and relations; for instance, if x is selected and given the property P, and if y is also selected and x is given the relation R to y, the model is of the possibility for x of being P and being R to y. Thus if x and y are given from the outset as different things, then using x in the model of a possible situation is different from using y.

A better defense of the principle that intrinsic and spatio-temporal duplication implies identity is to query the logic of the supposed counter-example. It is natural to view (4) as a modal case of a paradox of vagueness, or a *Sorites* paradox (see Chapter 18, SORITES). More familiar examples involves vague predicates like "tall" or "bald", or color words. For example, suppose 1,001 people are arranged in descending order of height, beginning with someone two meters tall and ending with someone one meter tall, adjacent people differing in height by one millimeter. The first person in this sequence is tall, the last is short. However, if we accept the seemingly plausible

(7) If x is tall then anyone not visibly distinguishable in height from x is tall

we easily derive, by repeated applications of (7), that the last person in the sequence is tall, though he or she is not. Case (4) is similar, the vague predicate being "_is a possible make-up for x". Whatever the problem is with relying on (7), then, the same difficulty should afflict (4).

However, it is one thing to know that a form of argument is untrustworthy, another to be able to say what theoretical flaw it embodies. There are various accounts of the mistake in the paradox of tallness, but a suggestive idea is that the argument depends on treating tallness as all or nothing: a person is either tall or not tall. Yet tallness is a matter of degree: someone can be tall, very tall, fairly tall, tallish, not exactly tall, and so on. Suppose we regard the various possible heights as correlated with *degrees of tallness* in such a way that different heights, even two that are not visibly discriminable, correspond to different degrees (unless they both qualify their bearers as tall *simpliciter* or not tall at all). The degree to which x is tall may be thought of as determining a *degree of truth* for the statement "x is tall", so that if we are somewhere in the upper third of our line-up, where the people are somewhat tall but also somewhat medium-sized, then "a is tall" will be true to a slightly higher degree than "b is tall" if a is one millimeter taller than b. Suppose also that the degree of truth of a conditional $p \rightarrow q$, when the antecedent has a higher degree of truth than the consequent, reflects the amount by which the truth of p exceeds the truth of q, the conditional's degree of truth dropping as the gap increases (in the limits, when p is not more true than q, $p \rightarrow q$ is wholly true, and when p is wholly true and q is wholly false, $p \rightarrow q$ is wholly false, as in classical logic; if we use the real numbers between 0 and 1 inclusive as degrees of truth, with 0 for complete falsehoods and 1 for absolute truths, then a clause for $\rightarrow$ which satisfies these conditions is: the degree of truth of $p \rightarrow q$, for short "$\text{deg}(p \rightarrow q)$", is $1 - [\text{deg}(p) - \text{deg}(q)]$ when $\text{deg}(p) > \text{deg}(q)$, otherwise $\text{deg}(p \rightarrow q) = 1$). The derivation of our conclusion that the one-meter-tall person in our line-up is tall can be represented as a chain of conditionals, "$\text{tall}(a_1) \rightarrow \text{tall}(a_2)$", "$\text{tall}(a_2) \rightarrow \text{tall}(a_3)$", and so on, the antecedent of the first conditional be-ing given. However, there is now no reason to accept the conclusion "a_{1001} is tall", since somewhere in the first third of these conditionals we encounter ones in which the degree of truth of the antecedent is slightly higher than the degree of truth of the consequent. These premises are not wholly true, so the argument is unsound.

If this is a reasonable resolution of the paradox of tallness, how does it carry over to (4)? There are two different ways in which the transfer might be done, according to whether or not we wish to retain the standard method of modelling possible situations described earlier, which is to begin with a stock of objects whose possibilities we wish to model, and to construct possible situations by selecting some of the objects and configuring them with atomic properties and relations. If we retain this approach, another of its constituents which we can employ is that of the *relative possibility* relation between different possible situations. To use Nathan Salmon's terminology, each self-contained configuration of objects with properties and relations can be regarded as a *way* for those objects to *be* (Salmon, 1989: what follows is my own perspective on the approach of Salmon, 1986, which is not necessarily one with which he would agree). So we might have three possible situations, w, u, and v, where it is part of w that x and $p_1, \ldots, p_{20}$ stand in the "made of" relation, part of u that x and $p_1, \ldots, p_{11}, p_{32}, \ldots, p_{40}$ stand in the "made of" relation, and part of v that x and $p_1, \ldots, p_{10}, p_{31}, \ldots, p_{40}$ stand in the "made of" relation. This gives us three different ways for x to be. But on top of this, we have to say which ways for x to be are possible relative to the various other possible situations, and this is a question which we can treat as a matter of degree. Relative to *u*, *v* has a high degree of possibility, indeed is perhaps *entirely* possible, since there is only a difference of one part in the make-ups of *x* in *u* and *v*. But relative to *w*, *v* can be stipulated to be not possible at all, while again relative to *w*, *u* may be regarded as a very remote possibility, though slightly more possible than *v*, because there is less difference in *x*. A possibility statement is read as asserting possibility relative to the actual world, so looking at (4) in this light, we construe it as saying that if a situation in which *x* has such-and-such a make-up is possible relative to the actual world, so is a situation in which *x* has a slightly different make-up. But analogously to the case of people of different heights, it is possible to choose two make-ups for *x* such that *x*'s having the second makes any situation which includes that as a way for *x* to be more remote from actuality than a situation which includes *x*'s having the first needs to be. Repeated applications of (4), then, essentially involve reasoning through a chain of conditionals, each conditional of the form "if such-and-such is possible for *x* then so is such-and-such", in which the antecedent can have a degree of truth that is slightly higher than that of the consequent, because the antecedent mentions something that is more possible for *x*, relative to the way things actually are, than the consequent does. Such a gap prevents the premises which manifest it from being wholly true, so an argument that depends on (4) in this way is unsound.

An alternative way of implementing the degree-of-truth idea is to use the counterpart-theoretic approach to the modelling of possibilities due to Lewis (1968 and 1986, ch. 1). To model possibilities for a collection of objects $a_1, \ldots, a_n$ one does not configure those objects with properties and relations, but rather, for each self-contained possibility for $a_1, \ldots, a_n$ which one wishes to model, one selects objects $b_1, \ldots, b_q$ to be the counterparts or representatives of $a_1, \ldots, a_n$ in the model, and then configures those counterparts with properties and relations. Its being possible for *a* to be f is then modelled by a set-up in which *a* has a counterpart *b* configured so that f is true of it (that is, of *b*).

This approach introduces certain degrees of freedom missing in the standard approach. For example, one of the a_i may have two or more representatives $b_{i_1}, \ldots, b_{i_j}$. Or two of the a_i may have the *same* counterpart b_j (thus, on this approach, we can make sense of the idea that actually distinct things could have been identical). However, more to the point in the present context is the fact that it makes good sense to treat the counterpart relation as a relation of degree. Repeating our previous example in the present context, we would have three possible situations, *w*, *u*, and *v*, such that it is part of *w* that *x* and $p_1, \ldots, p_{20}$ stand in the "made of" relation, part of *u* that a counterpart *y* of *x* and counterparts of $p_1, \ldots, p_{11}, p_{32}, \ldots, p_{40}$ stand in the "made of" relation, and part of *v* that a counterpart *z* of *x* and counterparts of $p_1, \ldots, p_{10}, p_{31}, \ldots, p_{40}$ stand in the "made of" relation. But while *y* and *z* can be counterparts of each other to the maximum degree, *x* can only be represented by either to a much lesser degree, because of the great difference in make-up. Still, *y* can qualify as a slightly stronger counterpart of *x* than *z* is, because *y* has more than half its parts in common with *x* while *z* only has half in common.

Returning to (4), we now read it as asserting that if there is a world where a counterpart of x has such-and-such a make-up, then there is a world where a counterpart of x has a slightly different make-up. Definition (4) generates such conditionals as

(8) If it is possible for x to be made of $p_1, \ldots, p_{11}, p_{32}, \ldots, p_{40}$, then it is possible for x to be made of $p_1, \ldots, p_{10}, p_{31}, \ldots, p_{40}$

which we interpret counterpart-theoretically as

(9) If there is a world where x has a counterpart made of (counterparts of) $p_1, \ldots, p_{11}, p_{32}, \ldots, p_{40}$, then there is a world where x has a counterpart made of (counterparts of) $p_1, \ldots, p_{10}, p_{31}, \ldots, p_{40}$.

But (9) has an antecedent "there is a world where x has a counterpart made of (counterparts of) $p_1, \ldots, p_{11}, p_{32}, \ldots, p_{40}$", which has a higher degree of truth than its consequent, "there is a world where x has a counterpart made of (counterparts of) $p_1, \ldots, p_{10}, p_{31}, \ldots, p_{40}$", because of the higher degree of counterparthood associated with the constitution closer to that of x. Again, therefore, the argument against the sufficiency of intrinsic and spatio-temporal duplication for identity that (4) seemed to support is shown to be unsound. Being a universal statement, (4) itself cannot be any more true than the least true of its instances. So on both the counterpart-theoretic and the relative possibility accounts, (4) comes out as at best slightly less than wholly true.

In passing, let us note that this apparatus solves the problem with which we ended § 2, the problem of how to make sense of the idea that an individual's natural essence might be vague. In the jargon of the counterpart-theoretic approach, we can understand the claim that it is part of the natural essence of x to be made of a *substantial proportion of* $p_1, \ldots, p_{20}$ as allowing that an object y which at another world w is made of counterparts of a substantial proportion of $p_1, \ldots, p_{20}$ can be fully a counterpart of x, while an object z not meeting this condition cannot (the vagueness of individual essence can also be accommodated by the relative possibility approach). Naturally, the solution generalizes to other respects in which things could have differed from the way they actually are to various degrees. For example, the previous considerations can be repeated with respect to the design of an artifact.

It is not appropriate here to attempt to adjudicate between the relative possibility and counterpart-theoretic diagnoses of the flaw in modal slippery-slope arguments, since this would take us rather far afield into some of the technical esoterica of modal logic and metaphysics (see Ramachandran, 1989). The point is simply that on both accounts, the argument against duplication as sufficient for identity is plausibly convicted of the same fallaciousness as affects the better-known Sorites paradoxes which do not involve modality. Thus, while we have not gone beyond intuition ourselves yet in defence of the sufficiency of duplication for identity across worlds, at least we have shown that the intuition is consistent with others that also have some force.

A different kind of objection to intrinsic and spatio-temporal duplication as sufficient for identity has been given by T. J. McKay (1986). McKay's example is a direct counter-example to the sufficiency condition that does not rely on any explicit supplementary argumentation for its force. Suppose we have an organism o_1 arising from a cell c. Then, even though highly improbable, it is conceivable that one way or another the molecules composing c should eventually detach themselves from o and reassemble to constitute a cell c' in which the same molecules are configured in the same way as in c. We shall suppose that $c' = c$, since if this is denied, c' and c may themselves be used in a McKay-style counter-example to the sufficiency of intrinsic and spatio-temporal duplication for identity across worlds. So in this story, what happens is that c reassembles.

But if c reassembles having given rise to o_1, we may suppose that c now gives rise to an organism o_2 by the same biological processes through which it gave rise to o_1. And so long as it does this while o_1 still exists, there is no doubt that $o_1 \neq o_2$. Indeed, logically we can have this phenomenon repeating itself as rapidly as we like to give as many organisms as we like, but two suffice to make the point. Organisms o_1 and o_2 are otherwise unexceptional, and so they both have the usual mundane range of possibilities open to them, concerning when they come into existence, what routes they trace through space, what food they ingest, what fate ultimately befalls them, and so on. Indeed, for any life which o_1 might have had, it seems that o_2 might have had the same life. Only possibilities which somehow involve one of the o_i rather than the other would be unsharable (for example, o_1 can exist in a world where o_2 does not exist, but o_2 cannot exist in such a world). However, if that is as much as the modal differences between the two amount to, then there are worlds u and v such that in u, o_1 leads such-and-such a life, and neither o_2 nor anything else originating from c exists; while in v, o_2 leads the same life, while neither o_1 nor anything else originating from c exists. Since there need be no other differences in context, it seems that the only required difference between u and v is in the mere identity of a certain organism. Thus, as it is in u, o_1 is intrinsically and spatio-temporally indistinguishable from o_2 as the latter is in v. But o_1 and o_2 are different things, hence the counter-example to the sufficiency of intrinsic and spatio-temporal duplication for identity across worlds.

The case has undeniable force. If we can correctly say "*this* one might have been thus-and-so" pointing at o_1, why cannot we equally well say "*that* one might also have been thus-and-so", pointing at o_2, when it is perfectly ordinary possibilities for organisms which fill out the "thus-and-so"? On the other hand, the idea that there are such worlds as u and v has the counter-intuitive consequence that the normal biological creation processes by which an o_i comes into existence do not settle *which* of the o_i it is which is coming into existence: some extra ingredient, the identity of the organism itself, remains to be added. In a well-known paper on personal identity, Chisholm propounded the view that if functionally equivalent hemispheres of a human brain were transplanted into separate bodies in such a way that no relation not presupposing identity distinguishes one of the new individuals from the other in terms of how he stands to the original owner of the brain ("Oldman"), there might nevertheless be a fact of the matter to the effect that one rather than the other of the new individuals is identical to Oldman (Chisholm, 1970). Since Chisholm is not positing anything like Cartesian substance, the idea that such an identity may hold in the absence of any distinguishing feature of the sort normally taken to be relevant to identity is difficult to understand. Similarly, confronted with o_1 and o_2, the idea that one rather than the other of these is identical to an organism which could have come into existence had things been thus-and-so is equally puzzling. To be able to point at o_1 and o_2 and intone "there could have been an organism which is thus-and-so and is identical to *this* organism, not that one" makes the consequences no more intelligible than they are in Chisholm's case if we point at one of the new individuals and say "*This* one, not *that* one, was Oldman".

However, a significan't difference between the modal case and the split-brain case is that in the former there is an inevitable asymmetry to which appeal can be made to justify exclusion of *v*. For in the actual world, o_2 is the second organism to originate from *c*, while in *v* it is the first, since it is stipulated to be the only organism which develops in *v* from *c*. The untoward consequences of admitting *v* may then be taken as an argument for its being *essential* to o_2 to be the second organism to originate from *c* rather than the first, or a later one, and *essential* to o_1 to be the first. We will call this the *essentiality of order*. Then if we count the fact that o_2 is the second to originate from *c* as being intrinsic to o_2, we can still have intrinsic and spatio-temporal duplication across worlds as a sufficient condition for identity.

"Intrinsic" is a term of art, and we are free to extend it in this way, but only if we apply it consistently, counting other properties relevantly like *being the second organism to develop from c* as intrinsic too. Yet earlier, we defended the essentiality origin in part by pointing out that some forms of skepticism about it allow the identity of an organism which develops from a certain cell at a world to turn on whether or not some *other* cell gives rise to an organism at that world. So we do not want to say that being in a world where such-and-such another cell does not give rise to an organism is intrinsic to a given organism. How, then, is it any better to allow the identity of an organism which develops from *c* at a world to turn on whether or not *c* has *already* given rise to an organism at that world?

There are two respects in which the cases differ. First, the proposal to allow the identity of the organism which develops from c_1 at *w* to turn on whether any organism develops from c_2 at *w* has consequences that the essentiality of order does not. The main one is that in *w*, on the former proposal, future facts play a role in fixing the identity of presently existing organisms, that is, facts about whether or not c_2 will give rise to an organism. And this seems wrong. Still, this only means that allowing the identity of an organism which develops from *c* to turn on whether it is the first, second, third, and so on to do so is not vulnerable to one particular objection; it does not make the classification of the order-property as intrinsic any more reasonable. However, on the positive side, we can note that there is a particularly intimate relationship between an organism and the cell from which it develops. The two cannot be said to be identical, since the cell ceases to exist when it divides while the organism is just beginning its existence. But there is another relation, variously known as temporary identity, or *coincidence*, or realization, which characterizes how the cell and the organism to which it gives rise stand to each other (Yablo, 1987). If having been coincident with a certain cell is an intrinsic feature of an organism at all, it seems a reasonable extension of the notion of intrinsicness to say that having been identical with a new, or an n-times-used, cell, is also intrinsic.

A move like this is partly terminological, designed mainly to keep the formulation of the sufficient condition for transworld identity simple: intrinsic and spatio-temporal duplication. The substantial issue is whether counting the order property as essential is justifiable; for if it is not, then arguments for the essentiality of a set's members, or an artifact's composition, or an organism's origin, are in trouble, since these apparently depend on constraints on identity that McKay's example, if conceded, would show to be incorrect. Yet these essentialist theses also have intuitive force. So there is an unavoidable trade-off here, unless we find a different way of justifying the essentialist theses.

4 The grounds of metaphysical necessity

Perhaps the most difficult question surrounding the topic of essentialism is the problem of how the kinds of necessities we have been discussing arise. It seems, on the face of it, that these necessities require us completely to rethink our received notions about the grounds of necessity. According to the traditional view, which receives its paradigm formulation in Hume's writings, there are no "necessary connections" between distinct existences. But this is inconsistent with a thesis such as the essentiality of origin, which postulates a connection between an organism and the cell from which it arose that is necessary *modulo* existence of the two entities. On the positive side, according to Hume, whatever necessities there are, are to be explained in terms of "relations of ideas". But again, this is inconsistent with such a thesis as that Wiggins is essentially human: even if a name such as "Wiggins" has a meaning, grasp of which is a condition for mastery of the name, it is not plausible that "human" would be part of the meaning of a name of a human. For example, in a society with advanced robotic or biotechnology, one might have complete mastery of an individual's name without knowing whether or not that individual is human. And it is completely implausible that some way of identifying the cell from which a named organism develops should be part of the content of any name of that organism. The overall problem for the traditional view is that the sorts of examples we have been discussing involve necessary truths which are a posteriori, while truths that are based on relations of ideas are supposed to be a priori.

However, our discussion in fact contains an implicit defense of the traditional association between the necessary and the a priori. For any specific essentialist thesis about a particular entity or entities, such as that Wiggins is human, is derived from two premises, one of which gives some a posteriori information about the relevant object or objects (such as that Wiggins *is* human) and the other of which states a modal principle to which objects of that sort must conform, such as the principle that the biological kind of an organism is essential to it. And the latter principle is a priori true if it is true at all. So the source of necessity may be in "relations of ideas" after all. This division of labor in the production of the necessary a posteriori renders essential properties a little less mysterious. The explanation of why some property of an object is temporary, or permanent, may have to do with the physical nature of the environment in which the object is situated, or with other physical features of the object; and it is hard to see how the explanation of why a property is accidental rather than essential or vice versa could make headway from similar resources. But it will not have to, if the status of a property as accidental or essential is settled by a priori principles.

On the other hand, for every alleged a priori truth which our defenses of certain essentialist theses have appealed to, there is a good question about the source of the truth of that principle. It would be convenient if the duplication-implies-identity principle or the no-bare-particulars principle could be accounted for as the product of definitions or decisions ("conventions"). But it is unsatisfactory to suppose that these truths are manufactured by stipulations, whether explicit or implicit. To the extent that one finds the principles plausible, they seem forced on us by the nature of our concepts. At this point, it looks as if the best one could hope for is a Strawsonian "descriptive metaphysics" which spells out the aspects of our concepts that account for the force of the principles.

It is surely no accident that essentialist theses are asserted for unified classes of things. We do not find any grounds for holding that there are *some* sets whose members belong to them accidentally, while others have their members essentially, or *some* organisms whose origin is essential to them and others whose origin is accidental. A hypothesis which would explain this is that we have a general conception of what a set is, or what an organism is, and the conception of a specific set, or a specific organism, as an instantiation of the general conception. That is, the general conception of a set, or an organism, has certain *parameters*, and our understanding of what is involved in the existence of a particular set, or organism, is simply that these parameters take on particular values: no less, *and* no more, is involved. In more detail, an organism is conceived of as a thing with a particular origin in some reproductive process, a particular nature deriving from the entities involved in that process, and a subsequent career that traces some continuous spatio-temporal path through the world; and any particular organism is simply a particular manner of instantiation of these parameters. There is, of course, no simple step from parameter-instantiation to essential property, as the inclusion of spatio-temporal path here illustrates. The point is, rather, that if there is no more to individuality than instantiation of the parameters of a general conception, then there is no sense to a notion of identity which transcends instantiation of parameters. But it seems that opposition to essentialist theses of the principles on which, we have argued, they rest inevitably leads to such a notion of identity. For example, on McKay's view, the parameters of the general conception of organism may be instantiated at a world without this being sufficient to fix which organism it is that results from the instantiations. And on a view that denies that the kind of a thing is essential to it, we arrive at a notion of bare particular, a thing which has a specific identity without, it seems, instantiating the parameters of any general conception at all.

The proposed scheme, then, if it is an accurate reflection of our concepts, offers some justification for some essentialist theses. What other kinds of justification are there? In § 1 of this chapter, we noted some technical difficulties in getting the definitions of "essential property" and "individual essence" exactly right. Fine has recently suggested that these problems are symptomatic of a deeper inadequacy in an approach to these concepts which tries to explain them in terms of what is possible and what is necessary (Fine, 1993). According to Fine, a truth of the form "*P* is essential to *x*" will certainly give rise to modal truths, such as that necessarily, if *x* exists then *x* has *P*. But simply because facts about what is essential give rise to such truths, it does not follow that essentialist concepts are modally explicable. And in fact they are not, he argues, since it is possible for the same range of modal facts to be determined by different, incompatible, collections of essentialist facts. For example, at least three competing views of the essentialist facts about persons, bodies, and minds might give rise to the same range of modal facts, the three views disagreeing over how a person, her body, and her mind are related. If a person *p* has a body *b* and a mind *m*, it may be true that, necessarily, if *p* exists *p* has *b* and *m*; but one philosopher might say that this is because persons are fundamental, though essentially possessing the bodies and minds they do, while another might say that this is because human bodies are fundamental, giving rise to persons when they (the bodies) realize sentience, but giving rise to the same mind and therefore the same person in any possible situation where they give rise to a mind. What this brings out, Fine says, is that an essentialist truth has its source in specific objects, but the modal truths to which essentialist truths give rise do not determine which particular objects are the sources of the essentialist truths.

What Fine is suggesting, then, is that modal concepts are insensitive to essentialist facts in much the same way as they are to intensional facts. It is familiar that analogs of intensional notions like proposition and belief can be defined in modal terms, using the possible-worlds apparatus; but if these analogs are taken to be the intensional notions themselves, there are various counter-intuitive consequences, such as that everyone believes all the logical consequences of their beliefs, and that there is only one necessarily true proposition. In a similar way, our definition (3), for example, has the consequence that an object can have more than one individual essence.

In place of the modal approach, Fine would put the Lockean idea of *real definition* in center stage for the explanation of essentialist concepts. We commonly think that it is words, or concepts, which admit of definition; but if we can make sense of ordinary things being definable as well, then the individual essence of a thing would be exactly what that thing's definition delivers. Correspondingly, essential properties would be those which flow from individual essence, and there would be no reason to expect existence, or being a member of $\{x\}$, to be essential to an ordinary material object *x*. With these ideas worked out in detail, we have a rival to the modal approach, and the project of resolving the problems with the modal definitions, if they can be resolved, takes on more urgency. So despite the fact that investigation of essence stretches back at least to Aristotle, we can expect lively and ongoing research to extend it; it is yet another subject whose history is definitely not at an end.

References

Aristotle 1928: Topica. In *The Works of Aristotle*, Vol. 1; ed. Sir David Ross, trans. W.A. Pickard-Cambridge. Oxford: Oxford University Press.
Chisholm, R. 1968: Identity through possible worlds: some questions. *Noûs*, 1, 1–8.
——1970: Identity through time. In *Language, Belief and Metaphysics*, eds. H.E. Kiefer and M. Munitz. New York: State University of New York Press, 163–82.
Chomsky, N. 1988: *Language and Problems of Knowledge*. Cambridge, Mass.: MIT Press.
Fine, K. 1977: Postscript. In *Worlds, Times and Selves*, A.N. Prior and K. Fine. London: Duckworth, 116–68.
——1981: First-order modal theories I – sets. *Noûs*, 15, 177–205.
——1994: The concept of essence. *Philosophical Perspectives*, Vol. 8, ed. James E. Tomberlin. Atascadero: Ridgeview Publishing Company.
Kripke, S. 1972: Naming and necessity. *Semantics of Natural Language*, ed. D. Davidson and G. Harman. Dordrecht: Reidel Publishing Company, pp. 252–355.
——1980: *Naming and Necessity*. Oxford: Basil Blackwell.
Lewis, D.K. 1968: Counterpart theory and quantified modal logic. *Journal of Philosophy*, 65, 113–26.
——1986: *On The Plurality of Worlds*. Oxford: Basil Blackwell.
McGinn, C. 1976: On the necessity of origin. *Journal of Philosophy*, 73, 127–35.
McKay, T.J. 1986: Against constitutional sufficiency principles. *Midwest Studies in Philosophy XI: Studies in Essentialism*, eds. P.A. French, T.E. Uehling, and H.K. Wettstein. Minneapolis: University of Minnesota Press, 295–304.
Putnam, H. 1975: The meaning of 'meaning'. In *Mind, Language and Reality: Philosophical Papers*, Vol. 2 by Hilary Putnam. Cambridge: Cambridge University Press, 215–71.
Ramachandran, M. 1989: An alternative translation scheme for counterpart theory. *Analysis*, 49, 131–41.
Salmon, N. 1986: Modal paradox: parts and counterparts, points and counterpoints. In *Midwest Studies in Philosophy XI: Studies in Essentialism*, eds. P.A. French, T.E. Uehling and H.K. Wettstein. Minneapolis: University of Minnesota Press, 75–120.
——1989: The logic of what might have been. *Philosophical Review*, 98, 3–34.
Wiggins, D. 1980: *Sameness and Substance*. Cambridge, Mass.: Harvard University Press.
Yablo, S. 1987: Identity, essence, and indiscernibility. *Journal of Philosophy*, 84, 293–314.

Further reading

Blackburn, S. 1987: Morals and modals. *Essays in Quasi-Realism* by Simon Blackburn. Oxford: Oxford University Press.
Fine, K. 1981: Model theory for modal logic Part III: existence and predication. *Journal of Philosophical Logic*, 10, 293–307.
Forbes, G. 1985: *The Metaphysics of Modality*. Clarendon Library of Logic and Philosophy, Oxford: Oxford University Press.
——1986: In defense of absolute essentialism. In *Midwest Studies in Philosophy XI: Studies in Essentialism*, eds. P.A. French, T.E. Uehling and H.K. Wettstein. Minneapolis: University of Minnesota Press, 3–31.
French, P.A., Uehling, T.E. and Wettstein, H.K. (eds) 1986: *Midwest Studies in Philosophy XI: Studies in Essentialism*. Minneapolis: University of Minnesota Press.

Mackie, J.L. 1974: *De* what *re* is *de re* modality? *Journal of Philosophy*, 71, 551–61.
Parsons, T. 1969: Essentialism and quantified modal logic. *Philosophical Review*, 78, 35–52.
Plantinga, A. 1974: *The Nature of Necessity*. Clarendon Library of Logic and Philosophy, Oxford: Oxford University Press.
Price, M. 1982: On the non-necessity of origin. *Canadian Journal of Philosophy*, 12, 33–45.
Sidelle, A. 1989: *Necessity, Essence and Individuation: A Defense of Conventionalism*. Ithaca, NY: Cornell University Press.
Simons, P. 1987: *Parts: A Study in Ontology*. Oxford: Oxford University Press.
Yablo, S. 1992: Cause and essence. *Synthese*, 93, 403–49.

21

Reference and necessity

ROBERT STALNAKER

Saul Kripke remarked, at the beginning of his lectures, *Naming and Necessity* (1972), that he hoped his audience would see some connection between the two topics mentioned in his title. In those lectures Kripke defended some bold theses, some about naming that belong to semantics and the philosophy of language, others about necessity that belong to metaphysics. It is clear that the arguments for the different theses were interrelated, but it remains a matter of debate just what the connections are, both in Kripke's argumentative strategy, and in the issues themselves. Kripke and Hilary Putnam were criticized for attempting to derive metaphysical conclusions – about the essential properties of things – from premises in the philosophy of language about the nature of reference and the semantics of proper names. One might instead think that the direction of Kripke's arguments go the other way: that conclusions about reference and proper names were derived in part from controversial metaphysical assumptions about possible worlds and essential properties. Either way, there is reason to be puzzled: on the one hand, one might be skeptical (to borrow the metaphor that Nathan Salmon used to express his puzzlement about this) that one could, without sleight of hand, pull a metaphysical rabbit out of a linguistic hat (see Salmon, 1981). On the other hand, one might wonder why a proper understanding of the way our language happens to work should require controversial assumptions about the metaphysical nature of the world that our language talks about. My aim in this chapter is to try to resolve some of this puzzlement by clarifying the relationship between theses and questions about reference and theses and questions about necessity and possibility. In the background of my discussion will be very general questions concerning how claims about the way we talk about the world relate to claims about what the world must be like, but in the foreground will be more specific questions concerning the relations between the different theses Kripke defends about individuals and their names. My main claim will be that Kripke's contribution was not to connect metaphysical and semantic issues, but to separate them: to provide a context in which questions about essences of things could be posed independently of assumptions about the semantic rules for the expressions used to refer to the things, and in which questions about how names refer could be addressed without making assumptions about the nature of the things referred to. I will argue that Kripke's theses about proper names and reference do not presuppose any metaphysical theses that ought to be controversial, though even stating those theses requires a framework that might be thought not to be metaphysically neutral. And I will argue that no metaphysical conclusions are derived from theses about reference and names, although clarification of the nature of reference helps in the rebuttals to arguments against metaphysical theses that Kripke defends.

I will start in section 1 by contrasting three kinds of questions that Kripke discusses in *Naming and Necessity* – two that belong to semantics and the philosophy of language, and one that belongs to metaphysics – and sketching the answers that Kripke defends, along with contrasting answers that he criticizes. Then, in section 2, I will discuss the apparatus that he uses to clarify his questions – the possible-worlds framework – and argue that it should be understood not as a metaphysical theory, but as a methodological framework in which alternative metaphysical and semantic theses can be stated. In sections 3 to 5 I will look in more detail at the arguments for the different theses and the way the three different kinds of issues interact. (See also Chapter 20, ESSENTIALISM; Chapter 22, RIGID DESIGNATION; and Chapter 19, MODALITY.)

1 Questions and theses

At this point my aim is just to set the stage by making some simple distinctions between questions, and stating, without much explanation or argument, some alternative answers to the questions. First there are questions of what I will call "descriptive semantics". A descriptive-semantic theory is a theory that says what the semantics for the language is, without saying what it is about the practice of using that language that explains why that semantics is the right one. A descriptive-semantic theory assigns *semantic values* to the expressions of the language, and explains how the semantic values of the complex expressions are a function of the semantic values of their parts. The term "semantic value," as I am using it, is a general and neutral term for whatever it is that a semantic theory associates with the expressions of the language it interprets: the things that, according to the semantics, provide the interpretations of simple expressions, and are the arguments and values of the functions defined by the compositional rules that interpret the complex expressions. If, for example, the semantic theory in question assigns senses or intensions to the names and predicates of a language, and explains the senses of complex expressions as a function of the senses or intensions of their parts, then as I am using the term, the semantic values of that semantic theory will be the senses or intensions. The particular descriptive semantic question we will be concerned with is the question, what kind of thing is the semantic value of a proper name?

Second, there are questions, which I will call questions of 'foundational semantics', about what the facts are that give expressions their semantic values, or more generally, about what makes it the case that the language spoken by a particular individual or community has a particular descriptive semantics. The specific question of this kind that we will focus on is the question, what is it about the situation, behavior, or mental states of a speaker that makes it the case that a particular proper name, as used by that speaker in a particular linguistic community, has the semantic value that it has? (See also Chapter 15, RULE-FOLLOWING,

OBJECTIVITY AND MEANING, section 2, and Chapter 5, A GUIDE TO NATURALIZING SEMANTICS.)

Third, there are questions about the capacities and potentialities of the things in the domain forming the subject-matter of some language; what, for example, might have been true of the things, such as persons and physical objects, that are the referents of some particular proper names?

Kripke's answer to the first question – the descriptive-semantic question about proper names – is the Millian answer: the semantic value of a name is simply its referent. The contrasting answer that he argued against is that the semantic value of a name is a general concept that mediates between a name and its referent: a concept of the kind that might be expressed by a definite description. According to this contrasting answer, the semantic value of the name – its sense or connotation – determines a referent for the name as a function of the facts: the referent, if there is one, is the unique individual that fits the concept, or perhaps the individual that best fits the concept.

Kripke's answer to the second question – the foundational-semantic question – is that a name has the referent that it has in virtue of a causal connection of a particular kind between the use of the name and the referent; the referent is the individual that plays the right role in the causal explanation of the fact that the name is being used, in the particular context in question, in the way that it is being used. In the case of this question, it is less clear what the contrasting thesis is, since the question is not explicitly addressed by the philosophers whom Kripke is criticizing. But what seems to be suggested is that the sense of a name is determined by the abilities and dispositions of the speaker to describe or identify a certain individual.

In response to the question about the capacities and potentialities of the things that we commonly refer to with names, Kripke defends the thesis that it makes sense to talk about the logical potential of an individual thing independently of how it is referred to, and that this potential is greater in certain ways, and less great in others, than some philosophers have supposed. For example, Shakespeare need not have been a playwright; he need not have written anything at all. He might have died in infancy, and been someone of whom we had never heard – even someone of whom all trace was lost after the seventeenth century. He might not have been called "Shakespeare," by us, or by anyone. His plays, or at least plays which are word-for-word just like his plays, really might have been written by someone else of the same name. On the other hand, Shakespeare could not possibly have been anything other than a human being, and he could not possibly have had parents other than the ones that he in fact had. In contrast, others have conceded that Shakespeare might have lacked any one of the attributes commonly attributed to him, but argued that he could not have lacked them all. Attributes not commonly known to apply to Shakespeare, such as having the particular parents that he in fact had, are all attributes that he might have lacked.

One thing I will argue is that while Kripke defends these theses about the descriptive semantics of names, the way the reference relation is determined, and the capacities and dispositions of human beings and physical objects (and I think he makes a persuasive case for each of them), his most important philosophical accomplishment is in the way he posed and clarified the questions, and not in the particular answers that he gave to them. I will suggest that we might buy Kripke's philosophical insights while rejecting all of the theses – while opting for a pure, Russellian description-theory of ordinary names, a non-causal account of the way names get associated with their values, and, in metaphysics, either for an anti-essentialist thesis according to which Shakespeare might have been a lamppost or a fried egg, or for a Leibnizian theory according to which Shakespeare had even his most apparently accidental properties essentially. The positive case for the theses that Kripke defends is not novel philosophical insight and argument, but naïve common sense. The philosophical work is done by diagnosing equivocations in the philosophical arguments for theses that conflict with naïve common sense, by making the distinctions that remove the obstacles to believing what it seems intuitively most natural to believe.

2 The possible-worlds framework

To accept what I will argue is Kripke's main philosophical contribution, you do have to buy a framework, an apparatus that he used to sharpen and clarify the contrasting theses, both semantic and metaphysical. I won't try to claim that the apparatus is either semantically or metaphysically neutral, but I will argue that the motivation and commitments of the framework are more methodological and conceptual than they are metaphysical. Philosophers often talk as if the decision to theorize with the help of this framework is, if one takes the claims one makes while using it seriously, a specific ontological commitment to a certain kind of entity. Some philosophers reject the framework because they reject the ontological commitment that its serious use makes. One hears, "I don't believe in possible worlds," as one might hear people say that they don't believe in transubstantiation, or flying saucers from other planets (commitments that some philosophers believe are about as plausible as the commitment to possible worlds). I think this attitude is based on a misconception (although I have to concede that it is a misconception that some defenders of possible worlds share with the critics). It is not that it is a misconception to think that serious talk about possibilities commits one to the existence of the possibilities one claims there are, just as it is not a misconception to think that the literal use of quantifiers commits one to the existence of things that one purports to quantify over. But it is not the framework itself that makes the specific commitments, just as it is not the semantics for first-order logic that makes any particular ontological commitment. Suppose someone were to reject the standard (extensional) semantics for first-order logic on the ground that he did not believe in individuals, to which that semantics is ontologically committed. The proper response would be to point out that first-order semantics is a framework for doing ontology, and not a particular thesis about what ontology is correct. Individuals are whatever there is to talk about; the semantic theory itself says nothing about what there is to talk about, and so makes no particular ontological commitments. Quine's slogan "To be is to be the value of a bound variable" is not an ontological thesis, but an attempt to promote a framework in which the ontological commitments of alternative philosophical and scientific theories can be stated without equivocation and compared.

The Leibnizian slogan "Necessity is truth in all possible worlds" should be understood in a similar spirit. This slogan and the possible-worlds framework that it presupposes should, I think, be understood not as an attempt to provide an ontological foundation for a reduction of modal notions, but as an attempt to formulate a theoretical language in which modal discourse can be regimented, its structure revealed, equivocation diagnosed and avoided. Modal discourse – speech that involves words such as "may," "might," and "must" – is notoriously complex and problematic, providing fertile ground for ambiguities, both ambiguities of scope, that arise because the semantic structure of modal statements is complicated and not simply reflected in surface syntax, and ambiguities that arise from alternative senses and context dependence of the modal words. Modal words interact with each other and with quantifiers, descriptions, temporal modifiers, and grammatical tense, aspect, and mood in complicated ways that are difficult to sort out. Philosophical puzzles about, for example, necessary connection and counterfactual dependence, reference to non-existent things, capacities, and dispositions, the ability to do otherwise, the necessity of the past and the openness of the future, will presumably not all be dissolved simply by getting clear about modal discourse; but everyone should agree that clarifying the discourse in which such problems are posed is an essential first step. It is important to separate disagreements based on contrasting interpretations of the way the language works from those about the claims that the language is being used to state. Whatever one's metaphysical beliefs about the reality that modal discourse purports to describe, one should agree that it would be nice to have a language that is free of some of the ambiguities that infect modal discourse, and in which the claims made with modal words and constructions might be paraphrased; a language that uses only parts of discourse that are relatively clear and uncontroversial (the indicative mood and quantifiers), but that still has the expressive power to make claims about what might, would, or must be true. Achieving such clarification does not require a reductive analysis of modal to non-modal concepts, and so it is not required that a canonical language in which we do modal semantics be built on some pure, non-modal foundation, any more than formal languages designed to clarify quantification needed to be built on some pure, non-quantificational foundation (whatever that would be). What is needed is only the kind of opportunistic departure from ordinary language involved in the boot-strap operation that Quine called "regimentation". In the kind of regimentation Quine recommends, we begin with *ad hoc* paraphrases to remove ambiguity, we introduce variables to facilitate cross-reference, and we adopt a syntax in which quantifier scopes are reflected in a simple and systematic way in the order of the symbols and the placement of parentheses. "The artificial notation of logic," Quine remarked, "is itself explained, of course, in ordinary language"(1960, p. 159). Similarly, the primitive resources of the possible-worlds framework are explained in ordinary modal language, and the explanations will be intelligible only to one who understands at least some of that part of language. A modal skeptic who doubts that anything both meaningful and true is said in modal discourse will doubt both the value and the intelligibility of a framework in which that discourse is clarified. But it may be that the source of the skepticism is in the equivocations and unclarities that the framework helps to remove.

The general strategy is to find a part of our modal discourse that seems relatively free of the particular equivocations and unclarities that infect modal discourse generally, a part that might be developed and used to clarify the rest. We look for a way of making modal claims that uses paraphrases to avoid problematic constructions, a way that uses forms of expression that may perhaps be stilted and less idiomatic than the familiar ones, but that will still be recognizable paraphrases of ordinary modal claims. The following assumption about what is, in any sense, possible points the way to one such strategy of paraphrase: if something might be true, then it might be true in some particular way. It would make no sense to affirm, for example, that there might be life elsewhere in our galaxy, while denying that it is possible that there be life in any particular part of the galaxy, or that there might be life of any particular kind – animal life, or non-animal life – elsewhere in the galaxy. If something is possible, then it is possible that it be realized in a concrete way – perhaps in many alternative ways. The possible-worlds framework begins with this simple assumption, and with the assumption that, in general, statements about what may or might be true can be described in terms of the ways a possibility might be realized. The framework takes alternative specific ways that possibilities might be realized as the primitive elements, out of which propositions – the things that are said to be possible, necessary, or true – are built, and in terms of which the modal properties of those propositions are defined. The main benefit of this move is that it permits one to paraphrase modal claims in an extensional language that has quantifiers, but no modal auxiliaries, and so in a language in which the semantic structure of the usual modal discourse can be discussed without begging controversial questions about that structure.

I have been arguing for the metaphysical neutrality of the possible worlds framework; but I should emphasize that I do not mean to suggest that the use of the framework is free of ontological commitment to possibilities (such as ways things might be, counterfactual situations, or possible states of the world). Regimentation clarifies one's commitments, but does not pretend to eliminate them. Furthermore, it must be conceded that the moves made in this regimentation of modal discourse (particularly the move that paraphrases "—might have been true in various particular ways" as "there are various particular ways that—might have been true") are not completely innocent (see Chapter 19, MODALITY, section 3.3). As Quine would be the first to emphasize, no strategy of regimentation is neutral in any absolute sense: "The quest of a simplest, clearest overall pattern of canonical notation is not to be distinguished from a quest of ultimate categories, a limning of the most general traits of reality"(Quine, 1960, p. 161). But it is a desideratum of any such project that it be able to accommodate and articulate a range of alternative responses to the questions and puzzles that motivated the project. I think the possible-worlds framework satisfies this desideratum, but the real test of this claim is not in some general methodological argument, but in the fruits of the work that is done with its help.

3 What are the semantic values of names?

The possible-worlds framework provides the resources to state and clarify both metaphysical and semantic theses. In both cases, I want to argue, the principal conceptual benefit of the apparatus is that it provides an account of a subject-matter that is independent of languages used to describe that subject-matter. Of course, whether the subject is geology or modal metaphysics, we never get away from language – it is just too hard to say very much without using it. But just as we want to distinguish rocks from words (even if we have to use words for rocks to do it), so it is useful to distinguish possibilities from the words used to describe them. To make this distinction is not to beg any questions against the philosophical thesis that the source of all necessity is in language; a conceptual distinction does not foreclose the possibility that one of the things distinguished may in the end be reduced to the other.

To see that possibilities are part of the subject-matter of semantics as well as of modal metaphysics one need only make the following assumptions: first, a central function of an assertion is to convey information, and information is conveyed by distinguishing between possibilities. Second, a principal goal of semantics is to explain how the expressions used to perform speech-acts, such as assertion, are used to convey information – to distinguish between possibilities – and how the way complex sentences distinguish between possibilities is a function of the semantic values of their parts. To understand what is said, for example, in an utterance of "The first dog born at sea was a basset hound," one needs to know what the world would have to be like in order for what was said in that utterance to be true.

These simple assumptions about the goal of semantics might be expressed in terms of truth conditions: semantics is concerned, among other things, with the truth conditions of statements, and the way their truth conditions are a function of the semantic values of their parts (where semantic values are whatever they must be in order to contribute appropriately to truth conditions). What are truth conditions? If we are looking for an answer to this question that identifies a non-linguistic object that semantics can associate with statements, it seems natural to say that the truth conditions of a statement are the possibilities that, if realized, would make the statement true. We want a conceptual distinction between truth conditions and any particular forms of expression in which those truth conditions might be stated, simply because it is useful to theorize about a language in a different language, and when we do so, we want to be able to talk not just about the inter-linguistic relations between the language we are theorizing about and the language we are theorizing in, but about the relation between the language we are theorizing about and the world.

The task of descriptive semantics, in this framework, is to say what kinds of things the semantic values of expressions of various categories are, and to explain how the truth conditions of sentences (or sentences in context) are a function of the semantic values of their constituents. So to give the semantic value of a proper name is to say what contribution a proper name makes to the truth conditions of the sentences containing it, where the truth conditions of a sentence, or a sentence in context, are represented by the set of possibilities that, if realized, would make what the sentence says in that context true. The two answers that Kripke compares – the Millian and the Fregean answers – are made precise in the following ways:

(1) the semantic value of a name is simply its referent; the proposition expressed by a simple sentence containing a name is the proposition that is true in a possible world if and only if that referent has the attribute expressed by the predicate of the sentence.

(2) the semantic value of a name is its sense, which is a concept that applies to, at most, one individual in each possible world (the kind of concept that might be expressed by a definite description). The proposition expressed by a simple sentence containing a name is the proposition that is true in a possible world if and only if the individual to which the concept expressed by the name applies in that world has the attribute expressed by the predicate of the sentence.

Thus far, I have talked only about a question and a framework for clarifying alternative answers to it, and not about arguments in support of one or the other of the answers. The framework is neutral on the question of which of these alternatives, if either, gives a correct account of the semantics of the expressions in English and other natural languages that we identify as proper names. This seems to be an empirical question of no particular philosophical interest, a question that philosophical analysis and argument are not relevant to answering. The way in which the alternative answers are articulated in the framework does point the way to some of the empirical considerations that may be relevant to settling the issue, by making clear what the consequences of those alternatives are; but it appears that no philosophical – certainly no metaphysical – issue hangs on which answer is right. Even though Kripke defended, on empirical grounds, the Millian answer, he nowhere suggested that things had to be this way. For all that he argues to the contrary, we might perfectly well have spoken a language with names that all referred only by having senses that determined referents. It just happens that we do not.

What needed philosophical defense was not the empirical adequacy of the Millian answer, but its coherence. While Kripke did not suggest that philosophical argument could establish that the answer he favored was correct, he had to answer philosophical arguments that purported to establish that it was incorrect. John Searle, for example, argued that

> the view that there could be a class of logically proper names, i.e. expressions whose very meaning is the object to which they are used to refer, is false. It isn't that there just do not happen to be any such expressions: there could not be any such expressions. . . . The view that proper names are 'unmeaning marks', that they have 'denotation' but not 'connotation', must be at a fundamental level wrong. (Searle, 1969, p. 93)

Michael Dummett makes a similar claim: "there cannot be a proper name whose whole sense consists in its having a certain object as referent, without the sense determining that object as referent in some particular way" (Dummett, 1973, p. 232). These claims are puzzling, in the light of Kripke's way of posing the problem of the descriptive semantics of proper names. It appears that he showed, simply in setting up the alternatives, how to give a coherent specification of a language containing "expressions whose very meaning is the object to which they are used to refer." What kind of argument could show not only that we do not in fact speak such a language, but that we could not possibly do so? To address this question, we need to turn to the second of the two kinds of issues in the philosophy of language that Kripke is concerned with.

4 How do names get their semantic values?

Why do Searle and Dummett think that we could not speak a language of the kind that Kripke described, in which the semantic value of a name is simply its referent? Searle's reason was that "if the utterance of the expressions communicated no descriptive content, then there could be no way of establishing a connection between the expression and the object," no way to answer the question, "What makes *this* expression refer to *that* object?" (Searle, 1969, p. 93). Dummett's reason is similar: "an object cannot be recognized as the referent of a proper name . . . unless it has first been singled out in some definite way" (Dummett, 1973, p. 232). In both cases, the reason for rejecting the possibility of a certain descriptive semantic thesis appeals to considerations that relate to the foundational question, which asks what it is about the capacities, customs, practices, or mental states of a speaker or community of speakers that makes it the case that an expression has the semantic value that it has. What seems to be suggested is that the hypothesis that a language has a Millian semantics poses a foundational question that cannot be given a satisfactory answer.

But this is not the way either Searle or Dummett put their claims, since they do not separate the two questions, "what is the semantics for names (or the semantic value of a particular name) in the language we speak?" and "what makes it the case that the language we speak (or a particular name in that language) has this semantics?" Once the two questions are separated, it is difficult to see what could rule out the *possibility* that we speak any language that has a well-defined semantics. If a Millian semantics for names can be articulated, why can't a community of speakers adopt the convention to speak such a language?

The assumption implicit in the rejection of the possibility of a Millian semantics is that the two questions we have separated should receive a single answer. Something like a Fregean sense should explain why a name has the particular referent it has, where this is interpreted to mean that it should explain both what it is about the capacities and attitudes of the speaker that give the name the referent it has, and also what it is that the speaker communicates or conveys in using the name. Kripke charged Frege with conflating these two questions:

> Frege should be criticized for using the term 'sense' in two senses. For he takes the sense of a designator to be its meaning and he also takes it to be the way its reference is determined. Identifying the two, he supposes that both are given by definite descriptions. (Kripke, 1972, p. 59)

Whether Frege is responsible for making this mistake is a question of textual interpretation that I will not comment on, but it is clear, I think, that Searle is concerned with both kinds of questions, and that he takes himself to be following Frege. Searle describes his axiom of identification, a principle that is supposed to be constitutive of singular definite reference, as "a generalization of Frege's dictum that every referring expression must have a sense"(Searle, 1969, p. 80). The principle is about what must be communicated or conveyed (or at least "appealed to" or "invoked") in the utterance of the referring expression; but it is also an attempt to say what it is about the capacities of speakers that explains why their referring expressions have the referents they have. "What I am trying to get at," he says, "is how noises identify objects"(Searle, 1969, p. 83 n.).

If we are implicitly looking for a semantic account of names that answers both questions at once, then the Millian theory that says that the semantic value of a name is simply its referent looks like a non-answer; it seems to be denying the obvious fact that there must be something about the capacities, behavior, or mental state of the users of the name that make it the case that the name has the referent that it has. On the other hand, the conflation of the two questions masks the fact that the sense theory, interpreted as an answer to the question of descriptive semantics, is also a non-answer to the foundational question. Suppose we were to accept the Fregean thesis that names have the referent that they have because they have a sense that determines a function whose value (at the actual world) is that referent. This simply raises the question: what is it about the capacities, behavior, or mental state of the users of the name that makes it the case that the name has the sense that it in fact has? Whether one is a Fregean or not, the two questions need to be distinguished; and once they are, the way is opened for answers to each that are less easily seen as possible answers to the other: the Millian answer to the descriptive question, and the causal account of reference that Kripke defends as an answer to the foundational question. This latter thesis – that what makes it the case that a name has a certain individual as its referent is that the individual plays a certain role in the causal or historical explanation of the speaker's use of the name – makes no sense as an attempt to specify a semantic value, a candidate to be the meaning or sense of a name, and so it can be taken seriously only after the two questions are distinguished.

Kripke and other defenders of a causal theory of reference were criticized for the vagueness of their thesis. Causal connections are ubiquitous, and it is obvious that there are a great many individuals that are causally implicated in the speaker's use of the name; but that are not by any stretch of the imagination plausible candidates to be the referent. A proper causal theory of reference would have to specify just what sort of causal connection is necessary and sufficient for reference, and that is a notoriously difficult demand. Kripke himself emphasized that he was presenting not a reductive analysis of reference, but only an alternative picture. To some skeptics, this sounded like an evasion. The suspicion was that any sufficiently specific and precise version of the causal theory would be subject to as many counter-examples as the description theory, and so that the plausibility of the positive alternative to the description theory rested on its lack of specificity. But I think this line of criticism misses the point. What is essential to the alternative picture was the separation of the questions, and the distinction between two different ways in which the extension of an expression might depend on the facts: first, what semantic value an expression has depends on the facts; second, if the semantic value is a sense, the extension of an expression with a given semantic value may depend on the facts. The philosophical work was done in making the distinctions that removed the obstacles to accepting the naïve answers to the questions that were distinguished. If we ask, what does one have to know to understand a name? the naïve answer is that one must know who or what it names – nothing more. (In contrast, no-one would be tempted to give this answer to the analogous question, of what one must know to understand a definite description.) And if we ask how a name comes to name what it names – what, for example, makes "Shakespeare" as we use it a name of the particular person Shakespeare – I think most people would be inclined to point to a historical narrative: his family was called "Shakespeare," or something like that, at the time, and knowledge of him, his plays, and his name were passed down through the generations to us. This is not a particularly exciting philosophical theory, but it doesn't seem wrong, and it does seem incompatible with the kind of answer implied by a description theory. Kripke's causal-chain story is just an articulation of the naïve answer, and one that does not add a lot of constructive detail to it. But by separating and clarifying the questions to which these naïve answers are answers, he brought out why the theoretical reasons for resisting those answers are bad reasons.

The diagnosis of equivocation is rarely the end of the matter in a philosophical argument. I will sketch a line of argument for the impossibility of a Millian semantics that recognizes the distinction between the two kinds of questions. I don't think this line of argument is successful, but it is instructive to see where it takes the debate.

If there is a credible defense of the thesis that a Millian language is impossible, I think it must challenge the assumption that any well-defined semantics might be the semantics of a language that is used by a speaker, or realized in a speech community. Here is one way that the assumption might be challenged: First, the following seems a reasonable general constraint on the correctness of a claim that a certain semantics is the semantics for the language spoken in a certain community of speakers: if the semantics is correct, then speakers must know, at least for the most part, what, according to the semantics, they are saying. A notion of saying might allow that in some cases one succeeds in saying things using words one does not understand; but it is hard to deny, first, that if one doesn't know what one is saying, then one does not mean what one says, and second, that according to a correct account of what people say in a given speech community, speakers generally mean what they say (not in the sense that they are sincere

– believe what they say – but just in the sense that what they say coincides with what they mean).

Second, we may note that it is possible to give a determinate specification of a semantic value without knowing what that value is, even without anyone knowing what the value is. Consider this example discussed by Gareth Evans: let "Julius" be a (rigid) proper name for the person (whoever he or she was) who invented the zip (Evans, 1982, p. 31). Then (assuming that some particular single individual invented the zip) a sentence such as "Julius was born in Minsk" expresses a determinate proposition about a particular individual, but we don't know who the individual is, so we don't know what proposition it is that is expressed. We understand a description of the proposition, and we understand, and may believe, metalinguistic statements about that proposition, such as 'What is said by "Julius was born in Minsk" is probably false.' We can have beliefs and make assertions about the truth or falsity of whatever proposition is expressed, but (according to this line of argument), we do not thereby assert or believe that Julius was or was not born in Minsk, and we cannot do so unless we know who invented the zip.

Now suppose that one could make a case that our mental relations to particular individuals are in all relevant respects like our relation to Julius – that since we can know individuals only by description, only as whoever or whatever it is that is presented to us in a certain way – we don't ever know, in the relevant sense, who or what it is that we are referring to with the names we use. Then it would seem to follow that, although we can define a language with a Millian semantics, we could never speak one, since we could not have the knowledge required to know what the sentences of such a language say.

I think the first premise of this argument should be conceded: a semantics for the language spoken by a community of speakers cannot be right if it implies that speakers generally do not know what they are saying. It should also be conceded that, according to the Millian semantics for names, as contrasted with the Fregean semantics, speakers do not know what they are saying when they use a name if they do not know who the referent of their name is. But what is it to know what one is referring to? At this point the battleground shifts from semantics and the philosophy of language to the philosophy of mind, where variations on some of the same battles are fought.

Underlying the contrasting answers to the foundational question about reference (what makes it the case that a name has the referent it has?) are contrasting strategies for answering parallel foundational questions about mental states: what makes it the case that a thought – a judgment or an intention – has the content it has, or is about what it is about? The argument sketched above against the possibility of a Millian semantics for an actual language rests on the assumption that thoughts can be about particular things only by expressing general concepts that apply to those individuals. If this were right, then the kind of causal-chain or historical-explanation story that Kripke and Keith Donnellan told to answer the foundational question about semantics would be an answer that detached the determination of the semantic values of expressions from the mental states and capacities of the users of the expressions, and so would be an answer that was vulnerable to this argument. But why should we think that thoughts, any more than names, can be about individuals only by expressing general concepts?

In defense of his principle of identification and his argument against the Millian theory, Searle asks:

> What is it to *mean* or *intend* a particular object to the exclusion of all others? Some facts incline us to think that it is a movement of the soul – but can I intend just one particular object independent of any description or other form of identification I could make of it? And if so, what makes my intention an intention directed at just *that* object and not at some other? Clearly the notion of what it is to intend to refer to a particular object forces us back on the notion of identification by description. (Searle, 1969, p. 87)

The suggestion implicit in these rhetorical questions is that an intention to refer to a particular individual must be explained as a behavioral capacity, the capacity to give a general description, or otherwise identify an individual who is, by fitting the description or being the object identified, the object meant or intended. The only alternative, it is implied, is some kind of obscurantist intentional magic, some kind of movement of the soul.

Even if Searle were right in his suggestion that intentions and other intentional states directed at particular individuals must be explained in terms of the capacities of the agent to identify the individual, this would still not give him the additional premise needed for the argument against the possibility of a Millian semantics for names. For Searle is not arguing that we cannot have intentions and other attitudes toward particular individuals; he is only arguing for a condition that is necessary for having such intentions and attitudes. What he needs for the argument is a constraint on the content of the attitudes we can have; but what he offers instead is a constraint on the conditions under which one can have attitudes with a certain kind of content. Whatever it is that constitutes intending and having knowledge and beliefs about a particular object, "to the exclusion of all others," so long as it is possible to have such intentions, knowledge, and beliefs, it will be possible to understand and speak a language with a Millian semantics.

But in any case, there is no real argument for the conclusion that mental magic is the only alternative to an explanation of intentionality in terms of an agent's capacities to identify. A causal account of intentional content – an explanation that looks back to how mental states came to be, rather than only forward to what those states dispose the agent to do – is equally compatible with a non-obscurantist account of intentionality. A causal account of intentions and beliefs seems, in fact, to be presupposed by the defense of a causal account of reference given by Kripke and Donnellan, since it is argued that speakers not only can refer, but can intend to refer, to particular individuals without being able to describe or identify those individuals. Causal and non-causal accounts of how names get their reference can share the assumption that reference is determined by intentions. The causal theory of reference is causal because it assumes a causal account of the content of the intentions that determine reference.

An argument of Michael Dummett's for the impossibility of a Millian semantics, like the argument I have sketched, bases this conclusion on the impossibility of a certain kind of knowledge: what Dummett calls *bare knowledge of reference*. Here is his characterization: "A *bare* knowledge of the reference of the name *a* will consist . . . in knowing, of some object, that *a* refers to it, where this is a *complete* characterization of this particular piece of knowledge" (Dummett, 1991, p. 127). I am not sure what Dummett means by a "particular piece of knowledge," or what it is for a characterization of such a piece to be complete; but if we interpret Dummett's arguments in the context of the possible-worlds conception of content, I think it is reasonable to identify his notion of bare knowledge of reference with knowledge of a singular proposition – the proposition that is true in a possible world if and only if a certain particular individual is the referent of the name *a*. An essential step in Dummett's argument for the impossibility of bare knowledge of reference is a claim that is essentially equivalent to Searle's principle of identification: we cannot have what Dummett calls knowledge-what – knowledge *of* a certain individual that it has some property F (for example, knowledge of a certain individual that it is the referent of the name *a*) – unless we have the capacity to describe or identify the object. More strongly, for any true knowledge-what ascription, there must be a true propositional-knowledge ascription whose content is a non-singular proposition that makes the method of identification explicit, and that entails the knowledge-what ascription: a propositional-knowledge ascription on which the knowledge-what ascription "*rests*" (Dummett, 1991, p. 130). Now, I am not persuaded that this claim is correct; but even if this much is granted, I don't think it gives one reason to reject the possibility of knowledge of singular propositions. Suppose we grant that one cannot know of some particular individual x that it is F unless for some G one identifies x as the G, and knows that the G is F. Further, suppose we grant that in a particular case the claim that y knows of x that it is F rests on, and is entailed by, the claim that y knows that the G is F. What has been granted is a claim that certain conditions are necessary, and others sufficient, for having knowledge of a certain kind; but nothing follows from this about the content of that kind of knowledge. If "bare knowledge" of some object, that *a* refers to it, is taken to mean knowledge that can exist in isolation, without knowing anything else about what *a* refers to, then we can grant that bare knowledge of reference is impossible; but that does not imply that knowledge of x, that *a* refers to it, is not knowledge of a particular proposition, a singular proposition, or that it is not possible to have knowledge of such propositions.

We can agree with Dummett that it is a difficult problem to say just what conditions must be met for one to know who or what the referent of a name *a* is, and that the problem is not solved simply by saying that to have such knowledge-what is to know a singular proposition of the form "x is the referent of *a*". But the problem is not that saying this would be wrong; it is just that specifying the content of a knowledge ascription is not the same as saying what it is for that knowledge ascription to be true.

The distinctions, on the level of both speech and thought, between questions about what content is and about how content comes to be determined, help to open up a place in conceptual space for a causal account of reference and of intentionality generally, and provide a rebuttal to arguments for the impossibility of a Millian semantics for a realized language. They do not, of course, end the debate. Once theoretical obstacles to such accounts are removed, examples and untheoretical considerations make a strong prima facie case for the claim that some such account is correct; but, as Gareth Evans reminded Kripke, "the deliverances of untutored linguistic intuition may have to be corrected in the light of considerations of theory" (Evans, 1982, p. 76). I think more theoretical considerations also support causal accounts of intentionality, but that is a different part of the story. I want to turn back now to questions about the relation between reference and metaphysical necessity.

5 Names and essences

Whatever the fate of the debate between them, we have a stark contrast between two pictures of the way we are related, both by speech and by thought, to particular things in the world. On one picture, we can think and talk directly about particular things in virtue of our causal interaction with those things; on the other, our mental and linguistic acts relate us to particular things only by our grasping and expressing purely qualitative concepts that may be instantiated by particular things. The question now is, do these pictures of mental and linguistic representation either presuppose or support some particular conception of the nature of the particular things that we talk and think about, or that instantiate our concepts? Specifically, does the conception of reference that Kripke argues for presuppose or support the particular brand of essentialism that he defends? The two kinds of issues, I will argue, are independent. The only role of the theory of reference in Kripke's arguments for metaphysical conclusions is to help diagnose and rebut fallacious arguments that rest on a conflation of the two kinds of issues.

One of Searle's arguments against the Millian account of proper names was that it (or at least an "uncritical acceptance" of it) leads us into some "metaphysical traps" (Searle, 1969, p. 163). It is suggested that this conception of proper names presupposes "a basic metaphysical distinction between objects and properties or aspects of objects" (p. 164). Actually, Searle's attitude toward the relation between the metaphysical and the semantic issues is not entirely clear. Does he locate the mistake in the premise – the Millian semantics for names – or in the inference from this premise to a metaphysical conclusion? On the one hand, we are warned against "the original sin of metaphysics, the attempt to read real or alleged features of language into the world" and "the metaphysical mistake of deriving ontological conclusions from linguistic theses" (p. 164); but on the other hand, the fact that the Millian account of names seems to presuppose this metaphysical distinction is part of an argument against that semantic account. It cannot be a good argument against a semantic account of proper names that someone has illegitimately drawn metaphysical conclusions from that account. So perhaps the view is that the Millian theory of names is already a covertly metaphysical thesis: that false metaphysical conclusions are validly drawn from it because the thesis is the result, rather than the occasion, for reading alleged features of language into the world. But if so, can't we separate the semantic from the metaphysical aspects of the thesis, and evaluate the semantic thesis independently of the metaphysical conclusions that are illegitimately drawn from it? If we couldn't make such a separation, then it would not be so clear that it was illegitimate to draw ontological conclusions from linguistic theses.

Searle's target is the Wittgenstein of the *Tractatus*, and not Kripke (whose lectures were given after Searle's book was published). But Kripke does make the kind of metaphysical distinction between objects and properties that Searle rejects; and, of course, he also defends the account of names that Searle argues is the illegitimate source of the metaphysical distinction. I will sketch the way Kripke makes the metaphysical distinction, and then argue that his metaphysical theses are compatible with the Fregean picture of mental and linguistic representation, and so do not presuppose the Millian semantics or the causal theory of reference. What is presupposed in the defense of Kripke's metaphysical conception is only that the two accounts of reference and intentionality not be conflated. I will conclude by considering whether there is a dependence that goes in the other direction: whether the semantic picture that Kripke defends presupposes his metaphysical theses about the relation between individuals and their properties. Here the issues are harder to disentangle, but I will argue that the Millian theory of names, and the causal theory of reference, are compatible with alternative metaphysical conceptions of individuals and their properties. There is no derivation of metaphysical conclusions from semantic premises.

What is it to make a basic distinction between objects and properties? Searle derided the metaphysical picture of an object as "a combination of its propertyless self and its properties," as well as the contrasting picture of an object as nothing but "a heap or collection of properties" (1969, p. 164); but what do these pictures really come to? Kripke also scorned the same two contrasting pictures, rejecting the assumption that objects are some kind of "bare particulars" or "propertyless substrata underlying the qualities," as well as the claim that they are nothing but bundles of qualities, "whatever that may mean" (Kripke, 1972, p. 52). The possible-worlds framework suggests a way to express the idea that a particular is conceptually separable from its properties without relying on the rejected picture of a bare particular. Properly understood, the issue concerns the modal properties of an individual. Intuitively, it seems clear that ordinary things might have had different properties from the ones they in fact have: Shakespeare might not have written plays, which, in the possible-worlds paraphrase, is to say that there is a possible world in which Shakespeare did not write plays. This possible world is one in which the very person who actually wrote the plays we know and love exists, and did not write plays. So (assuming the modal claim is right) the property of writing plays is not essential to a particular person who has this property. The same goes for lots of other ordinary properties ascribed to ordinary persons and things; but not to all of them. Shakespeare obviously could not have been someone other than Shakespeare (although he could have been called something else), and according to Kripke he could not have been a member of a different species, or even have had different parents. Now these simple modal claims say nothing about names or reference; but in stating them I am using the proper name "Shakespeare," so the content of what I am saying about counterfactual possibilities might be thought to depend on the semantics for names. If "Shakespeare" were an abbreviation for a definite description, as Russell argued, then the statement that Shakespeare might not have written plays, and its paraphrase, that there is a possible world in which Shakespeare did not write plays, would both be ambiguous. If, for example, "Shakespeare" were an abbreviation for "the most famous Elizabethan playwright," then on one interpretation the claim that Shakespeare might not have written plays would be the claim that there is a possible world in which the person who is the most famous Elizabethan playwright in that world did not write plays. This, of course, is not the claim that Kripke intended to make, and it does not seem, intuitively, that the words used to make the claim are open to such an interpretation. The modal claims, in either their ordinary form or in their possible-worlds paraphrases, do not seem ambiguous, but that is a linguistic intuition which is separable from the modal intuition about the person who is the referent, by whatever means, of the name "Shakespeare," the claim that is expressed by the other reading of the claim that the most famous Elizabethan playwright might not have written plays. Now on what I have been calling the Fregean conception of mental representation, perhaps we cannot have such modal intuitions about particular individuals, since perhaps, on that conception, the only way we can have any thoughts at all about an individual is to have beliefs about whoever it is that is presented to us in some particular way. But this does not matter to the issue, since the metaphysical intuition can be expressed in a perfectly general way: whoever the person is who fits our Shakespeare concept, that person might have been someone who didn't write plays. So the modal theses stand or fall independently of the success or failure of the defense of theses either about the semantics for proper names, or about the way our thoughts relate us to the individuals that are the referents of those names.

If both the Fregean conception of reference and intentionality that Searle favors and the alternative semantic conceptions that he criticizes are compatible with the metaphysical distinction between particulars and their properties, what is the source of his objections to this distinction? I think they derive from a conflation of the two semantic conceptions. By equivocating between the two semantic theses, one can argue from semantic assumptions to a metaphysical conclusion: On the Fregean picture, there is an analytic, and so necessary connection between the name "Aristotle" and a cluster of properties, and so it is legitimate to conclude, as Searle does, that "it is a necessary truth that Aristotle has the logical sum [inclusive disjunction] of the properties commonly attributed to him" (Searle, 1969, p. 173). This claim, by itself implies nothing about what must be true of the person Aristotle, and so raises no problems about the traditional distinction between objects and their properties. On the unequivocal Fregean picture, "Aristotle" means, roughly, whoever satisfies the cluster; so according to this semantic hypothesis, if the person Aristotle hadn't satisfied the cluster, he would not have been Aristotle, but he might still have existed. It is only when one combines the Fregean premise with the assumption incompatible with it that the name "Aristotle" is a Millian name that one can take the next step in the argument, the inference from the claim that

Aristotle satisfies the cluster, to the conclusion that it is true *of* Aristotle that he satisfies the cluster. As Searle says, "I wish to argue that though no single one of them is analytically true of Aristotle, their disjunction is" (p. 169). It is only when one has the conclusion that the person Aristotle is necessarily connected with the properties used to identify him that one has reason for skepticism about substance, and for the claim that "it is misleading, if not downright false, to construe the facts which one must possess in order to refer as always facts *about* the object referred to, for that suggests that they are facts about some *independently* identified object" (p. 93).

To make a positive case for his modal theses about individuals, all Kripke does is to develop the framework in which the theses can be formulated clearly and separated from theses about names and reference. The rest of the work is done simply by pointing out what seems from an intuitive point of view obviously true, once it is clear what the alternatives are. If Kripke's rhetorical style had been a little different, he might have made this point by saying that he was just assembling reminders, not putting forward theses. What philosophy does, he might have said, is simply to put everything before us (Wittgenstein, 1953, §§ 126–8).

Not all of the metaphysical claims about individuals that Kripke defends on intuitive grounds are equally compelling. On the one hand, it seems hard to deny that we can make intuitive sense of questions about the potentialities of particular individuals independently of the means used to refer to them. To suppose that Shakespeare never wrote plays is to envision a counterfactual situation in which Shakespeare – the man himself – wrote no plays. Other theses Kripke defends are more controversial from an intuitive point of view, particularly theses that deny that certain things are possible, or equivalently, that affirm that particular things have certain essential properties. Can I coherently suppose that Shakespeare – the man himself – had different parents from the ones he in fact had, or that he was born in a different century? Kripke would argue that if we think we can suppose these things, we are confused: if we think clearly about what we are trying to suppose we will see that these are not coherent counterfactual possibilities. Not everyone will share these intuitions, even after setting aside the bad reasons for resisting them that Kripke points out. The possible-worlds framework does not settle such metaphysical questions, or even tell us how they should be settled; its job is to raise them, and to make clearer what the alternative answers say.

I have argued that Kripke's metaphysical theses do not presuppose his theses on reference and intentionality. What about the other direction? Does the Millian semantics for proper names or the causal account of reference and intentionality presuppose the metaphysical picture that Kripke defends? The theses about names can easily be separated from the more specific essentialist theses, but the general metaphysical issues about the identification of individuals across possible worlds are more difficult to disentangle from the thesis that names are rigid designators whose reference is established by causal interaction between the speaker and the referent. A rigid designator is one which denotes the same individual in all possible worlds; doesn't this presuppose that the same individuals can be found in different possible worlds?

Consider the following anti-essentialist metaphysical picture, a version of the "bundle of qualities" conception of an individual rejected by both Kripke and Searle. According to this conception, a particular individual is just the coinstantiation of a certain set of qualities. If individuals are identified across possible worlds at all, it is only in virtue of some counterpart relation which is definable in terms of the relations between the bundles of qualities coinstantiated in the different worlds. Consider first the pure Leibnizian version of this metaphysical picture, according to which particular individuals have all of their properties, including their relational properties, essentially. On this conception, not only is it a mistake to think that we can coherently suppose that Shakespeare – the person himself – had different parents, we cannot even make sense of a counterfactual possibility in which he ate a slightly different breakfast than he in fact ate on a certain morning, or even lived in a world in which slightly different events took place years after his death. The thesis that names are rigid designators is perfectly compatible with this uncompromising metaphysics, but the combination of metaphysical and semantic theses has no plausibility. It gives us the conclusion, for example, that the proposition expressed by the statement that Shakespeare wrote plays is one that is true only in the actual world, and so is one that entails every true proposition. Only God could know that Shakespeare wrote plays. We more limited creatures can know that "Shakespeare wrote plays" expresses a true proposition, and we can know that, whatever proposition it expresses, it is necessarily equivalent to the proposition expressed by "Elvis Presley played the guitar;" but so long as we are ignorant of any fact, we cannot know which proposition it is that these sentences express.

Giving up the Millian theory of names would not resolve the problem, since there is no plausibility in the assumption that however we refer to him, Shakespeare – the man himself – could not possibly have failed to write plays, or to eat what he in fact ate for breakfast. A less uncompromising version of this metaphysical picture gives a different account of what it is for an individual to have a property essentially. According to the liberal Leibnizian (Lewis, 1986, ch. 4), to say that Shakespeare – the person himself – might not have written plays is to say that a counterpart of that person in some possible world did not write plays, where the counterpart relation is reducible to some kind of qualitative similarity. The counterpart variation of the Leibnizian metaphysics of individuals is not a thesis about names, but is about the modal properties of individuals, however they are referred to. The difference between the unreconstructed Leibnizian theory and the counterpart version might still be construed as a semantic rather than a metaphysical difference, but it is a difference in the way complex predicates involving modality are to be interpreted, and by itself says nothing about how names are to be understood. But the absurd consequences drawn from the combination of the Leibnizian metaphysics and the Millian account of names were about the propositions expressed by simple sentences involving non-modal predicates. If "Shakespeare" is a Millian name, then "Shakespeare wrote plays" is true in a possible world only if Shakespeare himself wrote plays in that world, which means only in the actual world. The fact that we construe "could have written no plays" in such a way that "Shakespeare could have written no plays" is also true in (and only in) the actual world is beside the point.

One might try to reconcile the Leibnizian metaphysics in its counterpart variation with a version of the Millian semantics for names by reinterpreting the concept of a rigid designator in a way that parallels the reinterpretation of modal predication. Suppose we say that a designator is *quasi-rigid* (relative to a possible world w) if its referent in any possible world w′ is a counterpart of some particular individual in w. Then if "Shakespeare" is a quasi-rigid designator, relative to the actual world, "Shakespeare wrote plays" might be true in some other possible worlds – worlds in which a counterpart of Shakespeare wrote plays. The thesis that names are quasi-rigid designators is a kind of compromise between the Millian theory and the sense theory that accounts for some of the phenomena Kripke brought to our attention, but there are problems with it. First, if (as David Lewis has argued) an individual may have more than one counterpart in the same world, then the semantic value of a name will not be determined by the individual. Suppose Shakespeare has two counterparts in some possible world, only one of whom wrote plays. Is "Shakespeare wrote plays" true in that possible world or not? To answer this we need to know which of two (or more) quasi-rigid concepts is expressed by "Shakespeare". Second, even if an individual has at most one counterpart in any possible world, a designator might be quasi-rigid relative to one possible world and not relative to another, since two counterparts of the same thing (in different possible worlds) need not be counterparts of each other.

Despite these problems, the basic Kripkean picture of the way the reference of names is determined might still be reconciled with this metaphysical theory. What is essential to Kripke's picture, I think, is the idea that the content of speech acts and mental attitudes may be determined as a function of particular things (and kinds) with which the speakers and thinkers interact. Whatever one's metaphysical presuppositions, it will be agreed that the way content and reference are determined by the facts will be context-dependent, and influenced by general beliefs, purposes, and assumptions. The counterpart-theorist's story about the background against which reference to a particular (world-bound) individual can determine a proposition will be different from the story Kripke might tell, but there is nothing in the counterpart-theorist's metaphysics that prevents him telling such a story.

The dialectic of this last discussion shows that metaphysical and semantic issues cannot be kept completely apart for at least two reasons. First, if semantic and metaphysical theses together yield implausible consequences, it may be a matter of dispute where the source of the problem lies. Second, some metaphysical theories may force a reformulation of claims about semantics and intentionality. But the possible-worlds framework helps to clarify the metaphysical alternatives, and to separate metaphysical from semantic issues so that each can be evaluated on its own terms.

References

Donnellan, Keith 1972: Names and identifying descriptions. In G. Harman and D. Davidson (eds), *Semantics for Natural Language*. Dordrecht-Holland: D. Reidel.

Dummett, Michael 1973: *Frege: Philosophy of Language*. London: Duckworth.

Dummett, Michael 1991: *The Logical Basis of Metaphysics*. Cambridge, MA: Harvard University Press.
Evans, Gareth 1982: *The Varieties of Reference*. Oxford and New York: Oxford University Press.
Kripke, Saul 1972: *Naming and Necessity*. Cambridge, MA: Harvard University Press.
Lewis, David 1986: *On the Plurality of Worlds*. Oxford: Basil Blackwell.
Quine, W.V. 1960: *Word and Object*. Cambridge, MA: MIT Press.
Salmon, Nathan 1981: *Reference and Essence*. Princeton, NJ: Princeton University Press.
Searle, John 1969: *Speech Acts*. Cambridge: Cambridge University Press.
Wittgenstein, Ludwig 1953: *Philosophical Investigations*. New York: Macmillan.

22

Names and rigid designation

JASON STANLEY

The fact that natural-language proper names are rigid designators is an empirical discovery about natural language. However, unlike other empirical discoveries about language made in the past few decades, it is one which has been taken to have great philosophical significance. One reason for this is that it has helped simplify the formal semantical representation of ordinary modal discourse. But the central reason is that the discovery threatens a certain picture, the descriptive picture, of the content of names, upon which a great deal of philosophy was premised. (See Chapter 21, REFERENCE AND NECESSITY.)

This paper is mainly intended to be a survey of both the background and contemporary discussion of this discovery. However, the survey takes place in the context of an evaluation of the extent to which the discovery that English proper names are rigid itself threatens the descriptive picture of the content of names. The goal is to show that the exact philosophical significance of the discovery that natural-language proper names are rigid designators is still, and should still be, a matter of controversy.

Section 1 discusses different explications of rigidity. Section 2 is devoted to a sketch of the development of the notion of rigidity. Section 3 is a discussion of the descriptive picture of the content of names. In Section 4, Kripke's argument for the thesis that natural-language proper names are rigid is outlined, as well as an argument based upon this thesis against the descriptive picture. Finally, the remaining three sections cover various possible defenses of the descriptive picture.

1 Rigidity

Rigidity is a semantic property of an expression. More specifically, it has to do with the evaluation of that expression with respect to other possible situations (or 'worlds'). There are many subtle issues involved in the notion of evaluating an expression with respect to a possible situation, some of which we will discuss in this paper. But there are also some simple confusions about this notion. Before we begin our discussion of rigidity, it is important to dispel one such confusion.

On one way of understanding evaluation of a sentence with respect to another possible world, a sentence is true with respect to another possible world just in case, if the sentence were uttered in that other possible world, it would be true. However, this is decidedly *not* how to understand the notion of evaluation with respect to another possible world which underlies our modal discourse.

The correct notion of evaluation of a sentence with respect to another possible world involves considering the sentence as uttered in the *actual world*, rather than as uttered in other possible worlds. When the sentence is uttered in the actual world, it expresses some semantic value which is determined by how the words are used by speakers in the actual world. This semantic value is then evaluated with respect to other possible worlds. What the nature of the entity is which is evaluated with respect to other possible worlds – whether it is a "proposition" (what is said by an utterance of the sentence) or some other entity – is a difficult question, and one which we will address at the end of this paper. But for now it is only important to note, as a preliminary to our discussion of rigidity, that what is at issue in evaluating a sentence with respect to another possible world does not involve considering that sentence as uttered in that other possible world, but rather considering the sentence as uttered in the actual world.

How an expression e is used by speakers in other possible situations is thus irrelevant to the question of what the extension of e is when evaluated with respect to those other possible situations. For instance, what the denotation of "Cayuga Lake" is with respect to another possible world is has nothing to do with how the speakers of that world – if there are any – use the expression "Cayuga Lake". It just has to do with which object Cayuga Lake is in that world. Now that this possible confusion has been eliminated, we may turn to the notion of rigidity.

According to Kripke's characterization of rigidity, "a designator d of an object x is rigid, if it designates x with respect to all possible worlds where x exists, and never designates an object other than x with respect to any possible world".[1] This characterization, as Kripke intends, is neutral on the issue of the extension of the designator d in possible worlds in which x does not exist. That is, if d is a designator which satisfies the above criteria, there are three possibilities left open for d's extension in worlds in which x does not exist. First, d could designate nothing with respect to such possible worlds. Second, d could designate x in all such possible worlds (despite x's non-existence in those possible worlds). Third, d could designate x with respect to some such worlds, and designate nothing with respect to other such worlds.

These three possibilities determine three different species of rigidity. However, only the first two species deserve discussion; a designator in the third class is a hybrid, and there is no reason to countenance such expressions. In the rest of our discussion, I will not consider designators in this third class left open by Kripke's characterization of rigidity.

The first species of rigidity, corresponding to the first of the above possibilities, includes all and only those designators d of an object x, which designate x in all worlds in which x exists, and designate nothing in worlds in which x does not exist. Following Nathan Salmon (1982, p. 4), let us call these *persistently rigid designators*.

The second species of rigidity, corresponding to the second of the above possibilities, includes all and only those designators d of an object x, which designate x in all worlds in which x exists, and designate x in all worlds in which x does not exist; or, more simply, designate x with respect to every possible world. Again following Salmon, let us call these *obstinately rigid designators.*[2]

There are expressions which are uncontroversially rigid in both of the above senses. For instance, consider Kripke's class of *strongly rigid designators* in *Naming and Necessity*.[3] This class contains the rigid designators of necessary existents. That is, this class contains all and only those designators d of an object x which exists in all possible worlds, which designate the same thing in all possible worlds (that is, x). For example, the descriptive phrase "the result of adding two and three" is a strongly rigid designator, since its actual denotation, namely the number five, exists in all possible worlds, and the phrase denotes that number with respect to all possible worlds. Strongly rigid designators clearly belong to both of the above classes.[4]

At several points in this paper considerations in support of the notion of obstinate rigid designation over that of persistent rigid designation will be advanced. However, it is unclear to what degree issues about persistent rigidity versus obstinate rigidity are substantive, rather than merely disguised terminological discussions about how best to use the expression "evaluation with respect to a world". There is a sense of this expression in which it seems to presuppose the existence of the denotation in the world; and if someone is using the expression in this sense, then persistent rigidity might be the more appropriate notion. If, on the other hand, one has a purely semantical understanding of "denotation with respect to a world", then the fact that the semantic rules directly assign a denotation to an expression might lead us to think that even in worlds in which that object does not exist, it is still the denotation of the relevant expression. But these are certainly just terminological issues.[5]

A further distinction is often made in discussions of rigidity: that of Kripke between *de jure* rigidity and *de facto* rigidity.[6] An expression is a *de jure* rigid designator of an object just in case the semantical rules of the language unmediately link it to that object. All other rigid designators of objects are *de facto* rigid designators of them. To give an example from Kripke, the description "the smallest prime" is supposed to be *de facto* rigid, because it is not metaphysically possible for there to be a smallest prime distinct from the actual smallest prime, that is, two. The fact that "the smallest prime" denotes the same object in every world flows not from semantics, but from the metaphysical fact that mathematical facts are true in all metaphysically possible worlds. If, on the other hand, the semantical rule for a term t takes the form of a stipulation that it denotes a certain object x, then t is *de jure* rigid, since it is part of the semantical rules that it denotes that object.

The intuitive content of *de jure* designation lies in the metaphor of "unmediated" reference. A rigid *de jure* designator is supposed to denote what it denotes without mediation by some concept or description. A *de facto* rigid designator, on the other hand, is supposed to denote what it denotes in virtue of its denotation meeting some condition. That is, a *de facto* rigid designator denotes via mediation of some concept or description.[7]

The core notion of rigidity has been taken by philosophers to be *de jure*, obstinate rigidity. This is the notion which lies at the center not only of Kripke's work, but also of David Kaplan's work on direct reference.[8] We will give some (albeit not so weighty) reasons in future sections for preferring obstinate rigidity over persistent rigidity. But we shall see already in the next section why the *de jure* character of rigidity is thought to be important. For rigidity arose in the development of the semantics of Quantified Modal Logic (henceforth QML), and in particular, as a part of the explanation of the proper treatment of variables in QML. In that context, there is no question that *de jure* rigidity is the relevant concept.

2 Rigid designation and quantified modal logic

The pre-theoretic notion of rigidity began its life as a concept in the semantics for QML. In particular, rigidity arose in connection with the 'objectual' interpretation of QML, where the quantifiers were taken to range over objects, rather than non-constant functions. Even more specifically, rigidity was relevant to issues concerning Quine's "modal paradoxes", raised as objections to the coherence of QML. In this section, I will attempt to show where the notion of rigidity enters into the attempt to give a coherent and natural semantic interpretation to QML.

One of the first issues which arose in QML was what the proper intended interpretation of quantification should be. The two camps in the 1940s were the conceptual interpretation, championed by Alonzo Church and Rudolf Carnap, and the objectual interpretation, championed by Ruth Barcan Marcus.[9] But while Church, Carnap, and Barcan Marcus and others were developing axiom systems for QML, Willard Van Orman Quine was busy attempting to demonstrate their incoherence.

Quine raised two influential objections to QML.[10] According to the first of these objections, quantification into modal contexts violated fundamental logical laws. According to the second (and obviously related) objection, if QML and its intended interpretation could be so formulated as to evade the first objection, then it would inexorably carry with it unpalatable metaphysical commitments.[11] Since the defenders of QML partially defined their own positions against the first of these objections, something must be briefly said about it here. Following this we will outline the conceptual interpretation of QML, and then the objectual interpretation, explaining how their original espousers evaded Quine's worry.[12]

According to the principle of substitution, for any terms a and b, if "a = b" is true, then for any formula ϕ containing "a", the result of replacing one or more occurrences of "a" by "b" does not change the truth-value of ϕ.[13] However, according to Quine, QML essentially involved a violation of this principle. For "nine = the number of planets" is true. Furthermore, "Necessarily, nine = nine" is true. But the result of substituting "the number of planets" for the first occurrence of "nine" in "Necessarily, nine = nine" yields a falsity, namely, "Necessarily, the number of planets = nine".

Quine took the failure of substitution in modal contexts also to demonstrate the failure of existential generalization in QML. That is, Quine took the failure of substitution to show that the inference from "$\Box$ Fa" to "$\exists x \Box Fx$" is illegitimate. The reason Quine thought that a failure of substitution demonstrated the failure of existential generalization is that he thought that substitutability by co-referential terms was a *criterion* for the legitimacy of quantifying in.[14]

Here is one reason why Quine thought that the substitutability of co-referential terms in a linguistic context C was a criterion for the legitimacy of quantification into C. Consider a quotational context, such as:

(1) The first sentence of the (English translation of the) *Duino Elegies* is "Who, if I cried out, would hear me among the angels' hierarchies?"

Inside such a quotational context, substitution of co-referential terms fails to preserve truth-value. For example, (1) is true, but (2), which results from (1) by the substitution of co-referential terms, is false:

(2) The first sentence of the (English translation of the) *Duino Elegies* is "Who, if Rilke cried out, would hear Rilke among the angels' hierarchies?"

Thus, substitution of co-referential terms fails in quotational contexts.

But it is also illegitimate, according to Quine, to quantify into such contexts. To see this, consider the sentence:

(3) There is something x such that "Who, if x cried out, would hear x among the angels' hierarchies?" is the first sentence of the *Duino Elegies*.

Sentence (3) is false. The reason (3) is false is, as Quine is fond of pointing out, that the quoted sentence in (3) names not some sentence which results from replacing 'x' by a term, but rather a sentence containing the symbol 'x'. That is, a quotation such as ' "x flies" ' denotes the result of concatenating the symbol 'x' with the word 'flies', not the concatenation of some replacement term for 'x' with "flies". Thus, for Quine, it is illegitimate to quantify into quotational contexts.[15]

But Quine does not simply conclude from the failure of both substitution and quantifying into quotational contexts that substitution is a criterion for quantifying in. For Quine, the failure of substitution in a linguistic context demonstrates a deep incoherence in quantifying into such contexts. For in giving the semantics of a quantified sentence, one must avail oneself of the notion of satisfaction; the sentence is true just in case some object satisfies the relevant open sentence. Yet, for Quine, the failure of substitution shows that there is no available notion of satisfaction in terms of which one can define the truth of such sentences. There is no notion of objectual satisfaction for quantifying into quotational contexts, for instance, because such contexts are sensitive not just to objects, but also to how they are named.

Thus, for Quine, the failure of substitution in modal contexts demonstrated that there was no appropriate notion of objectual satisfaction for open formulas such as "$\Box Fx$". For the failure of substitution seemed to show that whether or not an object satisfied an open, modalized formula depended upon how the object was named. Quine hence thought there was a similarity between modal and quotational contexts: in both cases, what matters is how the object is named, rather than just the object itself. Quine concluded that there was no way of giving a coherent semantics for sentences such as "$\exists x \Box Fx$", since there was no available notion of satisfaction in terms of which one could define the truth of the sentence. He hence declared that quantification into modal contexts was illegitimate (since incoherent), and that existential generalization fails.

There is also a historical reason for Quine's analogy between modal and quotational contexts: for Quine's target, Carnap, wished to explicate necessity in terms of the analyticity of certain sentences. That is, Carnap in *Meaning and Necessity* believed that to say that a certain proposition was necessary was "really" to say, of a certain sentence, that it was analytic.[16] Thus, according to Carnap, a construction such as (a) "really" expressed (b):

(a) Necessarily, bachelors are unmarried men.
(b) "Bachelors are unmarried men" is analytic.

So, according to Carnap, modal contexts were really disguised quotational contexts. If so, then quantifying into modal contexts seems tantamount to quantifying into quotational contexts.

There are several responses which have been given to Quine's challenge. One response stems from the interpretation of QML which emerged from the work of Church and Carnap. According to this approach, variables in modal languages ranged over individual concepts, describable (in contemporary terms) as functions (possibly non-constant) from possible worlds to extensions. The principle of substitution, on this approach, was interpreted as licensing not substitution of terms for two extensionally equivalent individual concepts (that is, functions which yield the same denotation in the actual world), but rather, substitution of terms which denote the same individual concept.

Now, "nine" and "the number of planets" do not express the same individual concept, for though they are extensionally equivalent, there are possible situations in which the extension of "the number of planets" is different from the extension of "nine". Thus, the principle of substitution does not license the substitution of "the number of planets" for "nine", on this account of QML. Furthermore, any two expressions which do express the same individual concept (are "L-equivalent", in Carnap's terms) will be substitutible, even in modal contexts.

This 'conceptual' interpretation of QML thus has a systematic, logically consistent account of the notion of the satisfaction of an open-modal formula (cf. Church, 1943, and Carnap, 1988, sections 43 and 44). On the conceptual interpretation of QML, one can take the quantifier in "$\exists x \, \Box Fx$" to range over individual concepts. In this case, the relevant notion of satisfaction is satisfaction by individual concepts, rather than objects.[17]

However, the conceptual interpretation of QML does not seem to accord with our natural interpretation of QML. The sentence:

(4) $\exists n$ ($\Box n$ numbers the planets)

is intuitively false on a natural reading of the quantifier (cf. Garson, 1984, pp. 265–7). The reason it seems false to us is that, according to a very natural reading of (4), what it asserts is that there is some object which necessarily numbers the planets. However, on the conceptual interpretation, (4) is true, because the individual concept expressed by "the number of planets" will satisfy the open formula:

(5) □n numbers the planets

since, in every possible world, the number of planets numbers the planets.

What such examples suggest is that the natural reading of quantification into modal contexts is as quantification over objects, rather than over individual concepts. If we wish to capture this intuition, then we should think of, say, an existential quantification into an open-modal formula (henceforth OMF) as true just in case some object satisfies the relevant modal condition.[18] On this account, which we shall call the objectual interpretation of QML, the first-order quantifiers range only over objects, rather than over concepts.

According to the objectual interpretation, a sentence such as "∃x □Fx" is true just in case some object is necessarily F. But what about Quine's worry? Can the objectual interpretation supply a natural account of the satisfaction of OMFs?

An OMF, such as "□Fx", is, on the objectual conception, satisfied by an assignment just in case the object which that assignment assigns to 'x' is necessarily F, that is, is F with respect to every possible situation, *irrespective of any names of that object*. We are not to understand the satisfaction of such an OMF "substitutionally", as satisfied by an assignment, just in case, for some name a of the object which that assignment assigns to 'x', the sentence, "□Fa" is true. Rather, we are to read "□Fx" as satisfied by an assignment s just in case the object which that assignment assigns to 'x' satisfies F with respect to every possible situation.

This understanding of the satisfaction clause for OMFs undercuts Quine's objection to the coherence of quantifying into modal contexts. For Quine's worry can only arise if objectual satisfaction is characterized in terms of the truth of closed sentences containing names of the alleged satisfiers. Only if objectual satisfaction is given such a substitutional construal is it relevant to the coherence of quantifying into modal contexts that two closed modalized sentences, differing only in containing different names for the same object, may differ in truth-value.[19]

If such a notion of an object satisfying a predicate necessarily indeed makes sense, then it is possible to quantify into modal contexts despite the failure of substitution. Of course, Quine's *other* objection to QML is that, where the necessity in question is metaphysical, this notion involves a dubious metaphysic of essentialism. But discussion of this question will take us too far away from the topic of rigidity (see Chapter 20, ESSENTIALISM, and Chapter 21, REFERENCE AND NECESSITY).

This construal of the satisfaction of OMFs, combined with possible-world semantics, naturally brings with it an interpretation of variables according to which they are *de jure* rigid designators. To see why this is so, consider a sentence of QML such as "∃x □(Exists(x) → Rational(x))".[20] According to the objectual interpretation of QML, this sentence is true just in case there is some assignment function which assigns to the variable 'x' an object o which, in every possible situation, satisfies the open formula "Exists(x) → Rational(x)". The evaluation of the truth of the sentence hence involves, relative to an assignment function, evaluating the open formula "Exists(x) → Rational(x)" with respect to every possible situation. Since, in each possible situation, we are considering whether or not the object o satisfies the formula, we need to ensure that the variable 'x' denotes o in all of the possible situations. That is, on the objectual interpretation of QML, when taken with respect to an assignment s, variables are rigid designators of the objects which s assigns to them. The reason that variables are *de jure* rigid designators is because there is nothing else to the semantics of variables besides the stipulation that, when taken with respect to an assignment s which assigns the object o to a variable, it designates o in every possible situation.[21]

If we understand variables as rigid designators (with respect to an assignment), then the following version of substitution is validated:

(6) $\forall x \forall y\, [x = y \rightarrow [\phi \leftrightarrow \psi]]$

(where ϕ differs from ψ only in containing free occurrences of "x" where the latter contains free occurrences of "y"). For even if ϕ and ψ contain modal operators, the rigidity of the variables will guarantee the intersubstitutability of "x" and "y".

The situation is slightly more complicated in the case of terms. Quine's challenge is to validate, not just (6), but also the fully schematic version of substitution:

(7) $t = s \rightarrow (\phi \leftrightarrow \psi)$

(where ϕ differs from ψ at most in containing occurrences of t where the latter contains occurrences of s, and no free variables in t and s become bound when t and s occur inside ϕ and ψ). But where t and s are replaceable by non-rigid designators, then (7) will, in the modal case, fail to be valid; thus the defender of the objectual interpretation who wishes to preserve full classical substitution must disallow non-rigid terms from her language.

There are also other motivations for restricting the class of terms to rigid ones on the objectual interpretation. For example, to do so would allow a uniform treatment of the class of terms. If all terms are rigid, then non-variables can be treated in the semantics as free variables whose interpretation does not depend on assignments.[22] Another reason is that, if one allowed non-rigid designators, one would have to restrict universal instantiation to rigid designators to retain (6), and some might hold that such a restricted UI rule is unappealing. Finally, non-rigid terms raise further technical problems which, though certainly solvable, nevertheless complicate the semantics.[23]

At this point the reason for the introduction of terms which directly represent objects is purely technical – it is a technical response to a logico-semantical dilemma. If one wishes to preserve classical substitution, as well as the objectual conception of satisfaction, then one must ensure that one's variables and terms are rigid. In availing ourselves of such terms, there is no commitment to thinking that any terms in ordinary language are rigid. Rigid terms only play the role, at this stage, of desirable formal-semantical tools, which allow us a better grasp of the objectual notion of satisfaction, as well as an explanation of the validity of classical substitution.

However, if we wish QML to serve as a representation of ordinary modal discourse, then the rigidity constraint on terms may seem problematic. Without a philosophical justification of this restriction, or a semantical argument to the effect that natural-language terms are rigid, this restriction is *ad hoc*. If natural-language singular terms are non-rigid, then the extra logico-semantical complexities which attend the addition of non-rigid terms into QML will either have to be accepted as realities or used as a basis for rejecting its coherence.[24]

Even in the late 1940s it was recognized that a philosophical/semantical argument demonstrating the rigidity of natural-language terms would be desirable.[25] However, it was not until the seminal work of Saul Kripke in 1970 that a fully explicit argument for this conclusion was forthcoming. But Kripke's ambitions went far beyond demonstrating that natural-language terms are rigid. For Kripke used the notion of rigidity as a basis for quite substantive claims about the nature of intentionality. It was thus with Kripke that the *philosophical* construal of rigidity began.

3 The descriptive picture

According to the picture of intentionality attacked by Kripke, the way our words hooked onto an extra-linguistic reality was via description. That is, a name such as "Aristotle" denoted the person, Aristotle, because the name was associated with a series of descriptions (such as "the last great philosopher of antiquity") which were uniquely satisfied by the person Aristotle. More relevant for our purposes, however, is Kripke's attack on the descriptive picture of the *content* of proper names. According to this, the content of a name was given by the description which fixed its referent. That is, what someone said when they uttered a sentence such as "Aristotle is F" was a descriptive proposition to the effect that, say, the last great philosopher of antiquity, whoever he was, is F.

Kripke (1980) first demonstrated that ordinary-language proper names were rigid. He then used this feature of names as part of a larger attack on a certain version of the above picture of content.

In the next section, we will discuss how Kripke used rigidity to attack the descriptive picture. But before we do so, it is important to gain an understanding of what the descriptive pictures of intentionality and content are. In particular, we will distinguish between two different versions of the descriptive picture which are often not distinguished in the literature.

The problem of linguistic intentionality, in one of its forms, is the question of what it is in virtue of which an expression has the reference it does. According to the first descriptive picture of linguistic intentionality, what it is in virtue of which a primitive expression has the referent it does is that it is associated with a set of descriptions, in purely general, non-indexical, or particular involving terms. These descriptions are uniquely satisfied by an entity which then counts as the reference of that term.

A less problematic and more commonly held version of the description theory dispenses with the requirement that the descriptions which fix referents must be given in purely general terms. According to this version, which is most explicit in the works of Strawson and Dummett, but at least implicit in Frege, the descriptions which fix referents can, and indeed often must, contain non-descriptive elements.[26]

It is worthwhile to mention briefly a motivation for the latter picture of intentionality. One might think that, in the case of demonstrative reference, one has reference without any description. But this is merely a myth. Suppose I point to a brown table, and say, "This is brown." It is not my pointing alone which fixes the reference of the occurrence of "this", for my finger will also be pointing at the edge of the table, or a small brown patch on the table. Rather, a factor in fixing the reference of my demonstrative is that I intend to be demonstrating some object whose identity criteria are those of tables, rather than those of small brown patches or edges. Such identity criteria play a crucial role in overcoming the massive indeterminacy of ostensive definition. It is for their specification that descriptive material is required.[27] But this insight in no way requires that we ignore the non-descriptive element inherent in true demonstrative reference[28] (see Chapter 24, OBJECTS AND CRITERIA OF IDENTITY).

A final relevant factor which distinguishes descriptive accounts of intentionality from each other has to do with the role of the social. According to Russell, as well as the account of descriptive intentionality attacked by Kripke (1980), a term refers, in the mouth of a speaker, to that object which satisfies the descriptions the *speaker* associates with the term. However, according to other traditional descriptive accounts, such as that of Strawson (1959, pp. 151ff.), what is relevant is not which descriptions the speaker associates with the term, but rather, which descriptions are associated with the term in the language community. On this latter, more plausible account, a use of a term in the mouth of a speaker refers to the object it does in virtue of her participation in a language community which associates certain descriptions with that term that are uniquely satisfied by the object in question.[29]

There are thus two different versions of the descriptive picture, one according to which the descriptions must be in general terms alone, and another in which they may contain irreducible occurrences of demonstrative and indexical expressions. Each of these two versions has two sub-versions; one according to which it is the descriptions the speaker associates with a term which are relevant for determining the reference of terms she uses, and the other according to which it is the descriptions the language community of the speaker associates with the term which determine the reference of the term when she uses it.

Each of these versions corresponds to a theory of the content of sentences containing proper names. On the first picture, utterances of sentences containing proper names express descriptive propositions, where the relevant descriptions only contain expressions for general concepts. According to the second version of the description theory, utterances of sentences containing proper names also express descriptive propositions. However, these descriptive propositions typically are also irreducibly indexical propositions. So, on this latter account, a sentence such as

"Bill Clinton is F" would state some proposition equivalent to what is expressed by "The *present* president around here of the United States is F".[30]

If the descriptive picture is true, then, for each expression in our language, we possess, a priori, uniquely identifying knowledge about its referent. Such a premise is more than just a useful tool in epistemological and metaphysical theorizing. For if the descriptive picture is true, then we have a rich store of a priori knowledge. This makes more plausible a classic picture of philosophy, according to which it proceeds by a priori methods. The Kripkean challenge to the descriptive picture is thus not merely a challenge to an empirical thesis, but also threatens to undermine deeply rooted conceptions of the nature of philosophy.

4 Kripke's argument and the rigidity thesis

I will not go into great detail in this paper about Kripke's larger critique of the descriptive picture of intentionality and content, as the issue is covered in another chapter in this volume (see Chapter 21, REFERENCE AND NECESSITY). In this section I will first describe an argument, due essentially to Kripke, for the thesis that names are rigid designators. I will then conclude with an argument from rigidity against the descriptive picture of content.

One of the central contributions of Kripke (1980) lay in the argument that natural-language proper names are rigid designators (where "rigid designator" is taken in the first, neutral sense of Section 1). In what follows, we will go through this argument. More exactly, what we will motivate is the following thesis, which I will call RN, the Rigid Name thesis:

(RN) If N designates x, then N designates x rigidly

where "N" is replaceable by names of English-language proper names. Throughout the argument for RN, it will be assumed that variables under assignments are rigid designators, and it will be argued from this assumption that natural-language proper names are also rigid designators.[31]

According to the neutral characterization of rigidity, a designator D of an object x is rigid just in case, for all possible worlds w, if x exists in w, then D designates x in w, and if x does not exist in w, then D does not designate something different from x in w. There are thus three ways in which a designator D of an object x could fail to be rigid:

(a) There could be a world in which x exists, but is not designated by D.
(b) There could be a world in which x exists, but D designates something else.
(c) There could be a world in which x does not exist, and D designates something other than x.

It will be argued that each of these possibilities is ruled out in the case in which D is a proper name.

Before we proceed with the argument, it is worth noting that no separate proof is required for (b). Given that proper names designate, at most, one thing in each world, any situation in which x exists, but D designates something else will be a situation in which D does not designate x. That is, every (b) situation is an (a) situation. Thus, the demonstration that (a) is incompatible with D being a proper name will suffice to show that (b) is incompatible with D being a proper name.

So let us first argue that if "a" is a proper name designating x, then, in any world in which x exists, x is designated by "a". Suppose not, that is, suppose "a" designates x, and (a) is true. Then the following is the case:

(8) $\exists x\, [x = a\ \&\ \Diamond\ (x \text{ exists}\ \&\ x \neq a)]$

But (8) seems false when "a" is a proper name. Plugging an actual proper name in for "a" in (8) should make this clear:

(9) There is someone who is Aristotle but he could exist without being identical with Aristotle.

This is intuitively false. Thus, it seems that if N is a proper name designating x, then, if x exists in a world, then N designates it. So, we are done with case (a) as well as (b).

Now, let us turn to the argument that if "a" is a proper name designating x, then, in any world in which x does not exist, "a" does not designate something other than x. Suppose not, that is, suppose "a" designates x, and (c) is true. Then the following is the case:

(10) $\exists x\, [x = a\ \&\ \Diamond\ (a \text{ exists and } a \neq x)]$

But (10), like (8), seems false when "a" is a proper name. Substituting an actual proper name for "a" in (10) should make this clear:

(11) There is someone who is Aristotle but Aristotle could exist without being him.

Like (9), (11) also seems intuitively false. Thus, it seems that if N is a proper name designating x, then, if x does not exist in a world, then N does not designate anything else. So we are done with case (c), and the argument for (RN).

The argument for (RN) exploits speaker's intuitions about the truth-value of instances of (8) and (10). In the case of normal proper names, it seems true that, when substituted for "a" in (8) and (10), a false sentence results. (RN) is thus an empirical claim about natural language. As such, it has been challenged. That is, some have maintained that there are true instances of (8) and (10). However, the proper names that are typically considered are somewhat elaborate, involving issues in metaphysics that are beyond the scope of this chapter. The literature on "contingent identity-statements" will thus not be discussed in what follows.[32]

In the above description of Kripke's argument, I have been using the expression "rigid designator" in the sense of a term which denotes its actual denotation in all possible worlds in which that denotation exists, and nothing else in other worlds. But there are also some considerations which some have felt mitigate in favor of the thesis that names are obstinately rigid designators. For instance, Kripke (1980, p. 78) gives as an example the sentence:

(12) Hitler might never have been born.

Sentence (12) is true. But (12) is true just in case the sentence, "Hitler was never born" is true when evaluated with respect to some possible world. If "Hitler" does not denote anything with respect to that world, then, unless one gives sentences containing non-denoting terms truth-values, it will be impossible to make the sentence "Hitler was never born" true in that world. But, if "Hitler" denotes Hitler in that world, then, despite the non-existence of Hitler in that world (or perhaps because of it), the sentence "Hitler was never born" can be true in that world.

This argument is, however, unimpressive. For it relies on the thesis that sentences containing non-denoting terms receive no truth-value. If one said that sentences containing non-denoting terms were false, then analyzing "Hitler was never born" as the negation of "Hitler was born" in a world in which "Hitler" is non-denoting would yield the correct prediction.[33]

Many have adverted, at this point, to a more indirect argument, one which exploits the analogy between tense and modality. A tense-logical obstinately rigid designator is one which denotes the same thing at all times, regardless of whether or not that thing exists at the time of evaluation. That proper names should be treated as tense-logical obstinate rigid designators is supported by the Montagovian example:

(13) John remembers Nixon.[34]

Example (14) can be true, as uttered in 1995, despite Nixon's non-existence at the time of utterance. Such evidence is taken, by the tight analogy between tense and modality, to support the modal logical obstinancy of proper names.[35]

However, examples such as (13) only demonstrate that proper names can denote individuals existing prior to, but not during, the time of evaluation. If proper names are to be true tense-logical obstinate rigid designators, then proper names of objects which exist subsequent to, but not during, the time of evaluation, should nonetheless denote at the time of evaluation. But this does not seem to be the case. For instance, consider the name "Sally", introduced in 1995 to denote the first child born in the twenty-first century. In the case of such a name, it is dubious that it denotes, as evaluated in 1995. For it is metaphysically likely that the future is open, and not already determined. If so, then there is no fact of the matter, in 1995, as to what the reference of "Sally" is now. Thus, it is unclear whether proper names are tense-logical obstinately rigid designators.

Whatever the outcome of the debate concerning the obstinancy of proper names is, it does seem that proper names are rigid designators. This would suggest that what fixes the referent of a proper name is not a non-rigid description, but rather something else. If so, then the descriptive account of intentionality would seem to be false.

This argument, as Kripke recognized, is, however, too swift. For it collapses once one makes Kripke's useful distinction between a description giving the content of a name and merely fixing its referent. If the description fixes the referent of a name then there is no commitment to saying that the name denotes an object in other possible worlds in virtue of that object satisfying the description. On this picture, the description fixes the referent, which is then the denotation of the proper name, even in worlds in which the referent does not satisfy the description. Thus, there is no direct argument from rigidity against the descriptive picture of intentionality.

The case differs, however, with the descriptive picture of content. For there does seem to be an argument from rigidity against the thesis that the content of a proper name is descriptive. For suppose that the content of the proper name "a" is descriptive. In particular, suppose that its content is given by the non-rigid description "DD". Then the content of a sentence which results from replacing "N" by "DD" should stay unchanged, since "N" and "DD" have the same content. But, given that "N" is rigid and "DD" is not rigid, (14) and (15) do not have the same content, as (14) is true and (15) is false:

(14) N might not have been DD.
(15) N might not have been N.

Therefore, substitution of "DD" for "N" does not preserve truth-value, and hence also does not preserve content. Hence "DD" and "N" do not, after all, have the same content.

Let us take a concrete example. Suppose that the name "Aristotle" has the same content as the description, "the last great philosopher of antiquity". Then, replacement of "Aristotle" by "the last great philosopher of antiquity" should preserve content. But:

(16) Aristotle might not have been the last great philosopher of antiquity.
(17) Aristotle might not have been Aristotle.

differ in content, since (16) has a true reading (for instance, there is a reading of (16) where it is true because Aristotle might have died as a child, in which case he never would have become a philosopher at all), and (17) has no true reading.[36] Thus, "Aristotle" and "the last great philosopher of antiquity" are not intersubstitutable, and hence do not have the same content.

It thus seems that Kripke's demonstration that proper names are rigid also shows that they do not have descriptive content. An obvious next step is the thesis, which Kripke attributes to John Stuart Mill, that the content of a proper name is simply its denotation. However, Kripke does not, from rigidity alone, conclude that Millianism is correct;[37] rather, he only commits himself to the following minimal thesis, which I shall henceforth call the *Rigidity Thesis*, or RT:

> The rigidity of proper names demonstrates that utterances of sentences containing proper names, and utterances of sentences differing from those sentences only in containing non-rigid descriptions in place of the proper names, differ in content.[38]

If RT is correct, then the descriptive account of content would seem to be false. In the rest of this paper, I shall focus on various ways of defending the descriptive account of content. In the next section, I will discuss a version of the descriptive account of content which is compatible with RT. After that, I will discuss critiques of RT.

5 The 'actualized' description theory

RT raises a *prima facie* difficulty for descriptive theories of content. Since the most plausible meaning-yielding descriptions seem to be non-rigid, RT seems to demonstrate that descriptive accounts of content are false. However, this appearance is misleading. RT does not demonstrate that all descriptive accounts of content are false. In particular, RT is only incompatible with one of the two descriptive accounts of content distinguished in Section 3. As we shall see in this section, though RT is indeed incompatible with the thesis that the content of proper names can be given by description in purely qualitative, general terms, it is not incompatible with the more traditional descriptive account of content, according to which the descriptions which give the content of proper names may contain indexical expressions.

RT is incompatible with the purely qualitative description-theory of the content of proper names. For consider plausible meaning-yielding descriptions for an ordinary proper name, such as "Aristotle". Since the meaning of an expression is what one knows in virtue of which one is competent with that expression, such descriptions must be the things that are known by those competent with the expression. Examples of such descriptions are "the last great philosopher of antiquity", or "the teacher of Alexander". But these are non-rigid descriptions. RT is incompatible with such descriptions matching proper names in content.

On the other descriptive account of content considered in Section 3, the descriptions which give the content of proper names may contain indexical expressions: that is, expressions occurrences of which denote fixed parameters of a context. For instance, "I" denotes the speaker of a context, "now" the time of the context, and "here" the place of the context. (See also Chapter 23, INDEXICALS AND DEMONSTRATIVES.) But once one broadens one's perspective to include modal evaluation, it seems natural to add the word "actual" to the list. That is, once one is in the context of possible-worlds semantics, "actual" indicates the world of the context.[39]

If so – that is, if "actual" is an indexical – it would be bizarre, on an account of content according to which the descriptions which give the content of proper names may contain indexical expressions, to disallow its appearance in the content-yielding descriptive expressions. But descriptions which contain the word "actual" are rigid. That is, a description such as "the actual F" rigidly denotes the object which is in fact F, even in worlds in which that object fails to be the unique F. Indeed, someone sympathetic with this account of the descriptive picture of content, as well as RT, would simply conclude that the descriptions which give the content of proper names must contain the indexical "actual". Furthermore, on this account of content, it would not even be a surprising fact that the relevant descriptions must be "actualized", since, on this account of content, the arguments for the thesis that meaning-yielding descriptions must contain indexical expressions (for instance, Strawson's consideration of symmetrical universes) straightforwardly generalize to the modal case.

Now, if proper names are *de jure* rigid designators, then even this descriptive account of content would be false, for actualized descriptions do not "unmediatedly" designate. That is, a description such as "The actual teacher of Alexander" designates Aristotle via mediation of some concepts.[40] There are several responses to this point.

The first response to this point is that the argument for RN given in Section 4 does *not* (and was not, by Kripke, intended to) demonstrate that proper names are *de jure* rigid, but merely that they are rigid. Secondly, given the metaphorical nature of the notion of mediation, it is difficult to see how one *could* argue for such a conclusion. Finally, there are examples of proper names which do seem, relatively uncontroversially, to rigidly designate what they designate "via mediation".

The first of these points is obvious. The statement of RN does not mention the notion of *de jure* designation. Furthermore, nothing in the argument for it would fail if proper names were only *de facto* rigid.

To grasp the second point, consider the case of indexicals, which are rigid designators. Does the word "I" designate what it designates via mediation, or not? Kaplan (1989a) seems to think it does not.[41] But "I", whenever it is used, designates the agent of the context. Though there are difficulties in making precise the notion of "agenthood" here, it is difficult to see how it could be that "I" designates "unmediately", given the linguistic rule that it is to designate the agent of the context. Perhaps there is a notion of mediation according to which "I" unmediatedly designates. But if so, it needs to be made more precise before an argument for such a conclusion can be evaluated.

Finally, there are examples of proper names which, if the notion of mediation is coherent, do seem to designate mediately what they designate. Consider, for example, the following example, due to Gareth Evans (1985b). Suppose we wish to discuss what the world would have been like if the zip had not been invented. In particular, we wish to discuss what would have happened if the inventor of the zip had died at birth. Not knowing who the inventor of the zip is, we introduce a name "Julius", by the following reference-fixing stipulation:

(S) Reference("Julius") = The inventor of the zip

and then go on to theorize about what would have happened had Julius died at birth, and had failed to invent the zip.

Evans's intuition is that "Julius" is a rigid designator. That is, according to Evans, (18) has no true reading, but (19) does:

(18) Julius might not have been Julius.
(19) Julius might not have been the inventor of the zip.

If so, then "Julius" is an example of a proper name which designates what it does via mediation, and is hence not *de jure* rigid.[42]

Given Evans's example, it seems implausible to maintain that it is a feature of the semantic category of proper names that they are *de jure* rigid. Of course, on the descriptivist account, *no* proper name is *de jure* rigid, which, given the slight oddity of "Julius"-type names, may seem worrisome. Nonetheless, what is important to note for our purposes is that there is no argument from rigidity alone against a traditional descriptive account of the content of proper names. Issues of rigidity are simply independent of the question of whether names have descriptive content.[43]

None of this would be news to Kripke. Kripke never argued that his modal considerations refuted every version of the descriptive account of content. Michael Dummett has, however, leveled more direct challenges to Kripke's conclusions.[44] Though Dummett agrees that Kripke has shown an important difference between English proper names and descriptions, he has challenged Kripke's contention that the difference in question always makes a difference to what is said. In particular, according to Dummett, the rigidity of proper names does not affect the content of modally "simple" sentences, that is, sentences not containing modal terms. In other words, Dummett challenges the truth of RT.

Dummett's early views on rigidity can be separated into two doctrines. The first, which is a negative doctrine, is that rigidity does not make a difference to the content of simple sentences. The second, which is a positive doctrine, is that the phenomena which the notion of rigidity is intended to capture can be accounted for by a stipulation that terms which Kripke would classify as rigid take an obligatory wide scope with respect to modal operators.

In the next section I will discuss Dummett's positive doctrine, as well as Kripke's decisive objection to it. In the final section I will turn to a more promising line of argument against RT along essentially Dummettian lines.

6 Names and wide-scope

Consider again (16) and (17), which were used to show that "Aristotle" and "the last great philosopher of antiquity" have different contents. As we saw in Section 4, (17) has no true reading, whereas (16) does. If one assumes that "Aristotle" is rigid, whereas "the last great philosopher of antiquity" is not, then one can account for this contrast between the two expressions.

The point of Dummett's positive doctrine is that one can account for the distinction between (16) and (17) without supposing a difference in semantic value between "Aristotle" and "the last great philosopher of antiquity". That is, one can account for the distinction without supposing that "Aristotle" is rigid, whereas "the last great philosopher of antiquity" is not. According to Dummett, all that the distinction between (16) and (17) demonstrates is that there is a *syntactic* constraint on terms such as "Aristotle", which forces them to take wide scope with respect to modal operators.

Here is how Dummett's positive doctrine accounts for the distinction between (16) and (17). (17), and (the true reading of) (16), properly regimented (and abstracting from irrelevant detail), come out, on Dummett's view, as:

(16′) For some x such that Aristotle = x [$\Diamond$ x $\neq$ the last great philosopher of antiquity]
(17′) For some x, y such that Aristotle = x and Aristotle = y [$\Diamond$ x $\neq$ y]

(16′) is true because there are possible situations in which the actual denotation of "Aristotle" died as a child; whereas, given the rigidity of variables, (17′) is false. Thus, Dummett's positive doctrine accounts for the distinction between (16) and (17) without postulating a semantic difference between proper names and definite descriptions. Indeed, if Dummett's positive doctrine is correct, proper names can be identified with definite descriptions which take an obligatory wide scope with respect to modal operators.

On Kripke's account, the difference between (16) and (17) is attributed to a difference in the semantic values of the expressions "Aristotle" and "the last great philosopher of antiquity". (17) has no true reading because "Aristotle" is rigid; that is, it is associated with a (perhaps partial) constant function from worlds to objects, whereas (16) does have a true reading, since "the last great philosopher of antiquity" is not rigid; that is, it is associated with a non-constant function from possible worlds to objects. On Dummett's account, no difference in semantic value is required in order to explain the distinction between (16) and (17). It is simply a syntactic feature of proper names that they take wide scope with respect to modal operators; but, in all semantic respects, proper names are like descriptions.

However, Dummett's positive account is problematic, as the following argument by Kripke demonstrates. Suppose "t" is an expression which Kripke would classify as rigid, and "t′" is a non-rigid description which, according to Dummett, has the same content as "t". Consider now the following discourse:

(20) t is t. That's necessary.
(21) t is t′. That's not necessary.

Both (20) and (21) are true, given that "t" is an expression which Kripke would classify as rigid and "t′" is not rigid. But on Dummett's account, it is difficult to see how this could be so.

The central issue in interpreting this discourse is what the content of the occurrence of 'that' is. There are two possibilities. First of all, the occurrences of 'that' might refer to some 'value' of the preceding sentences, either the proposition it expresses ('what it says'), or some other semantic feature. The second possibility is that the occurrence of 'that' refers to the preceding sentences themselves, that is, it is replaceable by a quote-name of the preceding sentences. In each case it is difficult to see how Dummett's account could make both (20) and (21) true.

Suppose the first of these possibilities to be the case. That is, suppose that the occurrence of 'that' in (20) denotes some value of the preceding sentence 't is t'. Then, since both discourses are true, by Leibniz's Law, the value denoted by the occurrence of 'that' in (20) must be different from the value denoted by the occurrence of 'that' in (21), since the values have different properties (one is necessary, while the other is not). But Dummett's positive doctrine gives us no explanation of this fact. According to Dummett, one can explain rigidity facts by a syntactic stipulation that certain terms – those which Kripke classifies as rigid – take an obligatory wide scope with respect to modal operators. But no such operators occur in the initial sentences of (20) and (21). Therefore, Dummett's positive account predicts that there should be no differences in semantic value between these two sentences. But if the two occurrences of 'that' denote some semantic value of the preceding sentences, then the two sentences are associated with different semantic values, *contra* the predictions of Dummett's positive account.

So let us suppose, then, the second of the above possibilities to be the case; that is, suppose that the occurrence of 'that' in (20) denotes the sentence, "t is t". Similarly, suppose that the occurrence of 'that' in (21) denotes the sentence, "t is t′". In this case, we could replace the second sentences in (20) and (21) by:

(22) "t is t" is necessary.
(23) "t is t′" is not necessary.

(22) and (23) are true. But again, on Dummett's positive account, it is not possible to see how this could be the case. For there is no way for any of the occurrences of the term "t" to take wide scope with respect to modal operators, since they all occur within quotation marks.[45]

What Kripke's argument seems to show is that no syntactic account of the distinction between proper names and definite descriptions is possible. Thus, the difference between proper names and definite descriptions must be attributed to a difference in the semantic values they receive. Indeed, one might use this argument of Kripke's to establish RT. For even in the case of unmodalized sentences, replacing a rigid designator by a non-rigid designator will typically result in a sentence which differs in truth-value in some possible world. One can exploit this to provide an argument for RT.

To see this, consider the following discourses, both true:

(24) Aristotle was not a philosopher. That would be true in a situation in which Aristotle died as a baby.
(25) The last great philosopher of antiquity was not a philosopher. That would not be true in a situation in which Aristotle died as a baby.

Using the same reasoning as in Kripke's argument, it follows that the sentences "Aristotle was not a philosopher" and "The last great philosopher of antiquity was not a philosopher" must have different semantic values. For one value, when evaluated with respect to a situation in which Aristotle died as a baby, is true, while the other, when evaluated with respect to that same situation, is not true. Thus, since the values have different properties – one is true with respect to the world in question, while the other is not true – by Leibniz's Law they must be different.

What this argument of Kripke's establishes is that whatever it is that is evaluated with respect to different metaphysically possible worlds in the case of "Aristotle was not a philosopher" differs from whatever it is that is evaluated with respect to different metaphysically possible worlds in the case of "The last great philosopher of antiquity was not a philosopher". Furthermore, it is clear that similar demonstrations can be given for other cases in which a non-rigid description might seem to have the same content as a rigid designator.

But RT might still seem worrisome. According to RT, sentences containing definite descriptions have different contents from the sentences which result from replacing those definite descriptions by any rigid expressions, even when the sentences are unmodalized. But there are *prima facie* counter-examples to this. For example, the sentences:

(26) The president of the USA came to dinner.
(27) The actual president of the USA came to dinner.

do not, on the face of it, seem to say different things; rather, the difference between utterances of (26) and (27) seems to lie in their pragmatic force. Yet "the president of the USA" is non-rigid, and "the actual president of the USA" is rigid.

Furthermore, (26) and (27) pose a problem for Kripke's argument in this section. For (26) and (27) differ in truth-value with respect to some metaphysically possible worlds. Utterance (26) is true in a world in which George Bush came to dinner, Bill Clinton did not, and George Bush won the 1992 election. Utterance (27) is not true with respect to such a situation. But it seems over-hasty to conclude from this that utterances of (26) and (27) say different things.

Examples such as (26) and (27) might lead one to the view that the semantic differences between rigid and non-rigid expressions do not imply that they must differ in content, as well as to the thesis that the differences in modal semantic value – that is, whatever is evaluated in other possible worlds – do not necessarily lead to a difference in content. Yet these reactions presuppose a distinction between semantic value and content which requires greater explication before it can be developed into a serious response to RT. It is to this task which we now turn.

7 Assertoric content and ingredient sense

In this section, I will introduce and motivate Dummett's distinction between assertoric content and ingredient sense. I will then use this distinction in briefly suggesting a line of critique against RT.

The *assertoric content* of an utterance of a sentence is what is said by that utterance; it is also the object of belief, doubt, and other propositional attitudes. (See Chapter 9, PROPOSITIONAL ATTITUDES.) Assertoric contents are the fundamental bearers of truth-value. They are not true or false relative to a time or a place. Mary's belief that the sun is shining is not true at some times, false at others. What Mary says when she says that the sun is shining is not true in America, false in Australia. It is true or false, as Frege says, *tertium non datur*.

The *ingredient sense* of a sentence is what that sentence contributes to more complex sentences of which it is a part. The ingredient sense of a sentence is thus that sentence's compositional semantic value. It is the semantic value we must assign to a sentence in order to predict correctly the conditions under which more complex constructions in which it occurs are true. As Dummett notes, ingredient sense is what formal semantic theories are concerned to explain.[46]

Once one makes the distinction between ingredient sense and assertoric content, the possibility arises that the ingredient sense of a sentence might differ from its assertoric content. There are several ways in which this possibility might be realized. First of all, it could be the case that sentences which have the same assertoric content none the less contribute different things to more complex sentences containing them.[47] That is, it could be the case that sentences with the same assertoric contents have different ingredient senses. Secondly, it could be the case that the ingredient sense of a sentence cannot serve as its assertoric content, because it is not the sort of object which is fit to be believed or asserted. As we shall soon see, both of these situations in fact obtain.

Consider, first, the former of these possibilities, that is, that two sentences which have the same assertoric content differ in ingredient sense. Each of (29)–(31) has the same assertoric content as (28):

(28) The president is Bill Clinton.
(29) The current president is Bill Clinton.
(30) The president here is Bill Clinton.
(31) The actual president is Bill Clinton.

The difference between each of (29)–(31) and (28) is not truth-conditional, but pragmatic. In each of (29)–(31), a presupposition is present which is not present in (28).

But these presuppositions are cancelable. The sentences can be true, even if the presuppositions fail. Indeed, in any context c, an utterance of each of (29)–(31) is true in c just in case an utterance of (28) is true in c. On a natural construal of the expression "truth-condition", each of (29)–(31) has the same truth-conditions as (28), and hence has the same assertoric content as (28).

However, as the following sentence-pairs demonstrate, the two sentences in each of the sentence-pairs have different *ingredient senses*:

(32) It will always be the case that the current president is Bill Clinton.
(33) It will always be the case that the president is Bill Clinton.

(34) Everywhere, it is the case that the president here is Bill Clinton.
(35) Everywhere, it is the case that the president is Bill Clinton.

(36) Necessarily, it is the case that the actual president is Bill Clinton.
(37) Necessarily, it is the case that the president is Bill Clinton.

In each of these sentence-pairs, the first sentence is true, but the second false. Thus, each of (29)–(31) contributes different things to more complex sentences of which they are a part than (28). But then, given that utterances of them have the same assertoric content as utterances of (28), we have shown that utterances of two sentences can have the same assertoric content, while none the less differing in ingredient sense.

Consider now the second of these possibilities, namely that ingredient senses are not the sort of objects which can be identified with assertoric contents, things believed and asserted. As the following examples show, and as Lewis (1981) points out, this too is the case:

(38) It will be the case that the sun is shining.
(39) Somewhere, the sun is shining.
(40) In the future, there might be a miracle somewhere.

In each case, what the embedded sentence contributes to the interpretation of the whole sentence is not something which could plausibly be identified with an assertoric content, something fit to be believed or asserted. In the case of (38), the embedded sentence "the sun is shining" must express a function from times to truth-values. In the case of (39), the embedded sentence must express a function from places to truth-values. Finally, in the case of (40), the embedded sentence must express a function from world, time, and place triples to truth-values.

But, as we have seen, functions from times or places to truth-values are not fit to be things believed or asserted. Mary's belief that the sun is shining does not vary in truth-value from one time to another, or from one place to another. It is true or false, *tertium non datur*. Therefore, ingredient senses are not fit to be assertoric contents.[48]

Let us now sum up our conclusions so far in this section. First, we have seen that sentences can have the same assertoric content, while differing in ingredient sense. Secondly, we have seen that ingredient senses are not the sort of objects which can be regarded as assertoric contents. Keeping these facts in mind, let us now turn to how these facts bear on RT.

In the original argument for RT, we inferred, from the fact that "Aristotle is Aristotle" and "Aristotle is the last great philosopher of antiquity" embed differently in modal contexts – that is, (16) and (17) differ in truth-value – that the two sentences have different contents, and hence that "Aristotle" and "the last great philosopher of antiquity" have different contents. Yet, once the assertoric-content/ingredient-sense distinction is made, it is clear that this sort of inference is invalid. From (16) and (17), it is only legitimate to infer that "Aristotle is Aristotle" and "Aristotle is the last great philosopher of antiquity" have differing ingredient senses. Similarly, it is only legitimate to infer from (16) and (17) that "Aristotle" and "the last great philosopher of antiquity" have different semantic values. But as we have seen, this does not demonstrate that replacement of one with the other typically yields a sentence with a different assertoric content. That is, such facts as (16) and (17) do not demonstrate the truth of RT.

But what about the Kripkean argument for RT given in the last section? In the case of (20) and (21), and (24) and (25), the initial sentences were not embedded in modal contexts. None the less, the Kripkean argument established that the sentence containing the rigid designator, and the sentence resulting from it by replacing the rigid designator by a non-rigid designator, corresponded to different values. However, the Kripkean argument only demonstrates RT if the values in question are assertoric contents, or propositions, rather than ingredient senses. For, as we have seen, it is perfectly possible for two sentences to differ in ingredient sense, yet for utterances of them to have the same assertoric content.

The fundamental question in evaluating the Kripkean argument is what the denotations of the occurrences of 'that' are in the relevant discourses. If such occurrences of 'that' denote the assertoric content of the preceding sentences, then the argument does indeed demonstrate RT. If, however, such occurrences of 'that' denote the ingredient senses of the preceding sentences, then the argument only demonstrates that the preceding sentences differ in ingredient sense, a fact perfectly consistent with their coinciding in assertoric content.

Now, there is no question that such occurrences of 'that' can denote the assertoric content of the occurrences of the preceding sentences. This is precisely what the denotation of 'that' is in such contexts as:

(41) The sun is shining. That's asserted by John.
(42) The sun is shining. That's believed by Mary.

Our question is thus: do all such uses of 'that' denote the assertoric contents of the occurrences of the preceding sentences, or do they sometimes denote the ingredient senses of the preceding sentences?

That the latter is the case can be seen from the following two examples:

(43) The sun is shining. That will be true, but it isn't true now.
(44) The sun is shining. That's true somewhere, but it isn't true here.

In order for (43) to be true, the occurrence of 'that' must denote a function from times to truth-values. Similarly, in order for (44) to be true, the occurrence of 'that' must denote a function from places to truth-values. But, as we have seen, such entities are certainly not assertoric contents, things believed and expressed. Such examples hence show that some such occurrences of the word 'that' denote the ingredient senses, rather than the assertoric contents, of the preceding sentences.[49]

The fact that the word 'that' sometimes denotes the ingredient sense, rather than the assertoric content, of the preceding sentence allows the Dummettian to respond to the Kripkean argument as follows. What she would maintain is that the occurrences of 'that' in (20), (21), (24), and (25) denote, not the assertoric content of the preceding sentences, as in the occurrences of 'that' in (41) and (42), but rather the ingredient sense. Since a difference in ingredient sense does not imply a difference in assertoric content, the Kripkean argument fails to demonstrate RT.

For the Dummettian, then, the Kripkean argument fares about as well as the following argument for the thesis that utterances of (28) and (29) always have different assertoric contents:

(45) The current president is Bill Clinton. That will always be true.
(46) The president is Bill Clinton. That won't always be true.

It would be over-hasty to conclude, from this argument, that utterances of (28) and (29) must have different assertoric contents.[50] Similarly, according to the Dummettian, it would be over-hasty to conclude, from (20) and (21) alone, that "t = t" and "t = t′ " have different assertoric contents.

What a friend of RT must show is some disanalogy between the argument from (20) and (21) to the conclusion that "t is t" and "t is t′ " do not have the same assertoric content, and the argument from (45) and (46) to the conclusion that (28) and (29) have different assertoric contents. There are two ways in which she could proceed. First, she could argue that, in modal contexts, the relevant uses of 'that' do denote the assertoric contents of the preceding sentences. Alternatively, she could argue that, unlike the case of (45) and (46), a difference in the particular ingredient sense, or semantic value, denoted by these occurrences entails a difference in assertoric content.

According to the opponent of RT, the object of modal evaluation, like the object of temporal evaluation, is not a proposition or assertoric content. To make her position clear, she must first provide some clear account of the assertoric-content/ingredient-sense distinction. Then, she must provide an account of assertoric content which distinguishes it in relevant ways from the object of modal evaluation.[51]

Conclusion

As we have seen, given the possibility of actualized descriptions, there is no argument from rigid designation against the description theory of names. The more interesting question, however, is the status of RT. What I have tried (ever so briefly) to motivate is the view that RT is not as innocent as many philosophers believe. The classic Kripkean argument in its favor fails. That is not to say that RT is false: for instance, it may be that the best theory of content entails it.[52] On the other hand, there may be substantive empirical or methodological objections against it. But I am afraid that these are issues which we must leave for future Philosophy of Language to decide.[53]

Notes

1 This characterization of rigidity is from a letter from Kripke to Kaplan, cited on p. 569 of Kaplan's "Afterthoughts" (1989b).

2 Ibid.
3 Kripke (1980, p. 48).
4 There is another notion of rigidity occasionally suggested in the literature according to which a term is rigid just in case it refers to the same object in all possible worlds in which it refers at all. But this is consistent with the actual denotation of a rigid designator existing in some possible world, yet unnamed by that designator. This possibility is ruled out by Kripke's general characterization of rigidity. In what follows, "rigidity" will instead be used in accordance with Kripke's general characterization.
5 Besides the issues that will be discussed in later sections, there are other issues in philosophical logic which may push one to prefer one or the other characterization of rigidity. For instance, if one defines necessity as truth in every world, then, to capture the intuitive necessity of "Bill Clinton = Bill Clinton", one might wish to allow "Bill Clinton" to denote Bill Clinton with respect to every possible world (in which case one would prefer the characterization of rigidity as obstinate rigidity). Alternatively, one could exploit another notion of necessity, viz. non-falsity in every world. This would allow "Bill Clinton = Bill Clinton" to lack a truth-value in some possible worlds without thereby becoming contingent, hence removing the need to treat designators as obstinately rigid to preserve the necessity of "Bill Clinton = Bill Clinton". Similar issues arise with respect to the characterization of validity. However, here, too, it is difficult to see any substantive issues. As Kripke (1963, p. 66) writes, "For the purposes of modal logic we hold that different answers to [these questions] represent alternative *conventions*. All are tenable."
6 See Kripke (1980, p. 21, n. 21).
7 However, eliminating the metaphor of mediation in the characterization of this distinction is no easy task. Furthermore, as will become clear in later sections, it is unclear how the distinction between *de jure* and *de facto* rigid designation generalizes to other expressions.
8 See Kripke (1980, p. 21, n. 21) Kaplan (1989a), and, most explicitly, pp. 569–71 of Kaplan (1989b). See also Chapter 23, INDEXICALS AND DEMONSTRATIVES.
9 Because of space considerations, I will not discuss the latter's use of substitutional quantification in explicating quantification into modal context.
10 Quine (1943). For discussions of Quine's objections, see Fine (1989) and Kaplan (1986). See also Richard (1987). There is a substantial body of contemporary literature on this topic.
11 So perhaps it is not really correct to call these two different objections.
12 I am here, as below, *not* using "objectual" in the sense of the distinction between objectual and *substitutional* quantification, but rather in the sense of the soon-to-be-explicated distinction between quantification over individuals *vs.* quantification over concepts.
13 Here, "a" and "b" and "ϕ" are being used as schematic letters replaceable by metalinguistic names for object language expressions, and '' is being used for quasi-quotation. I will use '' as normal quotation and quasi-quotation, leaving it to context to disambiguate. In general, I will be lax about use/mention.
14 Kaplan (1986) calls this "Quine's Theorem". See pp. 231–8 for a reconstruction of Quine's (1943) arguments, and Kaplan's critique of it. See also Fine (1989).
15 It is illegitimate *simpliciter* to quantify into contexts in which the quotation is ordinary English quotation. However, Kaplan (1986) introduces a new quotation device, which he called 'arc quotes', and showed how to make sense of quantification into them (see Section 7ff.).

16 Carnap (1988, p. 174).

17 Furthermore, on the conceptual interpretation of QML, there are ways to rescue substitution of co-extensional expressions in extensional contexts, and even to rescue a quantified version of extensional substitution of the form:

(*) $\forall x \forall y\, (x = y \rightarrow (\phi \leftrightarrow \psi))$

(where ϕ differs from ψ in containing free occurrences of 'x' where ψ contains free occurrences of 'y', and ϕ and ψ are extensional). According to Carnap, for example, both terms and variables are systematically ambiguous. To each term, there corresponds both an extension and an intension (something which yields, at every possible world, an extension). In addition, to each variable, there correspond both *value extensions* and *value intensions*. The value intensions of a variable are the set of intensions of expressions which are admissible substitution instances of that variable, and the value extensions are the set of extensions of expressions which are admissible substitution instances of that variable (see Carnap, 1988, Section 10). Since in extensional contexts all that is relevant are the value-extensions of variables and the extensions of terms, once the notion of "extensional context" has been appropriately inductively defined (say, as a wff of non-modal first or higher-order calculus), both the fully schematic version of extensional substitution, as well as the version of substitution containing quantifiers, can be preserved. This is Carnap's *Method of Extension and Intension* (1988, ch. 1). Church avoids having to give expressions and variables a double interpretation, choosing instead to follow Frege in relativizing their interpretations to contexts. For a discussion of these matters, see Fine (1989, pp. 267ff.). For an old attack on the *metaphysical* coherence of the conceptual interpretation, see Quine (1947).

18 For simplicity's sake, I am speaking here only of non-vacuous existential quantifications into modal formulas with one free variable (so it is appropriate to speak of truth and falsity, rather than satisfaction). I will occasionally make such simplifying assumptions without comment.

19 Of course, such a primitive relational sense of necessity is analogous to Quine's (1956) primitive relational sense of propositional attitude verbs. Quine himself later noticed (1977) that his reconstruction of quantification into propositional attitude contexts could be used in this way to defend the coherence of quantification into modal contexts.

20 Here, "exists" is a primitive predicate which is true of an object with respect to a possible situation just in case that object is in the domain of the possible situation.

21 Missing this point, Quine (1977, p. 8) asserted that the notion of rigidity by itself presupposes the notion of an essential property: "A rigid designator differs from others in that it picks out its object by essential traits." A careful reading of Kripke's discussions of transworld identification (e.g. 1980, p. 44) might have dispelled his belief in this.

22 This is for non-complex terms. If the language contains rigid complex terms – rigid descriptions – the interpretation of terms which are not variables may, of course, depend upon an assignment function.

23 For instance, even the free-logical rule of universal instantiation can fail for languages with non-rigid terms (cf. Garson, 1984, pp. 262–3). Furthermore, the introduction of non-rigid terms complicates completeness proofs for systems of QML, since standard completeness proofs rely on substitution facts (cf. Garson, 1984, pp. 287–9).

24 In retrospect, the latter option seems only to be motivated if one accepts Quine's rather curious idolatry of classical quantification theory. There are many ways of restricting classical substitution to account for non-rigid terms, either by restricting substitution to atomic formulas, or by reformulating quantification theory in terms of complex predicates and restricting substitution to complex predications (for this latter option, see Robert Stalnaker, 1977 and 1995). See also, for a development of the appropriate proof theory for a language with complex predicates and non-rigid designators, Fitting (1993, section 3, as well as 1991).

25 For instance, Arthur Smullyan (1947, 1948) argued, against Quine's logico-semantical objection to QML, that once one recognizes that descriptions are to be treated on Russellian lines, rather than as terms, then Quine's objection fails. Smullyan is thus the first person explicitly to suggest that natural language terms are such that classical substitution holds for them. However, since Smullyan wrote years before Kripke's development of the semantics of QML, he cannot be credited with the discovery that natural-language names are rigid, since he did not possess the resources to define the notion of rigidity. Furthermore, he provided no argument to the effect that natural-language terms are rigid. A similar point holds for Barcan Marcus. Though she derived (quantified) versions of the necessity of identity (1947; see esp. theorem 2.32), she did not, at that time, have the notion of rigidity, since she had neither an explicit semantics in mind, nor any sort of philosophical or semantic argument about natural language. She does suggest (1961) that natural language names are mere "tags" for objects, but she neither provides the sort of arguments required for the establishment of this thesis, nor possesses the semantical apparatus necessary to characterize the notion of rigidity. None the less, the work of Smullyan, Marcus, and also Frederick Fitch certainly provided much of the necessary impetus for the later development of these notions. For an excellent discussion of their role in the history of the notion of rigidity, see Scott Soames (1995).

26 For instance, for Strawson, descriptive identification is based upon demonstrative identification:

> [The supposition that where the particular to be identified cannot be directly located, its identification must rest ultimately on description in general terms] is false. For even though the particular in question cannot itself be demonstratively identified, it may be identified by a description which relates it uniquely to another particular which can be demonstratively identified. (1959, p. 21)

None the less, for Strawson's anti-skeptical arguments to succeed, he must be assuming that successful reference requires uniquely identifying knowledge given by description. Dummett directly challenges the thesis that for Frege, the sense of each proper name can be given by a description (see, to cite one example, the Appendix to chapter 5 of his 1981a). For Frege, his belief that a change in reference entails a change in sense demonstrates that he did not ascribe to the "description in general terms alone" account.

27 The case is more difficult in the case of "I" and "here", for their reference is "guaranteed". See Evans (1982, chapters 6 and 7), for an attempt to fit an account of these words into a model more closely paralleling perceptual demonstratives than seems, prima facie, to be possible, and see Lucy O'Brien (1995) for a recent critique of Evans's account.

28 Though see Kripke (1980, n. 58) for a challenge to this paragraph.

29 This distinction between different descriptive pictures of intentionality is relevant for Kripke's epistemological critique of descriptive theories of intentionality, though not his argument from rigidity.

30 Of course, to bring this fully in line with the description theory, we would also have to analyze the place name "the United States".

31 Furthermore, I will use "possibilist" quantifiers (that is, quantifiers whose domains are not restricted to worlds, but rather range over all actual and possible objects) as well as a primitive existence predicate ("x exists") which is true of an object at a world just in case that object is in the domain of that world (i.e. exists in that world).

32 See, for example, Allan Gibbard's discussion (1975) of "Goliath" and "Lumpl".

33 To rescue the necessity of identity, one would be forced to reformulate some clause in the semantics. One method is to replace the identity axiom schema by its free-logical counterpart. Alternatively, one could redefine the necessity operator, as in, for instance, van Benthem (1983, chapter 12, pp. 136–7) to restrict evaluation of the embedded sentence to worlds at which there exist the denotations of constants in the sentence, and values of the free variables of the sentence.

34 See Montague (1974, p. 126). This example, too, is not fully convincing, since "remembers" is intensional. A slightly better example is "Aristotle is currently the most-read philosopher".

35 Cf. Salmon (1982, pp. 37–9) for a longer discussion. Evans (1985a) has challenged the analogy between tense and modality.

36 That is, (18) has no true reading where the possibility in question is *metaphysical* possibility. Throughout, all occurrences of modal expressions should be read as expressing metaphysical possibility.

37 Kripke's argument that the content of a proper name is only its denotation depends more on the epistemological arguments he gives in Lecture II (1980). We will not discuss these arguments here.

38 This is only a rough statement of the actual thesis. For one may have a coarse-grained account of content, where, say, logical contradictions say the same thing. In this case, utterances of sentences which express logical contradictions, such as "John is tall and it is not the case that John is tall", would say the same thing as utterances of sentences with the name replaced by a non-rigid designator. But this is obviously not an objection to Kripke, for if such an account of content is endorsed, then the statement of the rigidity thesis would have to be modified to capture more adequately Kripke's intention.

39 Formally, the logic of the sentential operator "actually", which is the modal logic analogue of the temporal indexical "now", has been much investigated. Classic papers in this area include Segerberg (1973), Davies and Humberstone (1980), and Hodes (1984a, 1984b). For recent books on the subject, see Graeme Forbes's excellent (1989), which uses rigidifying operators such as "actually" to dispense with quantification over (and hence ontological commitment to) possible worlds, as well as Max Cresswell (1990) for an argument against a Forbes-like position.

40 However, if one characterizes the notion of *de jure* rigidity in terms of an expression being rigid "in virtue of the semantical rules of the language", then, given that the semantical rules of the language state that "actual" is a rigidifying operator, actualized descriptions *will* count as *de jure* rigid designators (cf. Almog 1986, pp. 223ff.). If *de jure* rigidity is so characterized, then the *de jure*/*de facto* distinction is simply irrelevant to the question of whether names have descriptive content.

41 However, Kaplan does add qualifications (1989a, p. 497).

42 See also, in this context, Kripke's discussion of "Cicero" and "Jack the Ripper" on (1980, p. 79). For an interesting challenge to the whole idea of a descriptive name, see Bostock (1988).

43 To make issues of rigidity relevant for arguments against descriptive accounts of content, one needs to argue that proper names are, in the sense of Evans (1985b), *deeply rigid designators*, where an expression e counts as a deeply rigid designator of an object o just in case, for every possible world w, e refers to o when considered as *uttered in w*. Actualized descriptions are thus not deeply rigid designators. There are few attempts to address the question of whether names are deeply rigid; though see Deutsch (1989). Thanks to Sanford Shieh for discussion here.

44 See e.g. the Appendix to chapter 5 of Dummett (1981a), Appendix 3 of his (1981b), and chapter 2 of his (1991). The arguments outlined in the final two sections have their sources in these passages.

45 There is a third possibility, that is, that the occurrences of "that" are unstructured names of the preceding sentence-tokens. But in this case it is even more difficult to see how "t" could take wide-scope with respect to the modal operator in the next sentence. The only way I can see to defend Dummett's positive account is by using Kaplan's (1986) device of "arc-quotes", maintaining that the "that" is replaceable by arc-quote names of the preceding sentences, which do license quantifying in.

46 See Dummett (1991, p. 48). By "formal semantic theory", I mean the project Robert Stalnaker calls "descriptive semantics" (see Chapter 21, REFERENCE AND NECESSITY).

47 I have characterized assertoric content as applying primarily to utterances rather than to sentence types. But we can, from this characterization, obtain an equivalence relation of sameness of assertoric content which holds between sentence types. Say that two sentence types, S and S′, have the same assertoric content, just in case, for every normal context c, utterances of S and S′ in that context have the same assertoric content (for the notion of "normal context", see Section I of my (1996)).

48 This is precisely Lewis's central conclusion (1981), albeit phrased in terms of Dummett's distinction between assertoric content and ingredient sense, rather than Lewis's vocabulary of "proposition" versus "semantic value" (1981, p. 95). Some of these facts have also been recognized (though used for different purposes) by Richard (1981, 1982) and Salmon (1986, chapter 2).

49 Ordinary language examples can, however, occasionally mislead here. For instance, the sentence "John believes something that was true yesterday, and false today" is perfectly acceptable. Yet the existence of such examples should not be taken as undermining the philosophical position that the objects of belief must be true or false absolutely. Such examples can be dealt with, as in Forbes (1989, p. 163), by interpreting the quantification substitutionally.

50 Similarly:

(a) The sun is shining. That's true now, but it won't be true tomorrow.
(b) The sun is shining. That's true here, but it's not true in Scotland.

51 According to Forbes (1989, Part II), whereas assertoric contents are to be identified with Fregean thoughts, states of affairs are the objects of modal evaluation. My own view (Stanley, 1996) is that modal semantic value comes from the speech act of supposition, rather than assertion.

52 The classical 'Russellian proposition' view of content, e.g. Kaplan (1989), Salmon

(1986), and Soames (1987) is one view which entails RT.

53 Robert Stalnaker and Timothy Williamson deserve the greatest thanks for helping me with this paper. In addition, extensive comments by Bob Hale and Crispin Wright substantively improved the paper. I would also like to thank Michael Dummett, Kit Fine, Richard Heck, and Susanna Siegel for discussion.

Bibliography

Almog, Joseph 1986: Naming without necessity. *Journal of Philosophy*, 83, 210–42.

Almog, Joseph, Perry, John, and Wettstein, Howard 1989: *Themes from Kaplan*. Oxford: Oxford University Press.

Barcan, Ruth 1947: The identity of individuals in a strict functional calculus of second order. *Journal of Symbolic Logic*, 12/1 (March), 12–15.

Barcan Marcus, Ruth 1961: Modalities and intensional languages. *Synthese*, 13, 303–22.

Bostock, David 1988: Necessary truth and a priori truth. *Mind*, 97/387 (July), 343–79.

Carnap, Rudolf 1988 (first publ. 1947): *Meaning and Necessity*. Chicago: University of Chicago Press.

Church, Alonzo 1943: Review of Quine's 'Notes on existence and necessity'. *Journal of Symbolic Logic*, 8 (1943), 45–7.

Cresswell, M.J. 1990: *Entities and Indices*. Dordrecht: Kluwer.

Davies, M. and Humberstone, L 1980: Two notions of necessity. *Philosophical Studies*, 38, 1–30.

Deutsch, Harry 1989: On direct reference. In Almog, Perry, and Wettstein (1989), pp. 167–95.

Dummett, Michael 1981a: *Frege: Philosophy of Language*. 2nd edn, London: Duckworth.

——1981b: *The Interpretation of Frege's Philosophy*. Cambridge, Mass.: Harvard University Press.

——1991: *The Logical Basis of Metaphysics*. Cambridge: Harvard University Press.

Evans, Gareth 1982: *The Varieties of Reference*. Oxford: Clarendon Press.

——1985a: Does tense logic rest upon a mistake? In *Collected Papers*, Oxford: Clarendon Press, pp. 343–63.

——1985b: Reference and contingency. In *Collected Papers*, Oxford: Clarendon Press, pp. 178–213.

Fine, Kit 1989: The problem of de re modality. In Almog, Perry, and Wettstein (1989), pp. 197–272.

Fitting, Melvin 1993: Basic modal logic. In *Handbook of Logic in Artificial Intelligence and Logic Programming*, Vol. 1. Oxford: Clarendon Press, pp. 365–448.

——1991: Modal logic should say more than it does. In Lassez and Plotkin (eds), *Computational Logic, Essays in Honor of Alan Robinson*. Cambridge, Mass.: MIT Press, pp. 113–35.

Forbes, Graeme 1989: *Languages of Possibility*. Oxford: Basil Blackwell.

Garson, James 1984: Quantification in modal logic. In *Handbook of Philosophical Logic*, ed. Gabbay and Guenthner, Dordrecht: Reidel, pp. 249–307.

Gibbard, Allan 1975: Contingent identity. *Journal of Philosophical Logic*, 4, pp. 187–221.

Hodes, Harold 1984a: Axioms for actuality. *Journal of Philosophical Logic*, 13, 27–34.

——1984b: On modal logics which enrich first-order S5. *Journal of Philosophical Logic*, 13, 423–54.

Kaplan, David 1986: Opacity. In *The Philosophy of W.V. Quine*, ed. Hahn and Schilpp, La

Salle, Ill.: Open Court, pp. 229–89.
——1989a: Demonstratives. In Almog, Perry, and Wettstein (1989), pp. 481–563.
——1989b: Afterthoughts. In Almog, Perry, and Wettstein (1989), pp. 567–614.
Kripke, Saul 1963: Semantical considerations on modal logic. *Acta Philosophica Fennica*, 16, 83–94.
——1980 (first publ. 1970): *Naming and Necessity*. Cambridge, Mass.: Harvard University Press.
Lewis, David 1981: Index, content, and context. In *Philosophy and Grammar*, ed. Stig Kanger and Sven Ohman, London: Reidel, pp. 79–100.
Montague, Richard 1974: Pragmatics and intensional logic. In *Formal Philosophy*, New Haven: Yale University Press, pp. 119–47.
O'Brien, Lucy 1995: Evans on self-identification. *Noûs*, 29/2 (June 1995), 232–47.
Quine, Willard 1943: Notes on existence and necessity. *Journal of Philosophy*, 40, 113–27.
——1947: The problem of interpreting modal logic. *Journal of Symbolic Logic*, 12, 43–8.
——1956: Quantifiers and propositional attitudes. *Journal of Philosophy*, 53, 177–87.
——1977: Intensions revisited. In *Midwest Studies in Philosophy*, Vol. 2, Morris, Minn.: University of Minnesota Press, pp. 5–11.
Richard, Mark 1981: Temporalism and externalism. *Philosophical Studies*, 39, 1–13.
——1982: Tense, propositions, and meanings. *Philosophical Studies*, 41, 337–51.
——1987: Quantification and Leibniz's law. *Philosophical Review*, 96 (October), 555–78.
Salmon, Nathan 1982: *Reference and Essence*. Oxford: Basil Blackwell.
——1986: *Frege's Puzzle*. Cambridge, Mass.: MIT Press.
Segerberg, Krister 1973: Two-dimensional modal logic. *Journal of Philosophical Logic*, 2, 77–96.
Smullyan, Arthur 1947: Review of Quine's 'The Problem of Interpreting Modal Logic'. *Journal of Symbolic Logic*, 12/4 (December), 139–41.
——1948: Modality and description. *Journal of Symbolic Logic*, 13/1 (March), 31–7.
Soames, Scott 1987: Direct reference, propositional attitudes, and semantic content. *Philosophical Topics*, 15, 47–87.
——1995: 'Revisionism about reference: a reply to Smith', *Synthese*, 104, 191–216
Stalnaker, Robert 1977: Complex predicates. *The Monist*, 60/3 (July), 327–39.
——1995: The interaction of modality with quantification and identity. In *Modality, Morality, and Belief: Essays in Honor of Ruth Barcan Marcus*. Cambridge: Cambridge University Press.
Stanley, Jason (forthcoming): Rigidity and content. In *Logic, Language, and Reality: Essays in Honour of Michael Dummett*, ed. R. Heck. Oxford: Oxford University Press.
Strawson, Peter 1959: *Individuals*. London: Methuen.
van Benthem, Johan 1983: *Modal logic and classical logic*. Napoli, Italy: Grafitalia.

23

Indexicals and demonstratives

JOHN PERRY

1 Introduction

When you use the word "I" it designates you; when I use the same word, it designates me. If you use "you" talking to me, it designates me; when I use it talking to you, it designates you. "I" and "you" are *indexicals*. The designation of an indexical *shifts* from speaker to speaker, time to time, place to place. Different utterances of the same indexical designate different things, because what is designated depends not only on the meaning associated with the expression, but also on facts about the utterance. An utterance of "I" designates the person who utters it; an utterance of "you" designates the person to whom it is addressed, an utterance of "here" designates the place at which the utterance is made, and so forth. Because indexicals shift their designation in this way, sentences containing indexicals can be used to say different things on different occasions. Suppose you say to me, "You are wrong and I am right about reference," and I reply with the same sentence. We have used the same sentence, with the same meaning, but said quite different and incompatible things.

In addition to "I" and "you", the standard list of indexicals includes the personal pronouns "my", "he", "his", "she", "it", the demonstrative pronouns "that" and "this", the adverbs "here", "now", "today", "yesterday", and "tomorrow" and the adjectives "actual" and "present". This list is from David Kaplan (1989a), whose work on the "logic of demonstratives" is responsible for much of the increased attention given to indexicals by philosophers of language in recent years. The words and aspects of words that indicate tense are also indexicals. And many other words, like "local", seem to have an indexical element.

Philosophers have found indexicals interesting for at least two reasons. First, such words as "I", "now", and "this" play crucial roles in arguments and paradoxes about such philosophically rich subjects as the self, the nature of time, and the nature of perception. Second, although the meanings of these words seem relatively straightforward, it has not been so obvious how to incorporate these meanings into semantical theory. I will focus on the second issue in this essay and, even with respect to that issue, will discuss only a few of the many topics that deserve attention. Among other things, I won't consider tense, or plurals,[1] or the relation of indexicality to anaphora,[2] or Castañeda's concept of quasi-indication.[3] I'll focus on the words Kaplan listed, and among those on singular terms.

In section 2 I fix some concepts and terms. In section 3 I develop a treatment of indexicals that I call the "Reflexive-referential theory". It is based on an account by Arthur Burks, and also incorporates ideas from Reichenbach, Kaplan, and a number of other authors.

2 Meaning, content and propositions

Meaning, as I shall use the term, is a property of expressions – that is, of *types* rather than tokens or utterances. Meaning is what is fixed by the conventions for the use of expressions that we learn when we learn a language. In contrast, *content* is a property of individual utterances. Content is tied to truth-conditions. The content of a statement – a specific use of a declarative sentence – is a proposition that embodies its truth-conditions. The contents of utterances of sub-sentential expressions – terms and predicates – is the contribution they make to truth-conditions; it's the things that utterances of names designate, and the conditions expressed by utterances of predicates and definite descriptions.

Any part of speech can have an indexical element, but I'll focus on the role of such expressions as "I", "you" and "that man" in simple statements. This will allow us to compare indexicals with the categories of expression most studied in the philosophy of language: proper names and definite descriptions – phrases of the form *the so-and-so*.

First I need to make some distinctions and develop some concepts about propositions. I will not need to adopt a specific and detailed ontology of propositions and their components for the purposes of this chapter. There are two main approaches to propositions in the literature today, the classic conception of a proposition as a set of possible worlds, and a number of conceptions of structured propositions. (See also Chapter 9, PROPOSITIONAL ATTITUDES.) I'll think of propositions structurally, but borrow the possible-worlds conception when convenient to get clear about things. The distinctions I need can be made in any number of more detailed approaches.

Consider:

(1) Jim was born in Lincoln

(1) is a statement of mine, referring to my son Jim Perry and to Lincoln, Nebraska. On the now-standard view of proper names (which I'll discuss below), (1) expresses a *singular* proposition, a proposition that is about Jim himself and Lincoln itself, rather than any descriptions or attributes of them. In some of the possible worlds in which this proposition is true Jim will not be named "Jim"; in some he will look different than he in fact does, act differently than he in fact does, have a different job than he in fact has, and so forth. And in some of the worlds Lincoln may be named "Davis" or "McClellan" and may not be the capital of Nebraska. As long as Jim was born in Lincoln in a given world then the proposition is true in that world, whatever he is like and whatever he is called in that world, and whatever Lincoln is like and whatever it is called.

On the possible-worlds conception of propositions, this proposition just *is* the set of worlds in which Jim was born in Lincoln. On a structural conception of propositions, one could think of the proposition expressed by (1) as an ordered pair of a sequence of objects and a condition:

⟨⟨Jim Perry, Lincoln⟩, *x* was born in *y*⟩

Such propositions are true if the sequences of objects in the first member of the pair meets the condition that is the second member. It is natural to say that Jim himself is a constituent of the proposition, on the structural conception. Although on this conception we don't identify the proposition with a set of worlds, it is still natural to talk about the worlds in which it is true.

In fact, Jim is the manager of Kinko's,[4] and Lincoln is the capital of Nebraska. So consider,

(2) The manager of Kinko's was born in the capital of Nebraska.

On the standard account of definite descriptions, (2) expresses a *general* proposition, a proposition that is not specifically about Jim and Lincoln, but about being the manager of Kinko's, and being the capital of Nebraska. This proposition is true in worlds in which someone – it doesn't have to be Jim – is the manager of Kinko's, and some city – it doesn't have to be Lincoln – is the capital of Nebraska, and the someone was born in the city. Consider the possible world in which Omaha is the capital of Nebraska, and Marlon Brando or Henry Fonda or Saul Kripke or some other native Omahan[5] manages the Kinko's in Lincoln. In these worlds (2) would be true, wherever my son might be born.

Let a *mode of presentation* be a condition that has uniqueness built into it, so that at most one thing can meet it, such as *x is the manager of Kinko's* or *x is the capital of Nebraska.* We can think of the proposition expressed by (2) as an ordered pair of a sequence of modes of presentation and a condition:

⟨⟨*x* is the manager of Kinko's, *y* is the capital of Nebraska⟩, *x* was born in *y*⟩

The distinction between singular and general propositions is helpful, but a bit too simple. Consider,

(3) Jim was born in the capital of Nebraska.

This would usually be called a singular proposition; being singular is sort of a dominant characteristic, so that if at least one argument role of a condition is filled by an object, the result is singular even if the other argument roles are filled by modes of presentation. I will speak this way, but we have to keep in mind that the basic concept is that of an argument role being filled either by an object or by a mode of presentation of an object.

Now consider,

(4) *x was born in Lincoln.*
(5) *x was born in the capital of Nebraska.*

Conditions (4) and (5) express conditions rather than propositions. But we need to draw a distinction between them: (4) is a singular condition, because it incorporates the city, Lincoln, as a constituent, while (5) is a general condition, with the mode of presentation *y is the capital of Nebraska* as a constituent.

For our final point, look closely at (2). It expresses a general proposition – both argument roles of the condition *x was born in y* are filled by modes of presentation. But these modes of presentation themselves are singular, involving Kinko's and Nebraska as constituents respectively. I'll say that a proposition or condition is *purely qualitative* if, as one goes down through the hierarchy of conditions involved in it, one never encounters an object, only more conditions. I'll call it *lumpy* if one encounters an object. The proposition expressed by (2), though general, is lumpy.

Now compare

(1) Jim was born in Lincoln.
(6) The manager of Kinko's was born in Lincoln.

I use "designate" as a general word for the relations between singular terms and the objects they stand for. Thus the subject terms of both (1) and (6) *designate* the same person, Jim Perry. Both (1) and (6) assert the same thing of the same person, and in that sense (1) and (6) have the same truth conditions.

In spite of this, (1) and (6) are quite different, because the singular terms in them work quite differently. I'll express this difference by saying "Jim", the name in (1), *names* and *refers to* Jim Perry, but neither *denotes* nor *describes* him. "The manager of Kinko's" *denotes* and *describes* him, but neither *names* him nor *refers to* him. Let me explain these terms.[6]

Denoting versus naming

Definite descriptions and names have quite different sorts of meaning. Language associates definite descriptions with modes of presentation. Definite descriptions are only indirectly associated with the objects they designate, as the objects that meet the mode of presentation associated by meaning. So, in virtue of its meaning, "The manager of Kinko's" is associated with a certain mode of presentation. It designates Jim Perry not simply in virtue of its meaning, but in virtue of its meaning and his job.

With names it is quite different. The convention I invoke when I use "Jim" to refer to my oldest son, is not a convention that associates the name with a condition which, as it happens, he fulfills. It's just a convention that says that "Jim" is his name – a convention established when he was born and that name was used on the birth certificate.[7]

There are then two quite different forms an answer to the question "Why does term *t* designate object *a*?" may take:

(i) The meaning of *t* associates it with a certain mode of presentation *C*, and
(ii) *a* is the object that satisfies *C*

or,

The meaning of *t* associates it directly with *a*

I use the terms *denoting* for the form of designation corresponding to the first, two-part, answer, and the term *naming* for the form of designation corresponding to the second, one-part, answer.

Describing versus referring

Our second distinction has to do with the contribution terms make to what I shall call "the official content" of a statement. The official content of a statement is what we would take the speaker as having asserted or said, or, as it is sometimes put, "what is said" by the statement.

On standard accounts, at least, the official contents of (1) and (6) are different. The proposition expressed by (1) is a singular proposition about Jim, while that expressed by (6) is a general proposition about being the manager of Kinko's. As we saw above, these are different propositions, true in different possible worlds.

I use "refers" and "describes" to mark this distinction. These terms pertain to the contribution a term makes to the official content of statements of which it is a part. Names *refer*; that is, they contribute to official content the individual they designate. Definite descriptions *describe*; that is, they contribute to official content the mode of presentation their meaning associates with them.[8]

If we ignore indexicals, confining our attention to names and definite descriptions, our two distinctions line up, and may seem to amount to the same thing.[9] Definite descriptions denote and describe, names name and refer. But in the case of indexicals the distinction is needed. For, as we shall see, indexicals are like definite descriptions in that they denote, but like names in that they refer.

3 The reflexive-referential theory

3.1 Burks's framework

In his pioneering work, Arthur Burks (1949) distinguishes the following aspects of an utterance containing indexicals:

- (i) The sign itself, which is a token that occurs at a spatio-temporal location and which belongs to a certain linguistic type.
- (ii) The existential relations of the token to other objects.
- (iii) The meaning associated with the type.
- (iv) The indexical meaning of the token, which, in the case of tokens involving indexicals, goes beyond the type meaning.[10]
- (v) The information conveyed by the sign.

Suppose, for example, Burks tells me, pointing to a house on Monroe Street in Ann Arbor: "I live in that house." (i) The sign itself is the token or burst of sound that

Burks utters; it is a token of an English sentence of a certain type, namely, "I live in that house", and it occurs at a certain spatio-temporal location. (ii) This token has "existential relations" to other objects. That is, *there is* a person who uttered it (Burks), *there is* a house at which that person was pointing at the time of utterance, and so forth. (iii) English associates a meaning with the type, the same for every token of it. Any token of "I live in that house" will be true if the speaker of that token lives in the house he or she points to at the time they produce the token. This is what all tokens of the type have in common. (iv) Each token also has an *indexical meaning*, which results from the combination of the type-meaning and the the particular token. Call the token Burks produced **t**. Imagine David Kaplan pointing to a house in Pacific Palasaides at some other time and producing a token **t′**. Tokens **t** and **t′** have the same type-meaning, but different indexical meanings. Token **t** will be true if the house Burks points to is the one he lives in, while **t′** will be true if the house Kaplan points at is the one he lives in.

Aspect (v) is the information conveyed by the sign. Let's add a third token to our example. Let **t″** be my token of "You live in that house", said to Burks, pointing to the house on Monroe Street. My token doesn't have the same symbolic meaning or the same indexical meaning as **t**, Burks's token of "I live in that house". But there is something important that my token and Burks's have in common. Each of them will be true if a certain person, Burks, lives in a certain house, the one on Monroe Street. Once we factor in the contextual or "existential" facts that are relevant to each token, they have the same truth-conditions. Their truth places the same conditions on the same objects. Burks calls this "conveying the same information".

The reflexive-referential theory that I advocate builds on Burks's basic framework. In sections 3.2–3.6 I go through the five aspects, usually starting with a discussion of Burks's basic idea. I discuss various issues, elaborating and qualifying the basic idea; the reflexive-referential theory is the account that emerges from this process. Here is an overview, highlighting the differences in terminology:

Aspect (i). Burks takes the sign itself to be the token. I think there is an ambiguity in "token"; it is sometimes used for the act, and sometimes for something produced by or at least used in the act. I'll use "utterance" for the first and reserve "token" for the second. In some kinds of discourse tokens are epistemically basic, but utterances are always semantically basic. (As I use the term "utterance" it does not have the implication of speech as opposed to writing.)

Aspect (ii). What Burks calls the "existential relations" is now usually referred to as the "context"; indexicals are expressions whose designation *shifts* from context to context. I will distinguish several different uses we make of context, and will distinguish various contextual factors that are relevant to different types of indexicals.

Aspect (iii). For Burks the "type meaning" is associated by language with expressions. I simply call this "meaning": I try to always use "meaning" for what the conventions of language associate with types. The key idea here in our account of the meaning of indexicals comes from Reichenbach, who emphasized the *reflexivity* of indexicals.

Aspects (iv) and (v). I take content to be a property of specific utterances. Burks recognizes two kinds of content, while I recognize (at least) three. What Burks calls "indexical meaning" I call "content given facts about meaning" or "content_M". What Burks calls "information conveyed" I call "content given facts about designation" or "content_D". I claim that neither of these is our official, intuitive notion of content; that is, neither corresponds to "what is said" by an utterance. That role is played by "content given facts about context," or "content_C". All three kinds of content, however, play important roles in the epistemology of language.

3.2 *Signs, tokens and utterances*

For Burks, the sign itself is simply the token. But the term "token" is used in two ways in the literature. Sometimes it is used for the *act* of speaking, writing, or otherwise using language. At other times, it is used for an object that is produced by, or at least used in, such an act. Reichenbach, for example, says that tokens are acts of speaking, but then talks about the position of a token on a page.

I use "utterance" for the first sense. Utterances are intentional acts. The term "utterance" often connotes spoken language, but as I use it an utterance may involve speech, writing, typing, gestures, or any other sort of linguistic activity.

I use "token" in the second sense, in the way Reichenbach used it when he said that a certain token was to be found on a certain page of a certain copy of a book. Tokens, in this sense, are traces left by utterances. They can be perceived when the utterances cannot, and can be used as evidence for them. Modern technology allows for their reproduction. The paradigm tokens are the ink marks produced in writing or typing. When we read, tokens are epistemically basic, and the utterances that produced them hardly thought of. But the utterances are semantically basic; it is from the intentional acts of speakers and writers that the content derives.

An utterance may involve a token, but not be the act of producing it. My wife Frenchie and I were once Resident Fellows in a dormitory at Stanford, eating with the students each evening in the cafeteria. If she went to dinner before I returned, she would write on a small blackboard on the counter, "I have gone to the cafeteria," and set it on the table near the front door of our apartment. I would put it back on the counter. There was no need for her to write out the message anew each time I was late; if the blackboard had not been used for something else in the interim, she could simply move it from the counter back to the table. Frenchie used the same token to say different things on different days. Each use of the token was a separate utterance.

One can imagine the same token being re-used as a token of a different type of sentence. Suppose there is a sign in a flying school, intended to warn would-be pilots: "Flying planes can be dangerous". The flying school goes bankrupt; the manager of a park near the airport buys the sign and puts it next to a sign that prohibits walking on high tightropes. In its new use the sign is a token of a type with a different syntax and a different meaning than in its original use. In principle, tokens could even be re-used for utterances in different languages; I leave finding such examples as an exercise for the reader.

In the case of spoken utterances in face-to-face communication, the utterance/token distinction becomes pretty subtle. One who hears the token will see the utterance which produces it. Writing brings with it the possibility of larger gaps between use and perception; letters are sent, books are put on shelves, to be read months or even years later, and so forth. The utterance/token distinction is most at home in the case of written text. It grows in importance as culture and technology develop. Modern technology allows for the storage and reproduction of both spoken and written tokens, and with such devices as email an utterance involves the production of numbers of tokens around the world.[11]

So, to review some distinctions and terminological decisions made thus far:

- *Tokens* are physical events or objects, bursts of sound or bits of written or electronic text, that are used by agents in their utterances.
- An *utterance* is an act that involves the use of a token and typically the production of a new token. Utterances can be spoken, written, typed, etc.
- A *statement* is an utterance of a declarative sentence.
- An *expression* is a type, either a word or a longer phrase such as a sentence.
- The utterances of expressions that are parts of utterances of larger expressions are *subutterances*; e.g. an utterance of "I was born in Lincoln" involves a subutterance of "I".

3.3 Context

What Burks calls the "existential relations" of a token or utterance is now usually referred to as its "context". The "context-dependence" of indexicals is often taken as their defining feature: what an indexical designates *shifts* from context to context. But there are many kinds of shiftiness, with corresponding conceptions of context. Until we clarify what we mean by "context", this defining feature remains unclear.

The key distinction is between pre-semantic and semantic uses of context. Sometimes we use context to figure out with which meaning a word is being used, or which of several words that look or sound alike is being used, or even which language is being spoken. These are *pre-semantic* uses of context. In the case of indexicals, however, context is used *semantically*. It remains relevant after the language, words, and meaning are all known; the meaning directs us to certain aspects of context.

Consider these utterances:

(7) Ich! (said by several teenagers at camp in response to the question, "Who would like some sauerkraut?").
(8) I forgot how good beer tastes.
(9) I saw her duck under the table.[12]

With (7), knowing that the utterance occurred in Frankfurt rather than San Francisco might help us determine that it was German teenagers expressing enthusiasm and not American teenagers expressing disgust.

With (8), knowing whether our speaker has just arrived from Germany or just arrived from Saudi Arabia might help us to decide what the syntactic structure of the sentence is, and whether "good" was being used as an adjective or an adverb.

With (9), knowing a little about the situation that this utterance is describing will help us to decide whether the person in question had lost her pet or was seeking security in an earthquake, and whether "duck" is a noun or a verb.

In each of these cases, the context, the environment of the utterance, the larger situation in which it occurs, helps us to determine what is said. But these cases differ from indexicals. In these cases it is a sort of accident, external to the utterance, that context is needed. We need the context to identify which name, syntactic structure, or meaning is used because the very same shapes and sounds happen to be shared by other words, structures, or meanings. In the case of indexicals we still need context *after* we determine which words, syntactic structures, and meanings are being used. The meanings *exploit* the context to perform their function. The meaning of the indexical "directs us" to certain features of the context, in order to fix the designation.

It seems, then, that a defining feature of indexicals is that the meanings of these words fix the designation of specific utterances of them in terms of facts about those specific utterances. The facts that the meaning of a particular indexical deems relevant are the contextual facts for particular uses of it. However, indexicality is not the only phenomenon in which context plays a semantic role. *Anaphora* provides another case.

In anaphora, what one word designates depends on what another word in the same bit of discourse, to which the word in question is anaphorically related, designates. Compare

(10) (Indicating a certain woman) She advocated subjective semantics in her UCLA dissertation.

(11) That woman wrote a very interesting dissertation at UCLA. She advocated subjective semantics.

The designation of "she" in (10) simply depends on a contextual fact, whom the speaker was indicating. But in (11) the designation of "she" depends on which previous word in the discourse is taken as its antecedent. In both anaphora and indexicality we have semantic use of context; the difference is in the sorts of contextual facts that are relevant.

What is the relation between the "she" used in (10) and the "she" used in (11)? No-one supposes they are mere homonyms. Many philosophers are at least tempted to suppose they are occurrences of a single ambiguous word, which sometimes functions as a variable and sometimes as an indexical (Kaplan, 1989a). Many linguists find this implausible, and would prefer an account that gives a uniform treatment of pronouns, bringing the relativity to linguistic and other contextual

Table 1: Types of indexicals

	Narrow	*Wide*
Automatic	I now*, here*	tomorrow, yea
Intentional	now, here	that, this man, there

factors into a single framework for a subject-matter called "deixis" (Partee, 1989). I have some sympathy with this point of view, but for the purposes of this essay I will set the issue of the precise connection of anaphoric and demonstrative uses of pronouns to one side.

3.3.1 Types of indexical contexts

With respect to contexts for indexicals I need to emphasize two distinctions, which together create the four categories exhibited in Table 1:

- Does designation depend on narrow or wide context?
- Is designation "automatic" given meaning and public contextual facts, or does it depend in part on the intentions of the speaker?

I'll show which expressions fit into these categories, and then explain them.

3.3.2 Narrow and wide context

The narrow context consists of the constitutive facts about the utterance, which I will take to be the agent, time, and position. These roles are filled with every utterance. The clearest case of an indexical that relies only on the narrow context is "I", whose designation depends on the agent and nothing else.

The wider context consists of those facts, plus anything else that might be relevant, according to the workings of a particular indexical.

The sorts of factors on which an indexical can be made to depend seem, in principle, limitless. For example,

> It is yea big.

means that it is as big as the space between the outstretched hands of the speaker, so this space is a contextual factor in the required sense for the indexical "yea".

3.3.3 Automatic versus intentional indexicals

When Rip Van Winkle says, "I fell asleep yesterday," he intended to designate (let us suppose) July 3, 1766. He in fact designated July 2, 1786, for he awoke 20 years to the day after he fell asleep. An utterance of "yesterday" designates the day before the utterance occurs, no matter what the speaker intends. Given the meaning and context, the designation is automatic. No further intention than that of using the words with their ordinary meaning is relevant.

The designation of an utterance of "that man", however, is not automatic. The speaker's intention is relevant. There may be several men standing across the street when I say, "That man stole my wallet." Which of them I refer to depends on my intention.

However, we need to be careful here. Suppose there are two men across the street, Harold, dressed in brown, and Fred, in blue. I think that Harold stole my wallet and I also think wrongly that the man dressed in blue is Harold. I intend to designate Harold *by* designating the man in blue. So I point towards the man in blue as I say "that man". In this case I designate the man in blue – even if my pointing is a bit off-target. My intention to point to the man in blue is relevant to the issue of whom I designate and what I say, but my intention to refer to Harold is not. In this case, I say something I don't intend to say: that Fred, the man in blue, stole my wallet; and fail to say what I intended to, that Harold did. So it is not just any referential intention that is relevant to demonstratives, but only the more basic ones, which I will call *directing intentions,* following Kaplan (1989b).

In a case like this I will typically perceive the man I refer to, and may often point to or otherwise demonstrate that person. But neither perceiving nor pointing seems necessary to referring with a demonstrative.

The indexicals "I", "now", and "here" are often given an honored place as "pure" or "essential" indexicals. Some writers emphasize the possibility of translating away other indexicals in favor of them: see Castañeda (1967) and Corazza (1995). In Table 1, this honored place is represented by the cell labelled "narrow" and "automatic". However, it is not clear that "now" and "here" deserve this status; hence the asterisks. With "here" there is the question of how large an area is to count, and with "now" the question of how large a stretch of time. If I say, "I left my pen here," I would be taken to designate a relatively small area, say the office in which I was looking. If I say, "The evenings are cooler than you expect here," I might mean to include the whole San Francisco Bay area. In "Now that we walk upright, we have lots of back problems," "now" would seem to designate a large, if, indefinite, period of time that includes the very instant of utterance, while in, "Why did you wait until now to tell me?" it seems to designate a considerably smaller stretch. It seems, then, that these indexicals really have an intentional element.

"Here" also has a demonstrative use. One can point to a place on a map and refer to it as "here" (Kaplan, 1989a). "Now" and the present tense can be used to draw attention to and confer immediacy on the time of a past or future event, as when a history teacher says, "Now Napoleon had a dilemma . . ." (Smith, 1989).

3.4 *Meaning*

To repeat: as I use the terms, *meaning* is what the rules of language associate with simple and complex expressions; *content* is an attribute of individual utterances. The simple theory into which I am trying to incorporate indexicals focuses on the contents of utterances of four kinds. The content of a statement is a proposition, incorporating the conditions of truth of the statement. The content of an utterance of a predicate (for our purposes, a declarative sentence with some of its terms replaced by variables) is a condition on objects. The content of an utterance of a definite description will be a mode of presentation. The content of the utterance of a name will be an individual. The contents of utterances of terms combine with the contents of utterances of predicates to yield propositions.

The contents of utterances derive from the meaning which language associates with expressions. The simplest way for this to happen is equisignificance: the meaning of an expression assigns the same content to each and every utterance of the expression.

But, as I explained in section 3.3, indexicals don't work this way. The meaning directs us to certain aspects of the context of the utterance, which are needed to determine the content. The object designated by an indexical will be the object that bears some more or less complicated relation to the utterance. Instead of the usual twofold distinction – *Sinn* and *Bedeutung*, meaning and denotation, intension and extension – we have a threefold one:

> The meaning provides us with a binary condition on objects and utterances, the condition of designation.
>
> The utterance itself fills the utterance parameter of this condition, yielding a unary condition on objects, or a mode of presentation.
>
> The object that meets this condition is the object designated by the indexical, or the *designatum*.

The *reflexivity* apparent in the second level has long been one of the major themes in the study of indexicals. Reichenbach put forward a *token-reflexive* theory in his *Introduction to Symbolic Logic* (1947).

Reichenbach claimed that token-reflexive words could be defined in terms of the token-reflexive phrase "this token", and in particular, as he put it, 'The word "I" . . . means the same as "the person who utters this token"' (p. 284).

If we take Reichenbach's claim as a literal claim of synonymy between "I" and "the person who utters this token", it is wrong. The two terms may be assigned the same condition, but "I" refers, whereas "the person who utters this token" describes. But Reichenbach was clearly on to something. There is an intimate connection between the meanings of "I" and "the person who utters this token", even if it falls short of synonymy. The second phrase does not *have* the meaning of "I", but it *gives* part of the meaning of "I". It supplies the condition of designation that English associates with "I". We can put this in a rule that brings out the reflexivity:

> If *u* is an utterance of "I", the condition of designation for *u* is *being the speaker of u*.

Here we see that the condition of designation assigned to an utterance *u* has that very utterance as a constituent, hence it is reflexive. (I discussed the reasons for using "utterance" rather than "token" above, in section 3.2.)

This rule does two things. First, it assigns a binary condition to the type, "I". The condition is that *x is the speaker of u*. This condition has a parameter for the object designated and one for utterances. Second, the rule assigns a unary condition, on objects, to each utterance of "I", by specifying that the utterance parameter is to be filled with that very utterance. To state this sort of rule in English, we would naturally make use of a reflexive pronoun:

> The designation of every utterance of "I" is the speaker of the utterance *itself.*

Here are the conditions of designation for some familiar indexicals, in line with the discussion in section 3.3.

I:	u designates x iff x is the speaker of u
you:	u designates y iff $\exists x$(x is the speaker of u & x addresses y with u)
now:	u designates t iff $\exists x$(x is the speaker of u & x directs u at t during part of t)
that:	u designates y iff $\exists$x(x is the speaker of u & x directs u towards y)

In considering the meanings of sentences, it is helpful to think of propositions as 0-ary conditions. English assigns 0-ary conditions, propositions, to indexical-free sentences, but assigns unary conditions on utterances to sentences with indexicals in them.

So our conditions of designation give rise to *conditions of truth* that are also reflexive. Meaning does not associate a proposition or 0-ary condition with a sentence containing an indexical, but a unary condition on utterances:

> An utterance u of the form $\phi(\alpha)$, where u' is the subutterance of an indexical α, is true iff $\exists y(u'$ designates y & $\phi(y))$.

So, for example,

> An utterance u of "You were born in Los Angeles", where u' is the subutterance of "you", is true iff $\exists y(u'$ designates y & y was born in Los Angeles);

that is, iff

> $\exists y\, \exists x$(x is the speaker of u' & x addresses y with u & y was born in Los Angeles).

On David Kaplan's approach, the meanings of expressions in languages with indexicals are regarded as characters. Characters are functions from contexts to contents. So the meaning of "I" is a function, whose value is a for contexts in which a is the speaker and the meaning of "I am sitting" is a function whose value is the singular proposition that a is sitting for such contexts. This theory neatly captures what is special about *context* in the case of indexicality; that it plays a semantic role, rather than merely a pre-semantic one. I don't think Kaplan's view does as well with what is special about *content* in the case of indexicals, however. Kaplan provides only one level of content – official content – where I agree with Burks that more than one level of content is needed in the case of indexical utterances. In the next two sections I will defend Burks's perspective.

3.5 *Content$_M$*

Reichenbach analyzed Luther's utterance, "Here I stand," in terms of the relation

speaks(x, θ, z)

where x is a person, θ is a token and z is a place. In

stands[(the x)(∃z(speaks(x, θ, z), (the z)∃x(speaks(x, θ, z)]

θ is Reichenbach's term for Luther's utterance; his analysis amounts to:

(12) The speaker of θ stands in the place where θ is made[13]

In our scheme, we have here a general proposition about two modes of presentation, *being the speaker of* θ and *being the place of* θ. Each of these modes is a singular condition, with θ as a constituent.

This proposition fits pretty well Burks's description of his fourth aspect, as what results from combining the meaning with the token or utterance. On the reflexive-referential account, the meaning of a sentence like Luther's is a condition on utterances, and Reichenbach's analysis fills the parameter of that condition with the utterance itself. It seems that Reichenbach's proposition, or something like it, deserves a central place in our account.

However, (12) is clearly not what Luther said. He didn't say anything about his own utterance, and he referred to himself with "I", rather than describing himself. (12) is not a good candidate for the official content of Luther's remark. Where, then, does it fit in?

On Kaplan's approach, the level of analysis represented by (12) and by Burks's fourth aspect is bypassed (1989a, 1989b). The meaning, or *character*, of an indexical is, on Kaplan's theory, a function from context to official content, to what is said. The approach Barwise and I took in *Situations and Attitudes* (1983) was similar, although we did compensate somewhat with what we called "inverse interpretation". Stalnaker complained that something was missing from such approaches (1981), and I have come to think that he and Burks were correct.[14] In fact, we need a variety of contents.

3.5.1 Varieties of truth-conditions

A problem that underlies the simple picture of meaning and content is now going to come to the surface. The problem is that the concept of "truth-conditions of an utterance" is a *relative concept*, although it is often treated as if it were absolute. Instead of thinking in terms of *the* truth-conditions of an utterance, we should think of the truth conditions of an utterance *given* various facts about it. And when we do this we are led to see that talking about *the* content of an utterance is an over-simplification.

Suppose that you are at an international philosophy meeting. During what seems a stupid lecture, the person next to you writes a note which he passes to you. It says, "Cet homme est brillant". He then whispers, in English, "Don't you agree?" You are a confirmed monolingual, and don't even recognize in which language the message is written. To avoid compounding ignorance with impertinence, you nod. All you can infer about the message is that it is a statement, with which one could agree or disagree. Do you know the truth-conditions of his message?

Given the ordinary philosophical concept of the truth-conditions of an utterance, you certainly do not. You have no idea what proposition is expressed. If you did, you wouldn't have nodded as if you agreed.

But you could list some conditions, such that, were they met, the message would be true. Call the message **m**. It is true if there is a proposition *P*, such that in the language in which **m** is written, its words have a certain meaning, and in the context in which **m** was written, words with that meaning express *P* and *P* is true.

It is fair to call these truth-conditions of **m**, because they are conditions such that, were they satisfied, **m** would be true. But they are not what philosophers usually have in mind when they talk about the truth-conditions or content of the message. They would have in mind the proposition that a certain person, the lecturer, was brilliant.

But this philosophical concept of truth-conditions is a special case of a more general one: the truth-conditions of an utterance *given* certain facts about it. What you know about **m** is its truth-conditions given only the barest facts about it, that it is a statement. You can specify conditions under which **m** would be true, but because you know so little about **m** itself, those conditions have a lot to do with **m**'s relation to the rest of the world, and say little about the world independently of **m**. The philosophical concept of truth-conditions corresponds to the case in which one knows a lot about **m**; in this case the conditions will pertain to the world outside **m**, not **m** itself.

If your high-school French started to return to you, you might reason as follows: '*Given* that the language of **m** is French, and *given* the meaning of "Cet homme est brillant" in French, and *given* the fact that the author of **m** intended to use the words "Cet homme" to refer to that person (looking at the lecturer), **m** is true iff *that person is brilliant*.' As you figure out more about **m**, fixing more of its linguistic properties, the conditions that had to be fulfilled for its truth become more focused on the world. The *additional* or *incremental* conditions required for the truth of **m**, given all that you knew about **m**, were conditions on a certain person, that he be brilliant. Our philosophical concept of truth-conditions of an utterance is that of the *incremental* conditions required for truth, given that all of these linguistic factors are fixed.

This picture of truth-conditions as relative is just a matter of treating them like other conditions we ask about. Whenever we ask about the conditions under which something has a certain property, we take certain facts as given. What we want to know is *what else*, what additional facts, have to obtain, for the thing to have that property, *given* the facts we assume. I ask you "Under what conditions will Clinton get re-elected?" and you say, "He has to carry California." You are taking for granted a number of things – that he will lose the South, do well in the Northeast, get at least two midwestern states. *Given all of this*, what *else* does he need to get re-elected?

It's the same with truth-conditions. What does the world have to be like for **m** to be true? That guy must be a brilliant lecturer. Right – *given* the facts about the language, the words, the meaning, and the context of **m**, that's what *else* is needed.

As I mentioned above, I use three different kinds of content in the account of indexicals. These correspond to three kinds of facts one might take as fixed in assessing truth-conditions:

> The content_M of an utterance corresponds to the truth-conditions of the utterance given the facts that fix the language of the utterance, the words involved, their syntax and their *meaning*.[15]
>
> The content_C of an utterance corresponds to the truth-conditions given all of these factors, plus the facts about the *context* of the utterance that are needed to fix the designation of indexicals.
>
> The content_D of an utterance corresponds to the truth-conditions given all of these factors, plus the additional facts that are needed to fix the *designation* of the terms that remain (definite descriptions in particular, but also possessives, etc.).

We shall see below that we need all three kinds of content to adequately describe the epistemology of indexicals and other terms.

3.5.2 Content_M as cognitively relevant content

As we saw in section 3.4, the meaning of an indexical or sentence containing indexicals provides a condition on utterances. We move from this condition to the content_M of an utterance of that type by filling the parameter of that condition with the utterance itself. In the case of indexical terms, we go from binary conditions on objects and utterances to 1-ary conditions on objects. In the case of sentences containing indexicals, we go from 1-ary conditions on utterances to 0-ary conditions, propositions. These are propositions *about* utterances.

Consider,

(13) You were born in the capital of Nebraska.

The content_M of (13) is a proposition about (13) itself:

$$\exists x\, \exists y(x \text{ is the addressee of (13) \& } y \text{ is the capital of Nebraska \& } x \text{ was born in } y)$$

As we noted, this proposition certainly does not seem to be the official content of (13), what the speaker said when he uttered (13) – a point I will emphasize in the next section.

Nevertheless, $content_M$ is very important in understanding the connection between meaning and cognition, how we use language to express our beliefs, and influence the beliefs of others. It is *cognitively relevant* content.

Imagine that I am standing next to W. V. O. Quine at a party. Consider the difference between my saying "I would like to shake your hand" and "John Perry would like to shake your hand." In response to the first, we would expect Quine to extend his hand; in response to the second, he might well ask, "Well, where is he?" (See Castañeda (1966), Perry (1979), Stalnaker (1981), and Perry (1993).)

If we ask what I hoped to accomplish by saying, "I'd like to shake your hand," we might just say that I wanted to make him aware that I wanted to shake his hand, so I said that I wanted to. This would be accurate, but incomplete. It leaves out many of my subgoals and my plans for achieving them. I spoke the sentence, rather than including it in a letter or email, because I realized that he was standing where he could hear me. I said it in English because I thought that he understood English. I wanted him to be aware of that, in order to get him to turn and offer his hand for me to shake. In order to get that effect, I wanted to produce a certain kind of thought in him. I wanted him to think that the person in front of him wanted to shake his hand. My plan might be summarized as follows:

Goal: To get Quine to turn towards me and offer his hand for me to shake.

Given: Quine knows English; he can hear me if I speak; he can see me and will recognize that the person he sees is the speaker of the utterance he hears; he knows how to shake hands with a person in front of him; he is good-natured and will try to shake the hand of someone next to him if he knows that this person would like him to.

Plan:

(i) Direct an utterance **u** of "I'd like to shake your hand" at Quine.

(ii) Quine will hear **u** and grasp its $content_M$, thinking, "That utterance is spoken by someone who wants to shake the hand of the person he or she is addressing."

(iii) Quine will think, "That person I see in front of me is the speaker of that utterance."

(iv) Quine will think, "I am the person the person I see in front of me is addressing."

(v) Quine will think, "That person I see in front of me wants to shake my hand."

(vi) Quine will extend his hand.

Now the $content_M$ of my utterance is the key to this plan. The $content_C$ of my utterance is simply the singular proposition that John Perry wants to shake W. V. O. Quine's hand. This is the same as the $content_C$ of "John Perry wants to shake your hand".[16] But there would be no reason to expect this utterance to have the desired effect, given my assumptions. The difference between them comes out at the level of $content_M$.

3.6 *Official content*

3.6.1 Content$_C$ as official content

Content$_M$ is a useful tool for understanding the motivation and impact of utterances. But it is not our ordinary concept of content. It is not what I have called official content, the content that corresponds to what the speaker says. There are two main arguments for this; the reader may be convinced by and familiar with the arguments, but I want to highlight them to help us reflect on just what they show.

The first and simplest I'll call the "samesaying argument". Consider my utterance, directed at my son Jim:

(14) You were born in Lincoln.

The content$_M$ of (14) is a proposition about (14). But we would ordinarily count me as having said the same thing to him as he said to me with his utterance:

(15) I was born in Lincoln.

And the same thing I say to a third party with my utterance

(1) Jim was born in Lincoln.

But these two utterances have quite different contents$_M$ than (14). The content$_M$ of (15) is a proposition about (15) itself, and the content$_M$ of (1) is just a singular proposition about Jim (since names name, their designation is fixed by their meaning). It seems, then, that it is the individual designated by the subutterance of "you", and not the condition of being the addressee of that subutterance, that makes it into the official content of (14).

The second argument I call the "counterfactual circumstances argument". To understand it, one needs to keep clearly in mind the difference between the conditions under which an utterance is true, and conditions under which *what is said by the utterance* (or perhaps better, *what the speaker says*, in virtue of making the utterance) is true. We can separate these, by considering counterfactual circumstances in which the utterance is false, but what is said by the utterance is true (Kaplan, 1989a).

Now suppose, contrary to fact, that when I uttered (14) I was mistaken, and was talking to my son Joe rather than Jim. In those circumstances, my utterance would have been false, since Joe was born in California. And what I would have said in those circumstances, that Joe was born in Lincoln, is false. But what I *actually* said, since I actually was talking to Jim, was that he was born in Lincoln. And that proposition, that Jim was born in Lincoln, would have been true, even if, when I uttered (14), I was talking to Joe.

The upshot of these arguments is that the official content of (14) is a singular proposition about Jim. This is the same proposition that Jim expressed with (15), and that I expressed with (1). And it is a proposition that would still be true even if I were talking to Joe rather than Jim, although of course then I would not have expressed this proposition, but a quite different and false one about Joe.

Our other two kinds of content, content_C and content_D, both assign this proposition to (14), (15), and (1). But these differ with respect to

(6) The manager of Kinko's was born in Lincoln.

Content_C, recall, corresponds to truth-conditions with the contextual facts fixed. The content_C of (6) is not a singular proposition about Jim. The first argument-role of *x was born in y* gets filled with a mode of presentation of Jim, not Jim himself.

Content_D corresponds to truth-conditions with *all* the facts that determine designation of terms fixed, including, in this case, the fact that Jim is the manager of Kinko's. So the content_D of (6) is our singular proposition about Jim.

Content_D corresponds to Burks's concept of "information conveyed". On this concept (14), (1), and (6) all convey the same information, "for they both refer to the same object and predicate the same property of it".

Which corresponds to official content, content_C or content_D? It depends on whether we think of definite descriptions as referring or describing. If they refer, then they contribute the objects they designate to official content, and the right answer is that content_D is official content. If they describe, then content_C is the right answer. For the purposes of this chapter, I have accepted the traditional account of definite descriptions as describing.[17]

With this understanding of definite descriptions, it seems that content_C corresponds to official content. When we compare what people say, and consider the counterfactual circumstances in which what they say is true, we fix the meaning and context, but let other facts vary, even the ones that fix the designation of definite descriptions. Consider,

(16) You were born in the capital of Nebraska

said to Jim. When we think of the possible worlds in which this is true, what do we require of them? Worlds in which Jim was born in Iowa, but "You were born in the capital of Nebraska" means that $2 + 2 = 4$ don't get in. We fix the meaning, before we consider the world. Worlds in which Jim was born in Iowa, but I am talking to Sue, who was born in the capital of Nebraska, don't get in. We fix the contextual facts, and so the designation of indexicals, before we consider the worlds. But worlds in which Jim was born in Omaha, and Omaha is the capital of Nebraska, do get in. We consider the worlds, before we fix the facts that determine the designation of definite descriptions.

3.6.2 Referentialism

In maintaining that content_C is official content, I agree with a movement in the philosophy of language I call "referentialism". The referentialist thinks that names and indexicals refer, and statements containing them express singular propositions. This set of views constitutes a movement because it had to overthrow an opposing orthodoxy, which dated back to Frege and Russell.

Frege was troubled by singular propositions.[18] How can a proposition have an object in it? Won't there always be different ways of thinking about the object? So won't a belief or desire or hope about an object always involve some specific way of thinking about it? Shouldn't the propositions we are worried about be ones that incorporate those ways of thinking – shouldn't propositions always have modes of presentation, not objects, as constituents?

This line of thinking led Frege and Russell away from singular propositions; Frege didn't have them at all, and Russell made less and less use of them as time went on. Both concluded that names were something like hidden definite descriptions; in our terminology, ordinary names denote and describe rather than name and refer.[19] And this became the standard view for the first two-thirds of the century, with some dissenters, like Burks and Ruth Marcus (Marcus, 1961, pp. 309–10). When Donnellan and Kripke attacked description-theories of names and argued that names referred and statements containing them expressed singular propositions, the feeling was that something like a conceptual revolution was occurring. And Kaplan's "direct reference" theory of indexicals seemed to turn the revolutionary doctrine into unassailable common sense (see Chapter 21, REFERENCE AND NECESSITY, and Chapter 22, RIGID DESIGNATION).

It seems to me that the referentialist movement was basically correct. Names and indexicals refer; they do not describe. Singular propositions may be sort of fishy, but they play a central role in the way that we classify content for the purpose of describing minds and utterances. Our concept of what is said is, as such things go, fairly robust.

Still, it is not entirely clear how far-reaching the philosophical consequences of this revolution are. There are three attitudes towards the referentialist treatment of "what is said" or official content:

The skeptic. Something is wrong with official content, for the reasons sketched above. The whole idea was really refuted by Frege, with his puzzles about identity. Consider the two cases we looked at in section 3.5. One can simply not give a coherent account of these cases, if one sticks to content_C or content_D. So the true contents must be something else.

The true believer. Referentialist arguments show what the true content of a statement is. We just have to live with any epistemological difficulties it raises. The proposition expressed by an utterance is its "semantic value", that which a competent speaker and hearer must grasp, and all the information that is semantically conveyed by the utterance is to be found in, or implied or implicated by, this proposition.

The moderate. Official content gets at an aspect of statements that is important for describing utterances, one that has shaped the concepts of "folk psychology" – but no more than that. There is no reason to postulate that an utterance has a unique "semantic content" that encapsulates all of the information it semantically conveys.

The third, reasonable-sounding view is, of course, my own. I call it "critical referentialism" – a term so ugly only moderates could like it. The critical referentialist believes that one commits "the fallacy of misplaced information" (Barwise and Perry, 1983) when one expects that all of the content a meaningful utterance carries can be found at the level of official content. Critical referentialism is simply referentialism without the fallacy. Free of the fallacy, the referentialist can employ other aspects of content, such as $content_M$, to explain the motivations and impact of language on semantically competent speakers and listeners, without having to elevate it to official content.

According to critical referentialism, the counterfactual test and samesaying tests identify the proposition that best fits our intuitive conception of *what is said* by an utterance or *what the speaker says* in making an utterance. There are many other propositions systematically associated with an utterance in virtue of the meaning of the words used in it, which can and must enter into the explanation of the significance the utterance has for competent speakers and listeners.

The "reflexive-referential" account of indexicals developed in this essay is an example of critical referentialism. We need to consider the $content_M$ of statements containing indexicals to deal with the sorts of cases that bothered Frege, such as our example of meeting Quine. But for other purposes, including those enshrined in our everyday concepts for describing utterances, the referentialist concept of what is said is useful and legitimate. Burks's original account was also critically referentialist; he recognized the importance of $content_D$ for certain purposes, and of $content_M$ for others.

The importance of the contextual or official level of content stems from the basic facts of communication and the purposes for which our ordinary tools for classifying and reporting content are adapted.

In the paradigm communicative situation, the speaker suits the message to the listener's knowledge of the context of utterance and the impact on belief he hopes to achieve. That is, he assumes the listener to know the relevant contextual facts, and tries to convey the incremental content. I assume that Quine will recognize the speaker of "I'd like to shake your hand," ("that person in front of me") and the addressee ("me"). Given this knowledge, the additional information he receives is: *that person* would like to shake *my* hand. The incremental content of my utterance, given the facts about context – the singular proposition that John Perry would like to shake Quine's hand – does a good job of characterizing what *additional* fact I am trying to convey to Quine, given what he knows and what will be obvious to him.

In a non-philosophical moment someone might explain Quine's action, of turning and extending his hand to me, by simply saying:

(17) Perry told Quine that he wanted to shake his hand.

The embedded sentence here, "he wanted to shake his hand", does not seem to identify any of the modes of presentation that were crucial to my plan and Quine's understanding, as explored in section 3.5. And yet (17) is a perfectly adequate explanation.

We have to see this as a *situated* explanation. In the background is the assumption that Quine and I were engaged in a normal case of face-to-face communication. The explainer tells what I was trying to *add to* what Quine knew and could easily perceive, and to do this it suffices to identify the singular proposition that is the content$_C$ of my utterance. This is what the ordinary report does.

Frege's insight was that there are multiple ways to cognize any object. Any utterance that adds to a listener's knowledge in a significant way will connect to the modes of presentation by which the listener already cognizes the object, or can easily do so, and the modes of presentation that connect with the ways the listener has for acting on the object or dealing with information about the object. To trace these interactions in a completely unsituated way, making no assumptions, dealing with the listener's thought-processes in a way that doesn't rely on the external world to suggest internal connections, would require what we might call completely "Fregean" content, totally without lumps. For practical purposes, what we need is "Fregean-enough" content. That is, we must specify the modes of presentation that are actually involved in cognition and the ways they are linked in the mind in so far as there is something in the context of explanation that suggests that the ordinary links might be broken.[20]

Thus when I raised, in section 3.5, the question of the difference between "I'd like to shake your hand" and "John Perry would like to shake your hand", I undermined the assumptions that make (17) an adequate explanation of Quine's action. I asked for an account of exactly what is taken for granted by (17), the planned connections between the modes of presentation involved in the utterance (being the speaker of it, being the addressee), and those involved in the cognitions the led to Quine's action (being the man he sees, being himself).[21]

When we retreat from the content$_C$ of my utterance to its content$_M$, to provide an explanation for the links now brought into question, we retreat to more Fregean, less lumpy content, in the sense that I and Quine are replaced by modes of presentation. But note that the content is not without lumps. For the content$_M$ of an utterance is also a singular proposition, about the utterance itself. The explanation I gave in section 3.5 is also situated; the assumption is that Quine hears my utterance in the usual way, as it comes out of my mouth. If we asked why I could get him to shake my hand by talking *to* him, but not by saying the same thing in such a manner that his first perception of my utterance was of an echo from a far room (details left to reader), we would have to revert to even more Fregean content, with modes of presentations of the utterance, rather than the utterance itself, appearing in the contents.

4 Conclusion

We can now contrast indexicals with other expressions. Indexicals differ from other shifters in the role that context plays. In the case of indexicality, context does not affect designation by providing evidence for what word is being used, with what meaning. Context plays its role after the words, syntax, and meanings are all fixed, for in the case of indexicals meaning determines content relative to contextual factors. Anaphors also use context semantically, but the relevant facts are relations between utterances, while with indexicals the relevant facts relate the utterance to non-linguistic items. Indexical pronouns are like definite descriptions in that they denote; they are like names in that they refer.

Our examination of the reflexive theory of indexicals leads to an important distinction, that between reflexivity and indexicality. Return for a moment to our example of the note saying "Cet homme est brillant", with which I introduced the concept of relative truth-conditions. I'll alter the note slightly, to get in a definite description: "Cet homme est l'homme le plus brillant dans cette salle". We could construct a whole hierarchy of relative truth-conditions for such a message, of the form, given that *such-and-such*, , **m** is true iff *so-and-so:*

1 Given that **m** is in French, **m** *is true iff* the meaning in French of the words on **m** is such that in the context of **m** they express a true proposition.

2 Given that **m** is in French, and the words are "Cet homme est l'homme le plus brillant dans cette salle," **m** *is true iff* these words have a meaning in French such that in the context of **m** they express a true proposition.

...

m (Content$_M$) Given that **m** is in French, the words are "Cet homme est l'homme le plus brillant dans cette salle," that in French these words mean that the man the speaker directly intends to refer to is the most brilliant man in the room, ***m*** *is true iff* there is a man the speaker of **m** directly intends to refer to and that man is the most brilliant man in the room.

m + 1 (Content$_C$) Given that **m** is in French, the words are "Cet homme est l'homme le plus brillant dans cette salle," that in French these words mean that the man the speaker directly intends to refer to is the most brilliant man in the room, and that the speaker of **m** directly intends to refer to Henri, **m** *is true iff* Henri is the most brilliant man in the room.

m + 2 (Content$_D$) Given that **m** is in French, the words are "Cet homme est l'homme le plus brillant dans cette salle," that in French these words mean that the man the speaker directly intends to refer to is the most brilliant man in the room, and that the speaker of **m** directly intends to refer to Henri, and given that the most brilliant man in the room is Jacques, **m** *is true iff* Henri is Jacques.

Perhaps, in line with our Fregean inclinations, even ending with something like:

m + ? Given that **m** is in French, the words are "Cet homme est l'homme le plus brillant dans cette salle," that in French these words mean that the man the speaker directly intends to refer to is the most brilliant man in the room, and that the speaker of **m** directly intends to refer to Henri, and given that the most brilliant man in the room is Jacques, and given that Henry is not Jacques, **m** *is true iff* The False.

We have reflexivity at point *m*. At *m* we get content_M; the meaning is fixed, but not the context and other facts relevant to designation and truth. That is, even given the meaning, we need context to get official content. That is indexicality.

But we have reflexivity at every stage up to and including *m*. That is, the truth-conditions, given what has been fixed, are still conditions on the utterance itself. That is reflexivity. Indexicality is, one might say, simply the highest form of reflexivity, reflexivity exploited by meaning.

Now the relative concepts of truth-conditions at each of the stages lower than *m* – the reflexive but pre-indexical stages – can give rise to a species of content, and all of these kinds of content can be put to good use in the epistemology of language. The epistemology of language is not just a matter of understanding how people who know all there is to know about the language in which a given utterance is couched go on from that point. It needs also to deal with how languages are recognized and learned, how new words are learned, how poorly pronounced or indistinctly heard words are recognized, how ambiguities are resolved and the like. In all of these inquiries, the proper kinds of content to represent the knowledge of the agent are reflexive.

One often hears that indexicality is pervasive, that practically every bit of language has a hidden indexicality. This is not quite right. Indexicality is widespread, but much of what passes for discoveries of new instances of indexicality are actually discoveries about the utility of reflexive content at a pre-indexical level in understanding how we understand language. The importance of indexicality is really that, as the highest form of reflexivity, it is the gateway to the riches of reflexivity.

Notes

1 See Nunberg (1992, 1993), Vallee (forthcoming).
2 See Partee (1989), Condoravdi and Gawron (1996).
3 See Castañeda (1967), Corazza (1995).
4 I use 'Kinko's' as a name for the Kinko's store on P street in Lincoln.
5 Actually, I'm not sure these famous people who grew up in Omaha were all born there.
6 The following distinctions, although not the terminology, I owe to Genoveva Marti, who presents them forcefully in Marti (1996). On this topic and elsewhere I also owe a great debt to Recanati's *Direct Reference* (1993), a work that can be profitably consulted on virtually any topic connected with indexicality and reference.
7 It is easy to be led astray here. Suppose you see Jim at a party, and ask him what his

name is. I tell you, and thus disclose to you a certain naming convention. Now you will be thinking of Jim Perry in a certain way at that point, perhaps as 'the man I am looking at and just asked the name of and heard saying something interesting about computers a minute ago'. So, when I tell you that man's name is 'Jim', the association in your mind may be between the name and a certain mode of presentation of him. This does not mean that the *convention* I have disclosed to you is one linking the name with the mode of presentation. The convention links the name with Jim; it has been around since he was born, and so long before he had anything interesting to say about computers; the mode of presentation comes in only because that is how you happen to be thinking of him; the mode of presentation is involved in your way of thinking of the convention, but not the convention itself.

8 More accurately, in terms introduced below, definite descriptions contribute the condition associated with them by meaning and context, their content_C.

9 Keith Donnellan's famous distinction between referential and attributive uses of definite descriptions could be interpreted as the claim that definite descriptions do sometimes refer. I'll basically ignore this idea in this chapter, simply to keep the focus on indexicals, but see also footnote 17.

10 Burks also uses the term 'symbolic meaning' for a property of tokens determined by the meaning of their type.

11 David Levy and Ken Olson (1992) argue that to develop an account of documents adequate for the age of duplicating machines and computers we need to distinguish types, tokens and *templates*.

12 Thanks to Ivan Sag for the examples.

13 More literally: The person such that there is a place where that person speaks q there stands at the place such that there is a person who speaks q there.

14 For a discussion of Stalnaker's approach and its relation to Reichenbach's approach and the current approach, see Perry (1993, pp. 51ff.). Evans's complaints (1981) about Perry (1977) are related. See Perry (1993), pp. 26ff.

15 Note that, given our assumption that names name rather than denote, this means that the designata of names is fixed at the level of content_M.

16 See footnote 15.

17 As noted in footnote 9, I am offically ignoring Donnellan's distinction between attributive and referential uses of definite descriptions. This is not to imply that there is anything absurd about the idea that definite descriptions refer. Recanati has a clear conception of this. He sees terms as having or lacking a certain feature, 'ref'. In my terms, a term that has this feature contributes the object it designates to official content, whether the term names or denotes. Indexicals have this feature in virtue of their meaning. On Recanati's view, definite descriptions do not have this feature built into their meaning, but it can be added at a pragmatic level in particular cases (1993). One can surmise that David Kaplan's 'dthat' operator (1979, 1989a) is a way of making the ref feature syntactially explicit; 'dthat' itself is, of course, open to various interpretations, even by its inventor (1989b).

18 See the discussion in Perry (1990).

19 Russell continued to recognize a category of 'logically proper names' that referred, but ordinary proper names weren't among them. Interestingly, they comprised such indexicals as 'this' and 'I'.

20 Compare what David Israel and I say (1991) on the issue of having 'narrow' enough content.

21 For more on these themes, see Israel, Perry, and Tutiya (1993).

Suggestions for further reading

Burks, Arthur 1949: Icon, Index and Symbol. *Philosophical and Phenomenological Research*, 9 (4), June: 673–89.

Castañeda, Hector-Neri 1966: 'He': A study in the logic of self-consciousness. *Ratio*, 8, 130–57.

Evans, Gareth 1981: Understanding demonstratives. In Herman Parret and Jacques Bouveresse (eds), *Meaning and Understanding*. Berlin and New York: Walter de Gruyter, 280–303.

Kaplan, David 1989: Demonstratives. In Almog, Joseph, John Perry and Howard Wettstein (eds), *Themes From Kaplan*. New York: Oxford University Press, 481–563.

Nunberg, Geoffrey 1993: Indexicality and deixis. *Linguistics and Philosophy*, 16, 1–43.

Perry, John 1993: *The Problem of the Essential Indexical and Other Essays*. New York: Oxford University Press.

Recanati, François 1993: *Direct Reference: From Language to Thought*. Oxford: Blackwell.

Yourgrau, Palle (ed.) 1990: *Demonstratives*. Oxford: Oxford University Press.

References

Almog, Joseph, John Perry and Howard Wettstein (eds) 1989: *Themes From Kaplan*. New York: Oxford University Press.

Barwise, Jon and John Perry 1983: *Situations and Attitudes*. Cambridge: MIT-Bradford.

Burks, Arthur 1949: Icon, Index and Symbol. *Philosophical and Phenomenological Research*, 9 (4), June: 673–89.

Castañeda, Hector-Neri 1966: 'He': A study in the logic of self-consciousness. *Ratio*, 8, 130–57.

——1967: Indicators and Quasi-Indicators. *American Philosophical Quarterly*, 4, 85–100.

Condoravdi, Cleo and Mark Gawron, 1996: The context dependency of impicit arguments. In *Quantifiers, Deduction and Context*, eds Makoto Kanazawa, Christopher Piñon, and Henriette de Swart. Stanford: CSLI.

Corazza, Eros, 1995: *Référence, Contexte et Attitudes*. Paris: Vrin.

Donnellan, Keith 1970: Proper Names and Identifying Descriptions. *Synthese*, 21, pp. 335–58.

——1966: Reference and Definite Descriptions. *Philosophical Review*, 75, 281–304.

Evans, Gareth 1981: Understanding Demonstratives. In Herman Parret and Jacques Bouveresse (eds), *Meaning and Understanding*. Berlin and New York: Walter de Gruyter, 280–303.

Frege, Gottlob 1960a: *Translations from the Philosophical Writings of Gottlob Frege*. Edited and translated by Peter Geach and Max Black. Oxford: Basil Blackwell.

——1960b: On Sense and Reference. In Frege (1960a), 56–78.

French, Peter A., Theodore E. Uehuling, Jr., and Howard K. Wettstein (eds) 1979: *Contemporary Perspectives in the Philosophy of Language*. Minneapolis: University of Minnesota Press.

Israel, David, John Perry, and Syun Tutiya 1993: Executions, Motivations and Accomplishments. *Philosophical Review*, 102 (October): 515–40.

Israel, David and John Perry 1990: What is information? In *Information, Language and Cognition*, ed. by Philip Hanson. Vancouver: University of British Columbia Press, 1–19.

Kaplan, David 1978: Dthat. In French et al. (1979), 383–400. Reprinted in Yourgrau (1990), 11–33.

——1979: On the logic of demonstratives. *Journal of Philosophical Logic*, 8, 81–98. Reprinted in French et al. (1979), 401–12.

——1989a: Demonstratives. In Almog (1989), 481–563.

——1989b: Afterthoughts. In Almog (1989), 565–614.

Kripke, Saul 1980: *Naming and Necessity*. Cambridge, Mass.: Harvard University Press.

Levy, David and Ken Olson 1992: Types, Tokens and Templates. CSLI Report CSLI-92-169.

Marcus, Ruth 1961: Modalities and Intensional Languages. *Synthese*, 13, 303–22.

Marti, Genoveva, 1995: The essence of genuine reference. *Journal of Philosophical Logic*, 24, 375–89.

Nunberg, Geoffrey 1992: Two kinds of indexicality. In Chris Barker and David Dowty (eds), *Proceedings of the Second Conference on Semantics and Linguistic Theory*. Columbus: Ohio State University, 283–301.

——1993: Indexicality and deixis. *Linguistics and Philosophy*, 16, 1–43.

Partee, Barbara 1989: Binding implicit variables in quantified contexts. *Papers of the Chicago Linguistic Society*, 25, 342–65.

Perry, John 1970: The Same *F*. *Philosophical Review*, 79 (2), 181–200.

——1977: Frege on Demonstratives. *Philosophical Review*, 86 (4), 474–97. Reprinted in Perry (1993, pp. 3–25).

——1979: The problem of the essential indexical, *Noûs*, 13 (1), 3–21. Reprinted in Perry (1993, 3–49).

——1980: A problem about continued belief. *Pacific Philosophical Quarterly*, 61(4), 317–22. Reprinted in Perry (1993, pp. 69–90).

——1990: Individuals in informational and intentional content. In Enrique Villaneueva (ed.), *Information, Semantics and Epistemology*. Oxford: Basil Blackwell, 172–89. Reprinted in Perry (1993, pp. 279–300).

——1993: *The Problem of the Essential Indexical and Other Essays*. New York: Oxford University Press.

——and David Israel 1991: Fodor and Psychological Explanation. In *Meaning and Mind*, ed. Barry Loewer and Georges Rey, Oxford: Basil Blackwell, 1991, 165–80. Reprinted in Perry (1993, pp. 301–21).

Recanati, François 1993: *Direct Reference: From Language to Thought*. Oxford: Blackwell.

Reichenbach, Hans 1947: Section 50: token-reflexive words. In *Elements of Symbolic Logic*. New York: Free Press, 284ff.

Smith, Quenton 1989: The multiple uses of indexicals. *Synthese*, 78, 167–91.

Stalnaker, Robert 1981: Indexical Belief. *Synthese*, 49, 129–51.

Vallee, Richard, forthcoming: Who Are We?

Yourgrau, Palle (ed.) 1990: *Demonstratives*. Oxford: Oxford University Press.

Wettstein, Howard 1986: Has Semantics Rested on a Mistake? *Journal of Philosophy*, 83 (4), 185–209.

24

Objects and criteria of identity

E. J. LOWE

1 Introduction

'Object' and 'criterion of identity' are philosophical terms of art whose application lies at a considerable theoretical remove from the surface phenomena of everyday linguistic usage. This partly explains their highly controversial status, for their point of application lies precisely where the concerns of linguists and philosophers of language merge with those of metaphysicians. The degree of controversy concerning these terms has indeed prompted some scepticism as to their utility (see, for example, Strawson, 1976), but a less pessimistic response would be to try to exercise greater care and discrimination in their use (cf. Lowe, 1989a). Both terms are undeniably slippery, especially 'object'. Our concern will be with the sense of 'object' in which it is interchangeable with 'thing', but it is important to see that this only coincides with a restricted sense of 'thing'. For we seem to use the word 'thing' in both a narrow and a broad sense, the former associated with the free-standing use of the word and the latter with its use in combination with quantifying adjectives to form unitary quantifier expressions like 'something' and 'everything' (cf. Teichmann, 1992, pp. 15–16 and 166–7). The difference is brought out by reflecting on the two non-equivalent sentences 'Every thing is a thing', which is trivially true, and 'Everything is a thing', which is metaphysically controversial. (The first sentence means 'Everything which is a thing is a thing', and is trivial in just the way that 'Every horse is a horse' is trivial; the second sentence, by contrast, is controversial in rather the way that 'Everything is a horse' would be.) As we shall see, some philosophical answers to the question 'What is a thing?' effectively ignore or deny this distinction. My own view is that the distinction is indeed a genuine one, and that it is the narrower sense of 'thing' that is ontologically significant. What is crucial to the status of 'thinghood' in this narrower sense is, I consider, the possession of determinate identity-conditions (see section 3 below). This is where the notion of a 'thing' or 'object' ties in with that of a *criterion of identity*, for one guarantee that something possesses determinate identity-conditions is that it falls under a general concept which supplies a definite criterion of identity for its instances. (Such a concept may be classed as a 'sortal'.)

As I have already implied, the term 'criterion of identity' is, unfortunately, itself the subject of considerable dispute. One problem is that candidates for this title typically take one or other of two quite different logical forms, whose difference turns on the mode of reference they involve to the objects for whose identity they provide a criterion (see section 5). Some objects are such that a canonical mode of reference to them by *functional* expressions of a quite specific kind is available. For instance, to use a famous example of Frege's (Frege, 1953, pp. 74f.), a particular *direction* may be canonically referred to as the direction *of* a particular line. (Any expression like this, of the form 'the F of x', may be called a functional expression.) In this particular case the object in question is, of course, not a *physical* but a geometrical one, and this fact may encourage the thought that it is a peculiarity of those objects for which a functional mode of reference is canonical that they are in some sense *abstract* objects, with logico-mathematical objects like directions, shapes, numbers and sets providing paradigm examples (cf. Dummett, 1981, p. 481). However, as we shall see, the distinction between 'abstract' and 'concrete' objects is itself a highly controversial one, and although it has indeed been argued that this distinction turns ultimately upon differences between the criteria of identity governing objects of these two broad categories (see section 10), it certainly does not appear to be simply related to the distinction between those criteria which do and those which do not involve functional modes of reference to the objects they concern. (For one thing, we have indisputably 'abstract' objects like sets, for which a criterion of identity is available which does *not* involve a functional mode of reference to them.) My own view, I should say, is that the distinction I have alluded to between the two types of identity criteria is not, at root, one of fundamental philosophical importance, in the sense of reflecting any basic metaphysical, semantic or epistemological distinction between the categories of objects to which they apply. This being so, however, one might expect to be able to supplant one or other type of criterion by the other, and I shall indeed try to show how such an expectation may be satisfied in specific cases (see sections 7 and 8).

Of course, the very *existence* of abstract objects is itself a matter of considerable philosophical controversy, though it would be inappropriate to engage in it here (but see further Hale, 1987, and Teichmann, 1992, for very contrasting views). However, one should at least be clear as to what is *meant* by 'abstract object' before one debates whether or not anything answers to that description. The putative examples I have so far mentioned – all of them logico-mathematical – are at least provided with clear-cut and unimpeachable criteria of identity; but other putative examples like propositions, facts and properties do not appear to be so favoured. This puts pressure on the idea that propositions and the like possess determinate identity-conditions at all, and correspondingly that they qualify as 'objects' or 'things' (in my narrow sense). That may seem no great loss, until we come to reflect that we can, ostensibly at least, *quantify over* and *refer to* propositions, facts and properties. However, perhaps we can plausibly represent such 'quantification' and 'reference' as convenient *façons de parler*, capable of being paraphrased away innocuously. I think that is correct, despite the fact that the strategy of paraphrastic elimination is one which must be handled with a good deal of caution, as we shall see (section 3). But before we can tackle such issues, we need to examine the role which criteria of identity play in our talk about objects of the least controversial varieties.

2 Sortals and counting

It is a familiar but none the less important philosophical point that an instruction simply to count how many *things* there are in a given room at a certain time is one that cannot be carried out: not because there will always be too many things to count, but because the instruction does not even make determinate sense, in the absence of a specification of the *sorts* or *kinds* of things that are to be counted (cf. Geach, 1980, p. 63f., Dummett, 1981, pp. 547ff., Wright, 1983, p. 3 and Lowe, 1989b, pp. 10ff.). It makes sense to ask how many *books* there are on a shelf, or how many *girls and boys* there are in a class, because in these cases an appropriate specification is supplied. But what exactly is the nature of such a specification, and what role does it play in conferring determinate sense on such a question? In brief, the point is this. If one is to *count* or *enumerate* items, one must at least be able to *identify* and *differentiate* them, because otherwise some things might be counted more than once. (Just what 'counting' *is* is something that we shall return to later, in section 9.) For instance, if I count the books on a certain shelf, I must count each book just once, so that I must be clear as to what differentiates one book from another. A crucial point here is that what differentiates one A from another may not be the same as what differentiates one B from another (where 'A' and 'B' are sortal terms – or, as the linguists appropriately call them, *count nouns* – like 'book' and 'child') – and this is because different sortal concepts supply different *criteria of identity* for the individuals falling under them. A graphic example is provided by an ambiguity in the term 'book' itself, whereby it may either denote a kind of physical object made out of paper, glue and thread or else a kind of abstract entity possessing certain semantic and syntactic properties. We might call an item of the former kind a 'copy' and an item of the latter kind a 'work'. On a given shelf there might be several copies 'of' the same work, and so the number of books on the shelf in the *former* sense of 'book' would be greater than the number of them there in the *latter* sense.

A further point which emerges from this example, and to which we must return, is that some sortals denote kinds of *concrete* object while others denote kinds of *abstract* object – a distinction of importance, but one whose definition is controversial (see section 10). Observe, incidentally, that I spoke above as though items of the abstract kind denoted by the term 'work' might literally occupy a position in space, for instance, a place on a bookshelf; but we shall see later that such talk should perhaps be interpreted in a more roundabout way. (What about *kinds* themselves: are they objects, and if so are they abstract objects? Again, this is something to which we shall return.)

Yet another point emerging from the problem of counting is this: although one must specify what *sorts* of things are to be counted in order to render determinate an instruction to count, it would be wrong to suppose that one can only meaningfully count things of the same kind (cf. Bennett and Alston, 1984, and Lowe, 1989b, p. 105). As an earlier example implied, one may count the *boys and girls* in a class, and these are not the same kinds. It is true that boys and girls are both *children*, but that is by the by: one could meaningfully count the *boys and books* in a room, even though there is no single kind (governed by a single criterion of identity) of which both boys and books are sub-kinds. What is crucial is that if one is to count the As and Bs, then (1) A and B must each supply determinate identity-conditions for their instances and (2) A and B must be *disjoint* kinds, so that nothing can be an instance of both (for example, one cannot meaningfully be asked to count the *dogs and animals* in a room).

Finally, I should remark that the fact that a general term conveys a criterion of identity for items to which it applies is not a sufficient condition for it to be possible, even in principle, to *count* such items. For *mass* terms like 'gold' and 'water' appear to convey criteria of identity – one can meaningfully ask whether the gold in this room (which might be scattered about it in the form of dust) is *the same* as the gold which formerly composed a certain ornament – even though it makes no sense to ask *how many* gold things, or portions of gold, are currently present in this room, not least because any portion of gold contains other portions of gold as proper parts (see further Simons, 1987, pp. 153ff.). (By contrast, it does make sense to ask *how much* gold there is in this room.) This shows that a criterion of identity is not exactly the same as a *principle of individuation*, though in the remainder of this chapter we shall chiefly be concerned with count nouns, for which this distinction does not emerge (but see further Woods, 1965). A principle of individuation, we may say, combines a criterion of *identity* with a principle of *unity*: countable items are singled out from others of their kind in a distinctive way that is determined by the sortal concept under which they fall, whereas portions of stuff can only be singled out in *ad hoc* ways, of which there are indefinitely many – as when a portion of gold is singled out as the gold composing a certain ring.

3 What is an object?

Of course, not all general terms are sortals, supplying a criterion of identity for items to which they apply: there are also 'adjectival' general terms (Geach) or 'characterizing' universals (Strawson), which supply no such criterion and are, indeed, applicable to things of many different kinds – for example, 'wise' and 'red thing' (see Geach, 1980, p. 63f. and Strawson, 1959, p. 168). 'Thing' itself is the most general such term, and is often used interchangeably with the term 'object', both sometimes being dubbed '*dummy* sortals' (cf. Wiggins, 1980, pp. 63f.). But what *is* an object, in the most general sense of that term? (I should perhaps stress that what we are seeking here is a satisfactory characterization of what is *meant* by 'object', not a general criterion for the *existence* of objects of whatever type.) This question is apt to prove confusing. One popular answer, which I shall call the 'Linguistic Answer', is that anything that can be referred to all – anything that can be made the *reference of a singular term* or be the *value of a variable of quantification* – is a 'thing' or 'object' (cf. Frege, 1952a, 1953, Wright, 1983, and Quine, 1953a, 1953b). Another possible answer, which I shall call the 'Metaphysical Answer', is that the term 'object' properly applies to any item which enjoys determinate identity-conditions, and hence any item falling under some sortal concept supplying a criterion of identity for its instances – so that, by this account, a particular *book* (whether a 'copy' or a 'work') or a particular *boy* would qualify as paradigm examples of 'objects'.

Now, it may be disputed whether these two answers really *are* different, in the sense of providing different extensions for the term 'object': for it may be contended that anything that can be referred to or quantified over must for that very reason fall under a sortal concept supplying a criterion of identity for its instances. A proponent of the Linguistic Answer endorsing this contention occupies a position which may be epitomized by the two Quinean dicta 'To be is to be the value of a variable' and 'No entity without identity' (see Quine, 1976, 1969 and 1990, p. 52). However, the contention in question is certainly open to dispute (cf. Strawson, 1976). For instance, we may apparently refer to the *fact* that such-and-such or the *proposition* that so-and-so, and indeed we may ostensibly quantify over facts and propositions (and likewise over properties, relations and so forth), but must we therefore be able to provide *criteria of identity* for such items? It is at the very least highly debatable whether we can, in the light of the interminable philosophical disputes as to what those criteria might be. This is a suspicion which is confirmed by the observation that, although 'fact' and 'proposition' are both grammatically count nouns, there appear to be no principled ways of *enumerating* facts and propositions.

A relevant consideration here may be that apparent reference to and quantification over facts, propositions and the like seem to be *eliminable by paraphrase*, whence it might be thought that our apparent inability to provide criteria of identity in such cases coincides neatly with the exposure of such 'reference' and 'quantification' as mere *façons de parler* or inflated uses of language. To illustrate these possibilities of paraphrase, instead of saying 'The fact that John was promoted pleased me greatly', I might less sententiously say 'I was greatly pleased that John was promoted'; and I might paraphrase 'John knows something that I don't' (ostensibly quantifying over propositions) as 'John is somewise more knowledgeable than I am'. (It may be deemed significant that the expression 'somewise' in the latter sentence – admittedly rather an archaism, but none the worse for that – is an *adverb*, in contrast with the *noun* 'something' which figures in the sentence being paraphrased.)

However, there are dangers in putting too much weight upon such possibilities of paraphrase. For one thing, paraphrase is a symmetrical relation, so the fact that reference to or quantification over items of certain kind can apparently be eliminated by paraphrase provides by itself no guide as to *which* of the classes of sentences so related are to be regarded as 'mere' *façons de parler* (cf. Wright, 1983, pp. 25ff.; but see also Teichmann, 1992, for a defence of the claim that a privileged direction of paraphrase may be discerned). Another point is that it may turn out to be possible to eliminate by paraphrase even reference to and quantification over such paradigm examples of objects as books and children (see, for example, Quine, 1966), but we obviously would not want to say in these cases that such a possibility threatened the status of such items as 'objects'. Certainly this would undermine the suggestion that there is a neat coincidence between cases in which reference to and quantification over items of a certain class are eliminable by paraphrase and cases in which such items cannot be provided with adequate criteria of identity.

The dialectical position we have arrived at now would seem to be as follows. If the Linguistic Answer is combined with an insistence that items referred to or quantified over must be provided with criteria of identity, it looks as though reference to and quantification over facts and propositions must be deemed *ersatz*, since such criteria do not appear to be forthcoming in these cases; however, the possibility of eliminating such reference and quantification by paraphrase provides, it seems, no independent confirmation of the *ersatz* status of such reference and quantification, since such elimination is possible even where criteria of identity *are* available. In the absence of any other independent confirmation, the judgement that such reference and quantification are *ersatz* looks suspiciously like an *ad hoc* manoeuvre to save the combined view at issue. On the other hand, if the Linguistic Answer is cut free of the demand for criteria of identity, it appears excessively liberal as regards the objects it is prepared to admit to our ontology. The moral which I am inclined to draw is that we should prefer the Metaphysical Answer to the question 'What is an object?', and reject the contention that the Linguistic Answer effectively determines the same extension for the term 'object', on the grounds that it fails to determine that extension effectively at all. My point would be that the devices of reference and quantification are exploited with immense prodigality in natural language, and resist any principled division into 'genuine' and 'spurious' (*ersatz*) cases save by appeal to extra-linguistic metaphysical considerations. *Given* the Metaphysical Answer, we are entitled to deny the status of 'objects' to facts and propositions (on the grounds that they lack determinate identity-conditions) and on *this* basis deem 'reference' to and 'quantification' over them mere *façons de parler*, supporting the latter claim by the provision of suitable modes of paraphrase.

4 Frege on concepts and objects

It would not do to leave the Linguistic Answer without some further discussion of the views of one of its most esteemed proponents, Gottlob Frege. For Frege, a crucial contrast is to be drawn between objects and *concepts*, the hallmark of the latter being their 'unsaturatedness' (see Frege, 1952a). (The term 'concept' has today a psychological ring which would be quite alien to Frege's intention; in more familiar terminology it may be said to cover both *properties* and *relations*.) In Frege's view, then, the object/concept distinction is a reflection of the linguistic distinction between *subject* and *predicate*. What he has in mind, however, is not the ordinary *grammatical*, but rather the *logical* distinction – the point being that not all grammatical subjects are object-denoting (for example, quantifier phrases, like 'some boy' and 'every book', are not). So what sort of subject-term *is* object-denoting, on this view? In a word, *names* (*Eigennamen*, in Frege's terminology). However, these must be very broadly construed to include not just ordinary proper names but also definite descriptions (in their 'referential' uses; see Donnellan, 1966), demonstratives, personal pronouns and so forth. All 'singular terms', then? Yes, but arguably more besides (even if Frege himself did not think so). For *plural* terms, like 'the books on my shelf' and 'the Joneses', can function as logical subjects, and surely qualify as object-denoting (see Sharvy, 1980, Boolos, 1984 and Lowe, 1991a). Moreover, we should not assume that all object-denoting terms denote *individual* objects, for there are *mass* terms and *kind* terms (like 'gold' and 'tiger' respectively) which apparently qualify as object-denoting despite not denoting *individuals* (particulars) – rather, they denote *sorts* or *kinds* (of stuff or things; see Lowe, 1989b, pp. 138ff., pp. 199ff. and 1991a).

Now sorts or kinds are universals, and therefore presumably *abstract* objects (of which more anon). But what about the adjectival or characterizing universals mentioned earlier: are *they* not likewise objects, at least according to the Fregean view now under examination? This is where we run into Frege's paradox of the concept *horse* (Frege, 1952a): though bearing in mind what I have just said, 'horse' is an ill-chosen example because it is very arguable that 'horse' *does* function as a name and denotes an abstract object, the horse kind; for it can function as a logical subject, as in 'Horses eat grass' and 'Horses are mammals', which I for one *don't* see (in the way Frege did) as involving quantification over individuals (see Lowe, 1989b, pp. 138ff. and 1991a). A better example, from my point of view, would be the concept (or, as we might more familiarly say, the property) *wise*. The point then is that '—is wise' functions as a *predicative* expression and so is not object-denoting by Frege's account, because what it expresses is 'unsaturated' (that is, demands 'completion' by an object to form a whole proposition). But if we try to *refer* to what it expresses (by speaking of 'the concept *wise*', or 'the property of wisdom', or even just 'what "—is wise" expresses'), then by Frege's own lights we only succeed, it seems, in referring to an *object* which perforce is *not* the concept in question, but a surrogate (see Dummett, 1981, pp. 211ff. and Palmer, 1988, pp. 36ff.). Quite what to make of this puzzle is far from clear, though Frege's own attitude to it (namely, that language prevents us from saying what we want to here, but that we can still somehow get the appropriate message across: Frege, 1952a) certainly does not appear at all satisfactory. I confess I am strongly tempted to see the paradox as an artefact of the Linguistic Answer to the question 'What is an object?', and hence to regard it as a further consideration (though perhaps only a minor one) in favour of the Metaphysical Answer. (According to the Metaphysical Answer, of course, what – if anything – excludes properties like wisdom from the realm of objects is that they lack determinate identity-conditions.)

Rather than pursue this dispute further, however, it may be more profitable to build upon the common ground which clearly exists between an advocate of the Metaphysical Answer, like myself, and most proponents of the Linguistic Answer (namely, those who also subscribe, with Frege and Quine, to the view that reference to and quantification over any class of items presupposes the availability of criteria of identity for those items). This common ground is that to all intents and purposes we can take an object to be any item falling under a sortal concept which supplies a well-defined criterion of identity for its instances. Our next task, then, is to attend to certain difficulties attaching to the very idea of a criterion of identity.

5 Two forms of identity criterion

The notion of a criterion of identity is one which, again, we owe largely to Frege (Frege, 1953, pp. 73ff.), though we can find antecedents to it in ancient and medieval discussions of the *principium individuationis* (see, for example, Anscombe, 1981 and Gracia, 1988) and in Locke's discussion of the idea of identity (Locke, 1975, pp. 328ff.). Foremost, perhaps, amongst the difficulties attaching to this notion is the question of what *form* such a criterion may or should take. There are two paradigms to be found in the literature, which we may distinguish (using the convenient nomenclature of Timothy Williamson, 1990, pp. 145ff.) as 'one-level' and 'two-level' identity criteria (see also Lowe, 1989a). Take the example of *sets*. A *one-level* criterion of identity for sets is provided by the Axiom of Extensionality, as follows:

(S1) $\forall x \forall y((\text{Set}(x) \,\&\, \text{Set}(y)) \rightarrow (x = y \leftrightarrow \forall z(z \in x \leftrightarrow z \in y)))$

In words: if x and y are sets, then x is identical with y if and only if x and y have the same members. A *two-level* criterion of identity for sets is provided by Frege's (fatal) Axiom V of the *Grundgesetze* (see Frege, 1952b, pp. 234ff. and Wright, 1983, p. 155):

(S2) $\forall F \forall G(\{x: Fx\} = \{x: Gx\} \leftrightarrow \forall x(Fx \leftrightarrow Gx))$

In words: the set of Fs is identical with the set of Gs if and only if all and only Fs are Gs. This axiom was the source of notorious difficulty for Frege, because unless a suitable restriction on possible values of 'F' and 'G' is specified, Russell's paradox can be generated from it (see Frege, 1952b). Other well-known Fregean two-level criteria of identity are his criterion of identity for *directions* (Frege, 1953, pp. 74f.):

(D2) $\forall x \forall y((\text{Line}(x) \,\&\, \text{Line}(y)) \rightarrow (dx = dy \leftrightarrow x \,//\, y))$

(the direction of line x is identical with the direction of line y if and only if lines x and y are parallel with one another) and his criterion of identity for *cardinal numbers* (ibid., pp. 73f.):

(N2) $\forall F \forall G(Nx{:}\, Fx = Nx{:}\, Gx \leftrightarrow \exists R(\{x: Fx\}\ 1 - 1_R\ \{x: Gx\}))$

(the number of Fs is identical with the number of Gs if and only if the set of Fs is one to one correlated with the set of Gs).

The key formal differences between one-level and two-level identity criteria may be described as follows. One-level criteria explicitly quantify over objects of the sort for which they supply a criterion of identity, and state that criterion in terms of a biconditional, one side of which contains a simple expression of identity between such objects and the other side of which expresses an equivalence relation obtaining between those identified objects. By contrast, two-level criteria quantify over items of a *different* kind from that of the objects for which they supply a criterion of identity, and state that criterion in terms of a biconditional, one side of which contains an expression of identity between such objects in which they are referred to by means of *functional* terms relating them to items of the kind quantified over, and the other side of which expresses an equivalence relation obtaining between the items to which the identified objects are thus related.

A difficulty which can beset either form of identity criterion is that of *impredicativity*, which threatens to render such criteria viciously circular. (An impredicative criterion is one which involves 'appeal to a totality that includes or depends on' the very objects whose identity is in question: Quine, 1985, p. 166.) It is important to recognize, however, that impredicativity does not *inevitably* give rise to vicious circularity. It doesn't, for instance, in the case of (S1), even if it is advanced in the context of 'pure' set theory of the Zermelo-Fraenkel type, in which all sets save the empty set only have other sets as members (see further Lowe, 1989c). But there certainly *can* be such circularity, as for instance in Donald Davidson's one-level criterion of identity for *events* (see Davidson, 1980, Quine, 1985, and Lowe, 1989a, 1989c):

(E1) $\forall x \forall y((\text{Event}(x) \,\&\, \text{Event}(y)) \rightarrow (x = y \leftrightarrow \forall z(\text{Event}(z) \rightarrow ((\text{Cause}(x, z) \leftrightarrow \text{Cause}(y, z)) \,\&\, (\text{Cause}(z, x) \leftrightarrow \text{Cause}(z, y))))))$

In words: if x and y are events, then x is identical with y if and only if x and y cause and are caused by the same events. This is circular inasmuch as what makes for sameness amongst events is precisely what a criterion of identity for events is supposed to convey, and yet a grasp of that is needed in order to understand what is expressed on the right-hand side of the main biconditional in (E1). (This is more obvious when (E1) is expressed in words as above than it is when logical symbolism is employed as in the formula (E1) itself: but there, too, we can see that the repetition of the variable 'z', understood as taking events as its values, is equivalent to an expression of event-identity.) A similar problem does not beset the criterion of set-identity (S1) despite the fact that sets may themselves be set-members, because – according to standard set theory, at least – sets belong to a cumulative hierarchy in which (S1) fixes the identity of each set recursively, beginning with sets which contain only non-sets as members, or with just the empty set in the case of 'pure' set theory (see further Lowe, 1989c).

Certain difficulties peculiar to two-level criteria arise from the fact that they utilize *functional* expressions to refer to the objects for which they supply a criterion. One difficulty is that this limits their scope of application quite considerably, at least in the absence of further theorizing. For instance, we need to be able to employ other means of referring to numbers than expressions of the form 'the number of Fs' – not least the numerals '1', '2', '3', and so on. Thus Frege's criterion (N2) doesn't of itself determine the truth-conditions of a statement like '1 + 2 = 3' or 'The number of books on my shelf is eighteen'. Another difficulty is that when we turn away from the sort of mathematical examples which interested Frege, we are often hard put to think of an appropriate two-level way of stating identity criteria. Consider, for instance, the problem of *personal* identity: the trouble is that there is no standard *functional* mode of referring to persons as there is to directions and numbers and sets. Directions are directions *of lines*, and numbers are numbers *of objects satisfying some condition*, as also are sets. But persons aren't at all obviously persons 'of' anything at all in this sense – in short, it isn't obvious what domain of entities ought to be invoked in order that an equivalence relation on *them* may be cited as a criterion of identity for persons (but see Williamson, 1990, pp. 116ff. for a two-level proposal concerning personal identity).

Even setting aside the foregoing difficulties, which may not seem very serious, it is clear that the two-level approach to identity criteria contains a built-in limitation inasmuch as any such criterion presupposes the identity of items of one kind in providing a criterion of identity for those of another. Thus (D2) presupposes the identity of lines in providing a criterion of identity for directions, and (N2) presupposes the identity of sets in providing a criterion of identity for cardinal numbers. (By saying that (D2) 'presupposes the identity of' lines I mean, of course, that in the absence of a further criterion of identity for *lines* (D2) does not provide a fully informative account of what distinguishes one direction from another.) One-level criteria are not inherently subject to this limitation, which suggests that they will in any case have to be invoked at some stage whenever two-level criteria are themselves invoked. This inevitably provokes a query as to whether two-level criteria are really needed at all, that is, as to whether the work which they do might not be equally well effected by one-level criteria. For unless there are compelling reasons for supposing that two-level criteria provide an indispensable service, considerations of simplicity and parsimony urge us in the direction of regarding one-level criteria as constituting the canonical form. Before we explore this issue, however, one or two preliminary remarks are in order concerning the logical status and role of identity criteria quite generally.

6 The logical status and role of identity criteria

The first thing to stress is that criteria of identity are to be thought of, for present purposes, as logico-metaphysical rather than heuristic or epistemic principles – they tell us, in Locke's words, 'wherein identity consists' for objects of a given kind (Locke, 1975, p. 335), *not* how we may set about discovering the truth or falsehood of an identity statement concerning such objects; though, obviously, they will not be totally irrelevant to the latter sort of issue (cf. Lowe, 1989b, pp. 15f.).

Secondly, identity criteria are not *definitions* – neither of *identity*, nor of *identity restricted to a certain sort or kind* (for identity is univocal), nor even of the *sortal terms* for which they supply criteria (cf. Lowe, 1989b, pp. 22ff. and Williamson, 1990, pp. 148ff.). Neither one-level nor two-level identity criteria are apt to provide definitions of the associated sortals ('direction', 'number', and so forth). For two-level criteria, as Frege recognized (Frege, 1953, pp. 77ff.), do not enable one to replace *all* occurrences of those sortals, only those in which they figure in functional expressions flanking an identity sign on both sides. And one-level criteria involve, as we have seen, reference to and indeed quantification over things of the very sort for which they provide a criterion, and accordingly presuppose some grasp of the associated sortals. (This is made quite explicit in the one-level criteria formulated above – (S1) and (E1) – in which the relevant sortal figures in the antecedent of the formula, instead of a restriction being imposed on the domain of quantification.) So, although it is true that criteria of identity can be construed as conveying semantic information about the sortal terms they relate to (and, certainly, a full grasp of the meaning of those sortal terms requires a grasp of their associated criteria of identity), they do not completely specify the meanings of those terms. This is a fact which, indeed, becomes obvious once it is realized that many *different* sortals are governed by the *same* criterion of identity. ('Cat' and 'dog', for example, are so governed – for cats and dogs both being kinds of animal, they necessarily both share the criterion of identity governing the sortal 'animal': it would be hard indeed if 'that dog' and 'the animal in that cage' conveyed different identity criteria, given that they may refer to one and the same object.)

Thirdly and finally, I should emphasize that it is not enough for a criterion of identity for As simply to state a logically necessary and sufficient condition for A-identity: it must state such a condition in an informative and, more particularly, a *non-circular* way – by which I mean that a grasp of A-identity must not already be needed in order to understand what is involved in the satisfaction of the condition in question (cf. Lowe, 1989b, pp. 20f.). As we saw earlier, Davidson's one-level criterion of identity for events, (E1), fell foul of this requirement.

7 One-level versus two-level identity criteria

Let us now return to the issue of whether two-level identity criteria are dispensable. One obvious thought is that they may be capable of reformulation in one-level style. (The reverse could not in general be true, in view of our remarks towards the end of section 5.) Consider (D2), then, the Fregean criterion of identity for directions, which tells us that the direction of line x is identical with the direction of line y if and only if lines x and y are parallel with one another. Why not reconstrue this in one-level style as the principle that directions are identical just in case any lines of which they are the directions are parallel with one another (cf. Lowe, 1989a)? That is:

$$\text{(D1)}\quad \forall x\forall y((\text{Direction}(x)\ \&\ \text{Direction}(y)) \rightarrow (x = y \leftrightarrow \forall w\forall z((\text{Line}(w)\ \&\ \text{Line}(z)\ \&\ \text{Of}(x, w)\ \&\ \text{Of}(y, z)) \rightarrow w\ //\ z)))$$

It may be objected (cf. Williamson, 1990, pp. 146f.) that (D1) cannot strictly say the same thing as (D2) because it exploits new terminology in the form of the expression 'Of' (which expresses the relation between a direction and a line of which it is the direction). But, first, exact synonymy is not our target anyway, or else there would be no real advantage in trying to 'reconstrue' two-level criteria in one-level terms; and, second, we might in any case urge that the meaning of 'Of' must be implicitly grasped by anyone who can understand the functional expression 'the direction of x', which is symbolized in (D2) by 'dx'. Here, however, it may be further objected that, indeed, 'Of(x, w)' in (D1) is *only* to be understood as a paraphrase for 'dw = x', so that it is an illusion to suppose that (D1) really dispenses with such functional expressions (cf. Williamson, 1990, pp. 146f.). But it is not at all clear to me that this suggestion is correct, and we have in any case noted already, in section 3, that a possibility of paraphrase does not of itself establish semantic priority (because paraphrase is a symmetrical relation).

Other objections may perhaps be raised against the attempt to reconstrue (D2) as (D1), though I shall not pursue them here (but see further Lowe, 1991c). I must, however, reject Williamson's charge that the Fregean approach of (D2) can, whereas the one-level approach of (D1) cannot, explain why directions and lengths have *different* criteria of identity. According to Williamson, the explanation is that they do so 'because two lines can have the same direction and different lengths, or *vice versa*' (Williamson, 1991, p. 195). But in reality this is no explanation at all, for if it were correct parity of reasoning would require us to say that *heights* and *widths* must have different criteria of identity because two plane figures can have the same height and different widths or *vice versa*, yet heights and widths are both kinds of lengths, being vertical and horizontal lengths respectively, and so must in fact share the *same* criterion of identity, namely, that of lengths in general. (Observe that this doesn't imply that any height can be *identified* with any width, any more than the fact that cats and dogs share the same criterion of identity implies that any cat can be identified with any dog.) As to the question of what, then, *is* the correct explanation for the fact that directions and lengths have different criteria of identity, I can only say that the search for an *explanation* of this sort of fact seems to me misplaced from the outset: criteria of identity are built into the very sense of sortal terms, so that to ask why things of the sort which a sortal term denotes are governed by the criterion which it conveys is comparable to asking, absurdly, why the sort of things which it denotes is the sort of things that it is.

The case of directions is not, however, of enough intrinsic importance for too much to hang upon it: Frege himself only introduced it for illustrative purposes. It would be more interesting and potentially fruitful to explore a more fundamental case, such as that of the criterion of identity for cardinal numbers. However, we should bear in mind that what is ultimately at issue is whether two-level identity criteria are dispensable, and to demonstrate that they are it is not necessary to show that they can always be *reconstrued* in one-level terms. Rather, it may suffice to show that we can always supply an adequate one-level criterion *in place of* any two-level criterion; for one criterion of identity is all we need for any given kind of objects, especially if we can also *derive* any correct two-level criterion from an adequate one-level criterion, perhaps with the aid of other necessary truths or definitions. (As we shall see, however, matters may not end quite there, since questions of epistemological and semantic priority may still remain outstanding.)

8 On the identity of cardinal numbers

Consider, then, the case of cardinal numbers. (I should stress that in what follows we shall only be concerned, as Frege himself was, with cardinals no larger than the smallest transfinite cardinal.) What might a one-level criterion to replace Frege's (N2) look like? Here is a possibility:

(N1) $\forall x \forall y((\text{Number}(x) \,\&\, \text{Number}(y)) \rightarrow (x = y \leftrightarrow \forall z(\text{Number}(z) \rightarrow (\text{Precede}(z, x) \leftrightarrow \text{Precede}(z, y)))))$

In words: if x and y are cardinal numbers, then x is identical with y if and only if all and only the cardinal numbers preceding x also precede y (precede, that is, in the series of cardinal numbers ⟨0, 1, 2, 3, . . .⟩). Of course, (N1) is 'impredicative' – but only in the harmless way in which (S1) is. No vicious circularity ensues. Criterion (N1) serves to identify 0 unambiguously as the cardinal number which has no predecessors (compare the empty set), and to identify all succeeding cardinal numbers in a recursive fashion (thus 1 is the cardinal number which has as its sole predecessor the cardinal number which has no predecessors, that is, 0, and so on). It is indisputable that (N1) cannot of itself convey the meaning of the sortal term 'cardinal number' to anyone not yet possessed of the concept, and so cannot be taken as providing anything like a definition of this term; but that, as we have seen, should not be regarded as part of the function of a criterion of identity in any case.

An interesting question to raise now is this: can we recover Frege's principle (N2) from (N1), supplemented with some further necessary truths or definitions? It appears that we can. First we need to define functional expressions of the sort used in (N2), 'Nx: Fx' – 'the number of Fs'. The obvious thing to say is that the number of Fs is the cardinal number the set of whose predecessors is one-to-one correlated with the set of Fs. More formally, we may adopt the following definition:

(Def N) $\text{Nx: Fx} =_{\text{df}} (\text{iy})(\text{Number(y)} \;\&\; \exists\text{R}(\{\text{z: Number(z)} \;\&\; \text{Precede(z, y)}\}$
$1 - 1_{\text{R}} \{\text{x: Fx}\}))$

In (Def N), I have used 'i' for Russell's definite description operator, so that '(iy)(. . . y . . .)' means 'the object y such that . . . y . . . ' and is analysed in Russell's way, according to which (in plain English) 'The object y such that . . . y . . . is thus and so' is taken as being equivalent to 'There is one and only one object y such that . . . y . . . and y is thus and so'. If in addition to (Def N) we adopt the existence postulate that there *is* a cardinal number which is the number of Fs, for any condition F (subject to certain necessary restrictions discussed below), that is:

(N*) $\forall\text{F}\exists\text{y}(\text{Number(y)} \;\&\; \text{Nx: Fx} = \text{y})$

then we are in a position to derive Frege's principle (N2). That is to say, (N1) in conjunction with (Def N) and (N*) entails (N2) (see Appendix). Or, in plain English, *given* that cardinal numbers are identical just in case they have the same predecessors, that the number of Fs is the cardinal number the set of whose predecessors is one-to-one correlated with the set of Fs, and that there *is* a cardinal number which is the number of Fs (and likewise a cardinal number which is the number of Gs), it *follows* that (Frege) the number of Fs is identical with the number of Gs if and only if the set of Fs and the set of Gs are one-to-one correlated.

9 Cardinal numbers and counting

But what precisely does the foregoing result serve to show? One's view of that will depend on what semantic and epistemological status one takes Frege's criterion

(N2) to have. Is it a principle which has to be grasped by anyone aspiring to a basic knowledge of the cardinal numbers and so of elementary arithmetic? It is not clear to me that it is (but see Wright, 1983, pp. 117ff., where an opposing view is expressed). Consider this: when children begin to learn about number they do so by learning to *count*. But what *is* 'counting'? It is a process of establishing a one-to-one correlation between a set of objects (for instance, the books on a certain shelf) and the set of predecessors of a certain cardinal number: a task which is accomplished by singling out each object just once (often by pointing to it) and uttering a numeral in sequence until every object has been accounted for. In practice, of course, we don't say 'zero' but rather 'one' as we point to the first object, but that is purely a matter of convention: the upshot is still that when we have finished the counting process we 'reach' a number which is the number of the objects being counted, in the sense just defined – that is, a number the set of whose predecessors is one-to-one correlated with the set of objects in question. It is arbitrary whether by 'reaching 3' we mean uttering the sequence of numerals '0', '1', '2' or, as is conventional, uttering the sequence of numerals '1', '2', '3'. Now, counting provides us with a means whereby to establish the *equinumerosity* of two sets of objects – for example, the books on a shelf and the children in a class – relying on the fact that one-to-one correlation is transitive. Such equinumerosity *can* sometimes be established directly (for instance, by giving each child one and only one book), but often this is impractical. It seems to me that the realization that one-to-one-correlated sets of objects are *equinumerous* is a more sophisticated achievement than the simple ability to *count* sets of objects, and consequently that we should not expect a grasp of Frege's criterion of identity for cardinal numbers to lie at the heart of our basic understanding of number. Indeed, it is a possible objection to Frege's approach that it gives no immediate insight into the relationship between cardinal numbers and the process of counting which is central to a child's induction into a grasp of the numbers (for an extended discussion of this and related matters, not always consonant with the views expressed here, see Dummett, 1991, pp. 143ff.).

This discussion of counting takes us back to some of the issues of section 2. We remarked there that we can only meaningfully be asked to *count* objects when supplied with appropriate sortal specifications. We can now see more clearly why this is so. Counting a set of objects is a process of establishing a one-to-one correlation between those objects and the set of predecessors of a certain cardinal number, which is then designated as the number of that set of objects. But this process demands that each object is identifiable and differentiable from the others, and supplying a criterion of identity for each such object (which is what a sortal specification will convey) normally enables this demand to be met. However, this should not be taken to preclude us from saying that *there are* objects that are uncountable even in principle: for example, the portions of gold, or the red things, currently present in this room. Incidentally, I remarked earlier that a restriction would have to be placed upon the postulate that for any condition F there is a cardinal number which is the number of objects satisfying that condition ((N*) of section 8). One reason why this is so is now clear: unless 'F' supplies a concept conveying a criterion of identity for each object falling under it, we cannot meaningfully assign those objects a number. Thus, where 'F' means 'book on this shelf', there is no difficulty in supposing that there is a number which is the number of Fs: but not so where 'F' means 'red thing currently present in this room'. Observe, though, that even if 'F' *does* supply a concept conveying a criterion of identity for objects falling under it, this does not guarantee that there is such a thing as the number of Fs. For instance, 'set' supplies such a criterion in the form of (S1), and yet we know that there are 'too many' sets for there to be a number of them (though there may, of course, be a number of sets *meeting some further specified condition*, such as the number of thirteen-membered sets of cards that can be dealt from a fifty-two-card pack: see, for example, Moore, 1990, pp. 147ff.). Again, there is a criterion of identity governing portions of gold, and yet, as we saw in section 2, no number can meaningfully be assigned to the portions of gold currently present in this room (because mass terms like 'gold' fail to supply a principle of *unity* for their instances). So, stating an appropriate restriction on 'F' in (N*) is no simple matter. How best to handle this problem I shall discuss no further here, beyond saying that one obvious strategy which will serve the purposes to which we put (N*) earlier is to replace (N*) by:

$$(\text{N}^{**}) \quad \forall F(\exists G \exists R(\{x: Fx\}\ 1-1_R\ \{x: Gx\}) \rightarrow \exists y(\text{Number}(y)\ \&\ \text{N}x: Fx = y))$$

In words: if the Fs are one-to-one correlated with the members of some set, then there is a cardinal number which is the number of Fs.

10 Abstract and concrete objects

One important issue which I have postponed until now is that of the distinction between 'abstract' and 'concrete' objects. I assume that numbers, sets and directions are uncontroversially abstract, while books and children are indisputably concrete. Of course, it may be asked how I *know* that numbers are abstract, when nothing I have said about them so far determines what they are. Indeed, it has been argued that numbers *could not* be 'objects' at all (see Benacerraf, 1983; but see also Wright, 1983, pp. 117ff., for criticism). My own view is that the natural numbers, at least, are *sorts* or *kinds* (of sets) and so *a fortiori* abstract (see Lowe, 1993). However, even if this is not accepted, perhaps we know enough about numbers to know that they would have to be abstract whatever they are – perhaps because there are too many of them for them to be concrete.

An obvious suggestion is that concrete objects are, while abstract objects are not, denizens of space-time (or, which perhaps amounts to the same thing, are/are not subject to causality: see, for example, Grossmann, 1992, p. 7). This has been queried, for instance by Bob Hale (1987, p. 49), on the grounds that objects such as *languages* are plausibly abstract and yet come into existence and undergo change and so presumably exist in time. (It won't do to classify them as abstract on the grounds that they *only* exist in time and not also in space – even if it were altogether plausible to say this of them – for we should want to classify Cartesian egos as 'concrete' despite ascribing only temporal, not spatial, existence to them.) Hale proposes instead, developing a suggestion of Harold Noonan's (see Noonan, 1976 and 1978), that abstract objects can be distinguished by reference to certain features of the criteria of identity which govern them. Specifically, he proposes (Hale, 1987, p. 61):

(A4) F is an abstract sortal iff, for any R that grounds F, either
 (i) R cannot hold between spatially located items at all or
 (ii) R can hold between things which are spatially, but not temporally, separated

where R is an equivalence relation and R *grounds* F iff, for any statement of identity linking F-denoting terms, there is some statement to the effect that R holds among certain things, the truth of which is (logically) necessary and sufficient for the truth of that statement of F-identity (Hale, 1987, p. 59).

As an example of a grounding relation, Hale cites the relation of parallelism between lines, which qualifies as such 'in virtue of the fact that lines have identical directions iff they are parallel' (ibid.). From this it appears that Hale is thinking primarily in terms of two-level ('Fregean') rather than one-level identity criteria; though he acknowledges that at least some sortals must be governed by one-level criteria (p. 57), and it is clear, indeed, that he intends (A4) to prescind from the distinction between one-level and two-level criteria.

Limitations of space prevent me from discussing the interesting reasoning behind Hale's ingenious proposal, but it appears in any case to be fatally flawed. This is most easily seen if one considers what it implies about *concrete* sortals (assuming that a sortal is 'concrete' if and only if it is not 'abstract'). Negating the right-hand side of (A4), we see that by Hale's account a sortal F qualifies as concrete iff there is some R that grounds F such that (i) R can hold between spatially located items and (ii) R cannot hold between things which are spatially, but not temporally, separated. Now consider the relation 'x and y coincide in their boundaries'. This is clearly a relation which serves to 'ground' the abstract sortal 'part of a geometrical figure', for it is evident that if x and y are parts of a geometrical figure (for example, semicircular parts of a circle), then they are, of logical necessity, identical parts if and only if they coincide in their boundaries. However, this is a relation which *can* also hold between spatially located items (for instance, Switzerland coincides in its boundaries with itself), but cannot hold between things which are spatially separated (and so *a fortiori* cannot hold between things which are spatially, but not temporally, separated). By Hale's account, therefore, the sortal 'part of a geometrical figure' is wrongly classified as concrete.

However, rather than attempt to refurbish Hale's proposal, let us look again at the previous suggestion that abstract objects are those that are not denizens of space-time. The supposed difficulty was that objects like languages are plausibly abstract and yet also plausibly come into existence and undergo change. But perhaps we need to make a distinction, which can best be brought out by analogy with a related case: that of biological species. These too are said to come into existence and undergo change – indeed, that they do so is crucial to the theory of evolution.

How then can species names denote universals, which are abstract entities and so, on the present proposal, timeless? The solution is to distinguish between biological *species*, which are *concrete individuals* consisting at any time of the mereological sum of their currently existing members (particular tigers or particular oaks), and biological *sorts* or *kinds*, which are universals instantiated by the members of those species (see Lowe, 1991a, and cf. Hull, 1976). Thus we can say that the horse *species* at one time did not exist and has evolved over millennia as its individual members have gradually taken on different morphological features, but that the *kind* horse which all these past and present individual horses instantiate never 'came into' existence and has not itself undergone change. In like manner, we may say that 'English', construed as denoting a kind of language, does not refer to an ephemeral and changeable entity, but that what have come and gone and been subject to change are the concrete processes of linguistic communication which, over the centuries of English history, have all qualified as manifestations of English. On this view, inasmuch as 'English' denotes something abstract it denotes a *kind* (a universal), not an individual. To the extent that we happily identify various *sub*-kinds of English – such as American English and Old English – this view seems reasonable, since only kinds (not individuals) can have sub-kinds.

11 The paradoxes of identity over time

This is a convenient place to address a final issue, which concerns the problem of *identity over time* and the paradoxes to which identity criteria often appear to give rise when time is brought into the picture. (There are also analogous *modal* paradoxes, which, however, I shall not discuss here; but see Lowe, 1986, and Williamson, 1990, pp. 126ff., as well as Chapter 25, RELATIVE IDENTITY.) The paradoxes arise because the identity criteria that we are intuitively led to adopt for various kinds of objects which persist through time permit these objects to change in certain respects while remaining numerically the same objects, and yet a series of small and acceptable changes can add up to a large change which we may intuitively feel to be incompatible with the retention of numerical identity for the object concerned. (Such paradoxes are, then, ostensibly a variety of sorites paradox: see Chapter 18, SORITES.)

In short: identity over time must be a *transitive* relation, and yet our intuitive identity criteria for objects persisting through time seem to rely on relations which are not strictly transitive.

For instance: we want to allow that a *ship* can persist identically through small changes in its component parts or in its overall design or structure, but a great many such successive changes may transform it into an object made of completely different materials put together in a completely different way; so that what we eventually have is no longer a ship at all, and so *a fortiori* not the *same* ship as the one we started with. Similar points have been made about *languages* (ignoring for the moment the bearing of my earlier denial that these may literally undergo change when conceived of as abstract entities). For example (see Williamson,

1990, p. 137), the language now spoken in Rome has, we may suppose, developed by small step-by-step changes from the language which was spoken in ancient Rome, such that no one of those changes amounted to the extinction of one language and the birth of a new one; and yet modern Italian is not numerically the same language, surely, as ancient Latin.

To cope with these problems we might attempt to refurbish what we take to be the intuitive identity criteria for artefacts like ships and languages, substituting strictly transitive relations for the non-transitive ones supposedly causing the trouble (cf. Williamson, 1990, pp. 139ff.). But before taking such drastic action we should explore the possibility that the problems are spurious ones, arising from a confusion between the identity criteria for individuals falling under given sortal concepts and the conditions for the correct application of those sortals to individuals. We need, I suggest, to allow for the possibility of *metamorphosis* (see also Lowe, 1989b, pp. 103f.), that is, a process whereby one and the same individual object can persist through a transformation from being an object of one sort A to being an object of another sort B, such that no object can *simultaneously* be both an A and a B. A logical restriction on such change is that A and B should supply the same criterion of identity for individuals instantiating them. But we have already noticed that very different sortal concepts can indeed convey the same identity criteria – for instance, the concepts *cat* and *dog* – and, indeed, that all sortals falling under the same higher-level sortals (as *cat* and *dog* both fall under *animal*) must, on pain of contradiction, supply the same identity criteria for individuals instantiating them. There can thus be no *logical* objection to the possibility of an individual animal surviving a change from being a cat to being a dog, even if such a transformation is *physically* impossible for biological reasons. In the case of artefacts like ships and languages such physical restraints are absent, and hence 'metamorphosis' may be expected to be a more common phenomenon amongst them. Thus, we can consistently react to the Italian/Latin example discussed earlier by saying that the same *individual language* has persisted identically in Rome from ancient to modern times, but that in the course of history it has changed from being an instance of the language-type *Latin* to being an instance of the language-type *Italian*, where these language-types are defined by certain important lexical and syntactic features. (It should be observed that this reaction is consistent with my earlier proposal that to the extent that language-names like 'Latin' and 'Italian' denote abstract entities, they denote kinds or types rather than individuals; furthermore, it may be conceded that the boundary between Latin and Italian is not a sharp one, and even that some sub-kinds of Latin equally qualify as sub-kinds of Italian.) Similarly, one and the same individual artefact might change from being a ship to being a hotel, provided both sortals convey the same criterion of identity.

If this solution is correct, the lesson would be that it is an error to suppose that the criterion of identity for, say, artefacts of a given sort necessarily embodies within it a condition to the effect that such an individual can only persist *as an individual of that sort*. We need to distinguish between the diachronic *identity* conditions of individuals and the conditions for their persistence as individuals *of a given sort* (what we might call 'sortal persistence conditions': cf. Lowe, 1991b, pp. 93f.).

Once this distinction is drawn, I surmise, many of the supposed temporal paradoxes of identity will dissolve, since they present no challenge to the transitivity of *identity*, and only serve to demonstrate that 'metamorphosis' is possible and, indeed, quite common. (There do exist puzzle cases, like that of the ship of Theseus, which genuinely concern identity and cannot be handled in the way just proposed: but I believe that most such puzzles are independently soluble in a quite straightforward fashion: see Lowe, 1983.) Of course, it may be said that we were already familiar with the possibility of metamorphosis from the case of transformations like that of a caterpillar into a butterfly or that of a tadpole into an adult frog: but in fact such transformations are not true cases of metamorphosis as I presently understand that term, because count nouns like 'caterpillar' and 'tadpole' – like also 'boy' and 'sapling' – are what Wiggins has called *phased* sortals, describing an individual as it is during one period of its natural development (see Wiggins, 1980, p. 24). True metamorphosis, such as that of a cat into a dog or that of a human being into a frog, would not be a natural process; nor can 'cat' and 'human being' properly be called phased sortals.

Appendix: informal proof of (N2)

We want to show that (N2) follows from the conjunction of (N1), (Def N) and (N*) (see section 8). Suppose, then, that

(1) Nx: Fx = Nx: Gx

that is, the number of Fs is identical with the number of Gs. Then, by (Def N), this implies that there is a number y, the set of whose predecessors is one-to-one correlated with the set of Fs, and a number w, the set of whose predecessors is one-to-one correlated with the set of Gs, and y = w. If y = w, then by (N1) y and w have exactly the same predecessors, and since we are given that the set of these predecessors is one-to-one correlated both with the set of Fs and with the set of Gs, it follows by the transitivity and symmetry of one-to-one correlation that the set of Fs is one-to-one correlated with the set of Gs, that is:

(2) $\exists R(\{x: Fx\}\ 1 - 1_R\ \{x: Gx\})$

So (2) follows from (1), and hence (N2) holds in the left-to-right direction. Next assume for the converse that (2) is true. Now, by (N*) we have that there is a number y, which is the number of Fs, and a number w, which is the number of Gs. That is to say, by (Def N), we have that there is a number y, the set of whose predecessors is one-to-one correlated with the set of Fs, and also a number w, the set of whose predecessors is one-to-one correlated with the set of Gs. But by (2) we have that the set of Fs is one-to-one correlated with the set of Gs, whence it follows by the transitivity and symmetry of one-to-one correlation that the set of y's predecessors is one-to-one correlated with the set of w's predecessors. From this it follows that y and w have exactly the same predecessors, and consequently by (N1) that y and w are the same number. But y and w are, respectively, the number of Fs and the number of Gs, which are therefore also identical, so that (2) follows and consequently (N2) holds in the right-to-left direction. *QED.* (Note that the proof will equally go through with (N**) of section 9 replacing (N*). It is crucial to the proof, incidentally, that – as stated at the beginning of section 8 – we are concerned with cardinals no larger than the smallest transfinite cardinal (for background information see Moore, 1990, pp. 147ff.)

Bibliography

Anscombe, G.E.M. 1981: The principle of individuation [1953]. In her *From Parmenides to Wittgenstein: Collected Philosophical Papers Volume I.* Oxford: Basil Blackwell.

Benacerraf, P. 1983: What numbers could not be [1965]. In P. Benacerraf and H. Putnam (eds), *Philosophy of Mathematics: Selected Readings*, 2nd edn, Cambridge: Cambridge University Press.

Bennett, J. and Alston, W. 1984: Identity and cardinality: Geach and Frege, *Philosophical Review*, 93, 553–67.

Boolos, G. 1984: To be is to be a value of a variable (or to be some values of some variables). *Journal of Philosophy*, 81, 430–49.

Davidson, D. 1980: The individuation of events [1969]. In his *Essays on Actions and Events.* Oxford: Clarendon Press.

Donnellan, K. 1966: Reference and definite descriptions. *Philosophical Review*, 75, 281–304.

Dummett, M. 1981: *Frege: Philosophy of Language*, 2nd edn, London: Duckworth.

——1991: *Frege: Philosophy of Mathematics.* London: Duckworth.

Frege, G. 1952a: On concept and object [1892]. In *Philosophical Writings of Gottlob Frege*, trans. P.T. Geach and M. Black. Oxford: Basil Blackwell.

——1952b: Frege on Russell's paradox [*Grundgesetze der Arithmetik*, Vol. ii, Appendix]. In *Philosophical Writings of Gottlob Frege*, trans. P.T. Geach and M. Black. Oxford: Basil Blackwell.

——1953: *The Foundations of Arithmetic* [1884], trans. J.L. Austin. Oxford: Basil Blackwell.

Geach, P.T. 1980: *Reference and Generality*, 3rd edn, Ithaca: Cornell University Press.

Gracia, J.J.E. 1988: *Introduction to the Problem of Individuation in the Early Middle Ages*, 2nd edn, Munich: Philosophia.

Grossmann, R. 1992: *The Existence of the World: An Introduction to Ontology.* London: Routledge.

Hale, B. 1987: *Abstract Objects.* Oxford: Basil Blackwell.

Hull, D.L. 1976: Are species really individuals? *Systematic Zoology*, 25, 174–91.

Locke, J. 1975: *An Essay Concerning Human Understanding* [1690], ed. P.H. Nidditch. Oxford: Clarendon Press.

Lowe, E.J. 1983: On the identity of artifacts. *Journal of Philosophy*, 80, 220–32.

——1986: On a supposed temporal/modal parallel. *Analysis*, 46, 195–7.

——1989a: What is a criterion of identity? *Philosophical Quarterly*, 39, 1–21.

——1989b: *Kinds of Being: A Study of Individuation, Identity and the Logic of Sortal Terms.* Oxford: Basil Blackwell.

——1989c: Impredicative identity criteria and Davidson's criterion of event identity. *Analysis*, 49, 178–81.

——1991a: Noun phrases, quantifiers, and generic names. *Philosophical Quarterly*, 41, 287–300.

——1991b: Real selves: persons as a substantial kind. In D. Cockburn (ed.), *Human Beings*. Cambridge: Cambridge University Press.

——1991c: One-level versus two-level identity criteria. *Analysis*, 51, 192–4.

——1993: Are the natural numbers individuals or sorts? *Analysis*, 53, 142–6.

Moore, A.W. 1990: *The Infinite*. London: Routledge.

Noonan, H.W. 1976: Dummett on abstract objects. *Analysis*, 36, 49–54.

——1978: Count nouns and mass nouns. *Analysis*, 38, 167–72.

Palmer, A. 1988: *Concept and Object*. London: Routledge.

Quine, W.V. 1953a: On what there is [1948]. In his *From a Logical Point of View*. New York: Harper and Row.

——1953b: Logic and the reification of universals. In his *From a Logical Point of View*. New York: Harper and Row.

——1966: Variables explained away. In his *Selected Logic Papers*, New York: Random House.

——1969: Speaking of objects [1958]. In his *Ontological Relativity and Other Essays*, New York: Columbia University Press.

——1976: A logistical approach to the ontological problem [1939]. In his *The Ways of Paradox and Other Essays*, revised edn, Cambridge, MA: Harvard University Press.

——1985: Events and reification. In E. LePore and B. McLaughlin (eds), *Actions and Events: Perspectives on the Philosophy of Donald Davidson*. Oxford: Basil Blackwell.

——1990: *Pursuit of Truth*. Cambridge, MA: Harvard University Press.

Sharvy, R. 1980: A more general theory of definite descriptions. *Philosophical Review*, 89, 607–24.

Simons, P. 1987: *Parts: A Study in Ontology*. Oxford: Clarendon Press.

Strawson, P.F. 1959: *Individuals: An Essay in Descriptive Metaphysics*. London: Methuen.

——1976: Entity and identity. In H.D. Lewis (ed.), *Contemporary British Philosophy, Fourth Series*. London: George Allen and Unwin.

Teichmann, R. 1992: *Abstract Entities*. Basingstoke: Macmillan.

Wiggins, D. 1980: *Sameness and Substance*. Oxford: Basil Blackwell.

Williamson, T. 1990: *Identity and Discrimination*. Oxford: Basil Blackwell.

——1991: Fregean directions. *Analysis*, 51, 194–5.

Woods, M.J. 1965: Identity and individuation. In R.J. Butler (ed.), *Analytical Philosophy, Second Series*. Oxford: Basil Blackwell.

Wright, C. 1983: *Frege's Conception of Numbers as Objects*. Aberdeen: Aberdeen University Press.

25

Relative identity

HAROLD NOONAN

Introduction

A piece of bronze is shaped into a statue of Napoleon and then some time later melted down and shaped into a statue of Winston Churchill. Thus the same *piece of bronze* is, at different times, different *statues*. A ship built entirely of timber undergoes over time a process of repair and replacement of parts so that eventually not a plank of the original ship remains. Thus the same *ship* is at different times two completely different *collections of planks*. Dr Jekyll drinks his potion and transforms himself into Mr Hyde. Thus the same *man*, at different times, is two different *persons* or *personalities*. I ask you to count the number of animals in the local zoo; you are unable to do so without further instruction since the zoo contains several individuals of the same species: Tiger Tim is the same *species of animal* as Tiger Tom, but a different *member* of the species. According to the doctrine of the Trinity, the Father, the Son and the Holy Ghost are the same *God*, but three different *Persons*.

These examples suggest that in a variety of circumstances one and the same A can be different Bs, and hence that there is some sort of incompleteness or indefiniteness in the unqualified statement that x and y are the same, which needs to be eliminated by answering the question 'the same *what?*'

One way of making these vague thoughts more precise is by appeal to the idea that *identity is relative*, which was first suggested to contemporary philosophers by Peter Geach (see Geach, 1962, 1967 and subsequent references). In the ensuing heated debate major contributions on the opposing side were those of David Wiggins (1967 and 1980) and Michael Dummett (1973, 1981 and 1991) in particular, whilst other writers who have put forward views similar to, or partly identical with, those of Geach included W. V. O. Quine (1963 and 1973), R. M. Chisholm (1969, 1970 and 1976), and David Lewis (1976). In what follows I shall set out and briefly attempt to evaluate Geach's main claims and arguments and the counter-arguments of his most significant opponents. I shall be considering Geach's claims solely as pertaining to the philosophy of language and to philosophical logic, but it should be noted that much of the interest of the concept of relative identity concerns its applicability to other areas of philosophical concern, in particular to the metaphysical controversy about *personal identity* and to the debate in philosophical theology centering on the doctrine of the Trinity: in this latter context see Geach's comments in his (1961) and (1977), and the papers by Richard Cartwright (1987), Peter Van Inwagen (1990) and James Cain (1989).

I shall first set out Geach's views under six headings: (1) the non-existence of absolute identity, (2) the sortal relativity of identity, (3) the derelativization thesis, (4) the counting thesis, (5) the thesis of the irreducibility of restricted quantification and (6) the name 'for' an A/ name 'of' an A distinction. I shall then look at the main arguments given by Geach and his opponents with regard to (1), (2) and (3), which are the core of his position. I begin with thesis (1).

The non-existence of absolute identity

On the classical view of identity it is an equivalence relation which everything has to itself and to nothing else and which therefore satisfies Leibniz's Law, i.e. if '=' expresses identity the schema '$(\forall x)(\forall y)(x = y \rightarrow (Fx \leftrightarrow Fy))$' is valid. Now these formal properties are sufficient to ensure that within any theory expressible by means of a fixed stock of one- or many-place predicates, quantifiers and truth-functional connectives, any two predicates which can be regarded as expressing identity will be extensionally equivalent. But they are not sufficient to ensure that a two-place predicate does express identity within a particular theory, for it may simply be that the descriptive resources of the theory are not rich enough to distinguish items between which the equivalence relation expressed by the predicate holds (see Geach, 1972, pp. 238–47).

Geach calls a two-place predicate which has these formal properties in some theory an 'I-predicate' relative to that theory. Relative to another, richer, theory the same predicate, interpreted in the same way, may not be an 'I-predicate'. If so it will not, and did not, even in the poorer theory, express identity.

However, Quine has suggested that when a predicate is an I-predicate in some theory only because the language in which the theory is expressed does not allow one to distinguish items between which it holds, one can reinterpret the sentences of the theory so that the I-predicate in the newly interpreted theory does express identity. Each sentence will have just the same truth-conditions under the new interpretation and the old, but the references of its sub-sentential parts will be different. Thus Quine suggests that if one has a language in which persons of the same income are indistinguishable, the predicates of the language may be reinterpreted so that the predicate which previously expressed *having the same income* comes now to express identity. The universe of discourse now consists of income groups, not people. The extensions of the monadic predicates are classes of income groups and, in general, the extension of an n-place predicate is a class of n-member sequences of income groups (see Quine, 1963, pp. 65–79). Any two-place predicate expressing an equivalence relation could be an I-predicate relative to some theory, and Quine's suggestion will be applicable to any such predicate if it is applicable at all.

In his (1967) (reprinted in his 1972, pp. 238–47) Geach objects to Quine's suggestion that applying this procedure leads to a 'baroque Meinongian ontology' and is thus inconsistent with Quine's own expressed preference for 'desert landscapes' (1972, p. 245). He concludes that the only tenable position is his own, that identity is relative.

What, then, is Geach's relative identity thesis?

In fact, there are several, logically independent, components to Geach's position, but we can begin by considering the following passages.

In the first Geach, as he often does, compares and contrasts his position with that of Frege:

> When one says 'x is identical with y' this, I hold, is an incomplete expression, it is short for 'x is the same A as y', where 'A' represents some count noun understood from the context of utterance – or else it is just a vague expression of a half-formed thought. Frege emphasized that 'x is *one*' is an incomplete way of saying 'x is one A, a single A' or else has no clear sense: since the connection of the concepts *one* and identity comes out just as much in the German 'ein und dasselbe' as in the English 'one and the same', it has always surprised me that Frege did not similarly maintain the parallel doctrine of relativized identity, which I have just briefly stated. (1967, p. 3)

Geach often associates his thesis that identity is relative with the notion of a *criterion of identity*: 'I maintain that it makes no sense to judge whether x and y are "the same" or whether x remains "the same" unless we add or understand some general term "same F". That in accordance with which we thus judge as to the identity, I call a *criterion* of identity.' And he takes his view to have the implication that 'x is the same A as y' does not 'split up' into 'x is an A (and y is an A) and x is the same as . . . y' (1962, pp. 39 and 152. On criteria of identity, see further Chapter 24, OBJECTS AND CRITERIA OF IDENTITY).

He also remarks (1980, p. 181), 'On my own view of identity I could not object in principle to different As being one and the same B; conceivably, two intentional objects could be one and the same man, as different heralds may be one and the same man.'

This last quotation gives us our first clue to understanding Geach. Let us say that an equivalence relation R is *absolute* if and only if, if x stands in it to y, there cannot be some other equivalence relation S, holding between anything and either x or y, but not holding between x and y. If an equivalence relation is not absolute it is *relative*. Now as an equivalence relation is any relation, like, say, *being the same size as*, which is symmetrical, transitive and reflexive, it is obvious that there are many relative equivalence relations, and no one can cavil at the idea. But now the question can be raised whether there are any *absolute* equivalence relations.

Geach's foremost contention is that there are not, that all equivalence relations are *relative* equivalence relations. This is vaguely stated, however. Given the definition of an absolute equivalence relation above, classical identity must be an absolute equivalence relation if it exists, as must any necessarily uninstantiated equivalence relation. Stated more precisely, then, Geach's main contention is that *any expression for an absolute equivalence relation in any possible language will have the null class as its extension*. This entails that *there can be no expression for classical identity in any possible language*, given that we understood classical identity as the relation everything stands in to itself and nothing else. This is the thesis Geach argues against Quine. We shall look at his argument later.

The sortal relativity of identity

If there is no such relation as classical identity in the sense just explained, then, of course, no statement of the form 'x is the same A as y' can be logically equivalent to 'x is an A and y is an A and x = y' where '=' expresses classical identity. Thus in this sense, 'x is the same A as y' cannot be 'split up'. However, even if this is so it need not be the case, as Geach claims, that x can be the same A as y but a different B – where 'A' and 'B' are two count nouns (or, more generally, two sortal terms). For it may be that whenever a term 'A' is interpretable as a sortal term in a language L the expression (interpretable as) 'x is the same A as y' in language L will be satisfied by a pair ⟨x,y⟩ only if the *I-predicate* of L is satisfied by ⟨x,y⟩. Then no truth of the form 'x and y are the same A but different Bs' will be expressible in the language. Geach's contention that this is a possibility is thus an additional thesis – the *thesis of the sortal relativity of identity* – which is not entailed by and, in fact, does not entail his thesis of the non-existence of absolute identity. It is this thesis which is the central one at issue between Geach and Wiggins (1967 and 1980), and which has attracted most attention. It entails that a relation expressible in the form 'x is the same A as y' in a language L need not entail indiscernibility even by the resources of L. Geach argues for it by illustrative examples – the cases of the cat on the mat (1980, p. 215), Heraclitus and the bath water (1962, pp. 150–1) and men and heralds (1980, p. 174ff.). We shall look at these later.

The derelativization thesis

Though an agreed example would suffice to establish it, the sortal relativity thesis depends for its significance on the distinction between sortal (or, as Geach calls them, 'substantival') terms and non-sortal (or 'adjectival') terms. For, of course, we can simply introduce *by abbreviative definition* an expression of the form 'x is the same A as y' to denote a relative equivalence relation R and, again by abbreviative definition, an expression of the form 'x is an A' to denote the property of being R to something or other, and then it may well turn out that in the language thus expanded some statement of the form 'x is an A, y is an A, x is the same A as y but x and y are different Bs' is true. This is the way, in fact, that Geach introduces the infamous concept of a surman. He first defines 'x is the same surman as y' to mean (by abbreviative definition) the same as 'x is a man and y is a man and x has the same single surname as y' and he then defines 'x is a surman' to mean the same as 'x is the same surman as something or other'. Given these definitions it cannot be denied that there are cases in which x is a surman, y is a surman, x is the same surman as y but x and y are different men. But this will cut no ice (as Geach is fully aware) with opponents of the sortal relativity thesis, who will simply deny that 'surman', so introduced, functions as a sortal term, that is, conveys a genuine criterion of identity. (See Chapter 24, OBJECTS AND CRITERIA OF IDENTITY.)

Geach's response to this line of objection is to offer his own account of the distinction between sortal terms and non-sortal terms – an account which is consistent with the thesis of the sortal relativity of identity.

The basic distinction, agreed on all sides, is between those terms 'A' such that 'same A' makes sense, and those terms of which this is not true. In his (1962) and (1967) Geach, following Aquinas, calls this the distinction between 'substantival' and 'adjectival' terms. He illustrates it by reference to Frege's remarks about the number of red things:

> Frege said that only such concepts as "sharply delimited" what they applied to, so that it was not "arbitrarily divisible", could serve as units for counting . . . Frege cagily remarks that in other cases, e.g. "red things", no finite number was determined. But, of course, the trouble about counting the red things in a room is not that you cannot make an end of counting them, but that you cannot make a beginning, you never know whether you have counted one already, because "the same red thing" supplies no criterion of identity. (1962, p. 63)

Thus, according to Geach, 'red thing' is an adjectival term because 'same red thing' provides no criterion of identity and hence makes no sense, whereas 'apple', say, and, as he goes on to mention, 'gold', are substantival terms because 'same apple' and 'same gold' do provide criteria of identity (the difference between the latter two terms is the difference between *count nouns* and *mass terms*, a difference which can be put in Geach's way by saying that though, in both cases, one can *begin* to count, only in the former can one make an end. See Chapter 24, OBJECTS AND CRITERIA OF IDENTITY).

But why does 'same red thing' not make sense, whereas 'same apple' does? And what is the relation in the latter case between the two-place predicate 'is the same apple as', and the one-place predicate 'is an apple'?

Geach's proposal is that the latter is derived from the former by what Quine has called *derelativization*. Quine writes: 'commonly the key word of a relative term is also used *derelativized*, as an absolute term to this effect, it is true of anything x if and only if the relative term is true of x with respect to at least one thing. Thus anyone is a brother if and only if there is someone of whom he is a brother' (1960, p. 106). It would be nonsense to suppose that the explanation could go the other way round; that we could start with 'is a brother' and then go on to explain 'is a brother of'. Just so, Geach claims, with respect to 'is an apple' and 'same apple'. 'Is an apple' is definable by derelativization as 'is the same apple as something', and 'the same' in 'the same apple as' is not a syntactically separable part but an index showing we have here a term for a relation with certain logical properties, just as the 'of' in 'is a brother of' does not signify a relation by itself (as if the phrase were 'is a brother, who belongs to'), but serves to show that the whole 'is a brother of' stands for a relation (1973, p. 291).

'A' is a substantival term, then, according to Geach, if 'is (an) A' is to be explained as formed by derelativization from 'is the same A as'. Otherwise it is an adjectival term. For, since 'the same' is merely an index of a certain type of relation, we cannot start with the monadic predicate 'is (an) A' and then explain the relational predicate 'is the same A as' in terms of it.

The manner in which he introduces talk of surmen is thus, according to Geach, not a mere trick, but a faithful representation of the way in which substantival terms in general are to be understood as acquired.

Of course, this does not commit Geach to claiming that 'surman', so introduced, *is* a substantival term. For he need not hold that every equivalence relation can serve in this way to introduce a substantival term; in fact, in his latest writing on identity (1991, p. 294ff.) Geach repudiates what he calls this 'false doctrine' and consequently disowns the 'surman' example. But what is central to Geach's position is the thesis that every substantival term is to be understood by derelativization from an expression for an equivalence relation. In addition he maintains that merely *relative* equivalence relations may serve in this role in relation to substantival terms, both mass and count (it is, in fact, count nouns about which Geach writes most frequently, but he has always been explicit that mass terms are also substantival terms).

To refute Geach, then, what his opponents must do is to point to features of the semantics of substantival terms which are incompatible with their being understood as derelativizations of expressions for relative equivalence relations. On the other hand, to establish his thesis Geach must demonstrate that there are no such features.

It is in the light of this that Geach's views on *counting* must be understood.

The counting thesis

It is obvious that in counting we must be able to distinguish and identify: we must distinguish items not yet counted from those already counted, and identify ones already counted as being among those already counted. Consequently it is a deeply ingrained conviction in many philosophical circles, in which the concept of relative identity is dismissed, that if x is an A and y is an A and x and y are not (classically) identical, then x and y can not be legitimately counted as *one* A. According to this philosophical view, when counting As one must count them as one if and only if they are identical. But, in fact, as Geach points out, it is perfectly possible to count by a relation weaker than, that is, not entailing, classical identity – a relative-equivalence relation. Suppose R is a relation weaker than identity which holds among As and which sorts the As into equivalence classes (as, for example, the relation *the same height as* sorts men into equivalence classes in respect of their height), then one can count As according to the rule that As x and y are to be counted as one just in case xRy. To do so one assigns the number *one* to any A and to any A which bears R to that A, and to no other A; one assigns the number *two* to any A to which a number has not yet been assigned, to any A which bears R to it and to no other A, and so on. The number finally arrived at will be the count of As under consideration when counting by R, and if it can be true that xRy even if x is not classically identical with y this number may obviously be smaller than the number arrived at when counting by classical identity.

It is, of course, a further question whether we ever do count by a relative equivalence relation, as Geach claims. But the correctness of Geach's counting thesis – the thesis that we *can* do so without falling into confusion or inconsistency

– is enough to show that the mere fact that a noun is a count noun does not suffice to show that it *cannot* be understood as a derelativization of an expression for a relative-equivalence relation. Moreover, in the light of this analysis of counting, Geach is in a position to demand that his opponents explain how, on their view, any term can be (logically) adjectival. For if the relation we count by is always identity, and if the distinction between substantival and adjectival terms is *not* that the former are, but that the latter are not, derelativizations of expressions for (possibly relative) equivalence relations, it is at first sight hard to see why the distinction between substantival and adjectival terms does not simply collapse, that is, it is hard to see how 'same A' can make any better sense in some cases (e.g. 'same man') than in others (e.g. 'same red thing').

The irreducibility of restricted quantification

An important component of Geach's position is his thesis that for any sortal term 'A' there is a distinction between restricted quantification over A's and unrestricted quantification over things that *are* As.

'Some man is F', Geach holds, is not equivalent to 'something is a man and is F', and 'every man is F' is not equivalent to 'everything, if it is a man, is F'. In the first pair the former is stronger, and in the second pair the latter is stronger.

Again, Geach maintains, if 'A' and 'B' are two sortal terms, 'Every (some) A is F' need not be equivalent to 'Every (some) B is F', even if 'Every A is B' and 'Every B is an A' are both true. Thus, for example, Geach claims 'Every (some) man is F' need not be equivalent to 'Every (some) herald is F' even if both 'Every man is a herald' and 'Every herald is a man' are true.

These claims about restricted quantification are, in fact, straightforward consequences of Geach's thesis of the sortal relativity of identity. We can see this by looking briefly at two of the examples he uses to argue for the sortal relativity thesis.

First, the case of the cat on the mat. If Tibbles is sitting on the mat and is the only cat sitting on the mat there will none the less, Geach claims, be a considerable number of distinct individuals on the mat which are cats and are the same cat as Tibbles. For each proper part of Tibbles which is smaller than Tibbles by just one hair is a cat and (since there is only *one* cat on the mat) the same cat as Tibbles. This description of the case is, of course, highly disputable. But the point at present is that if we *do* accept Geach's description of this case then we must also accept that 'Some cat is F' is not equivalent to 'something is a cat and is F'. For, in this situation, if every (or any) proper part of Tibbles differing in size from Tibbles by just one hair is a cat, it is true that *something which is a cat* is a proper part of Tibbles, but, indisputably, it is false that *some cat* is a proper part of Tibbles – that is something no one would wish to say. Again, if Tibbles has exactly 1,000 hairs it is false that *everything which is a cat* on the mat has exactly 1,000 hairs, but indisputably true that *every cat* on the mat has 1,000 hairs (since Tibbles is the only cat on the mat and has 1,000 hairs).

The same point can be seen by reflecting on Geach's example of Heraclitus's bathe in the river. If Heraclitus bathes in the river on two occasions and, as Geach claims, the river is at any moment a collection of water molecules and so is the same water as the collection of water molecules then in the river bed (since there are not two collections of water molecules occupying exactly that space), then it will be true that Heraclitus bathes in *something which is water* on two successive occasions, but it will be false (since new waters are ever flowing in) that there is *some water* that Heraclitus bathes in on two successive occasions.

If one accepts the sortal relativity of identity, then, one has no choice but to accept Geach's thesis of the irreducibility of restricted quantification. On the other hand, it is important to note, one can accept the latter thesis without accepting the former.

The 'name for an A'/'name of an A' distinction

The distinction between restricted and unrestricted quantification, if accepted, carries with it a distinction between two senses in which a name may name an A: a name may name *something which is an A*; more strongly, it may name *some A*. In the former case Geach calls it a name *of* an A; in the latter case a name *for* an A. Thus any non-empty name *for* an A is also a name *of* an A, but, if restricted quantification is irreducible, a name *of* an A need not be a name *for* an A. In the Tibbles case, for example, 'Tibbles' is both a name *for* a cat and a name *of* a cat, but if 'c' names a proper part of Tibbles which qualifies as a cat, it will be a name *of* a cat, but not a name *for* a cat.

With this distinction made Geach is able to explain the truth-conditions of statements containing restricted quantification and their relation to the truth-conditions of statements containing unrestricted quantification as follows:

'F (some A)' is true iff 'F(a)' is true for some interpretation of 'a' as a name *of* and *for* an A;
'F (any A)' is true iff 'F(a)' is true for any interpretation of 'a' as a name *of* and *for* an A.

If we delete from the above truth-conditions for 'F(some A)' and 'F(any A)' the restriction to proper names *of* and *for* an A we obtain truth-conditions for 'For some x, Fx' and 'For any x, Fx' respectively. It is worth noting that Geach does *not* intend that these explanations should be read as employing substitutional quantification; see Geach (1978) for an emphatic statement of the point.

Thus, we can say, a name 'a' which names something which is an A is a name *for* an 'A' if 'F(a)' is a sufficient condition for the truth of 'F (some A)' otherwise it is merely a name *of* an A.

(A complication which needs to be mentioned here is that Geach holds that there is no absolute distinction between general and proper names, since a name may be at the same time a name of several As and a name of just one B. Consequently, Geach would say, in the Tibbles case 'Tibbles' is a proper name *for* and *of* a cat, but is also a general name *of* each proper part of Tibbles which qualifies as a cat. This is a position which Geach stoutly maintains, but it does not appear to be logically required by his other views. If 'Tibbles' names Tibbles, and Tibbles is the same cat as c (a proper part of Tibbles which qualifies as a cat), why must we infer that 'Tibbles' names c? If *same cat* was an absolute equivalence relation, this inference would be obligatory. But, by hypothesis, it is not. In the sequel, therefore, I will concentrate on Geach's views about identity and leave aside his views on general and proper names.)

This account of the name *for* an A/name *of* an A distinction, of course, takes for granted the distinction between restricted and unrestricted quantification. However, Geach thinks that the former distinction can be explained independently and thus can be used to cast light on the latter. A name *for* an A, Geach suggests, can be explained as: a name associated with the *criterion of identity same A*. A name of an A which is not a name *for* an A, on the other hand, is a name which names something which is an A but is not associated with the criterion of identity *same A*.

The idea of a criterion of identity is a much-stressed element of Geach's conceptual repertoire, which he derives from Frege and Wittgenstein, but it is an idea which he shares with many philosophers, including strong opponents of his views on relative identity. It is a standard, though not wholly uncontroversial view that reference is only possible against the background of a criterion of identity, and hence that any proper name must have a sense (not necessarily an individuating sense of the sort attacked by Kripke, 1980) which has a criterion of identity as a component (see Chapter 24, OBJECTS AND CRITERIA OF IDENTITY).

The general idea can be understood as follows. To introduce a name, to assign it a use, is to determine its contribution to the truth-conditions of the sentences in which it occurs. (We can introduce a name by saying what it stands for, without making an explicit mention of the contribution it makes to the truth-conditions of the sentences in which it occurs, but this is only because we are acquainted with the form of stipulation 'name X stands for Y' and know in general how to determine the truth-conditions of sentences containing X, given the information that X stands for Y and the truth-conditions of sentences containing 'Y'.) The contention that the introduction of a name requires its association with a criterion of identity is, then, the contention that one cannot make a determinate assignment of a contribution to truth-conditions to a name unless one associates with it a relation to serve as a criterion of identity for the object named.

To consider precisely why this is thought to be the case and the arguments for and against this position would take us too far afield. But, evidently enough, if this standard view is accepted the legitimacy of Geach's notion of a name *for* an A cannot be rejected; what remains disputable, however, is whether a name *of* an A – a name which names something which is an A – can *fail* to be a name *for* an A.

I now turn to an examination of the main arguments for and against Geach's claims.

Geach versus Quine: a baroque meinongian ontology

Geach argues for his thesis (1), that absolute identity does not exist, by trying to show that absurdities result from Quine's claim that one can always reinterpret the range of the quantifiers in a language L in such a way as to ensure that the I-predicate of L expresses absolute identity, and not merely indistinguishability by the stock of predicates contained in L. To be relevant to its target the argument must be read as assuming that *if* absolute identity is expressible in language at all *then* one can always reinterpret the range of the quantifiers in any language L in such a way as to ensure that the I-predicate of L expresses absolute identity; but this assumption seems unexceptionable.

Geach argues that this Quinean claim leads to a 'baroque Meinongian ontology'. There are, however, two versions of Geach's argument, an earlier one and a later one, and these need to be considered separately, since the earlier argument is vulnerable to a criticism which does not apply to the later one.

In its earlier version the argument goes as follows. Suppose we have a language L containing a number of expressions for equivalence relations E1, E2, E3 and a theory T expressible in L in which these expressions are employed. Then, for each such expression En we can consider that sub-language of L (Ln) in which that expression is an I-predicate, and that fragment of T (Tn) expressible in that sub-language. Adopting Quine's suggestion, we can then reconstrue the range of the quantifiers in each Ln and reinterpret the predicates of Ln in such a way that while each true sentence of T which is also a sentence of Tn remains true in Tn, En in Ln no longer expresses a relation which holds between distinct items, but rather the relation of absolute identity. The range of the quantifiers in each Ln will now be different from their range in any other Ln, and also different from their range in L. For instance, if we start off with a language in which we quantify over token words, and in which the predicates 'is the same token word as', 'is equiform to' and 'has the same dictionary entry as' all occur, we may consider fragments of this language, and correspondingly fragments of theories expressible in this language, in which these various predicates qualify as I-predicates.

Following Quine's suggestion we may then reconstrue the quantifiers and reinterpret the predicates in these various language-fragments in a way that ensures, for example, that 'has the same dictionary entry as' expresses absolute identity in the language fragment in which it is the I-predicate. One way of doing this is to regard the quantifiers in this language-fragment as ranging over classes of words which have the same dictionary entry. Similarly, one may regard the quantifiers in the language-fragment in which 'is equiform to' is the I-predicate as ranging over classes of equiform words. Since equiform words need not have the same dictionary entry, nor words with the same dictionary entry be equiform, the ranges of the quantifiers in these two language-fragments will now be different, and different again, of course, from the range of the quantifiers in the original language, in which neither 'has the same dictionary entry as' nor 'is equiform to' is an I-predicate.

Now Geach does not claim, in the earlier version of his argument, that interpreting quantifiers in this way, so as to get at a relation of absolute identity, involves one in logical incoherences or absurdities – merely that it sins against a highly intuitive methodological programme enunciated by Quine himself, namely that 'as our knowledge expands we should unhesitatingly expand our ideology, our stock of predicables, but should be much more wary about altering our ontology, the interpretation of our bound name variables' (1972, p. 243), and that it has a consequence possibly unwelcome to a lover of desert landscapes, namely that

> since a rich language L may allow for our carving many sub-languages, L1, L2, L3 . . . out of it, users of L are committed to the existence, not only of a realm of objects for which the I-predicable of L itself gives the criterion of absolute identity, but also for each of these possible sub-languages Ln, of a distinct realm of objects for which the I-predicable of Ln gives the criterion of absolute identity. (1972, p. 248)

Geach's argument is thus that in view of the mere *possibility* of carving L1, L2, L3 . . . out of L, if the thesis maintained by Quine is right, users of L will be ontologically committed to any number of entities which are not spoken of, or quantified over, in L. They will be so committed because any sentence of L which is also a sentence of some sub-language Ln will have just the same truth-conditions in L and Ln and hence also in any theory T expressible in L and any theory got from T by mere omission of the sentences of L which are not sentences of Ln, but '[it] is, of course, flatly inconsistent to say that as a member of a larger theory a sentence retains its truth-conditions but not its ontological commitment' (1973, p. 299).

The crucial premiss of this argument, it therefore emerges, is the claim that sameness of truth-conditions entails sameness of ontological commitment. But, however it may be with other notions of ontological commitment, this is not true of Quine's. For Quine, the ontological commitments of a theory are those entities which must *lie within the domain of quantification* of the theory if the theory is to be true; or, alternatively expressed, those entities the predicates of the theory have to be true of if the theory is to be true. A theory is not, if I may so express it, ontologically committed to what is required to be in *the universe* if it is to be true, but merely to what it is required to be in *its universe* if it is to be true. Because this is so there is no argument from sameness of truth-conditions to sameness of ontological commitments.

Thus, as an *ad hominem* argument against Quine (which is how he himself describes it) Geach's argument, in the earlier version now being discussed, has to be judged a failure.

Matters stand differently with the later version of the argument, though it, too, I shall argue, in the end turns out not to be cogent (the criticism following is indebted to Dummett, 1991). The difference between the earlier and later version is that in the later (to be found in Geach, 1973) Geach's claim is not merely that Quine's thesis about the interpretation of quantification has a consequence which is unpalatable and 'possibly unwelcome to a lover of desert landscapes', but that it leads to an out-and-out logical absurdity, the existence of *absolute* surmen. Because Geach is now making this stronger claim, the objection that his argument depends upon the incorrect assumption that sameness of truth-conditions entails sameness of ontological commitments is no longer relevant. In order to make out his case Geach has to establish just two points. First, that there are sentences of English (supplemented by the predicate 'is the same surman as') which are evidently true and which, considered as sentences of that fragment of English in which 'is the same surman as' is an I-predicate, when this is interpreted in the way Quine suggests, can be true only if absolute surmen exist. And second, that the existence of absolute surmen (entities for which 'is the same surman as' expresses absolute identity) is absurd.

But in the end Geach fails to establish these two points. Quine would say that, for the fragment of English in question, the domain of the variables can be considered as consisting of classes of men with the same surname and the predicates interpreted as holding of such classes. Thus, the predicate 'is the same surman as' will no longer be true of *men* if we adopt Quine's suggestion (I am writing, remember, in English, not in the fragment of English under discussion), but rather of classes of men with the same surname – these, then, will be the entities which are Geach's 'absolute surmen'. Now, Geach attempts to rule out such a suggestion by the argument that 'Whatever is a surman is by definition a man'. But this argument fails. The predicate 'is a man' will also be in the language-fragment in which 'is the same surman as' is the I-predicate; and so it, too, will be reinterpreted, if we follow Quine's suggestion, as holding of classes of men with the same surname. Thus the sentence 'Whatever is a surman is a man' will be true in the language-fragment interpreted in Quine's way, just as it is in English as a whole. What will *not* be true, however, is that whatever the predicate 'is a surman' is true of, *as it occurs in the language-fragment reinterpreted in Quine's way*, is a thing of which 'is a man', *as it occurs in English as a whole*, is true of. But Geach has no right to demand that this should be the case. Even so, this demand can in fact be met. For the domain of the interpretation of the language-fragment in which 'is the same surman as' in the I-predicate can, in fact, be taken to consist of men, namely to be a class containing exactly one representative man for each class of men with the same surname. Thus, as Geach says, 'absolute surmen will be just some among men' (1973, p. 300). Geach goes on, 'There will, for example, be just one surman with the surname "Jones"; but if this is an absolute surman, and he is a certain man, then which of the Jones boys is he?' But this question, which is, of course, only answerable using predicates which belong to the part of English not included in the language-fragment in which 'is the same surman as' is the I-predicate, is not an impossible one to answer. It is merely that the answer will depend upon the particular interpretation which the language-fragment has, in fact, been given. Geach is, therefore, not entitled to go on 'Surely we have run into absurdity'. It thus seems that his argument for the non-existence of absolute identity fails.

Cats, rivers and heralds

Geach's thesis (2) – his sortal relativity thesis – is, however, another matter. For, as we saw, it is neither entailed by, nor entails, the thesis of the non-existence of absolute identity. Geach argues for it by appeal to a variety of well-known examples: the case of the cat on the mat, the Heraclitus and the river example and the men and heralds case. I shall concentrate on the case of the cat on the mat, but the points I shall make about this will obviously generalize.

There are two versions of the argument about the cat on the mat. One version goes like this (see Wiggins, 1968, for the first appearance of this version of the argument in present-day philosophical literature). Suppose a cat, Tibbles, is sitting on a mat. Now consider that portion of Tibbles which includes everything except her tail, and give the name Tib to that portion (Tibbles's 'puss', we can call it). Since Tibbles and Tib do not occupy exactly the same space at the same time, they are non-identical. But what if we amputate Tibbles's tail? Tibbles and Tib now occupy exactly the same space. If Tibbles is still a cat, it is hard to see by what criterion one could deny that Tib is a cat. Yet they are distinct individuals, because their histories are different. (For example, it may be true of Tibbles that she once had her tail run over, but it cannot be true of Tib – the tail was never part of her.) But there is just *one* cat in the place they now both occupy. So they cannot be distinct *cats*. They must be the same cat, even though they are distinct individuals; and so identity under the sortal concept *cat* must be a relative identity relation, that is, a relation which does not ensure the indiscernibility of its terms.

The second version (presented by Geach, 1980) goes as follows. Tibbles is sitting on the mat, and is the only cat sitting on the mat. But Tibbles has at least 1,000 hairs. Geach continues:

> Now let c be the largest continuous mass of feline tissue on the mat. Then for any of our 1,000 hairs, say h_n, there is a proper part c_n of c which contains precisely all of c except that hair h_n; and every such part c_n differs in a describable way both from any other such part say c_m, and from c as a whole. Moreover, fuzzy as the concept *cat* may be, it is clear that not only is c a cat, but also any part c_n is a cat: c_n would clearly be a cat were the hair h_n to be plucked out, and we cannot reasonably suppose that plucking out a hair *generates* a cat, so c_n must already have been a cat.

The conclusion, of course, is the same as in the previous version of the argument: there is only one cat on the mat, so all the distinct entities which qualify as cats must be the same cat, and *same cat* must be a merely relative identity relation.

These two versions of the argument are worth distinguishing because the second version is vulnerable to an objection – that the concept of *cat* satisfies a maximality requirement: that nothing can be *both* a proper part of a cat *and* a cat – which does not apply to the first version. But it is clear that neither version will convince an opponent, who will simply deny that any of the entities distinct from Tibbles in the situation *is* a cat, pointing out in support of this denial that there are modal and historical properties possessed by Tibbles not possessed by the other entities.

On the other hand a defender of Geach's position will want to know with what right it is assumed that possession of some of *these* properties is regarded as essential to being a cat.

In fact, it is clear that there are three possible lines of solution to the puzzle of the cat on the mat (and that these solutions are applicable *mutatis mutandis* to any of the other examples Geach employs):

(1) One can just say that Geach is wrong, and that the correct definition of 'cat' applies to *none* of the entities present except for Tibbles herself. If one takes this

line one may appeal to David Wiggins's 'is' of constitution, (1968) and (1980), to explain why, despite this, it is correct to *say*, for example, of each of the continuous lumps of feline tissue c1, c2, c3 . . . that it 'is' a cat.

(2) One can say, with Geach, that what the puzzle shows is that it is a mistake to suppose that in everyday life counting is always by identity: that x and y are to be counted as one just in case x = y. In fact, in counting cats we count, as the puzzle shows, by a weaker equivalence relation R. This equivalence relation obtains between each of c1, c2, c3 and the next, and between each of these and Tibbles. Consequently, we are speaking correctly when we describe the situation as one in which there is just one cat, even though the situation contains 1,001 distinct objects, each of which qualifies as a cat. But, of course, in counting cats the relation we count by can be none other than the one we express by 'is the same cat as'. This, then, must be the relevant relation R. Thus 'is the same cat as' is an expression for a relation which does not ensure the indiscernibility of its terms, that is, a relative equivalence relation.

(3) Finally, one can say that the solution to the puzzle lies in recognizing that in counting cats not everything that qualifies as a cat should be included in the count. 'There is just one cat on the mat' means 'some cat is on the mat and every cat which is on the mat is identical with that one'. Thus, the only entities to be counted when counting cats are those which fall within the range of the natural-language quantifying expressions, 'some cat' and 'every cat'. But it is only if 'some cat is F' is equivalent to 'something is a cat and is F' and 'every cat is F' is equivalent to 'everything, if it is a cat, is F' that these quantifying expressions must be taken to range over everything which qualifies as a cat. A solution to the puzzle can thus be found in denying these equivalences, and maintaining that, of the 1,001 items in the situation which qualify as cats, only one – Tibbles herself – falls within the range of 'some cat' and 'every cat'.

It seems clear that the linguistic facts are consistent with each of these solutions, and so the puzzle cannot count *decisively* either for or against Geach's view. But the availability of the third line of solution also makes it evident that no example of this type could even provide a *reason* for embracing the sortal relativity thesis, since the distinction between restricted and unrestricted qualification which is all that the type (3) solution relies upon is something to which a proponent of a Geachian type (2) solution is already committed. On grounds of economy, then, it seems that type (3) solutions to problems of the sort Geach describes must always be preferable to type (2) solutions.

The availability of the type (3) solution also puts the position of the proponent of the type (1) solution in a clearer light. It makes it clear that opposition to the concept of relative identity, by itself, provides no motive for insisting on the type (1) solution or for endorsing the 'is' of constitution. What is required for providing such a motive is an argument for rejecting the thesis of the irreducibility of restricted (sortal) qualification to unrestricted quantification, but it is hard to see what form such an argument might take. The crucial point at issue between the proponent of the type (1) solution and the proponent of the type (3) solution is whether *'is a cat', understood as a syntactically simple predicate in which the 'is' is merely the 'is' of predication – a mere fragment of a predicate which expresses no property or relation by itself – applies univocally both to Tibbles and to (at least one of) the entities present in the situation described which are distinct from Tibbles.* If so, the type (3) solution can be accepted; if not, the type (1) solution must be accepted. But how this issue might be decided is wholly unclear.

The verdict on Geach's sortal relativity thesis must, then, be that it is not proven, and possibly unprovable; on the other hand, there seems to be no argument which weighs conclusively *against* the sortal relativity thesis.

Substantival terms and the derelativization thesis

This is not the case, however, with Geach's derelativization thesis: that every substantival term is to be explained as the derelativization of an expression for an equivalence relation. In this case it does seem clear that Geach's contention is over-ambitious, as Dummett (see 1981 and 1991) demonstrates.

The first class of counter-examples to the derelativization thesis to which Dummett draws attention is the class of what he calls *derivative* count nouns, where a count noun 'A' is a derivative count noun when there is some count noun 'B' such that 'is the same A as' may be satisfactorily explained as 'is an A and is the same B as'.

As Dummett points out, ironically enough Geach himself draws attention to counter-examples of this class when he introduces the derelativization thesis. If Geach is right, as he evidently is, that 'is a brother' is derived from 'is a brother of', it cannot be also be understood as derived from 'is the same brother as'. Rather, we have to understand the latter as derived from 'is a brother' (or else, implausibly, reject it as meaningless); and the evident explanation is that 'is the same brother as' means 'is a brother and is the same man as'.

Once this exception to the derelativization thesis is admitted, no reason remains for not allowing others. As Dummett argues, such nouns as 'postman' and 'baker' also seem to be exceptions. We understand 'is the same postman as' as meaning 'is a postman and is the same man as'. We do not have to learn 'is the same postman as' before we understand 'is a postman' and we cannot be thought of as required to derive the latter from the former by derelativization.

A second class of counter-examples to the derelativization thesis which Dummett draws attention to is the class of abstract nouns.

Consider first the noun 'shape'. This is certainly a count noun, but it seems clear that Geach's derelativization thesis does not give the correct account of its semantics. The reason is that there is a competing account which is far more plausible, namely the account sketched out by Frege in the *Grundlagen*, using the concept of direction as his model. According to this account, the noun 'shape' may be thought of as introduced into the language as follows: we begin by introducing an expression 'has the same shape as' for an equivalence relation between material objects; we then introduce the functional expression 'the shape of', explained in such a way as to yield the equivalence of 'the shape of x is the same as the shape of y' and 'x has the same shape as y'; and finally we explain 'x is a shape' to mean 'for some y, x is the shape of y'. We can supplement this account by stipulating that 'x is the same shape as y' is to mean 'x is a shape and x is the same as y', which is equivalent to 'for some z, for some u, x is the shape of z and y is the shape of u, and z has the same shape as u'.

The reason why this account seems superior to Geach's is that it reflects the necessary order of language acquisition. There *could not* be a language in which it was possible to make reference to shapes but which did not contain any functional expression with the sense of 'the shape of'. This is because shapes, unlike, say, colours, are not possible objects of ostension: even against the background of an appropriate criterion of identity one cannot pick out a shape by pointing and saying 'this'. The only way to refer to a shape is as the shape of some already-identified object or region. Thus, a language could not contain the predicates 'is a shape' and 'is the same shape as' unless it also contained the functional expression 'the shape of', and the Fregean account is in accord with this fact.

Another example for which the Fregean account seems plausible is 'nationality'. Here, too, it seems that we understand 'x is a nationality' and 'x is the same nationality as y', respectively, to mean 'for some x, x is the nationality of y' and 'for some z, for some u, x is the nationality of z and y is the nationality of u and z has the same nationality as u', understanding 'the nationality of' in such a way as ensures the equivalence of 'the nationality of x is the same as the nationality of y' and 'x has the same nationality as y', that is, 'x is a citizen of the same country as y'. But the reason in this case seems slightly different from the reason in the previous case. For while shapes are not possible objects of ostension, nationalities are. If I point towards a man and say 'this nationality', there may well be no choice, given the criterion of identity I have invoked, of objects to which I can be referring. But if I point and say 'this shape' there will always be more than one (if there is even one) choice of object of reference compatible with the criterion of identity I have invoked. Nevertheless, it does seem that a language could not contain any means of making reference to nationalities – and hence could not contain the predicates 'is a nationality' and 'is the same nationality as' – unless it also contained a functional expression with the sense of 'the nationality of'. This is presumably because no one could understand the notion of 'a nationality' without being aware of those relations among human beings in which there being such things as nationalities consists; and he could not be aware of these without being able to refer to individual human beings and their nationalities.

Once we recognize, with Dummett, that abstract nouns are counter-examples to Geach's derelativization thesis, it quickly becomes plausible that mass terms are also.

Consider the mass noun 'gold'. Like shape, and unlike colours or nationalities, parcels of gold are not possible objects of ostension. Pointing and saying 'this gold' will not determine which object I am referring to. This is because any proper part of a parcel of gold is itself a parcel of gold, but is a distinct parcel from that of which it is a proper part. Thus, just as in order to identify shapes we must relate them to some other, already-identified objects or regions – as the shapes *of* those objects or regions – so, in order to identify a parcel of gold, one must relate it to some already-identified object as the gold *of* that object; just as one may identify a shape as the *shape* of so-and-so's wedding ring, so one may identify a parcel of gold as the *gold* of her wedding ring; and, as the possibility of reference to shapes depends upon the existence of such means of identification, the same holds of the possibility of reference to parcels of gold. And so a language *could not* contain the means of making reference to parcels of gold – and hence could not contain the predicates 'is gold' and 'is the same gold as' (understood as applicable to parcels of gold) – unless it contained a functional expression with the sense of 'the gold of', as it occurs in 'the gold of her wedding ring'.

But in the light of this, the Fregean pattern of explanation seems to have as much plausibility for 'gold' as it has for 'shape' or 'nationality'. The predicate 'x is gold' is to be understood as meaning 'for some y, x is the gold of y' and 'x is the same gold as y' as 'for some z, for some u, x is the gold of z and y is the gold of u and z is constituted of the same gold as u', understanding 'the gold of' in such a way as ensures the equivalence of 'the gold of x is the same as the gold of y' and 'x is constituted of the same gold as y', where 'is constituted of the same gold as' expresses an epistemologically prior relation in the same way as do 'has the same shape as' and 'has the same nationality as'.

If these suggestions are correct, Geach's derelativization thesis is far too ambitious: there are many substantival terms which are counter-examples. It does not follow, of course, that there are no substantival terms to which it *does* apply. And, in fact, it might seem that it must apply to what, following Dummett, can be called 'basic count nouns'; that is, substantival terms which are (a) not abstract nouns (like 'nationality' and 'shape'), (b) not mass nouns (like 'gold') and (c) not derivative count nouns (like 'father' or 'postman'). For in the case of such basic count nouns it seems that the association with a criterion of identity which is definitive of a substantival term can be made in no other way: it cannot, as in the case of derivative count nouns, be derived from an association with a second count noun in terms of which the first is defined; nor can it, as in the case of abstract nouns and mass terms, be made in the way the Fregean pattern suggests, which requires that the associated criterion of identity be an equivalence relation between objects *other than* those to which the count noun applies.

However, once again Dummett suggests an alternative pattern of explanation. In the case of basic count nouns, he suggests (1981 and 1991) the crucial point to recognize is that the associated criterion of identity is not an equivalence *relation* at all (where a relation is thought of as holding between *objects*).

We cannot give a correct representation of that level of our language at which we quantify over and refer to objects, Dummett thinks, unless we recognize a lower level at which no reference to or quantification over objects exists; formalized languages serve only to regiment the higher level. At the lower level, what takes the place of the use, at the higher level, of proper names and other singular terms to refer to objects is the use of demonstrative pronouns in what Dummett calls 'crude predications'. The distinctive feature of this use of demonstratives is that no criterion of identity has to be invoked to make their utterance understood; no answer to the question 'This what?' need be available. In such crude predications the predicate cannot, therefore, be one applicable to an object, but must be one expressing what Strawson has called a 'feature-placing concept'. Examples of such crude predications are 'This is sticky', 'This is red' and 'This is smooth'.

The transition to the higher level, at which reference to and quantification over objects takes place, Dummett suggests, is mediated by what he calls 'statements of identification', that is, statements of the form, 'This is the same X as that' where 'X' is a basic count noun. A child does not actually acquire the word 'cat' in the first place by learning to point simultaneously to say, the head and tail of a cat, and to say, 'That is the same cat as that'. But this, nevertheless, correctly represents what is involved in the move from the lower level of language to the higher, namely the acquisition of a criterion of identity by which we can determine where one cat leaves off and another begins.

But a statement of identification, like a crude predication, does not *itself* involve any reference to objects, since in itself it is merely a crude relational statement like 'This is darker than that'. Hence the criterion of identity associated with a basic count noun is not an equivalence relation between objects, either objects of the sort to which the count noun applies, or objects of another sort: '. . . is the same X as . . .', as used in statements of identification, is *like* an expression for an equivalence relation, but it does not stand for such a relation, since it is not, at this stage, used to express a relation between *objects* at all. To grasp the criterion of identity associated with a basic count noun, it is thus not necessary to have any prior conception of objects of any sort. To think otherwise, Dummett suggests, is Geach's basic mistake.

These suggestions of Dummett's seem entirely correct, and the insights they contain into the semantics of substantival terms appear highly illuminating. But it is important also to see the extent of the agreement between Dummett and Geach. The main emphasis of Geach's work on identity has always been on the uselessness of the notion of absolute identity, and on its inability to provide any usable *criterion* of identity. If Dummett's suggestions are correct, then this point of Geach's is vindicated: the criterion of identity associated with a general term (and hence, derivatively, with a proper name) must either be given by an expression for a relative equivalence relation not holding between the objects to which the general term applies (as in the case of abstract nouns and mass nouns), or it must be given by an expression which does not designate a relation between objects at all – and *a fortiori* does not designate an absolute equivalence relation. This, I would suggest, is the most important lesson to learn from Geach's work, and it is one that so far has gone generally unappreciated.

References

Cain, J. 1989: The doctrine of the Trinity and the logic of relative identity. *Religious Studies*, 25, 141–52.

Cartwright, R. 1987: On the logical problem of the Trinity. In Cartwright, R., *Philosophical Essays*. Cambridge, Mass.: MIT Press.

Chisholm, R.M. 1969: The loose and popular and strict and philosophical senses of identity. In Case, N. and Grim, R.H. (eds), *Perception and Personal Identity*. Cleveland, Oh.: Ohio University Press.
——1970: Identity through time. In H.E. Kiefer and M.K. Munitz (eds), *Language, Belief and Metaphysics*. Albany, NY: State University of New York Press.
——1976: *Person and Object*. London: Allen and Unwin.
Dummett, M. 1973: *Frege: Philosophy of Language*. Second edition, with index and textual references added, 1981. London: Duckworth.
——1981: *The Interpretation of Frege's Philosophy*. Cambridge, Mass.: Harvard University Press.
——1991: Does quantification involve identity? In Lewis, H.A. (ed.), *Peter Geach: Philosophical Encounters*. Dordrecht: Kluwer Academic Publishers.
Geach, P.T. (with G.E.M. Anscombe) 1961: *Three Philosophers*. Ithaca, New York and London: Cornell University Press.
——1962: *Reference and Generality*. (Third edition, 1980). Ithaca, NY: Cornell University Press.
——1967: Identity. *Review of Metaphysics*, 21, 3–12. Reprinted in Geach (1972, pp. 238–47.)
——1972: *Logic Matters*. Basil Blackwell, Oxford.
——1973: Ontological relativity and relative identity. In M.K. Munitz (ed.), *Logic and Ontology*. New York: New York University Press.
——1975: Names and identity. In S. Guttenplan (ed.), *Mind and Language: Wolfson College Lectures 1974*. Oxford: Clarendon Press.
——1977: *The Virtues: The Stanton Lectures 1973–4*. Cambridge: Cambridge University Press.
——1978: Evans on quantifiers. *Canadian Journal of Philosophy*, 8, pp. 375–8.
——1979: Existential or particular quantifier? In P. Weingartner and E. Mascher (eds), *Ontology and Logic* (Proceedings of an International Colloquium, Salzburg, 21–4 September 1976). Berlin: Duncker and Humblot.
——1980: *Reference and Generality* (3rd edition). Ithaca, NY: Cornell University Press.
——1991: Replies. In Lewis H.A. (ed.), *Peter Geach: Philosophical Encounters*. Dordrecht: Kluwer Academic Publishers.
Kripke, S. 1980: *Naming and Necessity*. Oxford: Basil Blackwell.
Lewis, D.K. 1976: Survival and identity. In Rorty, A. (ed.), *The Identities of Persons*. California: University of California Press. Reprinted in Lewis, D.K. (1983), *Philosophical Papers*, Vol. 1. Oxford: Oxford University Press.
Quine, W.V.O. 1960: *Word and Object*. Cambridge, Mass.: MIT Press.
——1963: *From a Logical Point of View*. New York: Harper and Row.
——1973: *The Roots of Reference*. La Salle, Illinois: Open Court.
Van Inwagen, P. 1990: And yet they are not three gods but one god. In Morris, T. (ed.), *Philosophy and Christian Faith*. Notre Dame, Ind.: University of Notre Dame Press.
Wiggins, D. 1967: *Identity and Spatio-temporal Continuity*. Oxford: Basil Blackwell.
——1968: On being in the same place at the same time. *Philosophical Review*, 77, 90–5.
——1980: *Sameness and Substance*. Oxford: Basil Blackwell.

Glossary

Absolute versus relative notions of necessity/possibility: When 'necessity' and 'possibility' are qualified by prefixing 'physical', 'natural', 'biological' or the like, the notions expressed are probably best understood as relative to the assumption of the laws of the discipline to which the adjective alludes. To say, for example, that it is physically necessary that P is to claim that, given the laws of physics, it must be true that P (i.e. that it is a logical consequence of the laws of physics that P). Similarly, the claim that it is physically possible that P would normally be understood as the claim that the laws of physics do not exclude its being true that P (i.e. that it is logically consistent with the laws of physics that P). If, as is plausible, we allow that the universe might have behaved according to different physical laws, so that what is physically necessary, as things are, might not have been true, our notion of physical necessity could be said to be merely relative. Sometimes, however, when we claim that it is necessary that P, we mean to deny that there is any possibility of things being otherwise – we are claiming absolute necessity. Such an absolute notion is probably intended in claims about logical or metaphysical necessity. In terms of possible worlds, it is absolutely necessary that P if P holds true at all possible worlds without qualification; whereas it suffices for it to be physically necessary that P that P holds true at all physically possible worlds (i.e. all possible worlds where the actual physical laws hold), and similarly for other relative kinds of necessity.

Absolute versus relative identity: the contrast between absolute and relative identity has its home in the debate over Peter Geach's Relative Identity Thesis, given in 'Identity', *Review of Metaphysics*, 21 (1967). An absolute-identity relation is an equivalence relation which satisfies Leibniz's Law; a relative-identity relation is an equivalence relation which does not. It is uncontroversial that some relations are mere relative-identity relations. In fact, of course, this is true of all equivalence relations not satisfying Leibniz's Law (q.v.). What is controversial is whether an equivalence relation expressible in the form '*x* is the same A as *y*', where 'A' is a sortal term, can be a mere relative-identity relation, and whether absolute identity is expressible at all. Geach answers the first of these questions affirmatively and the second negatively.

Abstract objects: The distinction between abstract and concrete entities is usually thought to be exhaustive and mutually exclusive. A popular view is that the hallmark of the concrete is existence in physical space and/or time. As a corollary of this, it is often held that abstract entities lack causal powers and are consequently incapable of entering into causal relations with other things (though this threatens to make our knowledge of them problematic). In opposition to this way of characterizing the abstract/concrete divide, others have been proposed: for instance, some philosophers characterize abstract entities as ones which depend logically for their existence upon the existence of certain other entities (as, for example, a smile is said to depend for its existence upon the face whose smile it is), while others characterize abstract entities as the products of some sort of mental or logical process of 'abstraction' from concepts (as when numbers and geometrical shapes are said to be such products).

Acquisition argument: Common term for an objection (associated particularly with Michael Dummett) to any semantic theory which allows the nature of speakers' private states (see Privacy) to influence the meaning of the words they use: it cannot explain how a learner ever acquires an understanding of the language. The argument turns on the point that the meanings to be learned would depend on the nature of the private states of the already-competent speaker, something which cannot, by definition, be known to anyone else. The Acquisition Argument is a close relation of the arguments from Communicability (q.v.) and Manifestation (q.v.). (See Chapter 6, MEANING AND PRIVACY.) Interest in these arguments has been aroused by Dummett's suggestion that they support an 'anti-realist' approach to semantics, shifting emphasis away from the conditions under which a sentence is true, perhaps evidence-transcendently (q.v.), towards those under which a speaker might properly assert it. (See also Chapter 12, REALISM AND ITS OPPOSITIONS.)

Analyses, reductive and reciprocal: An analysis of a concept breaks up a given concept (the analysandum concept) into its component concepts (the analysans concepts). An analysis is represented by a biconditional, thus (in the case of meaning): X means that p iff . . . [favoured analysans concepts]. Analyses are usually taken to be reductive in nature, which is to say that the analysans concepts are held to be more fundamental or basic (in some sense to be specified) than the analysandum concept. But analyses may also be reciprocal in nature, meaning that the concepts on either side of the biconditional are seen as on a par – the idea being that whilst the proposed analysis is non-reductive, it illuminates the concepts involved by drawing out important links between them.

Asymmetric Dependence Theory (ADT): ADT is a development of the intuitive idea that the truth-conditions of a thought are resilient with respect to other causes of the thought. According to asymmetric dependence theory a Mentalese (q.v.) predicate C refers to the property P if C locks onto P (Fodor, *Psychosemantics*, MIT Press, 1987; *A Theory of Content*, MIT Press, 1990). C locks onto P just in case (i) it is a law that Ps cause Cs, (ii) there is some Q other than P such that Qs cause Cs, and for any Q distinct from P, if Qs causes Cs then the causal connection between Qs and Cs depends on the Ps-cause-Cs law, but not the other way round. In other words, if Qs failed to cause Cs it would still be the case that Ps caused Cs; but if Ps failed to cause Cs then Qs wouldn't cause them either. ADT solves the disjunction problem (q.v.), since not all the causes of C constitute its reference. However, the theory is difficult to evaluate, since it is not clear exactly what the dependence relation between laws (or causal relations) is, and whether it is naturalistic.

Bivalence: The Principle of Bivalence asserts that every statement is true or false. It should be distinguished from the Law of Excluded Middle, according to which every instance of the schema 'P or not-P' is true. Under the assumption that any false statement's negation is true, Bivalence entails Excluded Middle. But Excluded Middle does not entail Bivalence, since many-valued and supervaluational semantics may validate the former but do not validate the latter (see **Law of Excluded Middle**). Unrestricted endorsement of Bivalence has been taken, especially by Michael Dummett, as the hallmark of a realist position with regard to statements of some given kind. On some views about vagueness, Bivalence fails for vague statements, which are held to be neither true nor false in borderline cases.

Causal theory of reference: A causal theory of reference is a theory that attempts to explain the nature of the relation between the use of a referring expression and the referent – to say what it is about the use of an expression in virtue of which it has the referent that it has. What all such theories have in common is the thesis that the reference relation should be explained in terms of a causal or explanatory connection between the object that is the referent and the speaker's use of the expression: the referent of a name, as used on a particular occasion, is that object which plays a certain role in the causal process that results in the speaker's use of the name on that occasion. The constructive task of such a theory is to say more specifically how an object must be causally related to the use of the expression in order to be the referent of the expression.

Character, meaning and content: The terms "meaning" and "content" are used in many ways in philosophy, and it is always important to check what a particular author may have in mind. In the usage of Chapter 23, INDEXICALS AND DEMONSTRATIVES, meanings are properties of types of expressions, fixed by the rules of language; contents are properties of specific utterances. In the case of indexicals and expressions containing indexicals, the content of an utterance will not be fully determined by the meaning of the expressions used, but will also depend on context. "Character" is often used instead of "meaning," following David Kaplan in his work on demonstratives.

Cognitive command: The cognitive-command constraint is proposed by Crispin Wright as one of several features or marks in virtue of which realism concerning the subject-matter of a given discourse whose characteristic statements qualify for at least minimal truth (q.v.) may be maintained. Roughly, a discourse satisfies this constraint just in case it is a priori that differences of opinion arising within it can be satisfactorily explained only in terms of something worth describing as a cognitive shortcoming in one or other of the disagreed parties – at least one of the parties to the disagreement is lacking relevant information, or her assessment of the data is distorted by prejudice or idiosyncratic standards, or some such. The intended contrast is with cases in which disagreement may persist after all the relevant information is in, say because the disagreed parties diverge in their affective (non-cognitive) reactions to the facts – as is plausibly the case with divergent judgements about what is beautiful or funny, for example. [See also **Euthyphro contrast, Wide cosmological role**.]

Coherence: Coherence theories of truth hold that the truth of a belief consists in its coherence with the main body of our beliefs; coherence theories of knowledge hold that a belief's justification (but not necessarily its truth) consists in the same coherence. Those who hold these theories vary over what they understand by "coherence". Usually it is agreed that a coherent system must be consistent, and the differences are over what further requirements there are; though clearly they must be determined by the main body of our beliefs. Breadth, together with some sort of overall simplicity, are often required. What these requirements amount to depends on the role assigned to experience. Some hold that the coherent system must fit (in some manner hard to specify) with the content of experience as presented pre-conceptually. Some hold that experience can bear on the coherent system only by providing us with experiential beliefs, but that these beliefs have a special status: their truth (or their justification) is direct, not a matter of coherence, though to all other beliefs the coherence theory applies. Some, again, hold that their truth (or their justification) does consist in coherence: perhaps the most consistent line for a coherence theorist.

Communicability argument: Common term for an objection (associated particularly with Michael Dummett) to any semantic theory which allows the nature of speakers' private states (see **Privacy**) to influence the meaning of the words they use: it cannot explain how there can be communication between speaker and hearer. For if the former's meaning depends on the nature of their private states, what they mean is (by the definition of a private state, see **Privacy**) unknowable to the hearer. Yet for communication to take place the hearer must know what the speaker means. The Communicability Argument is a close relation of the arguments from Acquisition (q.v.) and Manifestation (q.v.). (See Chapter 6, MEANING AND PRIVACY.) Interest in these arguments has been aroused by Dummett's suggestion that they support an 'anti-realist' approach to semantics, shifting emphasis away from the conditions under which a sentence is true – perhaps evidence-transcendently (q.v.) – towards those under which a speaker might properly assert it.

Compositionality: A theory of meaning is said to be compositional when (a) it has only finitely many axioms and (b) delivers up meaning-specifying theorems on the basis of those axioms in such a way that the semantic structure of the sentences of the language is thereby exhibited. Intuitively, a compositional theory of meaning would serve up a meaning-specifying theorem for "The man with the red nose is drinking whisky" on the basis of the meanings of its constituent words and their mode of syntactic combination. An example of a non-compositional theory of meaning for a language with only finitely many sentences would be a long list of meaning-specifying theorems, one for each sentence of the language; an example of a non-compositional theory of meaning for a language with infinitely many sentences would be provided by an infinitary axiom schema such as *A is True iff P*, where "*P*" could be replaced by any declarative sentence of the language concerned and "*A*" by the quotational name of that sentence (assuming, for simplicity, that the correct form of a meaning-specification is a statement of truth-conditions). The construction of compositional theories of meaning is thought by some philosophers to throw light on such phenomena as Semantic creativity and the learnability (q.v.) of natural languages.

Context: The context of an utterance is the situation in which it occurs. The context is often needed to resolve questions about what words stand for. Context can be relevant, however, in different ways. Sometimes it is relevant to determining which expressions are used. Sometimes it is relevant to the resolution of ambiguities: to determine with which meanings expressions have been used. In the case of indexicals, context remains relevant when both the identity and the meaning of expressions are known, for the meanings of the expressions are rules that fix the designation of the expressions relative to contextual factors.

Context Principle: A principle enunciated in several forms by Frege in his *Foundations of Arithmetic* (1884: Eng. trans. 1959), asserting that it is only in the context of a complete sentence or proposition that a word has meaning (*Bedeutung*). In *Foundations*, Frege undoubtedly appeals to the principle to justify his view that it is not necessary for a word to have meaning that we should be able to point to what it stands for, and thence in arguing against psychologistic tendencies which seek to identify the meaning of number-words with mental entities. It is also taken by him, at least during his middle period, as justifying the procedure of defining terms contextually. Both its interpretation and its wider bearing upon issues in the philosophy of language and ontology are controversial. This is in part because, at the time of writing *Foundations*, Frege had not explicitly drawn his celebrated distinction between sense (*Sinn*) and reference (*Bedeutung*), so that it is unclear whether the principle should be taken as applying to sense, or to reference, or to both. Taken as applying to sense, the principle may be seen as underpinning his view that the sense of subsentential expressions consists in their contribution to the sense of complete sentences containing them, and so as supporting a position intermediate between semantic atomism at one extreme and semantic holism (q.v.) at the other. Taken as applying to reference, the principle may be seen as underpinning the view (to which Frege also subscribes) that it suffices for terms to have reference that they figure as parts of more complex expressions (e.g. sentences) which have reference.

Convention: The fundamental idea in the application of the notion of convention to language is to capture the arbitrary nature of the association between a word and its meaning. This *idea* is not in dispute by philosophers, despite the fact that at least one philosopher does deny that language is conventional. To understand this it is necessary to understand that the concept of convention has come to be associated with the idea of a kind of rational control by speakers over the meaning of their words. It is this that some philosophers dispute. Thus one finds two positions in the literature: (1) language is conventional in the sense of being both arbitrary and under speakers' rational control, and (2) language is conventional only in the sense of being arbitrary. At least one philosopher (Davidson) claims to reject the idea of language as governed by conventions altogether; however, on closer inspection one finds that the idea that meaning is arbitrary is still retained (only the association between this idea and convention is abandoned).

Convention T: see **Criterion of material adequacy**

Counterpart theory: An alternative semantics for quantified modal logic, due to David Lewis. In standard semantics, a sentence '*Possibly, Fa*' is true iff there is a possible world in which *a* is *F*. In counterpart-theoretic semantics, '*Possibly, Fa*' is true iff there is a possible world in which some counterpart of *a* is *F*. In Lewis's own version the counterpart relation is determined by similarity, but this philosophical view about the nature of counterparthood is only one of many that are consistent with the semantics.

Criterion of identity: The general notion of a criterion of identity is the notion of a standard by which identity is to be judged. A paradigm is Frege's example: the criterion of identity for directions is parallelism of lines. In this case the criterion of identity for one type of object is a relation between objects of another type. One question about criteria of identity is whether this must always be the case, or whether a criterion of identity for one type of object can be a relation between objects of the same type. A second question is whether a criterion of identity needs to be a relation at all. A standard, though controversial view is that reference to an object is only possible against the background of a criterion of identity, and hence that any proper name must have as part of its sense a criterion of identity.

Criterion of material adequacy: When Tarski set out to define "true sentence of language L", by the systematic determination of its extension, he stipulated that the definition should be formally rigorous, should make no use of semantic notions, and should in addition be *materially adequate*, or, in other words, should grasp the current meaning of the notion of truth as it is known intuitively. The definition must be faithful to the substance of the notion, in other words. What this involved (see Chapter 1, MEANING AND TRUTH-CONDITIONS, §16–17) was that the definition should *entail*, for each sentence of the language for which "true sentence" is to be defined, a biconditional of the form:

True x if and only if p

where the "x" holds a place for a designation of the sentence in question, and "p" holds a place for a translation of the sentence into the metalanguage in which the definition is being constructed. In the case where the object-language is a proper part of the metalanguage, the object-language sentence will count as a translation of itself. The same sentence, say "snow is white", is then referred to on the left-hand side and used on the right-hand side of the biconditional that the truth-definition must entail.

NB. A biconditional such as '"snow is white" is true if and only if snow is white' would be called in propositional logic a material equivalence. This use of the word "material" in logic has absolutely nothing to do with what Tarski means by material adequacy in his statement of Convention T. The material adequacy of a truth-definition involves the fidelity of the definition to the intuitive notion of truth. Material adequacy is seen by Tarski as a *substantial* requirement.

***De dicto* and *de re* ascriptions:** One can ascribe a property – or a "mode" of having a property, such as having it necessarily – to what a sentence says (a *dictum*) or to an individual (a *res*). Ascriptions of the first sort are *de dicto*, of the latter *de re*. To say that the claim that my mother had no children is possibly true is to make a (silly) *de dicto* ascription; to say, of my mother, that she might have been childless, is to make a (true) *de re* one. *De re*, but not *de dicto*, modal ascriptions have implications about the essential properties of an object. Sentences with quantifier phrases and operators (such as 'my mother might not have had a child') are often ambiguous between a *de dicto* and a *de re* reading. Some, such as Quine, have challenged the intelligibility of *de re* modal claims and of devices, such as quantification into modal contexts, typically used to make them.

De dicto and *de re* propositional-attitude ascriptions are distinguished as above: the first relates one to a *dictum* (a proposition); the latter to an individual and an attribute. In a *de re* ascription, such as 'Kristen believes, of my mother, that she is childless', the position which picks out the *res* (here, that of 'my mother') is transparent; in a *de dicto* reading of 'Kristen believes that my mother is childless', the position of 'my mother' is opaque. It is a matter of dispute whether this distinction, between ways of *talking* about attitudes, corresponds to a distinction between *kinds* of attitudes – whether, for example, there is a special kind of *de re* belief which involves an epistemically significant connection or acquaintance with an object.

***De re* senses:** A *de re* sense is a mode of presentation of an object which cannot be entertained if that object does not exist. *De re* senses were first introduced as such in the works of John McDowell, such as "On the Sense and Reference of a Proper Name", *Mind*, 86 (1977), pp. 159–85, and Gareth Evans, as in "Understanding Demonstratives", in *Meaning and Understanding*, H. Parret and J. Bouveresse (Berlin: W. de Gruyter, 1981) and *The Varieties of Reference* (Oxford: Clarendon Press, 1982), in which they attributed the notion to Frege.

According to *de-re*-sense theorists there are classes of terms which, when used, express *de re* senses, if they have content at all. If an occurrence of a term in such a class does not denote, then it does not have a sense, and hence is contentless. The most plausible candidates for terms, occurrences of which express *de re* senses, are demonstratives and indexicals. For instance, according to Evans (1982, chapter 6), grasp of the sense of an occurrence of a demonstrative, such as "this", is constituted in part by the existence of an "information link" between the denotation of that occurrence of "this" and the subject. If an occurrence of "this" does not denote, then there is no such information link, and hence nothing that would count as grasping the sense of that occurrence. But a sense which is such that there is nothing for it to be grasped is not a sense at all. Hence, if an occurrence of "this" does not denote, then according to Evans's account, it lacks a sense, and so is contentless.

Deflationary conception of truth: The view that the predicate 'true' does not stand for any real property, but, excepting its use in indirect endorsements (e.g. 'Fermat's last theorem is true') or compendious ones (e.g. 'Everything he said is true'), is no more than a device of disquotation (q.v.).

Degree of truth: If two things are borderline cases of red, but one is redder than the other, the redder one is, intuitively, a better candidate for being something of which "red" is true. One might try to capture this idea in terms of "red" being more true of the redder object than of the less red. This gives one an ordering. One might try to use this, along with further data (e.g. comparisons between closeness of pairs in the order) to create a scale. Finally, one might find end-points, to correspond to definite truth and definite falsehood. The points on such a closed scale are degrees of truth. Applied to vagueness, a degrees-of-truth theory does good justice to our feeling that a vague statement is not completely true, but encounters many difficulties, including ones relating to the assignment of degrees to complex sentences, and ones relating to higher-order vagueness.

Denoting versus naming: see **Referentialism**

Describing versus referring: see **Referentialism**

Direct reference: 1. Say that a term (or its use) is *Fregean* if its reference at each possible situation s is what is presented or described, at s, by the term's sense (or by some descriptive condition which the term supplies). A *directly referential* term is one whose uses are *non*-Fregean, since the term's referent, at each situation, is semantically constrained to be the actual referent. David Kaplan, who introduced the terminology, argued that demonstratives and proper names are devices of direct reference. Note that, on this use, a directly referential term may make a "descriptive contribution" to what a sentence says, so long as that contribution is truth-conditionally irrelevant.

2. On another usage, a directly referential term is one whose sole contribution to what a sentence says is its referent; sentences with such terms express singular propositions. Direct-reference accounts of propositional-attitude talk take demonstratives and names to be thus directly referential, and take attitude ascriptions to ascribe (only) relations to the propositions determined by their complements.

Disjunction problem: The disjunction problem is a problem for crude causal accounts of reference and truth-conditions. On a crude causal account the truth-condition of a belief-type B is the type of states of affairs that cause B. The difficulty is that if the state of affairs S causes the belief B, and the state of affairs S* causes the belief B, then the disjunctive state of affairs S or S* causes B. That is, according to the theory B's truth-conditions are the disjunction of all its causes. This makes error impossible. Naturalistic semantic theories attempt to deal with the problem by specifying a distinction between those causes that constitute B's truth-conditions and those that don't.

Disquotation: According to the disquotational principle for the predicate 'true', a true biconditional results whatever sentence is substituted for the variable 'P' in the scheme:

'P' is true if and only if P

If it is granted that truth is properly predicated of sentences (as distinct from the thoughts or propositions which sentences may be used to express), and provided that the sentence quoted in the left-hand component of the biconditional is taken to be (a quoted version of) the sentence used in the right-hand component, it appears indisputable that this principle captures a fundamental feature of the notion of truth, since the principle, so understood, appears to be no more than a metalinguistic version of what is usually called the Equivalence Thesis: It is true that P if and only if P. An associated – but much more controversial – thesis is that the predicate 'true' does not stand for a genuine property, and is little more than a device of disquotation, needed only for the purpose of indirect or compendious endorsement (as in 'Pythagoras's Theorem is true' and 'Whatever Aristotle says is true', respectively) – this is the Deflationary Conception of Truth. Closely related is the famous Redundancy Theory, according to which there is no more to (the concept of) truth than is involved in accepting all instances of the disquotation principle, or the equivalence thesis.

Effectively decidable: A statement is effectively decidable if there is a routine procedure which can be followed in any given case and which is guaranteed to lead to a correct decision as to the statement's truth-value. Derivatively, a predicate is said to be (effectively) decidable if there is a routine procedure for determining, with regard to an object (or sequence of objects, in case of an n-place predicate for $n \geq 2$) whether it satisfies that predicate – equivalently, whether the predicate is true of that object (or sequence of objects). Effectively decidable statements are, by their very nature, incapable of being undetectably – or evidence-transcendently (q.v.) – true.

Epistemic conception of meaning: In one usage, this denotes the view that to understand a word or sentence is to know rules (i.e. conventions) which govern its role in our language practices, in particular of assertion and inference. Rules governing the use of words take the form of conventions for introducing and eliminating terms in a language; they in turn determine when a sentence is assertible and what is inferable from it.

In another distinct, but perhaps related usage, an epistemic conception of meaning is any view which insists that sentence-meanings be given in terms of conditions whose satisfaction is always, at least in principle, a recognizable matter – such as conditions of warranted assertion, rather than Evidence-transcendent (q.v.) truth.

Epistemic conception of vagueness: This is the view that vague statements are either true or false (and not both) in borderline cases, although we cannot know which (see **Bivalence**). Similarly, on this view, the major premise of a sorites paradox, e.g. 'For all n, if n + 1 grains make a heap then n grains make a heap', is falsified by some number n, although we cannot know which. The epistemic view permits the retention of classical logic, truth-conditional semantics and disquotational principles about truth (q.v.) for vague languages. It is not implied that every unknowable truth is vague. Rather, the view identifies vagueness with a particular kind of unknowability whose origin is conceptual.

Epistemic possibility/necessity: Modal words ('possible', 'necessary', 'may', 'must', etc.) are sometimes used to express claims about what is possible, or necessary, given our state of knowledge or information. Thus when we say of some acquaintance whose intentions are as yet unclear to us, and are perhaps not yet determinate, that she may come to the party, we are probably not merely claiming that it is a bare logical possibility that she will come, but that we know of nothing from which it can safely be inferred that she will not come. If so, our claim is one of epistemic possibility. A correlative use of 'must' to express epistemic necessity is perhaps exemplified when we say, when the person we are expecting to meet conspicuously fails to alight from the train, that she must have missed it. This use of modal words needs to be carefully distinguished from their use to express other kinds of necessity and possibility, since what is epistemically possible may well not be, for example, logically or metaphysically possible. Thus it is plausible, at least, that whichever of Goldbach's Conjecture (that every even number greater than 2 is the sum of two prime numbers) and its negation is true, is necessarily true. But in our present state of knowledge, both the Conjecture and its negation are epistemically possible.

Error theories: An error theory for a given area of discourse maintains that statements belonging to the discourse are aimed at truth, but are systematically false, owing to the failure of some presupposition – usually ontological in character – of the discourse as a whole. Thus an error theory contrasts with certain other types of anti-realist position, according to which statements of the seemingly problematic kind are to be reinterpreted in some way; for example, by reductive translation into statements of some other unproblematic type, or, quite differently, by construing them as having some other than assertoric function (as on the emotivist theory of ethical utterances, according to which they are aimed not at stating facts but at evincing feelings or attitudes). In the classic example, John Mackie maintained that ordinary moral discourse is error-ridden because there do not exist the distinctively non-natural properties or moral facts required for the truth of its statements. Other examples are the view that mathematical statements are uniformly false because their truth would call for the existence of number, sets or other kinds of abstract entity (denied by the error theorist, in this case a nominalist); and eliminativist views about 'folk'-psychological discourse.

Essentiality of origin: A thesis due to Kripke and sometimes called 'the necessity of origin'. It claims that the origins of things of certain specified kinds are essential to them. For instance, an individual human being may be said to originate essentially from the zygote he or she in fact originated from. The thesis can also be applied to more abstract entities to which the notion of origin is applicable, such as species.

Essential property: A property P is traditionally said to be an essential property of an object x if x could not lack P, or, better, if x could not exist while lacking P. Without the qualification about existence, no property would be essential to a contingently existing object if possession of the property by an object required the object to exist. Unfortunately, with the qualification about existence, existence itself becomes an essential property, which is not the intent of the traditional notion.

Euthyphro contrast: The Euthyphro contrast, prominent in a good deal or recent discussion of realism and opposed positions, and especially in the work of Crispin Wright, concerns whether our best judgements in a given area are to be regarded as tracking an independently constituted realm of facts (the realist view) or whether, rather, we should view truth for the discourse's statements as somehow determined by, or constituted out of, our best judgements (the anti-realist option). The label recalls Plato's dialogue, which has Plato maintaining that pious acts are thought to be so by the gods because those acts are pious, while Euthyphro contends for the opposed view, that pious acts are so because the gods take them to be so. Realist and anti-realist may be presumed to agree that there will be a coincidence between the facts of the matter and our judgements made under optimal conditions. The issue then concerns the direction of dependence: are such judgements true because they match up with independently constituted facts, or are those facts themselves no more than a reflection of our best judgements? [See also **Cognitive command, Wide cosmological role**.]

Evidence transcendence: To hold that statements of some kind may be evidence-transcendently true or false is to claim that such statements may have determinate truth-values without its being possible, even in principle, for us to discover what those truth-values are. It is standardly taken to be a mark of a certain type of realism with respect to a class of statements to maintain that those statements may be evidence-transcendently true, or false. A realist of this kind holds that the meanings of (at least some of) our sentences are to be given in terms of truth-conditions, the satisfaction of which is a potentially evidence-transcendent matter. The opposed anti-realist contention is that the only notions of truth and falsehood which we may justifiably employ are evidentially or epistemically constrained notions – notions according to which there is an essential connection between truth-values and evidence (and hence between sentence meaning/truth-conditions and evidence). [See also **Bivalence**.]

Expressivism: An expressivist treatment of a given region of discourse maintains that, whatever the surface grammatical form of its characteristic utterances may suggest to the contrary, those utterances are not genuinely assertoric or descriptive, aimed at conveying truths concerning a certain subject matter, but are instead properly to be understood as serving to express feelings or attitudes. A classic example is the logical-positivists' treatment of ethical utterances – anticipated by David Hume and generally known as the emotive theory – as serving to evince feelings of moral approval or disapproval.

Extension/Intension: *Extension* is a generalization of the notion of reference. Standardly, the extension of a singular term is its referent; of an adjective, noun, or verb, it is the collection of things of which it is true; of a sentence, it is its truth-value. Extensions can be assigned to other meaningful expressions, such as quantifiers.

Some languages are *extensional*. Substitution of expressions with the same extension doesn't change the extension of the whole. (Interpreted) versions of first-order logic are examples: Replacing term *t* with term *s* in a sentence can't change the sentence's extension (truth-value) in such languages, if *t* and *s* have the same extension (referent); likewise, interchange of co-extensive predicates cannot alter a sentence's truth-value. Natural languages certainly don't *seem* extensional (though some have claimed otherwise): 'centaur' and 'unicorn' have the same extension; 'wanted to see a centaur' and 'wanted to see a unicorn' do not.

Intension is used in a variety of ways. A standard use identifies an expression's intension with some aspect of meaning which determines extension. A technical but important use is from possible-worlds semantics, where expressions receive extensions relative to "possible worlds"; an expression's intension is the rule or function assigning its extension at each world. Modal languages are typically intensional – the intension of an expression being determined by the intensions of its parts – but not extensional. David Lewis, Richard Montague and Robert Stalnaker have identified propositions and properties with possible-worlds intensions.

Externalism: Externalism is the view that semantic properties of at least some concepts and thoughts, especially the properties of making reference to certain entities and of having certain truth-conditions, do not supervene on intrinsic properties of mental or neural states. Arguments for externalism are mostly appeals to intuitions concerning thought-experiments in which thinkers are supposed to be identical with respect to their intrinsic properties, but are in different environmental contexts: see Hilary Putnam, *Mind, Language and Reality: Philosophical Papers Vol. II* (Cambridge, 1975), pp. 223–9. If externalism is true then the facts in virtue of which the semantic properties of concepts and thoughts are instantiated must involve relations between the thinker and her environment.

External realism: see **Metaphysical realism**

Facts: Our conception of a fact is ambivalent, in a philosophically confusing way. On the one hand, facts belong to the world and are not of our making (except in so far as we have made the world as it is: the fact that there is coffee here is due to something I did). In the traditional version of the correspondence theory of truth, facts in the world are what true propositions correspond with. On the other hand, many people think the fact that Caesar crossed the Rubicon is a different fact from the fact that the conqueror of Gaul crossed the Rubicon, even though there must be a sense in which only one thing happened. There is a case for saying that ordinary language encourages us to individuate facts as finely as we individuate statements or propositions; hence Strawson's (1950) thought that facts are just what true statements state. This can mislead people into thinking that, since facts are individuated by the concepts we use to express them, the reality to which true statements correspond cannot be fully independent of how we think about it and the concepts we employ. It might be better to give up calling that reality "the facts".

First-order languages: By a first-order language is meant, primarily, a formal language whose logical vocabulary comprises sentential connectives (usually negation, conjunction, disjunction, the conditional and the biconditional), together with quantifiers binding just individual- or name-variables. It is the latter condition which determines the order of the language. Higher-order languages contain, additionally, quantifiers binding variables ranging over entities of other kinds, such as properties and relations. Thus '$\forall xFx$' and '$\exists x\exists yGxy$' might be sentences of a first-order language, since they involve only quantification over individuals; but '$\forall F\forall x(Fx \vee \neg Fx)$' must belong to a language of (at least) the second order, since it involves quantification over properties of individuals. A language will be second-order if it permits quantification over properties and relations of individuals, but not quantification over entities of any 'higher' type, such as properties of properties of individuals, etc. By a natural extension, 'first- (or second-, etc.) language' may be used to refer to natural languages whose logical vocabulary does not exceed that of first- (or second-, etc.) formal languages.

Frege's Puzzle: Frege's Puzzle is this: How can (uses of) sentences which differ only by terms referring to the same thing differ epistemically (for example, in how informative they are)? This is a puzzle for anyone who believes (a) what a sentence-use says is individuated in terms of what the user speaks of in using the sentence (so that what 'Loetze wrote' says turns on the reference, not the sense, of 'Loetze'); and (b) that the epistemic properties of a sentence supervene on what it says. Frege's puzzle is the occasion for Frege's introduction of the notion of sense; it is seen as a major embarrassment for contemporary "direct reference" accounts of assertion.

Full-blooded vs. modest theory of meaning: Contrast introduced by Michael Dummett. A modest theory of meaning for a language is, as he puts it in *The Seas of Language* (Oxford, 1993), p. viii, not intended to "convey the concepts expressible" in it, but to "convey an understanding of that language to one who already had those concepts". A full-blooded theory should also specify what it is for a speaker of the language "to possess the concept it expresses".

Generality Constraint: The Generality Constraint is a version of the principle of compositionality. Applied to linguistic understanding, it entails that the ability to understand, say, a simple subject–predicate sentence Fa is composed of distinct abilities, the ability to understand a and the ability to understand F. These abilities must, furthermore, be manifested in the understanding of other sentences involving a and F.

A more exact characterization of the Generality Constraint (as applied to linguistic understanding) is as follows. Let e be an expression. If someone understands e, then that person possesses the ability to understand every sentence S which results from placing e into the open position of some linguistic string L which satisfies the following conditions: (1) that person understands all the expressions in L (and the person has a mastery of the relevant ways of composing the elements of the resulting sentence); (2) the result is syntactically and semantically well-formed; and (3) the result is not too complex to be processed by the speaker.

For example, suppose it is claimed that someone understands the predicate, "feels pain". If the Generality Constraint is true, then that person must also have the ability to understand sentences such as "I feel pain" and "Bill feels pain", if she grasps the first-person pronoun, the name "Bill", and predication. (Thus, the possibility that someone has an understanding of their own mental self-ascriptions, and third-personal physical ascriptions, but no understanding of third-personal mental ascriptions, is inconsistent with the Generality Constraint.)

Traditionally, the Generality Constraint is formulated as a prerequisite for possessing the ability to entertain thoughts, rather than in terms of linguistic understanding. The Generality Constraint was first introduced and put to use in chapter 3 of Strawson's *Individuals* (Methuen, 1959), though it is implicit in many defences of the compositionality of language and thought.

Higher-order vagueness: The word 'heap' has first-order vagueness because it can have borderline cases; it has second-order vagueness because the expression 'borderline case of "heap"' can itself have borderline cases. More formally, suppose that there is a standard way of constructing a metalanguage for any given language, in which any vagueness in the latter can appropriately be described. Given a language L, inductively define a sequence of languages L_1, L_2, L_3, . . . by letting L_1 be L itself and L_{n+1} be the metalanguage for L_n. Then L is nth-order vague if and only if L_n is vague in the ordinary sense; L is higher-order vague if and only if it is nth-order vague for some $n \geq 2$. Corresponding notions of vagueness can be defined for individual expressions. It is plausible that all natural languages are nth-order vague for all n. Theories of vagueness often have difficulty in accommodating higher-order vagueness because they treat the metalanguage for a vague language as though it were precise.

Homophonic specification of meaning or of reference, or of truth-conditions: When the object-language (containing the expressions whose meaning/reference/truth-conditions are to be given) forms part of the metalanguage (in which the specification is to be effected), those meanings, etc., may be specified homophonically, by using those very expressions themselves. Thus:

'cat' means cat
'mice' refers to mice
'cats eat mice' is true if and only if cats eat mice.

Hyperintensional: 1. Properties and propositions (thought of as what predicates and sentences express) are sometimes identified with constructions out of things such as possible worlds. *Hyperintensional* theories hold that propositions (and/or properties) are basic entities, not reducible to constructions from worlds or the like, and that they are more fine-grained than constructions from possible worlds (since, for instance, predicates can express different properties although they have the same intension).

2. Linguistic contexts in which expressions with the same (possible-worlds) intension are not inter-substitutable *salva veritate* are sometimes called *hyperintensional*. Propositional-attitude contexts are the paradigm of such linguistic contexts.

Indeterminacy of translation is the thesis, associated with Quine, that the methods of radical translation (q.v.) do not uniquely determine a single translation from one language to another. In other words, no matter how much linguistic–behavioural data radical translators of a given language have to go on – indeed, even if they had access to all such data available in principle – they could still arrive at distinct manuals of translation which, while making optimum sense of the native speakers' linguistic behaviour, were in conflict with each other about the correct translation of particular expressions. The thesis of the indeterminacy of translation proper maintains that this conflict can take the form of a divergence over the *truth-conditions* of certain sentences, so that one optimal manual of translation may represent a particular utterance as saying something true, while another represents it as saying something false. In a weaker form, however, the thesis is that the assignment of reference to the constituents of a sentence – singular terms and predicates, for instance, occurring within it – can vary, even though the truth-conditions of the sentence be fixed (see **Inscrutability of reference**).

Indexicals: Indexicals are words such as "I", "you", "here" and "now". The designation of such words (what they "stand for") shifts from use to use, depending on various contextual factors. The designation of "I" depends on who the speaker is; the designation of "you" on the intended audience; the designation of "now" on the time, and so forth. Demonstratives such as "this" and "that", and demonstrative phrases such as "that man" or "this computer" are usually reckoned to be a subclass of indexicals.

Indiscriminability: To discriminate between x and y is to recognize a difference between x and y. Thus x and y are indiscriminable if and only if no difference is recognizable between them. Things may be indiscriminable in one respect and not in another (e.g. in colour but not in shape), by one means and not by another (e.g. by chemical analysis but not by touch), by one person and not by another, when presented in one way and not when presented in another, and so on. In general, indiscriminability is a reflexive and symmetric, but not transitive relation: each term in a series may be indiscriminable from its neighbours, even though the first and last terms are easily discriminable. Sorites paradoxes (q.v.) result from the assumption that whenever two things are indiscriminable, an observational term correctly applicable to one must also be correctly applicable to the other.

Individual essence: Intuitively, the individual essence of a thing are those features of it which in some sense make it what it is, or constitute its identity. A collection of essential properties is an individual essence of an object x if it is not possible for any object other than x to possess them all. However, this definition is consistent with a thing's having more than one individual essence, and so does not entirely capture the traditional notion.

Informational theories of truth-conditional content: According to informational theories, the truth-condition of a belief-state B is the information that B carries, or would carry under certain circumstances: see F. Dretske, *Knowledge and the Flow of Information* (MIT Press, 1981). Different accounts result from different specifications of the circumstances in which information determines truth-conditions. For example, optimal-conditions theories specify the conditions as ones which are epistemically optimal: see R. Stalnaker, *Inquiry* (MIT Press, 1984), J. Fodor, "Psychosemantics, or Where Do Truth Conditions Come From?" in *Mind and Cognition*, ed. W. Lycan (Blackwell, 1990). These are conditions in which B is tokened if and only if it is true. Certain teleological theories specify the truth-condition-constituting information as the information that it is B's biological function to carry: see R. Millikan, "Biosemantics", *Journal of Philosophy*, 86 (1989) and D. Papineau, *Philosophical Naturalism* (Oxford: Blackwell, 1993). The accounts so far devised seem either to appeal to intentional specifications of truth-condition-constituting circumstances or to fail to assign determinate truth-conditions.

Inscrutability of reference (see also **Indeterminacy of translation**): The thesis that the truth-condition of a sentence, and hence its truth-value across all possible worlds, may be held constant consistently with variations in the assignment of reference to its constituents, in particular to the singular terms and common nouns which it may contain. That the thesis holds is the gist of Quine's famous 'gavagai' argument, and is ostensibly established in a very general form by Putnam's permutation argument (see **Permutation argument**).

Intension: see **Extension/Intension**

Intensionality: A context is intensional just if its truth-value is liable to be altered by the substitution within it of expressions which have the same Extension (q.v.) as those for which they are substituted. The principal examples of such contexts are modal sentences, sentences ascribing intentional attitudes (see **Intentionality**), and contexts of direct quotation. Thus, it is necessary that nine is greater than seven, but not necessary that the number of planets is greater than seven, although "nine" and "the number of planets" have the same extension (i.e. reference.) Again, someone may believe that all lions have hearts without believing that all lions have kidneys, although "has a heart" and "has kidneys" have the same extension (i.e. are true of the same things). Likewise, 'Richard was called "Cœur de Lion" because of his bravery' may be true, while 'Richard was called "Richard I" because of his bravery' is doubtless false, although "Cœur de Lion" and "Richard I" have the same reference.

Intentionality: That characteristic of mental states which consists in their being *about* something, in their being directed upon some particular (putative) object or state of affairs. The term was coined in this technical sense by the Scholastics (from the Latin *intendo*, "to point") and revived by Brentano, who held that intentionality defines the distinction between the mental and the physical, and constitutes a decisive barrier to any kind of reduction of the former to the latter. Brentano held, more specifically, that the intentionality of the mental shows itself in two characteristics: mental states may be indifferent to the non-existence of their objects – the mere fact that the Holy Grail does not exist is no barrier to Gawain's being correctly described as hoping to find it – and they are typically sensitive to variation in the mode of presentation of the object they concern: Lois Lane may hope to marry Superman, but not hope to marry Clark Kent, for instance, even though they are one and the same.

Derivatively, certain kinds of psychological sentences are described as intentional when they exhibit corresponding linguistic features, i.e. do not sustain wide-scope existential generalization and are prone to the kind of substitution failures associated with Intensionality (q.v.). Ascriptions of propositional attitude – belief, desire, hope, fear, intention and so on – are paradigms of such intentional contexts.

Intention-based semantics: Intention-based semantics is a term that has been used by Stephen Schiffer to refer to Grice's analysis of meaning. The title captures the centrality given to the concept of intention in this analysis. This title also brings out the way in which Schiffer once used Grice's work as part of a larger programme of reducing semantics to psychology and psychology to the physical-cum-functional.

Interpretation: In general terms, an interpretation of a language is an assignment of meanings to the expressions of the language. In the context of the semantic study of formal languages employed in logic, the term 'interpretation' bears a somewhat more precise meaning, which may be illustrated here for the case of a First-order language (q.v.) with logical vocabulary comprising the usual sentential connectives and quantifiers binding individual variables. Giving an interpretation, then, consists in specifying a (non-empty) set – the domain of the interpretation – and, on this basis, assigning references to the various items of primitive non-logical vocabulary, which will always include a selection of predicates, and may also include functional expressions and individual constants. The general idea is that these assignments should be made in such a way as to induce, via the fixed meanings of the logical expressions, truth-values on the sentences of the language, which are then said to be true, or false, relative to that interpretation. The individual variables range over the specified domain, i.e. they may take any of its elements as values. Each 1-place predicate is assigned a subset of the domain – intuitively, the objects in the domain of which it is stipulated to be true on that interpretation; 2-place predicates are assigned sets of ordered pairs of elements of the domain, 3-place predicates sets of ordered triples, and so on. Individual constants are assigned elements of the domain, and functional expressions are assigned functions taking objects in the domain as arguments and yielding objects in the domain as values. Thus a simple sentence 'Rab' will be true under an interpretation I if and only if the ordered pair of elements of I's domain assigned to the constants 'a' and 'b' respectively belongs to the set (of ordered pairs) assigned to the 2-place predicate 'R'. The universally quantified sentence '$\forall$xFx' will be true under I if and only if 'Fx' is true no matter which element of I's domain is taken to be the value of the variable 'x' (i.e. iff every element of the domain belongs to the set assigned to 'F'). A conjunction of sentences 'A & B' will be true under I iff both 'A' and 'B' are separately true under I. And so on.

In terms of these basic ideas, certain further important semantic concepts may be defined. For example, an interpretation I is said to be a model of a set of sentences Γ iff every sentence in Γ is true under I. An inference $\Gamma \vdash A$ is valid iff every model of G is also a model of $\{A\}$. A sentence A is logically true iff every interpretation of A's language is a model of $\{A\}$.

Kinds: Kinds are Universals (q.v.), having Particulars (q.v.) as their instances. Terms denoting kinds belong to the more general categories of Sortal terms (q.v.) and Mass terms (q.v.). Examples belonging to the former category are 'tiger' and 'lemon', while examples belonging to the latter are 'gold' and 'water'. All of these are examples of *natural*-kind terms, which are to be contrasted with terms for *artefactual* kinds, such as 'pencil' and 'yacht'. A distinguishing feature of natural, as opposed to artefactual, kinds is that they are typically subjects of natural scientific law (for example, it is a natural law that gold consists of atoms containing seventy-nine protons in their nuclei). It is nowadays widely held that natural-kind terms are Rigid designators (q.v.) and consequently not definable by means of complex descriptions in the way that empiricist philosophers such as John Locke believed them to be.

Law of excluded middle: The law claims that every instance of "P or not-P" is true, or is a theorem. This is guaranteed by Bivalence (q.v.), given that "not" toggles truth values. However, it can hold without bivalence, for example in a three-valued system in which "not" turns any non-truth into a truth. Among theories of vagueness, supervaluation theories maintain the Law of Excluded Middle, while departing from bivalence: some sentences are neither true (that is, true-on-all-valuations) nor false (that is, false-on-all-valuations); but every instance of "P or not-P" is true-on-all-valuations and so true.

Leibniz's Law: Leibniz's Law is the principle that if *a* is identical with *b* every property of *a* is a property of *b*. It is what distinguishes *absolute* from any form of *relative* identity. There are many apparent counter-examples involving psychological and modal properties, but these cannot be genuine counter-examples, since Leibniz's Law is definitive of absolute identity. Thus Leibniz's Law must be sharply distinguished from the false principle of substitutivity that if '*a*' and '*b*' are two singular terms for the same object, then replacement of '*a*' by '*b*' will be possible *salva veritate* in any context. Leibniz's Law is not in formal conflict with the Relative Identity Thesis (q.v.) of Peter Geach, since the latter entails not that Leibniz's Law is false, but that it is inexpressible, since no language can contain an expression for absolute identity.

Locutionary/Illocutionary/Perlocutionary acts: This threefold distinction was adopted by Austin after he abandoned his constative–performative distinction (see **Performative utterances**). A locutionary act is the act of saying something, characterized by him as a matter of uttering certain words 'with a certain "meaning" in the favourite philosophical sense of that word, i.e. with a certain sense and with a certain reference': see Austin, *How to Do Things with Words* (Oxford, 1962), p. 94. An illocutionary act is the performance of an act *in* saying something in this sense, such as giving a warning, making a promise, etc. A perlocutionary act is an act – such as drawing someone's attention to a bull or reassuring them – performed *through* or *by* the illocutionary act.

Löwenheim–Skolem theorems: These are some theorems in the model theory of first-order logic, established originally in several versions by Leopold Löwenheim and Thoralf Skolem, which disclose limitations on the expressive capacity of first-order languages. The Downward Löwenhiem–Skolem Theorem asserts that if a set of first-order sentences has a model at all, that is, an Interpretation (q.v.) in which all the sentences in the set come out true, then it has a countably infinite model (i.e. a model whose domain has exactly as many elements as there are natural numbers). The Upward Theorem asserts that if such a set of sentences has a model in any infinite cardinality, it has models in every infinite cardinality. The theorems have played a central role in one of Hilary Putnam's arguments directed against the position he calls external or Metaphysical realism (q.v.).

Malin génie: The point of the *malin génie* in Descartes's first *Meditation* is to introduce the most extreme scepticism possible. Some recent philosophers replace the *génie* with a scientist who keeps my brain in a vat, controlling it and all its inputs. The point is the same. No argument could show that I am not being deceived by a *génie*, because the *génie* could make me think arguments sound when they are not; so could the scientist. One can try to undermine the sceptical hypothesis, but one will get nowhere by arguing (as some have) that at least the *génie*/scientist must know some truths; for the *génie*/scientist is only a dramatization of the possibility that our belief-system wholly fails to match the world. The coherence theory of truth attempts to get round it by suggesting that our belief-system, or an idealization of it, determines how the world is. If that were so, there could be no general failure of match. Of course the doubt could still be raised that any particular beliefs (e.g. my present ones) might be mistaken – even my belief that they cohere may yet be false. Perhaps that doubt should not worry us.

Manifestation argument: Common term for an objection (associated particularly with Michael Dummett) to any semantic theory which allows the nature of speakers' private states (see **Privacy**) to influence the meaning of the words they use: it cannot explain how a language-learner could ever show their competence in the language to be learnt. For competence would involve associating the right kind of private state with the words of the language, and whether they are doing this or not can never (by the definition of a private state) be known to anyone else. The Manifestation Argument is a close relation of the arguments from Acquisition (q.v.) and Communicability (q.v.). (See Chapter 6, MEANING AND PRIVACY.) Interest in these arguments has been aroused by Dummett's suggestion that they support an 'anti-realist' approach to semantics, shifting emphasis away from the conditions under which a sentence is true, perhaps Evidence-transcendently (q.v.) towards those under which a speaker might properly assert it.

Mass terms: Mass terms, such as 'water' and 'gold', differ from Sortal terms (q.v.) in being dissective: gold is divisible into parts which are themselves gold, unlike the parts of a horse, which are not themselves horses. They also differ from sortal terms in not supplying principles of enumeration for their instances. Thus, whereas it makes sense to ask *how many* horses there are in a field, it only makes sense to ask *how much* water or gold there is in a room. Even so, mass terms do clearly have Criteria of identity (q.v.) governing their use, for it makes sense to ask whether the gold now in this room is the *same* gold as was in this room yesterday.

Meaning-truth platitude: This is the (allegedly platitudinous, and certainly widely endorsed) principle that 'the truth-value of a statement depends only upon its meaning and the state of the world in relevant respects', a formulation which, along with the term, comes from Crispin Wright's 'Kripke's Account of the Argument against Private Language', *Journal of Philosophy*, 81:12 (1984), pp. 759–78. The principle plays a central role in his argument that Semantic irrealism (q.v.)

leads to an untenable global irrealism. (For discussion, see Chapter 15, RULE-FOLLOWING, OBJECTIVITY AND MEANING, section 3.)

Mentalese: Mentalese is the name of the hypothesized language in which we think. According to advocates of the existence of Mentalese, e.g. J. Fodor, *The Language of Thought* (Harvester, 1976) to think a thought, form a belief or remember a fact, is to produce, in one way or another (which way depending on whether it is a belief, a memory, etc.), a sentence in an internal language. The existence of Mentalese explains the semantic properties of mental states in terms of the semantic properties of their component Mentalese expressions. This language, unlike natural languages, does not possess its semantics in virtue of the intentions or conventions of its users. Semantic naturalists think that the expressions of Mentalese possess their semantic properties in virtue of natural relations, especially causal and nomological relations, to extra-mental items. The Mentalese hypothesis is usually defended as being part of the best explanation for certain features of thought. The two most prominent features are productivity (a thinker can think complex thoughts) and logical inference: J. Fodor, *Psychosemantics: The Problem of Meaning in the Philosophy of Mind* (MIT Press, 1987).

Metaphysical realism: This term, along with 'external realism', is employed by Hilary Putnam to refer to an amalgam of several closely associated philosophical ideas about the relations between language and reality, and between truth and knowledge or justifiable belief. One component on which Putnam places considerable emphasis is that even an ideal theory (a theory that is '*epistemically* ideal *for humans*', ideal by the lights of the operational criteria by which we assess the merit of theories) may nevertheless be, in reality, false. More commonly, Putnam characterizes metaphysical realism in terms of three other theses, of which he takes this feature to be a consequence: that 'the world consists of a fixed totality of mind-independent objects', that 'there is exactly one true description of the way the world is' and that 'truth involves some sort of correspondence between words or thought-signs and external things and sets of things'. Putnam attacks this kind of realism, advocating instead what he terms 'internal realism'.

Millian semantics (Direct-reference theory): A Millian, or direct-reference, semantic theory is a hypothesis according to which the semantic value of a proper name (the contribution that it makes to the determination of the content of utterances containing it) is simply the referent of the name. According to this hypothesis, the thought or proposition expressed by a sentence containing a proper name is determined as a function of the individual named, perhaps by containing that individual as a constituent. The contrasting hypothesis is that reference or denotation is mediated by a sense or connotation. According to the contrasting theory, the semantics for the name provides some kind of abstract object – a sense or mode of presentation – which is a constituent or determinant of the thought or proposition expressed, and which also determines a referent.

Minimal truth: The term 'minimalism' is sometimes used to refer to a doctrine about truth not readily distinguishable, if indeed distinct at all, from the Deflationary view (q.v.). However, the term has also been employed (especially in recent work by Crispin Wright, and discussions that this has generated) for a characterization of truth intended to be neutral as between realists and their various opponents. According to this account, it suffices for a predicate T to be or function as a truth-predicate that it satisfy the Disquotation Scheme: '"P" is T if and only if P' and that it exhibit certain features embodied in or derivable from certain 'platitudes', as Wright describes them: centrally, that to assert a statement is to present it as true, and that any truth-apt content has a significant negation which is likewise truth-apt.

Modal realism: There are two quite distinct doctrines about modality to which the label 'modal realism' may be applied. Modal realism, in one reasonable sense of the term, is the view that there are irreducible modal truths or modal facts expressible by sentences featuring modal operators or equivalent devices, such as 'Necessarily 17 is prime', 'Uncles cannot but be brothers', etc. Realism in this sense is opposed by any view which denies the existence of a distinctive class of modal facts, either by rejecting modal talk altogether, or by giving a reductive account of it, or by accepting such talk as irreducible but arguing that, properly understood, it has some quite different, non-fact-stating role, as on a Non-cognitivist view (q.v.). In a quite different sense, 'modal realism' denotes a view about the existence of possible worlds. In its extreme form, as famously advocated by David Lewis, this second kind of modal realist holds that there literally are many other possible worlds besides the world we inhabit, each such world being spatially and temporally (and therefore causally) isolated from all other possible worlds. More moderate forms of realism about possible worlds have also been defended, most notably by Robert Stalnaker. It is clear that modal realism in the first sense does not require modal realism in the second. Indeed, since possible-worlds realists favour a reductive analysis of modal idioms to quantification over a domain of possible worlds, the two forms of realism appear incompatible. (For discussion, see Chapter 19, MODALITY.)

Model-theoretic arguments: Model theory is the branch of mathematical logic which studies the interpretation of formal languages (see **Interpretation**). Thus a model-theoretic argument might be any argument that draws on the results or techniques of model theory. In the philosophy of language, model-theoretic arguments which appeal to the Löwenheim–Skolem Theorems (q.v.) and to Permutation results (q.v.) have been deployed by Hilary Putnam, W. V. O. Quine, Donald Davidson and others in support of conclusions about indeterminacy of reference or meaning. (See Chapter 17, PUTNAM'S MODEL-THEORETIC ARGUMENT AGAINST METAPHYSICAL REALISM, for discussion of Putnam's use of these arguments.)

Myth of the museum: a term used by Quine to stigmatize the idea that there can be facts about the meanings a speaker assigns to particular expressions transcending anything that might in principle be determined as a correct translation of that speaker's utterances by a radical translator. [See **Radical translation**.]

Natural and non-natural meaning: The distinction, drawn in these terms at least, derives from Grice, 'Meaning', *Philosophical Review*, 66 (1957). Natural meaning (meaning$_n$) is the sort of meaning possessed by things in nature such as clouds (mean rain), or smoke (means fire), or wounds (mean damage). Non-natural meaning (meaning$_{nn}$) is possessed by our words and sentences, and by some of our actions and gestures. Grice draws attention to a number of differences between the two kinds of meaning; these include the fact that while "x means$_n$ that p" entails that p, the entailment fails for meaning$_{nn}$.

Necessity of identity: A thesis defended by Marcus, Wiggins, Kripke and other philosophers, according to which, if objects *x* and *y* are the same, they are necessarily the same. Instances may be formed in ordinary language by replacing the variables '*x*' and '*y*' with proper names or demonstratives, as in 'if Superman is Clark Kent then, necessarily, Superman is Clark Kent'. Since Superman *is* Clark Kent (treating the fiction as fact) it follows that it is necessary that Superman is Clark Kent, a surprising result if one expects everything that is necessary to be discoverable a priori. Marcus, Wiggins, Kripke and others conclude that some necessities are a posteriori.

Necessity of origin: see **Essentiality of origin**

Non-cognitivism: 'Non-cognitivism' is probably best understood as a generic term for any of a variety of views concerning some specified region of discourse according to which, to the extent that the surface syntax of its characteristic utterances suggest that they are aimed at recording discoveries (or cognitive achievements), this appearance is misleading. So understood, the non-cognitivist's thesis is a purely negative one – to the effect that the characteristic utterances of the discourse in question do not serve to depict or represent possible objects of knowledge – and is therefore compatible with a variety of positive theses about the function of those utterances. In particular, while it is consistent with, it does not require, the adoption of an expressivist or projectivist theory of the discourse.

Normativity of meaning: It is a central ingredient in understanding an expression to grasp that there are associated with it conditions for its correct application. Put another way, it is essential to any expression's possessing whatever meaning it does, that there are rules for its correct use. In this sense, meaning is normative. The normativity of meaning is frequently emphasized in the later writing of Wittgenstein, and especially in his discussions of rule-following: see *Philosophical Investigations* (1953), §§ 143–242; *Remarks on the Foundations of Mathematics* (second edn, 1956, part VI). It is a common theme in subsequent discussion, and especially in Saul Kripke's interpretation of Wittgenstein on rules, where certain attempts to explicate the notion of meaning in naturalistic terms (such as dispositional theories) are criticized as being incapable of accounting for the normative aspect of meaning.

Ontological conception of vagueness: This is the view that not all vagueness arises in thought and talk; at least some of it arises in what is thought and talked about, independently of its being thought or talked about. On this view, it may be vague what the spatio-temporal boundaries of an object are, whether one object is part of another, whether objects are identical, or whether a given object has a given property. Such borderline cases are held to result in the failure of the corresponding statements to be either true or false. Some technical treatments of vagueness consistent with the Semantic conception of vagueness (q.v.) are also consistent with the ontological conception.

Ontology: Ontology is the branch of metaphysics which is concerned with the study of being in general. As such, it concerns such matters as the nature of existence and the categorial structure of reality. That all entities occupy distinctive places within a categorial hierarchy is an idea traceable at least as far back as Aristotle. Different systems of ontology propose different categorial schemes. For instance, some schemes regard the distinction between concrete and Abstract objects (q.v.) as being most fundamental, while others accord this status to the distinction between Universals (q.v.) and Particulars (q.v.). Again, some schemes take the category of substance to be more basic than the category of events, whilst others take the converse view. Yet other schemes take 'particularized qualities' or 'tropes' to be the most fundamental category of physical entities. Ontological categories need to be clearly distinguished from Natural kinds (see **Kinds**).

Opacity: An opaque construction turns a position open to the substitutivity of identity into one not open thereto. Take the *doubts that* construction. It maps the word 'Alice' and the sentence

(1) Tully was an orator

to the sentence

(2) Alice doubts that Tully was an orator.

The construction seems opaque. For the position of 'Tully' in (1) is open to substitutivity, since from e.g.

(3) a = Tully

and (1) the sentence 'a was an orator' follows. But 'Tully' in (2) is not so open, since 'Alice believes that a is an orator' does not follow from (2) and (3). Constructions not opaque are called *transparent*. (Definition and terminology are due to Quine.)

Not all non-extensional contexts are opaque. For example, given that descriptions are quantifiers, and that proper names and demonstratives are rigid designators (and so, if co-referential, can be substituted in modal contexts *salva veritate*), modal constructions such as *it is necessary that S* are not opaque. But they are non-extensional.

As opacity is a property of constructions, its presence depends upon the presence of grammatical complexity. Quotation, for example, does *not* involve opacity if quotation names are spelling names. For then "Bob" is short for

'B' plus 'o' plus 'b'

which does not contain the word "Bob".

Openness and mutual knowledge: Mutual knowledge is knowledge possessed by two or more individuals. It is a form of iterated knowledge where it is held that A knows that p & A knows that B knows that p & A knows that B knows that A knows that p &. . . . The iteration here is potentially infinite. Despite the iteration involved in the account of mutual knowledge, some philosophers have held that the regress involved is perfectly harmless, and that it is obviously present in many cases of knowledge. Furthermore, it is taken by some to be a condition of knowledge. Some Griceans have employed a condition of mutual knowledge as a way of ensuring the sufficiency of their analysis of meaning. Without some such condition, the analysis is open to counter-examples based on deception. The concept of openness is designed to do the same work as that of mutual knowledge. Without appeal to an infinite regress of knowledge, the openness condition is meant to ensure that the speaker intend that all her intentions are recognized. In this way the deception which threatens the sufficiency of the analysis is blocked.

Parataxis: On Davidson's paratactic account of

(1) Gettier said that Sleigh slept

grammatical form masks semantical form. To utter (1) is to utter the complete sentence 'Gettier said that,' whose 'that' is a demonstrative; its reference is the ensuing utterance of 'Sleigh slept'. The point of the latter utterance is not to assert that Sleigh slept, but merely to provide a referent for 'that'; the force of the whole thing is something like

(2) An utterance of Gettier said-the-same-as *this*: Sleigh slept.

Among the virtues of this view are that it absolves sentences such as (1) from the charge that they violate the principle of substitutivity; and it apparently allows an account of such sentences to get by with only extensional semantic values. Among its apparent vices are that, in many cases (e.g. 'each author said that he would autograph his book'), it is implausible that we relate individuals to utterances; it seems, instead, that we relate them to *interpretations* of (possible) utterances.

Particulars: Particulars are normally contrasted with Universals (q.v.), the former being instances of the latter: for example, a particular apple is an instance of the universal *apple*, which in this case is a Natural kind (see **Kinds**). Particulars may be concrete objects, as in this case, or they may be Abstract objects (q.v.), such as numbers and sets. However, there may also be particulars which do not seem to qualify as 'objects' or 'Things' (q.v.) at all, in any very robust sense, such as the particular smile on someone's face, or the particular colour of this apple. Items like these are sometimes called 'particularized properties' or 'tropes'.

Performative utterances: J. L. Austin's term, designed to capture the fact that we do things with words. Austin distinguished performative utterances from what he labelled *constatives*. Austin once believed that only constatives could be said to be true or false; performatives are, by contrast, felicitous or infelicitous. The utterance of a performative was thought by Austin to be not so much a saying of something as a doing of something. Thus, in his view, to utter the words 'I do' or 'I promise to be there', in appropriate circumstances, is to bind oneself in marriage or to promise to be there, rather than to state that one is doing so. The precise drawing of this distinction gave Austin much trouble, and he eventually abandoned it.

Permutation argument: A permutation of a set of objects is any one-to-one function mapping that set on to itself. Under certain assumptions about the structure of a language, it can be shown that given one Interpretation (q.v.) or scheme of reference stipulations for the language, and given any permutation of its domain, there is an alternative, 'unintended' interpretation of the language based on that permutation, which makes quite different referential assignments to its singular terms and predicates, but which induces the same truth-values on the sentences of the language as does the given interpretation. This has been taken by some philosophers (especially W. V. O. Quine and Donald Davidson) to imply indeterminacy, or inscrutability, of reference, or (by Hilary Putnam) to raise insuperable difficulties for 'external' or 'Metaphysical' realism (q.v.).

Physicalism: The thesis that reality is nothing more than physical reality, and hence that physical science can, in principle, give a complete description of all that there is. The doctrine is widespread, and influential in the philosophy of language in so far as widely conceived as enjoining some form of reductive or reconstructive account of those areas of discourse – about values, or semantics, or intentional psychology, or modality, for instance – whose subject-matter does not appear to be physical in any straightforward sense. Physicalism has been a driving force in Quine's philosophy of language in particular, and a target of Putnam's writing since the mid-1970s.

Platonism: In the theory of meaning, this term is often applied to the view that the meanings of terms and sentences are (1) concepts and propositions which (2) are non-spatio-temporal entities known by non-perceptual intuition.

Possible world: A possible world is a way the world might be, a complete possible situation or state of affairs. The concept of a possible world has diverse formal and philosophical uses, and has been given very different philosophical explanations by different philosophers. In abstract formal semantics, possible worlds are primitive elements that are constituents of the models used to define the semantic values for expressions of the language of modal logic. Philosophers have appealed to them to formulate metaphysical theses and to give philosophical analyses of epistemological, semantic and metaphysical concepts such as supervenience, counterfactual conditionals, dependence and independence of various kinds, potentiality, essence, information, obligation and ability. According to some, possible worlds are literally worlds, universes parallel to our own; according to others, they are maximal properties that the world might have, or maximal propositions, or complex abstract structures whose elements are actual individuals, properties and relations.

Principle of Charity: The Principle of Charity is a supposed important constraint, invoked by Davidson, on the interpretation of the thoughts of others. The Principle says that interpretation must proceed in such a way that the judgements attributed to the others come out, for the most part, as true. It is argued to follow from the idea that we can disagree with someone, i.e. identify a thought of hers and label it false, only against a background of substantial agreement. This in turn is said to follow from Semantic holism (q.v.). Some philosophers take the Principle of Charity to be implausibly strong, and do not see why a person or persons should not, for example through the bad luck of being faced with many cases of misleading evidence, end up with beliefs which are largely false. Some philosophers, for this reason, prefer to see interpretation constrained by the Principle of Humanity (q.v.).

Principle of Humanity: The Principle of Humanity is preferred by some (e.g. Grandy and Lewis) to the Principle of Charity (see **Principle of Charity**) as a guiding constraint on interpretation. The Principle of Humanity says that we should interpret others as thinking and saying what we would have thought or said had we been in their circumstances, e.g. if we had had their sensory equipment, undergone their upbringing, been through their life experiences, etc.

Privacy: As it is understood in the philosophy of mind, the term 'privacy' is used to mean the property of being knowable to one person only. Certain mental states or events, it can plausibly be thought, can be known only to the person in whose mind they take place; nobody else can know what they are like. Whether there are any private states in this sense, and if so which, and what makes them private, are central questions in the philosophy of mind and the theory of knowledge. In the philosophy of language the main questions about privacy are (1) whether the nature of speakers' private states can affect the meanings of their words, or whether meaning is constituted solely by publicly knowable features of speakers and their behaviour; and (2) whether there could be a Private language (q.v.).

Private language: A private language is a language which a person uses to record thoughts about their own private states (see **Privacy**); it is often also understood to be a language which, in principle, only that person can understand. The most famous discussion of private language occurs in Wittgenstein's *Philosophical Investigations*, §§ 242–58, the burden of which is that no such language is possible, since it would not satisfy the conditions under which terms can have a meaning, even a private one. Wittgenstein's introduction of the notion of a private language (*Philosophical Investigations*, § 243) appears to use both the above definitions simultaneously; this may indicate a (contestable) assumption that the first entails the second.

Projectivism: A projectivist theory of a given region of discourse maintains that in casting its characteristic claims in assertoric or propositional style, we are not properly understood as attempting correctly to describe mind-independently constituted facts or states of affairs, but are instead 'projecting' our own feelings, attitudes or other affective (as distinct from cognitive) psychological states onto the world. Hume's treatment of moral judgements (according to which morals are "more properly felt than judg'd of") and judgements of causal necessity (as expressive of a felt determination of the mind to infer effect from cause, rather than record some objective necessary connection) are often regarded as classic examples of projectivist theories. As the first example suggests, projectivist theories are often developments of Expressivist (q.v.) accounts of a region of discourse (see also **Quasi-realism**).

Proposition: A proposition is what is said in a speech act, and also the content of a mental act or attitude – for example, a belief or desire state, or a mental act of judgement. A theory that appeals to propositions usually begins by factoring a speech act into content and force. An assertion – for example, a statement that the window is closed – differs in force, but might have the same content as a request that the window be closed. Different theorists differ about what a proposition is, though it is usually assumed to be an abstract object explained in terms of a set of truth-conditions: propositions might be identified either with truth-conditions themselves, or with a structure that represents a recursive procedure for determining a set of truth-conditions.

Propositional attitudes and subdoxastic states: Propositional attitudes are states such as beliefs, desires, hopes and wishes. The general form of a propositional-attitude ascription can be represented as follows: S j's that P, where "S" stands for the subject to whom the attitude is attributed (John, Jim), "j" for the type of attitude ascribed (belief, desire), and "P" for the informational content of the attitude (that Belhaven is brewed in Dunbar, that Raith Rovers sign Paul Gascoigne). Examples of propositional attitudes are thus John's belief that Belhaven is brewed in Dunbar, or Jim's desire that Raith Rovers sign Paul Gascoigne. Philosophers have attempted to delineate a related but distinct category of mental state, called subdoxastic states: these are like propositional attitudes in so far as they possess informational content, but different from propositional attitudes in so far as they are not ordinarily available to consciousness, and are inferentially insulated from the rest of their possessors' cognitive states: S. Stich, "Beliefs and Subdoxastic States", *Philosophy of Science*, 45 (1978); M. Davies, "Tacit Knowledge and Subdoxastic States", in A. George (ed.), *Reflections on Chomsky* (1989). Philosophers such as Davies, who are impressed by the arguments of Evans – "Semantic Theory and Tacit Knowledge", in S. Holtzmann and C. Leich (eds), *Wittgenstein: To Follow a Rule* (Routledge, 1981) – to the effect that states of tacit knowledge of semantic axioms cannot be propositional attitudes, have attempted to construe states of tacit knowledge as subdoxastic in this sense.

Public language: So called by contrast with Private language (q.v.), a public language is any language in which two or more speakers can communicate with each other. All existing natural languages may be presumed public languages in this sense. The philosophical use and interest of this concept lies in the questions (1) whether the fact that a language is public may not rule out certain accounts of the meaning of its words, and (2) whether being a language at all may not necessitate being a public language. (See Chapter 6, MEANING AND PRIVACY.)

Quantifying in: In (extensions of) first-order logic, a sentence involves *quantifying into* a construction when there is a variable within the scope of the construction bound by a operator without. For example, the sentence

(1) $\forall x(Fx \rightarrow \Box Fx)$

involves quantification into the necessitation construction (the construction which maps a sentence S to '$\Box$S'), as the last 'x' in (1) is in the scope of the construction, and is bound by the initial quantifier, which is not.

One often speaks of quantification in natural language; an example of such is

(2) Each spy believed that the man next to him was a spy

when 'him' is anaphoric on 'each spy'. One may understand such talk in terms of regimentation – a sentence involves quantification into construction c if its regimentation involves quantification into c('s regimentation). A first stab at a direct definition might be: S involves quantification into c when it contains pronouns (or the like) within c, bound to or anaphoric on expressions which occur outside of c.

Quasi-realism: 'Quasi-Realism' is the name conferred upon a species of anti-realism by its principal proponent, Simon Blackburn. As applied to moral discourse, the quasi-realist maintains, with the Expressivist (q.v.), that to construe moral utterances as descriptive of moral facts or states of affairs is a philosophical error – such utterances are to be understood as expressive of moral feelings or attitudes which we project on to the world, rather than as aimed at recording aspects of an independently constituted moral reality. Blackburn's distinctive aim is to show that the absence of a special realm of non-natural properties or facts to render moral judgements true or false does not – as on an Error theory (q.v.) – entail that such discourse is inherently defective, and that we can quite properly, and consistently with anti-realist scruples and with a Projectivist (q.v.) theory of morality, present our moral sentiments 'in propositional style', as if they were genuine judgements with truth-conditions.

Radical interpretation: To interpret an item , e.g. a sound, mark or gesture, is to assign a meaning to it. When we hear a remark in a familiar language we usually interpret it easily in the light of our knowledge of the language and/or of the person speaking. But Radical interpretation is the enterprise of working out the meanings of what we take to be some set of utterances, when we start with no prior semantic knowledge at all, such as information about the structure of the language, the meanings of any words, or the beliefs, interests etc. of the speakers. It is closely related to the enterprise of Radical translation introduced by Quine; but it differs in that it is to issue not just in claims that a certain sentence (of the native language) and this sentence (of my language) are synonymous, but in actual statements of the meaning of the sentence in the native language. It is thought that reflecting on how we might establish semantic hypotheses from non-semantic starting points could be a useful philosophical tool in throwing light on the metaphysics and epistemology of meaning.

Radical translation: The process of translating a foreign language in circumstances where no prior knowledge of its syntax, or the etymology and/or likely meaning of any of its expressions can be assumed, and where no assistance is to be had from bilinguals. Thus the assumption is that the radical translator is restricted, at least initially, to data which exclusively concern the linguistic behaviour of the native speakers of the foreign language. It is usually assumed, in addition, that the translator is able from the outset to identify natives' expressions of assent and dissent. It is an important assumption of Quine's philosophy of language that there cannot be more to meanings than can be detected under such constraints. (See also **Radical interpretation** and **Myth of the museum**.)

Referentialism: The term "Referentialism" is used for the movement in the philosophy of language that rejects the Fregean doctrine that the content of a term (definite description, name or indexical) is a mode of presentation or an identifying condition. Referentialists such as Marcus, Kaplan, Donnellan and Kripke claim that, at least for names and indexicals, this is not so. In Chapter 23, INDEXICALS AND DEMONSTRATIVES, a pair of distinctions are made, assigning rather special meanings to some well-worn terms from the philosophy of language, to further clarify this thesis.

Denoting versus naming: An expression denotes when the rules of language assign specific conditions to the expression that an object must meet to be designated by it. We say the expression denotes the object that meets these conditions, if any. Expressions that denote are contrasted with those that name. The rules of language assign specific objects to names, rather than conditions.

Describing versus referring: A term describes if it denotes, and contributes the condition assigned to it by the rules of language, rather than the object denoted, to the content of statements containing it. Describing is contrasted with referring. A term refers if it contributes the object it designates (denotes or names) to the content of statements containing it.

Given this terminology, we can say that referentialism is the doctrine that indexicals and names refer rather than describe: indexicals denote and refer, names name and refer.

Relative identity thesis: The Relative identity thesis is the thesis formulated by Peter Geach in 'Identity', *Review of Metaphysics*, 21 (1967), that identity is relative. The thesis has several components. The most ambitious contention Geach puts forward is that absolute identity is inexpressible; a language may contain a predicate expressing indistinguishability by the predicates it contains, but no language can contain a predicate expressing indistinguishability *simpliciter*. Additionally, Geach maintains that identity under a sortal concept (*being the same* A where 'A' is a sortal term) need not entail indistinguishability even by all the predicates contained in a language in which such sortal-relative identity is expressed. Thus objects may be identical under one sortal concept, distinct under another.

Restricted versus unrestricted quantification: The notion of restricted quantification is a significant element in the package of ideas put forward by Peter Geach under the heading of 'relative identity' in 'Identity', *Review of Metaphysics*, 21 (1967). It is an important part of his position that sortal terms, in subject position, are names, on a par with proper names; and he takes this to imply that where 'A' is a sortal term 'some A is F' is stronger than 'something is A and F', and 'every A is F' is weaker than 'everything, if it is an A, is F'. If Geach's thesis that identity under a sortal concept need not be absolute identity is accepted, the irreducibility of restricted quantification follows. Otherwise there is no argument for it.

Rigidity: Rigidity is a semantic property of expressions. Where e is an expression, let e-c denote the occurrence of e in the context c. e-c is rigid with respect to a class of points of evaluation (e.g. possible worlds, or times) just in case, for some x, the designation of e-c is x, and at every point of evaluation in which x exists, the designation of e-c is x, and e-c has no designation other than x at points of evaluation at which x does not exist. For example, the expression "I" when uttered by Frank is rigid with respect to the class of possible worlds, since in any possible world in which Frank exists, that occurrence of "I" designates Frank, and designates nothing else in worlds in which Frank does not exist. An expression can be said to be rigid just in case the denoting occurrences of it are.

The concept of rigidity has proved to be a useful tool in gaining an understanding of the complex semantical interactions between intensional operators and certain classes of expressions, such as names, indexicals and pronouns. Rigidity is also important in the model theory of quantified intensional logic, where it is used as a restriction on variables.

S4 principle: The distinctive theorem schema of C. I. Lewis and C. H. Langford's system S4 of modal logic can informally be stated thus: if it is necessary that P, then it is necessary that it is necessary that P. This is expressed by the formula $\Box p \rightarrow \Box\Box p$. Readings of the symbol $\Box$ other than 'it is necessary that . . .' give what may also be described as S4 principles. For example, if $\Box$ is read as 'it is clear that . . .', the result is the principle that if it is clear that P, then it is clear that it is clear that P, a principle to which Higher-order vagueness (q.v.) may provide counter-examples. In possible-worlds semantics the S4 principle corresponds to the condition that if a world z is possible from the standpoint of a world y, and y is possible from the standpoint of a world x, then z is possible from the standpoint of x, i.e. relative possibility is transitive.

S5 principle: The distinctive theorem schema of C. I. Lewis and C. H. Langford's system S5 of modal logic can informally be stated thus: if it is possible that P, then it is necessary that it is possible that P. An equivalent schema is: if it is not necessary that P, then it is necessary that it is not necessary that P. This is expressed by the formula $\neg\Box p \rightarrow \Box\neg\Box p$. Readings of the symbol $\Box$ other than 'it is necessary that . . .' give what may also be described as S5 principles. For example, if $\Box$ is read as 'it is clear that . . .', the result is the principle that if it is not clear that P, then it is clear that it is not clear that P, a principle to which Higher-order vagueness (q.v.) may provide counter-examples. In possible-worlds semantics, the S5 principle corresponds to the condition that if worlds y and z are possible from the standpoint of a world x, then z is possible from the standpoint of y. Given that relative possibility is reflexive, this is equivalent to the condition that it should also be both symmetric and transitive.

Second-order languages: see **First-order languages**

Semantic conception of vagueness: What distinguishes this view from the Ontological conception of vagueness (q.v.) is the claim that all vagueness arises in thought and talk, not in what is thought and talked about (in so far as it is not itself thought and talk). What distinguishes the semantic conception from the Epistemic conception (q.v.) is the claim that vagueness results in the failure to make a statement that is either true or false (and not both) in borderline cases. There is either no truth-value at all, or one of a non-standard kind, e.g. 'neutral', 'true to degree 0.7' or 'both true and false'. Such behaviour may be attributed either to gaps and defects in the meanings of vague expressions, or to positive meanings of an alternative kind, for instance as given by prototypical examples uncircumscribed by boundaries. Many different technical treatments of vagueness are consistent with the semantic conception. [See **Degrees of truth**, **Supervaluations**.]

Semantic creativity and learnability: Speakers of a natural language display semantic creativity in so far as they are able to understand novel utterances, that is, utterances of sentences which they have never before encountered. For example, your understanding of "Napoleon's grandfather wore purple pyjamas" is (almost certainly) a manifestation of semantic creativity. A related idea is that of the learnability of natural languages: a natural language is said to be learnable when a speaker needs only explicit training with, or exposure to, a small part of the language, in order to secure competence with a larger and more extensive part.

Semantic holism: Semantic holism is the view that meaningful items (1) must necessarily occur as part of some whole, i.e. a large set of such items, and (2) are such that the meaning of each item is somehow bound up with, constrains and is constrained by, the meanings of the other items. It comes in various different versions (often not distinguished as sharply as would be useful) depending on whether the items are taken to be sentences and the whole the language of which they are elements, or whether the items are sentences and the whole a theory they jointly compose, or whether the items are thoughts and the whole a mind of which they are the contents.

Semantic irrealism: Semantic irrealism is the thesis that there are no semantic facts and hence, in particular, no facts about what any expression means. Outrageous and even paradoxical as it may seem, this thesis has been seriously advanced and defended: most famously, perhaps, Saul Kripke takes it to be established by the sceptical argument he extracts from Wittgenstein's remarks on rule-following; and W. V. O. Quine draws a similar conclusion from his arguments for the indeterminacy of translation. Note that the semantic irrealist should not be seen as claiming that all expressions are meaningless, since the fact that an expression lacks meaning would be just as much a semantic fact as would the fact that it means such-and-such. Nor is the semantic irrealist necessarily committed to denying that semantic sentences have any proper use – though Quine certainly denies that they can have any part in serious science. The essential irrealist claim is that such sentences – in contrast with, say, sentences belonging to physics, for example, or geography – do not have meaning by being associated with truth-conditions. This leaves room to hold that semantic sentences have meaning in some other way, just as denying that there are moral facts leaves room to hold that moral utterances have meaning in some non-truth-conditional way. (See Chapter 16, THE INDETERMINACY OF TRANSLATION, for discussion of Quine's position, and Chapter 15, RULE-FOLLOWING, OBJECTIVITY AND MEANING, for discussion of Kripke's.)

Semantic naturalism: Semantic naturalism is the view that semantic and intentional properties and relations, especially the properties of referring to something and of having such-and-such a truth-condition, are part of the natural order. They are instantiated in virtue of the instantiation of natural properties and relations. Natural properties and relations are ones that are reducible to (or realized by) properties and relations expressible in the vocabulary of the natural sciences (physics, chemistry and biology) and the causal and nomological facts involving them. Most contemporary semantic naturalists think that the semantic properties of natural-language expressions can be explained in terms of the semantic properties of the mental states of users of the language, and that the semantic properties of mental states can be explained in terms of causal relations between them and various extra-mental items.

Semantic physicalism: see **Semantic naturalism**

Semantic value: A semantic value for an expression is an object that a semantic theory that interprets the language assigns to the expression. The term is intended to be abstract and neutral, leaving open what kind of objects a semantic theory uses to interpret its expressions. Semantic values for whole sentences may include the propositional content or thought expressed by the sentence, or a function that determines content as a function of context. The semantic values of words and other constituents of sentences will be whatever, according to the semantics, they must be to determine the semantic values of the expressions that contain them as constituents. In extensional theories, semantic values will be extensions.

Sense: Sense is that with which meaningful expressions are invested, and that in virtue of which they make reference to non-linguistic items (or, speaking more generally, have semantic values). Frege introduced the idea of the sense of an expression to be correlative with the idea of a speaker's understanding of the expression (see Chapter 1, MEANING AND TRUTH CONDITIONS, especially § 2). The sense of an expression is, then, the expression's *contribution* to the sense of any larger unit which can be used to say something true or false. In the limiting case of a sentence, the sense is the truth-condition. Or better (postponing commitment to senses as entities): to know what is the sense of a sentence is to know under what conditions the sentence has the semantic value of truth. Frege calls the sense of a sentence, which is very much the same thing as many philosophers have intended by "proposition", a *thought*. (The psychologistic overtones of the English word must be carefully kept out here. The thought is something public and non-psychological.)

Another special case of sense is that of the sense of a singular term. (Frege sets out from this case in "On Sense and Reference" in *Philosophical Writings of Gottlob Frege*, eds P. Geach and M. Black, Blackwell, 1952.) A singular term has its sense by standing for – or presenting – its reference, which is an object. Different singular terms may present one and the same object by different "modes of presentation". Wherever this is the case, the singular terms in question will make different contributions to the overall sense of the various sentences in which they figure. To grasp the sense of a proper name fully and correctly, then, is to know which object the name stands for, and to know this in virtue of being party to a particular way of thinking of this object. Different ways may call into being different proper names with different senses, which may contribute to different thoughts about one and the same thing, and may thereby contribute to an explanation of the possibility of informative statements of identity. This feature of the Fregean scheme has attracted the scepticism of those who see problems in the individuation of different ways of thinking of an item, and of those who see naming as irreducible to describing, and believe that different ways of thinking of a thing collapse into different descriptions of the thing.

Singular proposition: Suppose that assertion and belief are relations; call their objects *propositions*. Broadly Fregean views of propositions see them composed and individuated in terms of "ways of thinking" of objects and properties; broadly Russellian and Millian accounts posit *singular propositions*, whose identity is a function simply of the objects and properties they concern. A Fregean representation of the proposition that Fichte weeps, pairs a way F of thinking of Fichte and a way W of thinking of the set of weepers; the singular proposition may be represented by pairing Fichte with the property weeping.

As propositions determine truth-conditions, one difference between the views is truth-conditional. The Fregean proposition's truth presumably turns on the object, which F presents, having the property W presents; the singular proposition is true just in case Fichte weeps. If F can present something other than what it in fact does (or fail to present Fichte, though he existed), the propositions have different truth-conditions. A second difference is this: if 'Fichte weeps' expresses the Fregean proposition, presumably one must think of Fichte in way F to think that Fichte weeps; if it expresses a singular proposition, this is not so.

Sortal concepts: The notion of a sortal concept is the notion of a concept which conveys a criterion of identity and thus determines a type of object for which it makes sense to ask whether objects of the type are the same or different. Although the notion of a sortal concept can be illustrated by standard examples – 'man', 'gold', 'number' and 'direction' stand for sortal concepts – it is controversial how it is to be explained. Geach's view, in 'Identity', *Review of Metaphysics*, 21 (1967), which is part of the package he offers under the title of 'relative identity', is that predicates expressing sortal concepts like 'is a man' are semantically derivative from relational predicates expressing equivalence relations, like 'is the same man as': 'is a man' must be understood as 'is the same man as something' just as 'is a brother' must be understood as 'is a brother of someone'. This view is opposed by Michael Dummett in 'Does Quantification involve Identity?', in H. A. Lewis (ed.), *Peter Geach: Philosophical Encounters* (Kluwer, 1991) who argues that in the case of many sortal predicates, such as 'is a number', they are rather to be understood as derivative from functors, for example 'the number of . . .'. Whatever the correct way to understand the notion of a sortal concept, it is generally accepted that both Mass terms (q.v.), which provide a criterion of identity but no principle for counting, and count nouns, which provide both, are sortal terms.

Speaker meaning: A statement of the form: 'By uttering x, U meant such-and-such' aims to report what an agent meant_{nn} (see **Natural and non-natural meaning**) by doing something (perhaps uttering certain words) on a particular occasion. This will be an instance of speakers' $\text{occasion-meaning}_{nn}$. By contrast, 'U means such-and-such by x' would ordinarily be used to say something about what U typically means_{nn} by x, whenever she utters x – this will be an example of speakers' 'timeless' meaning, in Grice's terminology. Speakers' occasion meaning is the analysandum concept in the Gricean analysis of meaning. It is what speakers mean that is analysed in the first instance. In Grice's approach, one builds up to the concept of linguistic meaning from that of speaker-meaning. The priority of speaker-meaning in this approach is evidence that the concept of meaning that Grice is concerned to analyse is somewhat *wider* than linguistic meaning.

Stimulus synonymy: Quine's behaviouristic, non-normative surrogate for synonymy as more ordinarily conceived. A pair of sentences are stimulus-synonymous just in case the same stimuli as provoke assent to (or dissent from) the one as provoke assent to (respectively, dissent from) the other; a pair of sub-sentential expressions are stimulus-synonymous just in case any sentence containing an occurrence of the one is stimulus-synonymous with the result of replacing that occurrence by one of the other.

Strict implication and equivalence: A statement A strictly implies a statement B if and only if it is necessarily true that if A then B (i.e. if and only if $\Box$ (A $\rightarrow$ B), where '$\rightarrow$' is the material or truth-functional conditional). A and B are strictly equivalent if and only if they strictly imply each other (equivalently, if and only if $\Box$ (A $\leftrightarrow$ B), where '$\leftrightarrow$' is the material or truth-functional biconditional).

Substitutional quantification: To understand "($\exists$x)Fx" substitutionally is to understand it as true iff there is some name (say *n*) which can be substituted for the "x" in "Fx" such that the resulting sentence F*n* is true. This contrasts with the more common objectual understanding of "($\exists$x)Fx", whereby it is true iff there is some object which is F. If the only object or objects which are F lack names, "($\exists$x)Fx" will be true on the objectual reading but false on the substitutional. This difference will disappear if one extends the substitutional account to include new names, arguing perhaps that any object can be *given* a name. That, however, looks suspiciously like reducing substitutional quantification to objectual after all. The substitutional account may seem to help with "Whatever the Pope says is true": for any value of *s*, if the Pope says "*s*", then *s*. But it must not be allowed to disguise the problem of whether "*s*" is functioning in two different ways here. A decision to read the quantifier substitutionally does nothing by itself to explain the relation between the two occurrences.

Substitutivity, principle of: see **Leibniz's Law**

Superassertibility: This is a notion proposed originally by Crispin Wright as an anti-realistically acceptable replacement for the realist notion of evidence-transcendent truth (q.v.). It is superassertible that P if and only if there is, or can be, warrant to assert that P, and some warrant to assert that P would survive arbitrarily close scrutiny of its credentials and arbitrarily extensive increments to, or other improvements upon, our state of information.

Supervaluation: Most generally, a supervaluation is a semantic property defined by quantification over valuations. The idea seems first to have been used in connection with philosophy of science, the name in connection with Liar paradoxes: for the history, see Williamson, *Vagueness* (London, Routledge, 1994), 5.2. In connection with vagueness, the valuations are classical assignments of sets to predicates ("sharpenings"); admissible valuations meet various constraints designed to ensure that between them they represent the meaning of the predicate, even if it is vague. (So, e.g., an admissible valuation does not assign to the extension of the predicate something to which, intuitively, it definitely does not apply.) Truth (or "supertruth") is defined as truth-upon-all-admissible-valuations, and falsehood as falsehood-upon-all-admissible-valuations. This leaves room for the possibility, supposedly indicative of vagueness, of sentences which are neither true nor false.

Supervenience: The basic idea is that one range of facts supervenes upon another (the base or subvening facts) iff there could be no differences among the supervening facts without a difference in the subvening ones. When it is said that meaning supervenes upon use, the idea is that there could not be two communities who count as speakers of different languages unless there were differences in how each used its language. In serious discussion, some account must at once be given of "use", else the claim is trivial. (For example, it is not very controversial that the meaning of a declarative sentence supervenes on what it can be correctly used to say.) The slogan is often associated, historically, with behaviourist views in semantics: those which regard use as capable of being specified wholly behaviouristically.

Tacit knowledge: Philosophers of language have invoked this notion in attempts to explain the Semantic creativity and learnability (q.v.) of natural language. The main idea is that if speakers of a language can be credited with tacit knowledge of a compositional semantic theory for their language (see **Compositionality**), we will have an explanation of semantic creativity (since the theory the speaker tacitly knows has the resources to generate a meaning-specifying theorem for the sentence uttered in the novel context) and an explanation of learnability (since the theory tacitly known can generate meaning-specifying theorems for a wide range of sentences on the basis of a narrower range of semantic axioms). Philosophers disagree as to the nature of states of tacit knowledge; in particular, they disagree as to whether they should be construed as bona fide propositional attitudes – see M. Dummett, "What is a Theory of Meaning? (II)", in G. Evans and J. McDowell (eds), *Truth and Meaning* (Oxford, 1976) – or as mere dispositional states: see G. Evans, "Semantic Theory and Tacit Knowledge", in S. Holtzmann and C. Leich (eds), *Wittgenstein: To Follow a Rule* (Routledge, 1981), or as subdoxastic information-containing states: see M. Davies, "Tacit Knowledge and the Structure of Thought and Language", in C. Travis (ed.), *Meaning and Interpretation* (Blackwell, 1986).

Theory of meaning: As it appears in discussions by philosophers of language, this phrase may be taken in at least two ways. In the more general of the two senses, it denotes a theory dealing with language in general, which attempts to analyse and elucidate the concept of meaning. In this sense, it can be applied to attempted analyses or conceptual elucidations of what it is for an item to have meaning, as for example in Grice's linkage of linguistic meaning with speakers' intentions or in verificationist-style accounts which insist that what we can think, and hence mean, is importantly constrained by what we can know (see **Epistemic conception of meaning**). In the more specific sense it denotes a theory dealing with a particular language, which generates a theorem specifying the meaning of each well-formed declarative sentence of that language. Philosophers disagree about the nature of these theorems (often called "meaning-specifying theorems"): some take them to be statements of sentences' truth-conditions (Davidson), while others take them to be statements of sentences' conditions of warranted assertibility (Dummett).

Theory of truth, Tarski-style: The phrase 'a Tarski-style theory of truth' is used to describe an assignment of semantic properties to words and constructions which enables us, given a specification of a sentence as built from certain words by certain constructions, to work out a biconditional stating truth-conditions of that sentence. Tarski himself insisted, for his purposes of giving the so-called 'semantic theory of truth', that the theory should issue in statements of truth-conditions in which the sentence which gives the truth-conditions has the same meaning as the sentence whose truth-conditions are given. (In the case where the metalanguage includes the object language, this results in the demand that the output of the theory should be theorems like the famous '"Snow is white" is true iff snow is white'.) But the idea of a 'Tarski-style theory of truth', as invoked, for example, by Davidson in the context of his project of Radical interpretation (q.v.), abandons that requirement; the idea is to use the formal apparatus devised by Tarski (e.g. of connectives or quantifiers) for a different purpose. (See also **Compositionality**.)

Things: There is a very weak sense of the term 'thing' according to which it is trivially true that *everything* is a thing. In this sense, any item which a system of Ontology (q.v.) acknowledges as existing at all may be accounted a 'thing' in that ontology. But for most purposes the term 'thing', or 'object', is used in a more robust sense, in which its application is restricted at least to the class of entities possessing well-defined identity-conditions, and hence to Kinds (q.v.) of entity for which Criteria of identity (q.v.) may be stated. Sometimes, however, 'thing' is used in an even more narrow sense than this, to refer to concrete, physical occupants of space which persist through time (otherwise called 'continuants') – a sense which excludes both Abstract objects (q.v.) and such physical entities as events. Clearly, if confusion is to be avoided in the use of the word 'thing', care must be taken to indicate which of these senses is in operation.

Thought: see **Sense**

Timeless Meaning: Timeless meaning is the meaning our utterances have when they are not tied to a particular occasion of utterance. Linguistic meaning is an instance of timeless meaning. If one takes it that linguistic meaning is necessarily structured (as philosophers do), then it is possible to have timeless meaning that is not linguistic. A system of communication based on (unstructured) gestures would be an example. Most – though not all – Griceans propose to build up to the notion of timeless meaning by adding the concept of convention to the analysis of Speaker meaning (q.v.).

Tokens: Consider this list: philosophy, art, history, philosophy. Are there three or four words on the list? Three types appear, but four tokens; there are two tokens of the type "philosophy". Sometimes "token" is used for a particular act of uttering an expression of a given type, but more often it is used for the object that is produced by such utterances: the particular ink-marks on a page, or the burst of sound that travels through the air. In this volume (see Chapter 23, INDEXICALS AND DEMONSTRATIVES) "token" is used in the second way, and "utterance" is reserved for acts. In this usage, a token is an effect of an utterance.

Truth-bearers: There has been much dispute over what the (primary) bearers of truth are. Candidates have included sentences, statements, judgements, propositions, thoughts and beliefs. The dispute has been partly verbal. A sentence can be true, but evidently what is true is the sentence *as* used on a particular occasion, to convey a particular message; in other words, to make a particular statement or to express a particular proposition. Hostility to statements and propositions has often arisen from thinking they must be entities of a peculiar metaphysical kind. Some defenders of propositions have indeed thought of them like that, but without such commitment one can legitimize talk of propositions if one can specify the conditions under which two utterances express the same proposition. Following Quine, some have maintained this cannot be done – a serious objection, if correct, but at least counter-intuitive. The objection to taking thoughts, judgements or beliefs to be primary truth-bearers is that they are subjective mental occurrences. But again, while beliefs (etc.) are held by individuals, there seems a good sense in which two people can be said to share the same belief – which they might voice by uttering sentences expressing the same proposition.

Truth-condition: see **Sense**

Underdetermination of empirical theory by data: The contention that any body of empirical evidence for a particular theory will be compatible with alternatives to that theory, and hence cannot constrain the selection of any particular one among a range of alternative empirical theories. The thesis is uncontentious if one restricts attention to finite accumulations of evidence. In Quine, however, it is generalized to cover *all possible* empirical data. A stronger version yet contends that even all possible data *plus* best scientific methodology – proper canons of simplicity, economy, . . . , integration, etc. in theory construction – never determine one particular empirical theory as uniquely best. The Underdetermination thesis is the main premise for Quine's principal argument for the Indeterminacy of translation (q.v.).

Universals: Universals are the (supposed) referents of general terms, such as 'red', 'car' and 'planet', conceived as entities distinct from any of the Particulars (q.v.) which instantiate them. As such, they are Abstract objects (q.v.). Whether such entities really exist has long been a matter for heated debate, those denying their existence usually being called 'nominalists' and their opponents 'realists'. There are two main schools of realism: Aristotelian or 'immanent' realism, which holds that universals exist 'in' particulars, and accordingly cannot exist if uninstantiated; and Platonic or 'transcendent' realism, which holds that universals exist 'separately' from particulars, and consequently may exist even if they have no instances.

Use theory of meaning: Use theories of meaning are sometimes referred to as communication or pragmatic theories. Grice's account of meaning is an example of a use theory. Such theories of meaning have their roots in the work of J. L. Austin (the idea that meaning is to be associated with use is also a theme in the later writings of Wittgenstein). Such approaches to meaning connect the concept primarily with the actions of speakers. The approach looks at the phenomenon of meaning quite widely, taking linguistic meaning to be a particular instance of the phenomenon. As a result, structure is accorded less emphasis.

Verificationism: The verifiability criterion of meaningfulness is the claim that a meaningful sentence is one which is capable of being verified or falsified. Even those who would generally find no inclination to hold such a view find themselves disposed to think that, if our vague predicates really do draw sharp boundaries, it would have to be possible for us to tell where these boundaries fall. Such theorists would do well to justify the specific view about vagueness on some basis other than the general verificationist claim, for this latter is now rarely thought defensible, at least in the crude form given here.

A verificationist theory of meaning holds, in general terms, that understanding a sentence consists in grasping what information states would verify it. An information state verifies a sentence just if a person in that state is warranted in asserting it. Strict forms of verification further require that the verifying information state should be indefeasible.

A verificationist view of truth holds that truth is verifiability. A sentence is true if and only if it is verifiable, that is, if and only if there is evidence warranting its assertion.

Wide cosmological role: One of several features or marks proposed by Crispin Wright, in virtue of which realism concerning the subject-matter of a given discourse whose characteristic statements qualify for at least Minimal truth (q.v.) may be maintained. A discourse exhibits wide cosmological role if the facts recorded in its characteristic claims have a role to play in explanations of further facts of other kinds, beyond facts about our beliefs and other attitudes, and can figure in such explanations other than as objects of those attitudes. It might be contended that while moral, or modal, beliefs, for example, are apt to figure in explanations of our actions, desires and other beliefs, moral or modal facts themselves exert no influence on other goings-on; in contrast, facts about the primary qualities of bodies, for example, exert causal influence in the world at large. To the extent that this is so, we might think that it justifies a kind of realism about facts of the latter kind which is unwarranted in regard to the former. (See **Cognitive Command**, **Euthyphro contrast**.)

INDEX

HALE & WRIGHT: *A Companion to the Philosophy of Language* Index compiled by Meg Davies (Registered Indexer) *Note:* Page references in **bold** type indicate chief discussion of major topics. References in *italics* lead to Glossary entries. Where names of contributors to the *Companion* are indexed, the references are to citations in articles other than their own.